THE LINGUISTIC ATLAS of ENGLAND

THE LINGUISTIC ATLAS of ENGLAND

Edited by

HAROLD ORTON, STEWART SANDERSON
AND JOHN WIDDOWSON

CROOM HELM LONDON HUMANITIES PRESS
MAX HUEBER VERLAG
SHUBUN INTERNATIONAL COMPANY, LIMITED

Croom Helm Ltd, 2-10 St John's Road, London SW11
ISBN 0-85664-294-0

British Library Cataloguing in Publication Data

The linguistic atlas of England.
1. English language – Dialects – England – Maps
I. Orton, Harold II. Sanderson, Stewart
III. Widdowson, John David Allison
912'.1427 PE1705

ISBN 0-85664-294-0

First published in the USA 1977 by
Humanities Press, Atlantic Highlands, N.J.
ISBN 0-391-00759-9

Published in West Germany by Max Hueber Verlag by
arrangement with Croom Helm Ltd, London.

ISBN: 3-19-00.2210-0

Published in Japan by Shubun International Company, Limited
by arrangement with Croom Helm Ltd, London

Printed in Great Britain by
Redwood Burn Limited, Trowbridge & Esher

CONTENTS

This volume is dedicated
by his co-editors
to the memory of

HAROLD ORTON
1898–1975

FOREWORD

The publication of this volume marks one of the culminating stages of the English Dialect Survey planned by Harold Orton and Eugen Dieth some thirty years ago. The organisational principles of the Survey and the title under which its main collecting apparatus was published—*A Questionnaire for a Linguistic Atlas of England*—testify to the sustained interest in linguistic geography of both these historically oriented scholars; and while it is true that the cartographic methods employed in the final publication differ considerably from those envisaged by Eugen Dieth, and were evolved over many years by Harold Orton, latterly in collaboration with myself, they nonetheless reflect and are conditioned by the theoretical stance of the *Questionnaire's* compilers.

The direction of the Survey, however, was solely Harold Orton's responsibility, and it was he who planned its publication programme, of which the first fruits were his *Introduction* (1962) and the volumes of *Basic Material* (1962–71) on which he worked with a number of co-editors and research assistants. In 1964 he retired from his Chair, whereupon both the editorial team and the Survey's archives, which are the copyright property of the University of Leeds, were incorporated in the University's newly founded Institute of Dialect and Folk Life Studies, whose Director became responsible for the prosecution of the programme of research and publication.

Although he was over 70 years of age when the last parts of the *Basic Material* volumes were nearing completion, and had had more than one indication of the possible consequences of overtaxing his energies, Harold Orton as editor-in-chief of the Survey's publications continued to address himself to the production of the *Linguistic Atlas of England* referred to in his *Introduction*. Always a realist in such matters, he was aware that he might not be able to bring the work to its conclusion himself, especially as the University was no longer in a position to provide him with editorial assistance as it had on a substantial scale for the first part of the publication programme. The existence of the Institute, however, was in itself a guarantee that the work would continue, if only slowly; and this guarantee had been reinforced by my undertaking early in 1968 to act as co-editor and to complete the atlas if he himself should be unable to do so. As our plans developed an invitation was formally extended in 1971 to Dr J D A Widdowson of the University of Sheffield to join us as a co-editor. Progress was further assured when my application to the Leverhulme Trust resulted in a research grant generous enough to allow for the appointment in 1972 of two research assistants for a three-year period, and a cartographic draughtsman for the two later years; and it was confidently expected that the atlas would be completed by the end of 1975.

Unhappily Harold Orton died in March of that year after a short illness. He had already selected the phonological maps and had made a first draft of that part of the Introduction dealing with them; and he had also made a preliminary selection of lexical, morphological and syntactical maps to be included. The final choice and running order of the maps, and the design of the legends, footnotes and appendices, have of necessity been modified from his original conception because of spatial and other technical limitations in printing and production; but in completing the work his co-editors have tried to develop the final form of the atlas in ways which he, the principal author and interpreter of the Survey, would have approved.

The editors wish to express their gratitude to the many individuals and institutions who have in one way or another helped them throughout their work, and in particular to the University of Leeds for the facilities of the Institute of Dialect and Folk Life Studies and for secretarial, administrative, and technical assistance; to the Trustees of the Leverhulme Trust, without whose support this atlas would have taken at least a decade to produce; to Mrs Sue Powell and Mr Clive Upton, whose scholarly commitment and loyalty to the project led them to give invaluable help long after their appointments as Research Assistants terminated; to Mrs Joan Orton, whose continuing interest after Professor Orton's death has encouraged and sustained the efforts of the editorial team; to Dr Nathalia Wright, of the University of Tennessee, who as co-author of *A Word Geography of England* assisted Professor Orton at an early stage with the preliminary drafting of lexical maps; to Dr R C Alston who readily placed his expertise in the techniques of photo-lithography and printing at our service; to Dr J MacGregor, the University Registrar, and members of his staff, and to the staff of the Bursar, including particularly Mr Edmund Williamson himself, for much help, interest, and wise advice; and not least to Mrs Philippa Pryor and Miss Hilary Darwent for skilfully typing a complicated manuscript. They also wish to pay tribute to the care and skill exercised by Typesetting Services in translating that manuscript into print, and above all to record their appreciation of the imaginative, scholarly, and decisive approach of their publishers, Croom Helm, to the whole project at every stage.

There is a further debt to be acknowledged. This atlas could not have been produced but for the careful and devoted labours of the eleven fieldworkers and their many informants during the years when the

English Dialect Survey's collections were being made. Together they compiled a record of the dialectal speech of the English countryman, and countrywoman, which generations of scholars will recognise as a mid-twentieth century landmark in the perspectives of the history of our language. It is on the authority of this record, itself an accumulation of acts of critical judgment on the part of all those involved, that the atlas is based; and so, while responsibility for the major task of scholarship—the interpretation and presentation of the material—rests with the editorial team, the informants and fieldworkers have also been in a real sense co-authors of this volume.

Stewart F Sanderson
Director
Institute of Dialect & Folk Life Studies
The University of Leeds
October 1976

ABBREVIATIONS

a	*ante*, before
adj	adjective
adv	adverb
AF	Anglo-French
AN	Anglo-Norman
Angl	Anglian
app	apparently
Bd	Bedfordshire
Bk	Buckinghamshire
Brk	Berkshire
C	consonant
c	*circa*, about
Celt	Celtic
cf	*confer*, compare
Ch	Cheshire
Co	Cornwall
conn	connected with
cons	consonantal
contr	contraction of
corr	corruption of
Cu	Cumberland
D	Devon
Db	Derbyshire
dimin	diminutive of
Do	Dorset
Du	Dutch (in etyms)
Du	Durham
Edd	*SED* editors
Eds	*LAE* editors
EME	Early Middle English
ENE	Early New English
Ess	Essex
etym dub	etymology dubious
f	from
F	French
famil	familiar form of
fem	feminine
foll	follow(s)
ft	foot, feet
fw	fieldworker
g	gesticulate
Gl	Gloucestershire
Ha	Hampshire
He	Herefordshire
HO	Harold Orton
Hrt	Hertfordshire
Hu	Huntingdonshire
i	imitate
I	Icelandic
im	incidental material
imp	imperative
in(s)	inch(es)
inc	included
inf	infinitive
interpr	interpreted
intr	intransitive
irr	irrelevant
K	Kent
L	Lincolnshire
L	lexical map (in map numbers)
La	Lancashire
LAE	*Linguistic Atlas of England*
Lat	Latin
Lei	Leicestershire
LME	Late Middle English
LOE	Late Old English
M	morphological map
Man	Isle of Man
masc	masculine
MDu	Middle Dutch
ME	Middle English
MED	*Middle English Dictionary*
MLG	Middle Low German
Mon	Monmouthshire
MxL	Middlesex and London
n	noun
Nb	Northumberland
nd	not defined
ndg	not defined grammatically
neg	negative
Nf	Norfolk
NME	Northern Middle English
npl	noun plural
nr	not recorded
Nt	Nottinghamshire
Nth	Northamptonshire
obs	obsolete
OE	Old English
OED	*Oxford English Dictionary*
OF	Old French
OI	Old Icelandic

ON	Old Norse
ONF	Old Norman French
onom	onomatopoeic
Ox	Oxfordshire
p	point to
perh	perhaps
Pg	Portuguese
Ph	phonological map
pl	plural
ppl adj	participial adjective
poss	possibly
pp	past participle
pref	prefers, preferred
pr	present
pres	presumably
prob	probably
pron	pronoun
prp	present participle
prt	present tense
pt	past tense
q	question
R	Rutland
r(r)	response(s),
r-col	*r*-coloured, *r*-colouring
rec	recorded
ref	refers to
rel	relative
repr	represent(s)
S	syntactical map
Scand	Scandinavian
Scot	Scots
Sa	Shropshire
SED	*Survey of English Dialects*
Sf	Suffolk
sg	singular
So	Somerset
Sp	Spanish
Sr	Surrey
St	Staffordshire
sw	suggested word
Sx	Sussex
V	vowel
v	verb
var	variant
vbl n	verbal noun
W	Wiltshire
Wa	Warwickshire
We	Westmorland
WM	West Midland
Wo	Worcestershire
Y	Yorkshire
*	hypothetical form
†	date first recorded in this sense in *OED/MED*
+	one response of two or more
1prsg	first person present singular
2prsg	second person present singular
3prsg	third person present singular
1prpl	first person present plural
2prpl	second person present plural
3prpl	third person present plural
3ptsg	third person past singular
2ptpl	second person past plural
3ptpl	third person past plural

LIST OF LOCALITIES

1 Nb
- 1 Lowick
- 2 Embleton
- 3 Thropton
- 4 Ellington
- 5 Wark
- 6 Earsdon
- 7 Haltwhistle
- 8 Heddon-on-the-Wall
- 9 Allendale

2 Cu
- 1 Longtown
- 2 Abbeytown
- 3 Brigham
- 4 Threlkeld
- 5 Hunsonby
- 6 Gosforth

3 Du
- 1 Washington
- 2 Ebchester
- 3 Wearhead
- 4 Witton-le-Wear
- 5 Bishop Middleham
- 6 Eggleston

4 We
- 1 Great Strickland
- 2 Patterdale
- 3 Soulby
- 4 Staveley-in-Kendal

5 La
- 1 Coniston
- 2 Cartmel
- 3 Yealand
- 4 Dolphinholme
- 5 Fleetwood
- 6 Pilling
- 7 Thistleton
- 8 Ribchester
- 9 Read
- 10 Marshside
- 11 Eccleston
- 12 Harwood
- 13 Bickerstaffe
- 14 Halewood

6 Y
- 1 Melsonby
- 2 Stokesley
- 3 Skelton
- 4 Egton
- 5 Dent
- 6 Muker
- 7 Askrigg
- 8 Bedale
- 9 Borrowby
- 10 Helmsley
- 11 Rillington
- 12 Burton-in-Lonsdale
- 13 Horton-in-Ribblesdale
- 14 Grassington
- 15 Pateley Bridge
- 16 Easingwold
- 17 Gargrave
- 18 Spofforth
- 19 York
- 20 Nafferton
- 21 Heptonstall
- 22 Wibsey
- 23 Leeds
- 24 Cawood
- 25 Newbald
- 26 Thornhill
- 27 Carleton
- 28 Welwick
- 29 Golcar
- 30 Holmbridge
- 31 Skelmanthorpe
- 32 Ecclesfield
- 33 Tickhill
- 34 Sheffield

6a Man
- 1 Andreas
- 2 Ronague

7 Ch
- 1 Kingsley
- 2 Rainow
- 3 Swettenham
- 4 Farndon
- 5 Audlem
- 6 Hanmer (Flintshire)

8 Db
- 1 Charlesworth
- 2 Bamford
- 3 Burbage
- 4 Youlgreave
- 5 Stonebroom
- 6 Kniveton
- 7 Sutton-on-the-Hill

9 Nt
- 1 North Wheatley
- 2 Cuckney
- 3 South Clifton
- 4 Oxton

10 L
- 1 Eastoft
- 2 Saxby
- 3 Keelby
- 4 Willoughton
- 5 Tealby
- 6 Wragby
- 7 Swaby
- 8 Old Bolingbroke
- 9 Scopwick
- 10 Beckingham
- 11 Fulbeck
- 12 Sutterton
- 13 Swinstead
- 14 Lutton
- 15 Crowland

11 Sa
- 1 Weston Rhyn
- 2 Prees
- 3 Llanymynech
- 4 Montford
- 5 Kinnersley
- 6 Chirbury
- 7 All Stretton
- 8 Hilton
- 9 Clun
- 10 Diddlebury
- 11 Kinlet

12 St
- 1 Warslow
- 2 Mow Cop
- 3 Alton
- 4 Barlaston
- 5 Ellenhall
- 6 Hoar Cross
- 7 Mavesyn Ridware
- 8 Lapley
- 9 Edingale
- 10 Wigginton
- 11 Himley

13 Lei
- 1 Harby
- 2 Hathern
- 3 Seagrave
- 4 Packington
- 5 Markfield
- 6 Great Dalby
- 7 Sheepy Magna
- 8 Goadby
- 9 Carlton Curlieu
- 10 Ullesthorpe

14 R
- 1 Empingham
- 2 Lyddington

15 He
- 1 Brimfield
- 2 Weobley
- 3 Cradley
- 4 Checkley
- 5 Longtown
- 6 Whitchurch

16 Wo
- 1 Romsley
- 2 Hartlebury
- 3 Hanbury
- 4 Clifton on Teme
- 5 Earls Croome
- 6 Offenham
- 7 Bretforton

17 Wa
- 1 Nether Whitacre
- 2 Hockley Heath
- 3 Stoneleigh
- 4 Napton-on-the-Hill
- 5 Aston Cantlow
- 6 Lighthorne
- 7 Shipston-on-Stour

18 Nth
- 1 Warmington
- 2 Welford
- 3 Little Harrowden
- 4 Kislingbury
- 5 Sulgrave

19 Hu
- 1 Warboys
- 2 Kimbolton

20 C
- 1 Little Downham
- 2 Elsworth

21 Nf
- 1 Docking
- 2 Great Snoring
- 3 Blickling
- 4 Grimston
- 5 North Elmham
- 6 Ludham
- 7 Outwell
- 8 Gooderstone
- 9 Shipdham
- 10 Ashwelthorpe
- 11 Reedham
- 12 Pulham St. Mary
- 13 Garboldisham

22 Sf
- 1 Tuddenham
- 2 Mendlesham
- 3 Yoxford
- 4 Kedington
- 5 Kersey

23 Mon
- 1 Skenfrith
- 2 Llanellen
- 3 Raglan
- 4 Cross Keys

5 Llanfrechfa
6 Shirenewton

24 Gl
1 Deerhurst
2 Gretton
3 Bream
4 Whiteshill
5 Sherborne
6 Slimbridge
7 Latteridge

25 Ox
1 Kingham
2 Steeple Aston
3 Islip
4 Eynsham
5 Cuxham
6 Binfield Heath

26 Bk
1 Tingewick
2 Stewkley
3 Long Crendon
4 Buckland
5 Coleshill
6 Horton

27 Beds
1 Turvey
2 Great Barford
3 Harlington

28 Herts
1 Therfield
2 Codicote
3 Wheathampstead

29 Ess
1 Great Chesterford
2 Belchamp Walter
3 Cornish Hall End
4 Henham
5 Stisted
6 West Bergholt
7 Little Bentley
8 High Easter
9 Tiptree
10 East Mersea
11 Netteswell
12 Little Baddow
13 Tillingham
14 Doddinghurst
15 Canewdon

30 Mx and London
1 Harmondsworth
2 Hackney

31 So
1 Weston
2 Blagdon
3 Wedmore
4 Coleford
5 Wootton Courtenay
6 Stogursey
7 Stogumber
8 Withypool
9 Brompton Regis
10 Stoke St. Gregory
11 Horsington
12 Pitminster
13 Merriott

32 W
1 Ashton Keynes
2 Sutton Benger[r]
3 Avebury
4 Burbage
5 Steeple Ashton
6 Netheravon
7 Sutton Veny
8 Fovant
9 Whiteparish

33 Berks
1 Buckland
2 Uffington
3 West Ilsley
4 Inkpen
5 Swallowfield

34 Sr
1 Walton-on-the-Hill
2 East Clandon
3 Coldharbour
4 Outwood
5 Thursley

35 K
1 Stoke
2 Farningham
3 Staple
4 Warren Street
5 Denton
6 Goudhurst
7 Appledore

36 Co
1 Kilkhampton
2 Altarnun
3 Egloshayle
4 St Ewe
5 Gwinear
6 St Buryan
7 Mullion

37 D
1 Parracombe
2 Swimbridge
3 Weare Giffard
4 Chawleigh
5 Gittisham
6 South Zeal
7 Kennford
8 Peter Tavy
9 Widdicombe
10 Cornwood
11 Blackawton

38 Do
1 Handley
2 Ansty
3 Whitchurch Canonicorum
4 Portesham
5 Kingston

39 Ha
1 Hatherden
2 Oakley
3 King's Somborne
4 Alresford
5 Hambledon
6 Burley
7 Whitwell (I. o. W.)

40 Sx
1 Warnham
2 Harting
3 Sutton
4 Fletching
5 Horam
6 Firle

THE INTERNATIONAL PHONETIC ALPHABET

		Bi-labial	Labio-dental	Dental and Alveolar	Retroflex	Palato-alveolar	Alveolo-palatal	Palatal	Velar	Uvular	Pharyngal	Glottal
CONSONANTS	Plosive	p b		t d	ʈ ɖ			c ɟ	k g	q ɢ		ʔ
	Nasal	m	ɱ	n	ɳ			ɲ	ŋ	ɴ		
	Lateral Fricative			ɬ ɮ								
	Lateral Non-fricative			l	ɭ			ʎ				
	Rolled			r						ʀ		
	Flapped			ɾ	ɽ					ʀ		
	Fricative	ɸ β	f v	θ ð | s z | ɹ	ʂ ʐ	ʃ ʒ	ɕ ʑ	ç ʝ	x ɣ	χ ʁ	ħ ʕ	h ɦ
	Frictionless Continuants and Semi-vowels	w | ɥ	ʋ	ɹ				j (ɥ)	(w)	ʁ		
VOWELS								Front	Central / Back			
	Close	(y ʉ u)						i y	ɨ ʉ / ɯ u			
	Half-close	(ø o)						e ø	ə / ɤ o			
	Half-open	(œ ɔ)						ɛ œ, æ	ɐ / ʌ ɔ			
	Open	(ɒ)							a / ɑ ɒ			

(Secondary articulations are shown by symbols in brackets.)

Other Sounds.—Palatalized consonants: ƫ, ᶁ, etc.; palatalized ʃ, ʒ: ᶋ, ᶾ. Velarized or pharyngalized consonants: ɫ, ᵭ, ᵶ, etc. Ejective consonants (with simultaneous glottal stop): p', t', etc. Implosive voiced consonants: ɓ, ɗ, etc. ɼ fricative trill. σ, ƍ (labialized θ, ð, or s, z). ʅ, ʓ (labialized ʃ, ʒ). ʇ, ʗ, ʖ (clicks, Zulu *c*, *q*, *x*). ɺ (a sound between r and l). ŋ Japanese syllabic nasal. ɧ (combination of x and ʃ). ʍ (voiceless w). ɩ, ʏ, ɷ (lowered varieties of i, y, u). ɜ (a variety of ə). ɵ (a vowel between ø and o).

Affricates are normally represented by groups of two consonants (ts, tʃ, dʒ, etc.), but, when necessary, ligatures are used (ʦ, ʧ, ʤ, etc.), or the marks ͡ or ͜ (t͡s or t͜s, etc.). ͡ ͜ also denote synchronic articulation (m͡ŋ = simultaneous m and ŋ). c, ɟ may occasionally be used in place of tʃ, dʒ, and ƾ, ƻ for ts, dz. Aspirated plosives: ph, th, etc. r-coloured vowels: eɹ, aɹ, ɔɹ, etc., or eʴ, aʴ, ɔʴ, etc., or ᶒ, ᶏ, ᶗ, etc.; r-coloured ə: əɹ or əʴ or ɹ or ᶕ or ɚ.

Length, Stress, Pitch.—ː (full length). ˑ (half length). ˈ (stress, placed at beginning of the stressed syllable). ˌ (secondary stress). ˉ (high level pitch); ˍ (low level); ˊ (high rising); ˏ (low rising); ˋ (high falling); ˎ (low falling); ˆ (rise-fall); ˇ (fall-rise).

Modifiers.—˜ nasality. ̥ breath (l̥ = breathed l). ̬ voice (s̬ = z). ʻ slight aspiration following p, t, etc. ̫ labialization (n̫ = labialized n). ̪ dental articulation (t̪ = dental t). ˙ palatalization (ż = ʑ). ̣ specially close vowel (ẹ = a very close e). ̨ specially open vowel (ę = a rather open e). ˔ tongue raised (e˔ or ẹ̝ = ẹ). ˕ tongue lowered (e˕ or ę̞ = ę). ˖ tongue advanced (u˖ or u̟ = an advanced u, t̟ = t̪). ˗ or ˍ tongue retracted (i˗ or i̠ = ɨ˖, t̠ = alveolar t). ˒ lips more rounded. ˓ lips more spread. Central vowels: ï (= ɨ), ü (= ʉ), ë (= ə˔), ö (= ɵ), ɛ̈, ɔ̈. ̩ (e.g. n̩) syllabic consonant. ˘ consonantal vowel. ʃˢ variety of ʃ resembling s, etc.

The phonetic symbols used by the Survey's fieldworkers and editors are drawn from the International Phonetic Association's chart reproduced above by kind permission of the Association. It should be noted that the Survey departs from the practice of the Association by employing the symbol [ɽ] to denote a retroflex frictionless continuant, the corresponding IPA symbol being [ɹ].

INTRODUCTION

THE ENGLISH DIALECT SURVEY

In the summer of 1945 Harold Orton received from Eugen Dieth, of the University of Zurich, a letter resuming correspondence which had been interrupted by the Second World War.[1] Beside miscellaneous news of his own activities and enquiries about those of friends and academic acquaintances in Britain, Dieth wrote:

> I hear[2] the idea of a linguistic atlas of England etc. has not been given up, although conditions in the meantime have not improved. On the contrary, the 6 years of war and mixing of peoples must have ploughed up a good deal of the linguistic ground.... Will you tell me what steps you have taken so far towards launching the scheme?

The letters exchanged between them in the following months, in the course of which Orton responded positively to an offer by Dieth to visit England and cooperate in the project,[3] effectively laid the foundations of this atlas and the English Dialect Survey which necessarily preceded it.

Dieth's allusion to an earlier atlas proposal relates immediately to the outcome of Hans Kurath's remarks in a paper delivered on 22 July 1935 to the Second International Congress of Phonetic Sciences held at University College, London. Discussing the historical background of New England speech, Kurath said:

> Unfortunately the lines leading back to the Mother Country, to England, and to Northern Ireland, will remain vague and tentative until a linguistic atlas of the British Isles is made,... for the great majority of colonists of the seventeenth century, whose descendants remained the most influential element in America during the eighteenth century and after, did not speak the cultivated speech of London, but various English dialects or provincial standards. These we know only very imperfectly through contemporary evidence. They must be reconstructed very largely on the basis of a linguistic atlas of English folk speech of the present day.[4]

Kurath was in fact reviving an earlier plea of Joseph Wright's, the editor of the *English Dialect Dictionary* (1898–1905). In 1923—when Orton incidentally was in close touch with him[5]—Wright had observed that in the current state of knowledge only an approximate classification of Middle English dialects could be made because it was impossible

> ... to fix the exact boundaries where one dialect ends and another begins. Nor shall we ever be able to remedy this defect until we possess a comprehensive atlas of the modern dialects such as has been produced by France and Germany of their dialects. An atlas of this kind would enable English scholars to fix the dialect boundaries far more accurately than is possible at present.[6]

Wright was taking an even longer historical view than Kurath in suggesting that regional dialect boundaries in the past could be reconstructed on the basis of modern evidence; but both scholars were making substantially the same case.

Orton and Dieth both attended the 1935 Phonetics Congress, as did Wilhelm Horn of the University of Berlin, who in the course of the proceedings invited the Congress to hold its third meeting in the German capital. On the initiative of Horn and Kurath a committee, which included Orton, was formed to prepare a memorandum on a linguistic atlas of the British Isles;[7] but the invitation to Berlin was declined at the Business Meeting of the Congress on 26 July[8] and the atlas committee was in the gathering circumstances destined to be ineffective.

When Orton's and Dieth's correspondence was first renewed in 1945, the former was in the process of returning from wartime service with the British Council to his post in the University of Sheffield, where he was Lecturer in charge of the Department of English Language. His research interests, perhaps even more particularly than Dieth's, lay in the field of spoken English dialects, and had led to the publication of a study of the dialect of his native village of Byers Green[9] and later, when he was on the staff of Armstrong College, Newcastle (then part of the University of Durham), to the collection of an extensive corpus of material covering the whole of Northumberland and selected localities in County Durham.[10] He was about to start on the analysis and publication of this regional survey when his research was interrupted by the war.[11] Dieth for his part had worked in Scotland.[12] He himself had published a study of the dialect of Buchan[13] and later supervised the research of two of his students who, at Orton's suggestion,[14] undertook micro-studies of the phonology of Morebattle in Roxburghshire and Chirnside in Berwickshire,[15] villages in counties bordering on Orton's Northumberland–Durham survey. On returning to Zurich in 1927 Dieth had also taken an active part in dialect studies in Switzerland: he became one of the editors of

Schweizerdeutsches Idiotikon, the Swiss German Dialect Dictionary, sought to promote the use of dialects in official and semi-official business,[16] and later was influenced by the ideas of Swiss dialect geographers.[17]

Harold Orton and Eugen Dieth thus had in common the experience of research into varieties of dialectal English, the same kind of theoretical orientation as historical philologists, and an interest in linguistic geography. The congruence of their past investigations and present concerns made them natural collaborators in planning a new survey of spoken dialects, one of whose principal objects would be the production of a linguistic atlas of England.

Accordingly they arranged to spend a brief period together in Sheffield in the summer of 1946, when they discussed the broad principles of their projected investigation[18] and laid plans for the first of several lengthier meetings in the University of Leeds, to which Orton was about to move on appointment to the Chair of English Language and Medieval Literature. They also took steps to arouse the interest of other scholars in their proposals. Orton, who had been a member of the Philological Society since 1932, sponsored Dieth's membership and arranged that they should read a joint paper entitled 'A New Survey of English Dialects' at a meeting of the Society to be held on 6 December 1946.[19] This they duly did, and the Society's Council simultaneously resolved to set up a Planning Committee to promote such a Survey. Dieth also addressed a wider audience by putting together a long and persuasive article[20] in which he reviewed the work of A. J. Ellis and Joseph Wright together with subsequent monographs on English and Scottish dialects, presented a number of maps based on Ellis's collections from the 1870's and 1880's, and commented on the shortcomings of Ellis's and Wright's material from the standpoint of the linguistic geographer.[21] Meanwhile the Philological Society's Council continued its discussions and in March 1947 resolved that steps should be taken to conduct a pilot survey 'in a limited number of selected areas with a limited questionnaire' and to publish the results in a handbook 'which would contain a history of the subject, a critique of methodology, directions to fieldworkers, a questionnaire and model maps'.[22] This was intended to be the prelude to a more elaborate and comprehensive exercise. The Society appointed three Survey Directors and Handbook Editors, Harold Orton in Leeds, John Orr in Edinburgh, and C. L. Wrenn in Oxford, each of whom was to carry out the work in his own area of the country. It also undertook to try to secure funds for each Director to have a Research Assistant and money for fieldwork expenses. In accepting appointment as a Director and Editor, Orton informed the Secretary of the Society that he would 'have preferred to have gone straight for the chief goal' immediately but accepted that there might be good reasons for limiting the initial steps.[23] He also expressed his disappointment that Dieth had not been included in the Society's plans, an omission rectified three years later when the Council resolved 'that Professor E. Dieth and Professor Angus McIntosh' (who had been appointed to the Forbes Chair of English Language and General Linguistics at Edinburgh University in 1948) 'should be added to the list of Directors of the Dialect Survey.'[24]

The main contribution of the Philological Society to the development of both the English Dialect Survey and the Linguistic Survey of Scotland seems to have been that of providing moral encouragement initially. The Society was not in a position to finance the work from its own resources, nor apparently was it able to procure funds from elsewhere. In these early years, the finance for the development of the Linguistic Survey of Scotland came from the University of Edinburgh's quinquennial budget (derived from the University Grants Committee) and from the Carnegie Trust for the Scottish Universities, and likewise the English Dialect Survey was financed almost entirely from the budget of the University of Leeds.[25] The members of the directing Committee of the Scottish Survey, and Orton as Director of the English Survey, were primarily responsible to their own universities; and since the objectives and scholarly problems confronting each Survey differed—Edinburgh was also concerned with Gaelic—and these differences were reflected organisationally and administratively, the Philological Society was bound to recognise that the two surveys would develop independently. Thus eventually in January 1953 the Society's Dialect Planning Committee made its final report to the Council and declared the Society's formal responsibility to be ended.[26] By this time the English Dialect Survey's questionnaire had been published and the programme of fieldwork was well under way.

When Orton and Dieth met in Leeds in the summer of 1947 they had already agreed on a number of fundamental principles. Confronted with many varieties of spoken vernacular English, ranging from the conservative forms typical of rural communities, through the mixed dialects of country towns and larger cities, to Standard English (which in terms of pronunciation especially was itself being redefined within a larger range of acceptability than formerly), they decided to set as their objective the oldest kind of traditional vernacular. If, as Dieth had observed in his letter to Orton in July 1945, increasing physical and social mobility during the war years must have undermined the stability of regional dialects, it was clear that these influences, together with radio and television, would continue to accelerate the process in the years to come. Their primary aim therefore must be to compile a corpus of the oldest and most conservative forms of dialect speech, which would both demonstrate the continuity and historical development of the language and also serve as a historical baseline against which future studies could be measured. Specimens of these dialect forms would best be found in rural areas amongst the farming community. Furthermore, the material should be collected systematically throughout the country with a view to the compilation of a linguistic atlas. This would present a synchronic view of mid-twentieth century regional distributions; but the Survey would be designed inherently with a strong historical bias so that its material could be exploited in various kinds of diachronic analysis including, through further surveys in the future, the study of linguistic change from the 1950s onwards. Finally, the material should be collected by direct investigation, using a questionnaire in the hands of 'trained investigators working on the spot in each of the localities of a carefully chosen network',[27] so as to achieve the maximum comparability possible.

By the end of the 1947 summer vacation Orton and

Dieth had compiled the first version of their questionnaire, comprising 800 notions. This was tested in the field and found to be insufficiently rigorous in its control of the precise form in which the questions were put to the informants by the field-workers. It was therefore modified in form, revised and enlarged, and subjected to further tests and revisions until it reached the sixth and final version in which it is reproduced as 'A Questionnaire for a Linguistic Atlas of England' by Eugen Dieth and Harold Orton, in Orton's *Introduction* (1962) to the Survey's series of publications.[28] The questionnaire, which was designed to be linguistically comprehensive in that it elicits information about lexical, phonological, morphological and syntactical features, contains in its final form over 1300 questions. Of these, 387 are phonological, 128 morphological, 77 syntactical, and the remaining 730 mainly lexical in intent, though as the commentary on the maps in this atlas notes, these categories, while adequate for practical working purposes, are not by any means mutually exclusive. The questionnaire itself is divided into nine 'Books' or sections of which the first eight are thematic in subject-matter (the farm; farming; animals; nature; the house and housekeeping; the human body; numbers, time and weather; social activities) while the ninth (states, actions, relations) is specifically concerned with parts of speech and grammatical and syntactical structures. The subject-matter of the questionnaire reflects the ordinary daily life and environment of the English countryman to whom it was addressed; and since the fieldworkers were all trained in the use of the questionnaire by Orton, and most of them in phonetics by Peter MacCarthy, Head of the Department of Phonetics at Leeds, a high degree of consistency was to be expected in the recording of the informants' responses. These were written down by the fieldworkers in the alphabet of the International Phonetic Association in standard notebooks, primary responses in the left-hand column of each page while the right-hand column was used for 'incidental material'. The latter included eg exemplification of the responses in proverbial phrases or other idiomatic contexts, sketches to illustrate items of material culture for lexical referents, critical observations by informants on the currency or obsolescence of the response, and so forth. It should be noted that the depth of the incidental material varies considerably from item to item, fieldworker to fieldworker, and locality to locality. The written field recordings, strictly controlled by the questionnaire, were supplemented after 1952 by tape-recordings of free conversation by the informants, usually on the subject of farmwork but sometimes on memories of incidents in childhood, the celebration of seasonal festivities, and local customs. Although ideally the questionnaire interviews should have been tape-recorded after the Survey acquired its first instrument, financial considerations made this impossible.

The field survey was undertaken mainly between 1950 and 1961, when altogether eleven people were engaged in investigating 313 localities throughout England. Stanley Ellis, the principal fieldworker, was responsible for 118 localities and also for the major part of the Survey's sound-recording programme. The other fieldworkers, listed alphabetically, were Michael V. Barry (27 localities plus 2 shared), Howard N. Bernsten (9), W. Nelson Francis (13), Peter H. Gibson (11), Marie Haslam (1), David Parry (3), Averil H. Playford (12), Donald R. Sykes (31), John T. Wright (48 plus 2 shared) and Peter Wright (38). The localities in which they operated were chosen on a combination of geographical and demographical characteristics. They are usually not more than 15 miles apart, and with four major exceptions preference was given to villages with a fairly stable population, normally around 400–500 inhabitants, principally engaged in agriculture. The exceptions were Leeds, York, Sheffield and Hackney (London).

The selection of the informants was made with especial care. The fieldworkers were instructed to seek out elderly men and women—more often men, since women seemed in general to encourage the social upgrading of the speech of their families—who were themselves natives of the place and both of whose parents were preferably natives also. They were to be over 60 years of age, with good mouths, teeth and hearing, and of the class of agricultural workers who would be familiar with the subject-matter of the questionnaire and capable of responding perceptively and authoritatively. Guidance for selection in these terms may seem a trifle less rigorous than is desirable in the light of developments in sociolinguistic theory since 1950; but as Ellis has pointed out it provided in practice a remarkably taut control of the sampling and indeed comprehensive representation of a particular socioeconomic class at that period of English history. Since the questionnaire with its range of topics took some 18 hours to complete and the fieldworkers therefore normally used more than one informant to cover the various sections, they 'were almost always using as their informants all of those in a given locality who conformed to the criteria'.[29] The sample in effect represented virtually the total of 'a restricted social class most likely to have retained the oldest form of local speech'.[30]

When eventually the fieldwork was completed, the questionnaire responses yielded a harvest of over 404,000 items of information. The next step was to analyse and publish the data. Orton's original plan as outlined in 1962[31] was modified in some respects in subsequent years,[32] as indeed were the proposals for the Survey's atlas which he delivered as his Presidential Address to Section H (Anthropology) of the British Association for the Advancement of Science in 1970.[33] The first parts of this massive publication programme, however, were completed between 1962 and 1971, when an *Introduction* and Volumes I–IV (each in three separate parts) of the Survey's *Basic Material* were issued by Orton and various co-editors.[34] All this series was published for the University of Leeds by E. J. Arnold and Son, the noted educational publishers and printers.

Harold Orton has described his editorial practice for the *Basic Material* volumes in his *Introduction* and in the prefatory matter to each volume, to which the reader is referred for details. In brief, the editors were chiefly concerned with treating the primary responses to the questionnaire, supplementing them by reference to the incidental material, which is quoted where critically relevant, and to the sound-recordings, which provide precise evidence for the evaluation of the transcriptional practices of the individual field-workers. Any editorial modifications of the transcriptions in the recording books are fully noted in the *Basic Material* volumes, and simply represent the accommodation of the transcriptional practices of all the fieldworkers to a consistent phonetic model. In this sense the *Basic Material* volumes are, in Orton's description, 'factual'.[35] The responses to each questionnaire item are presented in the International Phonetic Alphabet in word-lists numbered according to the network of localities; and it is thus possible for the student to map the distribution, locality by locality, of any item in the *Basic Material*.

The implications of the patterns of distribution of these items, however, are matters open to interpretation; and whereas linguistic atlases on the model of Gilliéron's pioneering *Atlas Linguistique de la France*,[36] where all the information is displayed directly on the map, are, like the English Dialect Survey's *Basic Material* volumes, factual in their purport, the Survey's *Linguistic Atlas of England* is concerned with an interpretive presentation of a selection of these linguistic facts. The interpretation is essentially, and properly, that of the Survey's Director and chief editor, Harold Orton.

EDITORIAL AND CARTOGRAPHICAL PRINCIPLES AND METHODS

The English Dialect Survey's questionnaire was designed with two interlinked purposes in mind. Firstly, it should elicit information about the current dialectal usages of the older members of the farming communities throughout rural England; and secondly, this information, when mapped, should illustrate the nature of the regional distributions of those features of their speech which had persisted from ancient times. In editing the Survey's collections for the *Basic Material* volumes, Orton and his collaborators were at pains to give the data full and consistent critical treatment by referring to both the incidental material and the sound-recordings, so that the published results would be directly usable as a basis for the compilation of maps.

The responses to any one question, however, are often too varied and numerous for comprehensive display on a single map; and furthermore there are many items whose distributions form patterns so scattered and broken that little is to be learnt from mapping them beyond the fact that the distributions are indeed highly complicated. To transpose the IPA representations of such complex material into cartographic symbols and transfer these from numbered listings to points on a map would be merely to substitute one set of graphic conventions for another, and the resultant impression of the distributions would be too confused to be very meaningful: this cartographic technique is useful in maps of linguistic and other cultural data only when the types of the data are restricted in number and the distributional areas of each type are clearly distinct. When the data are complex, some process of selection is necessary if cartographic presentation is to be effective and useful. The main principles of selection adopted in this atlas are as follows: that the items should show contrastive features each with clear distributional areas; that these contrasts should illustrate aspects of the development of vocabulary, pronunciation, grammar and syntax; and that the maps, being selective and interpretive, should make a significant contribution to our understanding of the history of English dialectology and should also suggest topics and problems for further research.

To these ends we have chosen to present on our maps a generalised treatment of the material. The detailed variation in the Survey's recordings is considerable and, if presented narrowly, tends to obscure the general patterns of distribution. We have therefore, when considering the cartographic presentation of typological variation, frequently subsumed subtypes of the data (eg lexical compounds, variations in vowel nuance or vowel length) under more broadly defined main types when this makes for greater clarity and legibility. The detailed variation, however, is also presented in the atlas. Where a mapped form subsumes minor variants these are noted, with other significant information, below the map.

The distributional areas on the maps are delineated by isoglosses, ie boundary lines between two adjacent areas characterised by contrasting linguistic forms.[37] The isoglosses are drawn on a base map which shows the county boundaries (before the Local Government reforms of 1974) and the network of the Survey's localities. It should be noted that the localities have been numbered, county by county and locality by locality within each county, from north to south and east to west, using the English Place-Name Society's county abbreviations (except that Oxfordshire is abbreviated to Ox, not O); and these locality abbreviations and numbers are used both in the *Basic Material* volumes and in the atlas as a code for tagging questionnaire responses geographically for data retrieval. (Reference to the list above shows that eg the code 6Y 7 refers to Askrigg in Yorkshire, 33Brk 2 to Uffington in Berkshire, and so forth. These codes tag the footnote material on each map. In this connection, it should be noted that if the locality code incorporates a superscript plus sign, eg 6Y $^{+}$7, this indicates that the item is one of two or more responses at that locality, either in the basic material or the incidental material, which has been cited in footnotes as fully as practicable.)

The isoglosses are drawn midway between adjacent localities which show contrastive forms. Thus they do not so much mark clefts between two distributional areas as indicate transitional areas in which the contrastive forms meet or merge.

The maps carry both 'labelled' and 'unlabelled' areas, the labelled distributional areas being referred to the map legends either by numbers or in the case of the phonological maps by IPA symbols: these legends are printed on the top right of the map. Each labelled area on a map shows the distribution of a dominant linguistic form. An unlabelled area, on the other hand, contains no dominant linguistic form of significance to this particular map, though it may sometimes exhibit one or more stray forms, or outliers, from a labelled area. It may also, of course, contain dominant forms which, while irrelevant to the point being made on the map in question, are of importance in the context of a different set of contrasts displayed on another map. This is an obvious corollary of the selective process.

In presenting interpretive maps one sometimes has to make arbitrary decisions about where to draw isoglosses. It was Harold Orton's usual practice, though not his invariable one, to emphasize the older forms or those forms which showed the greater deviation from Standard English; and his co-editors have attempted to maintain his practice when translating the drafts to finished drawings. The map of

earth-closet L32b is an example of how this may be done. There are six distributional areas for the word **shit-house**, scattered from Devon in the South-West as far east as Suffolk and as far north as Yorkshire. This pattern suggested to Orton that the term was 'obviously once wide-spread.'[38] The isoglosses for these areas have therefore been drawn to emphasize this view, passing for instance between 6Y 15 and 6Y 18 so as to link up 6Y 17 and 6Y 22 with the larger area running north-east to the coast, and between 20C 2 and 28 Hrt 1/29Ess 1 to enlarge the impression of the distributional area by linking the two Suffolk localities to the group of localities further west. Instances of this kind of treatment will be found very occasionally elsewhere in the atlas: in each case the facts are clear, but the presentation is designed to suggest a particular interpretation of the facts.

It is essential that the reader should fully grasp a particular feature of our cartographic method, which Orton and Wright used also in their *Word Geography of England*. In labelled areas only, the locality dot on the base map represents the occurrence of the labelled form: thus in an area labelled 1 all locality dots denote that the fieldworker elicited form 1 in the map legend. If he did not, the dot is cancelled by a small St Andrew's cross, ×. Sometimes the fieldworker elicited an alternative response which occurs on the map in another distributional area with a different identifying label, say 2. In such cases, the map legend will incorporate a symbol after label 2, say ∩. The presence of form 2 at a locality in area 1 is shown on the map by printing the symbol ∩ centred on the dot: thus ⟁ denotes the existence of both forms at the locality, while ⊼ denotes that form 2 alone is found at this particular locality in the form 1 distributional area. Reference to any of the lexical maps will rapidly make the reader familiar with the convention: **tip** L8b is a simple example.

Occasionally more than one alternative to the labelled form may occur, in which case our normal practice is to place the second alternative symbol to the left of the first, the third—rarely found—above the first, and the fourth—rarer still—above the second. Thus one may find composite groups of symbols like

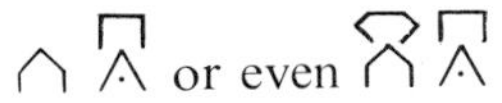

∩ Π/Λ or even ∩/∩ Π/Λ

though this standard arrangement has very occasionally been altered because of spatial restrictions on a given map.

There is one further point to be borne in mind. In unlabelled areas the only function of the locality dot is to provide geographical orientation: here the dot does not represent the occurrence of any particular form. But since the maps are concerned with the display of selected forms, if an outlier from a labelled area occurs at a locality in an unlabelled area, the appropriate symbol is printed at that locality. In unlabelled areas, however, the symbols are not centred on the dot but depend from it, the apex or central point of the top line of the symbol being placed on the locality dot so as to mask it. This convention is designed to help the reader to differentiate more easily between labelled and unlabelled areas, and is well illustrated on **stretcher** L4a and **trace-horse** L5a.

It is appropriate to mention here that the symbols used on the lexical, morphological and syntactical maps differ from those used on the phonological maps, which because of the greater complexity of the material are more numerous. Each set has its own logical progression of design. The simpler series is illustrated in its entirety in the legend for **brew** L42. As many symbols as are required are brought into use, always in the same sequence, on each lexical, morphological and syntactical map. In these sections of the atlas the symbolisation on each map has only an internal reference to that map legend. On the phonological maps on the other hand, the symbols, both IPA and others, have not only a fixed internal reference to the individual map legend, but also in general a constant external reference to all the maps in the phonological section. The symbols have been carefully devised to reflect, in their design and the way they face, the location of the vowels as represented on the chart of cardinal vowels in Daniel Jones's *Outline of English Phonetics*;[39] and while the complexity of some of the phonological maps has necessitated occasional departures from absolute consistency of practice, readers interested in this kind of technical problem may find in the design of these maps additional matter on which to exercise their critical ingenuity.

The lexical maps provide a suitable introduction to our editorial practice in the lay-out of the legends. The number for the labelled area, with a corresponding symbol where required, is followed by the selected form in capital letters. In the next line appears the etymology, and below that the first recorded date in English, prefixed with † if the date refers to the first instance of the word in the sense portrayed on the map. The etymologies are taken from OED and its available *Supplements*, with occasional references to MED which are always thus noted. For some ten words in the atlas the *Oxford Etymological Dictionary* supplies more modern etymologies than OED; but we have thought it best, for editorial consistency, to rely throughout on OED with its fuller historical documentation, even if its advice on etymology is now sometimes outdated. Words not listed in OED or MED are therefore not etymologised in the atlas.

On the lexical maps the words are normally listed in alphabetical order. Here again we have not felt we should be bound by inflexible rules when some freedom in ordering the entries makes for better display of the material. Thus in the legend for **goose-grass** L12b for example, items 3 and 4, **clide** and **clite,** are grouped together as monosyllabic responses, while 5–7, **cliden, clider** and **cliver,** are grouped as disyllabic derivatives. However, such departures from normal practice are rare, and the design of the legends should cause no difficulties in reading and assimilating the information on the maps.

The footnotes on each lexical map give full details of our practice in subsuming compounds or other variants under the form represented on the labelled distributional area, together with brief comments where necessary on the interpretation of the responses.

The map legends for the morphological and syntactical sections of the atlas follow in general the pattern of the lexical legends and should be self-explanatory, though a note on the ordering of the entries in the morphological section may be useful. These are presented according to a system devised by Harold Orton. In general, the Standard English response (as found in the headword above the map) comes first, and other forms are ranked according to the degree of their deviation from Standard, the items within individual sub-groups being ordered alphabetically. But the ordering is inevitably somewhat arbitrary because of the nature of the variations, as for instance in **dare not** M32, where it was thought appropriate to display the maximum variation of forms even though these are often of a phonological rather than morphological kind. Here the solution suggested by Orton was to attempt to relate the variations to the form from which each set has developed. Again, in **have got** M45 there are two distinct sets of forms, and it seems logical to list the material alphabetically within each set, while in **cursing** M56 and **doing** M57, for example, the order has been determined on the basis of phonological groupings.

Further comment is necessary on our editorial practice in dealing with the phonological maps. Reference has been made above to the accommodation of the fieldworkers' phonetic transcriptions to a consistent model in the *Basic Material* volumes and also to the practice in the atlas of subsuming minor variations under major forms when this leads to greater cartographic clarity. These editorial practices are of relevance to the legends on the phonological maps. Although further reference to the sound-recordings suggests that there may be room for reappraisal, the *Basic Material* transcriptions have been reproduced faithfully in the legends with two exceptions. These are /ɩ/ and /ɷ/ in stressed syllables, for which we have substituted respectively /i/ and /u/ on the assumption that these latter symbols used without length-marks sufficiently represent the vowels in question. In unstressed syllables, however, the fieldworkers frequently made a distinction between /ɩ/ and /i/, especially in the South, and clearly recognised a significant qualitative difference between them. We have therefore retained the distinction between /ɩ/ and /i/ on the maps in these instances.

The footnotes to the phonological maps report our practice in subsuming minor variation and follow the plan of the lexical footnotes. We suggest, however, that phoneticians who wish to make an even closer study of specific sounds should, if in doubt, also consult the relevant *Basic Material* volumes with their editorial preambles and the Survey's sound-recordings.

Some further details of editorial practice in compiling the phonological maps should also be noted.

Sporadic half-long vowels in a short-vowel enclave are regarded as conditioned shorts, but are treated as conditioned longs in a long-vowel enclave. Such instances are ignored in the footnotes. Marks indicating full length attached to the second elements of diphthongs with a considerable range of tongue movement are deemed to be negligible when they occur sporadically. They are therefore ignored on the maps, but are reproduced in the footnotes for information. Thus /əu:, au:, ɛu:/ and the like are mapped as respectively /əu, au, ɛu/. However, the lengthening of the second element in /iu:, iʉ:, jʉ:, iʏ:, jʏ:/ is thought to be sufficiently significant to warrant mapping as such. Occurrences of the short forms of these diphthongs are subsumed and listed in the footnotes.

Close diphthongs with a narrow range of tongue movement, with only marginal qualitative differences between the two elements, are regarded for mapping purposes as negligible variants of the syllabic vowels when lengthened and are therefore mapped as long vowels. Thus /ɩi, ɩi:, ᶥi:/ and /ɷu, ɷu:, ᵚu:/ are mapped as /i:/ and /u:/ respectively, without mention in the footnotes.

Close diphthongs with long first elements and short second elements qualitatively unlike the first, as eg /e:ᶥ, e:ɩ, o:ᵚ, o:ɷ/ are taken to represent long monophthongs in enclaves where such monophthongs are dominant. If, however, the enclaves are characterised by diphthongs, the close diphthongs are treated as being genuinely diphthongal, ie as /ei/ and /ou/ respectively (note the editorial substitution of /i, u/ for transcriptional /ɩ, ɷ/).

Long vowels followed by a centring off-glide are regarded as conditioned variants of the first element when they occur in long-vowel areas, or as full diphthongs in corresponding diphthongal areas. Thus /i:ᵊ, e:ᵊ, ɛ:ᵊ, ɔ:ᵊ, o:ᵊ, u:ᵊ/ in areas dominated by the first element are mapped as /i:, e:, ɛ:, ɔ:, o:, u:/. But when the dominating vowel elements are the diphthongs /iə, eə, ɛə, ɔə, uə/ the centring off-glide in question is mapped as the second element of a full diphthong without diacritics. However, when a long first element is the predominant form in an area it is mapped as such.

The maps are provided with footnotes which specify details of the evidence on which our interpretations are based. Evaluations of these interpretations may sometimes need to take account of the precise form in which the fieldworkers elicited the information. Accordingly we have listed the questionnaire items in Appendix 1 of the atlas: reference to this is important for some of the phonological and morphological maps in particular, as the context reveals whether the informant's response is enunciated with strong stress or with a significant degree of emphasis. Appendices 2 and 3 supplement the lexical section of the atlas, the first by adding a range of contextual information, usually of a semantic or sociolinguistic nature, the second by providing, for each headword in the lexical maps, a complete listing of those responses in the Survey's collections which have been ignored in the selection made for mapping. Each Appendix is introduced by an explanatory note.

PHONOLOGICAL MAPS

Vowels

In this discussion of maps illustrating the development of the ME phonological system, the chief aim is to call attention to the existing boundaries between the major dialects. Its three main sections deal firstly with stressed vowels, both in isolation and in combination with adjacent consonants, secondly with unstressed vowels, and thirdly with some of the more prominent consonantal developments. Although limitations of space necessarily curtail the discussion, the maps are fully representative of the principal features of the phonological evolution of English dialects.

MIDDLE ENGLISH SHORT VOWELS

ME a

Apples Ph1 and **carrots** Ph2 show that ME isolative **a** has undergone three main developments. In most of the country it appears as an /a/ sound, but in enclaves of considerable size in the South West, East Anglia and the Home Counties /æ/ regularly emerges; and in Kent the historical vowel in **apples** and **carrots** has been raised to /ɛ/.

Chaff Ph3 and **last** Ph4 clearly demonstrate that ME **a** before **s, f** and **th** respectively has mostly developed into a lengthened vowel in the southern half of England. In the northern half, however, it has retained its shortness.

Man Ph5 while in some areas testifying to the threefold development of ME isolative **a,** shows a quite different result in the West Midlands. Here OE **a,** which was normally rounded before **n** to an /ɔ/ sound, is seen to preserve its pre-Conquest rounding to this day. Yet the traditional sound is obviously under strong pressure from Standard English and is giving way to /a/, the local equivalent of Standard /æ/. **Wrong** Ph6 (a late OE loan from ON **wrangr*) and **among** Ph7 reveal divergent developments of considerable interest. The **a** sound in both words underwent rounding in OE. As with **man,** the vowel was unrounded again in the North and persistently retains this quality to this day. Elsewhere the rounding was not only maintained into ME but was intensified, with accompanying raising, into Modern English. Today both **wrong** and **among,** and especially the latter, testify to this widespread development in the West Midlands. It is noteworthy that in both cases the new **u** sound emerged early enough for it to be lowered and unrounded like the further development of ME **u,** namely to /ʌ/ (cf **butter** Ph50 and **tongue** Ph52). The change affected **among** to a much greater extent than **wrong** and its consequences are nowadays observable in both the South West and the South East.

Arm Ph11 and **arse** Ph12 exemplify the treatment of ME **ar**+ consonant and confirm that the group, except for **arm** in the extreme North, underwent the same further development as ME **er**+ consonant, see **darning** Ph19, **farmer** Ph20 and **farthings** Ph21.

Calf Ph9 and **half** Ph10 reveal substantial distributional variations separately and jointly and underline the point that each word has its own history.

ME e

Wednesday Ph13 is a typical example of the maintenance of ME **e** as an /ɛ/ sound when uninfluenced by neighbouring consonants. **Fellies** Ph15a,b gives evidence of an unexpected **a** sound as the present-day development of the **e** in the combination **el** preceding a vowel.

Darning Ph19, **farmer** Ph20 and **farthings** Ph21 all have **er** followed by a consonant in early ME. In late ME however, the **e** was lowered to an **a** sound and the group was then levelled with ME **ar** in the same circumstances. **Herrings** Ph22 is of interest because of the variations in the treatment, especially in the South-west Midlands, of ME **e** followed by **r** + vowel. The diphthong which occurs in a restricted measure in the North presupposes descent from the ME alternative with an unshortened **ē**. **Elm** Ph16a,b, **shelf** Ph17a,b and **twelve** Ph18a,b all display chiefly in the South East a diphthong of the /ɛu/ type derived from a ME parent form containing **el** followed by another consonant. The **l** has here become vocalised in the NE period. **Twelve** also shows the intermediate stage /ɛul/, cf also, for example, **silver** Ph28a,b, **bull** Ph53a, b, **wool** Ph54a,b, in all of which an etymological **l** has been similarly affected. **Buried** Ph23 shows that OE *byrgan,* which became ME *birien, berien* and *burien,* has undergone an unusual development in current vernacular, as indeed it has in Modern English.

ME i

Cinders Ph26, **thimble** Ph27 and **silver**[40] Ph28a,b demonstrate that ME isolative **i** has normally become, with only rare exceptions, short /i/.[41]

Third Ph30 and **birds** Ph31 show complex developments. Some of the present-day correspondences have long vowels both with and without *r*-colouring, and shortening in some has taken place in eastern England, apparently when the vowel was not affected by *r*-colour. The /ri/ forms of **birds,** however, do not add to this apparent confusion: they are all unmetathesised and derive direct from ME **brid**.

Only the disyllabic forms of **squirrel** Ph32 have been mapped here, the monosyllabic forms, which will be of special interest in the USA where they are frequently encountered, being listed in a footnote. The map reveals an extensive range of vowel nuances. **Light** Ph33, **night** Ph34, **right-**(handed) Ph35 and **sight** Ph36 all exhibit a consistent and well-defined profile and imply genuine and well-marked dialectal areas.

ME o

Bonnet Ph37 and **holly** Ph38 exemplify the survival of ME isolative **o** as a short vowel of the /ɔ/ type. On the other hand, **fox** Ph39 exhibits not only the same general pattern of short vowels, but also the development of a lengthened, as well as an unrounded, vowel in east Norfolk and again on both sides of the Upper Severn Estuary. Similar features, though more extensive, are found in **dog** Ph40. **Colt** Ph41a,b and **gold** Ph42a,b show more or less the same picture, implying that the parent vowel in the **gold** forms was, with one recorded exception, short **o** in the OE period. The present-day representatives of **yolk** Ph43a,b,c present a bewildering complexity of forms.

Off Ph44, **cross** Ph45 and **broth** Ph46 all testify, with minor deviations, to the occasional appearance of a lengthened vowel in the northern half of the country. In the southern half the equivalent vowel is usually long, but a short vowel is evidently established in **cross** and **broth** in south eastern England.

Forks Ph47 shows a distinctive and perhaps typical distributional pattern of development which differs significantly from those of **corn** Ph48 and **ford** Ph49. In both of these words the existing confusion very likely depends upon the quantity of the vowel in the ME parent forms whether short **o** or long **ǭ,** which is due to lengthening in late OE. At first sight it looks as if the /uə/ forms in **ford** derive from ME **ǭ,** but the problems involved require investigation.

ME u

Butter Ph50 and **thunder** Ph51 both show with great clarity the division between the dialects in which ME isolative **u** has remained relatively stable as a close-round vowel and those in which it has been unrounded and lowered to an /ʌ/ sound. Roughly, in the North and North Midlands it appears as an /u/ sound, in the South Midlands as an /ʌ/ type. **Tongue** Ph52, however, in one respect reveals a curious and, on first hearing, an unexpected departure from the pattern noted above, namely the widespread occurrence of an /ɔ/ form in the Midlands, presumably a spelling pronunciation.

In **bull** Ph53a,b and **wool** Ph54a,b the historical sound has mostly been preserved, except in the South West where it has been fronted. In both words the final **l** has been vocalised in the South East.

Furrow Ph57a,b has undergone two types of development, one being disyllabic and characterised by a short stem vowel, the other being monophthongal. In the latter case the vowel element is usually long with *r*-colouring, or diphthongal with /ə/ as second element, which itself may sometimes evidence *r*-colour. Lastly, **worms** Ph58 probably illustrates the typical development of ME **ur** + consonant, whereas **cursing** Ph59 shows much complexity involving a variety of shortenings.

MIDDLE ENGLISH LONG VOWELS

The maps showing the distribution of the current representatives of ME long vowels reveal that two types of development must have taken place, namely the formation of both closing and centring diphthongs. ME **ī** and **ū** not unexpectedly became closing diphthongs, the first part of the sound in each case becoming unstable and then lowered, whereas the second part retained its quality, the resultant diphthong then becoming wider and subsequently, in some areas, a monophthong because of the weakening and eventual loss of the second element. The historical Northern dialects, however, provide an exception to the rule. Here the maps imply that NME **ū** remained a close-back vowel for a considerable time and only then became diphthongal through the increasing instability of the first part.

On the other hand, the more open front vowels developed in two ways. In some regions they became closing diphthongs through increasing the tension on the latter part of the vowel. The new glide sound became established as an /i/ or the like. In other regions they might become centring diphthongs as a result of decreasing the tension in the second part of the sound, the result being /ə/. The /ɛ:/ arising early out of ME **ā** was similarly affected. The back vowels also might develop into diphthongs of two kinds. One was closing, with an /u/ sound, or its further development, as second element; and the other a centring diphthong ending in /ə/.

The maps discussed below clearly demonstrate that the developments of the ME long vowels **ā, ǭ** and **ū** were quite different in the dialects of the North from those of the Midlands and South. These differences stand out more distinctly when the material for each vowel is presented separately on two maps. But in the case of **ā** it is obvious that the traditional pronunciations with /ɩ, ɩɛ, ɩa, ja/ and /ea/ (from earlier /ia/) are rapidly disappearing. Similarly, the /i:/ which probably represented ME medial **ā** fairly extensively in the North-west Midlands was rarely recorded.

ME ā

Spade Ph60 and **naked** Ph61 are our best examples of the development of ME isolative **ā** over the country as a whole. They expose the characteristic Northern forms more clearly than any of the other maps. The profile of **hames** Ph62a,b, however, is complicated by changes dependent upon the loss of the initial **h** and the consequent treatment of the following **ā** as an initial sound. The West Midland forms of **hames** presuppose **ǭ** as the stem vowel and are therefore irrelevant to the development of ME **ā. Grave** Ph63 and **bacon** Ph64 only occasionally reveal traditional Northern forms. The maps of **April** Ph65, 66 seem to disclose no regular Northernisms. The /iə/ forms recorded in a small north-eastern enclave (see Ph66) are more likely to be loans from Standard English with /e:/ that locally became /eə/ and subsequently /iə/. The forms with /a/ noted on the same map are attributable to early shortening. **Make** Ph69a,b and **take** Ph70a,b also still exhibit traces of historical Northern forms, but both have characteristic short vowels in the upper half of the country, namely /a/ and /ɛ/, the former being the more northerly. The treatment of ME final **ār** is illustrated in **hare** Ph68, which seems to reveal traditional usages only in the North-west. **Waistcoat** Ph71a,b is included especially for its evidence of the extensive use of its shortened stem vowels, /ɛ/ being most frequent. But traditional /iə/ forms still persist in the North.

ME open ę̄ (/ɛ:/)

ME open **ę̄**, formerly contained in **beans** Ph72, **grease** Ph74 and **team** Ph75, has provided four differentiating features. In the extreme North it has become an /i:/-sound, thus evidencing present-day levelling with ME close **ẹ̄**. A little further south it appears as /ɛi/, thus differing from the concurrent /i:/ from ME close **ẹ̄**. In the South West and South-west Midlands it has produced both /e:/ and /ɛi/, the /ɛi/ apparently being a differentiating characteristic. Unexpectedly, **east** Ph73 exhibits /i:/ in almost the whole of the South and in the West Midlands, probably due to Standard English influence.

Peas Ph76 and **pea** Ph77 manifest the same vowel nuances throughout. The OE etymon *pise* may be assumed to become *pēse* in the North through lengthening and lowering in an open syllable, and apparently in the East Midlands too. This new **ę̄** would presumably become /i:/ in current vernacular, but not /iə/ or /ɛi/. These latter vowels presuppose ME open **ǭ** (from OE *peosan, piosan, pisan*).

In view of both origin and late entry into English, **tea** Ph78 might well be expected to reveal confusing variations in pronunciation, but the regional source of the present Standard pronunciation can scarcely be doubted, while the older Standard pronunciation /te:/ still occurs frequently in the vernacular.

Speaks Ph79 and **meat** Ph81 both had open **ę̄** in ME derived from short **e** lengthened in open syllables. They exhibit more or less the same vowel patterns of today. So does **eat** Ph80 with a similar earlier history in ME, though the present forms with initial /j/ in the West Midlands might seem to deny this assumption. However the consonant obviously derives from earlier initial /i/. The closing diphthong /ɛi/ in both south Lancashire and south-west Yorkshire is obviously exceptional and characteristic. These pronunciations distinguish the dialects in these localities most sharply from these in adjacent areas. They consequently presuppose a development entirely different from that which gave rise to /iə/ from the ME open **ę̄** that normally arose from OE **ēa** and **ǣ** (the i-mutation of **ā**). The southern forms of **meal** = flour Ph82a,b seem perplexing only because of the diphthong influence of the thick **l** which gave rise to a strong glide sound between itself and the preceding vowel (cf **wheel** Ph100a,b.)

The ME vowel **ę̄** in **break** Ph85a,b, **drain** Ph86 and **great** Ph87a,b shows an exceptional change to /ei/ in

Standard English: /i:/ would have been normal. This fact alone is sufficient to add to the special interest of the corresponding treatment in the regional dialects. These maps demonstrate that the three words in question have undergone more or less identical developments, although the short vowels often found in **break** and **great** obscure the picture. In the case of **great** the metathesized forms are evidently derived from a ME base containing short /ɛ/ from earlier /ɛ:/ (from OE **ēa**).

The map of **dead** Ph88 is included because it suggests the relationship between the many present-day correspondences of the ME stem vowel. On the other hand **deaf** Ph89 is readily intelligible, but the reader will note that in an extensive area stretching southwards from the northern counties, but excluding the South West, the ME open **ę̄** has been shortened to /ɛ/, thus accounting for the presence of this vowel in the Standard pronunciation.

The map of **fleas** Ph90a,b presents intricate problems. The existing forms with short /ɛ/ point back to a ME stem *fleh-* (shortened from OE *flēah*), in which the final consonant later became either /f/ or /k/, whereas the /ɛn/ form presupposes ME *flen* shortened from *flēn*, representing the OE weak plural *flēan* (earlier *flēahan*). The pronunciations ending in /z/ seem to descend from the OE *flēah* + -ES. The gap in the Yorkshire material results from the occurrence of the Scandinavian loanword *lop*.

Heat Ph91 exhibits features usually found in words formerly containing ME **ę̄**, but the forms with initial prosthetic /j/ are noteworthy. **Sheaf** Ph92 at first sight seems puzzling until it is realised that the apparently abnormal forms in both the West Midlands and East Anglia have a Dutch source.

ME close ẹ̄ (/e:/)

The forms of **geese** Ph93, **green** Ph94, **cheese** Ph95, **weeds** Ph96 and **creep** Ph97 all tend to demonstrate that ME **ẹ̄** uninfluenced by neighbouring sounds was normally raised throughout the country to /i:/ and that this sound is in process of changing into an upgliding diphthong which is becoming wider. In the South, however, a wellmarked deviation in /e:/ emerges. Comparisons with the dialectal treatment of ME open **ę̄** clearly show that both **ẹ̄** and **ę̄** are represented by an /i:/ sound not only in a broad belt stretching from coast to coast in the far North, but also—and very significantly for the history of Standard English—in most of the East Midlands and South. ME final **ẹ̄** in **see** Ph99 has developed like ME isolative **ẹ̄.**

The vowels in **week** Ph98 presuppose two separate paths of change, one from ME **ẹ̄,** the other from ME **i,** which vowel seemingly underwent no lengthening in the ME period. The long /i:/, as one would expect, is dominant in the North, and the short /i/ both in the West Midlands and in the South. The forms of **wheel** Ph100a,b may at first sight seem strange. They often show an ingliding diphthong of the /iə/ type, and in the South /iu/ appears. No doubt the cause is the final **l,** which is actually absorbed by the new /u/ south of the London area.

ME long ī

Ice Ph103, **knife** Ph104 and **white** Ph105, all of which in ME had a long **ī** sound followed by a voiceless consonant, have obviously followed the same path of change which, in most respects, is identical with that taken by old **ī** before a voiced consonant. As we may expect, the products are mostly closing diphthongs. South-eastern dialects then retract and round the first element of the diphthong /ai/; other dialects, namely in the North and the South West, display a tendency to monophthongise the closing diphthongs mentioned above. **Sky** Ph111, in which the ME vowel occurred finally, testifies to the same development as that of the vowel when medial.

Fire Ph112 illustrates the treatment of ME **ī** affected by final **r. Blind** Ph109 and **find** Ph110, except in the North, also exemplify the normal development of **ī** medially. The Northern short vowel /i/ points back to ME **i**. This obvious current contrast of short vowel versus a diphthong, or more recently developed monophthong, provides a significant distinction between Northern and non-Northern vernacular English.

Died Ph113, **eye** Ph114, **flies** Ph115 and **thigh** Ph116 all exhibit a convincing unanimity of vowel sounds which points to the existence of two different bases in ME. One had **ẹ̄h** or **ẹ̄g**(-); the other had **ī.** The former, with **ẹ̄,** characterised the North; the latter, with **ī,** was non-Northern. The **ẹ̄** became /i:/ with loss of **-h** or **-g**; and the **ī** became the diphthongs /æi, əi, ai, ɑi, ɒi/. It is evident that present-day /i:/ is losing ground in these words, presumably under Standard English pressure. The form /i:n/ Ph114 is evidently firmly entrenched in Northern English. In a restricted enclave embracing parts of Suffolk and Essex, the forms of **mice** Ph117 and **lice** Ph118 demonstrate undoubted descent from ME precursors containing **ẹ̄.** Thus ME **ẹ̄** is derived from OE **ȳ,** a change that is a well-known feature of south-eastern English. Otherwise the patterns of distribution are like those of any other reflex on ME **ī.**

ME long ǭ (/ɔ:/)

ME **ǭ** had two main sources. One was OE **ā,** the other OE and OF short **o** that underwent lengthening in EME open syllables in disyllabic words. OE **ā** in the North pursued an independent course: it survived as an unrounded vowel and absorbed the long **ā** that arose from OE and OF short **a** through lengthening in open syllables in disyllabic words. Further, it is evident from its subsequent history that this EME short **o** in restricted and adjacent parts of South Lancashire and South Yorkshire did not become merged with the open **ǭ** that normally arose from OE **ā** by rounding (see below). In the case of words formerly containing long **ā** in OE the material is best displayed on separate maps, one concerned with ME **ǭ** and the other with ME **ā.** This has been done here.

Both Ph119a,b, **comb** Ph120a,b, **loaf** Ph121a,b and **spokes** Ph122a,b exemplify the treatment of ME open **ǭ.** In many respects the developments of **both** and **loaf** in the non-Northern regions are seen to be very similar. Nevertheless the traditional sound /iə/ in eastern Yorkshire and /jɛ/ to the north in Northumberland is clearly being supplanted by /uə/ that originates from the North-east Midlands. On the other hand in the western parts of the North **comb** has clearly abandoned its historical forms.

Oak Ph124a,b strikingly preserves traditional Northern forms. **One** (the numeral) Ph125a,b is highly complicated, but the division between the Northern and non-Northern regions is well-marked. In this latter area the /w/ forms showing many vowel nuances are wide-spread. The Northern form of the adjective **one** Ph126b without final /n/ is distinctive. **None** Ph128a,b is notable on the one hand for its preservation, in the North, of /iə/, which in the same region normally represents ME **ā**, and on the other for the frequent vowel shortenings, in this respect often resembling **one** without prothetic /w/. The vowels in **once** Ph127a,b corresponding to ME **ā** are very like those of the numeral **one** Ph125a,b.

Home Ph129a,b,c,d exhibits non-Northern forms with prothetic /w/ which no doubt became established after the loss of the initial **h.** Similarly in the North the disappearance of the **h** seems to have consolidated the /ja/ and /jɛ/ forms. The shortened vowels in the East Midlands and East Anglia are notable; some of them presuppose that here ME **ǭ** became /u:/ first and was then shortened. OE final **ā** as represented in the North by **toes** Ph130a,b displays in the most northerly areas exceptional vowel counterparts. **Two** Ph131a,b also had final **ā** in OE and indicates an involved history that in non-Northern areas has been complicated by the preceding **w.** In the North, however, the **w** has survived.

The mapping of **cold** Ph132a,b,c and **old** Ph133a,b,c, has presented difficulties, not only because of the well-defined differences in the treatment of LOE *-āld* in Northern and non-Northern areas but also because of the evident infiltrations of non-indigenous forms both from neighbouring dialects (as in the North East) and from early and current Standard English. Thus the Survey's material enables us at present to do no more than hint at the nature of the distribution of the phonological development of LOE-*āld,* and these maps should therefore be treated with caution.

ME long close ọ̄ (/o:/)

Boots Ph138, **goose** Ph139, **moon** Ph140, **roof** Ph141, **foot** Ph143 and **school** Ph144a,b together demonstrate convincingly how the ME stem vowel concerned, namely long close **ọ̄**, has developed dialectally. Moreover the boundary between traditional Northern and non-Northern forms emerges very clearly: in the traditional Northern dialects close **ọ̄** normally appears medially as /iu, iʏ, iə/. Further, a very unusual diphthong /ui/, difficult enough in this context to explain historically,[42] is still firmly established in South-west Yorkshire. A long fronted vowel /ʏ:/ is also observable: it is doubtless regularly descended from /u:/ from ME **ọ̄**. The long close central /ʉ:/, a stage in the path of development from **ọ̄** to /ʏ:/, survives in Norfolk and to a certain extent in the Central Midlands. Under the influence of the final **l** in **school,** a schwa has set in after the vowel element in two distinct enclaves. **Hoof** Ph142 is additionally characterised by a shortened vowel-sound in the Midlands.

The forms of **floor** Ph145 have proved unusually difficult to classify, but those containing /iə/ and /iu:ə/ are undoubtedly genuinely Northern. Further, **door** Ph146 may reasonably be included here for comparison with **floor** because the present-day vowel sounds in both are essentially the same, though the ME bases concerned, except in the North, had dissimilar vowels.

Plough Ph147, in respect of its /iəf/ form, shows the normal development of ME final **-ọ̄h,** the **h** being represented by /f/. The /u:/ form apparently descends from **ọ̄h** via late ME **ūh,** whereas the /iu/ type derives from a late ME **iu** from earlier **-ọ̄ȝ-** which arose in the oblique cases. The /au/ type and its derivatives /æu, œu/ point to the same development as that of ME **ū. Boughs** Ph148 is probably not as perplexing as it seems. The assumption of a LME base in **-ū-** regularly developed from uninflected **ọ̄h** would probably explain all the various forms except the Yorkshire /iu/, the source of which is doubtless ME **ew, iw,** normally developed from ME **ọ̄ȝ-**.

ME long ū

House Ph149, **louse** Ph150, **snout** Ph151 and **clouds** Ph152 exemplify the vernacular developments of ME **ū** medially. They reveal that the dialects of the North East have in general preserved its monophthongal quality, or almost so. Indeed, the maps demonstrate that the on-glide of the vowel is beginning to establish itself as a distinct /ə/, thus pointing to late diphthonging. In the non-Northern dialects, however, it is equally clear that the diphthonging of old **ū** is early, has given rise to wide diphthongs, and is extensive. Moreover, in some areas in the North-west Midlands these diphthongs have even become monophthongs again. One sizable enclave in the same general area is outstanding for the presence of a diphthong of the /ai/ type. On the other hand, in some localities in the South-west Midlands ME **ū** seems to have remained relatively unchanged. ME final **-ū,** as represented today by **cow** Ph154, apparently developed like **ū** medially. Yet no /ai/ forms were recorded.

Drought Ph153 shows several vowel variants quite unlike the normal correspondences of ME medial **ū.** In two of its enclaves the final consonant in the OE etymon *drūgað* is now represented by /f/. Further, the old long vowel has apparently been shortened to /ɔ/ and later lengthened to /ɔ:/ before the **f,** a normal process in the southern half of the country.

Flour Ph155, **flowers** Ph156 and **hour** Ph157, though exhibiting a complexity of vowel correspondence for which *r*-colouring is largely responsible, show much the same profile. If the schwa-component is ignored, it accords with that characterising ME **ū** medially.

ME ai (ei)

Daisy Ph159, **faint** Ph160, **rain** Ph161 and **tail** Ph165a,b all exhibit the development of ME medial **ai.** Their sound patterns are essentially identical. All of the items point to the levelling of ME **ai** with ME **ā,** and all reveal the existence of a fairly large enclave in the North-west Midlands where the diphthong is still represented by /i:/. It should be recalled that ME **ā** has also given rise to /i:/ forms, but the enclaves in question are much smaller. It should be noted that part of the Northern evidence for **rain** Ph161 is not available because in the initial stages of the Survey the fieldworkers were required to elicit only **began.** After August 1953 they were asked to elicit the complete phrase **began to rain.**

The verb **lay** Ph163, which in ME times contained **ai** finally, shows the same picture, including the /i:/-enclave. So does **lay** Ph163, when recorded as the 3rd singular past tense of **lie. Key** Ph162, **whey** Ph166 and **weak** Ph168 have obviously undergone very complicated changes. The pronunciations of **weak** with /e:/, /ɛ:/ and /iə/ require further investigation, whereas the wide distribution of the mapped /i:/ forms of **weak** indicates the source of the current vowel in the standard language. **Whey** Ph166 reveals perplexing nuances of vowel sounds, which contrast with those of the homophonous **weigh** Ph167. The forms of **chair** Ph169 are equally confusing, the *r*-colouring adding to the problem.

ME au

The development of ME **au** is only sparsely exemplified in our material. Yet **saw**-(dust) Ph170 and **slaughter**-(house) Ph171 exhibit much the same profiles, the vowel /ɔ:/ dominating the whole country except in two main areas. In the West Midlands the newly developed /ɔ:/ sound has been unrounded, and further has sometimes acquired *r*-colouring by analogy; and the North East favours the monophthong /a:/ as an alternative to /ɔ:/.

Straw Ph172 displays the same, presumably the normal, development of ME **au** as exemplified by **saw**-(dust) and **slaughter-**(house) discussed above. It should be noted, however, that in the four most northerly counties, the current forms presuppose a base containing ME **ā**, the source of which is ON *strá*.

Thawing Ph173 has evidently had a curious history since the OE period. The North continues to employ an /a:/ or its derivative /æ:/, as well as /ɒu/ and /ɑu/ types, both of which point to ME **ou,** as in **daughter** Ph194. The non-Northern vowel-types, however, seem very confused and present a different appearance from that arising from ME **ǫu.**

Aunt Ph174 deserves mention. The northern half of the country prefers a short vowel, and the southern half a long vowel. The parent ME vowel is in each case **a,** though the Northern short /ɒ/ may prove to be a reduction of an earlier /ɔ:/ that normally developed from ME **au.**

ME eu

ME **eu,** which here includes both **ęu** and **eu,** has apparently undergone the same development in both **blue** Ph175 and **suet** Ph176. On the other hand **ewe** Ph177 has evidently undergone two developments, one of them presupposing ME **eu-**, the other pointing back to a ME **you,** with stress shifting. **Dew** Ph178 has also developed like **blue** and **suet** but, as will be seen, the combination of the /d/ and /i/ has partly obscured the normal profile. The South-west Midlands forms of **few** Ph179, 180 in /jau/ or the like seem well established and characteristic, but are difficult to account for historically. Forms without /j/ are also often found. The vowel qualities of the remainder are similar to those in words of the type under consideration.

ME iu

Only four words are available here to illustrate the treatment of ME **iu: new** Ph181, **suit** Ph182, **Tuesday** Ph183 and **tune** Ph184. **New** and **suit** may be assumed to exemplify the usual development, but **Tuesday** and **tune,** in respect of an initial combinative change, show a late departure from the norm. **New** and **suit** in general exemplify the retention of /iu/, but certain enclaves, more extensive in the case of **new,** have lost the first element of the diphthong and accordingly show /u:/ or its further development /ʏ:/. On the other hand, the original diphthong in **Tuesday** and **tune** has developed in three ways: first, /iu/ normally, second, /u:/ roughly in the same area as with **new** and **suit,** and third, the widely recorded /u:/, or its later development /ʏ:/, which remained after the preceding /i/ had combined with the initial /t/ to produce /tʃ/.

ME oi

The development of ME **oi** can be deduced from the history of three words, namely **boiling** Ph185a,b, **oil** Ph186a,b and **voice** Ph187. **Boiling** and **boil** both exhibit /bw/ forms which are detailed in the footnotes. The profile of **oil** is very much the same as that of **boiling.** But the final **l** of the former is occasionally seen to develop a schwa between itself and the preceding vowel, or else to became vocalised. **Voice** seems less involved than the other words, though the variant vowels emerging in the north-west Midlands are striking and presuppose the levelling of ME **oi** with old **ī.**

The word **onion** Ph188 has obviously had an exceptional evolution. It presupposes two types of vowel development, namely short monophthongs and diphthongs. The latter occur in the South-west Midlands and obviously derive direct from ME **oi.**

ME ou

Three maps, **mow** Ph189a,b, **snow** Ph190a,b and **throwing** Ph191a,b, all present the same general pattern and therefore show fairly consistently how OE medial **āw** has normally developed in vernacular English. In the North, **āw** became **au** in ME, whereas further south the long vowel was rounded to **ǭ** and then combined with **w** to produce **ǫu.** Northern **au** then changed sometimes to /a:/ or the like, but most commonly to /ɔ:/. Non-Northern ME **ou** on the other hand mostly remains as a diphthong in eastern England, but in the west it was extensively monophthongised. **Mow** and **snow** in a smaller enclave in the North West now display /u:/, and so call to mind the change of ME **ai (ei)** to /i:/. The vowel /ø:/ registered in the extreme North East presupposes earlier /o:/ and undoubtedly originated as an infiltration from Standard English.

Daughter Ph194 and **daughter-**(in-law) Ph195, so far as it was recorded, both show more or less the same vernacular development, but, surprisingly, this differs from the changes undergone both by ME **ǫu** from OE **āw** and by the ME diphthong resulting from the **ōw** in OE *grōwan,* the forerunner of **grow** Ph192.

Four Ph193 displays a great variety of vowel forms in a large number of small distribution areas. While the map shows this clearly enough, the effectiveness of cartographic techniques in demonstrating linguistic and other cultural data diminishes as the complexity of the variants and distributional patterns increases; and **four** with its many variants, like some other items in the Survey (eg the lexical responses for **left-handed** VI.7.13), would perhaps respond better to treatment by a detailed discussion supported by a series of maps in which related forms are grouped and contrasted.

Consonants

The historical development and modern distribution patterns of consonants, as expected, present a much less complex picture than that of the vowels. Nevertheless, a number of interesting consonantal features of regional speech are revealed by the Survey and their distribution is particularly amenable to the cartographic technique. The maps clearly demonstrate, for example, the persistence of the initial voicing of /f/, /s/,

/θ/ and /ʃ/ in the South West. The strength of this feature is best seen in **furrow** Ph215 where the voiced forms extend eastwards to Sussex and northwards to Herefordshire. The maps of **finger** Ph214, **from** Ph218, **Friday** Ph219, **saddle** Ph226, **seven** Ph227, **thigh** Ph232 and **thimble** Ph233, however, show that voiceless forms are well established in south-east Cornwall and also in other enclaves within the main area of voiced forms in the maps of **fleas** Ph216, **floor** Ph217, **sweat** Ph231, **three** Ph234 and **thread** Ph235. The standard voiceless forms are obviously gaining ground in **sure** Ph228, **snow** Ph229 and **swearing** Ph230, where the voiced forms are isolated in two or three small areas.

The maps of **hand** Ph220 and **hearse** Ph221 show that the initial aspirate, typically lost in English regional speech, is retained in three well defined areas: the extreme north, an area from East Anglia to north Sussex, and a smaller enclave in the South West. Initial /hw/ in **white** Ph223 is confined to the North East whereas in **wheel** Ph222 it extends west along the Border into north Cumberland and is also found in the Isle of Man. Here, as elsewhere, the graphic nature of the mapping technique makes for easy identification of individual and contrastive patterns of distribution.

In the maps of **rat** Ph224 and **red** Ph225 ME initial **r** is realised by four principal forms in the dialects: the velar /ʁ/ in the extreme North East, the retroflex /ɽ/ in the South West, the trilled /r/ in the Isle of Man (and also in the extreme North East in **red** Ph225), and the alveolar fricative /ɹ/ in virtually all the rest of England except for a small enclave in Somerset; here the glottal aspirate /h/ precedes the retroflex /ɽ/ in the map of **rat** Ph224.

Medial /d/ in **ladder** Ph236 is represented by /ð/ and occasionally /dð/ in several small enclaves in the Midlands and North. In **father** Ph237 and **mother** Ph238, on the other hand, medial /ð/ has virtually supplanted the /d/ and /dð/ forms which are still found in isolated enclaves in the extreme North West and in north-west Yorkshire and eastern Shropshire respectively. Medial /d/ also occurs in **father** Ph237 in much of Norfolk but here the consonant is sometimes lost altogether. In **butter** Ph239 medial /t/ is voiced to /d/ in the South West and in a very small enclave from mid-Cambridgeshire to north-west Essex. It is replaced by /ʔ/ in an area of the south-east Midlands and much of East Anglia while /tθ/ remains isolated in south Lancashire. The map of **finger** Ph240 graphically demonstrates the dominance of medial /ŋg/ roughly south of a line from the Humber to the Ribble, with the exception of an area of south-west Yorkshire and also the Isle of Man. **Hungry** Ph241 shows the /ŋ/ forms even more reduced, with a further /ŋg/ enclave in the extreme North East. In final position /ŋg/ in **tongue** Ph242 persists in a large area of the North-west Midlands and an isolated pocket in mid-Essex, while the plural form /ŋgz/ in **tongs** Ph243 continues in a smaller North-west Midlands area and in most of Kent.

The persistence of a variety of /r/ forms in late twentieth century English regional dialects is nowhere better demonstrated than in the pronunciation of final /r/ in unstressed syllables. Although **butter** Ph244 and **farmer** Ph245 both testify to the dominance of pronunciation without final /r/ in a broad band from northern Kent to the North West, three main variants of the consonant are strongly represented in other parts of the country. First, in the South West along the south coast /əʵː/ forms are dominant, while in Sussex, south Surrey and eastern Hampshire, and also in the south-west Midlands /əʵ/ forms are found, with isolated pockets of /r/-less forms in Monmouthshire and an area extending from Northamptonshire to south-east Gloucestershire. Second, /əʴ/ pronunciations continue in two small enclaves in the South East and also in the North-west Midlands and northern Lincolnshire. In east and north-east Yorkshire the /əʴ/ in **butter** Ph224 is evidently losing ground, though significantly less so in **farmer** Ph245. In both words the characteristic Northumberland /ɔʶ/ is still the normal pronunciation in most of the country, but a variant form /əʶ/ appears in a small area of south Northumberland and north Durham, perhaps representing a degree of compromise with standard /ə/. Final /l/ is 'clear' and syllabic in **uncle** Ph246 in the northern half of the country while in the south its syllabic forms are 'dark'. The labialisation in parts of the South East and the central South results either in the intermediate form /uɫ/ or the loss of the lateral altogether. The distribution of these forms in **weasel** Ph247 is more complex: the northern area has syllabic 'clear' /l/, though with considerable evidence of /əl/ forms. The southern half of the country is again characteristically dominated by syllabic 'dark' /ɫ/, with enclaves of /əɫ/ and /uɫ/, the latter resulting in loss of /ɫ/ in much of the South East. The Standard voiced affricate /dʒ/ is advancing at the expense of its voiceless equivalent in **cabbage** Ph248 but /tʃ/ still continues in the East Midlands, while the North has /ʃ/. The ME voiceless velar fricative in **drought** Ph249 has been lost in most of the county although /ft/ is still found in two very small enclaves, one to the west of the Thames estuary and the other on the Nottinghamshire-Lincolnshire border. The influence of the ME forms is also seen in the forms with final glottal stop recorded in an area of Buckinghamshire and south-eastern Oxfordshire, and the old pronunciation with /x/, noted at the foot of the map, is still within living memory in East Lancashire.

LEXICAL MAPS

Although the interpretation of phonological material is a central focus of the atlas, a representative selection of lexical, morphological and syntactical maps is included. In selecting the lexical maps from the full range of responses in the Basic Material the editors have borne in mind the 251 maps already published in *A Word Geography of England*, which concentrates on the lexis. The 80 maps of 65 notions have therefore been chosen to illustrate something of the range of variant forms and distributional problems revealed in the Survey. They cover a number of common items of vocabulary used by the countryman as he goes about his daily work or in his leisure hours—terms for buildings, gates and hedges, animals and their management, wild flowers, plants and insects, food, drink, clothing, for example. Many such items are of course to be found in other sections of the atlas, where they have been treated in their phonological and morphological aspects; and the reader can deduce from these maps further information about their distribution. In the lexical section, however, they are examined mainly from the standpoint of the variations in their origins and development from the different dialects of Old English, from Scandinavian loans in the period of Viking settlement, and from French, Dutch, Low German and other sources, the date of their entry into the language also being noted. Accordingly this selection of maps shows how some very old words are competing for survival, several others are evidently being replaced by words of foreign origin, a small number of Scandinavian words point to early Viking settlement, and a few words are derived directly from French, Dutch and Low German.

The lexical maps begin with expressions for **farmstead** L1, referring to the main buildings on a farm, but not to the fields. In this meaning the word **farm,** of French origin, is widespread not only as a simplex but also in the compound **farmstead,** prevalent in eastern England and the North West, but not the West Midlands or the South West. **Farm-house** is used somewhat restrictedly in both the East and West Midlands, as well as in the South West, but not in the North, where in the extreme North East the word **onstead** is used, which significantly the *English Dialect Dictionary* records mainly from Lowland Scotland.

Cartman L2 is itself rarely applied to the man in charge of the vehicles on the farm. The North on the whole uses **horseman,** but east Yorkshire seems to have abandoned it in favour of the Dutch loanword **wagoner.** Further north, in a comparatively restricted area, we find **cartman.** Still further north and east we encounter **hind,** of OE origin, heard frequently in Scotland and the North of England, but with the much wider meaning of 'farm servant' and (in northern England) of 'farm bailiff'. **Wagoner** is also favoured in the East Midlands, but further south the term **carter** is dominant.

The notion **stretcher** L4a,b, the wooden rod that prevents the traces from chafing the leading horse in a team, reveals at least four distinct and firmly established regional forms. The North, excepting the North West, employs the firmly established **stretcher,** whereas **spreader** dominates the whole of the region west of old Watling Street. East Anglia is the focal centre of **setstick,** with **cobble-stick** to the west in the North Midlands. A **trace-horse** L5b is the leader in a team of horses. The term itself is actually used in the North, but more especially in the east of the region, as well as in East Anglia and the South. A strong competitor is **chain-horse,** which prevails in the western counties as far south as the central West Midlands. Both expressions have as their first element words of French origin. However, they are late compounds first recorded only in the 19th century. Perhaps the most striking name is **gear-horse,** its first element evidently deriving from a Scandinavian etymon. A lesser known term is **forrest,** originally the superlative of **fore,** of OE derivation. This is restricted to a smallish South-east Midland region north of London.

The **tire** L7 of a cart-wheel is so called extensively in the South East and in the South-east Midlands and East Anglia. The word is derived from French. Further north, in the West Midlands and northern England, its chief competitor **hoop,** from OE, prevails. In the South West, **bond** is normal. This raises an important point about the value of linguistic cartography. When linguistic material is demonstrated graphically on maps, these often bring to light problems which escape notice when the items are presented orthographically; and the mapping of the response **bond,** like many other items in the Survey's data, reveals evidence for an alternative, in this case etymological, interpretation of the history of this form. Though OED suggests a Scandinavian origin for **bond,** the distribution area on the map is both sizable and far removed from the area of Scandinavian settlement. One might therefore, on the evidence of the map, presuppose an etymon from OE **bindan,** past tense **band,** rather than a Scandinavian loan. This map also reveals an interesting semantic development in that a very old usage **strakes,** formerly designating the individual sections of a tire, persists in a very small enclave in the central West Midlands where it now refers to the hoop tire which was introduced towards the end of the nineteenth century.

To **tip** L8a a cart in order to empty it quickly is mainly expressed by this word, which occurs throughout most of western England, the Central Midlands and down into the South East as far as Kent and east Sussex. Its origin is obscure, and so is its variant **tipe,** recorded in Lincolnshire. An alternative, **skell,** is well established further north, and in view of its form and distribution is probably of Scandinavian origin, while in the North East **cowp,** probably from French, is regularly used, as it is over the Border in eastern Scotland.

Dung L9 contrasts with **muck.** The former word is found mainly south of the Thames, whereas the Scandinavian form **muck** not only occurs in the North but has extended still further northwards beyond the Danelaw and, perhaps surprisingly, southwards right down to the Thames.

Couch-grass L10 derives its first element from OE *cwice*. This has given rise to many striking variants, all of which have well defined enclaves. The most extensively distributed are **twitch** in the East Midlands and North West, **wicks** in Yorkshire and Lancashire, and **wickens** in the North East. **Couch** is preferred in the South, excluding Devon and Cornwall. **Bindweed** L11a,b, or in its Latin designation convolvulus, denotes its chief characteristic, climbing tendrils, in its first element, while the synonymous **bear-bind,** a West Midland word, and **corn-bind** in the East Midlands relate this characteristic to particular cereal plants (bear = barley). In most of Norfolk the simplex **bind** suffices, while **withwind** and **withywind,** the first element meaning 'willow', are predominantly south-western.

Carting L14, referring to the conveyance of corn from the cornfield to eg the stackyard, has produced four main expressions. **Leading** is found in the North and North-east Midlands, **carting** in East Anglia and the South East, and **hauling** in the South West exclusive of Devon, where **saving,** apparently a very old usage from French, still survives.

Mole L26 shows a well-marked distribution of synonyms. **Want,** a native word, is widespread in a substantial area extending from Shropshire to Cornwall, excluding central Devon, but **mole**(-) and **moudy**(-), both ultimately of Low German origin, are deeply entrenched in the north West Midlands, Central Midlands, East Anglia and the South East, as well as northern England. A fourth synonym, **mould,** appears in widely separated enclaves in the Central Midlands and an area of Hampshire and East Dorset. It would seem that **mould** is under very strong pressure from the Standard **mole** which predominates in eastern England and is apparently extending northwards.

Ants L30 has produced a very distinctive contrast between its derivatives in (-)**ant** and (-)**emmet** (and variants). Both terms are derived from OE *aemete*. Compounded or not, (-)**emmet** is seen to be firmly established in southern England, whereas (-)**ant** dominates almost the whole of the rest of the country. Several small enclaves exhibiting compounds with a first element **piss,** 'from the urinous smell of an anthill' (OED), are scattered mainly in the old Danelaw or the neighbouring areas. The northern occurrences often have a second element from Scandinavian sources.

Threshold L31, which has an unusually complicated etymological and phonological background, exhibits three main enclaves. **Threshold** is mainly used in eastern England as far southwards as the Thames, with phonetic variants **drashold** and **dressol** in the South West. The differences of pronunciation in these forms, though minor, are such that they have become virtually separate words and are therefore so treated in the map: another typical example of this mode of interpretation is to be found in **freckles** L50a,b. An alternative synonym **threshwood** is well established in most of Yorkshire outside the West Riding, though it has been ousted by **threshold** in the North Riding. Northumberland shows the shortening **thresh.**

Kindling-wood L33a,b itself alternates with **kindling.** The latter has a Scandinavian first element, is widespread in the Danelaw, and is found in such widely separated areas as the north of the Welsh Marches and the extreme South East of England. **Kindling** compounded with **-wood** is found in a small enclave centred in south-west Yorkshire and also in a narrow band running from Berkshire to Sussex. The late date of the first recorded appearance of the compound (†1883) suggests that it has developed independently in these two widely separated areas. Other responses include **bavins,** of unknown origin, and the French loanword **faggots,** which occur in adjacent areas of the South East, while further west as far as south Cornwall the French word is often compounded with Old English to give **faggot-wood.**

A few terms concerning food and drink, revealing synonyms with well-marked enclaves, may be mentioned here.

Sad L35a,b, applied to bread or pastry not properly risen, is itself the commonest word for this condition, though mainly in the North and the central Midlands. Its chief competitor is **heavy,** which flourishes in East Anglia, the South East and the South-west Midlands, and appears to be infiltrating, presumably from Standard English, into the South West.

The term **girdle** L36, for the iron plate used in baking, and itself a word of French origin, is now widespread in the North but only somewhat scantily represented in isolated pockets in the South Midlands and South. By comparison, its Standard variant **griddle** is recorded only rarely, chiefly in the South. There are etymological and semantic problems with these two forms. The OED dating of **griddle** (1352) is here preferred to MED's ?a1300; for the latter citation, a gloss for *craticula*, evidently refers to an openwork iron grill rather than a flat plate. The questionnaire item (V.7.4) specifies an 'iron plate that cakes were baked on over the fire'. The responses, however, include **bakestone** and its variant **backstone** which, according to OED and the *English Dialect Dictionary*, could refer to either an iron plate or a flat stone. In a widespread but so far imprecisely determined area backstones were often built in to the fireplace itself rather than being placed over the fire. Although the evidence from the *English Dialect Dictionary* shows that the word **backstone** was widespread in northern and western England, the map on the other hand shows a distribution of both **backstone** and **bakestone** which is western rather than northern: it extends with one interruption from north-west Yorkshire to the Severn estuary. Clearly much work remains to be done both on the definition of the object itself with its typological variants, and on the patterns of distribution of these variants and their nomenclature.

Bacon fat L38 is so named throughout the whole of England. In Yorkshire, however, the word **dip** is used, except in the north-western parts of the county, where besides the Standard **bacon fat** there is also a small region where **collop-fat** preserves in its first element a word of obscure, perhaps Scandinavian, origin. The synonym **bacon-liquor,** with its interesting second element, occurs in the central West Midlands, and **grease** is virtually confined to Northumberland.

The notion of **insipid** L39, with reference to food, is widely expressed in the North (excluding west Yorkshire), the West Midlands and the South East, by Standard English **tasteless.** The etymologically obscure **wairsh** is favoured in the North East, while **walsh,** from OE, occurs in the North, with a less frequent variant **welsh** in northern Cumberland. Both are contractions of **wallowish,** the first element of which occurs independently in the North West. In the South West **fresh,** of French origin, is dominant. **Flash,** recorded in this sense in a restricted area of the eastern counties, is noteworthy, and so is **flat,** from a Scandinavian source, in a small area further to the west.

Shelling L41a,b, as in shelling peas, stretches from the South West through the Midlands into the more northerly parts of England, with variants **shilling,** found in the North-east Midlands, and **shulling** in the North-west Midlands. **Shelling** also appears in the south-eastern and south-western corners of the country. Enclaves of **sheeling, shucking** and **hucking** occur in south-east England, and **hulling** in the North-west Midlands.

To **brew** L42, which originally applied to the making of beer but about a century ago semantically widened to include tea, is extensively used in this newer meaning in the Midlands and North. Its synonyms **mash** and the more northerly variant **mas(k),** also originally brewing expressions, are widespread, the former extending from the North Midlands to the North West and the latter in the extreme North. Similarly **steep,** also used of malting, is now transferred to tea-making here and there. Much more recently **wet** has developed the same meaning in the South, while in the extreme South West the corresponding term is **soak. Scald,** found in the West Midlands, refers to pouring boiling water onto the tea-leaves; this, the only French loanword, is unique among the responses in that it is not a brewing term.

The wealth and variety of English vocabulary, so richly illustrated in Appendix 3 of this Atlas, demands much fuller discussion than is possible here; but a few more comments of a general nature may be offered before moving more specifically to the matter of loanwords.

The map of **headache** L46 is a good example of the competition of vocabulary items, where a Standard word contrasts with regional alternatives. **Headache** is employed almost everywhere except in the North and in a restricted area in East Anglia, with **skull-ache** persisting southwards. The North has the very distinctive **head-wark** over a wide area, with a characteristic variant **head-warch** mainly in south Lancashire. Northumberland prefers the descriptive collocation **sore head.** Expressions for a **loose piece of skin** L49a,b, show great variety and are distributed in several largish enclaves. The most widespread is **ang-nail,** dating from the OE period. It is centred, with or without initial aspiration, on East Anglia and the South East, as well as in a narrow belt in the western parts of the North, where **nail-spring** is localised in the south-west corner. **Back-friend** is the usual term in the West Midlands, and two compounds with the same second element, **idle-back** and **revel-back** with etymologically obscure first elements, occur in Lincolnshire and northwards across the Humber, as well as in south-western England. **Stepmother,** occurring in this form as well as compounded in the possessive singular with **blessing** and **jag,** is notable in the southerly parts of the North. Finally, such maps as **top and tail** L13, **pegs (for thatch)** L17, **donkey** L20a,b, **chip (of eggs hatching)** L28, **chapped** L48, and **bogey** L64, each exhibit a considerable variety of synonyms, while others, eg **hens** L27, **anything** L44, **something** L45 and **hungry** L51, show the distribution of conflicting synonyms of OE origin.

Following the Viking invasions and the establishment of the Danelaw, numerous Scandinavian loan-words came into English. Many of these are still very much in evidence today in the local dialects of the north of England, more particularly in Cumberland, Westmorland, north Lancashire, and the North and East Ridings of Yorkshire. However, they do not appear to be so strongly represented nowadays in other parts of the Danelaw, namely in Derbyshire, Nottinghamshire, Staffordshire, Leicestershire, Lincolnshire and East Anglia. Doubtless the losses have resulted from the pressure of Standard English. Although a decline of the Scandinavian element in our dialects seems inevitable, many Scandinavian loan-words are still holding their ground fairly well and several of those mapped here still seem relatively secure.

The **shaft** of a cart L6 is still a **stang** in a small enclave in the North West, but is evidently receding as **shaft,** the most common native word, extends its territory.

In the East Midlands and a little further north, the **ridge** of a stack L15 and of a house-roof L16 is spoken of as a **rigg.** The same word is also the first element of its more northerly competitor, **rigging.** The distribution areas of these terms show considerable correspondence on both maps, but **rigging** with reference to the stack is evidently falling out of use and being replaced by **rigg.** Two more Scandinavian loanwords designate the **ropes** tying the thatching to the stack, L18. They are **bands,** still firmly established in the North East and East Midlands, and **simes,** confined to a much smaller area in the North West. **Bands** and its variant **bonds** have become extensively established in the Midlands and South.

Geld, used in the specialised sense **not in calf** L19, is still strongly represented in north-western England and has even spread north-eastwards. Its chief rival further south is the French loanword **barren,** and its derivative noun **barrener** is found in parts of Berk-shire, Hampshire, Sussex, Dorset and the Isle of Wight.

To **plash** (a hedge) L22 is expressed by **lig** in much of Yorkshire, Lancashire and Cumberland, and in Westmorland. In the North East, however, its native cognate **lay,** which is widely used in the Midlands and South, is also often found. **Lig,** this time meaning **lie** (down) L61, is found in a considerably more extensive though similar area to that mapped in L22, and remains firmly established between those regions where the much more widely distributed standard **lie** is dominant. Nevertheless, the native word **lay,** wide-spread in south-eastern England, is seen, from the numerous examples of variant occurrences in northern Lincolnshire and Yorkshire, to be pressing northwards at the expense of **lig.**

The word **bait** seems to pose a problem. It is mapped here in two meanings, **snack** L56a,b, referring to food taken between breakfast and the mid-day meal, and **meal out** L57, applied to food taken to work as a meal. Both senses are frequently recorded in the North East, though the word shows contraction westwards, south-wards, and especially eastwards, where it appears to have been supplanted, when meaning 'snack', by the French loanword **allowance.** Further, **bait** in both senses occurs in profusion in the south West Midlands. The picture then is complicated and calls for more intensive study.

Icicles L58 has revealed a wide variety of synonyms including **ice-shockles** and its variants, which again seem to have spread northwards but to have lost ground eastwards and southwards. **From** L59 is still widely represented in the North by **fro,** but is obviously giving way to its native counterpart **from** from the Midlands and South. **Flayed** in the sense of **afraid** L65 shows signs of having a much wider distribution in the past than today. It is clearly being displaced by the native **frightened,** a shortened cognate of which, namely **frit,** still persists in the Midlands.

Several other maps in this section exhibit lexical items presupposing Scandinavian origin. They include **gear-** for **trace-** (horse) L5b, **muck** for **dung** L9, **smoot** for **sheep-hole** L23, **hinging-** for **hanging-**(post) L24a, **stoop** for **hanging-post** L24b, **kindling** for **kindling-wood** L33a, **flat** for **insipid** L39, and **freckles** L50a,b.

The French loanwords, unlike those from Scandinavian sources whose distributions reflect settlement patterns, occur in enclaves which are some-times neighbouring and sometimes widely scattered.

French **manger,** for example, when applied to the cowstall **trough** L3, is widespread in the East Midlands and parts of the South and South West, but has so far made little progress into the North East. On both sides of the River Humber **crib** from OE still persists.

The verb **brush** meaning **trim** (a hedge) L21a, now well established apparently at the expense of the native **trim** in the West Midlands, but less strongly in the South-east, seems unusual, but the form also exists as a noun meaning 'hedge clippings' both in English and American regional dialects and also as the first element in **brushwood.** Another term probably borrowed from French, though rather recently, is the north-country **slash** L21b.

Slice (of bread) L34 has almost swept the country, its main alternatives being the Low German loan

shive, now under great pressure, and the native **round** which at the time of the Survey was confined in traditional dialect usage to a section of East Anglia, though the word is still used extensively today with reference to sandwiches in the public-house bar catering trade.

Coat for **jacket** L53 is much preferred in the North, although **jacket,** which has no serious rival in the rest of the country, is strongly supplanting **coat,** despite its being a late loan. **Vest** L55 is usual in the South for the garment worn by a man next to his skin, and **singlet,** an older usage in this meaning, now preponderates in the North. The old Scandinavian word (-)**sark** survives in the sense of **vest** in the extreme North and is found even more extensively with the meaning **shirt** L54 in Cumberland, Northumberland and Durham.

Married L59 nowadays dominates the South and Midlands, as well as the extreme North. It is eviently displacing the once popular native word **wed(ded)** in the North and has already done so in east Yorkshire. Lastly, **stay** (at home) L62 is clearly expanding at the expense of the native **stop,** which is widespread in the North and Midlands. It has a foothold in the South East and part of the north Midlands and has extended into Yorkshire. Other French words are found, for example, in the maps for **farmstead** L1, **trace-horse** L5b, **carting** L14, **plash** L22, **girdle** L36, **smack** L56b and **afraid** L65.

Several maps exemplify the occurrence of loanwords from Low German sources, ie Middle Dutch, Flemish and Old Saxon. Reference to the individual items in the *English Dialect Dictionary* shows that most of them, unless also established in the Standard language, are now very much restricted geographically. None perhaps can be held to imply any precise early settlement by those who used the languages concerned. Amongst those words in regional dialects which derive ultimately from these sources, the term **flipe** is used for **brim** (of hat) L52 in a restricted area of north-east Yorkshire, while the word **poke** occurs very occasionally in the Midlands.

Other Old Low German derivations include **wagoner** for **cartman** L2, **switch** for **trim** (v) L21b, **stump** for **(hanging-)post** L24b and **snap(ping)** for meal out L56b.

MORPHOLOGICAL MAPS

Within the terms of the Orton–Dieth methodology, the morphological questions were principally intended to elicit certain features of grammatical variation. These include, for example, positive and negative forms of the present tense of verbs, the forms of past tenses and past participles, and plural possessive case inflections. It is, however, inevitable that, just as some phonological variation underlies lexical variation, it is often difficult to distinguish between ranges of vocabulary items and grammatical features. Forms of the first person singular of the verb **be** M1, for instance, include **I am, I are, I be, I bin** and **I is,** which derive from different OE etymons. Maps M1–M8 present ample evidence for the persistence of these forms and their analogues, with different patterns of distribution in the first, second and third persons singular and the first person plural of the present tense. The Standard forms are evidently gaining ground and in M3, M4, M7 and M8 are now the norm in most of the country. This is also substantially true for the 'linking' forms of the verb **be** in the present tense as seen in M16–M19 and the interrogative **am (I)** M28 and **are (they married)** M30. However in **(they) are** M4, and **(we) are** (emphatic) M8, for example, **be** remains firmly entrenched in south-western areas and extends eastwards to the Sussex-Kent border and northwards to central Warwickshire, with cognate **bin** forms in adjacent West Midland enclaves. **Be** forms also continue in a similar area in M16 and M18, while M2, M6, and M36 incidentally illustrate the persistence of all four forms of the second person pronoun.

The remarkable diversity of present tense negative forms is amply demonstrated in M9–M15 and again in M26 and M27. The distribution patterns are much more intricate than those of the positive forms and show much greater resistance to the encroachment of Standard English. The past tense forms of the verb **be,** mapped in M20–M23, also reveal that the use of **was** and **were** is still far from conforming with the Standard and the old weak form **weren** still persists in a small area of the West Midlands. Similar patterns also characterise **(if she) were** M24 and **(if we) were** M25.

Both the present and past tense negative forms of the verb **dare** M32–33b exhibit considerable variation, both morphological and phonological, and show that the two tenses share several forms, the tense markers therefore remaining indistinct. In **(he) does** (emphatic) M34 Standard **does** not only predominates but is also strongly represented in the South and South West. In **does (he)** M35 it is also dominant, but **done** is found in a small enclave in southern Shropshire. **Done** occurs more extensively in the West Midlands in **do you** (2prsg) M36, and the old second person singular form **dost** also survives in neighbouring areas of the North-west Midlands and the South-west Midlands. In the map of **done** M39 the old past participles **a-done** and **a-doed** in the South West are clearly being ousted by **done.** Among the other modal auxiliary verbs the variants of **must not** M46 indicate the many forms which such verbs may have in regional speech today. This map shows the Old Norse **mun** forms and their derivatives to be north of a line from the Humber to mid Herefordshire, apart from **maan't** which occurs in a small section of the South-east Midlands. The contracted Standard **musn't** is predominant in the southern half of the country.

The past tense forms in **(he) came** M51, **caught** M52, and **(they) grew** (v intr) M53 show some interesting variation. The Standard **came** is the norm in most of England but several sizable enclaves of **come** and **comed** are to be found in the eastern half of the country and in small sections of the West Midlands. **Caught** M52 has a similar distribution pattern with **catched** as the minority choice. In the map of **(they) grew** (v intr) M53, on the other hand, we find that **growed** remains well established in the South West and most of the Midlands, with further enclaves in the South East and in north-eastern Norfolk. The old weak past participle **putten** is seen to be receding northwards in M54, and **put** is the sole form in the Midlands and South. On the other hand the old strong past participle **took** is the most common form for **taken** M55 in the Midlands and South, with taken itself recorded in seven small areas, mainly in the southern half of the country, and **tayn** persisting as the most usual form north of the Humber. In the present participles **cursing** M56, **doing**

M57 and **laughing** M58 and the verbal noun **writing** M59 final /ŋ/ is notably absent except for a few isolated individual localities, while the distinctive /ŋg/ usage in **writing** M59 occurs only in a small area north west of Birmingham. As elsewhere in the atlas, a feature which is essentially phonological emerges alongside various morphological markers, since we are here concerned with the presentation of participial forms.

Morphemes marking the plural of nouns mapped in M60–M64 are seen to conform with the Standard over most of the country. In the map of **eyes** M60 the old weak form **een** persists in northerly areas, but the strong form with **-s** is clearly moving northwards and is already established along the Scottish border and in the North East. The map of **cows** M61 shows that the weak plural **kine** is confined to Cheshire, while **kye(s)** is evidently receding northwards under pressure from the Standard form. Double plural morphemes for **bellows** M63 are still found in an area extending north east from the Yorkshire-Lancashire border and in two south-western enclaves. The same is true for **hames** M64 in most of the South West. The **-s** morpheme marking the possessive case singular in **father's (boots)** M65 is absent in a broad band from coast to coast through most of Yorkshire, Lancashire and Westmorland, although the Standard marked form is obviously challenging it. This challenge is seen even more clearly in the map of **cow's (legs)** M66 where the morpheme is absent in a much narrower band.

The third person pronouns in M67–M73 again illustrate the strength of non-Standard forms in regional dialects. **She** M68 and **(is) she?** M69, for example, are represented by **her** in much of western England and the South West, while **shoo** persists in Lancashire, Cheshire, North Derbyshire and south west Yorkshire, **hoo** being confined to an isolated pocket on the eastern border of the **shoo** area. The reduced form **en,** expressing both **him** and **it** in M70 and M71 respectively, is restricted to the South West. **En** is strongly challenged by **it** in M71 and is now confined to south Cornwall with reference to broth in **(tasted) it** M72. This map also presents evidence of the survival of the plural form **them** for broth in the North West and in east Durham, while M73 shows that over a more extensive area of the North West and along the Scottish border the plural subject case form **they** replaces **it** with reference to porridge.

In the first person plural pronoun the Standard **us** M74 occurs in most of the country, with **we** in south-western areas, the Suffolk-Essex border and the Isle of Man. In **(with) our (eyes)** M75, however, **us** is confined to a single area in the North Midlands extending into southern Yorkshire, while the Standard **our** is the norm elsewhere.

Among third person singular possessive pronouns **hisn** and **hern** still typify the central southern area in the maps **his** M76 and **hers** M77. Cognate weak forms, **yourn** and **theirn,** are found in a broadly similar area for **yours** (sg) M78 and **theirs** M79, although in M78 **thine** remains the most common form in regional usage.

The demonstratives **these** M82 and **those** M83 are each realised by four principal lexical forms plus such variants as **these here, them there** and **they over there** and also several alternatives listed in the notes at the foot of each map. Just as lexical variation is a feature of these morphological maps, among others, so also some features of syntax inevitably appear in phrases such as **they over there** which are also distinguished from the simplexes such as **these** and **those** by their individual patterns of distribution.

SYNTACTICAL MAPS

Whereas the syntactical variants featuring in the morphological maps are in general of fixed linear order, those to be discussed here often exhibit various different patterns of word order within each phrase structure. In some of the syntactical maps the distribution patterns are clear cut. Map S1, for example, demonstrates that the word order **give me it** is the norm in the north and most of eastern England, whereas **give it me** is strongly represented in western and central areas, with enclaves in the South East and South West. The form with a preposition, **give it to me,** is well established in the South West, along with three small enclaves around the Thames estuary and in East Anglia. The word order of **we put the light on** S2 is clearly dominant over most of the country while **we put on the light** is confined to the South West. The decline of **go see** is particularly obvious in S4 where it survives in only two relic areas, each bearing strong evidence of the alternative form **go and see** which, apart from isolated individual locations, is supreme in the rest of the country. The map of **to whom** S6 shows that **who . . . to** is firmly established in most of England, with the simplex **who** preferred in much of the South West, the South East and the South-west Midlands. The form **who to** remains in Sussex and south-western Essex, and the old Northern **who . . . till** still persists in Cumberland and Westmorland. In the contention between **twenty-five (to three)** S7 and **five-and-twenty (to three)** the latter appears dominant in regional speech. The principal dialectal variant of **did not do** S9 is the contracted form **didn't do** which appears to be ousting the alternatives **didno' do** in the West Midlands and **never done** in five small enclaves south of a line from the Severn to the Wash.

The problems of mapping syntactical features are apparent in **(came) to (see)** S3, **who** S5 and **on Friday week** S8. Although the main distribution patterns of the forms of **(came) to (see)** are clear, the alternatives recorded in the various enclaves indicate that in these areas this feature is in a state of flux, one or more alternatives being used apparently indiscriminately. It is obvious, for example, that the older purposive form **for to** in much of Yorkshire and in South Cheshire and North Derbyshire is being challenged in almost every fieldwork locality by the simplex **to** which is also very common in the other **for to** area along the south coast. This map therefore enables us to see the encroachment of the dominant **to** into the few remaining relic areas and at the same time indicates the historical alternatives which are now in rapid decline. Similar features are also in evidence in the map of **who** S5, but here no single form is supreme, although **as** is in a strong position in the West and the Midlands. The pronoun is seen to be absent in individual locations in many parts of the country but this feature is not sufficiently frequent to be mapped as separate enclaves. The notes at the foot of the map illustrate some of the problems of interpretation and presentation involved in mapping complex distribution patterns, especially when alternative responses were often elicited by the fieldworkers in a given location.

Again we can see in this map the struggle for supremacy between the various contenders and in this case none has yet emerged as predominant.

On Friday week S8 presents similar problems, although here each distribution area in a complex map is clear cut and interpretation less hindered by the existence of alternative responses. The remarkable feature of this map, as of others, is that no less than seven principal syntactic variants and several minor alternatives continue in everyday usage and the cartographic technique allows us to see something of the extraordinary complexity of their mid-twentieth century distribution.

In conclusion, we have shown, in building up a comprehensive picture of the older kind of regional speech at this stage in the history of the English language, how some contrastive patterns in phonology, lexis, morphology and syntax are sharply delineated while others are more diffuse.

Perhaps nowhere is the complexity of elicited forms and their distributions more strikingly demonstrated than in the phonological maps which form the major part of this atlas. Here the extraordinary variety of forms, although presenting some cartographical problems, illustrates the diversity of this important aspect of contemporary speech and provides countless opportunities for further investigation and interpretation. A knowledge of the sound system is fundamental to a study of linguistic forms; and the essence of Harold Orton's approach to dialectology is to be found in the substantial portion of this atlas devoted to phonological features, where his considered interpretation of their historical development, their present-day realisations, and the implications of their distributions are presented.

The lexical section of the atlas is more accessible to a wider range of readers. It is of particular interest for the historical view it gives of the various linguistic stocks which contribute to the richness and flexibility of regional vocabulary and which account for its semantic variety and precision. This material relates also to patterns of settlement, of agricultural practice, and of domestic life which have important implications for ethnologists, historians, historical geographers and others in the fields of the social sciences.

It is moreover inevitable, from the very nature of the field data, that aspects of both phonology and vocabulary are also displayed in those maps concerned primarily with morphology and syntax. The reader will therefore find in the latter sections further material to complement the information in the first two sections. Once more in the maps dealing with morphology and syntax in the terms of the Orton-Dieth questionnaire, a great diversity of usage is illustrated. Grammatical markers for number and tense, for example, exhibit the persistence of many older forms as well as more recent developments and the encroachment of Standard forms, while many syntactical variations also show the continuity of modes of expression typical of the speech of rural England.

The wealth of material in the English Dialect Survey's collections has been exploited and displayed only in small measure in the pages of this atlas. It was Harold Orton's hope, as it is that of his co-editors, that this volume will stimulate a wide variety of further research into English dialects, not just in England alone but wherever the English language is spoken.

NOTES

1. The letter, dated 21 July, 1945, 'is the answer to yours of May 14th 1940', which Dieth had kept on his desk with other 'last letters' from Britain until 'the day when things would be normal again.' Orton's files containing the renewed correspondence are preserved in the archives of the Institute of Dialect and Folk Life Studies, University of Leeds.

2. Presumably from Professor H. Straumann of Zurich, who (as Dieth mentions at the beginning of this letter) had recently brought him news of Orton.

3. Dieth to Orton, 19 November 1945.

4. Hans Kurath, 'The Linguistic Atlas of the United States and Canada', in *Proceedings of the Second International Congress of Phonetic Sciences,* edited by Daniel Jones and D. B. Fry (Cambridge, 1936), pp. 18–22 (p. 20).

5. In 1923 Wright acted as one of the examiners of Orton's B.Litt. thesis, written under the supervision of H. C. Wyld.

6. Joseph Wright and Elizabeth Mary Wright, *Elementary Middle English Grammar* (Oxford, 1923), pp. 2–3.

7. The other members were Wilhelm Horn, University of Berlin, Chairman; Miles L. Hanley, University of Wisconsin; Hans Kurath, Brown University; and John Orr, University of Edinburgh. For further information see Hans Kurath, 'Progress of the Linguistic Atlas', *Dialect Notes,* 6 (1935), 481–5.

8. *Proceedings of the Second International Congress,* p. 253.

9. H. Orton, *The Phonology of a South Durham Dialect* (London, 1933).

10. For a preliminary account of this survey see H. Orton, 'Northumberland Dialect Research: First Report', *Proceedings of the University of Durham Philosophical Society,* VIII (1937), 127–35.

11. Bertil Hedevind of the University of Uppsala is undertaking an analysis of this material, which should reveal important comparisons with Guy Lowman's survey in the Midlands and South of England (1937–8), for which see Wolfgang Viereck, *Lexicalische und grammatische Ergebnisse des Lowman Survey von Mittel- und Südengland,* 2 vols. (Munich, 1975).

12. From 1922–7 he was a Lecturer in German in the University of Aberdeen, a post which gave him the opportunity for fieldwork in the North-East of Scotland.

13. E. Dieth, *A Grammar of the Buchan Dialect, Vol. I (Phonology and Accidence)* (Cambridge, 1932).

14. Eugen Dieth, 'A New Survey of English Dialects', *Essays and Studies by members of the English Association,* edited by Basil Willey, XXXII (1946), (Oxford, 1947), 74–104 (p. 78).

15. For further information on these and other Scottish dialect studies see especially the bibliography in Angus McIntosh, *An Introduction to a Survey of Scottish Dialects,* (Edinburgh, 1952) and the Introduction to *The Linguistic Atlas of Scotland: Scots Section, Volume 1,* edited by J. Y. Mather and H. H. Speitel (London, 1975).

16. See dedicatory note by H. Straumann and E. Leisi to *English Studies,* 34, No. 6 (1953), 241–3 (p. 242).

17. Dieth to Orton, 19 November 1945: 'I think I told you in my last letter that I had taken to studying linguistic geography . . . Just now we're studying all the available atlases (Wenker, ALF, AIS, Kloeke's Dutch atlas and LANE). Examining the Taalatlas Van Nord- en Zuid Nederland you feel tickled to tackle the English. Did I tell you that my friend and colleague J. Jud tried to induce me to take up the matter?'

18. Harold Orton, 'An English Dialect Survey: Linguistic Atlas of England', *Orbis,* IX (1960), 331–41 (p. 331).

19. Annual Report for 1946, *Transactions of the Philological Society,* 1947, (London, 1948), 156.

20. Eugen Dieth, 'A New Survey of English Dialects', *Essays and Studies by members of the English Association,* XXXII (1946), (Oxford, 1947), 74–104.

21. A notable omission in Dieth's comprehensive review is the absence of any reference to the two dialect maps in Prince Louis Lucien Bonaparte, 'On the Dialects of Eleven Southern and South-Western Counties, with a New Classification of the English Dialects', *English Dialect Society Series D, Miscellaneous,* Miscellanies II (1877), 13–24. The earlier version of these maps,

which differ only in minor detail, is reproduced in Stewart F. Sanderson, 'Language on the Map', *The University of Leeds Review*, 20 (1977), 160–71.

22. Letter from L. R. Palmer, Honorary Secretary of the Philological Society, to Orton, 15 March 1947.

23. Orton to Palmer, 18 March 1947.

24. Minutes of the Council of the Philological Society, 10 February 1950. The statement in Sever Pop, *La Dialectologie*, 2 vols. (Louvain, 1950), II, 913, based on information apparently supplied by Dieth, that 'La *Philological Society* a confié dans sa séance du 17 Fevrier 1950, au savant suisse Eugen Dieth, la direction de l'Atlas linguistique de la Grande-Bretagne', is not supported by the Society's minutes. The Council meeting of 10 February was followed by an ordinary meeting on 11 February, according to the Society's Annual Report. The only reference to Dieth is that quoted here in the first of four Council resolutions dealing with the Survey: the others relate to the projected questionnaire, handbook, and students' guide to dialect studies.

25. The University of Zurich provided funds for Dieth's research and his travel and subsistence on visits to England; but in view of the misrepresentation of the roles of both Orton and the University of Leeds in Sever Pop, *La Dialectologie*, (1950), p. 913, and in the dedicatory note by Straumann and Leisi in *English Studies*, vol. 34 (1953), p. 242, it must be stressed that the responsibility for financing, staffing, organising and directing the English Dialect Survey rested solely with Orton and the University of Leeds and that all proprietary rights in the Survey's collections are vested in the University. The collaboration between Orton and Dieth was purely personal and was not an arrangement between the Universities of Leeds and Zurich. It is necessary to set the record straight here as the above-mentioned misrepresentations have more than once led to misunderstanding.

26. Annual Report for 1953, *Transactions of the Philological Society*, 1954, (Oxford, 1955), 206–7.

27. Harold Orton, 'An English Dialect Survey: Linguistic Atlas of England', *Orbis*, IX (1960), p. 332.

28. An earlier version had been published in 1952, a reprint with separate pagination of the *Proceedings of the Leeds Philosophical and Literary Society*, VI, Part IX (1952). For accounts of the development of the questionnaire see Harold Orton and Eugen Dieth, 'The New Survey of Dialectal English', in *English Studies Today*, edited by C. L. Wrenn and G. Bullough, (Oxford, 1951), pp. 63–73, and Harold Orton, *Orbis*, IX (1960), pp. 333–5.

29. Stanley Ellis, 'Regional, Social and Economic Influences on Speech: Leeds University Studies', in *Sprachliches Handeln—Soziales Verhalten*, edited by Wolfgang Viereck, (Munich, 1976), pp. 93–103, (pp. 94–5).

30. *ibid.*, p. 95.

31. Harold Orton, *Survey of English Dialects, Introduction* (Leeds 1962), pp. 21–2.

32. For instance, there were changes in the co-editorship of the *Basic Material* volumes. It should also be noted that E. Kolb's completion of Dieth's phonological maps of the six northern counties, referred to in Orton's footnote, *Introduction*, p. 22, was not published, as had been expected, in association with the *Survey of English Dialects* volumes.

33. Harold Orton, 'A Linguistic Atlas of England', *Advancement of Science*, 27 (1970), 80–96.

34. In tribute to the memory of his original collaborator, Orton published these volumes under the general rubric '*Survey of English Dialects* by Harold Orton and Eugen Dieth (1893–1956)'. The volumes are as follows: (a) Harold Orton, *Introduction* (Leeds 1962). (b) *The Basic Material:* Vol. I, *The Six Northern Counties and the Isle of Man*, edited by Harold Orton and Wilfred J. Halliday, 3 parts (Leeds 1962–3); Vol. II, *The West Midland Counties*, edited by Harold Orton and Michael V. Barry, 3 parts (Leeds 1969–71); Vol. III, *The East Midland Counties and East Anglia*, edited by Harold Orton and Philip M. Tilling, 3 parts (Leeds 1969–71); Vol. IV, *The Southern Counties*, edited by Harold Orton and Martyn F. Wakelin, 3 parts (Leeds 1966–7). With the completion of the *Linguistic Atlas of England*, the next priority in the Survey's publication programme is the issue of a selection of material from the Survey's sound-recordings.

35. This is not inconsistent with Abercrombie's view that field transcriptions are themselves acts of interpretation. See David Abercrombie, 'The Recording of Dialect Material', *Orbis*, III (1954), 231–5.

36. J. Gilliéron and E. Edmont, *L'Atlas Linguistique de la France*, 7 vols. (Paris, 1902–10).

37. On strict bases of etymology and analogy with concepts such as the isobar, isoglosses should join localities distinguished by identical forms. For boundary lines separating contrasting forms, a more precise description would be 'heteroglosses'; but see the next paragraph for justification of our compliance with the accepted usage.

38. H.O.'s manuscript note on the draft map.

39. Daniel Jones, *An Outline of English Phonetics*, 3rd edn (Cambridge, 1932), p. 63.

40. The forms with /iu/ are due to the following *l*.

41. This is confirmed by the Basic Material data for *fifth* VII.2.5 and *wrist* VI.6.9. The vowel variation in *bristles* Ph29, which derives from an OE **brystel*, presupposes a history quite different from *wrist* (OE *wrist*) VI.6.9.

42. It is noteworthy that in this same region a closing diphthong ending in /i/ also represents both EME short *e* and *o* when lengthened in open syllables in disyllabic words.

Phonological Maps

a: 38Do 2, ä: 29Ess $^{+}$14, ɑ 6Y 1, 16Wo $^{+}$7,
ɑ: 16Wo $^{+}$7 under a
æ: 21Nf 3, 29Ess $^{+}$4, 30MxL $^{+}$1, 40Sx $^{+}$2 under æ
ε: 40Sx $^{+}$2 under ε
ɔ 16Wo $^{+}$7, 17Wa $^{+}$2 under ɒ

APPLE- 12St 11; -APPLES 40Sx $^{+}$2

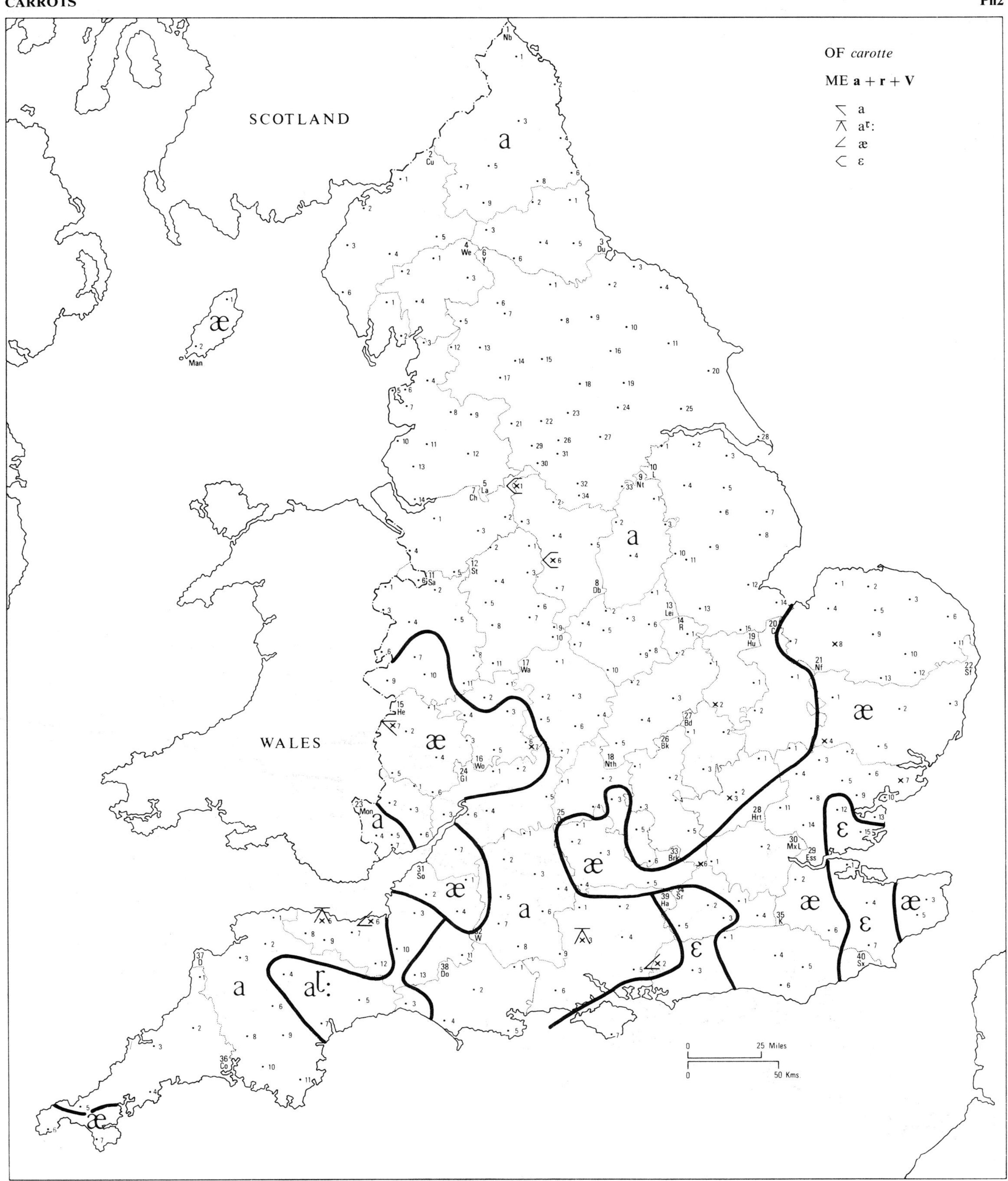

aʵ 31So 3 under aʵ:
æ: 21Nf 5 under æ

ɛə 29Ess 7
ə 16Wo 7

kæ:ɹ̵t 21Nf 5, kaʵ:ʈʂ 38Do 3,
kȩdʒəts (sic) 29Ess ⁺11
kj- 7Ch 2, 8Db 6/7, 12St 3, 15He 2–6, 24Gl 5,
27Bd 1, kʲ- 15He 7, kᶥ- 16Wo 3–5

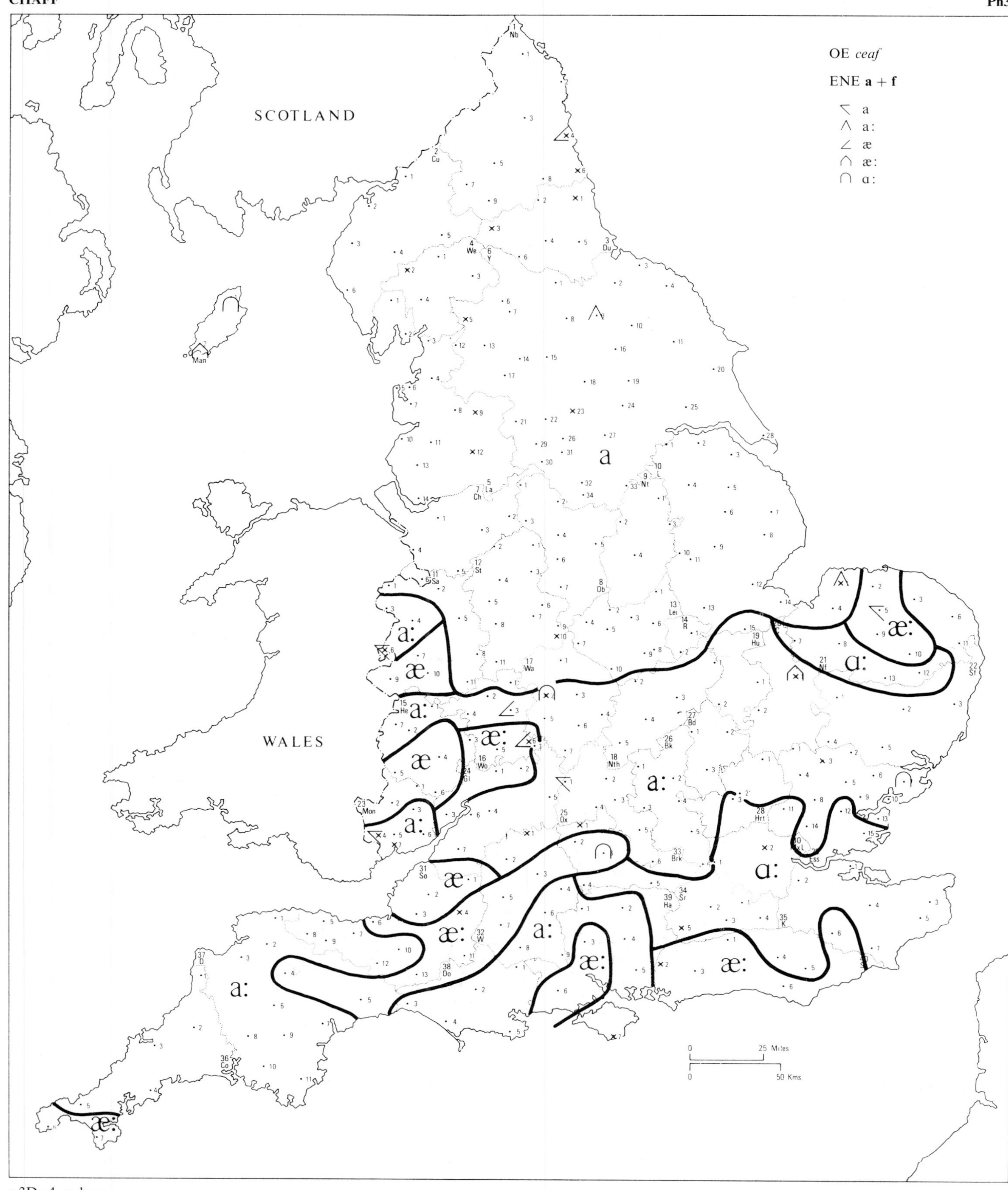

ɑ 3Du 4 under a
ạ:ᵊ 29Ess 6 under a:
æᵊ 1Nb 4 under æ
æ:ᵊ 21Nf +2, æ˙ᵊ Man 2, ɛ: 40Sx 3,
ɛ̨ 40Sx 1 under æ:

CHAFF- 25Ox +1

no -f 33Brk +3, 35K 1, 40Sx 5

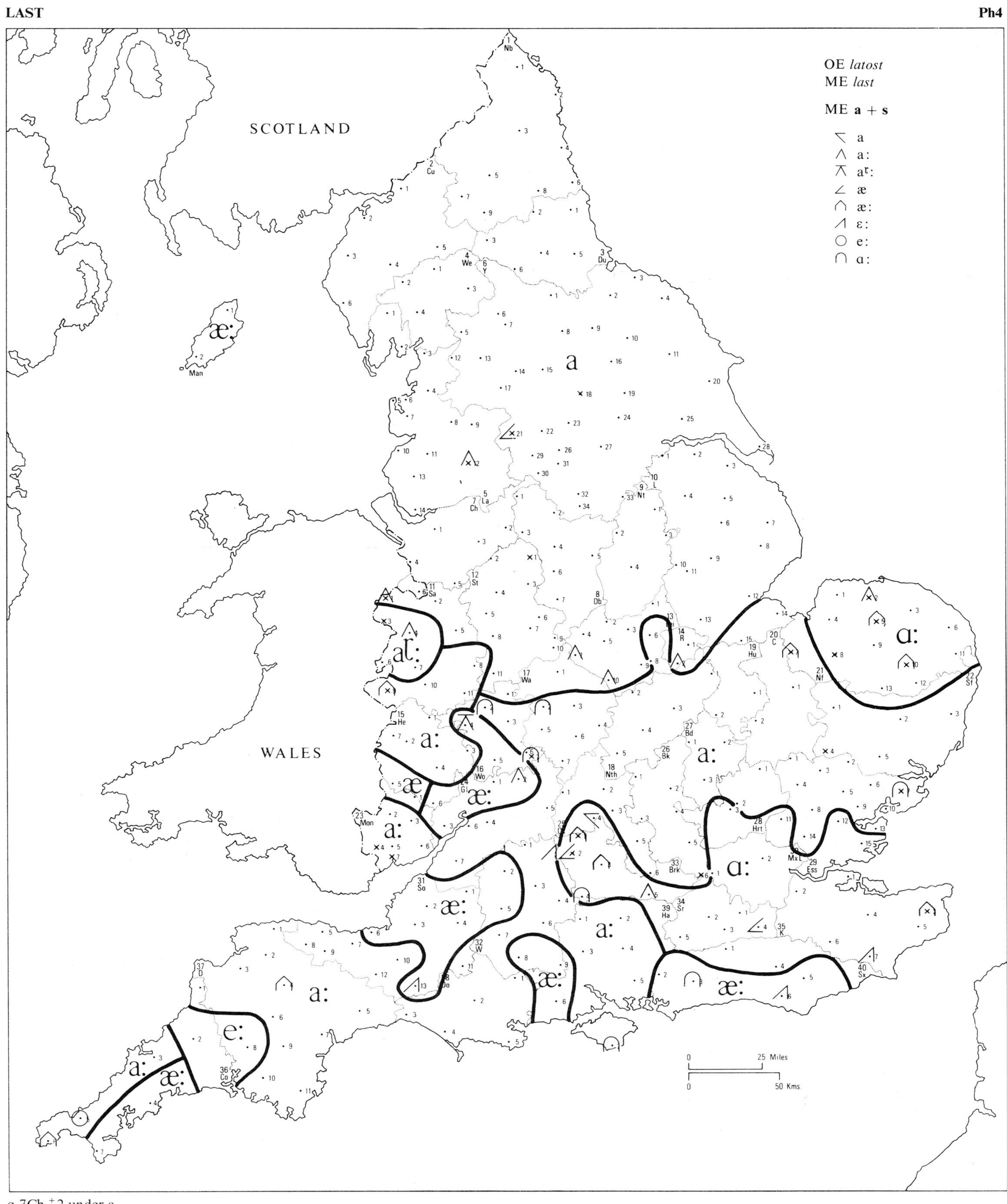

ɑ 7Ch ⁺2 under a
æᵊ Man 2, æ:ᶥ 31So ⁺13 under æ:
ɑ 29Ess ⁺12 under ɑ:

ɑ̊ᵗ: 34Sr ⁺5

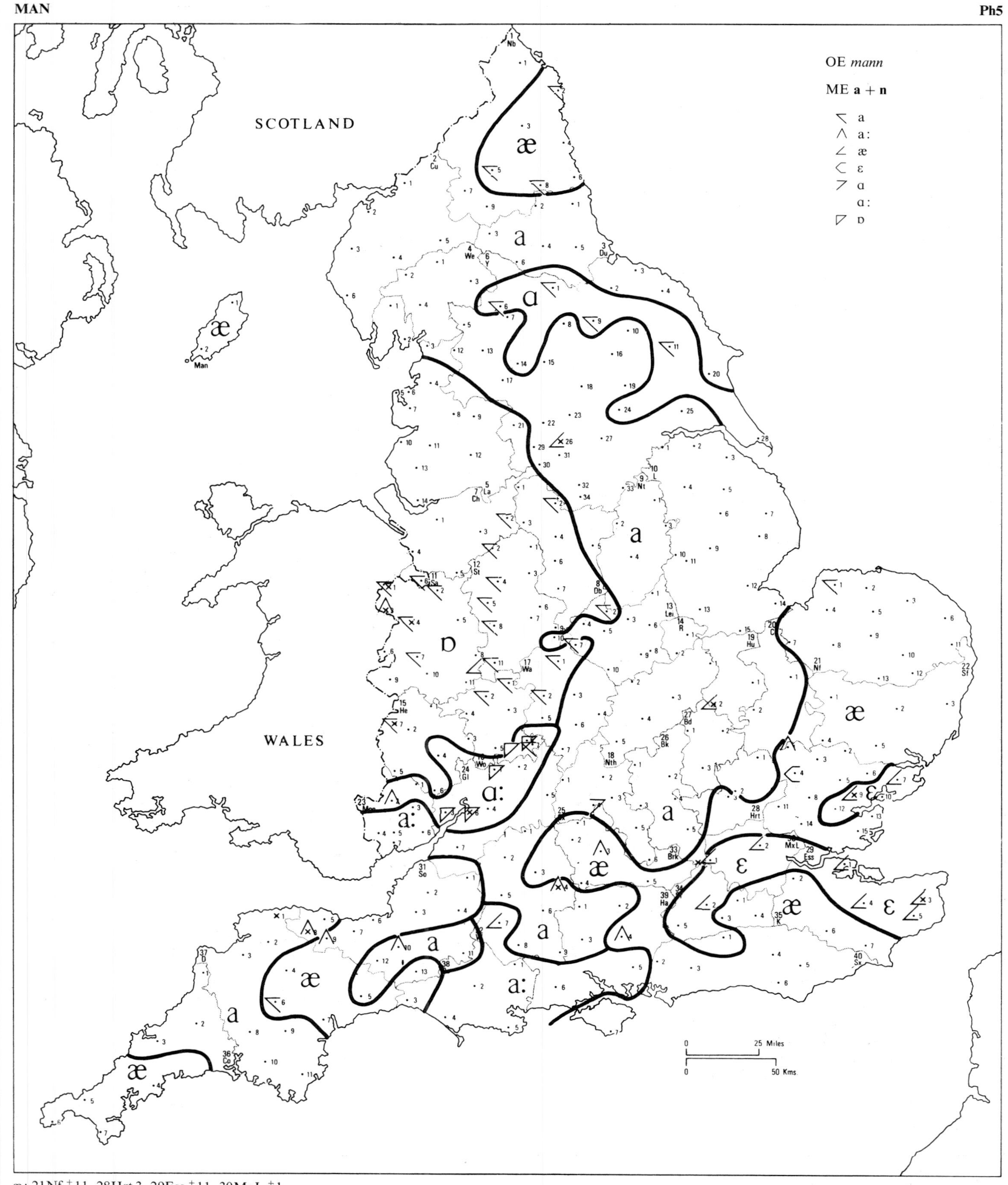

æ: 21Nf +11, 28Hrt 3, 29Ess +11, 30MxL +1,
31So 2/4, æ̠: 33Brk +3, æ̨: 39Ha +4,
æ̨̃: 21Nf +3, æᵊ 1Nb 4/+8, Man +2, 22Sf 4,
æ˙ᵊ 1Nb +5, Man +2, æ:ᵊ 1Nb 6, 21Nf +2,
æᶦ 31So 13 under æ
ɛ̨: 30MxL +2, ɛ̨̃: 30MxL +2, ɛə 29Ess +7,
ɛ:ə 29Ess +7, ɛ̨ᶦ 29Ess +4 under ɛ
ɔ 5La 7, 7Ch +2, 16Wo +7, 17Wa +2,
ɔ˙ 16Wo +7 under ɒ

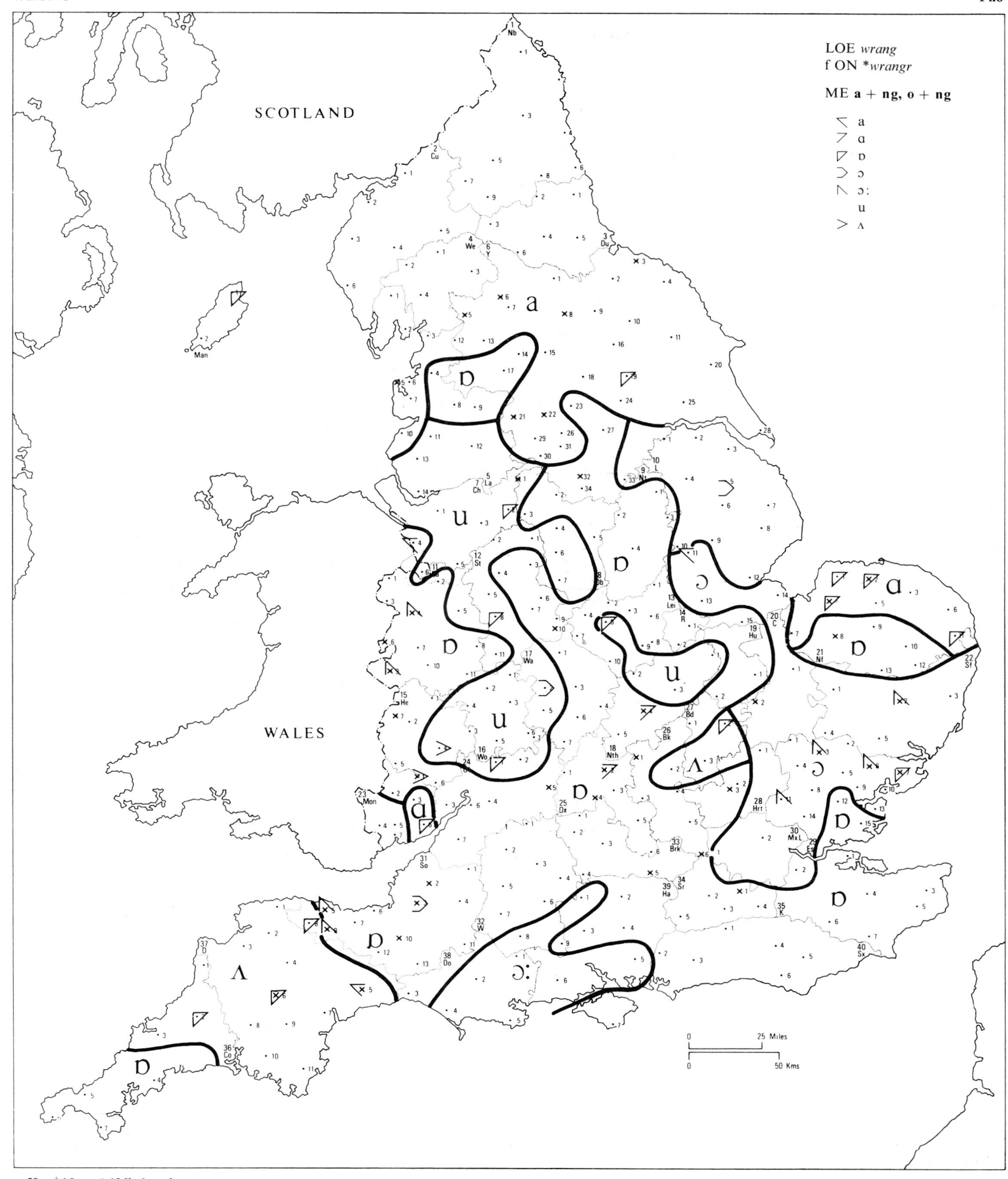

æ 5La [+]10, æ:ᵊ 1Nb 6 under a
ɑ: 21Nf [+]11, 23Mon 3/[+]6 under ɑ
ɒ̜: 34Sr [+]3 under ɒ
ɔ̜:ᵊ 22Sf 2 under ɔ:
ʊ: 15He 3, 24Gl [+]1 under u

ɛ 6Y 22

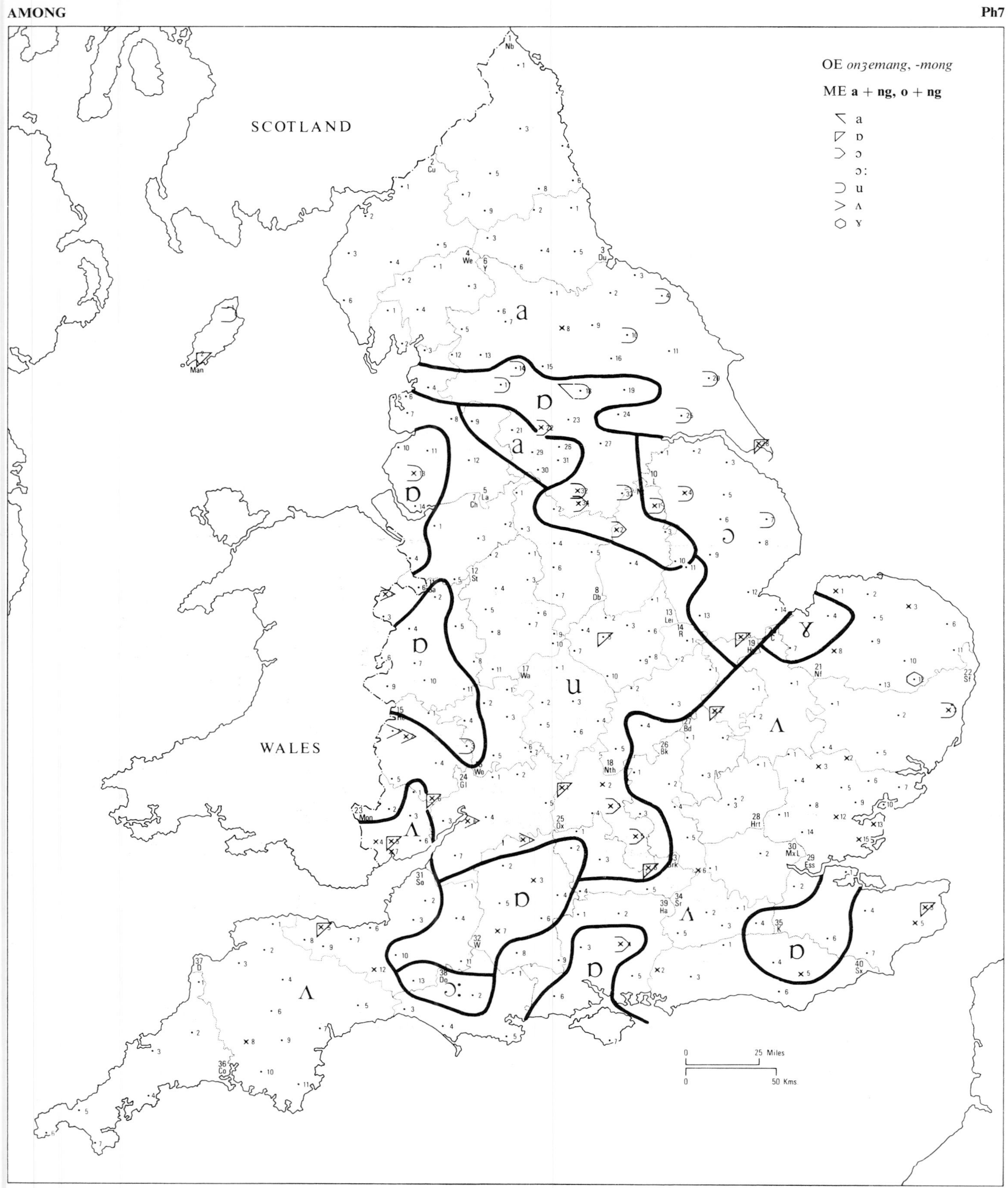

ɔ 24Gl6 under ʌ

ɑ 25Ox 2

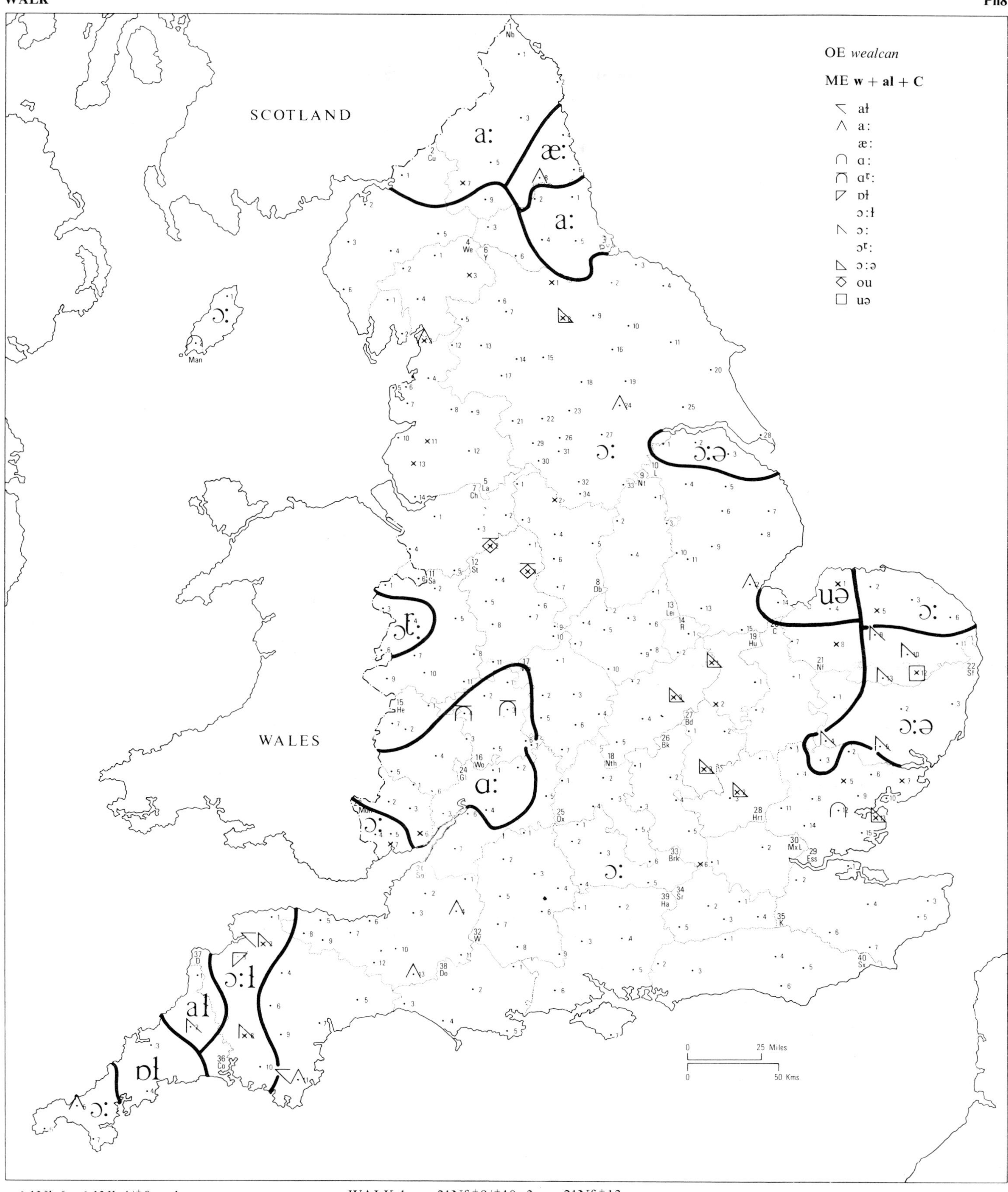

æ:ᵊ 1Nb 6, æᵊ 1Nb 4/$^{+}$8 under æ:
ǫ: 1Nb $^{+}$9 under ɔ:
ɔə 21Nf $^{+}$9 under ɔ:ə

aᵗ: 37D $^{+}$5
ɒ 13Lei $^{+}$5, ɔ 29Ess 5
ɒɷ 12St $^{+}$3
ɔl 10L $^{+}$11
o: 8Db 2, ö̩:ə 21Nf 1
ɤ:ə 21Nf $^{+}$11, ɤ̜:ə 21Nf 5
ǫ̈: (sic) 1Nb 7

WALK 1prsg 21Nf $^{+}$9/$^{+}$10; 3prsg 21Nf $^{+}$13; 2prpl 37D $^{+}$11; 3prpl 10L $^{+}$11; n 1Nb 1/$^{+}$8; ndg 1Nb $^{+}$8, 13Lei $^{+}$5, 21Nf $^{+}$11, 31So $^{+}$13; -WALK n 1Nb 1; WALKED 2ptpl 16Wo $^{+}$4; pt 37D $^{+}$2; WALKER n 1Nb $^{+}$9; WALKING prp 29Ess $^{+}$12, 36Co $^{+}$2; WALKS 3prsg Man $^{+}$2, 37D $^{+}$3

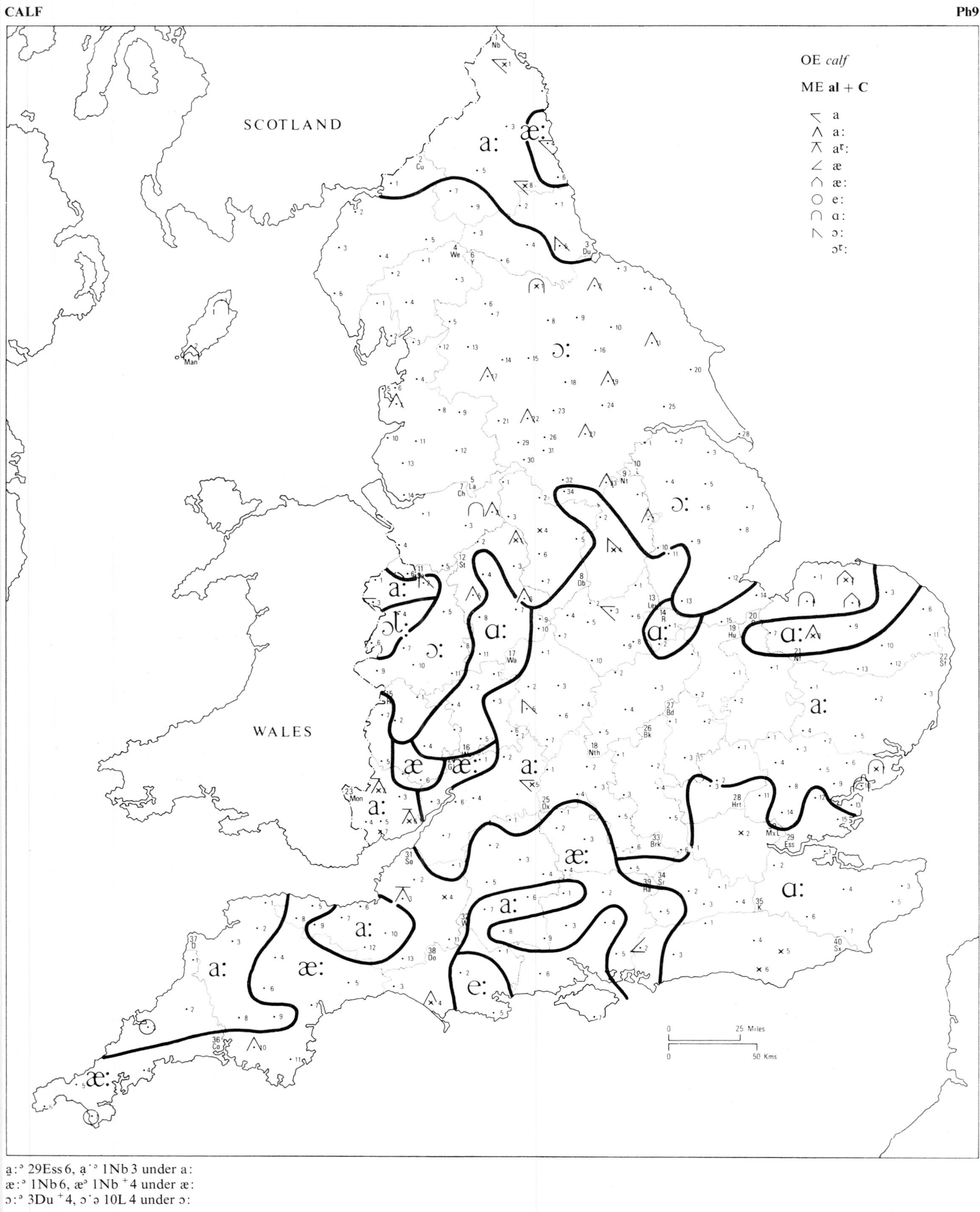

a̠:ᵊ 29Ess 6, ạˑᵊ 1Nb 3 under a:
æ:ᵊ 1Nb 6, æᵊ 1Nb $^{+}$4 under æ:
ɔ:ᵊ 3Du $^{+}$4, ɔˑə 10L 4 under ɔ:

ɛ: 40Sx 6
ɒ: 40Sx 5
ɒɷ 8Db 4
ɷə (sic, "very old") 1Nb $^{+}$5

CALF- 6Y $^{+}$2, 11Sa $^{+}$2, 13Lei $^{+}$3;
-CALF 7Ch $^{+}$2, 9Nt $^{+}$3, 13Lei $^{+}$3, 17Wa $^{+}$5, 37D $^{+}$10

kæ̈: Man 2, kɑ̈: Man 1

kɩ- 11Sa 1, kᶥ- 16Wo 5, kj- 7Ch $^{+}$2, 24Gl 5–7, 27Bd 2

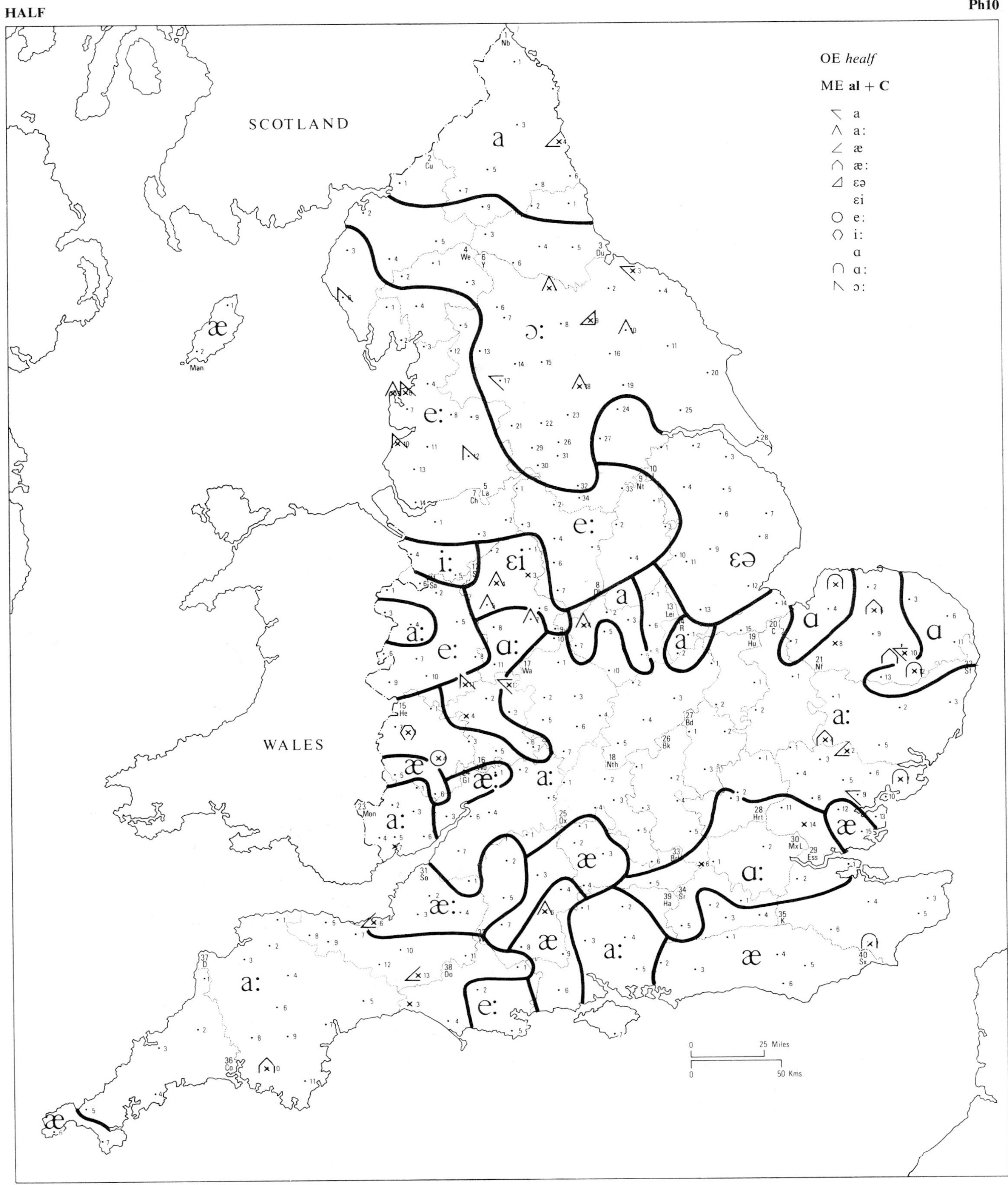

æ^{ə} 1Nb 4 under æ
ẹ:^{ə} 2Cu 3, e˙ə 2Cu $^{+}$6, 5La 4, 6Y 5, e:^{ı} 8Db 6,
e˙ɩ 8 Db 7 under e:

ɛ: 38Do 3
a^{r}: 16Wo 4
oɷ 12St 3
ə 29Ess 14

foll by AFTER: 6Y 2, 21Nf 5/$^{+}$10/11/12, 22Sf 1–5, 25Ox 2, 26Bk 1, 28Hrt 1, 29Ess 1/$^{+}$9/10/13, 31So 4/$^{+}$7/$^{+}$13, 32W 5/6/$^{+}$8/9, 38Do 2, 39Ha $^{+}$1/3/7

no -f Man 1/2, 12St 2/$^{+}$7/11, 13Lei 2/4/7/9, 14R 1/2, 15He 1–3/5–7, 16Wo 5/7, 17Wa 3/5–7, 18Nth 1/2/4, 19Hu 1/2, 20C 1, 21Nf 1–4/6/7/9/$^{+}$10/13, 23Mon 1/2/5/6, 24Gl 1/2/4–7, 25Ox 1/3/6, 26Bk 2–5, 27Bd 1–3, 28Hrt 2, 29Ess 2–4/6–8/$^{+}$9/11/12/14/15, 30MxL 2, 31So 1–3/5/6/$^{+}$7/8–12, 32W 1–4/7/$^{+}$8, 33Brk 1/3–5, 34Sr 1–3/5, 35K 2/4, 36Co 1–7, 37D 1–11, 38Do 1/3/4, 39Ha $^{+}$1/2/4/5, 40Sx 1

-p 34Sr 4, 35K 1/5/6, 40Sx 2–4/6

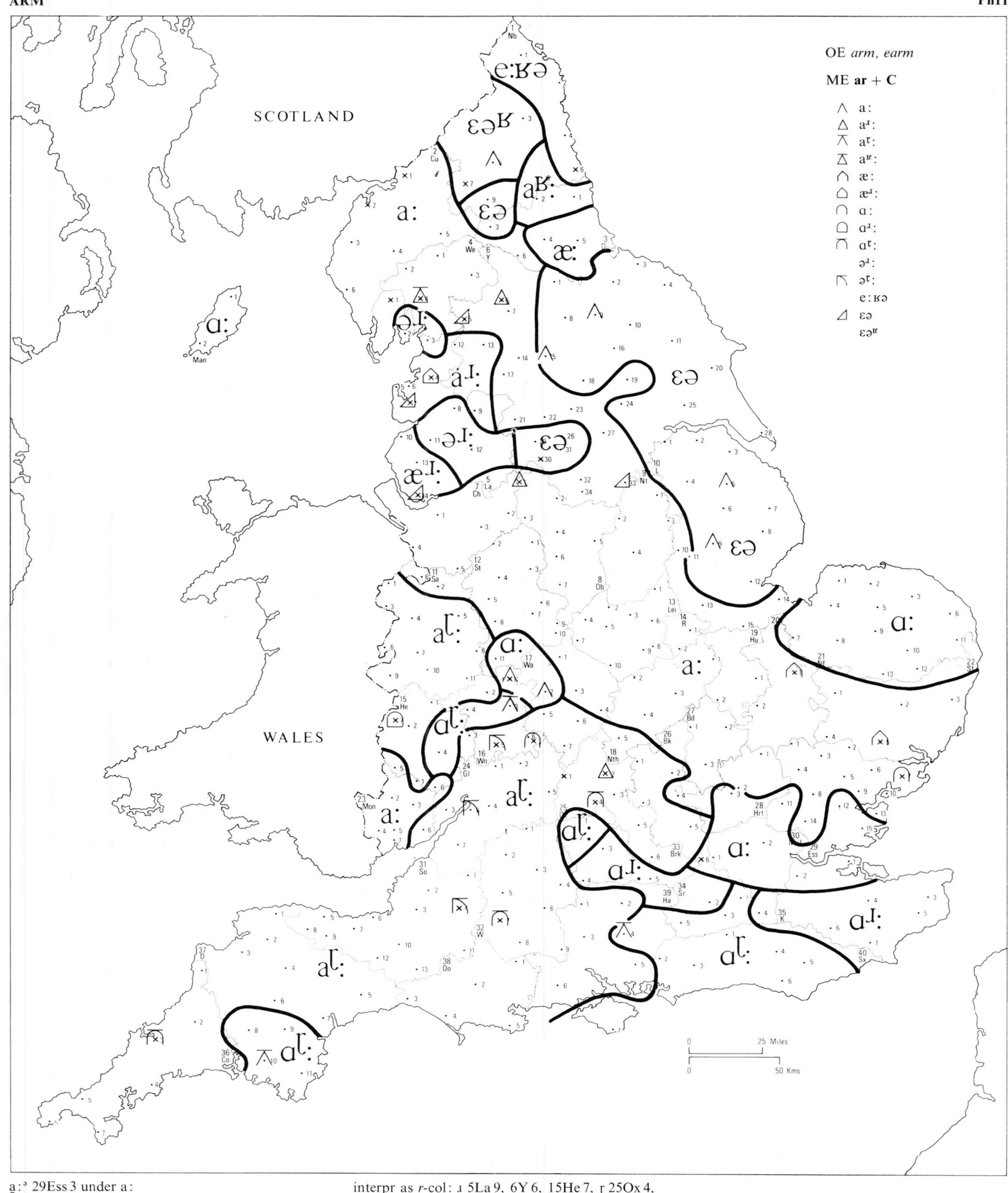

a̰:ᵊ 29Ess 3 under a:
aɹ 6Y 6, a:ɹə 2Cu 2 under aʴ:
aʵɽ 25Ox 3, ạʵ:ᵊ 26Bk 3 under aʵ:
æə 3Du ⁺3 under ɛə
æ˙ᵊʶʁ 1Nb 3 under ɛəʶ
ɑ:ᵊ 28Hrt 3, ɑ̇:ᵊ Man 2 under ɑ:
ɑɹ 15He ⁺7, ɑ:əʴ 33Brk 3, 34Sr 2/4 under ɑʴ:
ɑ:əʵ 34Sr 3/⁺5 under ɑʵ:
ɜʴ: 5La 3, ɜʴ:ɹ 5La 2/11/12, ɜ̈ʴ:ɹ 5La 8 under əʴ:

eəʁ 1Nb 6, e˙əʶ 1Nb 7
ɛ: 6Y ⁺19
ɛ:rə 2Cu 1
ɛəɹ 6Y 30
æʵ: 25Ox 1
a:ɹə 2Cu 2

interpr as *r*-col: ɹ 5La 9, 6Y 6, 15He 7, ɽ 25Ox 4, ʁ 1Nb 1/2/4
cons *r* foll *r*-col V: ɹ 5La 2/8/11/12, ɽ 25Ox 3/5, 32W 7, 33Brk 1/2, 40Sx 1–6, ʁ 1Nb 3

ARM- 1Nb ⁺5

j- 24Gl ⁺6/7, 31So 3/4, 32W 4/7/8, 33Brk 1/2, 39Ha 7

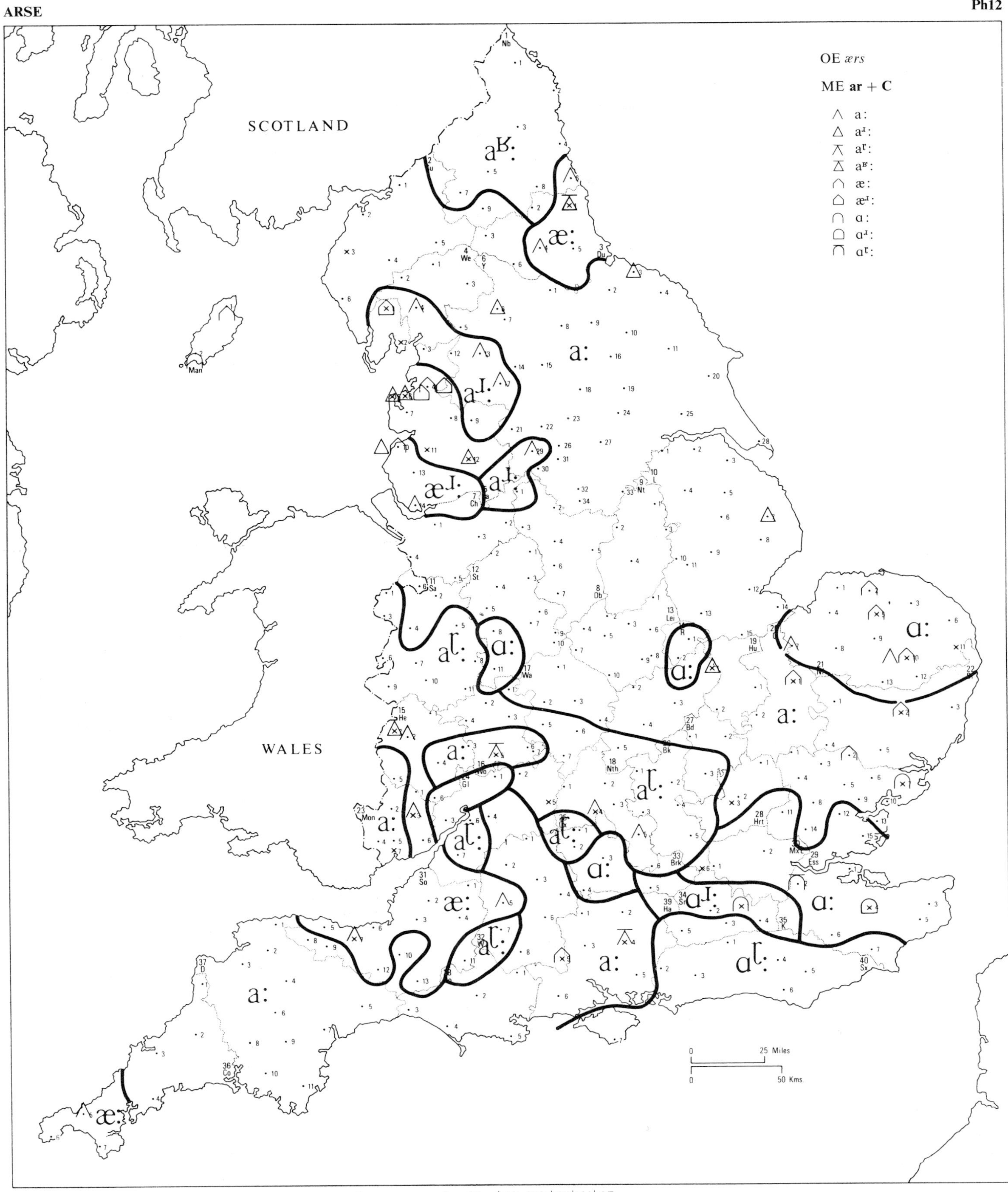

a 6Y 15, 32W 2/4, ä:ᵊ 29Ess 6 under a:
aɹ 6Y +3/+6 under aʴ:
äɽ 39Ha 4 under aɽ:
aʁ 1Nb 7 under aʶ:
æ 15He 6, 21Nf +2/+10, 29Ess +2, 31So +1/2/4,
æ:ᵊ 1Nb +6 under æ:
ɑ:əʴ 34Sr 2/4 under ɑʴ:
ɑɽ:ə 34Sr 5, ɑ:əɽ 40Sx 1, ɑ:əɽɽ 34Sr 3 under ɑɽ:

e: 5La 11
ɛ: 5La +12
ɛ·ə 10L +2
æɽ: 24Gl 5
aɾ 6Y +5, ar 2Cu 3, a·r 2Cu +1, a:r 2Cu +1
ɜʴ:ɹ 5La 2

interpr as *r*-col: ɹ 5La +12, 6Y +3/+6/+17,
15He 7, 18Nth 1, ʁ 1Nb 7
cons *r* foll *r*-col V: ɹ 5La 2/9/+10, ɽ 33Brk 1/2,
34Sr 3, 39Ha 7, 40Sx 2–6

-ARSE 21Nf +2; ARSE inf 10L +7

WEDNESDAY Ph13

KETTLE Ph14

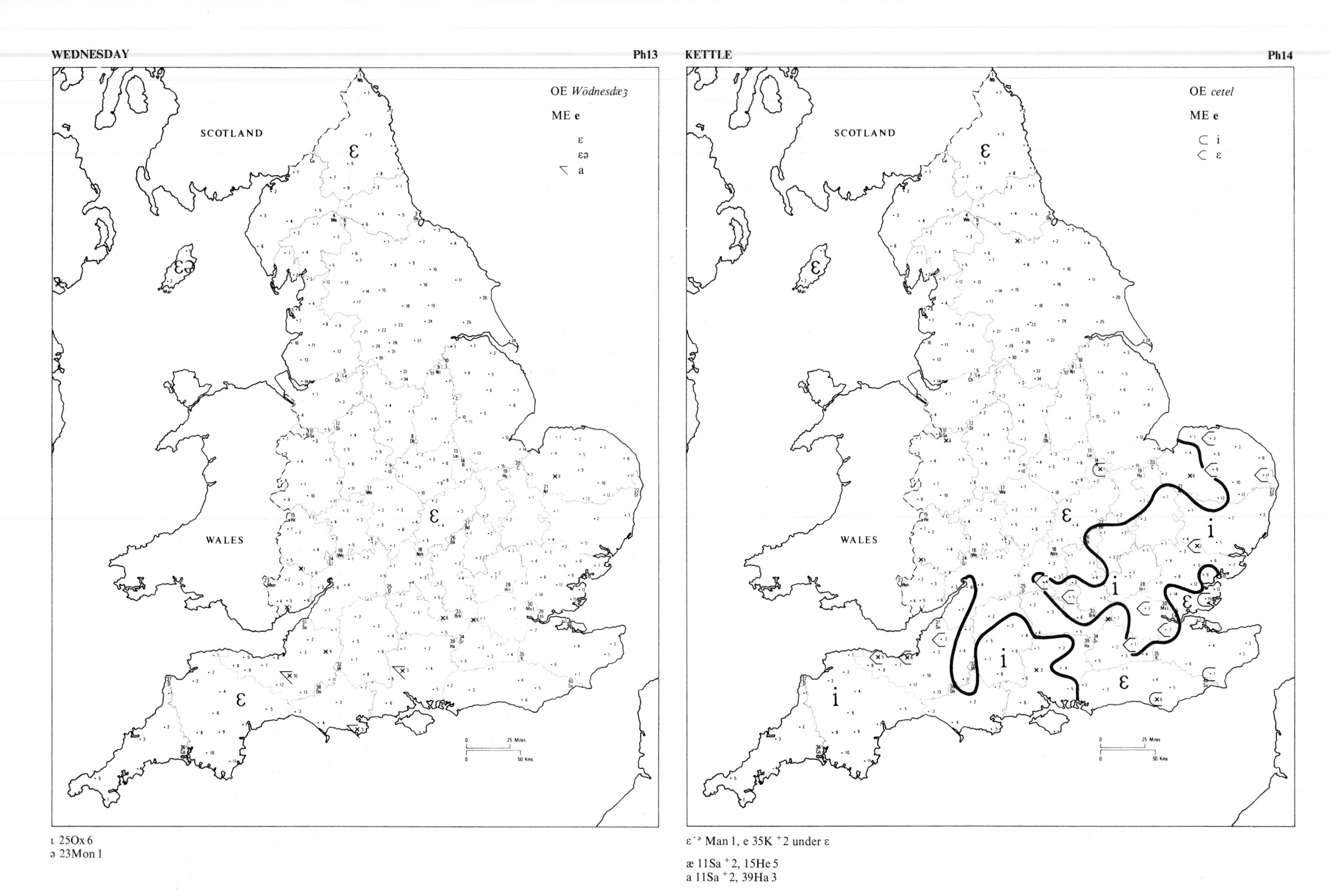

ι 25Ox 6
ə 23Mon 1

ε˙ᵊ Man 1, e 35K ⁺2 under ε

æ 11Sa ⁺2, 15He 5
a 11Sa ⁺2, 39Ha 3

-KETTLE 18Nth 5

kj- 7Ch 2, 15He 4–6, 24Gl 5, kᶦ- 15He 3, 16Wo 4/6

FELLIES **Ph15a**

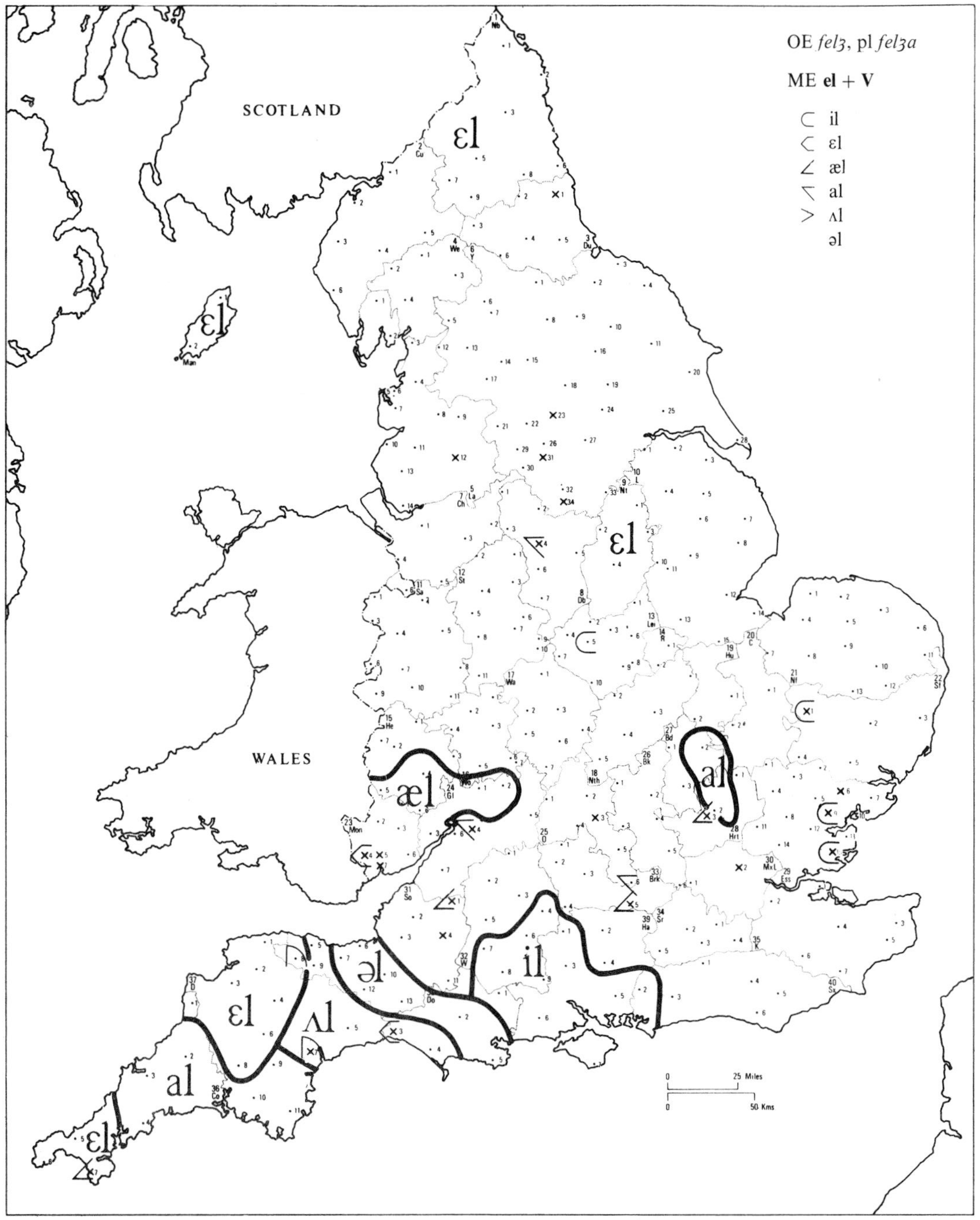

OE *felʒ*, pl *felʒa*

ME **el + V**

⊂ il
< ɛl
∠ æl
⊼ al
> ʌl
əl

SCOTLAND

WALES

ɛl æl al il əl ʌl

0 25 Miles
0 50 Kms

FELLIES **Ph15b**

l-quality

1 ∧ l
2 ⊓ ɫ

SCOTLAND

WALES

1 2

0 25 Miles
0 50 Kms

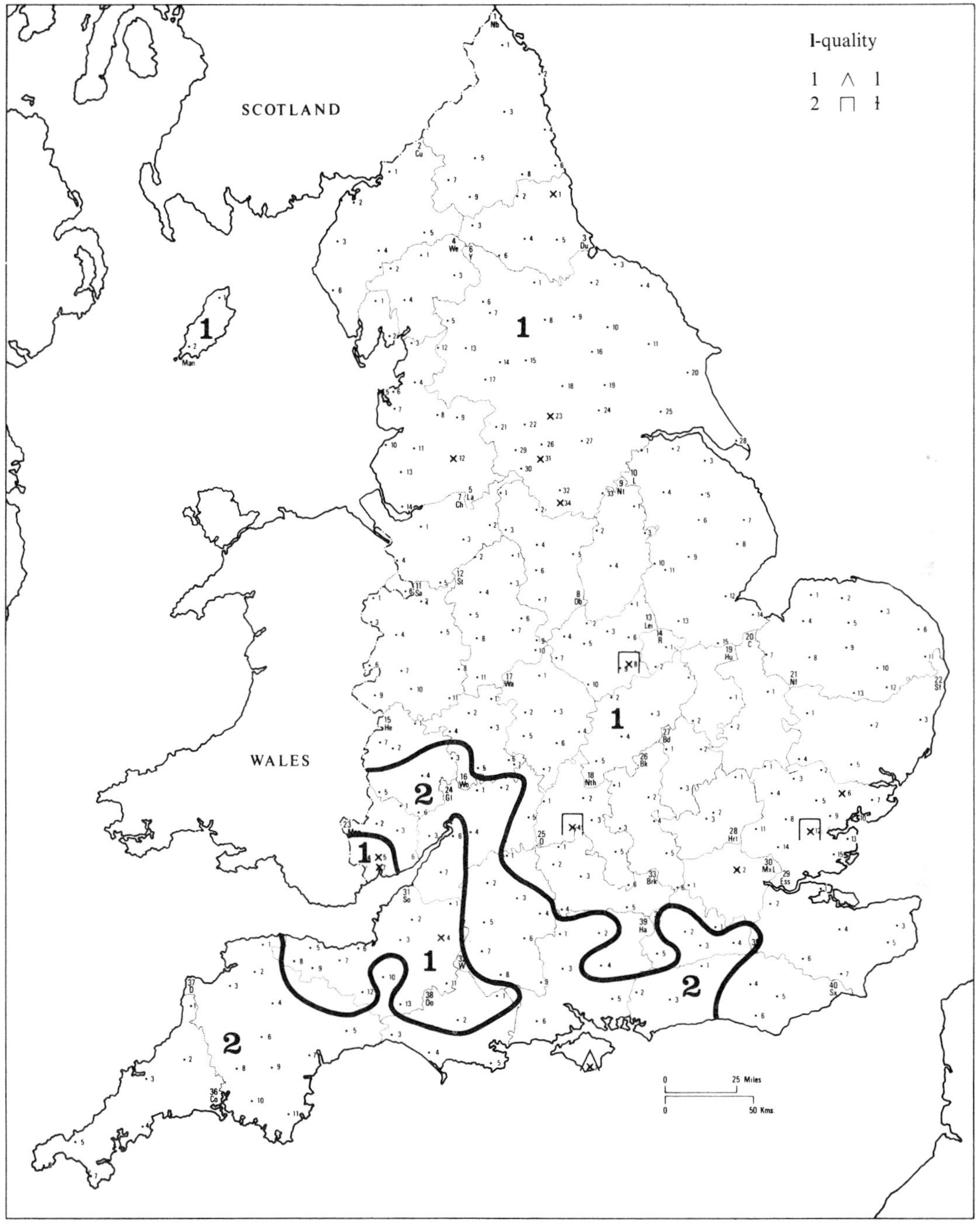

al 25Ox3

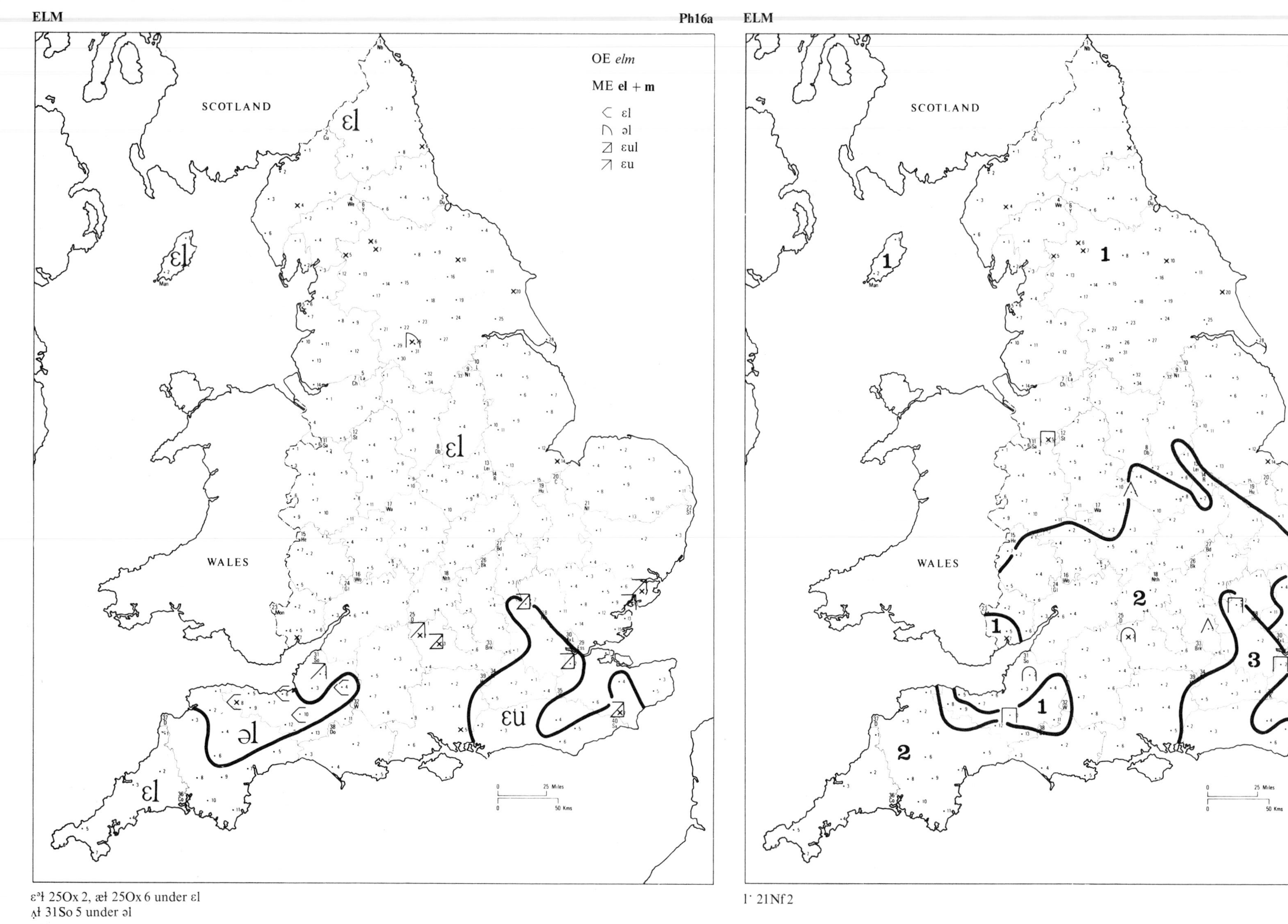

ɛᵊɫ 25Ox 2, æɫ 25Ox 6 under ɛl
ʌ̣ɫ 31So 5 under əl

al 26Bk ⁺5, aɫ 39Ha 5

j- 32W ⁺1/4

repr ON *álmr*: ɔ:m 4We ⁺1, 6Y 6/7/⁺9/10, ɔ˙əm 6Y 20,
o:m 6Y 5

? irr r ɛlə 2Cu 4

l˙ 21Nf 2

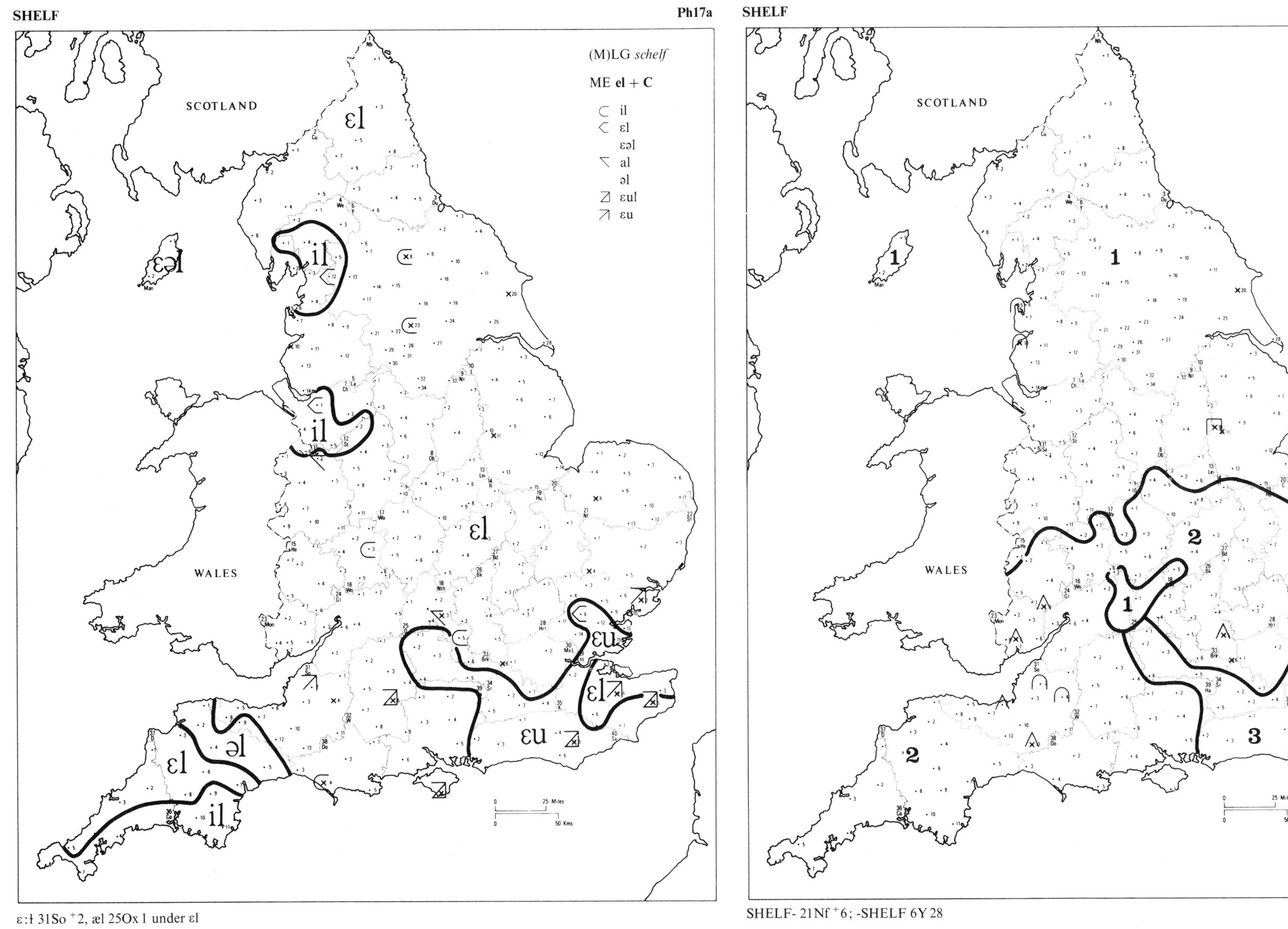

ɛ:ɫ 31So $^{+}$2, æl 25Ox 1 under ɛl

ɩɷ 31So $^{+}$4
ɩɷɫ 31So $^{+}$4
ɷ (obs) 5La $^{+}$5, ᵊu: 5La $^{+}$10, ᵊü: 5La $^{+}$10

-SHELF 5La $^{+}$10, 6Y 28, 11Sa $^{+}$2; SHELVES pl 15He 5, 23Mon 7, 33Brk 4, 34Sr 2/4, 35K 3

-f dropped 33Brk 3/5, 40Sx 4/5

SHELF- 21Nf $^{+}$6; -SHELF 6Y 28

l· 21Nf $^{+}$6/9/10, l: 21Nf 1/11

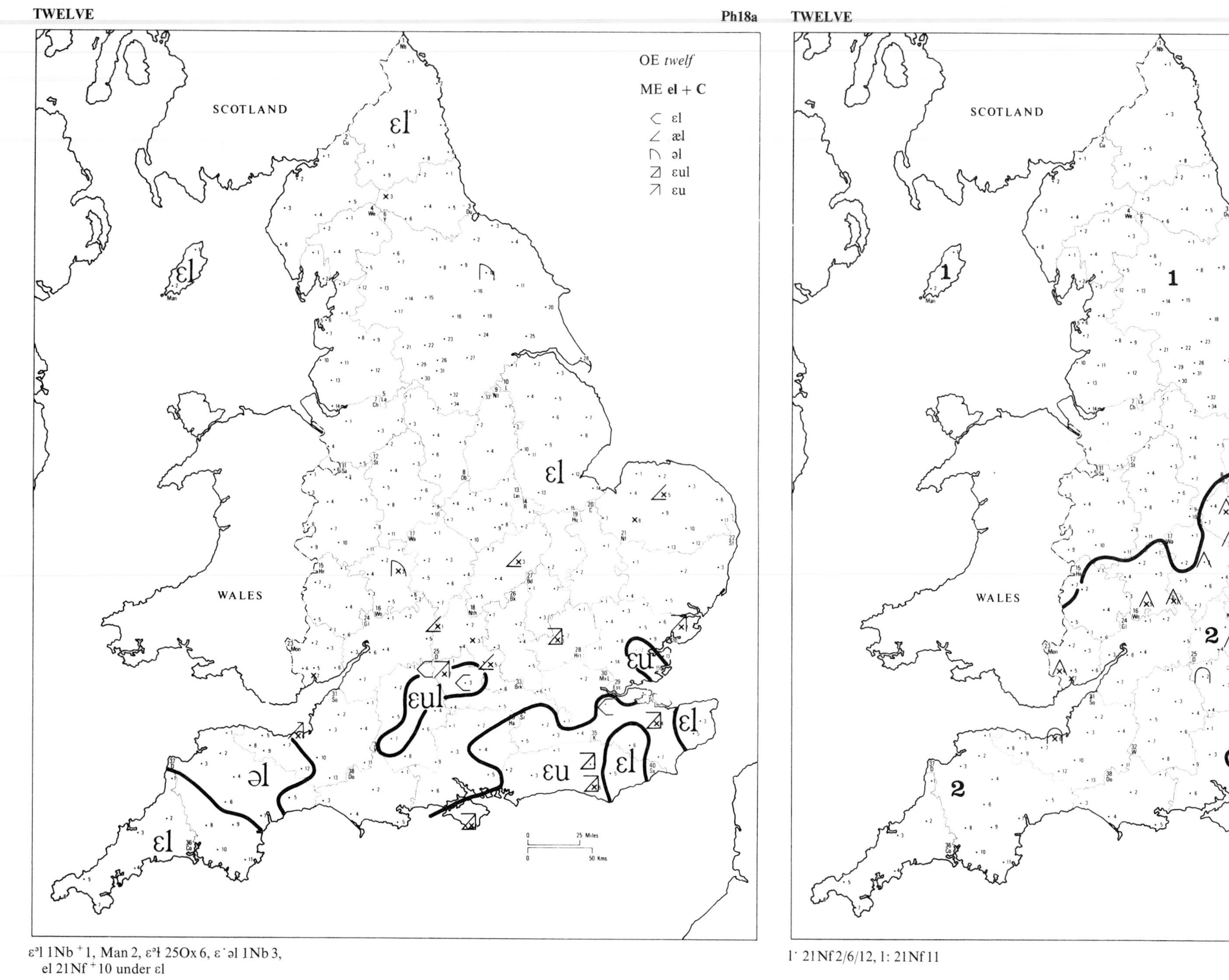

ɛ^{ə}l 1Nb $^{+}$1, Man 2, ɛ^{ə}ɫ 25Ox 6, ɛˑəl 1Nb 3,
el 21Nf $^{+}$10 under ɛl

al 8Db $^{+}$4, aɫ 25Ox $^{+}$3
ɑl 25Ox $^{+}$3
ɒl 6Y $^{+}$6
ɷl 3Du 3

lˑ 21Nf 2/6/12, l: 21Nf 11

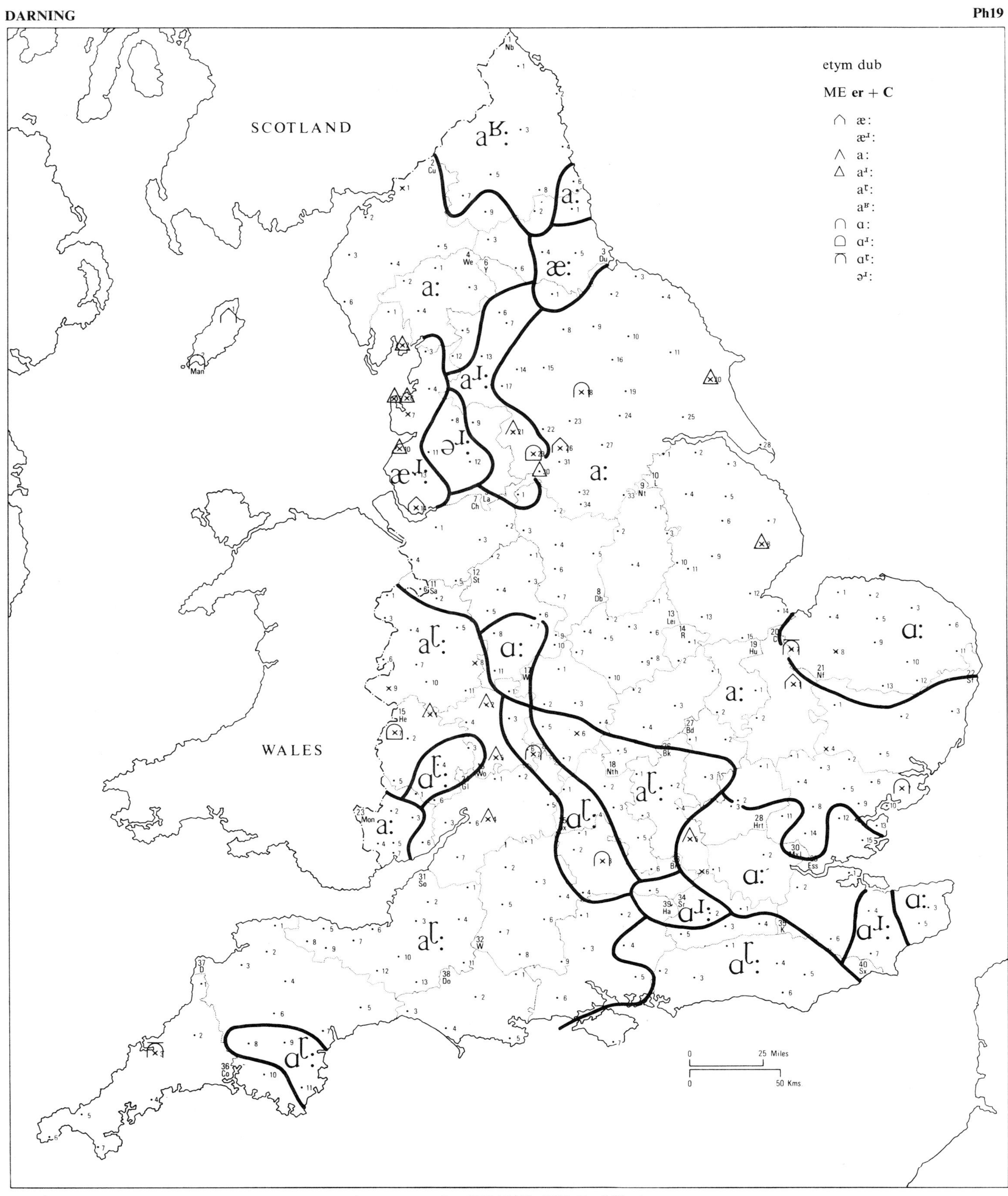

a 6Y ⁺30, ˌa: 16Wo 5 under a:
aɹ 6Y 6/⁺7/⁺30 under aʴ:
ạʵ 26Bk 3, äʵ 26Bk 2, ˌaʵ: 16Wo 4 under aʵ:
ɑ̈ɹ 15He 7 under ɑʴ:
ɑ̈ʵ 39Ha 4, ɑɽ 25Ox 4, ɑ:əʵ 34Sr 5,
ɑ̇:əʵɽ 34Sr 4 under ɑʵ:
ɜʴ:ɹ 5La 8/11/12 under əʴ:

æʵ: 17Wa 6
a˙r 2Cu 1
ɔʵ: 11Sa 8
əʵ: 11Sa 9

interpr as *r*-col: ɹ 6Y 6/7/⁺30, 15He 7, ɽ 25Ox 4,
33Brk 1/2, 40Sx 1, ʁ 1Nb 2
cons *r* foll *r*-col V: ɹ 5La 2/4/8–12, ɽ 34Sr 4,
39Ha 7, 40Sx 2/4–6

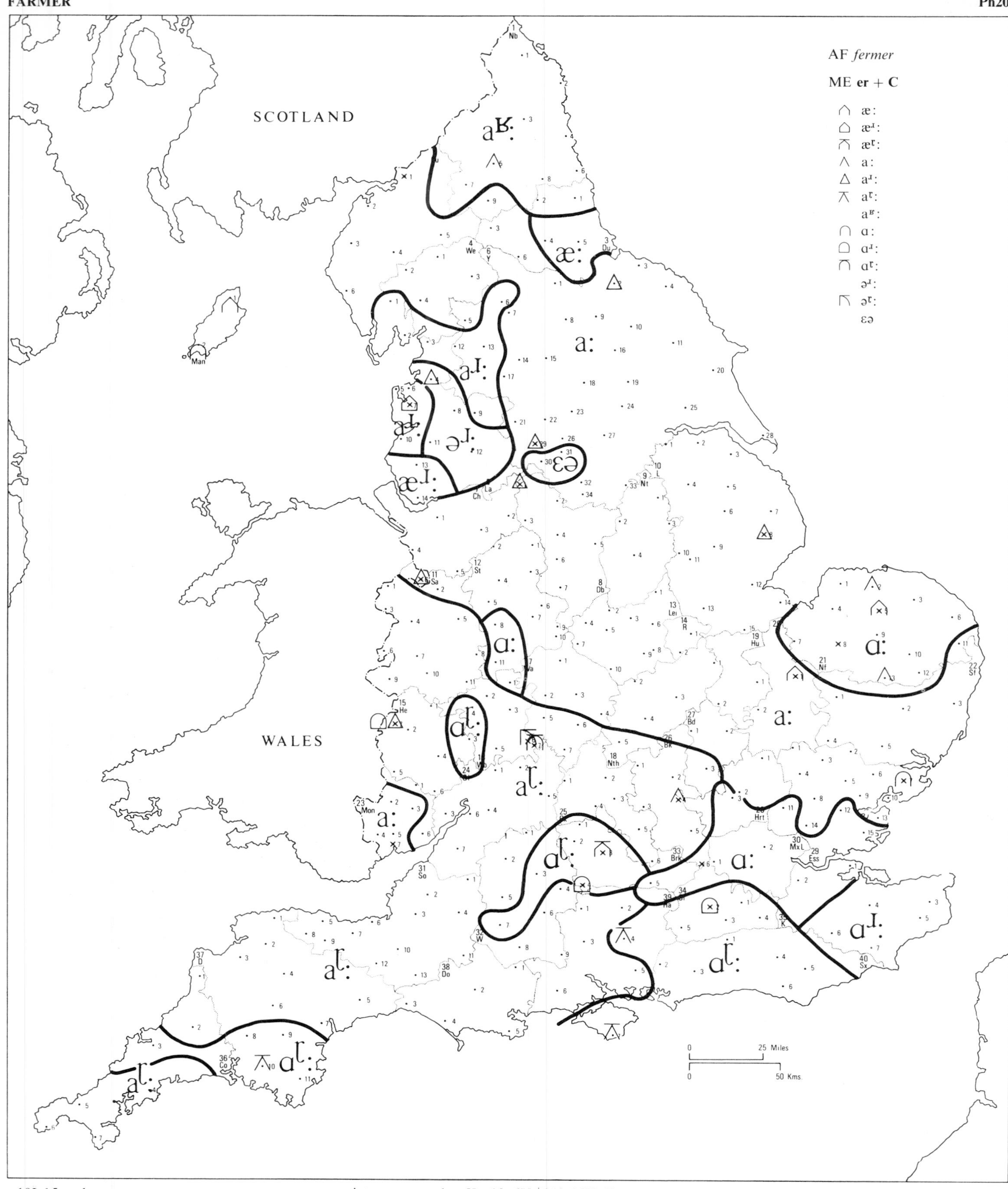

a 10L 15 under a:
aɹ 6Y +2/6, 15He +7 under aʴ:
a˞ 25Ox +3, 39Ha +4, ä˞ 39Ha +4, a˞ɽ 25Ox +3,
  aɽ 25Ox +4 under a˞:
ɑ̊ 12St 11 under ɑ:
ɑɹ 15He +7 under ɑʴ:
ɑ˞ 16Wo 7, 39Ha +4 under ɑ˞:
ɜʴ:ɹ 5La +4/8/11/12 under əʴ:

æ˙ɽ 33Brk 3
a:r 2Cu 1

interpr as *r*-col: ɹ 5La 10, 6Y +2/6, 15He 7,
  ɽ 25Ox 4/5, 34Sr 3/4, 40Sx 1
cons *r* foll *r*-col V: ɹ 5La 4/8/9/11/12, ɽ 25Ox +3,
  32W 3/7, 39Ha 7, 40Sx 2–6

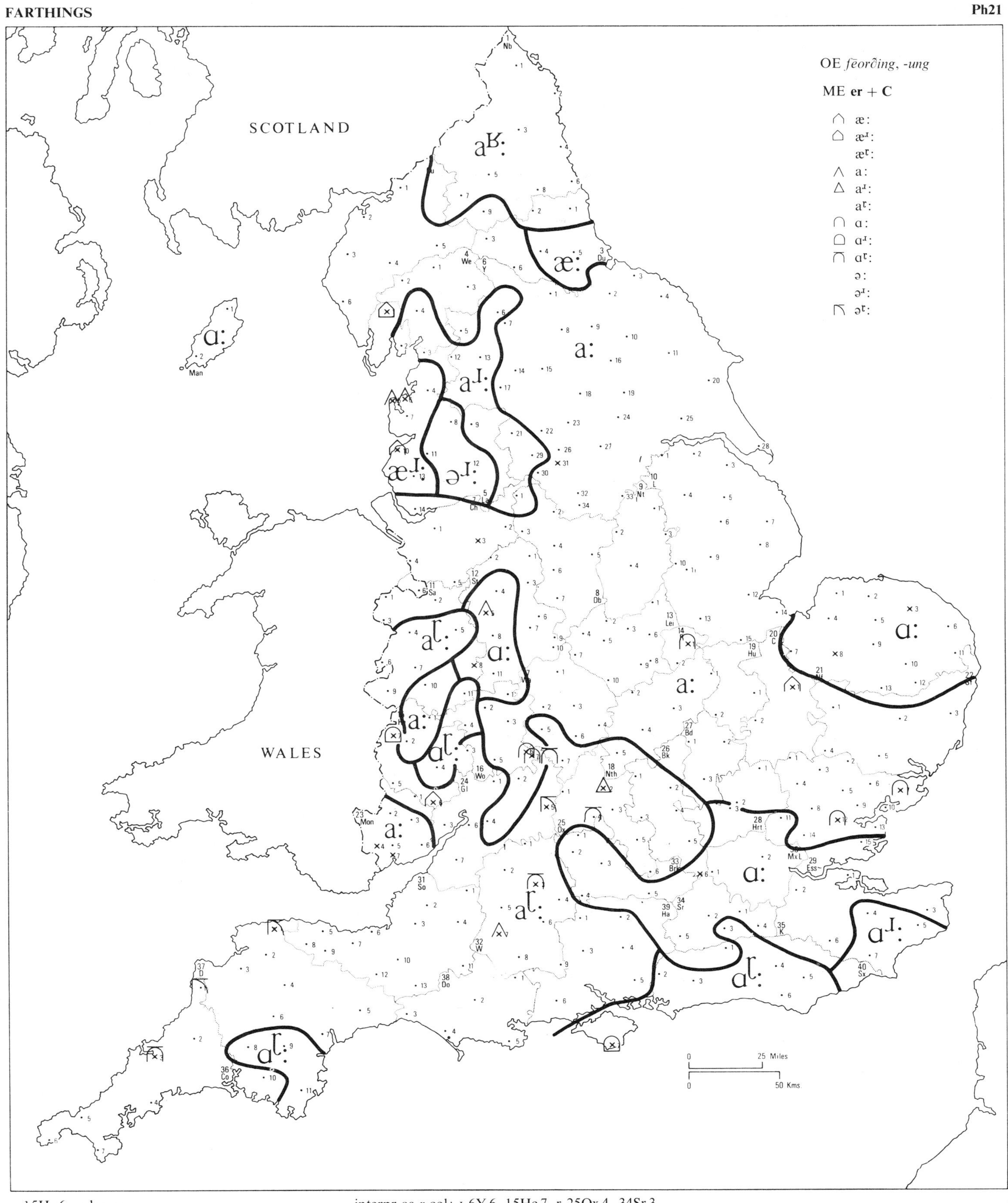

æ 15He 6 under æː
ä 29Ess 6 under aː
aɹ 6Y 6 under a˞ː
a˞ 25Ox 3, aɽ 25Ox +4 under a˞ː
ɑɹ 15He 7 under ɑ˞ː
ɑ̊ːəɽ 34Sr 3, ɑ˞ 16Wo +7, ɑɽ 25Ox +4 under ɑ˞ː
ɜ˞ːɹ 5La 8/11/12 under ə˞ː

eː 7Ch 3
ɛ˙ə 6Y 31
ɑ˞ːə˞ 40Sx +4
ɔː 11Sa 8
ɔ˞ː 11Sa 11

interpr as *r*-col: ɹ 6Y 6, 15He 7, ɽ 25Ox 4, 34Sr 3
cons *r* foll *r*-col V: ɹ 5La 8/9/11/12,
ɽ 40Sx 2/3/+4/5/6

-ð- dropped 7Ch 5

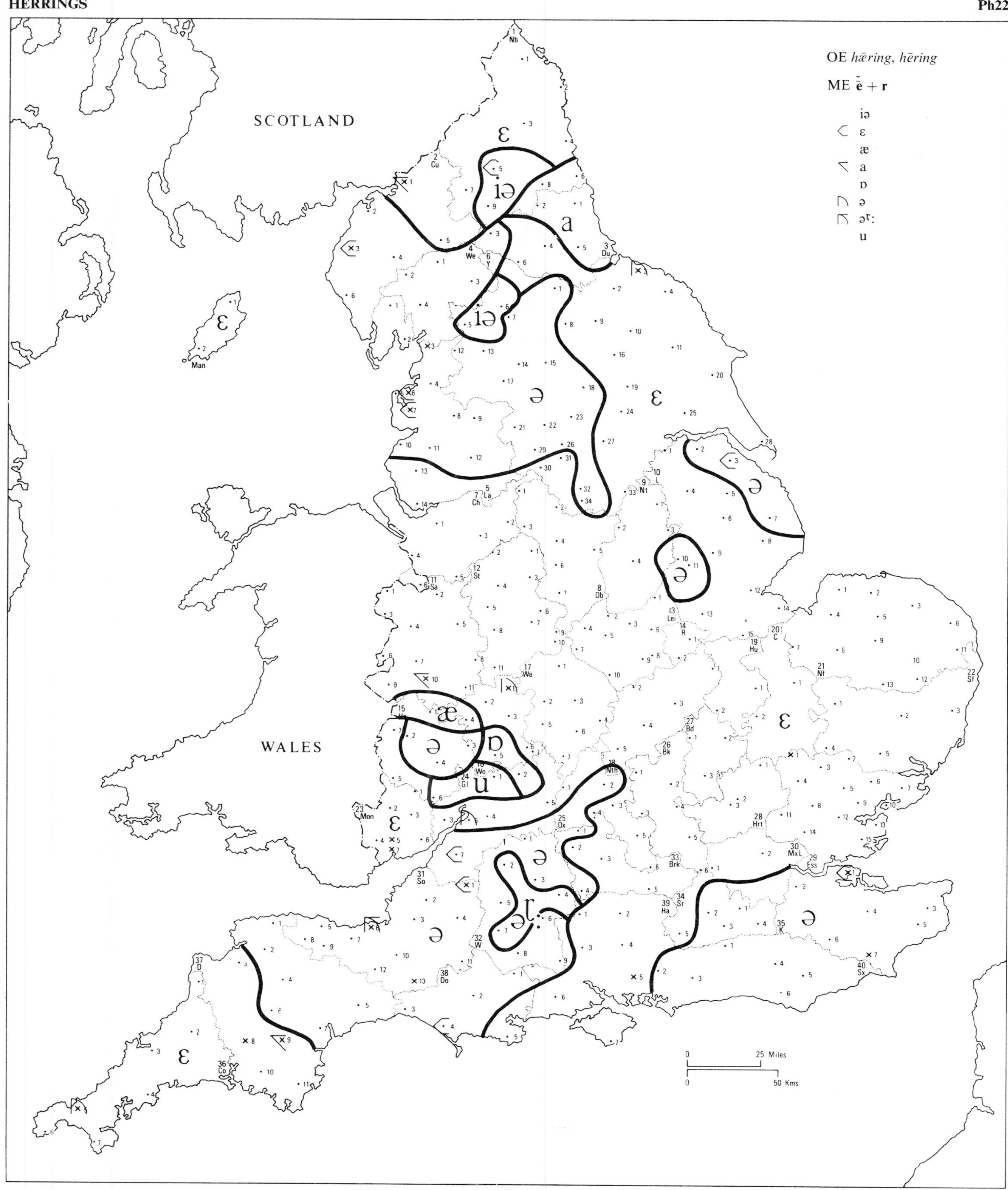

εᵊ 22Sf 4, εə 29Ess 12, ε˙ə 17Wa 5 under ε
ɔ: 31So 4, ʌ 15He 2/4 under ə

ι 29Ess 1
aʳ: 39Ha 5

-HERRING 3Du 5

həʳɳʐ 35K 7

prothetic j- foll loss of h- 3Du 4, 5La 12, 6Y 8/21/$^{+}$26/29/$^{+}$30/31, 11Sa 5/8/10/11, 15He 1–4/6, 16Wo 1/2/4/5, 24Gl 1–4/$^{+}$6/$^{+}$7, 31So $^{+}$3/4/6/7/$^{+}$8/9/$^{+}$10/12, 32W 1/3/4, 39Ha 5

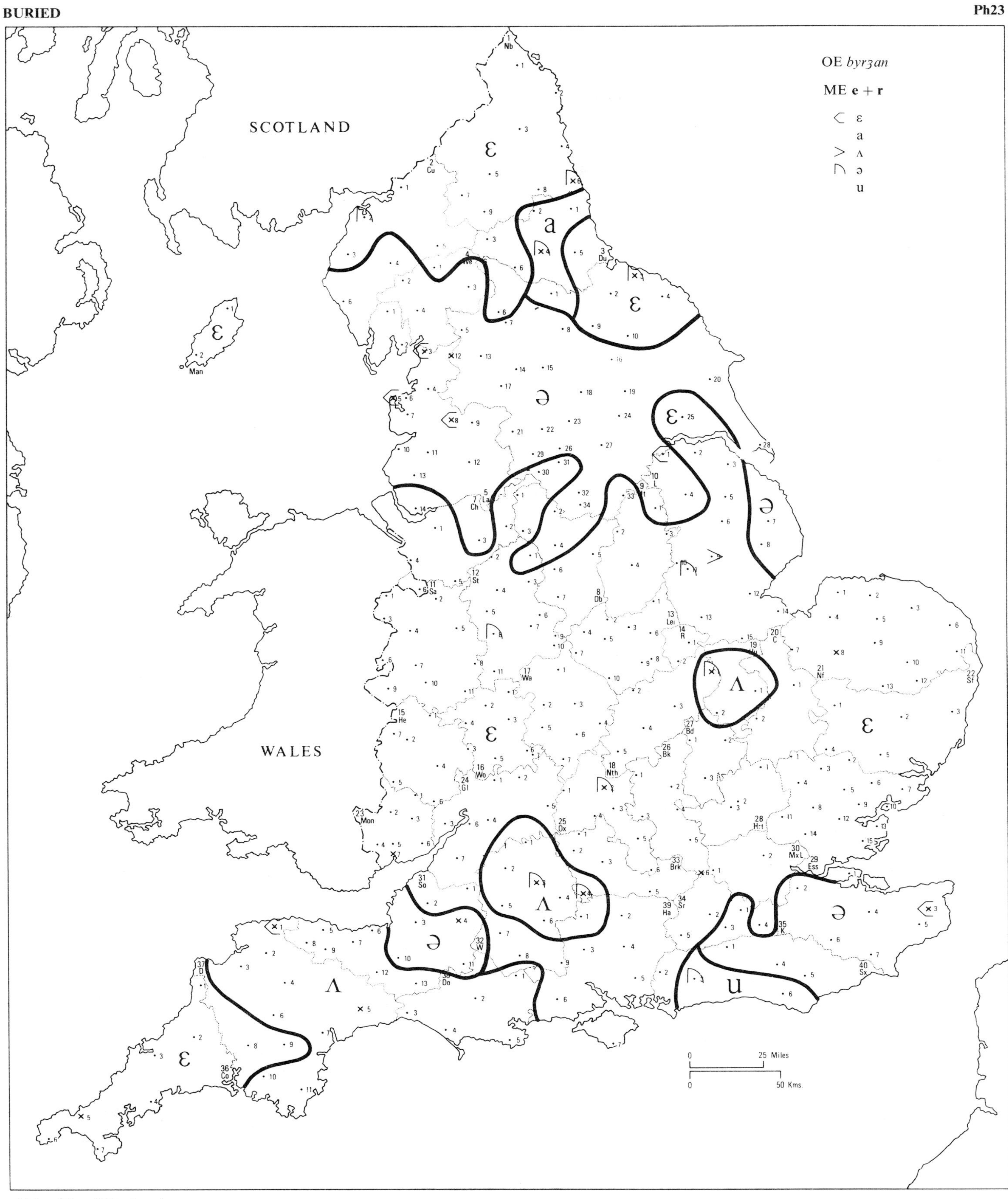

ε^{ə} Man $^{+}$2, æ 25Ox 5 under ε

eɪə Man $^{+}$2
ε^{r}: 36Co 5
ə^{r} 31So 4

bə^{r}:ɖ 37D 5

BURY inf 10L $^{+}$9; 1prpl 40Sx $^{+}$3; v 10L $^{+}$1;
BURIES 3prsg 12St $^{+}$8

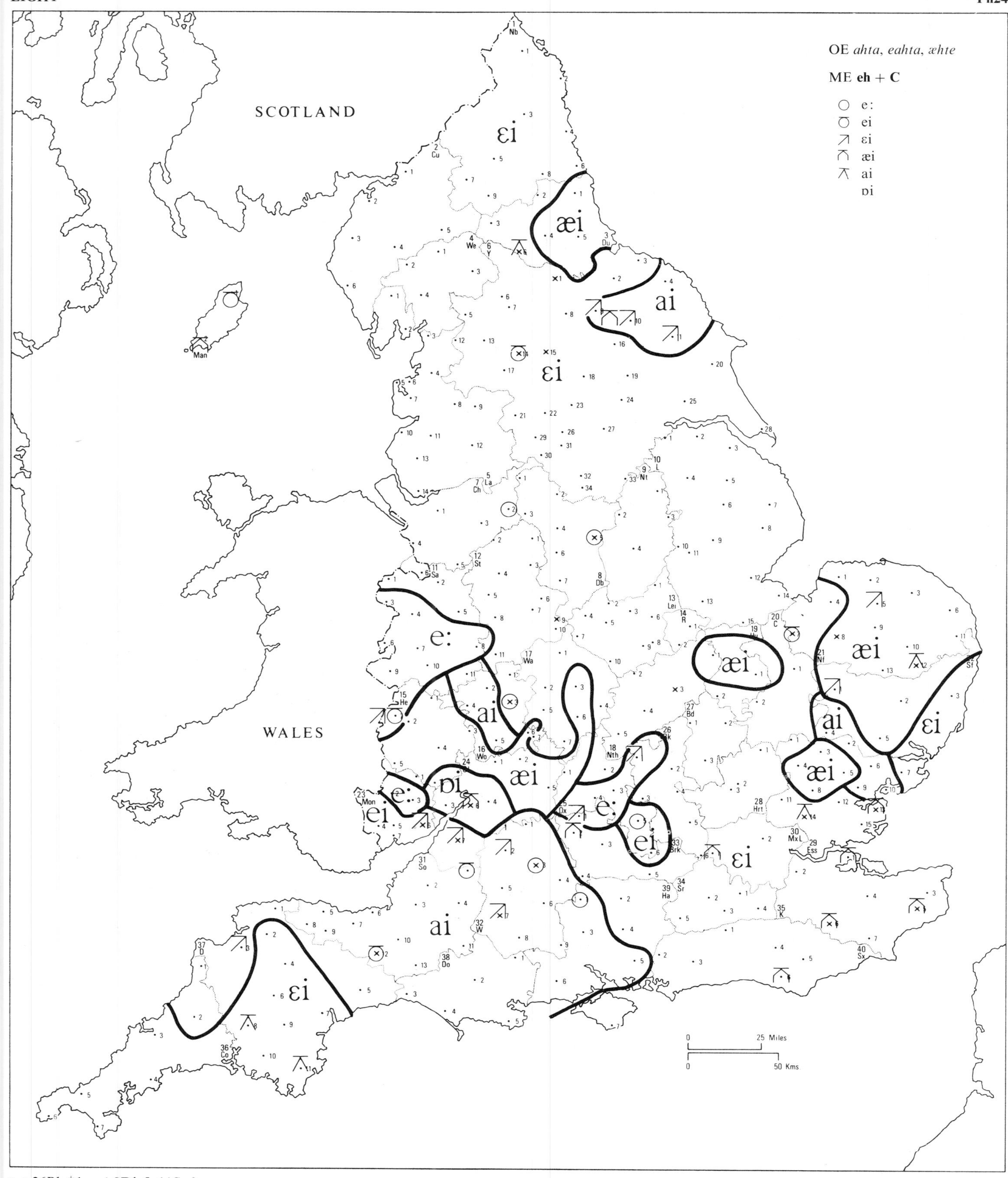

e ə 26Bk +1, e:[ɩ] 8Db 5, 11Sa 3,
e:ɩ 16Wo 3 under e:

ɛɩ[ə] 20C 1, ɛ̜ɩ[ə] 20C 2, ɛ:ɩ 13Lei +1, 21Nf +5,
39Ha 7 under ɛi

æɩ[ə] 24Gl 1 under æi

aɩj 31So 2 under ai

ɛ: 12St 9

ɛə 40Sx +4, ɛˑə 18Nth 3

ɑɩ 6Y 1, ɑ:ɩ 15He +5

əɩ 6Y 15

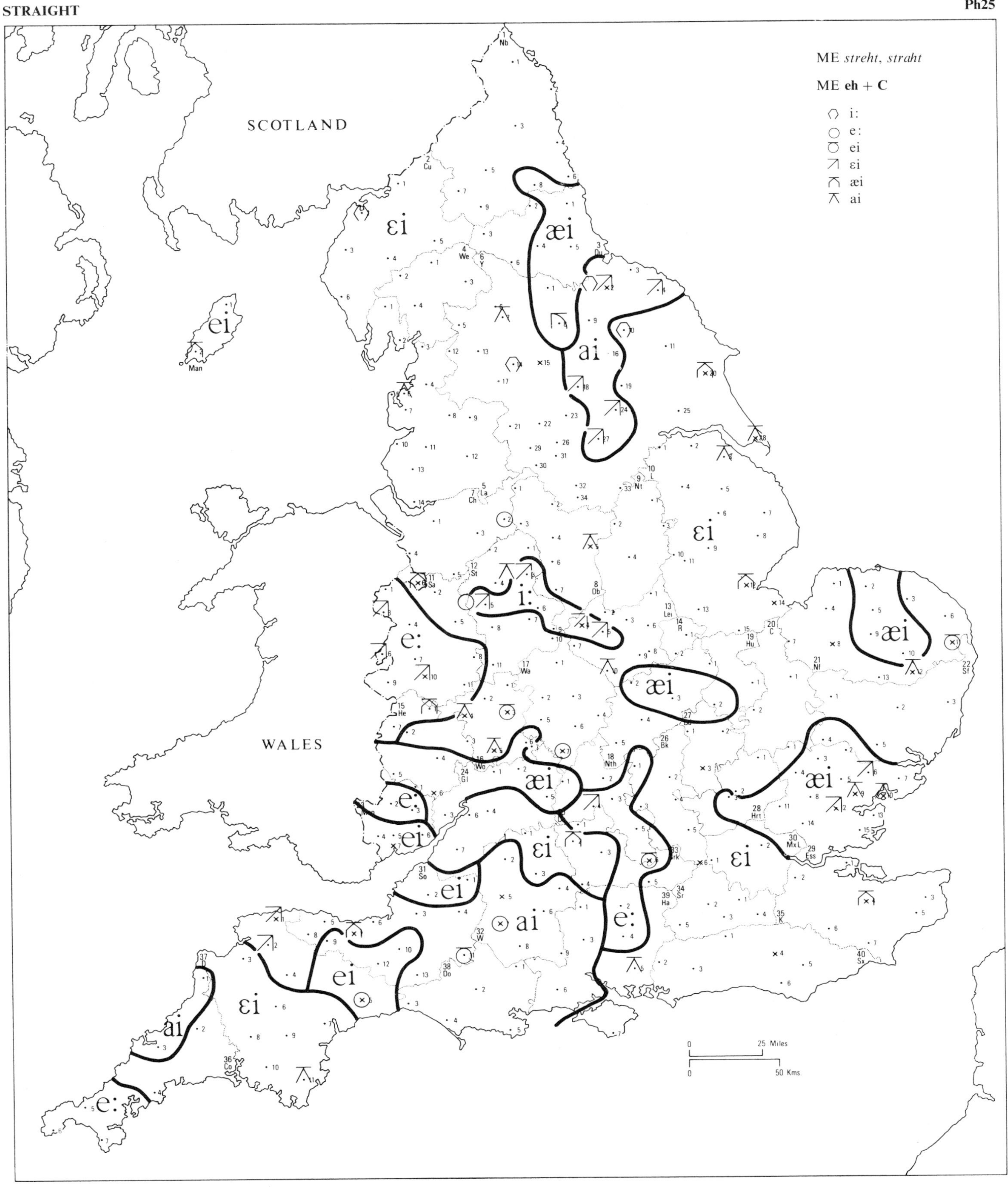

e:^{ə} 17Wa 7, e˙ə 26Bk 1, e:^{ι} 11Sa 8, 15He $^{+}$1/7,
39Ha 4 under e:

e:ι 16Wo 3, 23Mon 6, 31So $^{+}$11,
ẹ:^{ι} 23Mon 4 under ei

ẹι^{ə} 20C 2 under εi

a:ι 31So $^{+}$3/4 under ai

ιə ("rare") 6Y $^{+}$10

ε: 32W 5

εə 40Sx 4, εə 18Nth $^{+}$3, ε˙ə 27Bd 3

ɒι 15He 6

ɔ̈ι 10L 14

əι 6Y $^{+}$5/15

STRAIGHT adv 10L $^{+}$3, 11Sa $^{+}$3/$^{+}$6, 13Lei $^{+}$5,
25Ox $^{+}$4, 33Brk $^{+}$2, 37D $^{+}$2/$^{+}$11, 39Ha $^{+}$5;
ndg 15He $^{+}$1

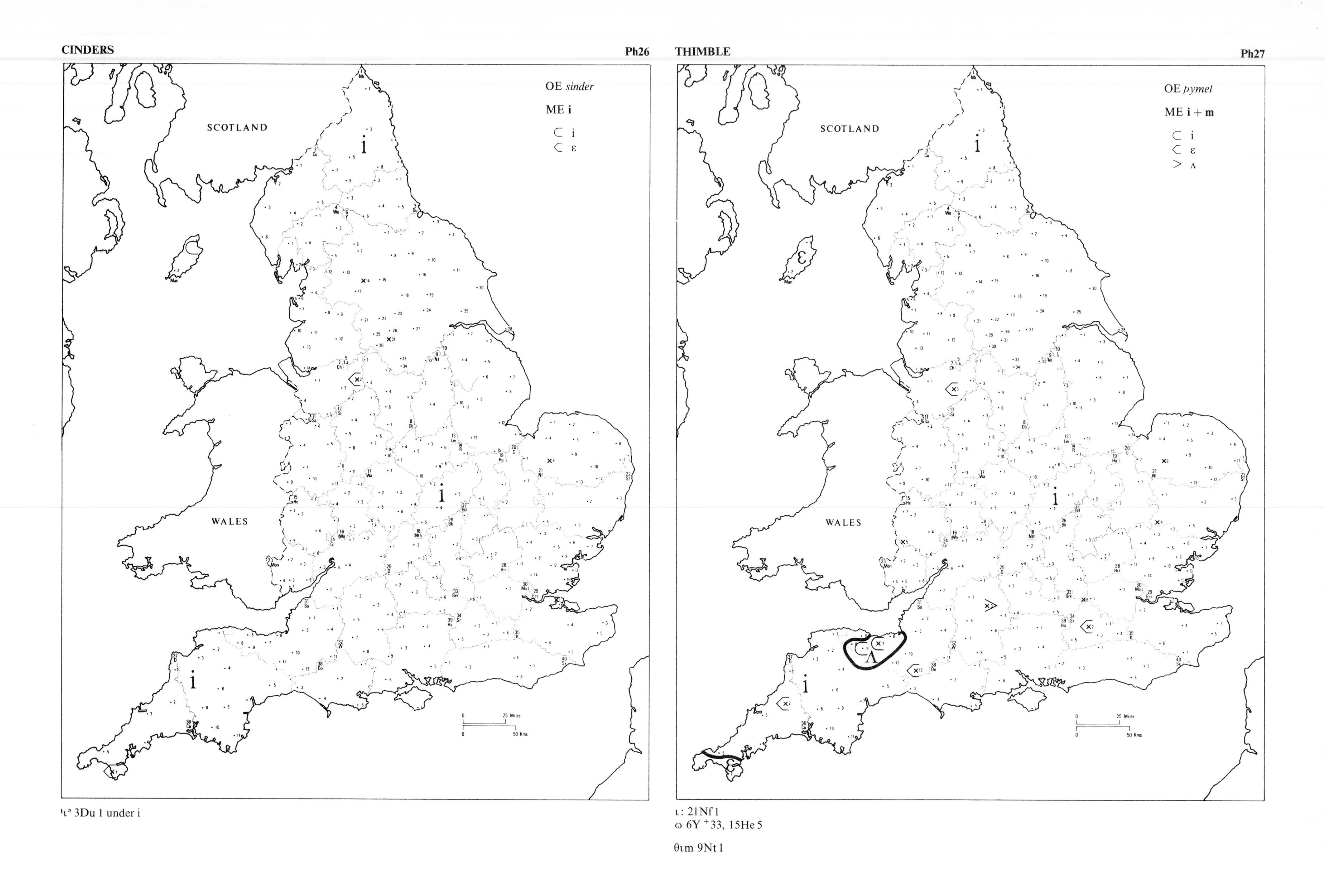

ɩᵊ 3Du 1 under i

ɩ: 21Nf 1
ɷ 6Y ⁺33, 15He 5

θɩm 9Nt 1

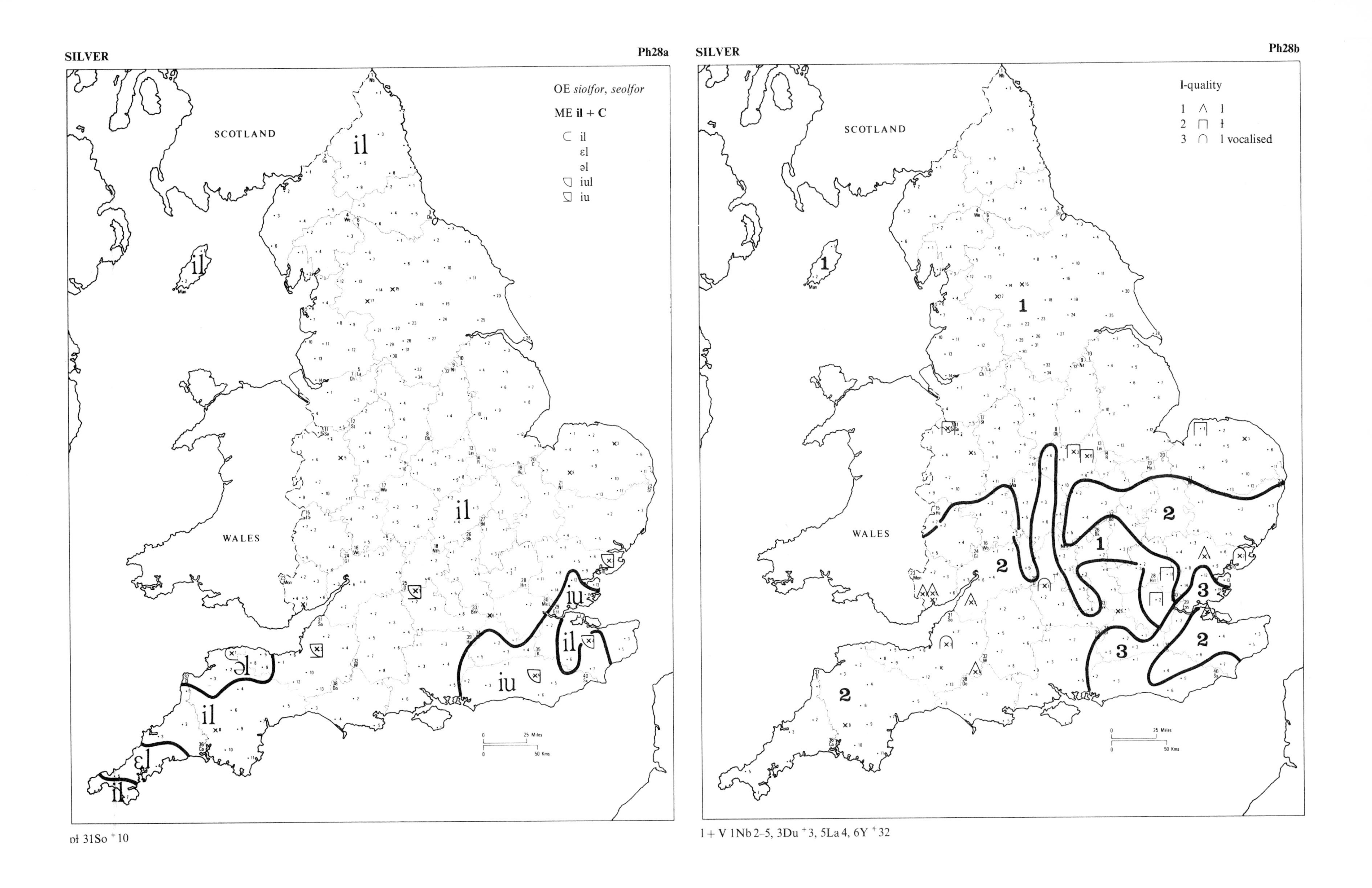

ɒɫ 31So $^{+}$10

l + V 1Nb 2–5, 3Du $^{+}$3, 5La 4, 6Y $^{+}$32

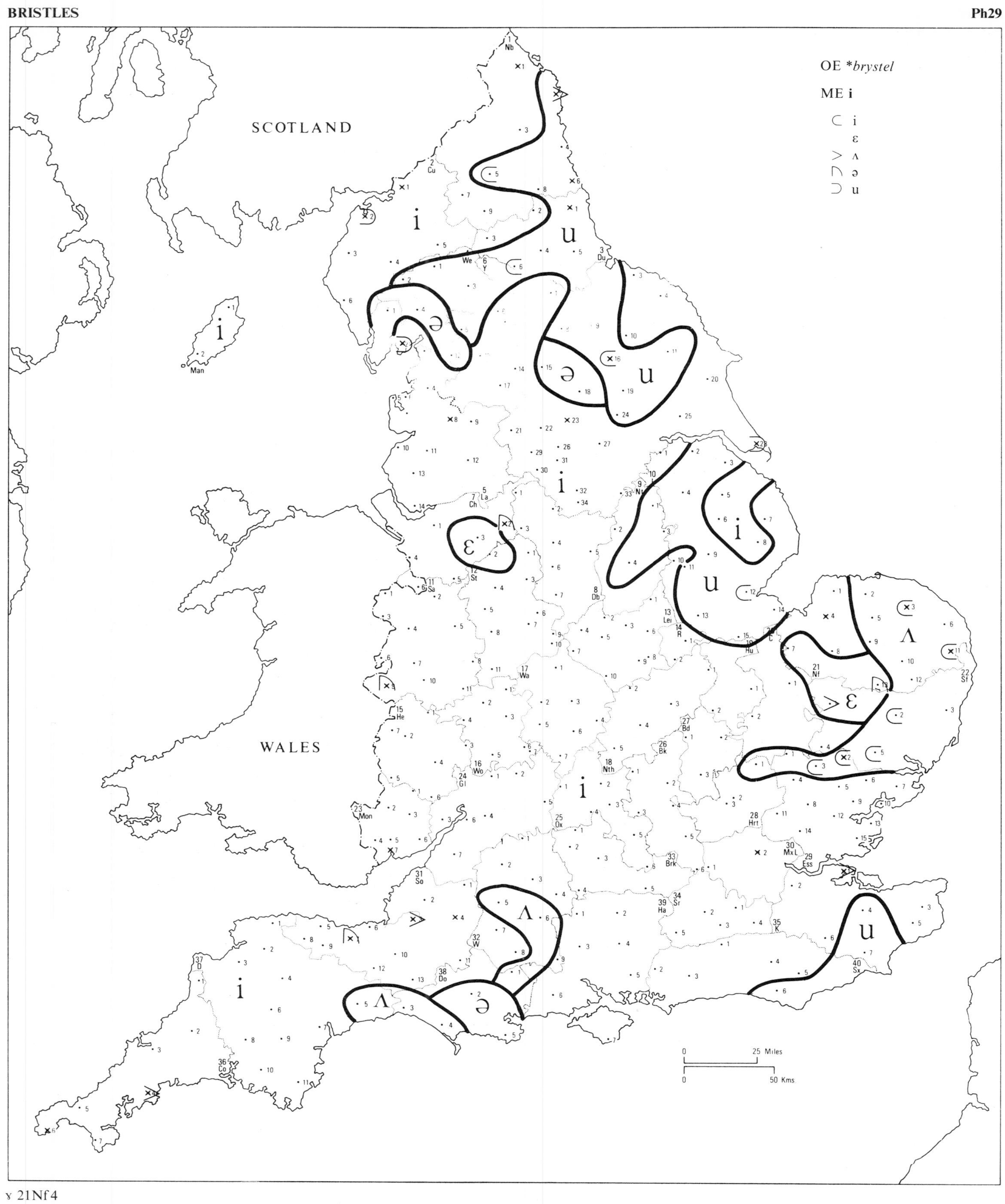

ɣ 21Nf 4

metathesised forms: bɔʁsɪz 3Du 1, bɜʴ:ɹslz 5La 8, bə:ɽʂɬʐ 33Brk ⁺5, bəʳ:ʂɬʐ 36Co 6

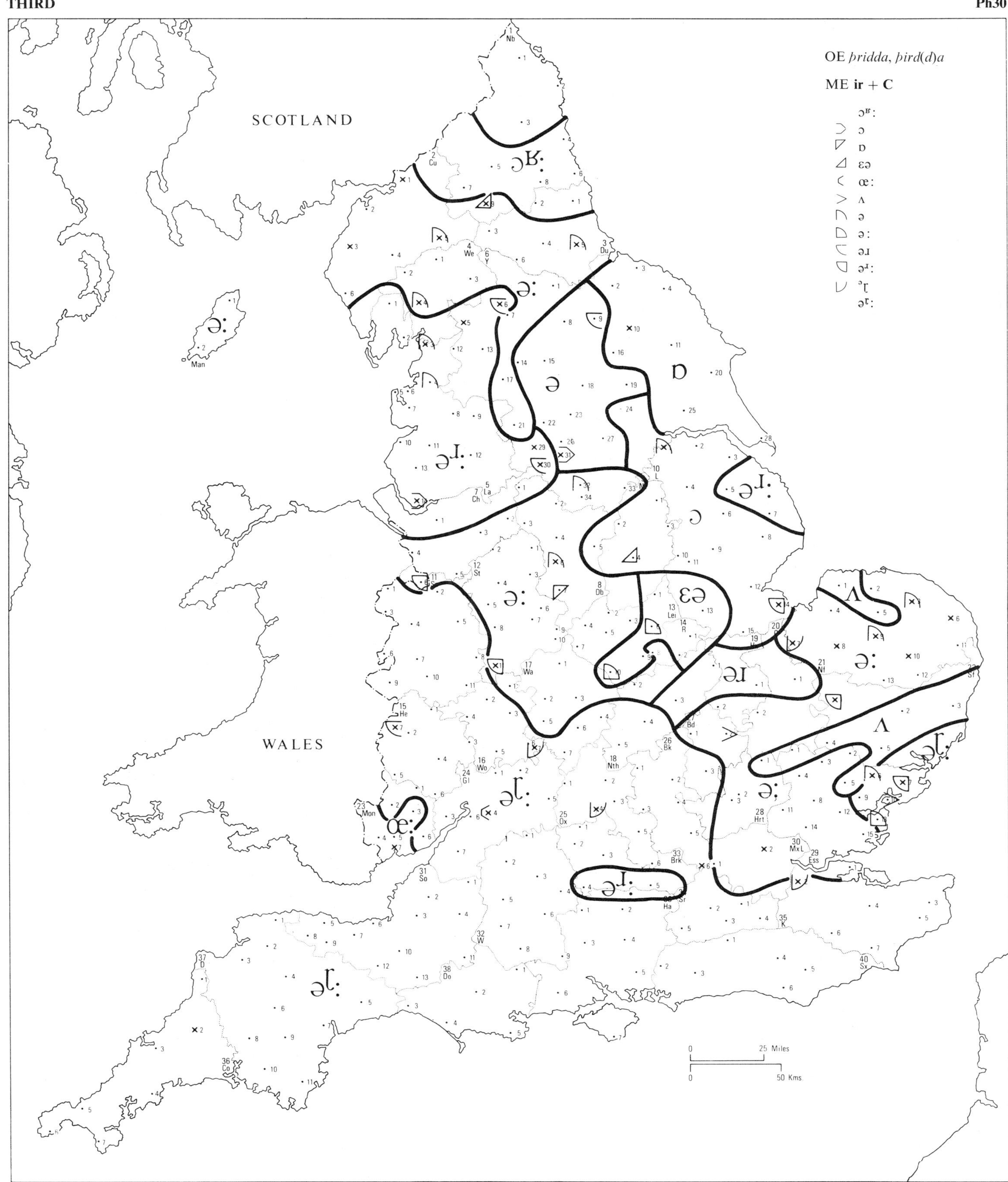

ɛ:ᵊ 9Nt +4 under ɛə
ʌ̈: 21Nf 1 under ʌ
ɐ 21Nf 9 under ə
ɐ: 21Nf 2/11, ɐˑ 21Nf +12, ɜ: Man 2,
ɜˑ Man 1 under ə:
ɜɹ: 5La 1/2/13, ɜɹ:ɹ 5La +4/8–12 under əɹ:
əɽ 16Wo 7, 35K 2 under əɽ
ˈəɽ: 16Wo 2 under əɽ:

ɛɽ: 36Co 2, ɛˑəʁ 1Nb 3
a̤ɹɹ 21Nf 10, aʁ: 1Nb 1
ɑ̤̈: 21Nf 6
ɒɹ 6Y 10
ɔɹ: 6Y 29, ɔʁə 1Nb +5
ɷr 2Cu 3
əɾ 6Y 5, ər 2Cu 1, əʁə 1Nb 2

interpr as *r*-col: ɹ 12St 11, 22Sf 1
cons *r* foll *r*-col V: ɹ 5La +4/8–12, ɽ 32W 3/7,
33Brk 1–3, 34Sr 3/4, 39Ha 7, 40Sx 1–6

parasitic ə in θəʁəd 1Nb 2, θɔʁəd 1Nb +5

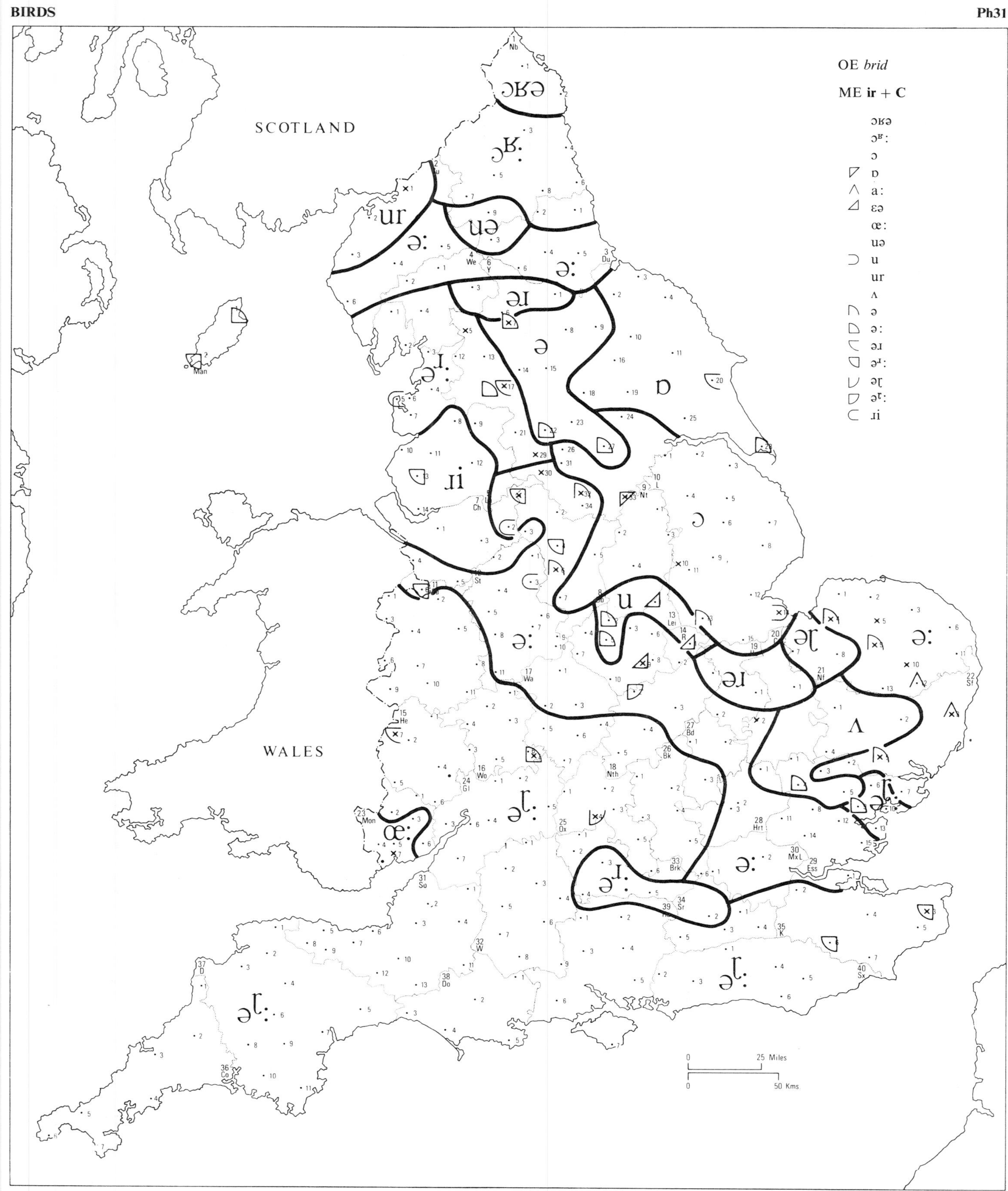

ọə 1Nb 9 under uə
ɐ: 21Nf 6, ɜ: Man 1 under ə:
ɜʴ: 5La 1–3/+13, ɜ:ʴ Man 2, ɜʴ:ɹ 5La 4/9,
  əʴ 10L 7 under əʴ:
əʳ 25Ox +6, 34Sr +1, 39Ha 4,
  əʳɽ 25Ox 3 under əʳ:

ɩˑə (sic) 10L 10
ˈəɽ: 16Wo +4
ɛ̈ˑ 21Nf 5
ɑ: 29Ess +7
ɒɹ 6Y 30
ɔʴ: 6Y 29
or 2Cu 1
əɾ 6Y 5

interpr as *r*-col: ɹ 20C 2
cons *r* foll *r*-col V: ɹ 5La 4/9, ɽ 25Ox 3, 32W +3,
  33Brk 1/2, 34Sr 4, 39Ha 7, 40Sx 2–6, ʁ 1Nb 3

BIRD- n 29Ess +9; BIRD(S)- v 13Lei +5, 14R +1,
  29Ess +7

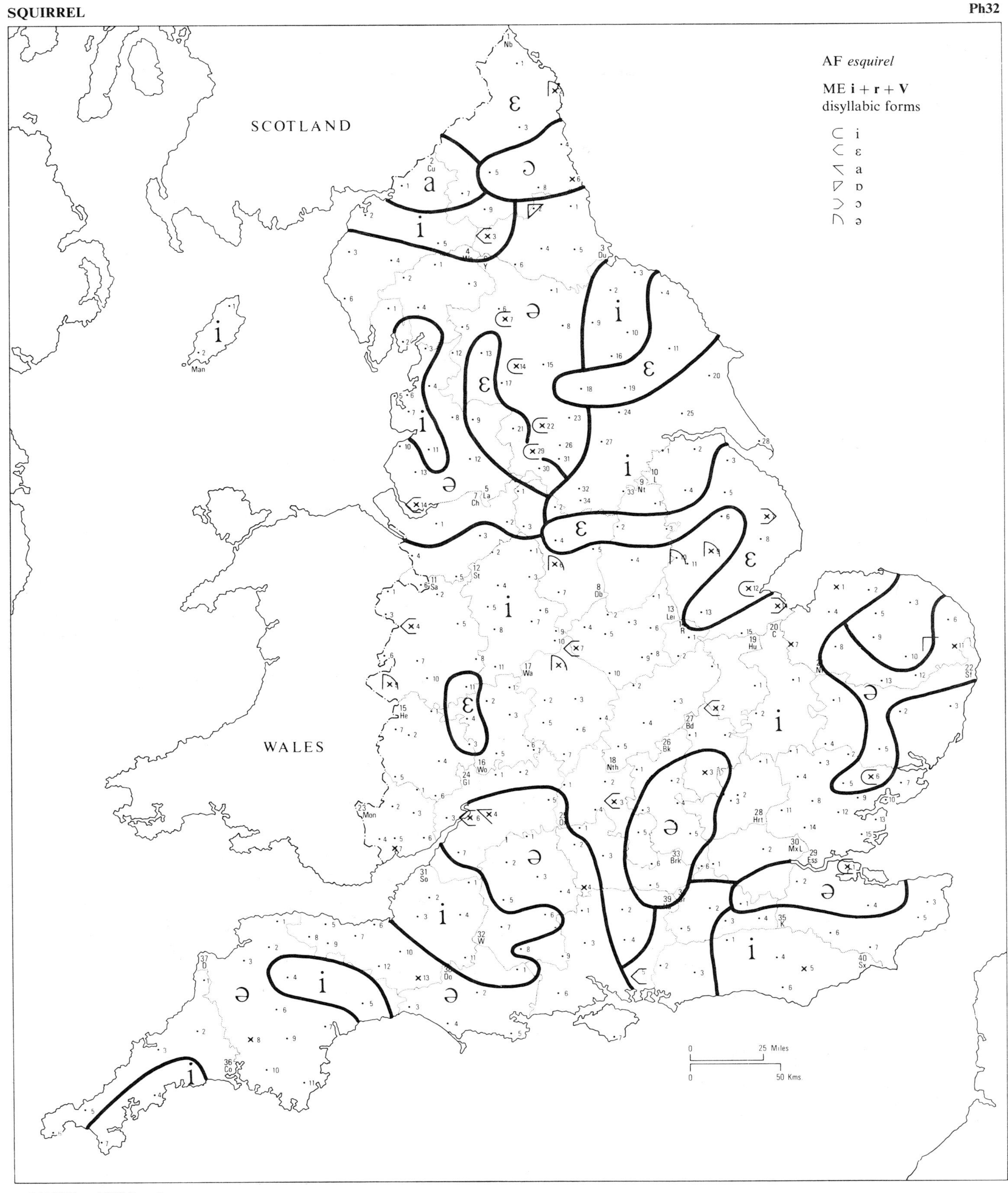

ə̣: 21Nf 12, ʌ̣ 32W 2 under ə

ɪ̈ˑ˞ 34Sr 5
ə̣˞ 21Nf 11, ə̣˞ˑ 21Nf 1
əʵ: 34Sr 2, 40Sx 2

skwəʵ:ɖɫ 31So ⁺13, skəɽət,
skwəɽəts(pl) 40Sx 5

monosyllabic forms: skwɩl 21Nf 7,
skwə:ɫ 27Bd 3, skwə̣:l 21Nf 10, skʷə̣:l 21Nf 9,
skwə̣ɹl 21Nf 3, skwəɽɭ 31So ⁺13,
skwəʵ:ɭ 37D 8, skəʵ:ɽɭ 40Sx 3, skwʌ̣ɹl 21Nf 5

sk- 13Lei 2, 17Wa 3, 35K ⁺6, 37D 4, 39Ha 7,
40Sx 1–3/⁺5, sw- Man 1/2, 12St 9, 16Wo ⁺7

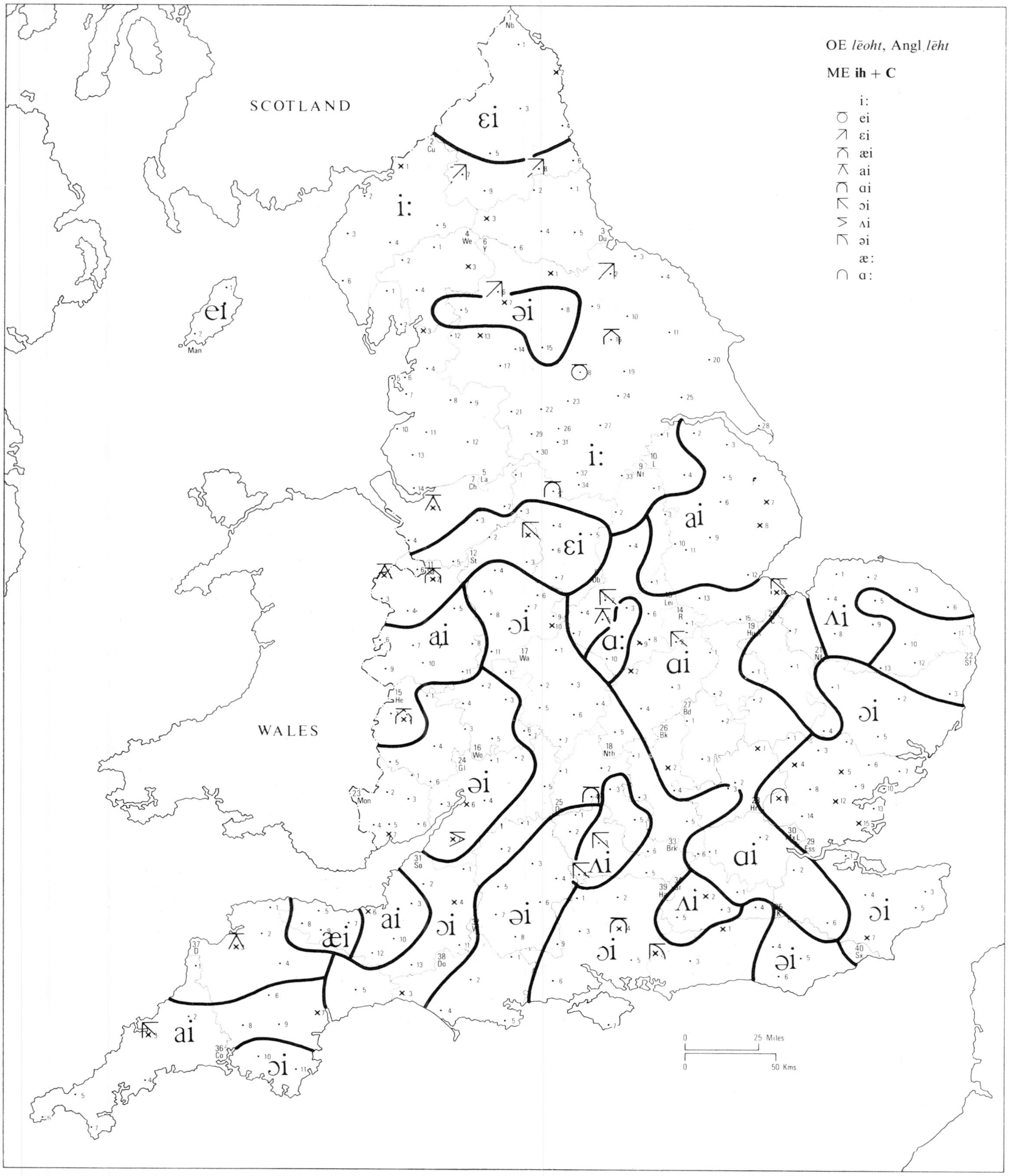

OE *lēoht*, Angl. *lēht*

ME **ih + C**

i:
ei
ɛi
æi
ai
ɑi
ɔi
ʌi
əi
æ:
ɑ:

SCOTLAND

WALES

a̱:ɩ 13Lei [+]5 under ai
ɒ:ɩ 12St 5/6/11̱ under ɔi
ʌʏ 25Ox 3/5 under ʌi
əi: 16Wo 3 under əi

-LIGHT(S) 6Y 12, 21Nf 4/8, 34Sr 5

lɩçt 6Y [+]21 informant "remembers an elderly native, a lady, saying this 50 years ago"

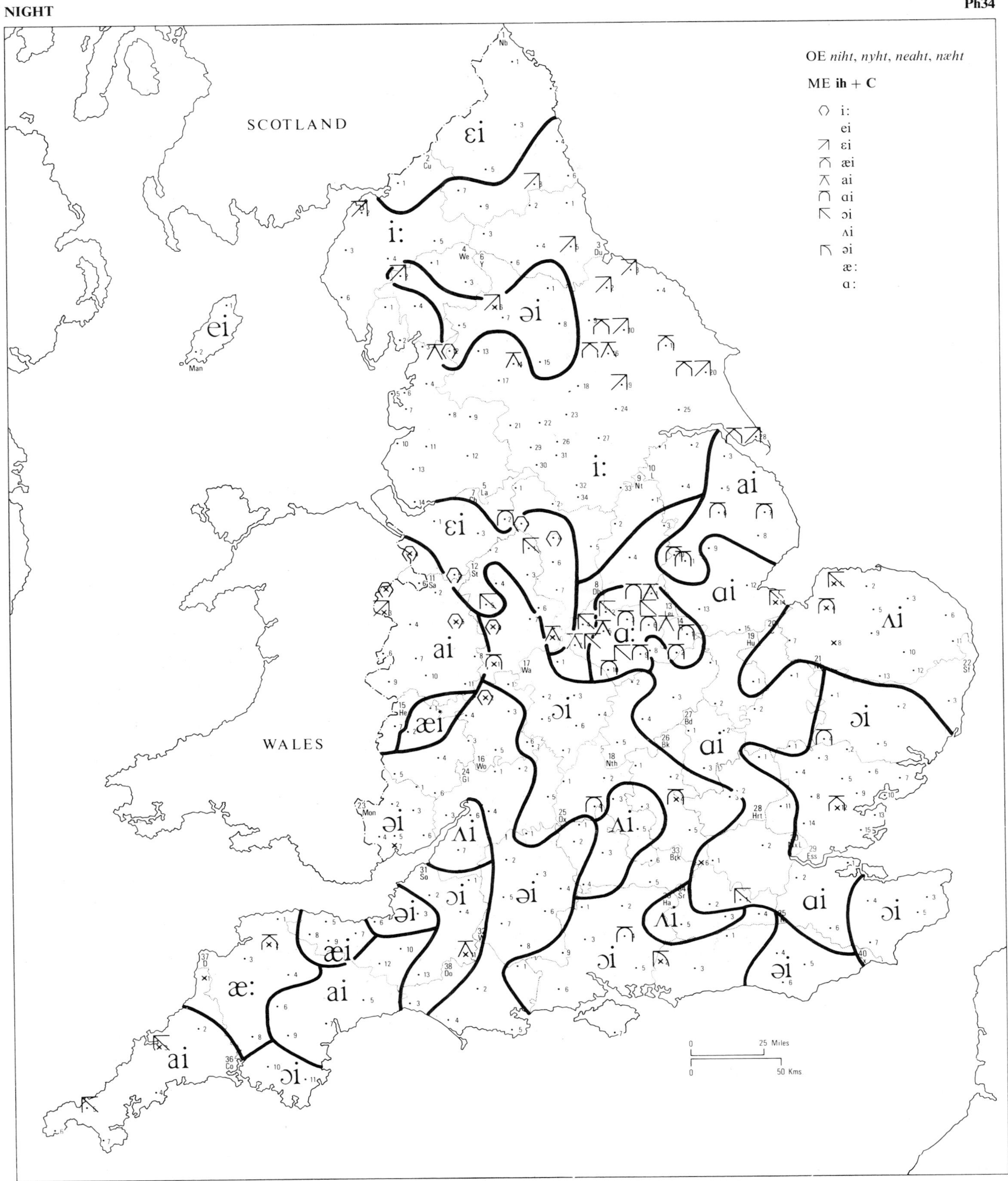

ᵊi: 3Du 3, 4We 1 under i:
ë̹ɩ 3Du +5 under εi
a:ɩ 10L +11, 12St 10 under ai
ɑ:ɩ 12St 11 under ɑi
ɒɩᵊ 16Wo +6, ɒ:ɩ 12St +5 under ɔi
ʌʏ 25Ox 3/5, ʌ̈ʏ 19Hu 1 under ʌi
əi: 16Wo 3 under əi

a: 36Co 1

-NIGHT 10L +6

niçt 6Y +21

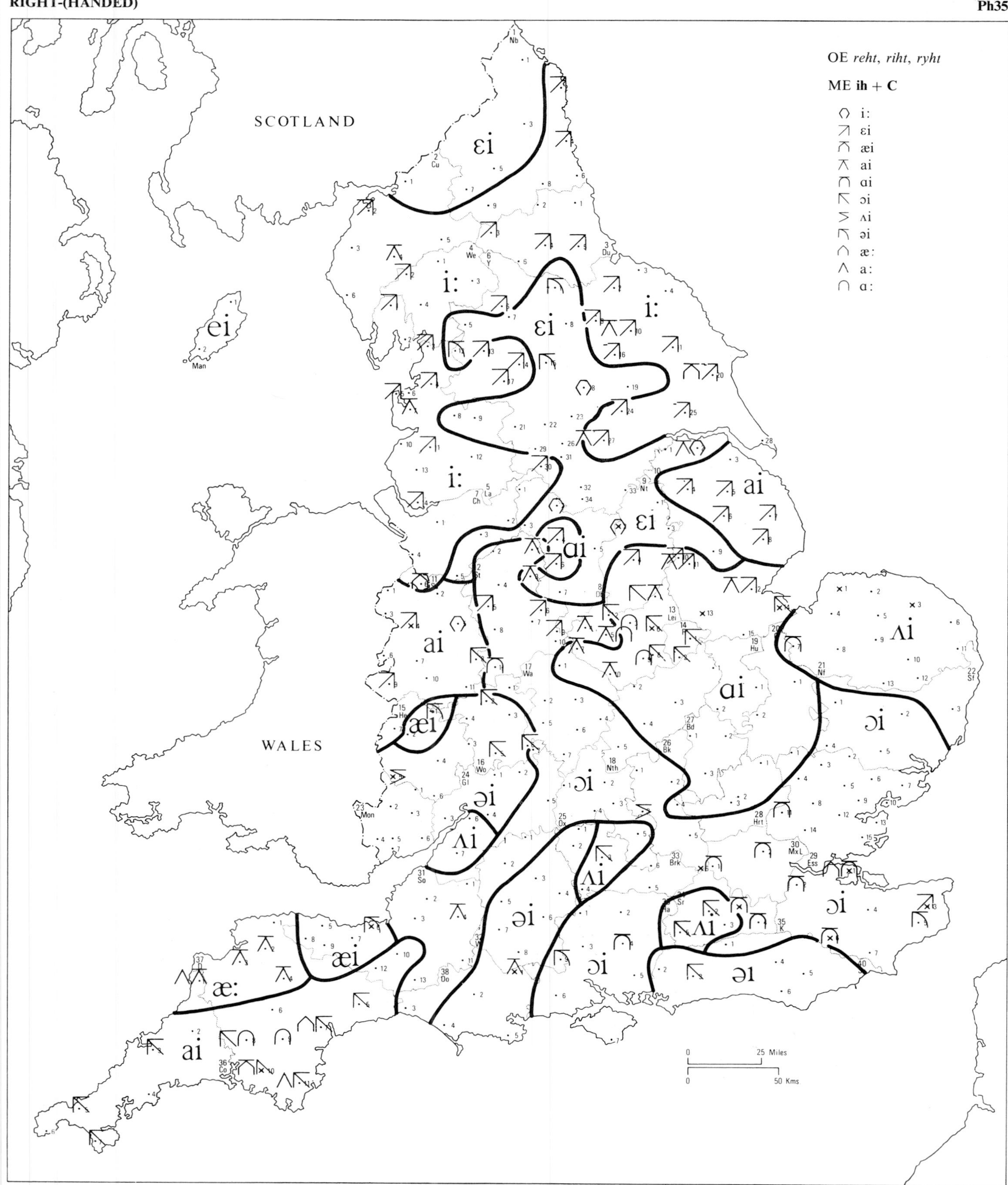

ẹ: 7Ch 1/$^{+}$4 under i:
ȩ̈ɩ 3Du $^{+}$5, ^{ë}ɩ 3Du $^{+}$5 under εi
ɑ:ɩ 12St $^{+}$11 under ɑi
ɔ:ɩ 12St $^{+}$11, ɒ:ɩ 12St $^{+}$6 under ɔi
ʌʏ 25Ox 5 under ʌi
əi: 16Wo 3, əɩ^{ə} 23Mon $^{+}$1, 24Gl 1 under əi

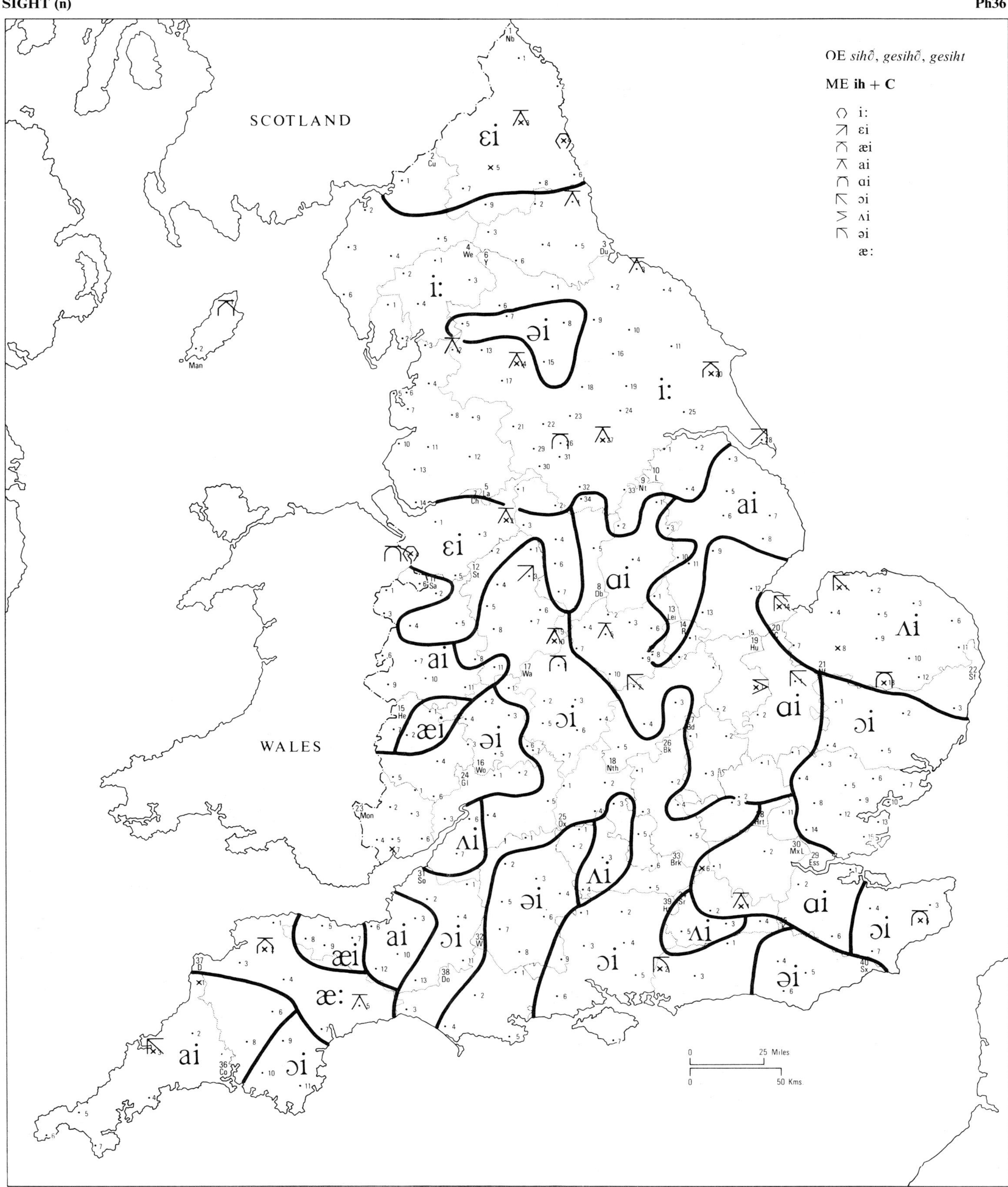

a:ɩ 12St 10/11 under ai
ɒ:ɩ 12St + 3/5/6, ɔɩᵊ 18Nth 3 under ɒi
ʌʏ 25Ox 3, ʌ̈ʏ 19Hu 1 under ʌi
əi: 16Wo 3 under əi

eɩ 1Nb 5, Man 2
a: 36Co 1
ɑ: 13Lei + 5

-SIGHT 13Lei + 5

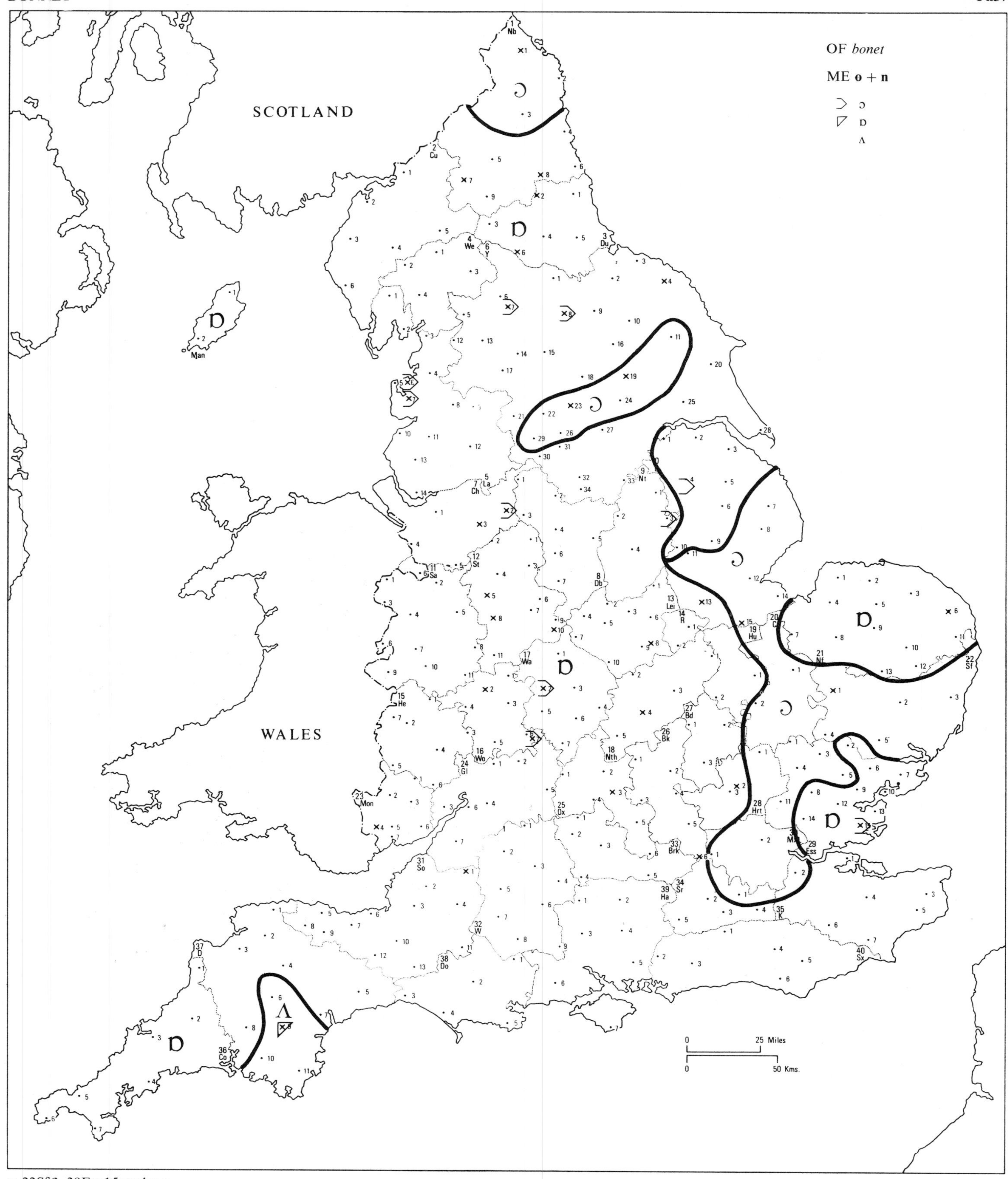

ɔ: 22Sf 2, 29Ess 15 under ɔ
ɒ: 35K +7 under ɒ

ɑ 16Wo 2, ɑ· 21Nf 6

-BONNET 8Db 4, 24Gl 3, 10L 8/12/14

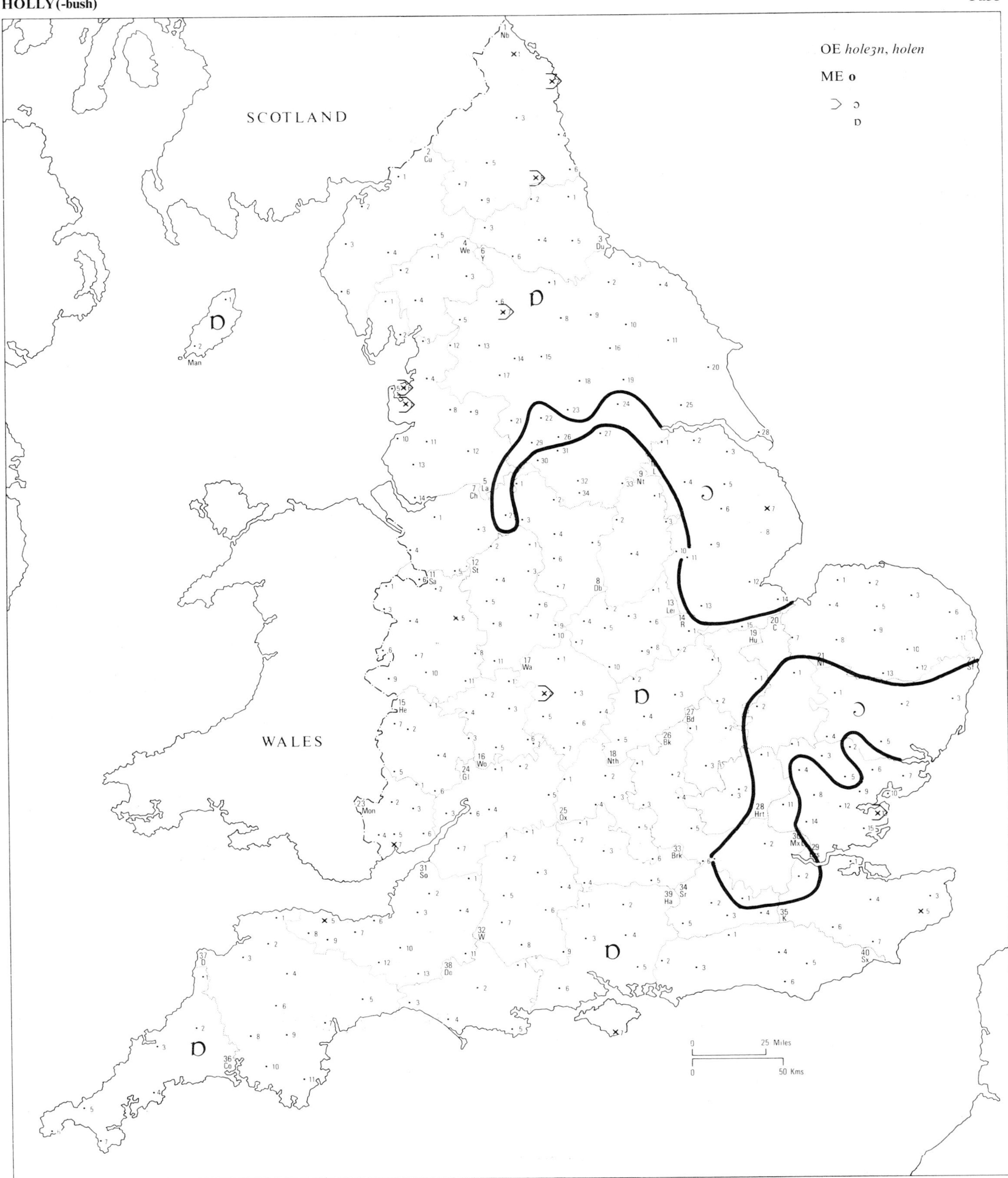

ɒ: 21Nf 6 under ɒ

œ 1Nb 1
æ› 39Ha 7
a i 1Sa 5, 31So 5

HOLLY- 5La 7, 6Y 1–3/$^{+}$4/6/$^{+}$10/14/$^{+}$16/17/
18/22/24/25/27–29/32/$^{+}$33, 7Ch 2, 10L 2/10,
15He 7, 16Wo 7, 17Wa 2, 21Nf 11, 25Ox 4,
30MxL 2, 31So 2, 34Sr 1, 35K 2, 39Ha 4;
-HOLLY 10L 5
HOLLIN 2Cu $^{+}$6, 4We 2, 5La 4/8/9/11,
6Y $^{+}$10/15/$^{+}$16, 8Db 1/2;
HOLLIN- 6Y $^{+}$4/5/9/11/21/30/$^{+}$33, Man 1

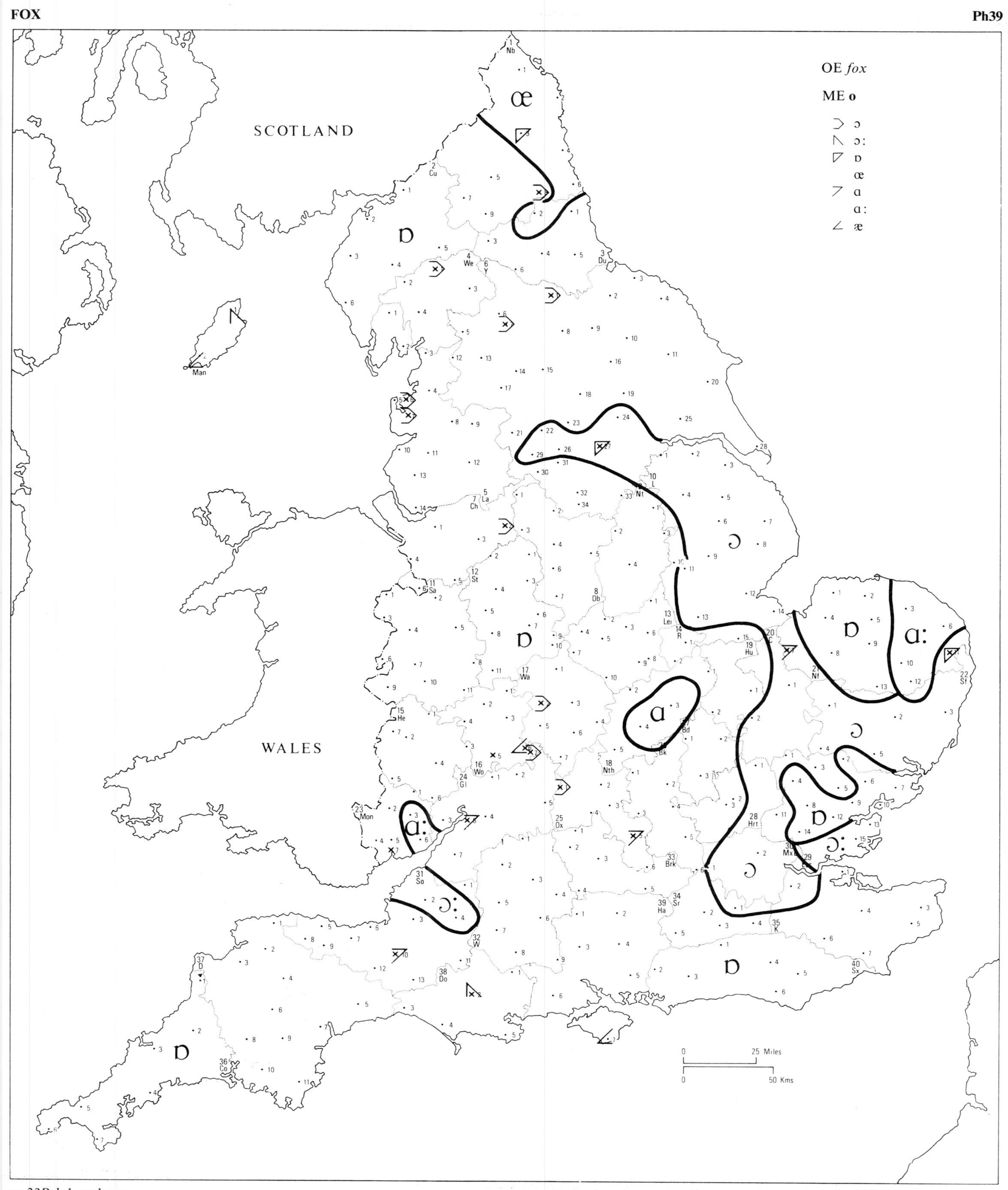

ɒ: 33Brk 1 under ɒ
œ: 1Nb 1/2/⁺3 under œ
ɑᵊ 21Nf 7 under ɑ

ɑʳ: 16Wo 5

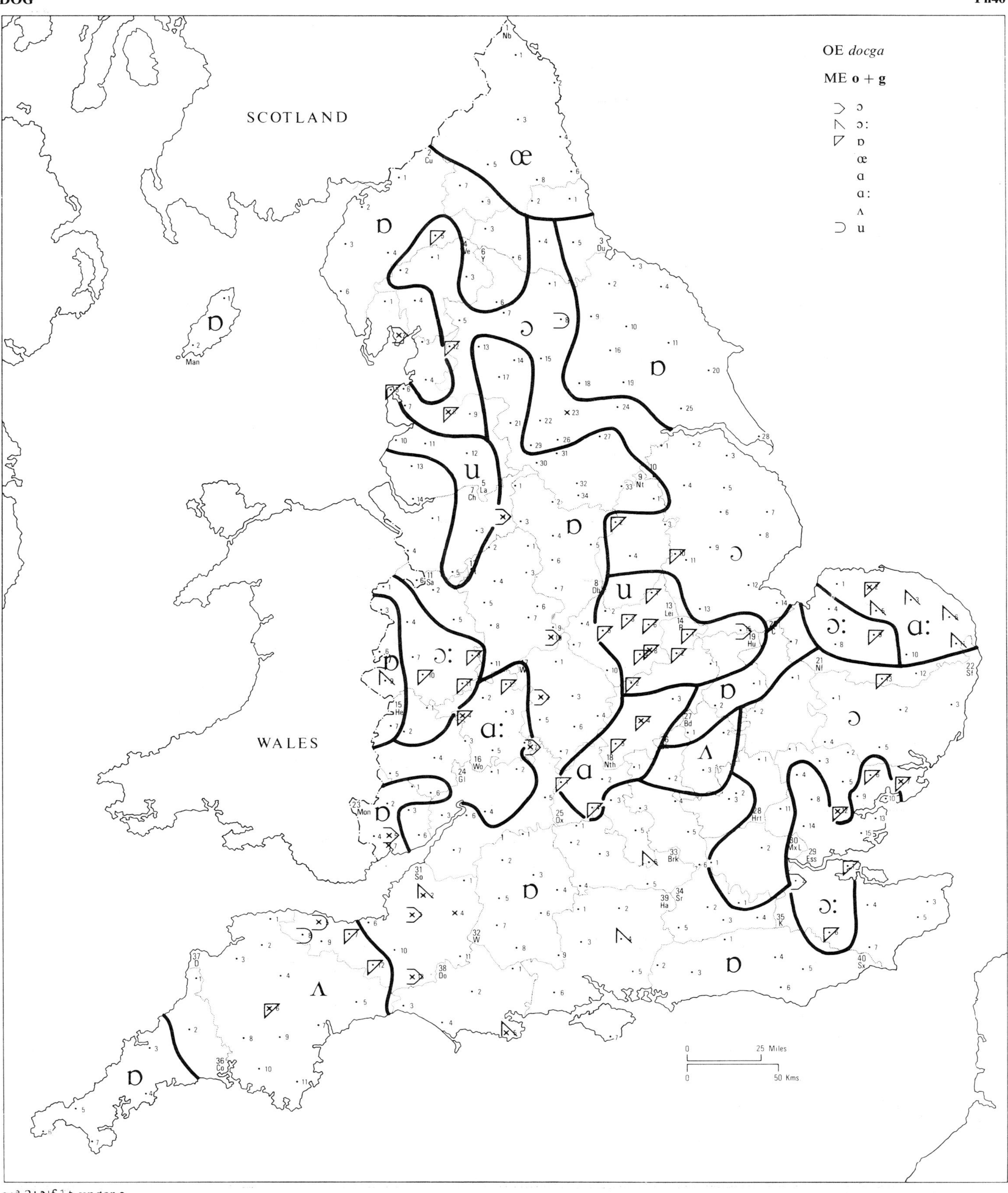

ɔ:ᵊ 21Nf $^{+}$5 under ɔ.
ɒ: 39Ha $^{+}$4, 40Sx $^{+}$3, ɒ̣: 34Sr 5 under ɒ
œ: 1Nb $^{+}$1/2/3/$^{+}$4/5 under œ
ɑ:ᵊ 21Nf $^{+}$11, ɑ˙ə 21Nf $^{+}$3, ˈɑ: 16Wo 2 under ɑ:
ọ 10L $^{+}$15 under u

æ 40Sx $^{+}$4

DOG- 11Sa $^{+}$8/$^{+}$11, 13Lei $^{+}$3, 16Wo $^{+}$1;
-DOG(S) 14R $^{+}$1, 21Nf $^{+}$11, 40Sx $^{+}$4

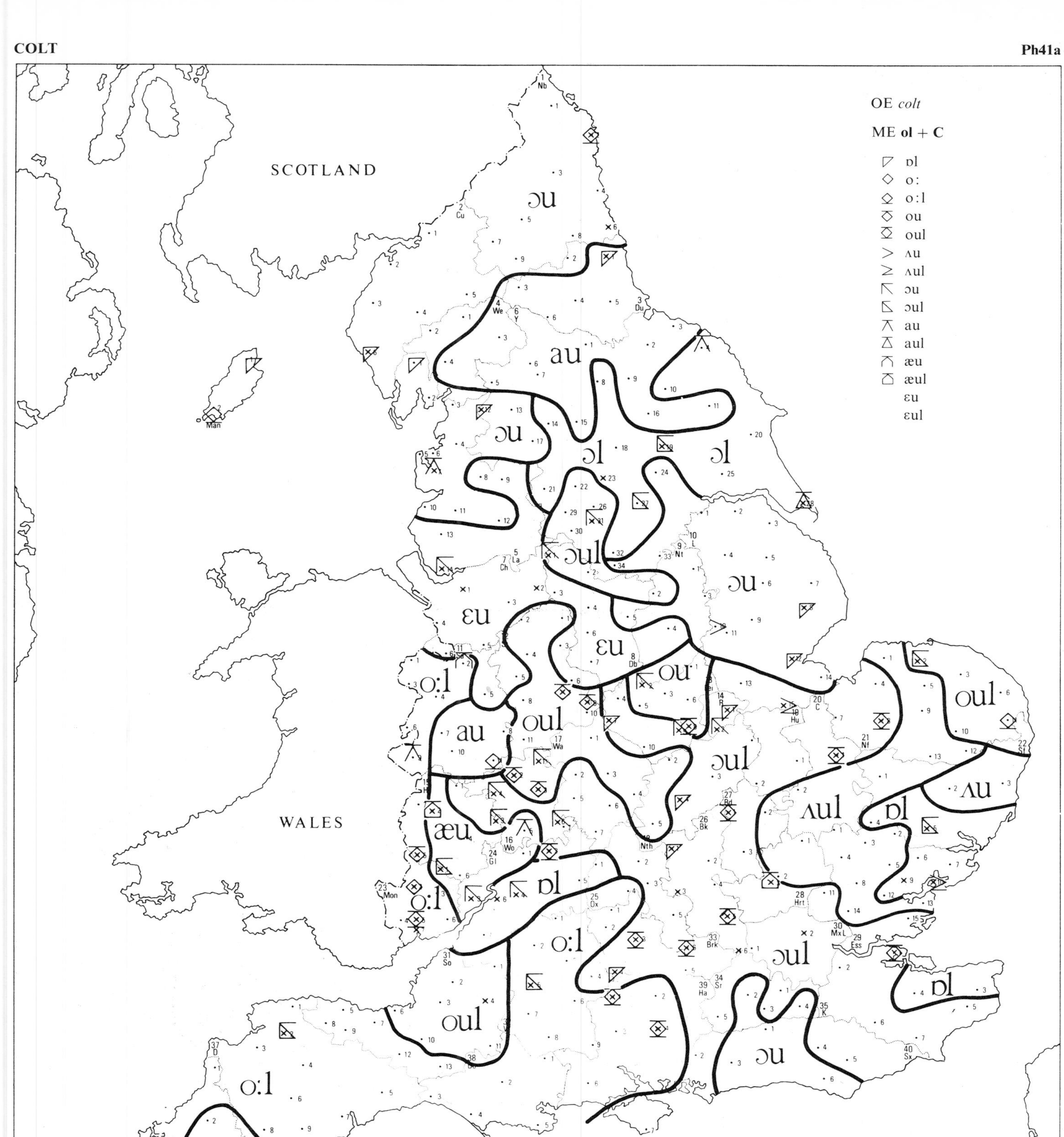

ɔl 10L 8/12, ɔɫ 22Sf 4, ɔ˂ɫ 29Ess 6 under ɒl
ol 11Sa 1, 21Nf $^{+}$11, oᵊl Man 2 under o:l
o:ɷɫ 24Gl 2 under oul
ɐɷl 10L 15 under ʌul
ɔw 10L 11 under ɔu
ɔ:ɷɫ 39Ha 7 under ɔul
ɑɷ 6Y 1/15 under au

ʌ̹ɫ 29Ess 9
ɷl 7Ch $^{+}$2, ɷ:l 7Ch $^{+}$2

COLT- 1Nb 5, 2Cu 3, 6Y 9/10/28/32, 26Bk 1, 35K 6; -COLT 5La 10, 18Nth 5, 21Nf 3, 22Sf 2, 24Gl 5/7, 25Ox 5/6, 26Bk 2/4/5, 27Bd 1/3, 28Hrt 2, 33Brk 1, 35K 4, 37D 7

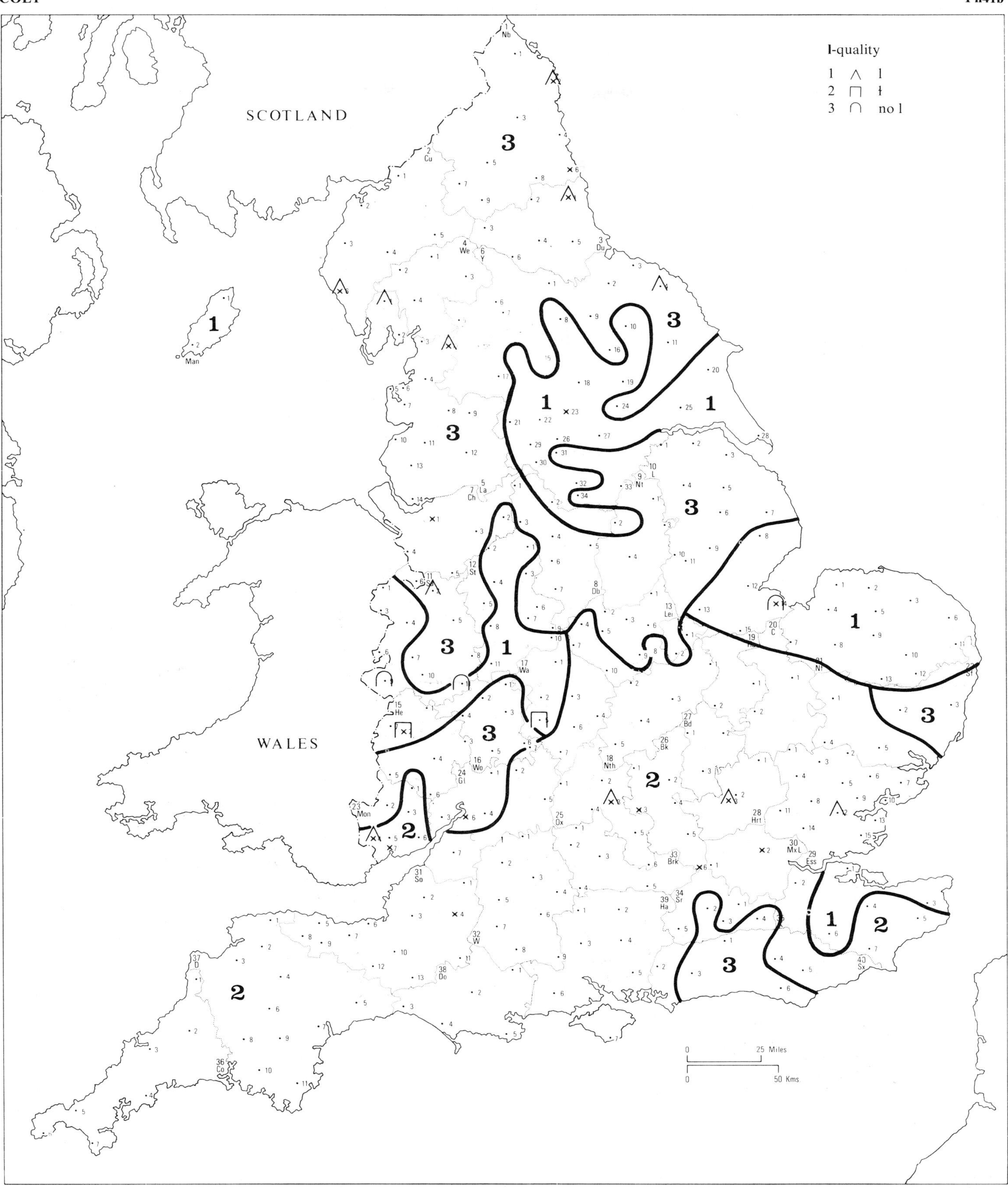

l 23Mon 4 under l

COLT- 1Nb 5, 2Cu 3, 6Y 9/10/28/32, 26Bk 1, 35K 6; -COLT 5La 10, 17Wa $^{+}$5, 18Nth 5, 21Nf 3, 22Sf 2, 24Gl 5/7, 25Ox 5/6, 26Bk 2/4/5, 27Bd 1/3, 28Hrt 2, 33Brk 1, 35K 4, 37D 7

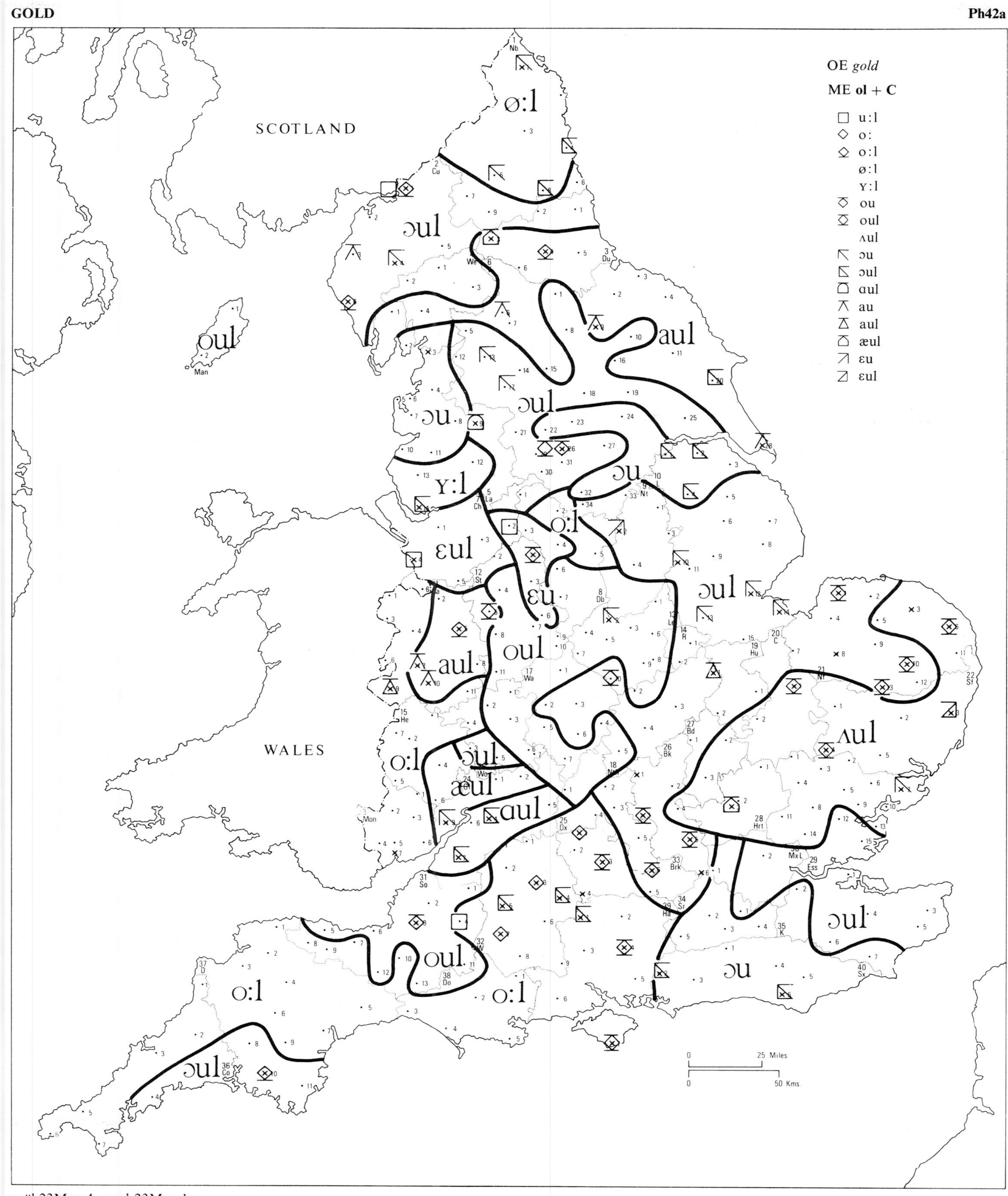

o:^{u}l 23Mon 4, o:ɷɫ 23Mon 1,
o:^{ɷ}l 15He 7 under o:l
øl 1Nb $^{+}$3/$^{+}$8, œ:l 1Nb $^{+}$4 under ø:l
ọ:ɷ 31So 3 under ou
o:^{ɷ}l 8Db 6 under oul
ʌɷ^{ə}ɫ 22Sf 2 under ʌul
ɒɷ^{ə} 24Gl 3 under ɔu
ɒɷ^{ə}ɫ 24Gl 7 under ɔul
æɷ^{ə}ɫ 24Gl 1 under æul
æɷ 7Ch $^{+}$2, æ̣ɷ 12St 3 under ɛu

a:l (sic) 5La 3
ɒɫ (sic) 26Bk 1
ɔ:l 6Y $^{+}$27, ɔ:ɫ 33Brk 4

ʏ:l 5La 12/13 presupposes ME *gōld* < LOE *gōld*

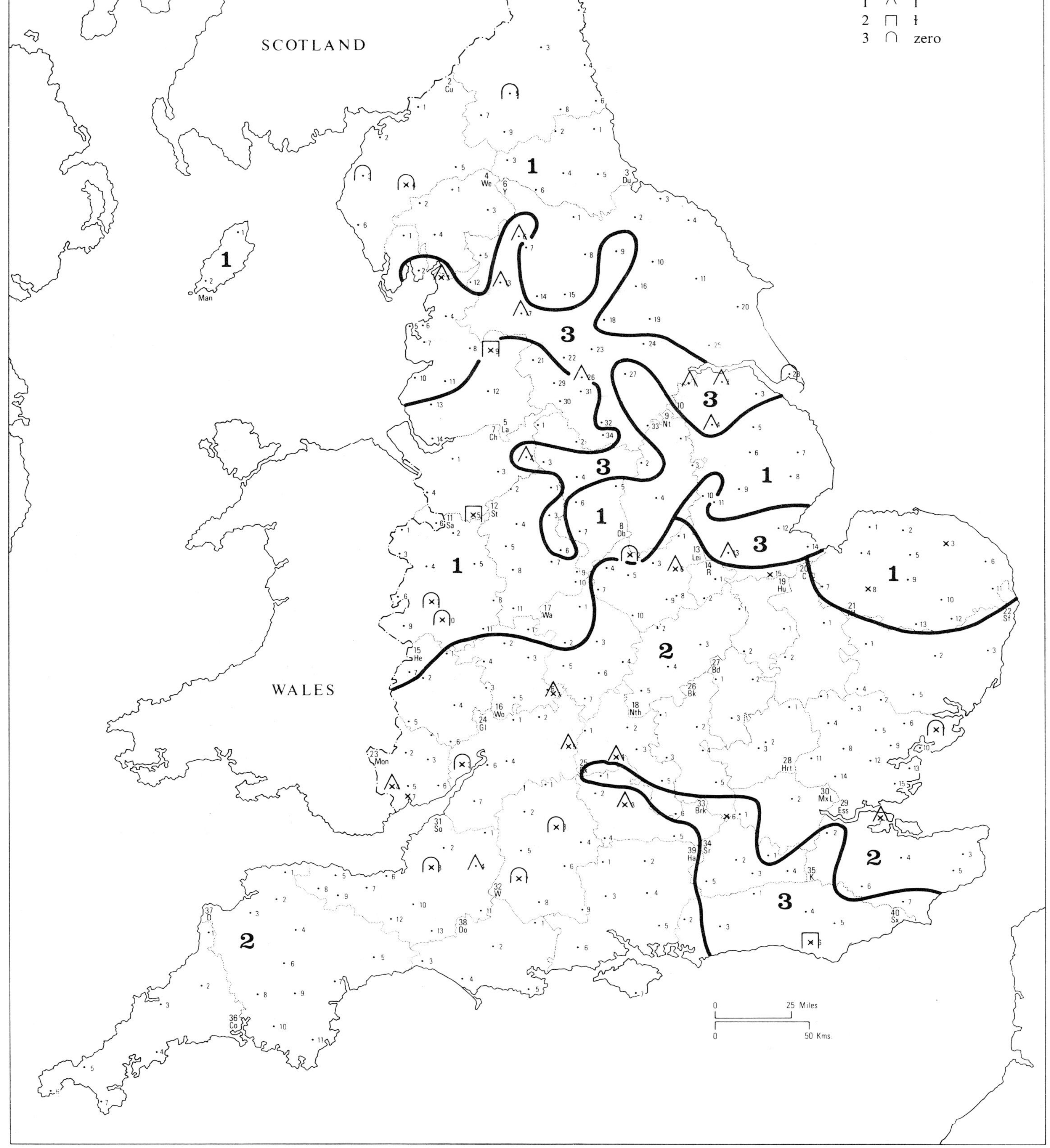
l-quality
1 ∧ l
2 ⊓ ɫ
3 ∩ zero
SCOTLAND
WALES
25 Miles
50 Kms

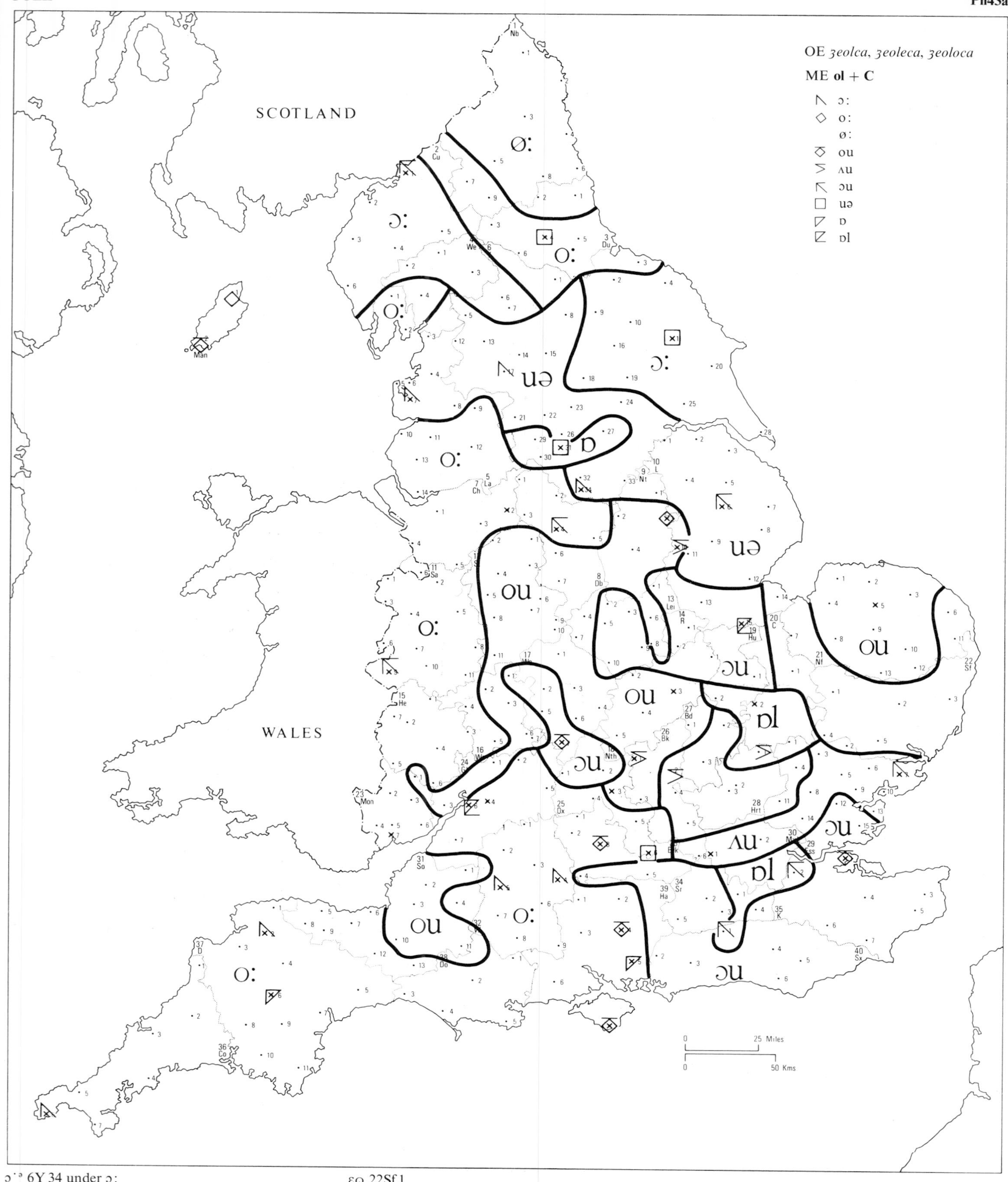

ɔ˙^{ə} 6Y 34 under ɔ:
o:^{ə} 3Du $^{+}$3, o:ə Man 1, o^{ə} 3Du $^{+}$3,
 o̜: 6Y 3 under o:
ø^{ə} 3Du 1, øə 3Du 2, œ: 1Nb 5/6 under ø:
o:u Man 2, o:ɷ 23Mon 1, 24Gl 1/3, 33Brk 3,
 o:^{ɷ} 8Db 6, 9Nt 2/4 under ou
ɔ:ɷ 33Brk $^{+}$4, 40Sx $^{+}$1 under ɔu
o̜ə 5La 8 under uə
ɔ 6Y 29 under ɒ
ɔɫ 28Hrt $^{+}$1, 29Ess 1, ɔ̈ɫ 34Sr 1, 35K $^{+}$2 under ɒl

ɛɷ 22Sf 1
æɷ 28Hrt 3
ɑ: 24Gl 4
ɔɷɫ 29Ess $^{+}$11, 30MxL 1
ʌɷɫ 29Ess $^{+}$11
ol 21Nf 11
ɷ˙ 7Ch 2

no j- 1Nb 3/9, 3Du 3

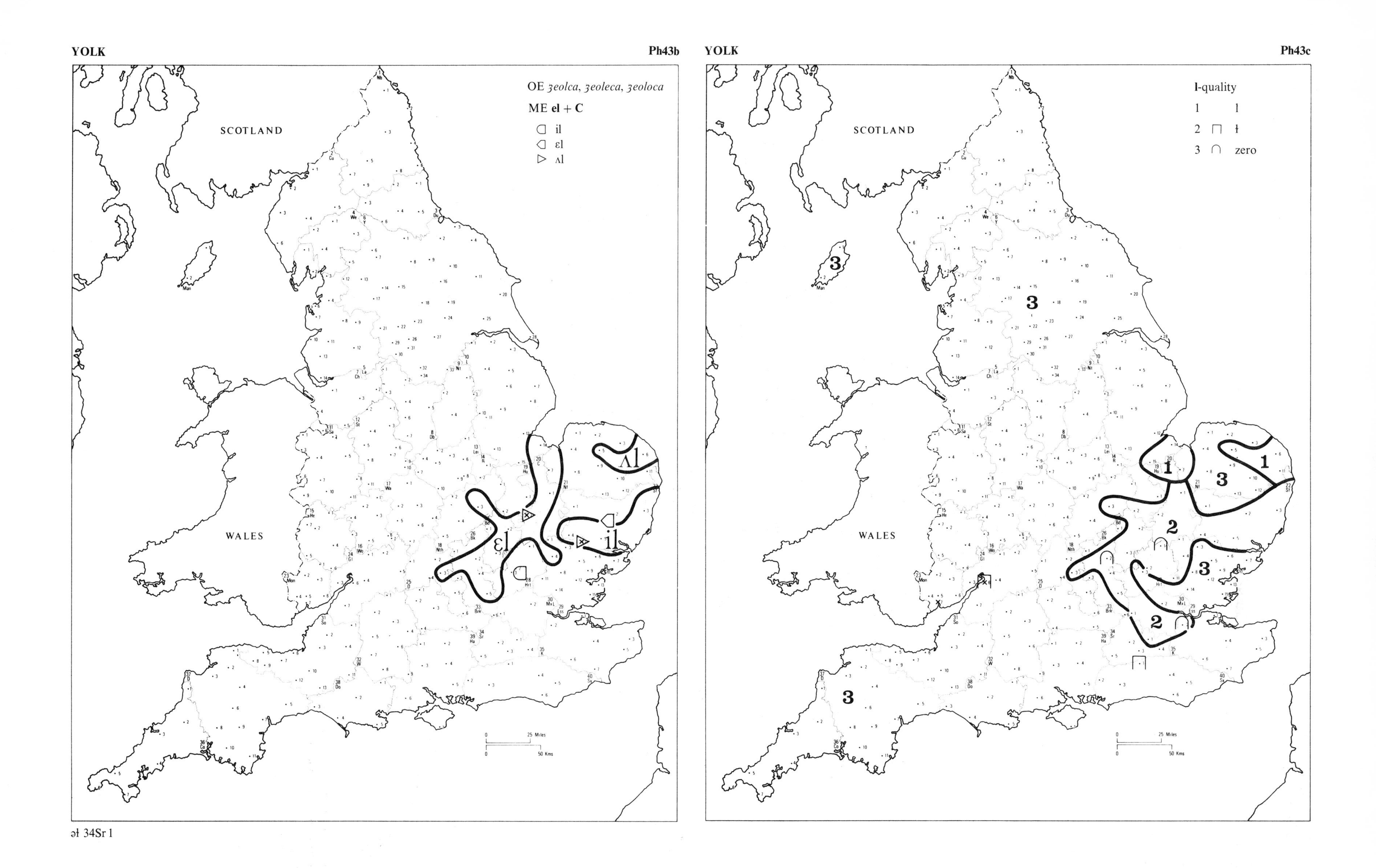
OE ʒeolca, ʒeoleca, ʒeoloca
ME el + C
il
εl
ʌl
SCOTLAND
WALES
I-quality
1 l
2 ɫ
3 zero
25 Miles
50 Kms

ɘɫ 34Sr 1

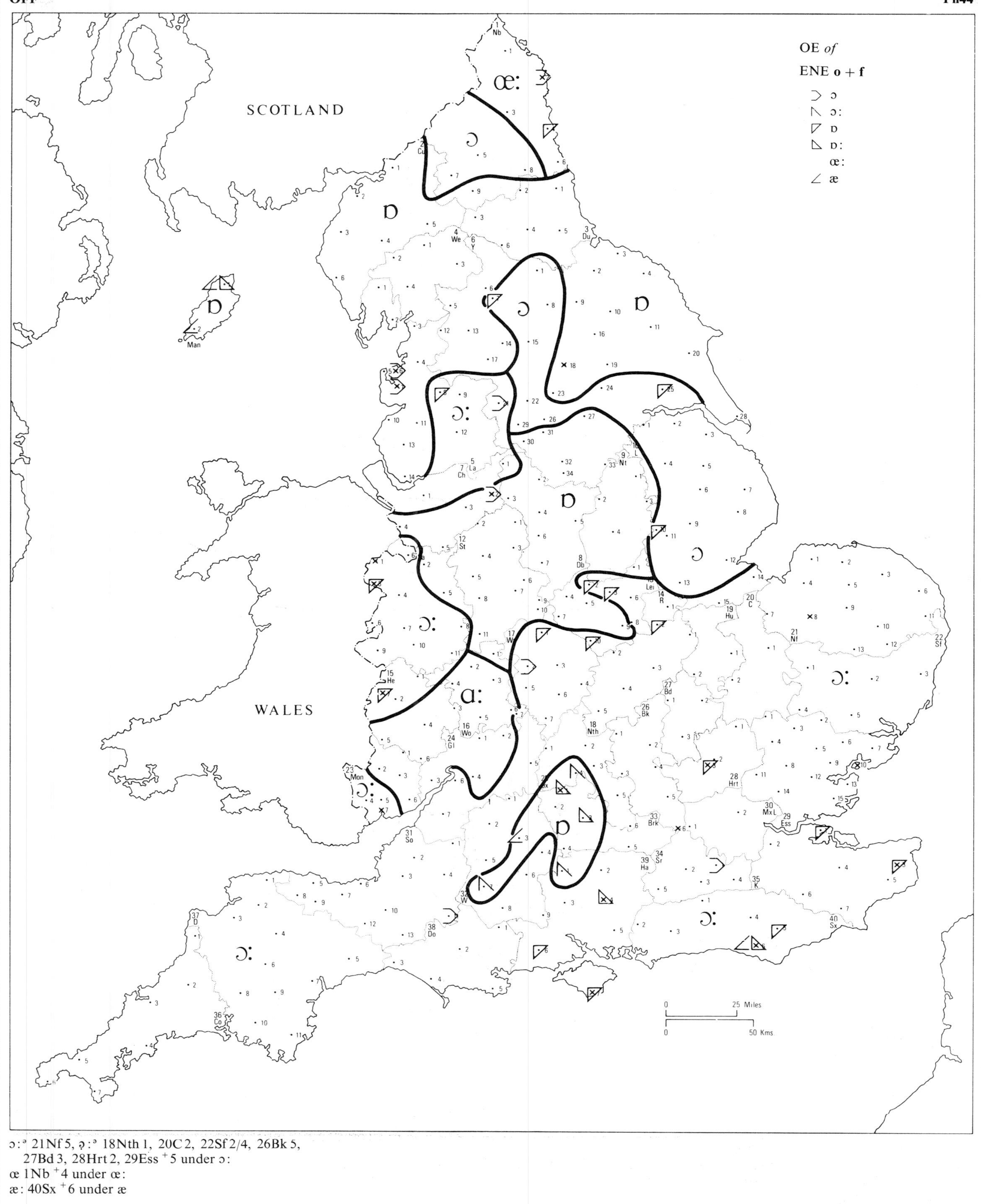

ɔ:ᵊ 21Nf 5, ɔ̝:ᵊ 18Nth 1, 20C 2, 22Sf 2/4, 26Bk 5, 27Bd 3, 28Hrt 2, 29Ess +5 under ɔ:
œ 1Nb +4 under œ:
æ: 40Sx +6 under æ

a Man +1
ɔʳ: 11Sa 1
oə 10L +14
ə 24Gl +1

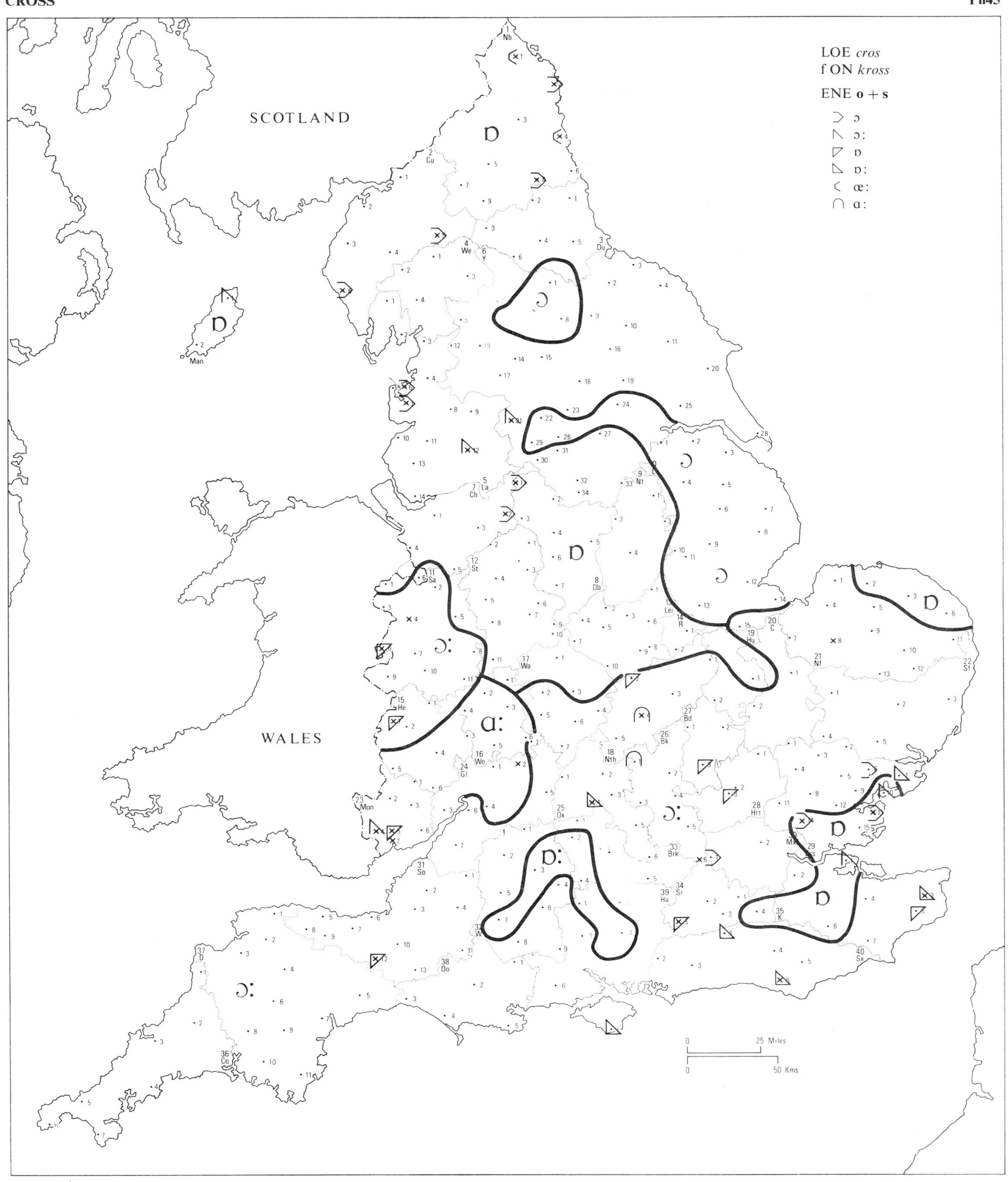

ɔ:[ə] 27Bd +3, 29Ess 4, ɔ̣:[ə] 18Nth 1/3, 19Hu 2,
22Sf 2, 26Bk 2, 27Bd 2, 28Hrt 1/2,
29Ess 5 under ɔ:
ɑ 26Bk +1 under ɑ:

a: 24Gl 2
ɔ[ɾ]: 11Sa 4
ə 10L +7

CROSS- 27Bd +3, 28Hrt +3, 40Sx +1;
CROSS v 35K +5; 3prpl 29Ess +7

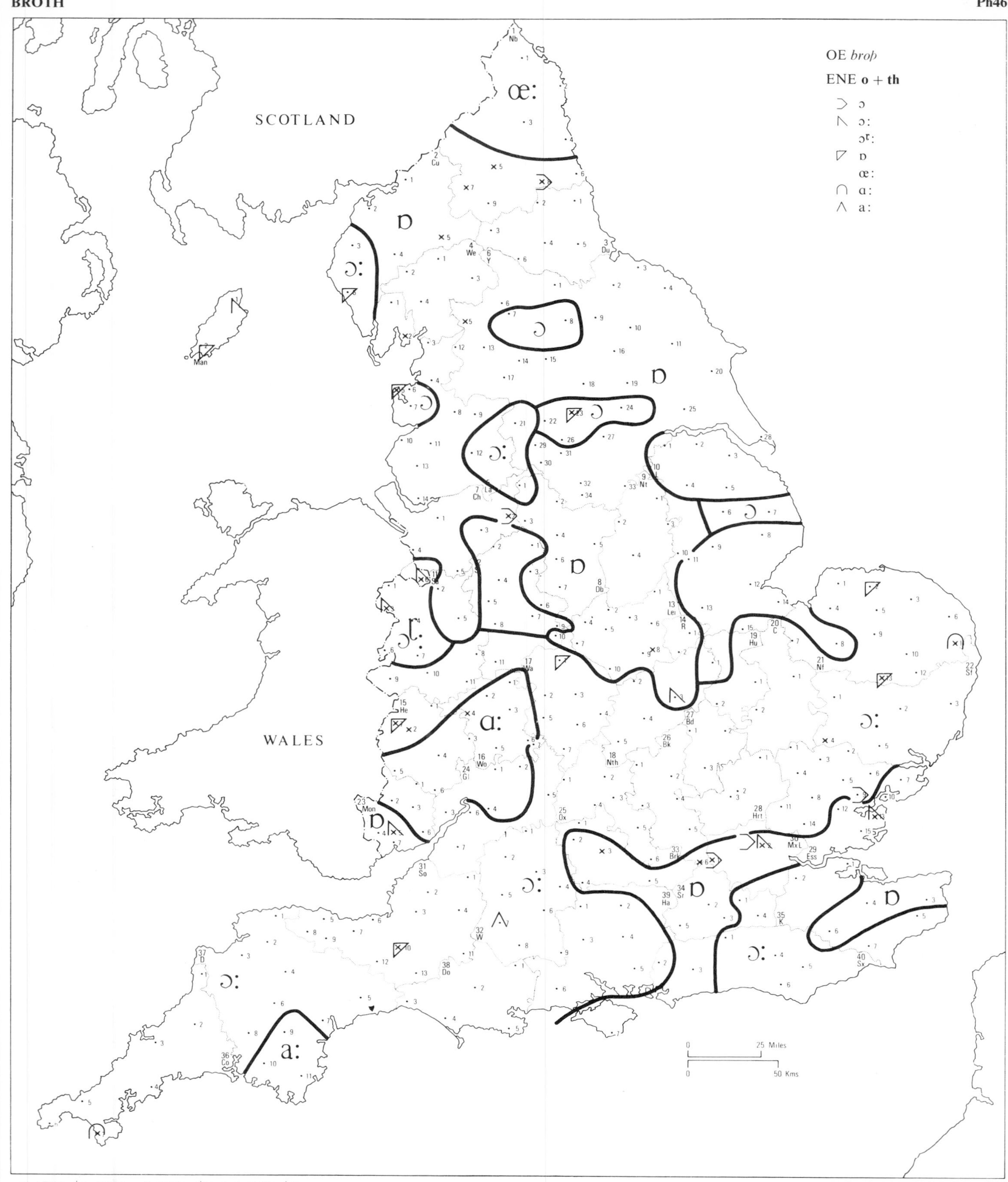

ɔ:ᵊ 17Wa +3, 23Mon 5, 29Ess +9, ɔ̣:ᵊ 17Wa +3,
22Sf 1/2, 26Bk 2, 28Hrt 2 under ɔ:

ɒ̇: Man 2, 33Brk 4, 34Sr 5, ɒ̣: 29Ess 7 under ɒ

œ 1Nb 4 under œ:

a Man +1

ɑʳ: 16Wo 4

oɷ 12St 2

-BROTH 17Wa +3, 22Sf 2, 24Gl 6, 37D 3/8

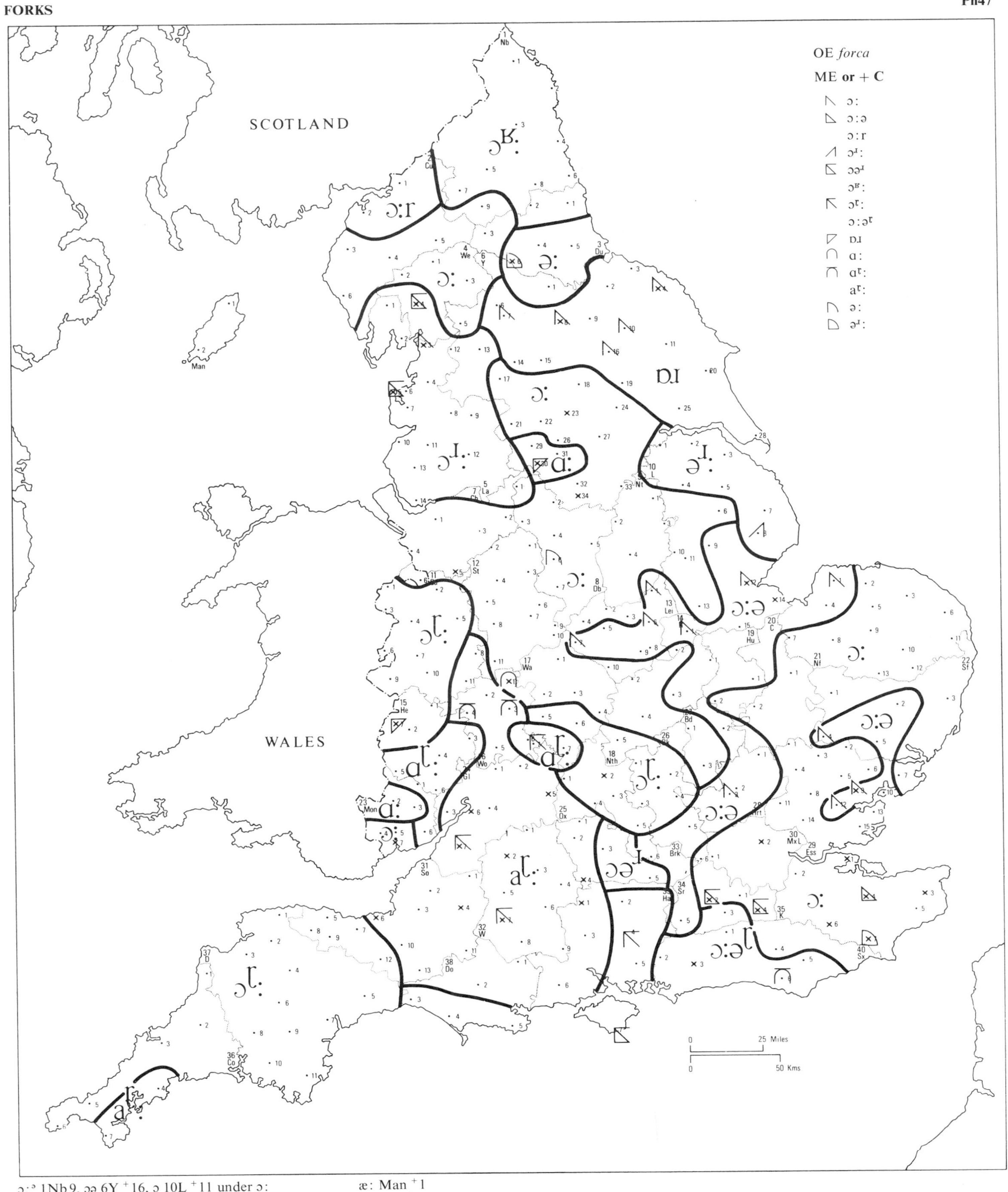

ɔ:ᵊ 1Nb 9, ɔə 6Y $^{+}$16, ɔ 10L $^{+}$11 under ɔ:
ɔᵊ 25Ox 6, ɔ̣ᵊ 10L 15 under ɔ:ə
ɔ̣r 2Cu 2 under ɔ:r
ɔ:əʴ 33Brk 5, 34Sr 2/4 under ɔəʴ
ɒ̈ʶ: 1Nb 2/5 under ɔʶ:
ɔ̣ʵ:ᵊ 26Bk 2/4, ɔʵ 16Wo $^{+}$7, ɒɽ 25Ox 4,
ɒʵ 39Ha 4 under ɔʵ:
ɔʵ:əʵ 40Sx $^{+}$6 under ɔ:əʵ
ɒʴ 6Y $^{+}$20, ɔɹ 6Y $^{+}$7, ɔ˙ɹ 6Y $^{+}$11 under ɒɹ
ɑʵ 16Wo $^{+}$7 under ɑʵ:
œ: 3Du $^{+}$5 under ə:
əɹ 3Du 6, 10L $^{+}$7 under əʴ:

æ: Man $^{+}$1
a: Man $^{+}$1
aʴ̠: 25Ox $^{+}$2
ɑʴ: 33Brk 4, ɑʴ̠: 25Ox $^{+}$2
ɒr 6Y $^{+}$14
ωə 10L 14, 13Lei $^{+}$2
əʵ: 24Gl 5, 25Ox $^{+}$1

interpr as *r*-col: ɹ 3Du 6, 6Y $^{+}$7, 10L $^{+}$7,
ɽ 25Ox 4, 33Brk 1/2
cons *r* foll *r*-col V: ɹ 5La 4/9/11/14, 6Y 13,
ɽ 40Sx 2

FORK- 13Lei $^{+}$1; -FORK(S) 6Y $^{+}$14/18,
10L $^{+}$11, 29Ess $^{+}$12, 31So 11;
FORK v 6Y $^{+}$3/$^{+}$10/$^{+}$20;
FORKING prp 10L $^{+}$8; ndg 6Y $^{+}$11;
FORKS 3prsg 6Y $^{+}$3

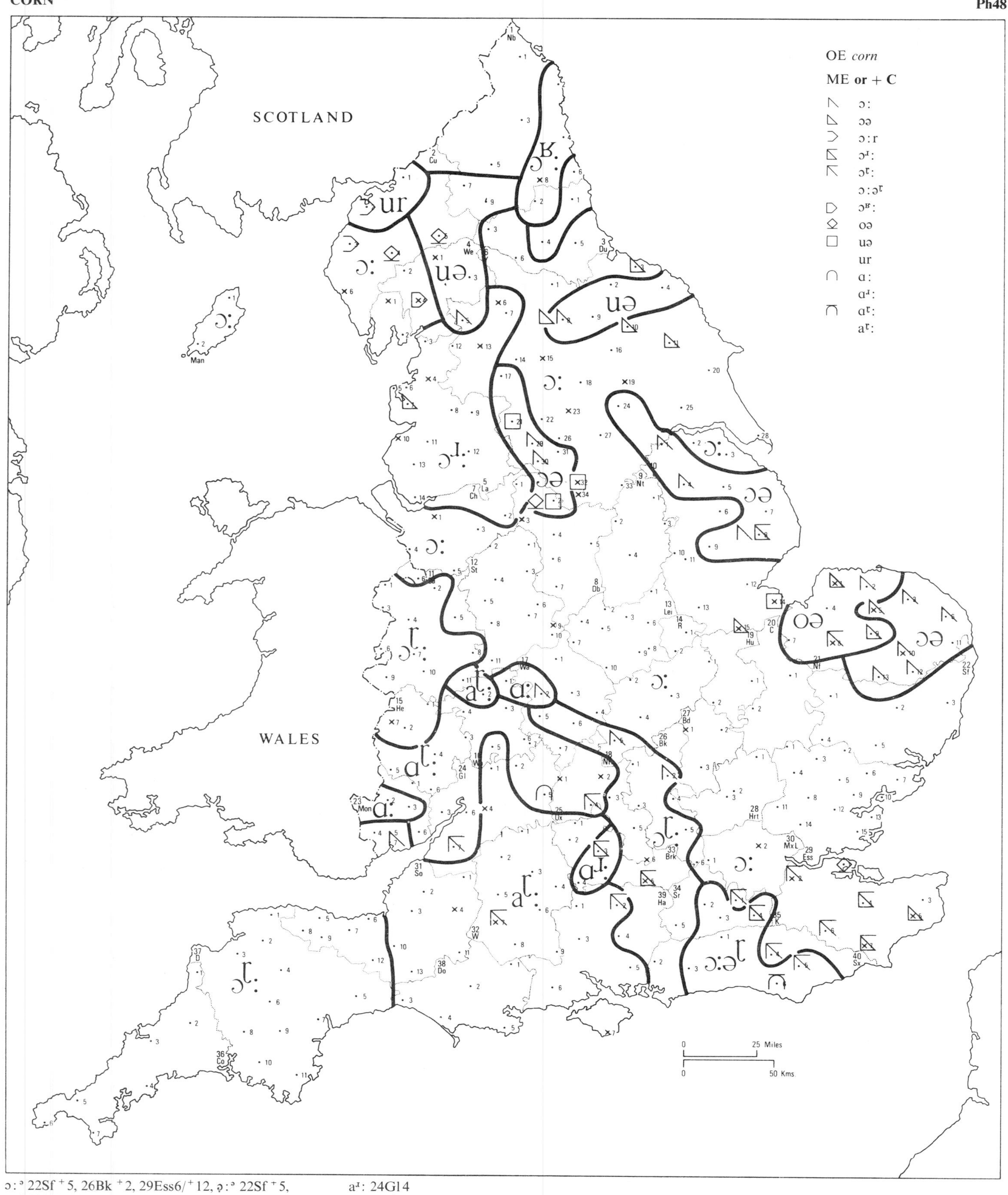

ɔːᵊ 22Sf +5, 26Bk +2, 29Ess6/+12, ɔ̣ːᵊ 22Sf +5, 26Bk 4, 28Hrt 1/2, ɔːə 29Ess +12, o̜ː 21Nf +5 under ɔː
ɔːə 6Y +29, 8Db +2 under ɔə
ɔɹ 7Ch 2, ɔɹ̠ 8Db 1, ɔəɹ 5La 5, 33Brk +3 under ɔɹ:
ɔʵːᵊ 11Sa 4, ɔ̣ʵːᵊ 26Bk +2, ɔʵ 39Ha +4, ɔɽ 25Ox +4 under ɔʵ:
ɔəʵɽ 40Sx +5, ɔʵːəʵɽ 40Sx +6 under ɔːəʵ
ɒ̈ʁ: 1Nb +2 under ɔʁ:
oːᵊ 8Db +2, o̜ːᵊ 35K +1 under oə
ọə 1Nb 9 under uə
ɑːᵊ 16Wo +1 under ɑː
ɑʵ 16Wo 7, ɑɽ 25Ox +4 under ɑʵ:

aɹ: 24Gl 4
ɒə 6Y +32
ɒɹ 6Y 6/+30, 15He +7
ɒɽ 25Ox +4, ɒʵ 39Ha +4, ɒʵˑ 39Ha +4
ə̹ɹ 15He +7
ɔʁə 1Nb 1
ɷəɹ 5La +8
əː 7Ch +4
əɹ 10L +7, əɹ: 7Ch 1

interpr as *r*-col: ɹ 6Y 7, 33Brk 5, ɽ 25Ox 4, 33Brk +2
cons *r* foll *r*-col V: ɹ 5La +8/9/11/14, ɽ 33Brk 1/+2, 34Sr 2/+4, 39Ha 7, 40Sx 2/3/+4/5/6

CORN- 2Cu +2, 6Y +29, 24Gl +7, 33Brk +3, 35K +6; -CORN 39Ha +4

kw- 2Cu +4

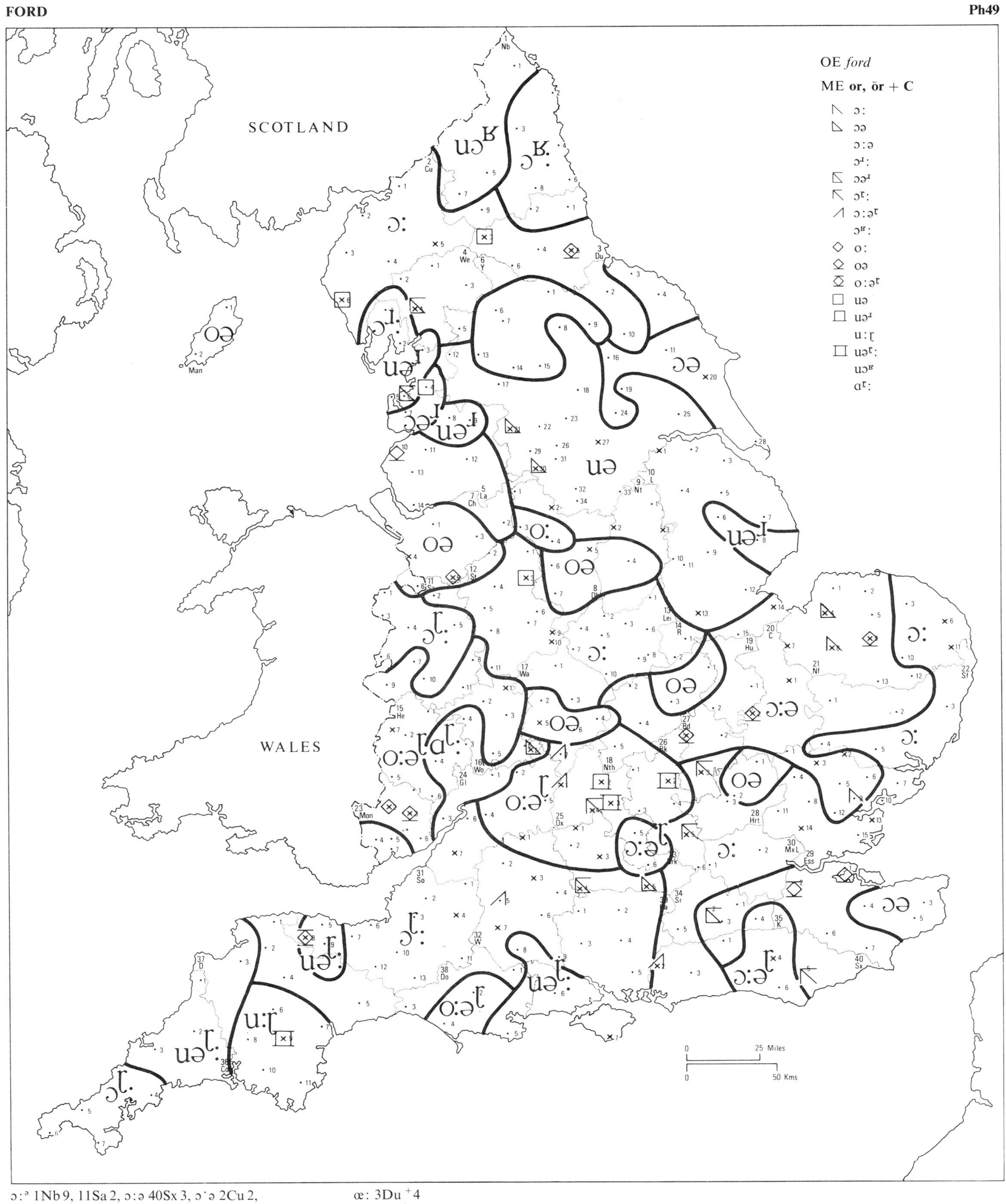

ɔ:ᵊ 1Nb 9, 11Sa 2, ɔ:ə 40Sx 3, ɔˑə 2Cu 2, 6Y 5 under ɔ:
ɔ:əʴ 34Sr 2 under ɔəʴ
ɔ̣ʵ:ᵊ 26Bk 5, ɔʵ:əʵ 11Sa 5 under ɔʵ:
ɔ:əʵ: 32W +5, ɔəʵ 25Ox 6, ɔᵊɻ 25Ox 1 under ɔ:əʵ
ϙʶ: 1Nb 2 under ɔʶ:
o:ə 7Ch 1, 23Mon 3, oωə 12St 2, ϙωə 18Nth 1, ouə Man 2 under oə
o:əʵ: 38Do 2, o:ωəʵ 17Wa +7, oəʵ 16Wo 5, 24Gl 5, 33Brk 2, 35K 2, oəʵ: 31So 8, 38Do 4 under o:əʵ
ωəʵ 25Ox 3, ϙəʵ 26Bk 2, u:əʵ: 31So 9, 38Do 5 under uəʵ:
ϙɔʶ 1Nb 5 under uɔʶ

œ: 3Du +4
a: 3Du +6
aʵ:əʵɻ 33Brk 1
ɑ:ə 16Wo 1
ɔɹ 15He 7
ɔωəʴ 33Brk 3
ɒωəʵ 17Wa 5
oəɹ 5La +14, o:əʴɹ 5La 12
oəʶ 1Nb +6

interpr as *r*-col: ɹ 5La +4/9, ɻ 25Ox 1/4/5
cons *r* foll *r*-col V: ɹ 5La 12, ɻ 33Brk 1, 34Sr 4, 40Sx 2/5

FORD- 3Du +6; -FORD 5La +6; FORDED pt 29Ess +9

fjωəθ ("older") 5La +14
-dʒ 5La +4, 16Wo 4, 24Gl 6, 29Ess 4/8/9

BUTTER Ph50

THUNDER Ph51

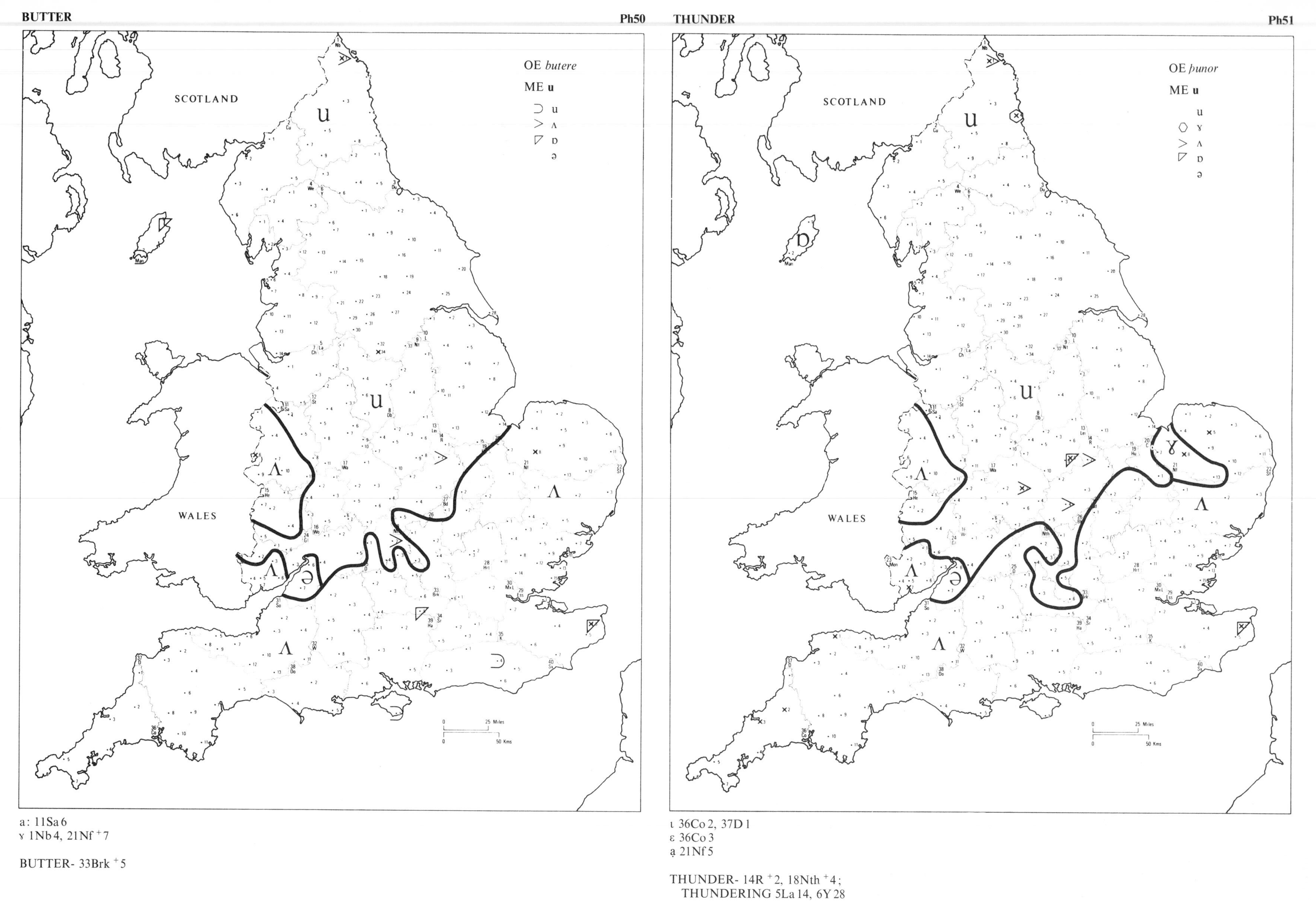

a: 11Sa 6
ʏ 1Nb 4, 21Nf +7

BUTTER- 33Brk +5

ι 36Co 2, 37D 1
ε 36Co 3
ạ 21Nf 5

THUNDER- 14R +2, 18Nth +4;
THUNDERING 5La 14, 6Y 28

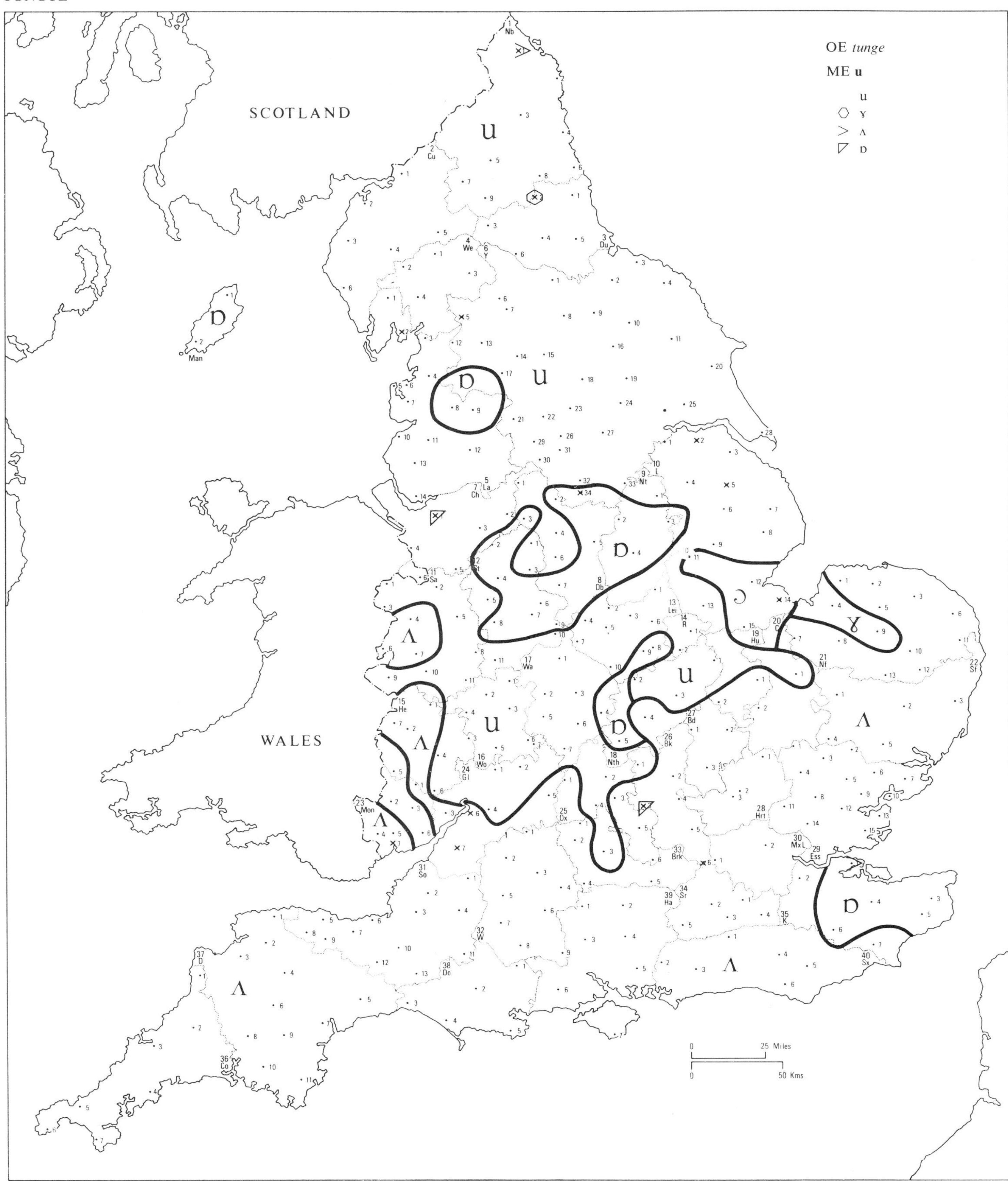

ɔ 24Gl 7

TONGUE- 6Y 2

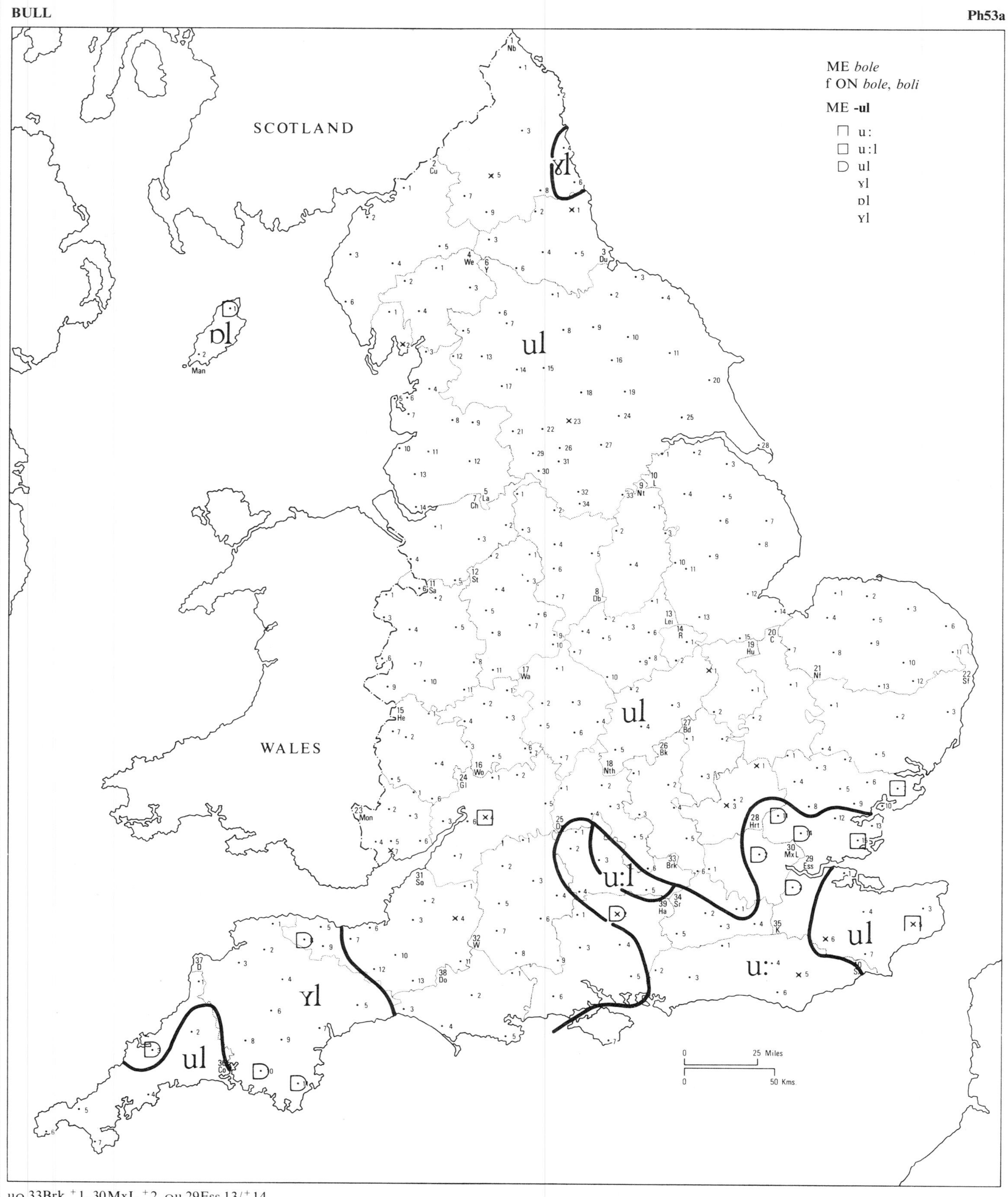

uọ 33Brk $^{+}$1, 30MxL $^{+}$2, ɷu 29Ess 13/$^{+}$14,
ɷọ 29Ess 12/$^{+}$15, 33Brk $^{+}$1/$^{+}$2/4, 34Sr 2–5,
39Ha 7, 40Sx 1–4/6 under u:
ᵚu:ɫ 24Gl 4, ɷọɫ 29Ess $^{+}$7/$^{+}$15 under u:l

œ:l 1Nb 5
ʌl 1Nb $^{+}$2, ʌɫ 35K 6
o: 33Brk $^{+}$2

BULL- 33Brk $^{+}$2; BULLS pl 30MxL 2, 31So $^{+}$8

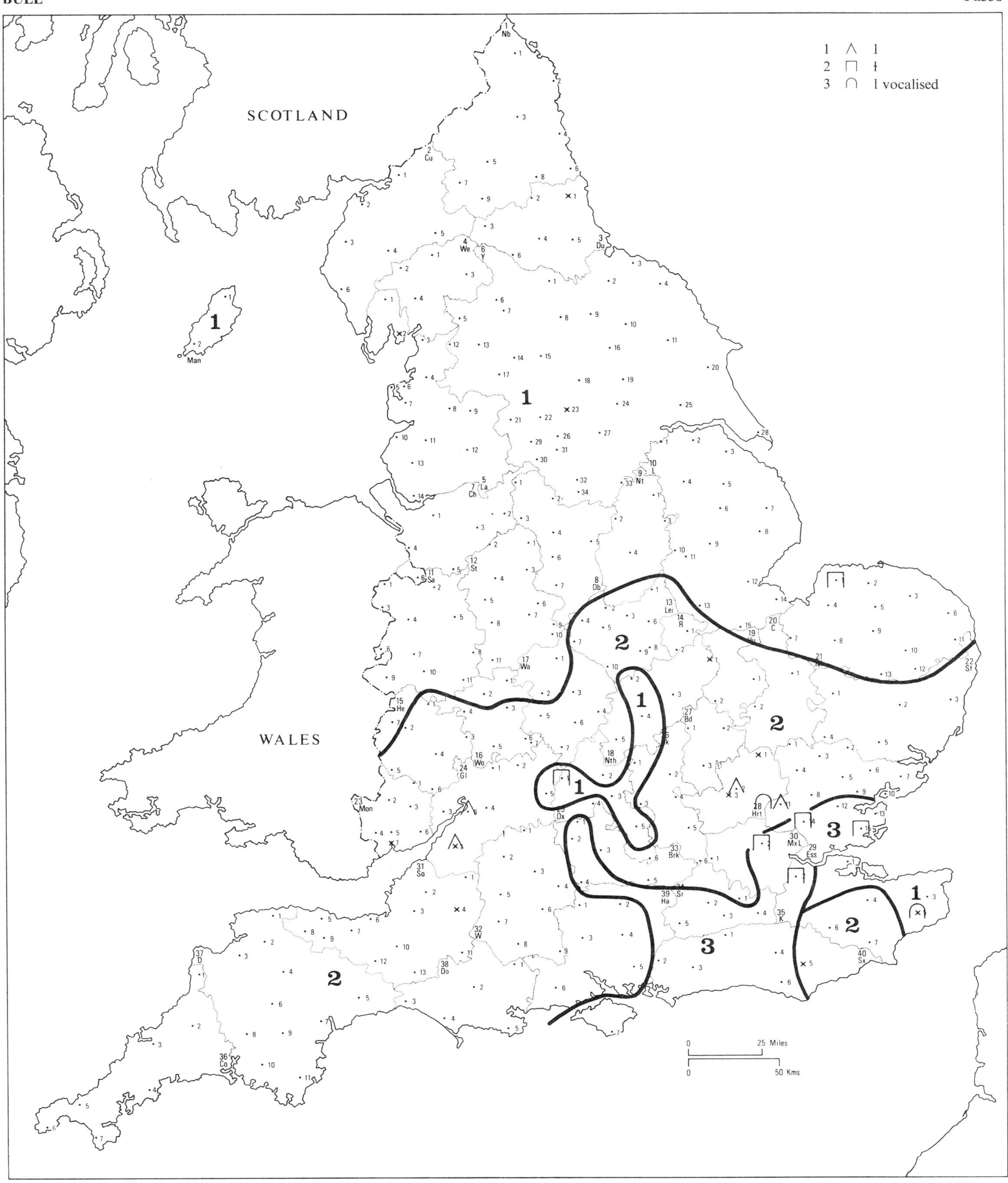

l· 21Nf 2/4/7/9/13, lː 21Nf 6/+10

BULL- 21Nf +1, 25Ox +1, 28Hrt +2

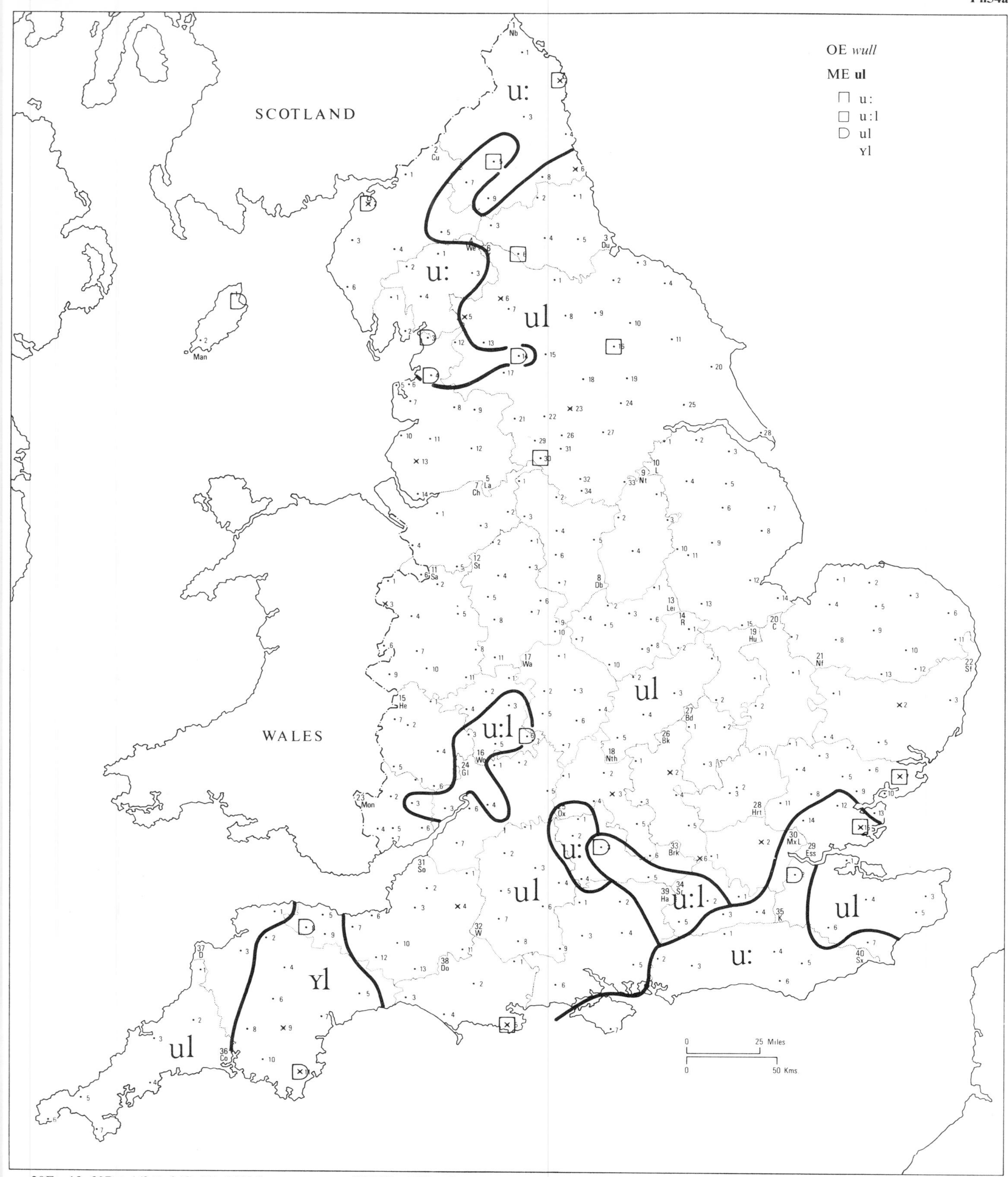

ωọ 29Ess 12, 33Brk 1/2/4, 34Sr 3/4, 35K 7, 39Ha 7, 40Sx 1–6, ωu 29Ess 14 under u:
ωωɫ 29Ess 7, ωọɫ 29Ess 15, 34Sr 2/5, ᵚu:ᵊɫ 24Gl 3 under u:l
ωᵊɫ 24Gl 7 under ul
ʏ:ɫ 37D 5 under ʏl

ɛ̈ωl 6Y $^+$6
äω 6Y 5
ɒl Man 2
ʌl 11Sa 3/$^+$7, ʌɫ 26Bk 2, ʌ̣ɫ 37D 9
oɫ 25Ox 3
əul 6Y $^+$6, əω 6Y $^+$7

WOOL- 11Sa 7

w- dropped 1Nb 1/3/4/$^+$5, 2Cu 1/6, 6Y $^+$30, 11Sa $^+$10/11, 15He 2–6, 16Wo 3/$^+$6, 17Wa 5/7, 23Mon 1, 24Gl 2–7, 25Ox 1–3/$^+$5, 26Bk $^+$1/2/3, 29Ess 1, 31So 2/3/5–7/$^+$8/9/10/$^+$12/13, 32W 2/3/6/8/9, 37D 5/7/10, 39Ha 5/6

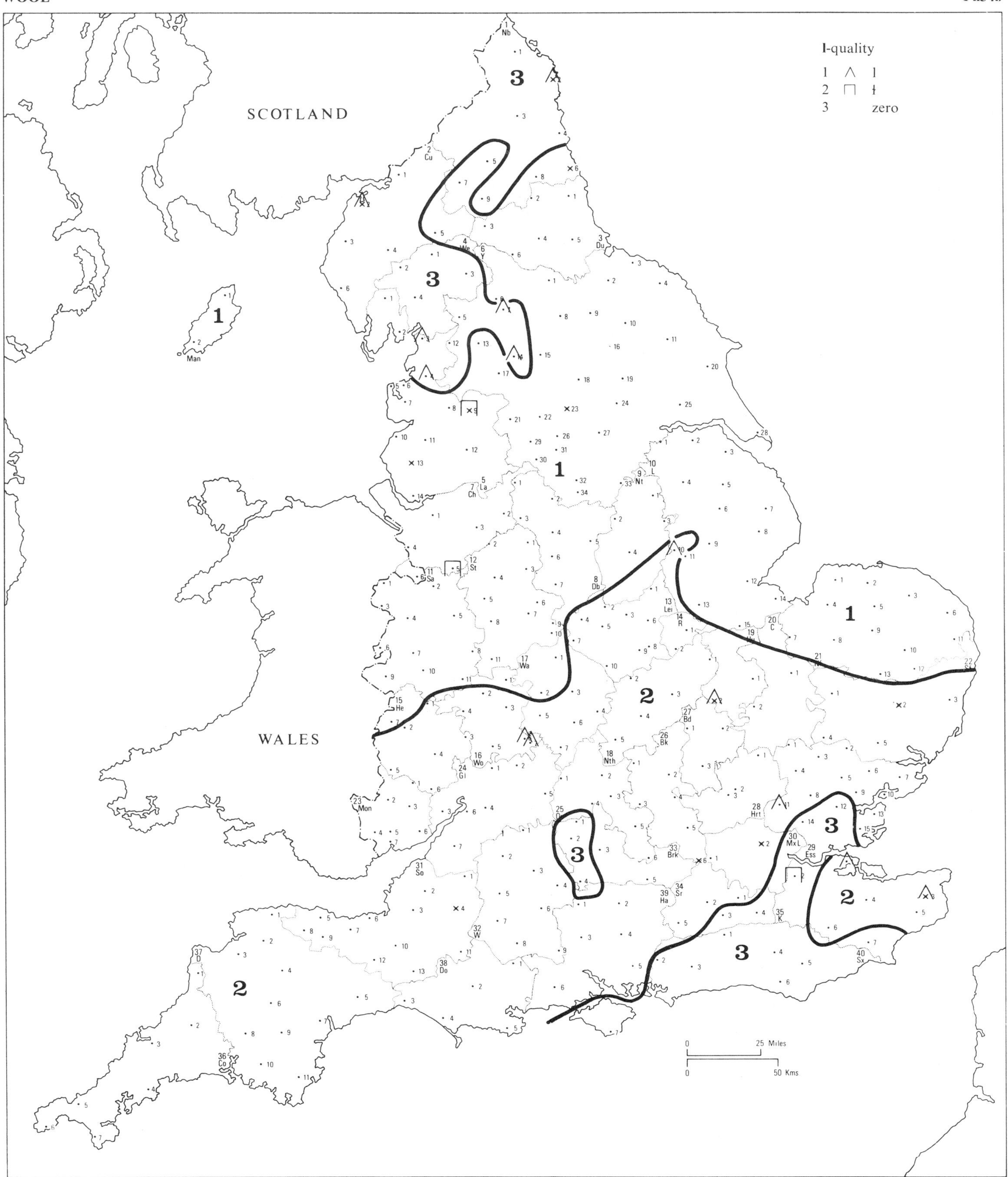

l˙ 21Nf 4/9/12/13, l: 21Nf 5/6/10, ɫ: 23Mon 4

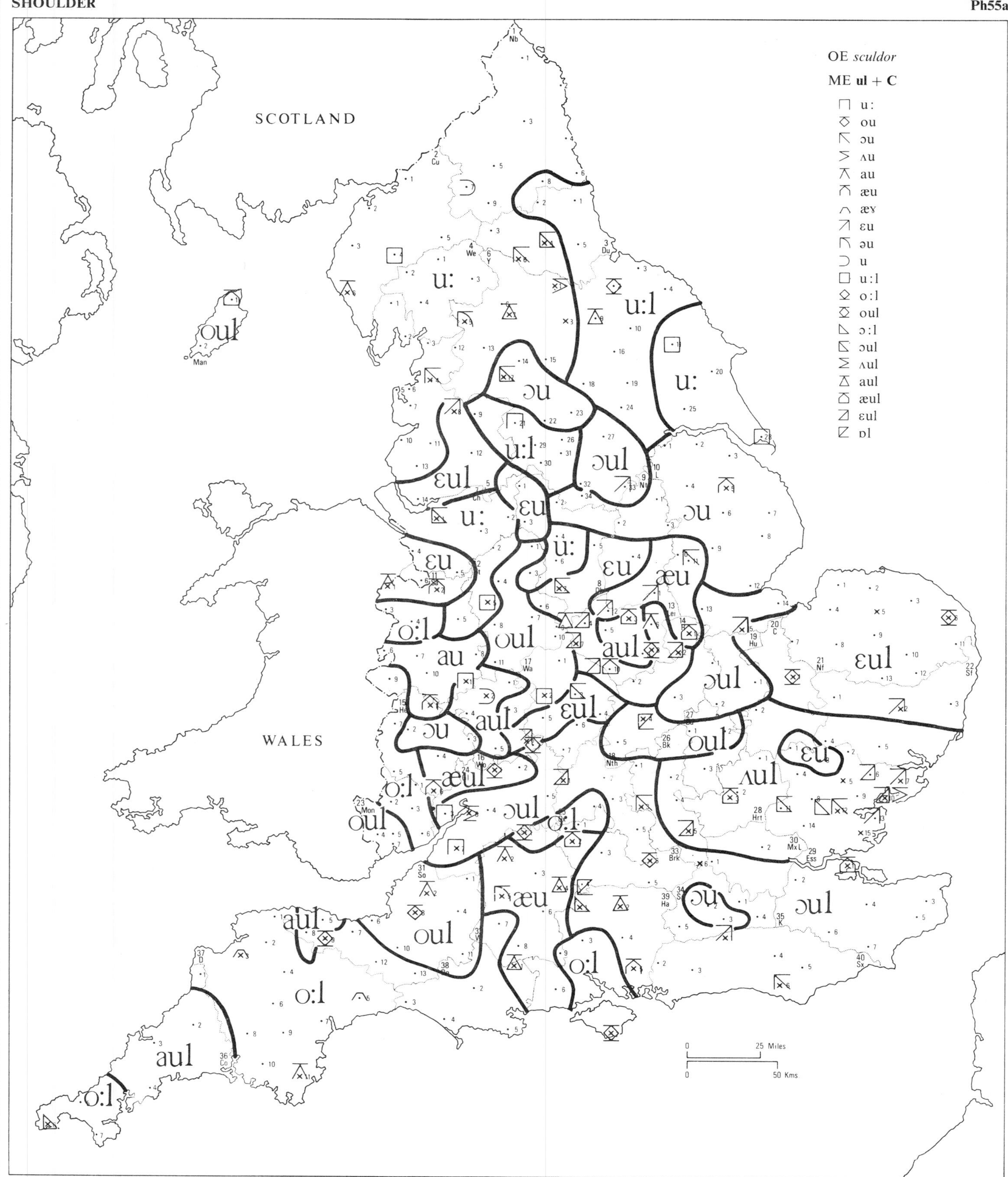

ᵊu: 3Du $^{+}$3, 4We 4, 6Y $^{+}$6/20, ᵊu˙ 6Y $^{+}$6,
  öu 5La 5, ɩü 7Ch 2 under u:
ɛu: 16Wo 6 under ɛu
ᵊu:l 3Du 5 under u:l
o:ᵚl 15He 7, o:ᵚɫ 23Mon 1, 25Ox 4,
  o:ɷɫ 24Gl 1 under o:l

ɑɷ 29Ess $^{+}$15
ɑɷɫ 29Ess $^{+}$15
ʌɫ 29Ess 5
ɷəl 10L $^{+}$12
əɷl 6Y 8, ə̣ɷl 21Nf 5

SHOULDER- 1Nb $^{+}$7, 3Du $^{+}$3, 6Y $^{+}$6/$^{+}$11,
  29Ess $^{+}$11; -SHOULDER 13Lei $^{+}$10

SHOULDER

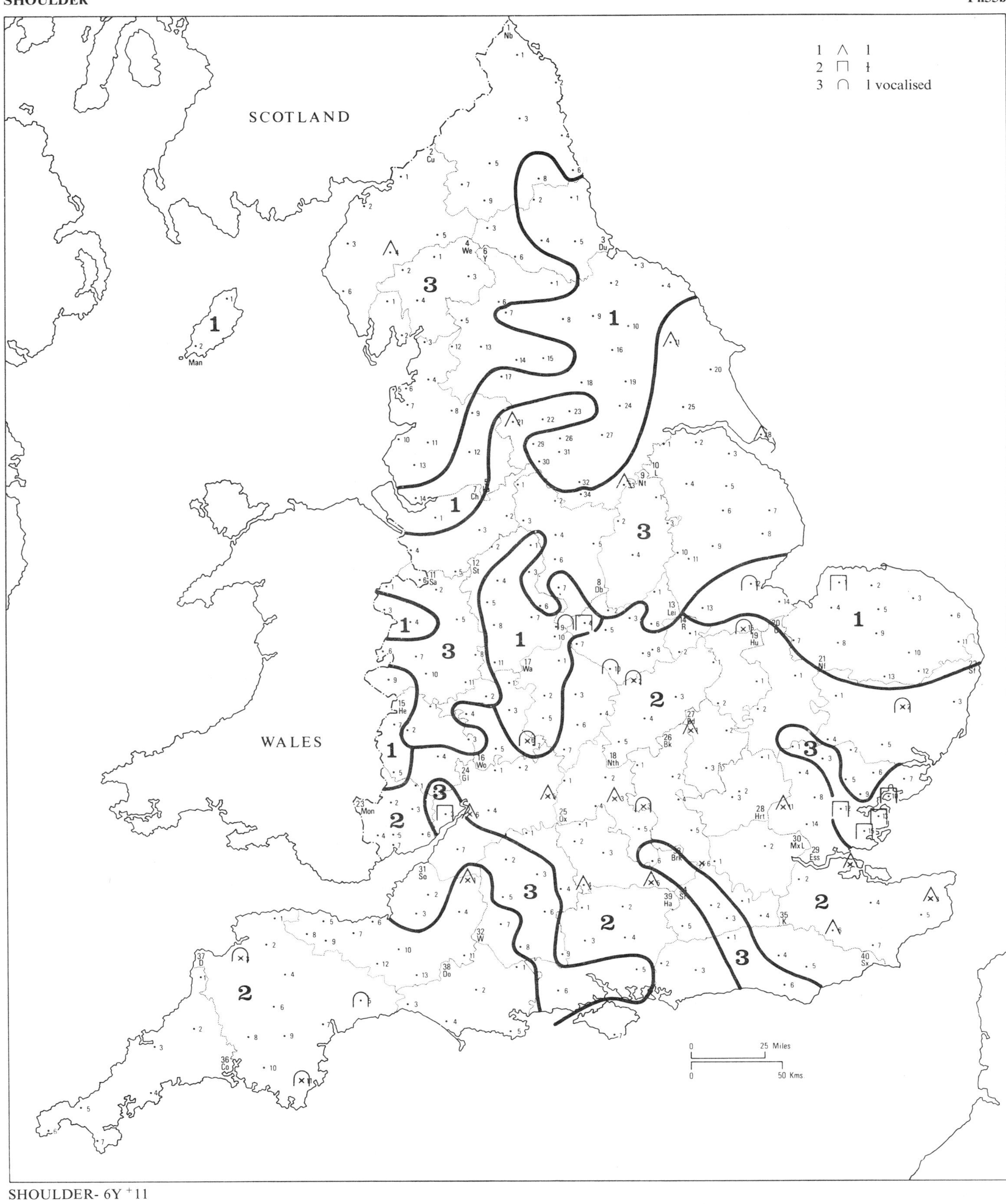

SHOULDER- 6Y $^{+}$11

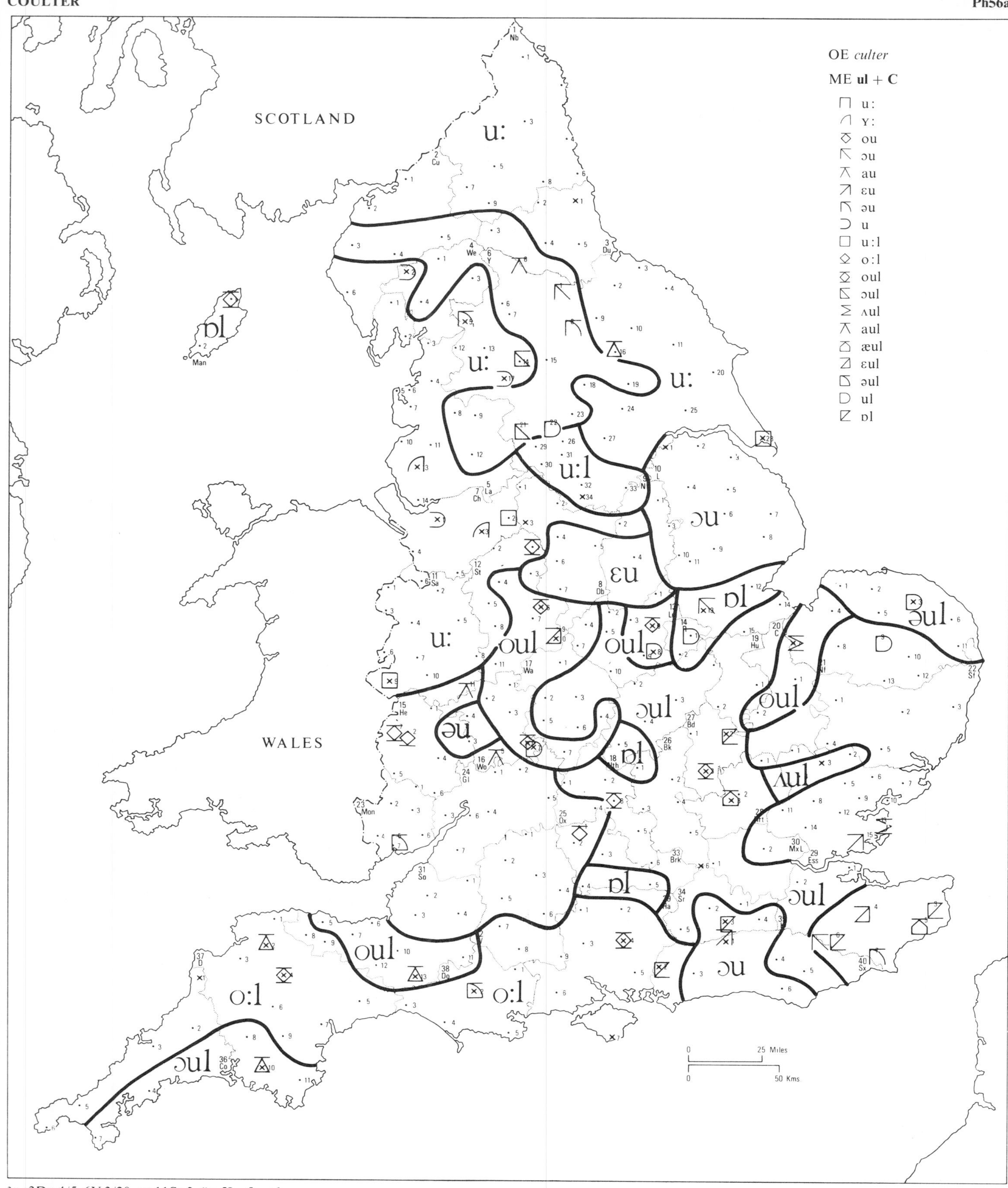

ᵊu: 3Du 4/5, 6Y 3/20, ʉ: 11Sa 2, öu 5La 5 under u:
əɷ: 16Wo 4 under əu
ɔl 10L 12 under ɒl

ɩɫ (sic) 36Co 1
ɔ: 39Ha 7
ʌl 15He 1, ʌɫ 29Ess 3
ʌɷ 26Bk 6

-COULTER 6Y +14
COULTERN 11Sa 11, 15He 2/3, 16Wo 4

kɩ- 11Sa 5, kʏ- 11Sa 2
kʌ̥tə 28Hrt +3, kʌ̥təᵗ: 31So 3 are taken to repr
CUTTER

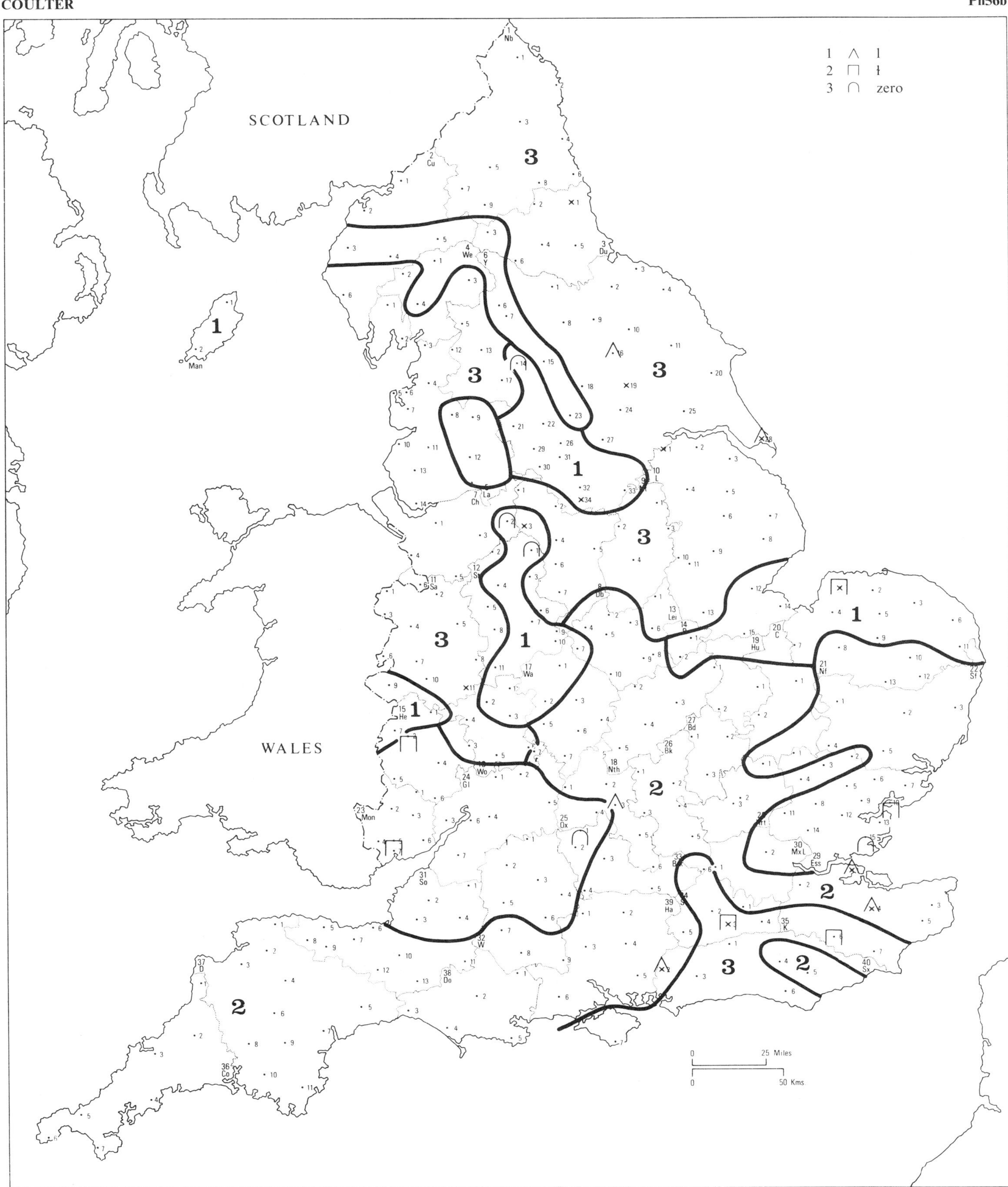

-COULTER 6Y [+]14

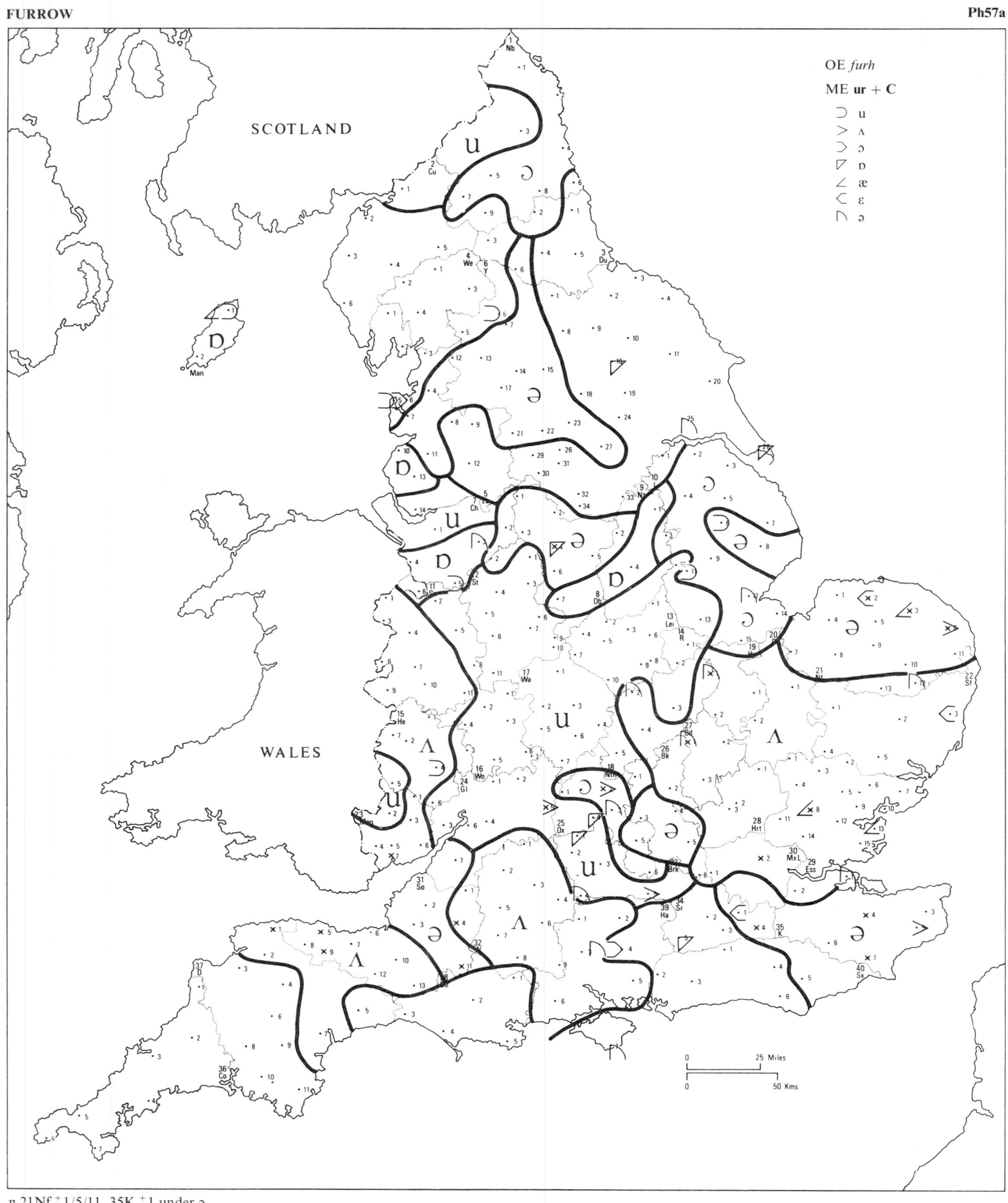

ɐ 21Nf +1/5/11, 35K +1 under ə

ɑ 21Nf +1, ɑː 29Ess +12
əɹ 33Brk +4
əʳ 35K +6, əʳː 31So 11

FURROW- 33Brk +5, 39Ha +4;
-FURROW 33Brk +4, 35K 3, 40Sx 5

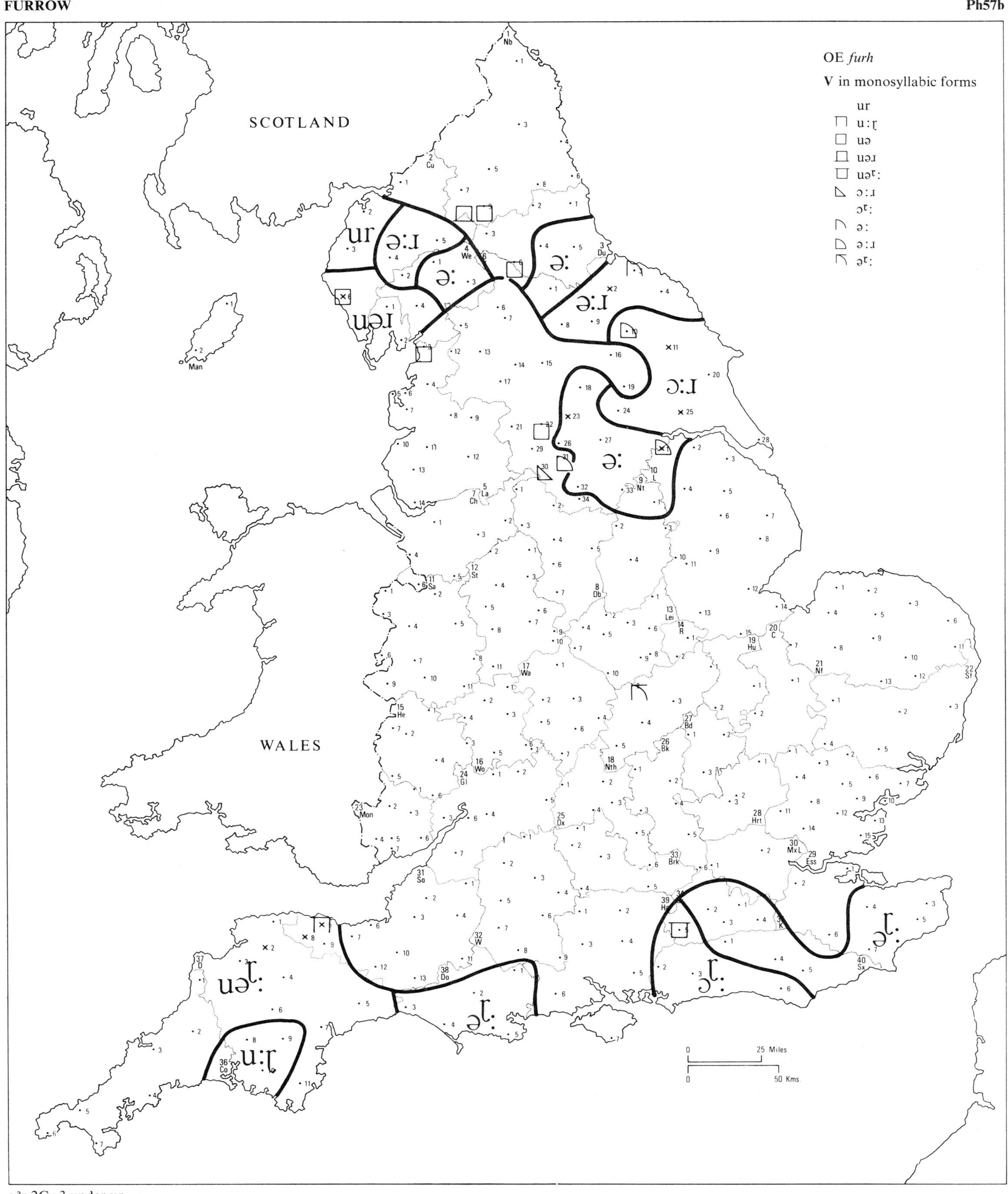

ɷ^{ə}r 2Cu 3 under ur
ọ˙ə 1Nb +9 under uə
ọəɹ 1Nb +9 under uəɹ
u:ə^{ɽ}: 37D +7, u:ə^{ɽ} 34Sr +5 under uə^{ɽ}:
ɔ^{ɹ}˙ 6Y 28, ɔɹ 6Y 24 under ɔ:ɹ
ɒ̣^{ɽ}: 34Sr +5 under ɔ^{ɽ}:
əɹ 6Y 8, 10L 1 under ə:ɹ
ə^{ɽ} 35K +3/+5 under ə^{ɽ}:

ɒ^{ɹ} 6Y 11
ɷ˙ɹ 6Y 2

interpr as *r*-col: ɽ 40Sx +4
cons *r* foll *r*-col V: ɽ 34Sr 2–4, 40Sx 1–3/+4/5/6

FURROW- 6Y +3; -FURROW 35K +5, 37D +7

fɷə^{ɹ}ð 5La 6, fɷəð 5La 7

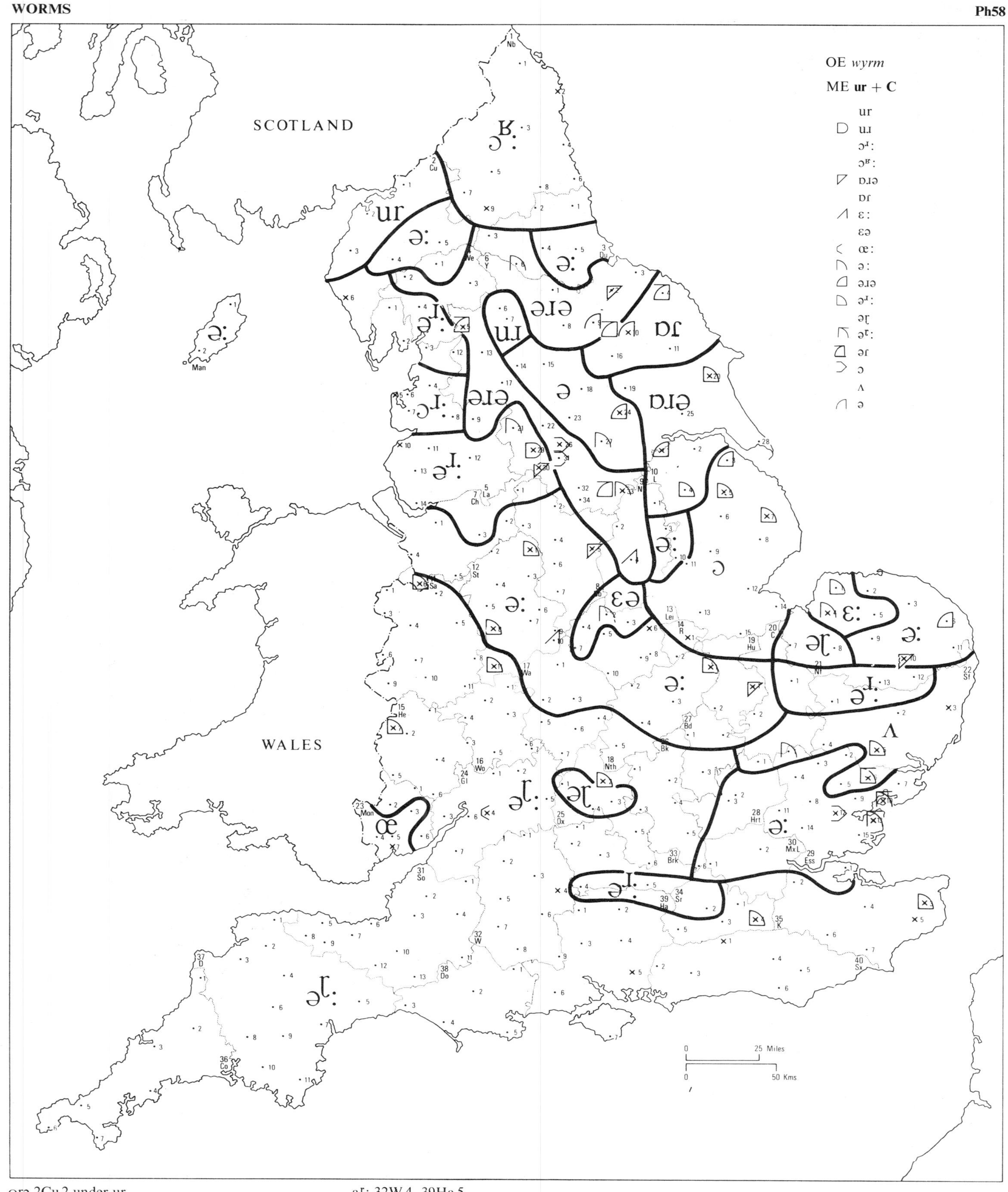

ɷɾə 2Cu 2 under ur
ɷɹə 6Y 29 under uɹ
ɔʶʁ 1Nb 3 under ɔʶ:
ɒɹ 6Y +25, ɔɹə 9Nt 1, 10L 2, ɔ̈ɹə 10L +4,
21Nf 10 under ɒɹə
ɒɾə 6Y 11 under ɒɾ
ɛ 21Nf +1 under ɛ:
œ 23Mon 4 under œ:
ɜ: 4We 1, Man 1/2 under ə:
ɜʴ: 5La 1–3/12/13, ɜʴ:ɹ 5La 11/14, ə̣ʴ:ɹᵊ 21Nf 12,
əʴ 10L 7, əɹ 15He 7 under əʴ:
əɽə 25Ox 3 under əɽ
əʵ:ɽə 32W 1, əʵ 16Wo +7, 34Sr 1, 35K +2/6,
39Ha 4 under əʵ:
əɾə 6Y +33 under əɾ
ɔ: 13Lei +1, 29Ess 12 under ɔ

aʵ: 32W 4, 39Ha 5
ɒ 6Y +18
ɒʵ 35K 5
ɔəʴ 5La 5
ɔ:ɽ 40Sx 1
ɔʁə 1Nb 2
ʌɹ 22Sf 3
ọə 1Nb 9
ɷ 13Lei +1, 14R 1
əʶ: 2Cu 6

interpr as *r*-col: ɹ 6Y 20, 12St 11, 15He 7,
18Nth 1, 20C 1, 22Sf 1/5, ɽ 33Brk 2/3, 39Ha 7
cons *r* foll *r*-col V: ɹ 5La 8/11/14, 21Nf 12,
ɹ˙ 21Nf 13, ɽ 32W 1, 33Brk 1, 40Sx 2/4–6,
ʁ 1Nb 3

WORM- 6Y +27; -WORM(S) 6Y +4/+9/+21,
7Ch 2, 16Wo +7, 35K +2

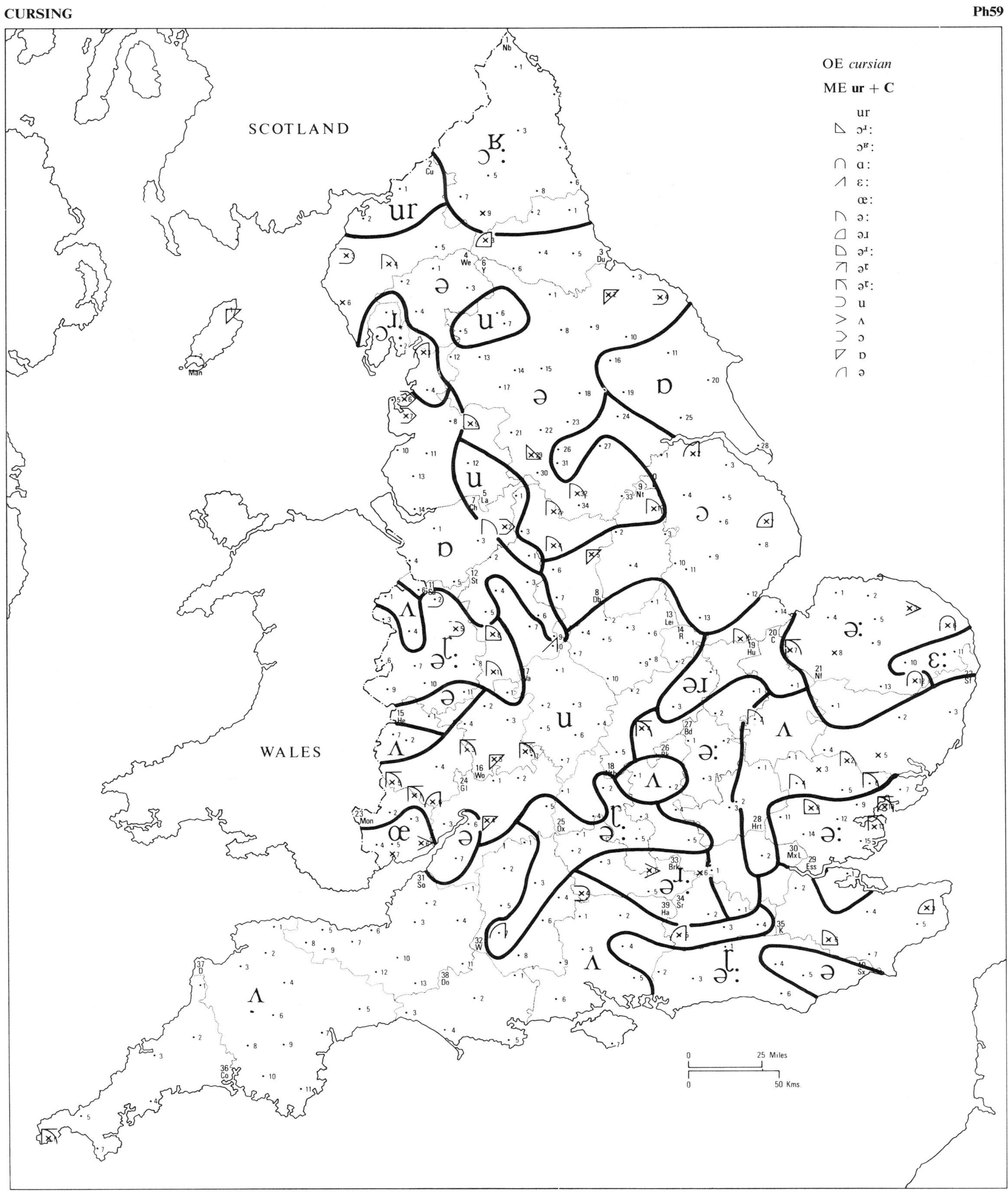

ɔʁ 1Nb +2 under ɔʁ:
ɛ̈ 21Nf 11 under ɛ:
əɹ 10L 7/14, 35K 3 under əɹ
ɜɹ:ɹ 5La 9 under əɹ:
əɽ 15He 3, 23Mon 1, 35K 2, 39Ha 4,
  ə̣ɽ 21Nf 7 under əɽ:

ä:ɹ 22Sf 5
ɔ: 1Nb 9
ər 2Cu 6

interpr as *r*-col: ɽ 21Nf 7, 33Brk +2
cons *r* foll *r*-col V: ɹ 5La 4/9, ɽ 32W 3/+7,
  33Brk 1/+2, 40Sx 1–3/6

CURSE inf 11 Sa +2; CURSES n 1Nb +2

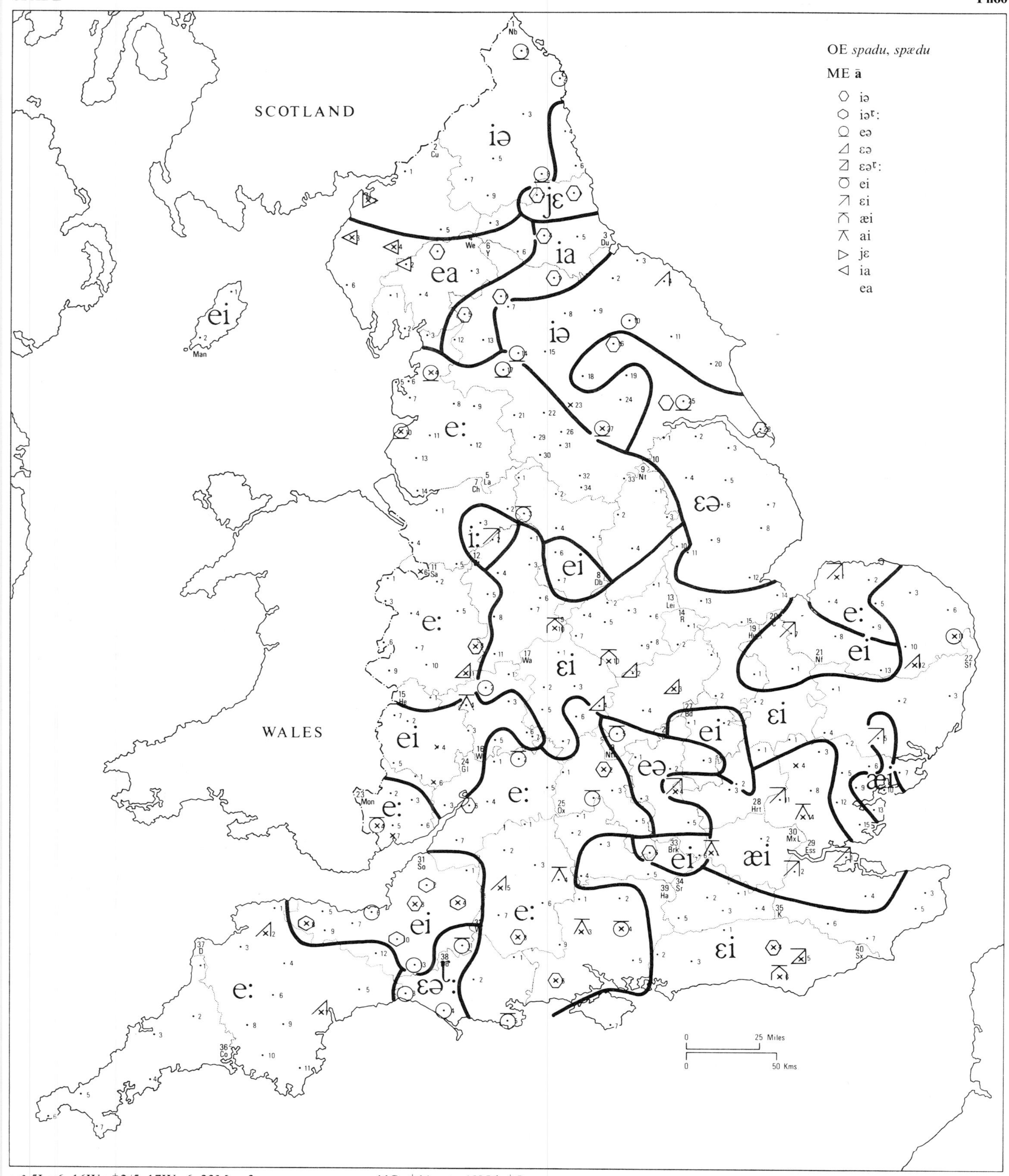

e:ᵊ 5La 6, 16Wo +2/5, 17Wa 6, 23Mon 3,
24Gl 1/+2, 25Ox +1, e:ə 36Co +1, 37D +3/4,
ᵊe: 21Nf 11 under e:
jə 24Gl +6 under iə
ɛ:ə 11Sa +11 under ɛə
ɛ:əʳ: 38Do +4, ɛəʳɽ 40Sx 5 under ɛəʳ:
e:ɩ 15He 3/5, 16Wo 3/+4/6, 23Mon 1,
31So +2/+5/+7, ẹ:ɩ 31So +13, e:ᶥ 8Db +3,
15He 2/+7, 24Gl +2/3, ẹ:ᶥ 8Db 6, eɩə Man +1,
ẹɩᵊ 20C 1, ᶥẹ:ᶥ 23Mon 4 under ei
ɛ:ᶥ 21Nf 5/10, ɛɩᵊ 16Wo +2, 22Sf +5,
ẹɩᵊ 20C 2 under ɛi
ɩɛ̈ 2Cu 2 under jɛ

e:a 11Sa +11, ẹˑa 18Nth +5
ɛ 15He 6

cons *r* foll *r*-col V: ɽ 40Sx 5

SPADE- 24Gl 6/7; -SPADE 6Y +5, 20C 1;
SPADE v 37D +3

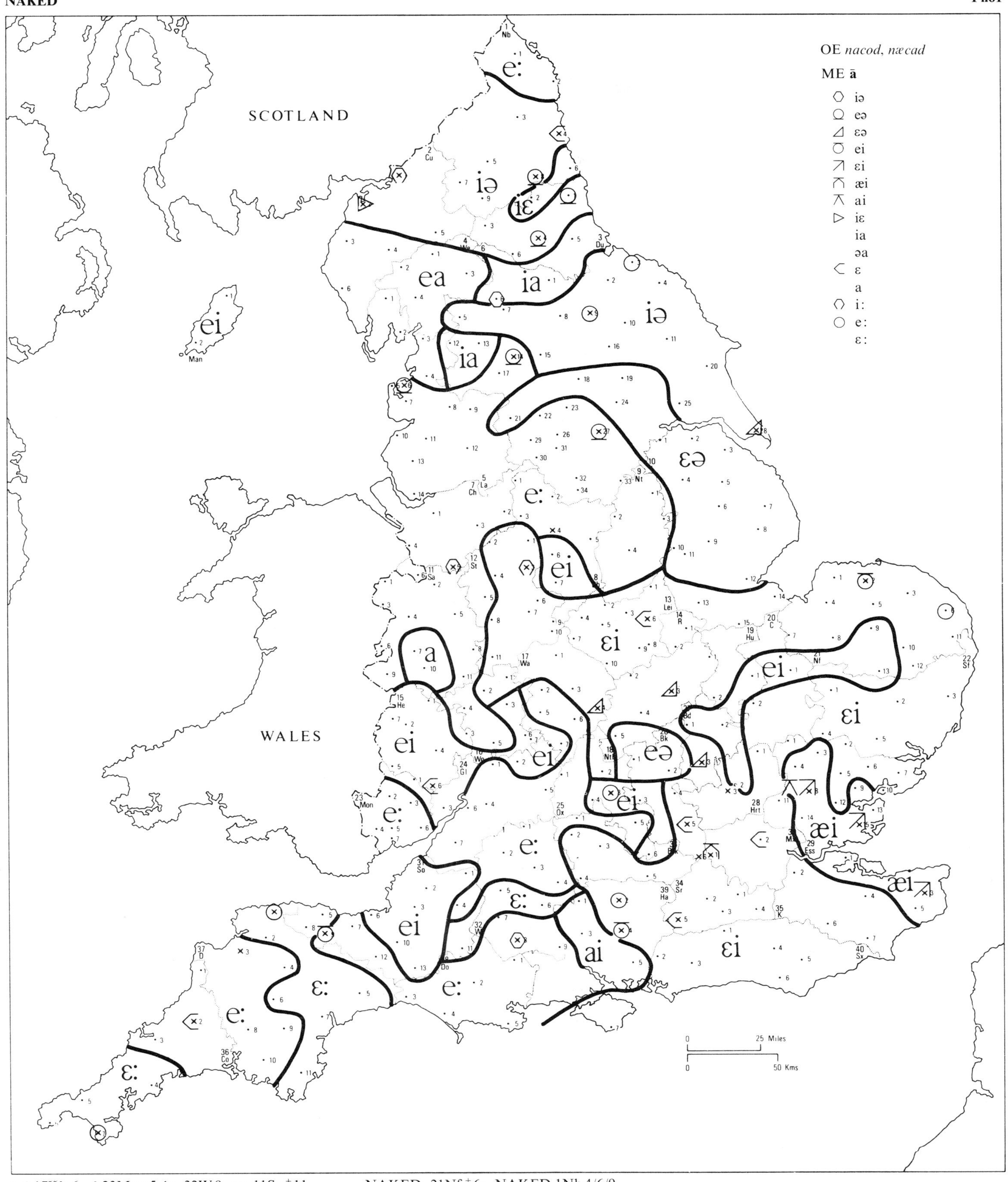

e:^{ə} 17Wa 6, ẹ^{ə} 23Mon 5, ˈẹ: 32W 9, ɩe: 11Sa $^{+}$11,
ɩ̆e: 11Sa $^{+}$11 under e:

ɛ̣:^{ə} 31So 8, ɛ:ə 31So 5 under ɛ:

je˙ə 18Nth 5 under eə

ɛ˙^{ə} 6Y 19 under ɛə

e:ɩ 15He 1/2/4/5, 16Wo 3/6, 23Mon 1, 24Gl 2,
31So 6/13, e:^{ɩ} 8Db 6, 21Nf 9, 24Gl 3,
25Ox 4, e^{ɩ}: (pres error for e:^{ɩ} Edd)
15He 7 under ei

ɛ:ɩ 21Nf 5, 33Brk 4, 40Sx 4 under ɛi

jɛ 1Nb 6 3Du 2

NAKED- 21Nf $^{+}$6; -NAKED 1Nb 4/6/9,
2Cu 1/4, 3Du $^{+}$1/3/4/6, 4We 2–4,
5La 1/2/4/7/8/11–13,
6Y 1/2/$^{+}$3/9/11/14/21/22/25/27/30,
7Ch 1/3–5, 8Db 1/2, 9Nt 4, 10L 7–9/13,
15He 7, 17Wa 7, 20C 1/2, 21Nf 8/10,
22Sf 3–5, 26Bk 2–4, 27Bd 2, 28Hrt 1/2,
35K 7

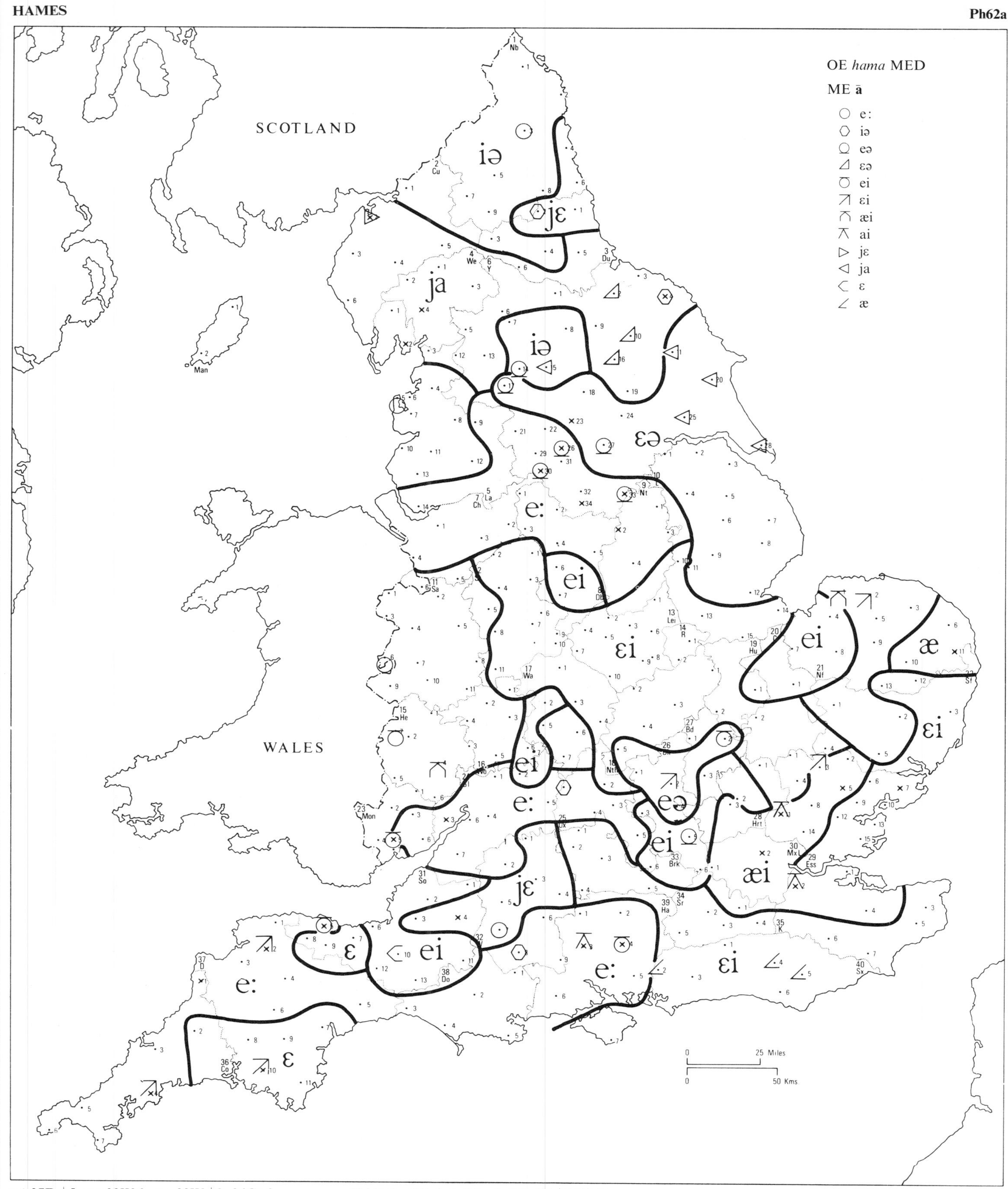

e:^{ə} 37D $^{+}$5, ę:^{ə} 32W 6, e:ə 32W $^{+}$8, 36Co 5, 37D 3/$^{+}$5, 39Ha 6 under e:
jə 6Y 8, 25Ox $^{+}$1 under iə
e:ɩ 16Wo 6, ę:ɩ 31So 13, e:^{ɩ} 8Db 6, 24Gl 2, e:ɩ^{ə} 31So 5, ęɩ^{ə} 20C 1 under ei
ɛ:ɩ 13Lei $^{+}$1, 33Brk 4, ɛ:$^{\ddot{ɩ}}$ 21Nf 12, ɛɩ^{ə} 18Nth 1, 20C 2 under ɛi
jɛ: 32W 1 under jɛ
ɩa 6Y 5/6/12/13, ea 5La 3 under ja
ɛ: 31So 9, 36Co 2, 37D 7 under ɛ

ɩ 11Sa 1
jeə 3Du $^{+}$4
a 4We 4, 5La 2, 36Co 1

HAME- 1Nb 1–9, 3Du 1–3/5, 6Y $^{+}$17/$^{+}$27, 34Sr 4, 40Sx $^{+}$4/$^{+}$5; -HAMESES 37D $^{+}$5

e:nz 23Mon 3
hɩəmz (= trouser-braces) 32W $^{+}$8

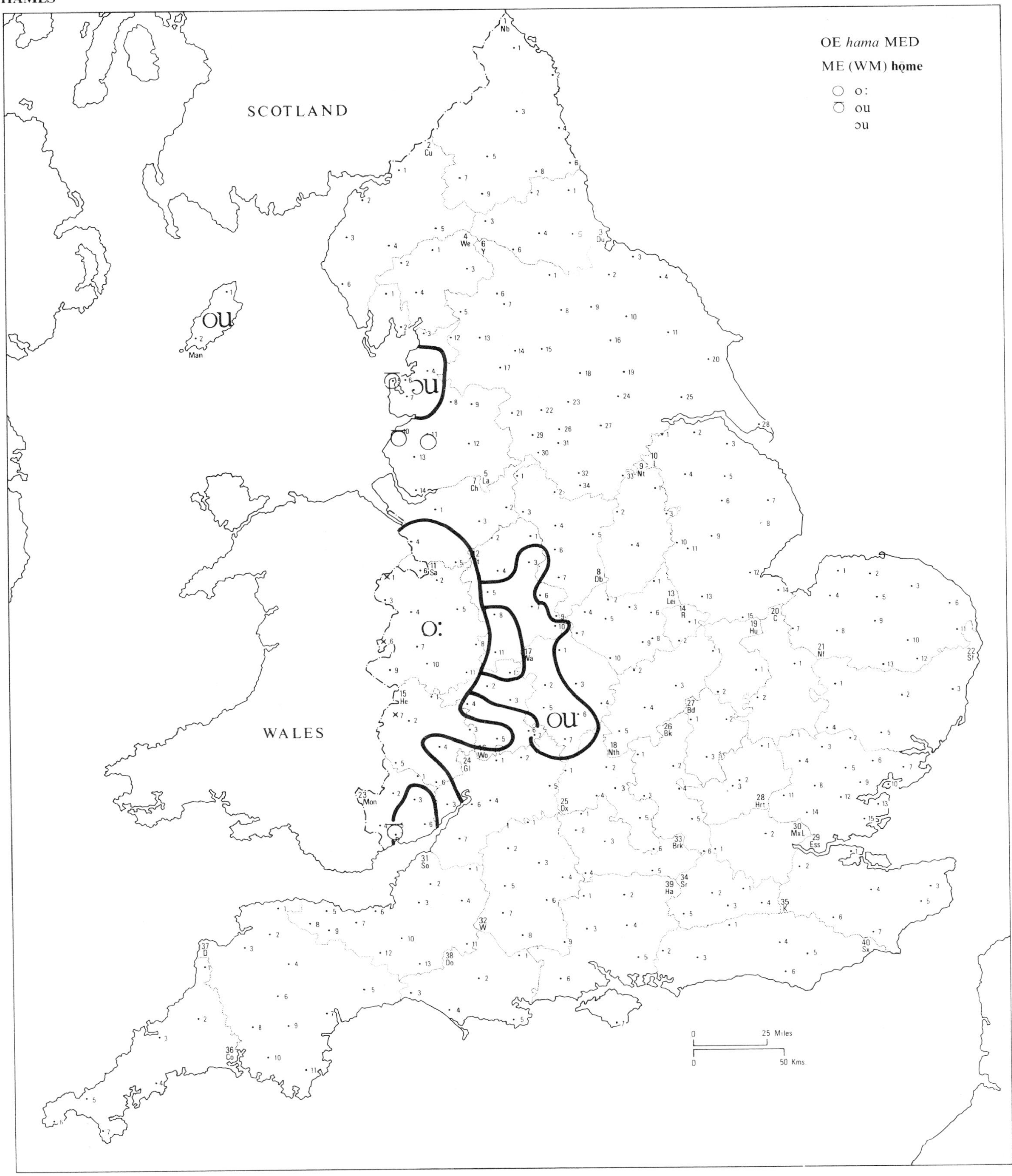

o:ɷ 15He 3, 23Mon 1, 24Gl 3 under o:
ɒɷ 5La 4/⁺5 under ɔu

ɛ̈ɷ 5La 8
ɔ: 24Gl 7
ɷ: 16Wo 4
ɷə 5La 10

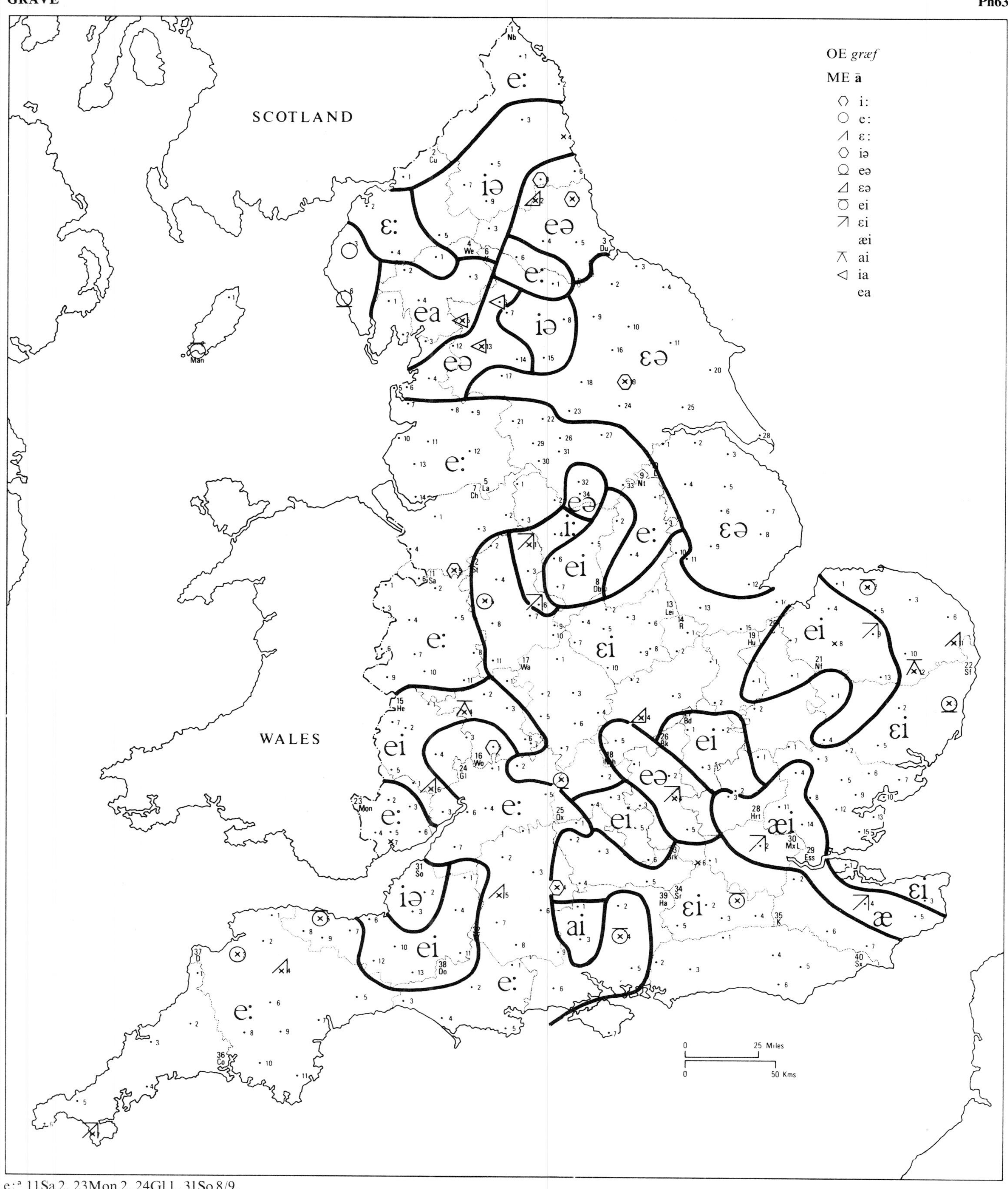

e:ᵊ 11Sa 2, 23Mon 2, 24Gl 1, 31So 8/9,
e:ə 37D 3 under e:
ɛ 15He 6 under ɛ:
i̜:ə 31So 3 under iə
e:ᵊ 1Nb 6, 22Sf 3, ẹ:ᵊ 6Y 34 under eə
ɛ:ᵊ, ɛ̣:ᵊ 6Y 23 under ɛə
eɩᵊ 21Nf 7, 31So 5, e̜ɩᵊ 22Sf 4, e:ɩ 15He 1/2/5,
16Wo 3/6, 23Mon 1, 31So 6/12/13, e:ᶥ 8Db 5/6,
9Nt 2, 16Wo 2, 24Gl 3, ẹ:ɩᵊ 31So 4 under ei
ɛɩᵊ 22Sf 5, ɛ:ɩ 21Nf 10, ɛ̜:ɩ 21Nf 5,
ɛ:-ɩ̜ (sic) 21Nf 3 under ɛi

GRAVE- 1Nb ⁺8, 6Y ⁺23, 21Nf ⁺9, 30MxL ⁺2

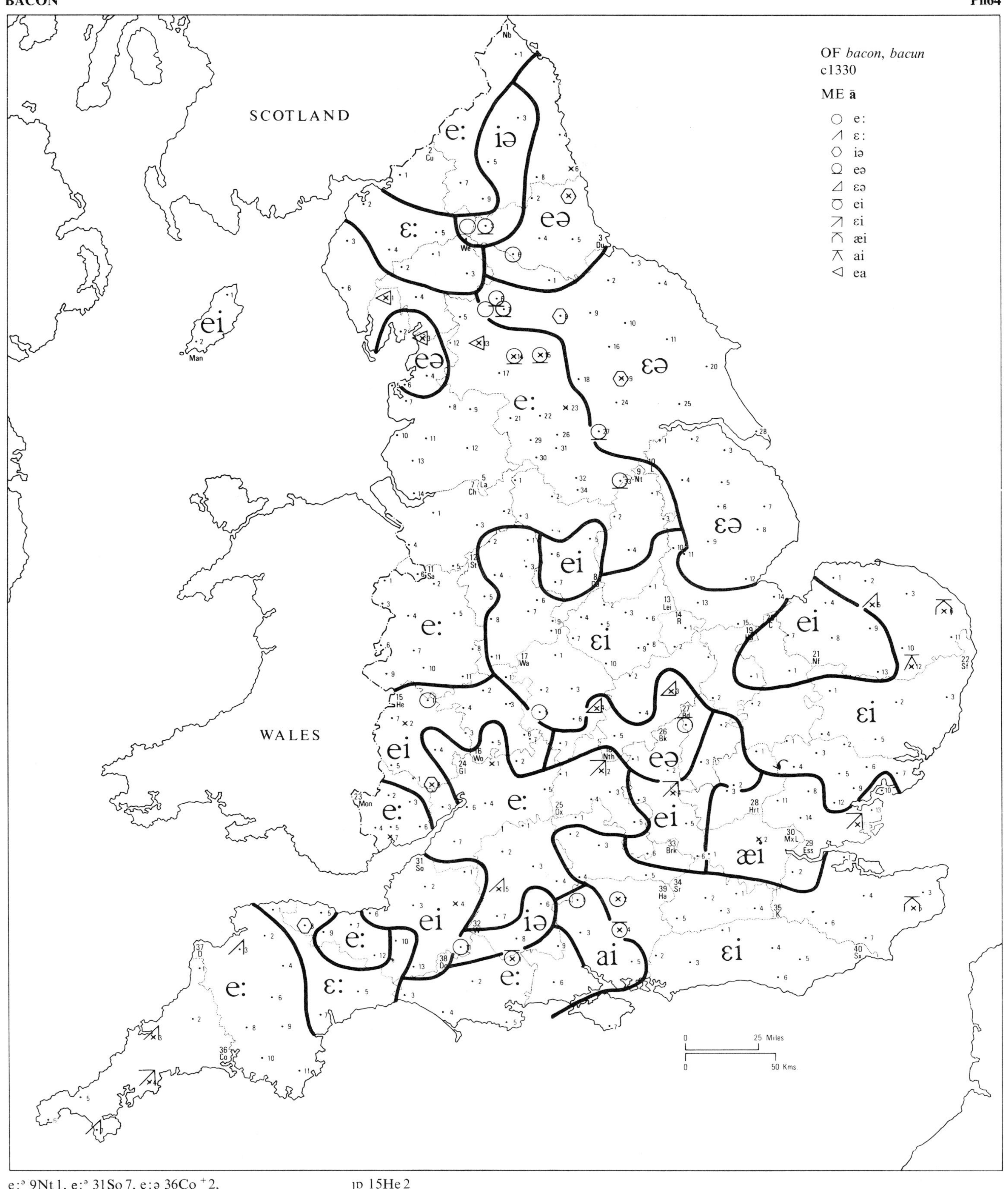

e:^{ə} 9Nt 1, ẹ:^{ə} 31So 7, e:ə 36Co $^{+}$2,
^{ι}ẹ: 32W 9 under e:
ɛ:ə 31So 5/$^{+}$8 under ɛ:
jə 15He 6 under iə
e:ə 3Du $^{+}$6, e:^{ə} 17Wa 7 under eə
e:ι 15He 3/5, 16Wo 3/4/6, 23Mon 1, 24Gl 2,
e:^{ι} 8Db 5/6, 15He $^{+}$1/$^{+}$7, 16Wo 2, 24Gl 3.
eι^{ə} 31So 6, ẹι^{ə} 31So 13 under ei
ɛ:ι 12St 11, 13Lei $^{+}$1, 21Nf 11, 33Brk $^{+}$5,
ɛ̧:ι 21Nf 1, ɛ:^{ι} 21Nf 2/3 under ɛi
ι̧ä 6Y 13 under ea

ɹɒ 15He 2
ɛ̣ä 6Y $^{+}$33

BACON- 15He $^{+}$7

błækɷn 24Gl 1

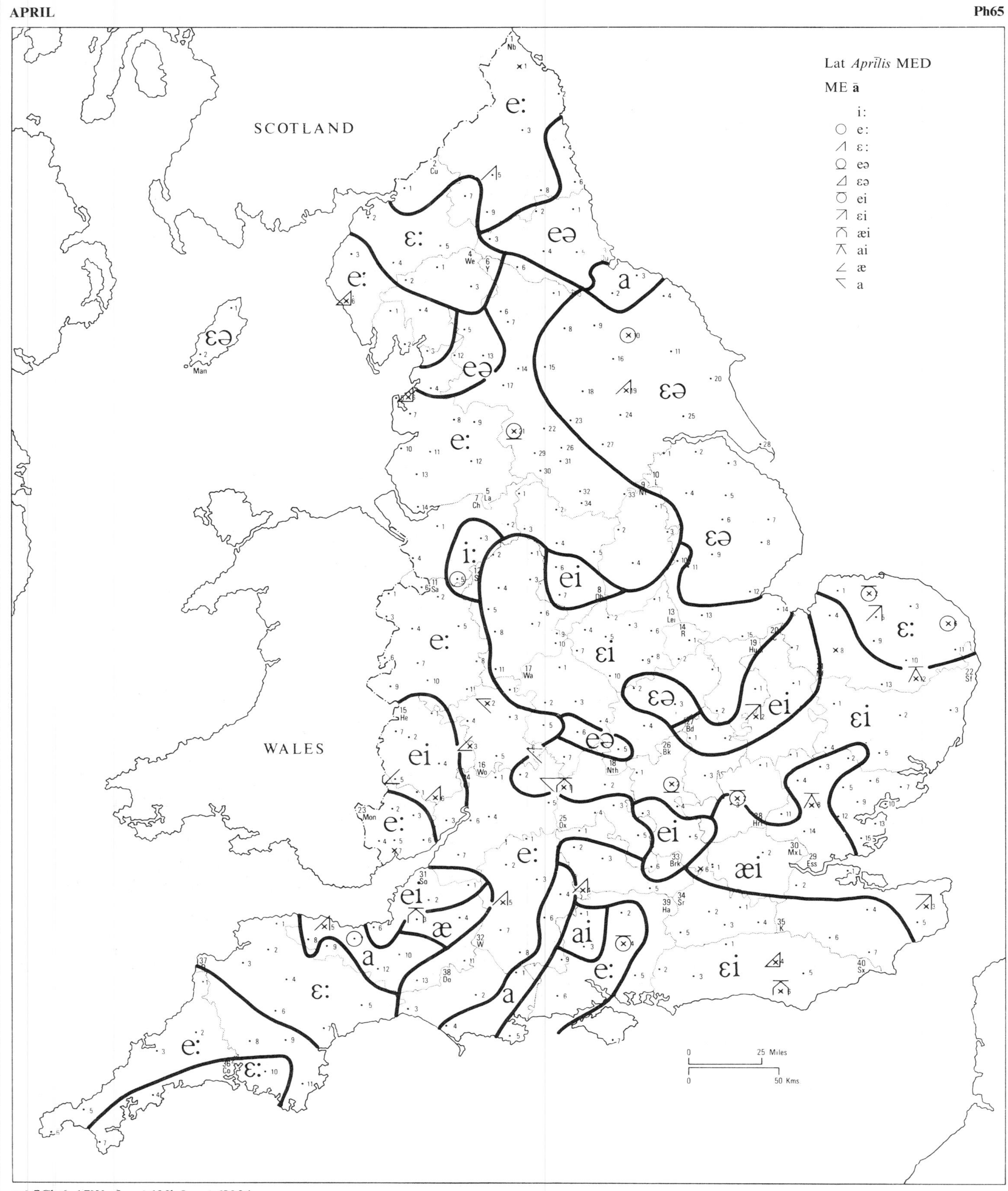

e:^{ə} 7Ch 6, 17Wa 5, ẹ:^{ə} 1Nb 8, ę:^{ə} 6Y 34,
e 11Sa 1 under e:
ɛ:^{ə} 31So 9, ɛ:ə 37D 4, ɛ 1Nb $^{+}$5/7, 15He 6,
31So 5, 37D 10 under ɛ:
ɩə 3Du 4 under eə
ɛ:^{ə} 6Y 23 under ɛə
e:ɩ 15He 1/2/4/$^{+}$5, 23Mon 1, e:^{ɩ} 8Db 6/7,
24Gl 3, eɩ^{ə} 31So 6 under ei
ɛ̧:ɩ 21Nf $^{+}$5, ɛ:^{ɩ} 21Nf 13 under ɛi

ə 1Nb 1

second syllable stressed: 1Nb 1, 5La 2,
6Y 13/23, 10L 4/$^{+}$5

prothetic j- 1Nb 7

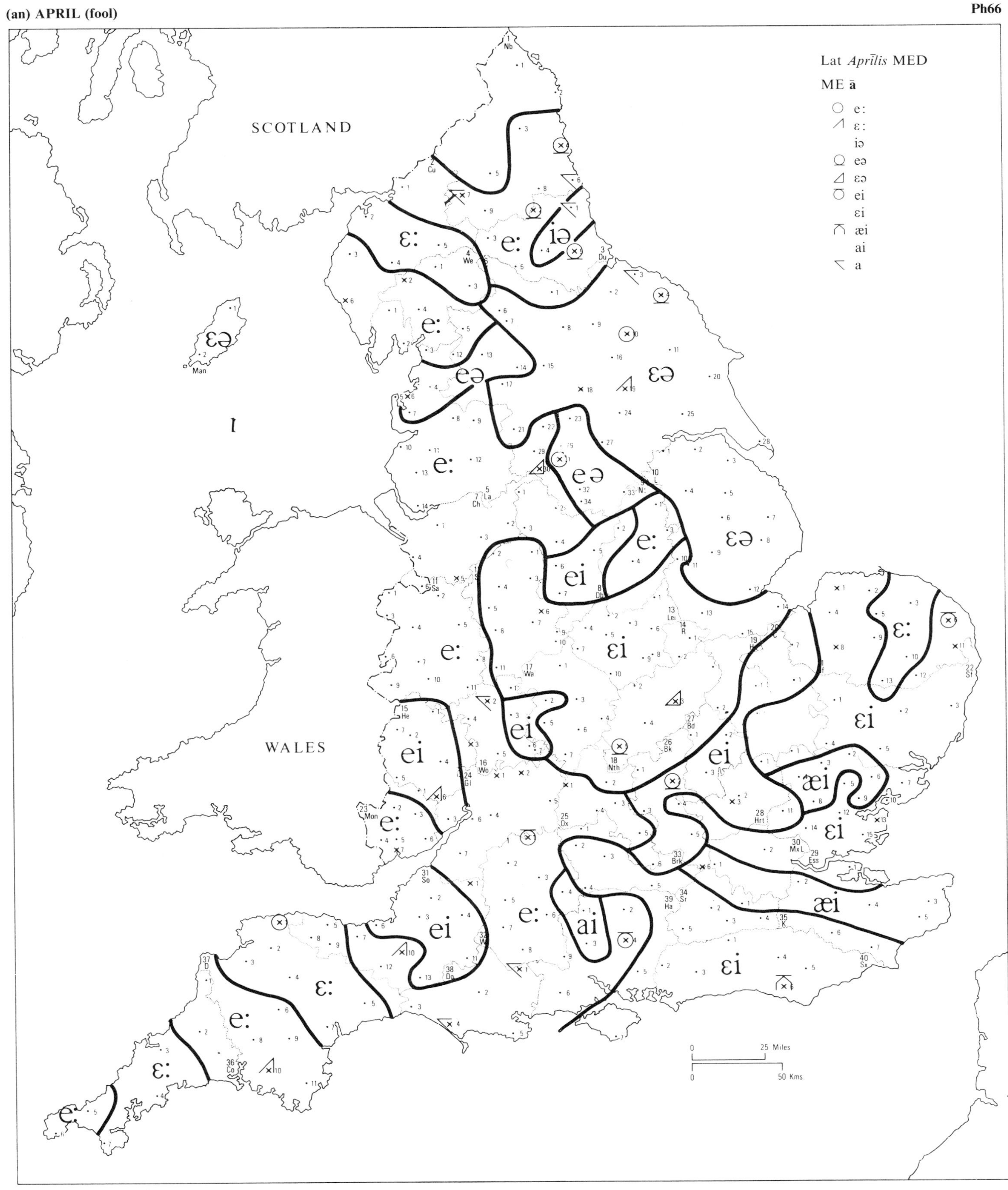

e:ᵊ 2Cu 3, 25Ox 5 under e:
ɛ 15He 6, 37D 10 under ɛ:
e:ᵊ 6Y 34 under eə
e:ɩ 15He 1/2/4/5, 16Wo 3/6, 23Mon 1,
e:ᶦ 8Db 5–7, 9Nt 2, 24Gl 3 under ei
ɛ:ᶦ 21Nf 9 under ɛi

i: 7Ch 5
æ 15He 3
ɔɩ 31So 1

prothetic j- 11Sa 8

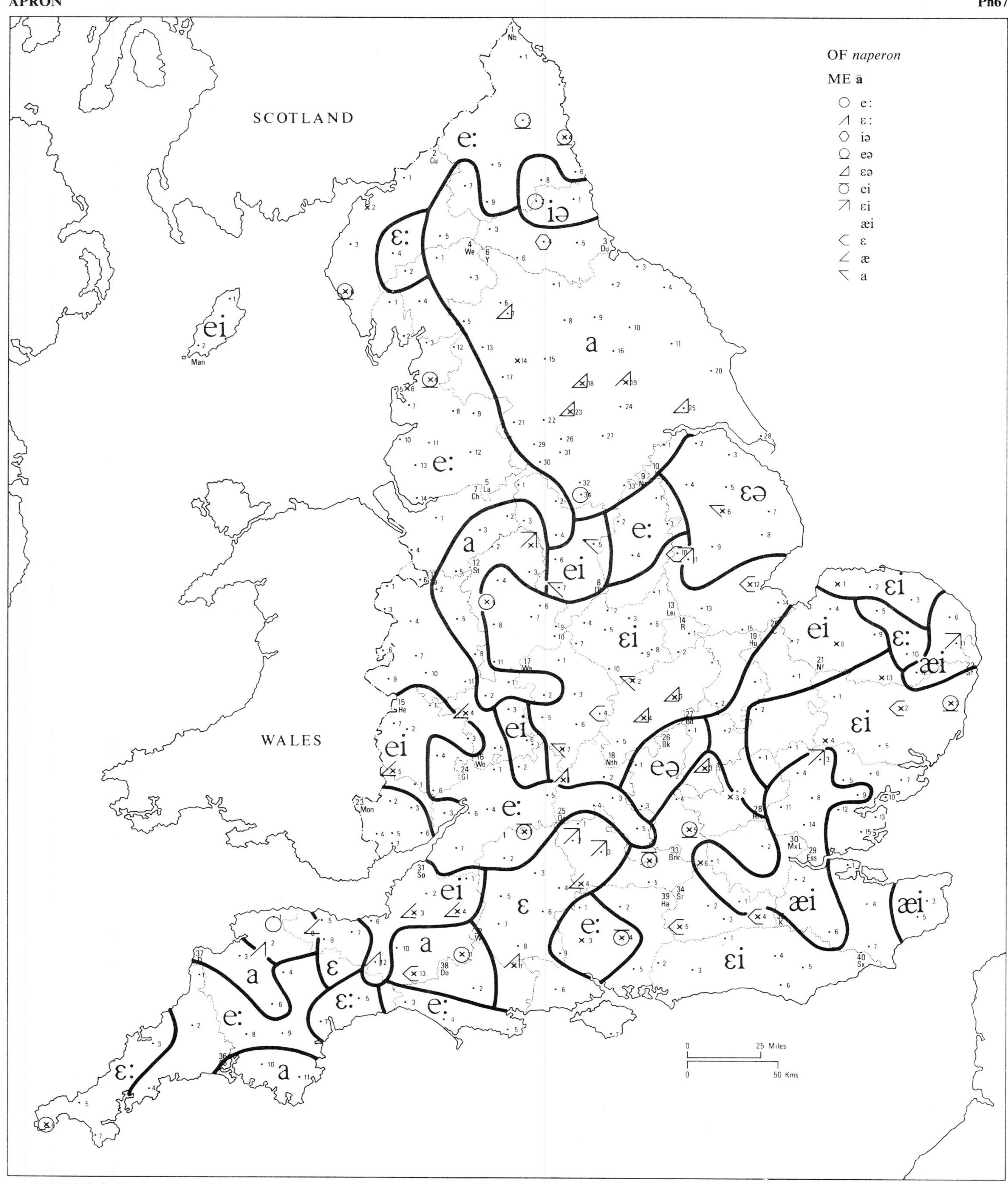

e:ᵊ 1Nb 6, 2Cu 3, 5La 3 under e:
e:ɩ 8Db $^{+}$6, 15He 1–3, 16Wo 3/6, 24Gl 2/3,
ẹ:ɩ 31So 2, e:ᶦ 8Db $^{+}$6, 23Mon 1 under ei

aɩ 39Ha 3

-APRON(S) 6Y 4/9/21, 8Db $^{+}$6/$^{+}$7, 10L 6/$^{+}$10, 11Sa 5/6, 15He 4, 17Wa 1, 21Nf $^{+}$11, 22Sf 1, 25Ox 4, 26Bk 1, 33Brk $^{+}$2, 34Sr 2, 37D 4, 40Sx 1

prothetic j- 31So 3/4/7/13, 32W 3/$^{+}$4/6–8, 37D $^{+}$11, 39Ha 6/7

n- 6Y 24, 21Nf $^{+}$7

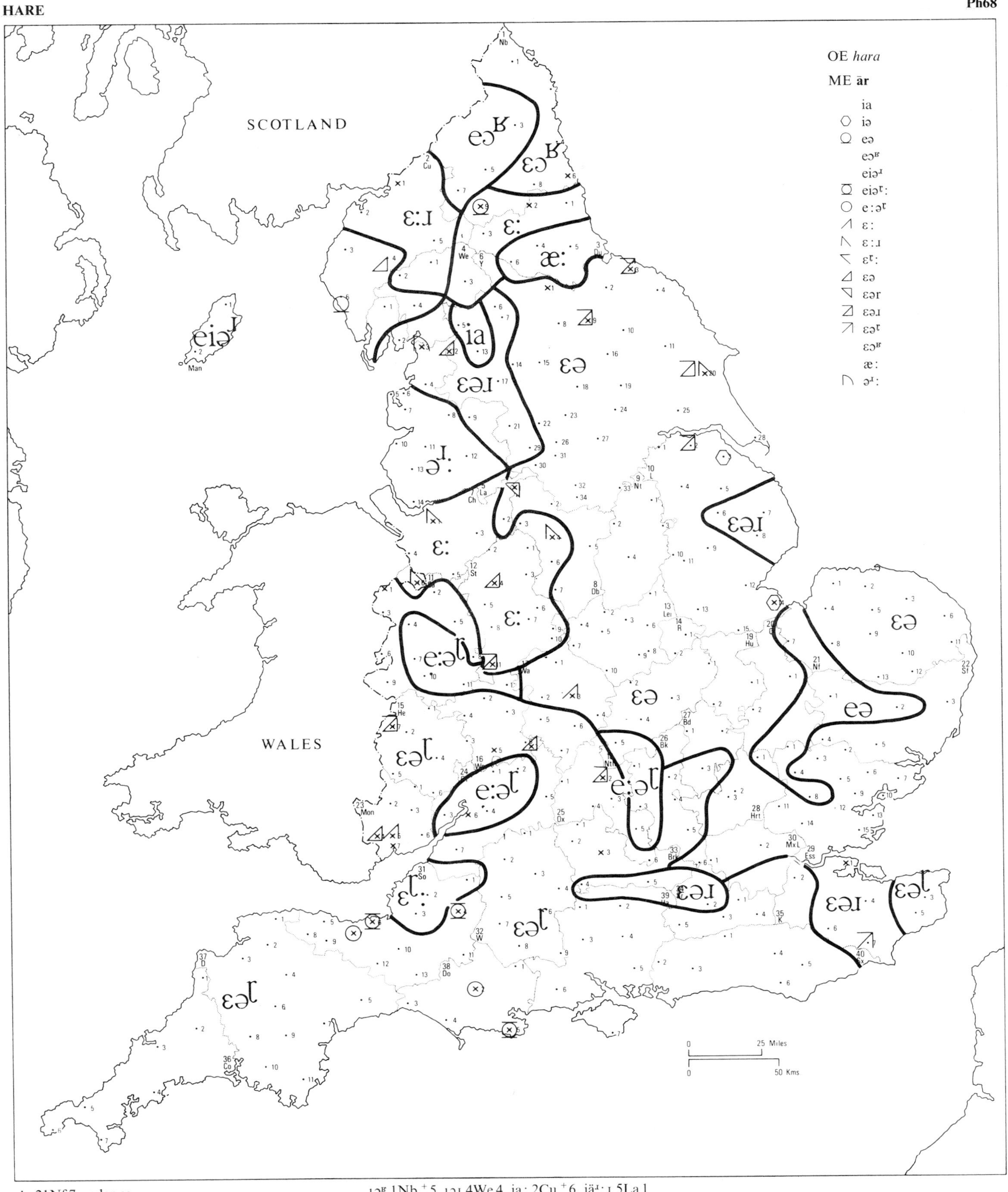

eˈə 21Nf 7 under eə
e:ɔʶ 1Nb 7 under eɔʶ
ɛ̣ɩəᵼ: 31So 6 under eiəᵼ:
e:əᵼ: 38Do 2, e˙əᵼ: 31So 7, eəᵼ 25Ox 5 under e:əᵼ
ɛ:ᵊ 3Du 1 under ɛ:
ɛɹ 6Y +20, æ:ɹ 2Cu 5, ɛᶦ: 8Db 4 under ɛ:ɹ
ɛ:ə 12St 4, 21Nf 3/11, ɛ:ᵊ 3Du 1, 17Wa 1,
23Mon 4 under ɛə
ɛ:əɹ 12St 11, ɛəʴ 6Y 21/29, 33Brk 4, 34Sr 2, 35K 4,
ɛəᶦ 25Ox 2, ɛ̣əʴ 35K +7, ɛ˙əʴ 10L 6,
ɛ̣ˈəʴ 35K 6 under ɛəɹ
ɛəᵼ: 11Sa 3/5/6, 16Wo 4, 31So 8/11,
32W 1/+2/3–9, 36Co 1–7, 37D 1–11,
38Do 1/3/4, 39Ha 1–3/5/6, ɛ̣əᵼ: 31So 10/13,
ɛ˙əᵼ: 31So 12, ɛ:əᵼ 11Sa 2/8, 16Wo 2, 24Gl 5,
ɛ:əᵼ: 31So 5/9, ɛ:əᵼɽ 17Wa 5 under ɛəᵼ
ɜʴ: 5La 3/13, ɜʴ:ɹ 5La 8/10–12/14 under əʴ:

ɩɔʶ 1Nb +5, ɩəɹ 4We 4, ja: 2Cu +6, jäʴ:ɹ 5La 1
e˙əʶ 1Nb 6
ɛ˙əʁ 1Nb +5, ɛəʶ 3Du 2, ɛər 2Cu 3, ɛ:ᵊr 2Cu 1,
ɛɩɐ 35K 1, ɛɩəʴ 33Brk 3
a: 6Y 1, a˙ɹ 6Y +6, aᵼ: 16Wo 5
əᵼ: 11Sa 1, 32W +2, jəᵼ: 24Gl +6,
jəᵼ (+C) 24Gl +6

interpr as *r*-col: ɽ 8Db 1, 25Ox 4, 31So 3
cons *r* foll *r*-col V: ɹ 5La 1/8/10–12/14, ɽ 17Wa 5,
34Sr 4, 39Ha 7, 40Sx 2/4/6

HARE- 1Nb +5

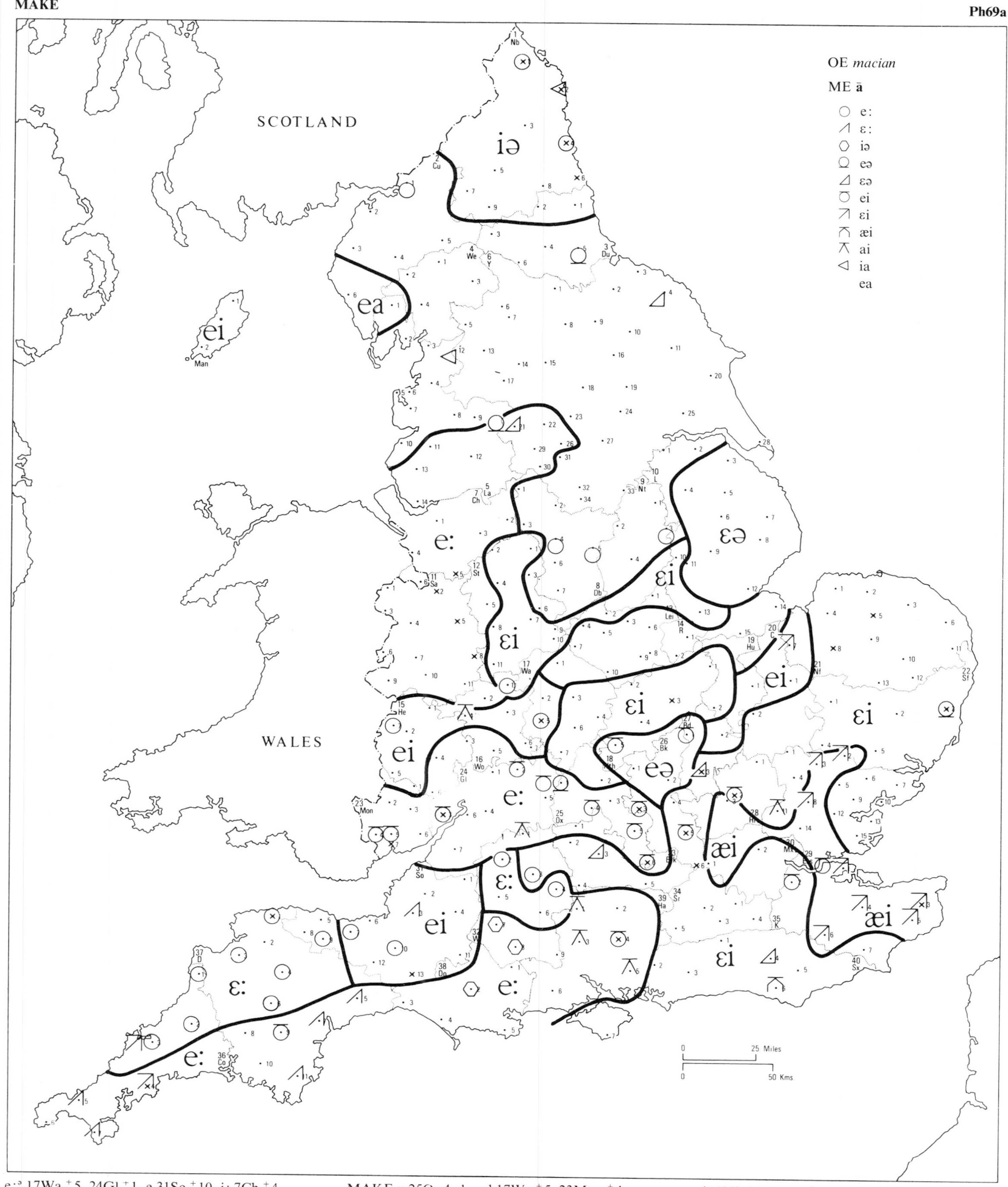

e:ᵊ 17Wa +5, 24Gl +1, e 31So +10, i̧: 7Ch +4,
e:ᶥ 8Db +5, e:ι 8Db +5 under e:
ɛ:ᵊ 31So 5/+8 under ɛ:
e:ι 15He 1/2/5̊, 16Wo 3/+6, 23Mon +1,
ę:ι 31So +7, e:ᶥ 16Wo +4/+6, 23Mon +1,
24Gl +2/3, 25Ox +5, ęιᵊ 31So +6 under ei
ɛ:ι 33Brk 4, ɛ:ᶥ 21Nf +1/+2/+9 under ɛi

i: 7Ch 5

MAKE v 25Ox 4; 1prpl 17Wa +5, 23Mon +4;
2prpl 6Y 12, 13Lei +2, 25Ox +1;
3prpl 6Y 22, 7Ch 3, 21Nf +9, 31So +7,
32W +2, 35K +1, 37D +11; imp 25Ox +5,
30MxL +1, 32W +4, 36Co +3; ndg 7Ch 6,
31So +6, 35K +6, 36Co +3, 39Ha +5,
40Sx +4; MAKE(S) 3prsg 3Du +5, 5La +12,
6Y +4/+21/26/+29, 7Ch 5, 8Db 4/+5,
12St +7, 13Lei +2, 16Wo +3, 24Gl +1,
25Ox +1/+5, 29Ess +2/+3/+8, 31So +3,
35K +5, 36Co +7, 37D +9, 39Ha +5, 40Sx +4;
MAKES ndg 12St +4, 16Wo +4, 24Gl +2;
(A-)MAKING prp 3Du 2, 12St +4/+7,
15He +7, 16Wo +3/+6, 23Mon +1, 27Bd +1,
31So +9, 32W +5, 35K +4/+6, 36Co +1/+7,
3̣7D +9, 40Sx +4; vbl n 10L 10, 32W +3;
ndg 1Nb 1, 31So +10, 35K +5

mj- 1Nb 4, 23Mon +5, mᶥ- 23Mon +4, 31So +10,
32W +5

no -k 5La +11/+12, 6Y +21/26/+29/30, 8Db 4/5

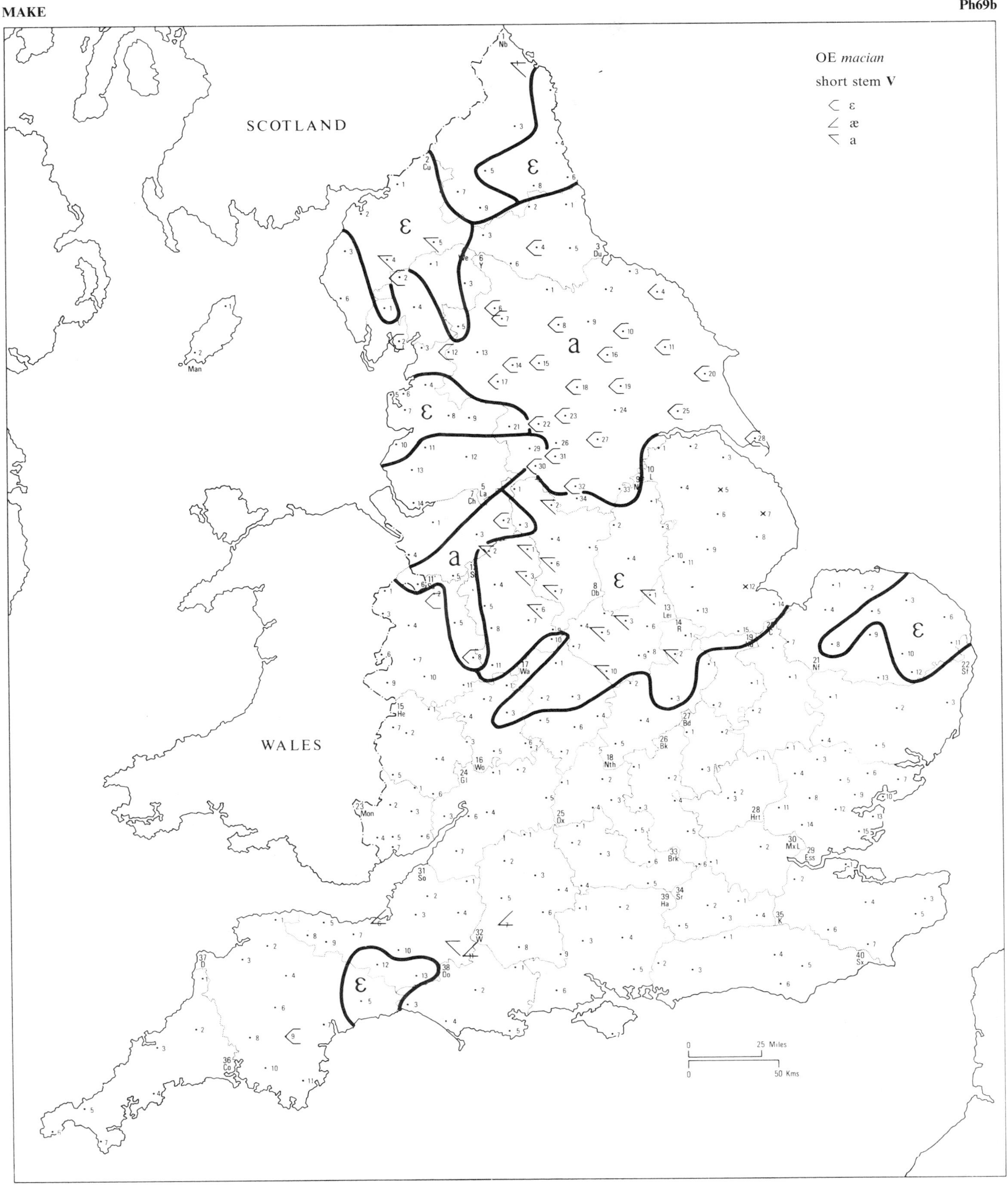

ε: 1Nb 5, 21Nf $^{+}$5/$^{+}$12 under ε

ι 13Lei $^{+}$2

-MAKING- 31So $^{+}$11; -MAKER 31So $^{+}$11; MAKE 2prpl 6Y $^{+}$6, 21Nf 11; 3prpl 12St $^{+}$5, 21Nf 10; imp 6Y $^{+}$15/$^{+}$25/$^{+}$32, 12St $^{+}$3, 31So 12; ndg 8Db $^{+}$6, 10L 8, 12St $^{+}$6; MAKE(S) 3prsg 1Nb 2, 2Cu 1, 3Du $^{+}$4, 4We $^{+}$2, 6Y $^{+}$14/$^{+}$19/$^{+}$25, 8Db $^{+}$2/$^{+}$7, 10L 3/6, 11Sa $^{+}$8, 12St $^{+}$5/11, 13Lei $^{+}$10, 33Brk 5; MAKING prp 5La 1, 6Y $^{+}$20, 11Sa $^{+}$8, 12St $^{+}$2, 21Nf 3; vbl n 21Nf 8

mj- 1Nb 4/6, mι- 31So $^{+}$11

e:ᵊ 17Wa +5, 24Gl 1, ȩ:ᵊ 1Nb +1,
e:ᶥ 8Db 5 under e:
ɛ:ᵊ 31So 5/+8 under ɛ:
e:ɩ 15He 1/2/+3/5, 16Wo 3, 31So 7/+11,
e:ᶥ 16Wo +4/6, 23Mon 1, 24Gl 2/3 under ei
ɛ:ɩ 21Nf +3/+11, ȩ:ɩ 21Nf +5,
ɛ:ᶥ 21Nf +1 under ɛi

ᶥi Man +2

TAKE 1prpl 22Sf +1; 2prpl 9Nt 2;
3prpl 1Nb +1/6, 35K +5, 40Sx +4;
imp 1Nb +3/+7 6Y 21, 17Wa +2, 21Nf +1,
29Ess +11, 32W +5, 36Co +3/+7, 37D +1/+5;
ndg 11Sa 2, 17Wa +5, 21Nf +1/+5, 25Ox 2,
29Ess +6/+11, 31So +13, 35K +6, 36Co +3,
37D +10/+11, 39Ha +4;
TAKE(S) 3prsg 1Nb +4, 6Y 31, 7Ch 6,
16Wo +4, 21Nf +3/+11, 29Ess +3/+8/+9,
31So +13, 32W +3/+6, 36Co +7;
TAKES ndg 8Db 4;
(A-)TAKING prp 1Nb +4, 17Wa +2,
23Mon 7, 32W +3, 40Sx +4; vbl n 21Nf +2;
ndg 37D +6

tj- 1Nb +4/8, tᶥ- 16Wo 5

no -k 6Y 21/26/30/31, 8Db 4/5

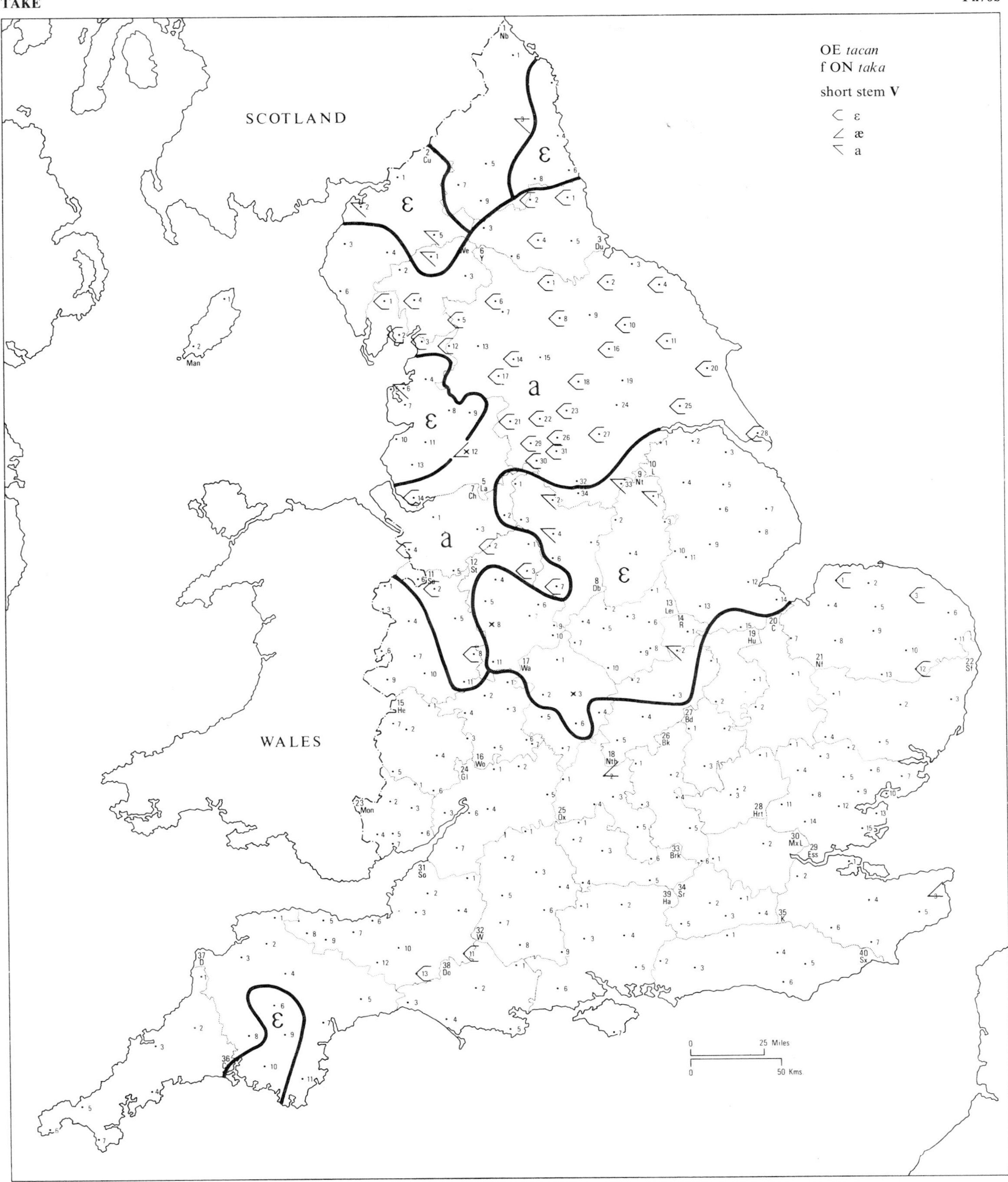

ε$^{\iota}$ 5La $^{+}$10, ẹ: 21Nf 1 under ε

TAKE 2prpl 1Nb $^{+}$2, 14R $^{+}$2; 3prpl 10L 7;
imp 2Cu $^{+}$2, 3Du $^{+}$1/$^{+}$2, 4We $^{+}$4, 5La $^{+}$3,
6Y $^{+}$1/$^{+}$8/$^{+}$16/$^{+}$21/$^{+}$23/$^{+}$26/$^{+}$28–$^{+}$31/$^{+}$33,
8Db $^{+}$2, 21Nf 12, 37D $^{+}$6/9/$^{+}$10; ndg 5La $^{+}$14,
18Nth 2, 35K 3, 37D $^{+}$10;
TAKES 3prsg 2Cu $^{+}$5, 3Du $^{+}$1, 4We $^{+}$1,
5La $^{+}$10/$^{+}$14, 6Y $^{+}$6/$^{+}$28, 8Db $^{+}$4, 11Sa $^{+}$2/$^{+}$8,
12St 11, 17Wa 6, 21Nf 1, 37D $^{+}$6;
TAKING prp 2Cu 1, 5La $^{+}$1, 6Y $^{+}$8, 8Db $^{+}$2,
12St $^{+}$3; ?vbl n 21Nf 3

tj- 1Nb $^{+}$2/4/6/$^{+}$8, 3Du $^{+}$1/$^{+}$2

no -k 5La $^{+}$11

e:ᶥ 39Ha 4, e:ɩ 15He 5, 23Mon 1,
e:a (sic) 11Sa 11, ẹ 2Cu 2 under e:
i:ᵊ 3Du 3 under iə
ɛ̣ə 17Wa 4, e:ᵊ 17Wa 6 under eə

i: 2Cu 1
eɩ 31So 1/9
ea 4We 3

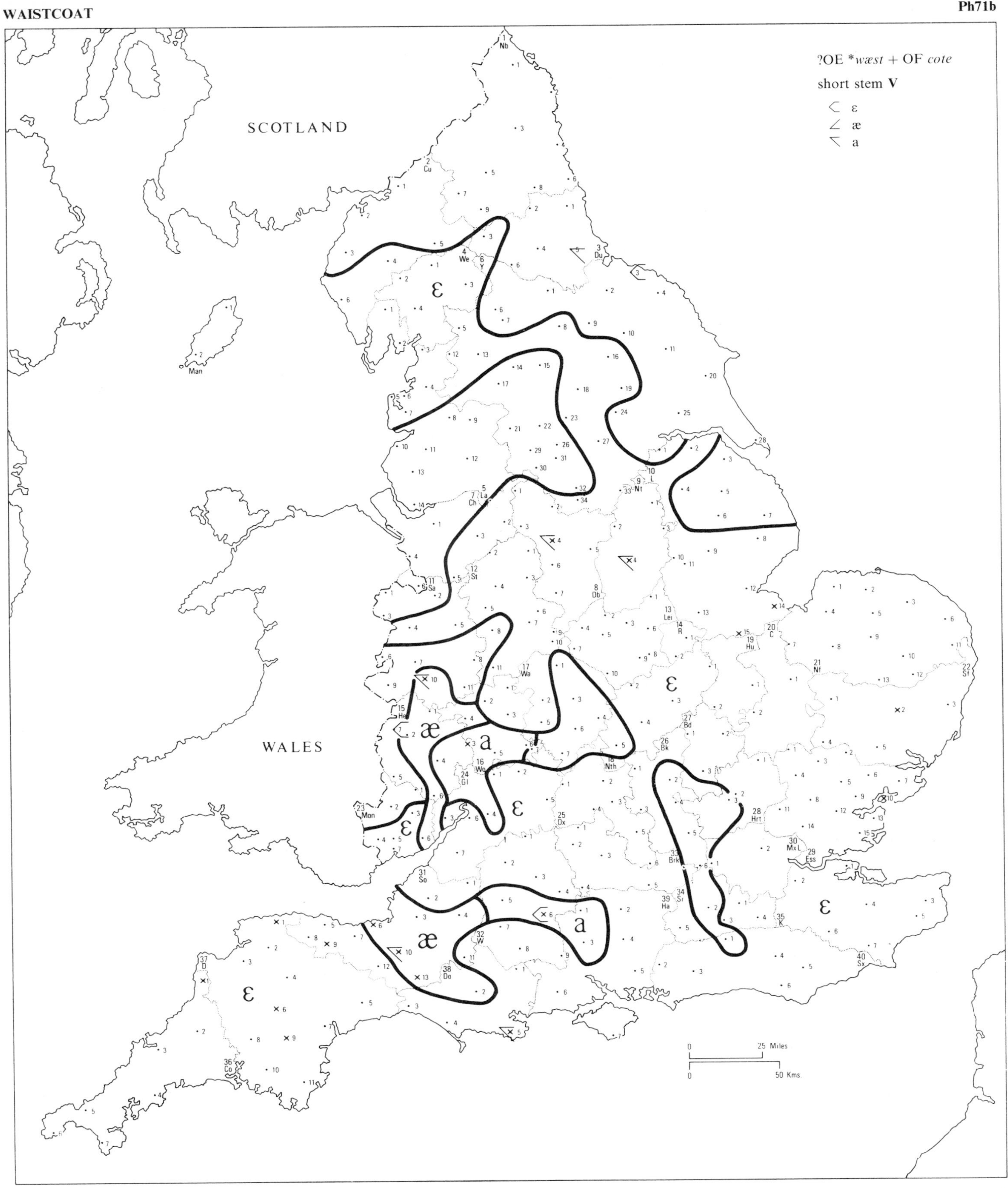

εə 40Sx 4, ε:ᵊ 16Wo 1, ε: 2Cu 4, 6Y 19, 12St 11,
31So 5, 37D 5/7, under ε
a: 15He 4, 16Wo 5/6 under a

ι 10L 14
ʌ 22Sf 2

wεstιk (sic) 6Y 16

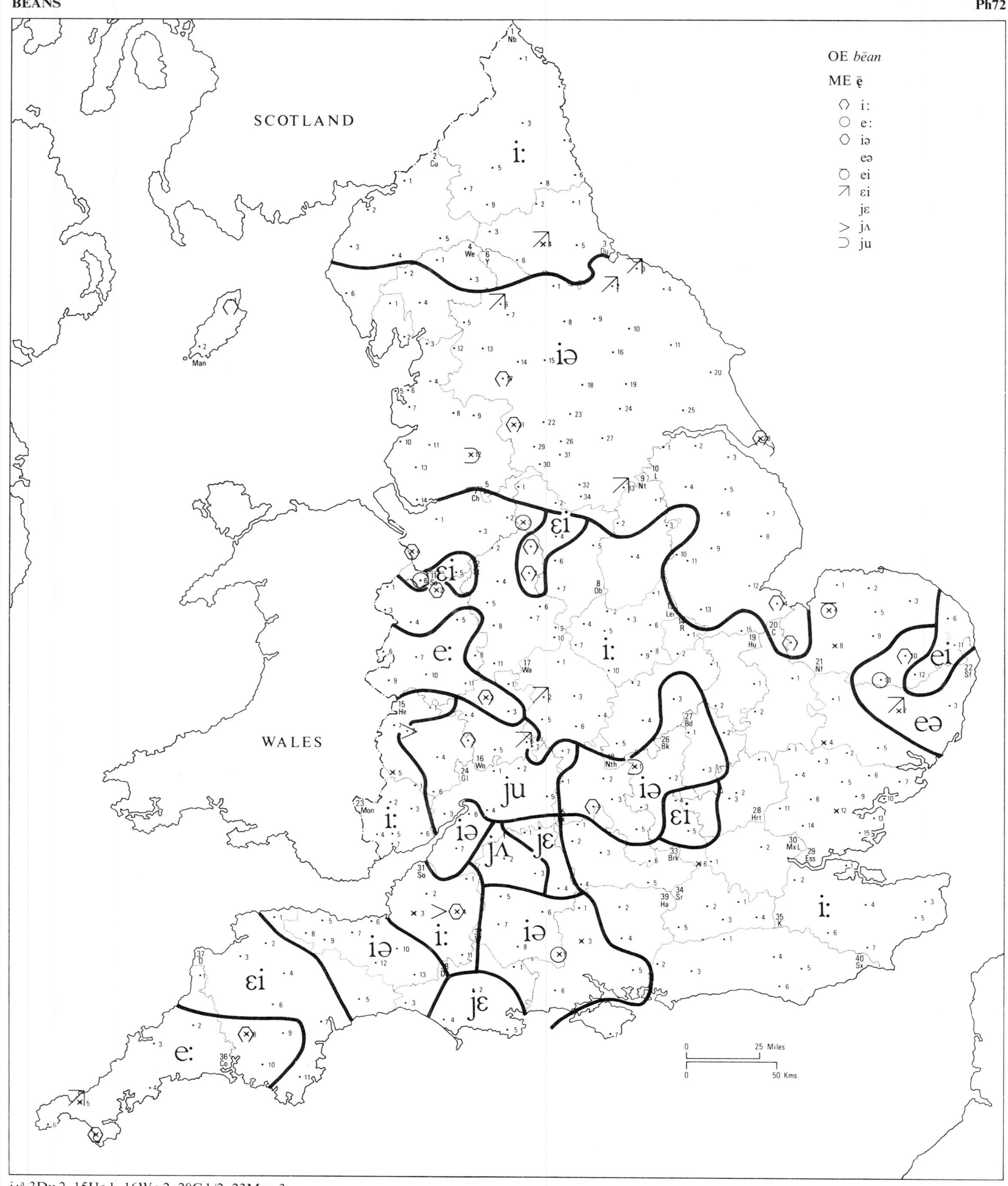

i:^{ə} 3Du 2, 15He 1, 16Wo 2, 20C 1/2, 23Mon 3, ɩ:^{ə} Man 1, ɩ·^{ə} 1Nb 8, ^{ə}i: 22Sf 5, 28Hrt 2, əi: 28Hrt 3, ẹ: 2Cu 1 under i:
e:ə 36Co 2/3, e:^{ɩ} 8Db 3, e:ɩ 16Wo 3 under e:
^{ə}ɩə 7Ch $^{+}$4, 27Bd 3, əɩə 7Ch $^{+}$4, jə 24Gl 6/7, 25Ox 1 under iə
ɛɩə 7Ch 5/$^{+}$6, ɛ̤̈ɩ 3Du 4 under ɛi
ɩjʌ̣ 31So 4, ɩʌ̣ 32W 2/3 under jʌ
ɩω 5La 12, 17Wa 7, 26Bk 1 under ju

ɛ: 37D 4
æɩ 15He 5
aɩ 39Ha 3
əɩ 6Y 1

-BEANS 5La 7, 6Y $^{+}$3/25/32, 21Nf 1

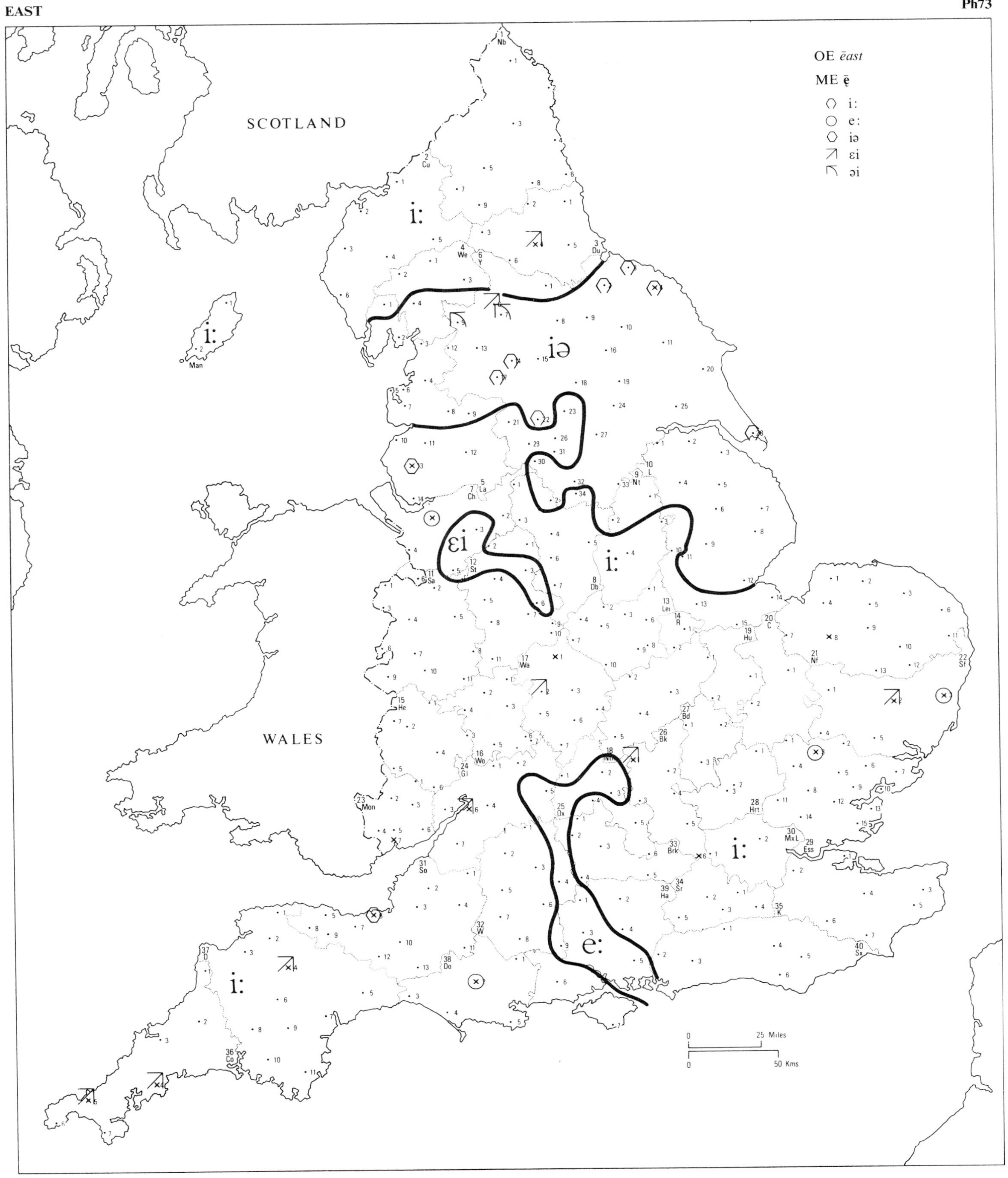

i:ᵊ 10L 14, 20C 2, ιi:ᵊ 6Y 34, ᵊi: 22Sf 4/5, 26Bk 2/4, 27Bd 1/2, 28Hrt 2/3, 29Ess 5 under i:
e:ᵊ 22Sf 3, eᶥ 25Ox 2 under e:
ę̈ι 3Du 4 under εi

jε̈ 6Y +6
jɷ 24Gl +5
ei: 17Wa 1

-EAST 6Y +14

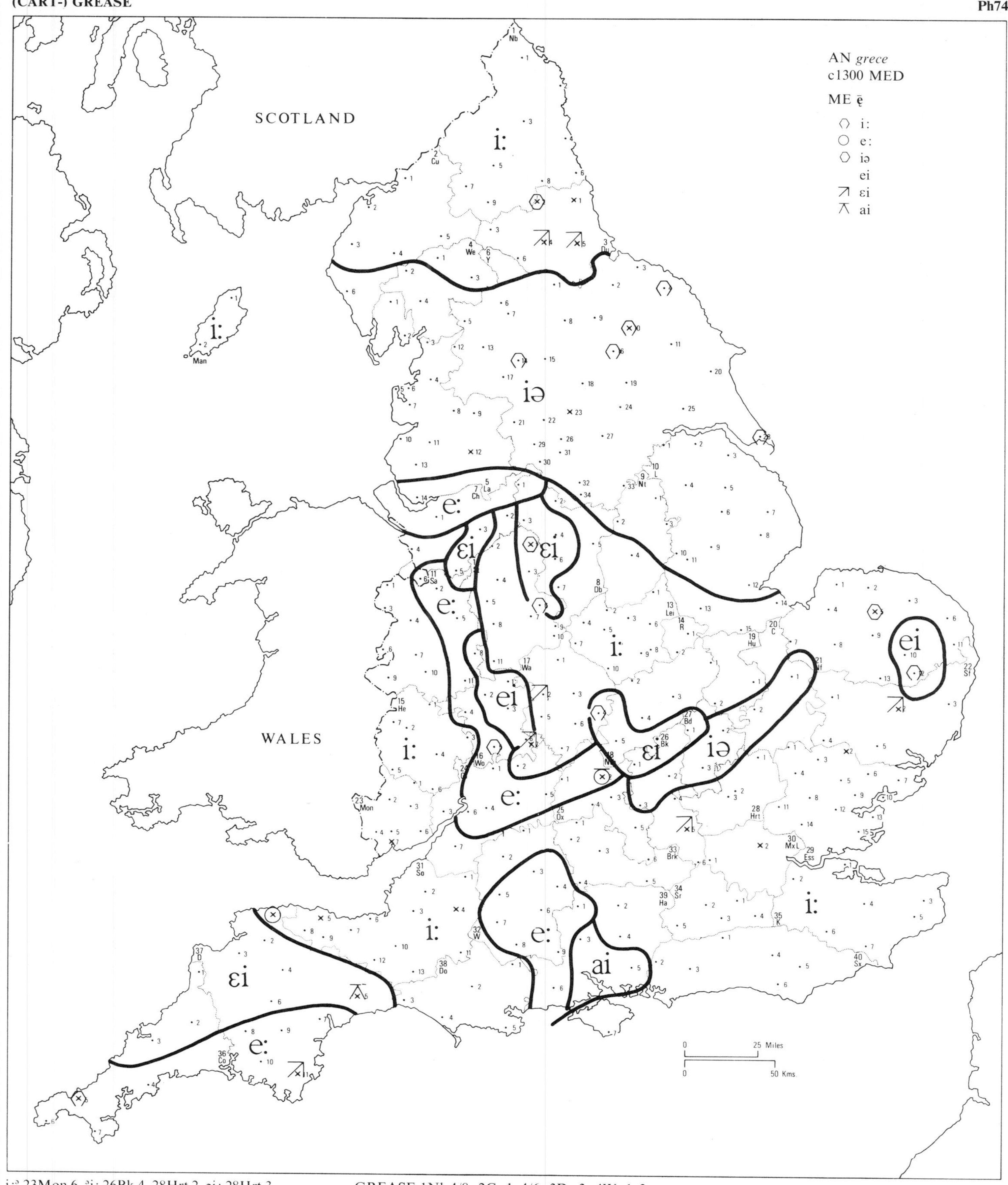

i:ᵊ 23Mon 6, ᵊi: 26Bk 4, 28Hrt 2, əi: 28Hrt 3,
ᵊi 22Sf 5, ẹɩ Man 1 under i:
e:ᵊ 24Gl 1, eˑᵊ 25Ox 1, e:ə 7Ch 6,
ẹ: 32W 6 under e:
i:ᵊ 20C +1, ᵊi:ᵊ 27Bd 2 under iə
e:ɩ 16Wo 3/6, e:ᶦ 11Sa 8, 16Wo 2 under ei
ẹ̈ɩ 3Du 5, ẹ̈i: 3Du 4 under ɛi

əɩ 31So 5

-GREASE 1Nb 4/8, 2Cu 1–4/6, 3Du 3, 4We 1–3, 6Y 3/7/+16/21/+28, Man 1, 7Ch 2, 9Nt 3, 10L 5/11, 11Sa 2, 13Lei 4, 14R 2, 15He 7, 16Wo 1/3/+5, 17Wa +4, 18Nth 2, 21Nf 2/6/8/10, 25Ox 4, 29Ess 3/6/8/10/13/15, 31So 9. 32W 6/9. 33Brk 2/3/5. 34Sr 1, 35K 2/3/5/7, 37D 9/10. 38Do 3, 39Ha 1/7, 40Sx 4; GREASE v 6Y +4, 20C +1, 21Nf +12, 32W 5; GREASING ndg 21Nf 3; GREASING- ppl adj 21Nf 9/+12; GREASY adj 12St +6, 16Wo +5

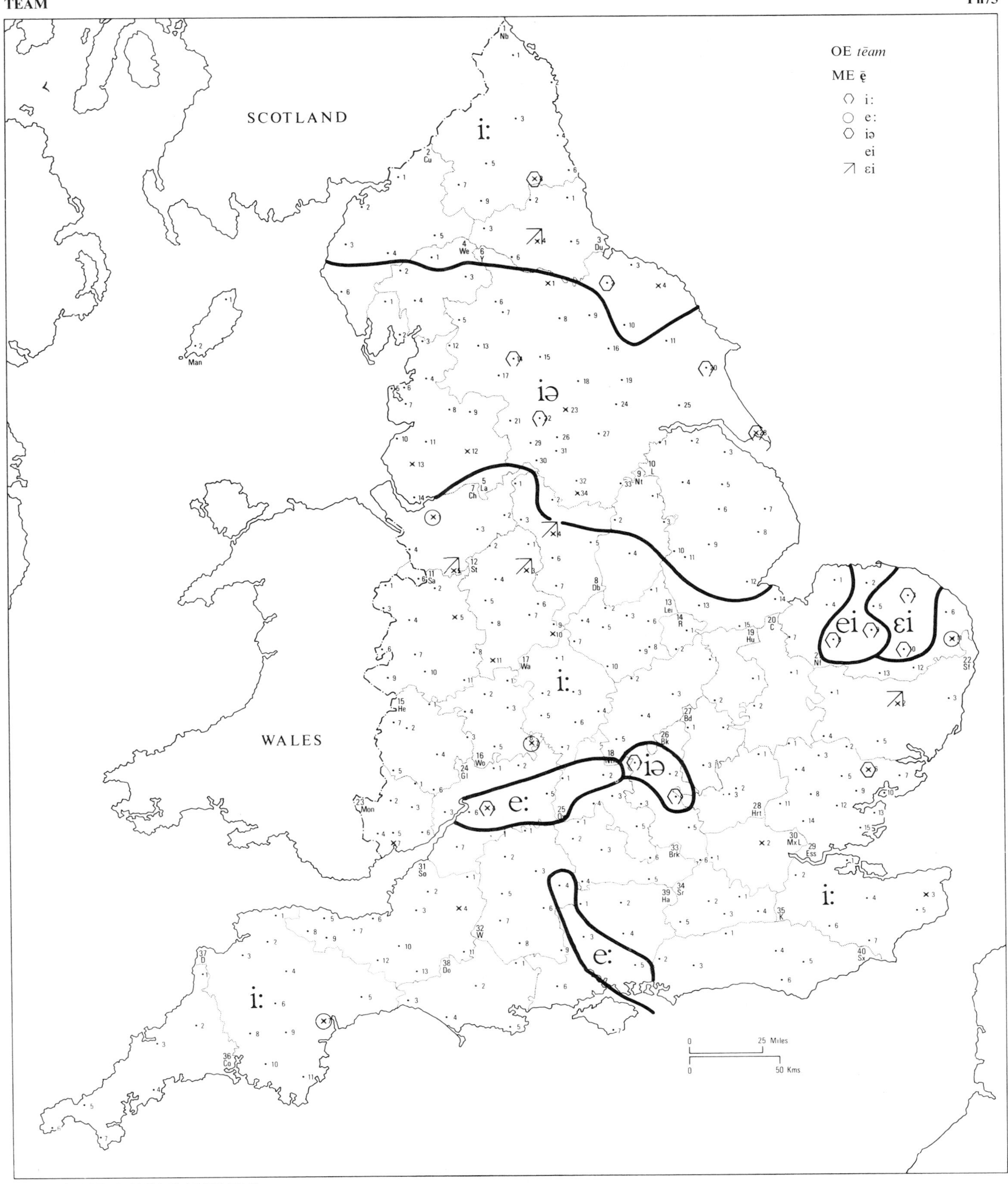

iːᵊ 3Du 2, 15He 1, 20C 1, ᶥiːᵊ 24Gl 1/3/4,
ᵊiː 22Sf +4/5, 26Bk +4, 27Bd 1/2, 28Hrt 2/+3,
29Ess 5, əiː 28Hrt +3, ᵉiː 17Wa 1 under iː
eːᶥ 16Wo 6 under eː
εːᶥ 21Nf +10, ë̞ɩ 3Du 4 under εi

əɩ 6Y 1

TEAM- 21Nf +3/+8–+10/12; TEAMER 6Y +22

tʃεm 11Sa 5

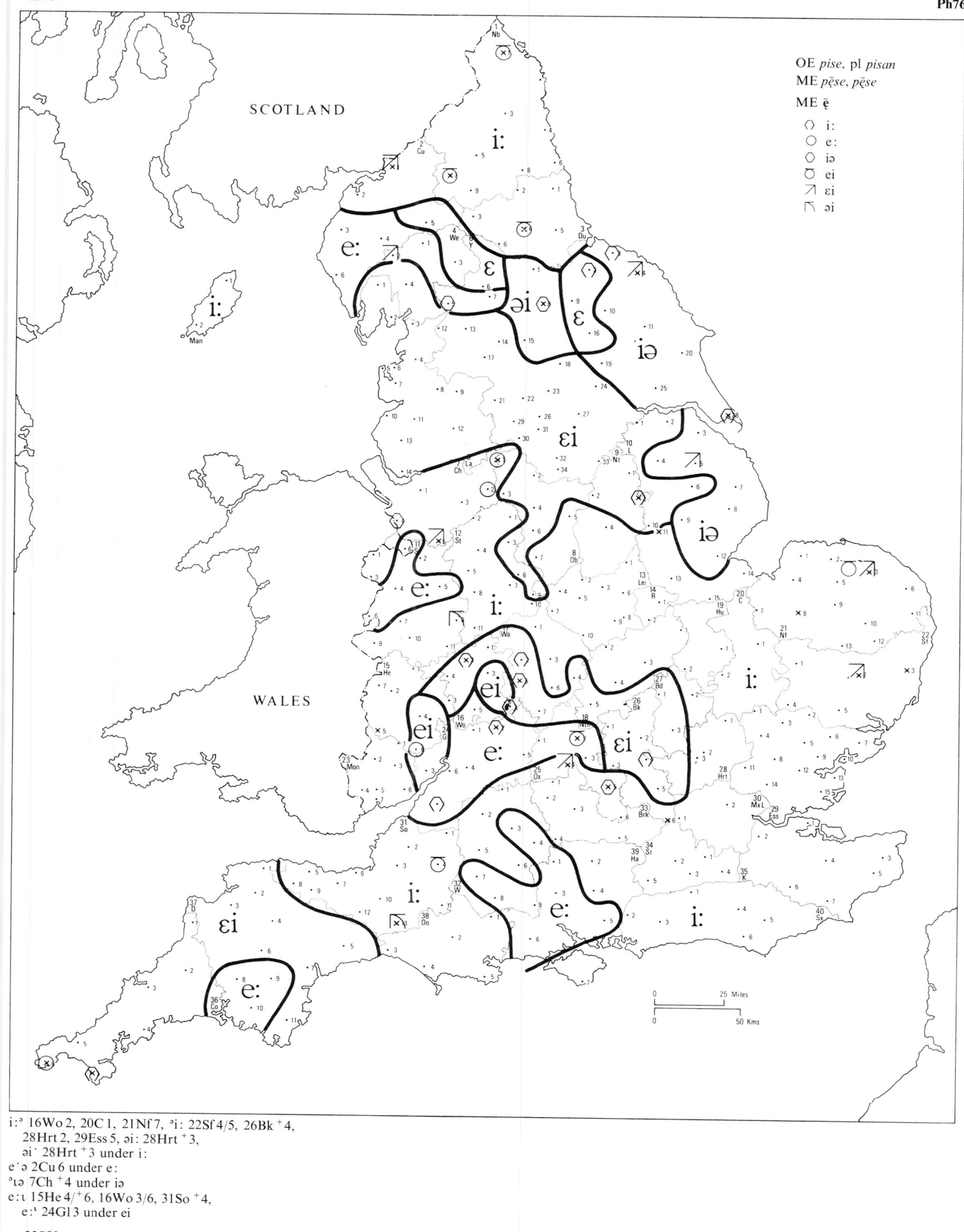

i:ᵊ 16Wo 2, 20C 1, 21Nf 7, ᵊi: 22Sf 4/5, 26Bk ⁺4,
28Hrt 2, 29Ess 5, əi: 28Hrt ⁺3,
əi˙ 28Hrt ⁺3 under i:
e˙ə 2Cu 6 under e:
ᵊɩə 7Ch ⁺4 under iə
e:ɩ 15He 4/⁺6, 16Wo 3/6, 31So ⁺4,
e:ᶦ 24Gl 3 under ei

ęə 22Sf 3
æɩ 15He 5

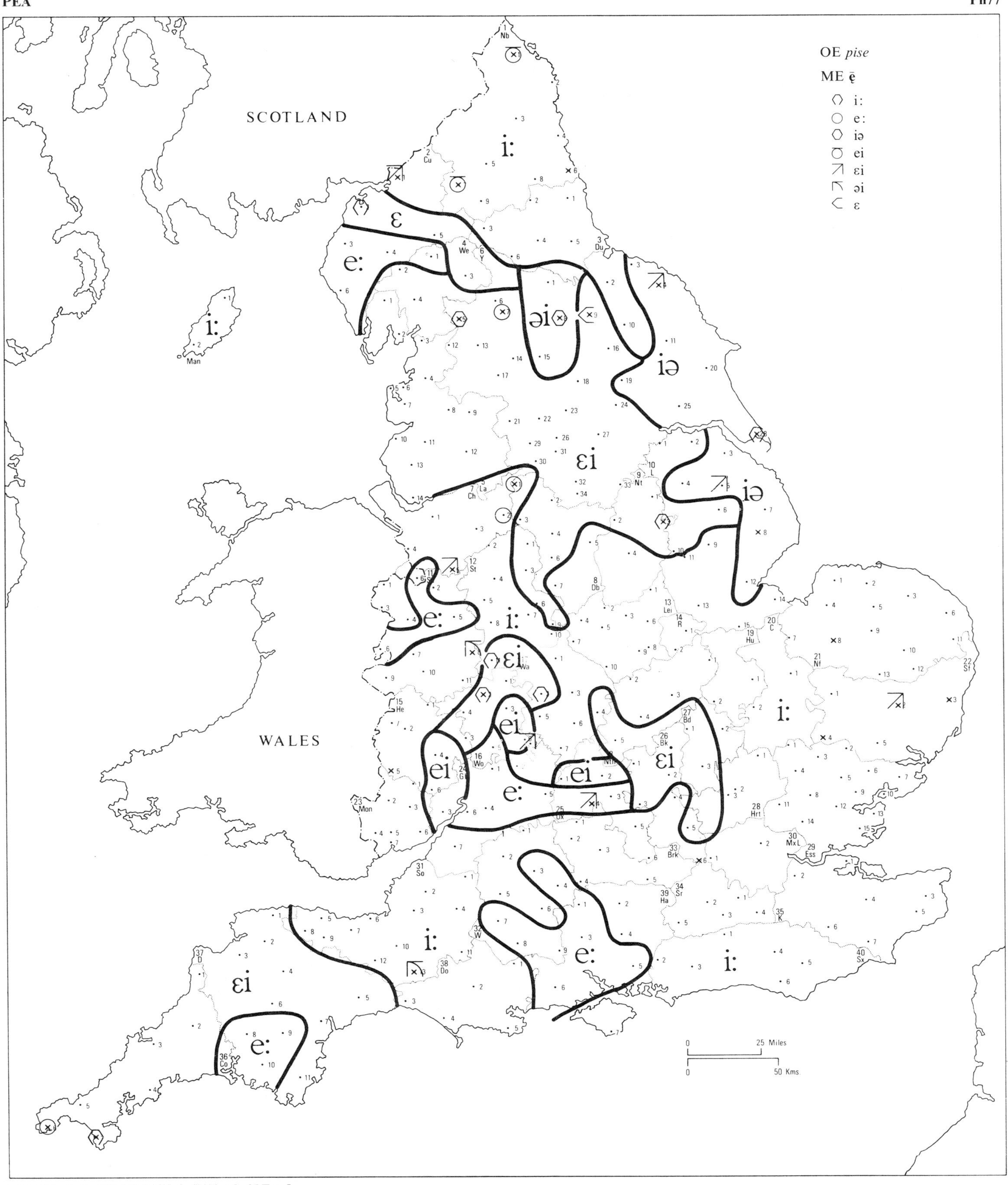

i:ᵊ 16Wo 2, ᵊi: 22Sf 5, 26Bk 4, 28Hrt 2, 29Ess 5,
əi: 28Hrt 3, ij 23Mon 5 under i:
e˙ə 2Cu 6 under e:
e:ɩ 15He 4/6, 16Wo 3/6, e:ᶦ 24Gl 3,
25Ox 1 under ei
ε: 2Cu $^{+}$2/5 under ε

ẹə 22Sf 3
æɩ 15He 5

PEA- 29Ess $^{+}$7/$^{+}$14, 35K $^{+}$4; PEASE- 2Cu $^{+}$2

-z retained 2Cu $^{+}$2, 3Du 5, 4We 1/3, 5La 1,
6Y 9/34, 9Nt 2, 25Ox 2 (?error for [peɩ] Edd)

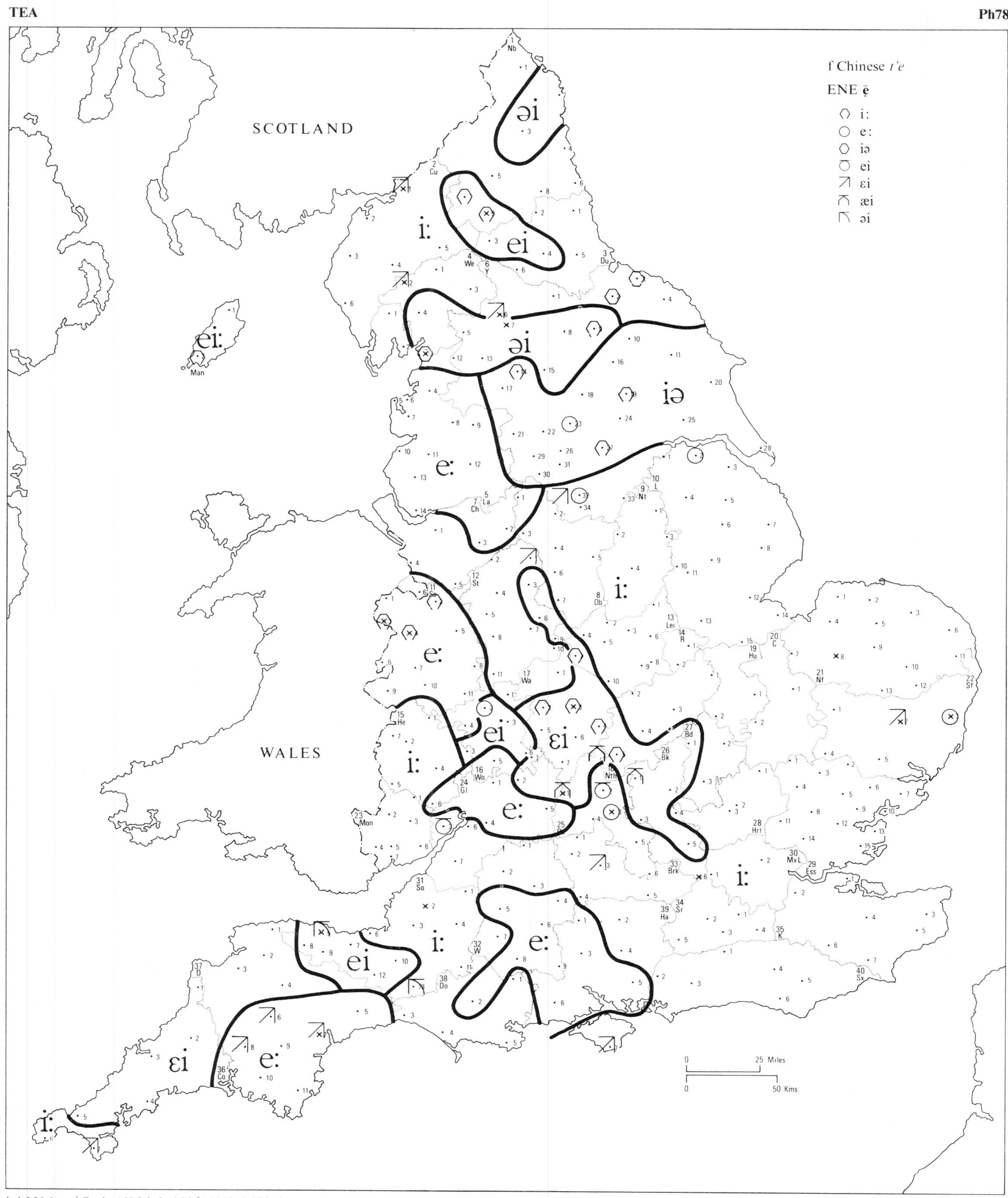

i:j 23Mon $^{+}$7, ^{ə}i: 18Nth 3, 22Sf 1/4/5, 26Bk 4, 27Bd 2, 28Hrt 2/$^{+}$3, 29Ess 5, əi: 28Hrt $^{+}$3, ə^{ɪ}ɩ 30MxL $^{+}$1, i 36Co $^{+}$6, ^{e}i: 17Wa 1 under i:
e:ɩ 15He 3, 16Wo 3/6, e:^{ɪ} 16Wo $^{+}$2, 24Gl $^{+}$3, 31So 10 under ei

aɩ 39Ha $^{+}$3

TEA- 6Y $^{+}$19, 16Wo $^{+}$7, 18Nth $^{+}$5, 23Mon $^{+}$7; -TEA 11Sa $^{+}$2

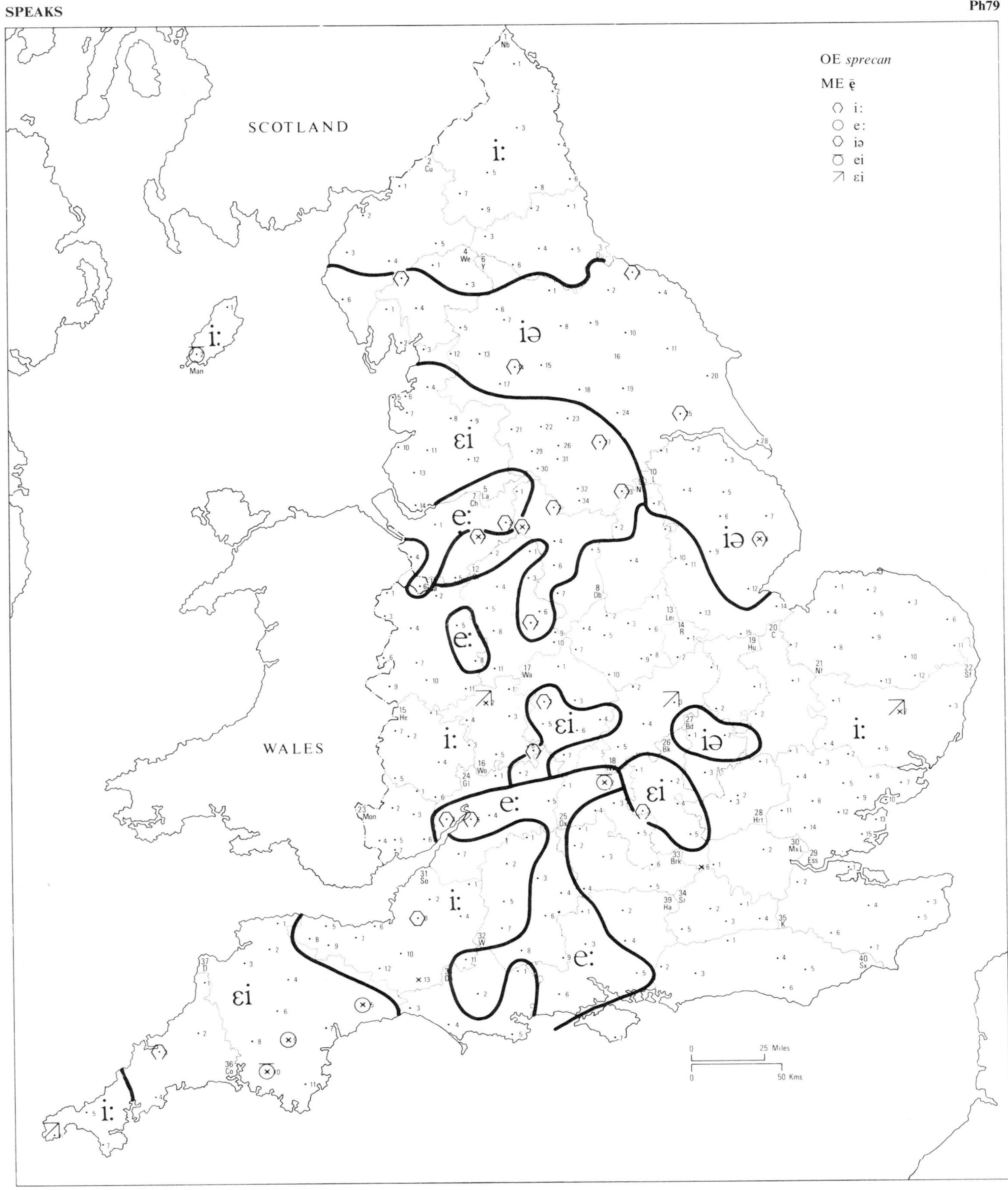

i:^{ə} 24Gl 1, ι$^{·ə}$ 29Ess 2, ^{ə}i: 18Nth +3, 22Sf 4/5,
28Hrt 2/3, 29Ess 5/14, ^{ë}ι 3Du +4/5, ι 15He 3,
31So +9/10, 36Co +3 under i:
e:^{ə} 7Ch 6, e:^{ι} 24Gl +3, 31So 11 under e:

aι 39Ha +3
əι 31So 13

SPEAK inf 1Nb 1/3/9, 2Cu 4, 3Du 5,
5La 6/7/9/11–13,
6Y +3/4/5/9–11/14/16/+18/19/20/22/25/27/28/
+29/32, Man +2, 7Ch +2, 12St +7, 24Gl +3/+6,
36Co +6; 1prsg 16Wo +7; 2prpl 36Co +3;
SPEAKING prp 6Y +18/+29, 36Co +3

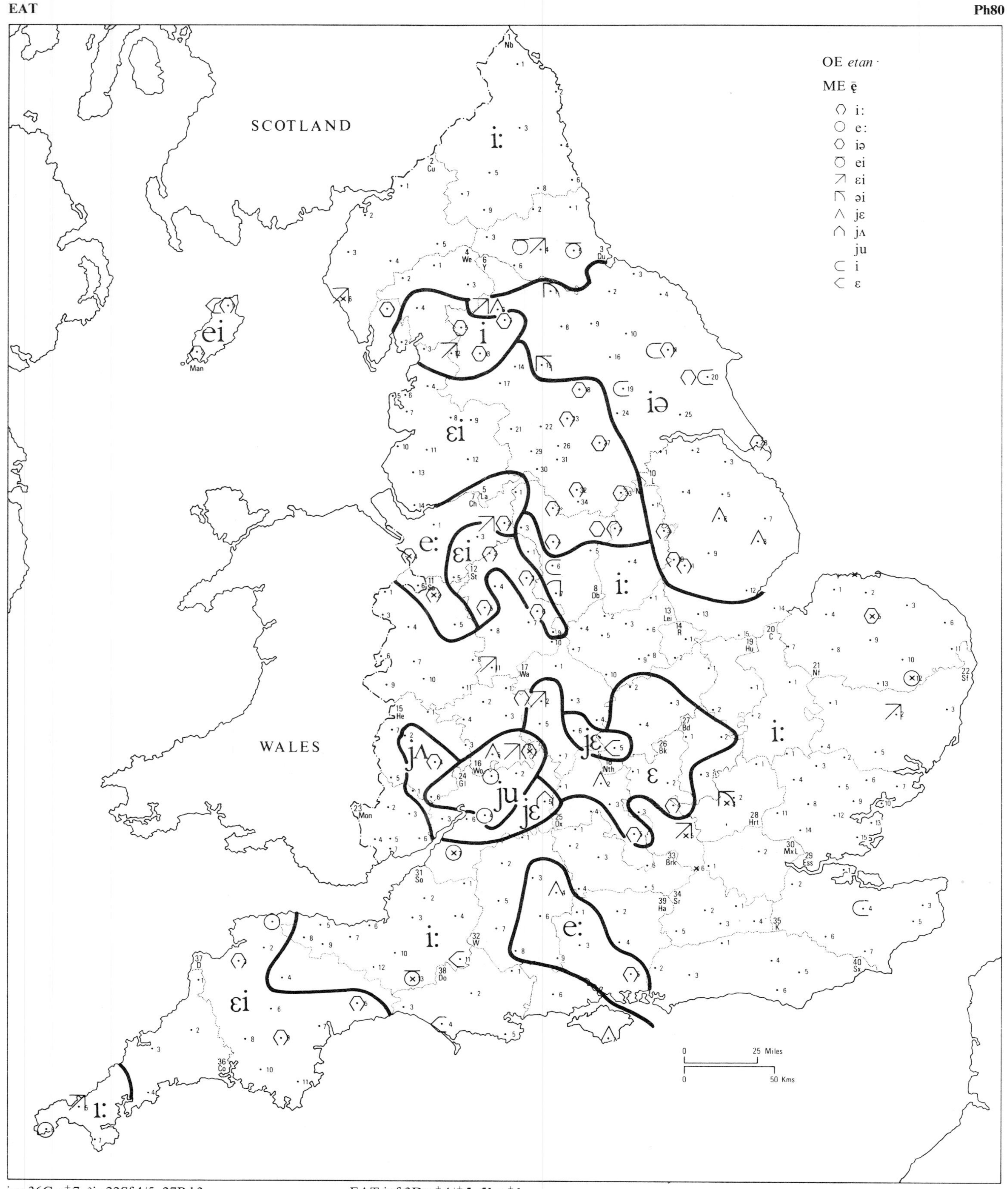

i:ə 36Co $^{+}$7, ᵊi: 22Sf 4/5, 27Bd 3,
29Ess 2/5/$^{+}$14 under i:
e:ᵊ 7Ch 6, e 24Gl 7 under e:
jə 6Y $^{+}$15 under iə
ɛi: 12St $^{+}$2 under ɛi
jə 15He $^{+}$4, 23Mon 1, 24Gl $^{+}$5 under jʌ

EAT inf 3Du $^{+}$4/$^{+}$5, 5La $^{+}$1,
6Y $^{+}$1/$^{+}$5/$^{+}$7/$^{+}$11/$^{+}$13/$^{+}$15/$^{+}$20/$^{+}$23/$^{+}$27,
Man $^{+}$1/$^{+}$2, 7Ch $^{+}$2, 8Db $^{+}$6, 9Nt $^{+}$2/$^{+}$3,
10L $^{+}$6, 12St $^{+}$2/$^{+}$3/$^{+}$5/$^{+}$11, 14R $^{+}$1, 15He $^{+}$4,
16Wo $^{+}$5, 17Wa $^{+}$2, 22Sf $^{+}$2, 24Gl $^{+}$1/$^{+}$4/$^{+}$5,
25Ox $^{+}$5, 26Bk $^{+}$4, 35K $^{+}$4, 36Co $^{+}$7, 37D $^{+}$3,
39Ha $^{+}$5/$^{+}$7; v 25Ox $^{+}$2/$^{+}$5; imp 29Ess $^{+}$14,
39Ha $^{+}$7; 1prpl 12St $^{+}$6; 2prpl Man $^{+}$2;
3prpl 3Du $^{+}$4, 8Db $^{+}$2, 10L $^{+}$6/$^{+}$10,
37D $^{+}$1/$^{+}$9; prt 7Ch $^{+}$2, 8Db $^{+}$2; ndg 6Y $^{+}$12,
10L $^{+}$6; EATEN 3prpl 8Db $^{+}$4;
EATING prp 6Y $^{+}$20/$^{+}$33, 8Db $^{+}$6, 10L $^{+}$11,
36Co $^{+}$6, 37D $^{+}$5; n 6Y $^{+}$13/$^{+}$33; ndg Man $^{+}$2,
10L $^{+}$8; EATS 3prsg 10L $^{+}$8; 3prpl 6Y $^{+}$7/$^{+}$32,
10L $^{+}$6

j- 6Y $^{+}$7, 14R $^{+}$1, 24Gl $^{+}$4/7

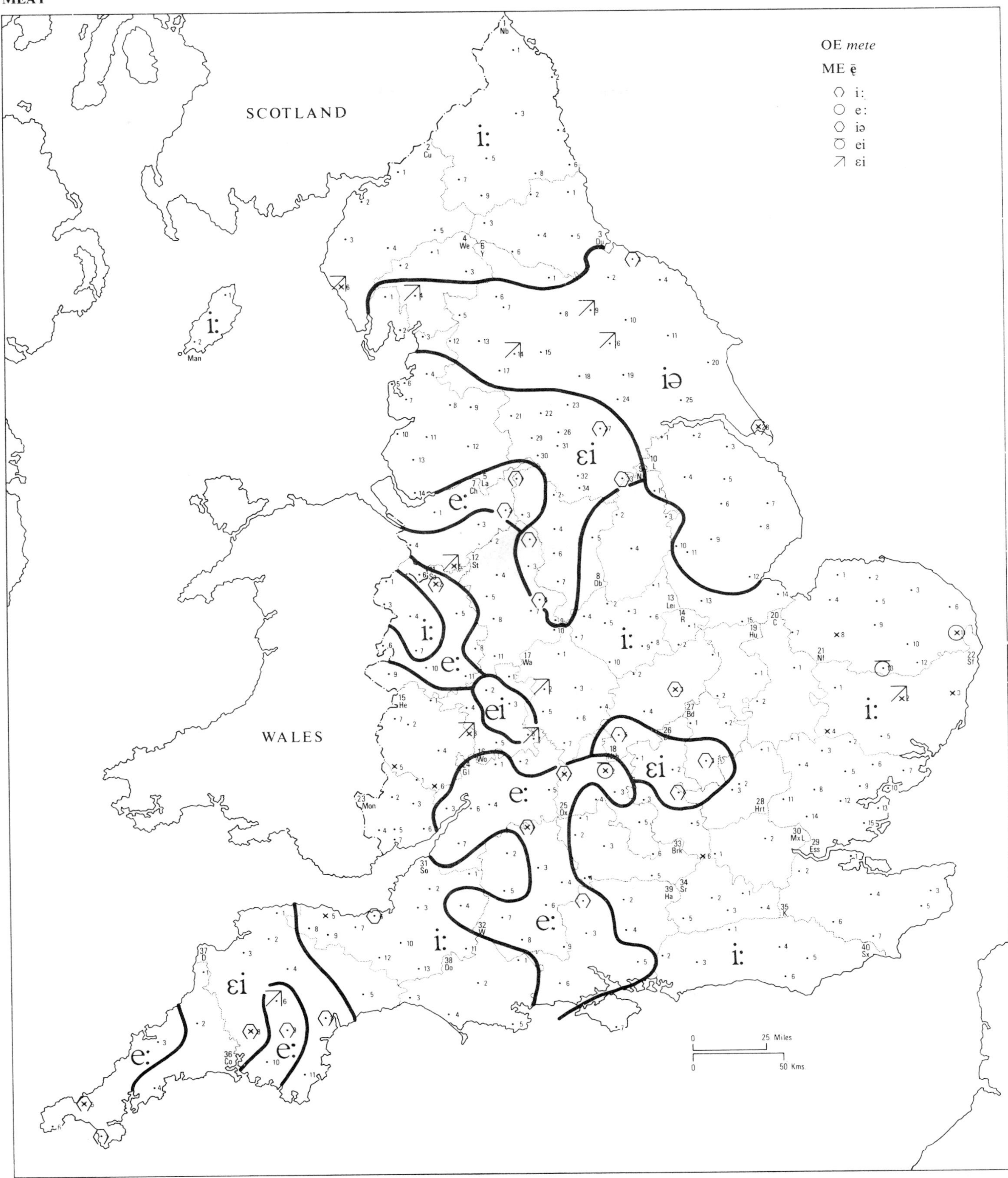

i:ᵊ 20C 1/$^{+}$2, ᵊi: 22Sf 5, 26Bk $^{+}$4, 27Bd 1/$^{+}$3, 28Hrt 2, 29Ess 5, əi: 28Hrt 3, əɩ 6Y 1, ᵉ̈ɩ̙˙ 3Du 4, ᵉɩ̣˙ 3Du 6, ę̈ɩ 3Du 5 under i:
e:ᵊ 7Ch 6, e:ᶥ 24Gl 3 under e:
e:ɩ 16Wo 3/6, e:ᶥ 16Wo 2 under ei

ɩɛ 38Do 4
e˙ə 22Sf 3
ɛ 15He 6
æɩ 15He 5
əɩ 31So 5/$^{+}$13

MEAT- 37D $^{+}$7; -MEAT 3Du 3, 12St $^{+}$6

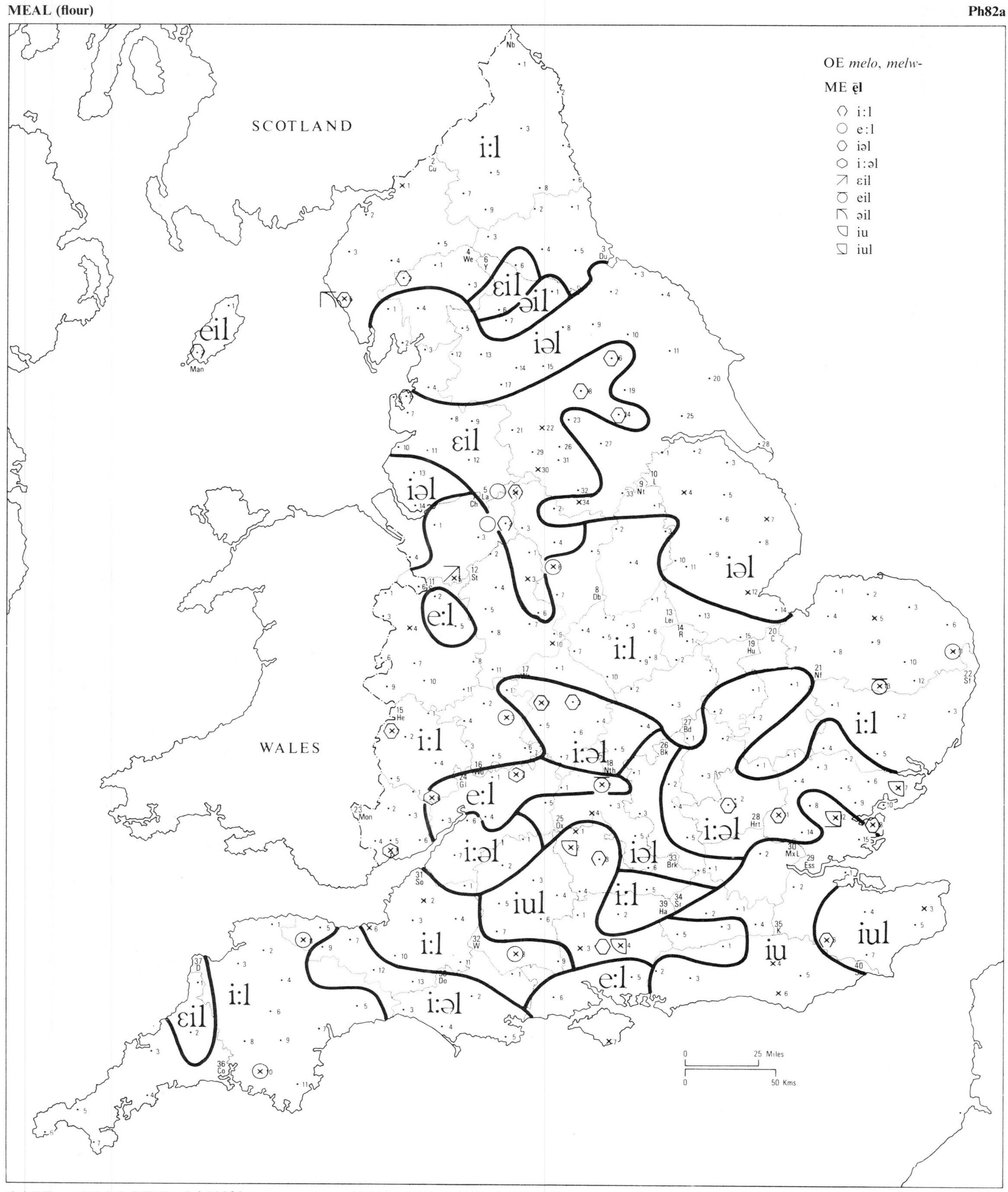

ᵊi:l 4We 1, 18Nth 3, 27Bd 1, ᵊi:ɫ 22Sf 5,
ᵊi˙l 2Cu 4, ᵉɩ˙l 3Du 4 under i:l
e:ᵊɫ 24Gl +1, 25Ox 1, ę:ᵊɫ 31So 8, e:əɫ 16Wo 3,
ę:ᶥl 8Db 6, ẹ:l 21Nf 5 under e:l
ᵊɩəl 7Ch 4, 28Hrt +3 under iəl
ᵊi:əɫ 28Hrt 2, ᵊi:ᵊɫ 27Bd 2,
əi:əɫ 28Hrt +3 under i:əl
ɩiɷ 40Sx 2, ɩiọ 33Brk 2, ɩi:ọ 40Sx +5,
ɩ̈i:ɷ 29Ess 7/8/15 under iu
i:ᵚɫ 32W 3–7, ɩ̈i:ɷɫ 29Ess 12 under iul

iɫ 35K 1, ɩɫ 24Gl +1
eəl 6Y +18
ẹ.l 21Nf 5, ɛ:ɷɫ 31So +4
aɩᵊɫ 39Ha 3

MEAL- 28Hrt 3, 29Ess 3, 39Ha +4;
-MEAL- 22Sf +2, 26Bk 5, 27Bd 3;
-MEAL 3Du 1, 4We +2/3,
6Y 1–3/6/7/9–11/+16/17/+18/+24/26/27/32,
7Ch +2/3, 9Nt 1, 10L 13/14, 11Sa 6/9,
12St 4/7/11, 13Lei 7, 15He 7, 17Wa 7,
21Nf 2/3/5/7/9–11, 22Sf +2/3, 23Mon 4–7,
24Gl +1, 29Ess 2/7/8/12/14/15, 31So +4,
33Brk 2/4, 34Sr 2–5, 37D 7, 40Sx 1;
MEALING- 33Brk +3

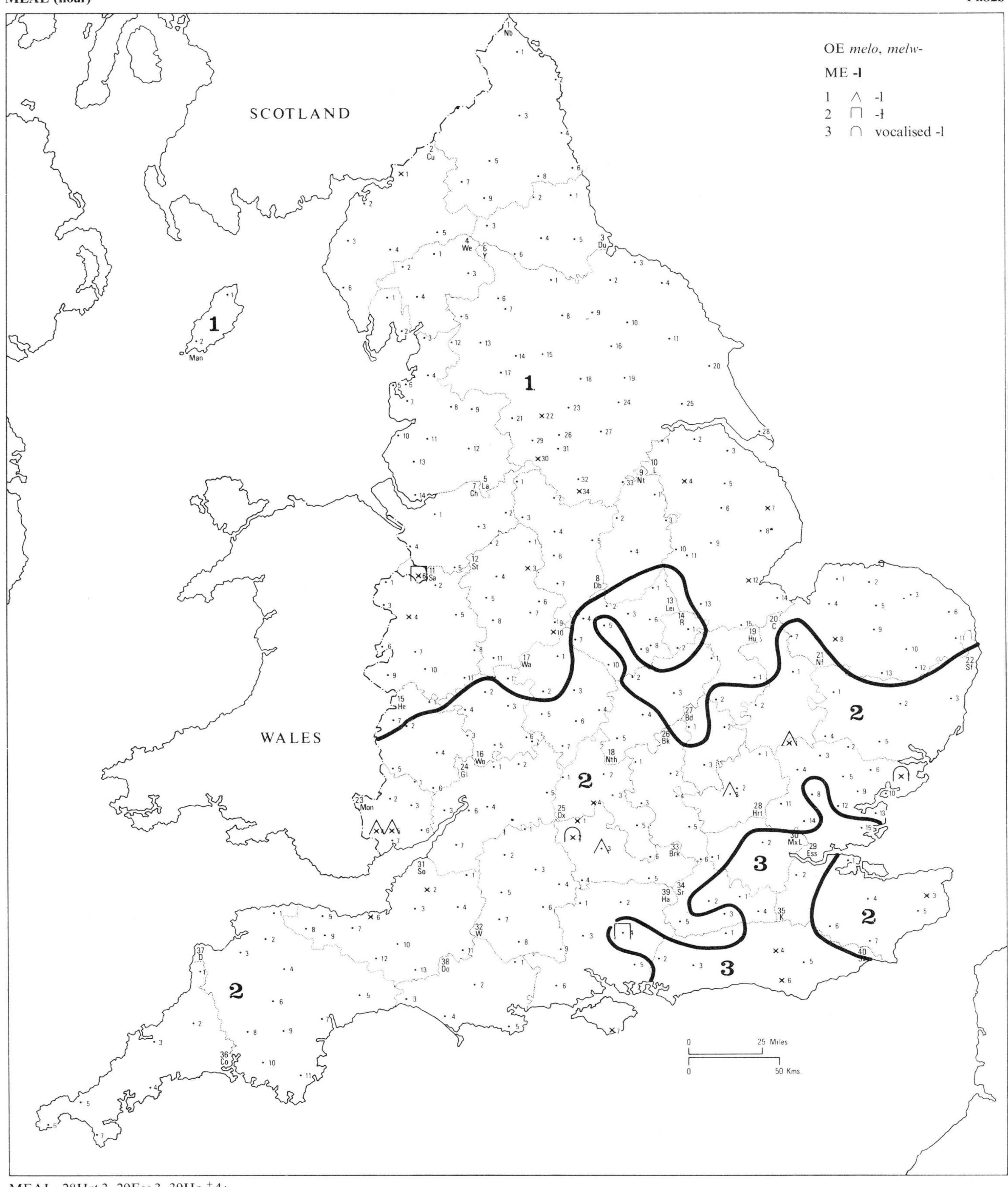

MEAL- 28Hrt 3, 29Ess 3, 39Ha +4;
MEALING- 33Brk +3; -MEAL- 22Sf +2,
26Bk 5, 27Bd 3; -MEAL 3Du 1/6, 4We 3,
6Y 1–3/6/7/9–11/17/26/27/32, 7Ch 3, 9Nt 1,
11Sa 6/9, 12St 4/7/11, 13Lei 7, 15He 7, 17Wa 7,
21Nf 2/3/5/7/9–11, 22Sf +2/3, 23Mon 4–7,
29Ess 2/7/8/12/14/15, 33Brk 2/4, 34Sr 2–5,
37D 7, 40Sx 1

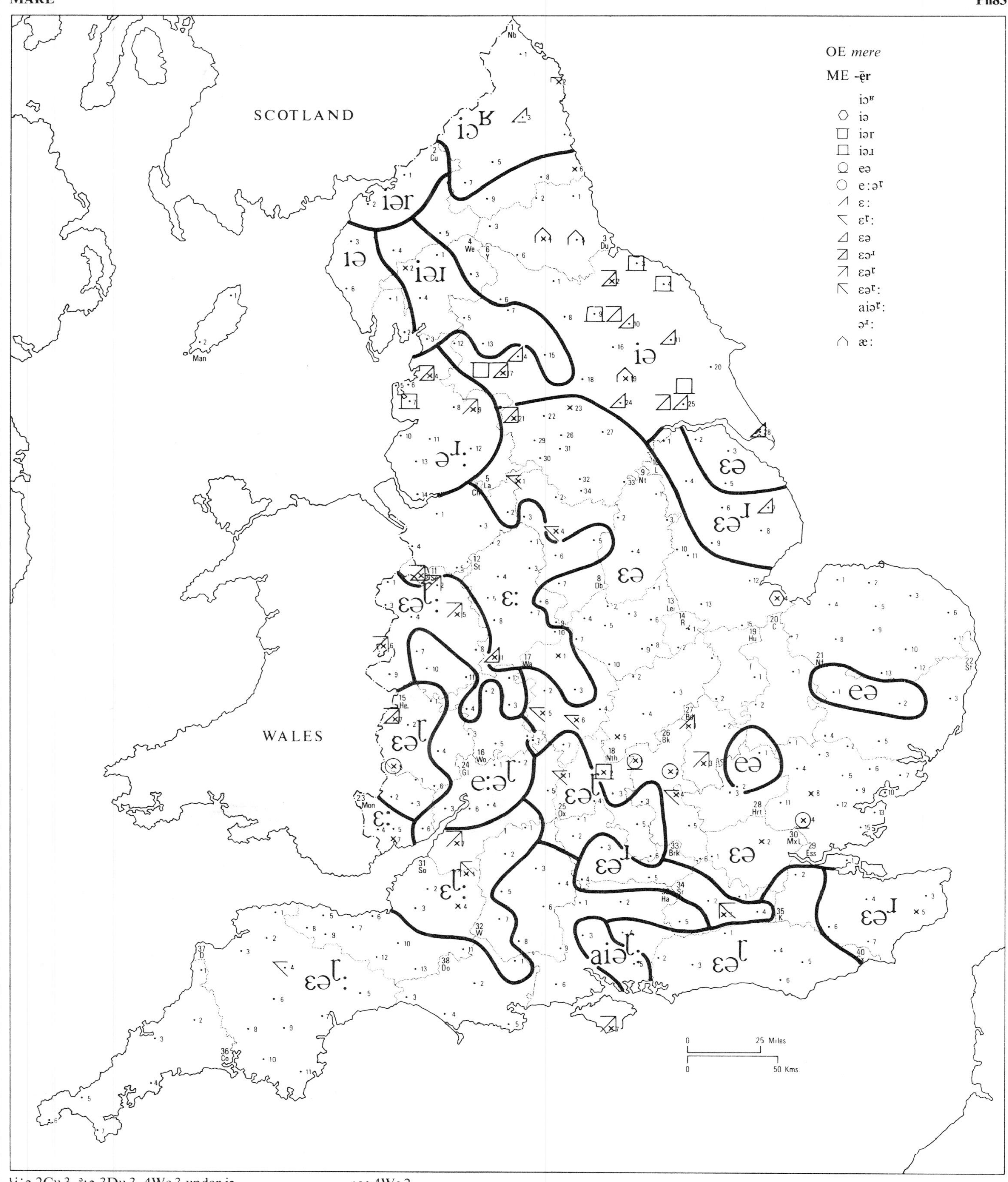

ˌi̜ˑə 2Cu 3, ᵊɩə 3Du 3, 4We 3 under iə
ᶦɩər 2Cu 2 under iər
ɩəɹ 5La 3/⁺7, 6Y ⁺20, ɩəɹ̠ 25Ox 2,
ᵊɩəɹ 4We 1 under iəɹ
ȩ:ə 29Ess 14 under eə
e:ɩəʳ 24Gl 3 under e:əʳ
ɛʳ:ᵊ 26Bk 4, ȩʳ:ᵊɽ 17Wa 5, æʳ: 25Ox 1 under ɛʳ:
ɛ:ə 12St 6/911, 18Nth 2, 21Nf 9/11/12, 29Ess 13,
ȩ:ə 21Nf 3/5, ɛ:ᵊ 8Db 7, ɛɩə 21Nf 10,
ȩᶦɐ 35K 1 under ɛə
ɛɩəɹ 35K 6 under ɛəɹ
ɛ:əʳ 11Sa ⁺2/8, 16Wo 1/3 under ɛəʳ
ɛ:əʳ: 31So 1/9/12, 38Do 2/5 under ɛəʳ:
ɜɹ: 5La 13, ɜɹ:ɹ 5La 8/10–12/14 under əɹ:
æ:ᵊ 6Y 19, æ:ə 3Du ⁺5 under æ:

ɩəɾ 4We 2
eɩə Man 2, ȩɩəɹ Man 1, eɩəɹ 35K 5
eˑəɹ 18Nth 5
ȩɔʁ 1Nb 2
ɛ:ɹ 17Wa 1
a: 6Y ⁺1
əʳ: 37D ⁺8
ɐ̧:ə 29Ess 8

interpr as *r*-col: ɹ 5La 4, 6Y 2/⁺9/⁺17, 10L 1/4/⁺7/8/9, 15He 7, 18Nth 5, ɽ 5La 9, 8Db 4, 25Ox 4
cons *r* foll *r*-col V: ɹ 5La 8/10–12/14, ɽ 8Db 1, 17Wa 5, 39Ha 7, 40Sx 1/3–5

MARE- 3Du 3

PEARS

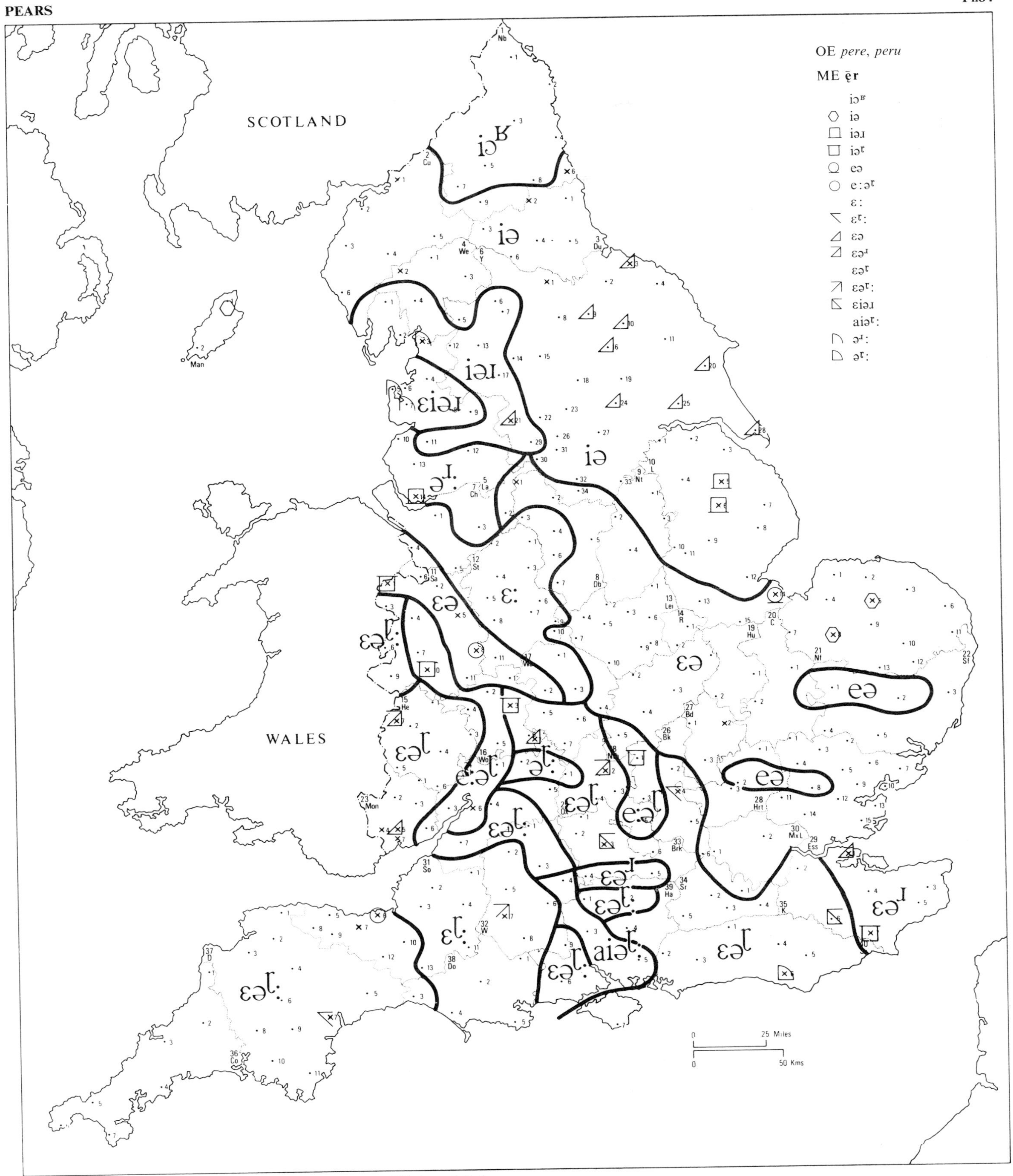

ᵉ̈ɩə 3Du 5, i:ə Man 1 under iə
ɩəɹ 4We 4, 6Y 12/13/29, 10L 6, ɩ˙əɹ 10L 5 under iəɹ
ɩəʵ: 11Sa 1/10 under iəʵ
ẹ:ᵊ 29Ess 8 under eə
eəʵ 25Ox 5, eəʵ: 31So 6, e˙əʵ: 11Sa 4 under e:əʵ
ɛʵ:ᵊ 26Bk 4 under ɛʵ:
ɛ:ə 11Sa 11, 12St 11, 16Wo 1, 21Nf 2, ẹ:ə 11Sa 2,
ɛ:ᵊ 18Nth 3, 23Mon 5, æᵊ 7Ch +2 under ɛə
ɛɩəʵ 35K +6 under ɛəʵ
ɛ:əʵ: 31So 8/9, 32W 7 under ɛəʵ:
ɛɩəɹ 5La +5/+7 under ɛiəɹ
ɜɹ: 5La 3/13, ɜɹ:ɹ 5La 10/12 under əɹ:

ɩəʶ 1Nb 6, ɩər 2Cu 1
ẹəʶ 3Du 2, ẹɩəɹ Man 2
ɛɷəɹ 5La +5
ɛɹ̠: 8Db 1
œ: 24Gl 4
a:ɹ 6Y 1, aʵ: 11Sa 5

interpr as *r*-col: ɹ 15He 7, ɽ 38Do 2/4/5
cons *r* foll *r*-col V: ɹ 5La 10/12, ɽ 33Brk 2,
34Sr 2–4, 39Ha 7, 40Sx 2–6

PEAR- 7Ch +2

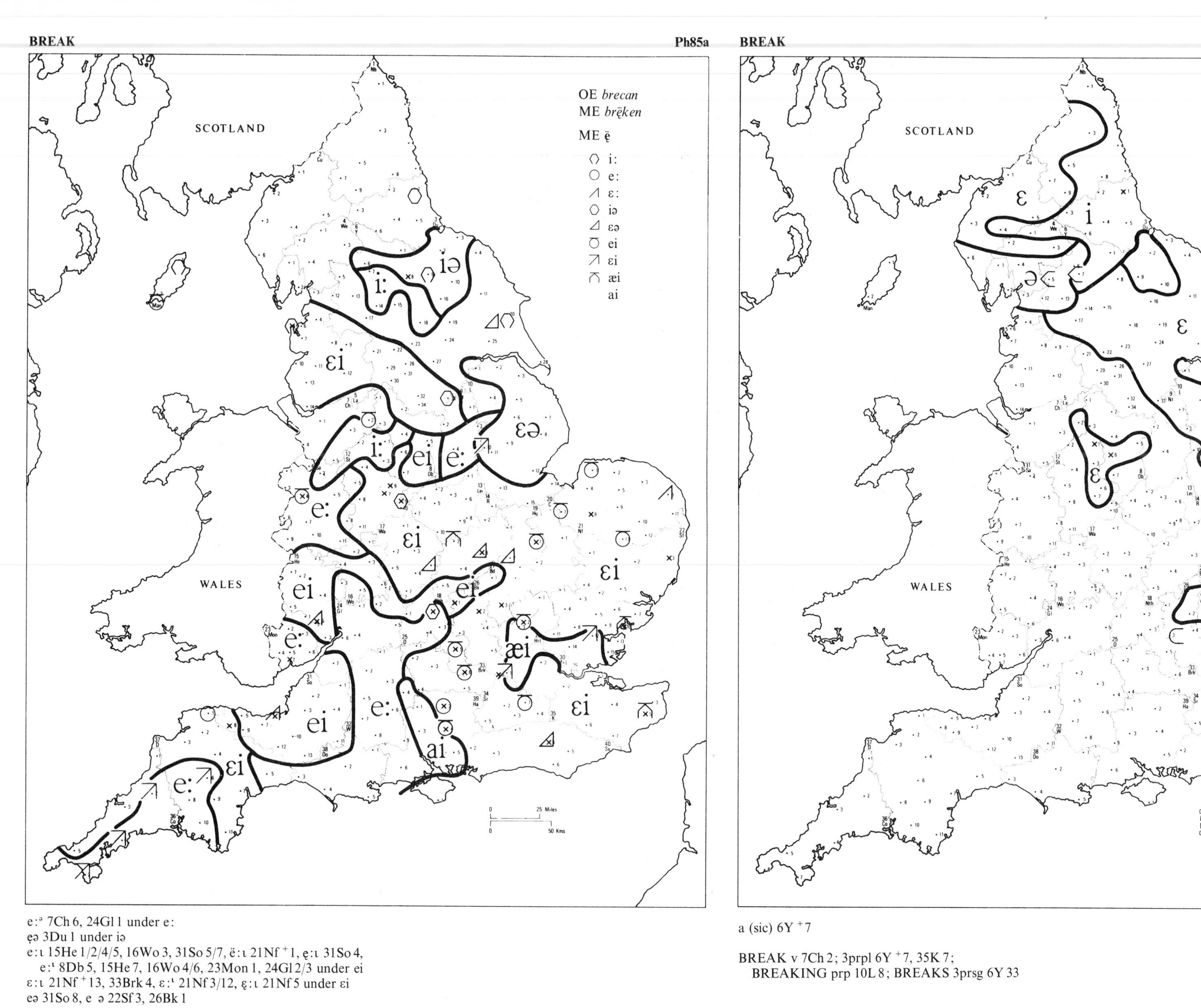

e:ᵊ 7Ch 6, 24Gl 1 under e:
ęə 3Du 1 under iə
e:ɩ 15He 1/2/4/5, 16Wo 3, 31So 5/7, ë:ɩ 21Nf +1, ę:ɩ 31So 4,
e:ᶦ 8Db 5, 15He 7, 16Wo 4/6, 23Mon 1, 24Gl 2/3 under ei
ɛ:ɩ 21Nf +13, 33Brk 4, ɛ:ᶦ 21Nf 3/12, ę:ɩ 21Nf 5 under ɛi
eə 31So 8, e ə 22Sf 3, 26Bk 1

BREAK v 17Wa +4; 2prpl 6Y 18; 3prpl 6Y 7; n 21Nf +13, 30MxL +1; ndg 29Ess +12; BREAKING prp 6Y +33, 10L +10, 36Co +2; vbl n 6Y 14; BREAKS 3prsg 6Y +33

bəɽ:k 36Co +6/+7

a (sic) 6Y +7

BREAK v 7Ch 2; 3prpl 6Y +7, 35K 7; BREAKING prp 10L 8; BREAKS 3prsg 6Y 33

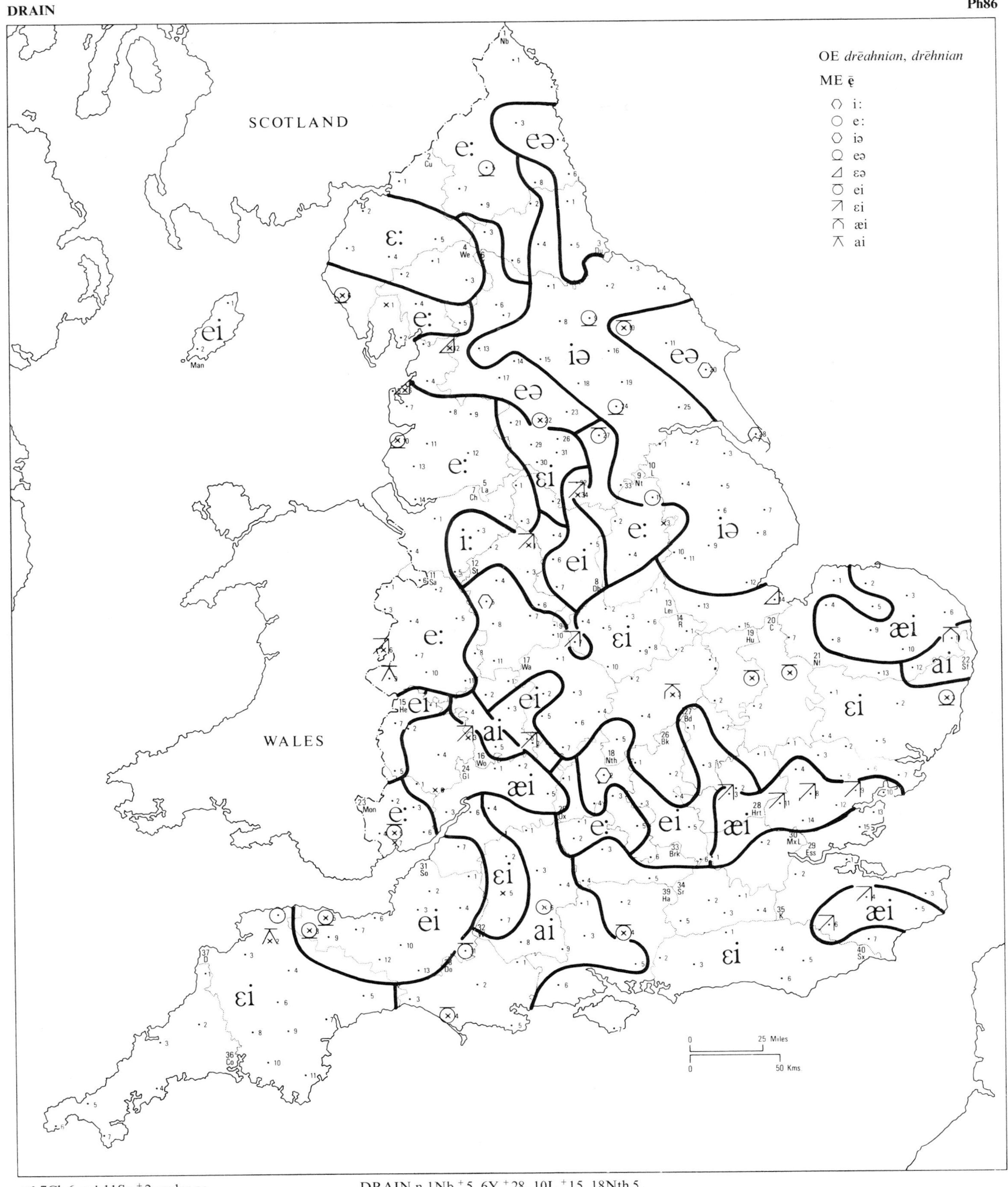

e:ᵊ 7Ch 6, ę:ᶥ 11Sa +2 under e:
e:ə 1Nb +5/6, 5La 10, 31So 8, e:ᵊ 6Y 6/7/23,
ę:ᵊ 31So 5 under eə
eɩᵊ 20C +1, ęɩᵊ 20C +1, e:ɩ 15He 5, 16Wo 3/6,
31So 6, ę:ɩ 38Do 4, e:ᶥ 8Db 5–7,
15He 1 under ei
ẹɩᵊ 19Hu 2, ɛɩə 10L +15, ɛ:ɩ 12St +9, ę:ɩ 21Nf 5,
ɛ:ᶥ 16Wo 2 under ɛi

ẹa 5La 1
ɛ: 6Y +28, 12St +9, 32W 5
ɑɩ 30MxL +2
ɒɩ 15He 6

DRAIN n 1Nb +5, 6Y +28, 10L +15, 18Nth 5,
20C +1, 21Nf +7, 29Ess +2;
DRAIN- n 6Y +27, 30MxL +2;
-DRAIN v 20C +1, 21Nf +7, 29Ess +2/+13;
n 29Ess +9; DRAINED 3ptpl 11Sa +9;
pp 31So +11, 37D +1; DRAINER n 7Ch +2;
DRAINING prp 29Ess +8; n 6Y 14/+28,
7Ch +2; vbl n 12St +9, 35K +4; ndg 6Y +20,
29Ess 4/+11/+13; DRAINS 3prsg 35K +4;
n 10L +14, 21Nf +11

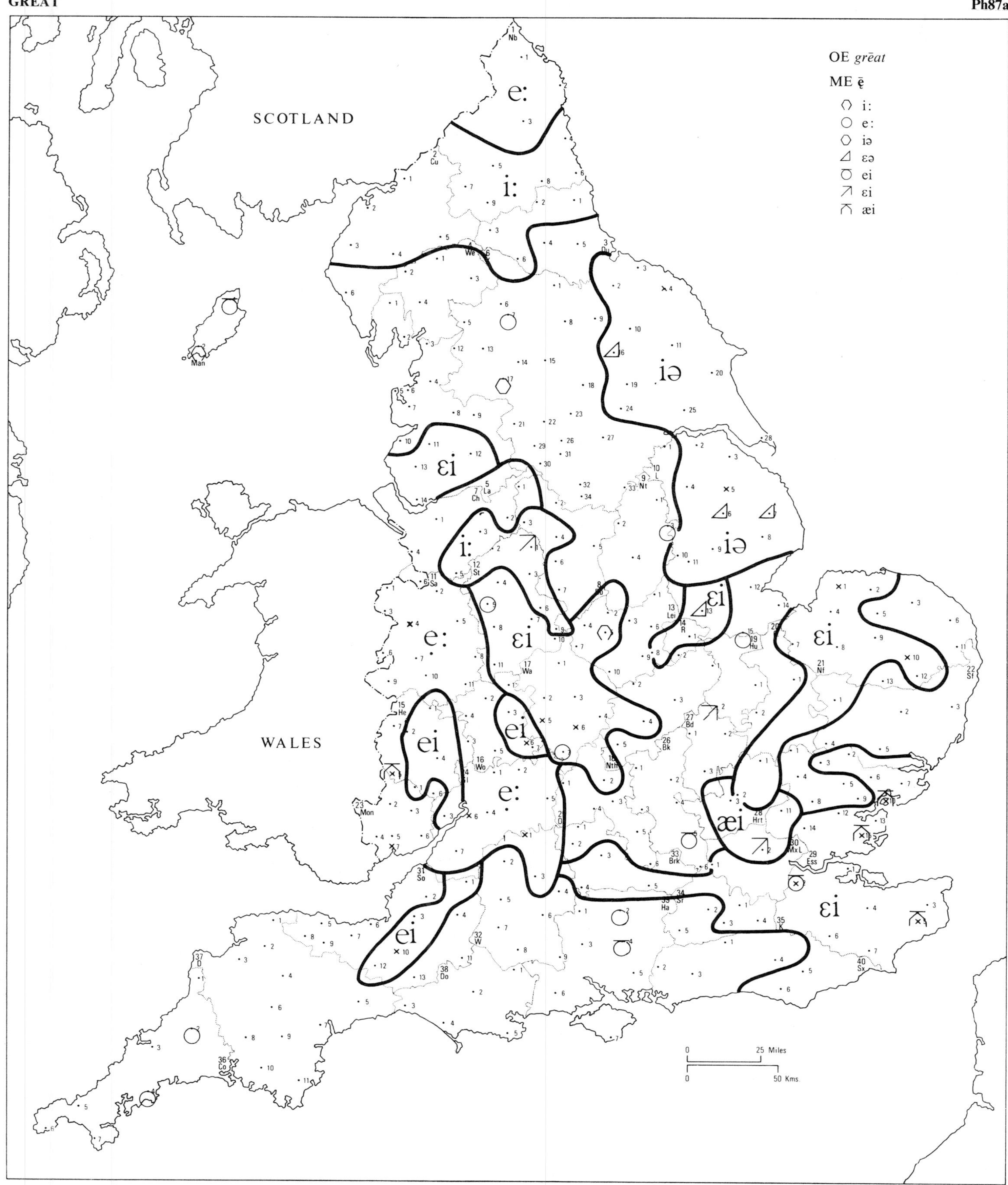

eːᵊ 7Ch 6, 17Wa ⁺7, 24Gl 1/2, e 10L 15,
e˙ə 1Nb 3 under eː
eːɩ 15He 1/2/4, 16Wo 3, 23Mon 1,
eːᶦ 24Gl 3 under ei

eə 6Y 4, eᵊ 6Y 32, e˙ə 22Sf 3

GREAT- 30MxL ⁺2; GREATLY 36Co 4

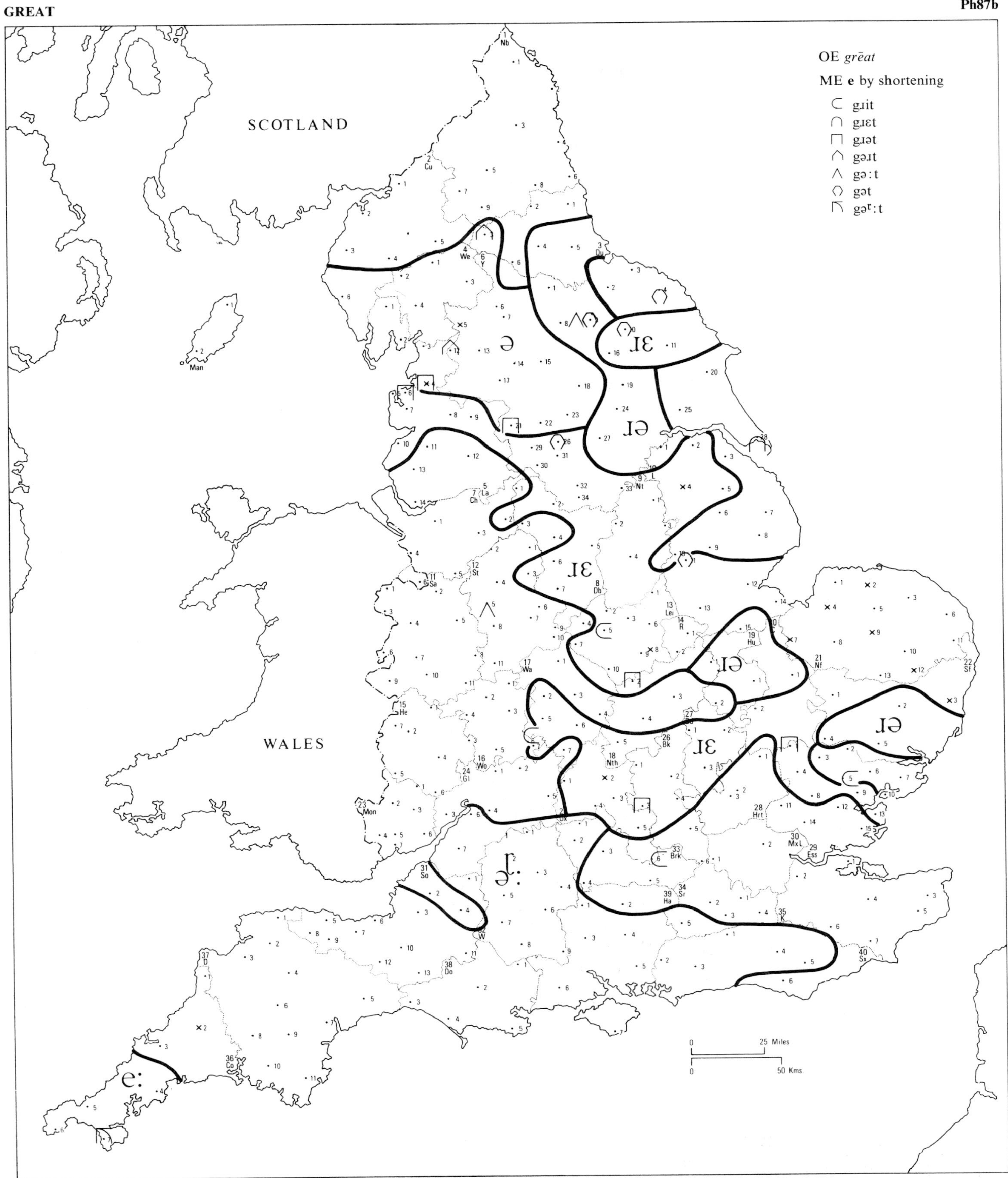

gɹɛ:t 21Nf 1/10, gɽɛ:t 25Ox 4 under gɹɛt
gɹʌt 22Sf 2 under gɹət
gəɹt 6Y +12 under gəɹt

gʁɩt 1Nb +5
gɹǫt 18Nth 3
gɛt 5La +6, 6Y +6
gɷt 14R +1
gəɹ:t 5La +5, 34Sr 2
gəɾt 6Y 5

interpr as *r*-col: ɽ 39Ha +7
cons *r* foll *r*-col V: ɽ 32W 7, 33Brk 1/2, 39Ha +7, 40Sx 1–5

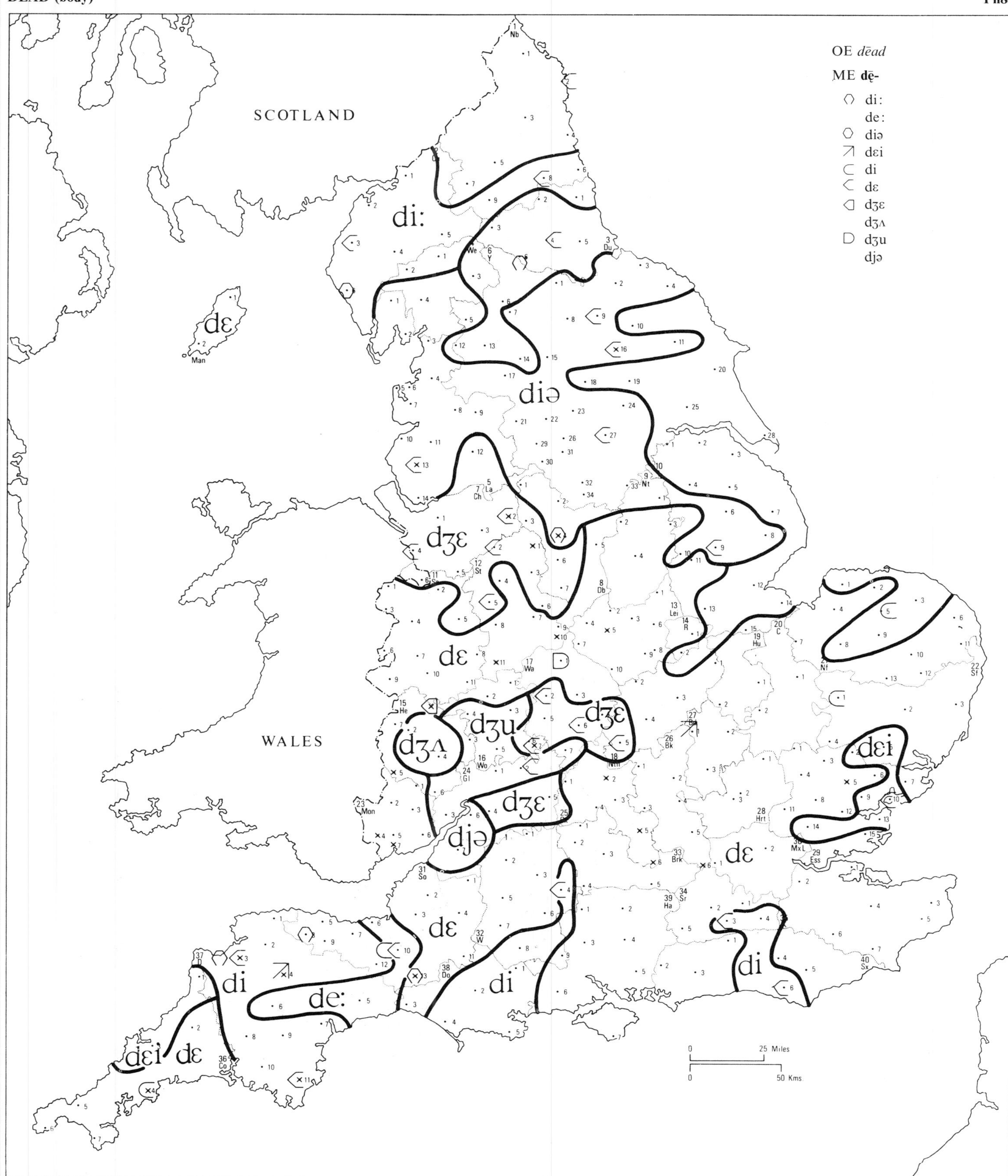

deɩ 37D 6, de 31So 6 under de:
dɛᵊ 1Nb +8, Man 1/+2, dɛ·ᵊ 35K 1, dę 30MxL +2,
35K +2 under dɛ
djɛ 17Wa +2, 18Nth +5 under dʒɛ
djʌ 15He +4 under dʒʌ
djɷ 16Wo 5, djɷ: 24Gl 1 under dʒu
dʒə 24Gl +6 under djə

dɩɷ 5La +12
deɩə Man +2
dæɩ 33Brk +5

DEAD adv 6Y 11

dɛdɩ 18Nth 3, dɛ bɒdɩ 31So 1

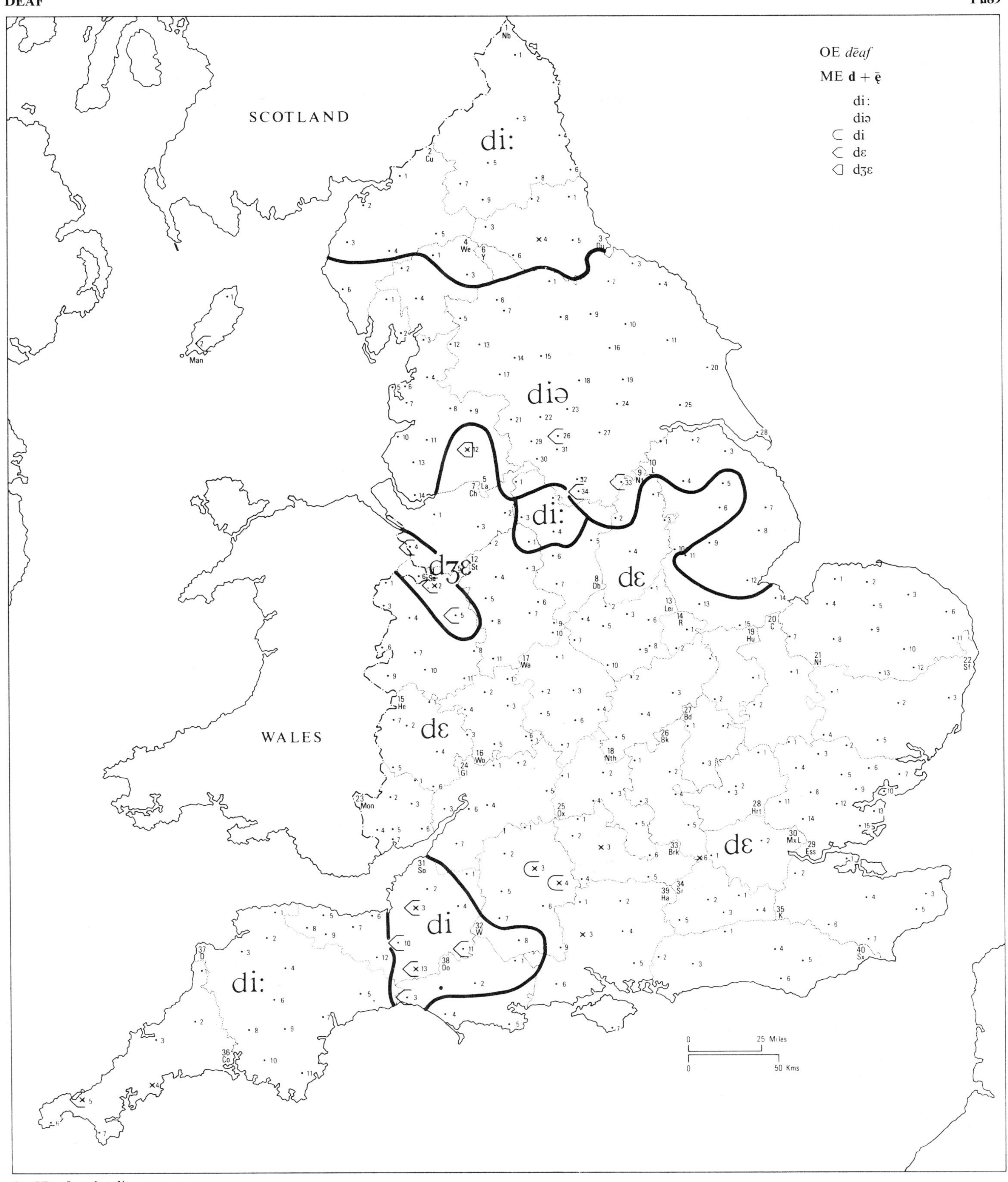

dę̈ɩ 3Du 5 under di:
dę̣ᵊ 35K 1, dɛə Man 2, 29Ess 7/15, 40Sx 1,
dę̣ə 29Ess 12, dɛ˙ᵊ 26Bk 2 under dɛ
djɛ 11Sa + 5 under dʒɛ

de: 7Ch + 1, de:ᵊ Man 1
da: 39Ha 3

-DEAF 10L 1, 22Sf 4

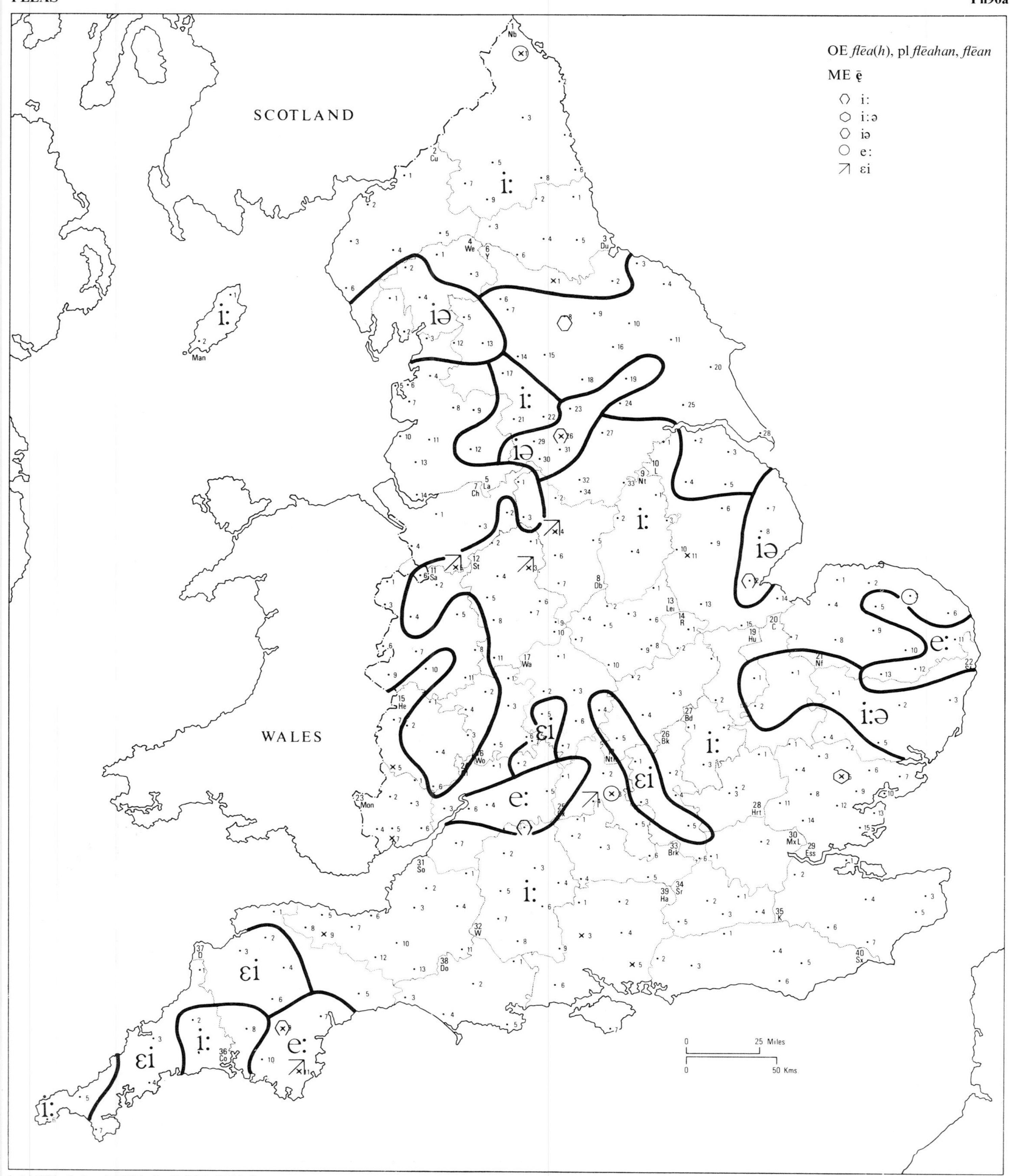

i:ᵊ 16Wo 3, i:ə 24Gl 1, ᵊi: 22Sf 4, 26Bk 2, 27Bd 1/2, 28Hrt 2/+3, əi: 12St 10, 28Hrt +3, ᵉi˙ 21Nf 8, ëɩ 1Nb 5, eɩ 1Nb 7 under i:

e˙ 21Nf 11, e˙ə 21Nf +3 ("old-fashioned"), e˙ɩ 21Nf 12/13, ẹ: 21Nf 5 under e:

aɩ 39Ha 3/5

əɩ 6Y 1, 31So 9, əɩə 7Ch 4

-FLEAS 6Y 26/27

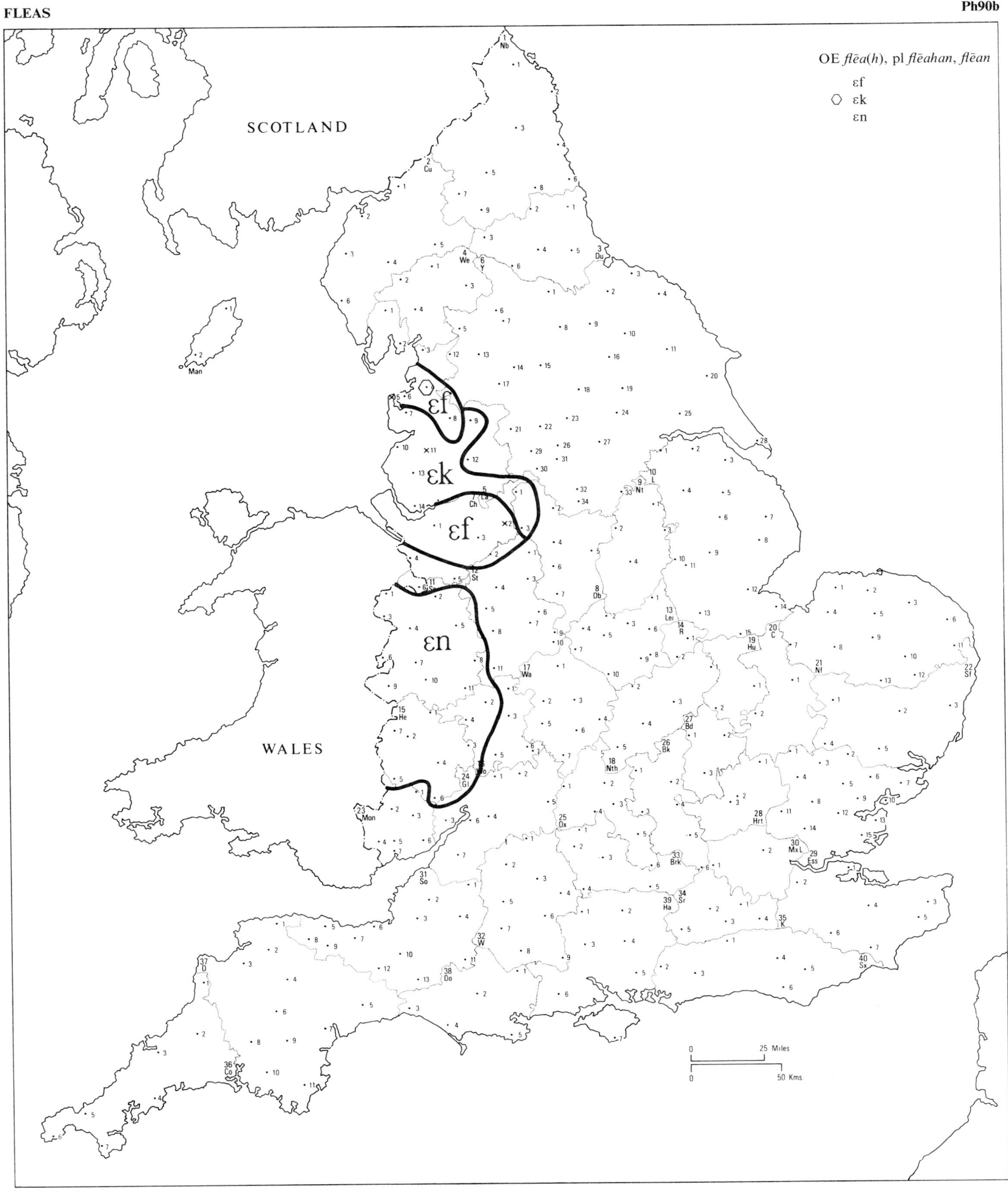

ɛ:n 15He 3 under ɛn

fjɒf ("usual") 11Sa 2, flɛɪθ 5La 11

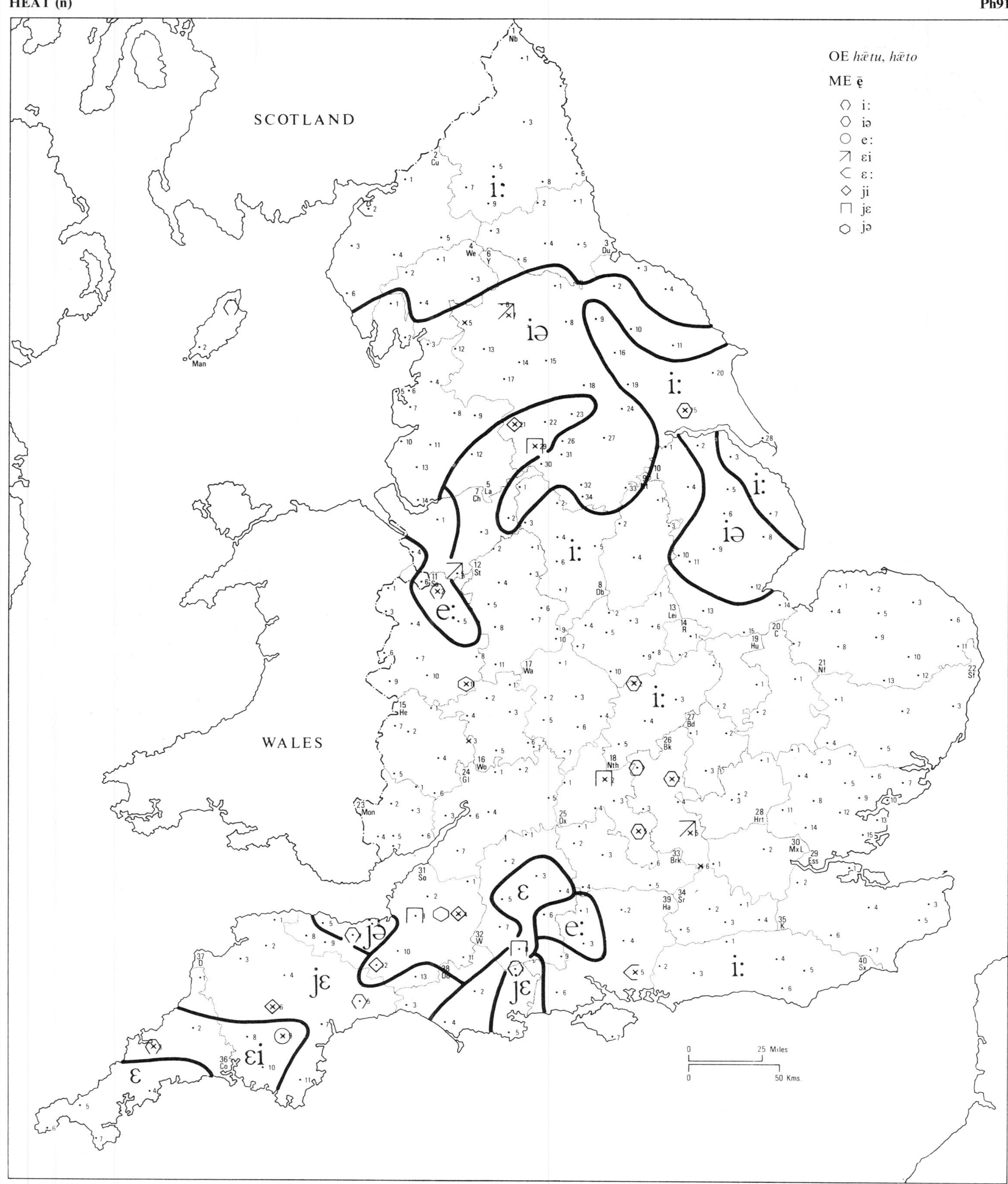

i:^{ə} 20C 1/$^{+}$2, ^{ə}i: 22Sf 1/4/5, 27Bd 1/2, 29Ess 5,
ë̜ɩ 3Du 4 under i:
e:^{ə} 7Ch 6, ę:ə 11Sa 5 under e:
εɩə 7Ch $^{+}$5 under εi

ɩ 31So $^{+}$11
ɩa 6Y 5
jɷ 15He 3
eɩ Man 2
əɩ 6Y $^{+}$7

hɒt 29Ess $^{+}$9, ɒʔ 25Ox $^{+}$5, ɔt 10L $^{+}$9

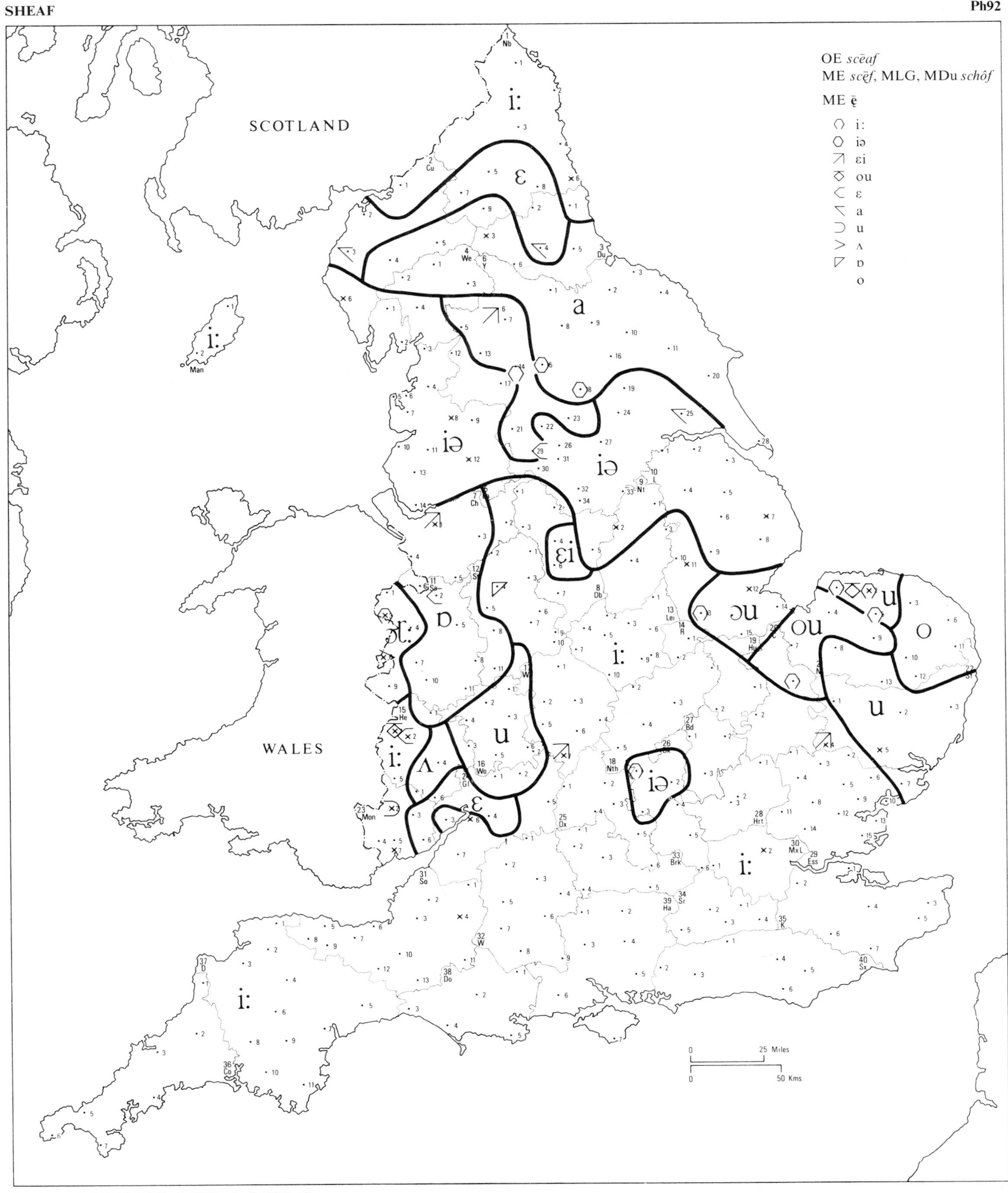

i:ᵊ 20C 2, ᵊi: 27Bd 1, 28Hrt 2, 29Ess 5, əi: 28Hrt 3,
i 35K 4, ɩ 1Nb ⁺2, ɩ̣ 1Nb ⁺2 under i:
ẹɩə 7Ch 1 under εi

ɩω 5La 12
eɩ 29Ess ⁺3
ẹa 2Cu 6
ε˙ə 10L 7
ɔ 22Sf 5
ə 24Gl 6

SHEAF- 6Y ⁺25

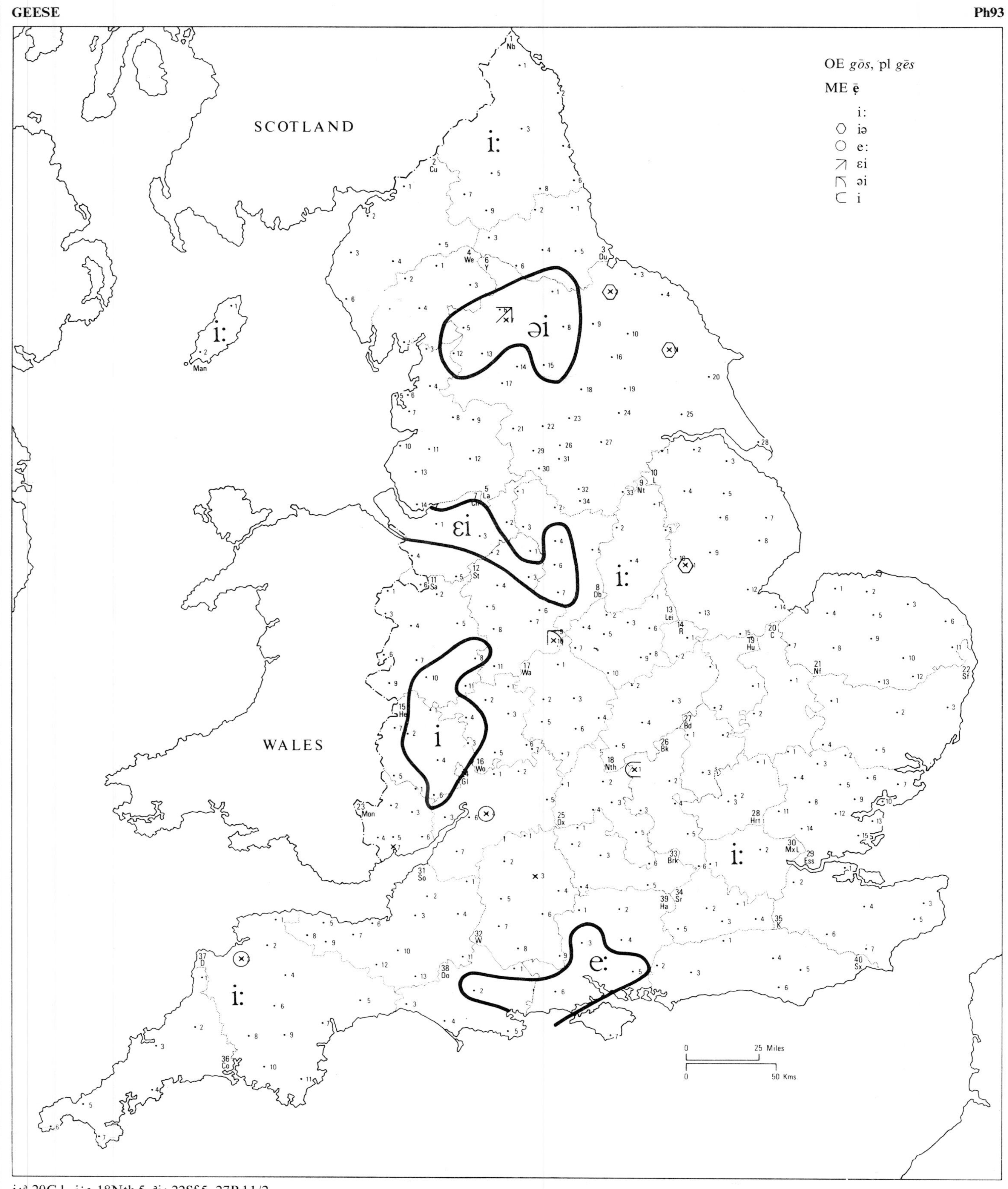

i:ᵊ 20C 1, i̜˙ə 18Nth 5, ᵊi: 22Sf 5, 27Bd 1/2, 28Hrt 2/⁺3, 29Ess 5, əi 28Hrt ⁺3, ëι 29Ess 12/15 under i:

ˌə 32W 3

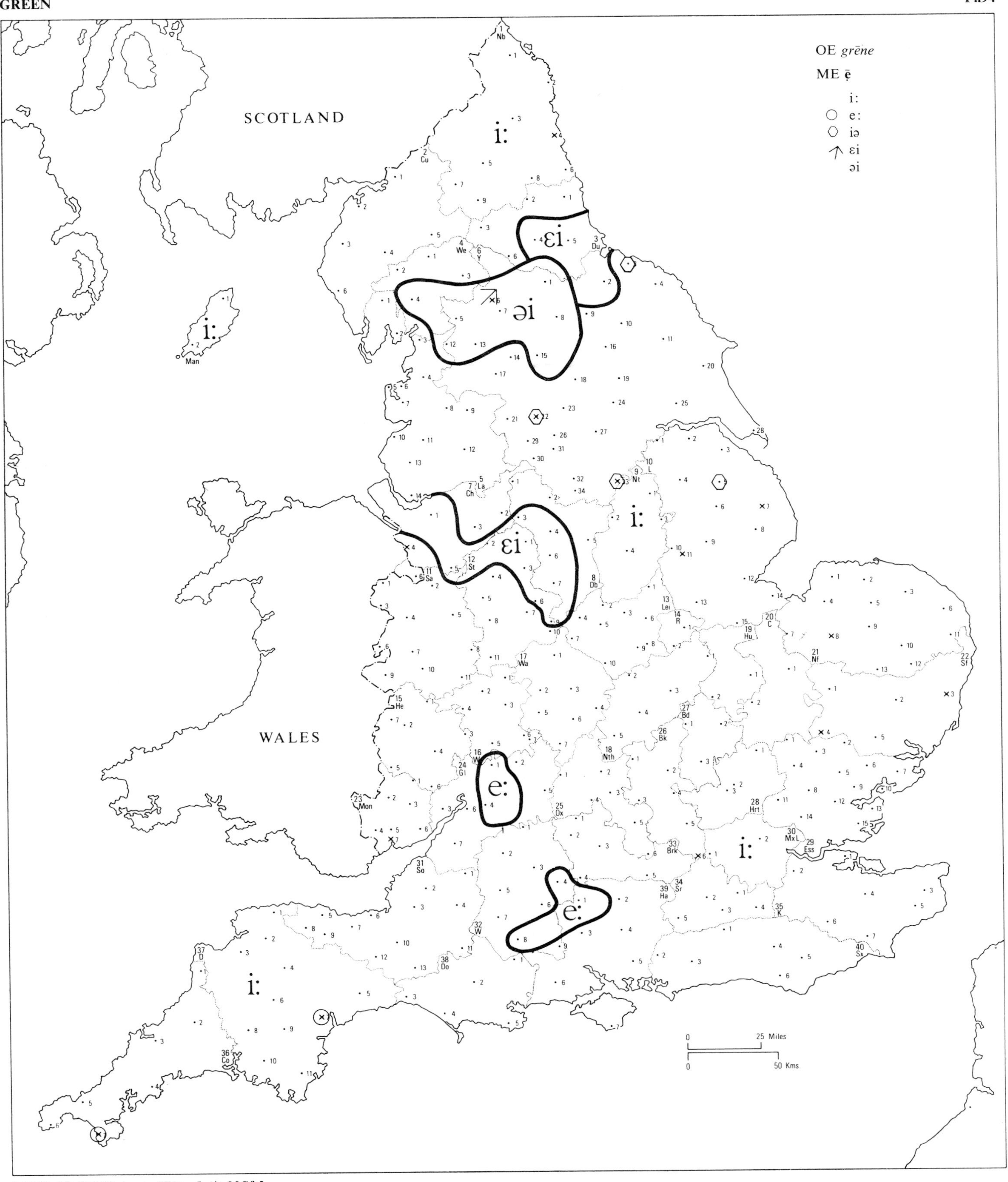

iː° 10L 13, 18Nth 1, ɪ̣ˑə 29Ess 5, °iː 22Sf 5,
26Bk 2, 27Bd 1–3, 28Hrt 2, əiː 28Hrt 3,
°iː° 22Sf 2 under iː

ë̜ɪ 3Du 5, ëiˑ 3Du 4 under εi

eˑə 22Sf 3

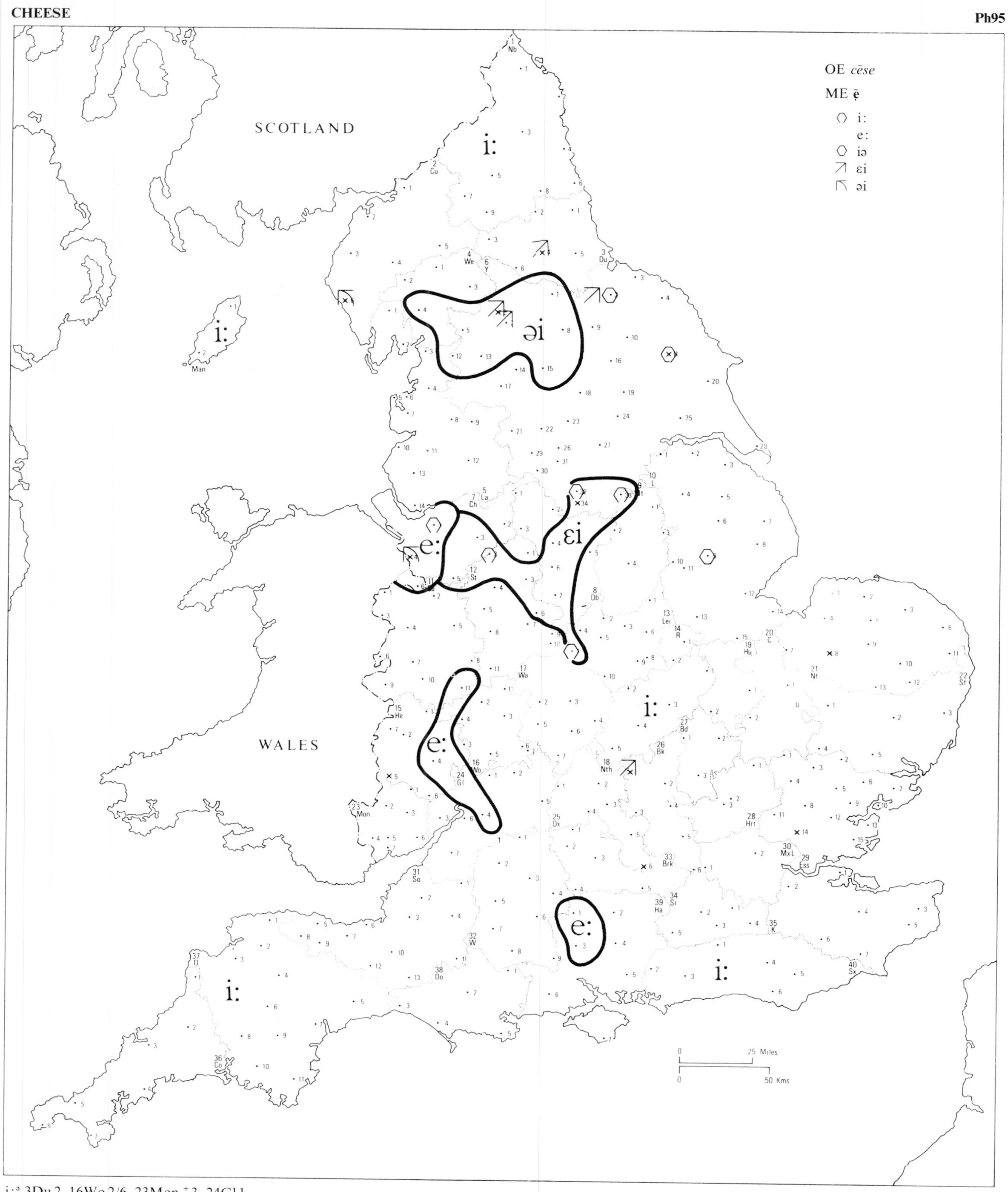

i:ᵊ 3Du 2, 16Wo 2/6, 23Mon +3, 24Gl 1,
ɩi:ᵊ 23Mon +1, ˡi:ᵊ 24Gl 3, i:ə 23Mon +3,
24Gl 2, ᵊi: 22Sf 2/4/5, 26Bk 2/4, 27Bd 1,
28Hrt 2/3 under i:
e:ᵊ 24Gl 4, e:ɩ 15He 4 under e:
ę̈ɩ 3Du 4 under εi

ε 6Y +2
æɩ 15He 5

CHEESE- 6Y +2

ɩ (in CHEESE-) 6Y +16/+28, 29Ess +10,
ε (in CHEESE-) 6Y +5/+11, 12St +1

WEEDS **Ph96**

CREEP **Ph97**

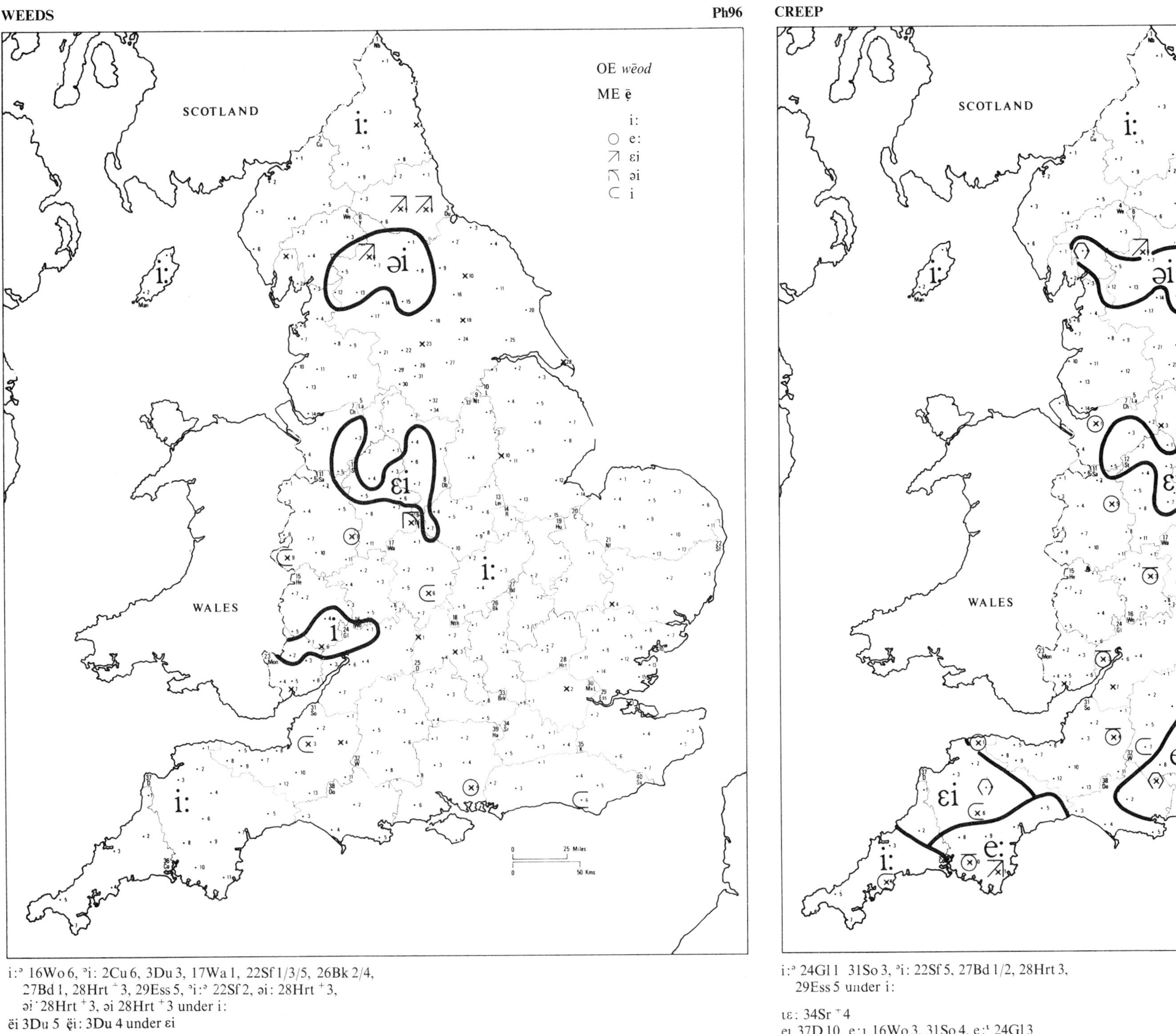

i:ᵊ 16Wo 6, ᵊi: 2Cu 6, 3Du 3, 17Wa 1, 22Sf 1/3/5, 26Bk 2/4,
27Bd 1, 28Hrt ⁺3, 29Ess 5, ᵊi:ᵊ 22Sf 2, əi: 28Hrt ⁺3,
əi˙ 28Hrt ⁺3, əi 28Hrt ⁺3 under i:
ëi 3Du 5 ę̈i: 3Du 4 under ɛi

ɛ 15He 6

-WEED 28Hrt ⁺3

i:ᵊ 24Gl 1 31So 3, ᵊi: 22Sf 5, 27Bd 1/2, 28Hrt 3,
29Ess 5 under i:

ɩɛ: 34Sr ⁺4
eɩ 37D 10, e:ɩ 16Wo 3, 31So 4, e:ᶥ 24Gl 3
eᵊ 39Ha ⁺4
ɛ̣ə 21Nf 1

CREEP 3prpl 4We ⁺4; -CREEPERS n 39Ha ⁺4;
CREEPING prp 2Cu 1, 4We 1,
6Y 2/7/9–11/14–17/20/22/24/25/27/⁺28/30/32/33,
7Ch 2, 10L 7, 12St 5, 16Wo 7, 17Wa 2, 21Nf 3/13,
29Ess ⁺15, 32W ⁺3/⁺7, 34Sr 2/⁺4, 39Ha 2, 40Sx ⁺5;
CREEPS 3prsg 32W ⁺3

ɩi erased by fw 33Brk ⁺2

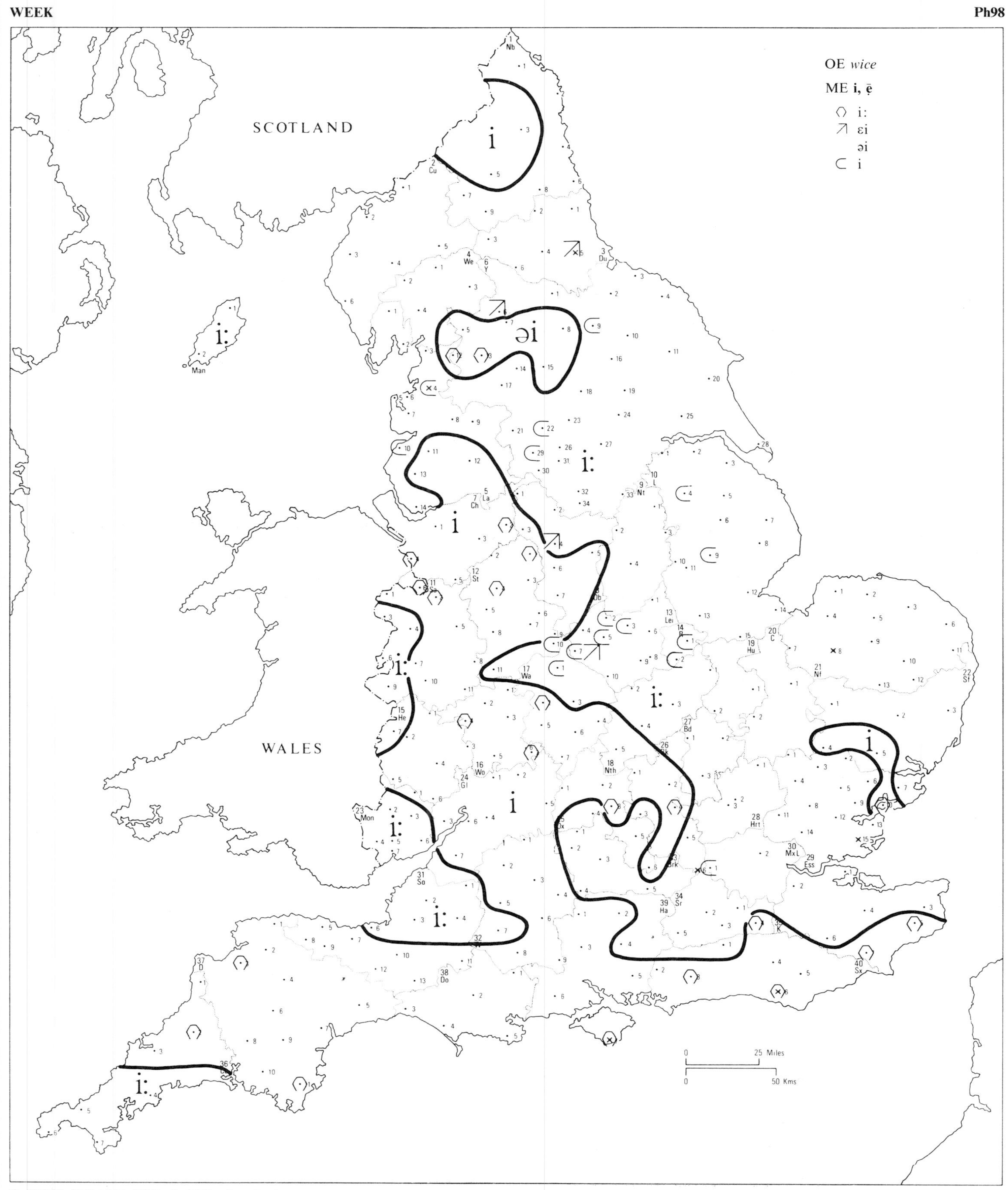

ᵊi: 22Sf 2, 27Bd 1/2, 28Hrt 3, 29Ess 5 under i:
ę̈ɩ 3Du 5 under εi

ɩə 6Y $^{+}$3/$^{+}$33, ɩ˙ə 10L $^{+}$10
e: 15He $^{+}$5
ëɩ 29Ess 15

WEEK- 6Y $^{+}$33, 10L $^{+}$10

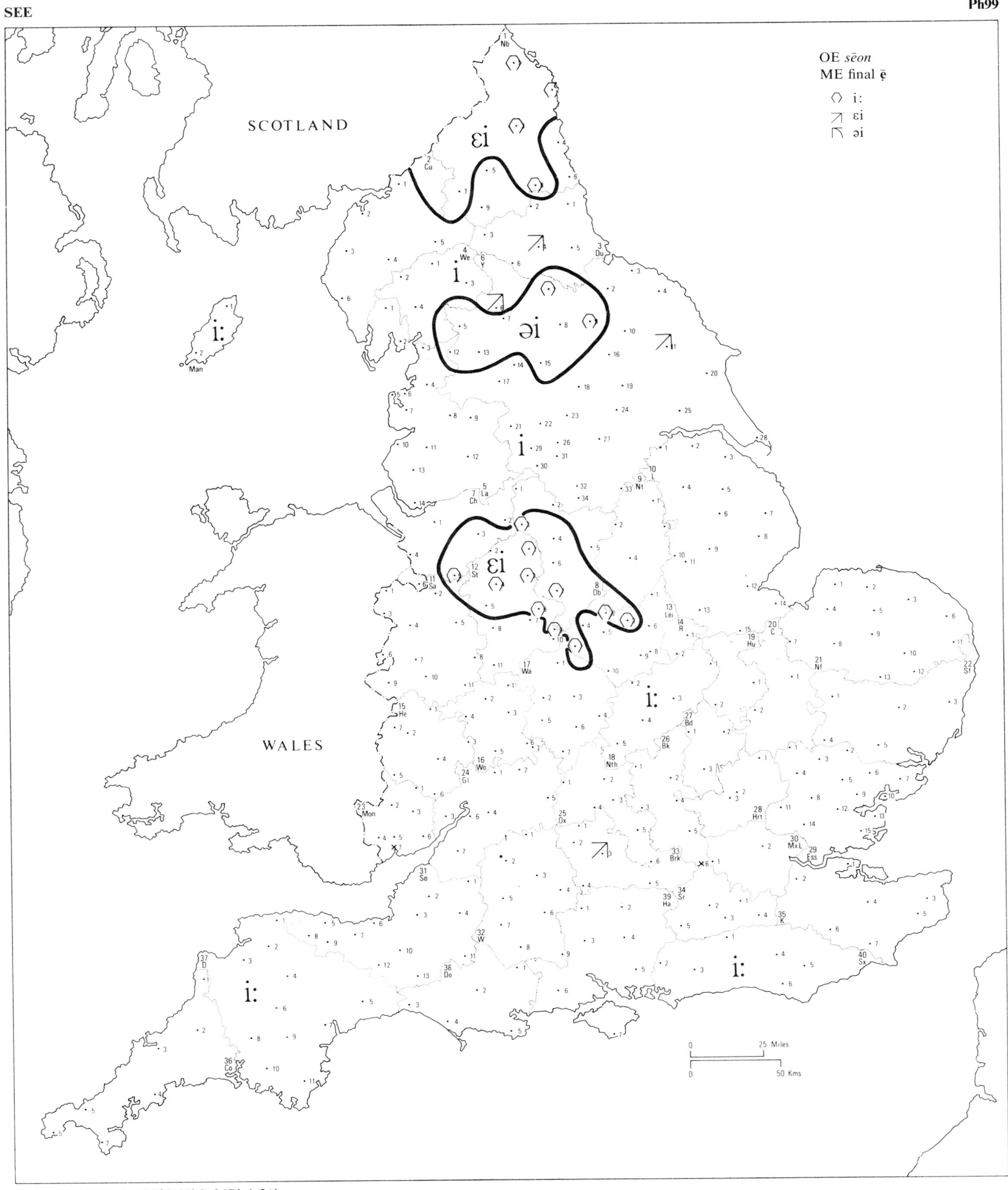

ᵊi: 4We 1, 18Nth 3, 22Sf 2/4/⁺5, 26Bk 1/2/4, 27Bd 1/2, 28Hrt 2/3, 29Ess 5, ᵊi̧: 7Ch ⁺4, 17Wa 5, ᵊɩ 7Ch ⁺4, ᵉi: 2Cu 1 under i:
ë̩ɩ 1Nb ⁺8, 3Du ⁺4, eɩ 1Nb ⁺1·/7, 6Y ⁺11 under εi

ëɩ 29Ess ⁺15

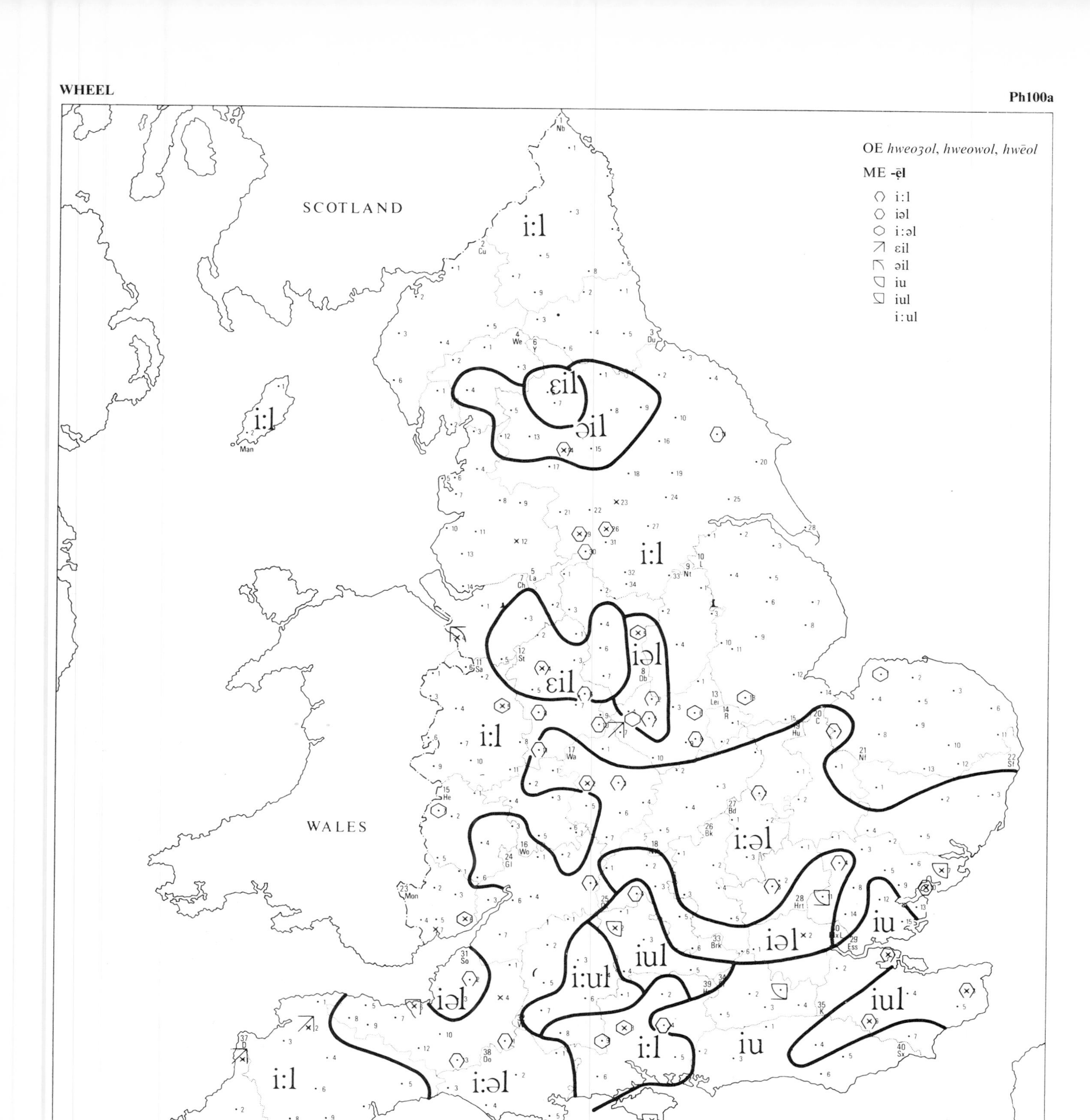

iɫ 35K $^{+}$1, ịɫ 29Ess $^{+}$4, ɩɫ 16Wo 4, 24Gl 3,
ɩɫ̣ 35K $^{+}$1, əi:ɫ 28Hrt $^{+}$3, ẹ:l 7Ch 1 under i:l
ᵊi:ᵊɫ 22Sf 4/5, 27Bd 1/2, əi:ᵊɫ 28Hrt $^{+}$3 under i:əl

ɩəɷ 31So $^{+}$3

WHEEL- 12St $^{+}$6, 21Nf $^{+}$7;
-WHEEL(S) 12St $^{+}$8, 13Lei $^{+}$5, 17Wa $^{+}$3,
25Ox $^{+}$4, 35K $^{+}$1

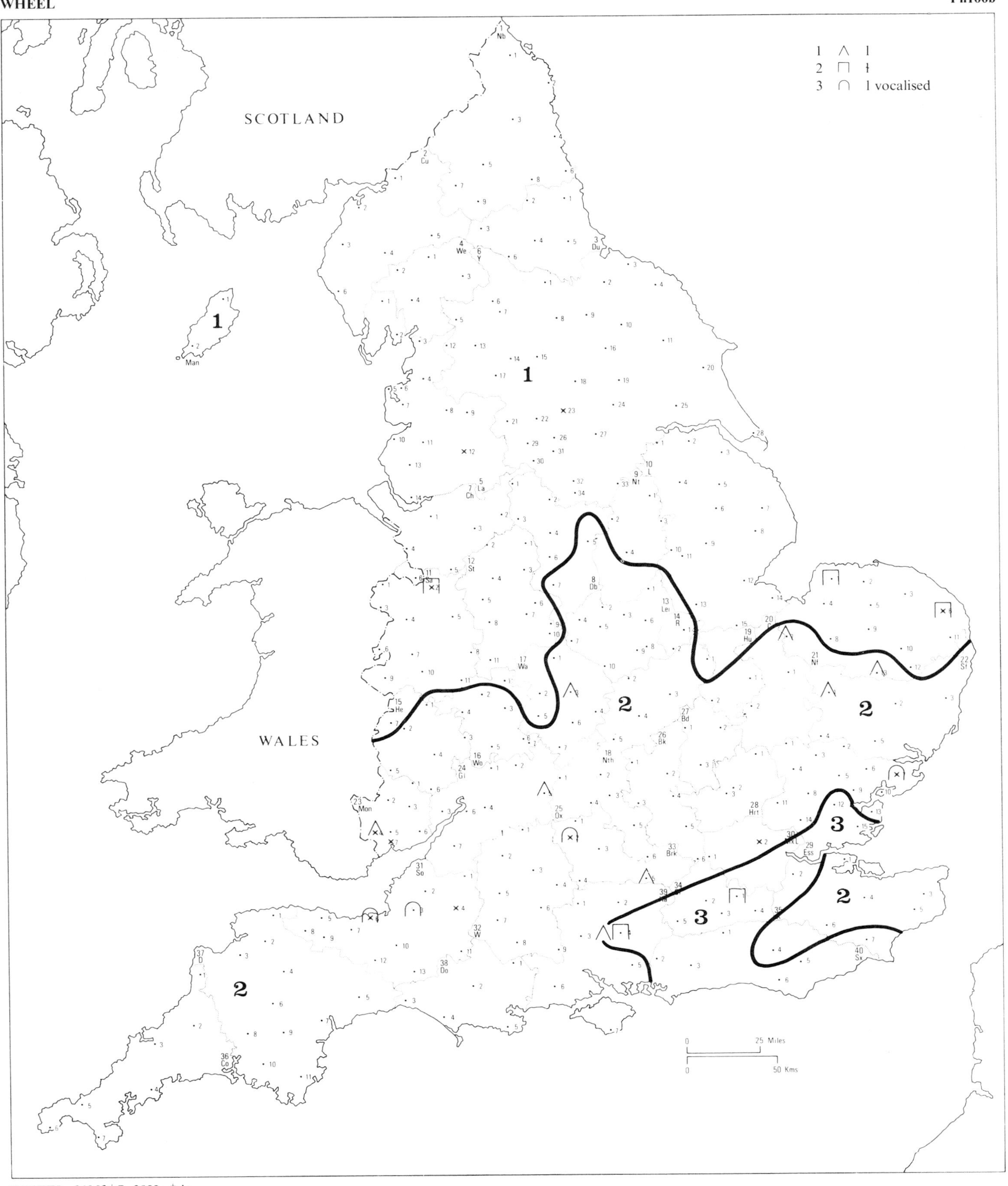

WHEEL- 21Nf $^{+}$7, 39Ha $^{+}$4;
-WHEEL 17Wa $^{+}$3, 21Nf $^{+}$13

+ V 24Gl $^{+}$5

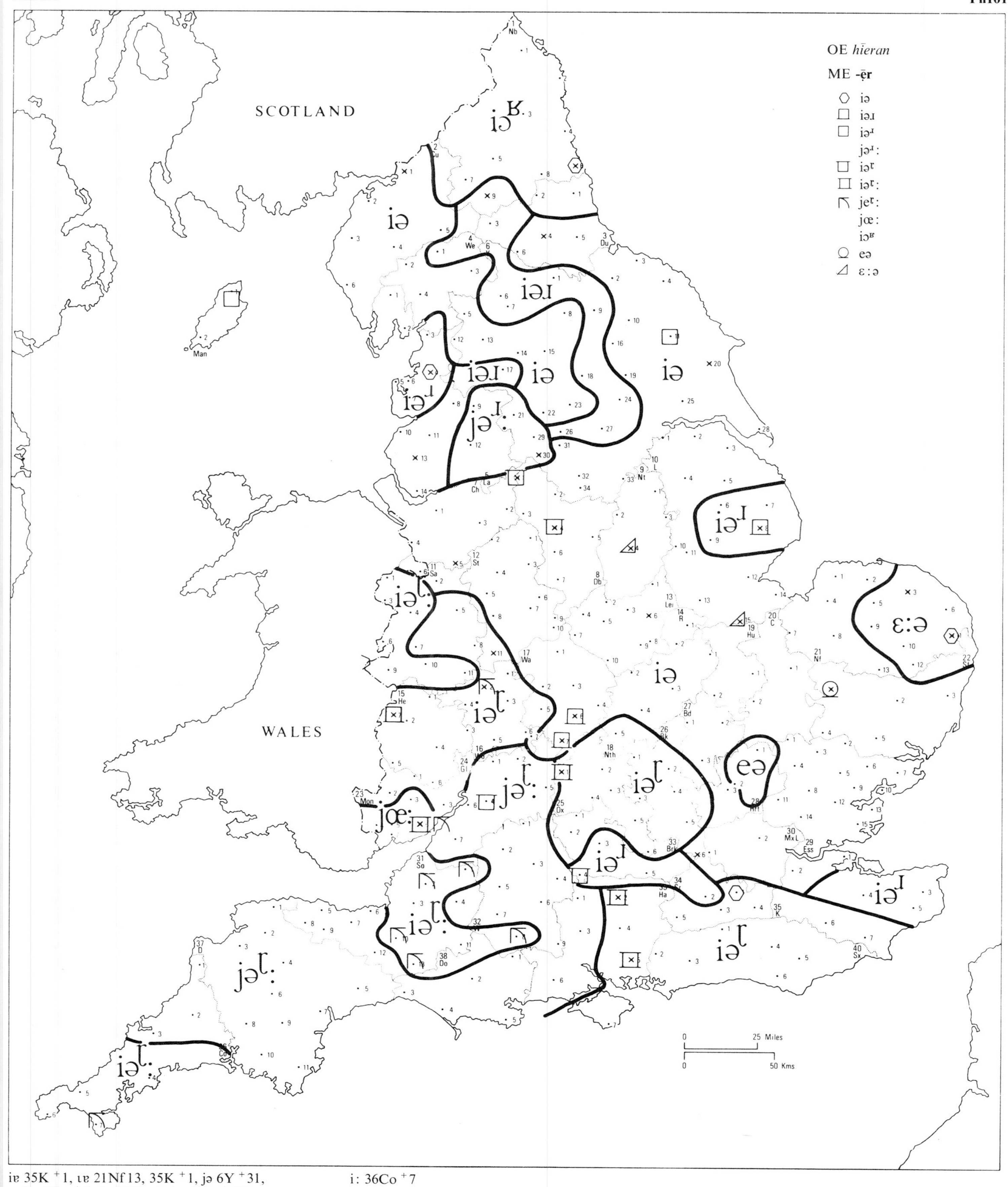

iɐ 35K +1, ɩɐ 21Nf 13, 35K +1, jə 6Y +31,
ëɩə 3Du +5, ᵊiə 28Hrt 3, ᵊɩə 3Du +5/6,
ɩ̯:ə 21Nf 11, ïi:ə 29Ess 15 under iə
jəɹ 6Y 26, 15He +7, ᵊɩəɹ 4We 1,
ᵊɩ˙əɹ 6Y 1 under iəɹ
jɩəʴ 33Brk +3/+4 under iəʴ
jɜ:ɹ 5La +12, jɜʴ:ɹ 5La 9/+12,
jəʴ 6Y 21 under jəʴ:
jəɽ 25Ox +4, jɩəɽɽ̤ 33Brk +4, 39Ha 7, 40Sx 3,
jɩəɽ 33Brk +2, ɩiəɽ 35K 6 under iəɽ
jœ̣:œ̣ (sic) 23Mon 5 under jœ:
ɛə 10L 15 under ɛ:ə

i: 36Co +7
iər 2Cu 1
ɩəʁ 1Nb 9
jɛɹ 6Y 30
eɩə Man 2
ɛɩə 7Ch 5; ëɩə 3Du 4
əʴ: 33Brk +5

interpr as *r*-col: ɹ 5La +12; ɽ 25Ox +4, 33Brk +2,
34Sr 3
cons *r* foll *r*-col V: ɹ 5La 9/+12, ɽ 32W 7,
33Brk +1/+2/+4, 34Sr 4, 39Ha 7, 40Sx 1–6

HEARS 1prsg 36Co +7, 1prpl 25Ox 1, 39Ha 1;
HEAR 2prpl 25Ox +4, 33Brk +1

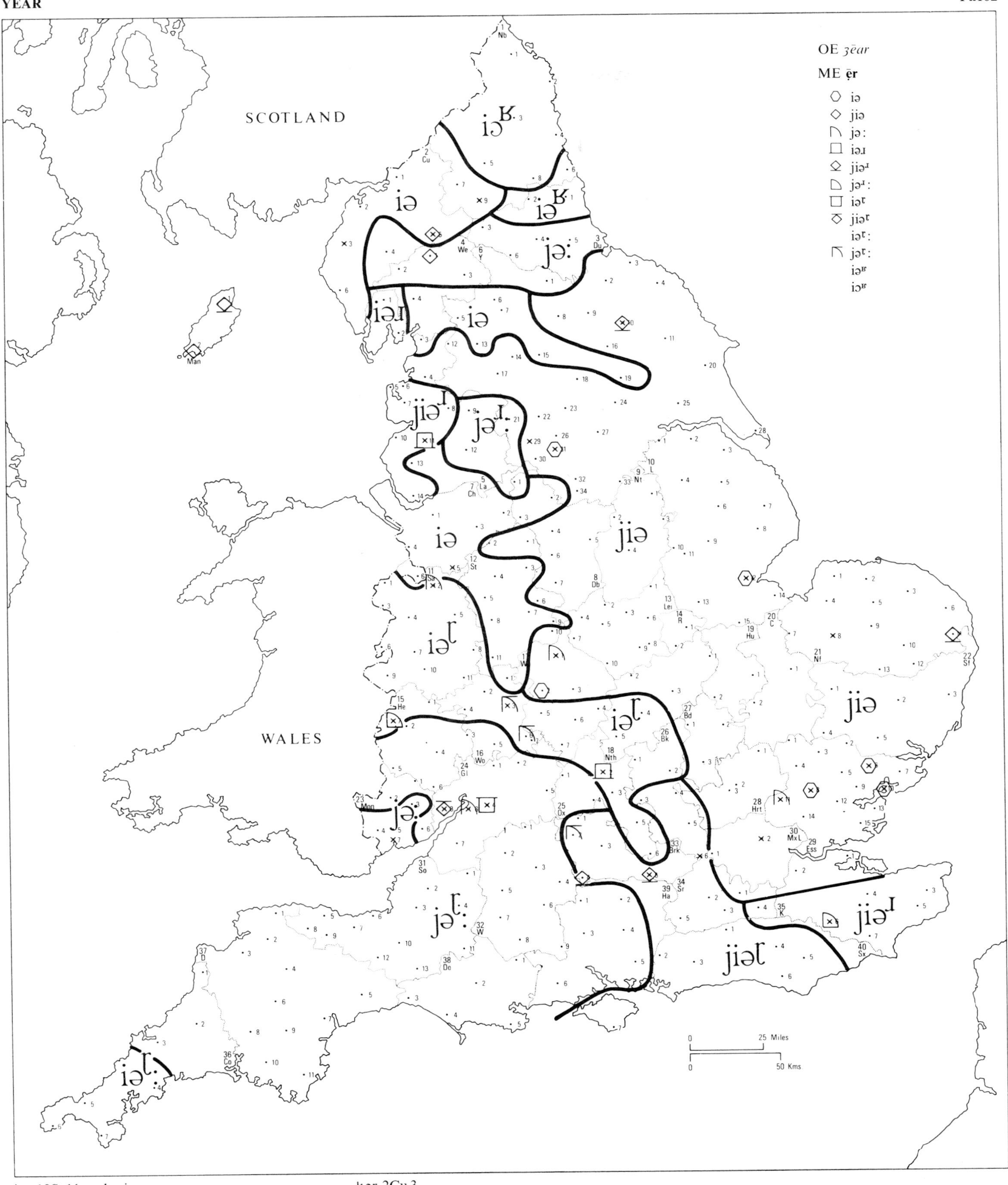

i:ə 12St 11 under iə
jɪɐ 29Ess 15, 35K 1, jïiə 29Ess 12,
  ji:ə 12St 1 under jiə
jə 23Mon 4, jɐ: 23Mon 5, jœ: 23Mon 3 under jə:
ɪəɹ 25Ox 2 under iəɹ
jɜɹ:ɹ 5La 9/12, jə˙ɹ 15He +7,
  jˡə˙ɹ 15He +7 under jəɹ:
i:əɽ 11Sa 4, i:əɽ˙ 11Sa 3 under iəɽ
jɪəɽ: 36Co 7 under iəɽ:
jəɽ 15He 5/6, 16Wo +7, 23Mon 1, 39Ha 4,
  jəɽ 25Ox 4 under jəɽ:
jɪəʁ 3Du 1 under iəʁ
jɪɔʁ 1Nb 2 under iɔʁ

ˡɪər 2Cu 3
jeə 1Nb 9
jɛɹ 6Y +30
ɛɪə 7Ch 5

interpr as *r*-col: ɹ 5La 8/10/14, 6Y 10, 15He 7,
  21Nf +11, ɽ 25Ox 4, 32W 7
cons *r* foll *r*-col V: ɹ 5La 9/12, ɽ 32W 3,
  33Brk +2/3/+4, 34Sr 2/3, 39Ha 7, 40Sx 1–4/6

TO-YEAR 6Y 10, 21Nf 5/6/+11

ʃɪə (after THIS) at 21Nf 1/2,
  29Ess 9/13 is taken to repr jiə.

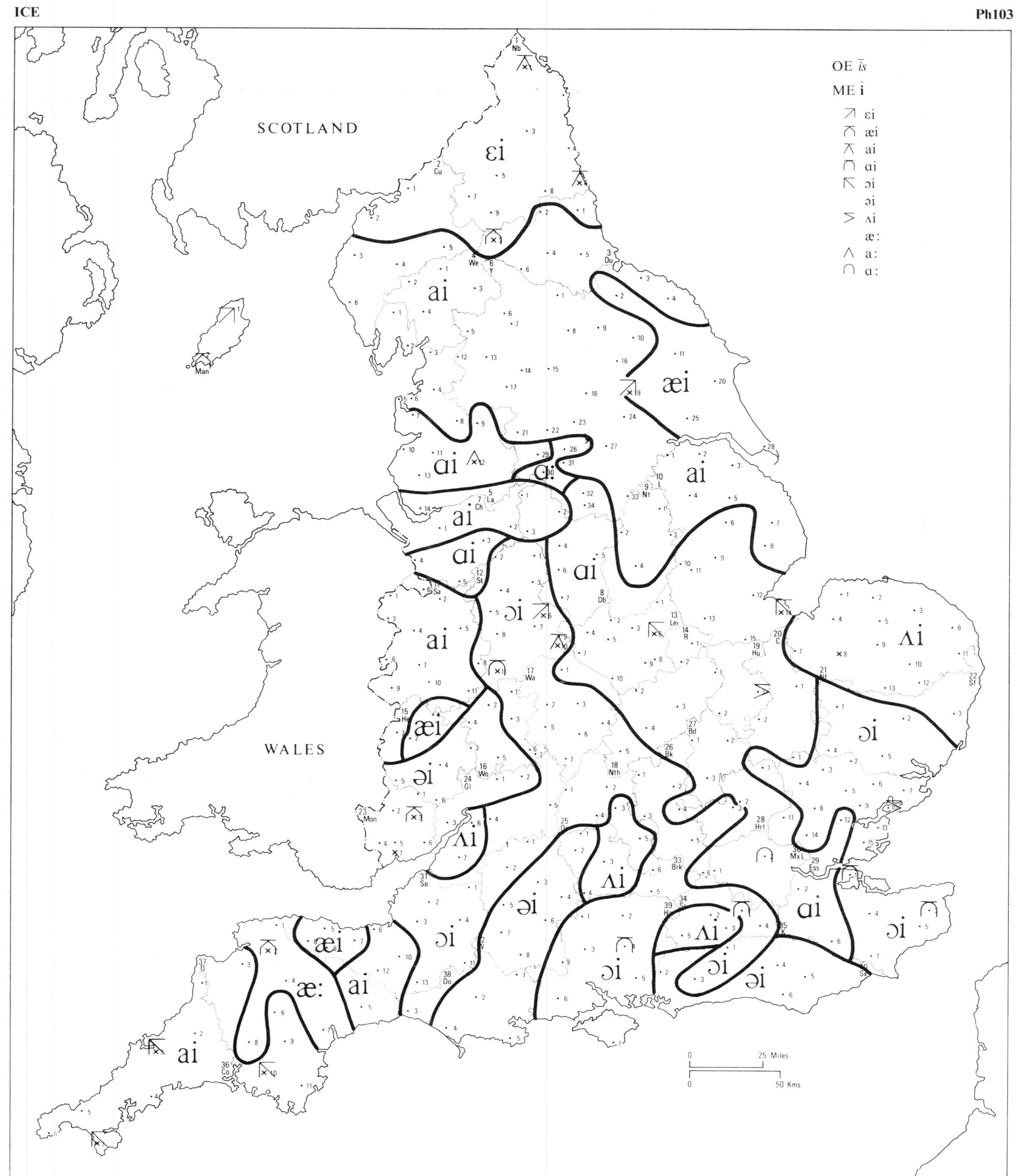

ɑ̂:ɩ 12St 11 under ai
ɒ:ɩ 12St 3/5 under ɔi
ʌ̈ʏ 19Hu 1 (according to informant used by father, native), ʌʏ 25Ox 3/5 under ʌi

ICE- 30MxL +2

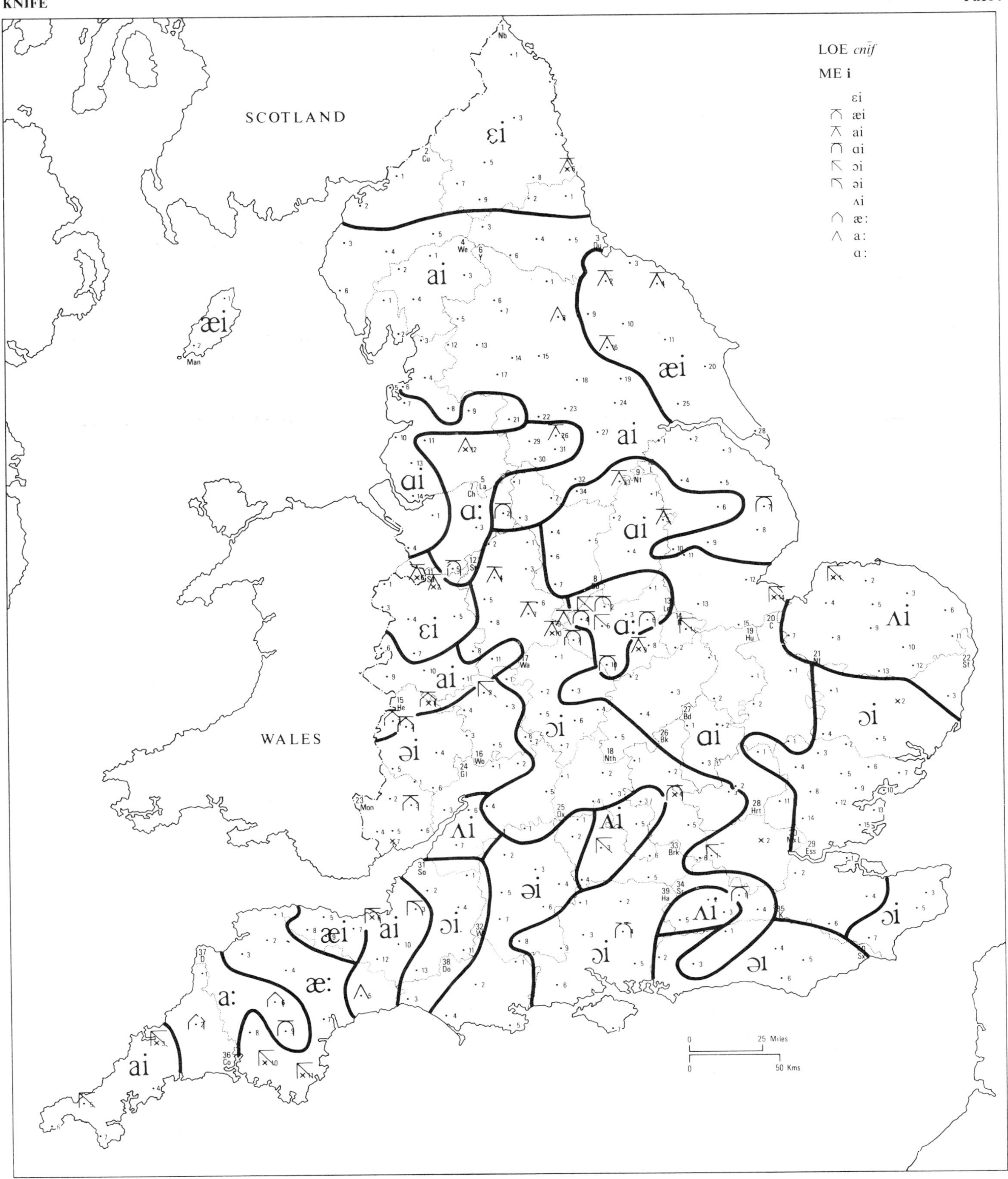

ɛɪ: 11Sa 4 under ɛi
aːɪ 12St +10/+11 under ai
ɑːɪ 37D +9 under ɑi
ɒːɪ 12St 3/5/6 under ɔi
əi: 16Wo 3 under əi
ʌʏ 25Ox 5 under ʌi

eɪ Man +2

-KNIFE 4We 1, 6Y +4/6/+16/30/32, 7Ch +2,
10L +7, 12St +11, 15He +7,
21Nf 1/3/4/8/9/13, 30MxL +1
KNIVES pl 6Y +8, 13Lei +2/+6

-v 36Co 1/2, 37D 1–3/+5/6, 38Do +3

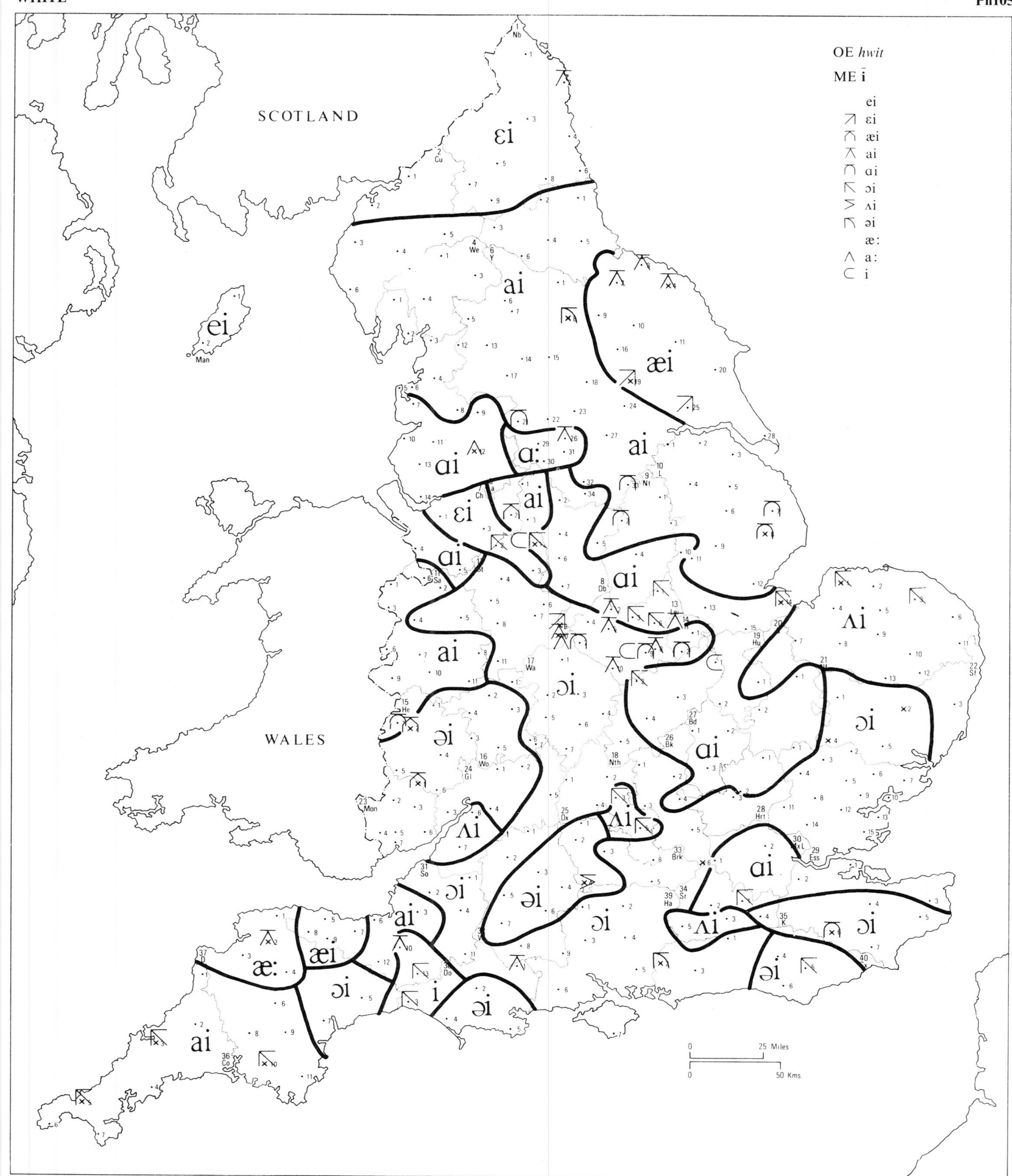

ɔɪ^{ə} 22Sf 5, ɒɪ^{ə} 11Sa $^+$5, ɒ:ɪ 12St 5 under ɔi
ʌʏ 25Ox 3/$^+$5, ʌ̆ʏ 19Hu 1 under ʌi
əɪ^{ə} 24Gl 1 under əi
i: 38Do $^+$3 under i

ɑ: 13Lei $^+$1/$^+$9

WHITE- 13Lei $^+$9, 18Nth $^+$1, 21Nf 8,
31So $^+$13, 38Do $^+$1

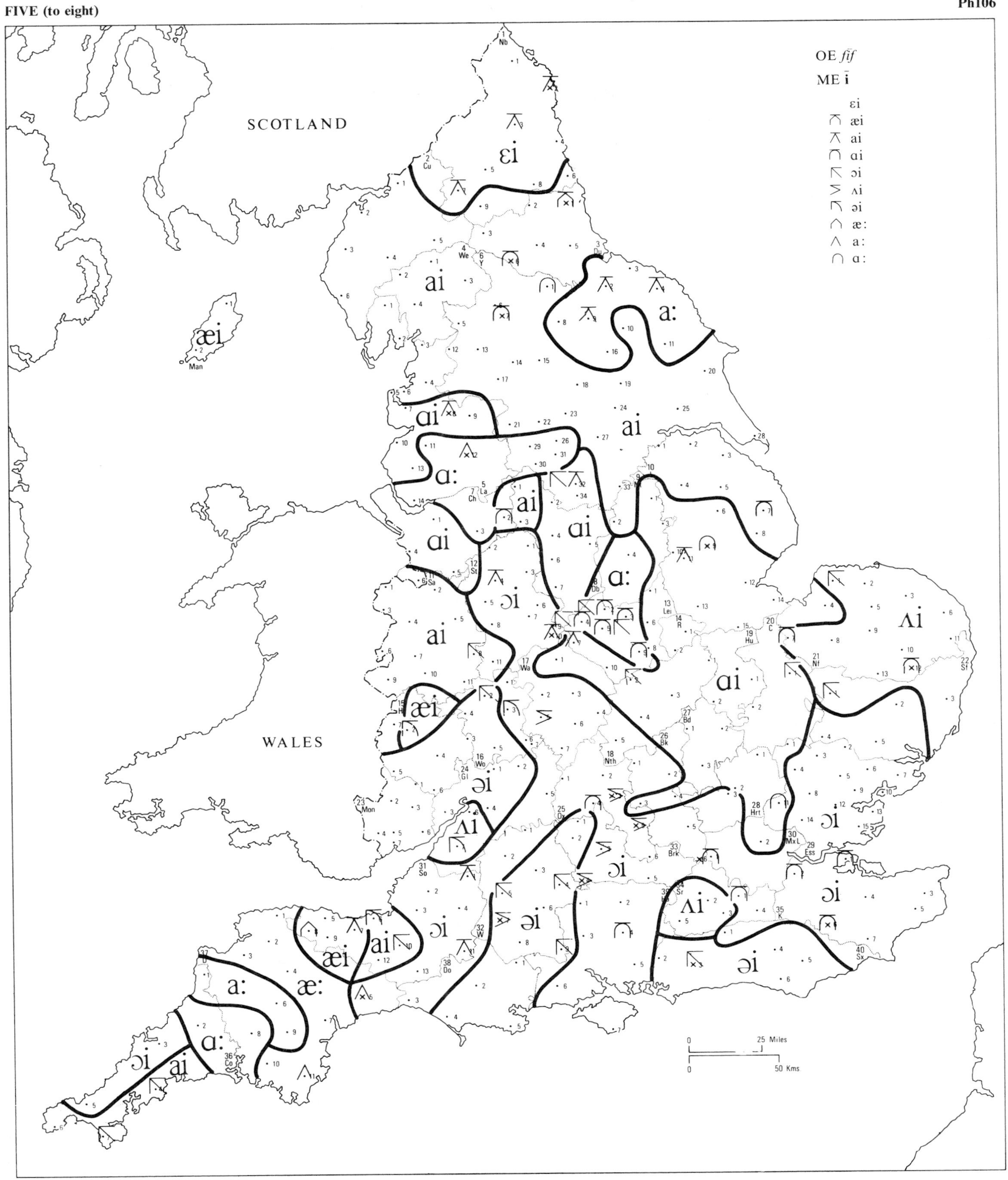

a:ɩ 12St +10/11 under ai
ɒ:ɩ 12St 3/6, ɒɩᵊ 16Wo +3 under ɔi
ʌʏ 25Ox 3/5 under ʌi
əi: 16Wo +3, əɩᵊ 15He +5, 16Wo +2/+5.
24Gl 1/+2–+4 under əi

ɩ 35K +1
eɩ 31So +7

FIVE- 31So +7; FIVE n 24Gl +7

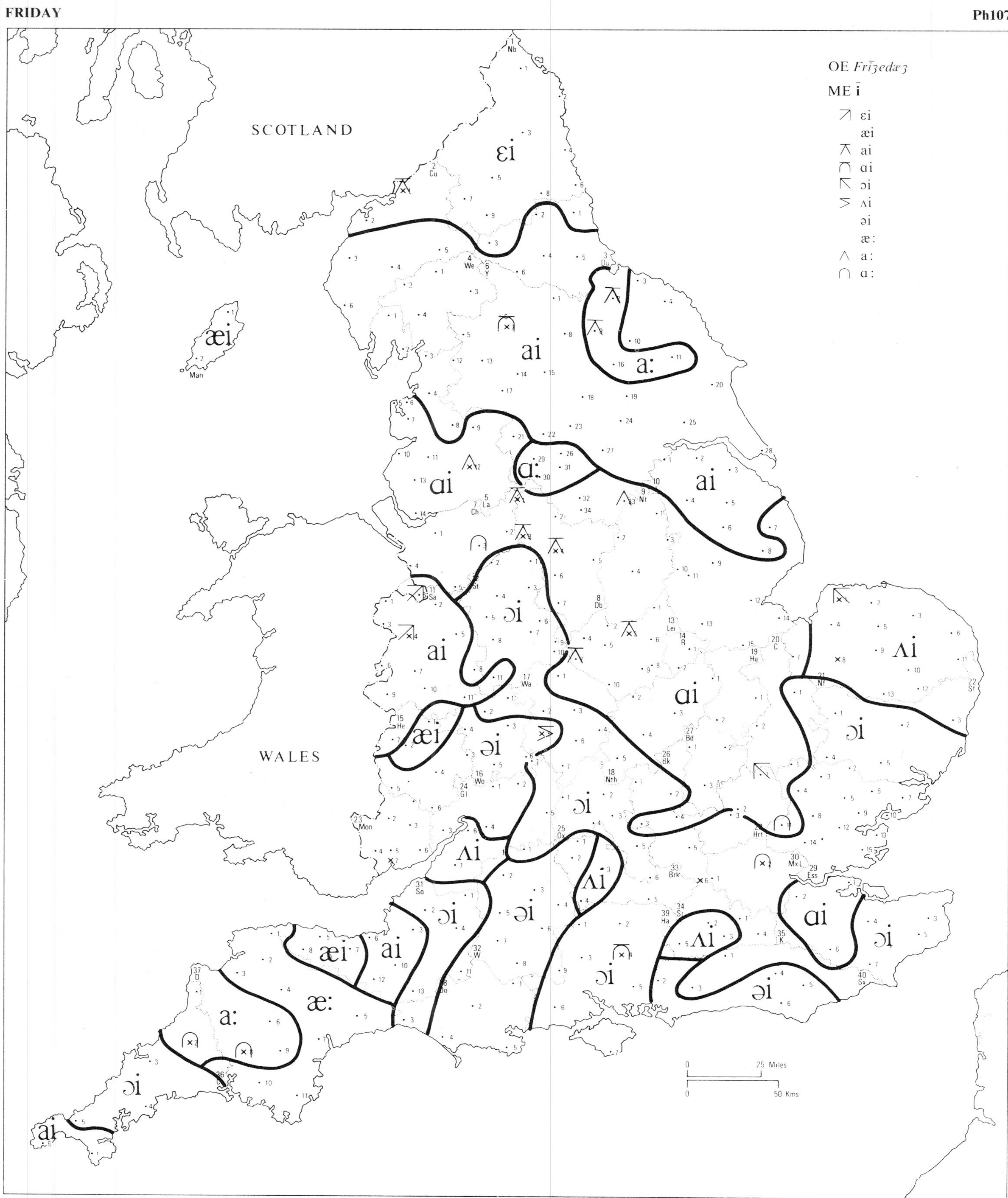

a̱:ɩ 12St 11 under ai
ɒ:ɩ 12St 3/5, ɒ̣:ɩ 12St 6 under ɔi

əi: 16Wo 3/6 under əi

31So ⁺3 gɷd fɽɒ̈di (? fw's error for fɽɒ̈ɩdi Edd)

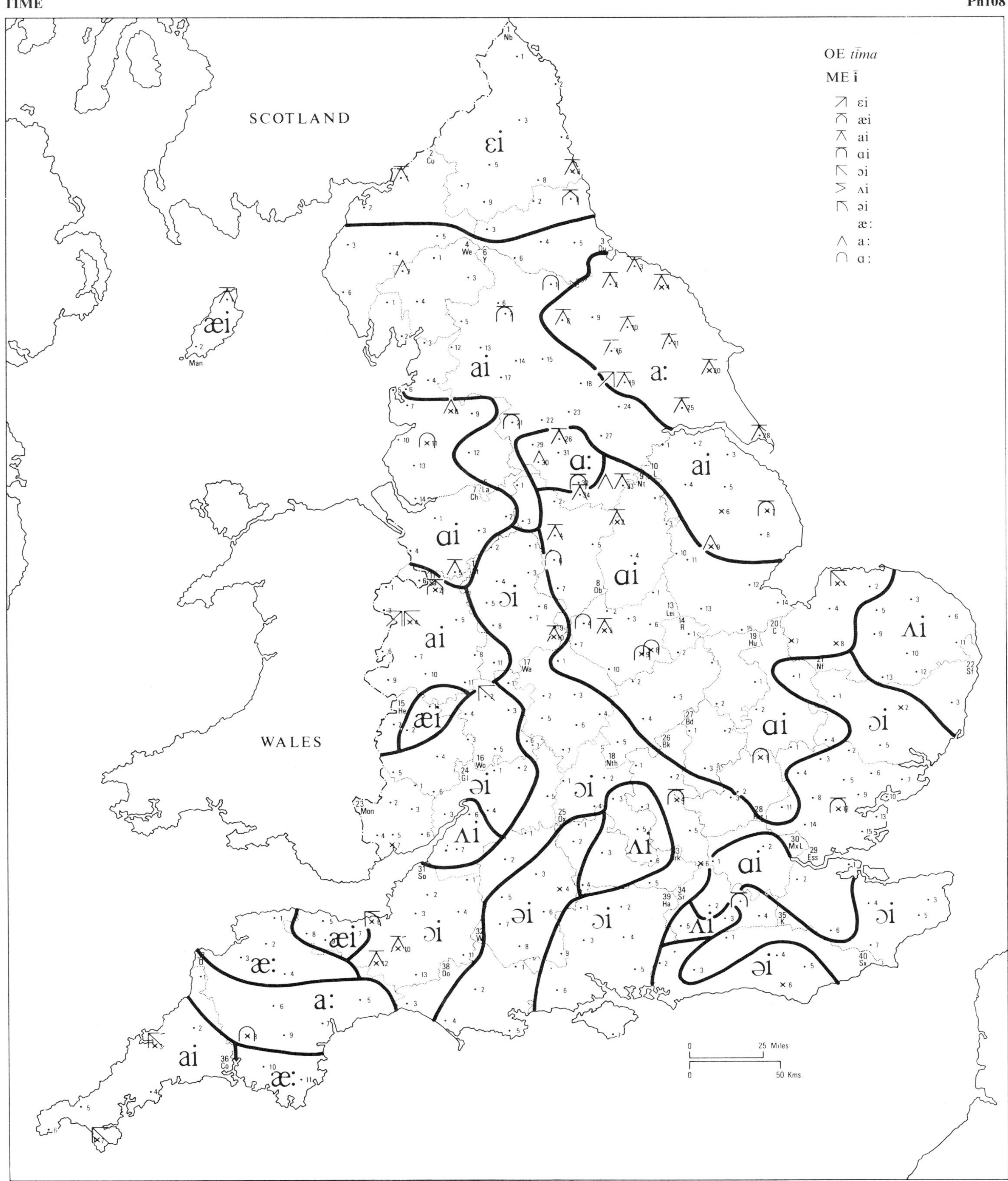

a:ɩ 12St +10, a̠:ɩ 12St 11, a:ᶥ 6Y +8/+11 under ai
ɑɩᵊ 18Nth 1, ɑ:ᶥ 7Ch +4 under ɑi
ɔɩᵊ 22Sf 5, ɒɩᵊ 16Wo +1, ɒ:ɩ 12St 3/5/6 under ɔi
ʌʏ 25Ox 3/5/6 under ʌi
əɩᵊ 24Gl 1, əi:ᵊ 16Wo 3 under əi
ɑ:ᵊ 28Hrt 1 under ɑ:

i: (sic) 1Nb +5
eɩ 32W 4, eɩ Man +1

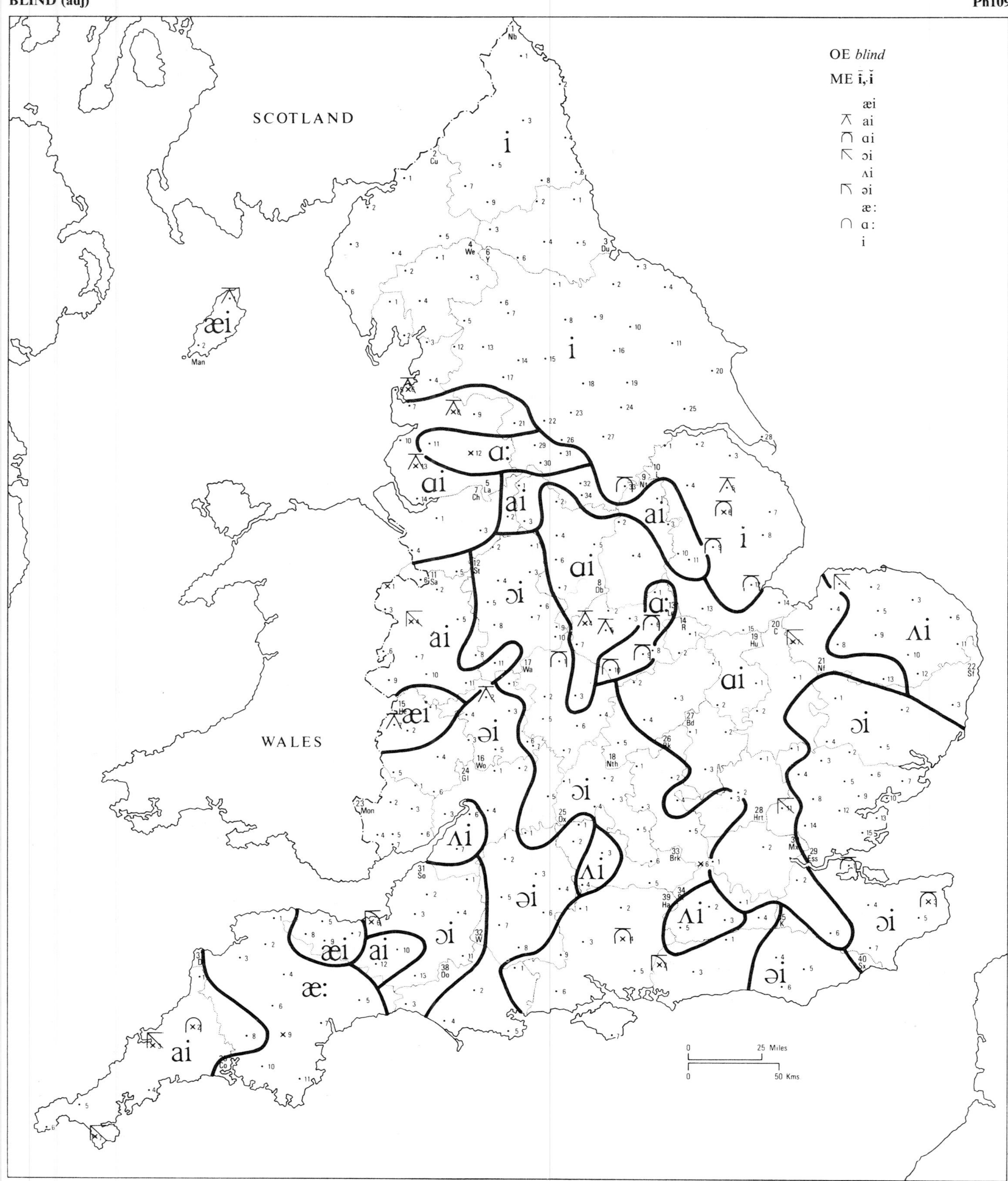

ɑ̈:ɩ 35K $^{+}$1 under ɑi
ɔ̣ɩ^{ə} 22Sf 2, ɒɩ^{ə} 16Wo 6, ɒ:ɩ 12St 3/5,
 ɒ̣:ɩ 12St 6 under ɔi
əi: 16Wo 3, əɩ^{ə} 16Wo $^{+}$2, 24Gl 1/$^{+}$4 under əi

a: 5La 12, 37D 9
ɛɩ 11Sa 1, 36Co $^{+}$2

BLIND- Man $^{+}$1, 15He $^{+}$7, 21Nf $^{+}$1, 29Ess $^{+}$11;
 -BLINDS n 16Wo $^{+}$2;
 BLINDING prp 17Wa $^{+}$1

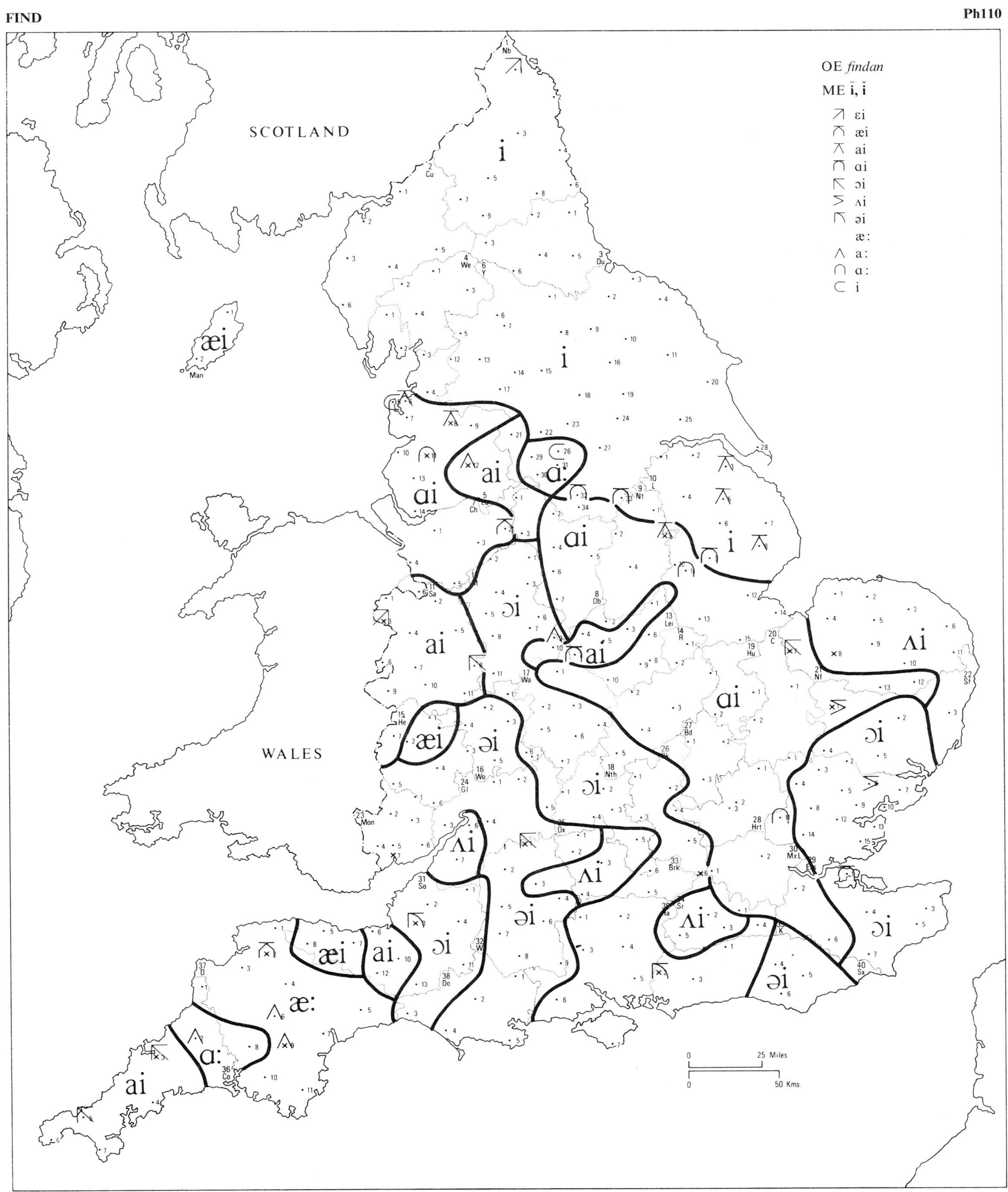

ɒ:ɩ 12St 3/5/6 under ɔi
ʌʏ 25Ox 5 under ʌi
əi: 16Wo 3, əɩ^{ə} 24Gl 1 under əi

FINDING prp 1Nb $^{+}$1

fɩn, fɷn ("older, but not used") 13Lei $^{+}$3

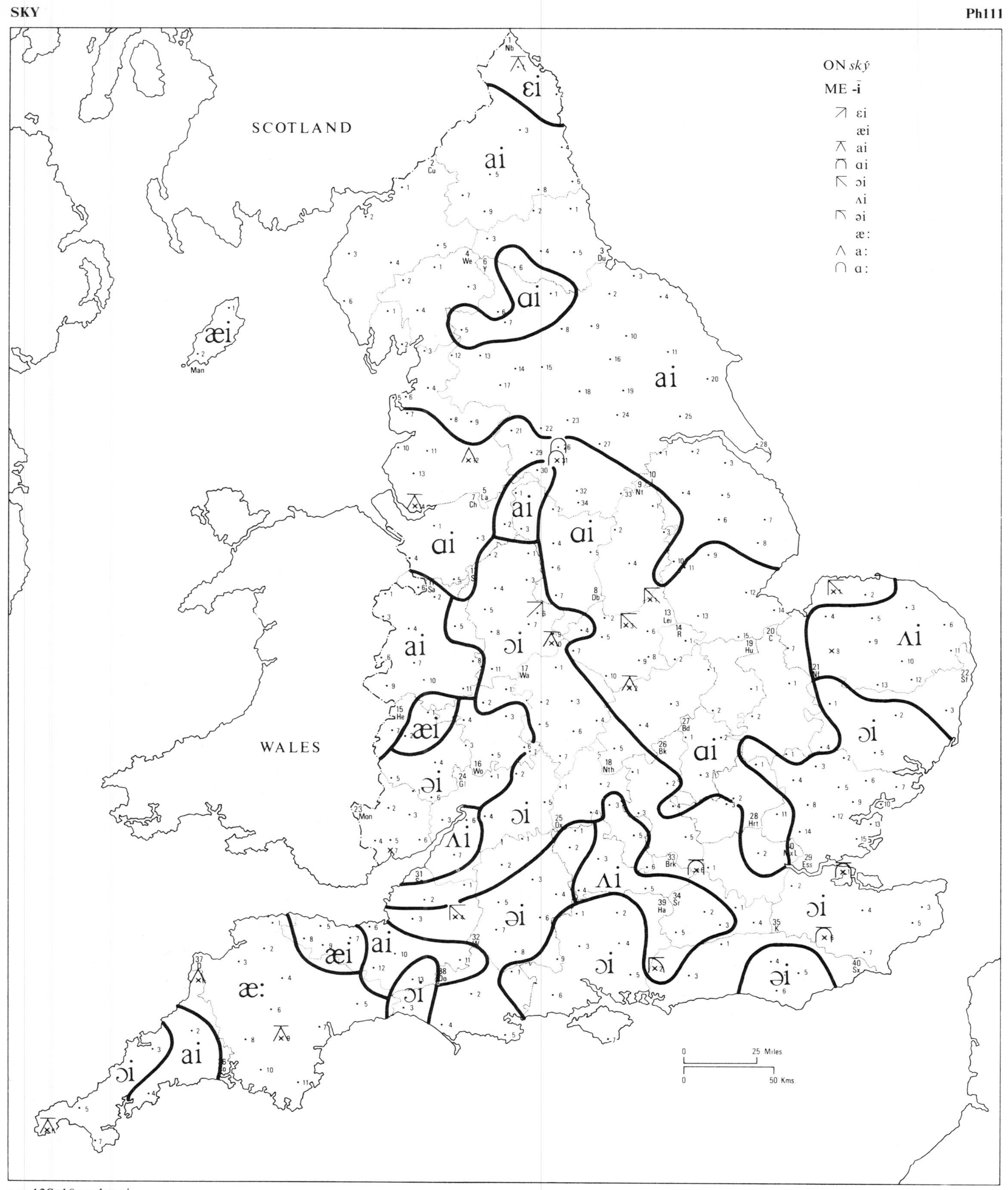

aːɩ 12St 10 under ai
ɑːɩ 13Lei 8 under ɑi
ɒːɩ 12St 3/5/+6 under ɔi
ʌʏ 25Ox 3/5 under ʌi
əiː 16Wo 3/6 under əi

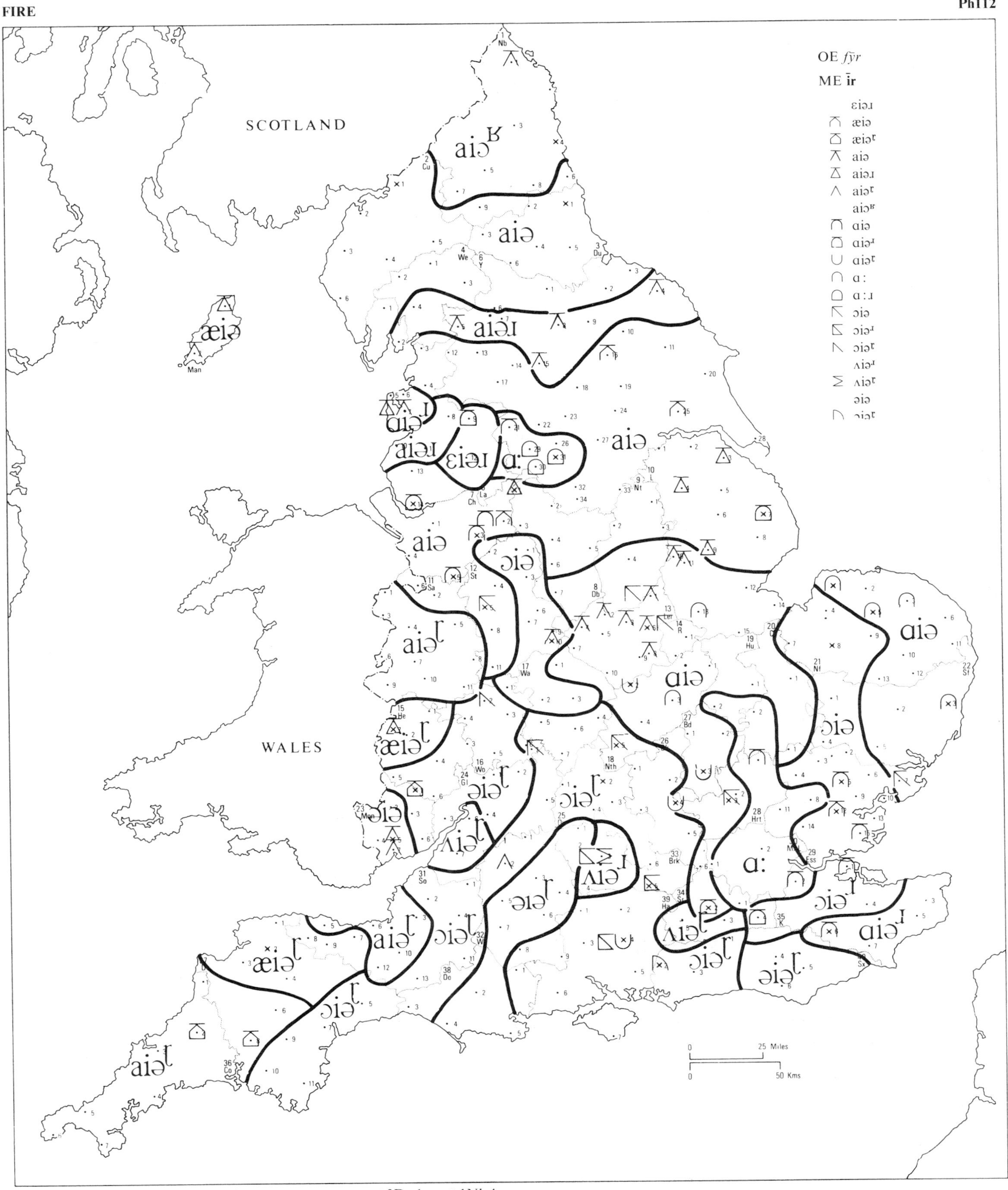

æɩəʵ: 31So 7–9, 36Co +2, 37D 1/3/4/+8 under æiəʵ
a:ɩə 12St +10/11 under aiə
aɩəʴ 5La +7, Man +1, 10L +3/+9,
aɩəʴ 8Db 1 under aiəɹ
aɩəʵ: 31So 5/6/10/12, 32W +2, 36Co 1/+2/3–7,
37D 6/+8, äɩəʵ: 31So 3 under aiəʵ
äɩɐ 35K +1, ɑ:ɩə 21Nf 13, ɑ:ˈə 29Ess 5 under ɑiə
ɑ:ᵊ 20C 2, 21Nf 1, 28Hrt +1, 30MxL 2,
ɑ:ə 19Hu 2, 21Nf 5, 22Sf +3, 29Ess 8,
ɑˑə 10L +13, 21Nf +3 under ɑ:
ɑ̣ɹ 6Y +30, ɑʴ: 6Y +29 under ɑ:ɹ
ɒ:ɩə 12St +3/6 under ɔiə
ɒɩəʵ: 31So +1/2/4/11/13, 32W 1/+2/8/9,
37D 5/7/9–11, 38Do 1/3,
39Ha 1–3/5/6 under ɔiəʵ
əɩəʵ: 32W 3–7, 38Do 2/4/5,
əi:əʵ 16Wo 3 under əiəʵ

ɛɩəʶ 3Du 1, ɛɩɔʶ 1Nb 4
æɩəʴ 6Y +20, Man +2, æ̩ɩəʴ 6Y +20, æ:əʵ: 37D 2
aɩr (sic) 2Cu 1
ɑʵ: 34Sr +1, ɑʵˑ 34Sr +1, ɑɩʴ 6Y +21, ɑ:ɩʴ 6Y +21
ɒ:ɩəɹ 12St +3
ɔ:ɹ 6Y +30, ɔ̆ɩ (sic) 25Ox 2, ɔɩɽ 25Ox +4
ə: (sic) 16Wo +7, əʵ: 34Sr +3, əʵ 34Sr +3,
əɩəʴ 35K +6

interpr as *r*-col: ɹ 5La +9/14, 10L 7, ɽ 25Ox +4
cons *r* foll *r*-col V: ɽ 33Brk +3, 39Ha 7, 40Sx +1/+2

FIRE- 6Y +21, Man +2, 10L +3/+13, 12St +10,
13Lei +4, 16Wo +2, 28Hrt +1, 29Ess +7,
34Sr +3, 39Ha +4; -FIRE 34Sr +3, 35K +2;
FIRE v 29Ess +15; FIRED 6Y +25;
FIRES 3prsg 10L +4, 18Nth +3, 33Brk +3;
AFIRE 6Y +15, 32W +2, 36Co +2

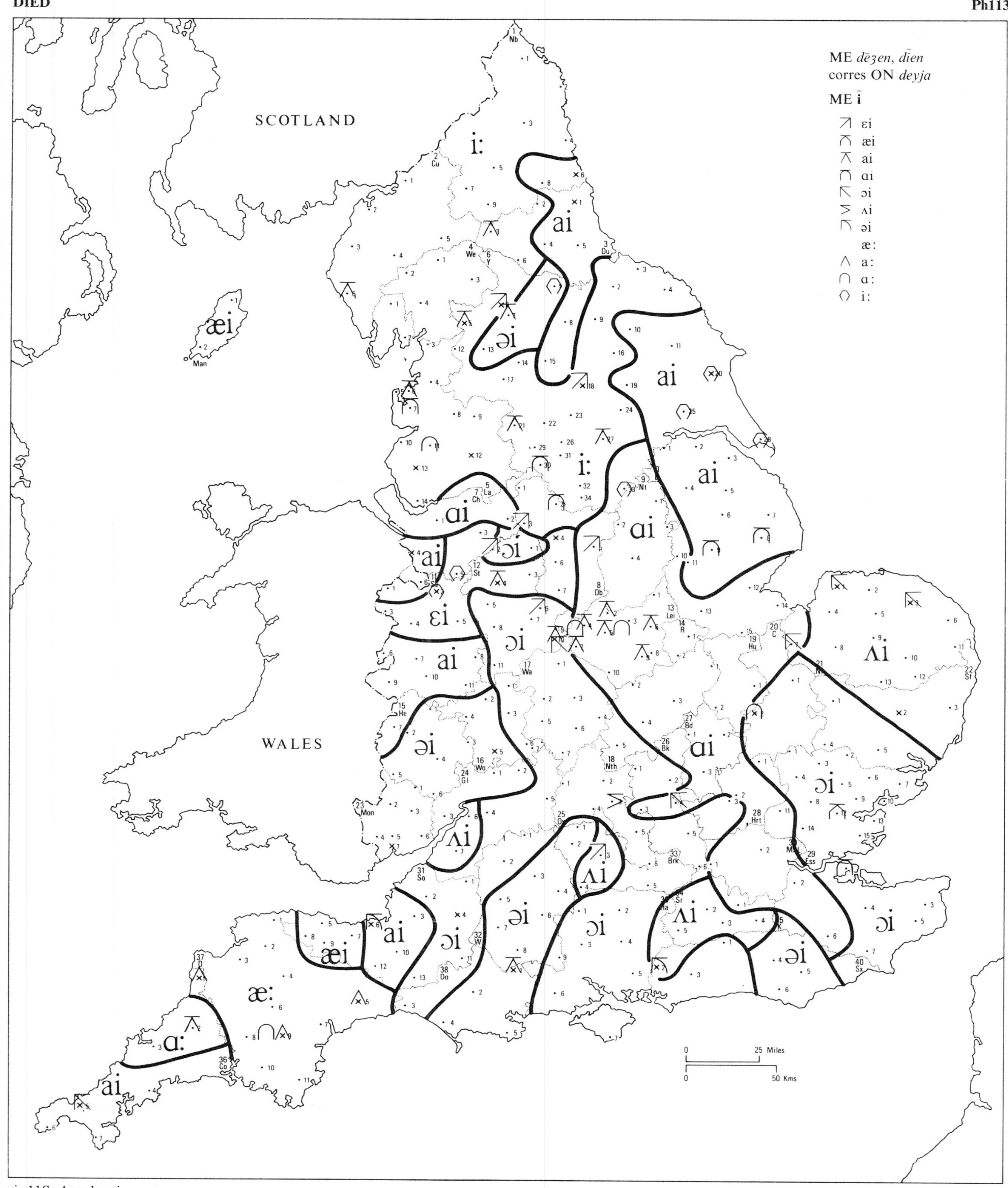

εi: 11Sa 4 under εi
ai: 11Sa $^{+}$10, a:ɩ 12St 10 under ai
ɒ:ɩ 12St 5/$^{+}$6/11 under ɔi
ʌ̣:ɩ 21Nf 5, ʌʏ 25Ox 3 under ʌi
ɑ:ᵊ 20C 2 under ɑ:
ᵊi: 4We $^{+}$1 under i:

ᶥω 16Wo 5
ɩə 5La $^{+}$1

DIE inf 8Db $^{+}$3, 12St $^{+}$6, 36Co $^{+}$2; pt 33Brk $^{+}$3;
v 5La $^{+}$11, 6Y $^{+}$21/$^{+}$28, 10L $^{+}$8;
DIED 3 ptpl 25Ox $^{+}$3; pp 7Ch $^{+}$5, 11Sa $^{+}$10,
12St $^{+}$2; pt 2Cu $^{+}$6, 5La $^{+}$7,
6Y $^{+}$21/$^{+}$30/$^{+}$33, 10L $^{+}$9, 13Lei $^{+}$2/$^{+}$4–$^{+}$7/$^{+}$9,
26Bk $^{+}$4; DYING prp 6Y $^{+}$1, 10L $^{+}$9,
29Ess $^{+}$12

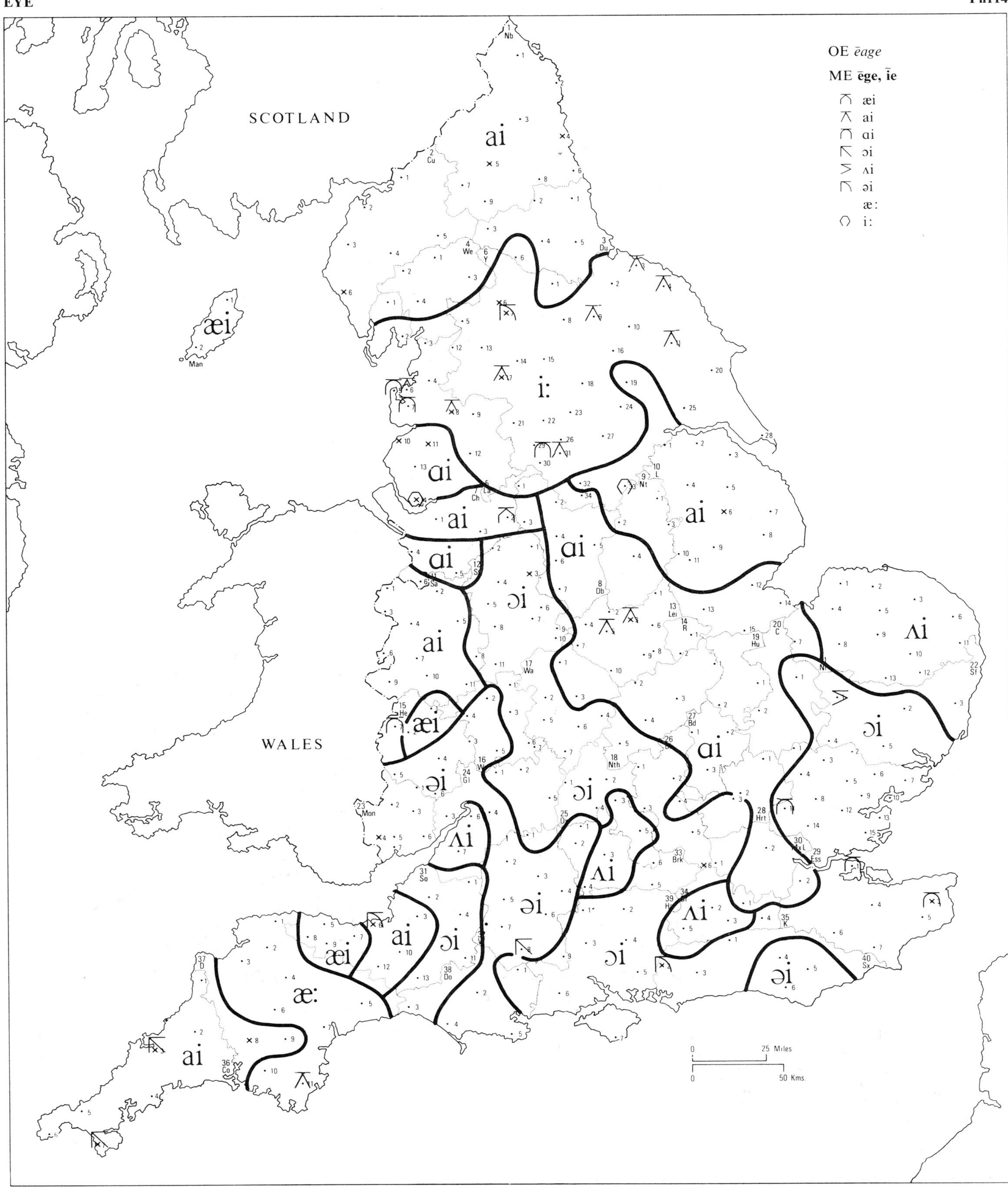

ai: 11Sa 10 under ai
ọ:ɩ 12St 10, ɒ:ɩ 12St 5/6 under ɔi
ʌʏ 25Ox 3/5 under ʌi
əij 23Mon 5 under əi

eij 23Mon 4
ɛɩ 12St 3, ẹɩ 6Y 6
ɑ: 5La 11, 37D 8

i:n 1Nb 4/5/$^{+}$9, 2Cu 6, 5La 10/$^{+}$12, 6Y $^{+}$17

EYE- 6Y $^{+}$3, 7Ch $^{+}$2, 15He $^{+}$7, 29Ess $^{+}$11, 37D $^{+}$11

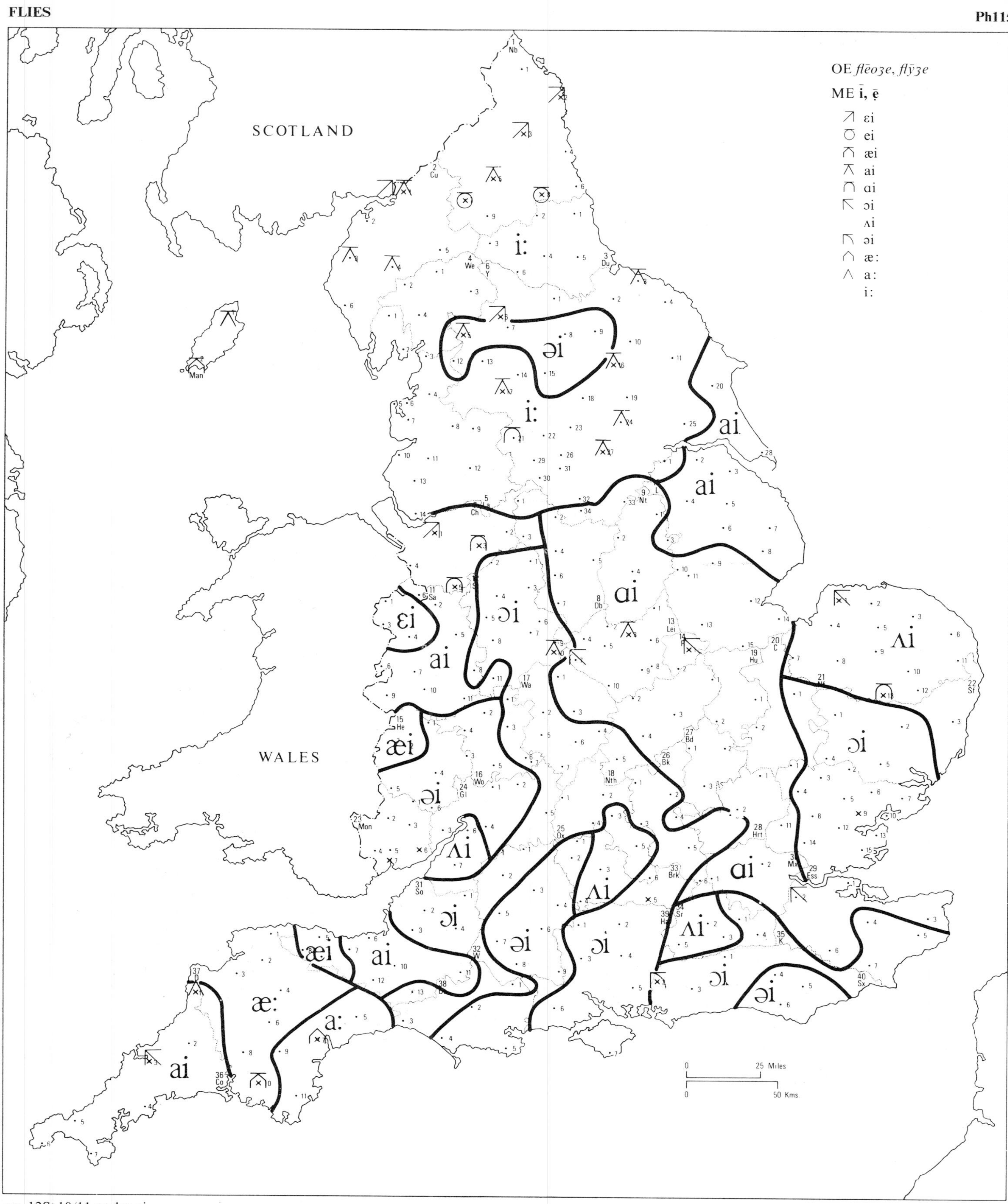

a:ɩ 12St 10/11 under ai
ɑ:ɩ 13Lei 6 under ɑi
ɒɩə 16Wo 1, ɒ:ɩ 12St 3/5/6 under ɔi
ʌʏ 25Ox 3/5 under ʌi
əɩə 24Gl 1 under əi

ǫɩ 29Ess 9

-FLIES 1Nb 3/4, 6Y 9/15/30, 10L 1/2/11, 21Nf 5/8, 31So 6, 35K 1/$^{+}$2; FLY sg 1Nb 2/7, 5La 12, 25Ox 6, 29Ess 12, 30MxL 1/2, 37D 11, 40Sx 3; FLY- 6Y $^{+}$21; -FLY 1Nb 7, 29Ess 12, 37D 11

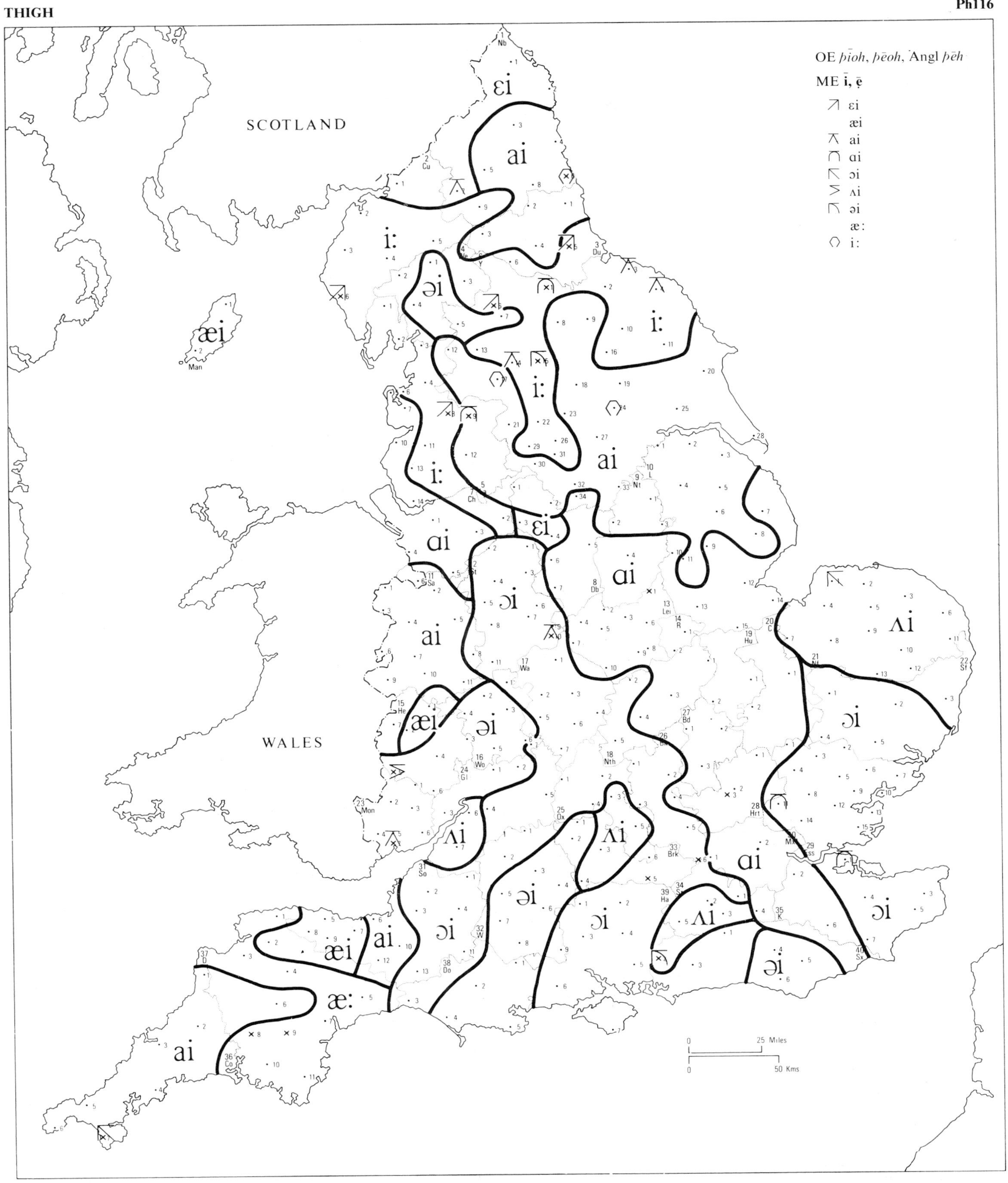

ë̞ɩ 3Du 5 under ɛi
a:ɩ 12St 10 under ai
ɒ:ɩ 12St 3/5/6 under ɔi
ʌʏ 25Ox 3/5 under ʌi
əi: 16Wo 3 under əi

a: 37D 9
ɑ: 37D 8
ɩx 6Y +21 ("used 40 years ago")

THIGH- 21Nf +1; THIGHS pl 29Ess +11

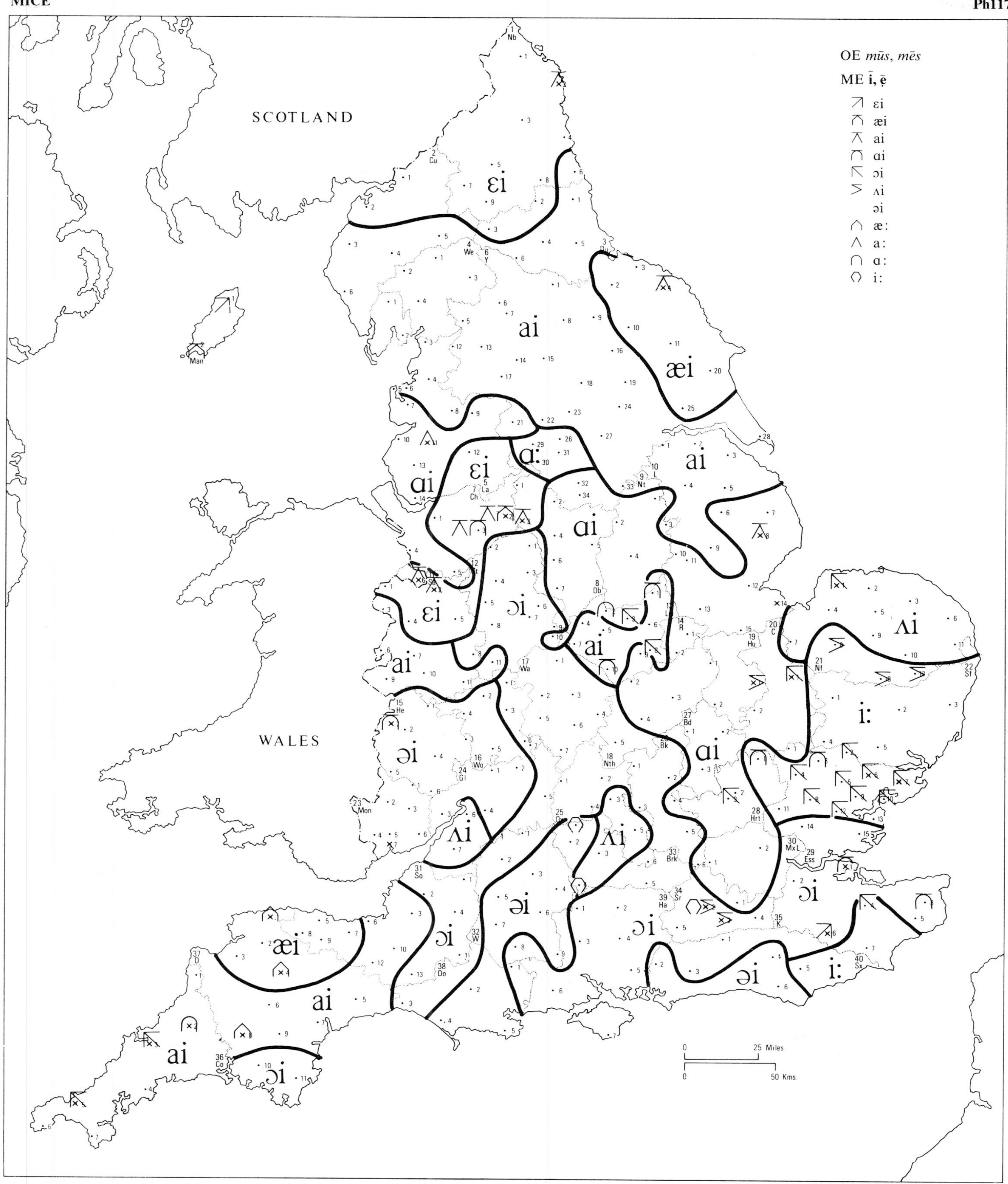

a:^{ɩ} 6Y 8, ai: 11Sa 11 under ai
ɑ:ɩ 12St 10 under ɑi
ɒ:ɩ 12St 3/5/6, ɒi: 16Wo 3, ^{w}ɒɩ 39Ha 5 under ɔi
ʌʏ 25Ox 3/5, ʌ̈ʏ 19Hu 1 under ʌi
^{ə}i: 22Sf $^+$4, ɩ 29Ess 11 under i:

ẹɩ Man 1

-MICE 13Lei $^+$8/$^+$10

double pl mɩəsɩz 6Y $^+$19, mu:sɩz 10L $^+$3,
maɷsɩz 10L $^+$9, mɑˑɩsɩz 14R $^+$1,
mi:sɩz 29Ess $^+$1, mæɷzi:z 31So $^+$13,
mʌɷsɩz 33Brk $^+$4, mæ̈ɤzɩz 36Co $^+$1, 37D $^+$3,
maɩsɩz 36Co $^+$7

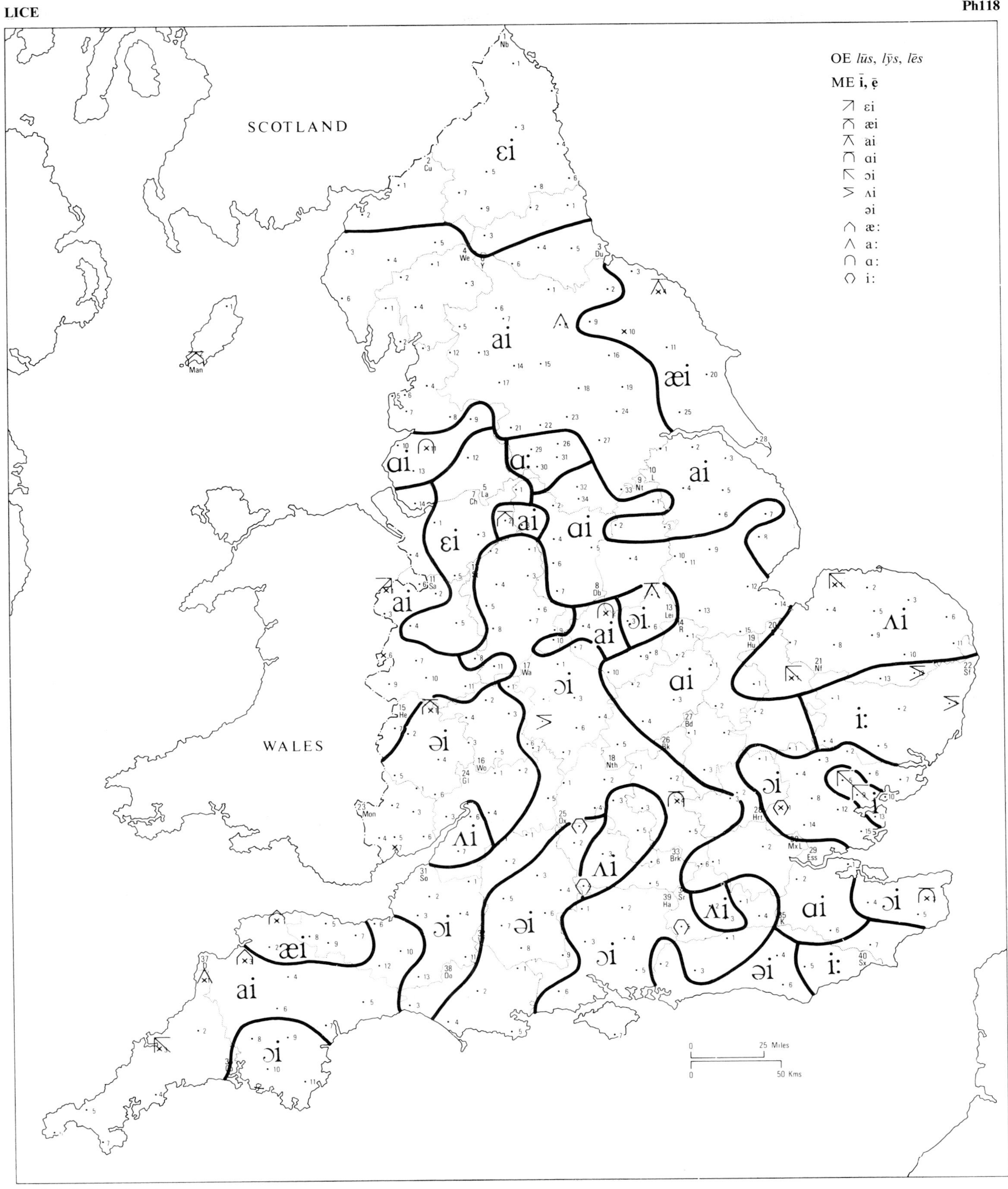

a:ɩ 12St 10/11 under ai
ɒ:ɩ 12St 3/5/6 under ɔi
ʌʏ 25Ox 3/5, ʌ̈ʏ 19Hu 1 under ʌi
əi: 16Wo 3 under əi

ẹ: 7Ch +1
ẹɩ Man 1

-LICE 6Y +8

double pl laɷ:zəz 11Sa 6, li:sɩz 29Ess +1

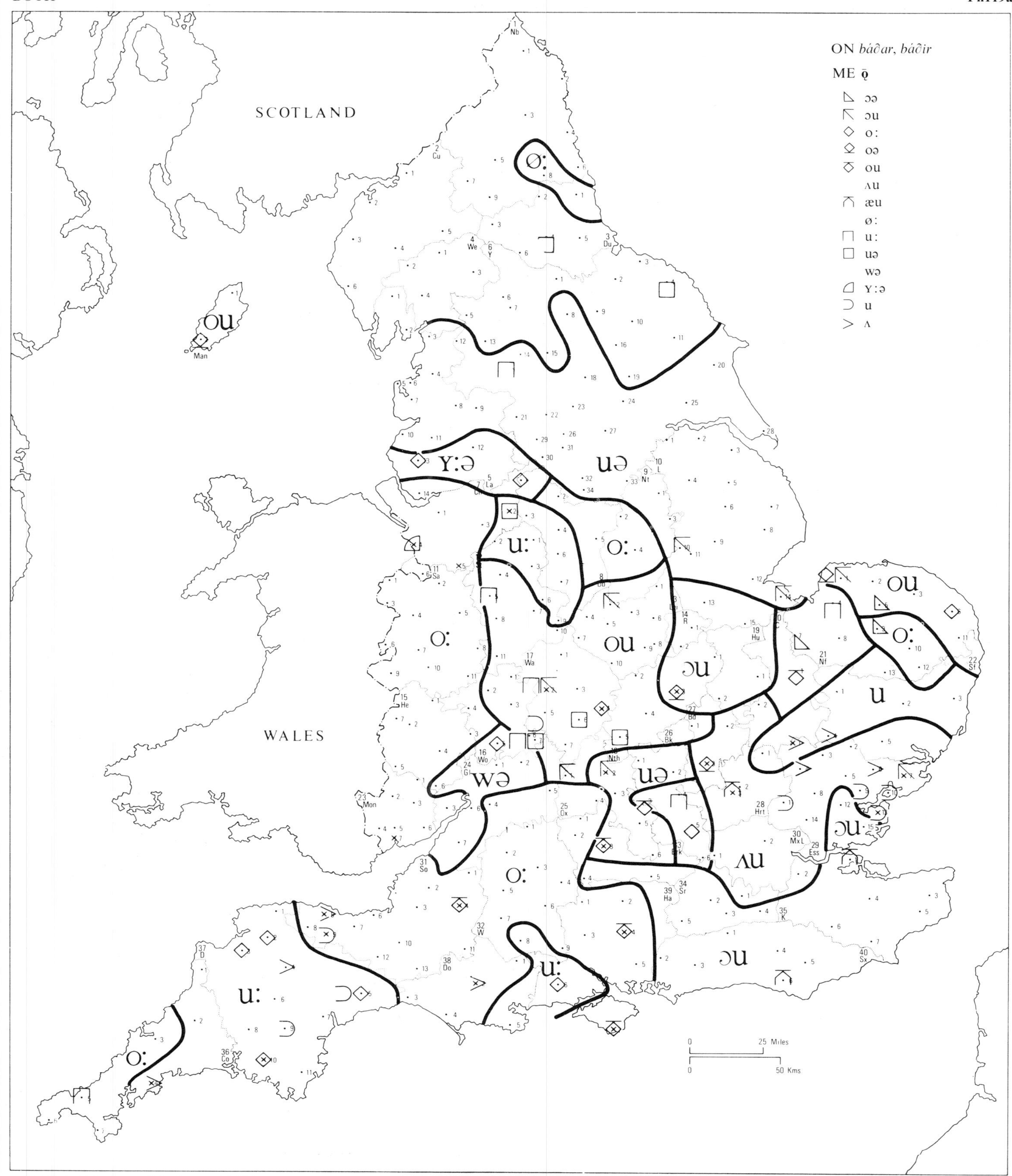

o:^{ə} 7Ch 6, 11Sa 4, ǫ:^{ə} 7Ch 1, o:ə 24Gl 4,
ọ:ə 17Wa 4, o:^{ɷ} 8Db 5, o:ɷ 23Mon 1, 24Gl 3,
ọ 21Nf $^{+}$6/10/$^{+}$12 under o:
əɷ 30MxL $^{+}$2 under ʌu
ø^{ə} 3Du 1 under ø:
wɷ 16Wo $^{+}$5, ^{w}ɷ 24Gl $^{+}$1 under wə

ɛɷə 7Ch 5
ɑɷ 29Ess $^{+}$15
ɔ 10L $^{+}$14

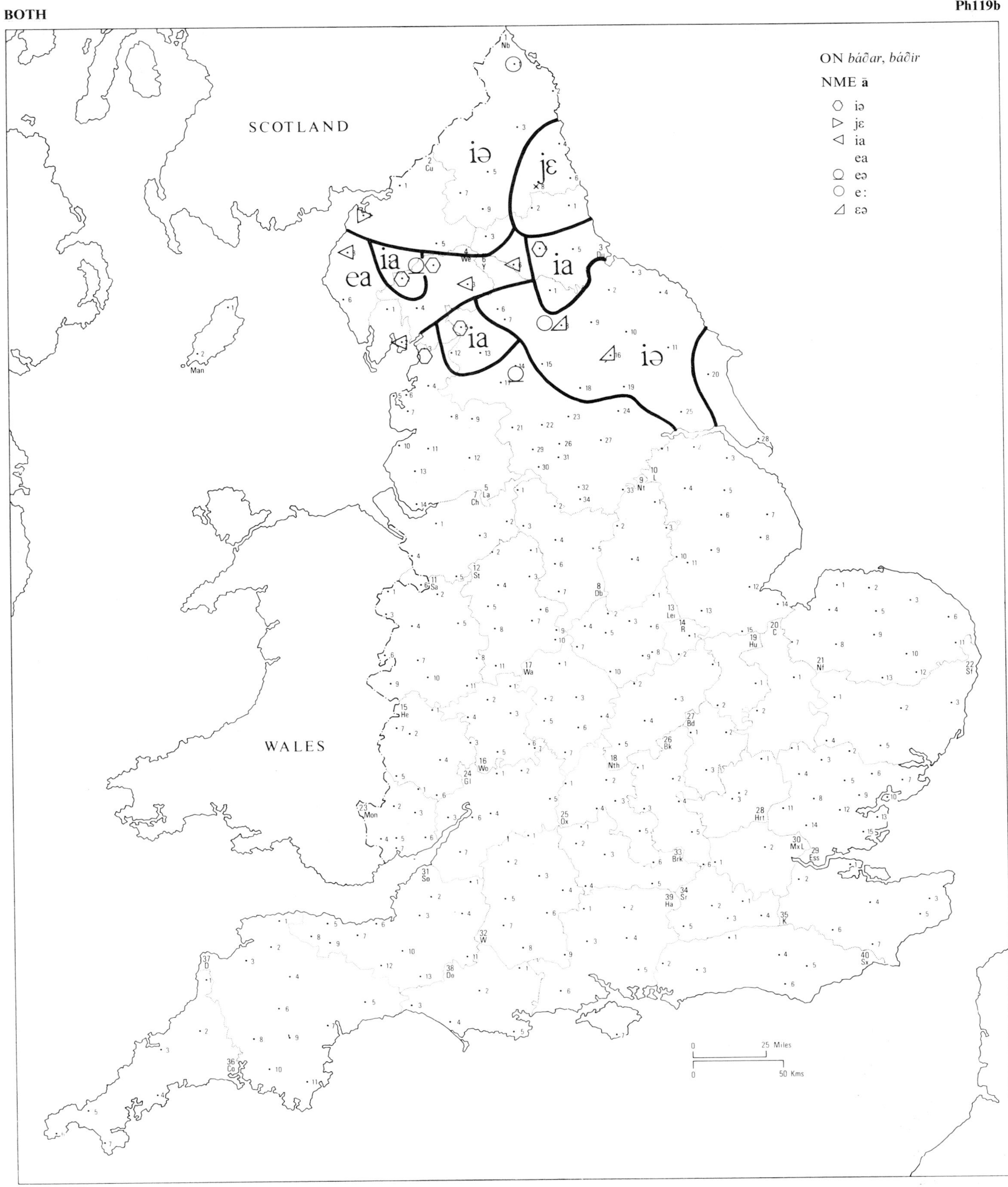

ɪɛ̃ 2Cu + 2 under jɛ

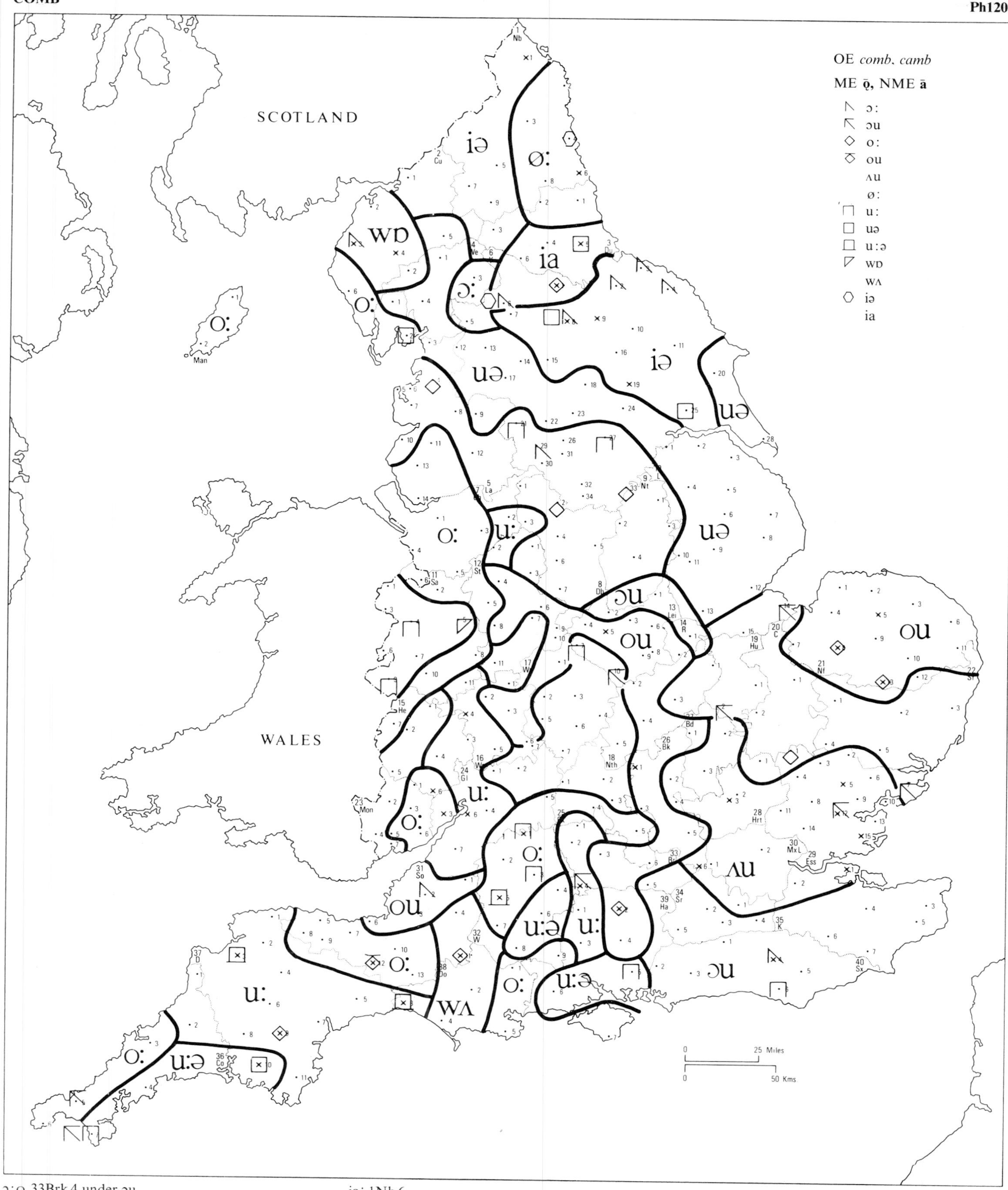

ɔ:ɷ 33Brk 4 under ɔu
o:ᵊ 31So 5, o˙ᵊ Man +1, o:ə 31So 13, 32W 9, 38Do 5, o˙ə Man +1, o:ᵚ 23Mon 1, o 5La 4, 21Nf 8, 24Gl 5, 29Ess 1 under o:
o:ɷ 16Wo +2, 31So 3/6 under ou
øə 1Nb 8, 3Du 1, øᵊ 3Du 2 under ø:
ọə 2Cu 5 under uə
wɒᵊ 2Cu 2 under wɒ
wə 31So 4 under wʌ
ẹə 1Nb 4 under iə

jɛ˙ 1Nb 6
ɛə 6Y +18, ẹə 6Y +18
æɷ 28Hrt 3, ᵆu 35K 1
ɑɷ 29Ess 15
ɒ: 5La 10

COMB(ED) pp 16Wo +2, 36Co +7, 39Ha +5;
COMBING n 6Y +18, 29Ess 3

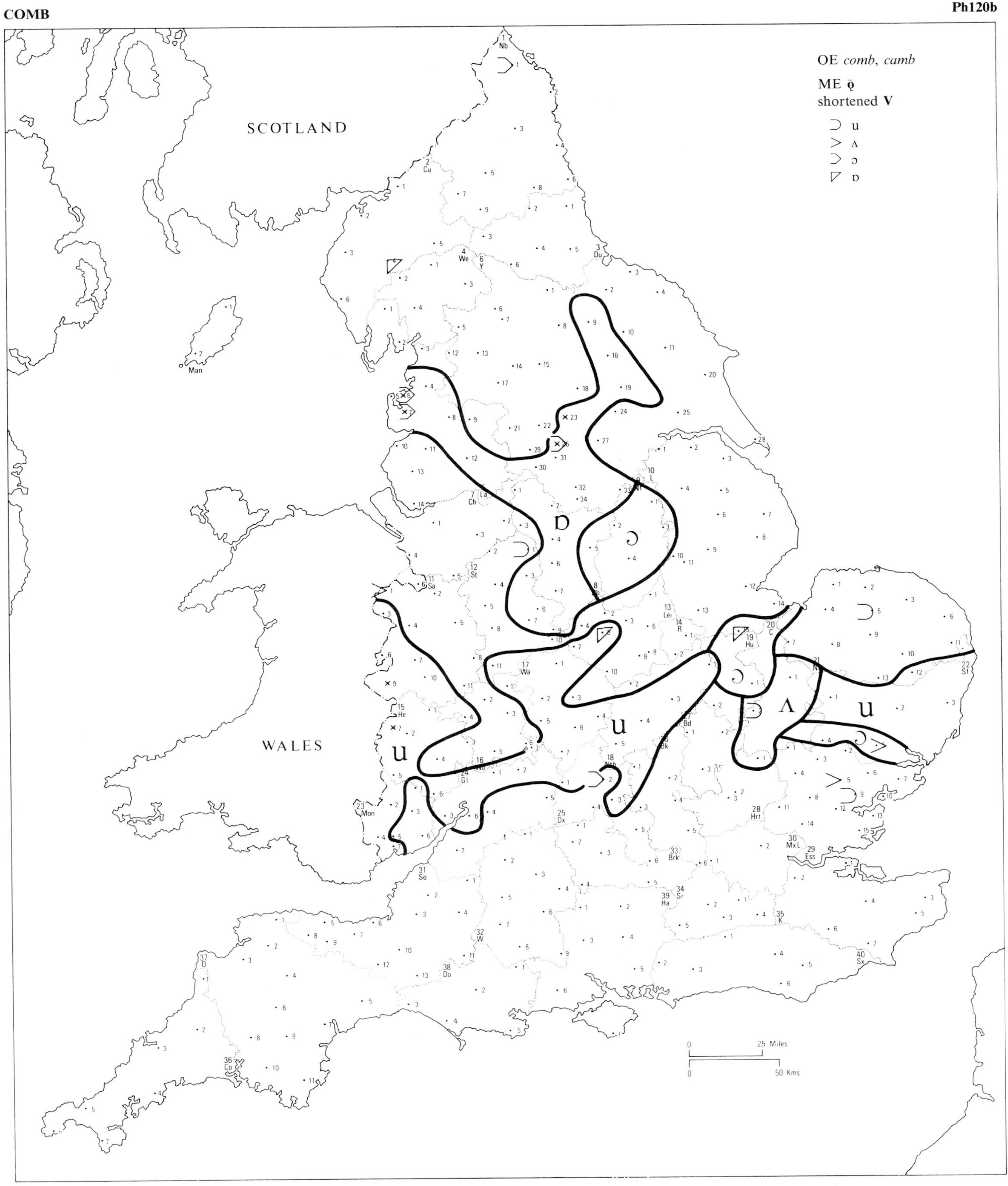

-COMB 16Wo 4; COMB v 13Lei 7;
COMBED pp 6Y 16

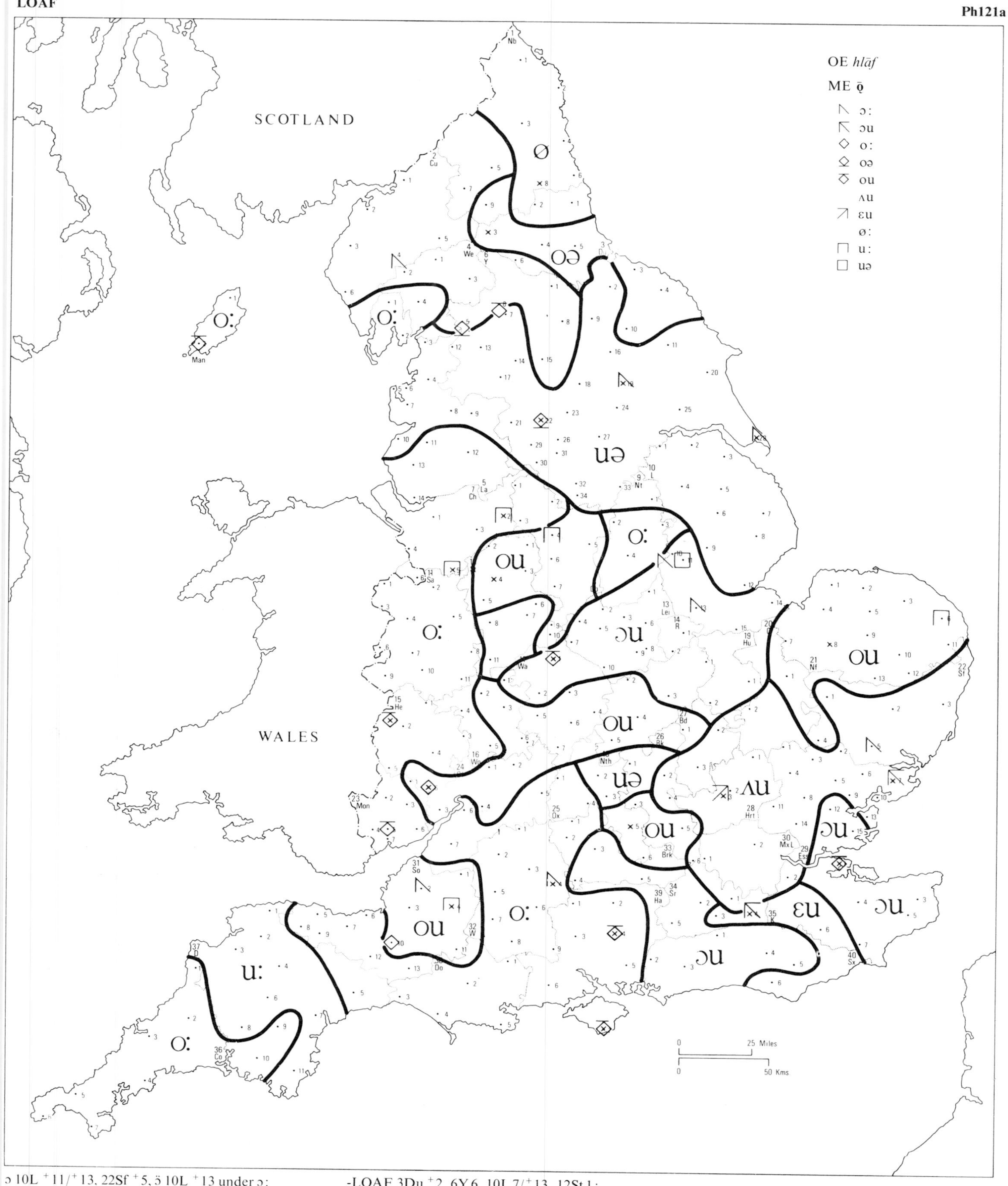

ɔ 10L $^{+}$11/$^{+}$13, 22Sf $^{+}$5, ɔ̈ 10L $^{+}$13 under ɔ:
o:^{ə} Man 1, 31So 13, o:ə 32W 6 under o:
ọ:^{ə} 3Du 4 under oə
o:ɷ 21Nf 1/5, 23Mon 1, 24Gl 1–4,
o:^{ɷ} 8Db $^{+}$4/5/6 under ou
æɷ 28Hrt 3, 40Sx 6 under ɛu
ø:^{ə} 1Nb 6, 3Du $^{+}$2, ø^{ə} 1Nb 4, 3Du 1/$^{+}$2 under ø:
u:^{ə} 31So 4 under u:

ɑ: (sic) 6Y $^{+}$2
ʌ 20C $^{+}$1

-LOAF 3Du $^{+}$2, 6Y 6, 10L 7/$^{+}$13, 12St 1;
-LOAVES 12St 9; LOAVES pl 12St 9, 21Nf 4, 23Mon $^{+}$5, 26Bk 2, 31So $^{+}$10, 34Sr 5, 40Sx 3

-v 5La 3, 10L $^{+}$11, 31So 8/9, 36Co 1/2, 37D 1–11

iːᵊ 2Cu 1 under iə

ɪɛ 2Cu 2
ɪa 6Y 1

-LOAF 6Y 28

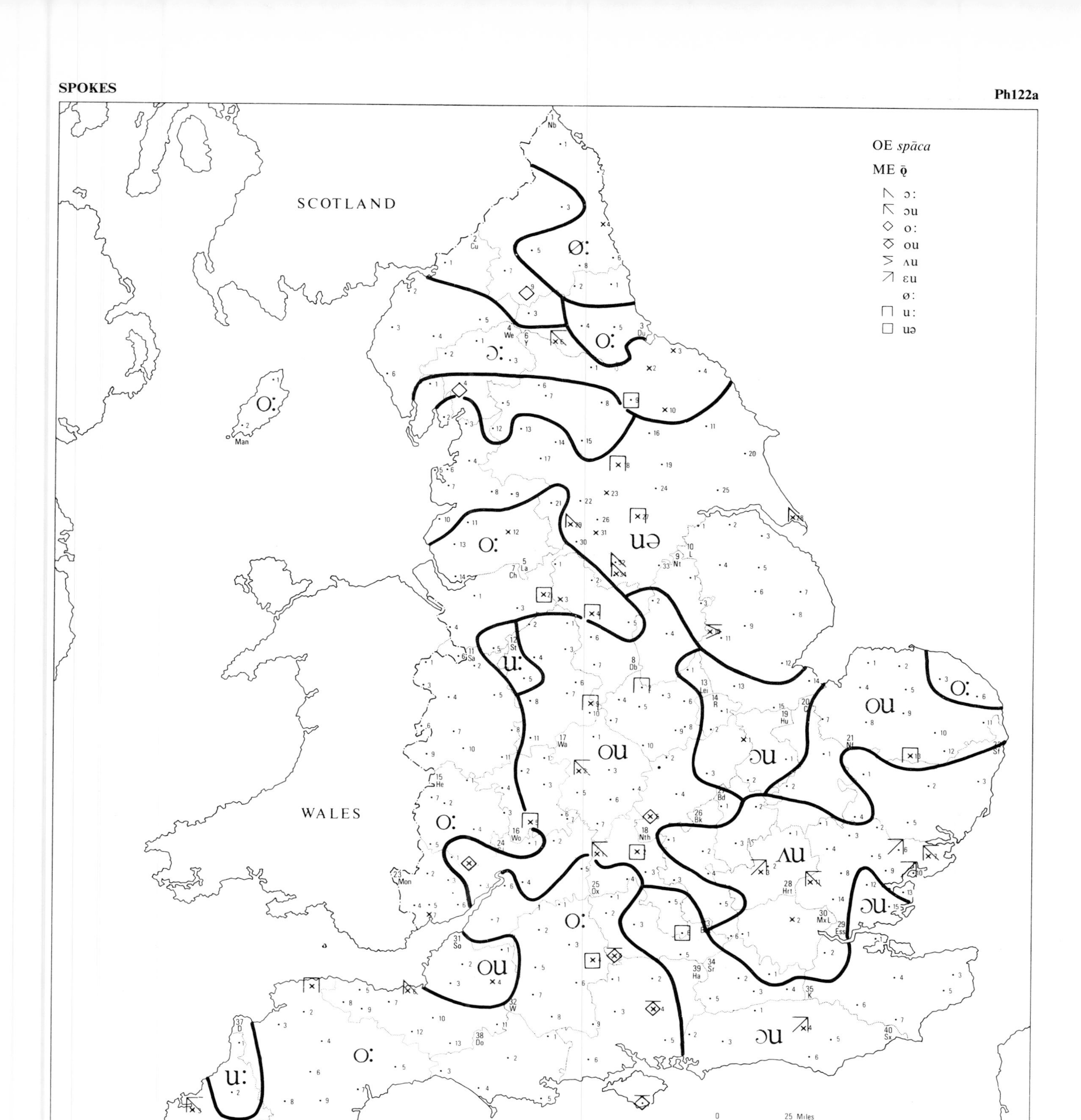

ɔ˙ə 6Y 34, ɔə 6Y 4/⁺9 under ɔ:
ọ:ᵊ 32W 5, o˙ə 18Nth 5 under o:
o:ɷ 23Mon 1, 24Gl 2–4, o:ᵚ 8Db 6, 9Nt 2/4,
  ǫ:ᵚ 8Db 7 under ou
æɷ 28Hrt 3 under ɛu
øə 3Du 1/2, ø 1Nb8, œ˙ᵊ 1Nb 1 under ø:
ɷ 13Lei ⁺2 under u:
u:ə 32W 4 under uə

äɷ 18Nth 1, ạ̈ɷ 29Ess ⁺11
wɷ 24Gl ⁺6

ɪɛ 1Nb 8 under jɛ

ɪa 6Y 5

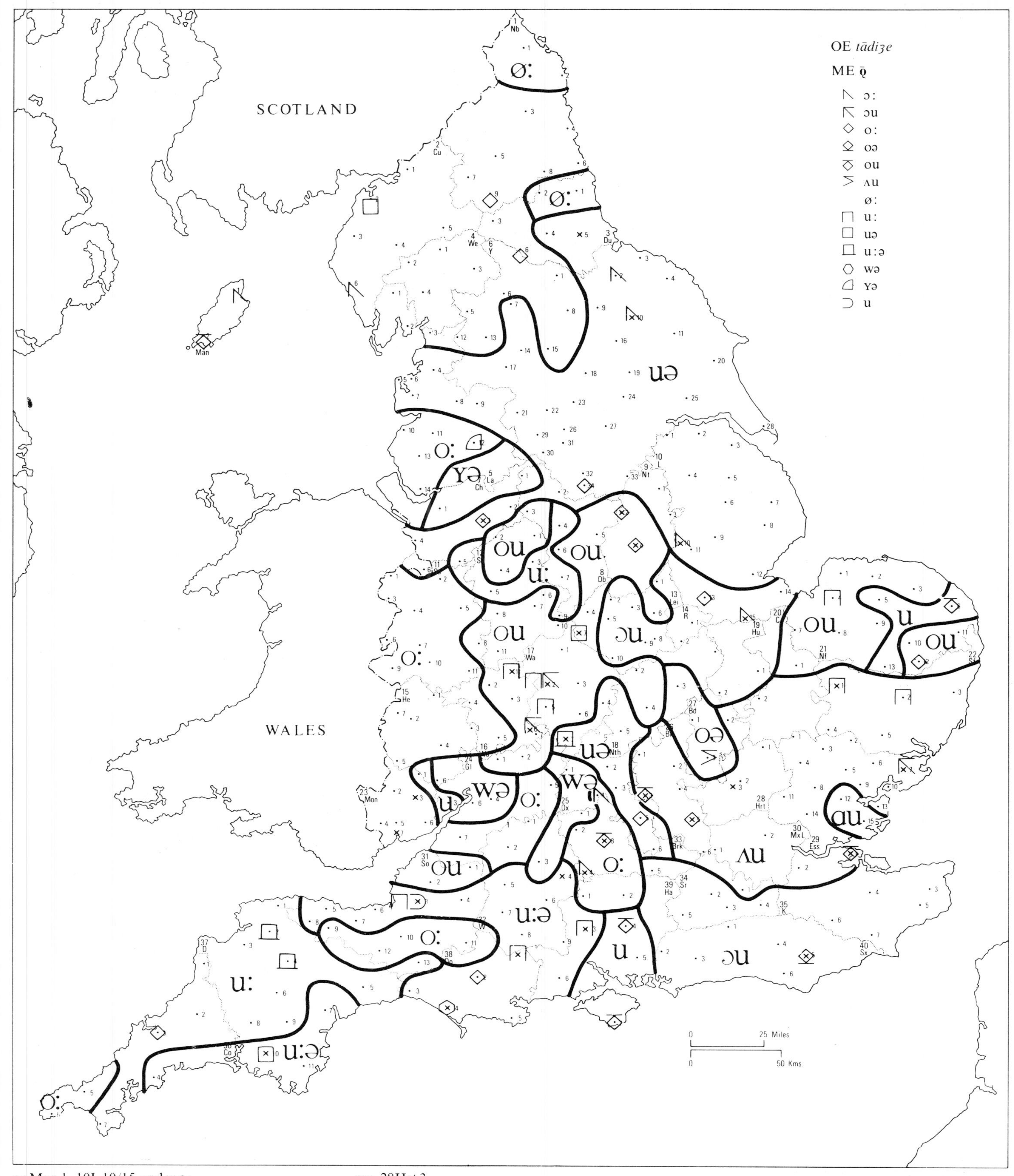

ɔə Man 1, 10L 10/15 under ɔ:
o:^{ə} 11Sa 3, 23Mon 4/5, ọ:^{ə} 31So 10, o:ə 31So 9,
o˙ə 9Nt 4, ^{w}o: 32W 1, wo: 38Do $^{+}$2 under o:
o:wə 40Sx 5 under oə
o:ɷ 21Nf $^{+}$1, 24Gl 1/2, 31So 2, o:^{u} Man 2,
o:^{ɷ} 8Db 3/5, 11Sa 8, ọ:^{ɷ} 8Db 6 under ou
ʌɷ^{ə} 29Ess 5, ʌɷə 28Hrt 2 under ʌu
ø^{ə} 3Du $^{+}$1/$^{+}$2 under ø:
ọə 2Cu 2, 17Wa 4, ɩuə 7Ch 6 under uə
wʌ̣ 38Do 4, wɷ̣ 24Gl 6, 33Brk 1, under wə
ɩʏ:ə 7Ch 1 under ʏə

æɷ 28Hrt 3
ɒ 3Du $^{+}$6, 23Mon 3
wɒ 32W 4

TOAD- 3Du $^{+}$6, 5La $^{+}$12, 6Y 10,
21Nf $^{+}$1/$^{+}$4/$^{+}$6/$^{+}$12, 25Ox $^{+}$4, 39Ha $^{+}$4/$^{+}$7

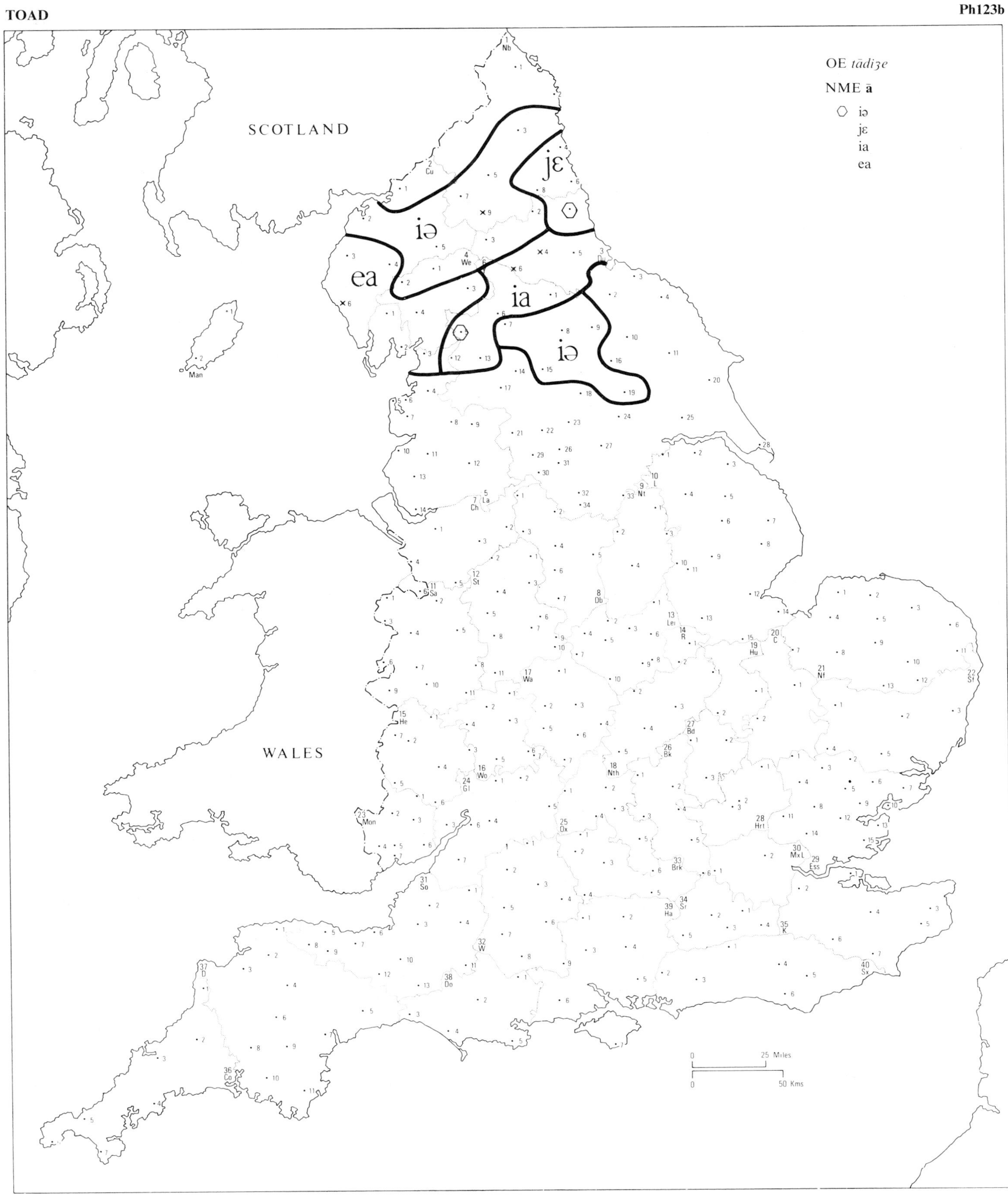

ẹ˙ə 4We 2, jə 3Du 1, jɤ 3Du 2 under iə

i: 2Cu 1
e:ᵊ 3Du 6

TOAD- 6Y ⁺5

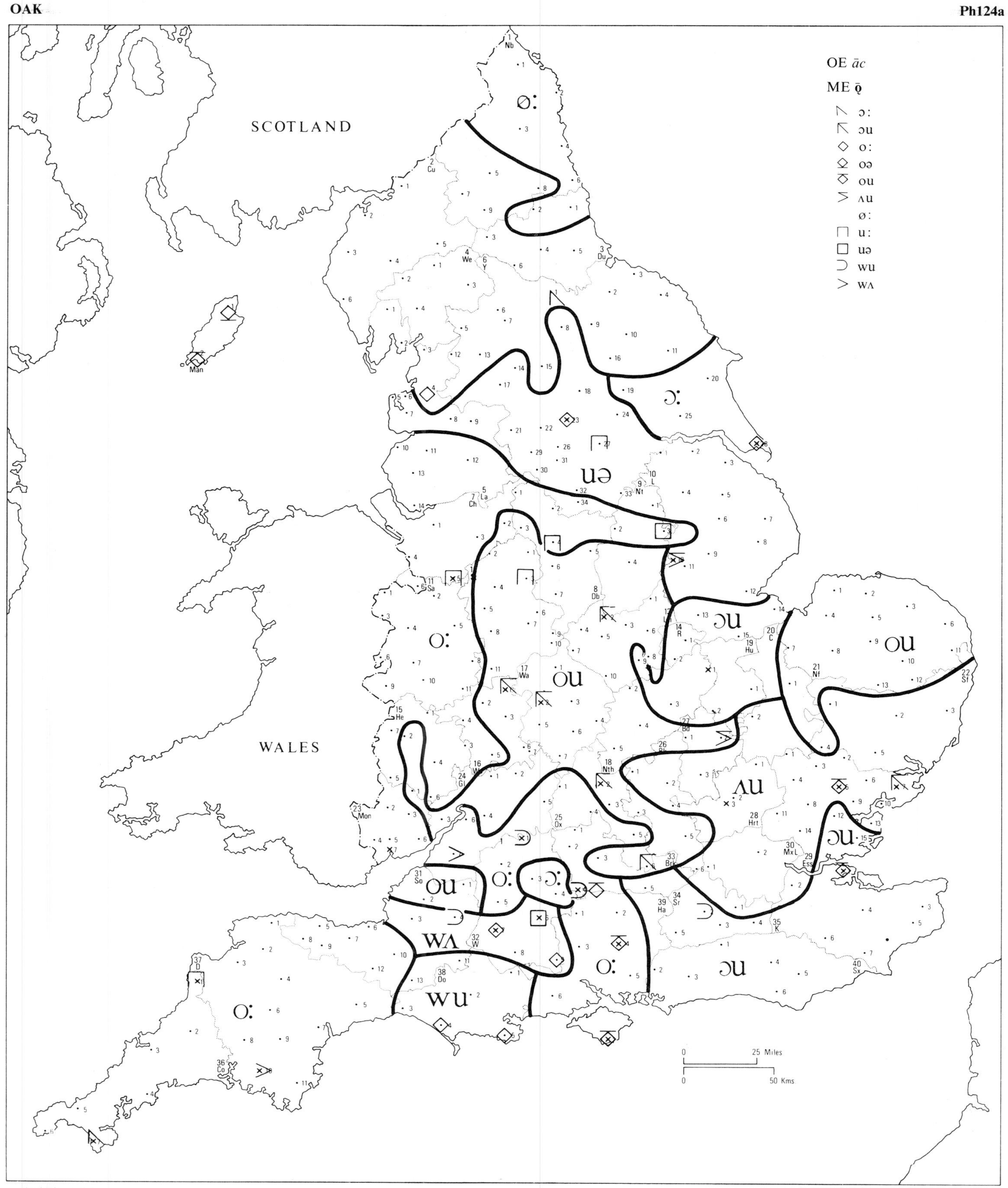

ɔə 6Y 20 under ɔ:
ǫ:^{ə} 31So 7, o˙ə Man 1, wo: 33Brk $^{+}$2,
39Ha $^{+}$6 under o:
oɷ: 12St $^{+}$5, o:ɷ 15He 2, 21Nf 1/5, 23Mon 1,
24Gl 1–4, o:^{u} Man 2, o:^{ɷ} 8Db 3/5–7, 9Nt 4,
woɷ 33Brk $^{+}$4 under ou
ø˙^{ə} 3Du 2, ø^{ə} 3Du 1 under ø:
u:ə 32W 6 under uə
wə 24Gl 7 under wʌ

æɷ 28Hrt 3
äɷ 18Nth 1
ɷ 40Sx $^{+}$5
^{ə}u 35K $^{+}$6

OAK- 6Y 8, 10L 14, 31So $^{+}$4, 33Brk $^{+}$2

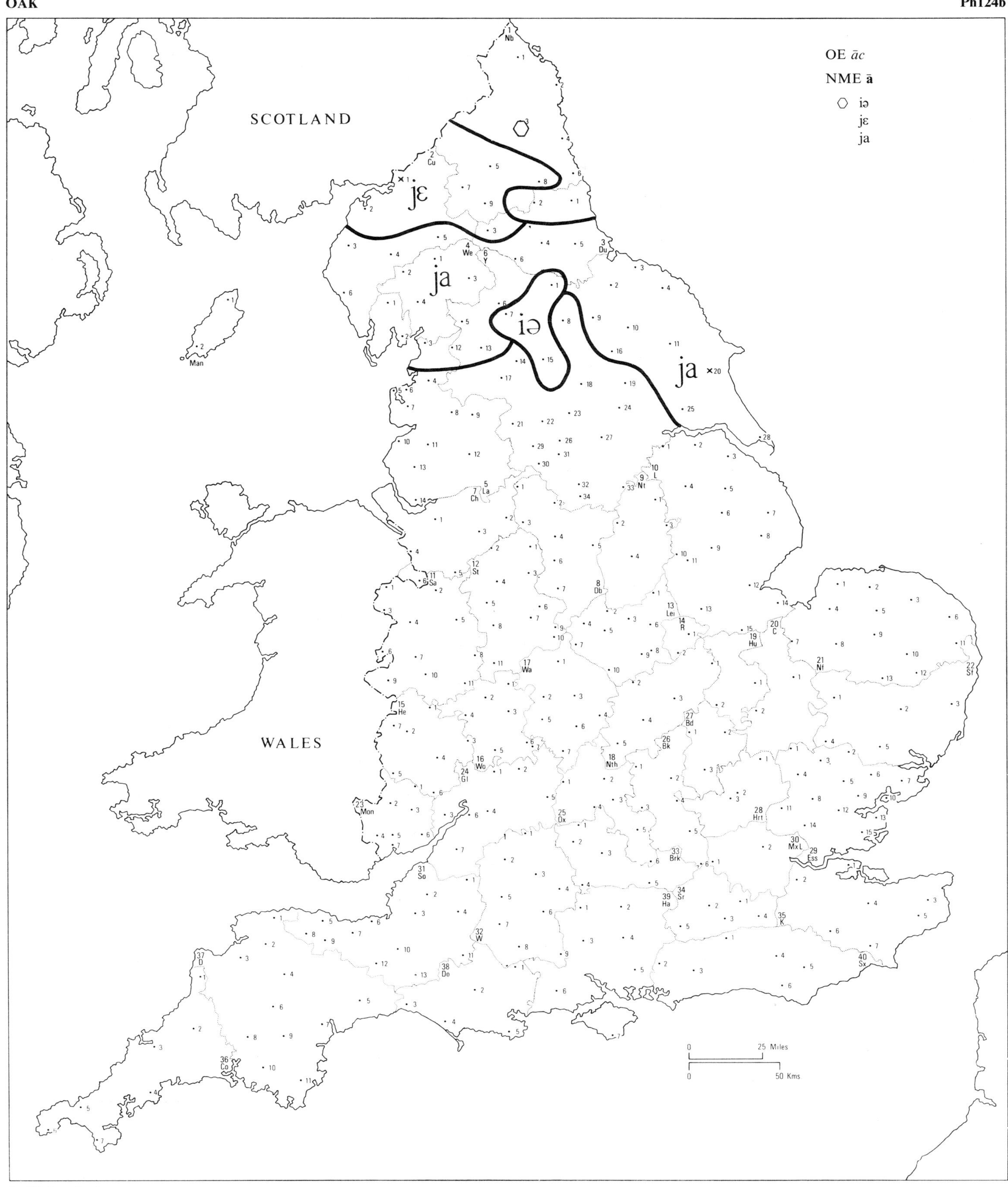

jə 6Y 1 under iə
ɩa 6Y 5/12, ɩa 6Y 12, ea 5La 3 under ja

jɩ 2Cu 1

OAK- 6Y 4/28

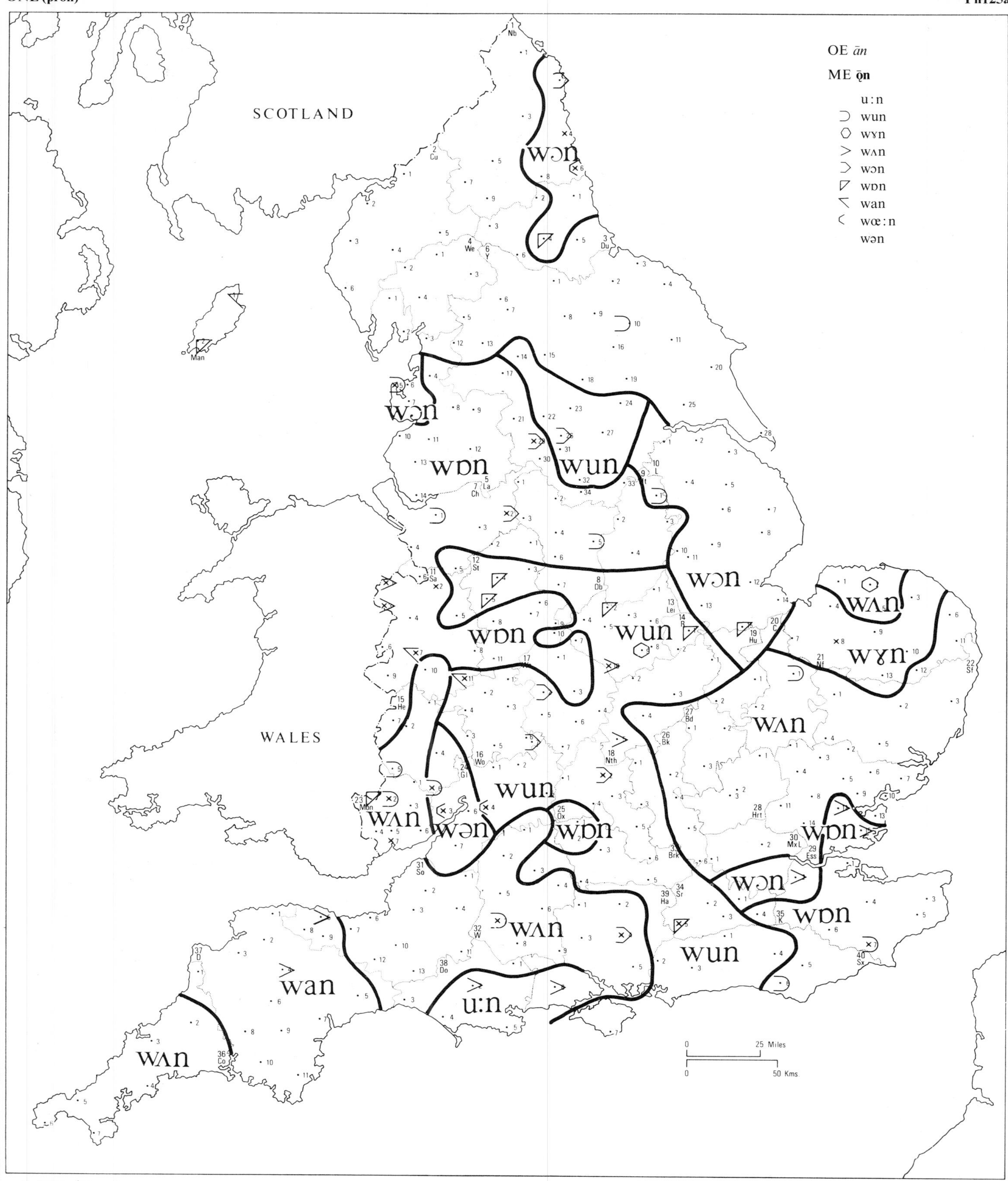

u:ᵊn 38Do ⁺5 under u:n
wɷ:n 16Wo ⁺6, 24Gl 1/2 under wun
wɔ˙ᵊn 1Nb 8 under wɔn
wa:n 11Sa 7/11, wæn Man ⁺1, 37D 6 under wan

wɑ:n 11 Sa 2

ONE (pron)

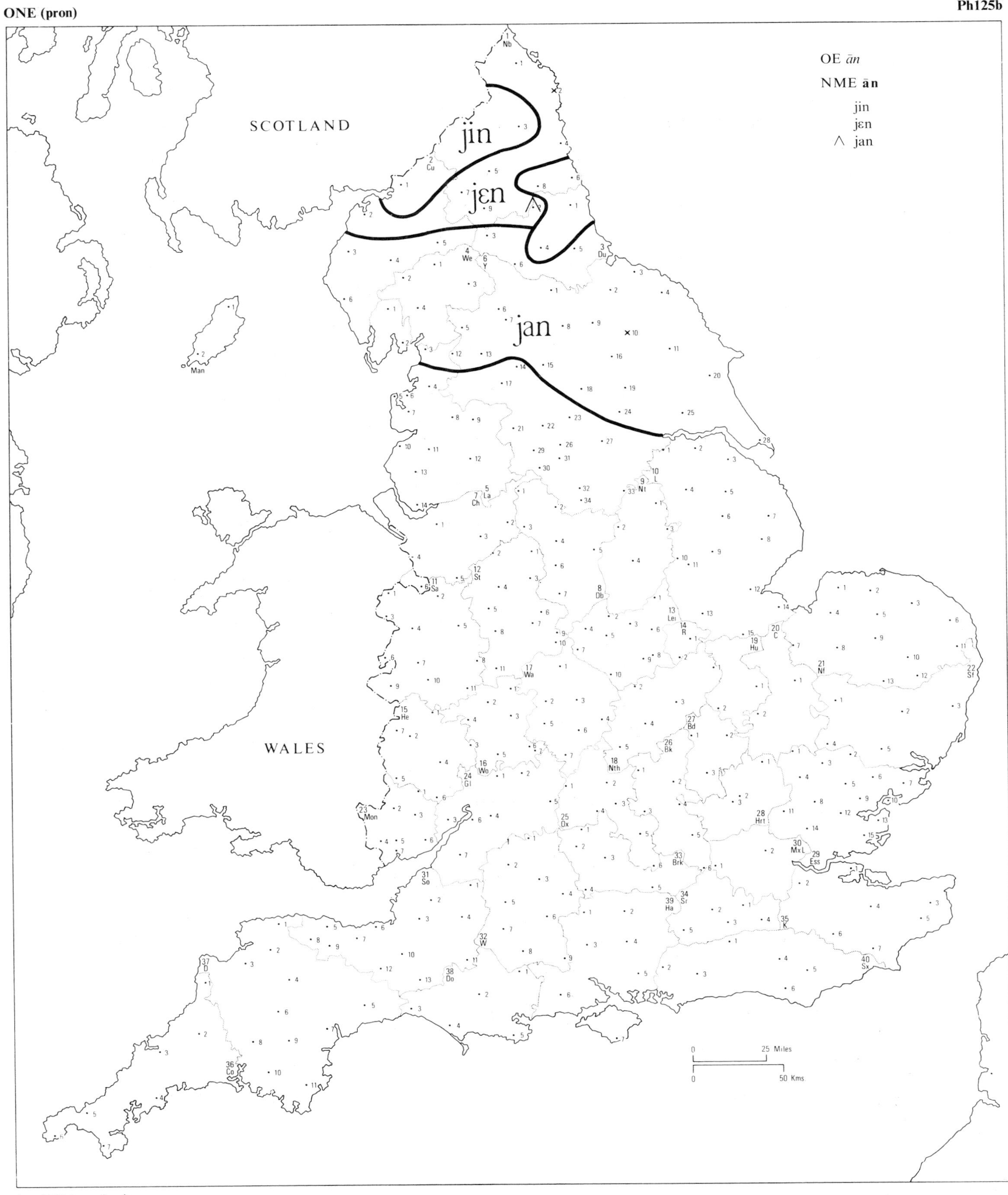

jen 1Nb1 under jɛn

ja: 6Y $^{+}$4

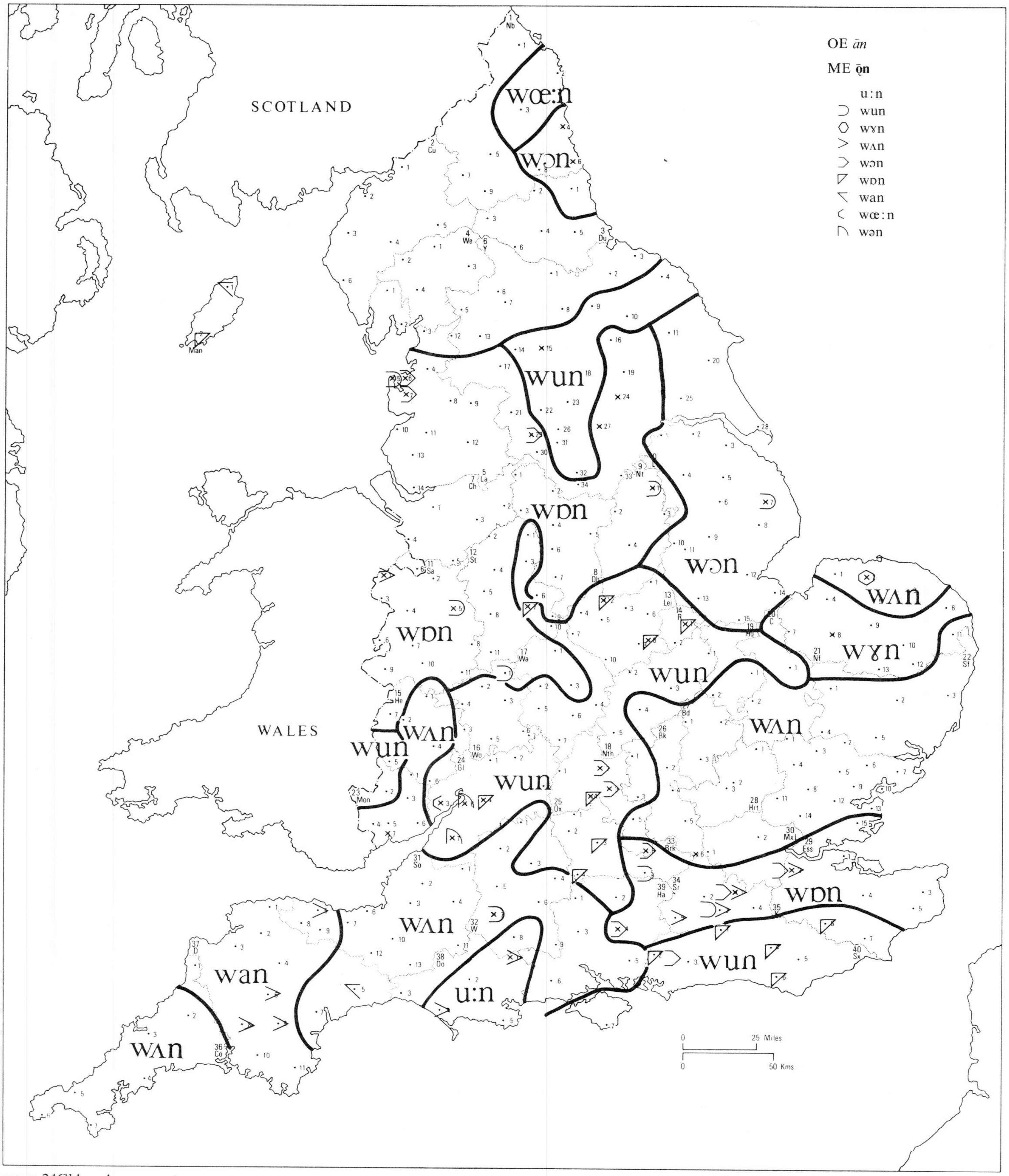

OE *ān*

ME **ǭn**

u:n
wun
wʏn
wʌn
wɔn
wɒn
wan
wœ:n
wən

SCOTLAND

WALES

wœ:n
wɔn
wun
wɒn
wɔn
wʌn
wʏn
wɒn
wun
wʌn
wʌn
wun
wun
wun
wɒn
wʌn
wan
u:n
wun
wʌn

0 25 Miles
0 50 Kms

wo:n 24Gl 1 under wun
wæ̜n Man 1 under wan

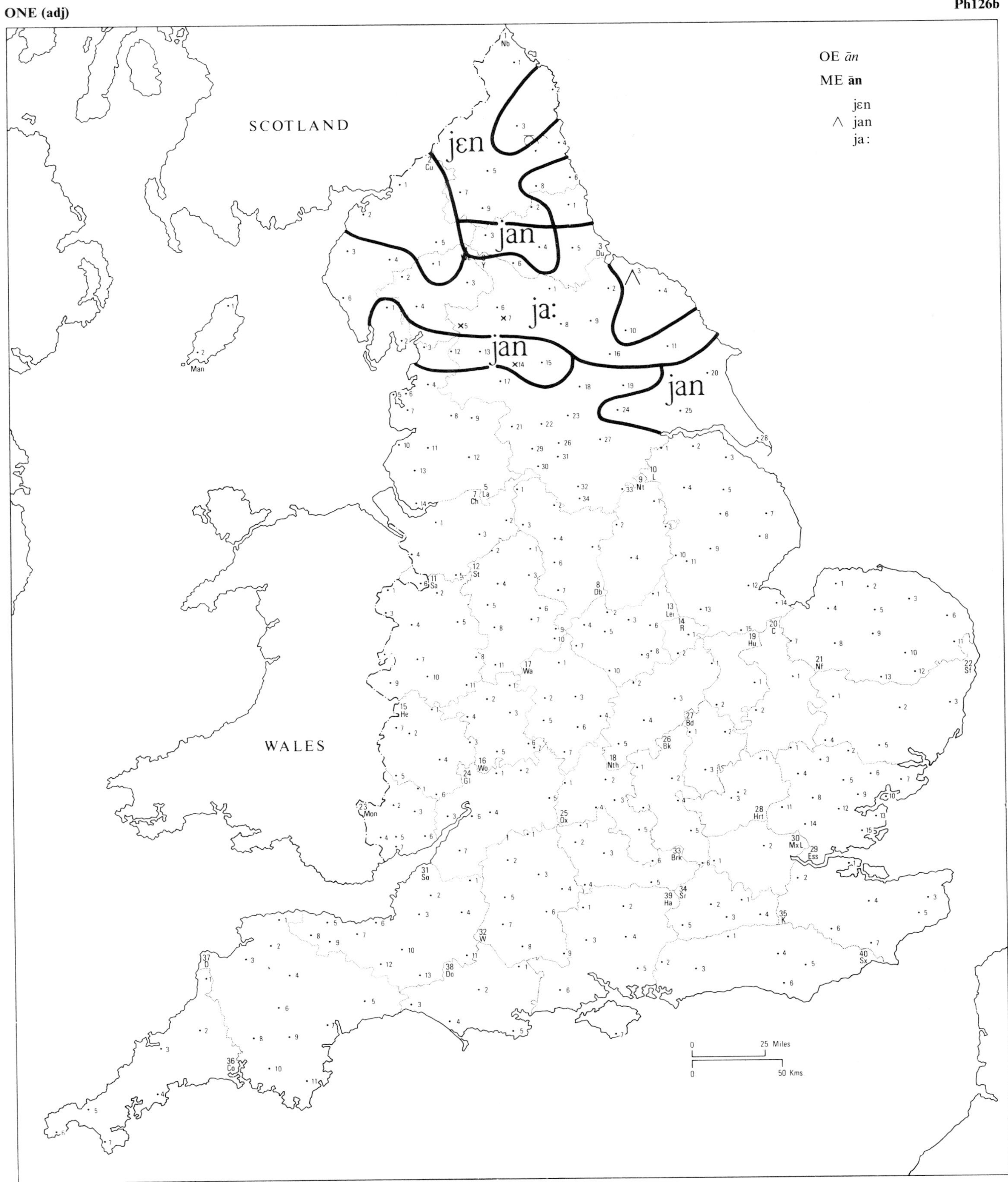

jen 1Nb 1 under jɛn

jɪn 2Cu 1
jɛ: 2Cu 2

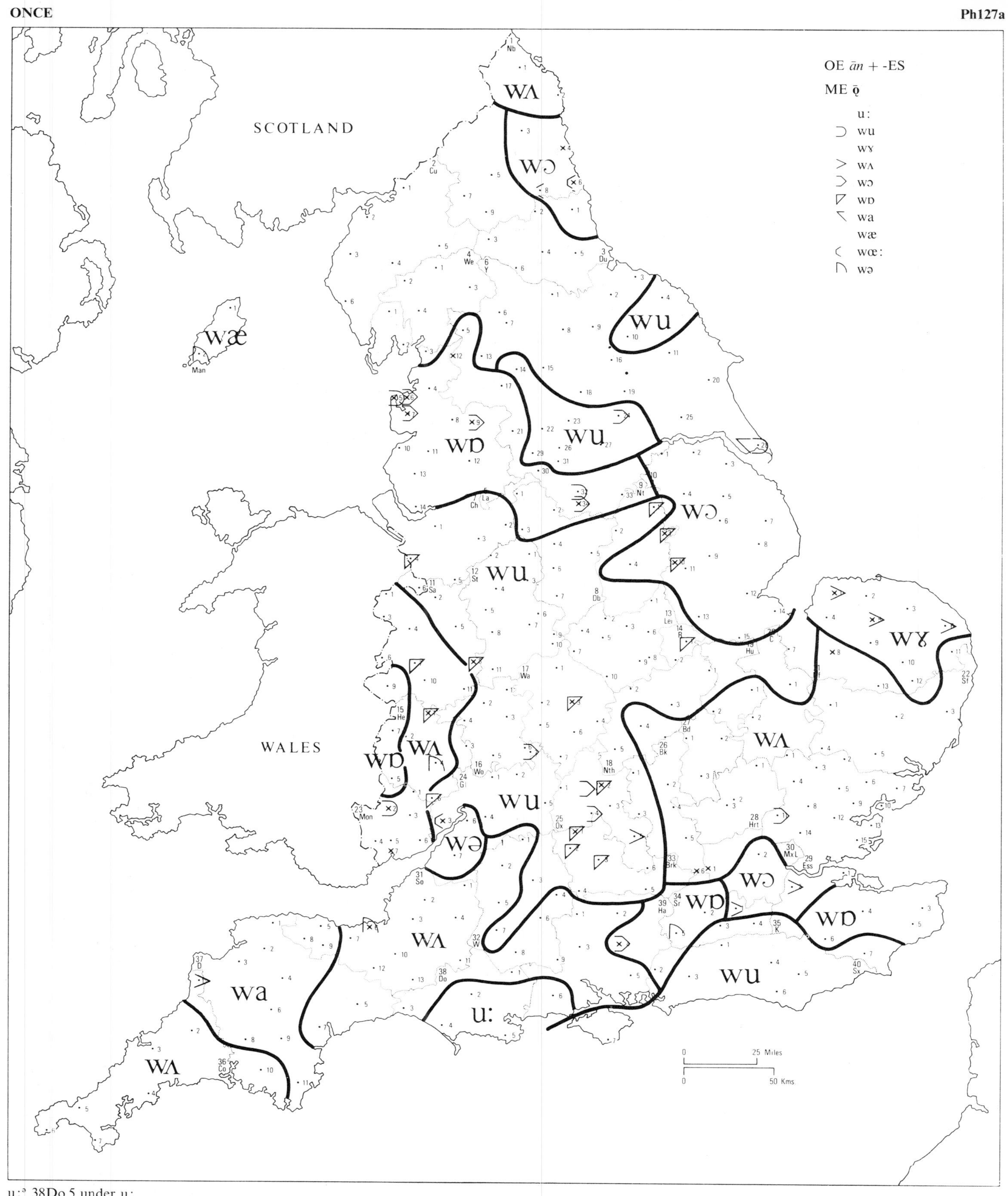

u:ᵊ 38Do 5 under u:
wɒ: 24Gl 1 under wu
wɐ 29Ess ⁺7 under wʌ

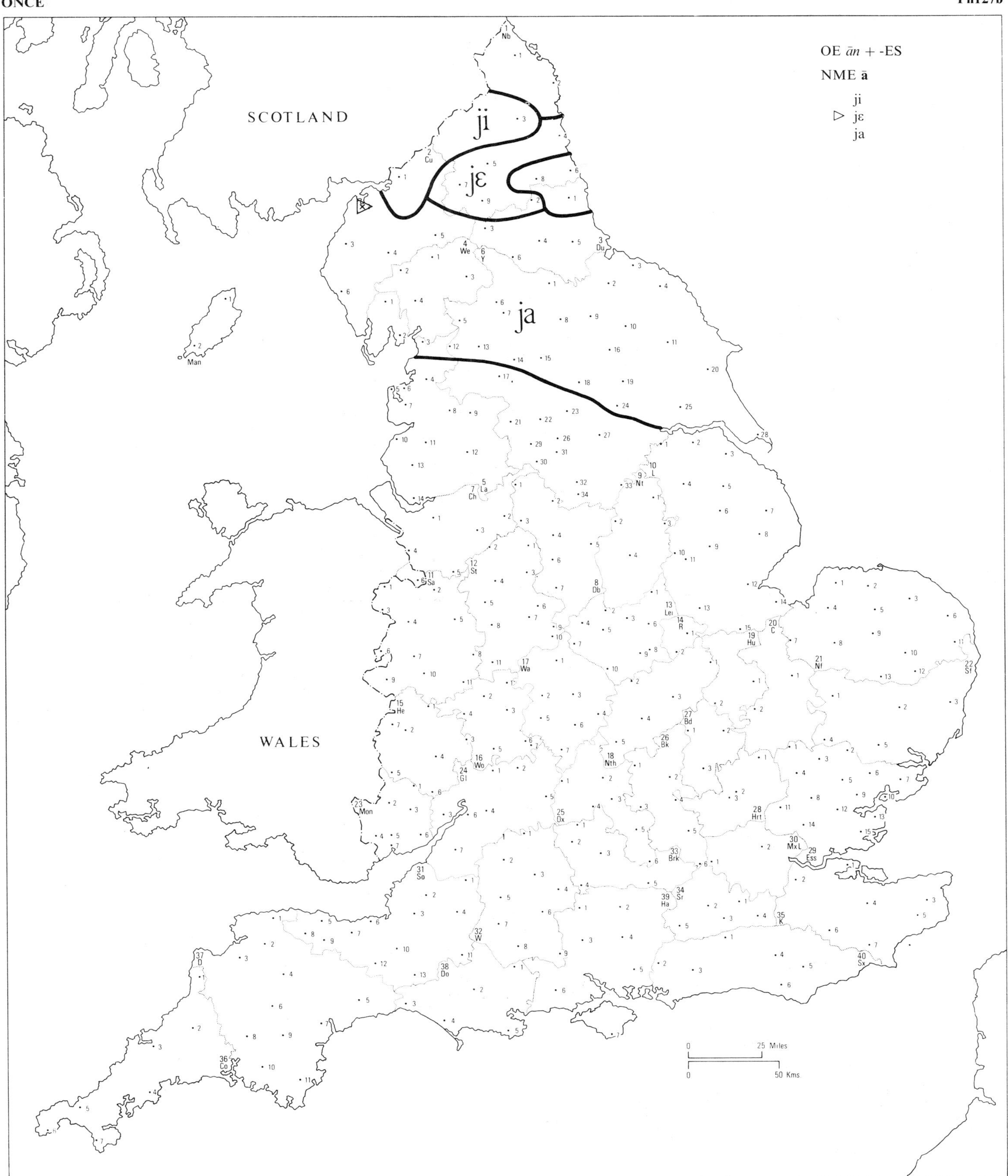
OE ān + -ES
NME ā
ji
▷ jɛ
ja
SCOTLAND
WALES
ji
jɛ
ja
0 25 Miles
0 50 Kms

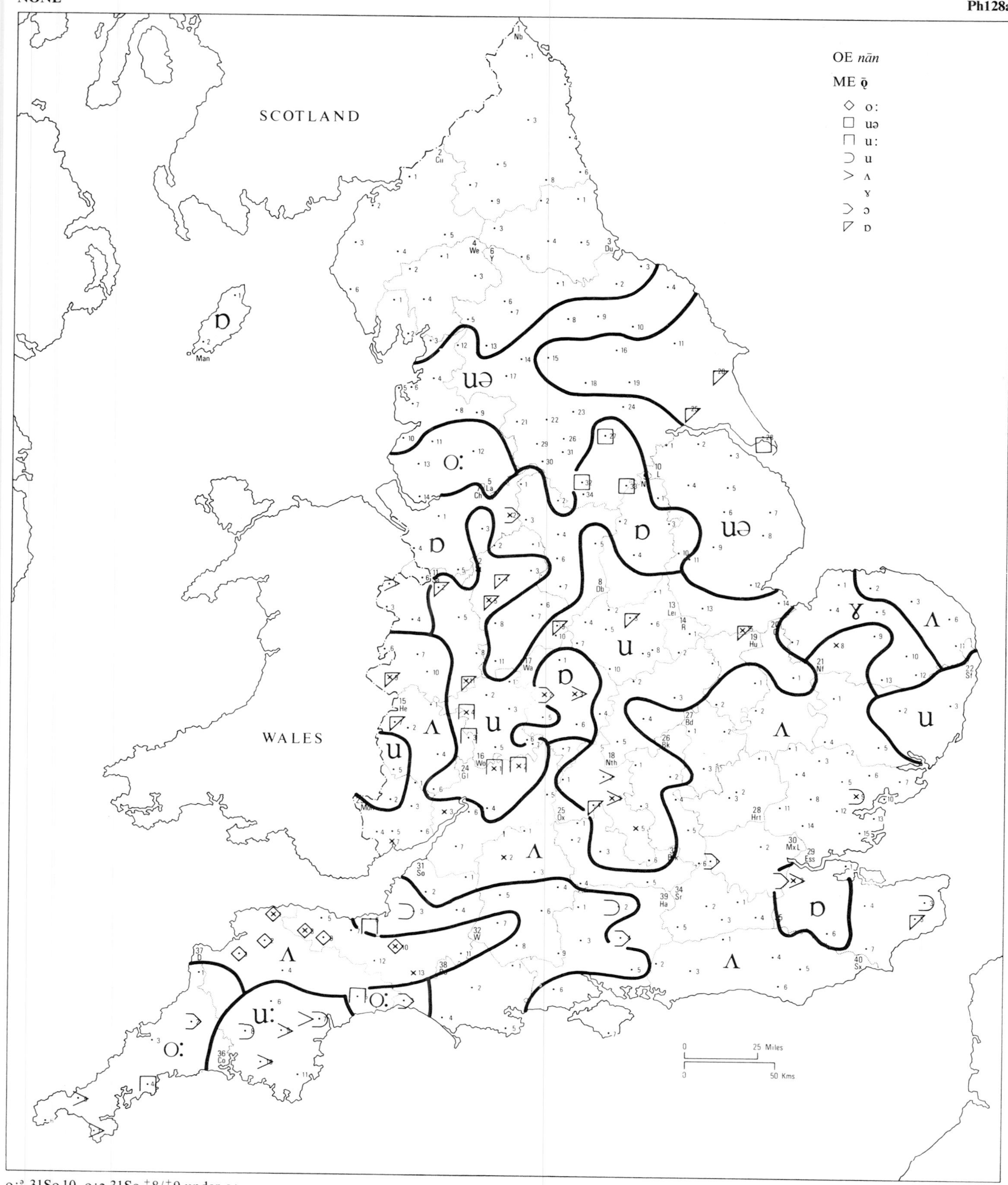

oːᵊ 31So 10, oːə 31So ⁺8/⁺9 under oː
uːə 31So 6, 37D ⁺5, ɷːᵊ 24Gl 1 under uː
ə 24Gl 7, 40Sx ⁺2/⁺4, ə˙ 24Gl 6 under ʌ
ɔː 36Co ⁺2, ɔ̣ː 38Do ⁺3 under ɔ

oɷ 16Wo ⁺6

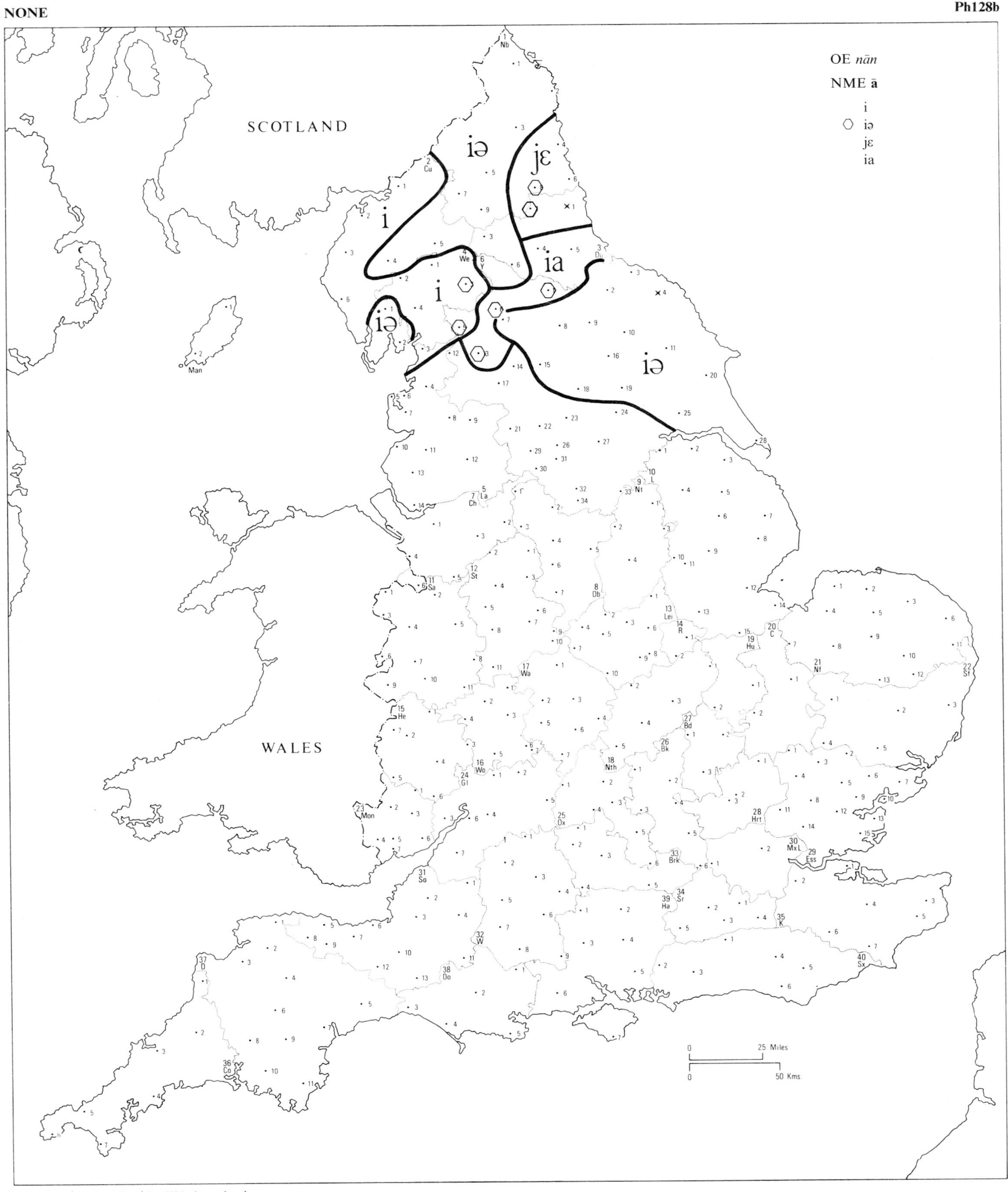

i: 2Cu 1/⁺3, ˈi: 2Cu ⁺3, 4We 2 under i
i:ə 3Du ⁺3, eˑə 3Du 6 under iə
ˈɛ 1Nb ⁺8 under jɛ
eˑa 3Du 4 under ia

jɩ 1Nb ⁺1
ɛˑᵊ 3Du 1

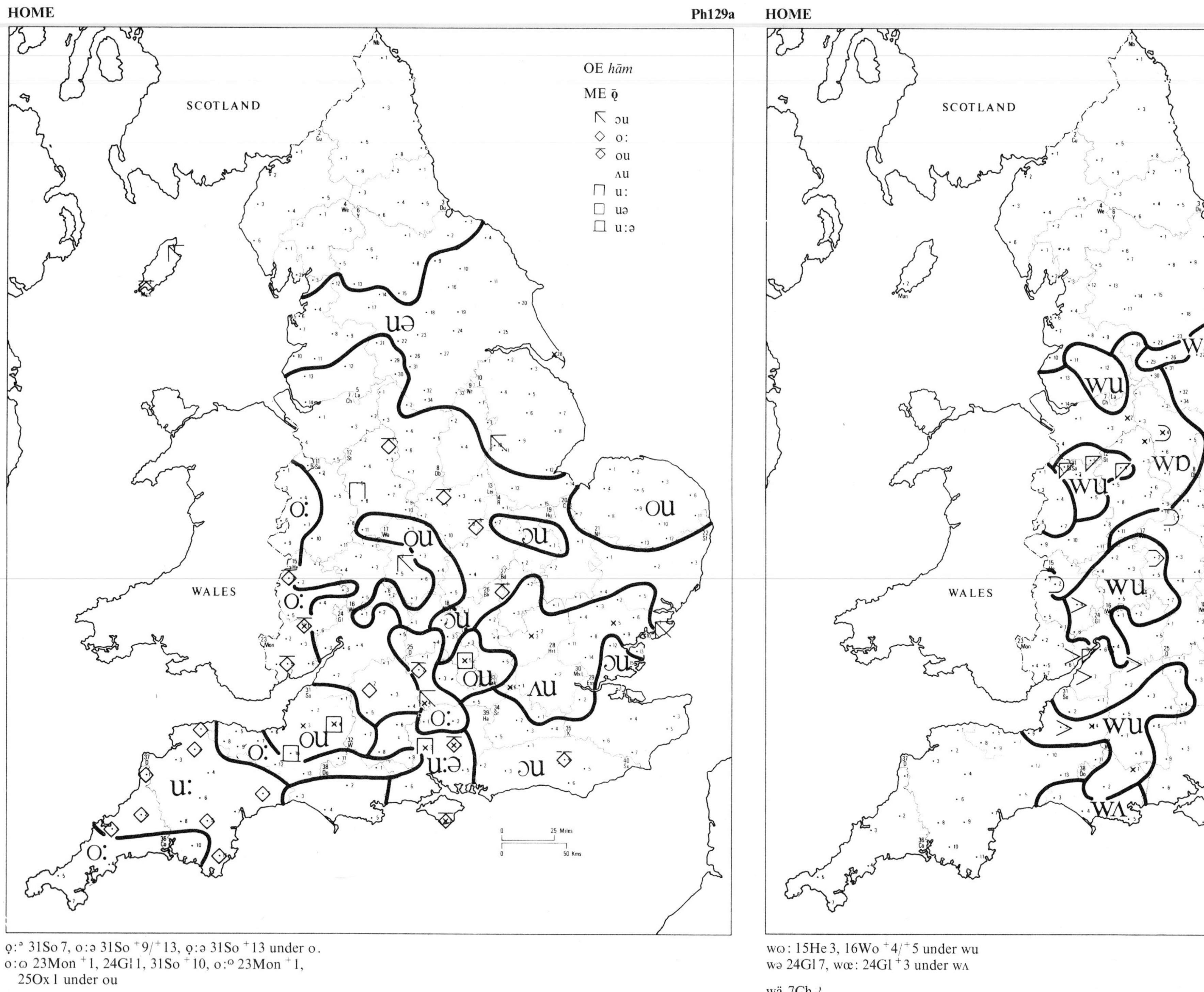

ǫ:ᵊ 31So 7, o:ə 31So $^{+}$9/$^{+}$13, ǫ:ə 31So $^{+}$13 under o.
o:ɷ 23Mon $^{+}$1, 24Gl 1, 31So $^{+}$10, o:ᵒ 23Mon $^{+}$1,
25Ox 1 under ou

æɷ 28Hrt 3
ɑɷ 29Ess $^{+}$12

HOME- 13Lei 2; HOMING- 10L $^{+}$10

wɷ: 15He 3, 16Wo $^{+}$4/$^{+}$5 under wu
wə 24Gl 7, wœ: 24Gl $^{+}$3 under wʌ

wä 7Ch 2
wɔ: 12St 1
wo: 39Ha 6
wɷə 24Gl 6

HOME- 6Y 26

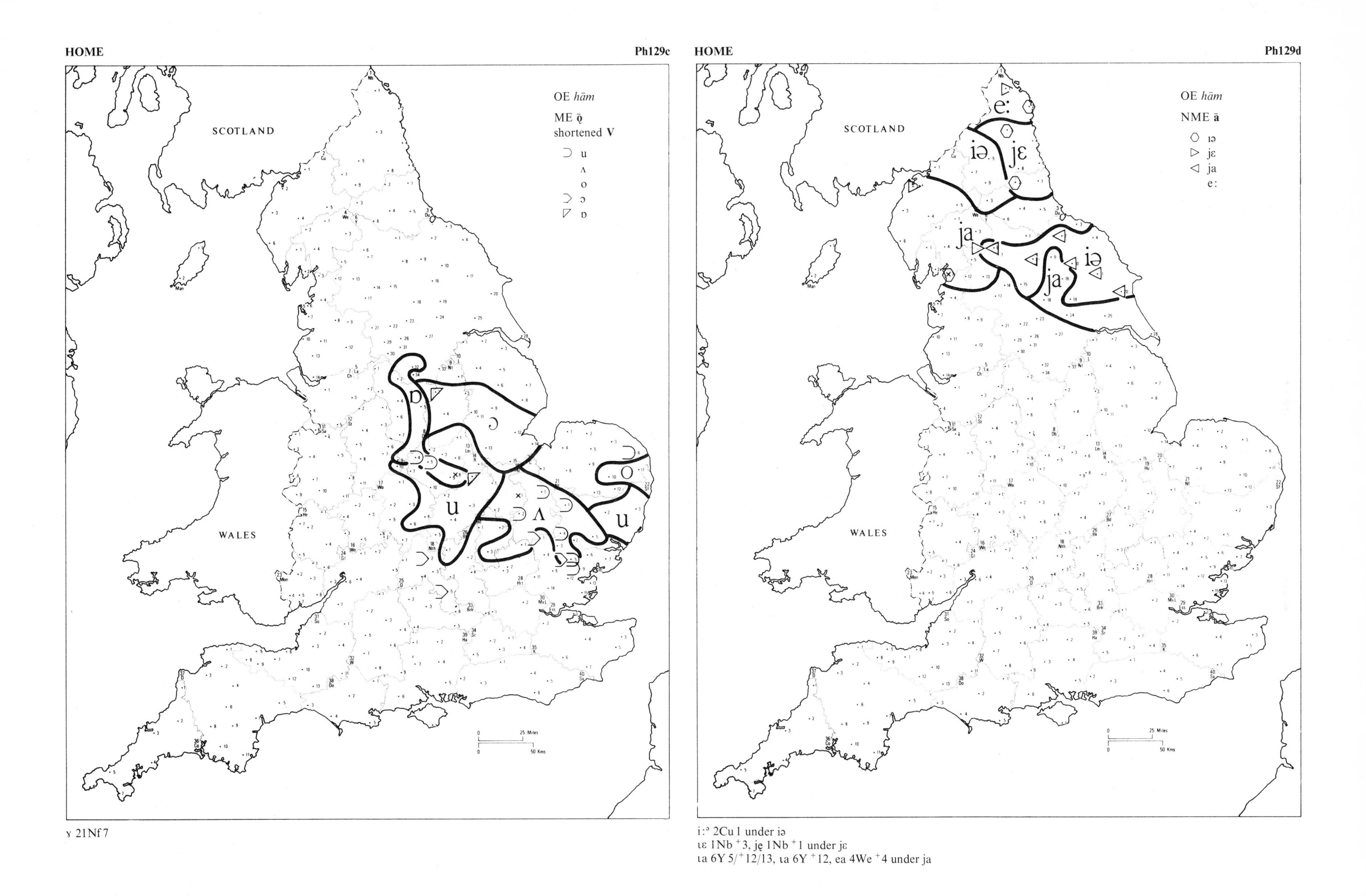

ɤ 21Nf7

iːᵊ 2Cu 1 under iə
ɪɛ 1Nb ⁺3, jɛ̨ 1Nb ⁺1 under jɛ
ɪa 6Y 5/⁺12/13, ɪa 6Y ⁺12, ea 4We ⁺4 under ja

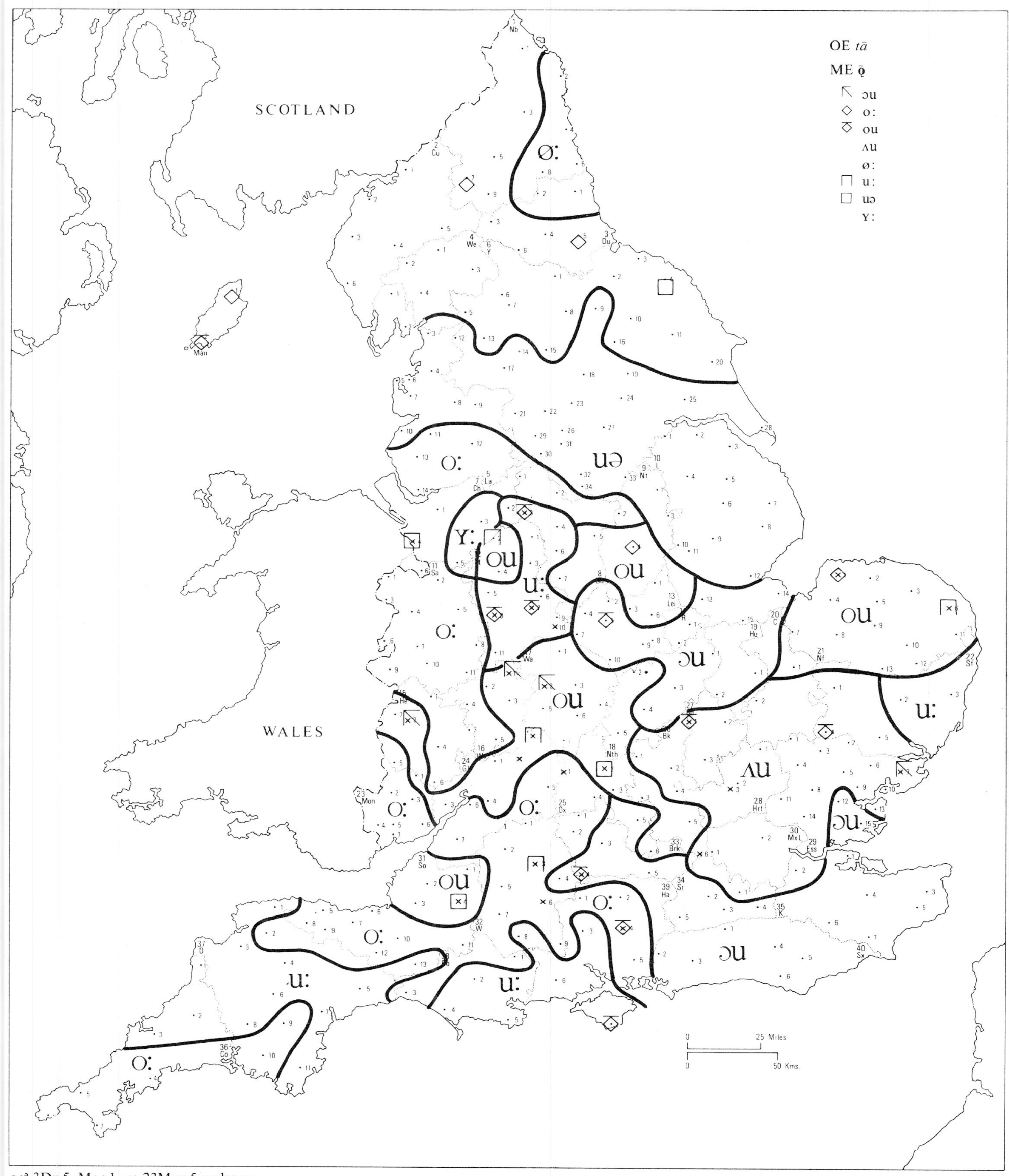

o:ᵊ 3Du 5, Man 1, oə 23Mon 5 under o:
oɷᵊ 16Wo 2, o:ɷ 24Gl 3/4, 31So 2/3, o:ɷᵊ 24Gl 1,
  ọ:ɷ 21Nf 5, o:ᵚ 8Db 3/5, 9Nt ⁺4, 15He 7,
  23Mon 1, 33Brk 4 under ou
øə 3Du 1 under ø:
u:ə 31So 4, ụ̈:ə 7Ch 4, ọə 6Y 19,
  oə 10L 4/8 under uə
ˡʏ:ə 7Ch 5 under ʏ:

ɛɷ 12St 10
æɷ 24Gl 2, 28Hrt 3
ɔ: 32W 6
ɷɩ (sic, ?for tɷəz, Edd) 3Du 4

TOE sg 6Y 19, 13Lei ⁺5, 22Sf ⁺4, 25Ox 6;
  TOE- 22Sf ⁺4

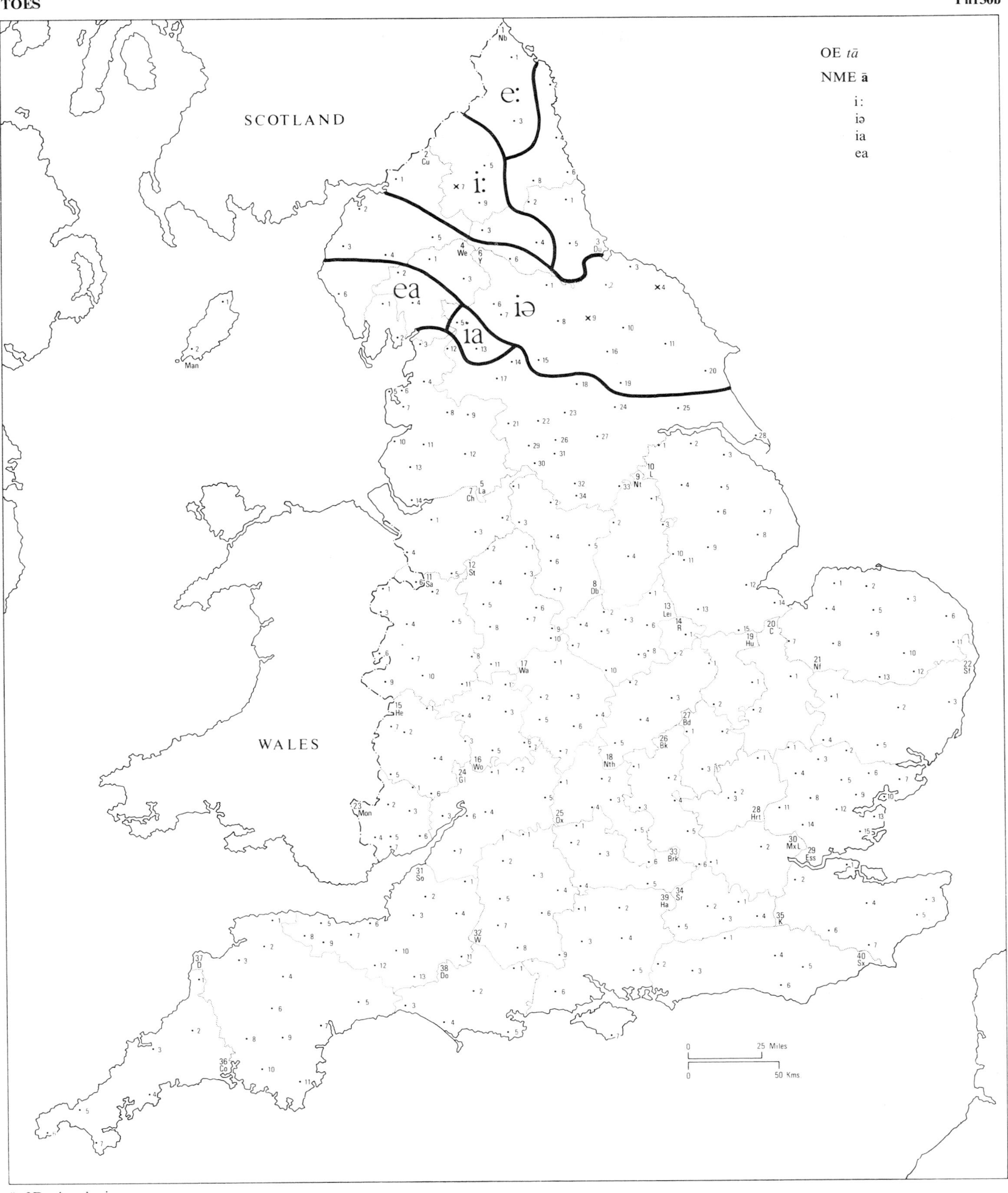

ę̈ɩ 3Du 4 under i:
ˈɩ̢ə 3Du ⁺6 under iə

ję 1Nb 4

-TOE 3Du ⁺6

u:ᵊ 24Gl +1, ᵊu: 6Y +9/+17/+20, 16Wo +3,
28Hrt 3, 35K +5, ᵊü: Man +2, əu: 10L +3,
40Sx +2, əü: 32W +3, 39Ha +7, öu 5La 5,
ᵋu: 16Wo +1 under u:

ʉ 21Nf +1–+3/+11, ʲʉ: 13Lei +5/+7/+9,
ʲʉ 13Lei +3/+6, 21Nf +1, ïʉ 21Nf +6/+11,
ɩʉ 21Nf +9 under ʉ:

y: 29Ess +11, ʏʉ: 11Sa +2, ʲʏ: 5La 11,
ʏ:ʷᵊ 5La +13 under ʏ:

ɩɷ: 12St +9 under iu:

ou 21Nf +7
ə̣ 21Nf +12, ə̣· 21Nf +10

TWO- 21Nf +9

no *tw*- forms were recorded

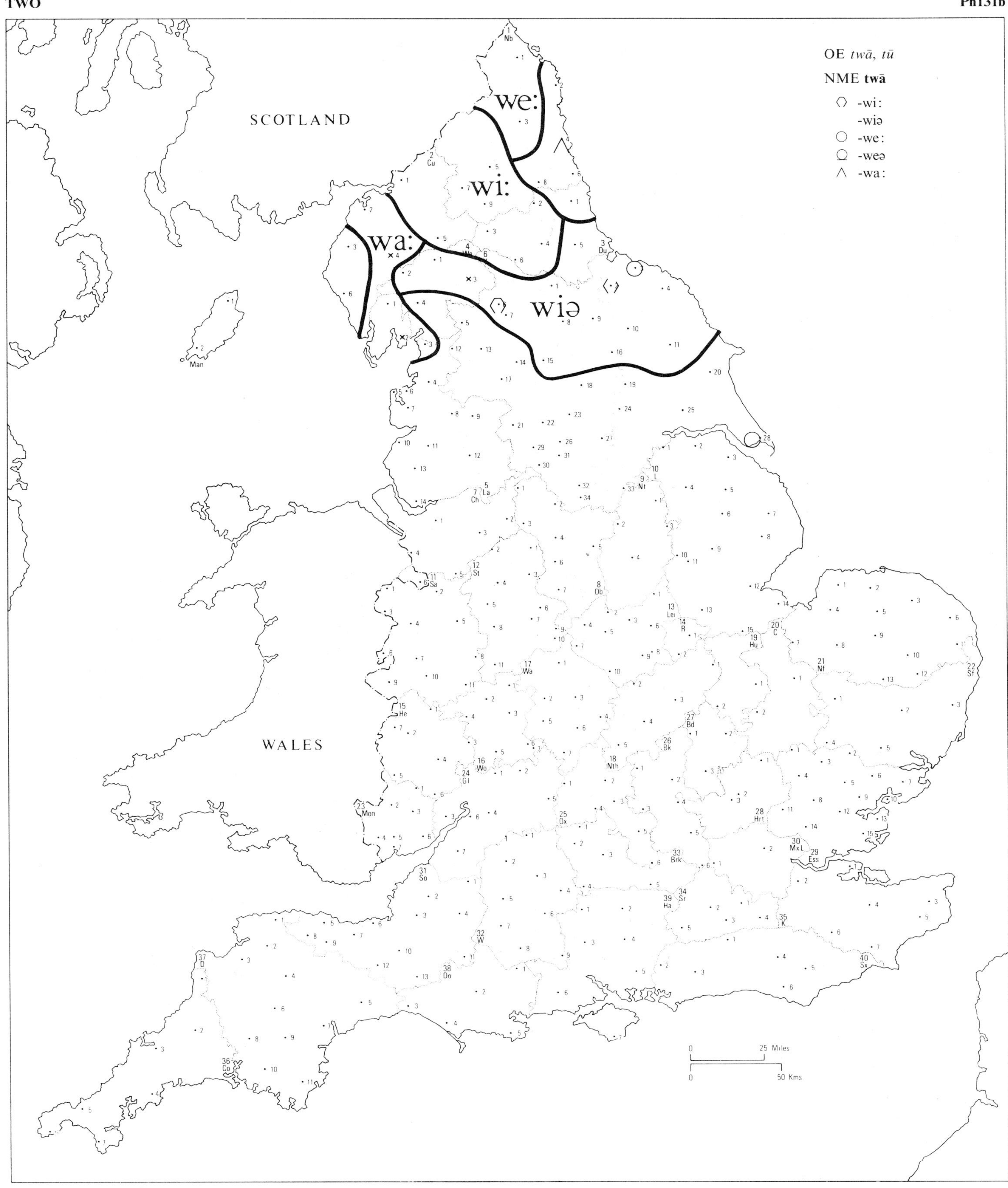

we˙ə 1Nb 3, weə 6Y +3 under we:
wa 1Nb +4 under wa:

i: 6Y +19
ɩə 6Y +19
wɛə 6Y 25

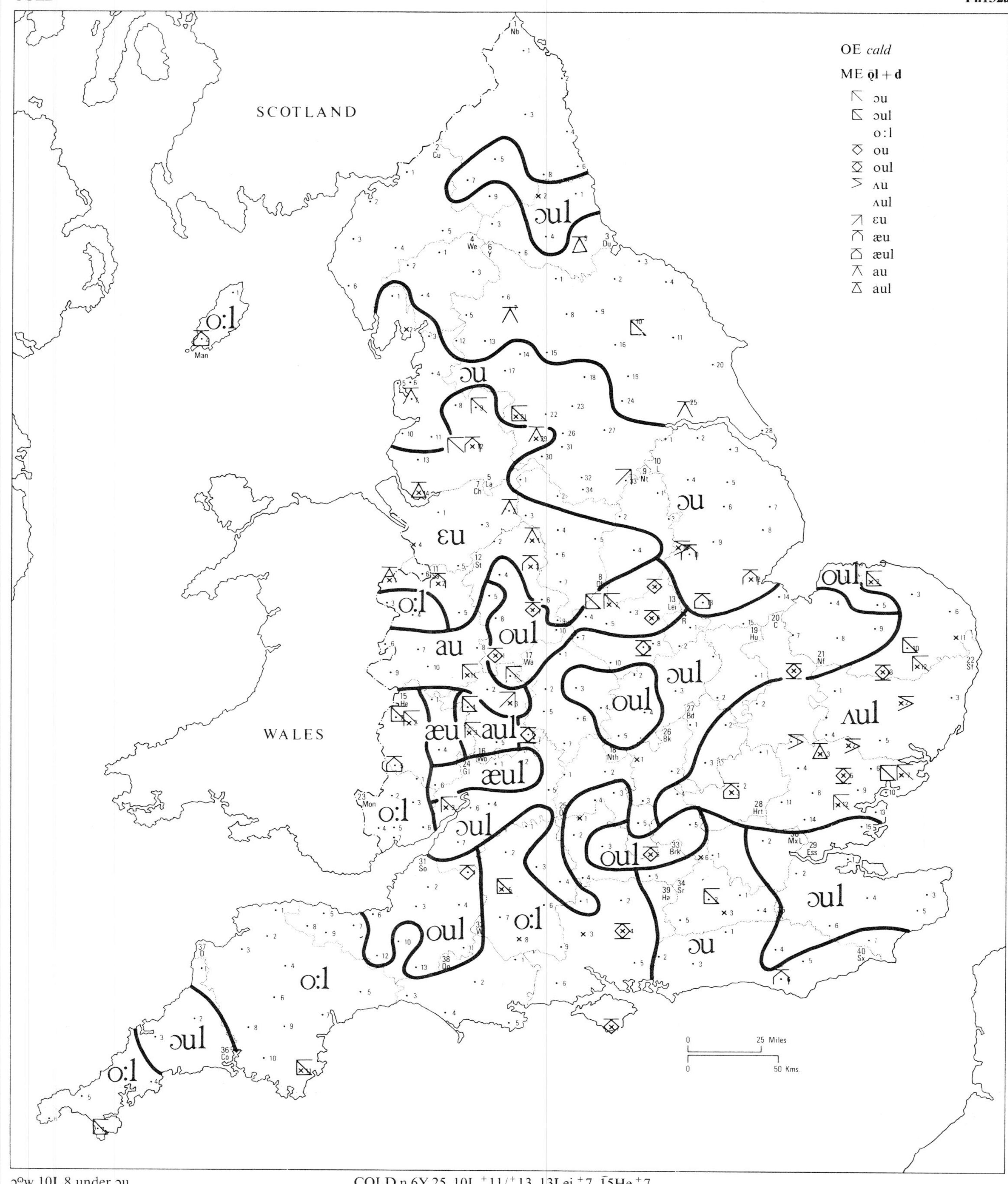

ɔ^{ɷ}w 10L 8 under ɔu
ɒɷ^{ə}ɫ 24Gl 6/7 under ɔul
o:^{ə}ɫ 23Mon 7, o˙^{ə}ɫ Man 1, o^{ə}l Man $^{+}$2,
o:^{ɷ}ɫ 25Ox 4, o:ɷɫ 23Mon 1 under o:l
o:ɷ 39Ha 7 under ou
ö:ɷl 21Nf 1, o:ɷl 21Nf 5 under oul
ɛu: 16Wo 3 under ɛu

ɛ̈ɷɫ 13Lei $^{+}$7
ä:l 15He $^{+}$7
ɑɷ 7Ch 4, ɑɷl 21Nf 11
ɒɫ 26Bk 1
o: 33Brk 1
u:ɫ 32W 8, 39Ha 3

COLD n 6Y 25, 10L $^{+}$11/$^{+}$13, 13Lei $^{+}$7, 1͡5He $^{+}$7, 16Wo $^{+}$1/$^{+}$6, 36Co $^{+}$7, 40Sx $^{+}$6; v 15He $^{+}$5

kɩ- 11Sa 1, kj- 12St $^{+}$3

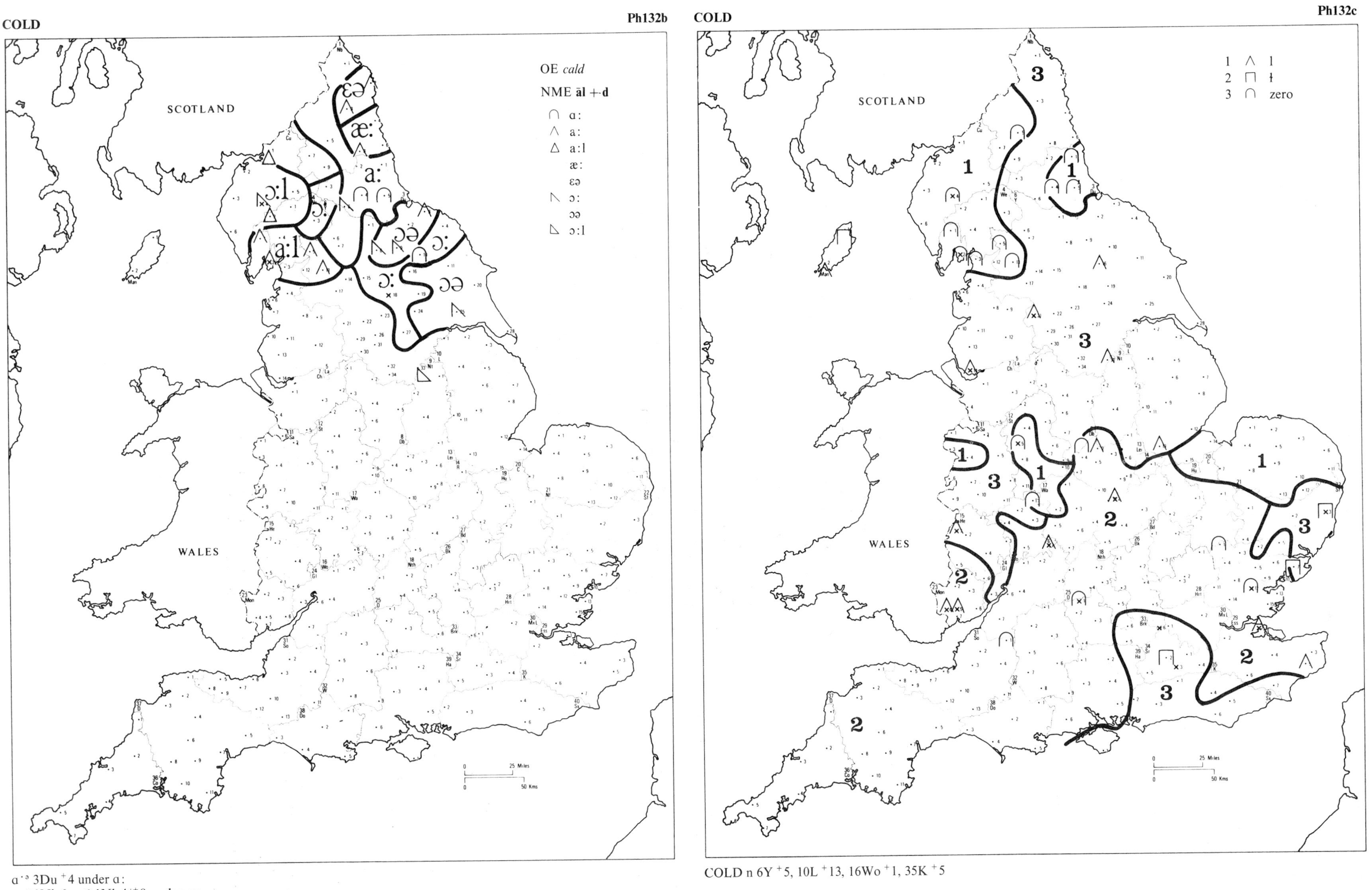

ɑ·ᵊ 3Du +4 under ɑ:
æ:ᵊ 1Nb6, æ·ᵊ 1Nb4/+8 under æ:

ǫ: 1Nb9

COLD n 6Y +5/+25/27

"I know that this ǫ: is the regular development at 1Nb9 (Allendale)" HO

COLD n 6Y +5, 10L +13, 16Wo +1, 35K +5

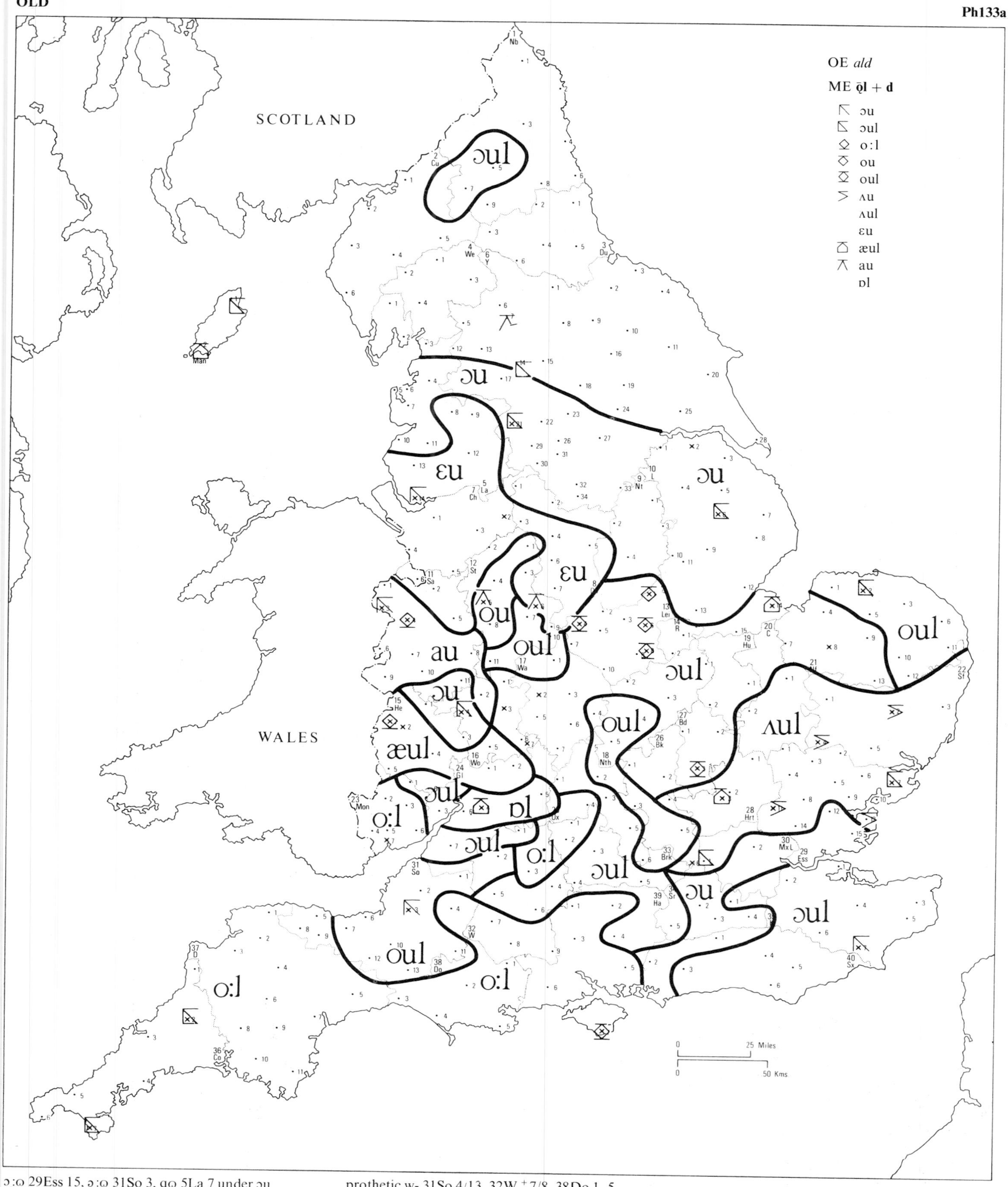

ɔ:ɷ 29Ess 15, ɔ̜:ɷ 31So 3, ɑɷ 5La 7 under ɔu
ɒɷᵊɫ 24Gl 3 under ɔul
o:ɷɫ 31So 12 under ou
æɷ 12St 3 under ɛu
ᵊæɷl 10L 14, æɷᵊɫ 24Gl 1, aɷɫ 16Wo 5,
24Gl 4 under æul
æɷ 16Wo 2 under au

ɛu:ɫ 16Wo 3
ɔ:ɫ 15He 2
u:ɫ 37D ⁺10

prothetic w- 31So 4/13, 32W ⁺7/8, 38Do 1–5,
39Ha 6

because of the unwieldy amount of im, no im
forms of OLD have been mapped

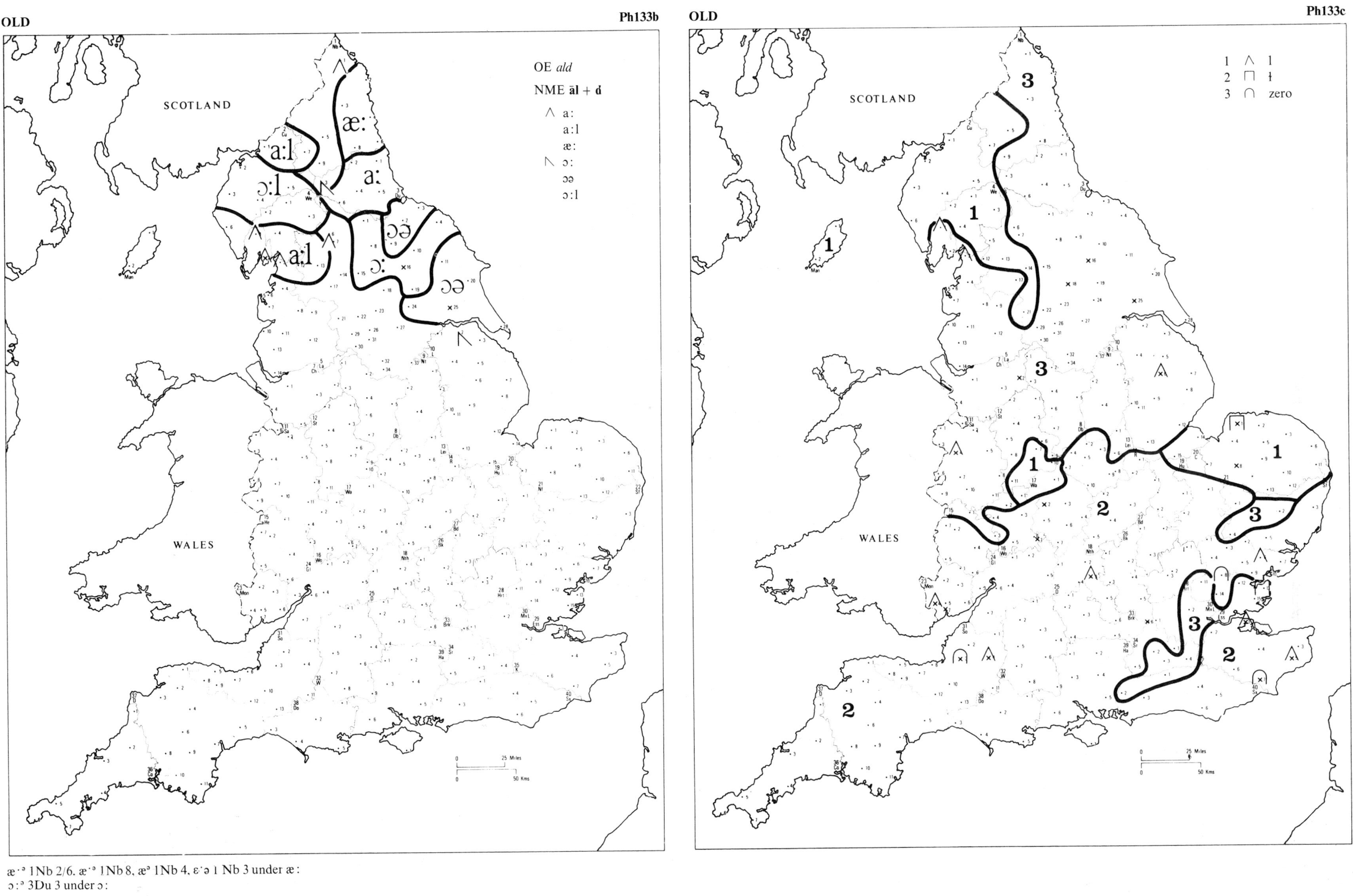

æ·ə 1Nb 2/6, æ·ə 1Nb 8, æə 1Nb 4, ɛ·ə 1 Nb 3 under æ:
ɔ:ə 3Du 3 under ɔ:

ǫ: 1Nb 9

"I know that this ǫ: is the regular development at 1 Nb 9 (Allendale)" HO

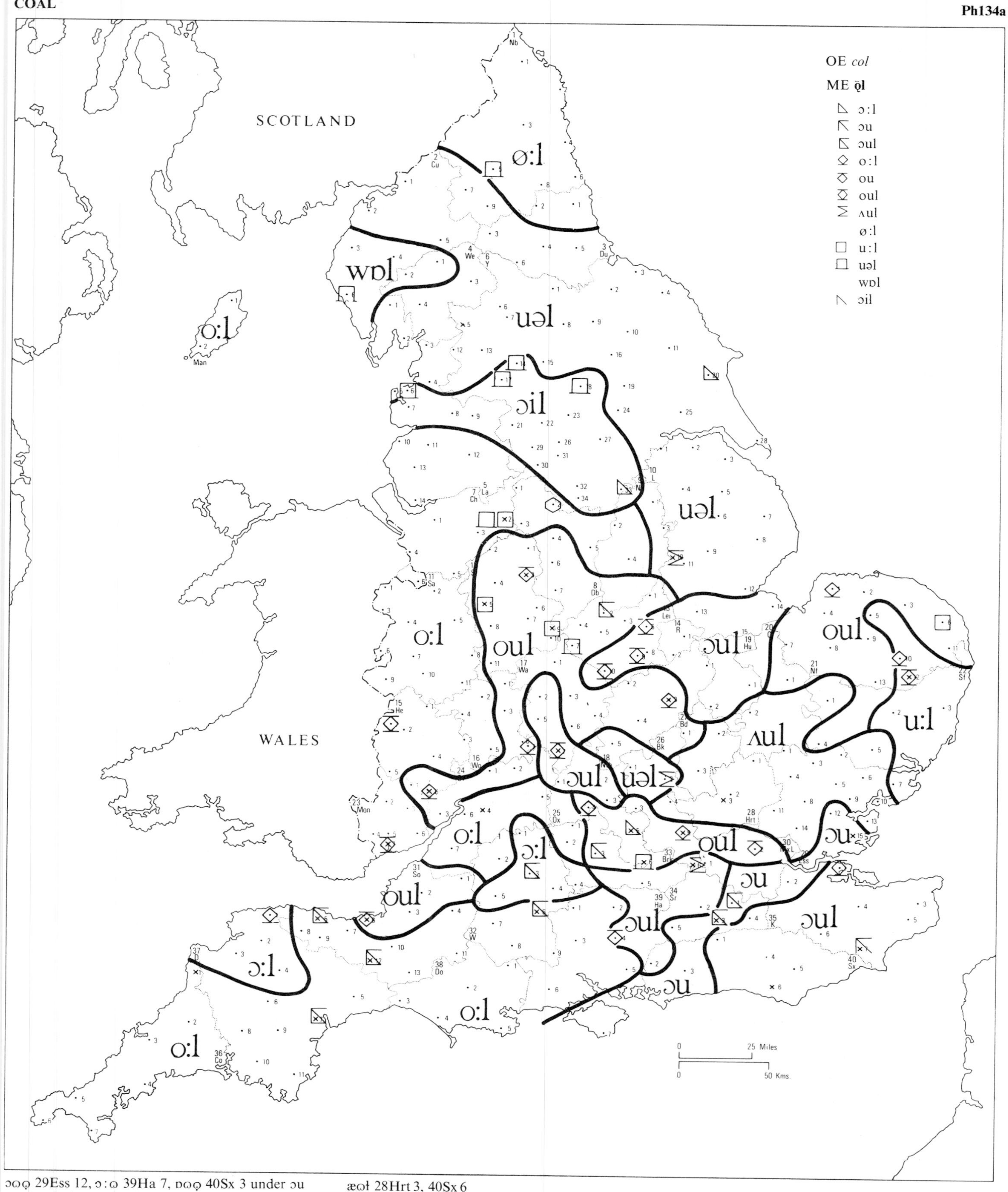

ɔɷǫ 29Ess 12, ɔ:ɷ 39Ha 7, ɒɷǫ 40Sx 3 under ɔu
ɔ:ɷɫ 32W +6, ɔ̣:ɷɫ 31So 5, ɔ:ᵚɫ 32W +6 under ɔul
o:ᵊl Man +2, 16Wo 2, 35K +1, ọ:ᵊɫ 23Mon 4,
o˙əl Man 1, o˙əɫ 21Nf +1, ọ˙əɫ 18Nth 3,
oəl 16Wo +7 under o:l
ǫ:ɷ 31So 6 under ou
oɷᵊɫ 20C 1, o:ɷl 8Db 7, 31So 3, o:ɷɫ 23Mon 1,
24Gl 2/3, o:ɷᵊɫ 24Gl 1, o:ᵚl 8Db 4/6 under oul
ø:ᵊl 1Nb +8, øᵊl 3Du 1, øəl 3Du 2 under ø:l
ᴧṻ:ɫ 22Sf 3 under u:l
ọəl 1Nb 9, 2Cu 2, 3Du +5, 6Y +19,
ʷọəl 4We 1 under uəl
ɷɒl 2Cu +4, wɔl 4We 2, wɔ:l 2Cu +4 under wɒl

æɷɫ 28Hrt 3, 40Sx 6
ɑ:ɫ 24Gl 4
ɑɷɫ 29Ess 15
o: 25Ox +4
ɷal 6Y 5

COAL- 6Y +33, 13Lei +9, 16Wo +7, 23Mon 7,
25Ox +4, 30MxL +2, 33Brk +3, 34Sr +1,
35K +1

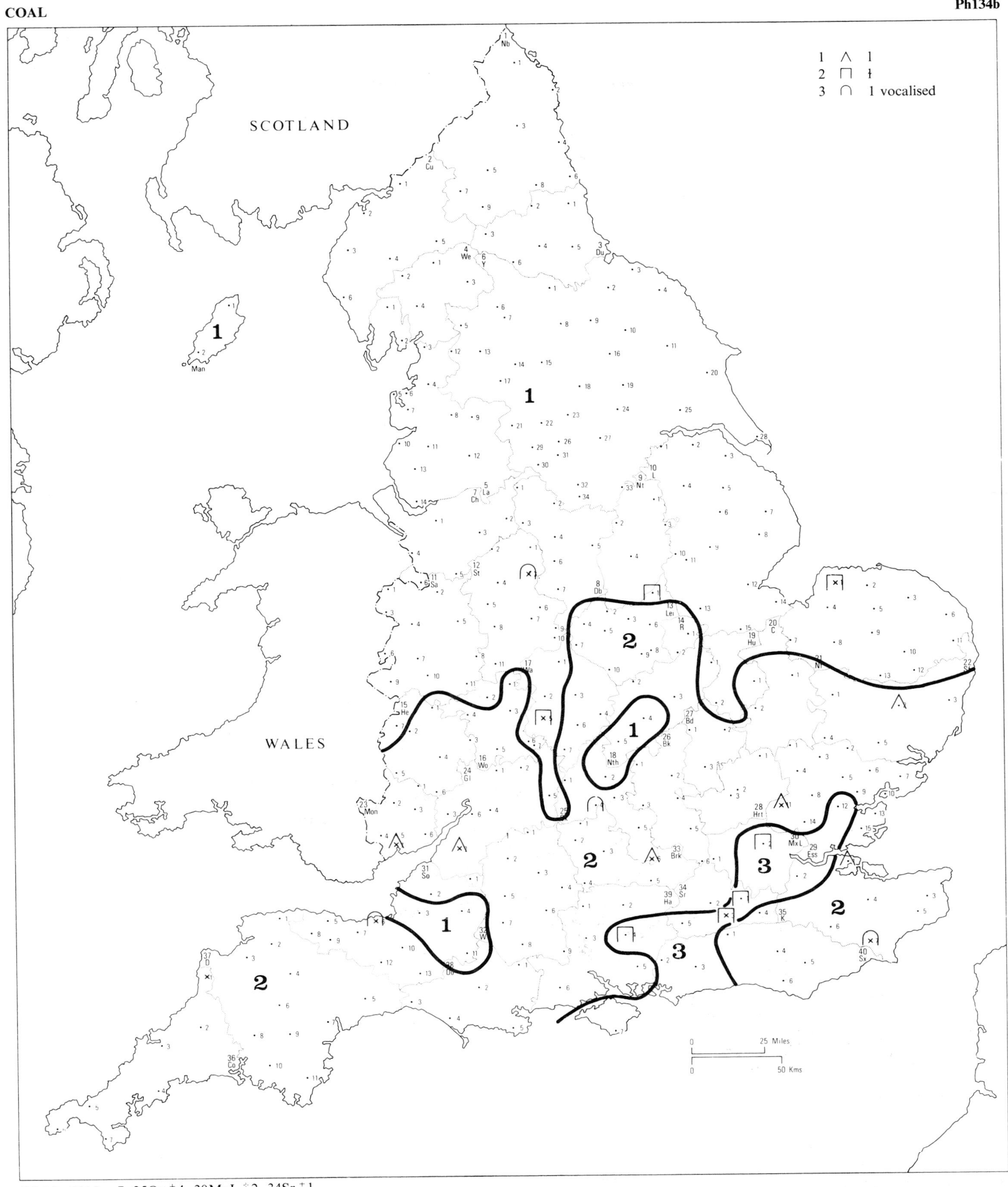

COAL- 23Mon 7, 25Ox ⁺4, 30MxL ⁺2, 34Sr ⁺1, 35K ⁺1

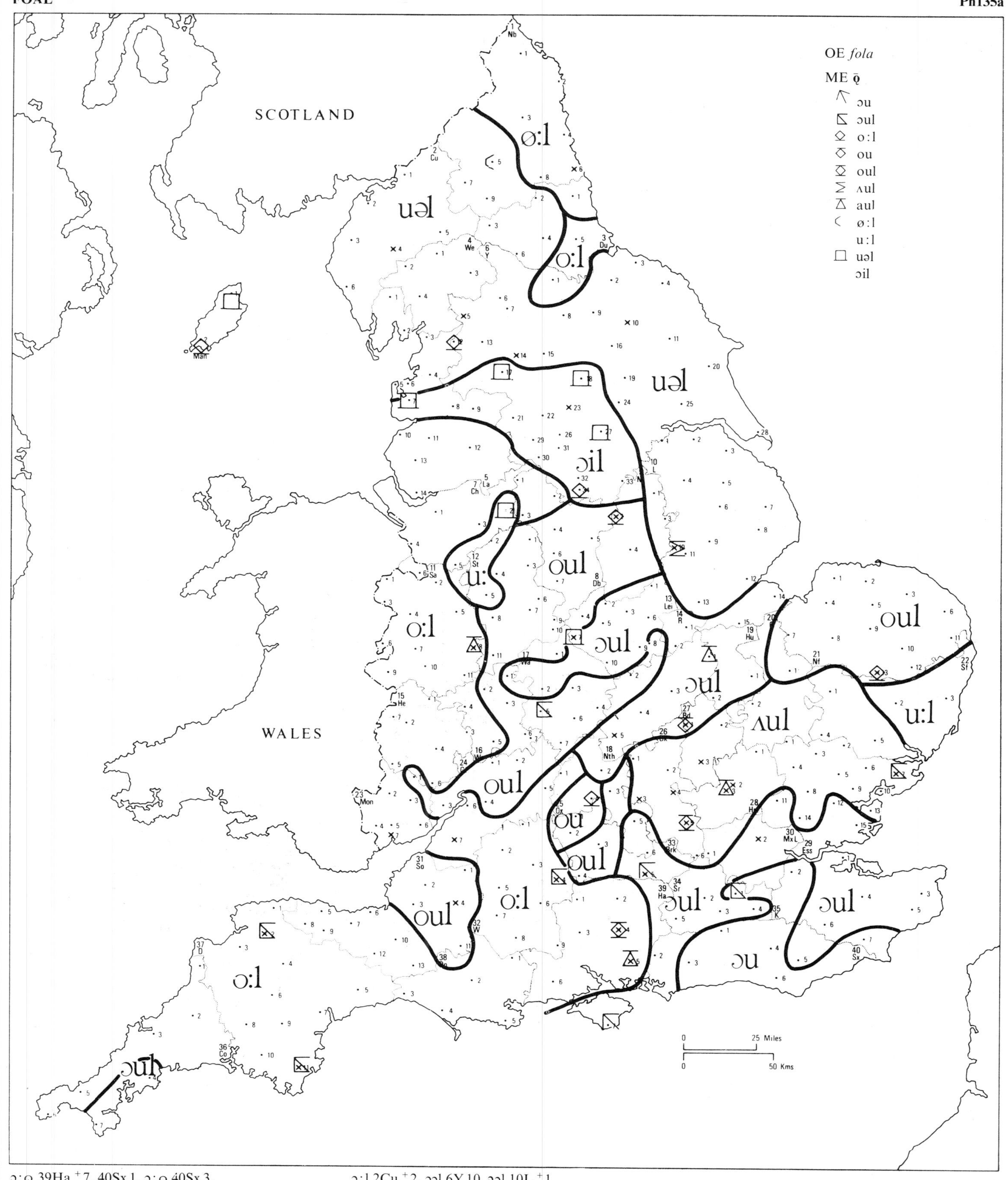

ɔ:ɷ 39Ha $^{+}$7, 40Sx 1, ɔ:ɷ̣ 40Sx 3,
 ɒɷɷ̣ 40Sx 4 under ɔu

ɔɷᵊl 10L 15, ɔ:ɷ̣ɫ 39Ha $^{+}$7,
 ɒ̈ɷᵊɫ 18Nth $^{+}$1 under ɔul

o:ᵊl 3Du 5, o:ᵊɫ 7Ch 6, 16Wo 4, 24Gl 6,
 o˙ᵊl 6Y $^{+}$34, Man 2 under o:l

o:ɷ 25Ox $^{+}$4, o:ɷ̣ 33Brk 1/2 under ou

ʊɷ:ɫ 16Wo 6, o:ɷl 21Nf $^{+}$1, 31So 11,
 o:ɷɫ 23Mon 1, 24Gl 1/2/4, 33Brk 4,
 o̧:ɷɫ 31So 3, o:ɷᵊɫ 24Gl 3, o:ᵚl 8Db 4–6,
 9Nt 4, o̧:ᵚl 8Db 7 under oul

əɷɫ 22Sf 5 under ʌul

ạ̈ɷᵊɫ 18Nth $^{+}$1, æɷɫ 28Hrt 3 under aul

øəl 1Nb 8, 3Du 1, œ:l 1Nb $^{+}$2,
 œ̣:l 1Nb $^{+}$2 under ø:l

wɷəl 6Y $^{+}$3, ọəl 1Nb 9, 2Cu $^{+}$2, 3Du 6,
 ọ˙əl 4We 1 under uəl

ɔ:l 2Cu $^{+}$2, ɔəl 6Y 10, ɔ̣əl 10L $^{+}$1
ɷal 2Cu 4, ɷ̣al 6Y 5

-FOAL 20C 1, 21Nf $^{+}$1; FOAL v 7Ch $^{+}$2;
 FOALDING prp 17Wa $^{+}$5

-d 16Wo 7, 17Wa 4/$^{+}$5/7, 24Gl 4, 31So 1,
 32W 3/5/7/9, 35K 6, 38Do 1/4/5, 39Ha 1–3/5/6

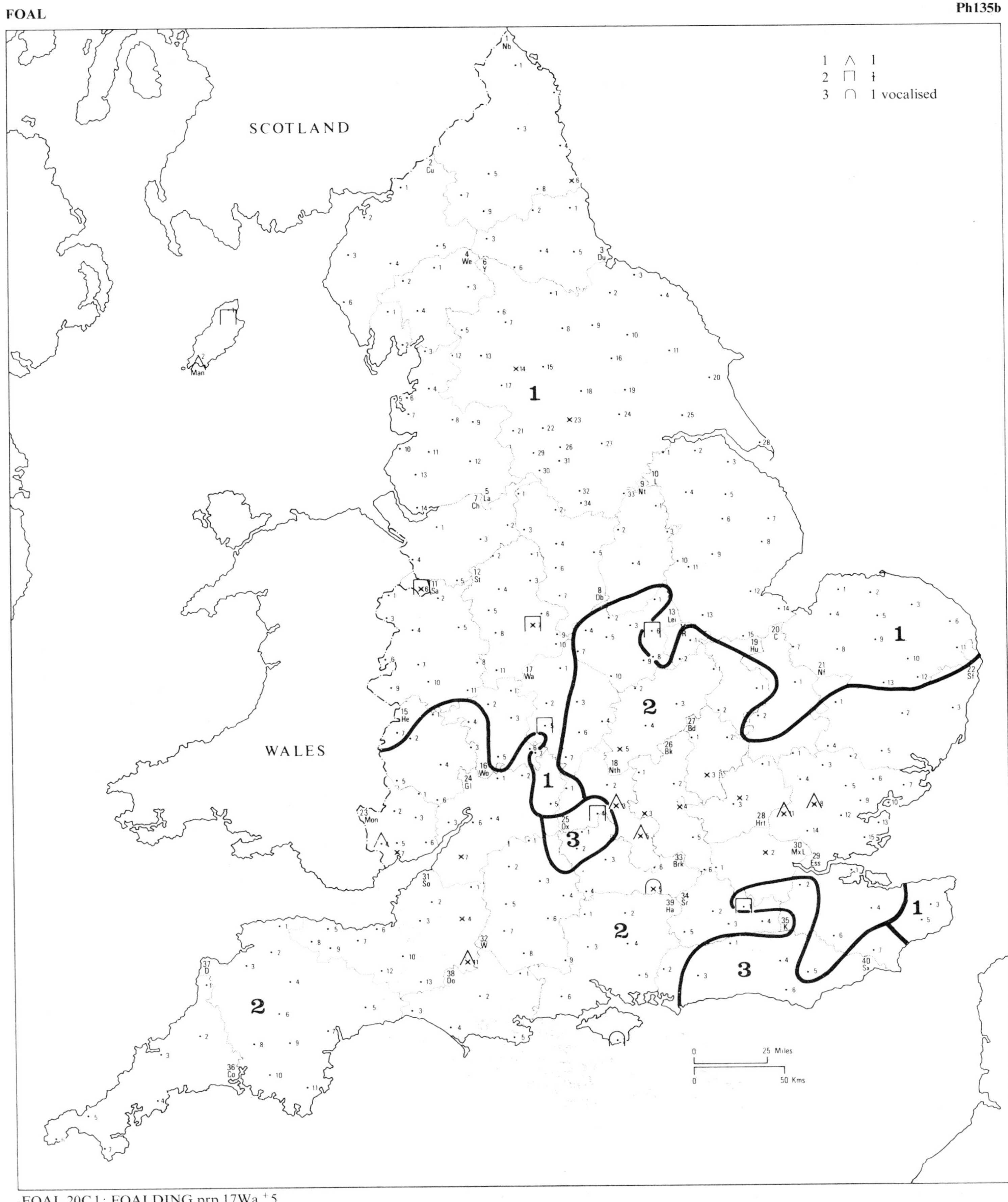

-FOAL 20C1; FOALDING prp 17Wa [+]5

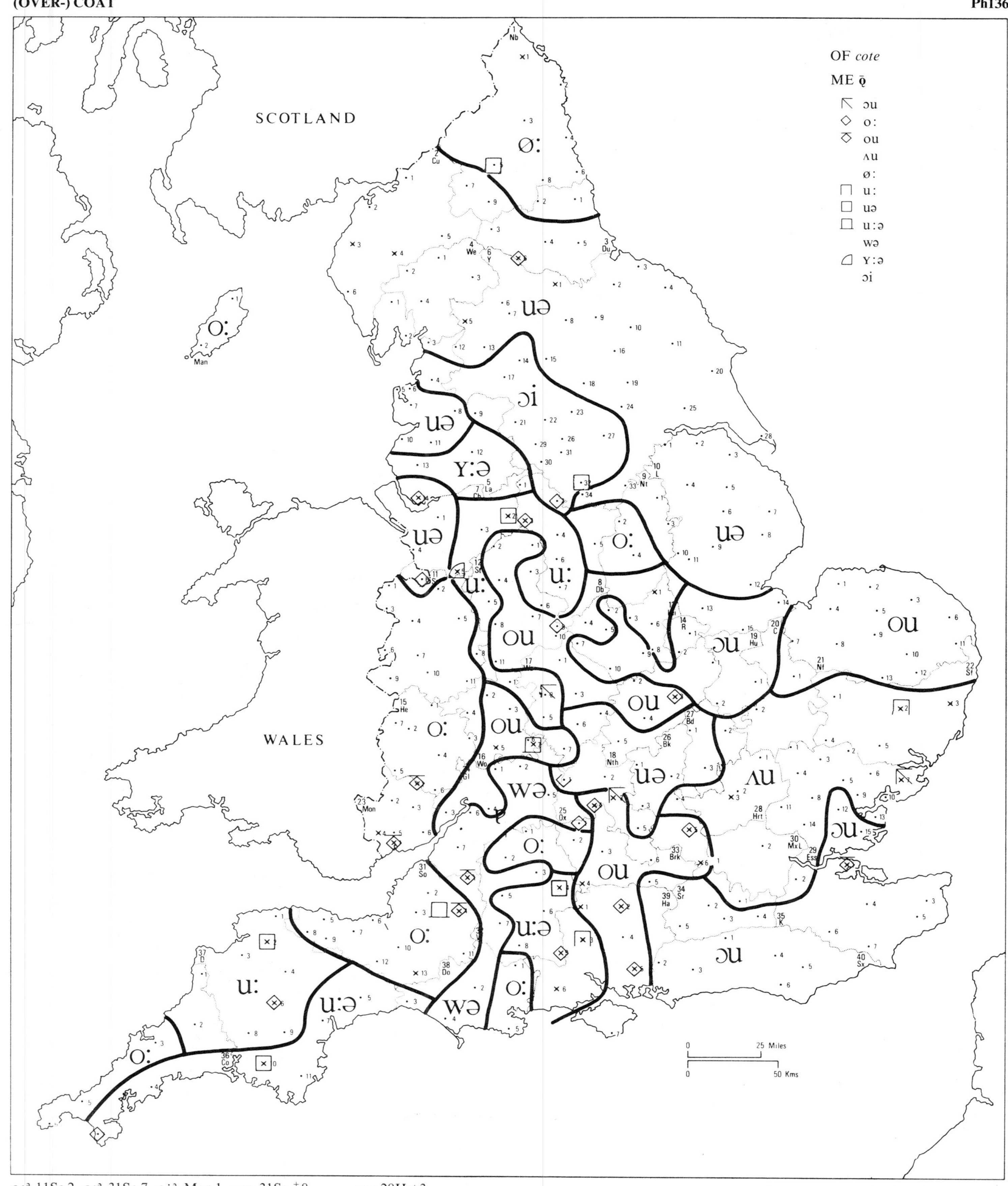

o:ᵊ 11Sa 2, ǫ:ᵊ 31So 7, o˙ᵊ Man 1, o:ə 31So +8, 36Co +7, 38Do 5, o˙ə 8Db 5, 18Nth 3, o:ᶷ 9Nt 2, o˙ᵘ Man 2, wǫ: 31So 3 under o:
oωᵊ 16Wo 2, o:ω 23Mon 1, 24Gl 3/4, woω, woωə 31So +4 under ou
ø˙ə 1Nb 8, øᵊ 3Du 1/2, œ:ᵊ 1Nb 6, œ˙ə 1Nb 3 under ø:
ᵊωə 7Ch 1, ᵊüə 7Ch 4, ᶷu˙ə 4We 4, ǫə 1Nb 9, 4We 1, 5La 2, 17Wa 4, 27Bd 1, ǫ˙ə 27Bd 3, oə 2Cu 1, wǫə 2Cu 2 under uə
wω 24Gl 5/6, 33Brk +1 under wə
ᶥY˙ə 7Ch 5, ιY:ə 5La 12 under Y:ə

æω 28Hrt 3
ɔ: 2Cu 4, 39Ha 1, ɔə 6Y +1, ɔ˙ə 6Y +1
ω 22Sf 3
ωa 6Y 5
wæ (sic) 31So 13
wɒ 2Cu 3, 33Brk 4, ʷɒ 16Wo 5
ə 1Nb 1, 13Lei 1

COAT 6Y 12, 7Ch +6, 8Db +2, 10L 14, 17Wa +2, 19Hu 2, 20C 2, 21Nf 3/9/12, 22Sf 2/5, 24Gl 5/7, 25Ox 3, 28Hrt 1, 29Ess 5, 31So +4, 36Co +7

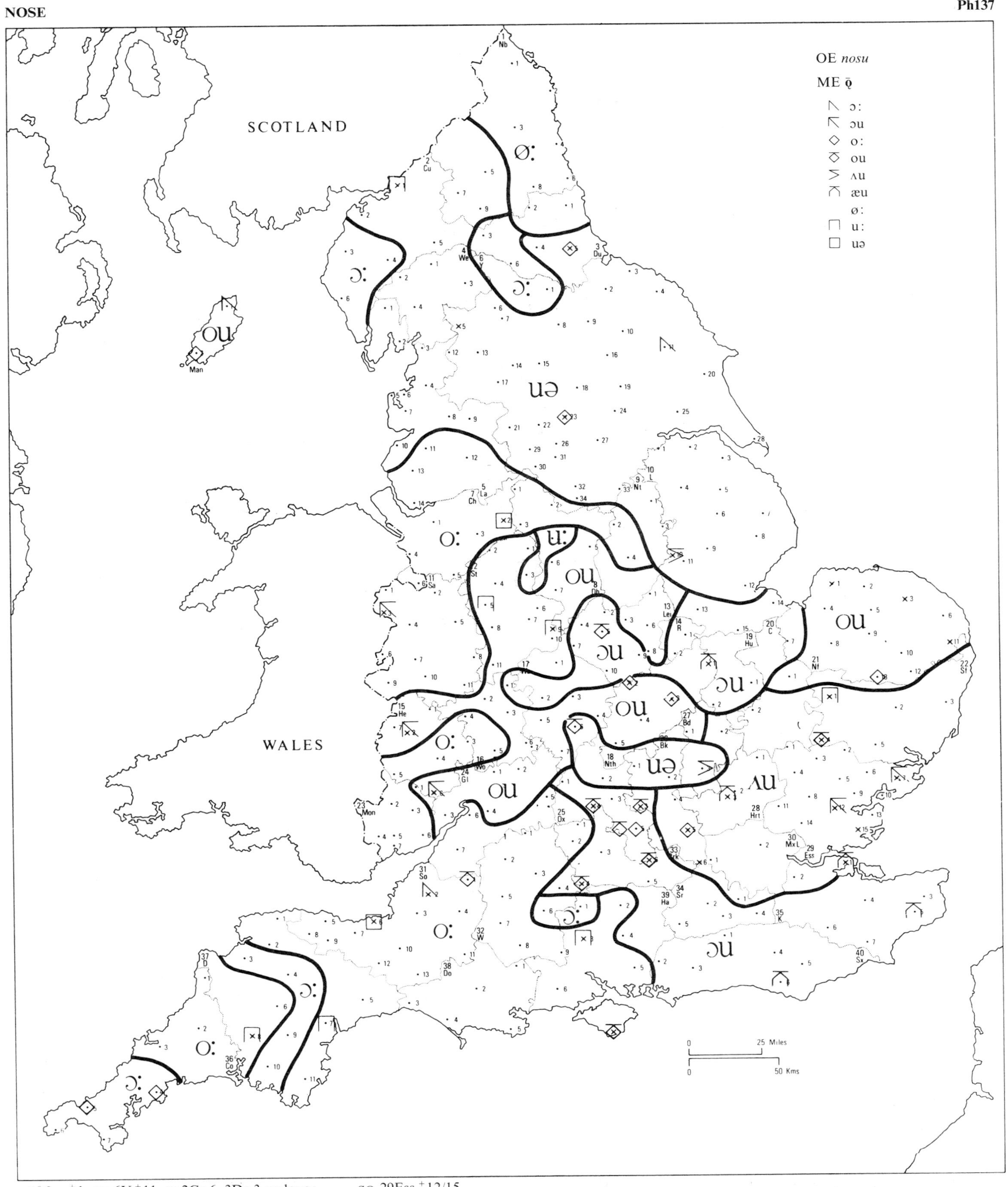

ɔ:^{ə} Man +1, ɔ˙ə 6Y +11, ọ: 2Cu 6, 3Du 3 under ɔ:
o:^{ə} 3Du 5, ö:^{ə} 23Mon +5, o˙ə 18Nth 2,
oə 23Mon +5 under o:
oɷ^{ə} 16Wo 2, o:ɷ 24Gl 3/4, 33Brk +4,
o:ɷ^{ə} 24Gl 1, o:^{ɷ} 8Db 5/6, 15He 7, 23Mon 1,
24Gl 2, 25Ox 4 under ou
äɷ 18Nth 1 under æu
ø:^{ə} 1Nb 6, ø^{ə} 3Du 1 under ø:
^{ə}ụ˙ə 4We 4, ụ:ə 31So 6, ọə 1Nb 9, 4We 1,
ọ˙ə 27Bd +3, oə 6Y 19, 10L 4 under uə

ɑɷ 29Ess +12/15
ɷa 4We +2, 6Y 5

NOSE- 21Nf +13, 29Ess +12; NOSE v 36Co +5;
NOSED 25Ox +5; -NOSED 25Ox +5;
NOSEY 27Bd +3, 35K +5

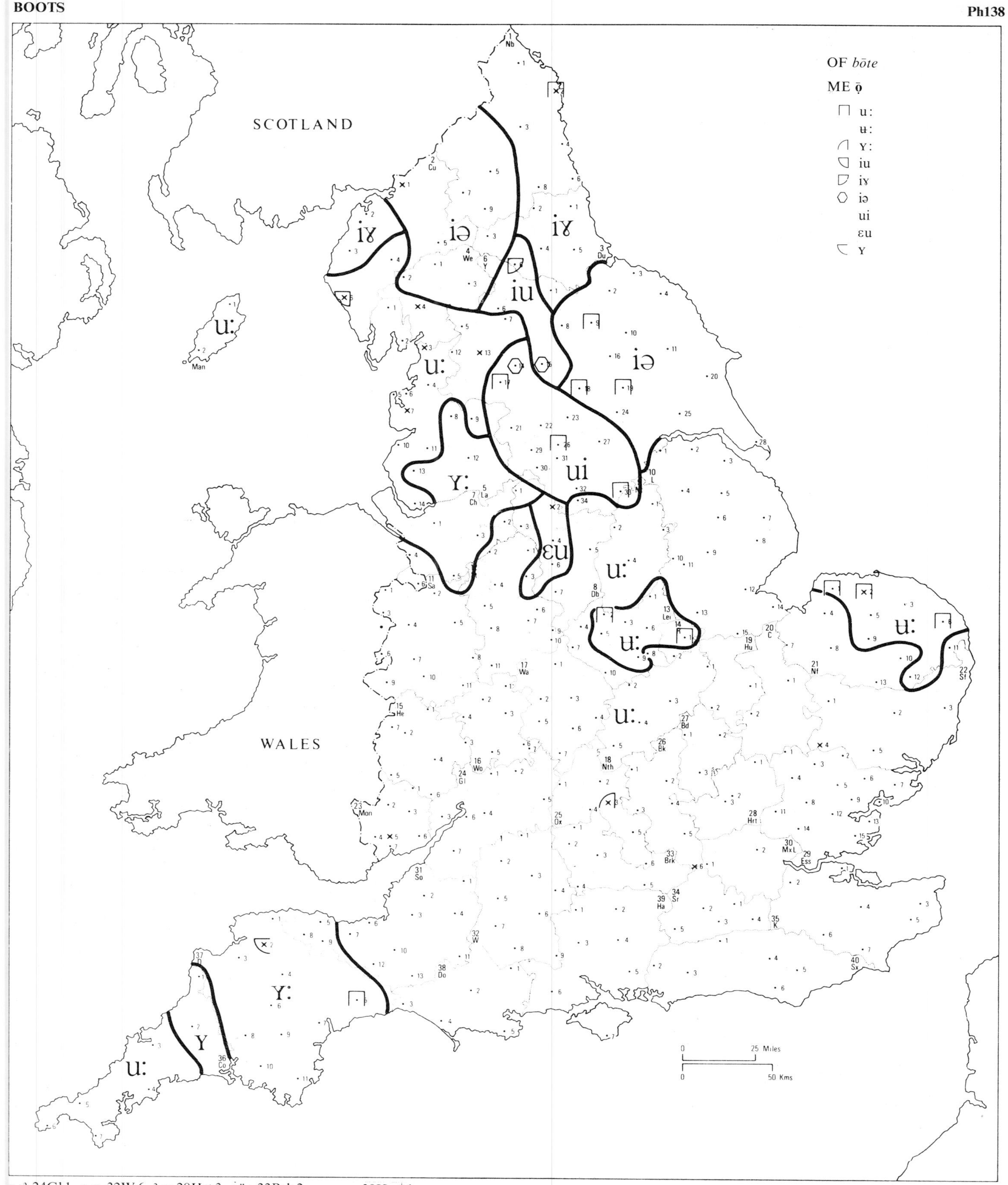

u:ᵊ 24Gl 1, u:ə 32W 6, ᵊu: 28Hrt 3, əü: 33Brk 2, əu˙ 21Nf +4, ᶥu: 8Db 5/7, 24Gl 2, ᶥü: 13Lei 8, 14R 2, ɩu: 11Sa 2/5, ïü: 33Brk +5, ɩü 21Nf 8, öu 5La 5, ü 29Ess +5, ɷ 31So 13, 38Do +5, 39Ha 7 under u:

ᶥʉ: 13Lei 1/+2/+6, 14R +1, ᶥʉ 21Nf +1, ɩʉ 21Nf 5, ʉ 21Nf +1 under ʉ:

ᶥʏ: 7Ch 5, y: 25Ox 3 under ʏ:

ɩu: 2Cu 6, 3Du +6, 6Y +15 under iu

jɤ 1Nb 6, 3Du 2/4/5, ɩø 1Nb 8, ɩɷ 2Cu 2/3, 6Y 1, ɩɷ̈ 1Nb 3, 3Du +6, jɷ 3Du 1 under iɤ

ʌ̣ 39Ha +1

ɷə 4We 4, 5La 3

-BOOTS 21Nf +1

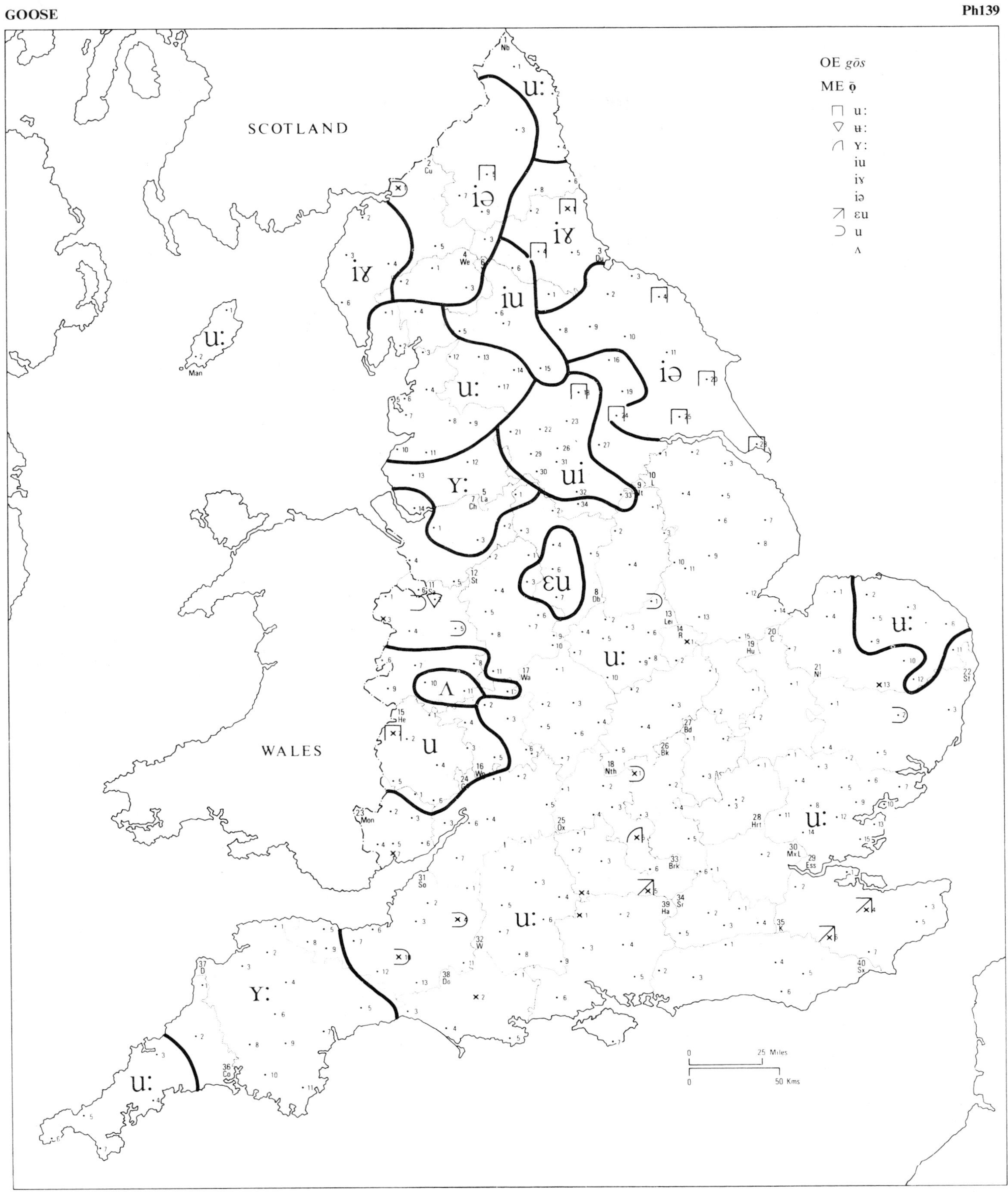

ᵊu: 28Hrt 3, 39Ha 7, ᵊü: 35K 5, öu 5La 5,
ou 21Nf 7, ᶥu: 8Db 5, ɩu: 11Sa ⁺5 under u:
ʉ 21Nf ⁺6, ɩʉ: 21Nf 5 under ʉ:
ɩu: 3Du 6, 6Y 5/15 under iu
jɤ 1Nb 6, 3Du 2/⁺4/5, ɩɷ 2Cu 2/3, ɩɷ̈ 2Cu 4,
6Y 1 under iɤ

o: 11Sa 3, o˙ 21Nf 13
əɷ 33Brk 4

GOOSE- 11Sa ⁺2/⁺5, 13Lei ⁺1, 21Nf ⁺6

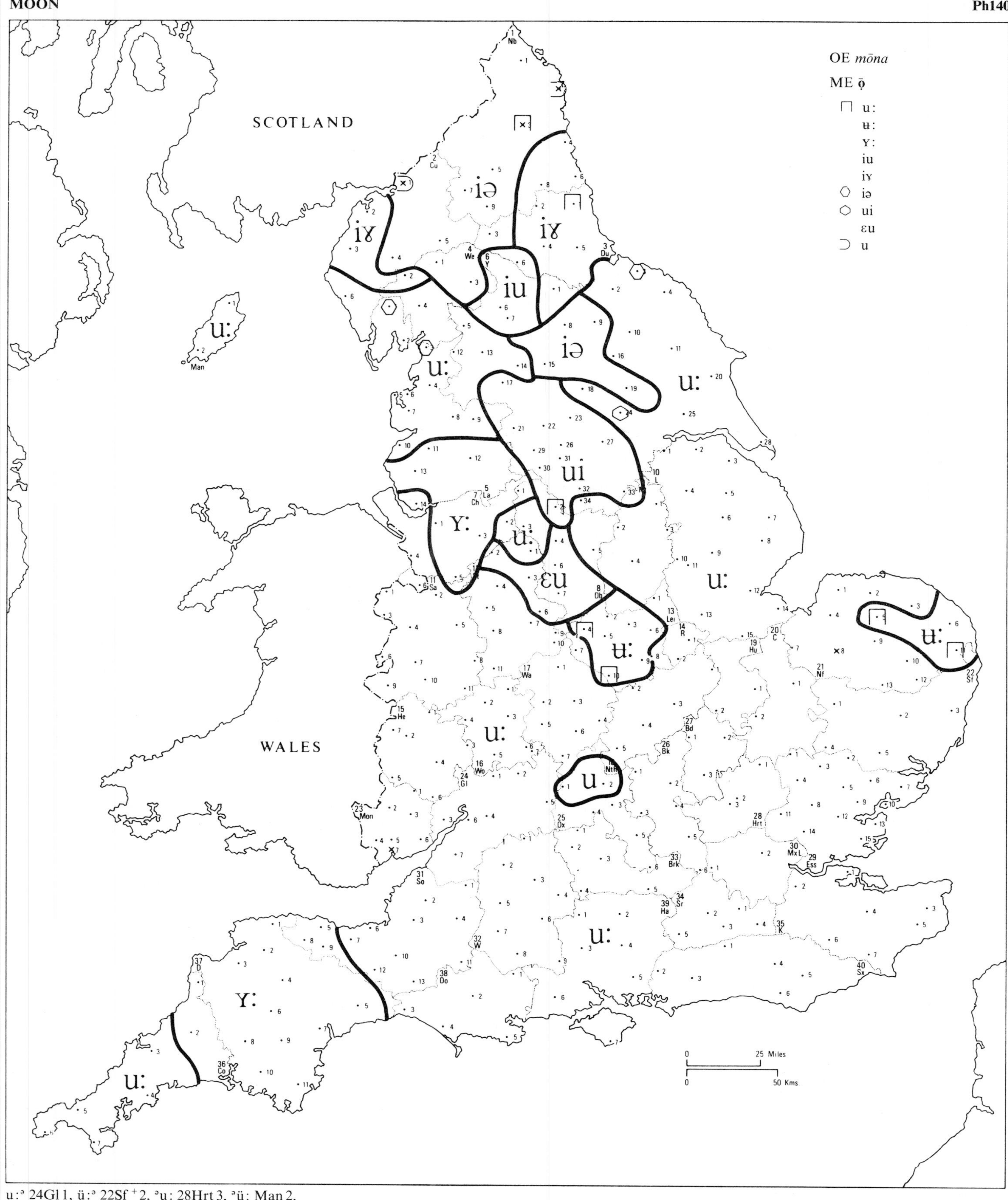

u:ᵊ 24Gl 1, ü:ᵊ 22Sf +2, ᵊu: 28Hrt 3, ᵊü: Man 2,
17Wa 3, əu: 32W 7, əü: 39Ha 7, əu˙ 21Nf +4,
əü˙ 35K 4, u 21Nf +7, öu 5La 5, ᶥu: 8Db 5,
11Sa 2, ᶥü̟: 29Ess +3, ᶥü: 13Lei 8, 22Sf +3,
29Ess 14, ɩu: 11Sa 5, ᶥü 29Ess +3,
ɩ̞u 21Nf +4 under u:
ᶥʉ: 13Lei 2/+3/+4/5/9/+10, ɩʉ: 21Nf +5 under ʉ:
ᶥʏ: 7Ch 5 under ʏ:
jɤ 1Nb 6, 3Du 4/5, ɩ̆ø 1Nb 8, ɩɷ 2Cu 2/3, 6Y 1,
ɩɷ̈ 4We 2, jɷ 3Du +1 under iɤ
i:ᵊ 3Du 3 under iə

aɷ 12St +1
ɤ 1Nb +2

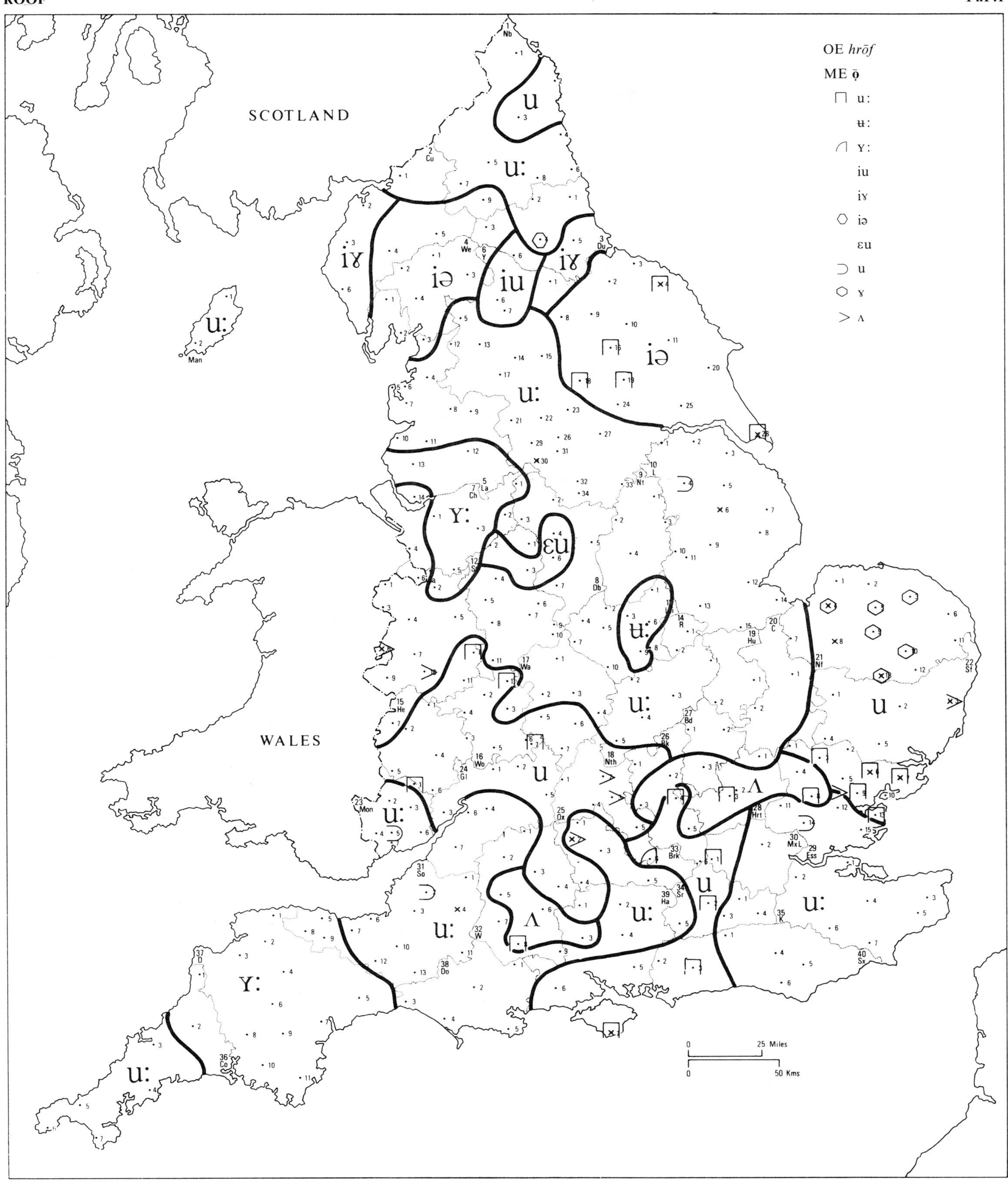

ᵊu: 28Hrt +3, ʉu: 29Ess 7, ᵒu: 6Y 12, öu 5La 5,
ou 21Nf +7, ˌu: 8Db 5, ˌu· 8Db 7,
ɩu: 11Sa 5 under u:
ˌʉ: 13Lei 1 under ʉ:
ˌʏ: 7Ch 5, ʏʉ: 11Sa 2, ʏ 37D 2 under ʏ:
ɩu: 3Du 6 under iu
ɩω 2Cu 2/3, ɩω̈ 6Y 1 under iɤ
i:ᵊ 3Du 3 under iə

ωɩ 6Y +22
ɘ: 31So 4

ROOFING 21Nf +5

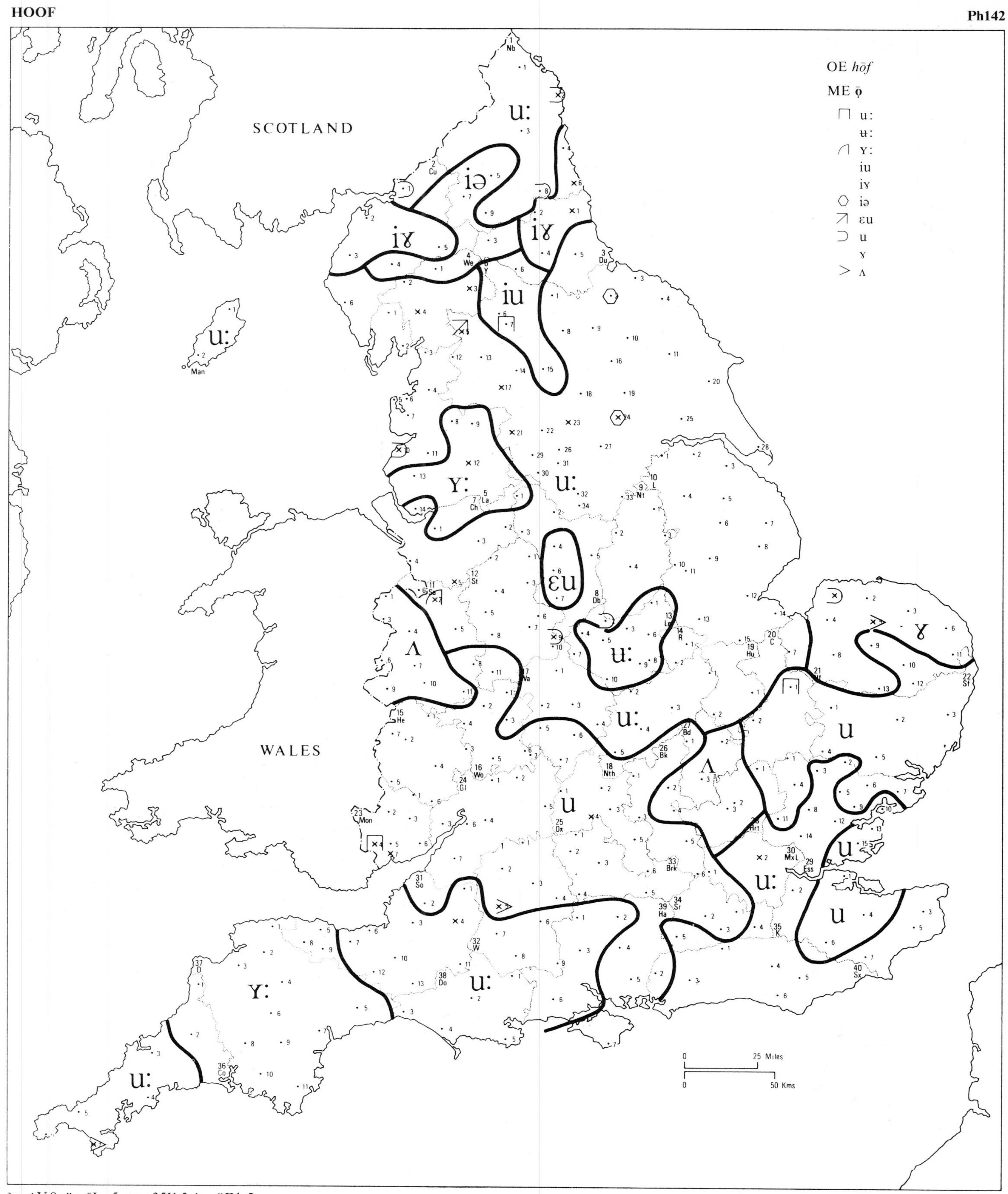

ᵊu: 6Y 9, öu 5La 5, ɒu: 35K 5, ᶥu: 8Db 5,
ɩu: 11Sa 5, ᵋu: 17Wa 1 under u:
ʏ 37D 4/10, ʏʉ: 11Sa 2 under ʏ:
ɩú: 3Du 6, 6Y 15 under iu
jɤ 3Du 2, ɩɷ 2Cu 3, jɷ 2Cu 2/5, 3Du 4 under iɤ
ɩɷ 12St 9 under u

h- retained 1Nb 1–5/7–9, 2Cu 1/3/5, 3Du 2/3/5/6, 4We 1/2, 6Y 1, Man 1/2, 11Sa 1, 20C 1, 21Nf 1–13, 22Sf 1–5, 29Ess 2–10/12–15, 30MxL 1, 31So 2/3/6/7/10–13, 32W 6/8/9, 33Brk 1, 34Sr 1/4/5, 35K 4/5/7, 38Do 3, 39Ha 2/6

-v 37D 2/6

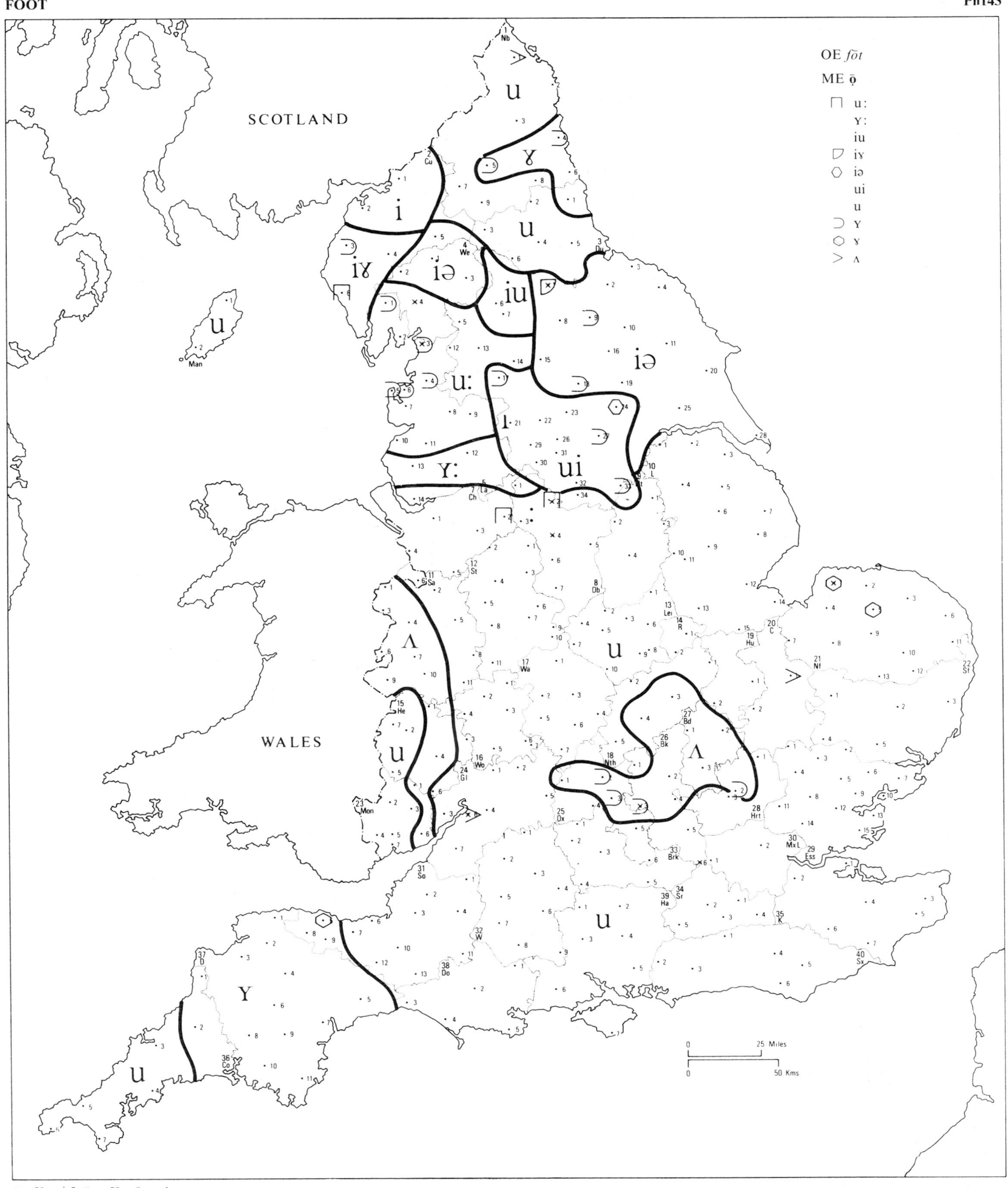

öu 5La +5, öω˙ 5La 8 under u:
ιω 2Cu +3, ιω̈ 2Cu 4, 6Y 1 under iɤ
ω: 16Wo +5 under u
ɤə 21Nf 1 under ɤ
ə 24Gl 6, 25Ox +3 under ʌ

ι 6Y +8, (sic) 32W +4
εω 8Db 4
ɒ Man +2
ωə 4We 4

FOOT- 6Y +8, Man +2, 20C +1;
-FOOT 31So +5; FOOT inf 16Wo +5

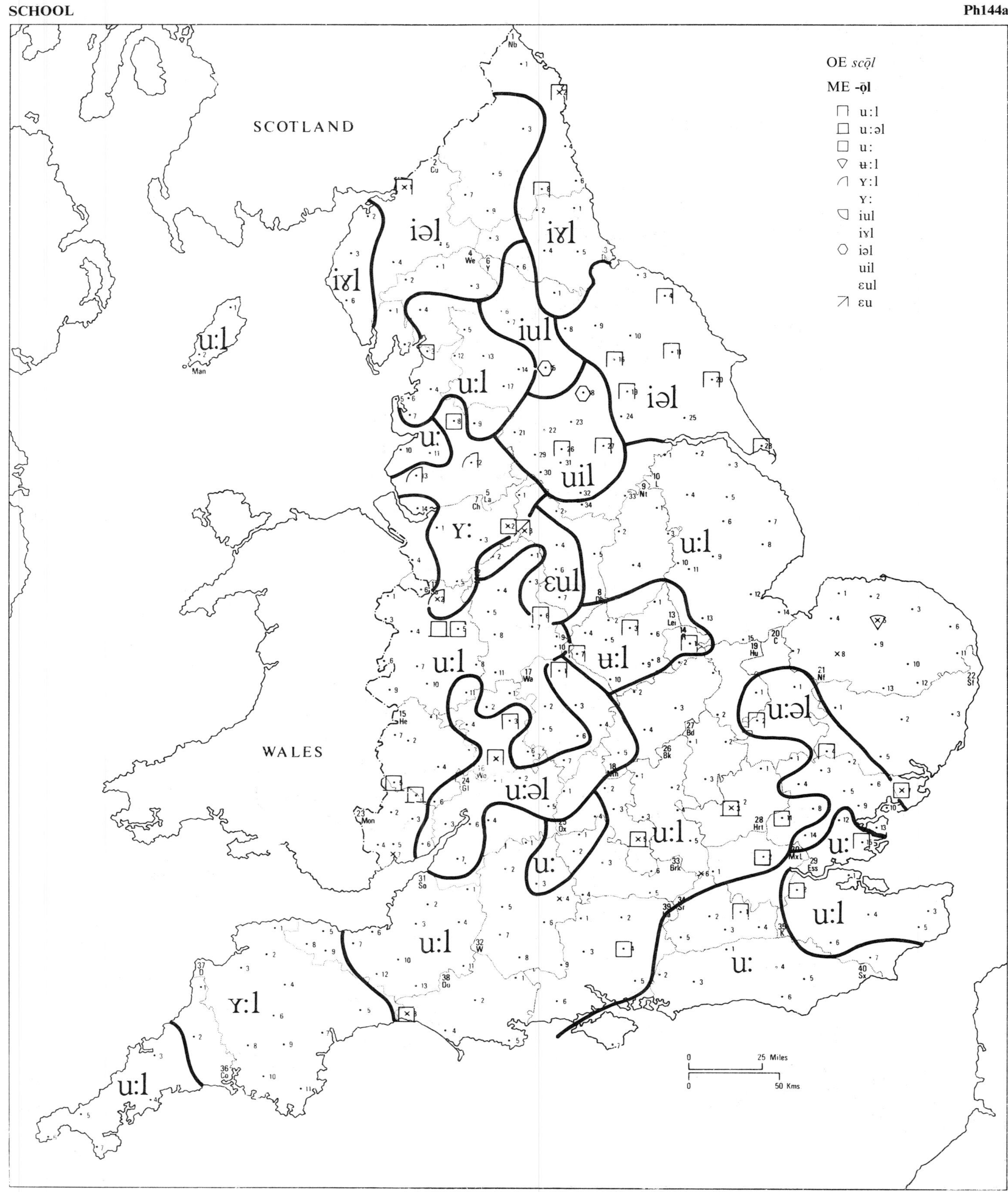

uɷl 15He +7, u:ɷɫ 33Brk 3/+4, ɷ̈ü:ɫ 33Brk +4,
ul 35K +1, ɷl 2Cu 1, 12St 9, 16Wo +7,
ɷɫ 16Wo +5, 29Ess +11, ə̣u:l 21Nf 2,
ə̣ul 21Nf 11 under u:l

ɷᵊɫ 25Ox 5 under u:əl

ᵊu: 7Ch +2, u:ᵚ 34Sr +1, u:ɷ 32W 3, 40Sx +2/6,
u:ọ 33Brk +1/2, 40Sx 3/+4/5, ü:ọ 39Ha 7,
u˙ɷ 25Ox +4, uɷ 34Sr +3/+5, 35K 7,
uọ 33Brk +1, 34Sr +5, 40Sx +2/+4, öu 5La 5,
ᵚu 5La +8, ɷọ 29Ess +15, ɷuɷ 34Sr +5,
ɷuọ 34Sr 2/+3, ɷ̈uọ 29Ess +7,
ɷu:ɷ 29Ess +7/12/+15, 34Sr +4/+5,
ɷu:ọ 34Sr +4, 40Sx 1 under u:

ʉɫ 13Lei +2 under ʉ:l
ʏʉ:l 11Sa 2 under ʏ:l
ᶥʏ: 7Ch 3, ɩʏ̈: 7Ch 5 under ʏ:
ɩu:l 3Du 6, 5La +3, 6Y +15 under iul
ɩɷl 2Cu 2/3, ɩɷ̈l 6Y 1, ɩøl 1Nb +8, jɷl 3Du 1/2/4,
jɤl 1Nb 6, 3Du 5 under iɤl
i:ᵊl 3Du 3 under iəl

o:ɫ 32W 4

SCHOOL- 16Wo +3/+7, 29Ess +11

kᶥ- 8Db 5, 13Lei 1/+2–+5/6/+7/8/+10, 14R +1/2,
kɩ- 11Sa 5, 12St 9, 16Wo 3, 21Nf 5

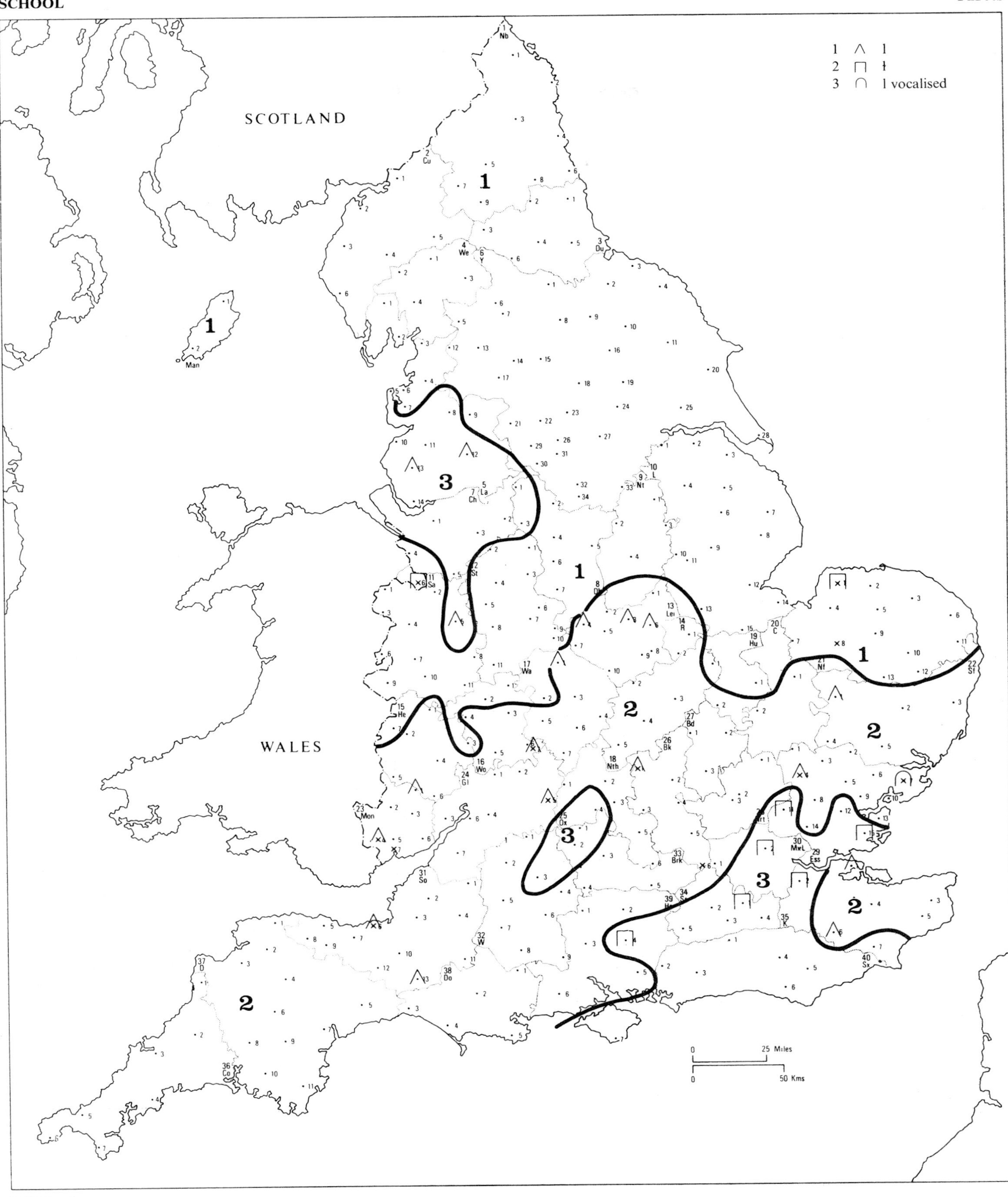
1 ∧ l
2 ⊓ ɫ
3 ∩ l vocalised
SCOTLAND
WALES
0 25 Miles
0 50 Kms

ɫ 23Mon 4

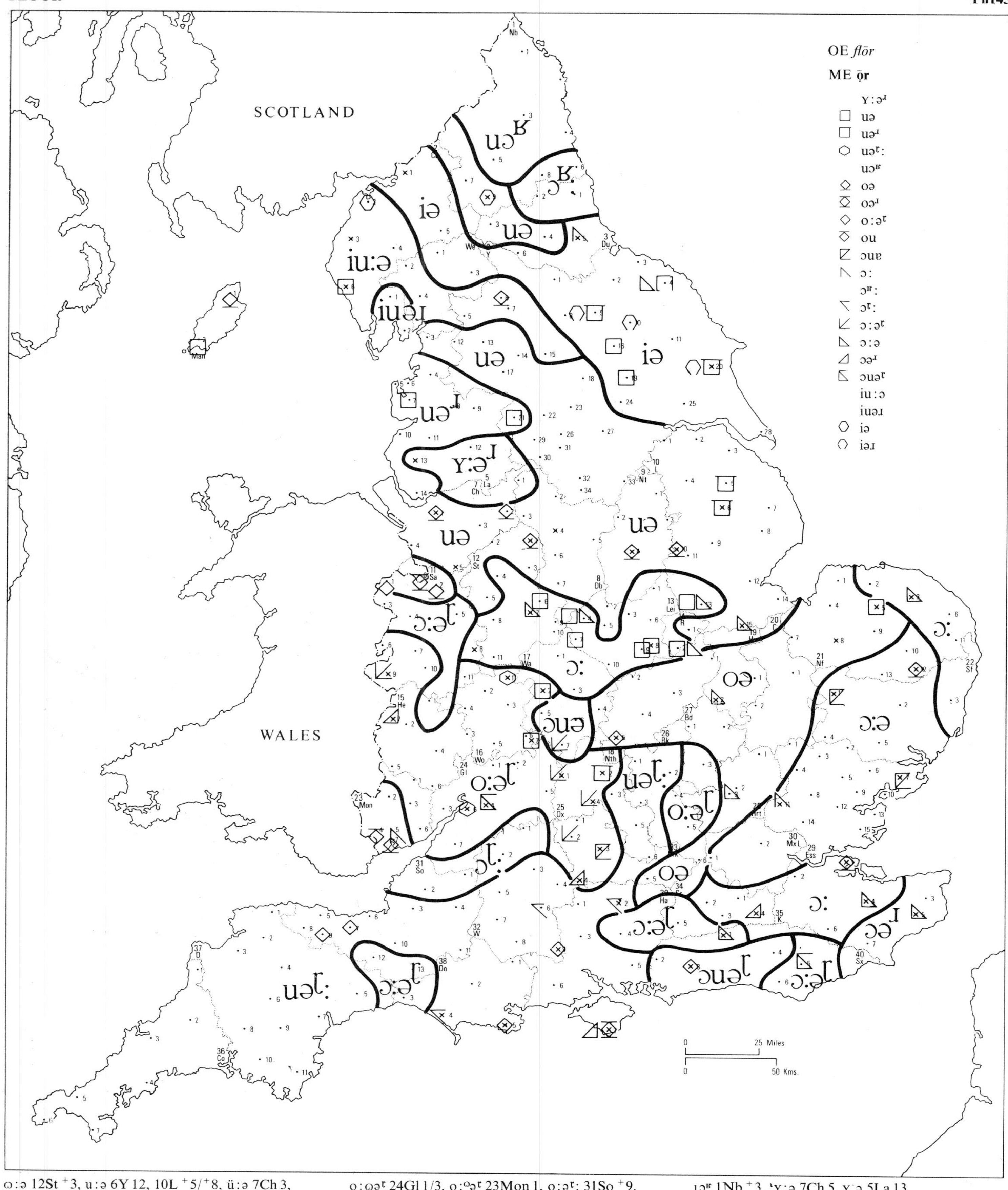

ɷ:ə 12St +3, u:ə 6Y 12, 10L +5/+8, ü:ə 7Ch 3,
ṷ:ə 21Nf 5, ü:ᵊ 13Lei +7, ɷu˙ə 6Y 13,
ɷu:ə 6Y 31 under uə
ᵚüəɹ 5La 11, ᵚu:əɹ 5La 14, ᵚü:əɹ 5La 8/9,
ü:əɹ 5La 10 under uəʴ
ɷəʵ 16Wo 1, 25Ox 5/6, 26Bk 3, ɷ̈əʵ 26Bk 1,
ǫ˙əʵ 26Bk 2, uəʵ 25Ox 3, u˙əʵ 24Gl 6,
u:əʵ 31So +3, u:əʵ: 31So +3/4–6/+9/10,
38Do +1, ü:əʵ: 31So +7,
ọəʵ: 32W +6 under uəʵ:
oɐ 35K +1, ouɐ 35K +1, oɷɐ 33Brk 5,
oɷə 12St +1, 29Ess +1, ǫɷə 18Nth 1,
o:ə 11Sa 2, 12St +1, 28Hrt +3,
ǫ:ə 21Nf 9 under oə
oɷəʴ 39Ha +7 under oəʴ

o:ɷəʵ 24Gl 1/3, o:ᵚəʵ 23Mon 1, o:əʵ: 31So +9,
38Do 5, o˙ɔʵ: 11Sa 1, ọ˙əʵ: 31So +7,
oəʵɽ 33Brk 1, ǫəʵ 33Brk +2, oəʵ: 32W 9,
oᵚəʵ 26Bk 5, oɷəʵ 16Wo 2/3,
oɷwəʵ 16Wo 6 under o:əʵ
ɔ ᵚə 22Sf 1 under ɔuɐ
ɔ:ɽ 38Do 4 under ɔʵ:
ɔ:əʵ: 38Do 3, ɔ˙əʵ: 31So 12, ɔʵ:əʵ 11Sa 3/4,
ɔəʵ: 31So 13, ɔəɽ 25Ox 4, ɔəʵɽ 25Ox 1,
40Sx +5 under ɔ:əʵ
ɔə 6Y +4, 13Lei +4, 14R +2, 30MxL 2, 35K 4/5,
ɔ̣ə 21Nf +13 under ɔ:ə
ɔ:əʴ 34Sr 4 under ɔəʴ
ɩuə 6Y +6/7 under iu:ə
ɩəʴ 6Y +20 under iəɹ

ɩɔʶ 1Nb +3, ˡʏ:ə 7Ch 5, ʏ˙ə 5La 13
ɛɷə 8Db 4, ɛɷəʵ 40Sx +4
œ:ᵊ 3Du +5
aɷəʵ 11Sa 8
ɑ: 23Mon +2
ɔ:r 2Cu +1, ɔ:ᵊr 2Cu +1
o: 23Mon +2, o:ɽ 38Do +1, ǫ:ɽ 38Do +1
u:ɽ 37D +11, u˙ər 2Cu 3

interpr as *r*-col: ɹ 5La 4/8–12/14, 6Y +9, 15He 7,
ɽ 25Ox 4, 38Do 4
cons *r* foll *r*-col V: ɽ 25Ox 1, 33Brk 1, 40Sx +5/6

-FLOOR 33Brk +2, 38Do +1;
FLOORS pl 13Lei +4, 38Do +1, 40Sx +1/+5

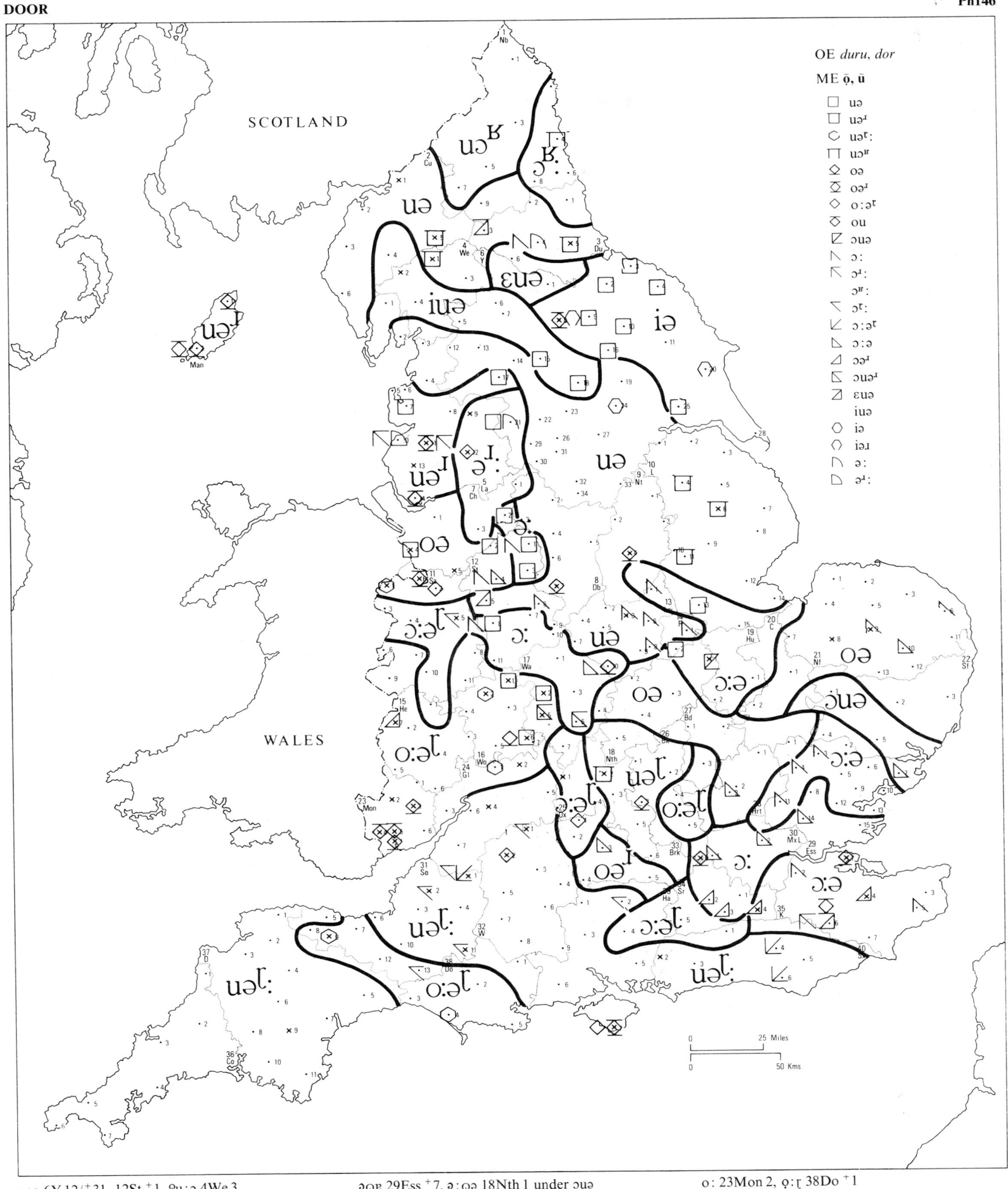

u:ə 6Y 12/+31, 12St +1, ᵚu:ə 4We 3,
ɷu:ə 6Y +31, ɷü:ə 8Db 4, ᵊu˙ə 3Du +3,
ᵊɷu˙ə 6Y 13, ɷ:ə 12St +5/+6,
ọə 1Nb 9 under uə

ᵚüəɹ 5La 8/+14, ᵚu˙əɹ 4We 1,
ᵊu:əɹ 3Du 5 under uəᴵ

u:əʳ: 31So 3/9/10, 32W 7, 38Do +1/+4,
u:əʳ 40Sx 3/+6, u˙əʳ 24Gl 5–7, uəʳ 25Ox 3,
40Sx 5/+6, uəʳɽ 40Sx +4, ɷəʳ 11Sa 1, 16Wo 2,
24Gl +1, 25Ox 5/6 under uəʳ:

oɐ 35K +1, ọɐ 35K +1, o:ə 11Sa +2, 23Mon 3,
28Hrt +3, ọ:ə 21Nf 5, ǫ:ᵊ 21Nf 2, o˙ᵚə 8Db 7,
oɷə 12St +2/+4, 29Ess 1, ǫɷə 13Lei +10,
ouə Man +2 under oə

oɷəᴵ 33Brk +3/5, 39Ha +7, ǫọəᴵ 33Brk 4,
ouəᴵ Man +2 under oəᴵ

o:əʳ: 31So 8, 32W 2, 38Do 3/+4,
ọ:əʳ: 31So 7/12/+13, 38Do 2/5, oəᴵ 33Brk +1,
39Ha +7, o:ᵚəʳ 23Mon 1, o:ɷəᴵ 24Gl +1/+3,
oɷəʳ 16Wo 3, oɷwəʳ 16Wo 6 under o:əʳ

ɔ̣ɷɐ 29Ess +7, ɔ̣:ɷə 18Nth 1 under ɔuə

ɔʶ:ᵊ 1Nb 2/8 under ɔʶ:

ɔəʳ 33Brk 2, 39Ha +4, ɔ̣əʳ 33Brk +1, ɔəɽ 25Ox +4,
40Sx +4, ɔəʳ: 31So 1, ɔ:ɽ 25Ox +4 under ɔ:əʳ

ɔə 13Lei +1/+10, 14R +2, 30MxL +1, 35K +5/7,
ɔ̣ə 35K 3, ɔɐ 33Brk +3 under ɔ:ə

ɔ:əɹ 15He +7, ɔ̣:əᴵ 34Sr +2, ɔ̣:əᴵɹ 34Sr +3,
ɔ̨:əᴵ 34Sr 4, ɒəᴵ 35K +6 under ɔəᴵ

æɷə 6Y +1 under ɛuə

ɩu:ə 4We 4, 6Y +15 under iuə

ɩəᴵ 6Y +20, ɩ̧iəɹ 6Y 8 under iəɹ

ɜᴵ:ɹ 5La +10, ɜ:ɹ 5La +12 under əᴵ:

ɩuəɹ 6Y +7, ɩu:əɹ 5La +1, ɩu:ər 4We 2

ʏ˙ə 8Db +1, ʏ˙əᴵ 5La 13, ʏ:əɹ 5La 9, ɩʏə 7Ch 5,
ɩʏə:ɹ 5La +11

ɛɷəɹ 3Du +3

aɷəʳ 24Gl 4

ɑ:əʳ 24Gl 2

ɔ:ᵊr 2Cu 1

ɔɷəʳ 40Sx 2

o: 23Mon 2, ọ:ɽ 38Do +1

ü: 7Ch +2, ɷɽ 25Ox 1, u:ɽ 37D +8/9

interpr as *r*-col V: ɹ 2Cu 5, 3Du 5, 4We 1,
5La 8/+10/+11/12/14, 6Y 17, 10L +4/+11,
15He 7, ɽ 25Ox 4

cons *r* foll *r*-col V: ɹ 5La +10, 34Sr +3,
ɽ 40Sx +1/+4

DOOR- 5La +12, 6Y +9/+17, 11Sa +2, 34Sr +3,
35K +5; -DOORS- 29Ess +11;
-DOOR 29Ess +4, 40Sx +6; -DOORS 35K +2,
39Ha +7, 40Sx +4;
DOORS pl 5La +1/+11/+14, 10L 10, 12St +6,
30MxL +1, 31So +1, 34Sr 4, 35K +1/+6

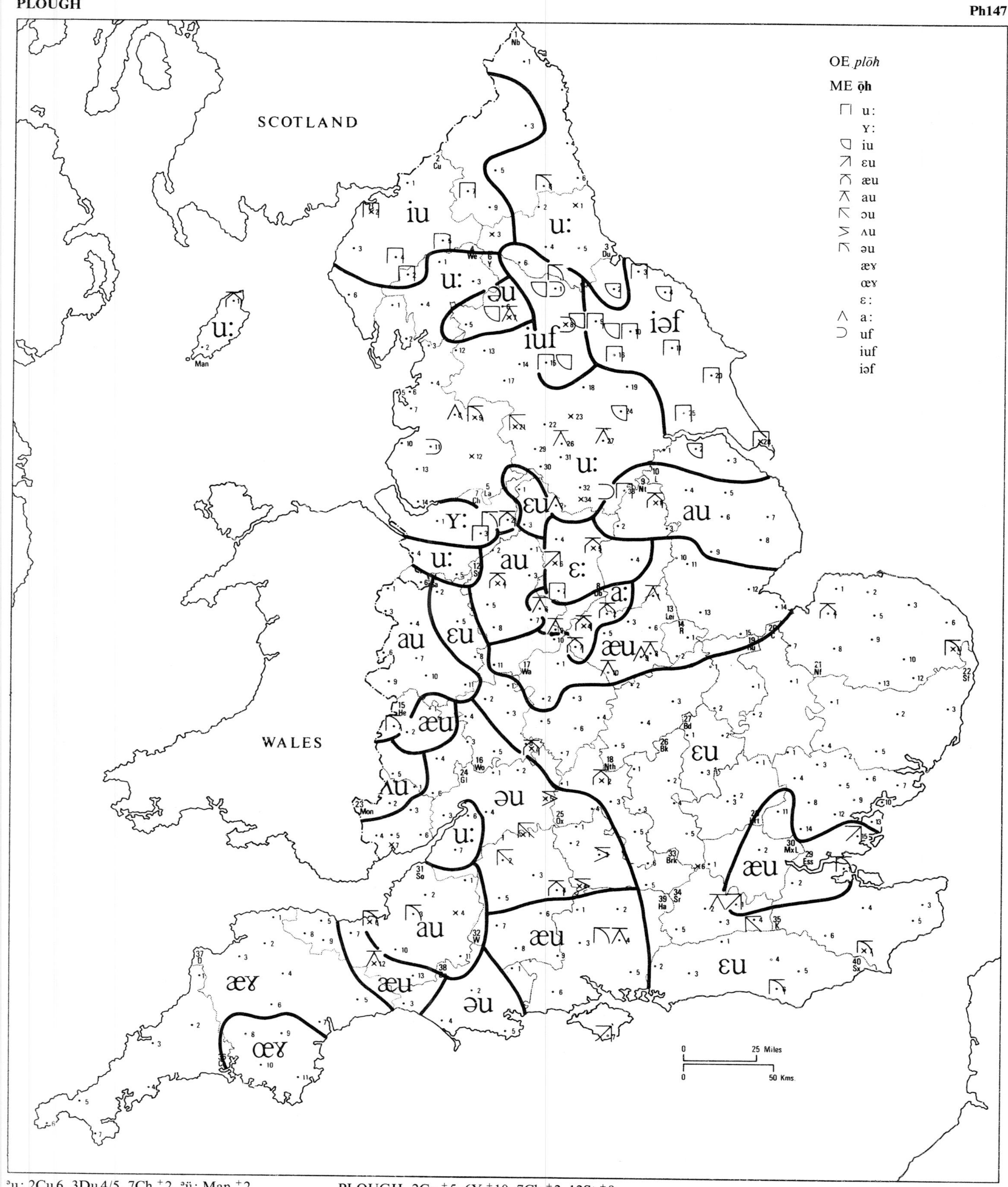

ᵊu: 2Cu 6, 3Du 4/5, 7Ch $^{+}$2, ᵊü: Man $^{+}$2,
u 2Cu $^{+}$5, 6Y $^{+}$28, ᵆü: Man 2, öu 5La 5 under u:
ᵊʏ: 7Ch 3 under ʏ:
ɩu: 1Nb 3/$^{+}$7/9, 2Cu 1/3/$^{+}$4/$^{+}$5, 4We $^{+}$2,
6Y $^{+}$1/$^{+}$15, 10L $^{+}$2 under iu
ɛu: 16Wo 3/6, eϖ̈ 21Nf $^{+}$7, ëϖ̈ 21Nf $^{+}$7 under ɛu
æ̣u: Man $^{+}$1, ᵊæϖ 10L 14 under æu
əϖ: 16Wo $^{+}$4/5, 24Gl 2, əϖᵊ 24Gl $^{+}$1,
əϖ:ᵊ 16Wo $^{+}$4, 24Gl $^{+}$1, ʌϖ 6Y $^{+}$1,
ᶺϖ 1Nb $^{+}$8 under əu
æ: 9Nt $^{+}$4, æ:ᵊ 9Nt $^{+}$4 under ɛ:
a̱:ᵊ 13Lei $^{+}$2/$^{+}$7/$^{+}$9 under a:
ɩu:f 3Du 6, 6Y $^{+}$15 under iuf

ɩɤf 3Du $^{+}$2
ɛʏ 31So $^{+}$8
ɑu 25Ox $^{+}$4

PLOUGH- 2Cu $^{+}$5, 6Y $^{+}$10, 7Ch $^{+}$2, 12St $^{+}$9,
15He $^{+}$7, 21Nf $^{+}$7, 31So $^{+}$3;
-PLOUGH Man $^{+}$2, 7Ch $^{+}$2, 12St $^{+}$10,
13Lei $^{+}$7/$^{+}$8, 29Ess 12, 33Brk $^{+}$3, 34Sr $^{+}$1,
35K $^{+}$1; PLOUGH 2prpl 34Sr $^{+}$1;
3prpl 34Sr $^{+}$4; imp 6Y $^{+}$33; v 2Cu $^{+}$4/$^{+}$5,
4 We $^{+}$2, 6Y $^{+}$3/$^{+}$9/$^{+}$15/$^{+}$16/$^{+}$24/$^{+}$33,
7Ch $^{+}$3, 21Nf $^{+}$7, 30MxL 2, 31So $^{+}$8, 34Sr $^{+}$1;
ndg 5La $^{+}$8; PLOUGHED pp 6Y $^{+}$1/$^{+}$10,
8Db $^{+}$2, 39Ha $^{+}$4; pp adj 1Nb $^{+}$8, 13Lei $^{+}$9;
pt 13Lei $^{+}$7/$^{+}$10; ndg 5La $^{+}$8;
PLOUGHING n 6Y $^{+}$2; vbl n 10L $^{+}$2,
39Ha $^{+}$4; prp 6Y $^{+}$15/$^{+}$27/$^{+}$33, 13Lei $^{+}$10;
(-)PLOUGHING ndg 5La 9, 6Y $^{+}$4/$^{+}$27/$^{+}$28,
8Db $^{+}$7, 34Sr $^{+}$1, 40Sx $^{+}$6;
PLOUGHS 3prpl 39Ha $^{+}$4

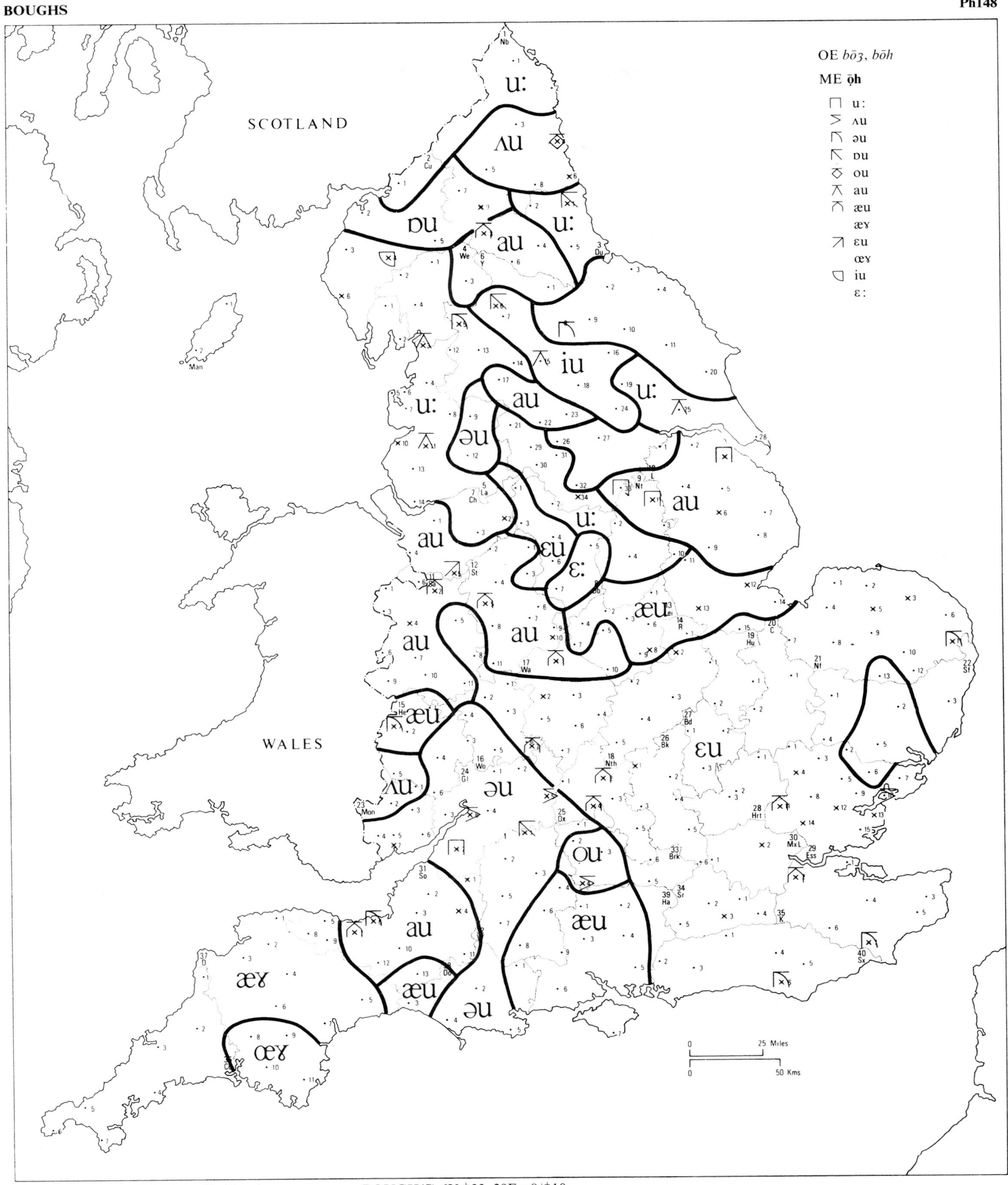

ᵊu: 3Du 5, 4We 4, 6Y +25, öu 5La 5 under u:
əɷ: 16Wo 4/5, 24Gl 3, əɷ:ᵊ 24Gl 1 under əu
au: 11Sa 1, a:ɷ 12St +11 under au
ᵊæɷ 10L 14 under æu
ɛu: 16Wo 3/6, ɛw 22Sf 4, eɷ 21Nf 7 under ɛu
ɩu: 2Cu 4, 6Y +15, ju: 6Y 16 under iu

ɛï 26Bk 1
a: 6Y 34, 12St 10, ạ: 30MxL 2, a̱:ᵊ 14R 2
ăọ 15He +7
o: 5La +12

-BOUGH(S) 6Y +33, 29Ess 8/+10;
BOUGH sg 2Cu 1, 3Du 1/3, 5La +12, 6Y 16/22/24, 7Ch 1, 8Db 2/7, 10L 11, 13Lei 4/6, 15He 1/+7, 16Wo 5, 17Wa 4/5, 23Mon 1/3, 24Gl 3/7, 27Bd 3, 29Ess 8/+10, 31So 2, 35K 2/4/5, 40Sx 2

bɩəfs 6Y 11

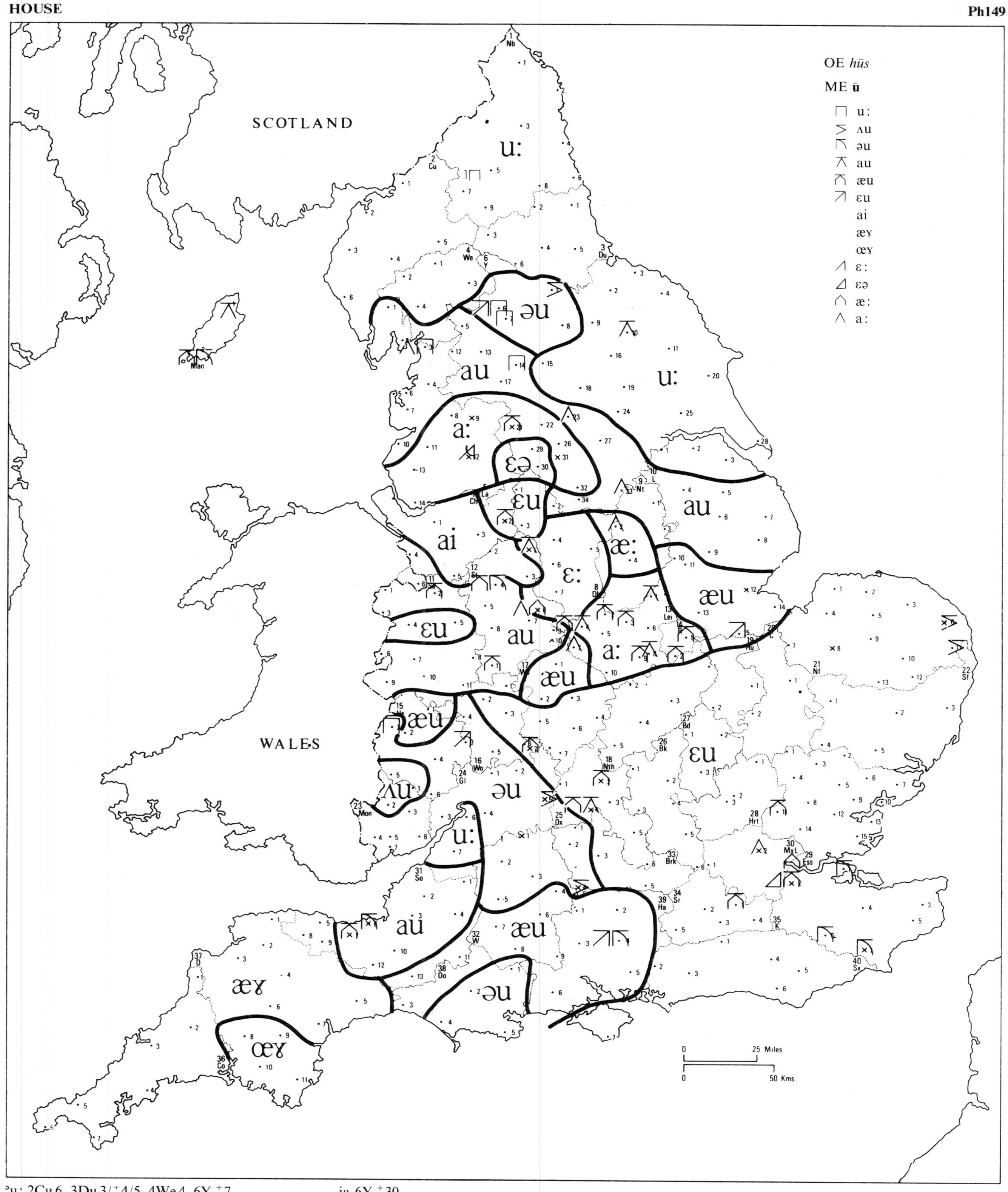

ᵊu: 2Cu 6, 3Du 3/$^{+}$4/5, 4We 4, 6Y $^{+}$7,
ᵊu̧: 15He $^{+}$7, ᵓu: 3Du 6 under u:
ɐu 21Nf 6 under ʌu
əɷ: 16Wo 4/5, 24Gl 2, əɷ:ᵊ 24Gl 1 under əu
au: 6Y $^{+}$14, 11Sa 11, a:ɷ 12St $^{+}$11 under au
ᵊæɷ 10L $^{+}$14 under æu
ɛu: 11Sa 4, 16Wo 3/6 under ɛu
æ̃:ᵊ 35K $^{+}$2 under æ:
a:ᵊ 13Lei $^{+}$3/$^{+}$4, a̱:ᵊ 13Lei $^{+}$1–$^{+}$4/5/6/$^{+}$7–$^{+}$9/10, 14R $^{+}$2 under a:

ja 6Y $^{+}$30
ᵋu: Man $^{+}$2
æ̣˙a 6Y $^{+}$31, æə 6Y $^{+}$31, æ̣ə 6Y $^{+}$31, æ˙ə 5La 9
ɑ: 6Y $^{+}$21
ɑu̧ 15He $^{+}$7
ɒɷ 32W 1
ou Man $^{+}$2
əɷzən (sg) 23Mon 3

HOUSE- 25Ox $^{+}$4, 35K $^{+}$6; -HOUSE Man $^{+}$2, 9Nt $^{+}$2/$^{+}$4, 10L $^{+}$15, 12St $^{+}$4, 13Lei $^{+}$4/$^{+}$7, 34Sr $^{+}$1, 35K $^{+}$2/$^{+}$6, 39Ha $^{+}$4

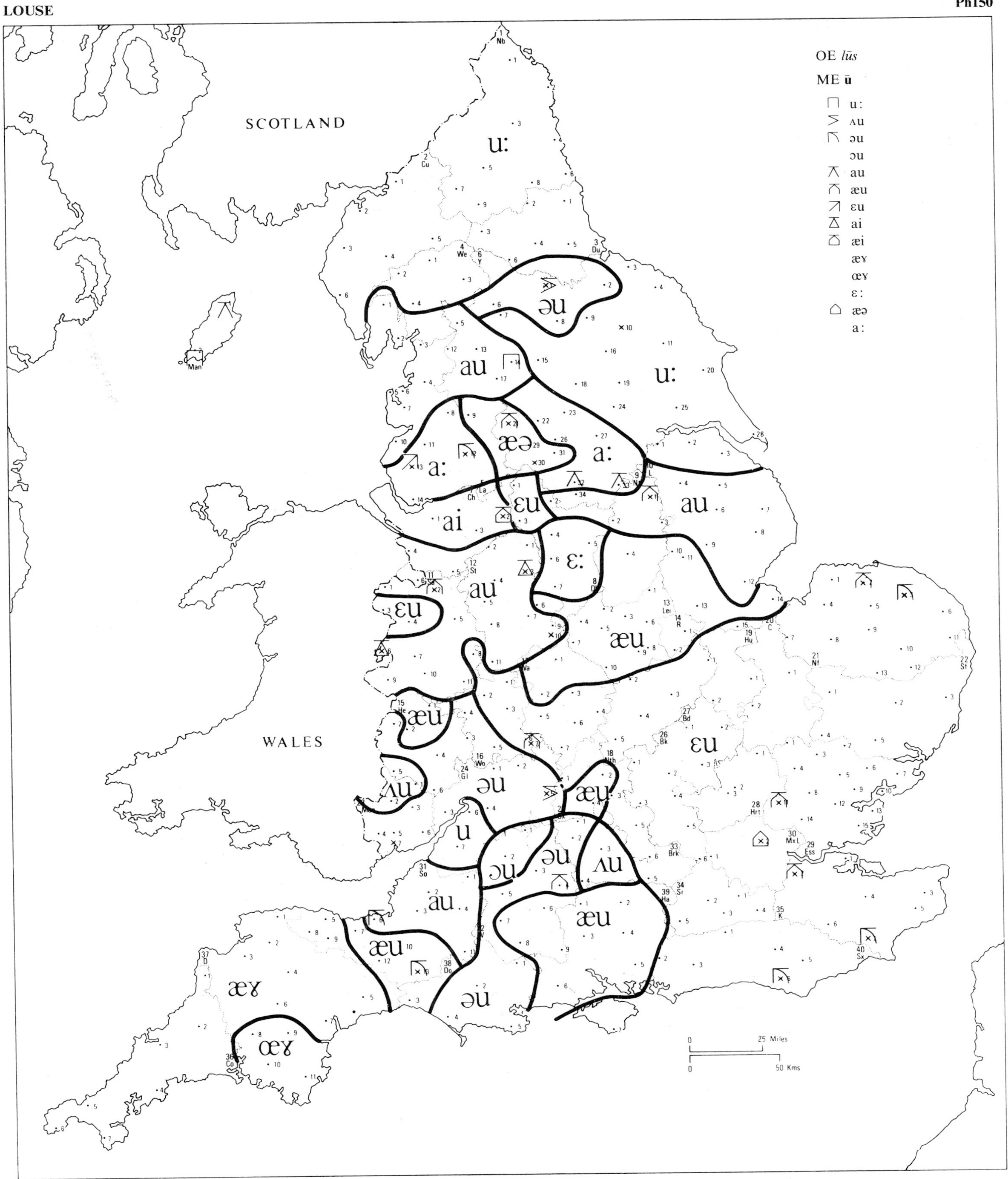

ᵊu: 2Cu 6, 3Du 4/5, 4We 4, 6Y +20, ᵊü: Man 2,
ᵓu: 3Du 6 under u:
əu: 33Brk 2, əɷ: 16Wo 4/5, əɷ:ᵊ 24Gl 1 under əu
au: 11Sa 10 under au
ᵊæɷ 10L 14 under æu
ɛu: 16Wo 3/6, ɛw 22Sf +4, ɛ̢w 22Sf +4,
eɷ̈ 21Nf 7 under ɛu
ɛə 6Y 29 under æə
a:ᵒ 6Y 27 under a:

ɛa 6Y 30
æ: 9Nt +4, æ:ᵊ 9Nt +4
ɑɩ 8Db +4
ɔɩ (sic) 28Hrt +3
ɔ̈ɷ 10L +1
oɷ 31So +1
əɤ̈ 31So +8

LOUSY adj 6Y +33, 9Nt +4, 10L +1, 18Nth 1,
31So +1/+6/+8, 32W +4

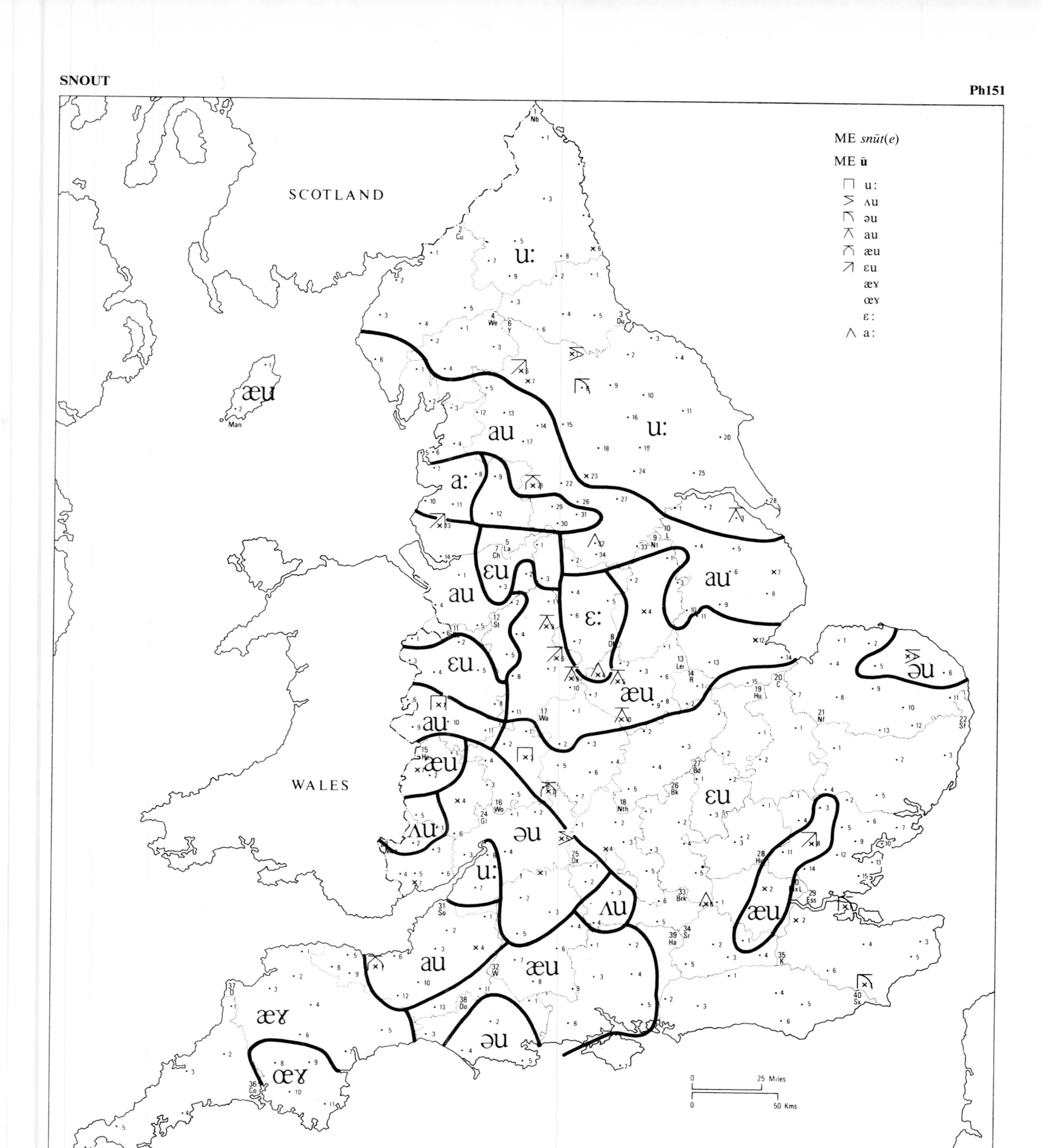

ᵊu: 3Du 3/4, əu: 3Du 5, ɩu: 16Wo 3,
ᵒu: 3Du 6 under u:
əɷ: 16Wo 4/5, 24Gl 1 under əu
au: 11Sa 10/11 under au
ᵊæɷ 10L 14 under æu
ɛu: 11Sa 4, 16Wo 6 under ɛu
a̠:ᵊ 13Lei 4 under a:

ᵊʏ: 5La 12
æ:ᵊ 9Nt 4, 35K 2, æ˙ə 5La 9, æ̣˙ə 6Y 31
ɑ̆ɷ 15He 7, ɑ̈ɷ 25Ox 4
ɒɷ 32W 1, ɔ̈ɷ 10L ⁺1
ɷ 15He 4

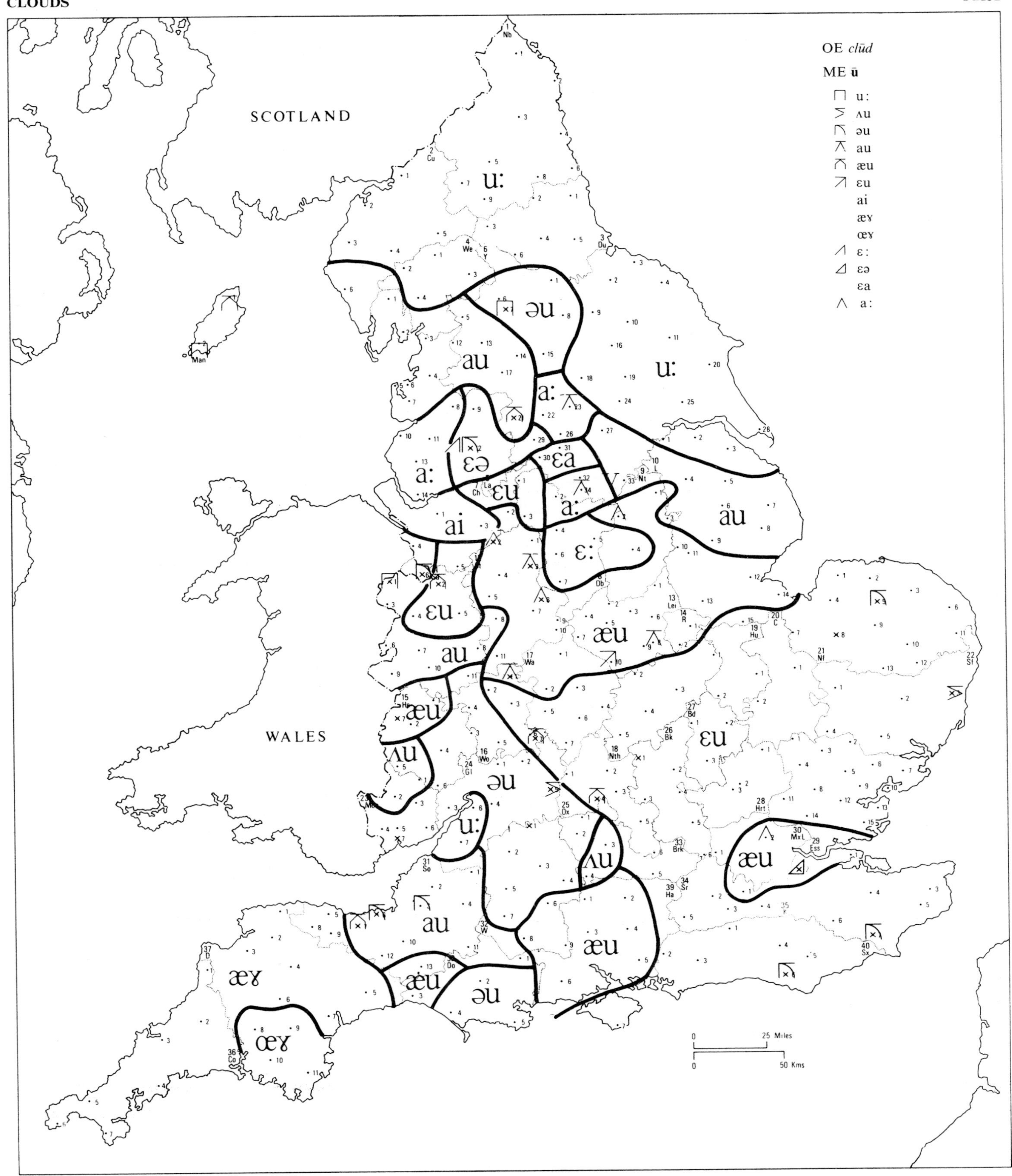

ᵊu: 3Du 3–5, 10L 2, ᵊü: Man 2, ᵊu: 3Du 6 under u:
əo̜ᵊ 24Gl 1, əo: 16Wo 4/5, 24Gl 2,
œo 7Ch 6 under əu
ᵊæo 10L 14 under æu
ɛw 22Sf 4, ɛu: 16Wo 3/6, eö 21Nf 7 under ɛu
ɛ̜:ᵊ 8Db 5, æ:ᵊ 9Nt 4 under ɛ:
æə 5La 9, 35K 2 under ɛə
æ̜a, æ̜·a 6Y 31 under ɛa

ɛĩ (sic) 26Bk 1
ɑ̆o 15He 7
ɒo 32W 1

CLOUDING prp 13Lei +10;
CLOUDY adj 6Y +23, 9Nt +2

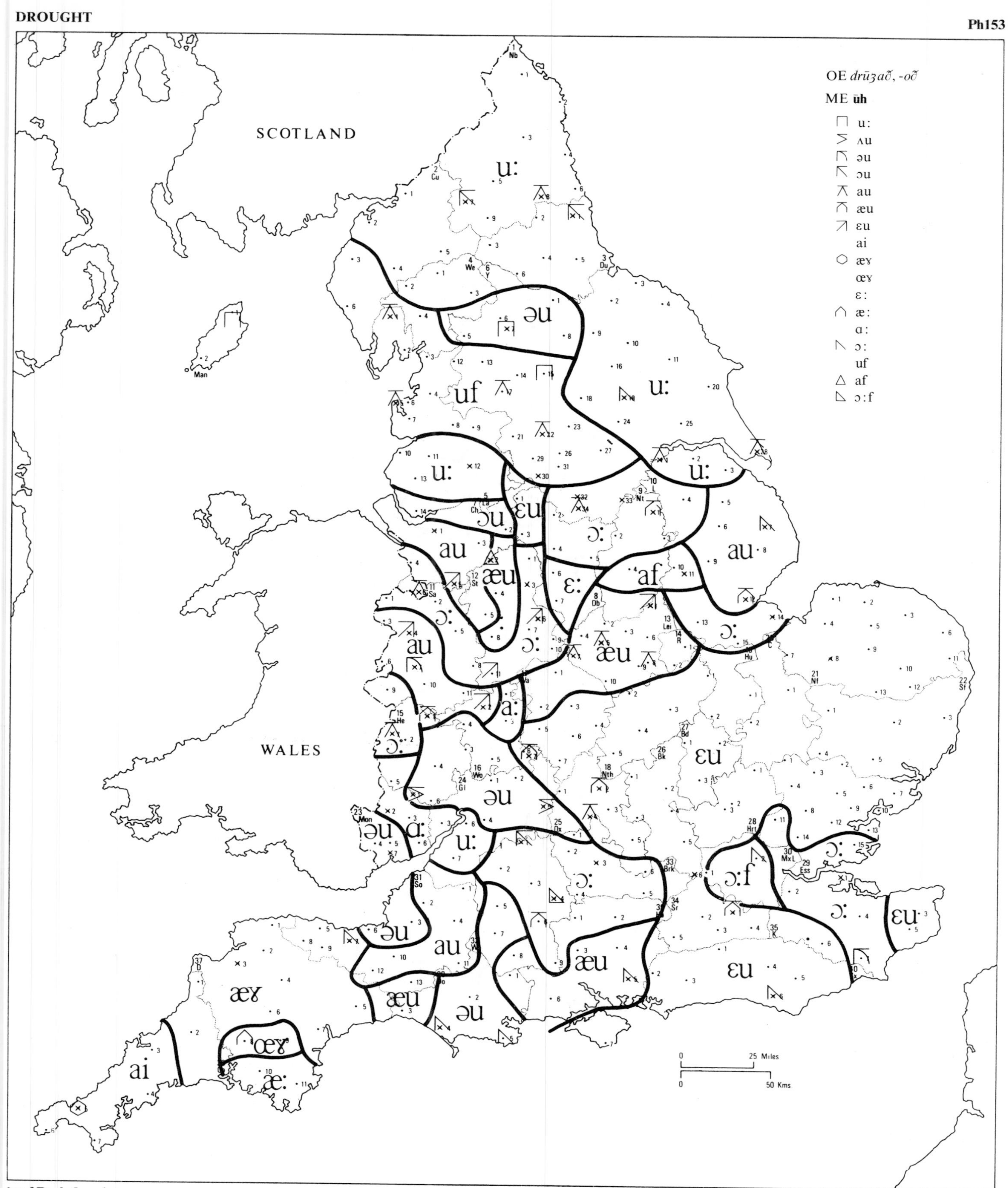

ᵊu: 3Du 3–5 under u:
əɷ: 24Gl 1, əu: 11Sa 7, 32W 7 under əu
a:ɷ 6Y 34, au: 11Sa 11 under au
ɛw 22Sf 4, 29Ess 5, ɛu: 11Sa 4, 16Wo 6,
eɷ̈ 21Nf 7 under ɛu
ɔ˙ə 10L 7/15 under ɔ:

ɛä 6Y 30
a: 6Y 32, ä: 26Bk 6
ɑɩ 7Ch 1, ɑ̈ɩ 35K 1
ɑɷ 1Nb +9
ɒ 37D 3
ɒɩ 36Co +7
oɷ 12St 3, ou Man 2
əɩ 23Mon 2

DROUGHTY 3Du 3

5La +9 (informant's father said dɹɷxt)

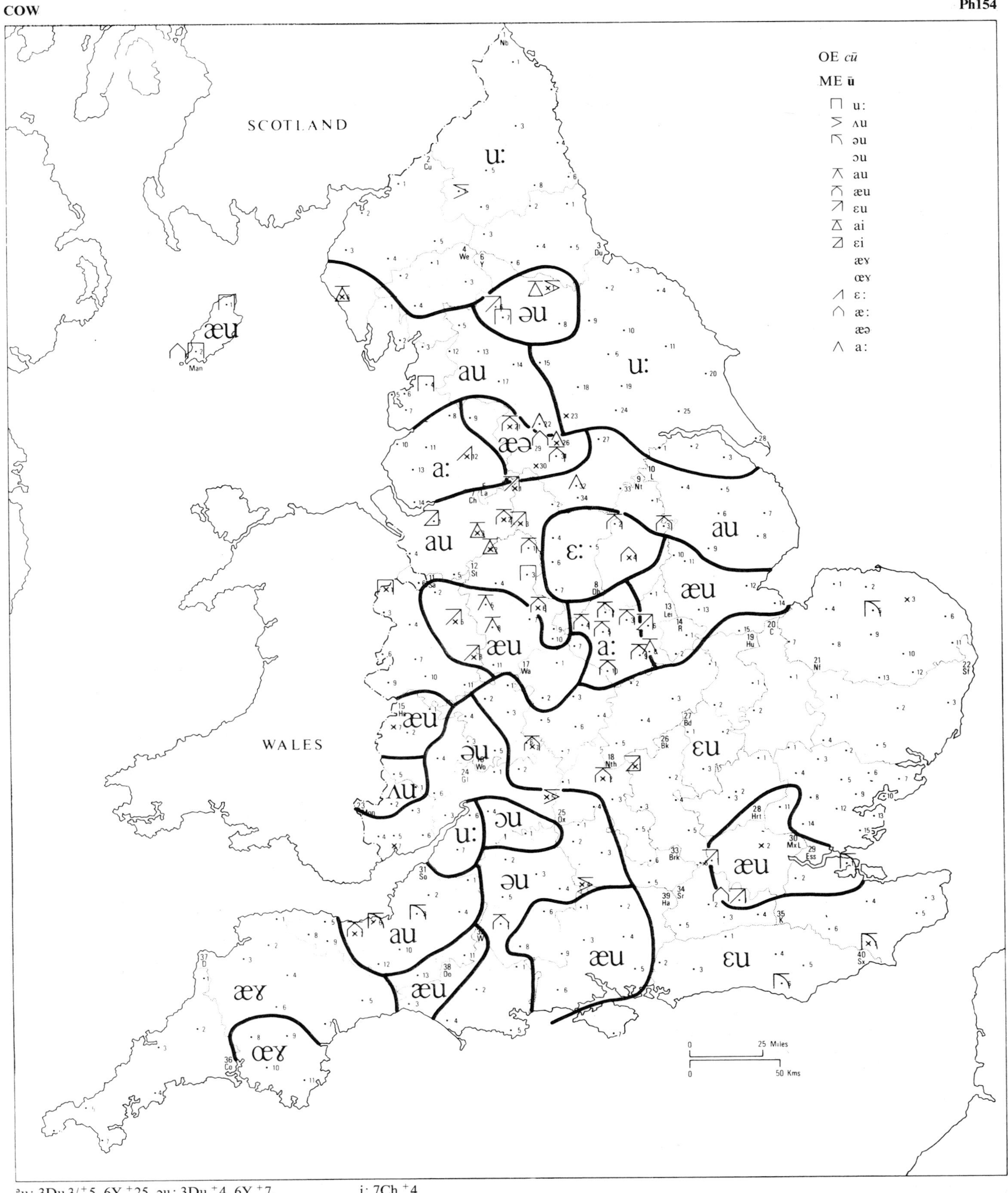

ᵊu: 3Du 3/+5, 6Y +25, əu: 3Du +4, 6Y +7,
ᵆu: Man +1, ᵆü: Man +2, ᵒu: 3Du 6 under u:
əɷ: 16Wo 4/5, 24Gl +1, əɷ:ᵊ 24Gl +1 under əu
au: 11Sa 4/10/11 under au
ᵊæɷ 10L +14 under æu

ɛu: 16Wo 3/6, ɛw 29Ess 5 under eu
ɛ:ᵊ 8Db 6 under ɛ:
æ̣:ᵓ 35K +2 under æ:
ɛə 6Y 29 under æə
a:ᵊ 13Lei +4, a̱:ᵊ 13Lei +2/+3/+5/+9/+10 under a:

i̜: 7Ch +4
ẹa 6Y +30
ɛa 6Y +30, ɛä 6Y +30
æ˙a 6Y +31
ɑɷ 25Ox +4, ɑ̆ɷ 15He 7, ạụ 21Nf3
ᵓɷ 3Du +5, ɔ̈ɷ 10L +1
oɷ 33Brk +3

COW- 6Y +25, 9Nt +3, 10L +14, 12St +3/+8,
13Lei +5, 31So 4, 33Brk +3; -COW 12St +1;
COW'S poss sg 9Nt +2, 13Lei +3–+5, 31So +3

kᶥ- 15He +1, kj- 7Ch +2, 12St +3, 27Bd 2

6Y +32 (informant says he heard ku: 60 years
ago from a native)

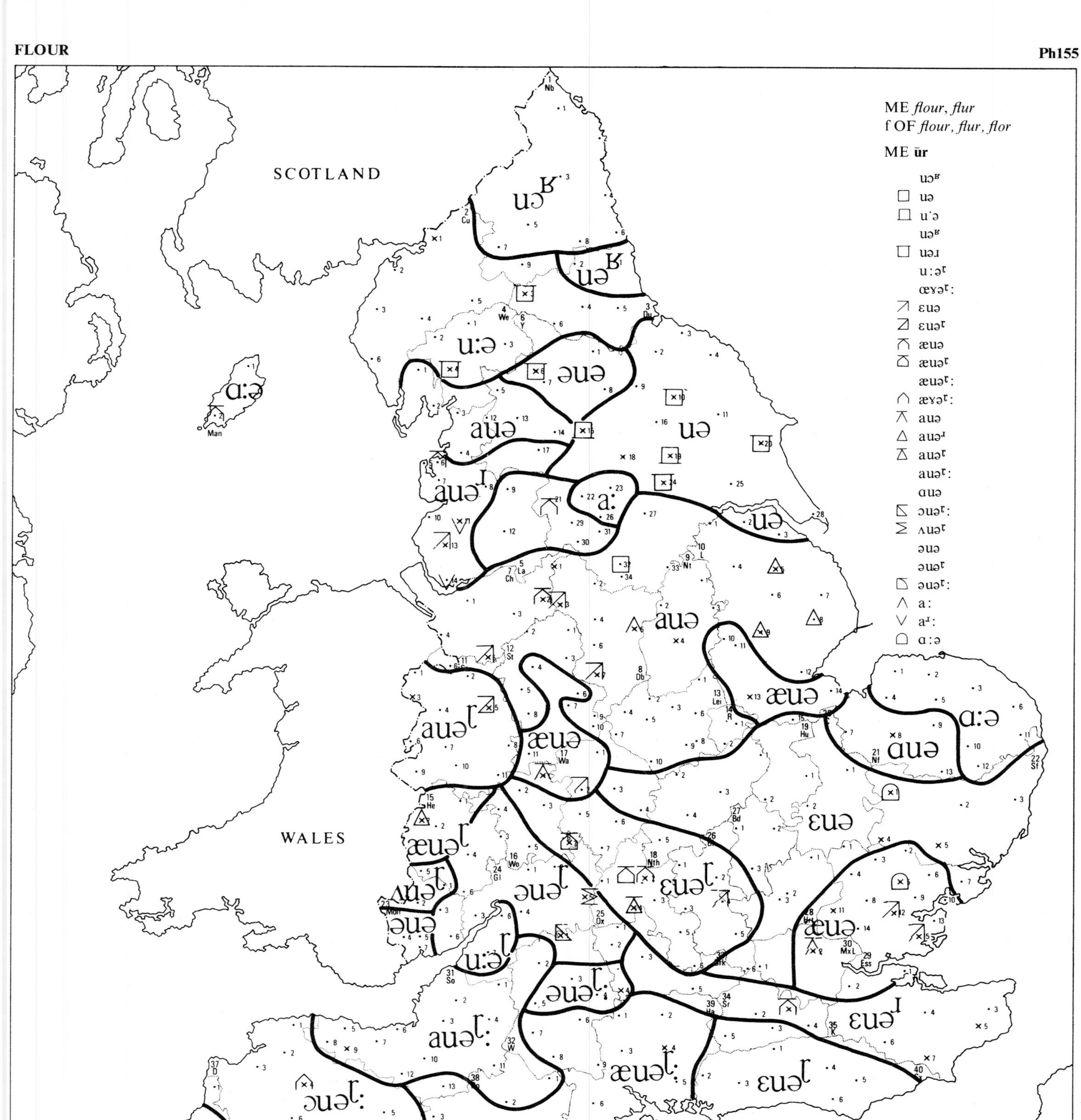

u:ɔʶ 1Nb 6 under uɔʶ
ᵊu:ə 4We 2, ᵊu·ə 3Du 4, ᵊu:ᵊ 3Du 5,
ᵓu:ə 3Du 6 under u:ə
ᵚu·əʶ 3Du 1 under uəʶ
ᵊu·əɹ 3Du 3, 4We 4 under uəɹ
εu:əʵ 16Wo 3/6 under εuəʵ
æɷwə 10L 11, ᵊæɷə 10L 14 under æuə
awə 10L 7 under auə
aɷwəɹ 10L 9 under auəʴ
ʌɷə 6Y 1 under əuə
əɷ:əʵ 16Wo 4/5, 24Gl 2, əɷ:ᵊɻ 24Gl 1 under əuəʵ
ɑ̊: Man ⁺2, ɑə 21Nf ⁺3 under ɑ:ə

ɩɷə (sic) 6Y 18
ea 6Y 30
εə 6Y 29, ε:ə 22Sf 4, ε:ᵊ 30MxL ⁺1, εɷəʴ 39Ha 7,
ε̧ɷə̇ʴ 8Db 1
æ̣ᵊ 29Ess 11, æ·ə 6Y ⁺31, 35K ⁺2, æ:ə 6Y ⁺31,
9Nt 4, æ·əɹ 5La 9, æʵ: 39Ha 4, æɷəɹ 10L 13
aɷ 10L ⁺5, aɷɩ (sic) 11Sa 3
ɑ: 35K 5
ɔ: 22Sf 5
ʌɷəʴ 33Brk 4
ǫ:əʵ: 31So 9
uər 2Cu 1
əɷəʴ 35K 7
ɜʴ:ɹ 5La 12

interpr as *r*-col: ɹ 5La 8/10/11/⁺14, 6Y 17,
10L ⁺8/9, 15He 7, ɻ 24Gl 1, 25Ox 4
cons *r* foll *r*-col V: ɹ 5La 12/⁺14, ɻ 40Sx 1

FLOUR- 35K ⁺2; -FLOUR 2Cu 2, 6Y 16/32
15He 7, 17Wa ⁺2, 21Nf 2/9, 29Ess 14

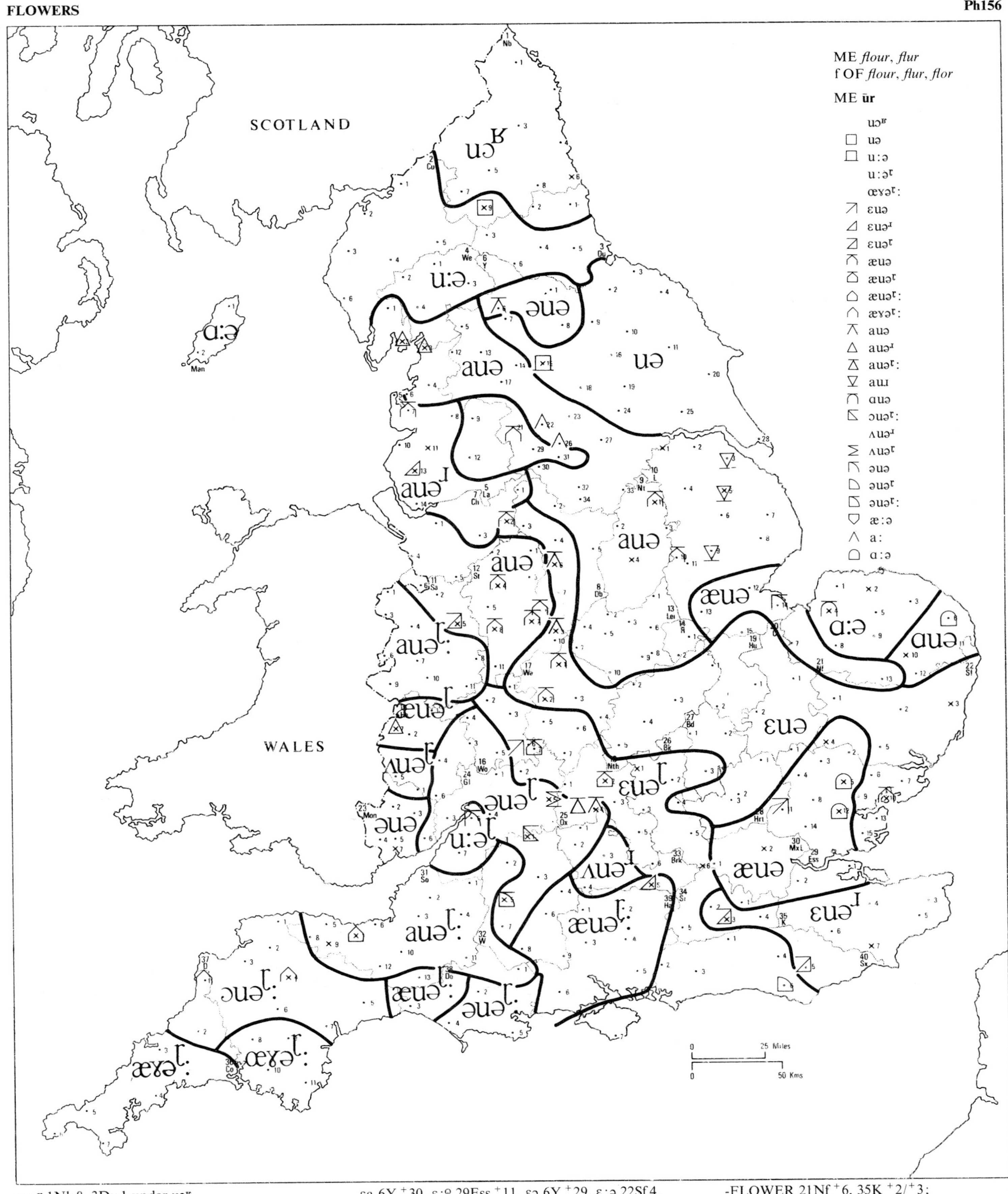

u:ɔʶ 1Nb 8, 3Du 1 under uɔʶ
ᵒu:ə 3Du 6, ᵊu:ə 2Cu 6, 3Du 3–5, 4We 2 under u:ə
ɛɷwə 12St 10 under ɛuə
æ̹uəʴ 35K $^+$3 under ɛuəʴ
ɛu:əʵ 16Wo 3/6 under ɛuəʵ
æɷwə 10L 12, ᵊæɷwə 10L $^+$14 under æuə
æɷəʵ 39Ha 4 under æuəʵ:
aɷwə 10L 4/8/$^+$9/11, awə 10L 7 under auə
aɷəʵ 11Sa 8, aɷəɽ 25Ox $^+$4 under auəʵ:
aɷwɹ 10L 5/$^+$9 under auɹ
ɑuwə 21Nf 12, ɑ˙wə 21Nf 4/11 under ɑuə
ʌɷə 6Y $^+$1, 23Mon 2, 24Gl $^+$6 under əuə
əɷ:əʵ 16Wo 5, 24Gl 1 under əuəʵ
ɑ: 21Nf 5/9, ɑ̱: (sic) Man $^+$1 under ɑ:ə

ɛa 6Y $^+$30, ɛ:ᵒ 29Ess $^+$11, ɛə 6Y $^+$29, ɛ:ə 22Sf 4, ɛəʴ 6Y $^+$29, ɛïəʵ 26Bk 1
æ: Man $^+$1, æ̹: 34Sr $^+$1, æ:ə 6Y 31, 9Nt 4, æ˙ə 35K $^+$2, æ:ᵒ 30MxL 2, æ˙əɹ 5La 9
ä:ə 29Ess $^+$5, a̹ʴ:ɹ 5La 11
ɑɔʶ 1Nb $^+$1, ɑɷəʵ: 31So 9
ɒ:ə 21Nf 10, ɒɷə 21Nf 2
ɔ: 22Sf $^+$5, ɔ̹:ᵊ 22Sf 3, ɔɷwə 10L 1
ᵒu:əʴ 4We $^+$4, u:əʶ 1Nb 6, u˙ər 2Cu $^+$1
ɜ:ɹ 5La 12, əɷəʴ 35K 7, ə̆uəɹ 15He $^+$7

interpr as *r*-col: ɹ 5La 2/8/10/14, 15He $^+$7, ɽ 25Ox $^+$4/5
cons *r* foll *r*-col V: ɹ 5La 11, 34Sr $^+$2, 40Sx $^+$5, ɽ 32W 3, 33Brk 1/2, 40Sx 2/$^+$3

-FLOWER 21Nf $^+$6, 35K $^+$2/$^+$3;
FLOWER sg 6Y $^+$22, Man $^+$1, 12St $^+$6, 21Nf $^+$6/8, 24Gl $^+$6, 29Ess $^+$5, 34Sr $^+$1/$^+$2, 35K $^+$3, 36Co $^+$1, 40Sx $^+$3/$^+$6;
FLOWERS 3prsg 6Y $^+$1

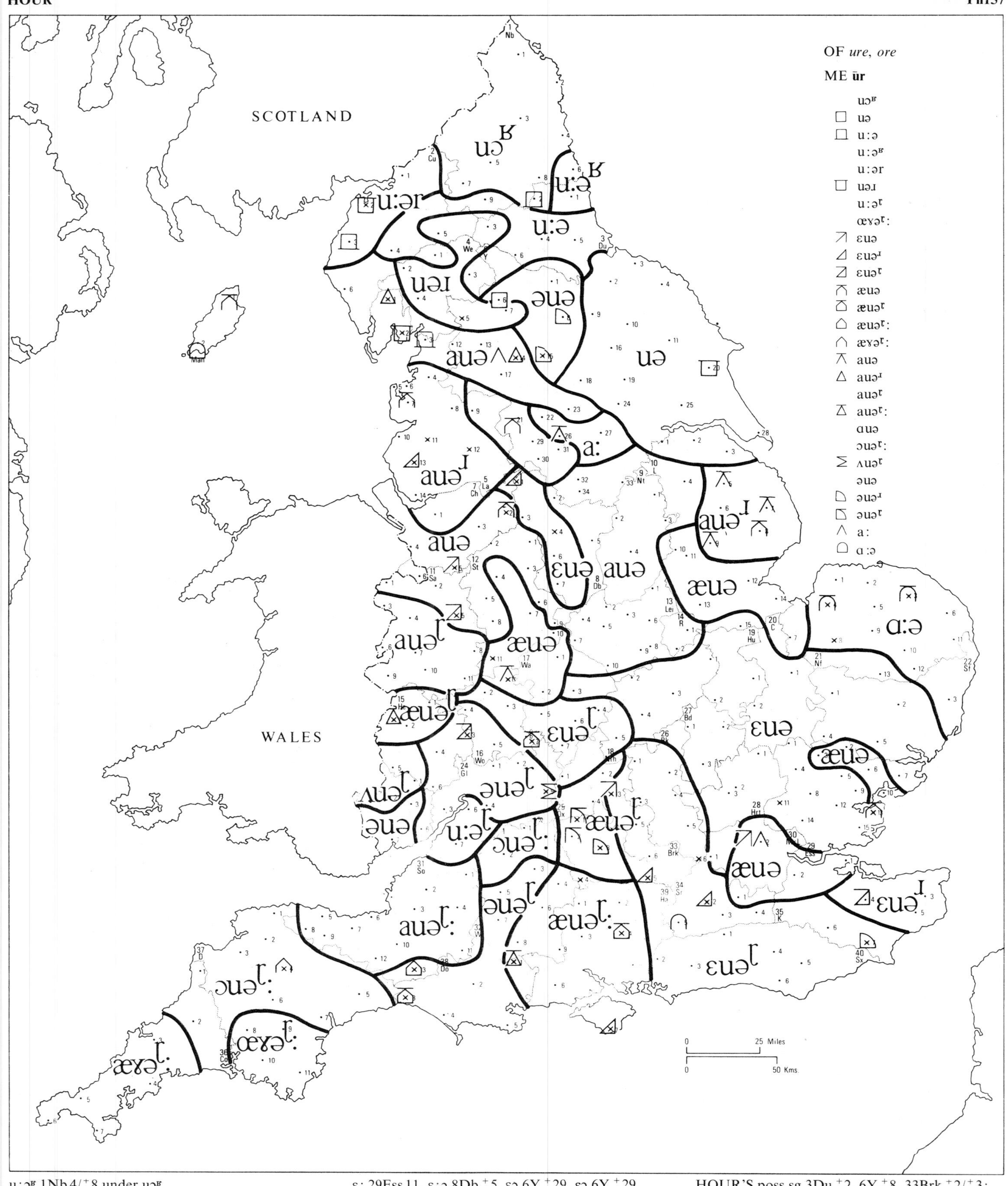

u:ɔʁ 1Nb 4/+8 under uɔʁ
ᵊu:ə 3Du 4/5, ᵓu:ə 3Du 6 under u:ə
ᵊu:ər 2Cu +3 under u:ər
ᵊu:əɹ 3Du 3, 4We 4 under uəɹ
ɛɷɐ 29Ess 7/15, ɛ:ᵚᵊ 22Sf +4 under ɛuə
æ̣uəɹ 35K 3 under ɛuəɹ
ɛu:əʈ 16Wo 3/6 under ɛuəʈ
æɷwə 10L +8/12, 12St 10, ᵊæɷə 10L 14,
æᵘɐ 35K +1 under æuə
aɷwə 10L +7, 11Sa 2 under auə
aɷwəɹ 10L +8, awəɹ 10L +7, aɷəɹ, awəɹ,
ɑ̆ɷəɹ 15He +7, æɷəɹ 5La +7 under auəɹ
ʌɷəɹ 33Brk +3 under əuəɹ
ɔɷ:əʈ 16Wo 4/5, 24Gl 1/2, əɷəʈ: 32W 5,
38Do 2/4 under əuəʈ
ɑ: 21Nf 1/5/12, 34Sr +5, ɑə Man 2 under ɑ:ə

ɛ̨: 29Ess 11, ɛ̨:ə 8Db +5, ɛə 6Y +29, ɛ̣ə 6Y +29,
ɛa 6Y 30, ɛ̨ɷ 29Ess +1
æ: 30MxL +2, æ̣ə 6Y 31, æˑəɹ 5La 9, æɷəɹ 12St 11
a:ɹ 6Y +14, ạ:ɹ 5La 11, aɷəɾ 6Y 5
ɔɷəɹ 33Brk +3
oɷəɹ 33Brk 4
ɜɹ:ɹ 5La 12

interpr as *r*-col: ɹ 5La 1/4/8/10/14, 6Y +8/+14/15,
10L +5/+8, 15He 7, ʈ 25Ox 4, 38Do 3/5
cons *r* foll *r*-col V: ɹ 5La 12, ʈ 32W 7, 34Sr 4,
40Sx 1/+2/3/+6

HOUR'S poss sg 3Du +2, 6Y +8, 33Brk +2/+3;
HOURS pl 2Cu +3, 6Y +6/+26, 10L +7/+9,
22Sf +4, 30MxL +2

h- 10L +14, 13Lei +9, 34Sr +5, 39Ha +4, 40Sx 5

n- 29Ess 1, 31So +7/10, 37D 10

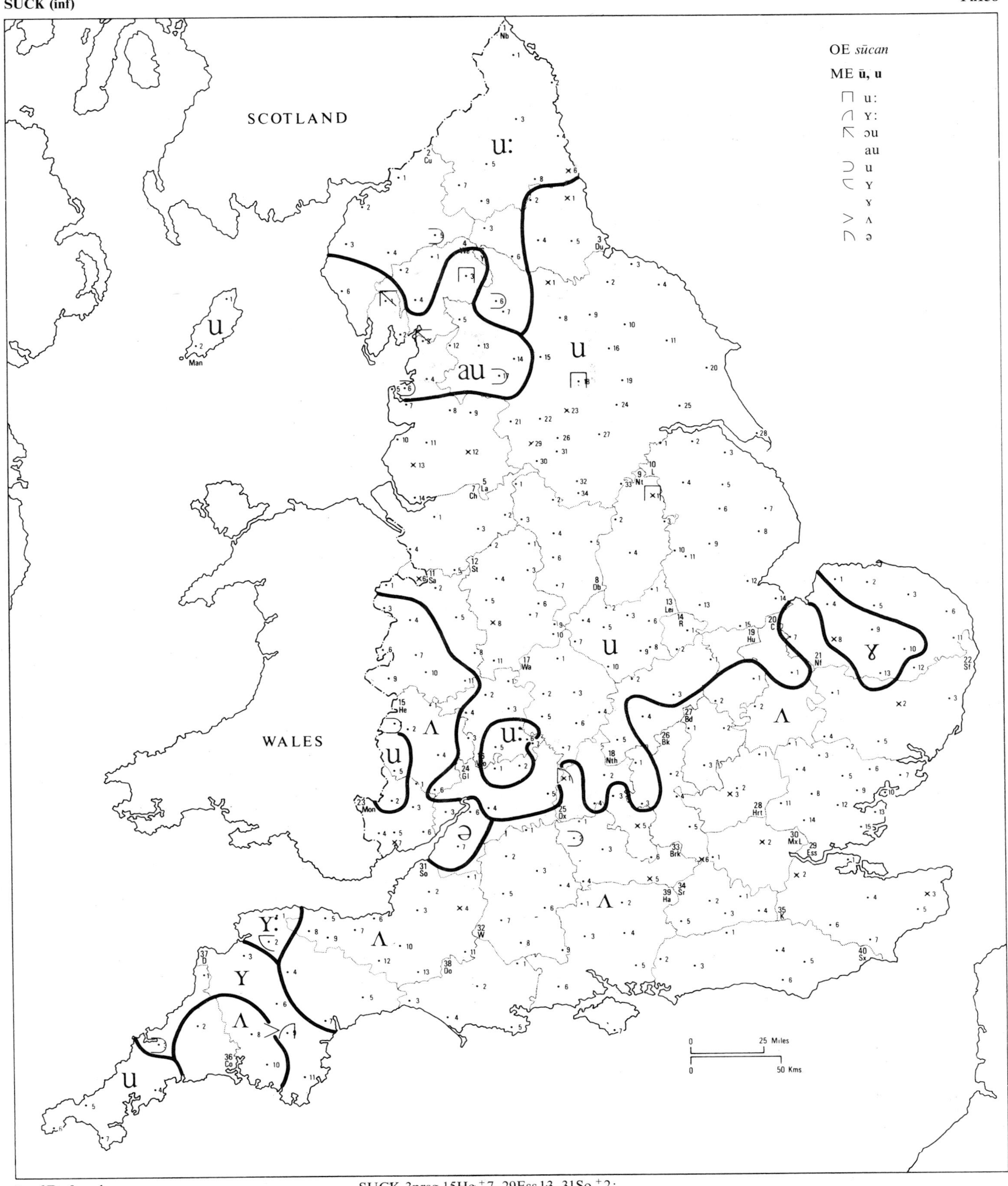

ᵊu: 3Du 3 under u:
ᵊu 6Y +6 under u

ɩu: 3Du +6, 6Y +15
εω 6Y +21, ε̈ω 6Y +6
œ: 24Gl +3
ɒ 33Brk 5

SUCK 3prsg 15He +7, 29Ess 13, 31So +2;
3prpl 6Y +26, 37D +2; n 4We +3, 31So +2;
SUCKED pp 6Y +6, 37D +11;
SUCKER(S) n 3Du +6, 5La +6, 15He +7, 22Sf 4, 33Brk +2, 37D +9;
SUCKING prp 2Cu +5, 6Y +6, 21Nf 5;
ndg 4We 2, 5La +3, 6Y +6/+15/16/31, 10L 4, 11Sa 2, 21Nf 3/11, 30MxL +1, 37D 3;
SUCKS 3prsg 5La 5/+6/7,
6Y 2–4/7/9–11/+17/+18/20/+21/22/25/+26/27/28/30/32/33, 7Ch 2, 10L 5/8/11, 12St 1–3/5, 16Wo 3/4/7, 17Wa 2, 21Nf 12, 25Ox 4, 29Ess 3/6/9/14/15, 30MxL +1, 31So 1/8/11/13, 32W 3/6, 33Brk +2/3/5, 34Sr 1/4, 35K 1, 36Co 6, 37D +9/10/+11, 38Do 4, 39Ha 2/4, 40Sx 3/6

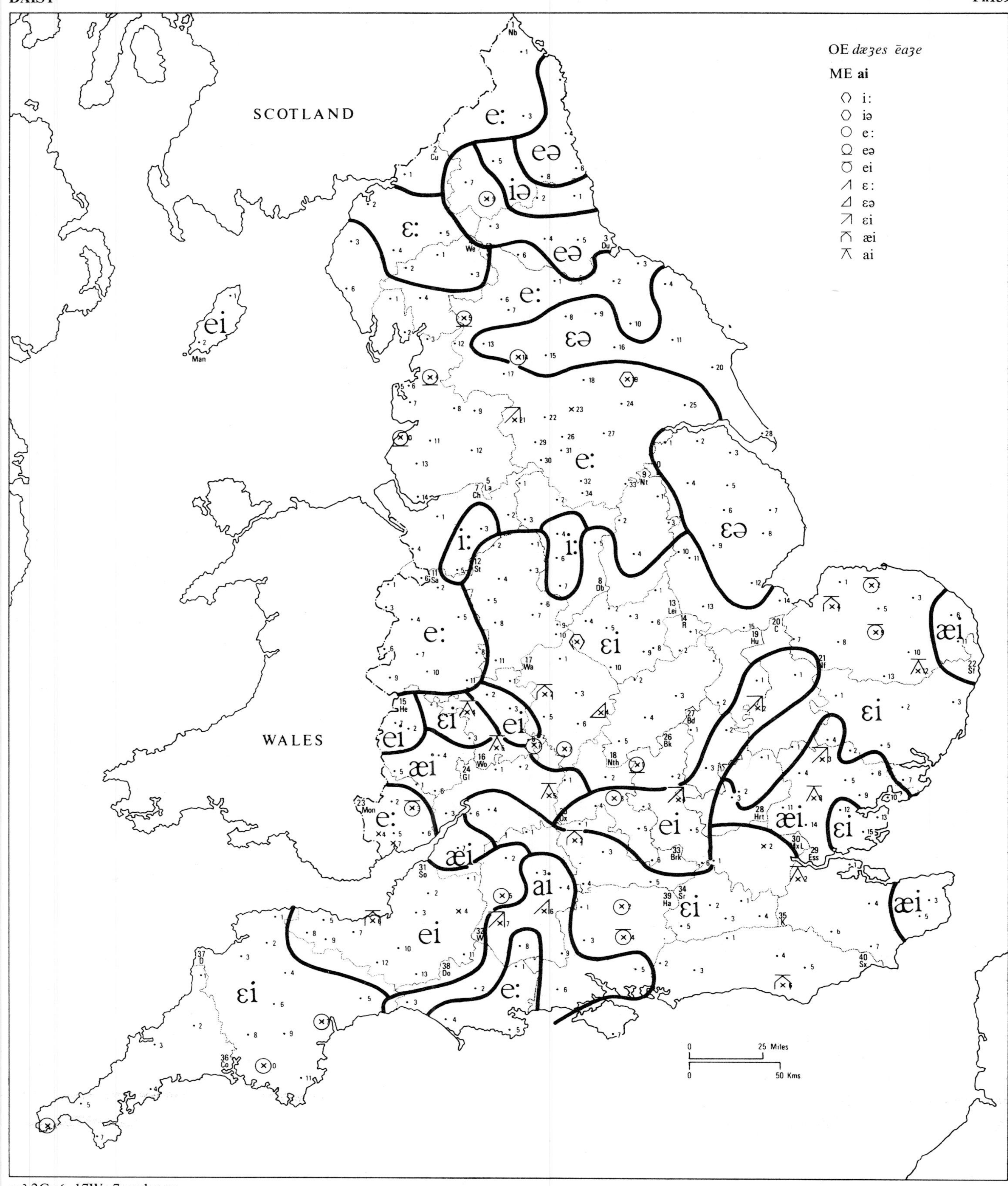

e:^{ə} 2Cu 6, 17Wa 7 under e:
ę:^{ə} 1Nb 6 under eə
e:ι 16Wo 2/3/6, e:^{ι} 15He 2, 23Mon 3, 25Ox 5,
ę:^{ι} 21Nf 2, eιə Man 2 under ei
ɛ:ι 13Lei $^{+}$1, ɛ:^{ι} 21Nf 10, ɛ̨:^{ι} 21Nf 5 under ɛi

ẹ˙a 5La $^{+}$1

-DAISY 10L 11, 32W 2, 33Brk 5

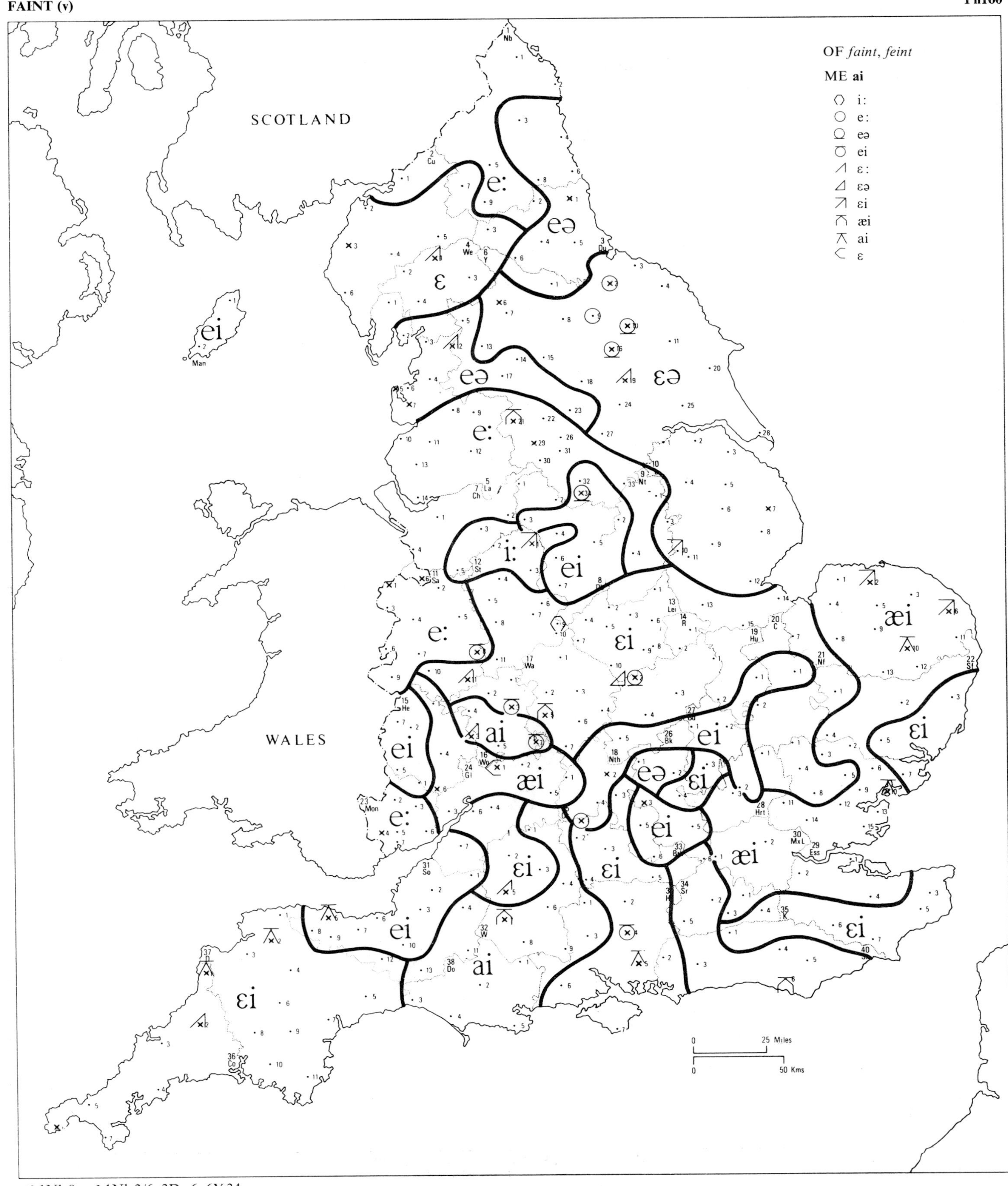

e˙ᵊ 1Nb 8, e:ᵊ 1Nb 3/6, 3Du 6, 6Y 34,
ẹ:ᵊ 18Nth +2 under eə
e:ι 16Wo 3, 23Mon 1, e:ᶥ 8Db 3/5, 9Nt 2, 11Sa 8,
15He 2/5, 25Ox 5, ẹ:ᶥ 8Db 7, ẹιə Man 1 under ei
ε:ι 11Sa +10, ειᵊ 16Wo 2, ε̣ιᵊ 20C 2 under εi

ι 2Cu 3
ιə 3Du 1, 25Ox 2
ɒι 15He 6

FAINTED pp 11Sa +10; pt 3Du 2, 6Y 7,
18Nth +2, 21Nf 11; FAINTING ndg 29Ess 6;
FAINTY adj 32W 7, 34Sr 3, 40Sx 6

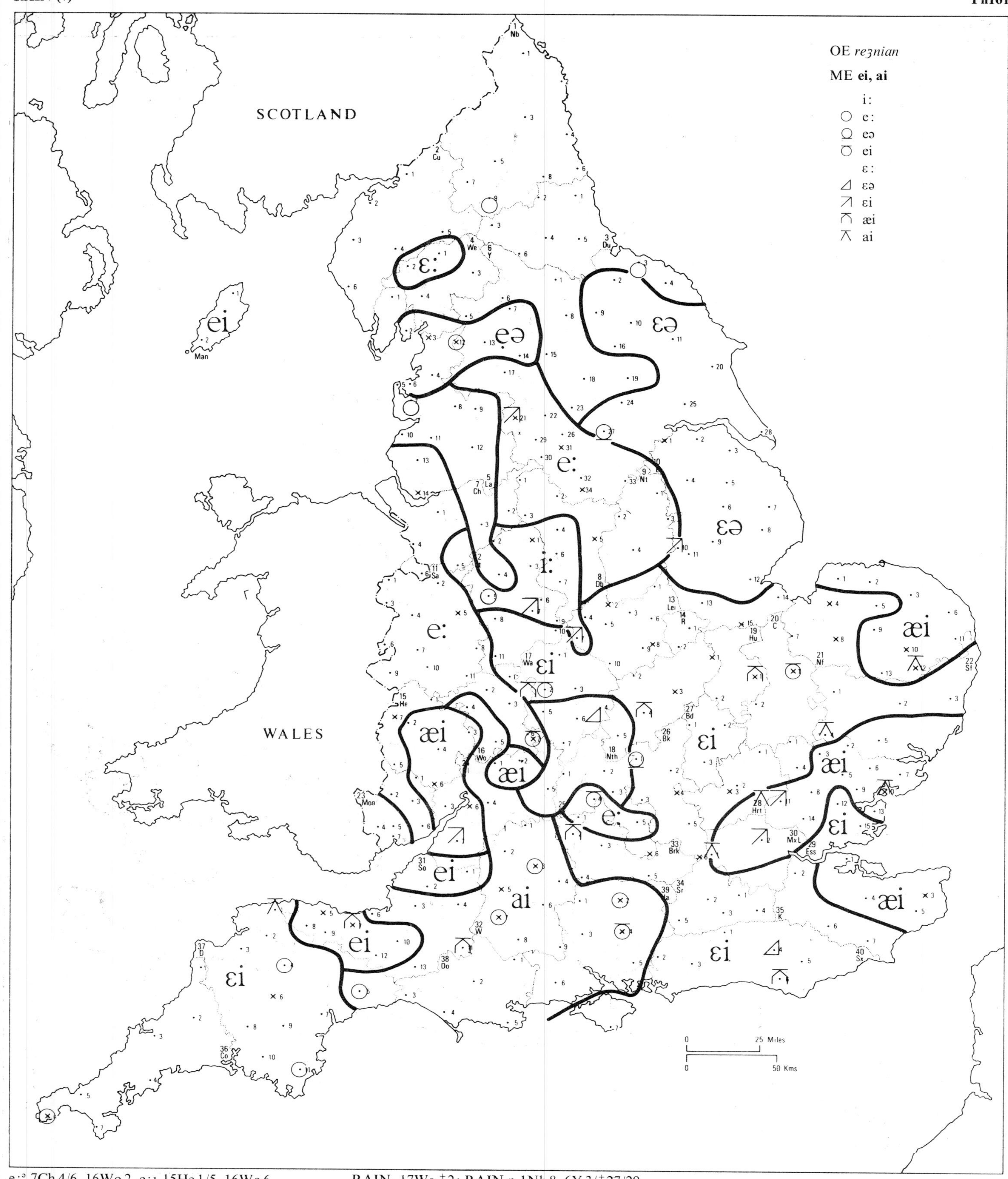

e:^{ə} 7Ch 4/6, 16Wo 2, e:ɩ 15He 1/5, 16Wo 6,
e:ɩ^{ə} 16Wo 3 under e:
eɩ^{ə} 20C 1 under ei
ɛɩə 20C $^{+}$2, ɛ̧ɩ^{ə} 20C $^{+}$2, ɛ̧ɩ 26Bk 3/5,
27Bd 2 under ɛi
æɩ^{ə} 24Gl 1 under æi

ɩə 1Nb 8
ea 5La 3
ɛ 15He $^{+}$6, ɛ: 32W 5
ɑɩ 22Sf $^{+}$4
ɒɩ 15He $^{+}$6

RAIN- 17Wa $^{+}$2; RAIN n 1Nb 8, 6Y 3/$^{+}$27/29, 10L $^{+}$10, 12St $^{+}$2/$^{+}$7/10, 13Lei 1, 17Wa $^{+}$2, 22Sf 2, 24Gl $^{+}$7, 25Ox $^{+}$4, 26Bk 2, 27Bd 1/3, 29Ess 1/4/$^{+}$11, 31So $^{+}$2, 33Brk $^{+}$2, 35K 1/6, 37D $^{+}$1; ndg 5La 4, 6Y 12, 10L $^{+}$10, 29Ess 6; RAIN(S) 3prsg 22Sf $^{+}$4, 25Ox 5, 31So $^{+}$11; RAINED 3ptsg 12St $^{+}$2, 31So $^{+}$2; pp 13Lei $^{+}$7, 37D $^{+}$5; pt 6Y 10, 30MxL $^{+}$1; RAINING prp 12St $^{+}$2, 22Sf $^{+}$4, 29Ess 3, 37D $^{+}$1; vbl n 6Y 13/$^{+}$27, 7Ch 1, 10L $^{+}$10, 12St $^{+}$2, 31So 1, 39Ha 3; ndg 10L $^{+}$10, 20C $^{+}$2

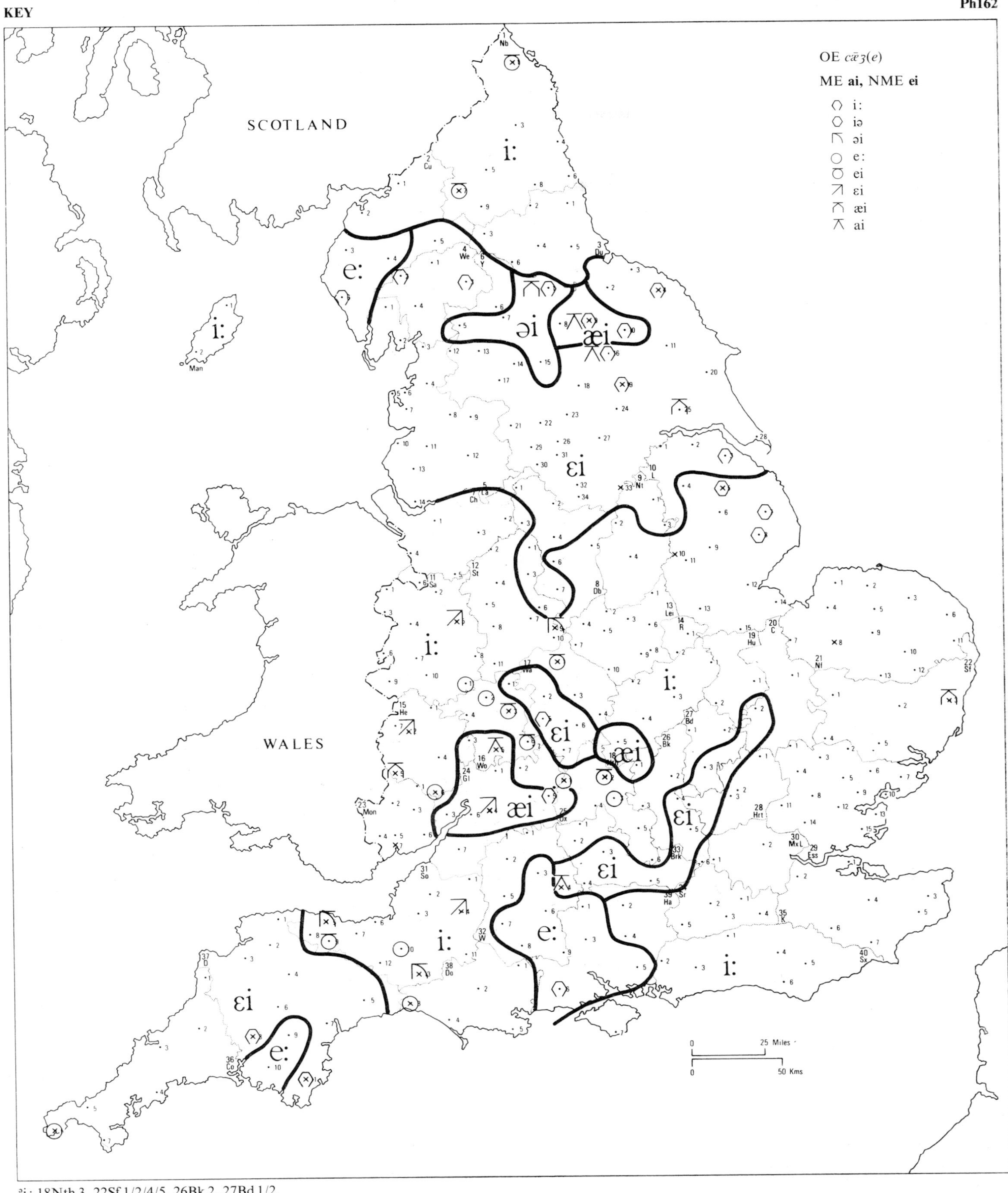

^{ə}i: 18Nth 3, 22Sf 1/2/4/5, 26Bk 2, 27Bd 1/2, 28Hrt 2/3, 29Ess 5, ë̜ɩ 3Du 4/5 under i:
e:^{ə} 2Cu $^{+}$6 under e:
e:ɩ 16Wo 3/$^{+}$6 under ei
ɛ̜:ɩ 31So 4 under ɛi

KEY-2Cu $^{+}$6, 4We $^{+}$2, 6Y $^{+}$1/$^{+}$9/$^{+}$10/$^{+}$16/$^{+}$25, 10L $^{+}$3/$^{+}$7/$^{+}$8, 16Wo $^{+}$6, 25Ox $^{+}$3, 31So $^{+}$9, 38Do 3; -KEY 21Nf 10

kɩ-15He 3, 16Wo 3/5, kj- 12St 3, 15He 2/5, 24Gl 1

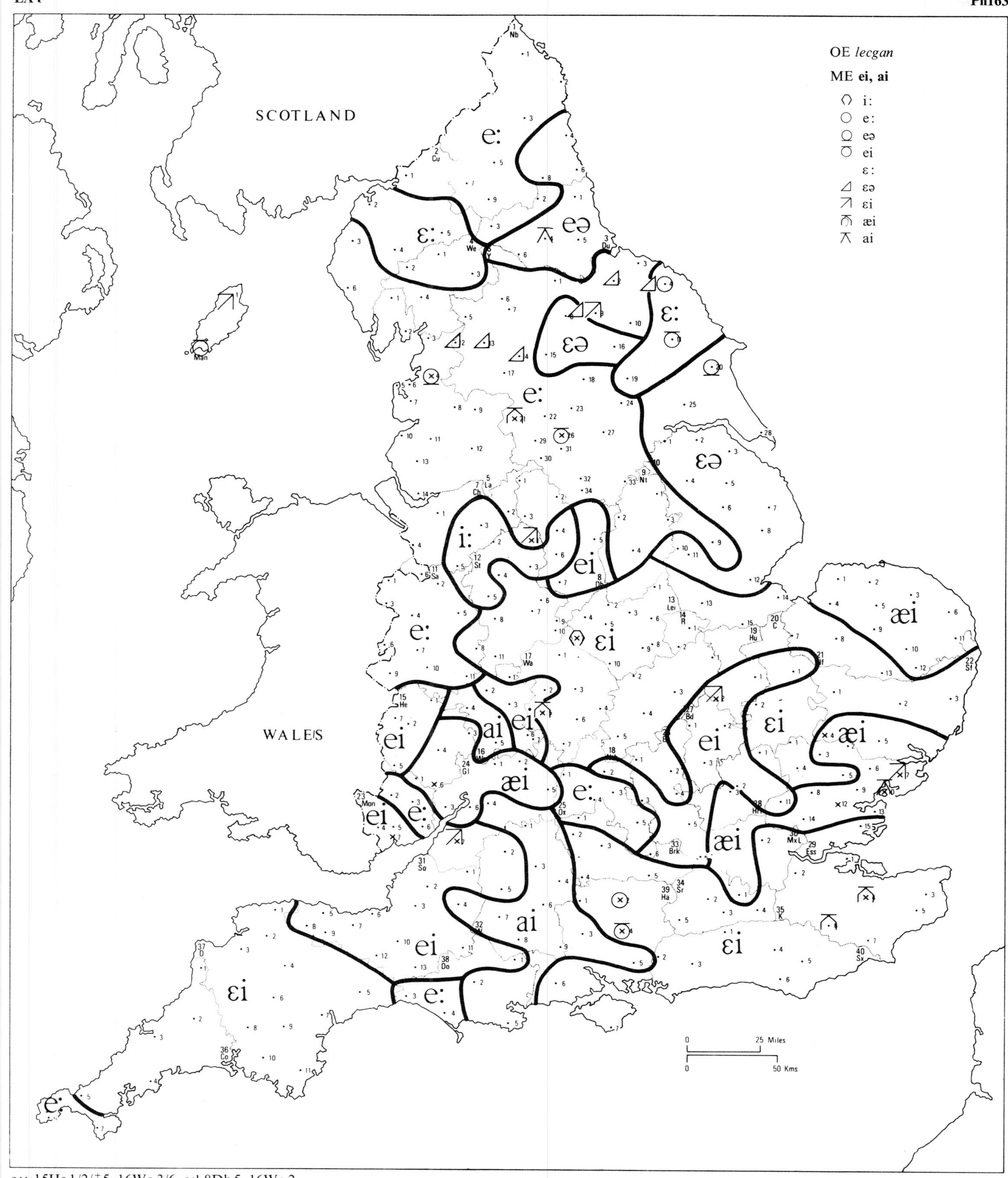

e:ɩ 15He 1/2/+5, 16Wo 3/6, e:ᶥ 8Db 5, 16Wo 2,
24Gl +7, ȩᶥ: 15He 7 under ei

ɩ·ə 6Y +1
ɛ 6Y +4, 39Ha +4/+5
a 39Ha +3
ɑɩ 22Sf 4
ɒɩ 15He 6

LAY 1prpl 6Y +9; v 6Y +11; LAYS 3prsg 6Y 7,
35K +6; LAID pp 6Y +1/+2/+4/+9/+12–+14,
39Ha +3–+5

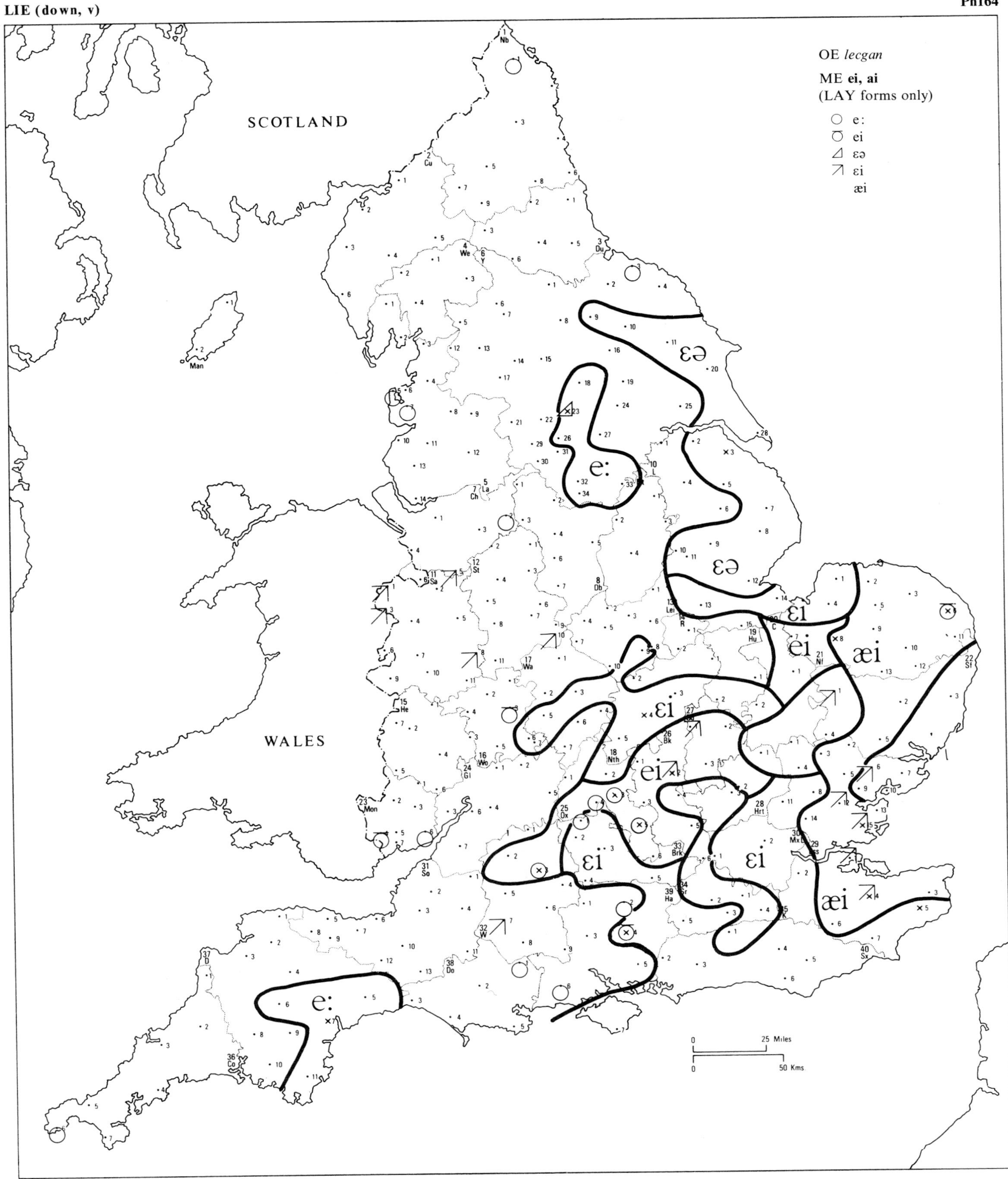

ẹə 6Y 23 under ɛə

ɛ̇ 25Ox +4, ɛ: 6Y 1̣9, 32W 5

LAY 3prpl 6Y 20; ndg 36Co 6; LAY- n 10L +11, 18Nth 3, 19Hu 2, 21Nf 11/13, 22Sf 5, 26Bk 3, 34Sr +5; LAYING prp 6Y 26, 27Bd +1; ndg 32W 7; LAYING-prp 23Mon 6; LAYS 3prsg 34Sr +5; 3prpl 10L +11; LAID 1ptsg 25Ox +4; pp 16Wo 3

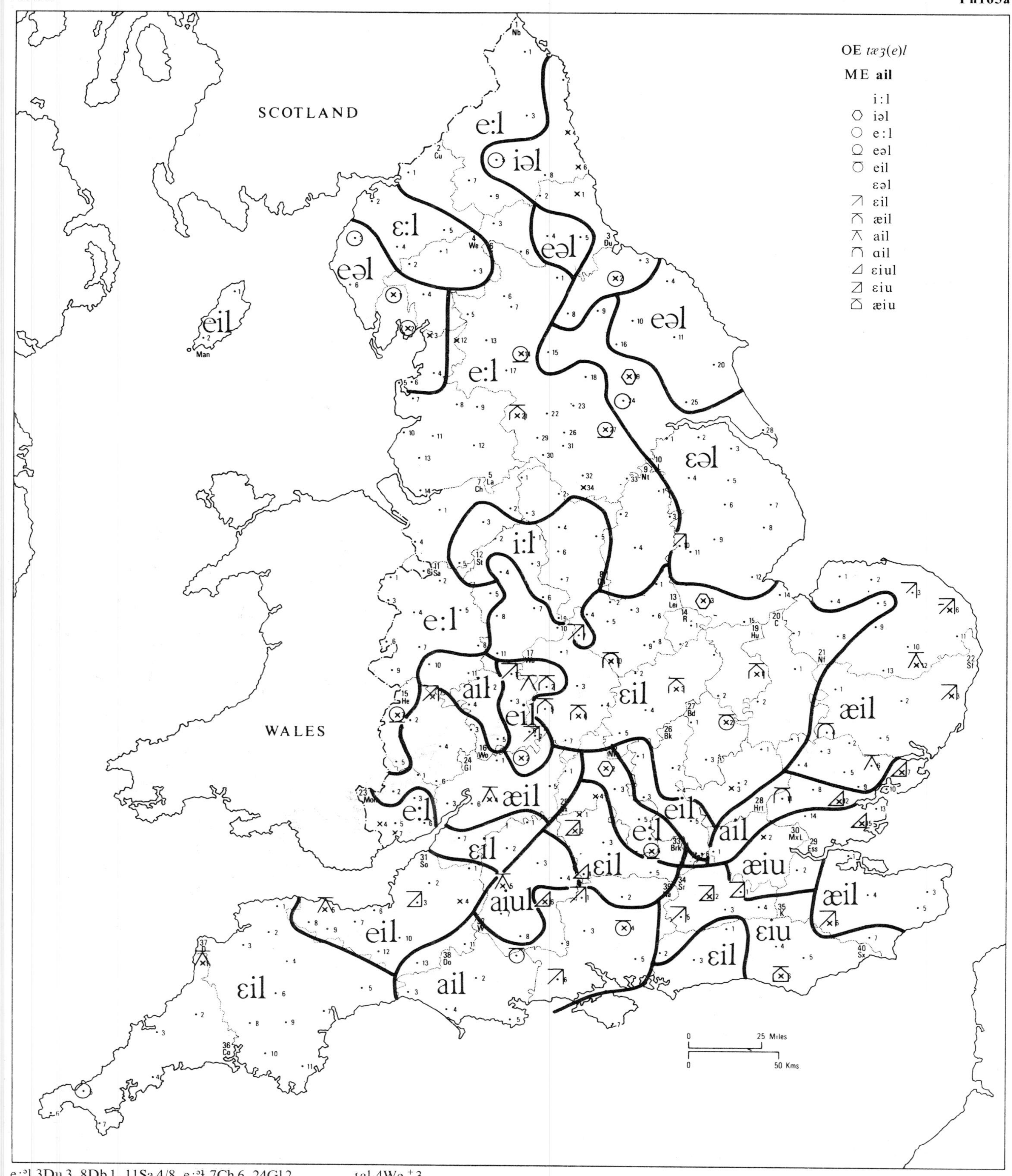

e:^{ə}l 3Du 3, 8Db 1, 11Sa 4/8, e:^{ə}ɫ 7Ch 6, 24Gl 2, 25Ox 3/5, ȩ:^{ə}l 11Sa $^{+}$2, e:ɩɫ 15He 5 under e:l

eɩ^{ə}ɫ 26Bk $^{+}$6, 31So 2/7–9/12, ȩɩ^{ə}ɫ 26Bk 1/3/5/$^{+}$6 27Bd 2, 38Do $^{+}$1, eɩəɫ 39Ha 4, e:ɩɫ 16Wo 6, e:ɩəɫ 16Wo 3, e:^{ɩ}l 16Wo $^{+}$1 under eil

ɛɩ^{ə}l 10L 15, 16Wo $^{+}$1, ɛɩ^{ə}ɫ 17Wa 3/4/$^{+}$5/7, 18Nth 1/2/4/5, 19Hu 2, 24Gl $^{+}$7, 28Hrt 1/2, 32W 1/2, 39Ha $^{+}$1, ȩɩ^{ə}ɫ 20C 2, ɛ̢ɩ^{ə}ɫ 24Gl $^{+}$7, 27Bd 1/3, ɛɩəɫ 26Bk 2/4, 29Ess 1, ɛ̢:ɩl 21Nf $^{+}$3. under eil

æɩ^{ə}ɫ 15He 6, 17Wa $^{+}$5/6, 19Hu 1, 22Sf 1/2/5, 24Gl 1/3/6, 29Ess 3/5/$^{+}$6 under æil

aɩ^{ə}ɫ 16Wo 5, 24Gl 4, 31So 13, 32W 5/$^{+}$9, 38Do 3–5, 39Ha $^{+}$1/3 under ail

æɩωɫ 29Ess $^{+}$7 under ɛiul

ɛɩəω 31So $^{+}$3 under ɛiu

ạɩω 34Sr $^{+}$1, 35K $^{+}$2, aɩω 35K $^{+}$2 under æiu

ɩal 4We $^{+}$3

jɛl 1Nb 4

ẹa! 5La 3

e:ωɫ 33Brk $^{+}$1

e:ω 33Brk $^{+}$1

ɛ:l 10L $^{+}$9, 11Sa $^{+}$10

ɛ˙ω 25Ox 4

TAIL- 24Gl $^{+}$7, 26Bk $^{+}$6; -TAIL(S) 6Y 21, 10L $^{+}$10, 21Nf $^{+}$3, 34Sr $^{+}$5; TAIL nd 34Sr $^{+}$1, 35K $^{+}$2

æɩω in -TAILED 29Ess $^{+}$7

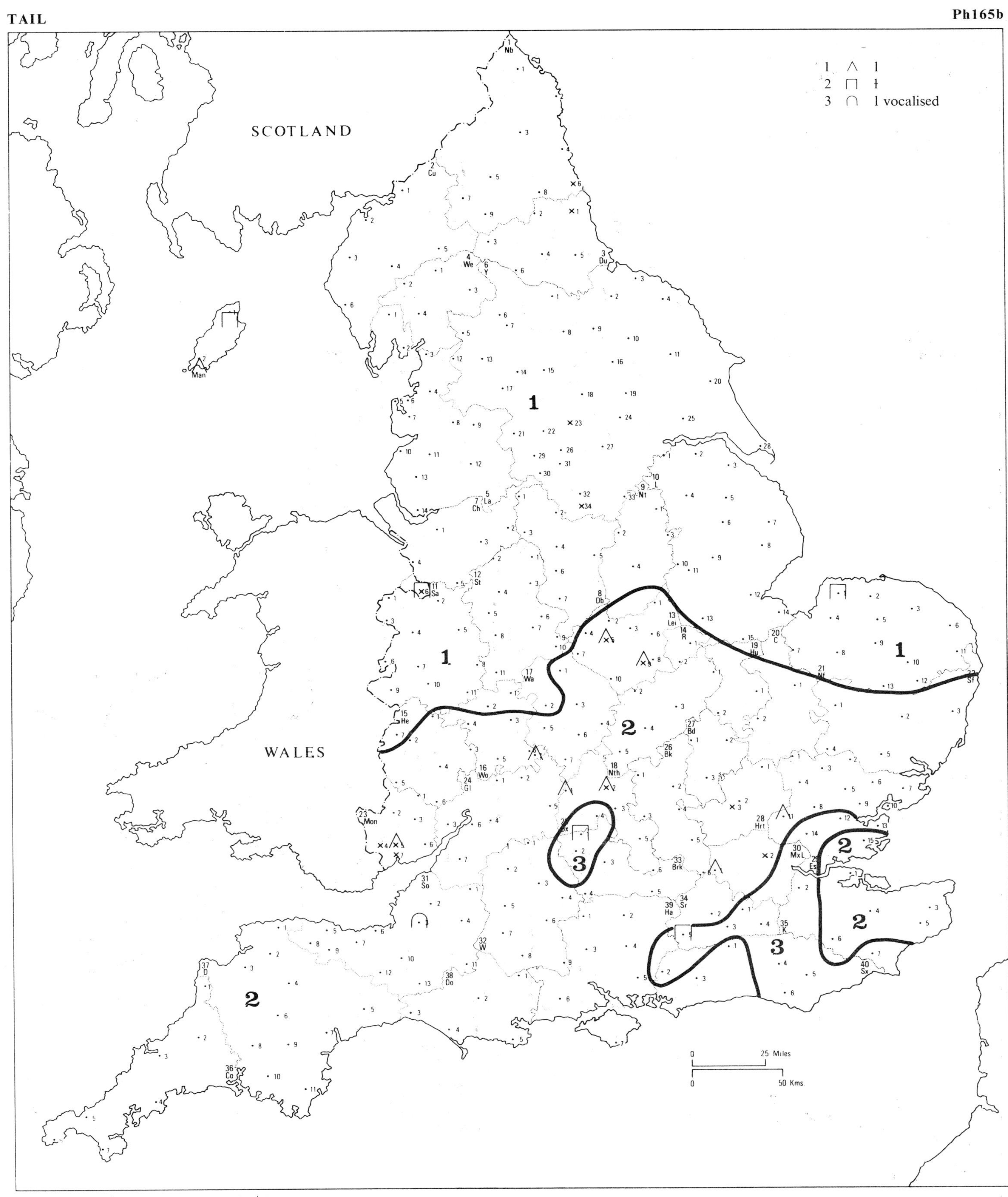

TAIL- 30MxL [+]1; -TAIL 6Y 21, 34Sr [+]5

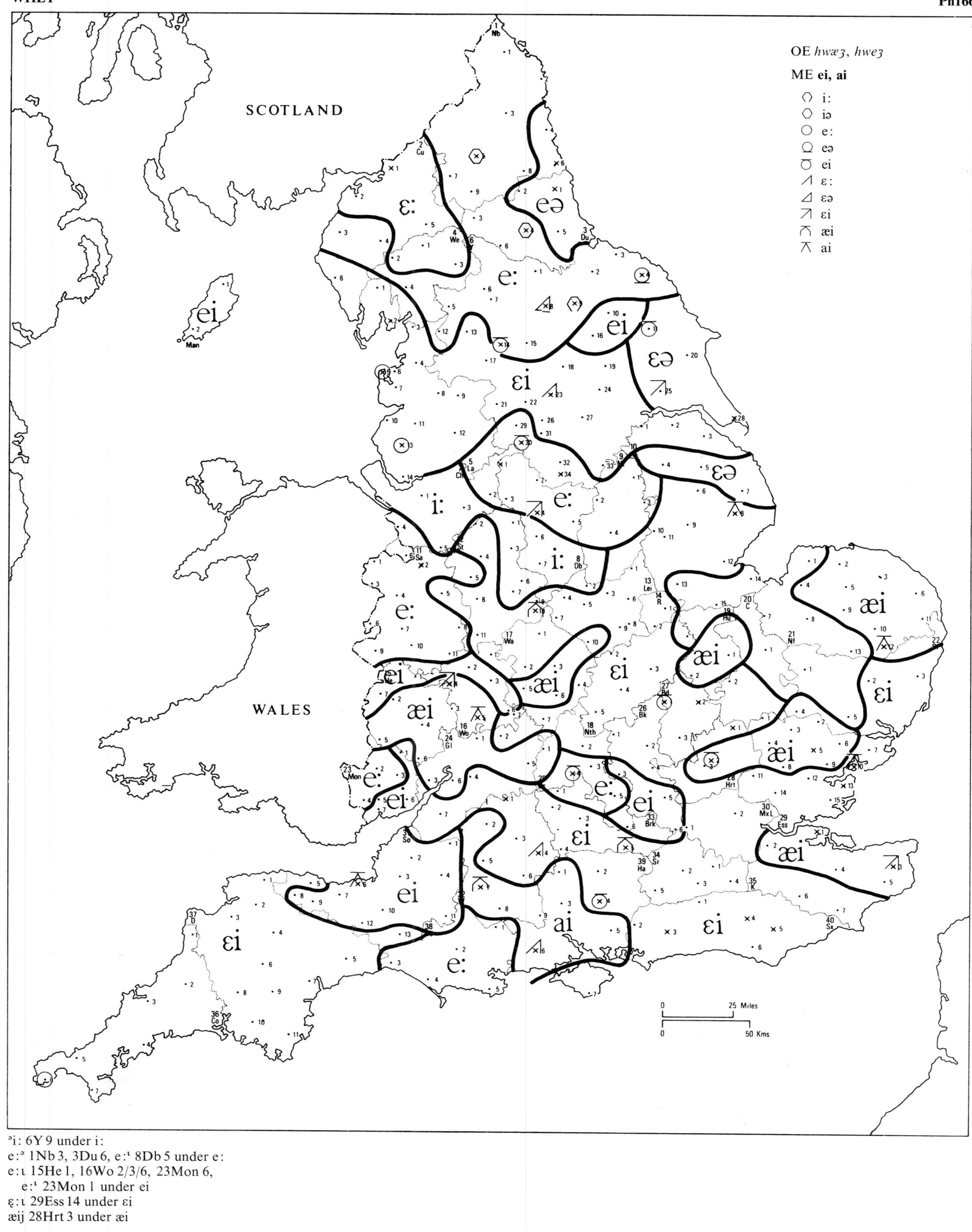

ᵊi: 6Y 9 under i:
e:ᵊ 1Nb 3, 3Du 6, e:ᵗ 8Db 5 under e:
e:ɩ 15He 1, 16Wo 2/3/6, 23Mon 6, e:ᵗ 23Mon 1 under ei
ɛ̧:ɩ 29Ess 14 under ɛi
æij 28Hrt 3 under æi

ɒɩ 32W 1

WHEY- 32W +7, 36Co +6

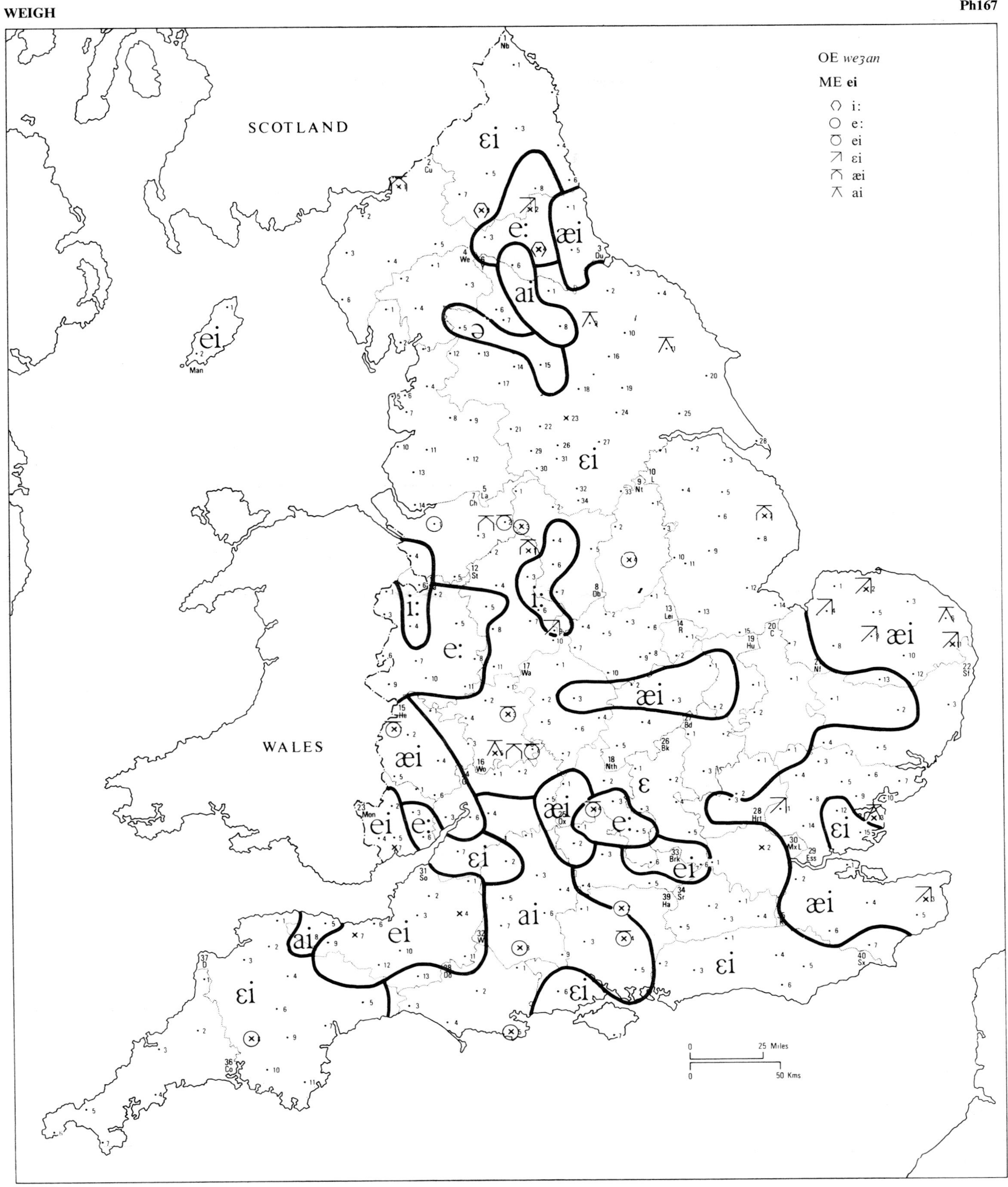

ę̈ɩ 3Du 4 under i:
e:ɩ Man 2, 23Mon 2, ę:i: 16Wo 3,
e:ɩj 23Mon 4 under ei
ɛ:ɩ 21Nf 2/11, ɛ:ɩ 21Nf +9 under ɛi
æɩj 28Hrt +3 under æi

ẹə 1Nb +4
ɛ: 21Nf +10
æ˙ 21Nf +13. æ: 21Nf 12
əɩ 31So 7

WEIGH 3prsg 21Nf +12;
WEIGHED pt 30MxL +1, 39Ha +4;
pp 6Y +9; WEIGHING vbl n 40Sx +3;
WEIGHING- 21Nf +6, 40Sx +3;
WEIGHS 3prsg 6Y +11; 2prpl 39Ha +4

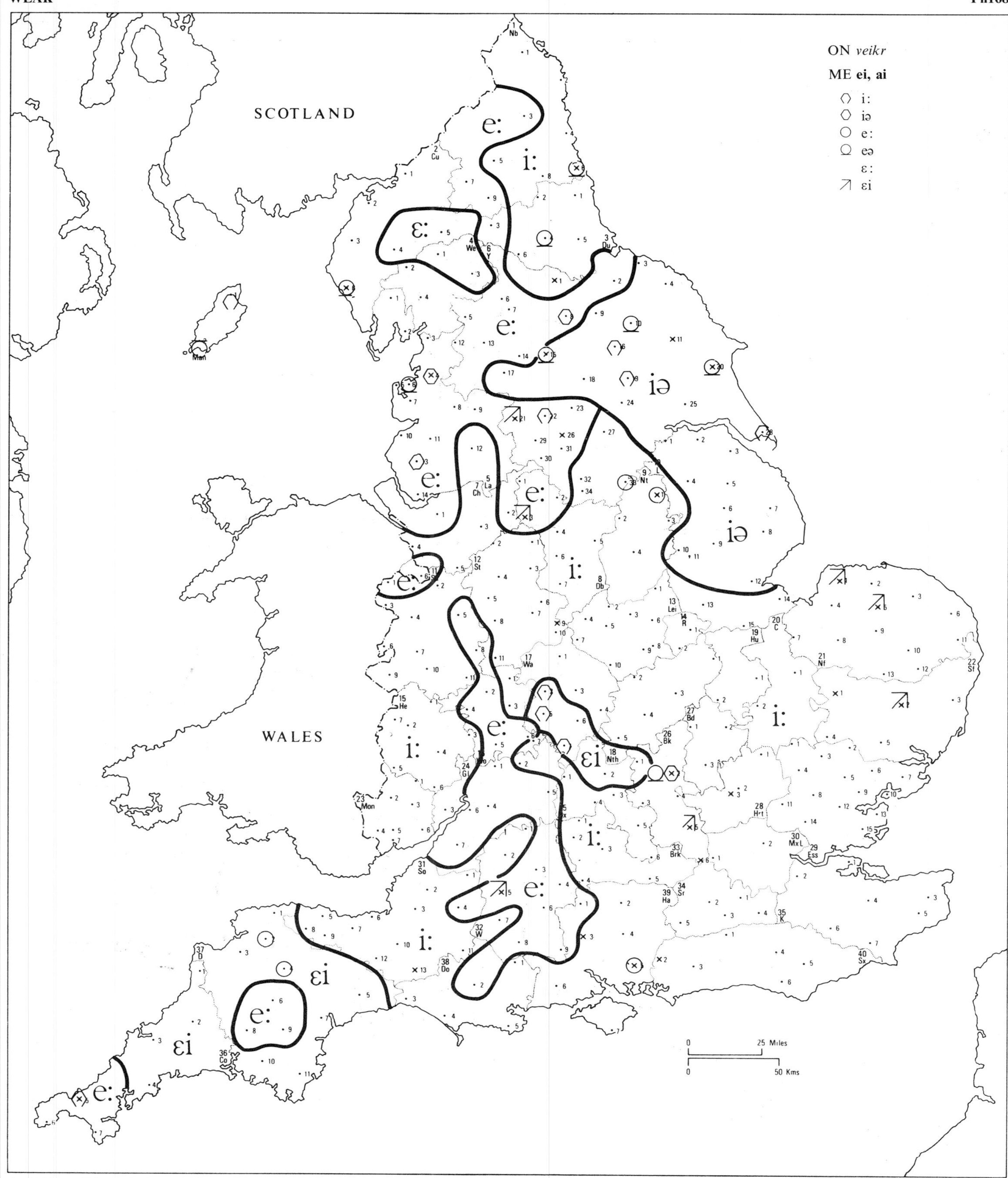

ᵊi: 22Sf 5, 26Bk 4, 27Bd 1–3, 29Ess 5,
ë̜ɩ 3Du 5 under i:
e:ᵊ 5La 2/3, 7Ch 6, 16Wo 2, e:ɩ 16Wo 6,
e̜:ɩ 31So 4 under e:
ɛ:ᵊ 4We 1 under ɛ:
e̜ɩ 25Ox 2, 32W 5 under ɛi

eɩ 31So 13
aɩ 39Ha 3
əɩ 6Y 1
ɛə· 6Y +9/11
ɛ 11Sa +8

WEAKLY adj 5La +6, 37D +4

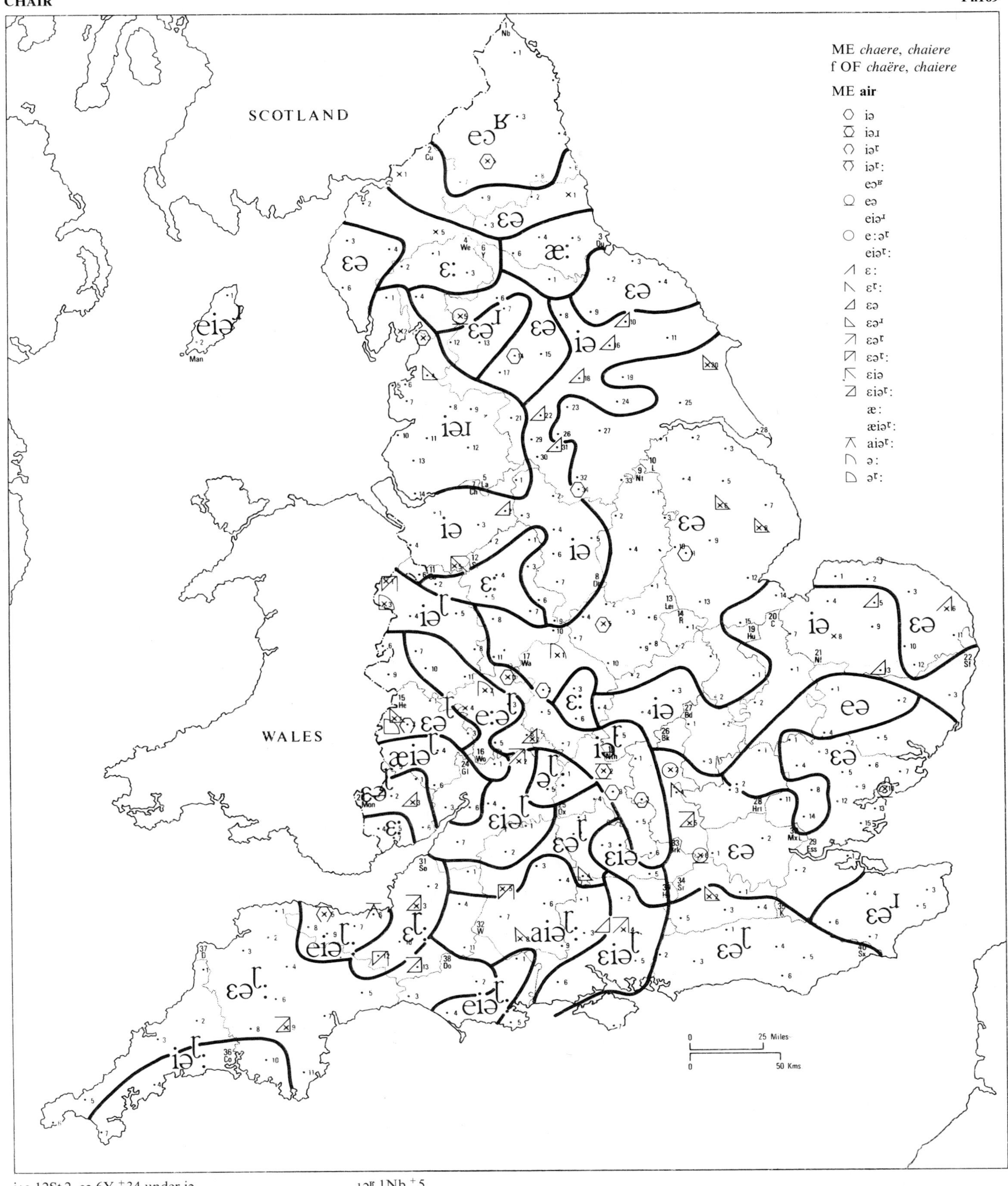

i:ə 12St 2, ẹə 6Y +34 under iə
ɩəɹ 5La 5–7/13, ɩəɹ̠ 8Db 1, 25Ox 2 under iəɹ
i:əʵ 11Sa 4 under iəʵ
ɛ˙ɔʁ 1Nb 7 under eɔʁ
ȩ:ə 1Nb 6, 29Ess 8 under eə
e:əʵ: 11Sa 7 under e:əʵ
ɛ:ᵊ 11Sa 2, ɛ 23Mon +7 under ɛ:
ɛʵ:ᵊ 26Bk +4 under ɛʵ:
ɛ:ə 21Nf 11, ɛɐ 35K +1, ȩɐ 35K +1, ɛ:ᵊ 26Bk +4,
ȩə 1Nb 9, ȩ:ə 1Nb 6 under ɛə
ɛ:əʵ 31So 1 under ɛəʵ
ɛɩɐ 33Brk 3/+5 under ɛiə
ɛɔʵ 24Gl 4, 26Bk 5, ȩɩəʵ 24Gl 7 under ɛiəʵ:
ɑ: 3Du 6 under æ:
a:ɩəʵ: 31So +4 under aiəʵ:

ɩɔʁ 1Nb +5
e˙əɹ 5La 2
ɛ:ɹ 2Cu 5, ɛəʁ 3Du 1, ɛər 2Cu 1, ɛɩɐɹ 33Brk +5
aʵ: 16Wo 4

interpr as *r*-col: ɹ 5La +4, 6Y 7/12, 10L 8,
15He 7, ɽ 25Ox 4
cons *r* foll *r*-col V: ɽ 33Brk 1/+4, 34Sr 4, 39Ha 7,
40Sx +2/4–6

CHAIR- 6Y +16/+31; -CHAIR 1Nb +5,
6Y 4/19/26, 21Nf +5/7/12, 23Mon 4, 25Ox 4;
CHAIRS pl 1Nb 6, 2Cu 2, 4We 2, 5La +4,
Man 2, 10L +11/12, 15He +2, 23Mon +7,
26Bk +4, 29Ess 15, 33Brk 1/+5, 34Sr 2–5,
35K 3/5/6, 39Ha 7, 40Sx 1/3/4/6

SAW(-DUST) Ph170

SLAUGHTER(-HOUSE) Ph171

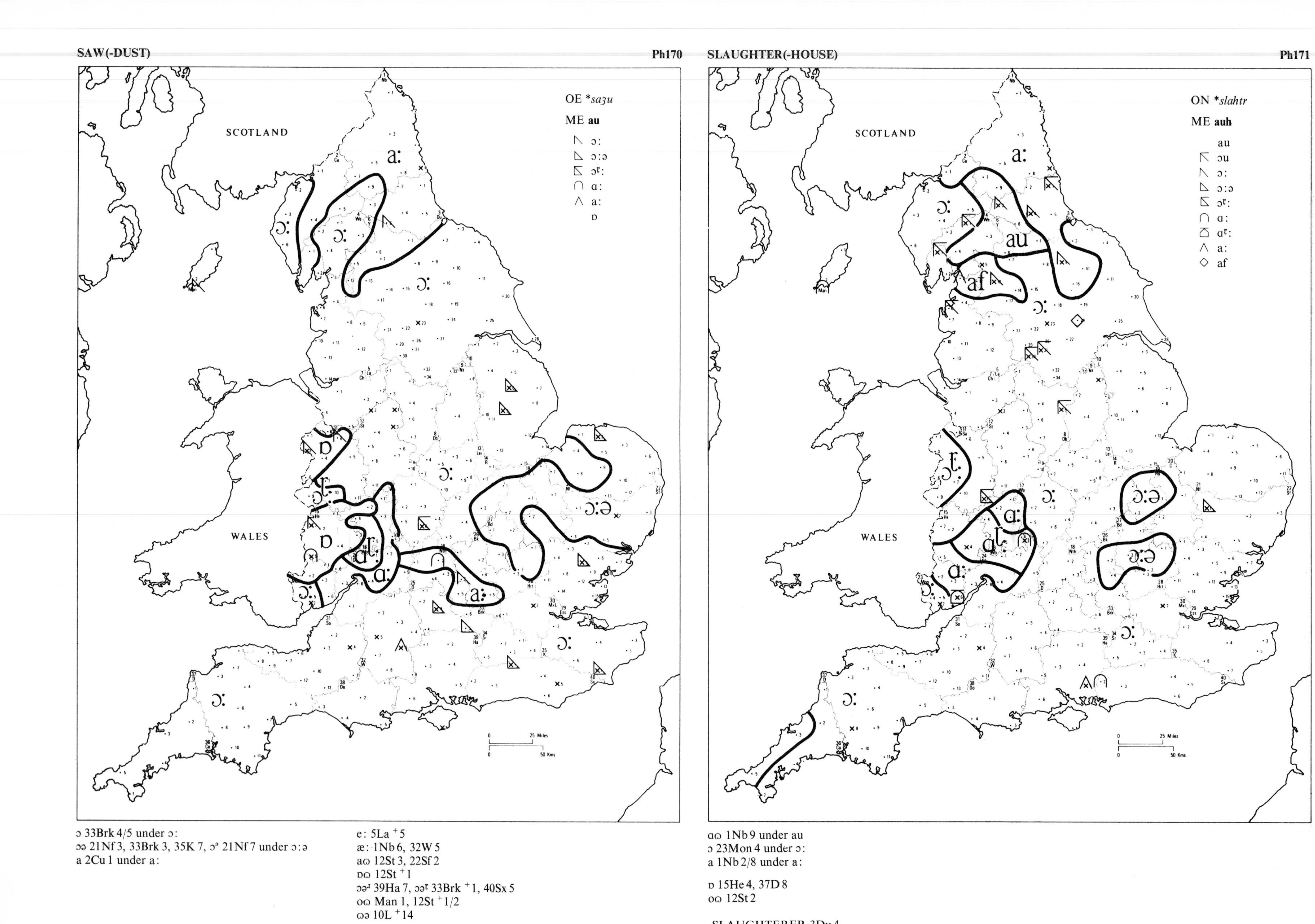

ɔ 33Brk 4/5 under ɔ:
ɔə 21Nf 3, 33Brk 3, 35K 7, ɔᵊ 21Nf 7 under ɔ:ə
a 2Cu 1 under a:

e: 5La $^+$5
æ: 1Nb 6, 32W 5
aʊ 12St 3, 22Sf 2
ɒʊ 12St $^+$1
ɔəʴ 39Ha 7, ɔəʳ 33Brk $^+$1, 40Sx 5
oʊ Man 1, 12St $^+$1/2
ʊə 10L $^+$14

SAW n 5La $^+$5, 33Brk $^+$1/$^+$5; v 12St $^+$1

se:g = SAW n 6Y $^+$21/$^+$30; v 6Y $^+$30;
se:gɪn = SAWING prp 6Y $^+$29/$^+$30; ndg 5La $^+$9

ɑʊ 1Nb 9 under au
ɔ 23Mon 4 under ɔ:
a 1Nb 2/8 under a:

ɒ 15He 4, 37D 8
oʊ 12St 2

-SLAUGHTERER 3Du 4

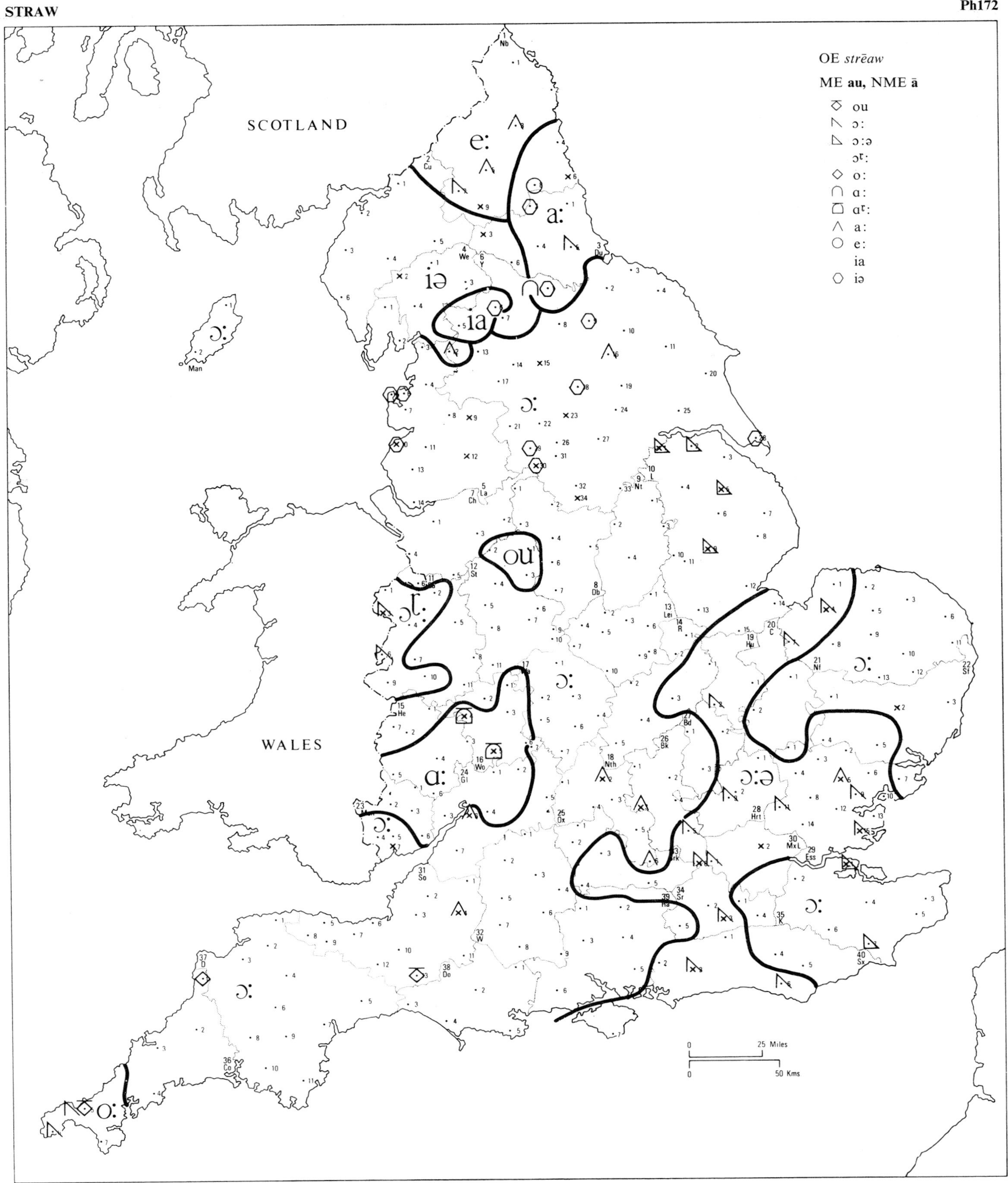

ɔ 28Hrt +3, ɔ̹:ᵒ 17Wa 1, ɒ: 21Nf +11 under ɔ:
ɔə 28Hrt +3, 29Ess 13, 30MxL +1, 33Brk 3/+4,
35K 7, ɔ˙ᵒə 18Nth 1, o̜˙ᵉ 35K 1 under ɔ:ə
e˙ə 1Nb +8, e:ᶦ 1Nb +5 under e:
ᶦɩə 4We 3 under iə

i: 1Nb 9
e̜ɩ 31So +3
æ: 32W +3
aɷ 22Sf 2
ɔɷ 6Y +33
ʌɷ 29Ess +10
ɷə 6Y 15/+28

STRAW- 6Y +16, 21Nf +7, 31So 4, 40Sx +6

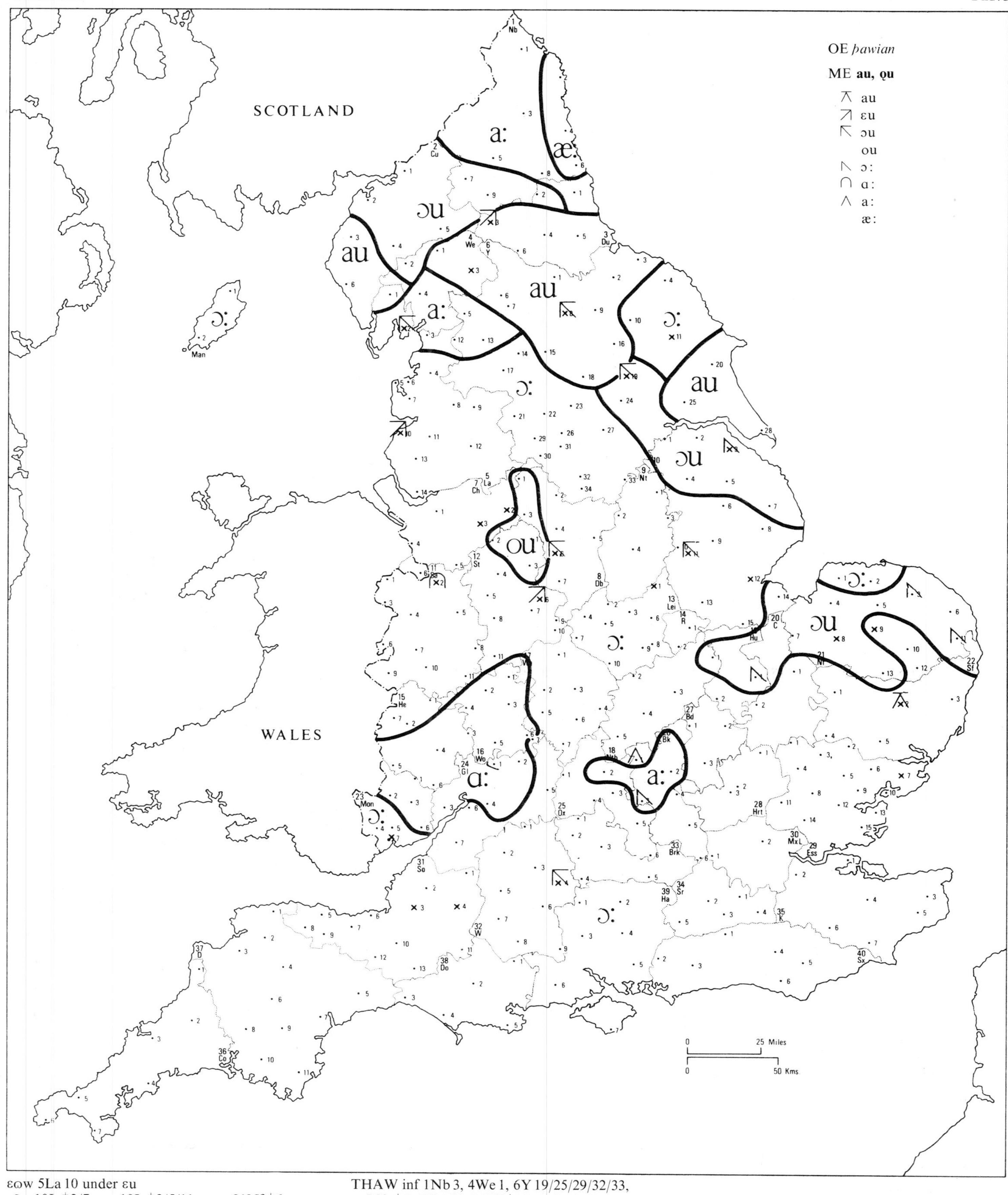

ɛɷw 5La 10 under ɛu
ɔᵒw 10L +2/7, ow 10L +2/5/11, ɒuw 21Nf +6, ɒɷw 6Y 8, 21Nf +5, ɒw 21Nf +3 under ɔu
o:ᵒw 8Db 3, o:w 8Db 1 under ou
ọ:ᵊ 18Nth 3, 28Hrt 1, ɔ:ə 34Sr 2, ɔˑə 30MxL +1, ɔə 30MxL +1, ɔ:w 12St 9/10, ɔ:ɷ 34Sr 3, 40Sx 2, ǫ 25Ox 4, ọ: 5La 11 under ɔ:
æ:ə 1Nb +6 under æ:

ɑɷ 6Y 11, 21Nf +1, 29Ess 7
ɒ: 21Nf 9
o: 13Lei 1, ọ: 7Ch 3
ɷu 7Ch 2, u: 10L 12
ə: (said by older people) 7Ch +4

THAW inf 1Nb 3, 4We 1, 6Y 19/25/29/32/33, 7Ch +4, 10L 7/8, 21Nf +11, 31So 6, 32W 7, 34Sr 2; n 1Nb +6, 6Y 11, 21Nf +6, 26Bk +1; THAWED 3ptsg 21Nf +5; pp 10L +2; THAWS 3prsg 6Y 28, Man 1, 30MxL +1

intrusive ɹ follows the stem vowel(s) at 12St 8, 17Wa 1/3/6/7, 18Nth 2–4, 19Hu +1/2, 20C 2, 21Nf 2/+3/+11/12, 22Sf 1/3/5, 23Mon 2/4/5, 27Bd 1–3, 28Hrt 1–3, 29Ess 1–6/8–15, 30MxL +1/2, 34Sr +1

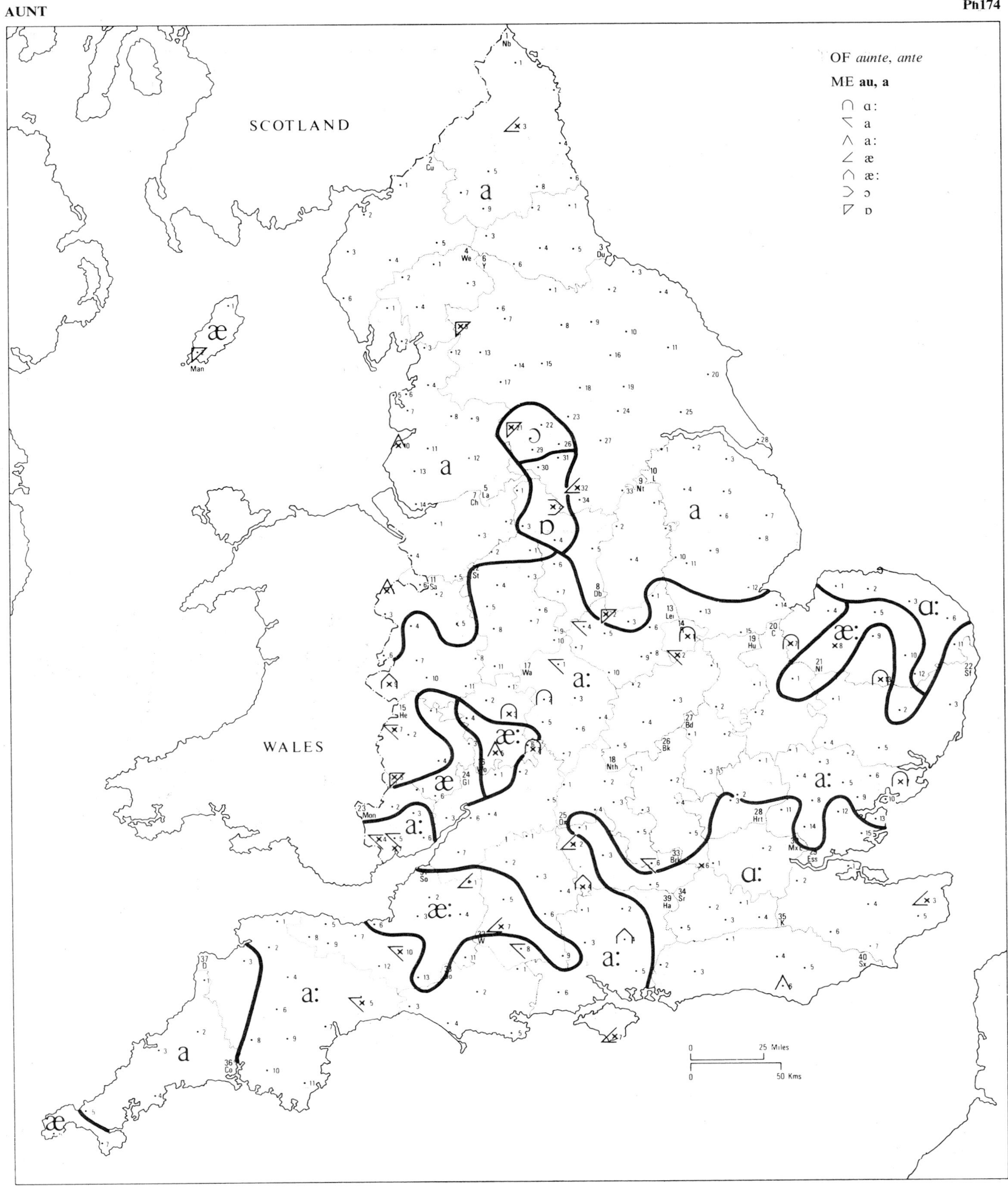

ɑ:ᵊ 28Hrt +3, ɑ̈ 21Nf 1 under ɑ:
ɑ 6Y 1 under a
æᵊ Man +2 under æ
æ:ᵊ 20C 1, æ˙ᵊ 22Sf 2, æ˙ᶦ 31So 13 under æ:

-AUNT 6Y + 6; AUNTIE 1Nb 4/7, 8Db 6, 12St 8, 15He 3/4, 16Wo 6, 17Wa +1, 28Hrt +3, 31So +1/7, 32W 4, 36Co 1–3/6/7, 37D 3/5, 38Do 2/4/5, 40Sx 3

n- 6Y +26/29/30, 7Ch 5, 8Db 1/2, 11Sa 5, 24Gl 3

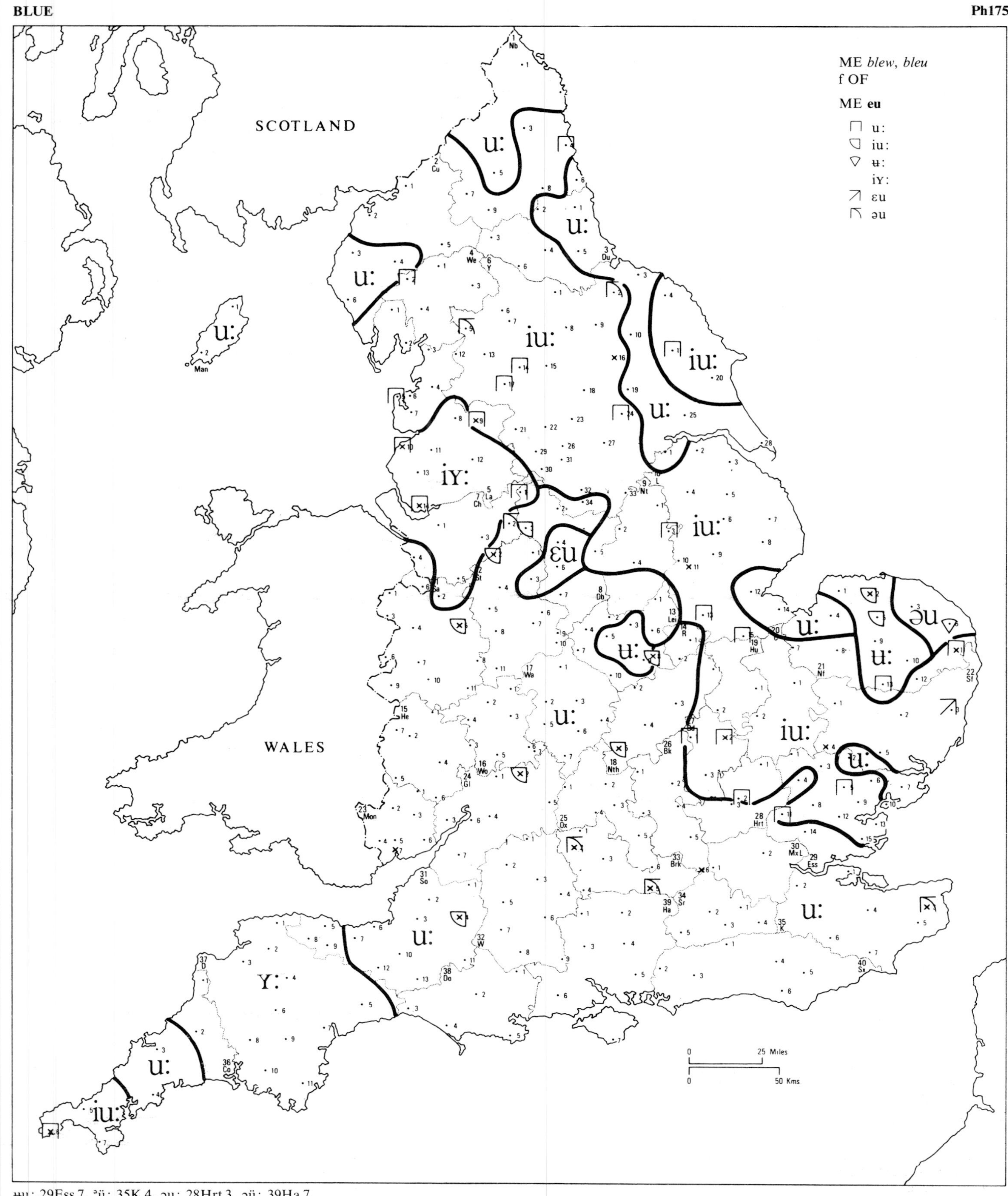

ʉu: 29Ess 7, ᵊü: 35K 4, əu: 28Hrt 3, əü: 39Ha 7,
ü 21Nf +13, öu 5La +5 under u:
ɩu 1Nb +9, 3Du +3, 5La +5/6/7,
6Y +2/+4/6/7/9/+11/+17/21/22/+24/26/29/
30/32/33, 21Nf 7/8, ɩü 29Ess 8/9/+11,
ˡü 22Sf +5, ɩω 6Y +11/+14/18/20/27, 12St 2,
31So 4, 36Co 5/7, ɩ̧ω 6Y 1 under iu:
ʉ 13Lei +3, 21Nf 1/+13, ˡʉ: 13Lei +9, ˡʉ 21Nf 10,
ɩʉ 21Nf +5/9 under ʉ:
ʏ: 5La 12/13, ʏʉ: 11Sa 2 under iʏ:
ʌω 6Y +5 under əu

ə̣: 21Nf +13

BLUE- 1Nb +4, 10L +13, 21Nf 8/+13,
29Ess +11

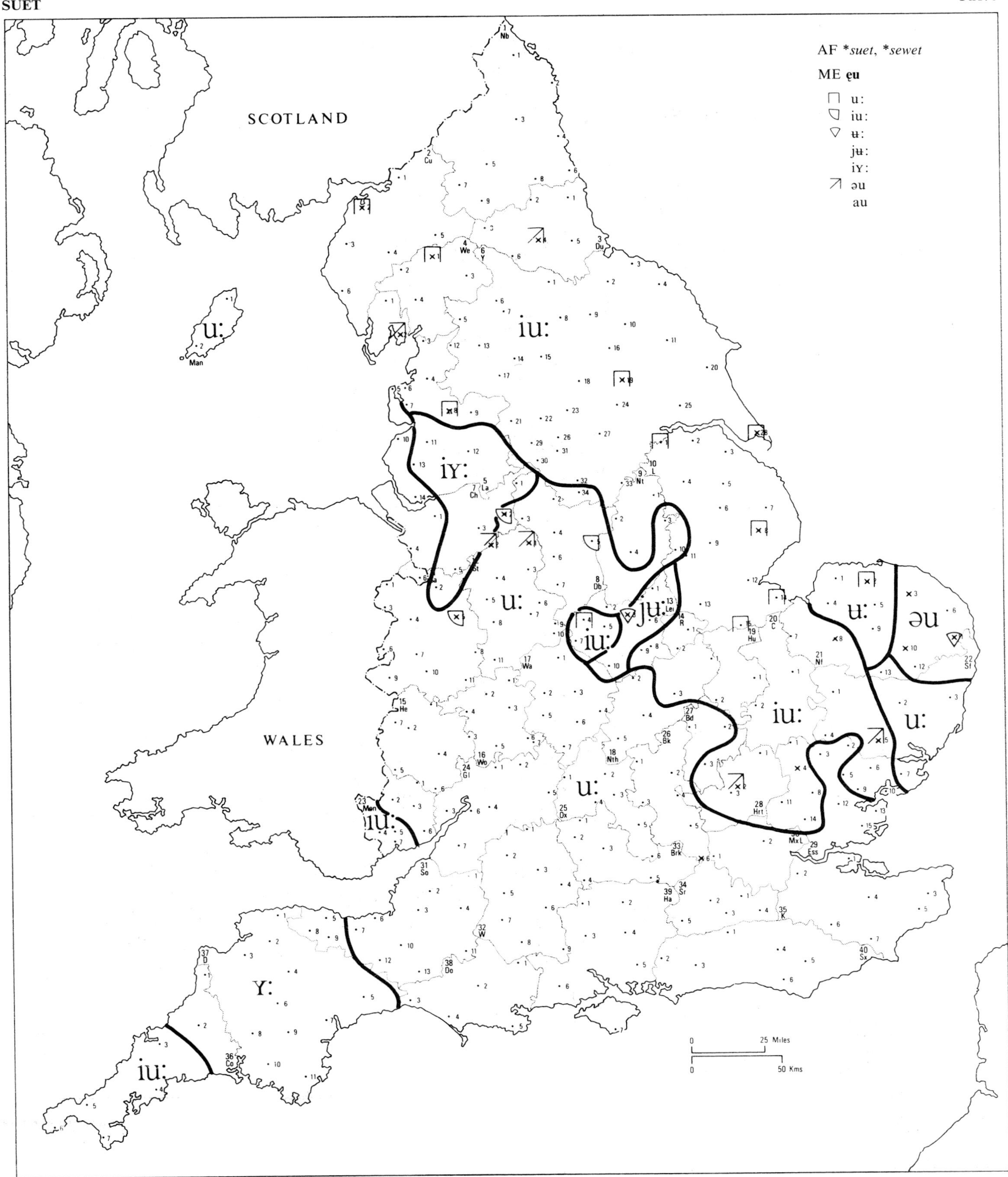

ʉu: 29Ess 7, uw 21Nf 2, əü: 39Ha 7, u 6Y 19, 7Ch 1, 10L +15, 25Ox 1–3/6, 31So 6/10/13, 32W 1/3, 35K 1/3–5, 38Do 3, 39Ha 5, ų 39Ha +4, ü 30MxL 1, ɷ 11Sa 1, 35K 2, öu 5La 5 under u:
ju: 13Lei +4/5/7–9, 14R 1/2, 23Mon 5, ju˙ 1Nb 8, 3Du 5, 10L +1/2/3/11, ɩu 1Nb 5, 3Du 2/3, 5La 1/6/7, 6Y 2–5/7/9/11/17/21/22/24–26/29/30/32/33, 10L +15, 23Mon 7, ɩü 6Y 6, ˡü 7Ch 2, 29Ess 11, ju 1Nb 1, 2Cu 5, 3Du 1, 10L 7, jü 1Nb 4, jiu 23Mon 4, ɩɷ 6Y 10/14/16/18/20/27, 36Co 3–7, jəu˙ 28Hrt 3, ɩ˙w 21Nf 7, ʉw 6Y 31 under iu:
ʉ 21Nf 1 under ʉ:
ˡŸ 5La 11, ʏʉ: 11Sa 2, ʏ˙ 5La 13, 8Db 1 under iʏ:

ø 21Nf 5
ə̣: 21Nf 10

SUET- 10L +14; -SUET 39Ha +4

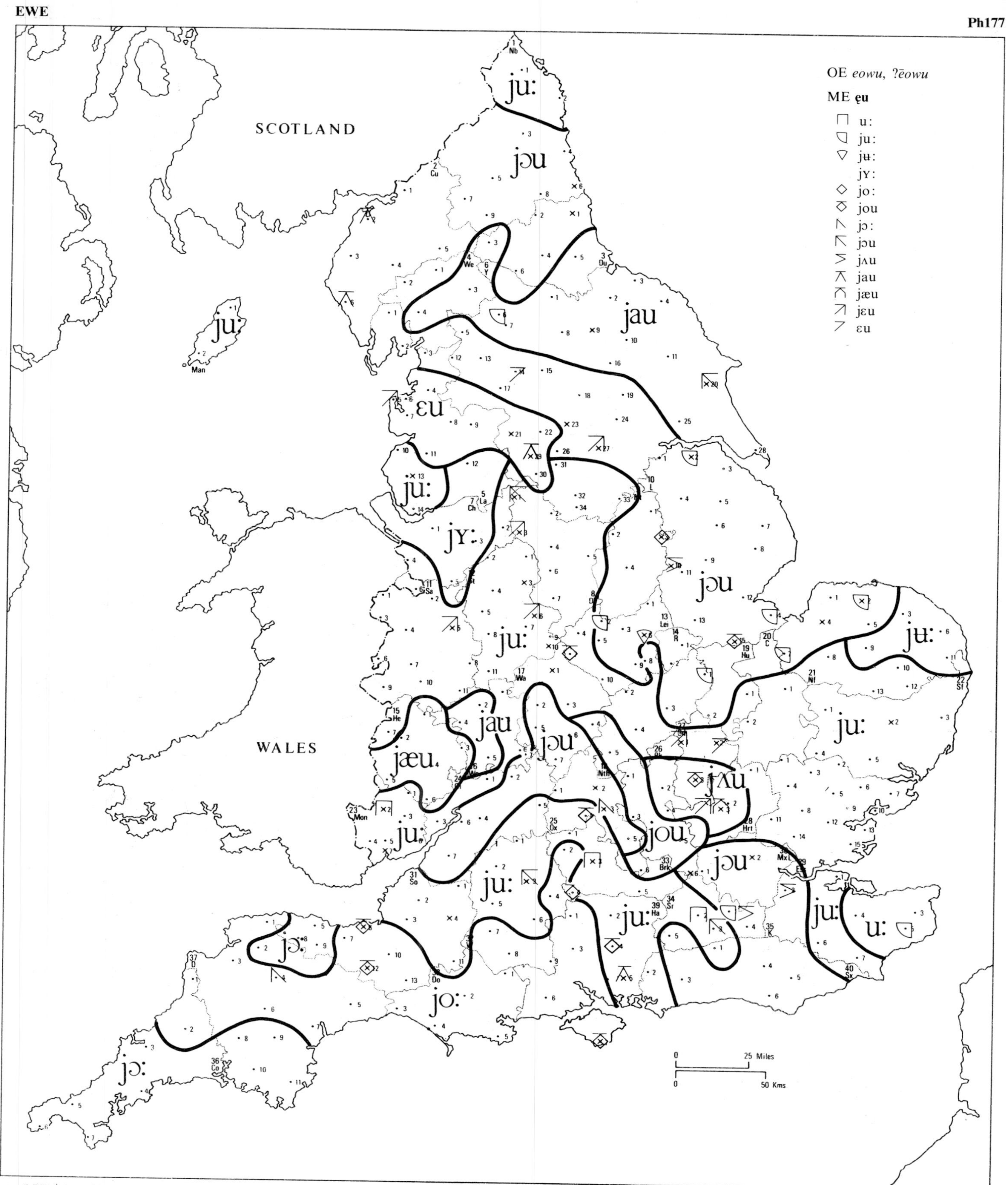

əu: 35K $^{+}$4 under u:
ɩu: 11Sa 3/6, 18Nth $^{+}$1, 19Hu 1, 20C 1/2, 21Nf $^{+}$7, 22Sf 5, 29Ess 1/7, ɩů: 29Ess 3/4/9, ɩü: 22Sf 4, 29Ess 5/10/14, ɩ̆ü: 29Ess 8, ɩɷu: 29Ess 12, ɩų: 28Hrt 1, ɩ̹ü: 21Nf 2, jəu: 33Brk 5, j^{ɩ}u: 8Db 5, 21Nf 8, j^{ɩ}ü: 8Db 7, jɩu: 10L $^{+}$14, jɩü: 7Ch 4, 22Sf 1, jɩu 23Mon 4/5, jü 5La 10, ɩu 6Y $^{+}$6/33, ʔɩu 35K 7, ɩü 29Ess $^{+}$6/11, ɩɷ 6Y 32, j^{ɛ}u: 35K 6 under ju:
ɩʉ˙ 21Nf 9, jɩʉ: 21Nf 11 under jʉ:
jɩʏ: 7Ch 1 under jʏ:
jo:^{ɑ} 25Ox $^{+}$4 under jou
jɑɷ 17Wa 2, 24Gl 6, jɔw 10L 8 under jɔu

ʏ: 36Co $^{+}$1
aɷ 6Y 21
oɷ 12St 3
ʉ: 13Lei $^{+}$6

EWES pl 2Cu 4/$^{+}$6, 4We 1/4, 5La 10, 6Y 5, 10L 1/3/5/8/13, 13Lei $^{+}$6/$^{+}$7, 18Nth $^{+}$1, 19Hu 2, 21Nf 6/9, 25Ox 3, 28Hrt $^{+}$3, 33Brk $^{+}$4, 40Sx 3/5

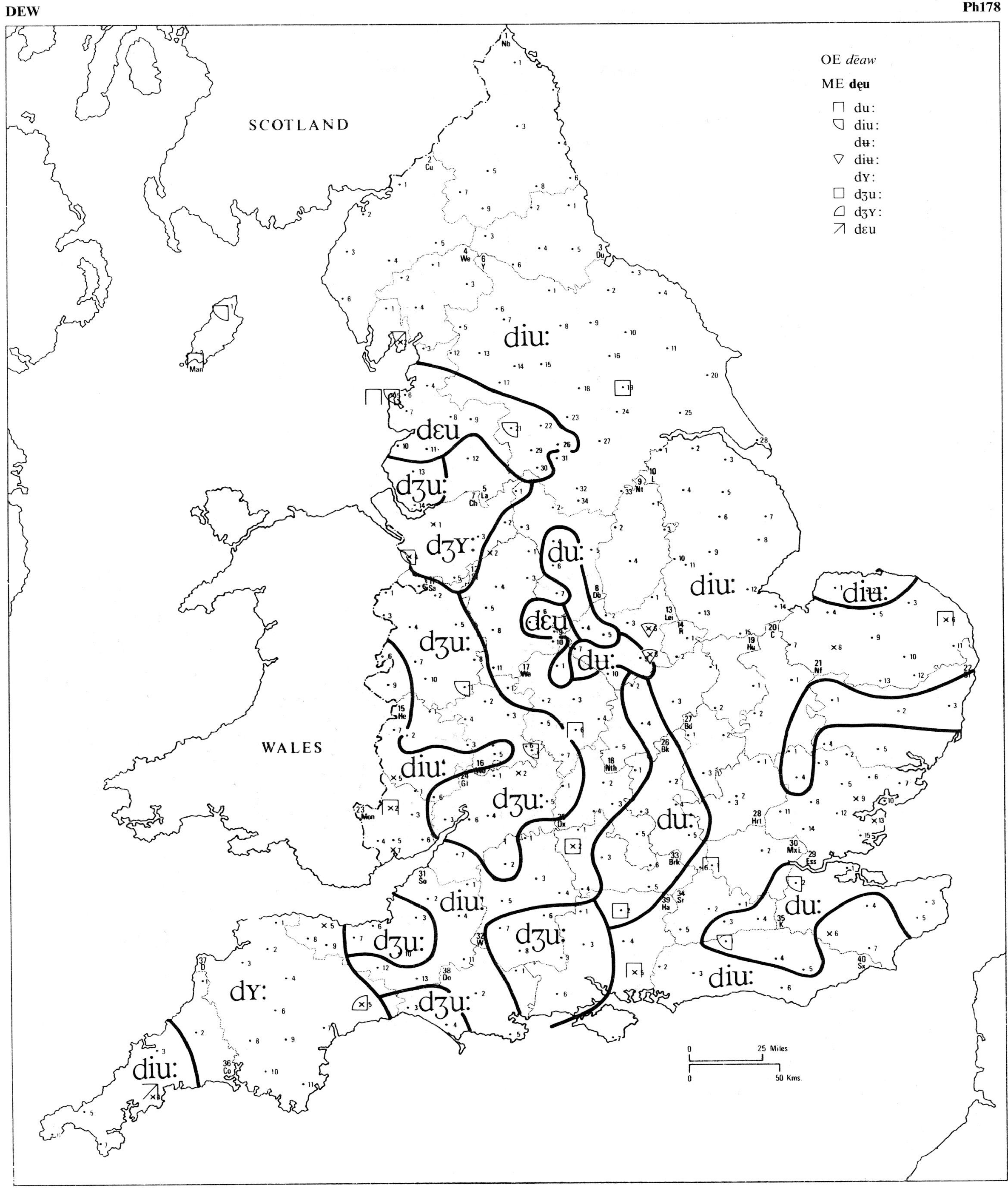

dᵊü: Man 2, döu 5La +5 under du:
dju: 1Nb 2/4, 2Cu 3, 3Du 1/2/5, 6Y 1/4/+19/20/25/+27/28, Man 1, 7Ch 4, 10L 11, 11Sa 5, 12St 3/4/7/8/11, 13Lei 1–3/10, 14R 1/2, 15He 4/7, 16Wo 5/+7, 17Wa 2/+6, 23Mon 3/4/6, 24Gl 7, 25Ox 3/4, 31So 1/11/12, 32W 1/3–5, 38Do 2/5, djü: 7Ch 2, 12St 5/10, 35K +2, djᵚu: 3Du 4, 23Mon 1, djɷu: 31So 2/4, djɷ̈ü: 33Brk 4, dɩ·əu: 28Hrt 3, djᶥu 23Mon 5, dɩu 2Cu 6, 5La +5, 6Y 2/3/6/9/17/+21/24/32, 11Sa +11, 25Ox 2, 30MxL +1, 34Sr 1/5, 35K 7, 39Ha 4, dɩ̆u 6Y 33, dɩü 21Nf 7, 29Ess 11, 30MxL 2, dɩ̆u 21Nf 13, dɩɷ 6Y 10/11/14/16/18/+27, 30MxL +1, 31So 13, 36Co 3/5–7 under diu:

djʉ: 13Lei 6/8, dɩʉ 21Nf 2 under diʉ:
dʒɩu: 11Sa 1, dʒᶥu: 15He 1, 16Wo 3, dʒəü: 32W 7 under dʒu:
dʒɩʏ: 5La 12 under dʒʏ:
dɛ̈u: 17Wa 1 under dɛu

djʏ: 7Ch 1, 31So 5
djɛɷ 12St 2
dʒæɷ 24Gl 2
dʒaɷ 32W +2
dʒʌɷ 15He 5
dʒɒɷ 24Gl +5
dɒɷ 40Sx +4
dəu 35K 6

DEW- 6Y +27, 16Wo +7; -DEW 40Sx +1

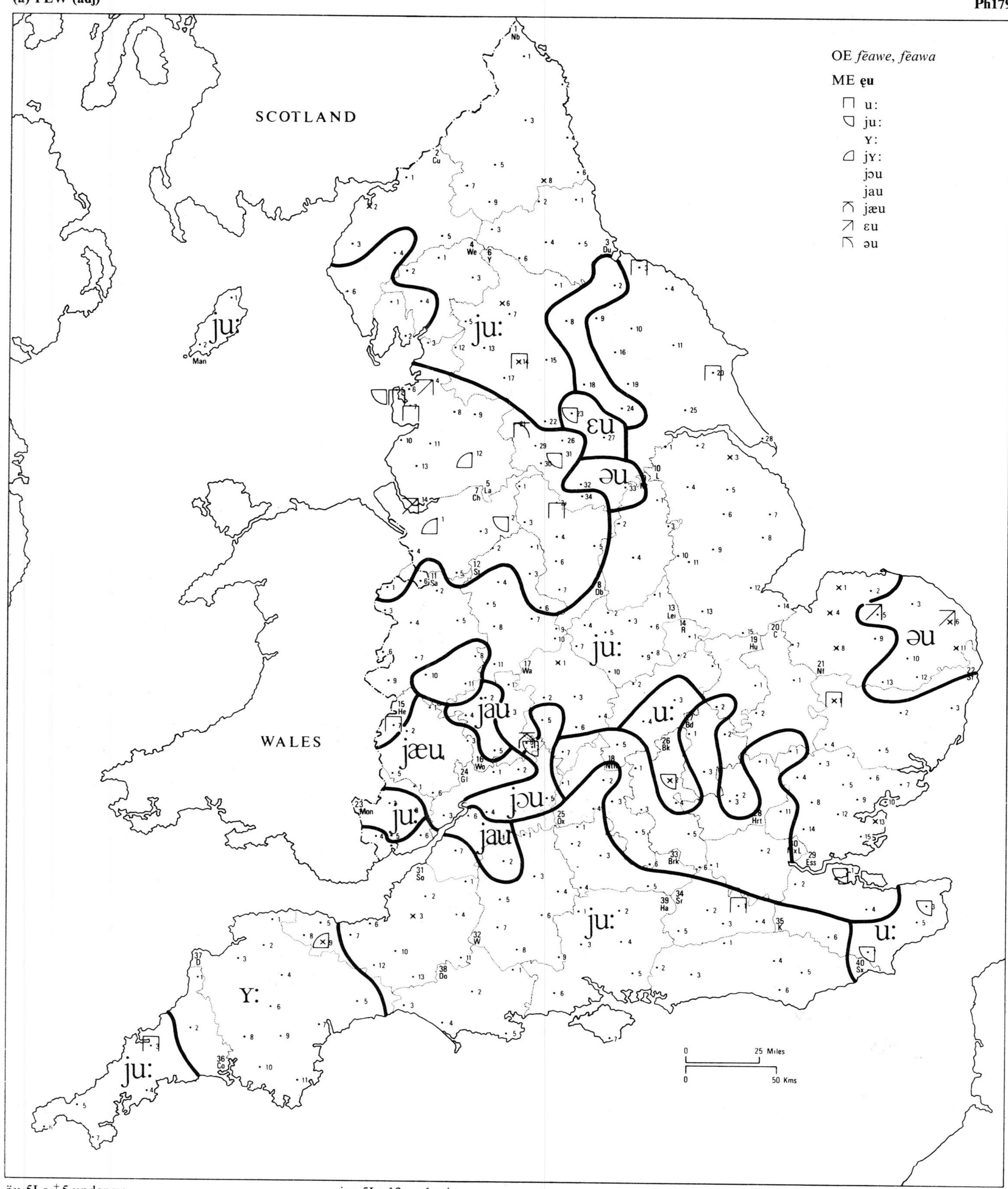

öu 5La $^+$5 under u:
jᵊu: 28Hrt 3, jəu: 33Brk $^+$4, jöu 5La $^+$5, jɩu 23Mon $^+$5, ju 10L $^+$14, 11Sa 7, 38Do $^+$1, 40Sx 2, jü 7Ch 2, 21Nf 7, 31So $^+$7, ɩu: 3Du $^+$3, 6Y 13, 10L 6/10/13/$^+$14/15, 11Sa 2–6/9, 12St 9, 16Wo 1, 18Nth 1/2, 19Hu 1, 20C 1/2, 22Sf 4, 29Ess 7/15, 32W $^+$7, 34Sr $^+$3/4/5, ɩ̣u: 1Nb 7, ị̆u: 1Nb 9, ɩu̇: 29Ess 2/3/8, ɩü: 22Sf 5, 29Ess 4/5/10, ɩɷu: 29Ess 12, ˈü: 22Sf 2/3, 26Bk 2, 28Hrt 2, 29Ess 9/14, ɩu 3Du $^+$3, 5La $^+$5, 6Y $^+$9/17/22, 35K $^+$7, 39Ha 7, ɩ̜u 21Nf 2/9, ɩü 29Ess 6, ɩɷ 6Y $^+$20, 36Co $^+$3/4/$^+$5/6/7 under ju:

jɩY 5La 12 under jY:
jɑɷ 24Gl 5 under jɔu
ɩaɷ 16Wo 2/$^+$5 under jau
ɩæɷ 16Wo $^+$6 under jæu

jɛɷ 16Wo $^+$7
aɷ 16Wo $^+$5

FEW ndg 3Du $^+$3, 6Y $^+$23, 21Nf $^+$5

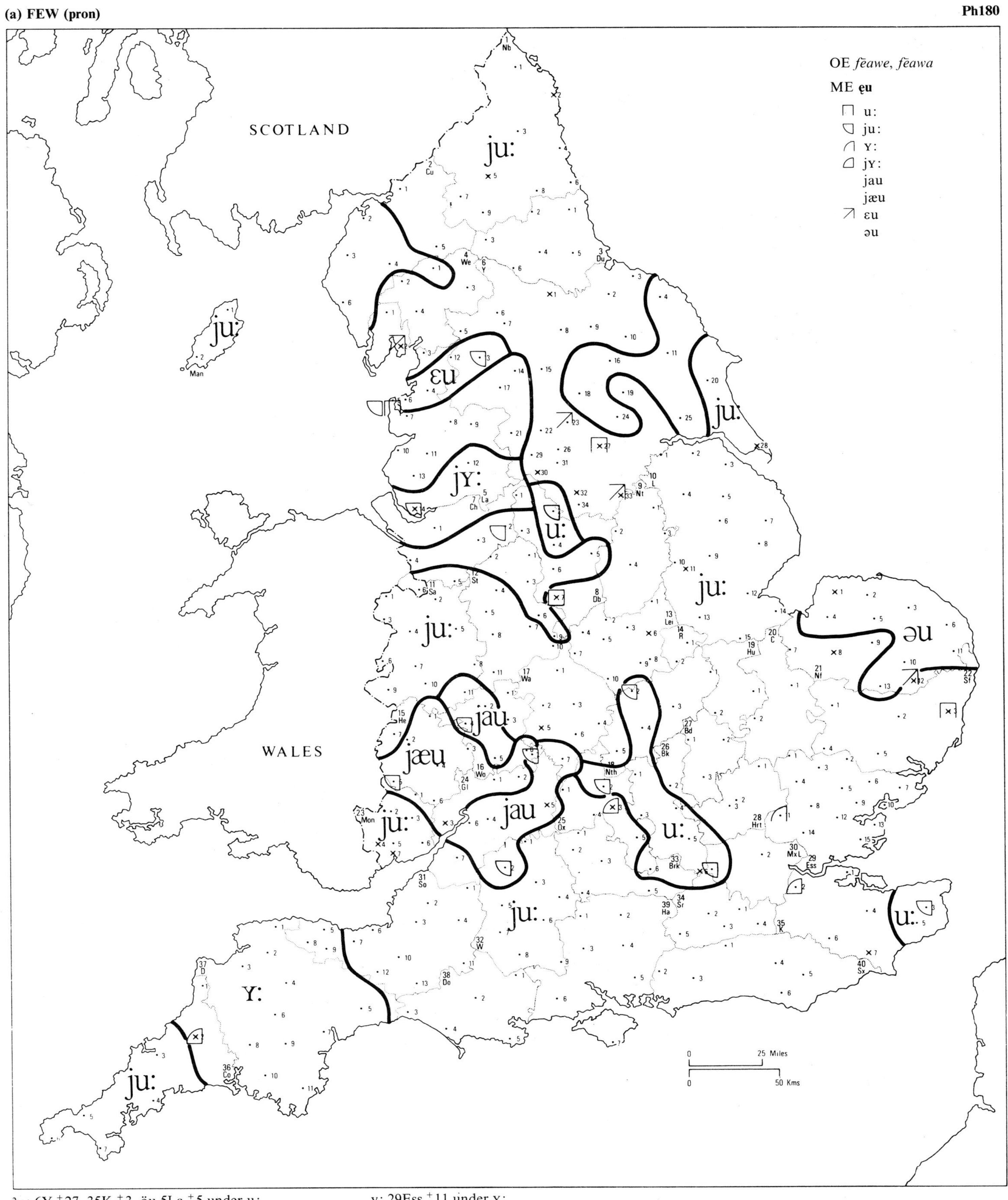

ᵊu: 6Y +27, 35K +3, öu 5La +5 under u:
jᵊu: 6Y 2, jəü: 32W +7, jᶥu: 18Nth 5, ju 6Y 8, jü 13Lei +4, jöu 5La +5, jɩu 23Mon 5, jɩɷ 31So +13, iu: 1Nb 9, ɩu: 1Nb +8, 2Cu 1, 3Du 3, 4We 4, 5La 1/3, 6Y +13/15/31/34, 9Nt 1–4, 10L +5/6/9/10/+13, 11Sa 3/4/6/9/10, 16Wo 1, 17Wa 4, 18Nth 1/+2, 19Hu 1/2, 20C 1/2, 22Sf 4, 27Bd 3, 29Ess 1/+7/12/15, 34Sr 5, 40Sx 1/2/6, ɩü: 22Sf 1, 27Bd 2, 29Ess 8/9/13, 39Ha +7, ɩʉ̇: 29Ess 2–4, ɩɷu: 29Ess +7, 34Sr +2/3/4, ᶥu: 11Sa 2, 18Nth 3, 27Bd 1, ᶥu: 28Hrt 1, ᶥü: 22Sf 2. 26Bk 2, 28Hrt 2, 29Ess 5/6/10/14, iˑəu: 28Hrt 3, ɩ̢ˑu: 1Nb 7, ɩuˑ 21Nf 9, ɩu 5La +5, 6Y 6/7/9/10/22/26/29, 21Nf 7, 39Ha 4, ɩü 22Sf 5, 29Ess +11, 35K 6, ɩ̣u 35K 4, ɩŭ 35K +2, ɩɷ 31So +13, 36Co 3–7, 39Ha +7 under ju:

y: 29Ess +11 under ʏ:
jy: 35K +2, ɩʏ: 5La 12, 7Ch 1 under jʏ:
ɩaɷ 16Wo +5 under jau

ɨ̢ʉ 21Nf 1, jʉ: 13Lei 6
jɑɷ 24Gl 5
jɒɷ 17Wa 5, 24Gl 3

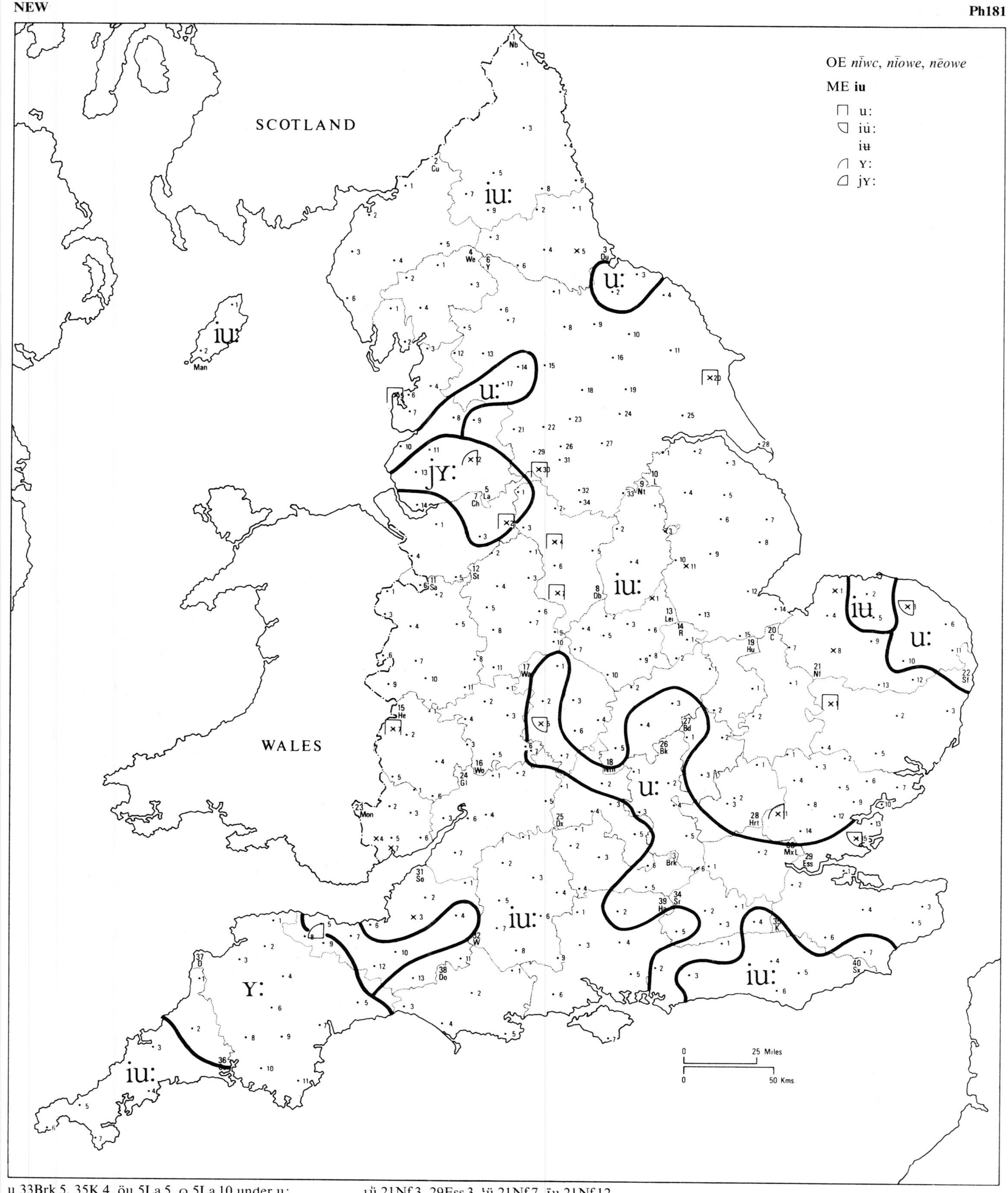

u 33Brk 5, 35K 4, öu 5La 5, ɷ 5La 10 under u:
ju: 1Nb 1–9, 2Cu 3–5, 3Du 1/2/4/6, 4We 1–3, 5La 2/4/9, 6Y 1/4/5/8/10/12/13/15/16/19/ 23/25/28/31/33/34, Man 1, 7Ch 1/4–6, 8Db 2, 9Nt 2/4, 10L 1–5/7/9/10/12–15, 11Sa 7–9/11, 12St 1–3/7–9/11, 13Lei 2–5/7–10, 14R 1/2, 15He 1/3–5, 16Wo 2–6, 17Wa 3/5/6, 18Nth 1/2, 22Sf 2, 23Mon 2/6, 24Gl 1/2/5–7, 25Ox 1/3–5, 27Bd 2, 31So 1/6/11/13, 32W 1–9, 33Brk 1/2, 38Do 1–5, 39Ha 1/3/5/6, 40Sx 4–6, jü: Man 2, 8Db 3/6, 12St 4/10, 22Sf 3/5, 28Hrt 2, jᵒu: 23Mon 1, 24Gl 3/4, jɷu: 31So 2, 34Sr 4, jɷu 40Sx 3, jɷ̈ü 33Brk 4, jəu: 28 Hrt 3, ju˙ 23Mon 5, ju 2Cu 2/6, 5La 1/14, 10L 8, 12St 5/6, 15He 2/6, 18Nth 5, 23Mon 3, 33Brk 3, jü 13Lei 6, ɩu 5La 6/7, 6Y 6/7/9/18/22/24/26/29/32, 11Sa 1, 21Nf 4/9/13, 34Sr 5, 35K 7, 39Ha 4/7, ɩü 21Nf 3, 29Ess 3, ˈü 21Nf 7, ïu 21Nf 12, ɩɷ 6Y 11/21/27, 36Co 3–7 under iu:
y: 29Ess 11 under ʏ:

jʉ: 13Lei 1
ʉ 21Nf 1/⁺11

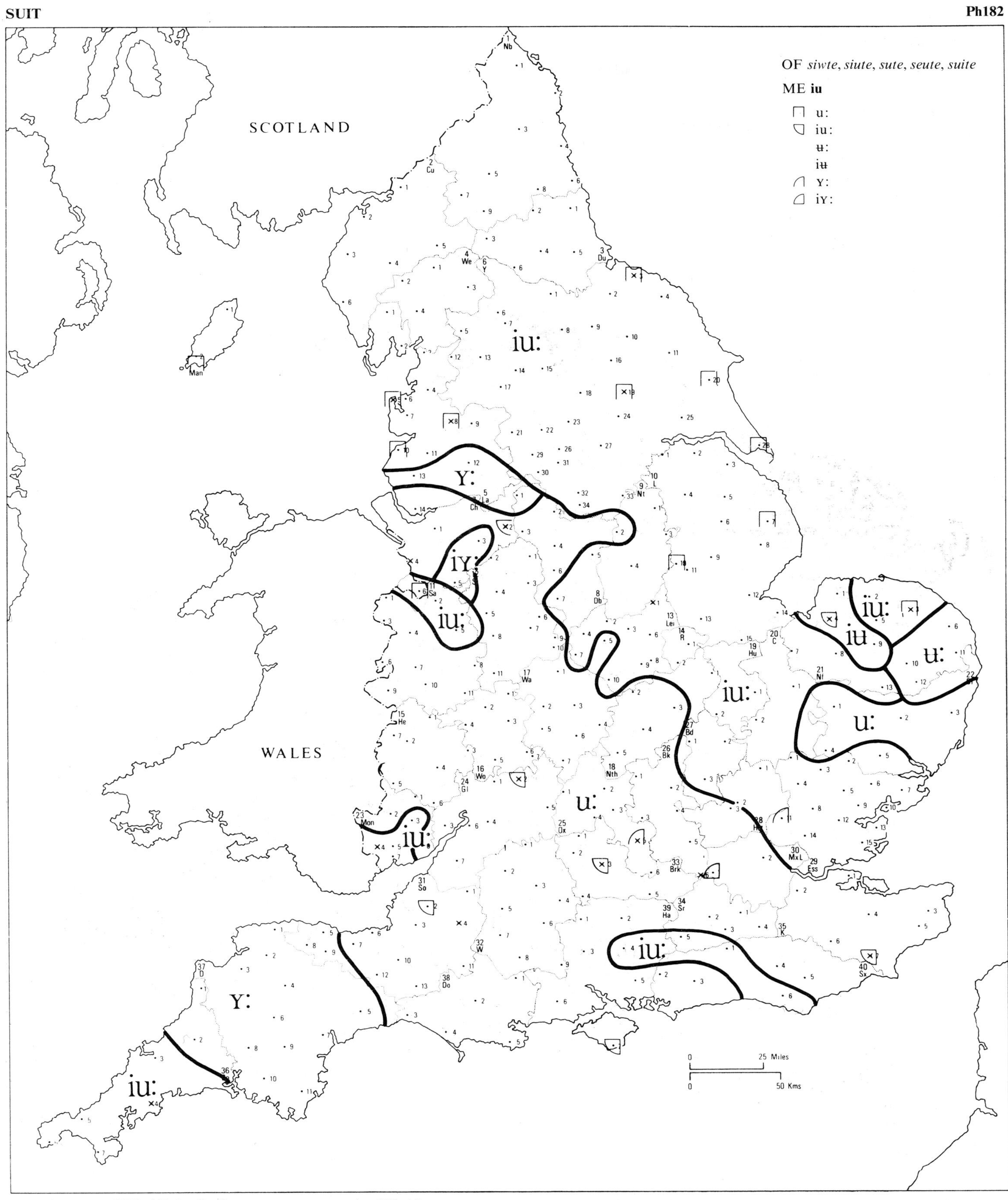

əu: 28Hrt 3, əü: 39Ha $^+$7, öu 5La 5,
ɷ 33Brk 1 under u:
ju: 1Nb 2/4/5, 2Cu 5, 3Du 1/2/5, 6Y 34,
10L 2–4/11, 13Lei 2–4/9, 14R 1/2,
ju‹: 13Lei 8/10, jü: 13Lei 6, ɩu 1Nb 1/6, 5La 6/7,
6Y 2/$^+$4/6/7/9/$^+$11/17/$^+$18/$^+$21/22/24/$^+$25/
26/$^+$28/29/30/32/33, 39Ha 4, ɩ̆u 6Y $^+$10,
ɩü 7Ch 2, 21Nf 4/7/8/13, 29Ess 5/8/9/$^+$11,
ˈü 27Bd 1,
ɩɷ 6Y $^+$4/$^+$10/$^+$11/14/16/$^+$18/$^+$21/$^+$25/27/$^+$28,
31So $^+$2, 36Co 3/5–7, ɩɷ̃ 6Y $^+$20,
jɩu 23Mon 5/7 under iu:
y: 25Ox 5, 29Ess $^+$11 under ʏ:
ɩy 30MxL $^+$1 under iʏ:

jʉ: 13Lei 1
ɛɷ 36Co 4
əɷ 32W $^+$7

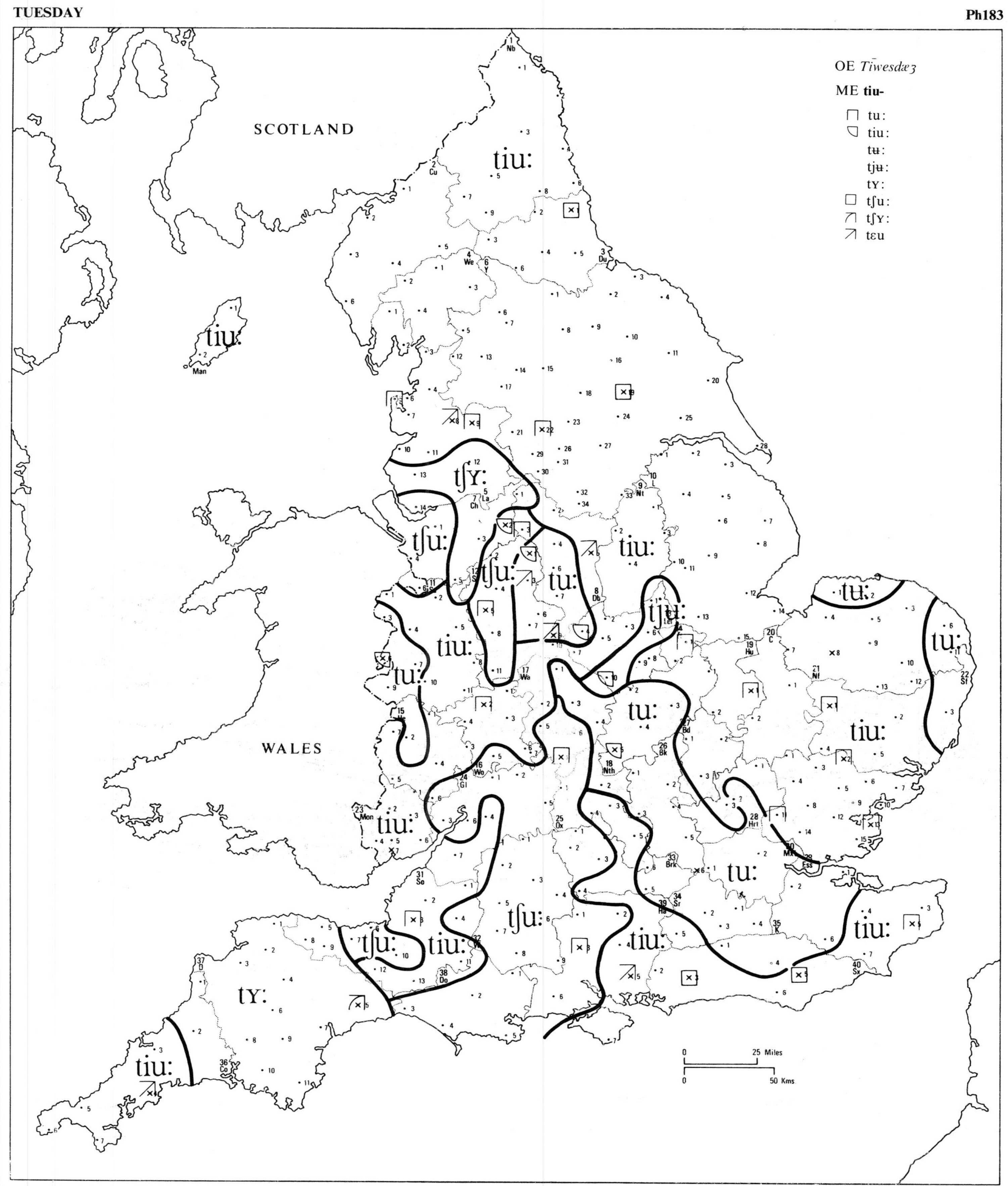

tü 21Nf 11, töu 5La +5, tᵊü˙ 29Ess +11 under tu:
tju: 1Nb 2/4, 2Cu 3/5, 3Du 2/4/5,
6Y 2/23/25/28/33, Man 1/2, 10L 2/11/12,
11Sa 8/10/11, 12St 1, 13Lei 2/3/+4/5/7–9/+10,
14R +1/2, 15He 1/3–5/7, 16Wo 3/4/6/7,
17Wa 2, 18Nth 5, 23Mon 2/3/5/6, 24Gl 7,
25Ox 3/4, 31So 1/2/11, 33Brk +4, 40Sx 2/6,
tju˙ 31So 12, tju˂:13Lei +10, tjü: 7Ch 2,
12St 10, tjᵚu: 23Mon 1, tjɷu: 24Gl 4,
tjɷ̈ü: 33Brk +4, tjᵊu: 6Y +20, 28Hrt 3,
tɩu 5La +5/6/7,
6Y 3/6/7/9/16/17/21/24/26/29/30,
10L 4/7/8, 21Nf 10/13, 29Ess 12, 35K 4/7,
39Ha 4/7, tᶥu 11Sa 1, tɩü 21Nf 3/5/7,
tɩ̈ü 21Nf 12, tɩ̧ü 21Nf 4, tɩ̆ü˙29Ess 8, tɩʉ 21Nf 9,
tᶥü 29Ess +11, tɩɷ 6Y 4/10/+11/18/27/32,
31So 13, 36Co 3/5–7, tɩ̆ɷ 6Y +20 under tiu:
tjʏ: 31So 5 under tʏ:

-TUESDAY 33Brk +4

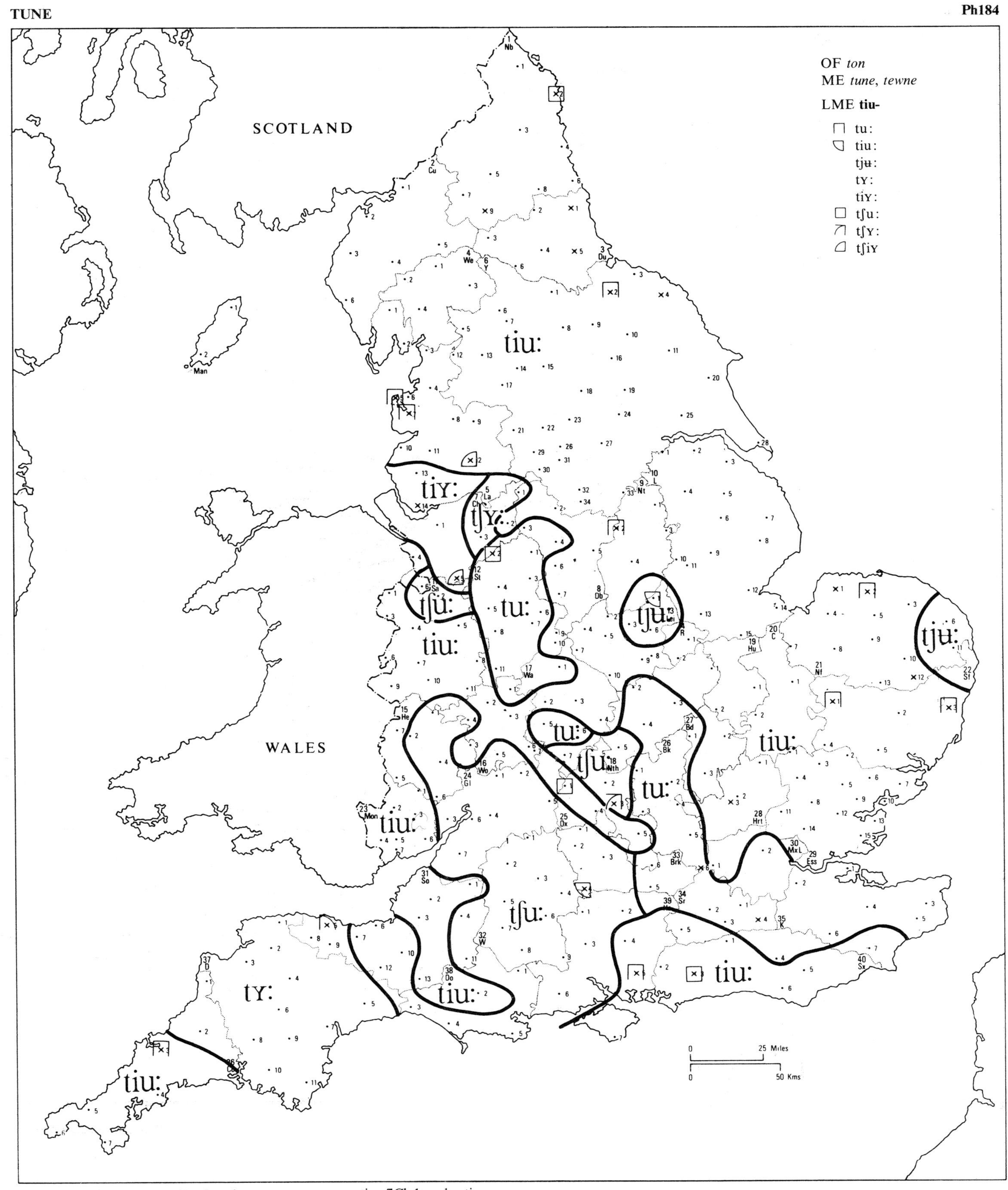

t^{ə}u: 5La 7, t^{ə}ü 35K 4, töu 5La 5 under tu:
tju: 1Nb 3, 2Cu 3, 3Du 2/4,
6Y 3/4/11/19/20/25/28/34, 7Ch 4, 8Db 2,
10L 1–3/8/9/11/$^{+}$13, 11Sa 3–8/10/11,
13Lei $^{+}$1/$^{+}$2/4/5/8/9, 14R 2, 15He 3/5/7,
16Wo 2/3/6/7, 17Wa 2, 23Mon 1/3–7,
25Ox $^{+}$1/4, 31So 1–3, 33Brk 4, 34Sr 5, 38Do 2,
40Sx 5, tjü: 7Ch 2, 12St 10, 13Lei 10, 14R 1,
tj^{ɷ}u: 23Mon 2, tɩu 5La 6,
6Y 6/9/17/22/24/26/29/30/32/33, 21Nf 4,
29Ess 11, 35K 7, 39Ha 4, tɩü 21Nf 7,
tĭu 21Nf 3/13, tɩ̦u 6Y 7,
tɩɷ 6Y 10/14/16/18/21/27, 31So 13,
36Co 5–7, tɩɷ̈ 4We 2
t^{ɩ}ü:^{ə} 22Sf 4, t^{e}u: 5La 8, tɛɷ 36Co 4 under tiu:
tɩʉ: 21Nf $^{+}$11, tɩʉ· 21Nf 6,
tĭʉ 21Nf $^{+}$11 under tjʉ:

tjʏ: 7Ch 1 under tiʏ:
tʃu:^{ə} 24Gl 1 under tʃu:
tʃy: 25Ox 3 under tʃʏ:

tɩə 1Nb 9
tjɤ 3Du 5, tjɤ: 5La 14
tʃɤ 3Du 1
tʉ: 21Nf 12

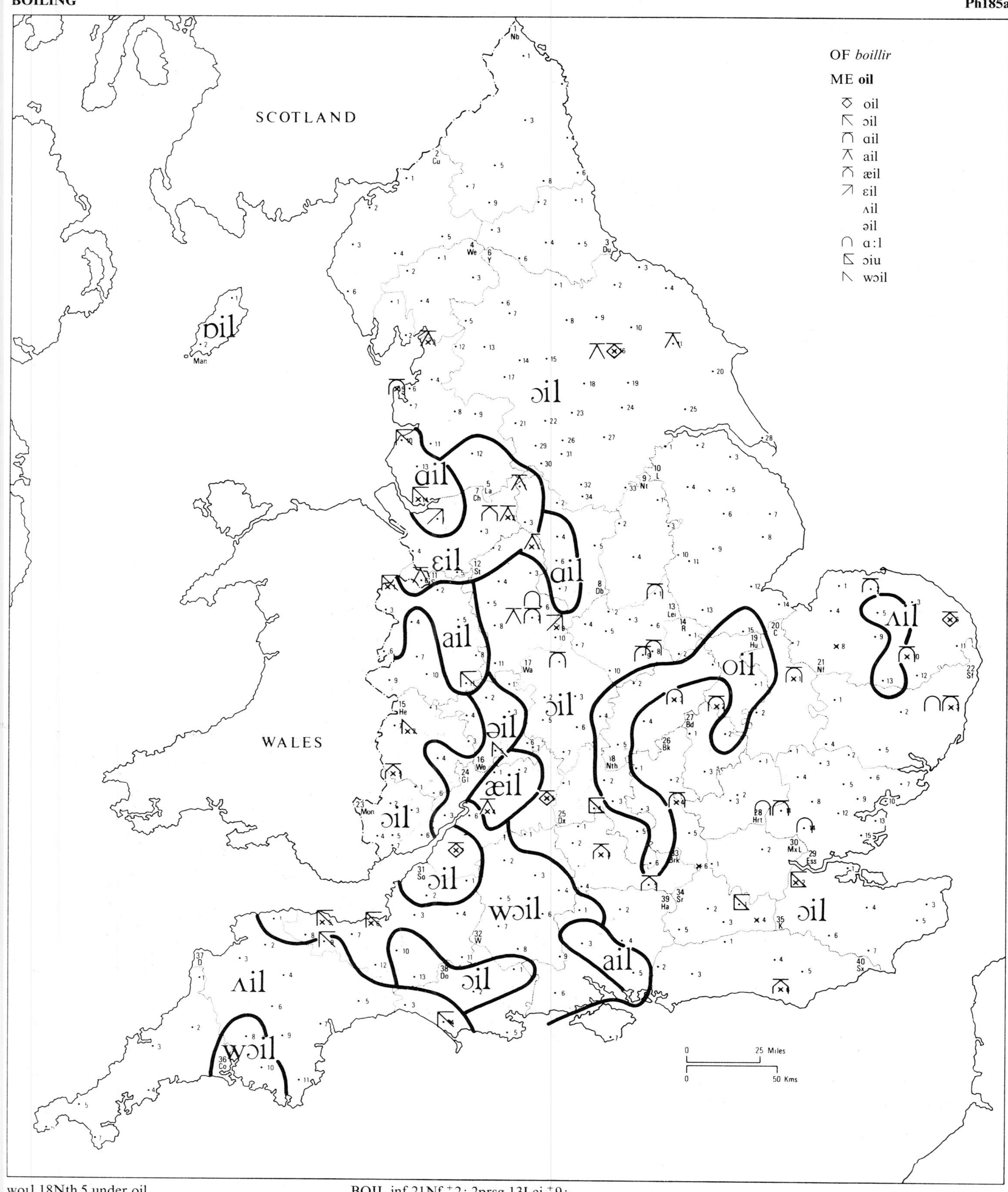

woɩl 18Nth 5 under oil
ɔɩᵊl 26Bk 1, ɔ̨ɩᵊɫ 22Sf +2, ɔ:ɩl 12St +4/8/11,
ǫɩl 3Du 3 under ɔil
əi:ɫ 16Wo 3, wəɩɫ 15He 4 under əil

ɔ: 35K +2
ɔɩ 34Sr +1
ɔ:ɫ 29Ess +4
ɷɩɫ 34Sr 4

BOIL inf 21Nf +2; 2prsg 13Lei +9;
3prsg 22Sf +2; 3prpl 35K +2;
v 5La 2/4/6/7/+10, 6Y 3/7/10/+11/14/15/+16/17/20/21/24/26/28–30/33, 8Db +1, 12St +7, 15He +7, 16Wo +5/+7, 22Sf +3, 25Ox +4, 29Ess +11, 30MxL 1, 31So 6, 34Sr 1, 35K +2; n 16Wo +7; BOILED pt 17Wa +1, 33Brk +5; pp 11Sa +11, 12St +4, 15He +7; ppl adj 6Y +16, 13Lei +8, 29Ess +4;
BOILER n 7Ch +2, 12St +7, 29Ess +11;
BOILING adj 7Ch +1

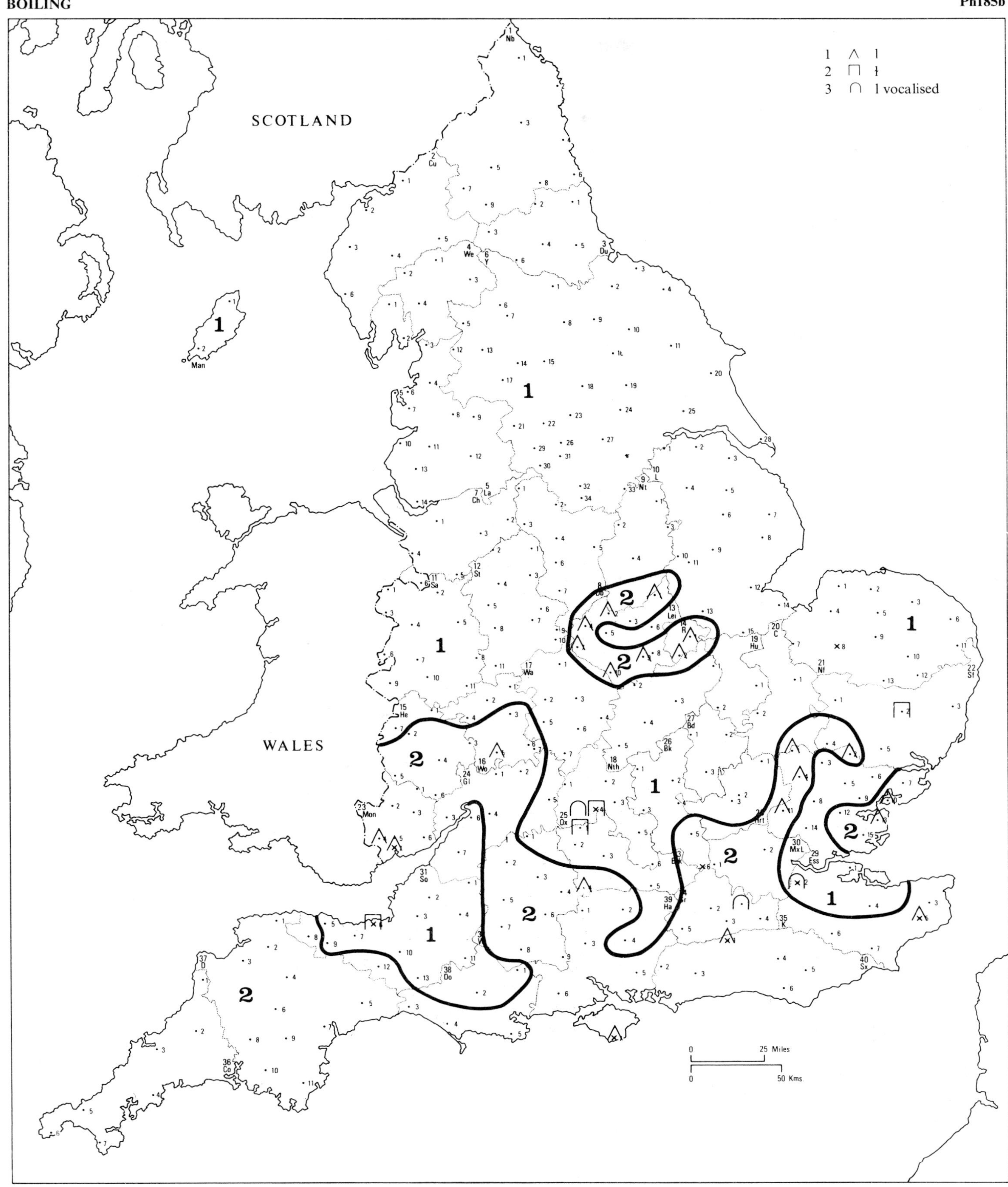

BOIL inf 13Lei +2/+4, 14R +1; 2prsg 13Lei +9;
3prsg 22Sf +2; 2prpl 33Brk +1; 3prpl 35K +2;
v 5La 2/4/6/7, 6Y 3/7/10/14/15/+16/17/20/
21/24/26/28–30/33, 13Lei +7, 15He +7, 16Wo +5/7,
23Mon +4, 25Ox +4, 29Ess +11, 30MxL 1,
31So 6, 34Sr 1, 35K +2; n 29Ess +10;
BOILED pp 13Lei +10, 14R +2, 15He +7,
29Ess +13, 33Brk +4; ppl adj 6Y +16,
13Lei +10, 14R +2, 29Ess +4; pt 29Ess +2;
BOILER n 29Ess +1/+11;
BOILER- n 29Ess +2

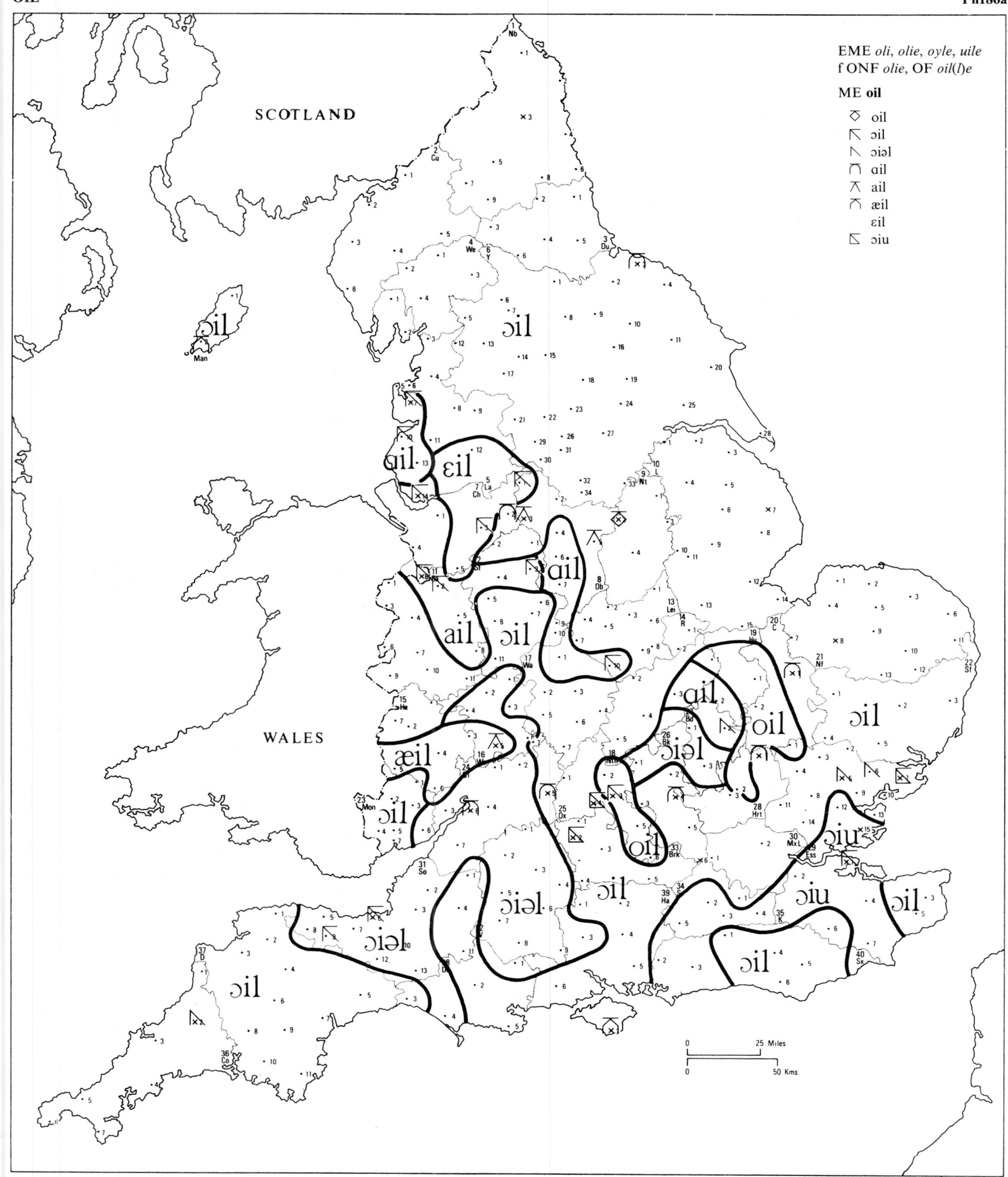

oɪ^{ə}ɫ 28Hrt 2 under oil
ɔːɪl 12St $^{+}$1/7/8/10, ɔːɪɫ 31So 4,
ɔ˂ːɪɫ 33Brk $^{+}$4 under ɔil
æɪ^{ə}l 15He $^{+}$6, æɪ^{ə}ɫ 15He 4 under æil

ɑːɫ 26Bk 6
œɪl 1Nb 3
ə̣ɪl 7Ch $^{+}$2

OIL- 1Nb 4, 5La 7, 6Y 25/27, 8Db $^{+}$1/$^{+}$5, 10L 11/13, 12St $^{+}$3, 13Lei $^{+}$10, 18Nth 3, 21Nf 1/7, 22Sf 3, 24Gl 5/7, 26Bk 4, 29Ess $^{+}$6/15, 31So $^{+}$9, 40Sx 3/5;
-OIL 6Y 3/4/7/14, 8Db $^{+}$1/6, 11Sa $^{+}$2, 13Lei 1/7/8, 19Hu 2, 40Sx 4

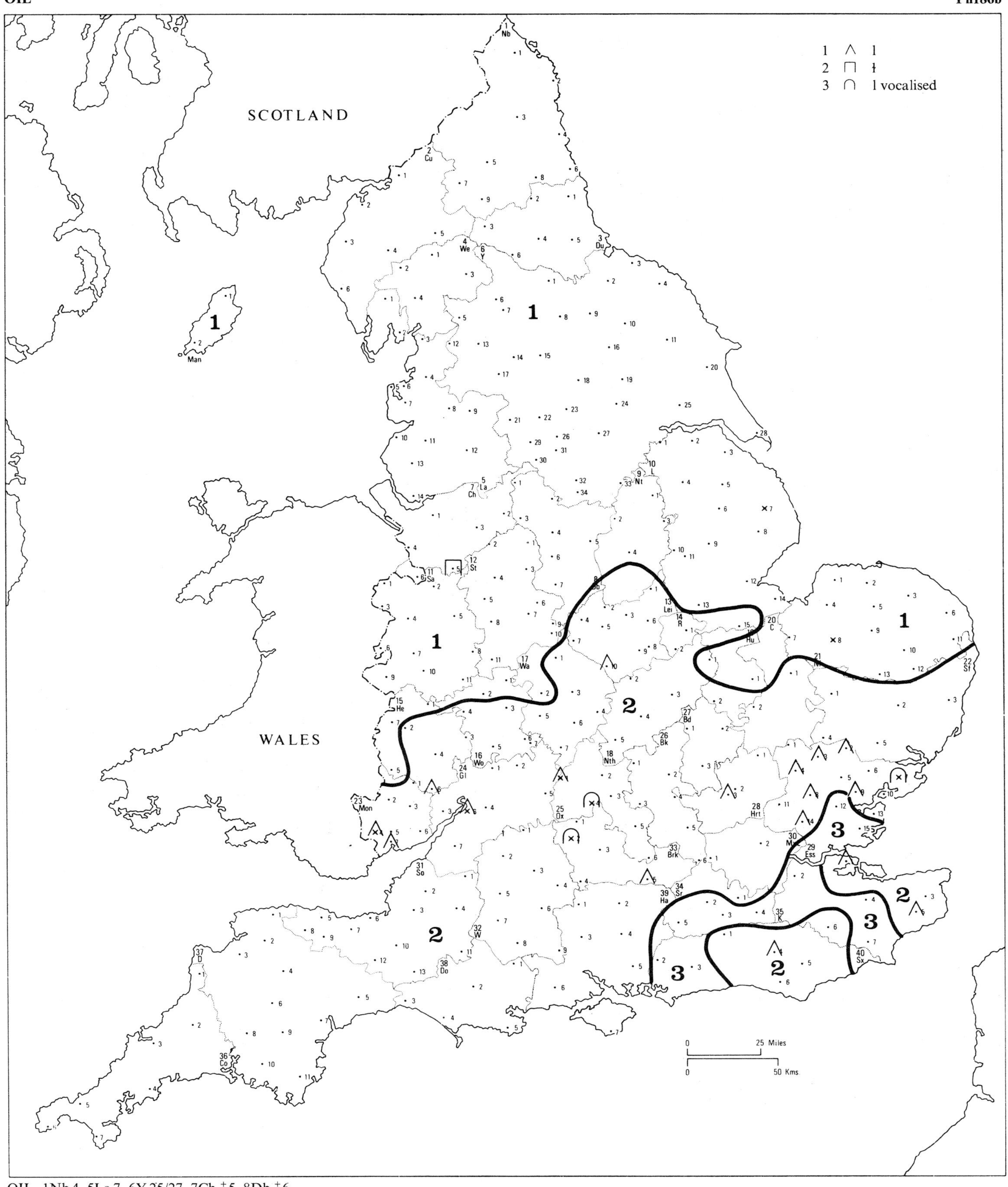

OIL- 1Nb 4, 5La 7, 6Y 25/27, 7Ch $^{+}$5, 8Db $^{+}$6, 10L 11/13, 13Lei $^{+}$7, 18Nth 3, 21Nf 1/7, 22Sf 3, 23Mon $^{+}$7, 24Gl 5/7, 26Bk 4, 28Hrt $^{+}$3, 29Ess $^{+}$2–$^{+}$4/$^{+}$8/$^{+}$9/$^{+}$14/15, 33Brk $^{+}$5, 35K $^{+}$5, 40Sx 3/$^{+}$4/5; -OIL 6Y 3/4/$^{+}$7/14, 8Db 1/6, 13Lei 1/$^{+}$7/8, 19Hu 2, 40Sx $^{+}$4; -OILED pt 13Lei $^{+}$10; OILING prp 6Y $^{+}$7

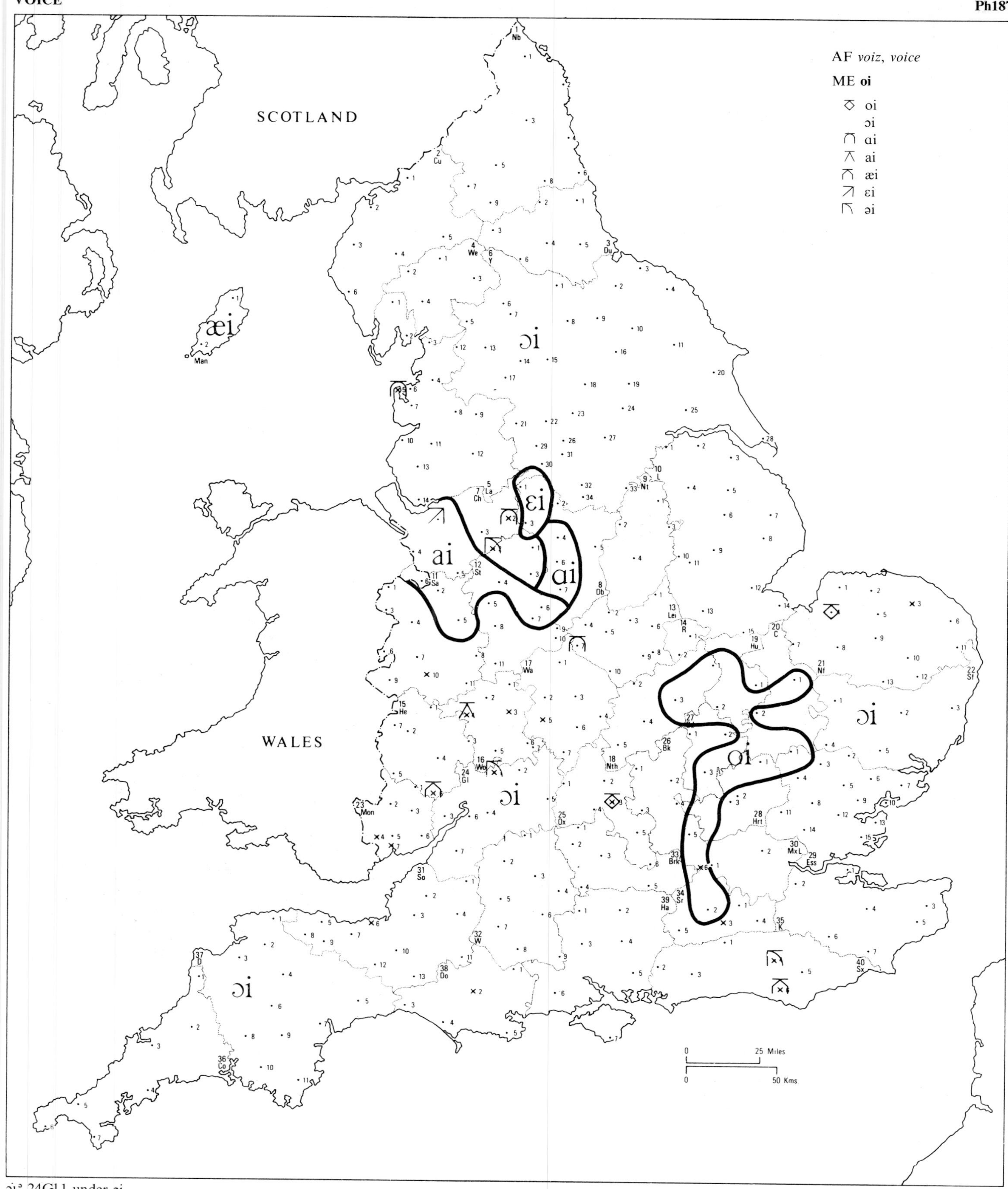

ə̇ɪᵊ 24Gl 1 under əi

ʌɪ 17Wa 5
ɷɪ 34Sr 3

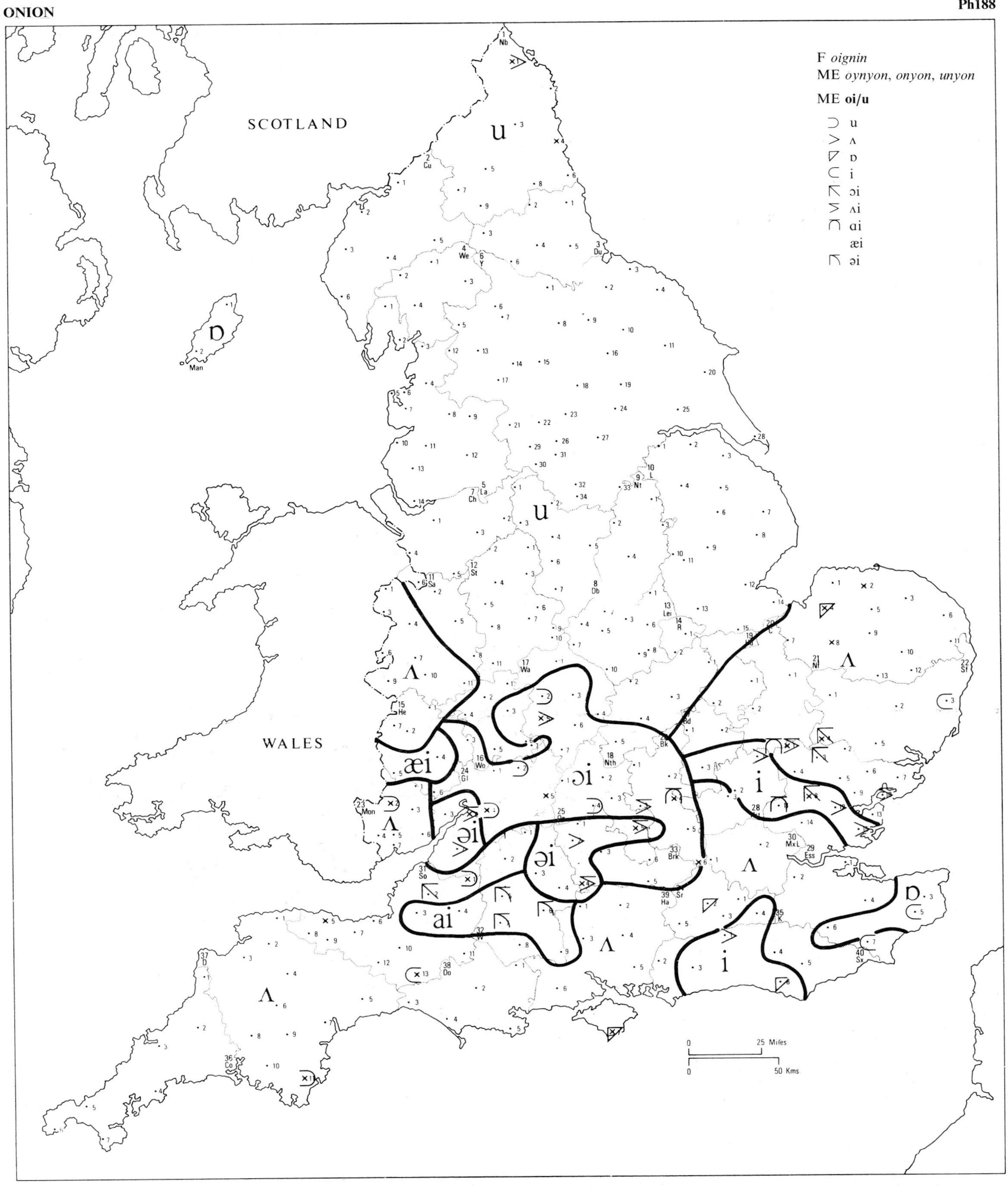

ə 24Gl 7 under ʌ
ʌʏ 25Ox 5 under ʌi

ɛ 27Bd +1, 31So 5
œ 1Nb 4
ʏ 21Nf 2/+9
ɒɩ 24Gl 5

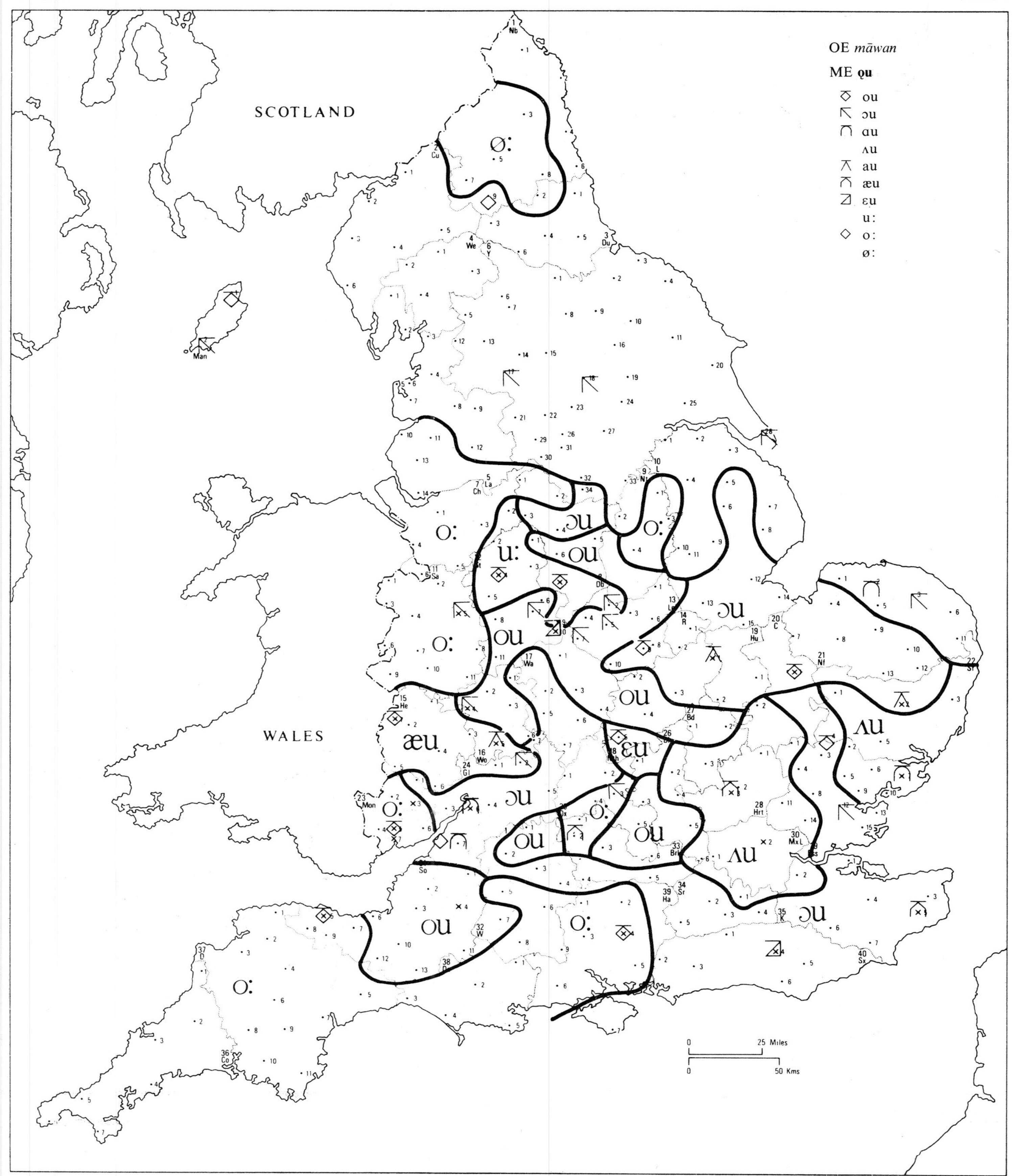

o:ɷ 31So 5, o:ᵒ 8Db 5–7 under ou
o 33Brk 1/$^+$2 under o:
œ: 1Nb 7 under ø:

ä: 29Ess $^+$5
ɑ: 21Nf $^+$2, 23Mon 3
ɒ˙ 21Nf 6
ɔ: 29Ess 15

MOW 2prpl 12St $^+$7; n 18Nth $^+$5;
MOWED pt 21Nf $^+$2;
MOWEN (pres 1prpl, Edd) 8Db 4;
MOWING prp 13Lei $^+$2/$^+$7/$^+$9;
(A-)MOWING ndg 3Du 2, Man 1, 21Nf 6, 24Gl $^+$2, 25Ox $^+$3, 33Brk 1/$^+$2/4, 34Sr 2–5, 35K 6/7, 39Ha 7, 40Sx 1–6;
MOWING- ppl adj 13Lei $^+$5;
-MOWING ndg 24Gl $^+$7;
MOWS 1 prpl 33Brk $^+$2

TO MOW

Ph189b

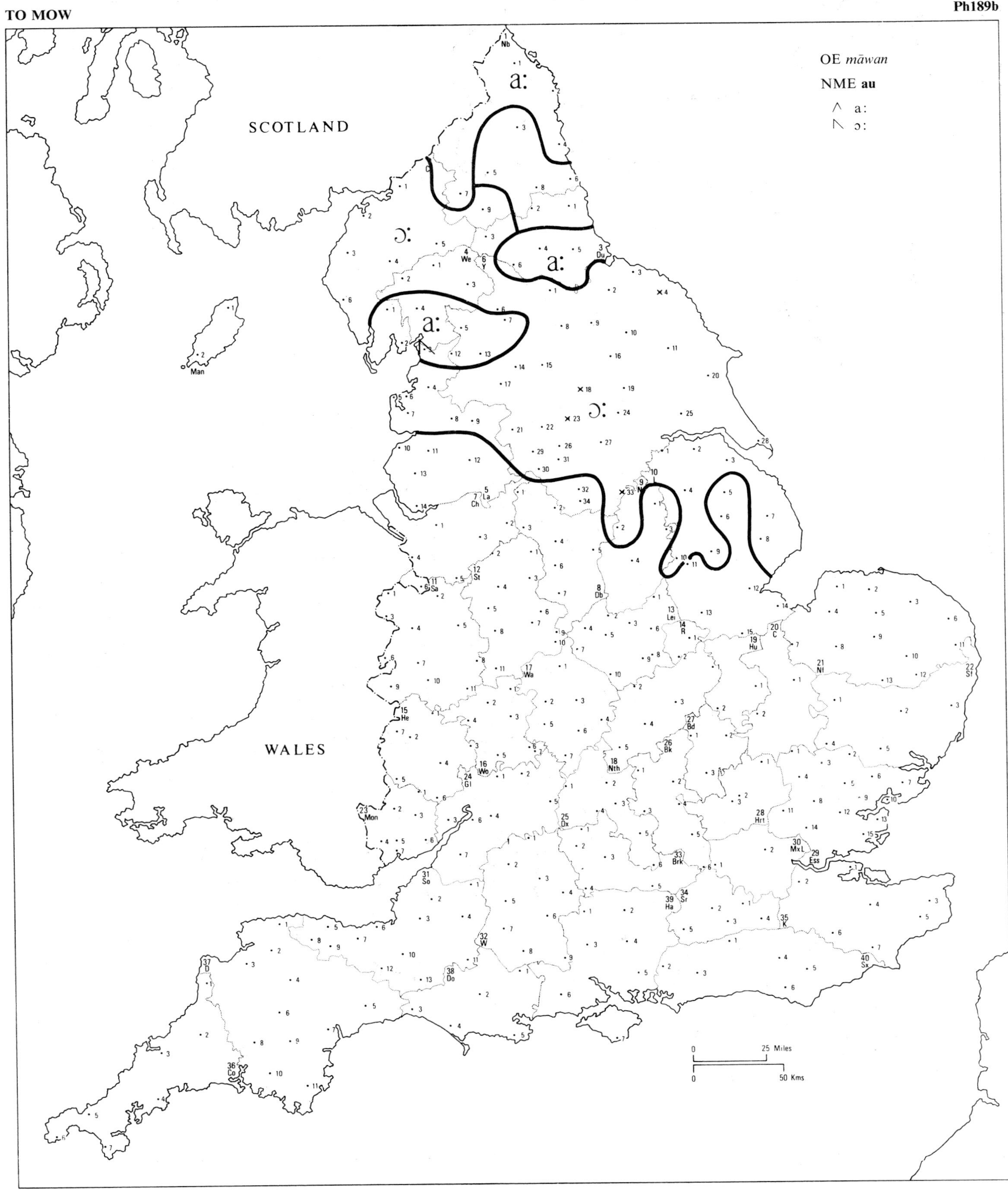

ɔ·ə 10L $^{+}$9 under ɔ:

ɑ: 6Y $^{+}$1

MOWS 3prpl 1Nb9

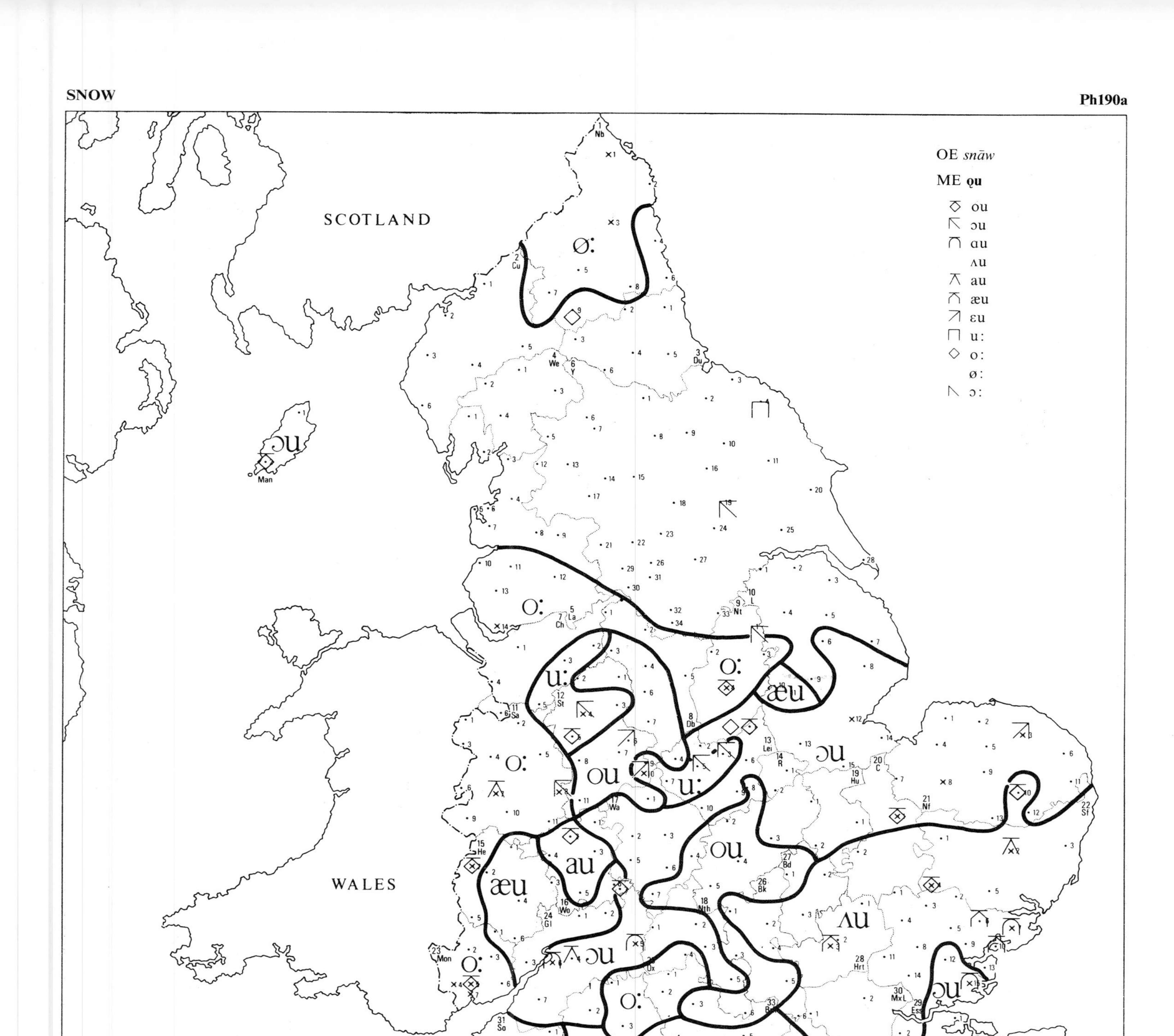

o:ɷ 31So 1/2/4, o:ᵒ 8Db 3/4/6 under ou
æɷ: 24Gl $^{+}$1 under æu
œ: 1Nb 2 under ø:

ä: 15He $^{+}$7
ɑ: 6Y 1/11
ɷə 10L 12

SNOWING prp 12St $^{+}$5, 13Lei $^{+}$1

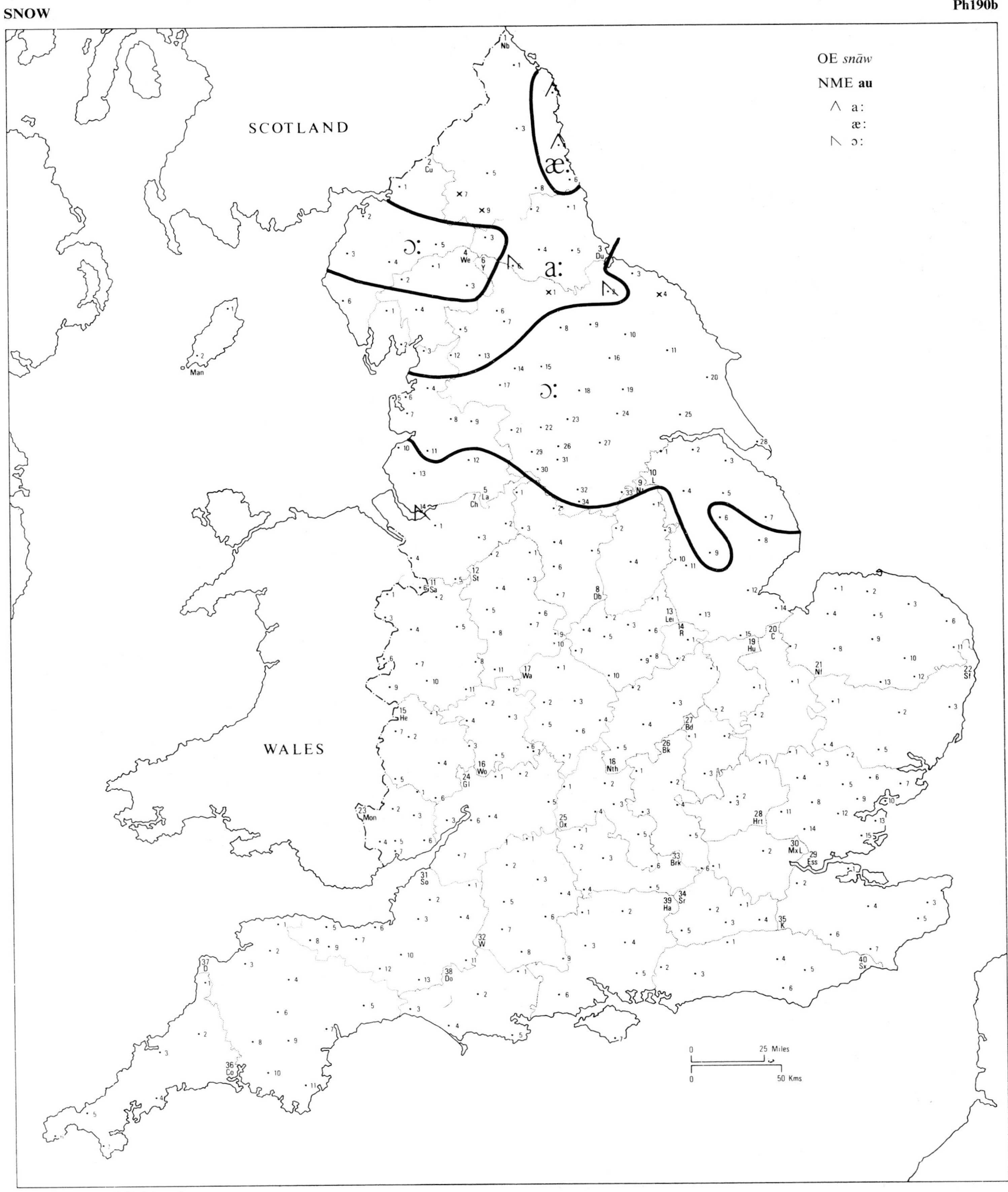

æ:ᵊ 1Nb 6, æ·ᵊ 1Nb ⁺4 under æ:
ɔ·ə 10L 1/5/7/9, ọ·ə 6Y 8 under ɔ:

SNOW- 3Du ⁺6, 6Y 19

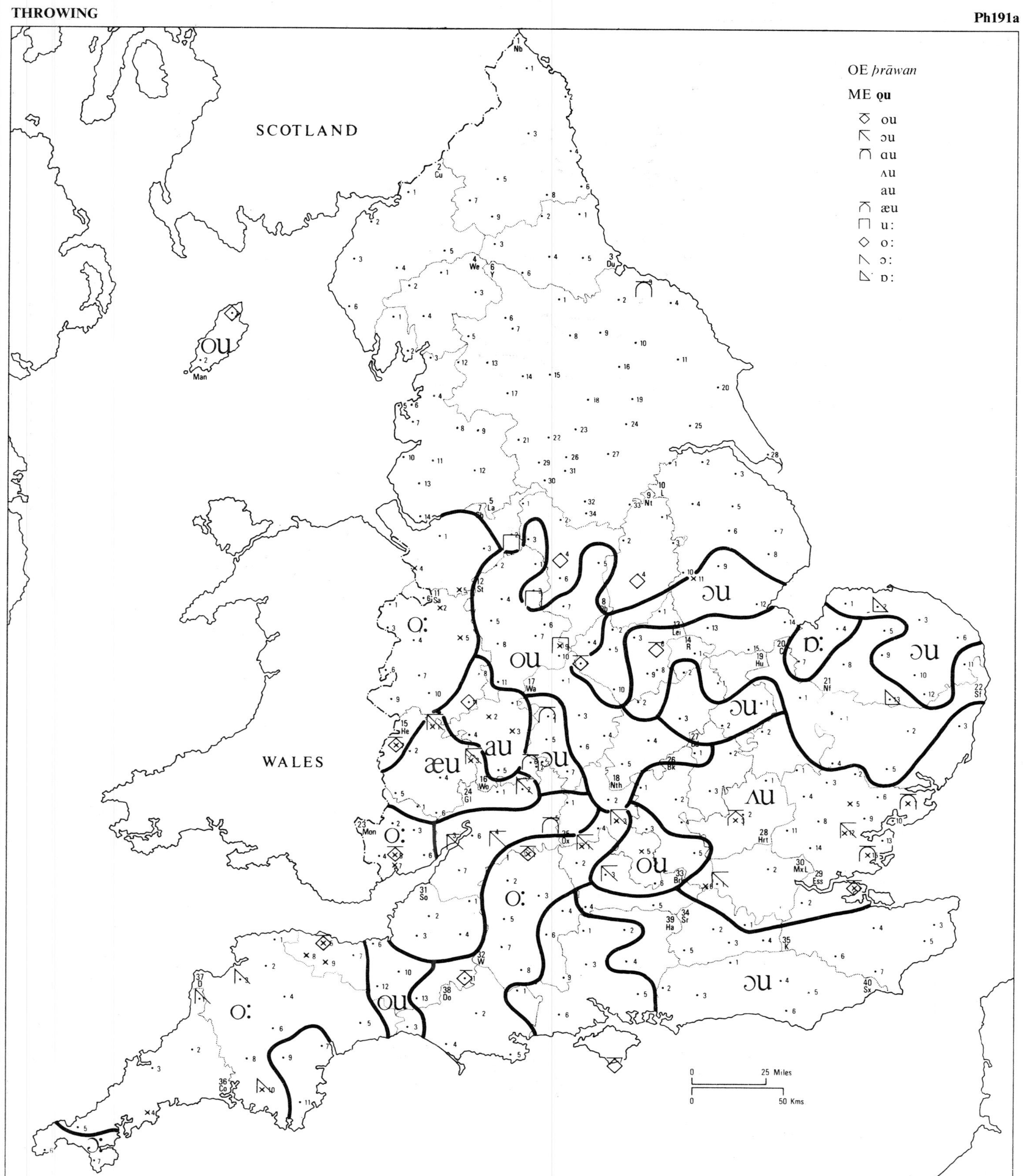

o:ɷ 8Db 5, 31So 5/6/10/$^{+}$11, o:w 8Db 3,
ɷw 12St 6/11 under ou
ɒ:ɷ 21Nf 1, ɒɷ: 40Sx $^{+}$6 under ɔu
o 11Sa 1 under o:

ø: 1Nb 7
e: 37D 11
a: 16Wo $^{+}$4
ɑ˙ 21Nf 11
əɷ 15He $^{+}$4, əu: 28Hrt $^{+}$3

THROWING ndg 21Nf $^{+}$2;
THROW inf 13Lei $^{+}$5/$^{+}$7, 16Wo $^{+}$7, 21Nf $^{+}$2/3, 23Mon $^{+}$5, 31So $^{+}$11, 37D $^{+}$3; 2prpl 15He 5, 40Sx $^{+}$6; 3prpl 10L 9/12; v 28Hrt $^{+}$3; ndg Man $^{+}$1/$^{+}$2, 11Sa $^{+}$4, 16Wo $^{+}$7, 17Wa $^{+}$2; 19Hu 2, 23Mon 4/$^{+}$5, 30MxL $^{+}$1, 35K 6, 36Co $^{+}$1;
THROWED pt 11Sa $^{+}$4/$^{+}$11, 13Lei 1/$^{+}$5, 24Gl $^{+}$2, pp 16Wo $^{+}$7, 25Ox 2, 33Brk $^{+}$3; ndg 13Lei 6, 16Wo $^{+}$7; THROWN pp Man $^{+}$2;
THROWS 3prsg 7Ch 2, 15He $^{+}$4, 34Sr 4; ndg 29Ess 12

no *-r-* 23Mon 1

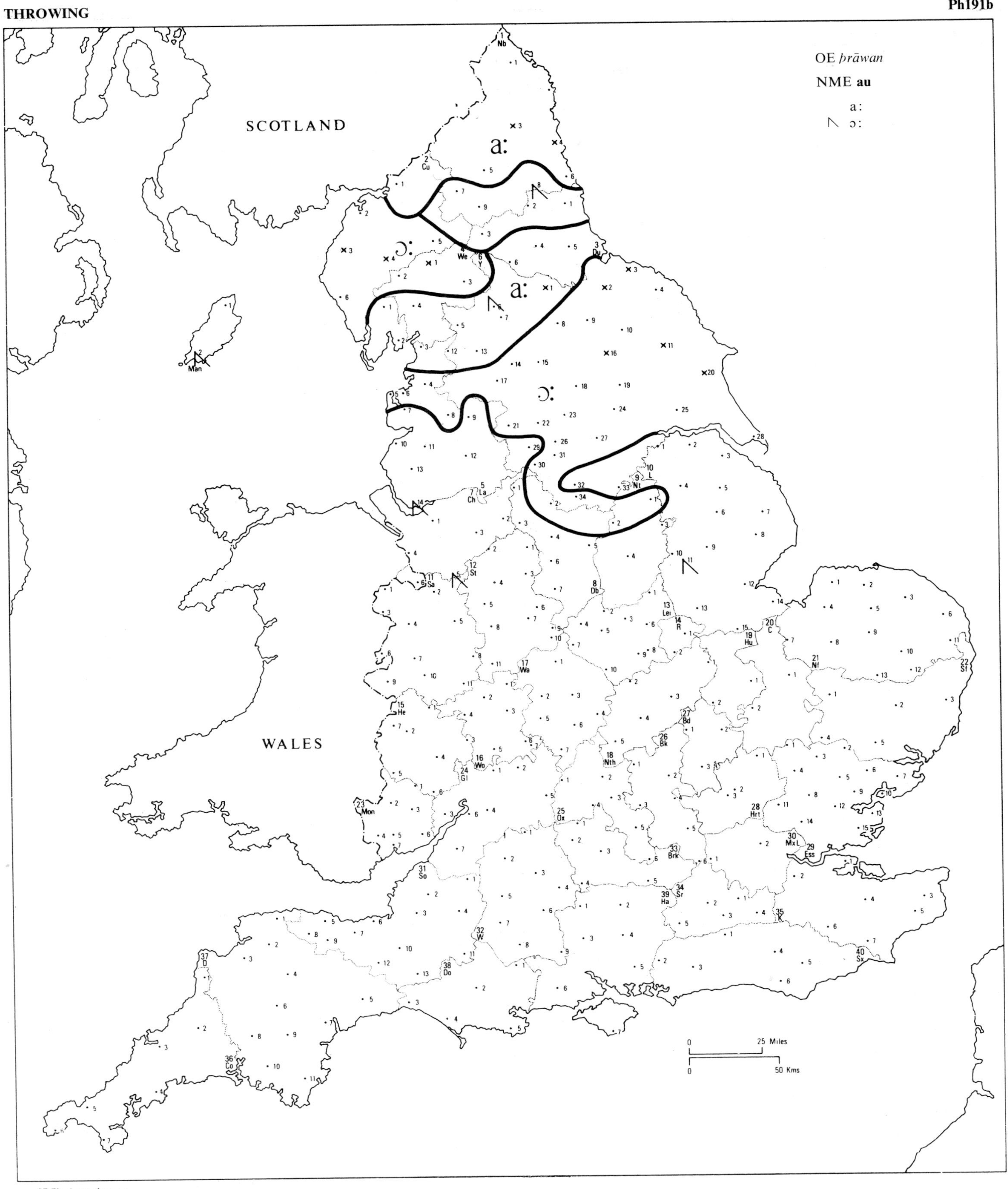

æ: 1Nb 6 under a:
ɒ: Man 2 under ɔ:

THROW ndg 1Nb 2/8, 4We 3/4,
6Y +6/+21/23/25/28/+30;
THROWS 1prpl 6Y +30;
THROWN pp 6Y +21

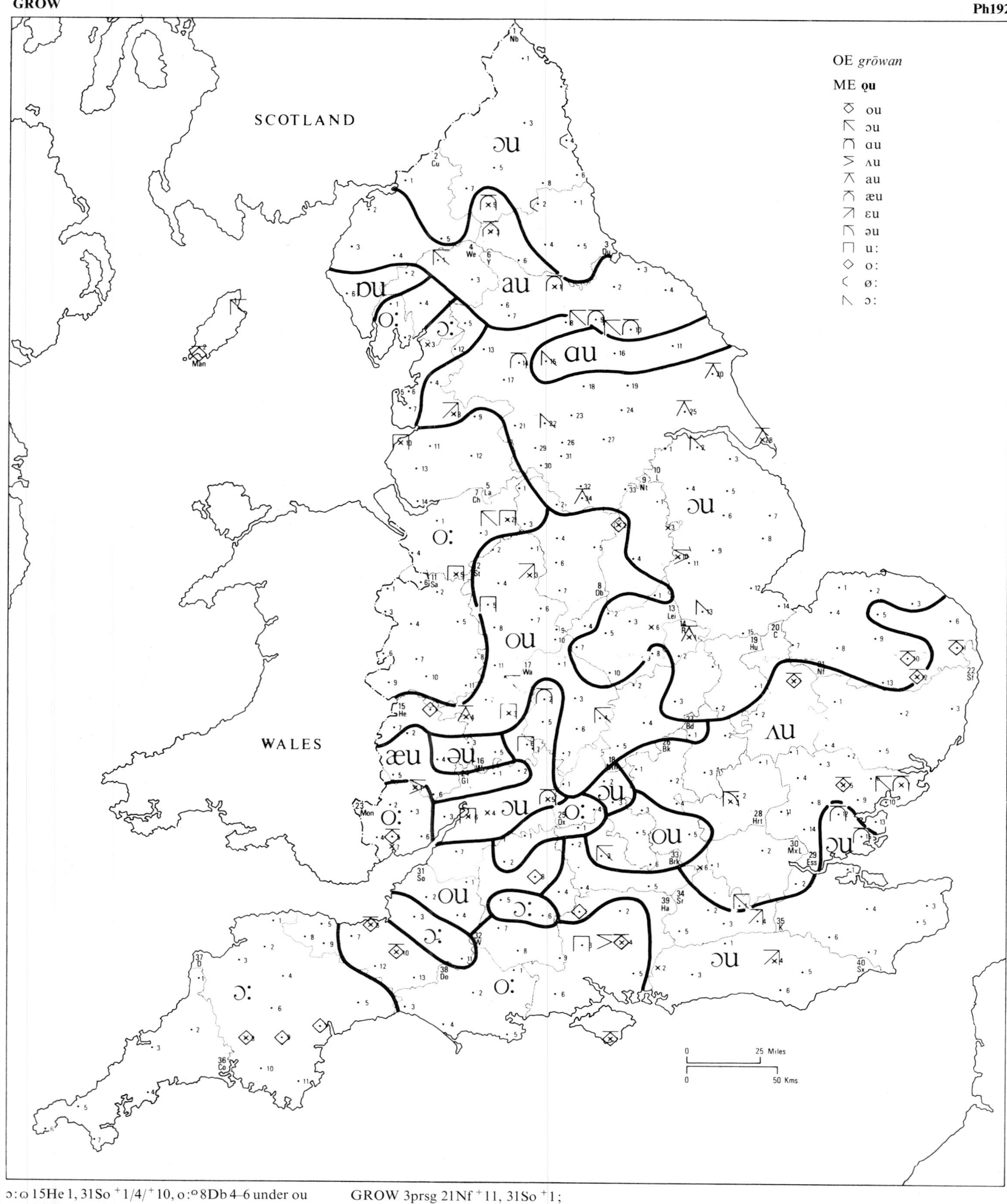

ɔ:ɷ 15He 1, 31So +1/4/+10, o:ᵒ 8Db 4–6 under ou
əɷ: 16Wo 5 under əu
ᵗu: 16Wo 3 under u:
ɔ·ᵊ 6Y 12 under ɔ:

a: 5La 3
ɒw Man +2
u 5La +6

GROW 3prsg 21Nf +11, 31So +1;
1 prpl 17Wa +2, 39Ha +4; 3prpl 3Du +2,
6Y +9/+14/+22, 10L +2, 16Wo +1,
21Nf +10, 31So +10; ndg 6Y +34;
GROWING prp 5La +6, 15He +1, 33Brk +3;
ndg 6Y +25, Man +2, 7Ch +2, 29Ess +15,
32W +3; GROWS 3prsg 1Nb +4,
6Y +9/+14/+15/+20, 10L +13, 17Wa +4,
29Ess +12, 39Ha +1; 3prpl 39Ha +3;
ndg 6Y +10

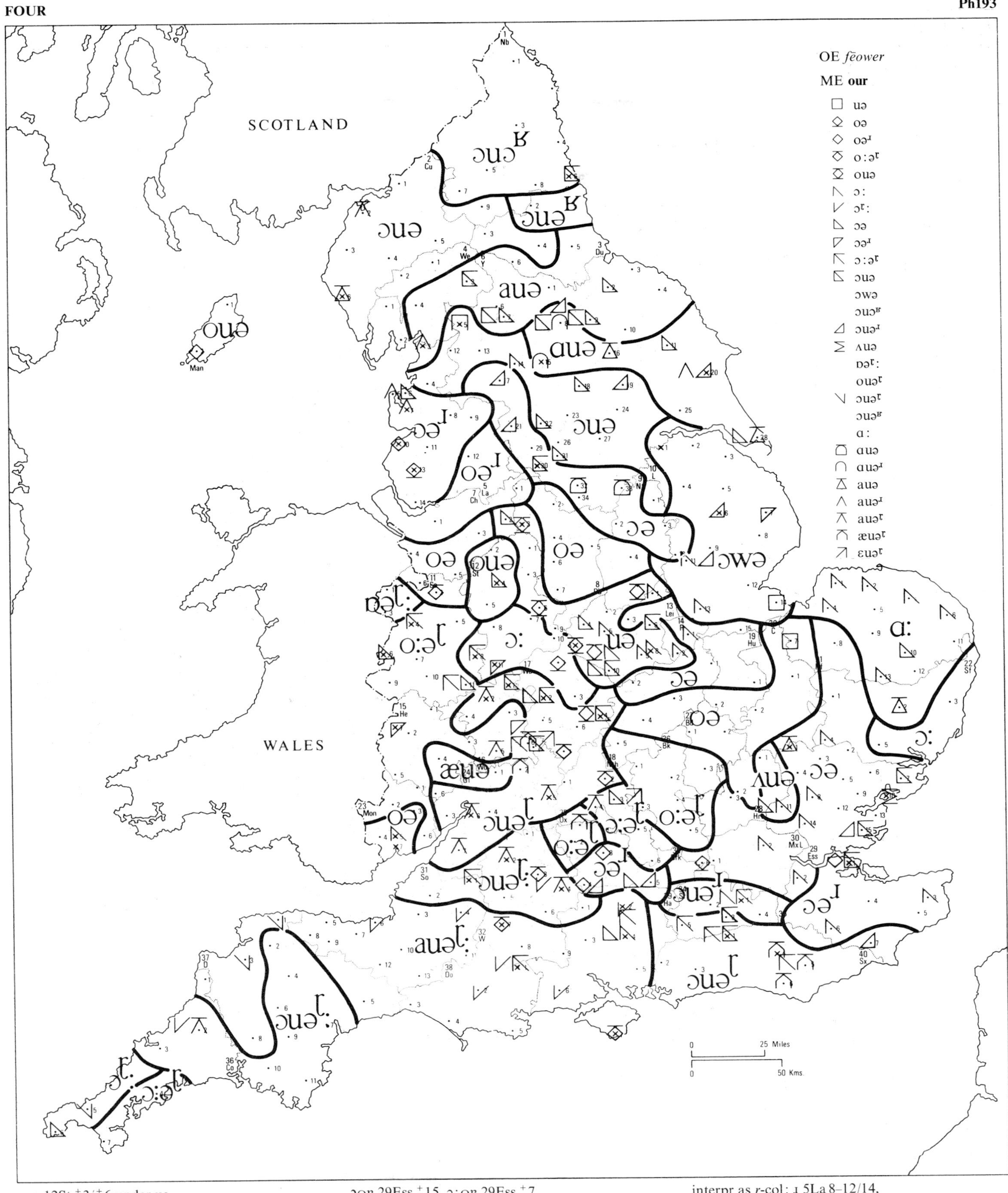

ɷ:ə 12St +3/+6 under uə
ọᵚə 18Nth 3, o:ə 11Sa +2, 23Mon 3,
o:ᵊ 5La 13 under oə
oɷəʴ 33Brk +3/+4, ouəʴ Man +2,
35K +1 under oəʴ
oə˞ 25Ox +2, 32W 7, 33Brk +1/+2, oᵚə˞ 26Bk 5,
oɷə˞ 16Wo +3, 17Wa +7, 32W +3,
oɷə˞ɽ 39Ha 7 under o:ə˞
o·ᵚwə 8Db 3 under ouə
ɔ:ə 11Sa 6/+11, 12St 4, 28Hrt 3,
29Ess 2/+7/+8/+14/+15, ɔ̣:ə 29Ess 3/+4,
ɔ̣:ᵚə 18Nth 1, ɔ:ᵊ 6Y +34, 10L 15, 13Lei 3,
29Ess 5/9/13, ɔ̣:ᵊ 22Sf 1, 26Bk +6,
29Ess 6 under ɔə
ɔ̣:əɹ 12St 11, ɔ:ɹ 5La 11, ɔ·ɹ 15He +7 under ɔəʴ
ɔ˞:ə˞ 11Sa 4, ɔə˞: 36Co 4/7, 38Do +1, ɔə˞ 25Ox +5,
39Ha +4 under ɔ:ə˞

ɔ̣ɷɐ 29Ess +15, ɔ:ɷɐ 29Ess +7,
ɒuɐ 35K +1 under ɔuə
ɔᵚwə 10L +2, ɔɷwə 10L 9 under ɔwə
ɔwəɹ 10L +11, ɒɷwəɹ 6Y 5 under ɔuəʴ
ɑ 21Nf +4, 22Sf +2, ɑ·ə 21Nf +2 under ɑ
aɷə˞ 16Wo 2/+5, 24Gl 6, aɷəɽ 25Ox +4,
ɑɷə˞: 31So +13, 37D 8, ɑɷə˞ 24Gl 5,
ɑɷəɾ 24Gl +7 under auə˞:
ɒɷəʴ 34Sr 2 under ɔuəʴ
ɛu:ə˞ 16Wo +6 under ɛuə˞

ɛ̈ɷə 7Ch +3
a· 21Nf +13, aw 30MxL +2, a̠˞ɽ 33Brk +1,
a˞: 35K +2
ɒ: 21Nf +1, ɒɹ 6Y +20
ɔwɹ̝ 10L 1, ɔᵚwɹ 10L +3
ʌɷ 27Bd +3
o: 23Mon +4 ɵu 23Mon +5

interpr as *r*-col: ɹ 5La 8–12/14,
6Y 5/+8/15/+17/+19/+21, 10L +11,
12St 11, 15He 7, 16Wo +7, 33Brk +5,
ɽ 24Gl +7, 25Ox +3/4
cons *r* foll *r*-col V: ɽ 39Ha 7

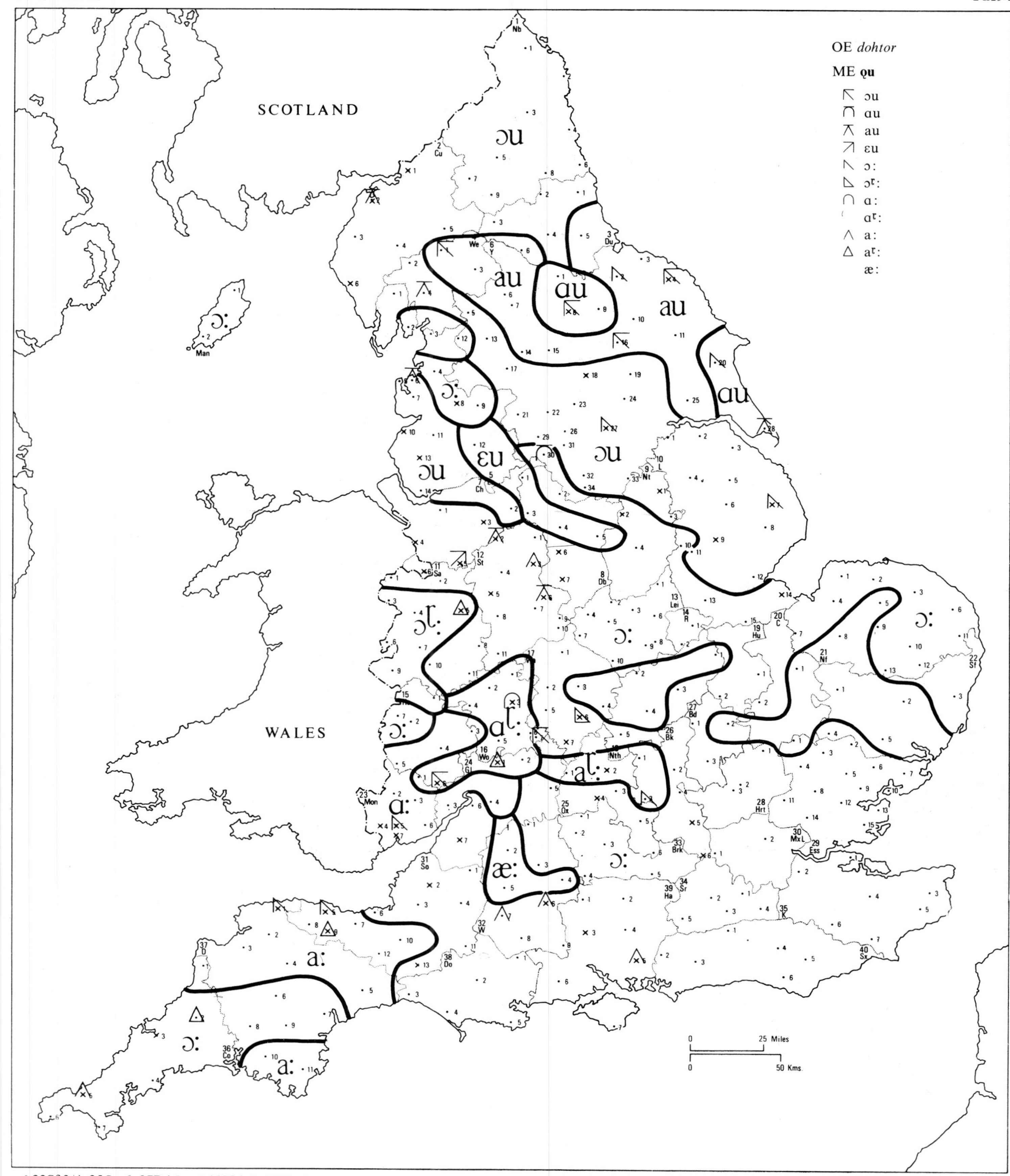

ɔːᵊ 22Sf 3/4, 25Ox 6, 27Bd 3. ɔ̣ːᵊ 18Nth 3, 19Hu 1,
26Bk 2/+3/4, 28Hrt 1/2, ɔˑᵊ 10L 15, 25Ox 3,
ɔ̣ˑᵊ 21Nf 1, ɔˑə 28Hrt +3, ɔᵊ 28Hrt +3,
ɔ̣ 21Nf 4 under ɔː

æɷ 12St +3
oɷ 12St 5
ɷə 10L 14
eː 39Ha 3
ɔɪ̠ː 25Ox 2

-DAUGHTER 5La +6, 6Y +28/32

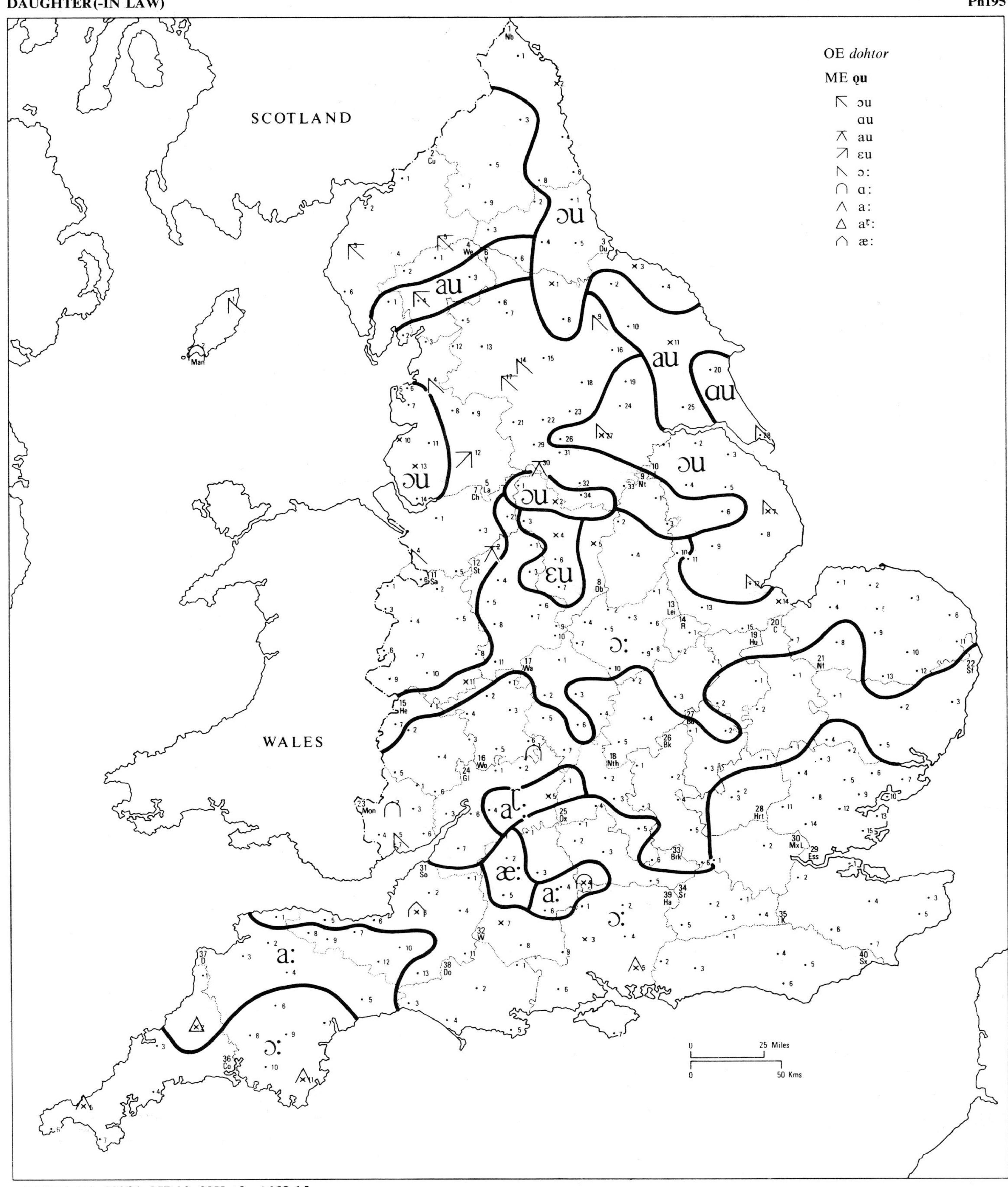

ǫ:ᵊ 18Nth 1/3, 22Sf 4, 27Bd 2, 28Hrt 2, ɔᵊ 10L 15,
ɔ 29Ess 8 under ɔ:

ɷə 10L 14
o˂ : 32W 7
ɑʳ: 15He 3, 23Mon 6
a̠ᶦ: 25Ox 2
ɔʳ: 11Sa 6
e: 39Ha 3

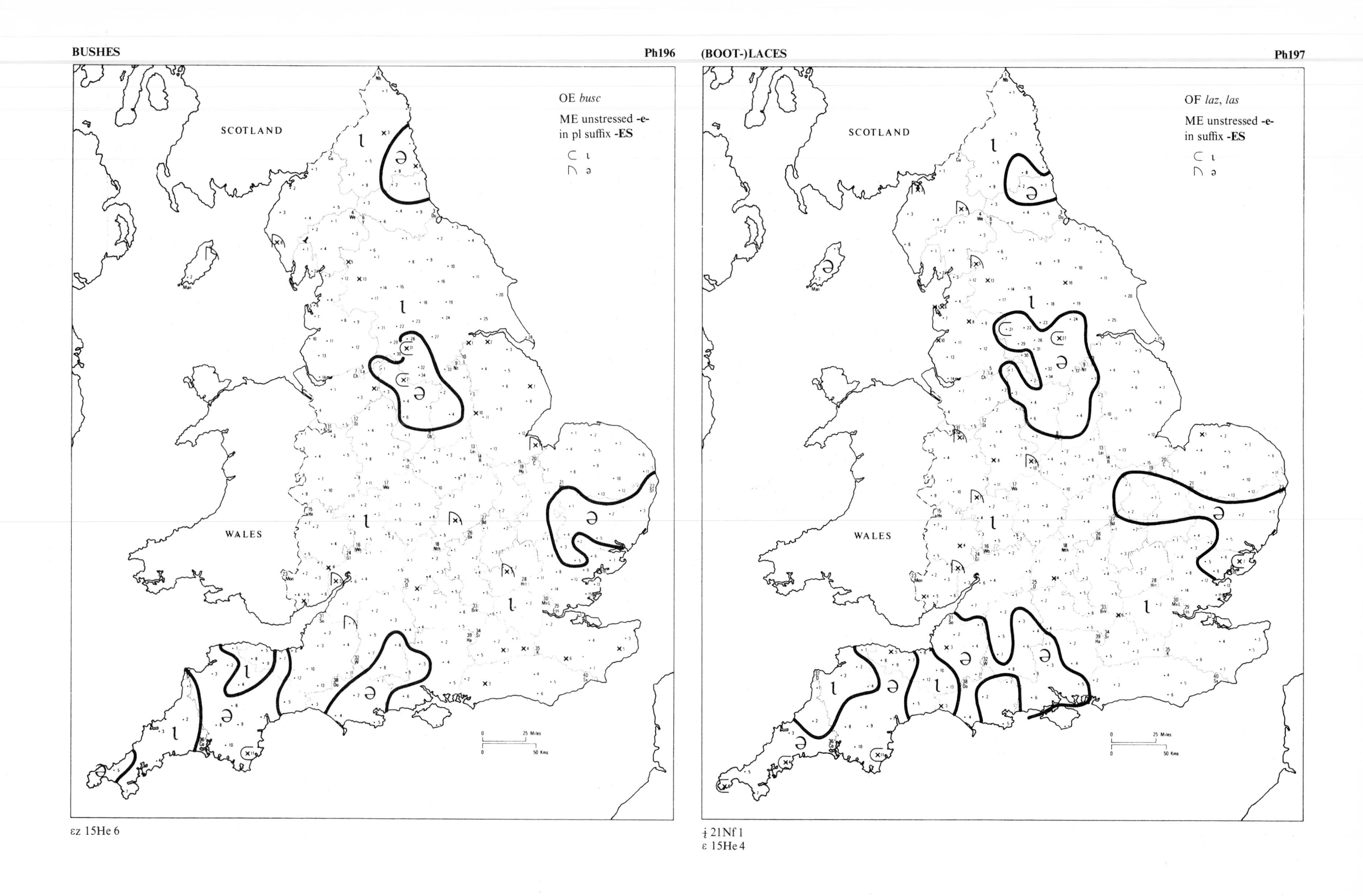

ɛz 15He 6

ɨ 21Nf 1
ɛ 15He 4

POCKETS Ph198

SUET Ph199

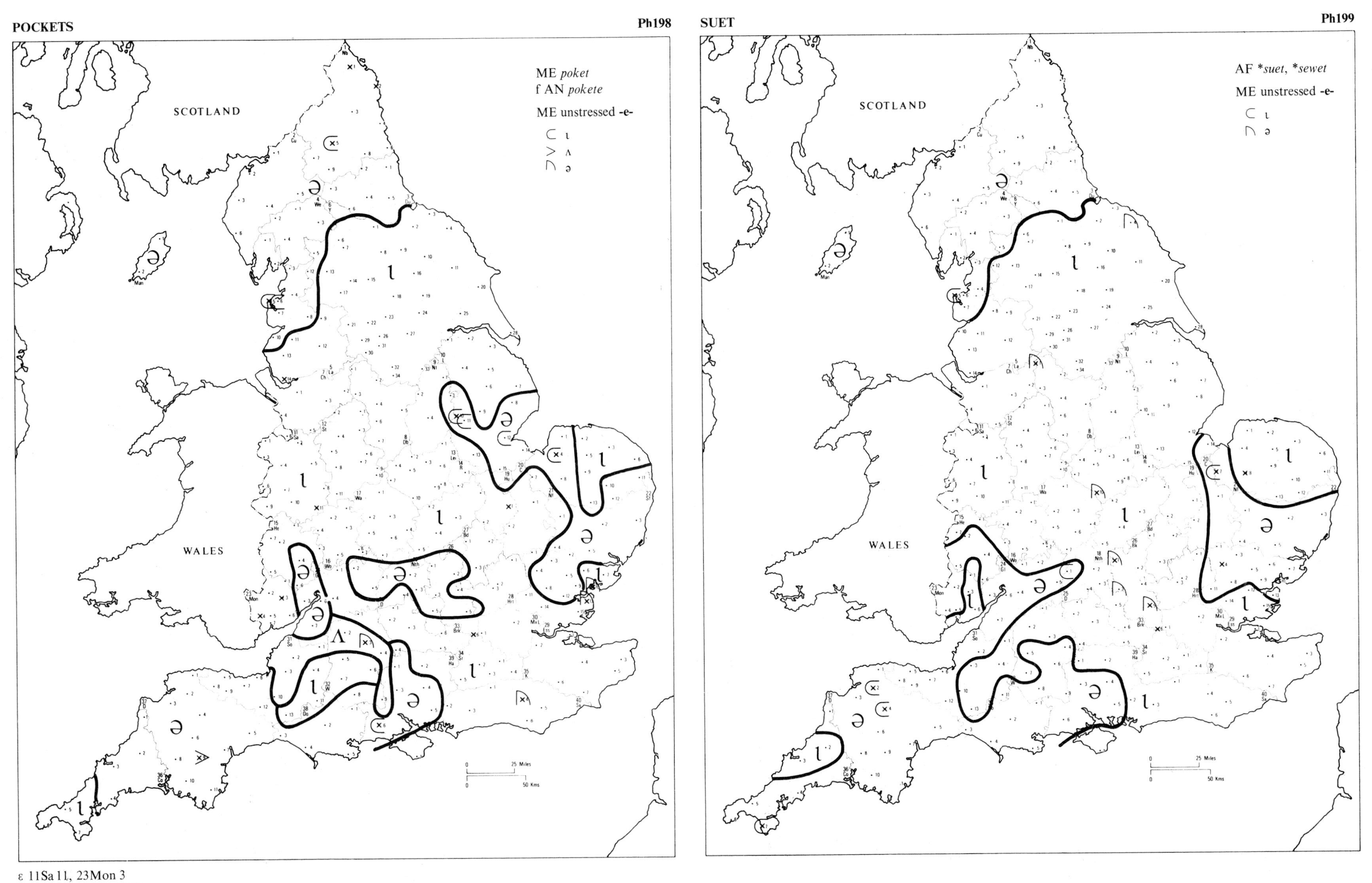

ɛ 11Sa 11, 23Mon 3
pɩkɩt, pɩkɩts (sic) 6Y 8

POCKET sg 5La 6/9–11, 6Y 2/27/31, Man 1/2, 8Db 6, 9Nt 3,.10L 5/7/⁺11/12/14, 11Sa 2/5, 12St 10, 15He 5, 18Nth 3, 21Nf 4, 22Sf 2/4, 24Gl 7, 25Ox 1, 31So 7, 34Sr 4, 39Ha 3, 40Sx 3

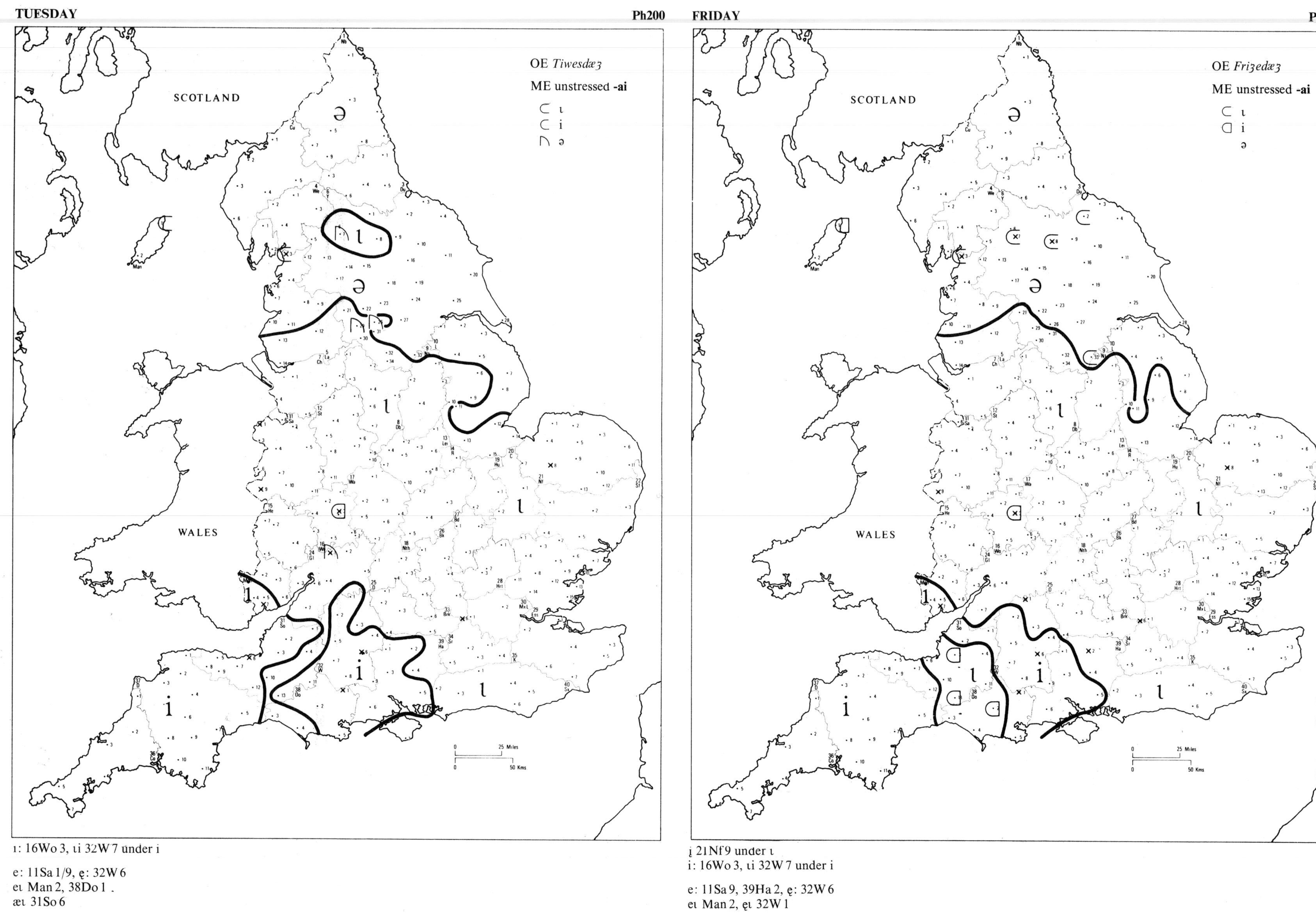

ɪ: 16Wo 3, ɩi 32W 7 under i

e: 11Sa 1/9, ẹ: 32W 6
eɩ Man 2, 38Do 1 .
æɩ 31So 6

į 21Nf 9 under ɩ
i: 16Wo 3, ɩi 32W 7 under i

e: 11Sa 9, 39Ha 2, ẹ: 32W 6
eɩ Man 2, ẹɩ 32W 1

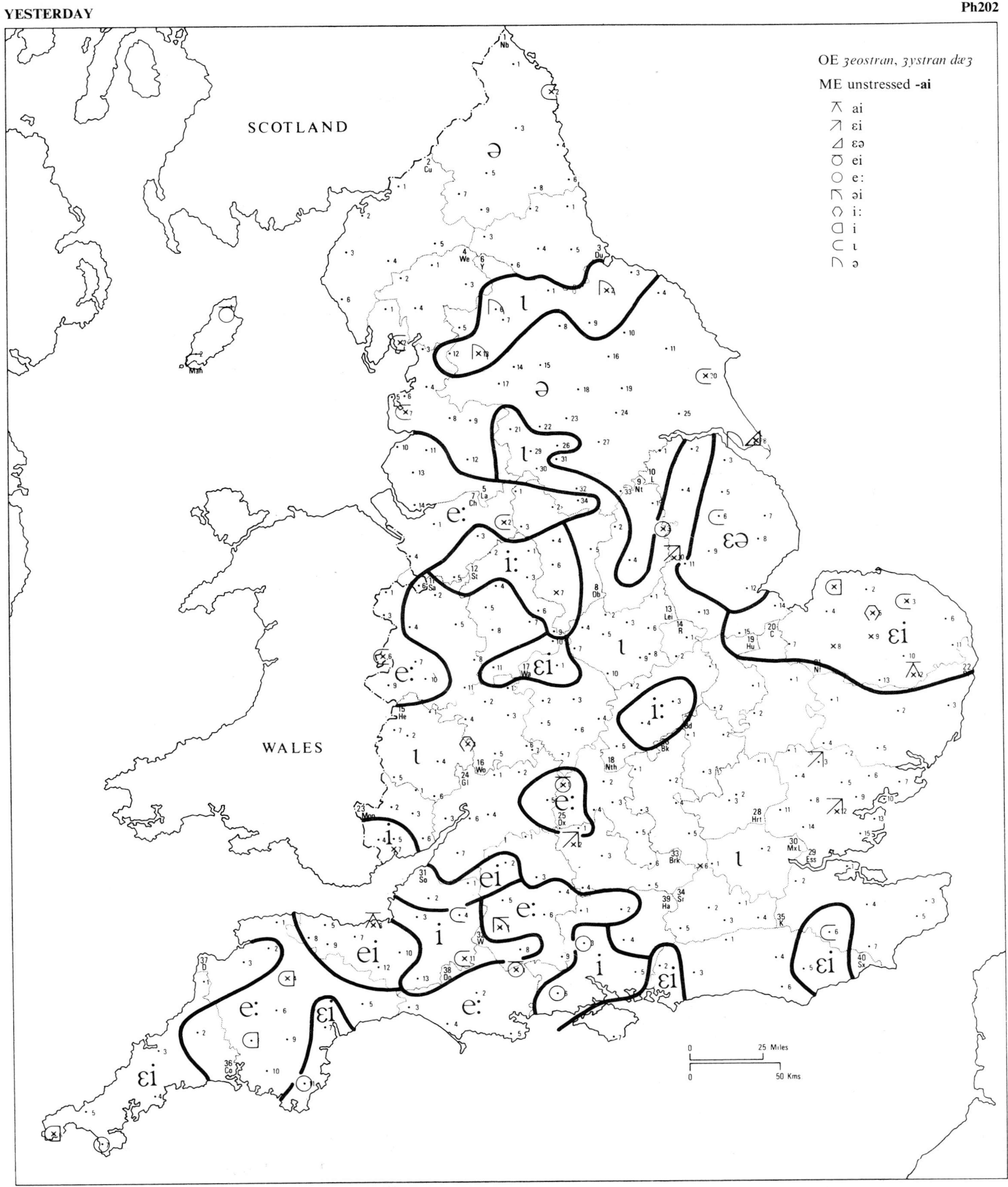

e:ɩ 31So +7 under ei
e 6Y 34 under e:

æɩ 21Nf 9, æi 21Nf +10

jɛstə⁴ɩ Man 2, jɩstədədɛə 6Y +28

EVERY Ph203

READY Ph204

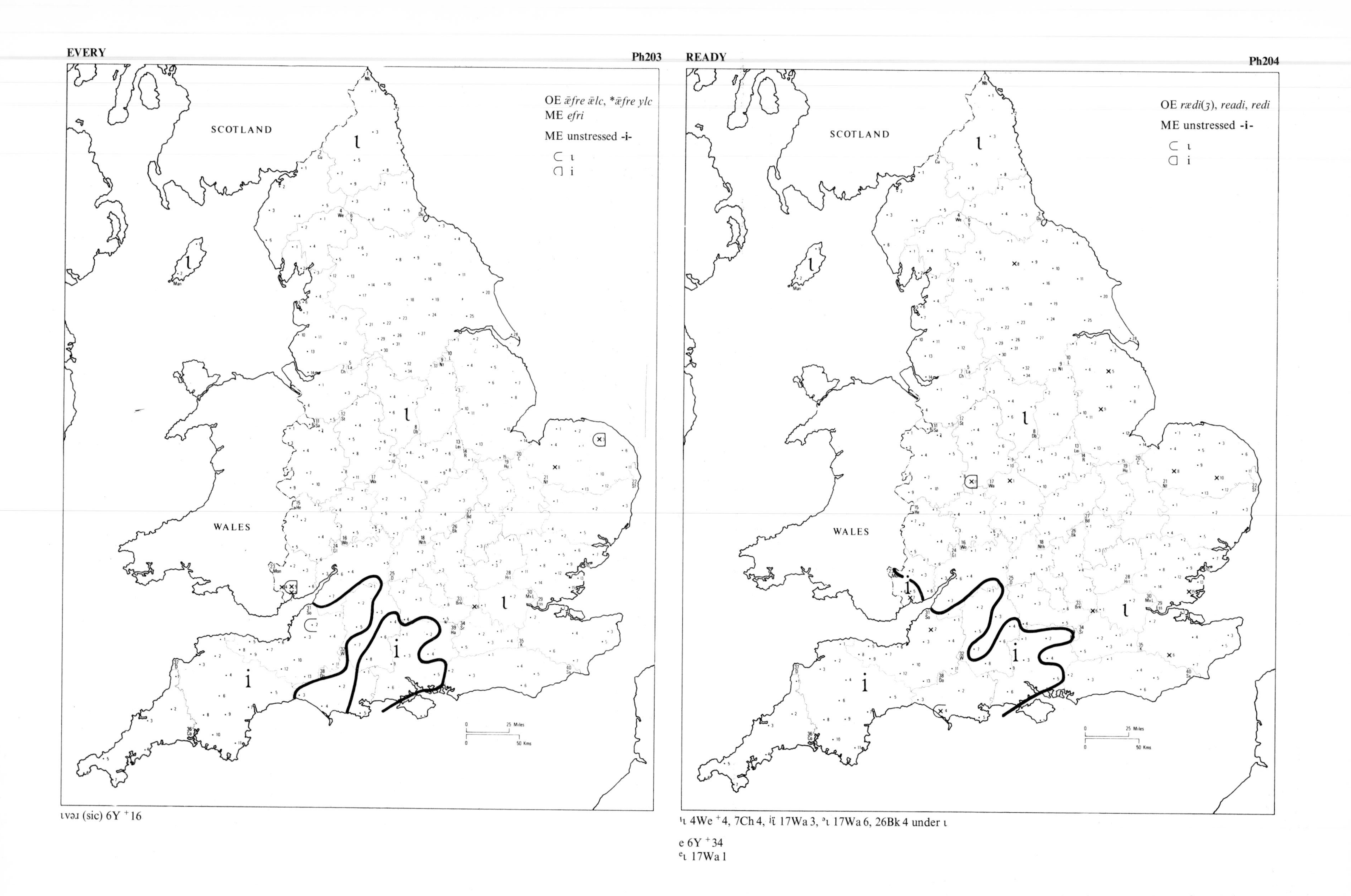

ɩvəɹ (sic) 6Y $^{+}$16

^{i}ɩ 4We $^{+}$4, 7Ch 4, ^{i}ɩ̆ 17Wa 3, ^{ə}ɩ 17Wa 6, 26Bk 4 under ɩ

e 6Y $^{+}$34

^{e}ɩ 17Wa 1

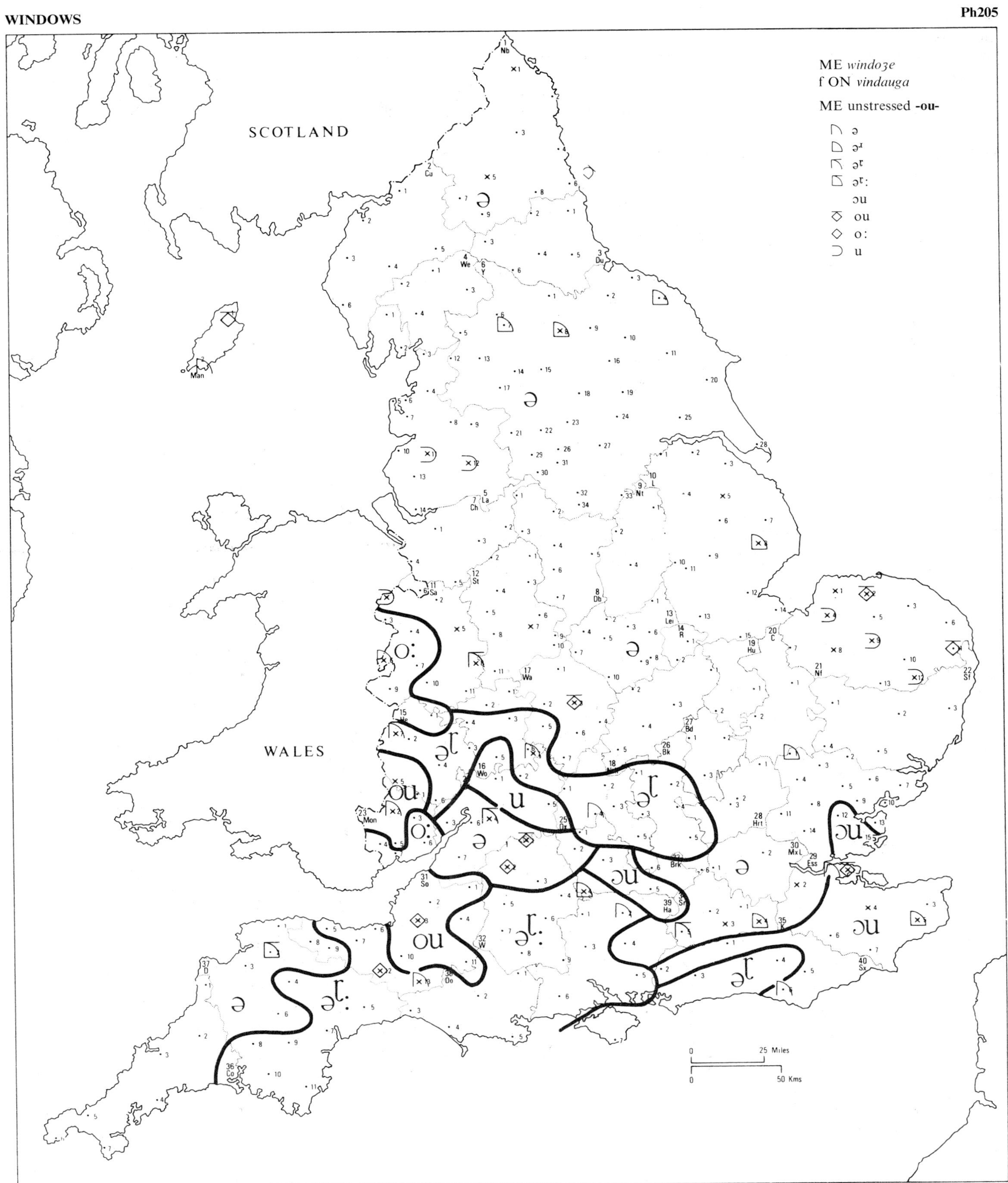

o:ᵚ 23Mon 1 under ou

ɩ 1Nb 1, 11Sa 5, ɨ 21Nf 1
εɷ 28Hrt ⁺3, 34Sr 3
ɔʁ 1Nb 5
ʌɷ 15He 5, 34Sr ⁺1, 35K 2
syllabic ɟ 10L 5

interpr as *r*-col: ɹ 6Y 4/⁺7/8, 29Ess ⁺1, ɽ 25Ox ⁺4

WINDOW- 6Y ⁺4

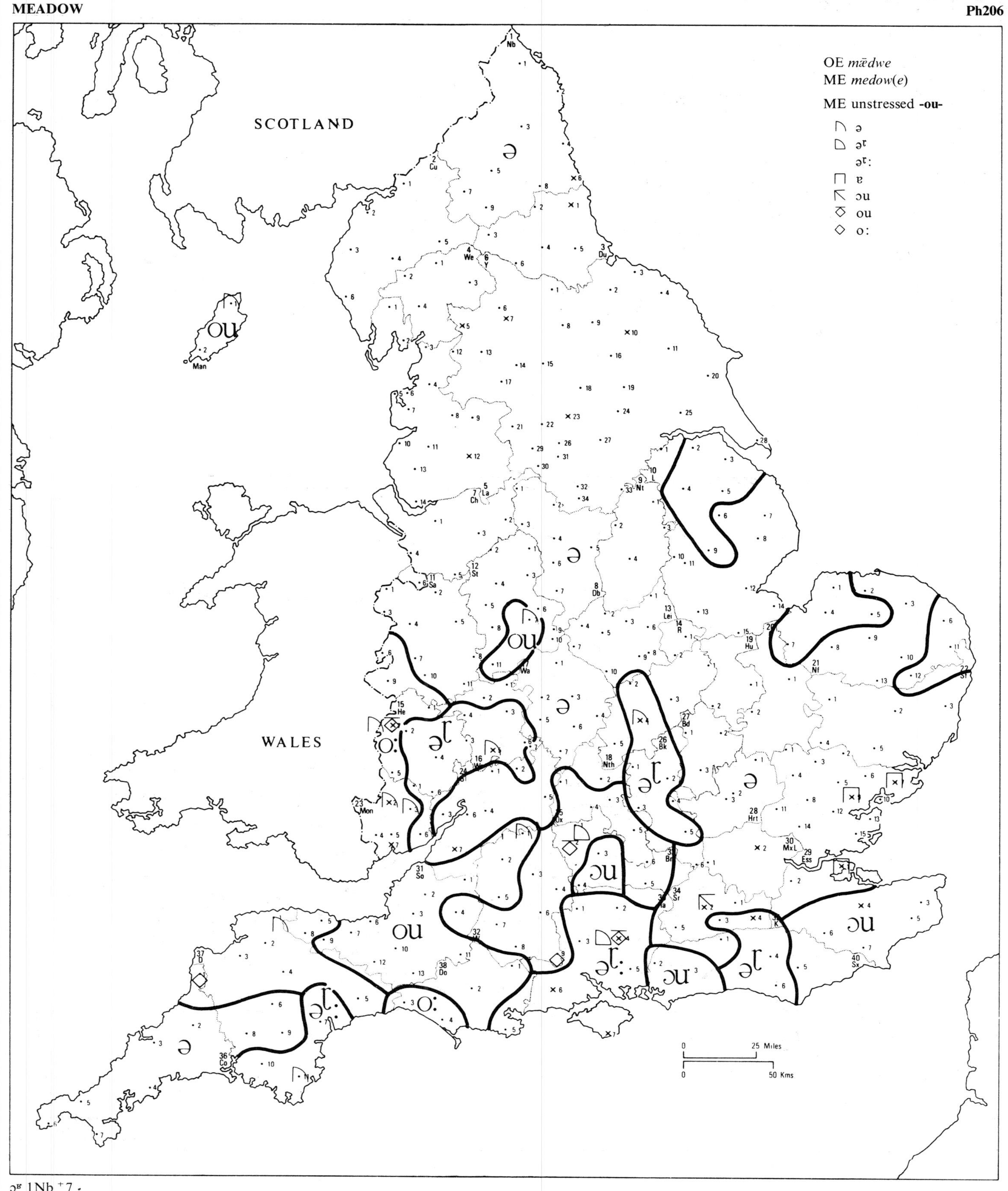

ɔʁ 1Nb +7 ‹
ʌɷ 35K +2
əɹ 33Brk +3, 34Sr 4, 35K 4

-MEADOW(S) 6Y 33, 10L 15, 15He 4/+7, 16Wo 5, 24Gl 4, 29Ess 7, 34Sr +4
MEADOWS pl 6Y 13, Man +1, 10L 10, 13Lei 2, 23Mon +3/6, 27Bd 3, 29Ess 6, 32W +1, 33Brk +3/4, 34Sr +4, 37D 1, 40Sx 2/3

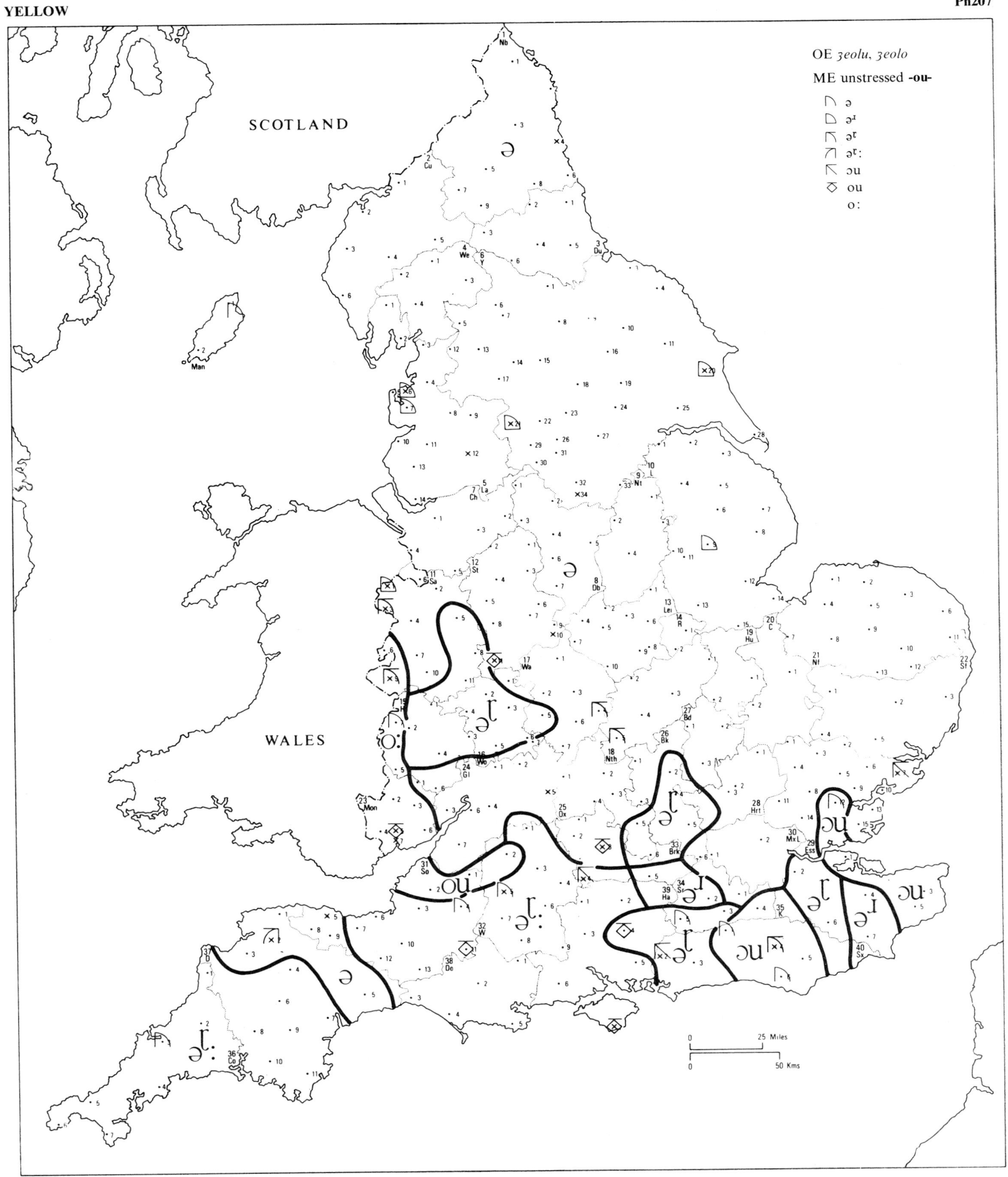

ɐ 29Ess 15 under ə
syllabic ɻ 10L +9 under əʴ
o 11Sa 6, 23Mon 4 under o:

ɩ 10L +4
æɷ 28Hrt +3
ɒ 6Y 34, Man 2
ɔʶ 1Nb 4
ʌɷ 30MxL +2
ɷ 5La 12, ö̥ 24Gl 5

interpr as *r*-col: ɹ 33Brk 5

SHILLING Ph208

MORNING Ph209

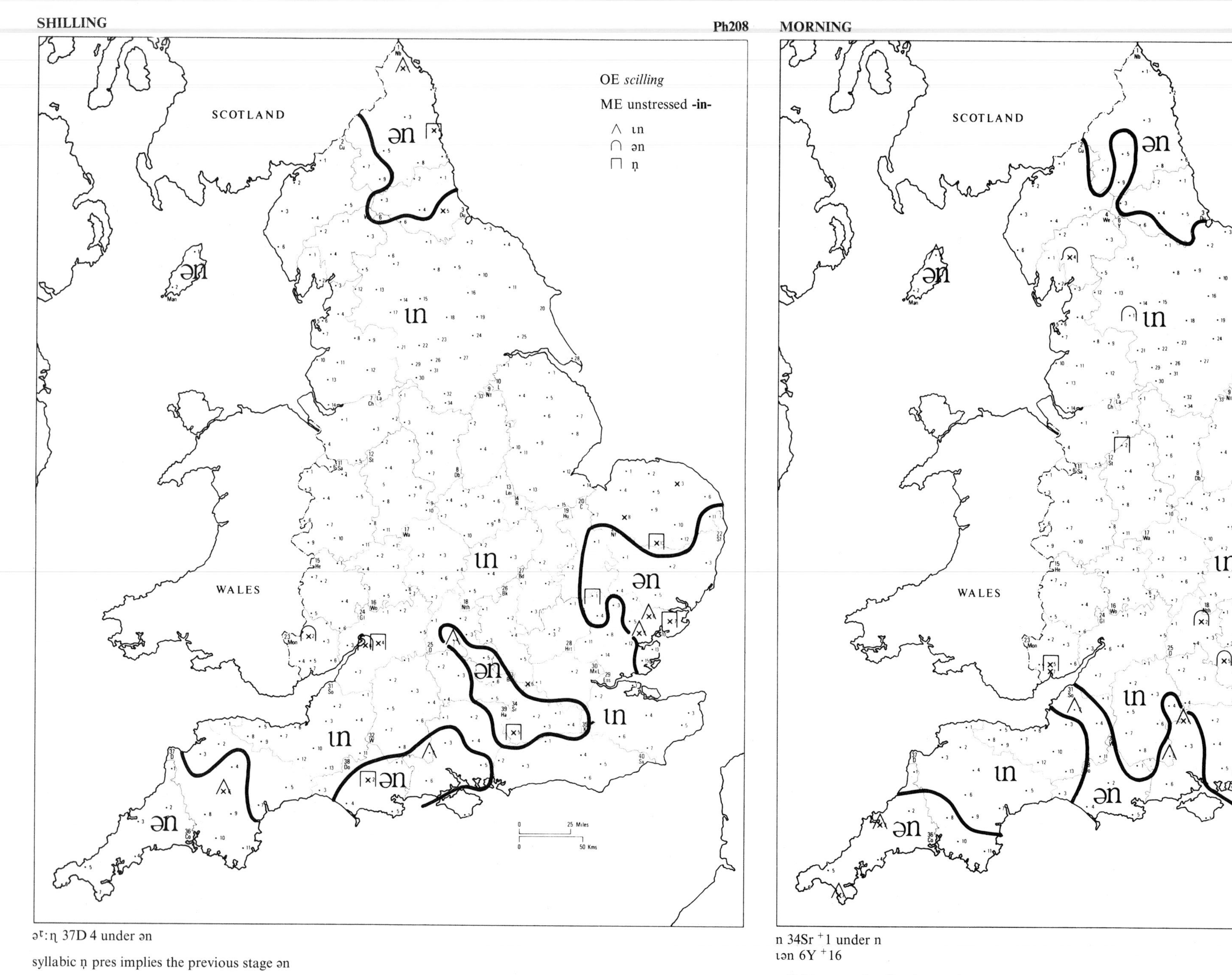

Ph208: əʳ:n̩ 37D 4 under ən

syllabic n̩ pres implies the previous stage ən

Ph209: n 34Sr $^{+1}$ under n
ɩən 6Y $^{+16}$

syllabic n̩ pres implies the previous stage ən

HERRINGS

Ph210

FARTHING

Ph211

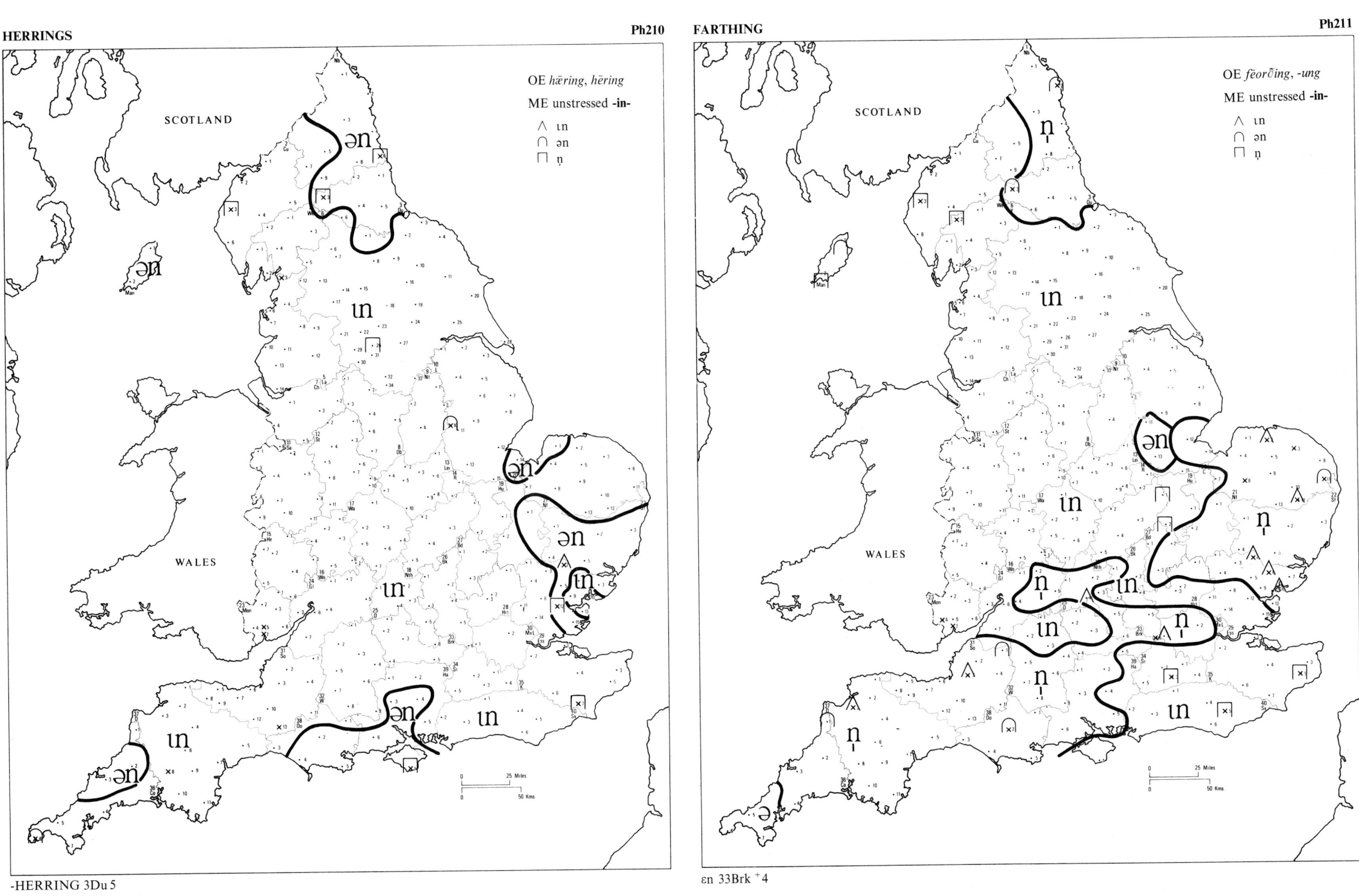

-HERRING 3Du 5

syllabic n̩ pres implies the previous stage ən

ɛn 33Brk ⁺4

syllabic n̩ pres implies the previous stage ən

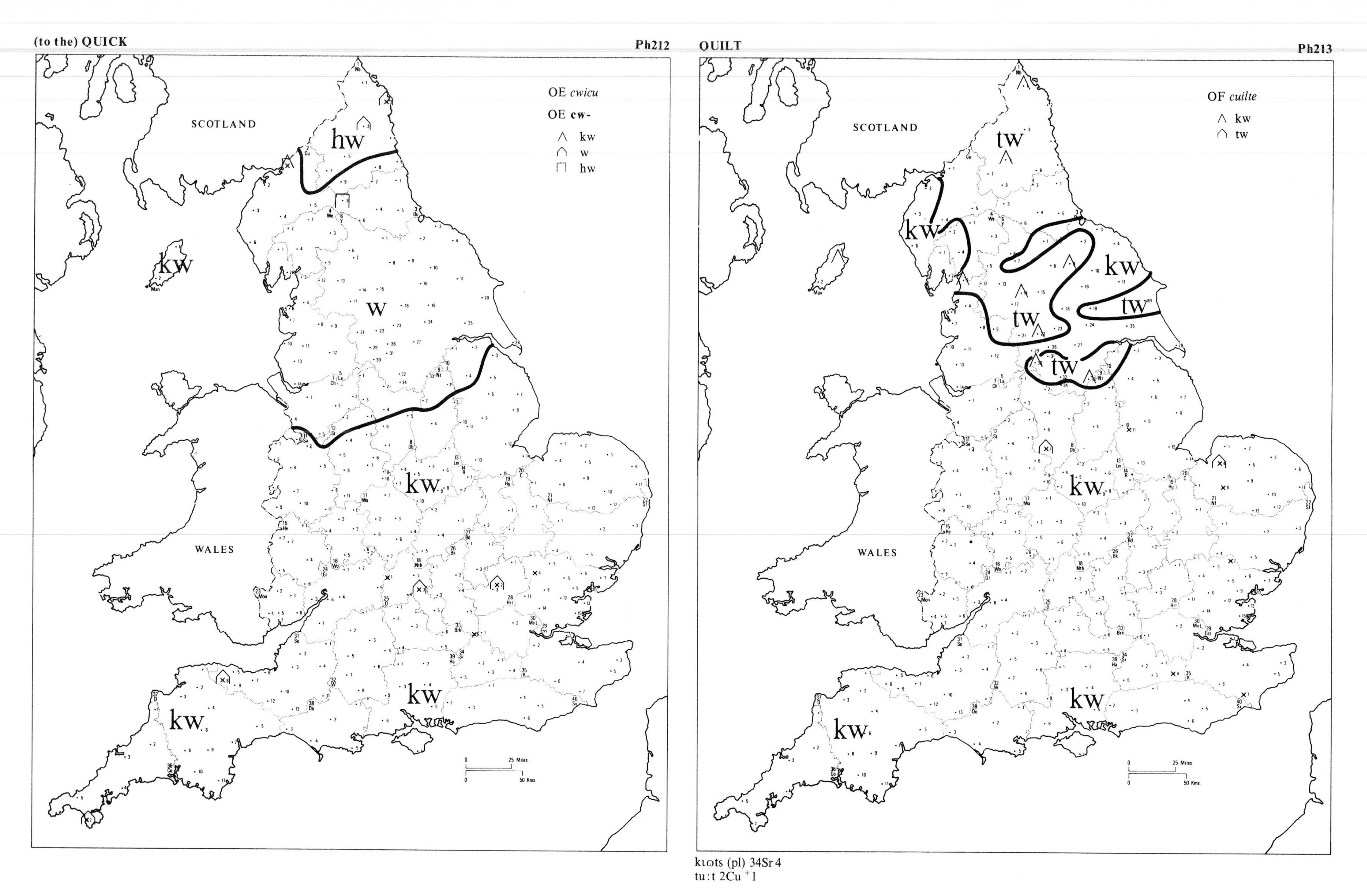

kɩɷts (pl) 34Sr 4
tu:t 2Cu $^{+}$1

-QUILT 6Y 5/6/$^{+}$30/32, 16Wo 7, 21Nf 6, 24Gl 5, 25Ox 4

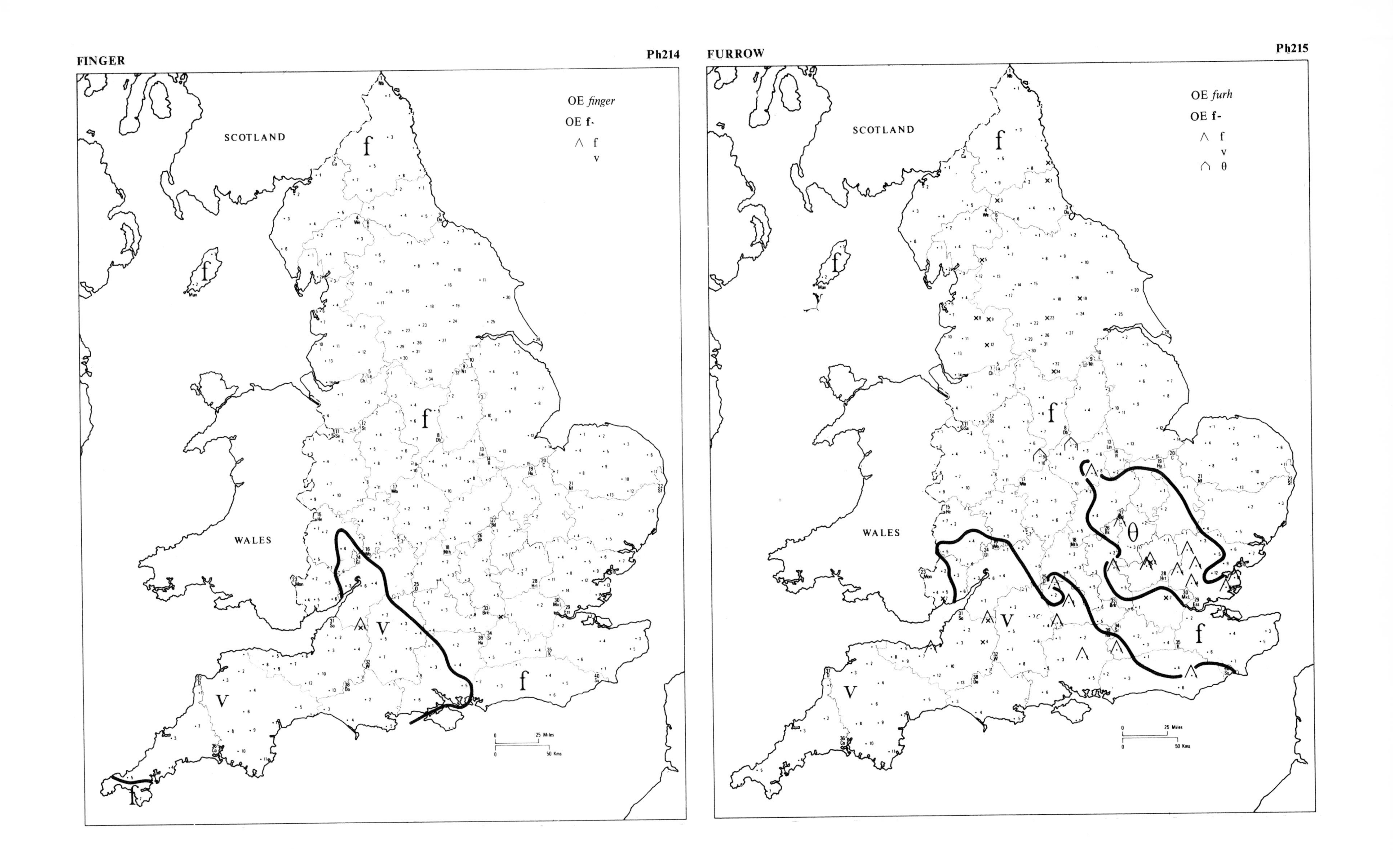
FINGER
Ph214
SCOTLAND
WALES
OE *finger*
OE **f**-
∧ f
v
25 Miles
50 Kms
FURROW
Ph215
SCOTLAND
WALES
OE *furh*
OE **f**-
∧ f
v
∩ θ
25 Miles
50 Kms

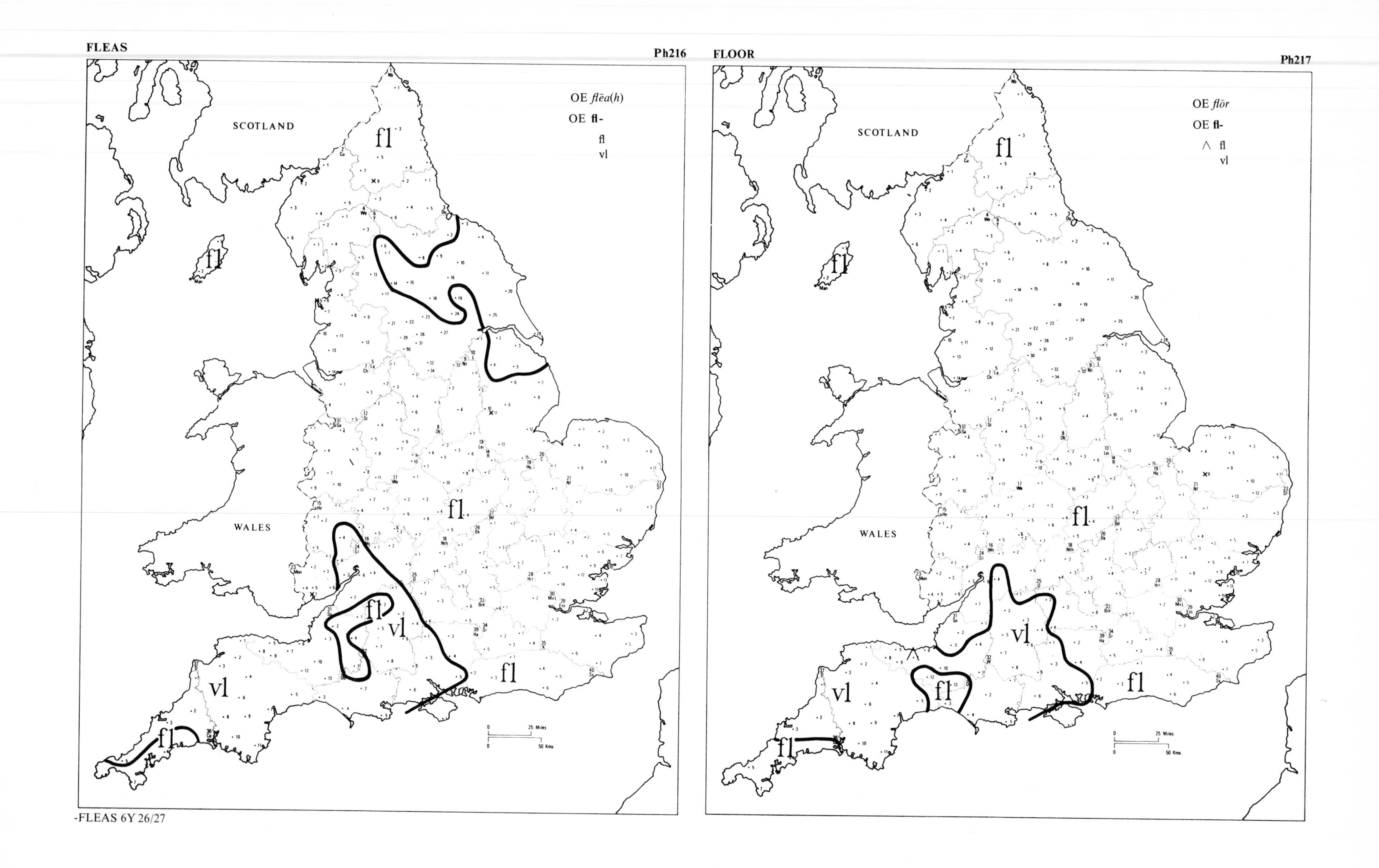

-FLEAS 6Y 26/27

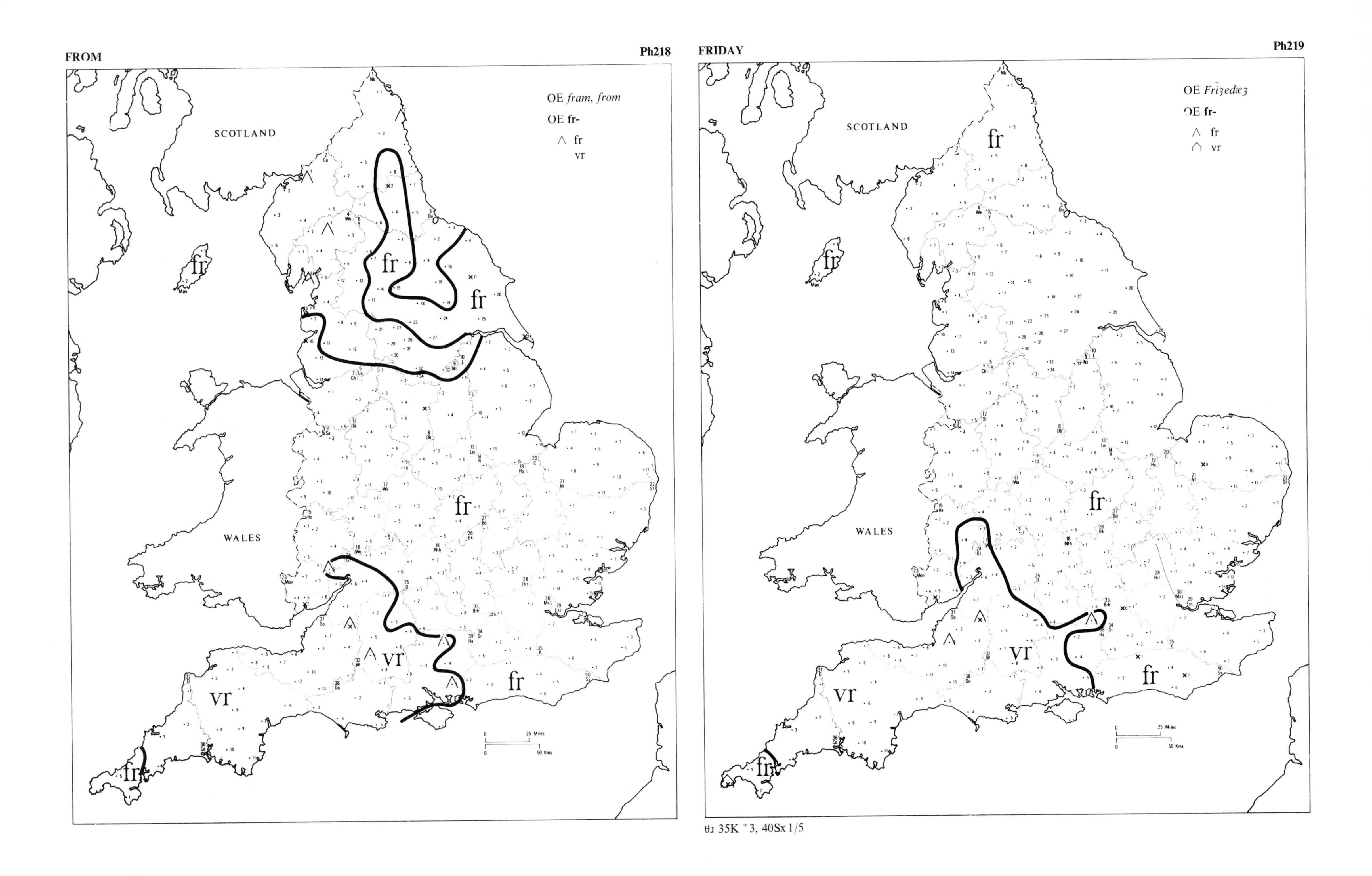
FROM
Ph218
OE *fram, from*
OE **fr-**
Λ fr
vr
SCOTLAND
WALES
fr
vr
25 Miles
50 Kms
FRIDAY
Ph219
OE *Frīʒedæʒ*
OE **fr-**
Λ fr
∩ vr
θɪ 35K ⁺3, 40Sx 1/5

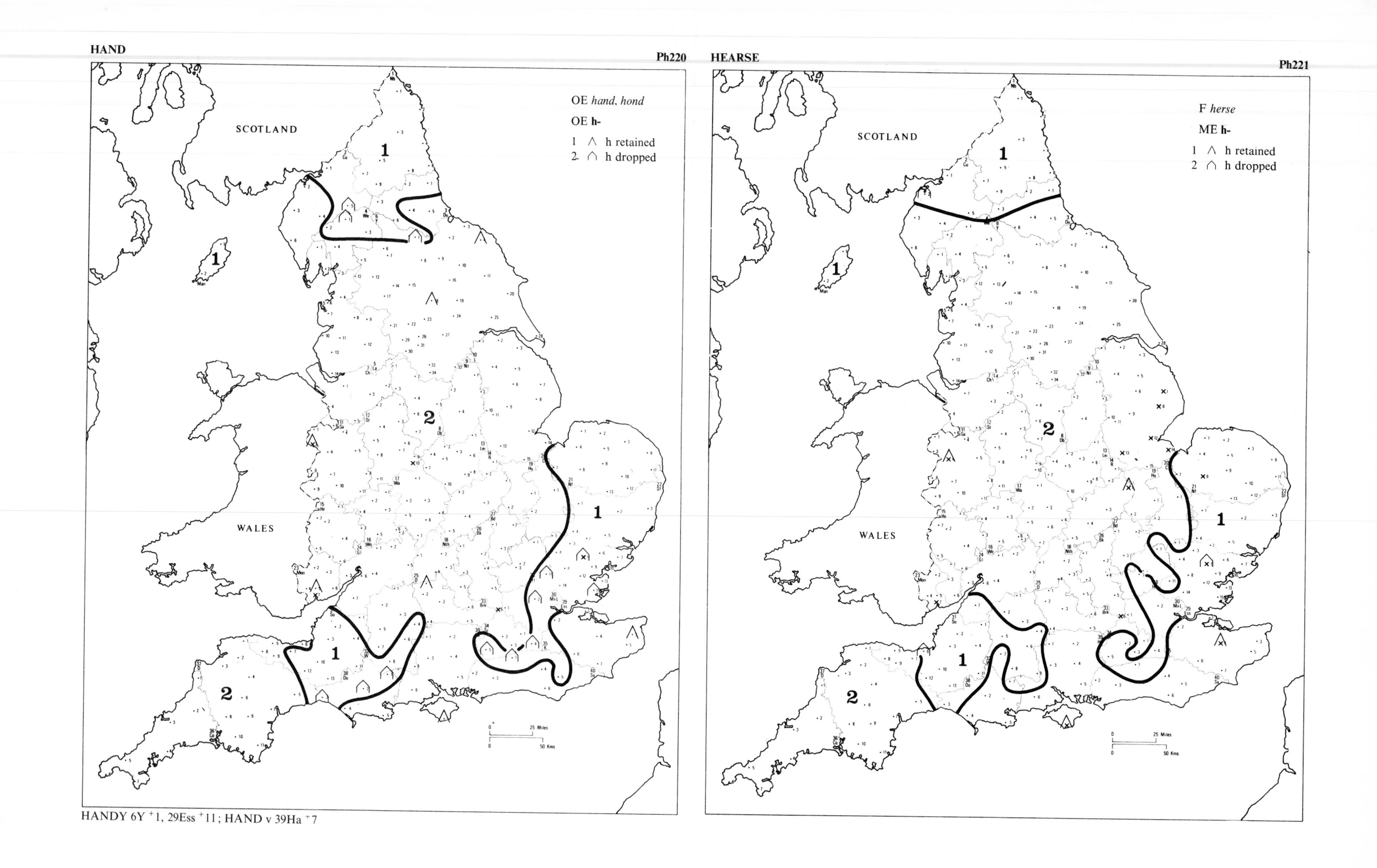

HANDY 6Y +1, 29Ess +11; HAND v 39Ha +7

WHEEL Ph222

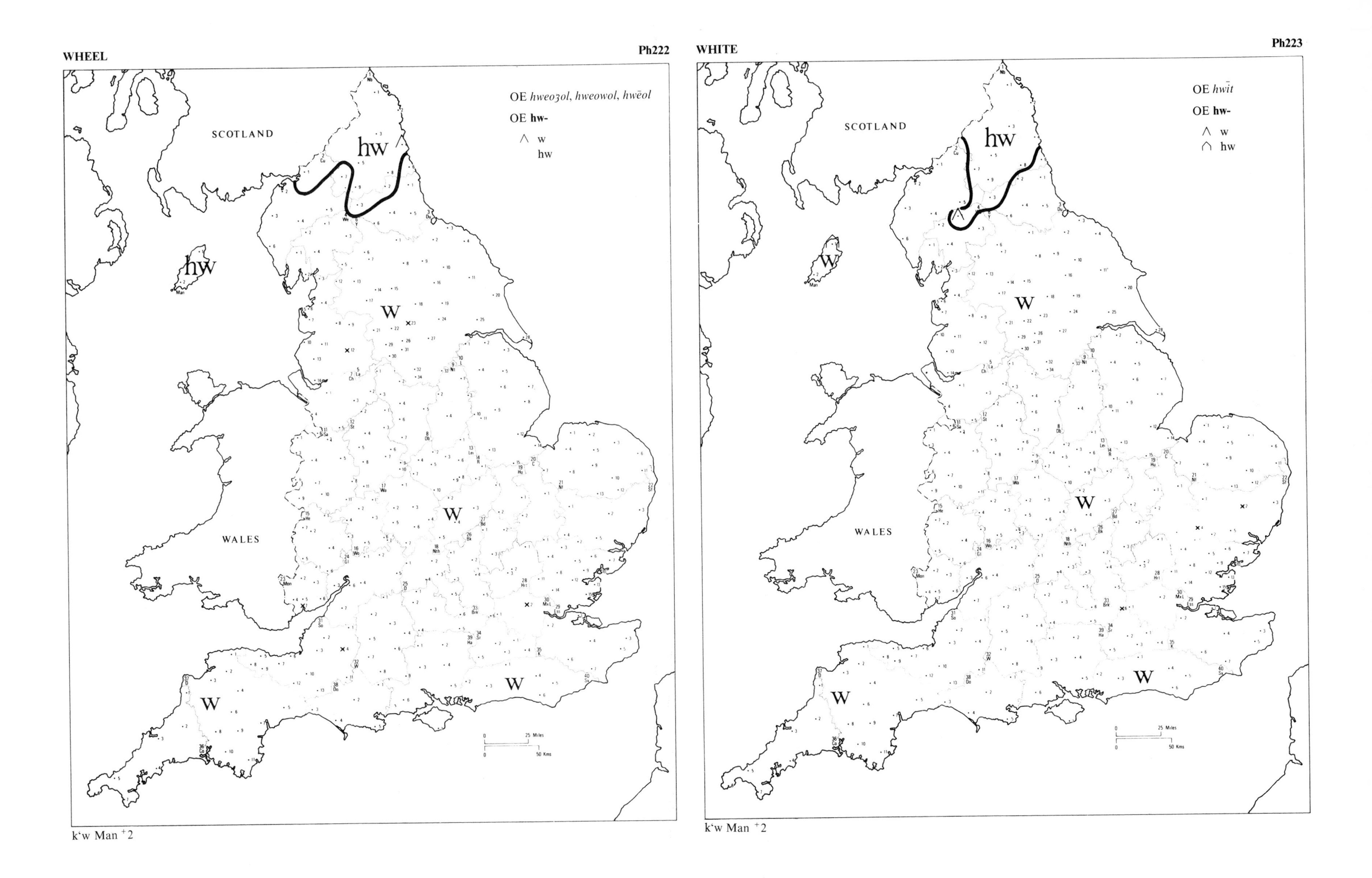

k'w Man +2

WHITE Ph223

k'w Man +2

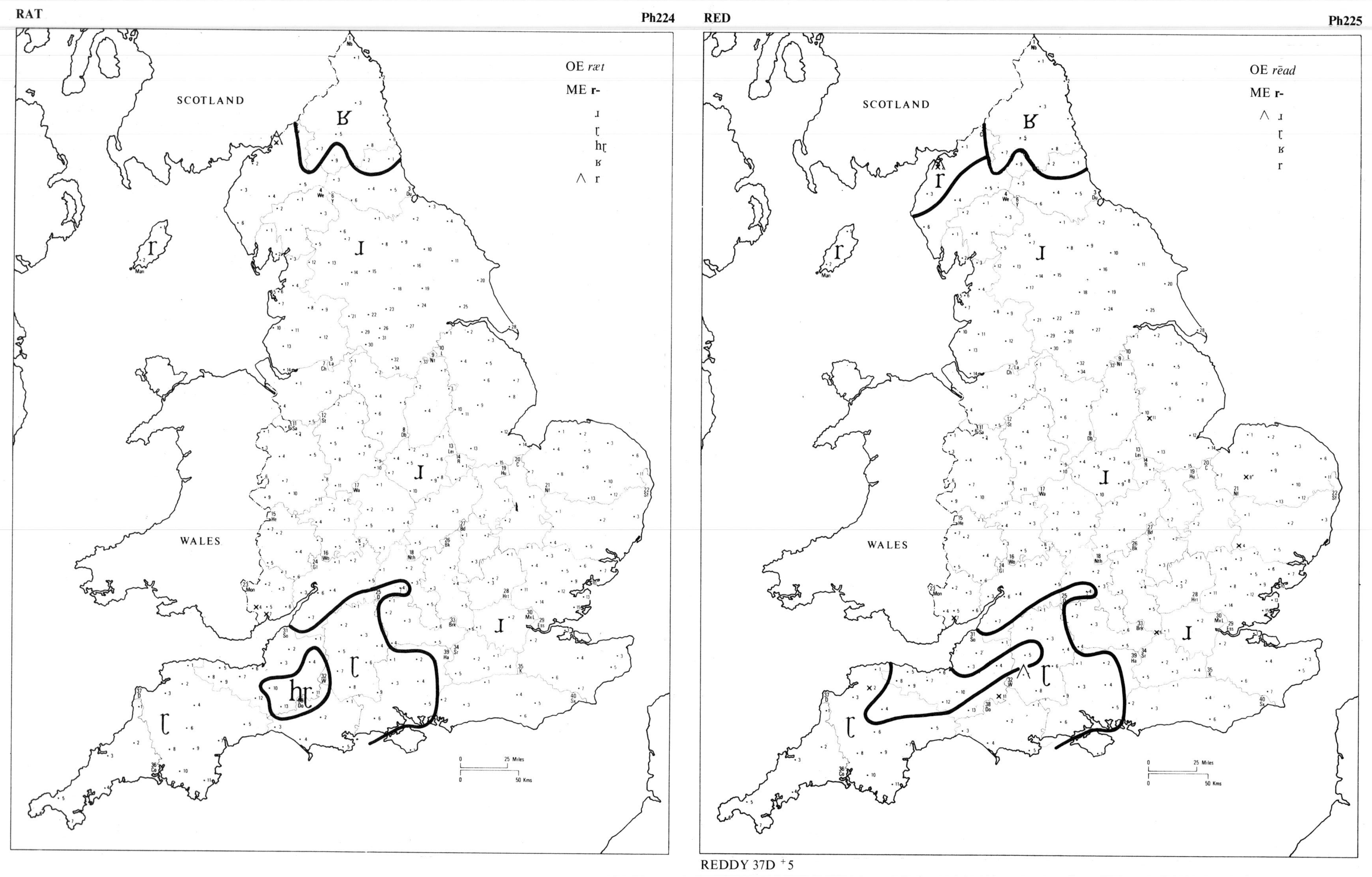

REDDY 37D $^+$5

həʳ:ɖ 31So 4/$^+$7/10/12, 32W 5, əʳ:ɖ 31So 5/6/$^+$7/8/9, 37D 2/4/$^+$5/$^+$6/7

SADDLE

Ph226

SEVEN

Ph227

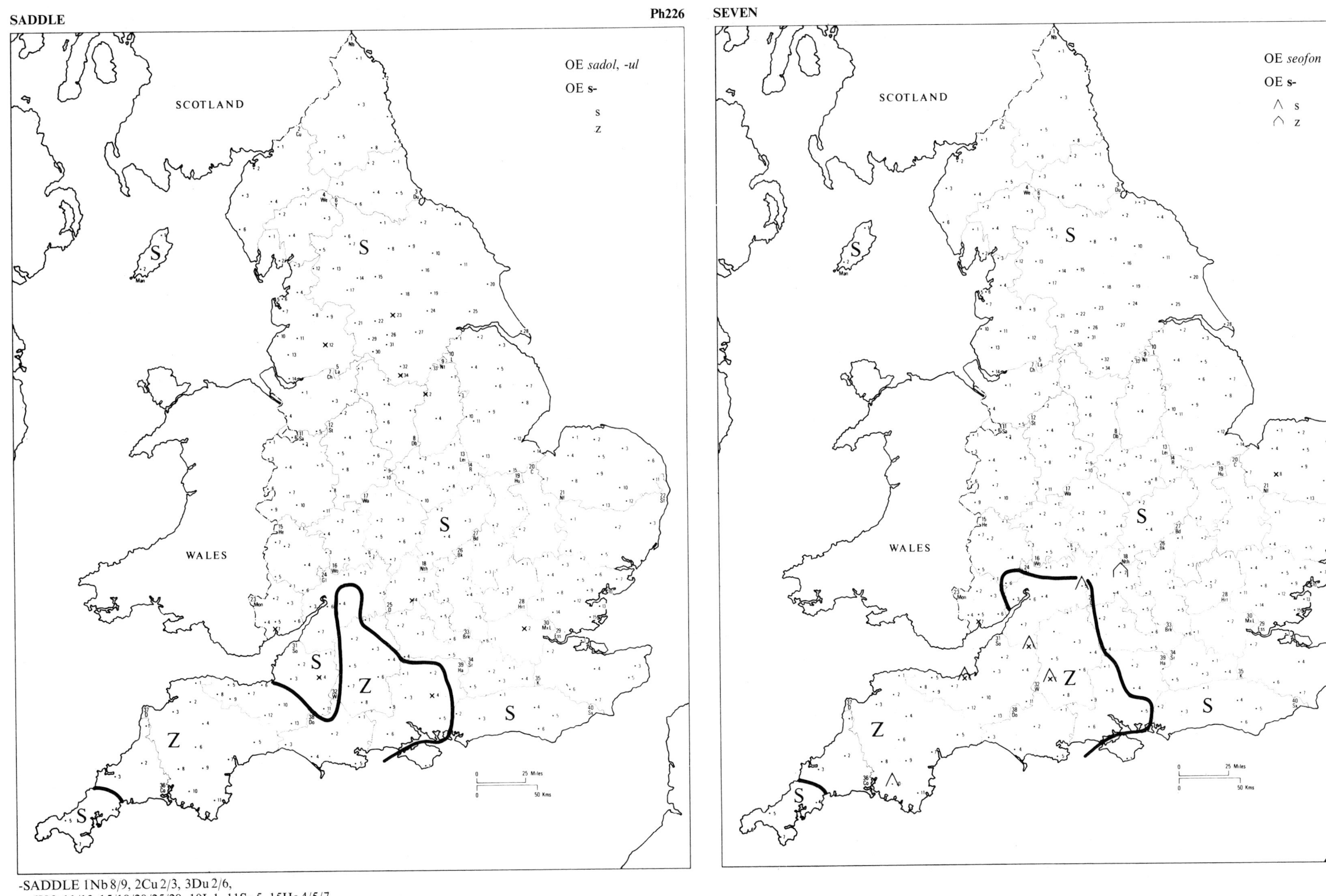

-SADDLE 1Nb 8/9, 2Cu 2/3, 3Du 2/6,
6Y 3–11/13–15/18/20/25/28, 10L 1, 11Sa 5, 15He 4/5/7,
16Wo 4/5, 17Wa 2, 21Nf 1/2/4/5/10, 23Mon 3/6, 24Gl 7,
25Ox 6, 29Ess 2, 31So 2/3/5–10/12, 32W 1

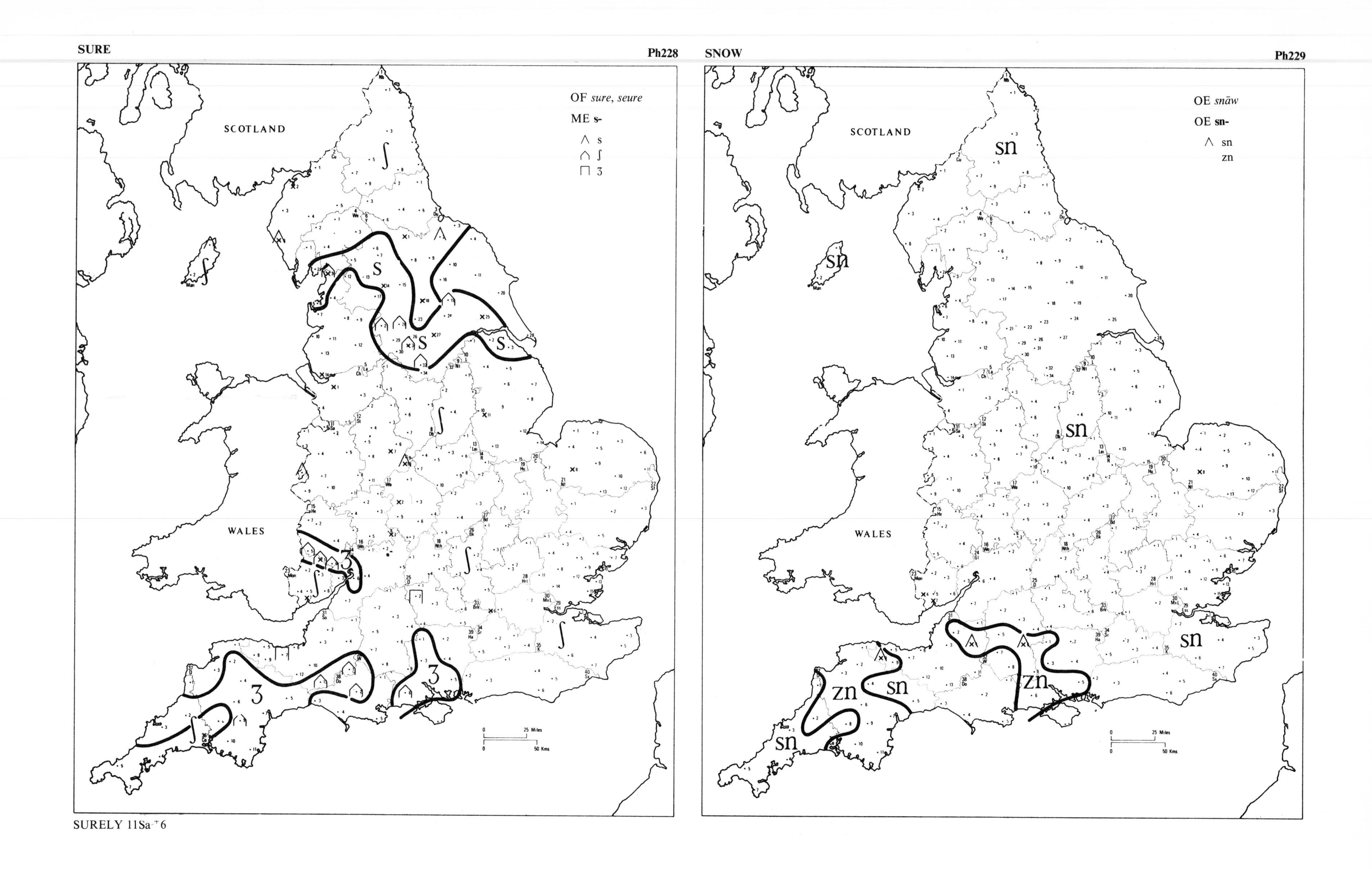

SURELY 11Sa⁺6

SWEARING **Ph230**

SWEAT **Ph231**

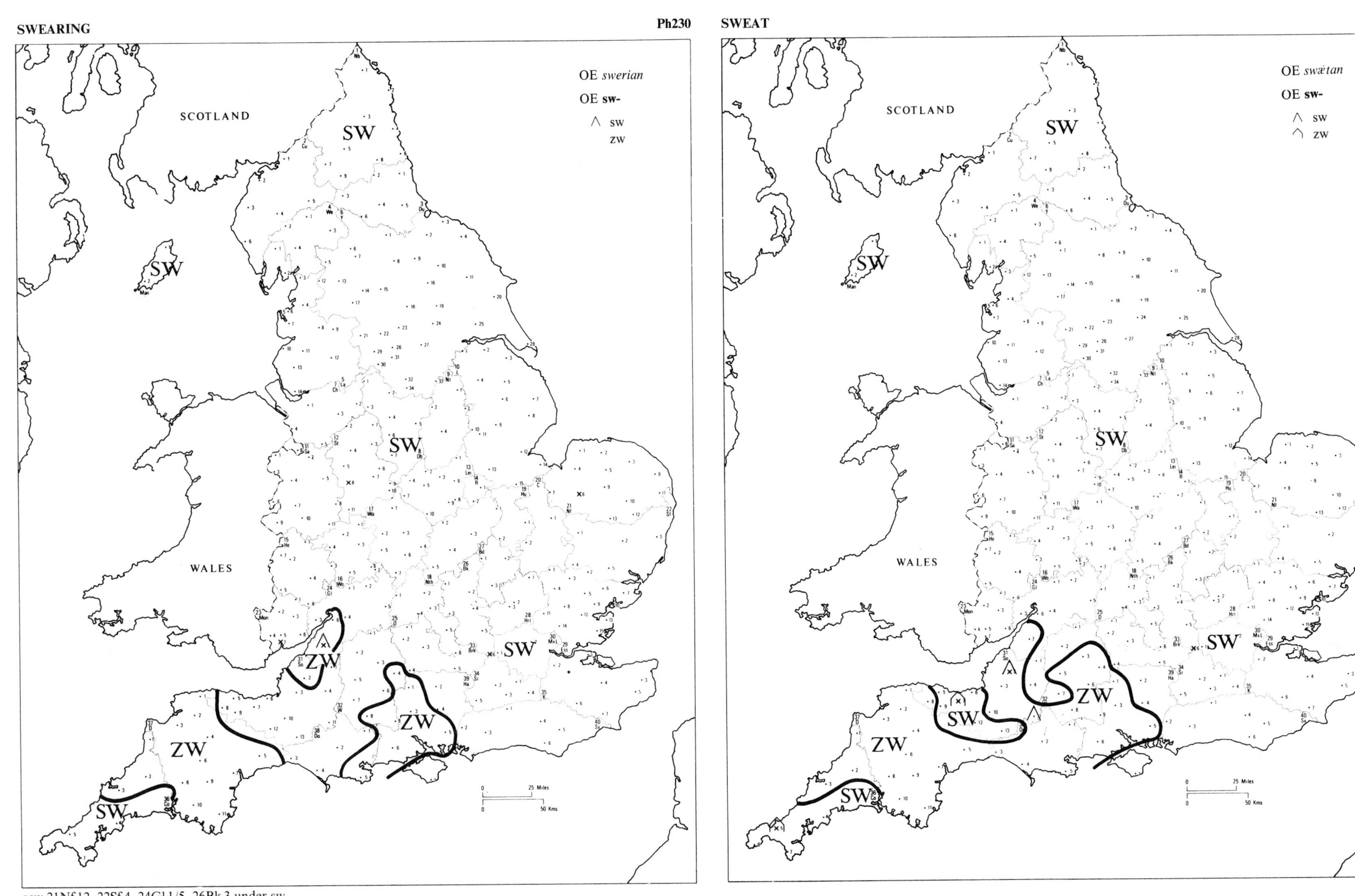

asw 21Nf 12, 22Sf 4. 24Gl 1/5, 26Bk 3 under sw

s 12St 8

sw in ASWORE pp 37D

THIGH Ph232

THIMBLE Ph233

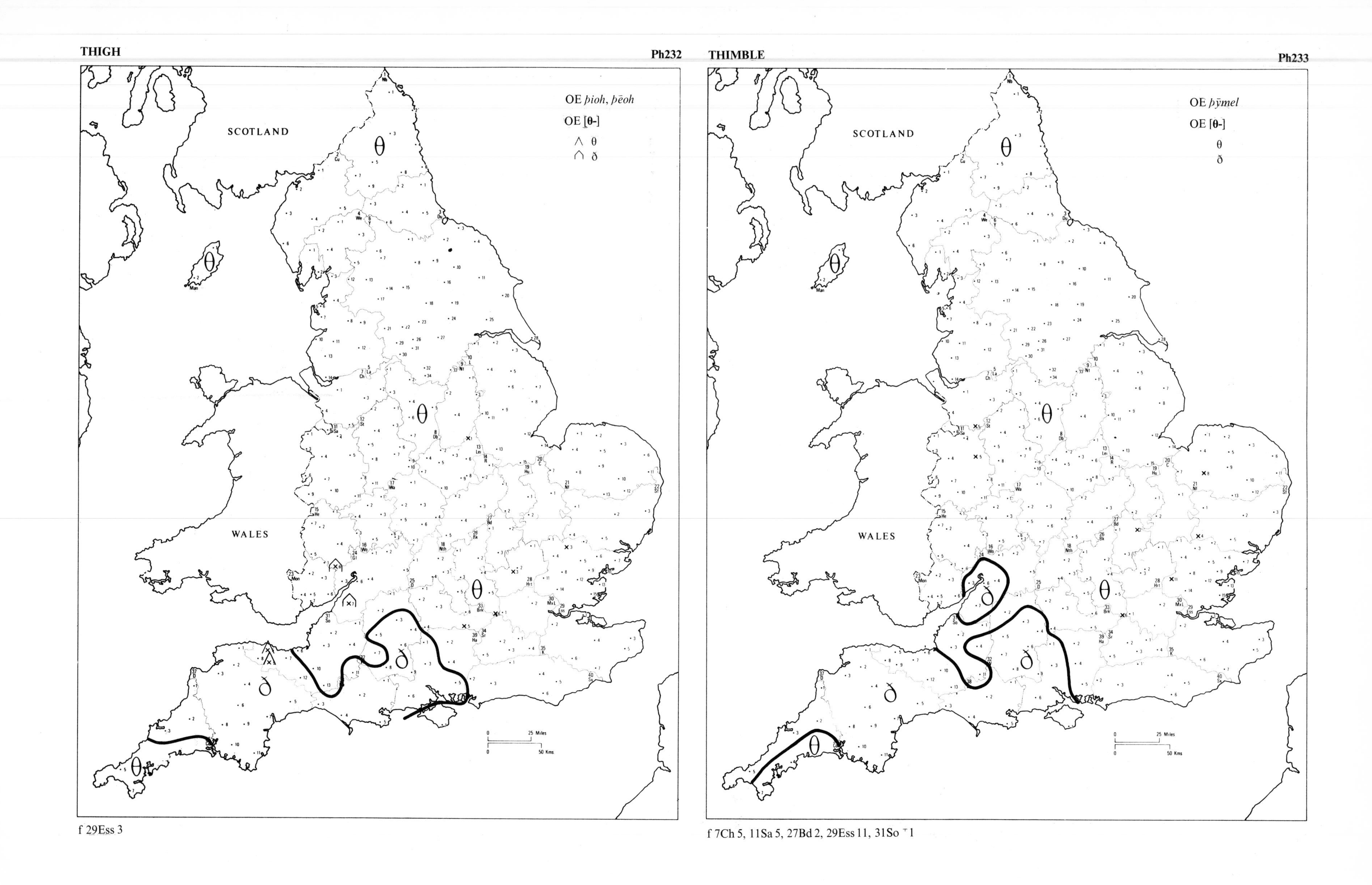

f 29Ess 3

f 7Ch 5, 11Sa 5, 27Bd 2, 29Ess 11, 31So ⁺1

THREE Ph234

THREAD Ph235

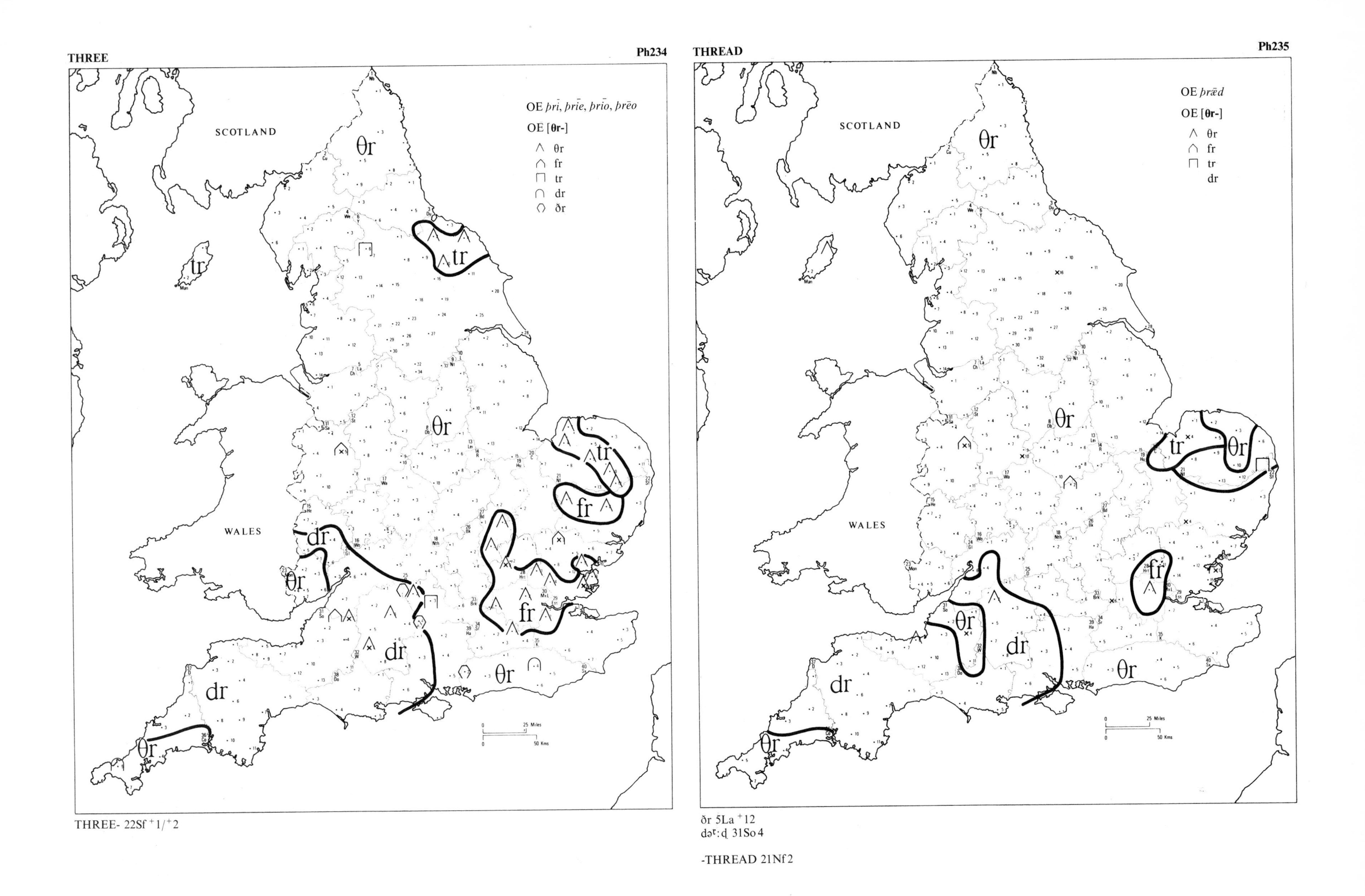

THREE- 22Sf $^{+}$1/$^{+}$2

ðr 5La $^{+}$12
dəʳ:d̨ 31So 4

-THREAD 21Nf 2

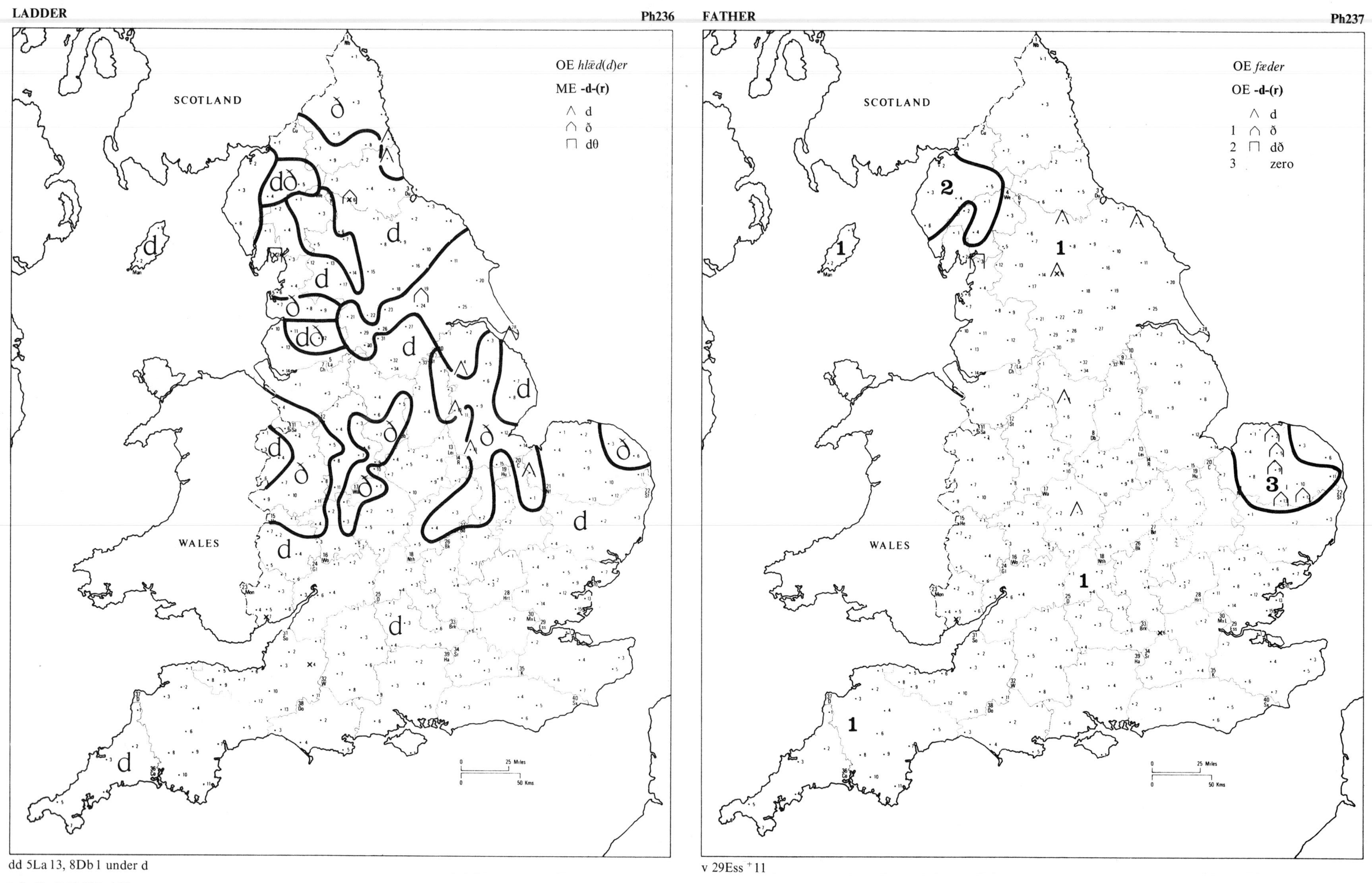

dd 5La 13, 8Db 1 under d

laðə ("stile") 12St +10

v 29Ess +11

MOTHER **Ph238**

BUTTER **Ph239**

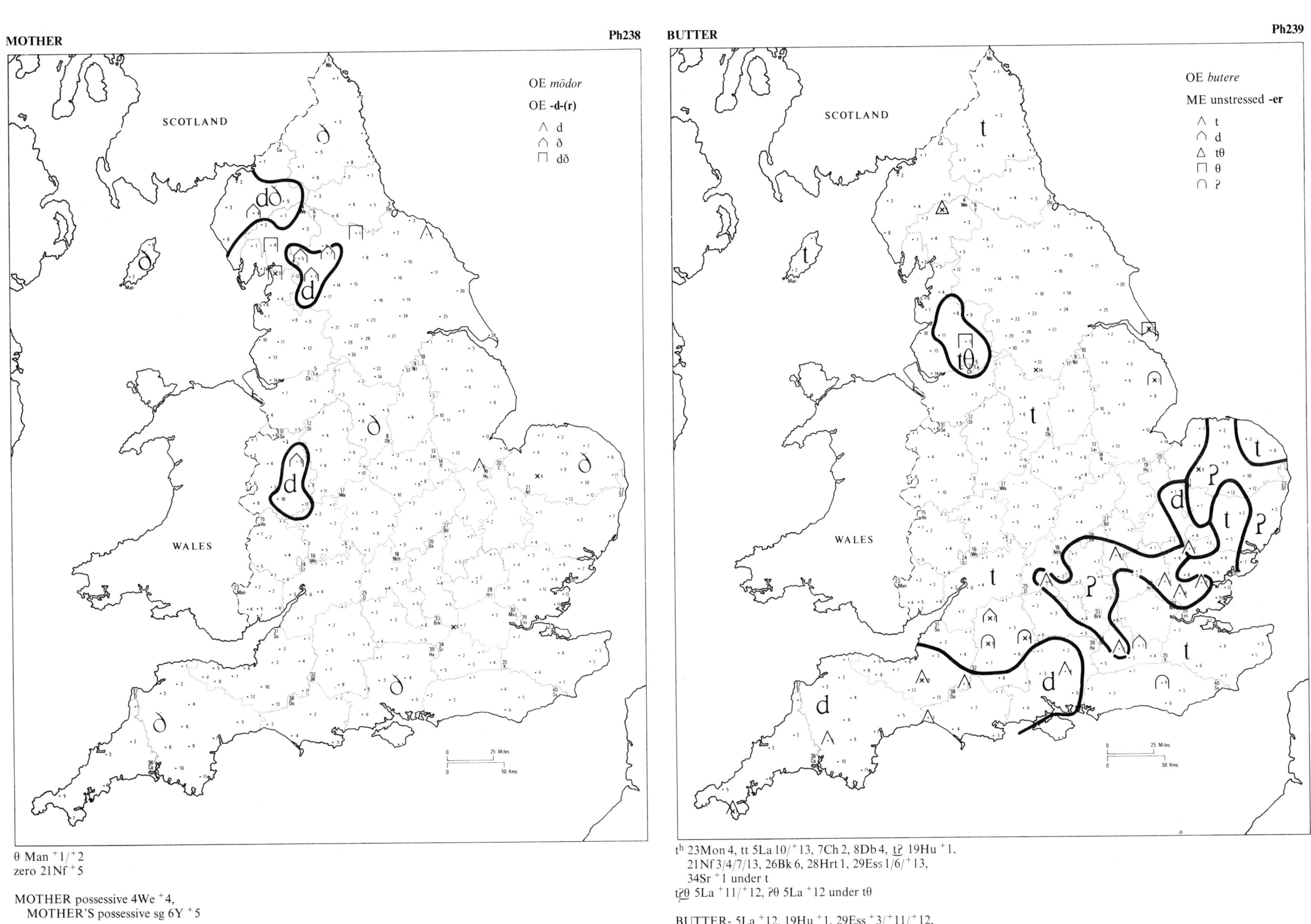

θ Man $^{+}$1/$^{+}$2
zero 21Nf $^{+}$5

MOTHER possessive 4We $^{+}$4,
MOTHER'S possessive sg 6Y $^{+}$5

t^{h} 23Mon 4, tt 5La 10/$^{+}$13, 7Ch 2, 8Db 4, tʔ 19Hu $^{+}$1.
21Nf 3/4/7/13, 26Bk 6, 28Hrt 1, 29Ess 1/6/$^{+}$13,
34Sr $^{+}$1 under t
tʔθ 5La $^{+}$11/$^{+}$12, ʔθ 5La $^{+}$12 under tθ

BUTTER- 5La $^{+}$12, 19Hu $^{+}$1, 29Ess $^{+}$3/$^{+}$11/$^{+}$12,
31So $^{+}$11, 34Sr $^{+}$2

FINGER Ph240 HUNGRY Ph241

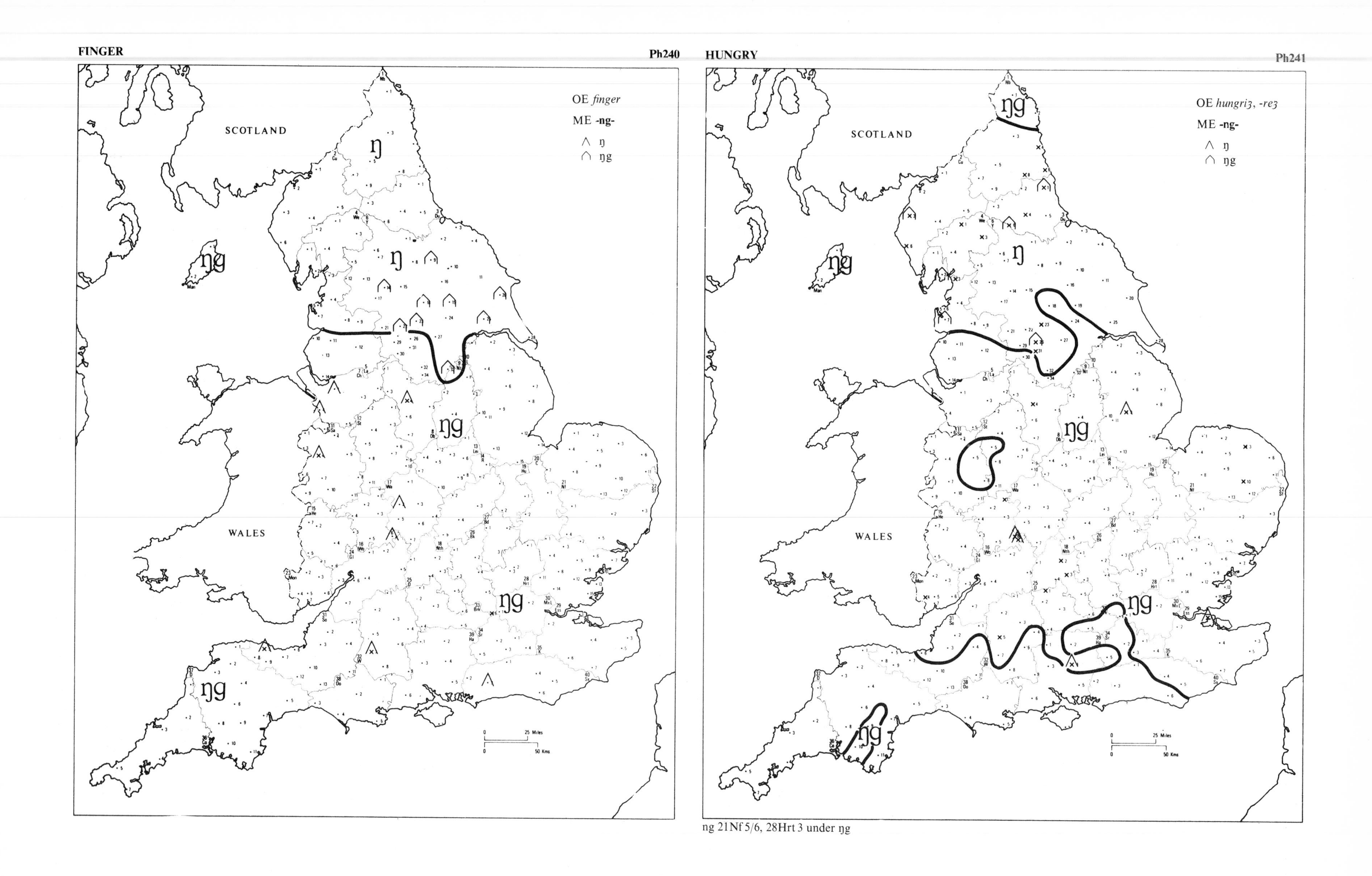

ng 21Nf 5/6, 28Hrt 3 under ŋg

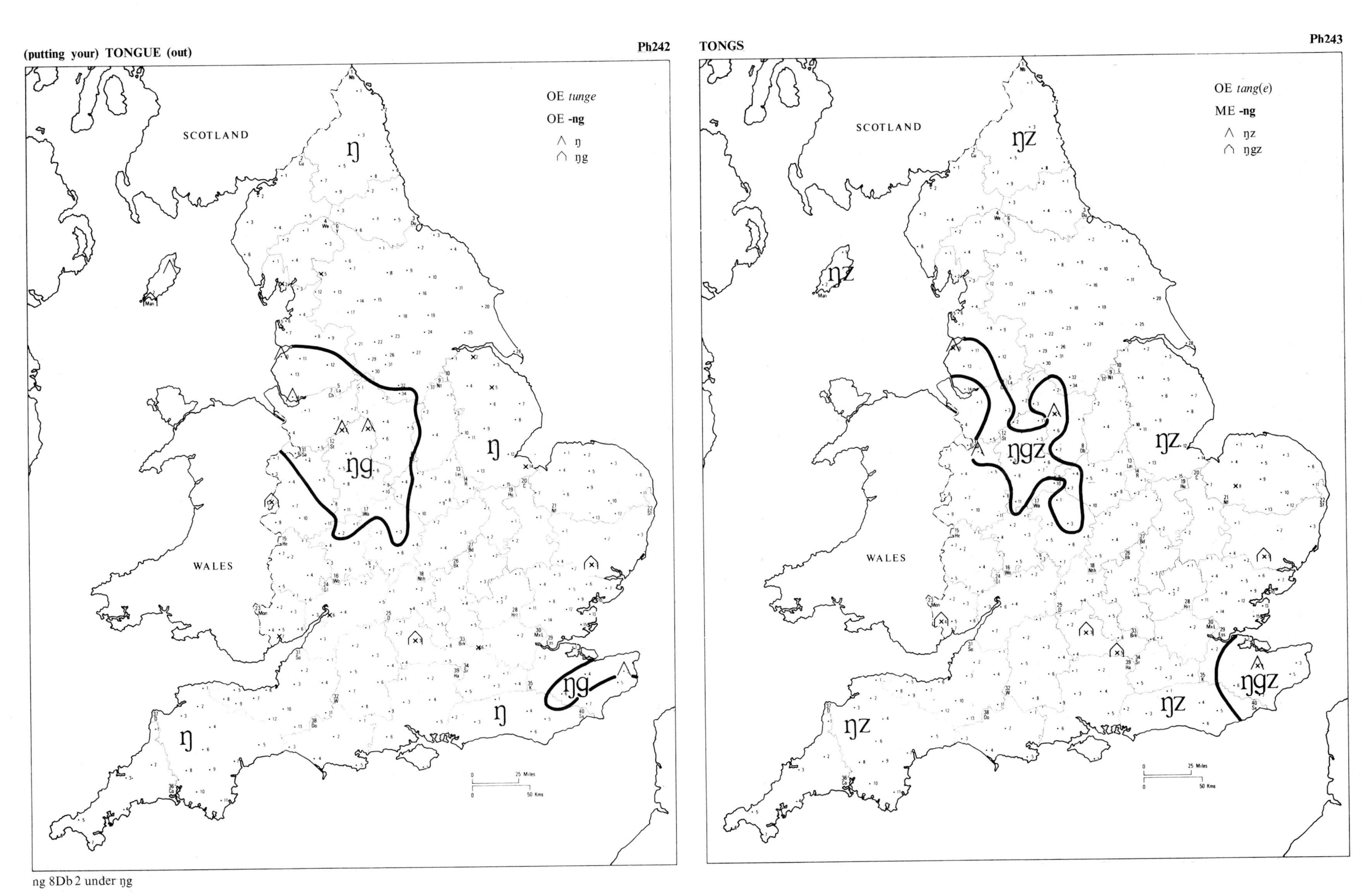

ng 8Db 2 under ŋg

TONGUE- 6Y 2

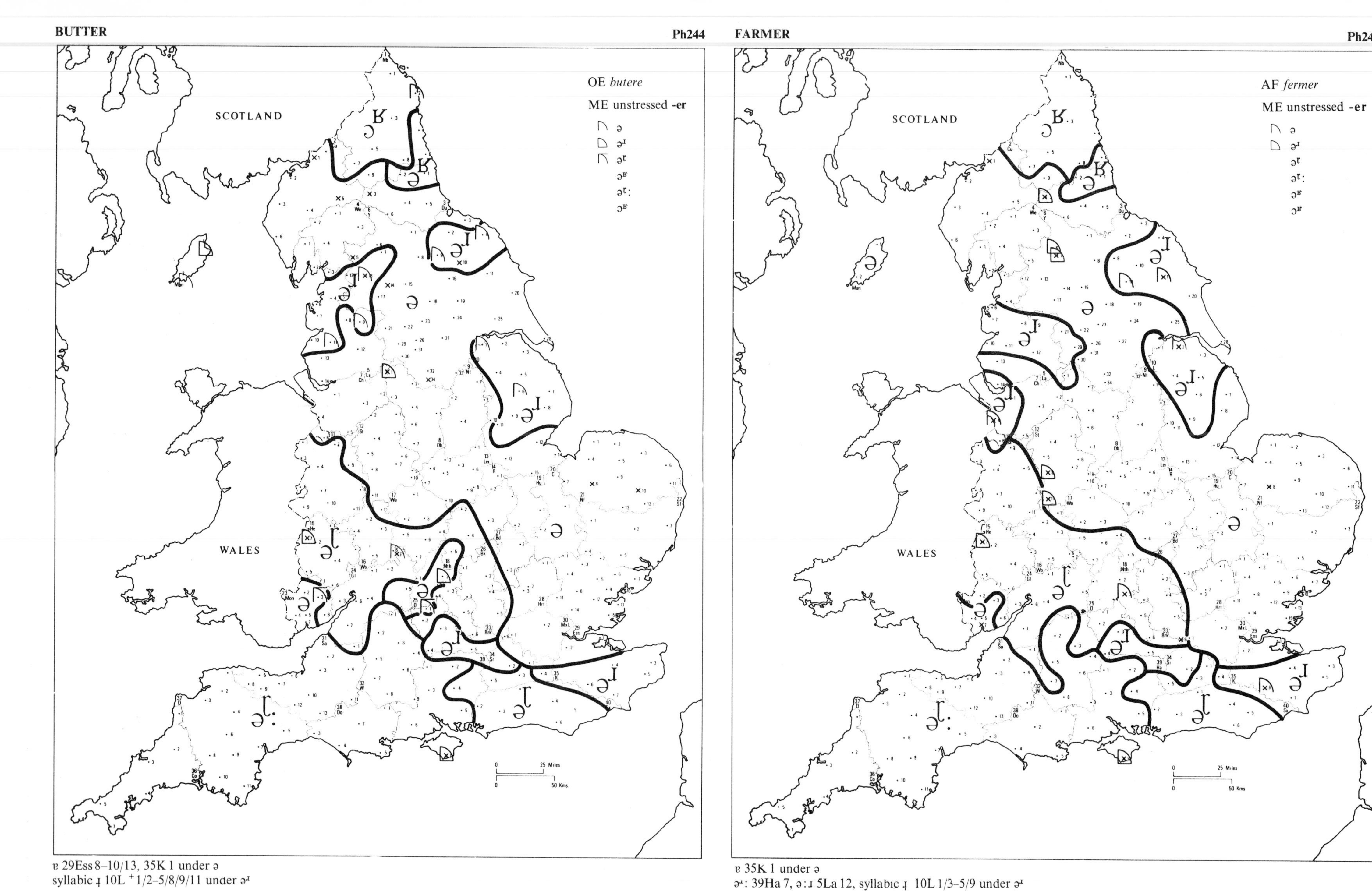

BUTTER — Ph244

ɐ 29Ess 8–10/13, 35K 1 under ə
syllabic ɻ 10L $^+$1/2–5/8/9/11 under əʴ

ɔr 2Cu 1, 3Du 3
əɾ 2Cu 5, 6Y 5/10/14/$^+$20

interpr as *r*-col: ɹ 5La 4/$^+$9/10/$^+$11, 6Y $^+$2/$^+$4/7/$^+$9, 10L $^+$1/2–5/8/9/11, 15He 7, 33Brk $^+$5, ɽ 25Ox 4/5
cons *r* foll *r*-col V: 40Sx $^+$1

BUTTER- 5La $^+$9, 33Brk $^+$5, 40Sx $^+$1

FARMER — Ph245

ɐ 35K 1 under ə
əʴ: 39Ha 7, ɔ:ɹ 5La 12, syllabic ɻ 10L 1/3–5/9 under əʴ

ər 2Cu 1

interpr as *r*-col: ɹ 3Du 3, 5La 8–12/14, 6Y 4/$^+$6/$^+$7/$^+$9/$^+$10, 10L 1/3–5/9, 12St 11, 15He 7, ɽ 25Ox 4

UNCLE Ph246

WEASEL Ph247

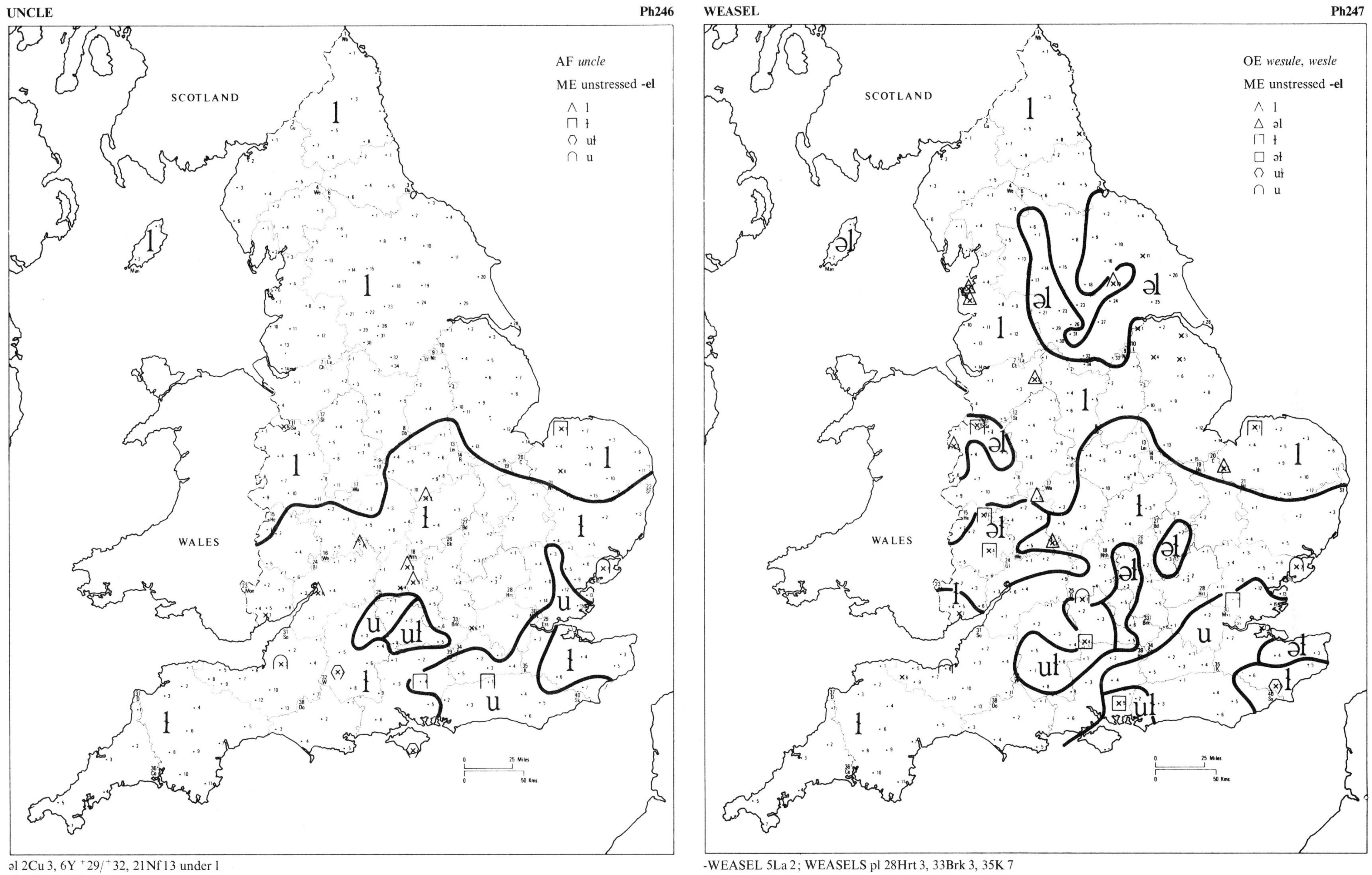

əl 2Cu 3, 6Y ⁺29/⁺32, 21Nf 13 under l
əɫ 26Bk 5 under ɫ

-WEASEL 5La 2; WEASELS pl 28Hrt 3, 33Brk 3, 35K 7

CABBAGE Ph248

DROUGHT Ph249

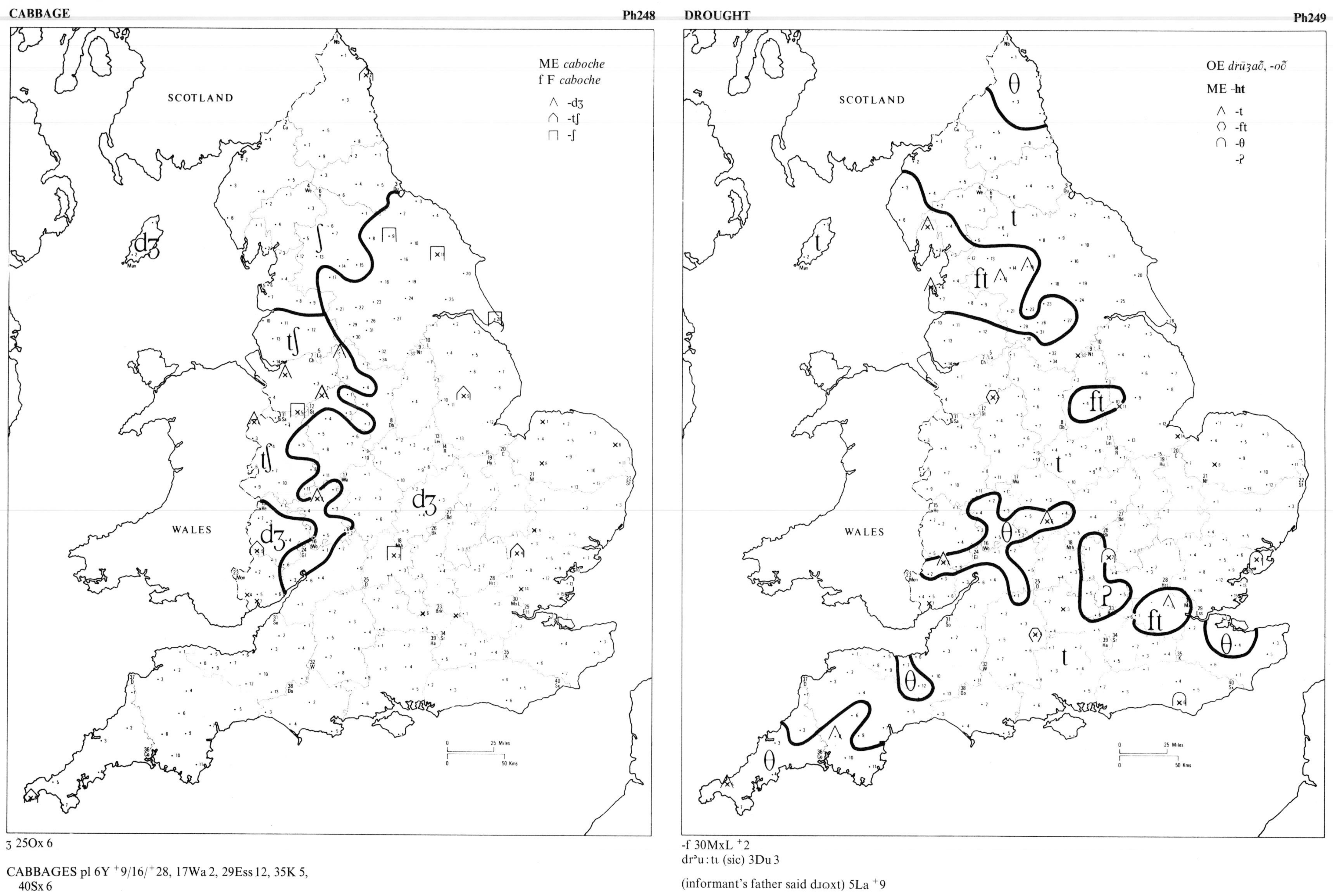

ʒ 25Ox 6

CABBAGES pl 6Y ⁺9/16/⁺28, 17Wa 2, 29Ess 12, 35K 5, 40Sx 6

-f 30MxL ⁺2

drᵊuːtɩ (sic) 3Du 3

(informant's father said dɹɒxt) 5La ⁺9

Lexical Maps

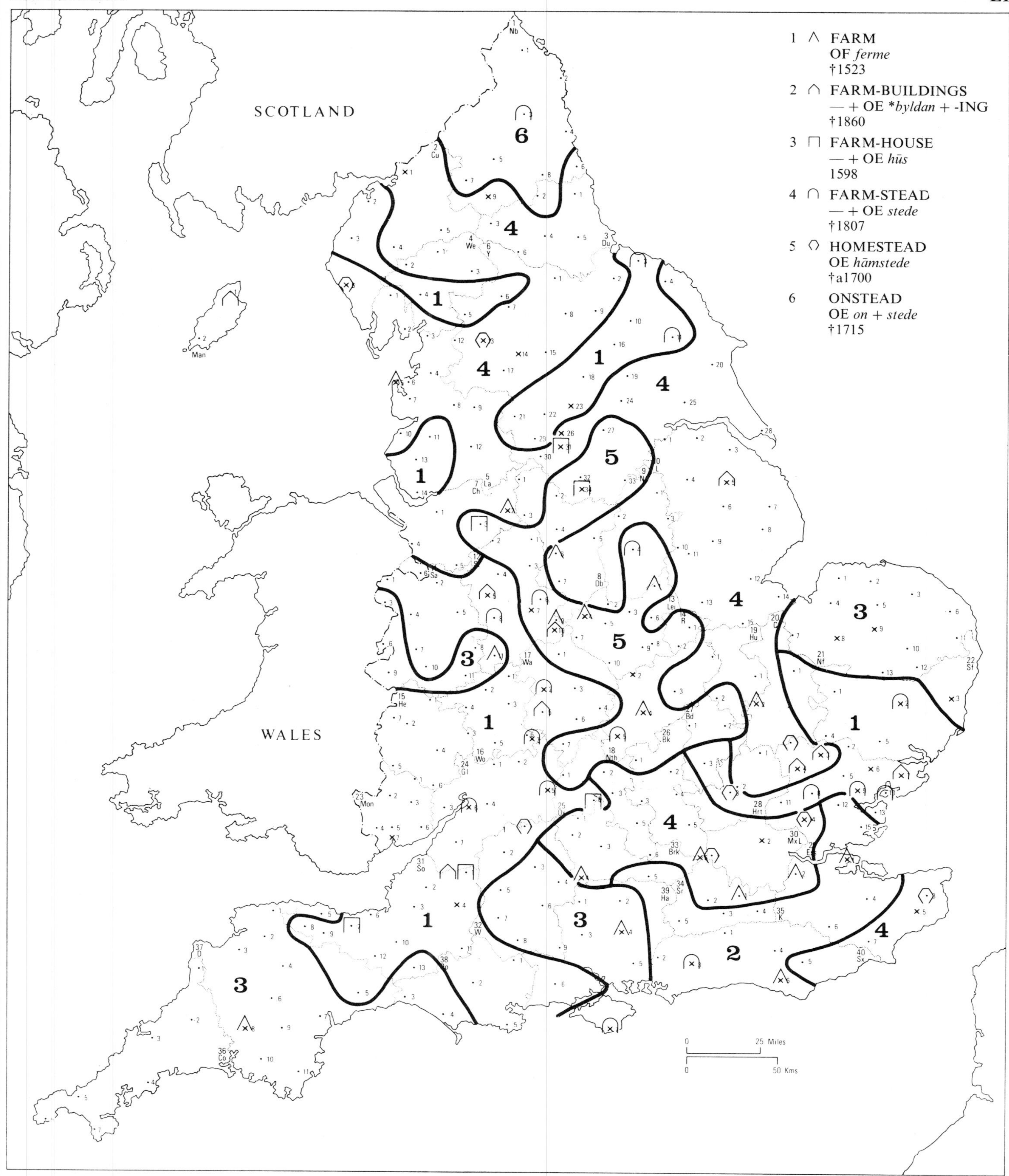

HOME(OE *hām*)-FARM 2OC 2 under FARM
FARM-BUILDING 34Sr 3,
BUILDINGS 29Ess 3 under
FARM-BUILDINGS
HOUSE 21Nf 2/4/12 under FARM-HOUSE

Although the question was designed to elicit a response meaning "a farm with the buildings on it", (FARM-)HOUSE apparently refers to the house only

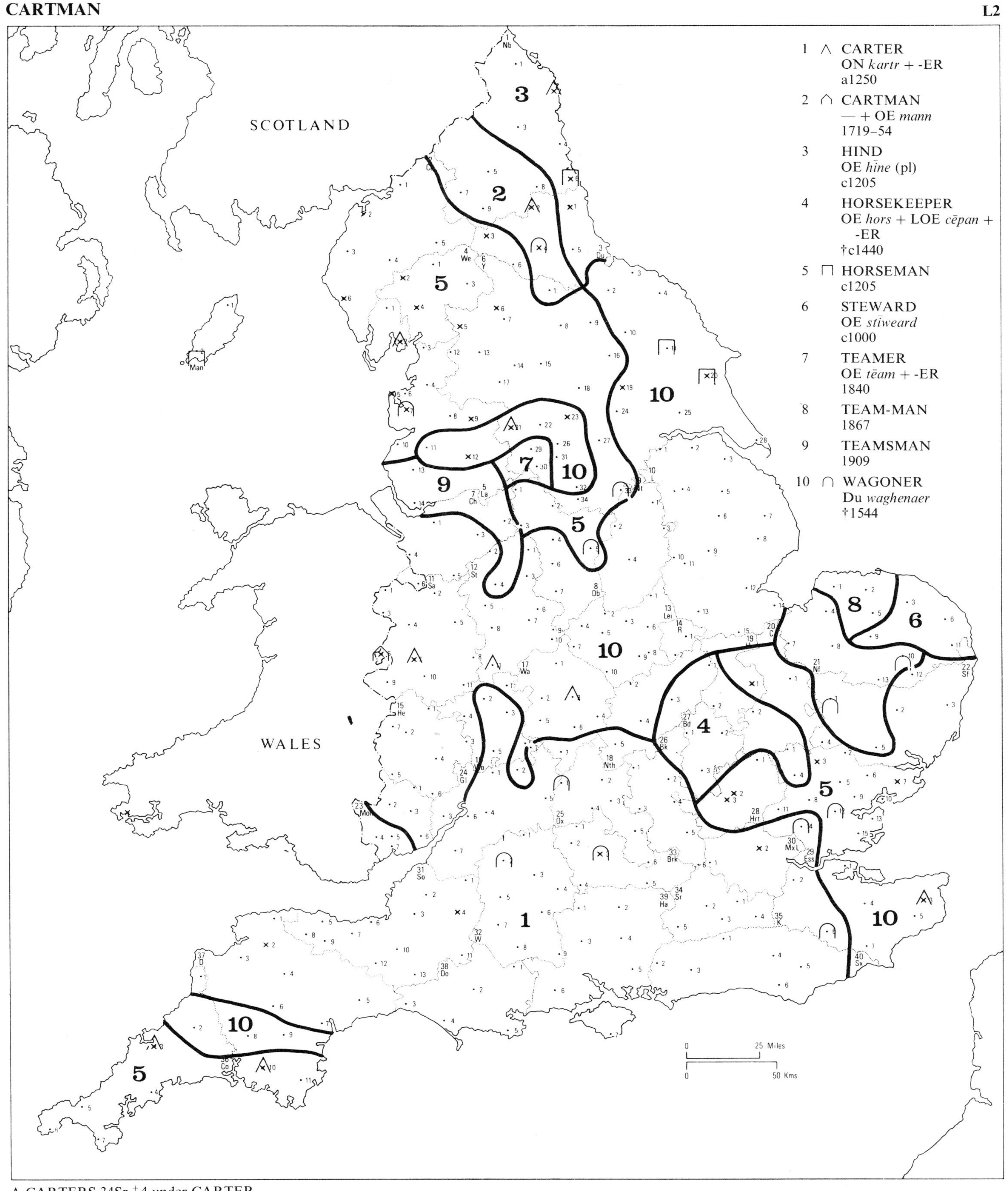

A CARTERS 34Sr ⁺4 under CARTER
HEAD(OE *hēafod*)-HORSEMAN 21Nf 12,
22Sf 2/⁺3, 29Ess 13 under HORSEMAN
A WAGONERS 33Brk 3,
HEAD WAGONER 11Sa ⁺5, 15He ⁺7,
WAG 6Y ⁺11 under WAGONER

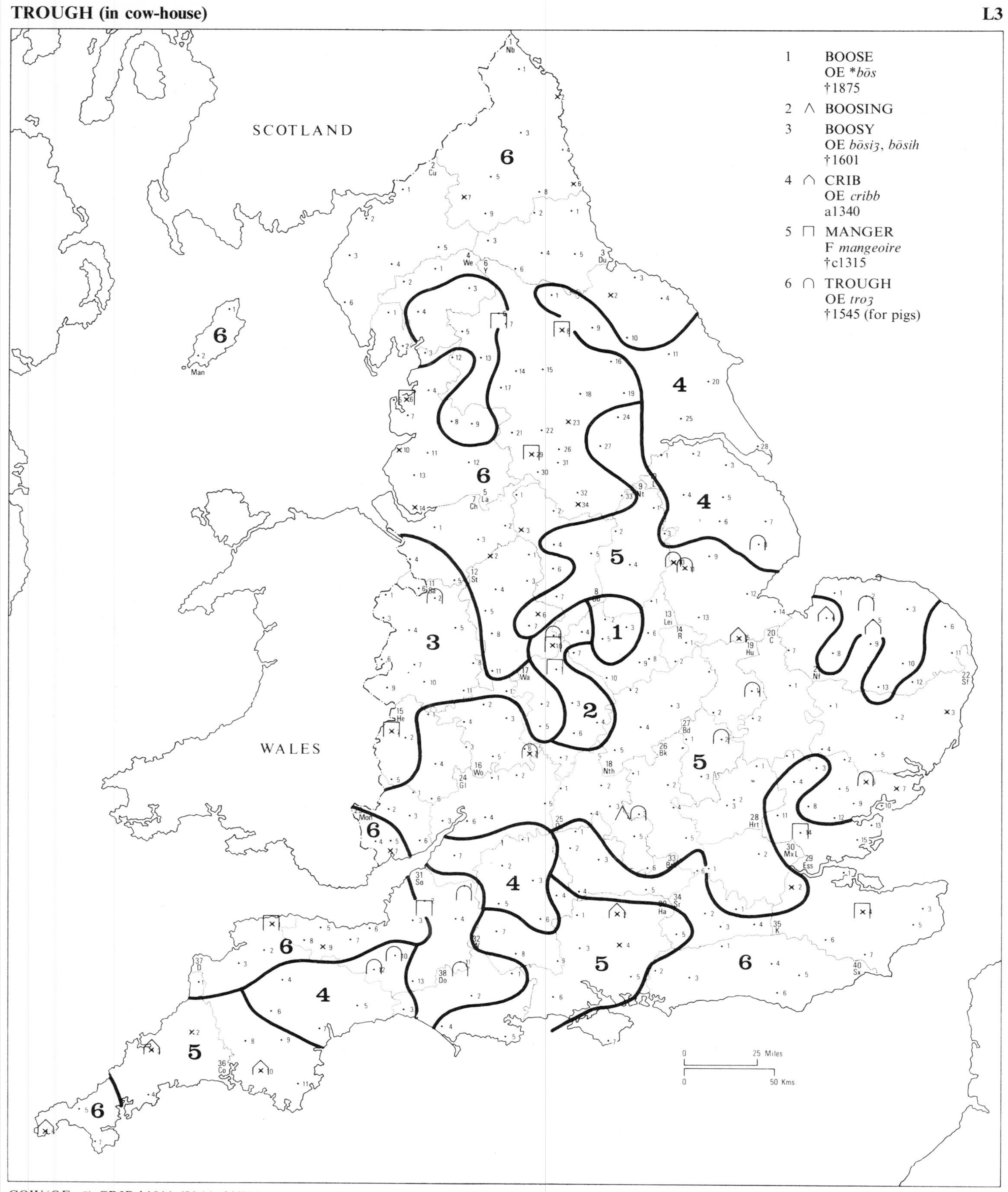

COW(OE *cū*)-CRIB †1811 6Y 11, 32W 1, 37D 5/⁺7 under CRIB
CATTLE(ME *catel* f ONF *catel*)-TROUGH †1887 6Y ⁺22, COW-TROUGH 6Y 30, FEEDING(OE *fedan*)-TROUGH 6Y 10, 29Ess 11, 36Co ⁺5, LICK(OE *liccian*)-TROUGH 6Y ⁺22, PROVIN(f F *provende*)-TROUGH 5La ⁺12 under TROUGH

STRETCHER (of harness) **L4a**

STRETCHER (of harness) **L4b**

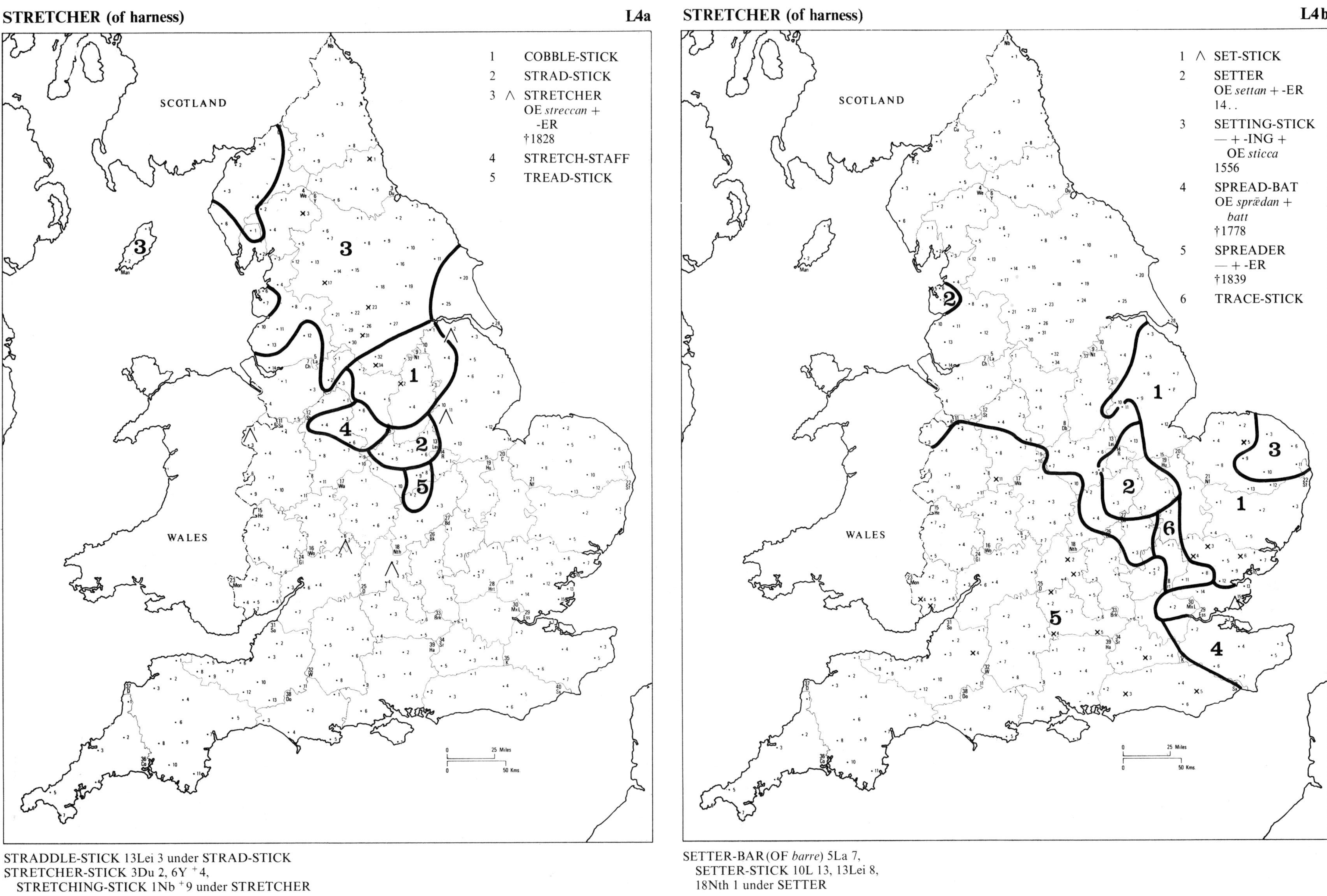

STRADDLE-STICK 13Lei 3 under STRAD-STICK
STRETCHER-STICK 3Du 2, 6Y +4,
STRETCHING-STICK 1Nb +9 under STRETCHER

stɛtʃstaf 12St 6 pres error for stɹɛtʃ Edd

SETTER-BAR (OF *barre*) 5La 7,
SETTER-STICK 10L 13, 13Lei 8,
18Nth 1 under SETTER

sɛtʃstik 21Nf 1 is taken to repr SET-STICK

TRACE-HORSE L5a

TRACE-HORSE L5b

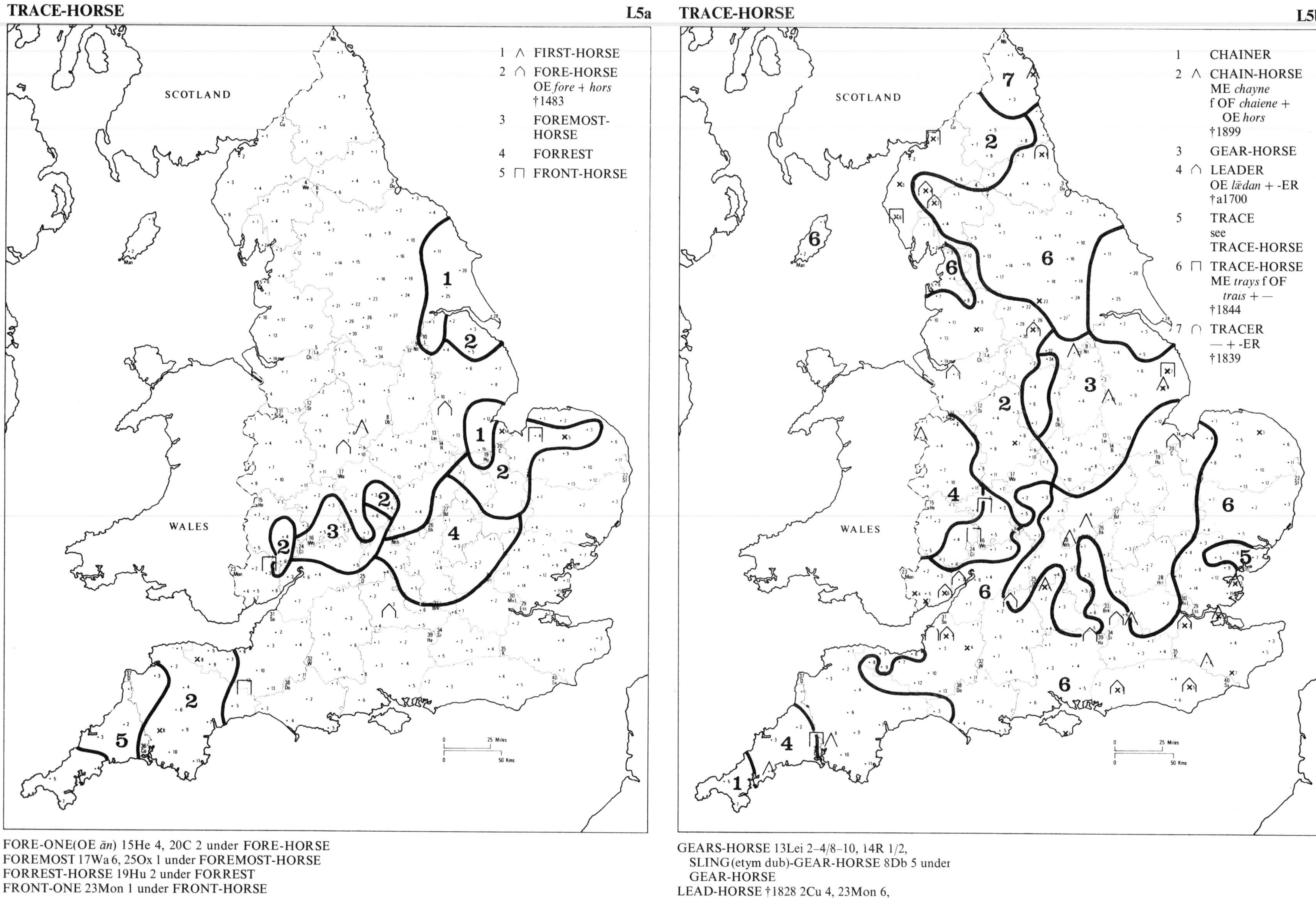

FORE-ONE(OE *ān*) 15He 4, 20C 2 under FORE-HORSE
FOREMOST 17Wa 6, 25Ox 1 under FOREMOST-HORSE
FORREST-HORSE 19Hu 2 under FORREST
FRONT-ONE 23Mon 1 under FRONT-HORSE

GEARS-HORSE 13Lei 2–4/8–10, 14R 1/2,
SLING(etym dub)-GEAR-HORSE 8Db 5 under GEAR-HORSE
LEAD-HORSE †1828 2Cu 4, 23Mon 6,
LEADING-HORSE 10L 14, 40Sx 3 under LEADER

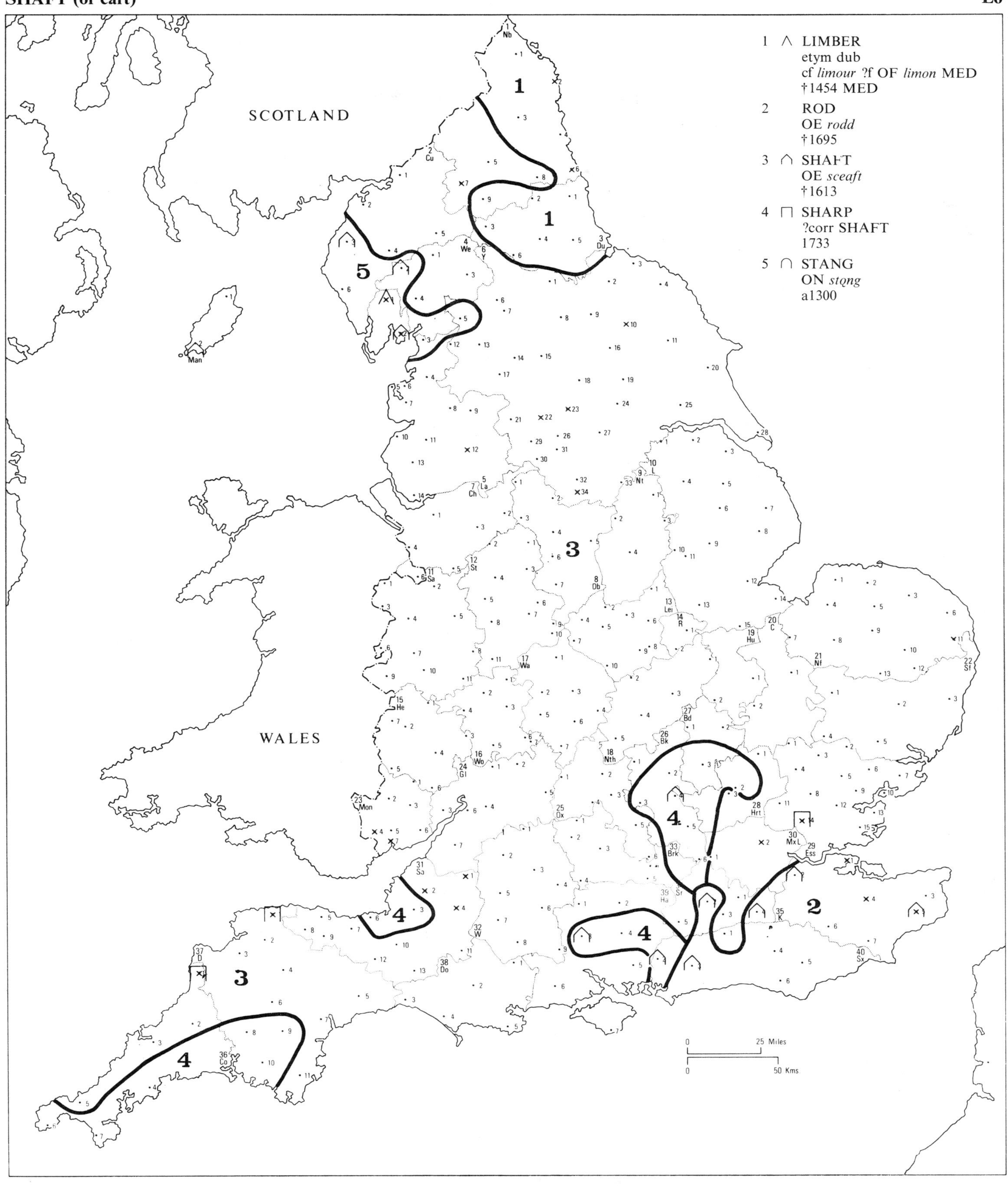
1 ∧ LIMBER
etym dub
cf *limour* ?f OF *limon* MED
†1454 MED
2 ROD
OE *rodd*
†1695
3 ∩ SHAFT
OE *sceaft*
†1613
4 ⊓ SHARP
?corr SHAFT
1733
5 ∩ STANG
ON *stǫng*
a1300
SCOTLAND
WALES
25 Miles
50 Kms

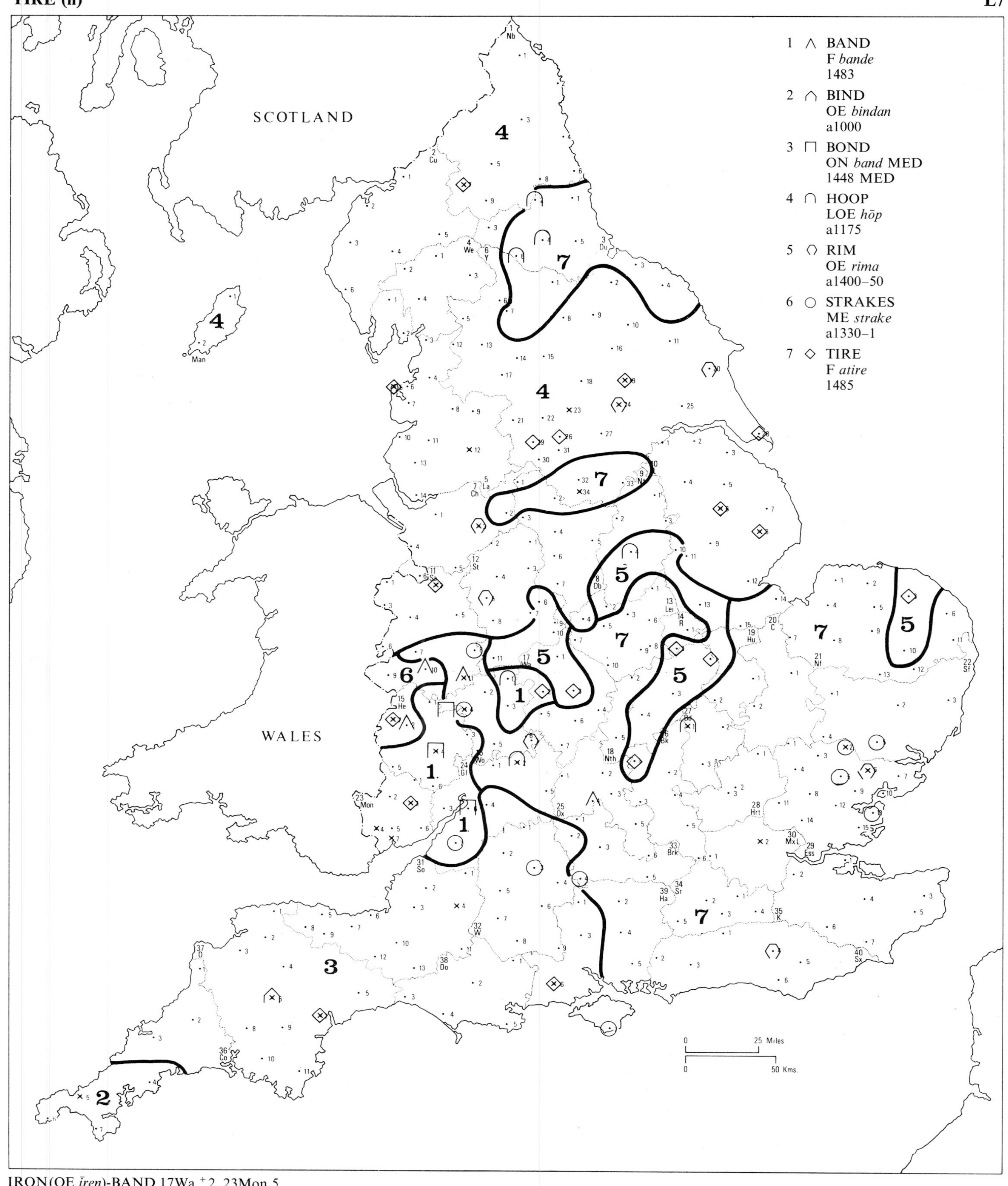

IRON(OE *īren*)-BAND 17Wa +2, 23Mon 5,
IRON-BANDING 16Wo 3 under BAND
BONDING 37D 5 under BOND
CART (ON *kartr*)-HOOP 6Y 27,
HOOPING 6Y 9 under HOOP
IRON-RIM 21Nf 10 under RIM
STREAKS 22Sf +5, 29Ess 2/+5/+13, 39Ha +7,
STRIGS (sic) 33Brk +4 under STRAKES
IRON-TIRE 13Lei 3, 29Ess 11, 30MxL 1,
SHOD(OE *scōgan*)-TIRE 18Nth +1 under
TIRE

TIP (v) L8a

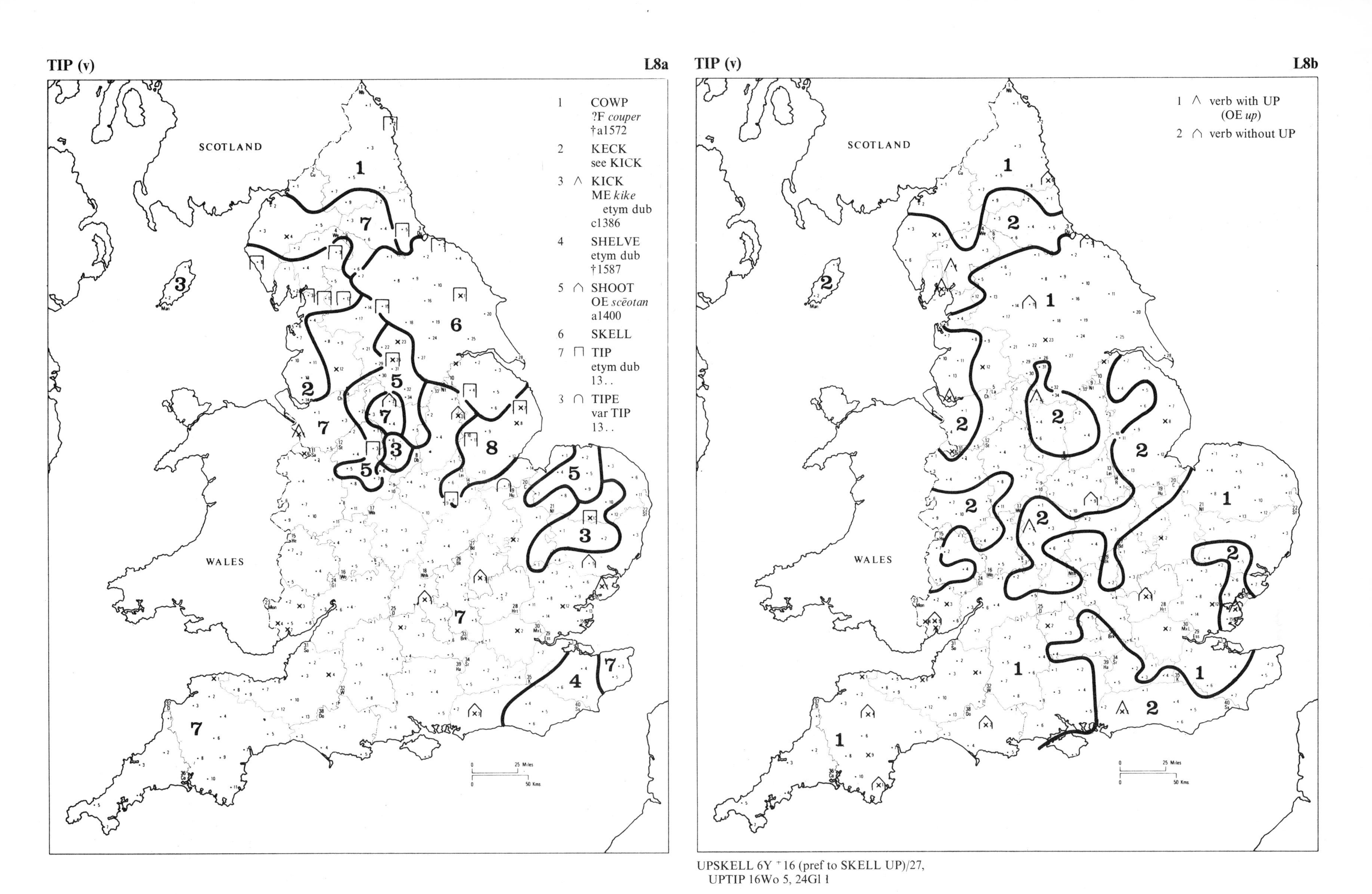

TIP (v) L8b

UPSKELL 6Y +16 (pref to SKELL UP)/27,
UPTIP 16Wo 5, 24Gl 1

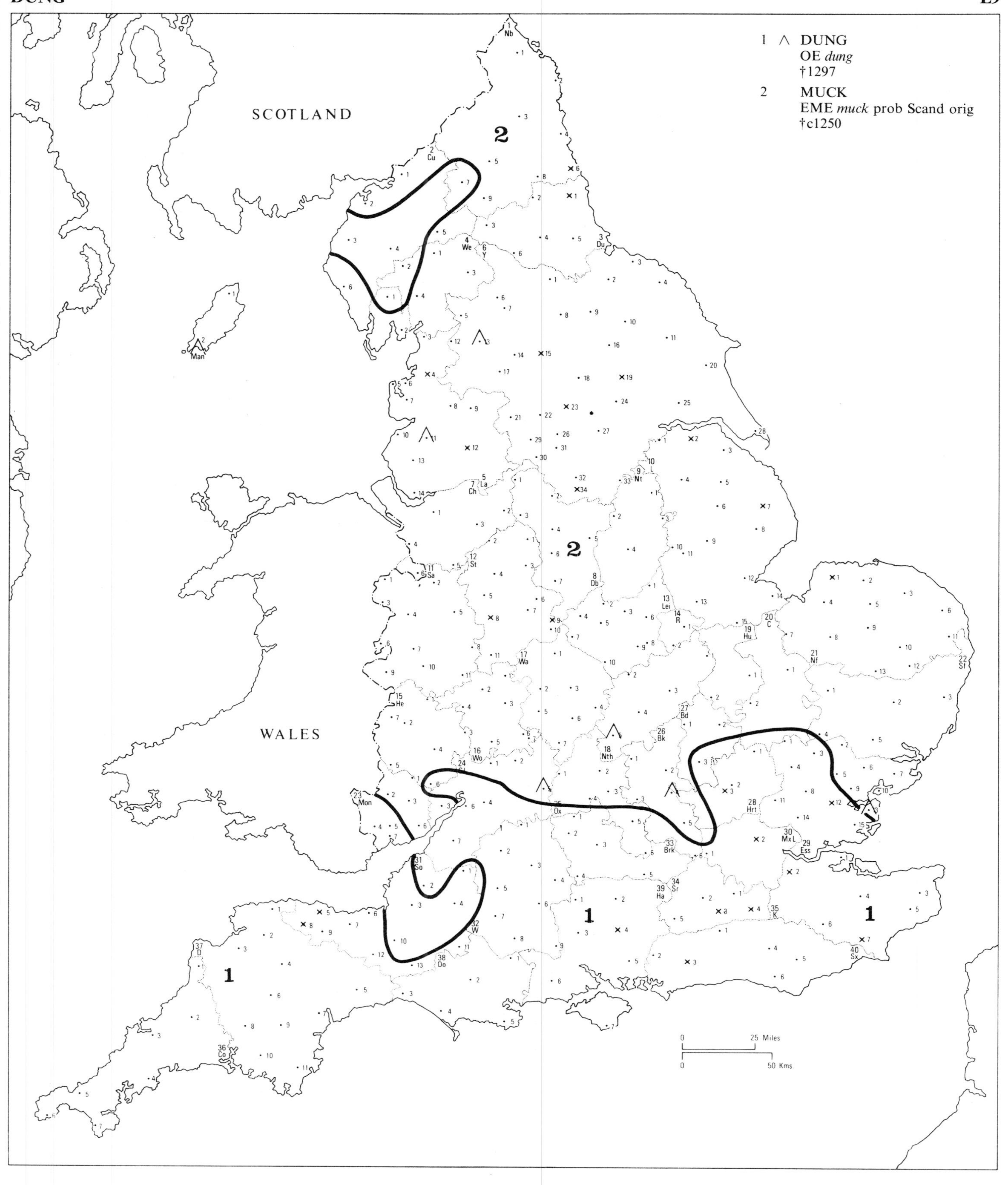
1 ∧ DUNG
OE *dung*
†1297
2 MUCK
EME *muck* prob Scand orig
†c1250
SCOTLAND
WALES
2
2
1
1
1
0 25 Miles
0 50 Kms

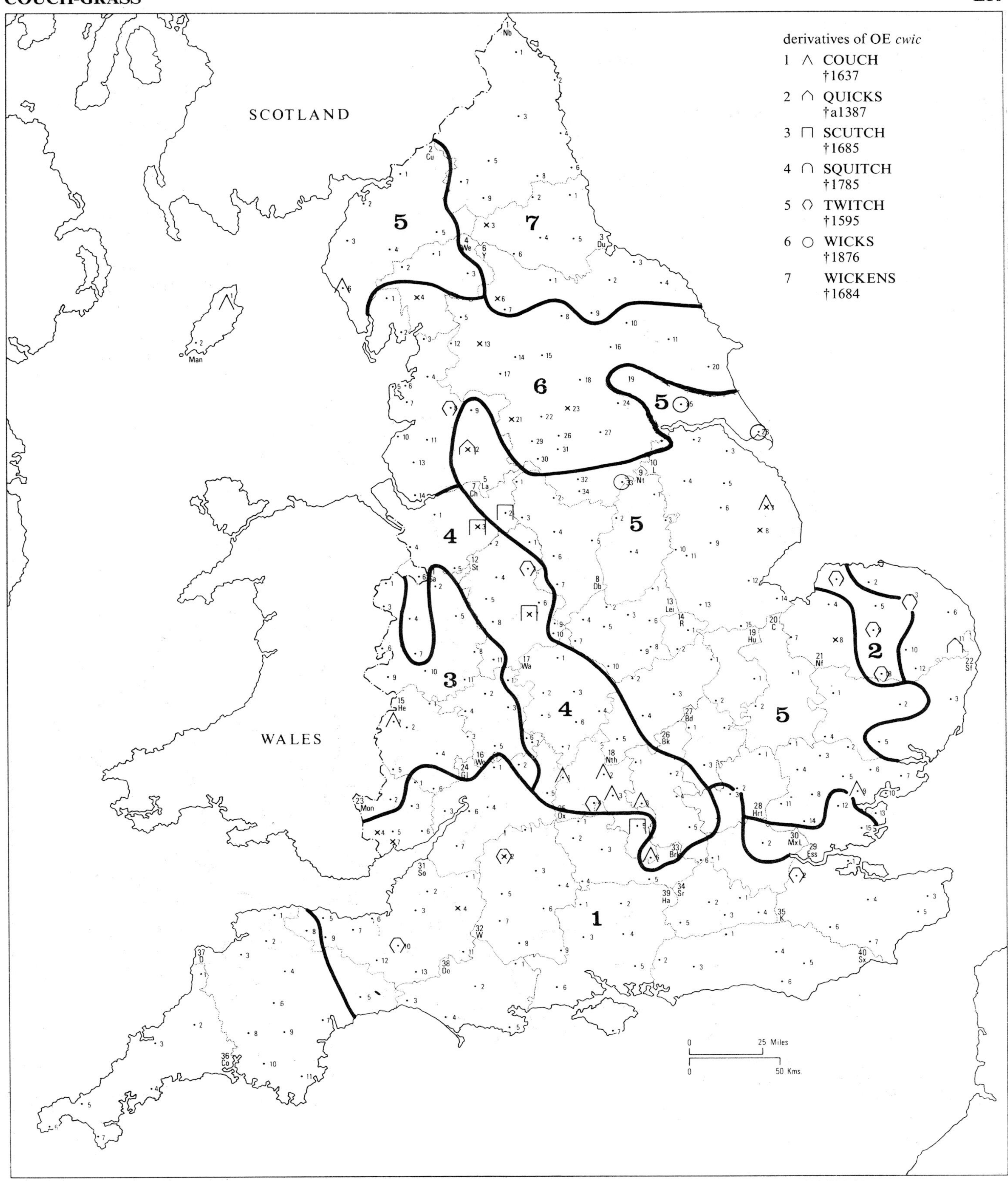

COUCH-GRASS(OE *græs*) †1578 Man 1, 10L 7, 15He +7, 23Mon 5, 29Ess +9, 30MxL 1, 31So 1–3/6/7/+10/12, 32W 1/7, 33Brk 2/5, 34Sr 5, 35K 1/3–5/7, 37D 5, 39Ha +5/6/7, 40Sx 2/3, STRING(OE *streng*)-COUCH (informant unsure) 24Gl 7 under COUCH
QUICK †1483 21Nf +13, QUICK-GRASS †1617 5La 12 under QUICKS

SCUTCH-GRASS †1685 15He +7, SCWUTCH 24Gl 2 under SCUTCH
SCITCH 16Wo 1, SQUITCH-GRASS †1846 17Wa 2 under SQUITCH
STRING-TWITCH 29Ess +2, TWITCH-GRASS †1707 6Y 32, 7Ch +2, 10L 3/13, 18Nth 1, 21Nf +4, 31So +10 under TWITCH

WICK †1876 5La 5, 6Y +8, WICK-GRASS 6Y 26/31/+33, WILKS 5La 4/6/7 under WICKS
WICKEN 1Nb 1–3, 6Y 7, WICKEN-GRASS †1858 3Du 1 under WICKENS

kwəːtʃ 28Hrt 3 pres repr COUCH

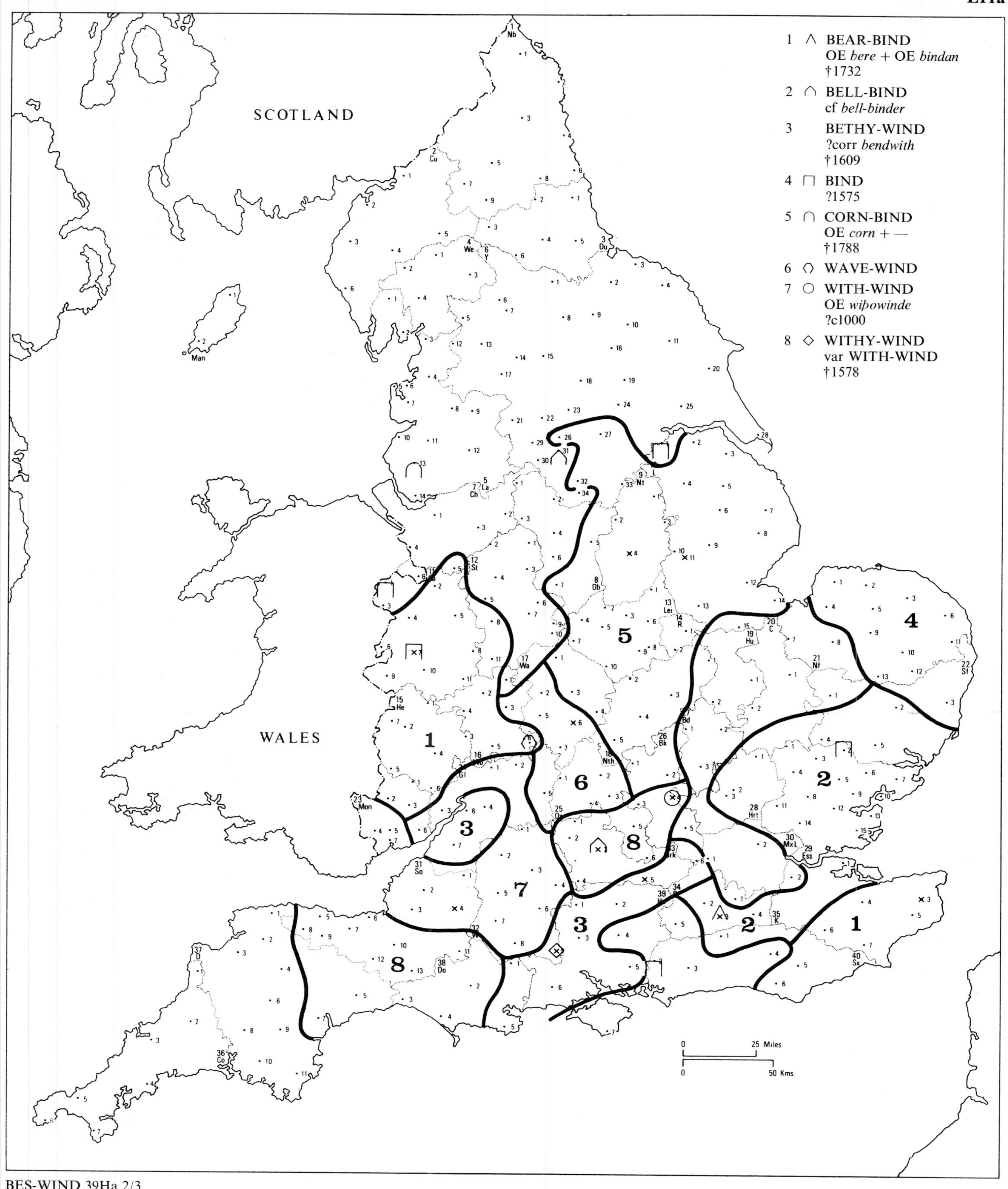

BES-WIND 39Ha 2/3,
BETH-WIND 26Bk 6,
BETTY-WIND 24Gl 4/6,
BITH-WIND 39Ha 1,
BITHY-WIND 38Do 1/5,
39Ha 6 under BETHY-WIND
WAY-WIND 16Wo 3, 17Wa 2/5/7,
25Ox 2–4 under WAVE-WIND
WID-WIND 31So 2–3, WIDDY-WIND 31So 5
under WITHY-WIND

wɛəʳwɒɪnd 16Wo 3 pres repr WAY-WIND

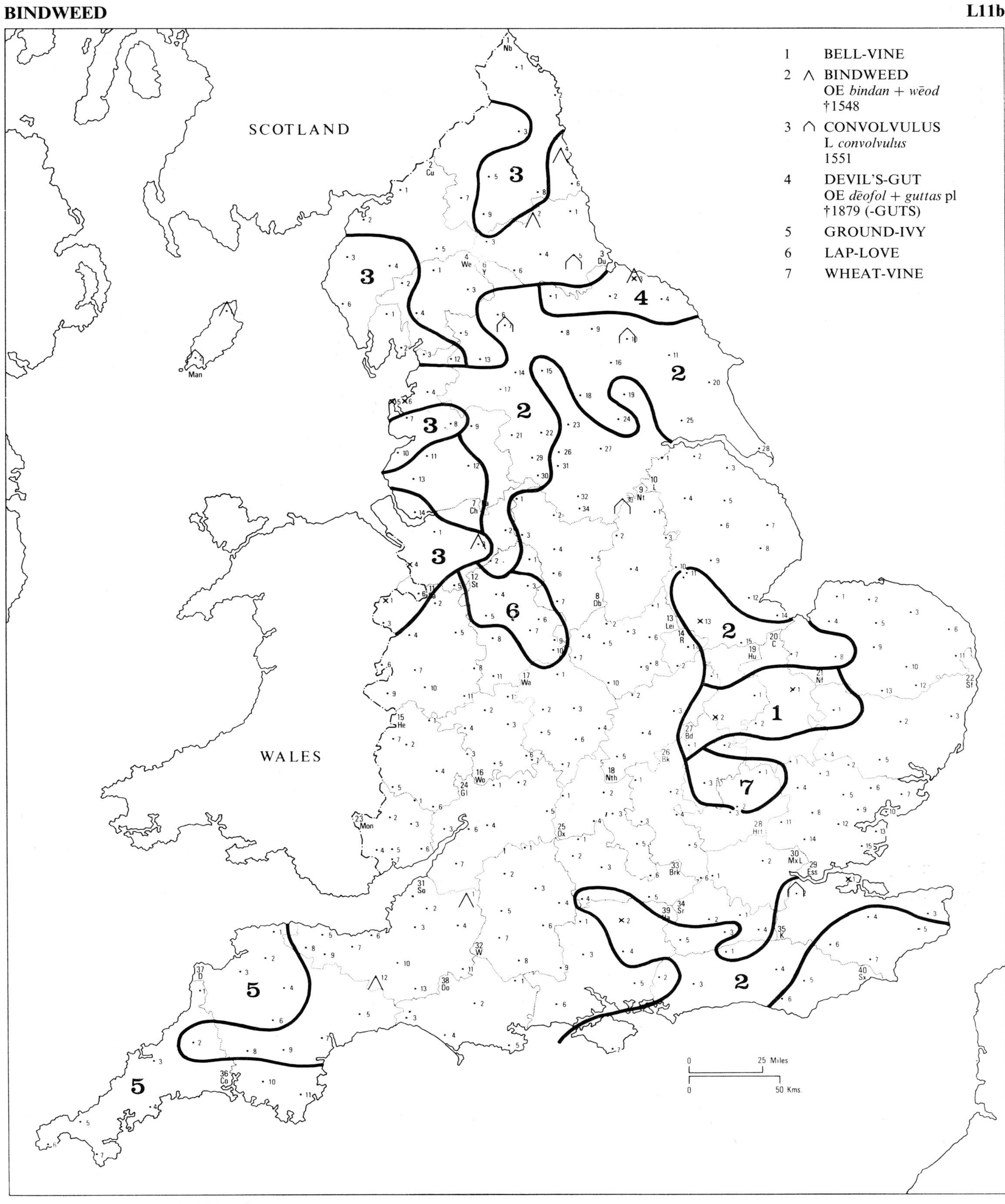

BIND-WOOD(OE *wudu*) 6Y 8/18 under
BIND-WEED
WILD(OE *wilde*) CONVOLVULUS
35K +2 under CONVOLVULUS

kɒlvɒdʒən 5La 8 pres repr CONVOLVULUS

GOOSE-GRASS L12a

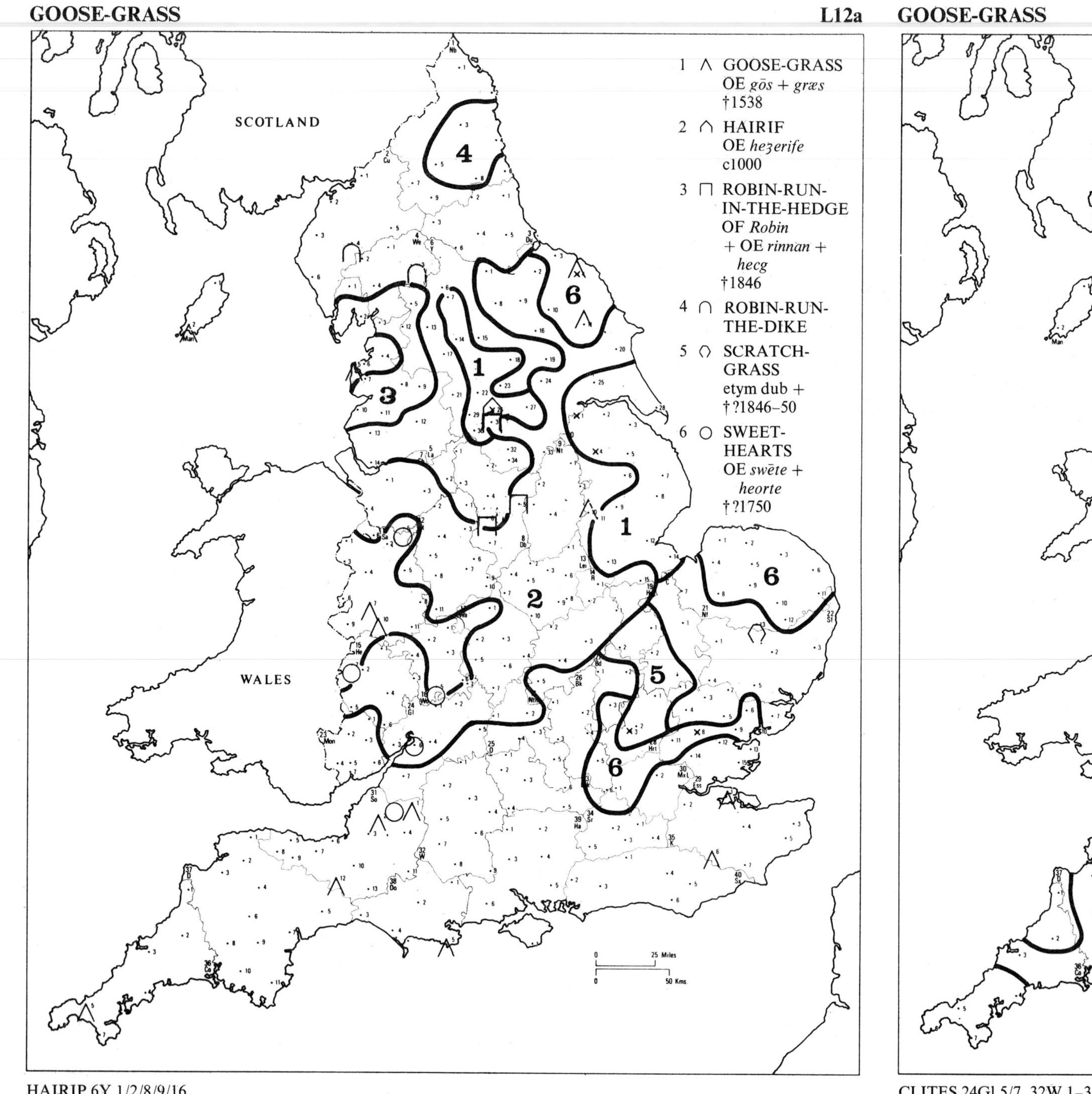

HAIRIP 6Y 1/2/8/9/16,
HAIRIS 6Y 26/⁺31 under HAIRIF
ROBIN-RUN-UP(OE *up*)-THE-DIKE 2Cu 4 under ROBIN-RUN-THE-DIKE
SCRATCH-WEED(OE *wēod*) 19Hu 1, 21Nf 13 under SCRATCH-GRASS
SWEETHEART 6Y 3/10, 21Nf 3/8/11/12, 26Bk 6, 29Ess 6/9 under SWEET-HEARTS

GOOSE-GRASS L12b

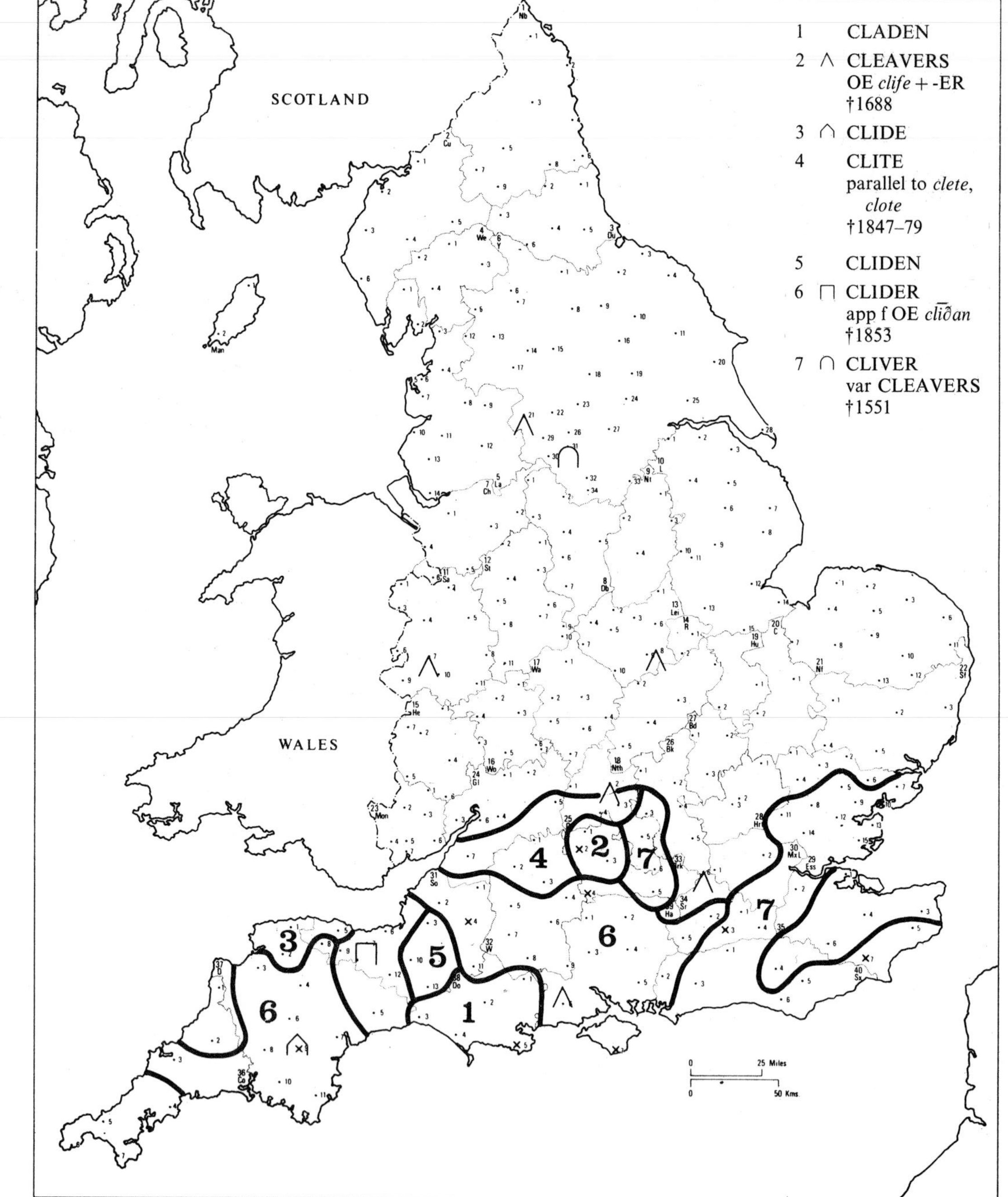

CLITES 24Gl 5/7, 32W 1–3 under CLITE
CLIDERS 32W 9, 34Sr 5, 39Ha 2/3/⁺6, 40Sx 2 under CLIDER
CLIVERS 6Y 31, 25Ox 5/6, 26Bk 3, 33Brk 5, 34Sr 4, 40Sx 3/6 under CLIVER

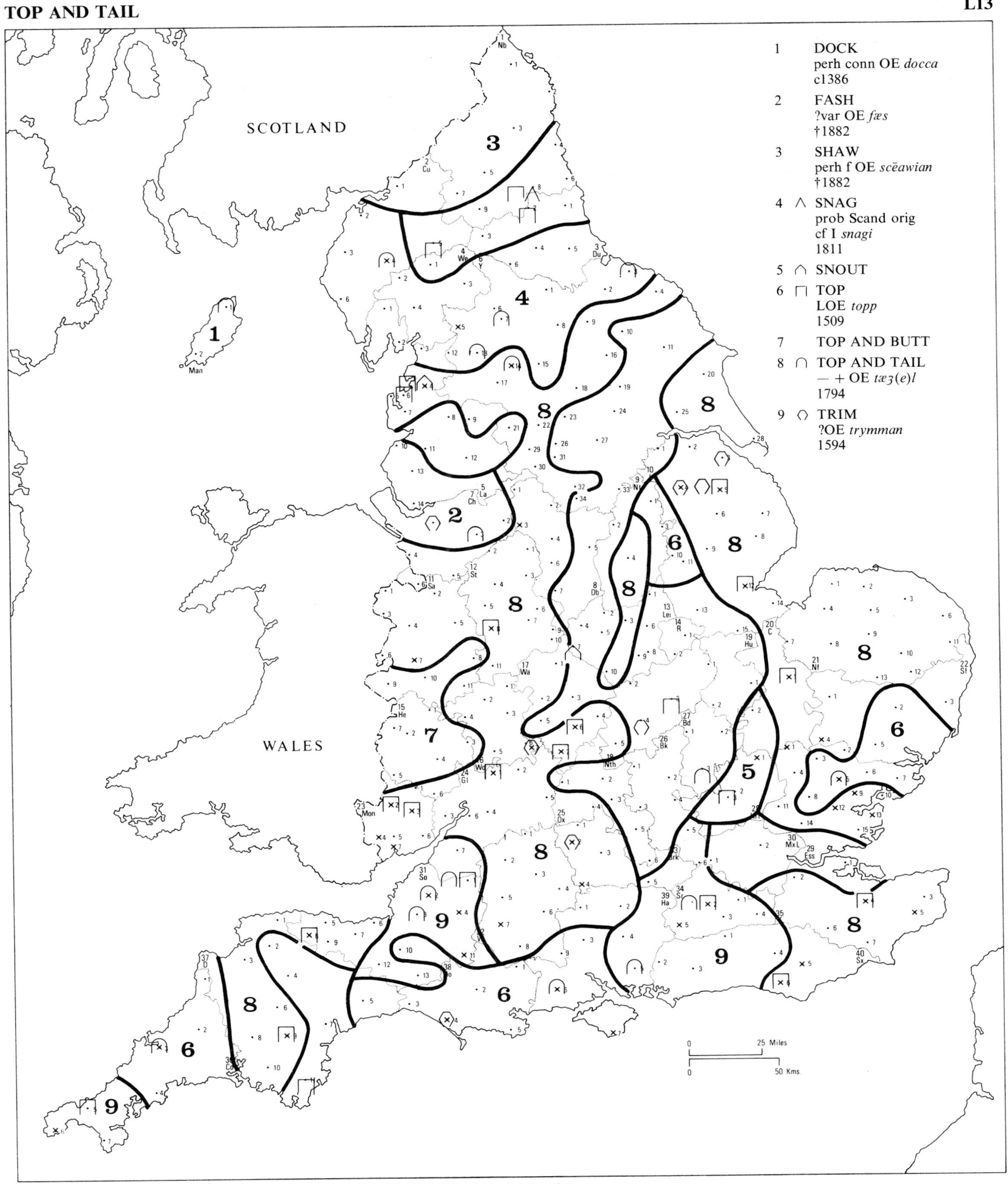

ROOT AND SHAW 1Nb 1/2 under SHAW
TOP AND SNOUT 5La 4 under SNOUT
CLEAN AND TOP 9Nt 1/3, 10L 10,
17Wa 6, 18Nth 3, MORE AND TOP 36Co 4,
ROOT AND TOP 1Nb +8, 2Cu 5, 3Du 2,
31So +1, 34Sr +2, TIP AND TOP 35K 4,
TOP AND BOTTOM 10L 11, 12St +8,
TOP AND MORE 37D 11,
TOP AND ROOT 36Co 1,
TOP AND SNOUT 5La 4,
TOP AND TRIM 10L 5,
TRIM AND TOP 36Co +5 under TOP

BUTT AND TOP 11Sa 9/10 under
TOP AND BUTT
HEAD AND TAIL 24Gl 6,
TAIL AND HEAD 35K 3,
TAIL AND TOP 13Lei 10,
17Wa 2 under TOP AND TAIL
SWEDE(f MLG, MDu *swede*)-TRIM 34Sr 4,
TOP AND TRIM 10L 5,
TRIM AND TOP 36Co +5,
TRIM OFF 31So +3, 39Ha 4,
TRIM UP 18Nth 4, 33Brk 2 under TRIM

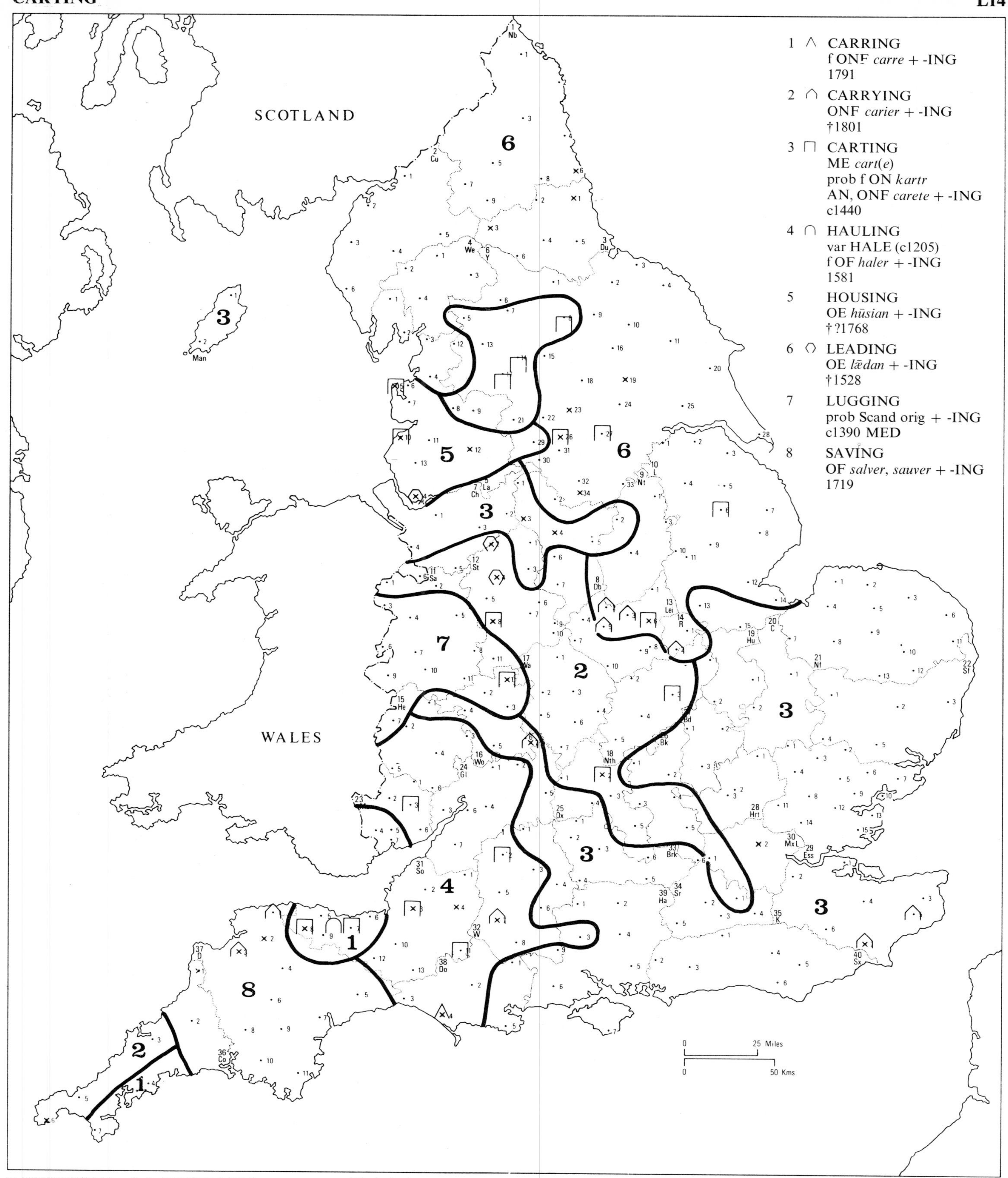

HARVEST(OE *hærfest*)-CARRY 35K 7 under CARRY

BARLEY(OE *bærlic*)-CART 32W ⁺6, 39Ha 5 im, CART CORN(OE *corn*) 21Nf 11, 29Ess 7, CART HOME(OE *hām*) 35K 4, CART OUT(OE *ūt*) 38Do 1, CORN-CART 12St 1, 33Brk 4, 39Ha 1/2/6, HARVEST-CART 32W 4, 33Brk 5, 34Sr 2, 40Sx 1, OAT(OE *āte*)-CART 39Ha 1im/5im, WHEAT(OE *hwǣte*)-CART 32W ⁺6, 39Ha 1im/5 under CART

CORN-HAUL 15He 3, 24Gl 1, 31So ⁺11 under HAUL

LEAD THE CORN 8Db 2, 13Lei ⁺2 under LEAD

LUG WHEAT 16Wo 3 under LUG

Though the response strictly required a verbal noun, the simple infinitive was frequently rec and responses have throughout been modified to this

Though it might seem to mean primarily "getting (the corn) under cover", HOUSE occurs so frequently as to warrant inclusion here as an appropriate response

kæ·ɽɩn, kæ·ɽᵗɩn 34Sr 1 are taken to represent CARRY(ING)

kjəʳ:ɽʔn 39Ha 7, kɑʳ:ɽʔɩn 40Sx 3 are taken to represent CART(ING)

RIDGE (of stack)

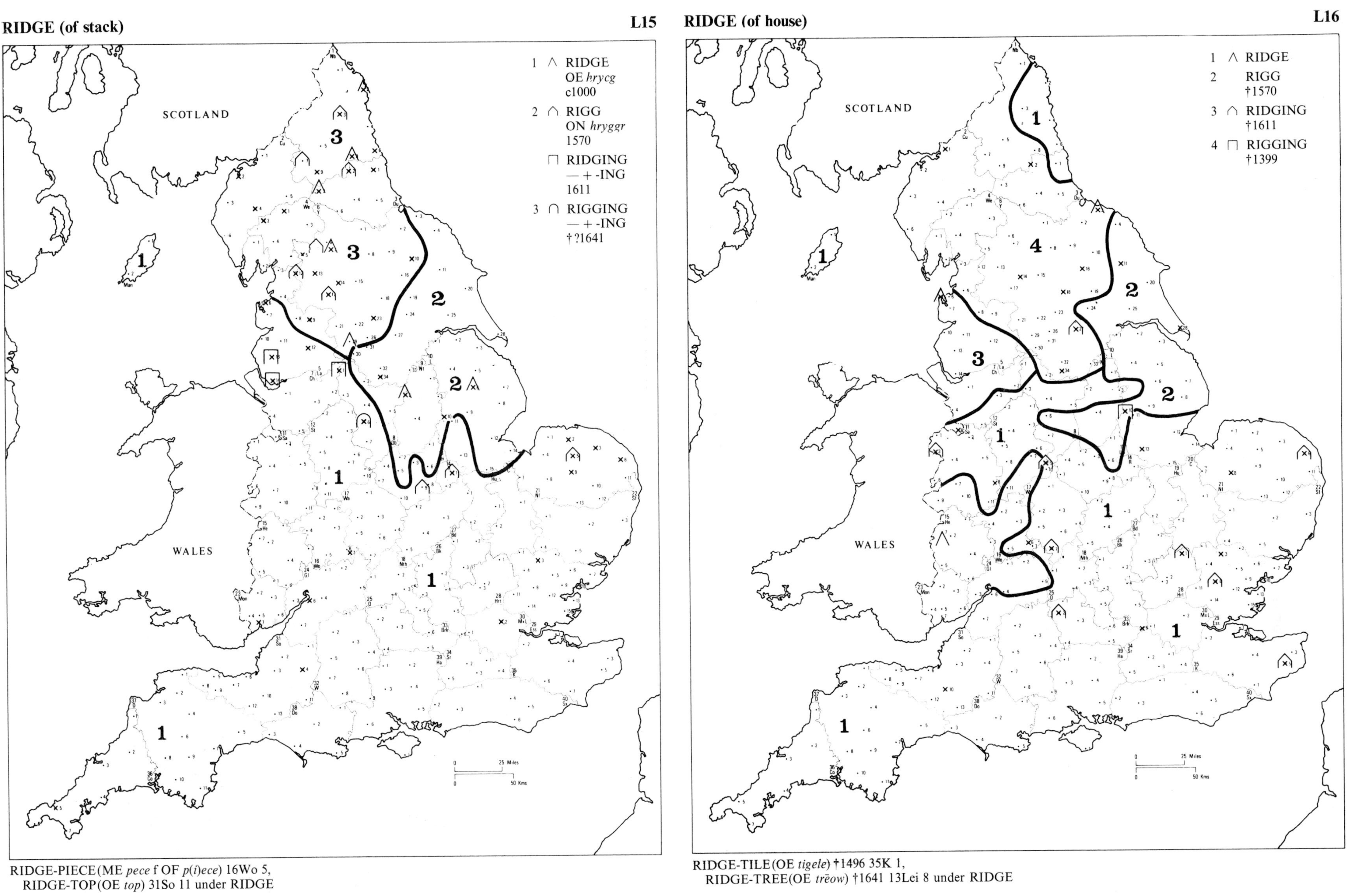

RIDGE-PIECE(ME *pece* f OF *p(i)ece*) 16Wo 5,
RIDGE-TOP(OE *top*) 31So 11 under RIDGE

RIDGE (of house)

RIDGE-TILE(OE *tigele*) †1496 35K 1,
RIDGE-TREE(OE *trēow*) †1641 13Lei 8 under RIDGE

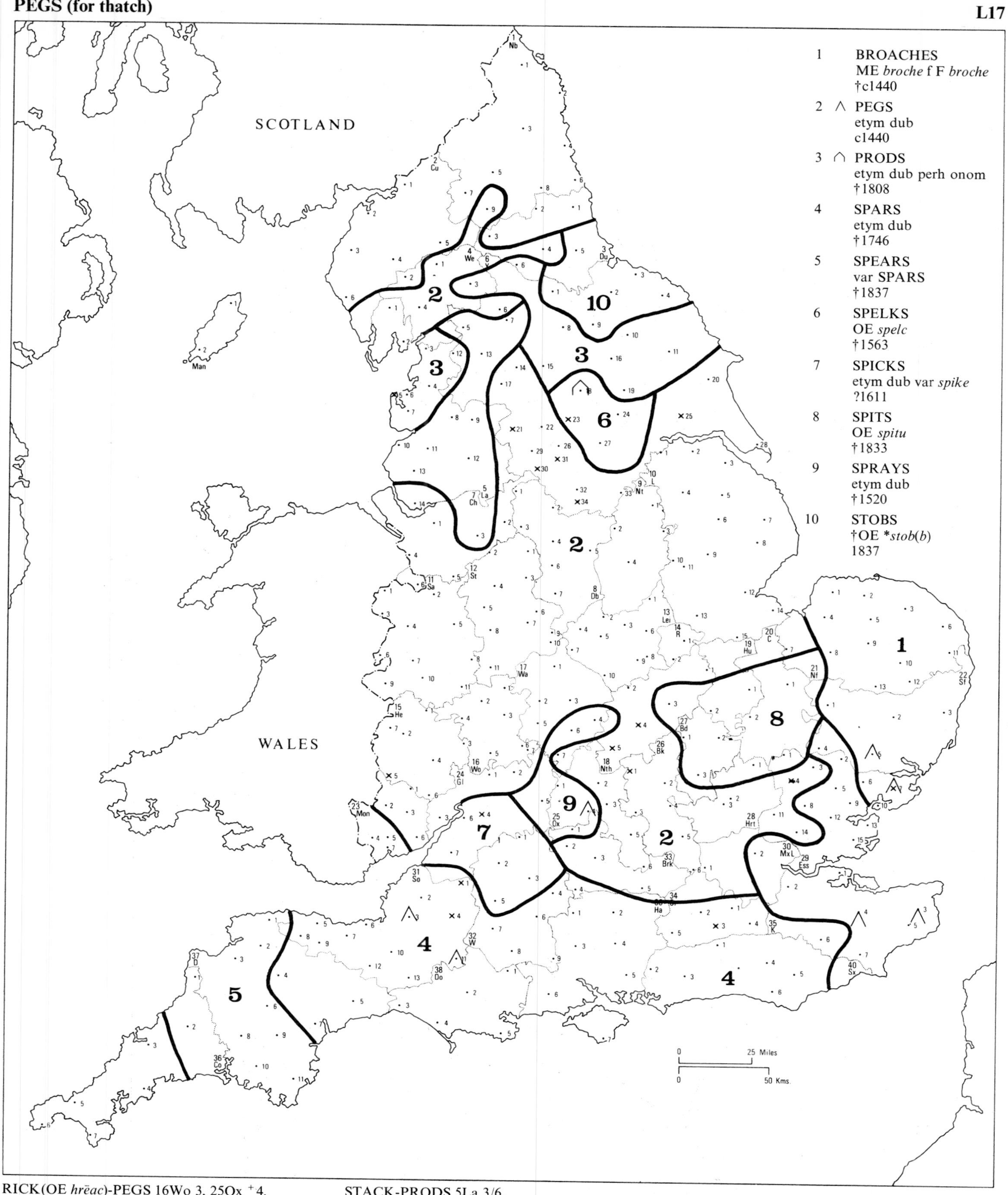

RICK(OE *hrēac*)-PEGS 16Wo 3, 25Ox $^{+}$4, 26Bk 3, 30MxL $^{+}$1,
STACK(ON *stakkr*)-PEGS 6Y 22, 10L 1/$^{+}$15, 21Nf 7,
THACK(OE *þæc*)-PEGS †1846 6Y 32, 8Db $^{+}$4, 9Nt $^{+}$1/$^{+}$4, 10L 4/6/7/9/10/$^{+}$12/14/$^{+}$15, 13Lei $^{+}$1/$^{+}$7,
THACKING-PEGS 6Y 17,
THATCH(f THACK)-PEGS †1897 7Ch 1/2, 8Db 6, 9Nt 2, 13Lei 6, 16Wo 1, 17Wa 2,
THATCHING-PEGS 6Y 29, 15He 7, 29Ess 14,
WITHY(OE *wiþig*)-PEGS 12St $^{+}$11 under PEGS

STACK-PRODS 5La 3/6, 6Y 11/12/16/$^{+}$18/19 under PRODS
RICK-SPARS 34Sr 2 under SPARS
STACK-SPELKS 6Y 24 under SPELKS
SPEAKS 24Gl 6, 32W 1/$^{+}$3 under SPICKS
RICK-SPRAYS 25Ox $^{+}$4 under SPRAYS
STACK-STOBS 6Y 3/4/9 under STOBS

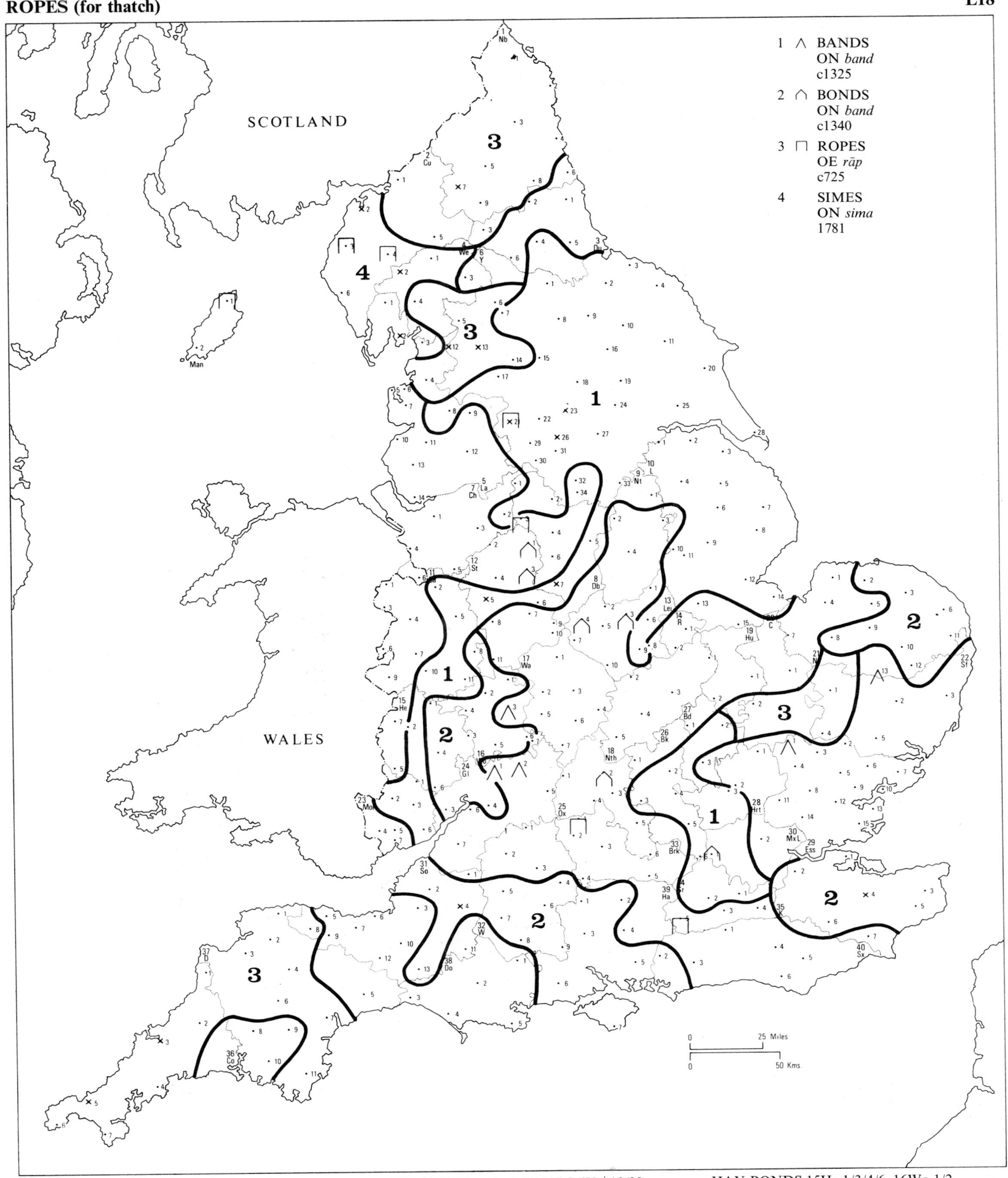

BILLY(pet name *William*)-BANDS 6Y +16, BINDER(OE *bindan* + -ER)-BANDS 6Y +18, 10L 11, COCONUT (f Pg and Sp *coco* + OE *hnutu*)-BANDS 6Y +16, 12St 6, HAY(OE *hēg*)-BANDS 6Y +8, 10L +9/10, 11Sa 5/10/11, 13Lei +9, 15He 2, 16Wo 3, 21Nf +13, 23Mon 1–3/6, 24Gl 1/2, 26Bk 2/3, HAZEL(OE *hæsel*)-BANDS 5La 8, PITCH(OE *pic*)-BANDS 29Ess 1, STACK (ON *stakkr*)-BANDS 6Y 7, STRAW(OE *strēaw*)-BANDS 6Y +10/20, 13Lei +9, 21Nf +13, 26Bk 4, 27Bd 2, 28Hrt 3, 34Sr 2, TAR(OE *te(o)ru*)-BANDS 6Y +11/15/+18/22/30, 9Nt 1, 10L +2/12, TAR-MARL(OF *marle*)-BANDS 10L 4/8, TARRED-BANDS 34Sr 1, TARRY-BANDS 6Y 24, THACKING(OE *þæc*)-BANDS 6Y +3/4/+11, 8Db 5, THATCH (f THACK)-BANDS 7Ch 2 under BANDS

HAY-BONDS 15He 1/3/4/6, 16Wo 1/2, 24Gl 3/4, 32W 9, 35K 5, STRAW-BONDS 21Nf 3/6/10/11, 32W 4–8, 35K 1–3/6, THUMB(OE *þūma*)-BONDS 21Nf 2 under BONDS

COIR(Malay *kayer*)-ROPES Man +1, 36Co 6, HAY-ROPES 6Y 6, OVER(OE ofer)-ROPES 2Cu +3, REED(OE *hrēod*)-ROPES 37D 2, REEDEN-ROPES 37D +6, STRAW-ROPES 1Nb 1/+8, 2Cu +4/+5, Man +1, 34Sr 5, 37D 4/7/11, TAR-ROPES 20C 2, 22Sf 1/4, THATCH-ROPES 8Db 3, THUMB-ROPES 5La 4 under ROPES

THUMB-SIMES 5La 1/3 under SIMES

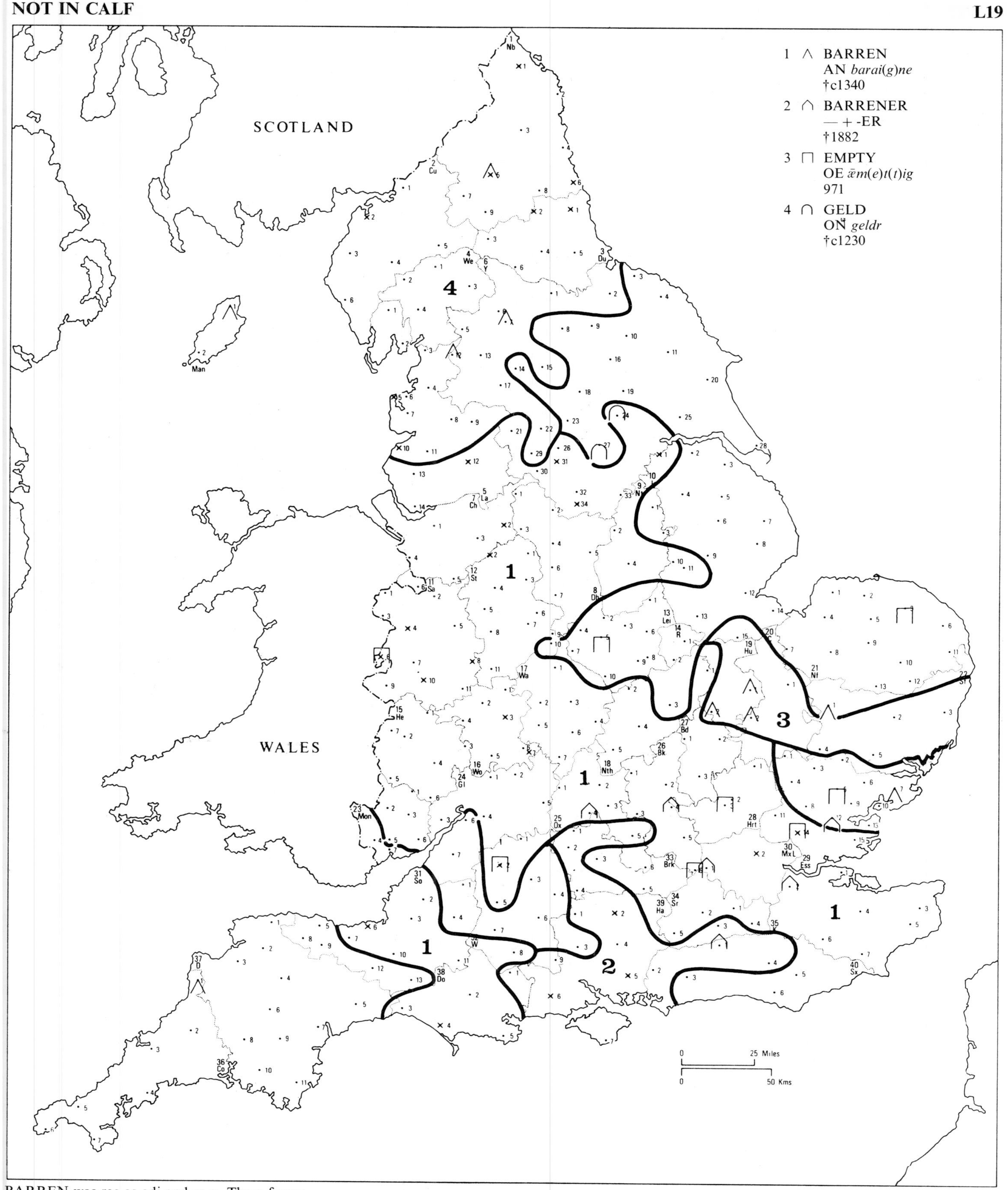

BARREN was rec as adj and as n. The n forms occur at 11Sa 1/3, 12St 5im, 15He 2, 23Mon 1, 40Sx 6. The first recorded date as n is c1420

BARRENER is rec only as n

DONKEY L20a

DONKEY L20b

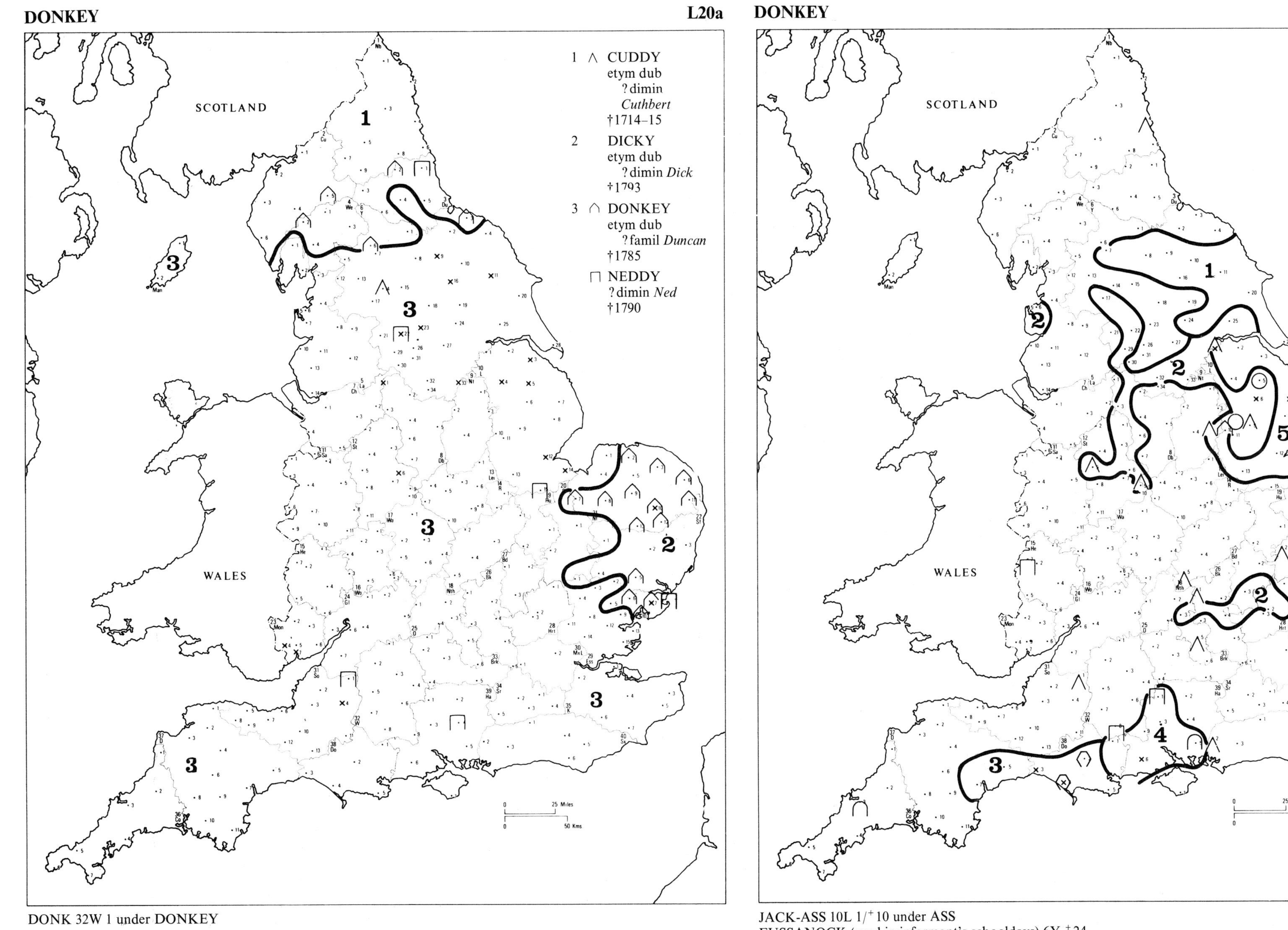

DONK 32W 1 under DONKEY

JACK-ASS 10L 1/+10 under ASS
FUSSANOCK (used in informant's schooldays) 6Y +24,
FUSSAZICK 10L +10 under FUSSOCK
MOKES sg 39Ha +1 under MOKE
JACK NIRRUP 39Ha +5 under NIRRUP
BRONKUS 10L 4/+5/+9/+10 under PRONKUS

SCOTLAND

WALES

1 ∧ BROWSE
?F *brouster*
1523

2 ∩ BRUSH
F *brosser*
†1845

3 ⊓ CROP
OE *crop(p)*
†a1225

4 ∩ CUT
OE **cyttan*
1419 MED

5 ⬡ DRESS
OF *dresser*
1526

6 ○ TOP
f OE *top*
†1509

0 25 Miles
0 50 Kms

BROWSE DOWN(OE *dūn*) 31So 8, 37D +1,
BROWSE OFF(OE *of*) 31So 5,
BROWSE OUT(OE *ūt*) 37D 4 under BROWSE
BRUSH UP(OE *up*) 8Db 5, 12St 10, 17Wa 2,
HEDGE(OE *hecg*)-BRUSH 12St 3/11,
13Lei 2/4/7, 15He 7, 16Wo 1,
17Wa 3 under BRUSH
HEDGE-CROP 24Gl +2 under CROP
CUT BACK(OE *bæc*) 6Y 26, 31So +13,
CUT DOWN 21Nf 7, 24Gl 4, 37D +1,
CUT OUT AND CHUCK(etym dub)
BACK 31So 4, HEDGE-CUT 21Nf 6
under CUT
HEDGE-TOP 10L 11,
TOP AND TWIG(f northern OE *twigge*
†1570) 10L 12 under TOP

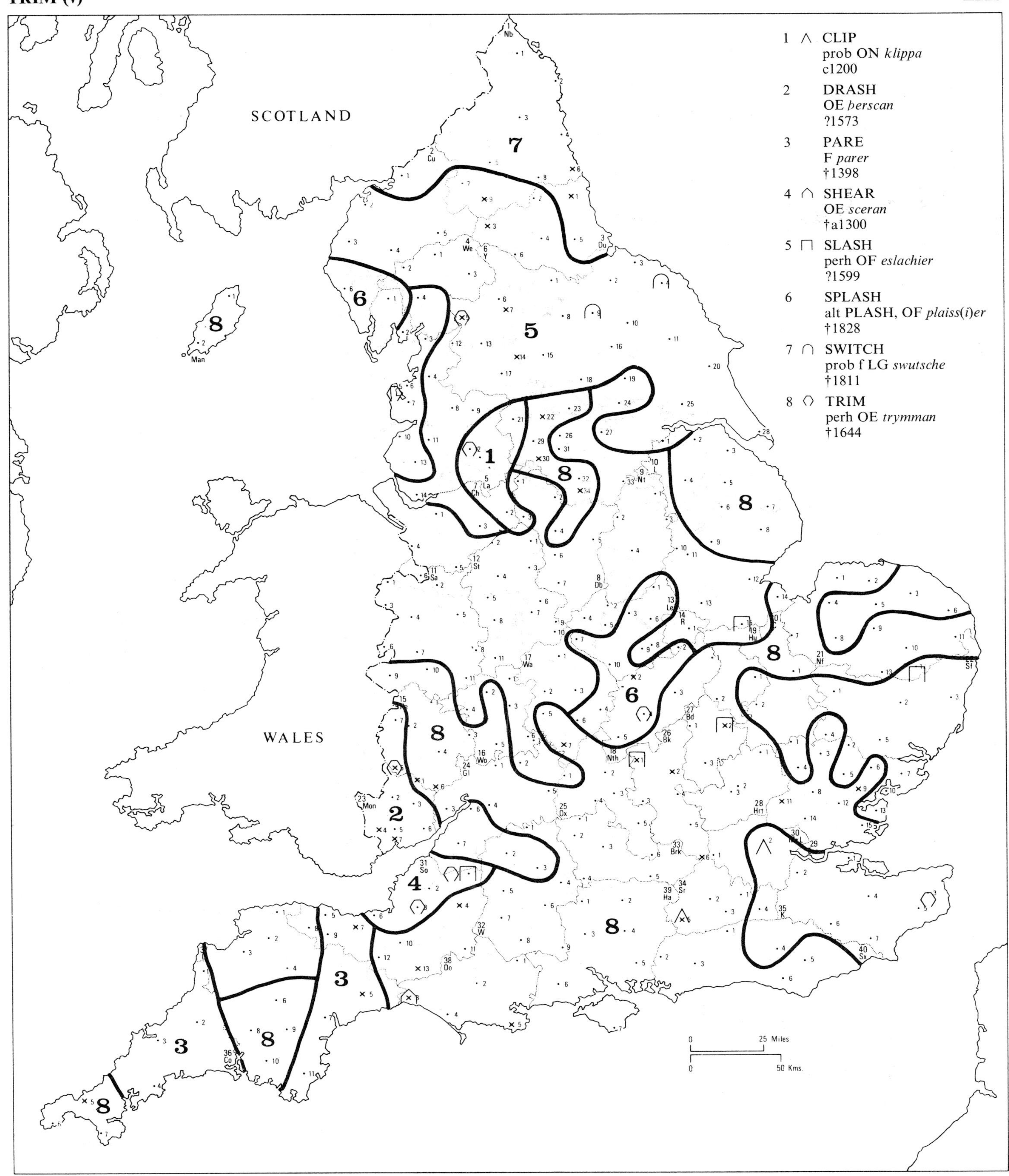

DRASH DOWN(OE *dūn*) 15He 7 under DRASH
SLASH DOWN 21Nf 12 under SLASH
SPLASH UP(OE *up*) 17Wa +6 under SPLASH
HEDGE(OE hecg)-TRIM 19Hu 2, 28Hrt 3,
TRIM BACK(OE *bæc*) 32W 7,
TRIM UP 21Nf 2, 24Gl 1,
29Ess 15 under TRIM

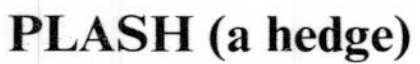

PLASH (a hedge)

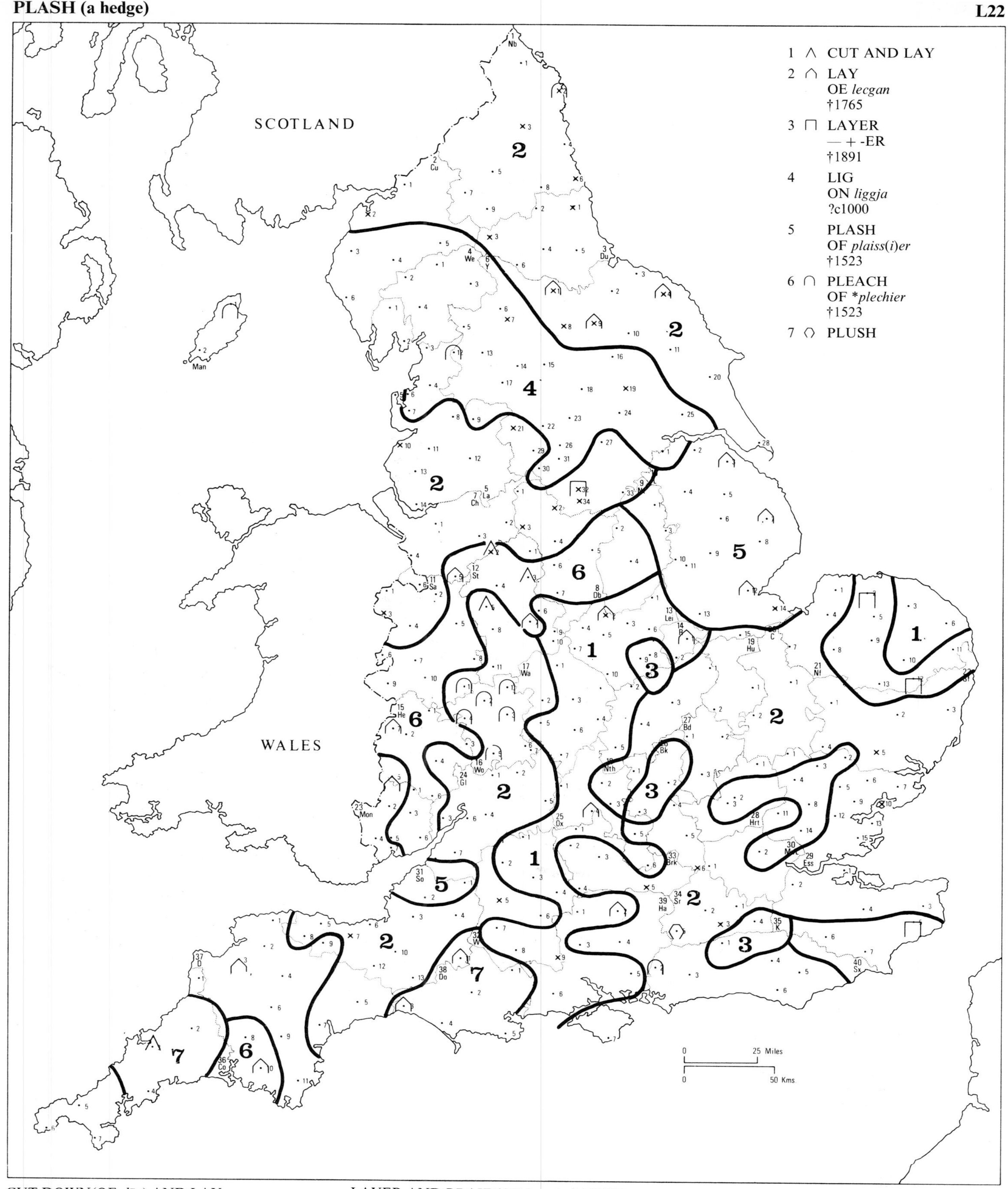

CUT DOWN(OE *dūn*) AND LAY
25Ox +4 under CUT AND LAY
BANK(f ME *banke* prob f ON **banke*, **banki*)
UP(OE *up*) AND LAY 31So 8,
BUCK-HEAD AND LAY 29Ess 6,
LAY DOWN 10L +7, 11Sa 4, 15He +7,
17Wa 2, 21Nf 1, 31So 4/+11, 39Ha +2/+3,
LAY OUT(OE *ūt*) 33Brk 3,
MAKE(OE *macian*) AND LAY 31So 5,
RE(Lat *re*)-LAY 29Ess 9 under LAY

LAYER AND BRAID(OE *bregdan*) 21Nf 5,
LAYER TO THE GROUND(OE *grund*)
26Bk +2 under LAYER
CUT AND LIG 6Y 16, FELL(OE *fellan*)
AND LIG 2Cu 5, LIG DOWN 6Y 25,
LIG IN(OE *in*) 6Y 24,
RE-LIG 6Y 14 under LIG
PLEACH DOWN 12St 3,
37D +10 under PLEACH
PLUSH DOWN 36Co 4, 38Do 2 under PLUSH

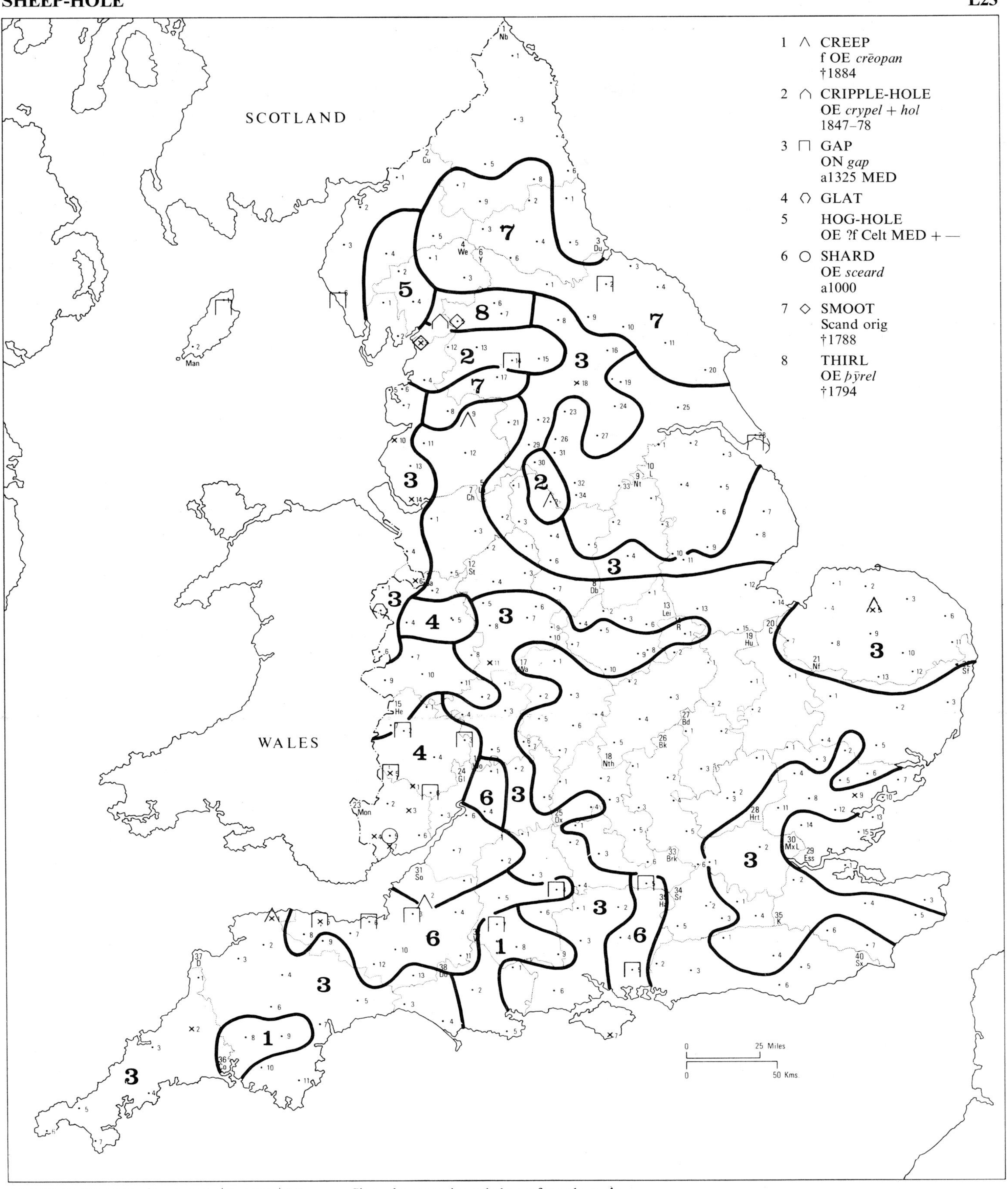

CREEP-HOLE †1646 5La 9, 8Db +2, 32W +7/8, 37D 9, SHEEP'S(OE *scēap*)-CREEP 37D 8 under CREEP
CRIPPER-GAP 7Ch 2, 8Db 1/3/4, 12St 1, CRIPPLE-GAP †1847–78 6Y +14, 8Db 6, GAP-STEAD(OE *stede*) †1644 6Y 8, 9Nt +4, GAP-WAY(OE *weg*) 33Brk 4, 39Ha +5, HOG-GAP 2Cu 6, SHEEP-GAP 13Lei 5/7–9, 14R 1 under GAP
SHARD-WAY 39Ha 4/+5 under SHARD
SHEEP'S-SMOOT 6Y 4, SMOOT-HOLE †1828 1Nb 7/8, 2Cu 5, 3Du 2/4/6, 4We 1/3, 5La 3/8, 6Y 1/10/11/17/20 under SMOOT
THIRL-HOLE 6Y +6/7 under THIRL

Since the q was intended to refer only to the artificial hole, the expressions rec for the animal-made hole were regarded as unwanted responses for mapping purposes, though they are noted in Appendix 2

smɷftɒɪl 5La 8 is taken to repr SMOOT-HOLE

kɽe:t 32W 7im (a smaller hole to allow lambs to graze the field before rest of flock) ?informant's error for kɽe:p

HANGING-POST (of gate)

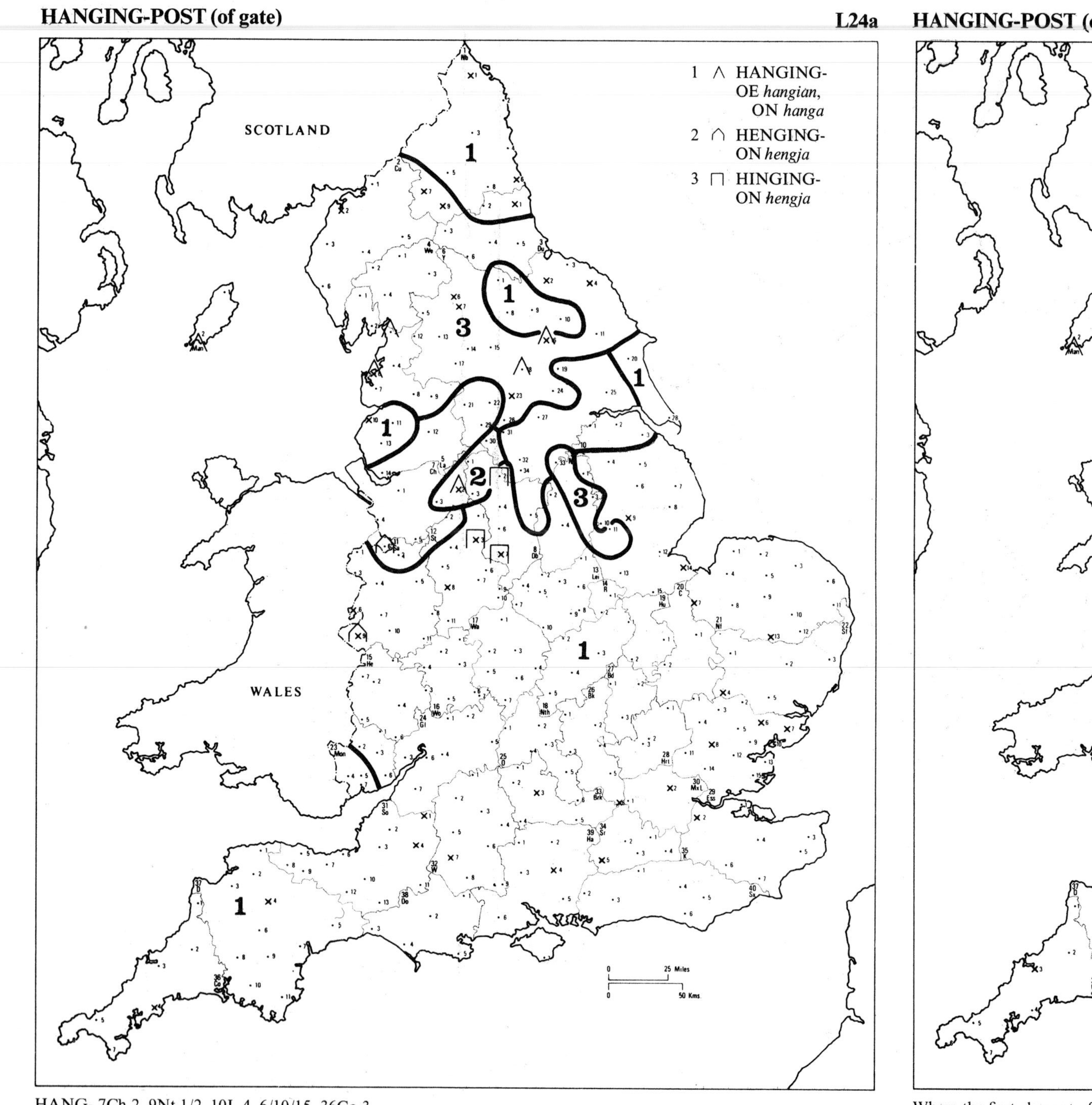

HANG- 7Ch 2, 9Nt 1/2, 10L 4–6/10/15, 36Co 3,
HENGING- 29Ess 11/12/15, 34Sr 2/4, K 1/3/5–7, 37D 10/11, 40Sx 1/2/4–6 under HANGING-
HING- 8Db 7 under HINGING-

At 36Co 3 the second element of the compound was BOW and at 7Ch 6 it was GATE. Elsewhere POST, STOOP, STUB and STUMP were rec, as shown on the next map.

HANGING-POST (of gate)

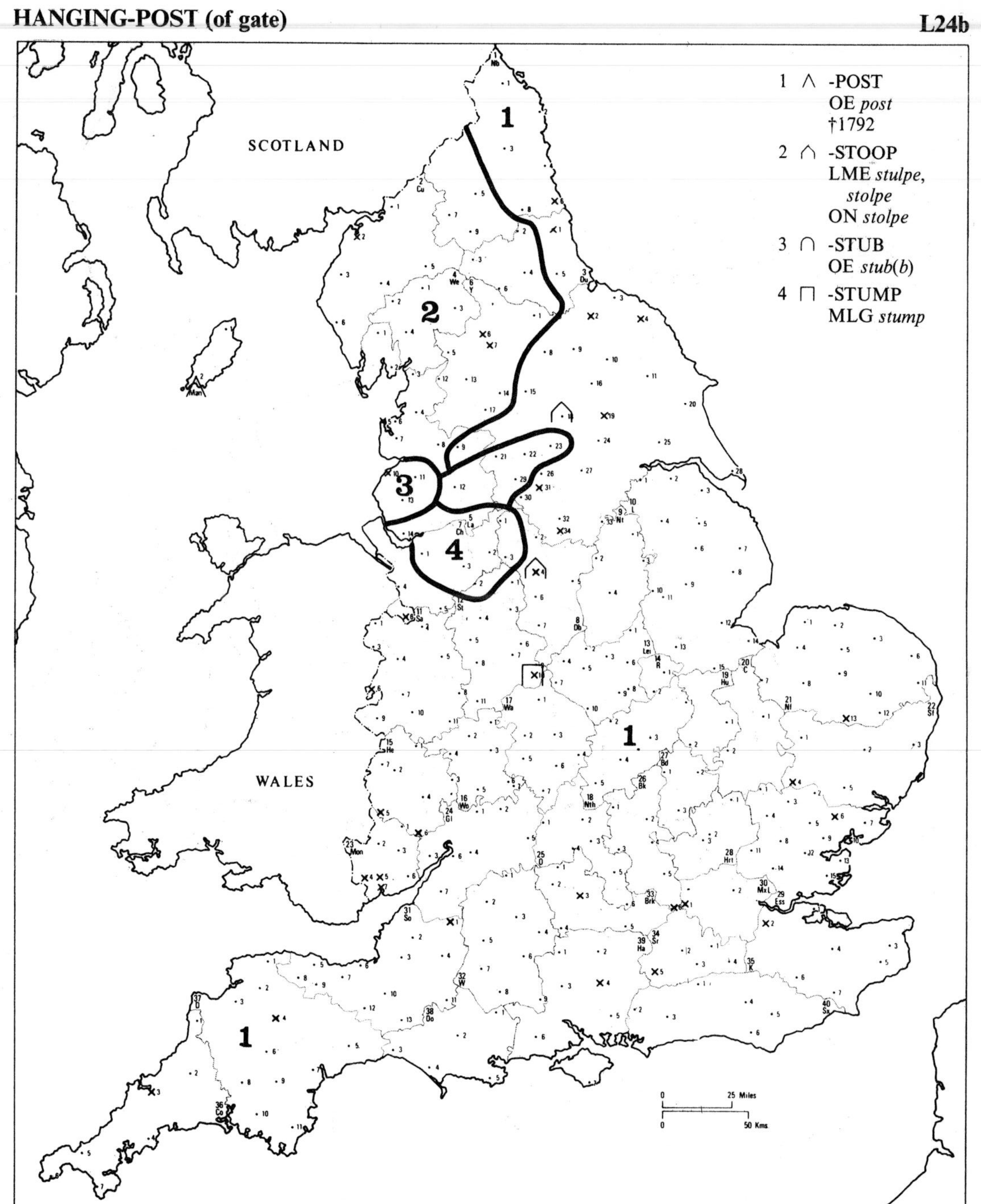

Where the first element of the compound was not HANG(ING), HENGING or HING(ING), as shown on the previous map, the following first elements were rec:
ARSE-END-(POST) 6Y ⁺3, BUTT-END-(POST) (politer than ARSE-END-POST) 6Y ⁺3,
CARRYING-(POST) 7Ch 4, FRONT-(POST) 29Ess 7,
GATE-(POST) 6Y 32, 21Nf 7, 31So 4,
HEAD-(POST) 10L 3, HEEL-(POST) 7Ch 5, 11Sa 2, 12St 8, 25Ox ⁺3 (ref "the bigger post"),
HIND-(POST) 36Co 4, HINGE-(POST) 32W 7,
STANDARD-(POST) (pref to HENGING-POST) 29Ess ⁺15, STAND-(POST) 10L 2,
STRINDING- (POST) 1Nb 1,
SWINGING-(POST) 6Y 25/⁺26, 21Nf ⁺3/⁺8, 29Ess 8, SWING-(POST) 8Db 5, 10L 1/9
CROOK-(STOOP) 1Nb 7, HINGE-(STOOP) 1Nb 9
FOOT-(STUMP) 7Ch 1, HEEL-(STUMP) 12St 2, HINGEING-(STUMP) 5La 14

The simplex POST was rec at 6Y 27 and BIG POST at 10L 14

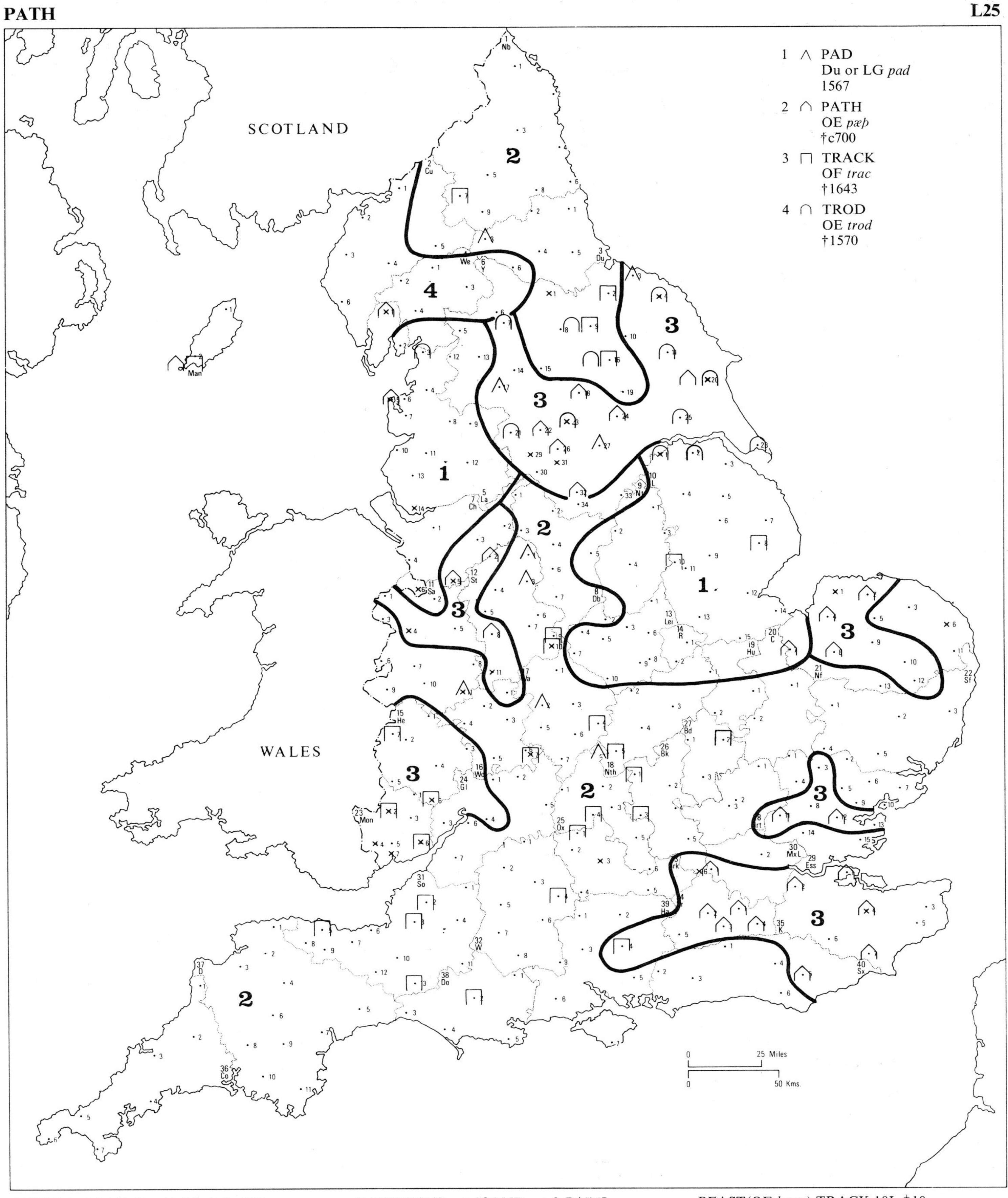

COW(OE *cū*)-PAD 5La +6/+7, 11Sa +11, 12St +3, FOOT(OE *fōt*)-PAD 5La +6/+7, 6Y 5/+17/+27, 7Ch +4, 8Db 5, 9Nt 1–4, 10L +2/4/5/9/+12/13/+14, 13Lei +1/+10, 18Nth +5, PADDING 17Wa +2, PAD-ROAD(OE *rād*) 5La +9, PAD-WALK(f OE *wealcan*) 5La 12, 6Y 12, 12St +3, SHEEP(OE *scēap*)-PAD 5La +6/+7, 12St +1 under PAD

CATTLE(ME *catel* f ONF *catel*)-PATH 30MxL +2, FOOT-PATH 1Nb 3–5, 2Cu 5, 3Du +3/5, 6Y +2/8/+9/15/+16/+18/+20/+22/+24/+26/+32/33, Man +2, 8Db 1/4, 12St +3/4/+6/7/+8, 15He +7, 17Wa 1/+2/3/+4, 18Nth 2–4/+5, 19Hu 1/2, 20C 2, 21Nf +2–+5/+7/+8, 22Sf 3/5, 24Gl 5/6, 25Ox 1/+3/+4/5/+6, 26Bk +1, 27Bd +1/3, 28Hrt 1/3, 29Ess 1/+6/+7/+12/15, 30MxL +1/+2, 31So 1/9/+13, 32W 1/3/9, 34Sr +1/+3/+4, 35K +2, 36Co 1, 37D 1/2/3/5/10, 38Do +1/3/+4, 39Ha +2/+4/5/7, 40Sx 1/3/6, PATH-WAY(OE *weg*) 21Nf 11, 29Ess 10 under PATH

BEAST(OF *beste*)-TRACK 10L +10, CATTLE-TRACK 6Y +26/+27, 34Sr +1, 39Ha +4, COW-TRACK 6Y +2/+3/+7/+9–+11/+17/+18/+21/+22/+24/+25/+30/+32, 7Ch +2, 12St +8, 15He +7, 16Wo +7, 25Ox +4, 27Bd +2, 29Ess +11, 30MxL +1, 38Do +2, FOOT-TRACK 1Nb +7, 33Brk +1, 35K 5/+7, SHEEP-TRACK 1Nb +7, 6Y +2/+3/+7/+9–+11/+14/+17/+18/+21/+22/+24/+25/+27/+30/+32, 7Ch +2, 10L +10, 12St +9, 15He +7, 16Wo +7, 17Wa +5, 25Ox +4, 27Bd +2, 29Ess +11/+12, 30MxL +1, 32W +4, 34Sr +2, TRACK-WAY 31So +13 under TRACK
FOOT-TROD 2Cu 1/2/+6, 6Y +16/+28 under TROD

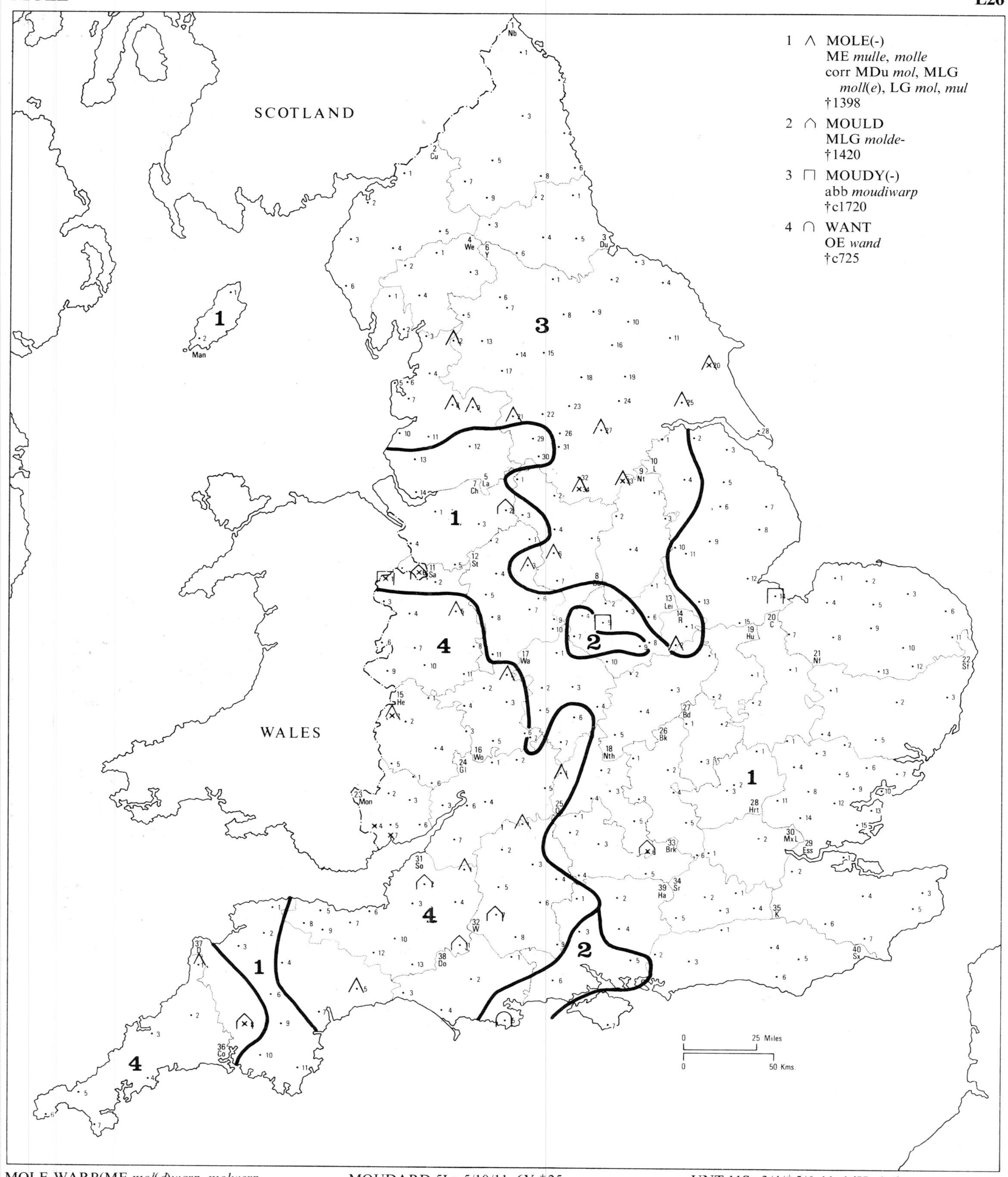

MOLE-WARP(ME *mol(d)warp, molwerp*, repr OE **moldweorp*) †c1380 5La +9, 6Y +21/29/30, MOW 12St 2/+3, 25Ox 4, 29Ess +11/15, 30MxL +2, 33Brk 1, 34Sr +1/4/5, 35K 2/7, 39Ha 7, 40Sx 1 under MOLE(-)
MOUD 25Ox 6 under MOULD

MOUDARD 5La 5/10/11, 6Y +25, MOUDY-RAT(OE *ræt*) 1Nb 4/5/8, 3Du 2, MOUDY-WARP †1577 2Cu 3, 3Du 5, 5La 4, 6Y 1–3/6–8/11/+12/15–17/+21, 8Db 1/+5/+7, 9Nt 1–4, 10L 1/4, 12St +3, 13Lei 1/+5, 14R 1/+2, MOUDY-WORM(OE *wyrm*) 11Sa 1, MOULDARD 6Y +25 (pref to MOLE). MOULDEN 17Wa +5 (older than MOLE), MOULDWARP †c1325, 6Y 26, MOULDY 6Y 28, MOULDY-WARP †c1380 6Y +4/19/22/23/+27/31/32, MOULY 6Y +10, 10L +14, MOULY-RAT 1Nb 6, 3Du 1, MOULY-WARP †1886 6Y +27 (very rare), 13Lei 6 under MOUDY(-)

UNT 11Sa 3/4/+5/6–11, 15He 1–6, 16Wo +1/2–6, 17Wa 7, 23Mon 1/2/5/6, 24Gl 1–7, 25Ox +1 (older than MOLE), 32W +1/+2, WONT 31So +1/+2/3/+4/6/7/10/+11/13, 32W 3–6/+7/8/9, 36Co 5–7, 37D 4/+5/7, 38Do 1–4/+5, 39Ha 1, WUNT 17Wa 6 (older than MOULD), 23Mon 3, 32W +2 under WANT

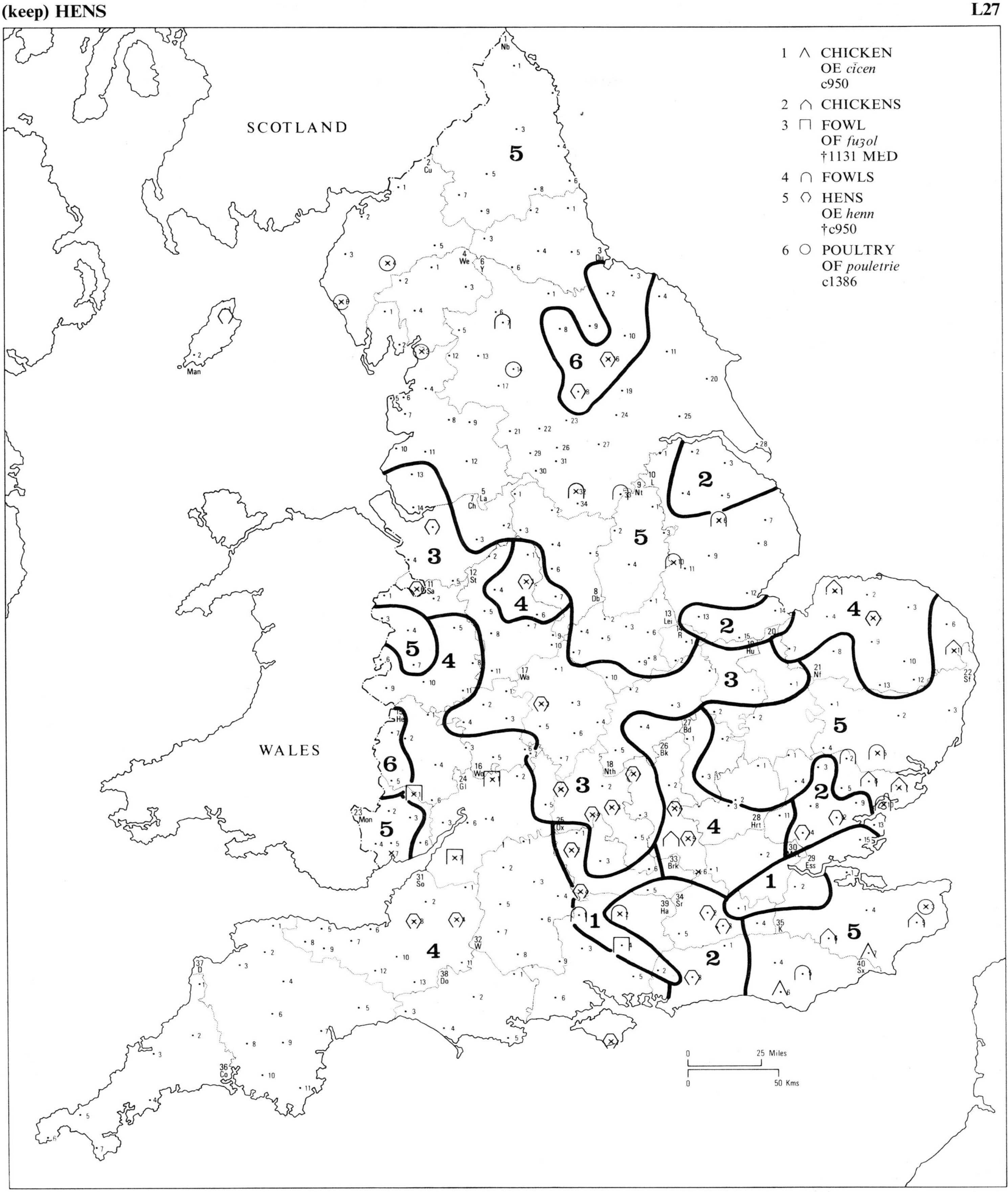

THEIR CHICKEN 34Sr 1 under CHICKEN
SOME CHICKENS 10L 5 under CHICKENS
A FEW FOWL 33Brk 3,
SOME FOWL 16Wo 1 under FOWL
FEW FOWLS 31So ⁺7, THE FOWLS 11Sa 6/9,
15He 4, THEIR FOWLS 11Sa 5, 24Gl 2/4,
31So 2 under FOWLS
A FEW HENS 5La 6, A LITE HENS 5La 7/⁺10,
THE OLD HENS 21Nf 5 under HENS
THEIR POULTRY 15He 7 under POULTRY

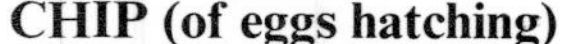

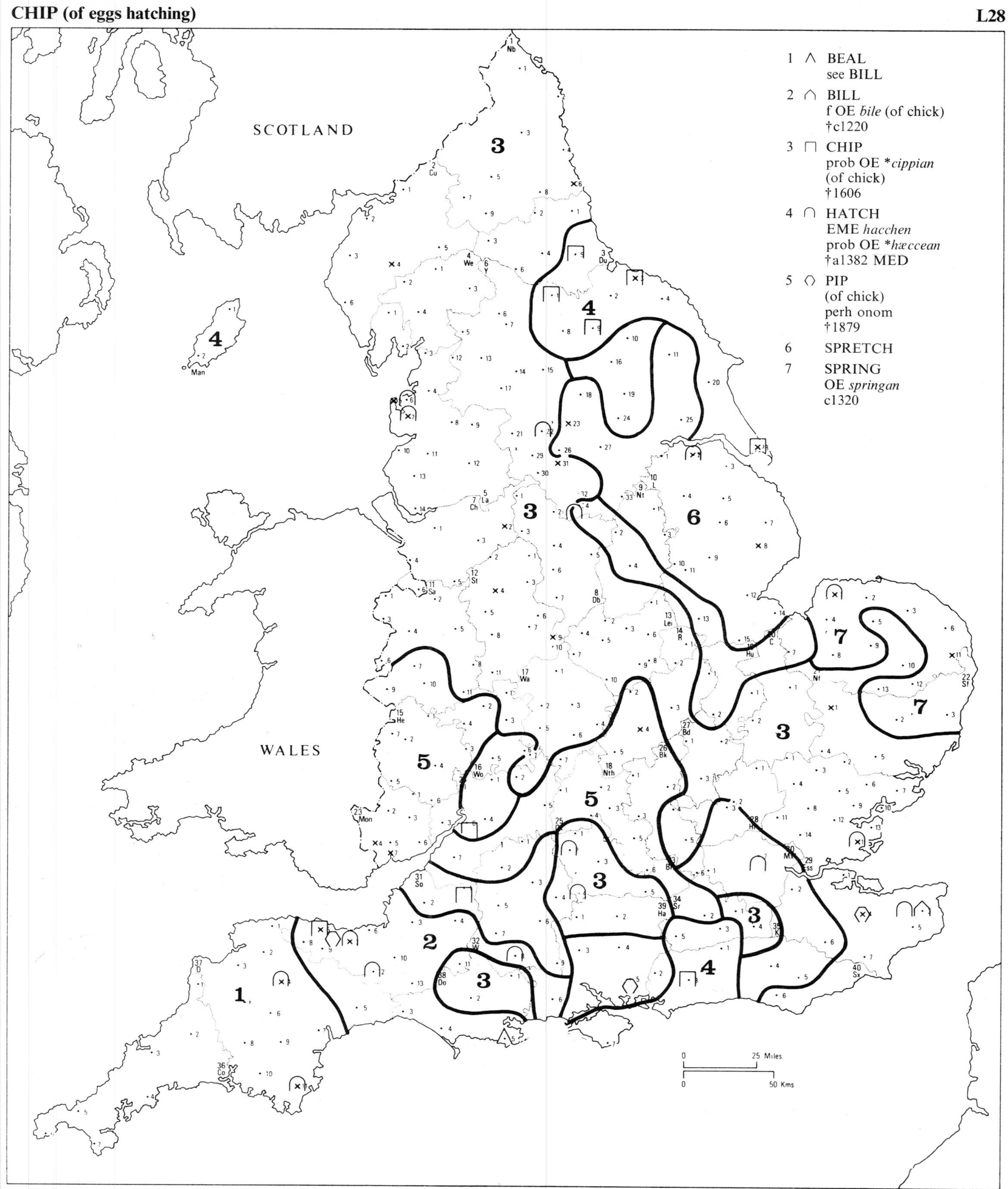

BEALD 36Co 3 under BEAL
BILD 31So 6/8/9/+12 (older than HATCH),
37D 5 under BILL
HATCH OFF(OE *of*) 21Nf 1,
HATCH OUT(OE *ūt*) 29Ess 15, 30MxL 2,
33Brk +2/+4, 34Sr 3, 35K +3,
37D 11 under HATCH

bɪdɪd (after tə *to*; pres form of *bild* Edd)
stɹɪtʃ (sic); older than HATCH
(?error for *spretch* Edd) 6Y +8

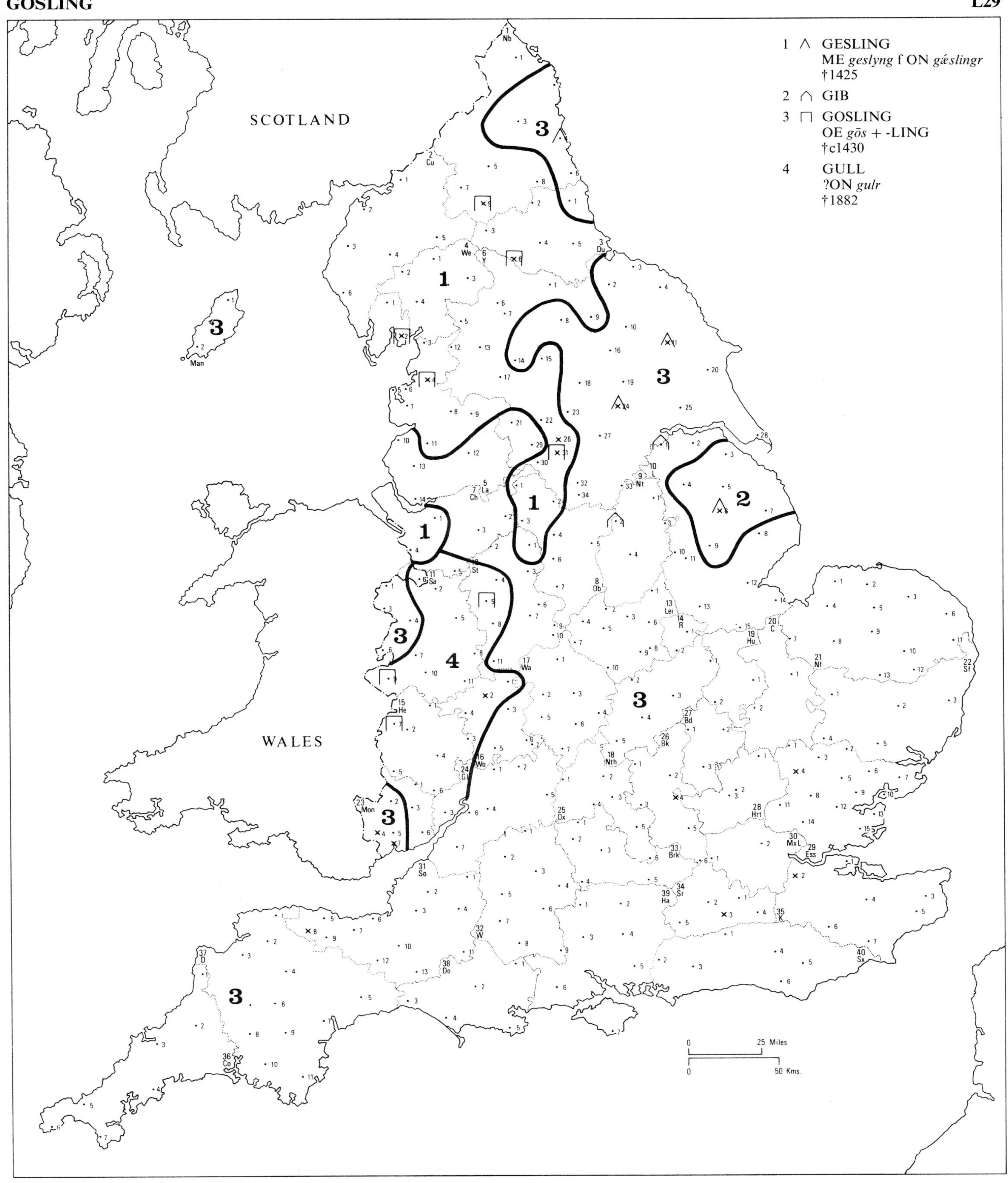

GOOSELING †1603 11Sa 4,
GUSLING 29Ess 14, 34Sr 5, 35K 7,
40Sx 3/6 under GOSLING
GULLY 7Ch 5/6, 11Sa 2/⁺ 5/7/10,
12St 4/⁺ 5/8 under GULL

gɒːdlɪŋz is taken to repr GOSLINGS

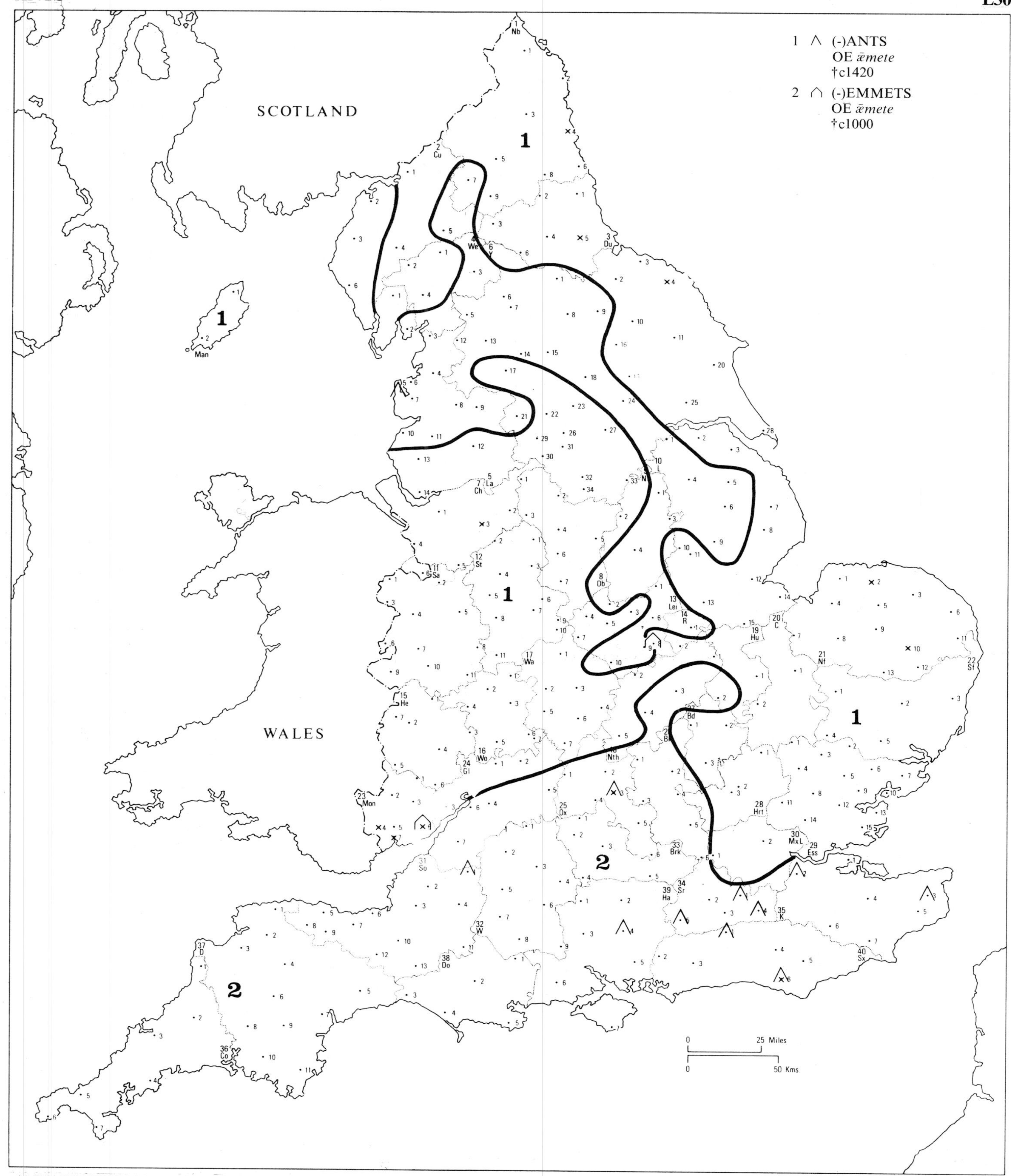

-ANNATS 7Ch 5, NANTS("common") 1Nb $^{+}$2 under (-)ANTS

The form of the legend indicates that responses were rec as both simplexes and compounds

Where -ANTS was rec as the second element of a compound, the first element was ARSE-(OE *ears*) at 24Gl 1, PEE- at 11Sa 8, PISS-(ME *pissen* f OF *pissier*) †1661 at 7Ch 5/6, 10L 14, 11Sa 2/4/6/9–11, 16Wo 3, 18Nth 20C 1/2, 21Nf 4, 22Sf $^{+}$1, 27Bd 1–3, 28Hrt 2, 29Ess 1/11, PISSY- at 11Sa 1

Where -EMMETS was rec as the second element of a compound, the first element was PISS- at 25Ox 5, 26Bk 1–4

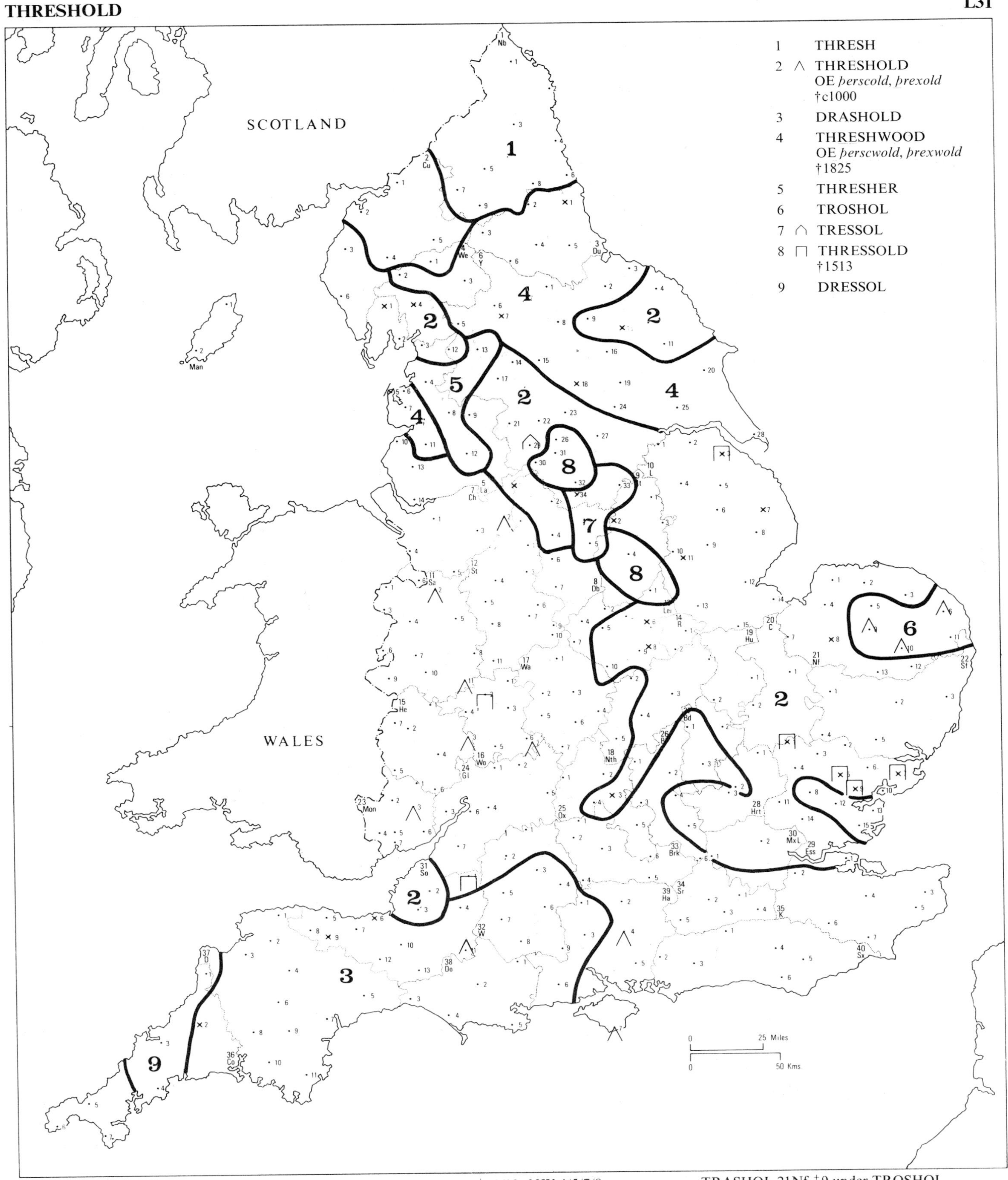

DOOR(OE *duru*)-THRESHOL 29Ess 2,
FRESHOL 27Bd 2, 29Ess 3,
THRAISHOL 31So +11,
THRASHOD 8Db 4,
THRASHOL 20C 1, 21Nf 1–3/+6/+10/13,
22Sf 1, 39Ha 4im, THRESHOD 6Y 23,
THRESHOL 6Y 14, 10L 1/2/4/12/15,
13Lei 5/9/10, 14R 1/2, 18Nth 1/3, 19Hu 1,
20C 2, 21Nf 7/+9, 22Sf 4/5, 25Ox +4,
26Bk 4, 28Hrt +3, 29Ess 4/6/10/11, 30MxL 2,
31So 3, 39Ha 7,
THRESHOL-BOARD(OE *bord*) 10L 13,
THRESHOL-DOOR 28Hrt 1,
THRESHOL-STONE(OE *stān*) †1805 10L 5,
THRESHOLT 2Cu 6, 5La 9, 6Y 12, 10L 8/+9,
11Sa 2, 31So +1, THRESHOW 31So 2,
THROSHOL 21Nf 4/12,
22Sf 2/3 under THRESHOLD

DRAISHOL 31So +11/13, 32W 4/5/7/8,
37D 2/3/5–8/10, 39Ha 1/3/6,
DRAISHOLD 37D 9, DRASHOL 31So 5/10,
32W 9, 38Do 1, DRASHOLD 31So 7,
38Do 4/5, DRASHOLT 31So 8/12,
38Do 2, DRESHOL 32W 3, 37D 1/4/11,
38Do 3, DRESHOLD 32W 6,
DRESHOW 31 Do 4 under DRASHOLD

DOOR-THRESHET 5La 6,
FRESHWOOD 6Y 2/3/6/8/19/20,
THRESHED 3Du 5, 6Y 15/24/28,
THRESHET 5La 7/11, 6Y 5,
THRESHET-BOARD 4We 3,
TRESHWOOD 6Y 25 under THRESHWOOD

TRASHOL 21Nf +9 under TROSHOL

DOOR-THRESSOL 29Ess +9,
FRESSOL 29Ess +1,
THRESSOL 6Y 31/32, 9Nt 4, 10L 3,
13Lei 1, 29Ess +1/5/+9 under THRESSOLD

DREXOL 36Co 4,
DREXTOL 36Co 1 under DRESSOL

EARTH-CLOSET

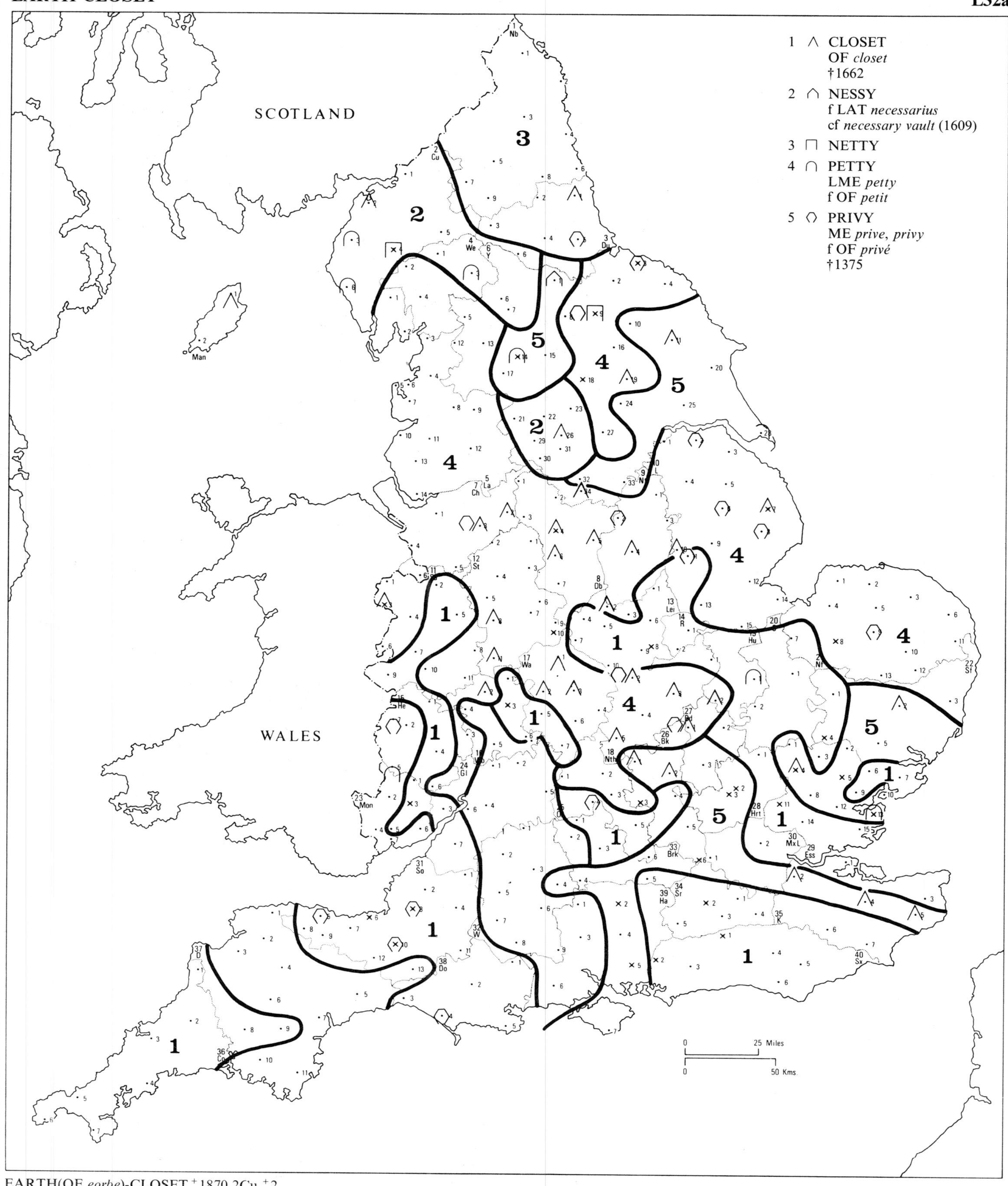

EARTH(OE *eorþe*)-CLOSET ⁺1870 2Cu ⁺2, 3Du ⁺1, 11Sa 2/7, 29Ess 15, 34Sr 3, 35K 1/⁺4 under CLOSET
NECESSARY †1756 6Y ⁺1 under NESSY
PETTY-HOLE(OE *hol*) 8Db ⁺5, PETTY-HOUSE(OE *hūs*) 15He 6 under PETTY

EARTH-CLOSET

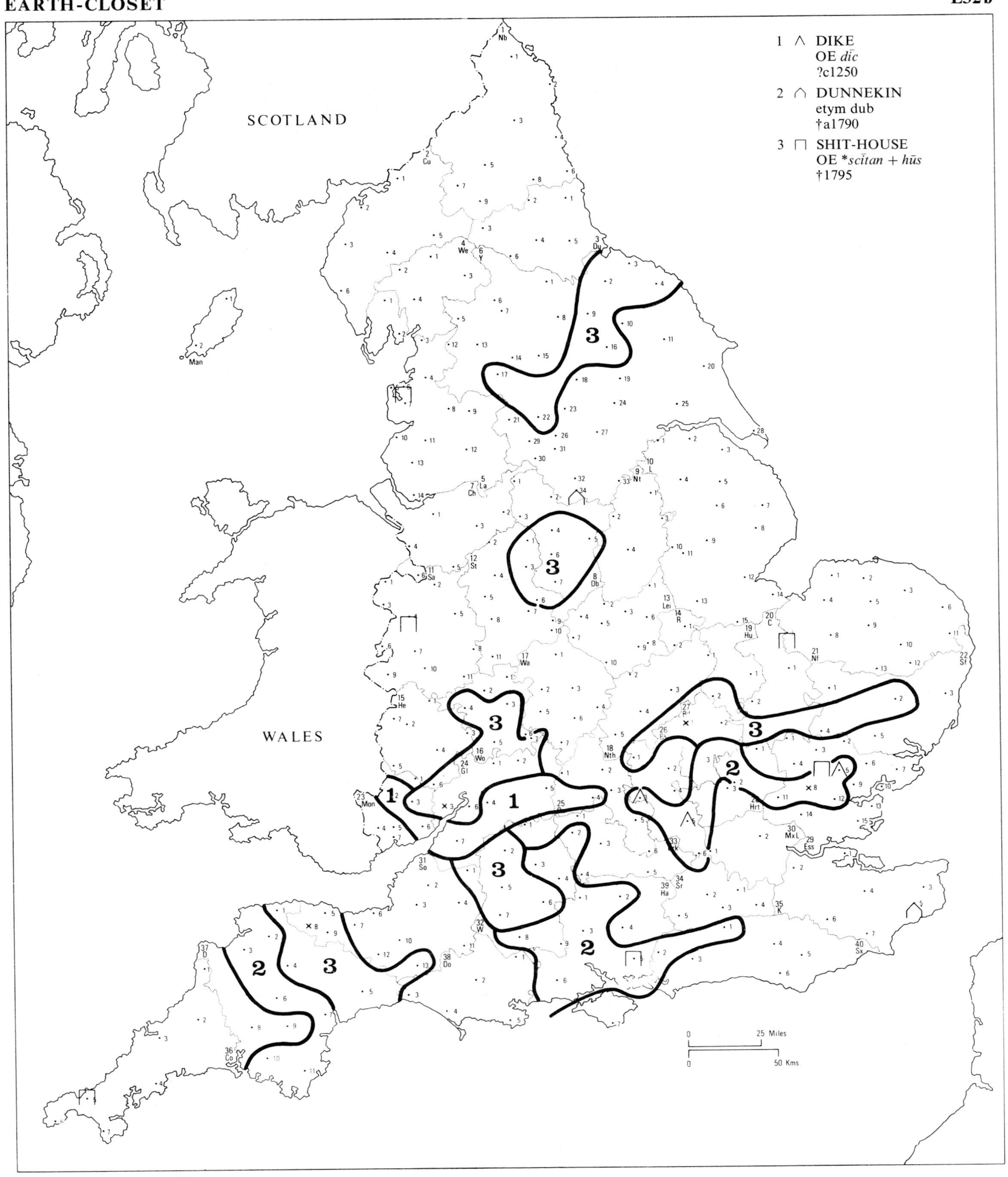

DUDDEKIN 29Ess 11, 32W 8,
DUNNEK 32W 4, 40Sx 1 under DUNNEKIN
SHITTING-HOUSE(OE *hūs*) 22Sf 2 under
SHIT-HOUSE

KINDLING-WOOD L33a

KINDLING-WOOD L33b

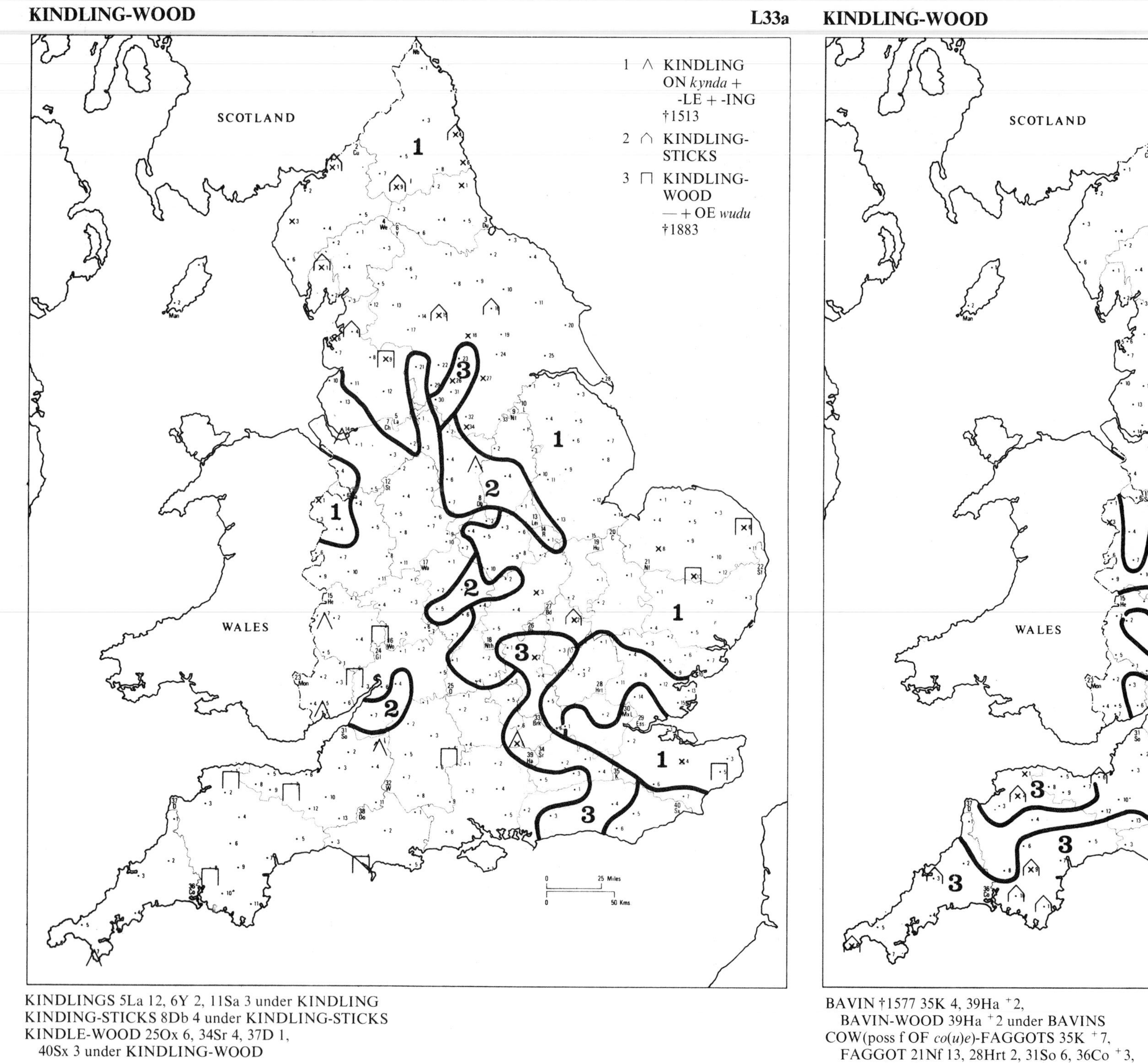

KINDLINGS 5La 12, 6Y 2, 11Sa 3 under KINDLING
KINDING-STICKS 8Db 4 under KINDLING-STICKS
KINDLE-WOOD 25Ox 6, 34Sr 4, 37D 1,
40Sx 3 under KINDLING-WOOD

BAVIN †1577 35K 4, 39Ha +2,
BAVIN-WOOD 39Ha +2 under BAVINS
COW(poss f OF *co(u)e*)-FAGGOTS 35K +7,
FAGGOT 21Nf 13, 28Hrt 2, 31So 6, 36Co +3,
37D 2/+10/+11, FURZEN-FAGGOT 36Co 6,
SCRAP(ON *skrap*)-FAGGOTS 29Ess +7,
SPRAY (etym dub)-FAGGOT 40Sx 1,
SPRAY-FAGGOTS 34Sr 3 under FAGGOTS
MORNING'S WOOD 24Gl +5, 29Ess 11, 32W 1,
40Sx 2, WOOD FOR MORNING 24Gl +5
under MORNING-WOOD

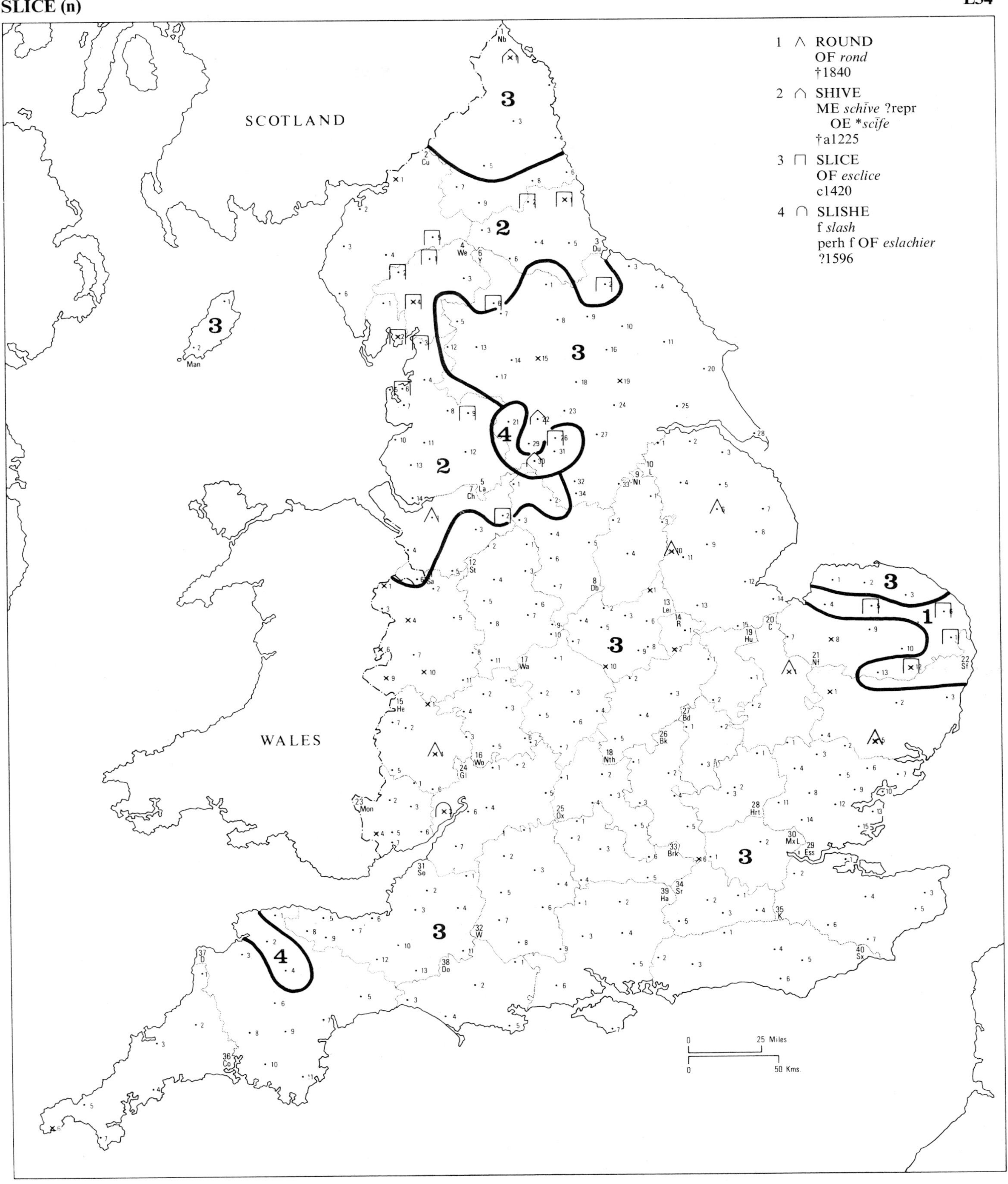

ROUNDEL 22Sf 5 under ROUND

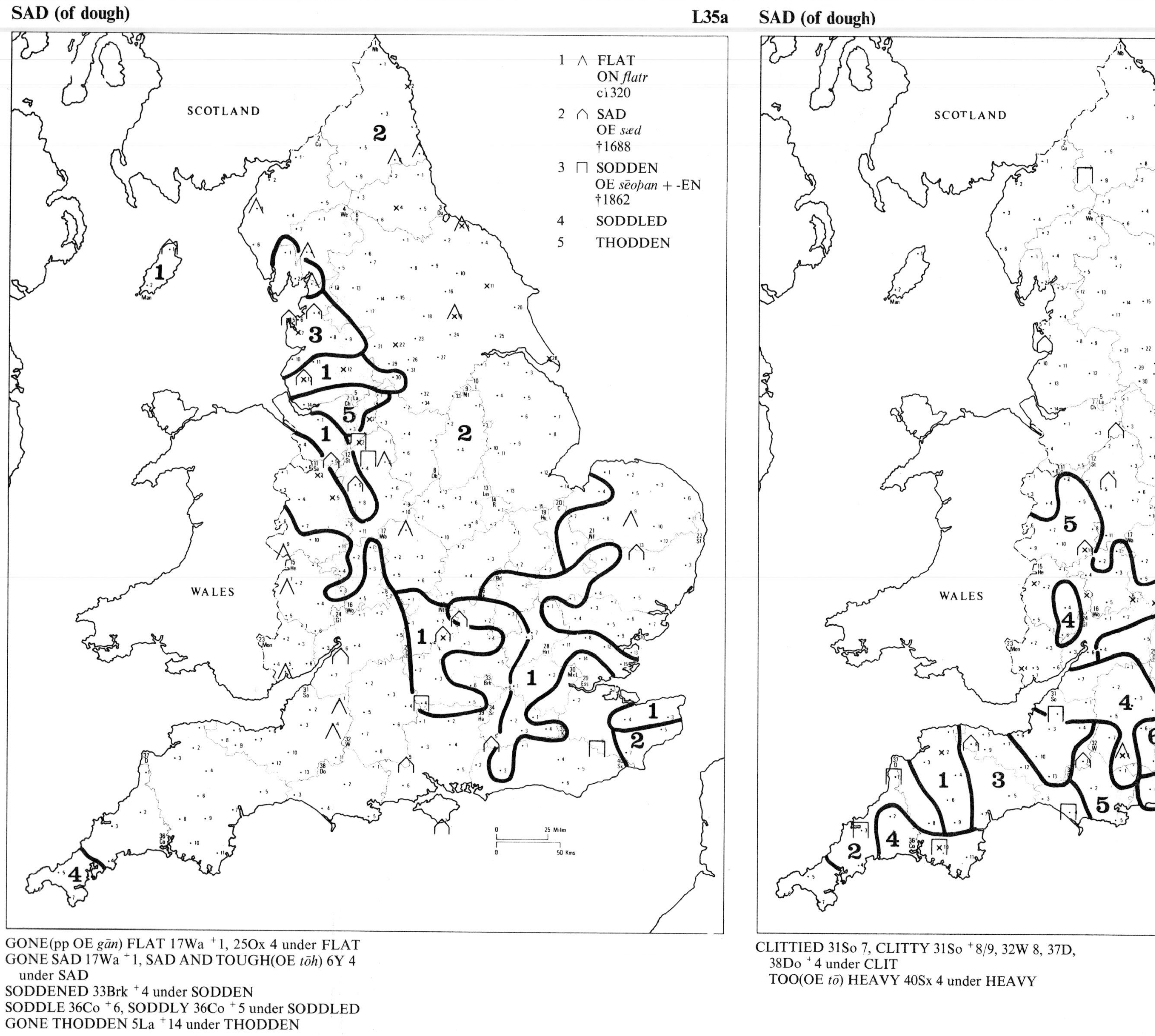

GONE(pp OE *gān*) FLAT 17Wa $^{+}$1, 25Ox 4 under FLAT
GONE SAD 17Wa $^{+}$1, SAD AND TOUGH(OE *tōh*) 6Y 4 under SAD
SODDENED 33Brk $^{+}$4 under SODDEN
SODDLE 36Co $^{+}$6, SODDLY 36Co $^{+}$5 under SODDLED
GONE THODDEN 5La $^{+}$14 under THODDEN

CLITTIED 31So 7, CLITTY 31So $^{+}$8/9, 32W 8, 37D, 38Do $^{+}$4 under CLIT
TOO(OE *tō*) HEAVY 40Sx 4 under HEAVY

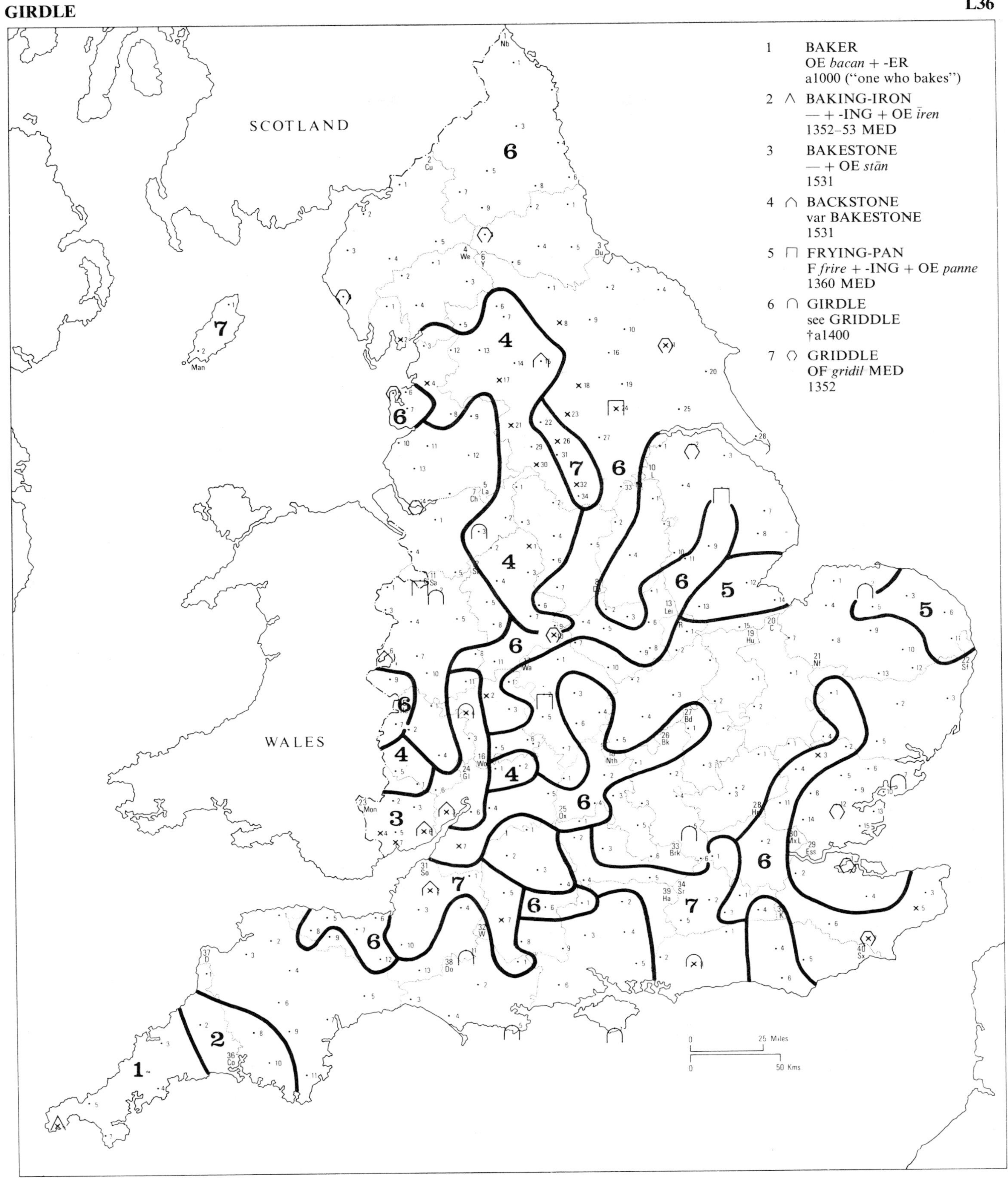

GIRDLE-PLATE(OF *plate*) 2Cu +6,
GIRDLE-STONE(OE *stān*) 12St 11
under GIRDLE

DRIPPING (n) L37

BACON FAT L38

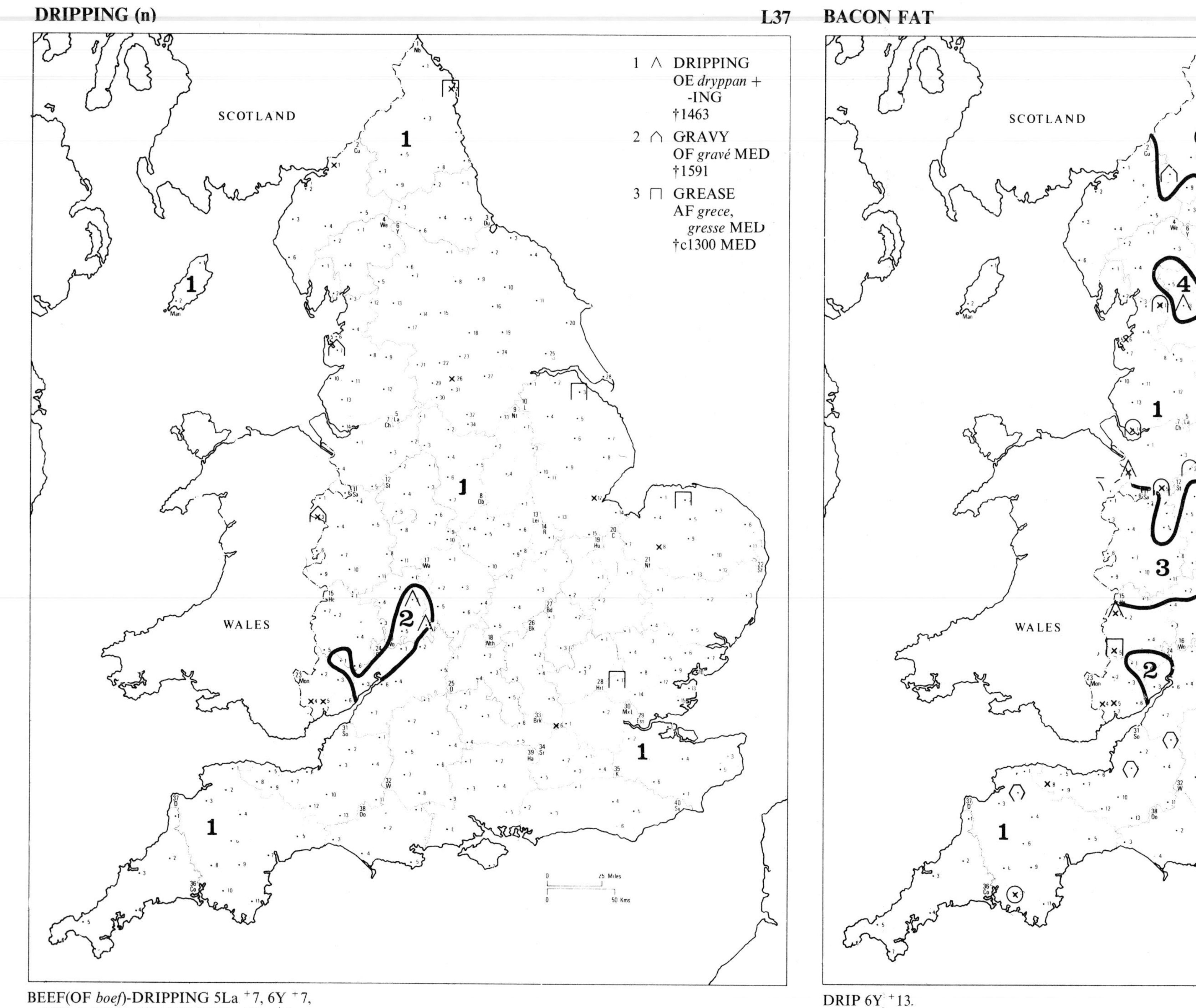

BEEF(OF *boef*)-DRIPPING 5La +7, 6Y +7, 26Bk 2, DRIP 6Y 21/22/29/33, 40Sx +5, DRIPPINGS 21Nf 1/11, DRIPPY 6Y 30 under DRIPPING

DRIP 6Y +13.
DRIPPING 21Nf 9 under BACON-DRIPPING
FAT 6Y +24, 13Lei 8, 20C 1, 21Nf 7, 32W 1, 34Sr 2, 35K 5, 38Do +1, 39Ha +3 under BACON-FAT
LIQUOR 7Ch 6 under BACON-LIQUOR
BACON-DIP 6Y +2/+11/26/27/+29, 7Ch 5, DIPPING 6Y 22, DIPPO 17Wa +4 under DIP
BACON-GREASE 1Nb 2/3, 29Ess 7, 39Ha +3 under GREASE

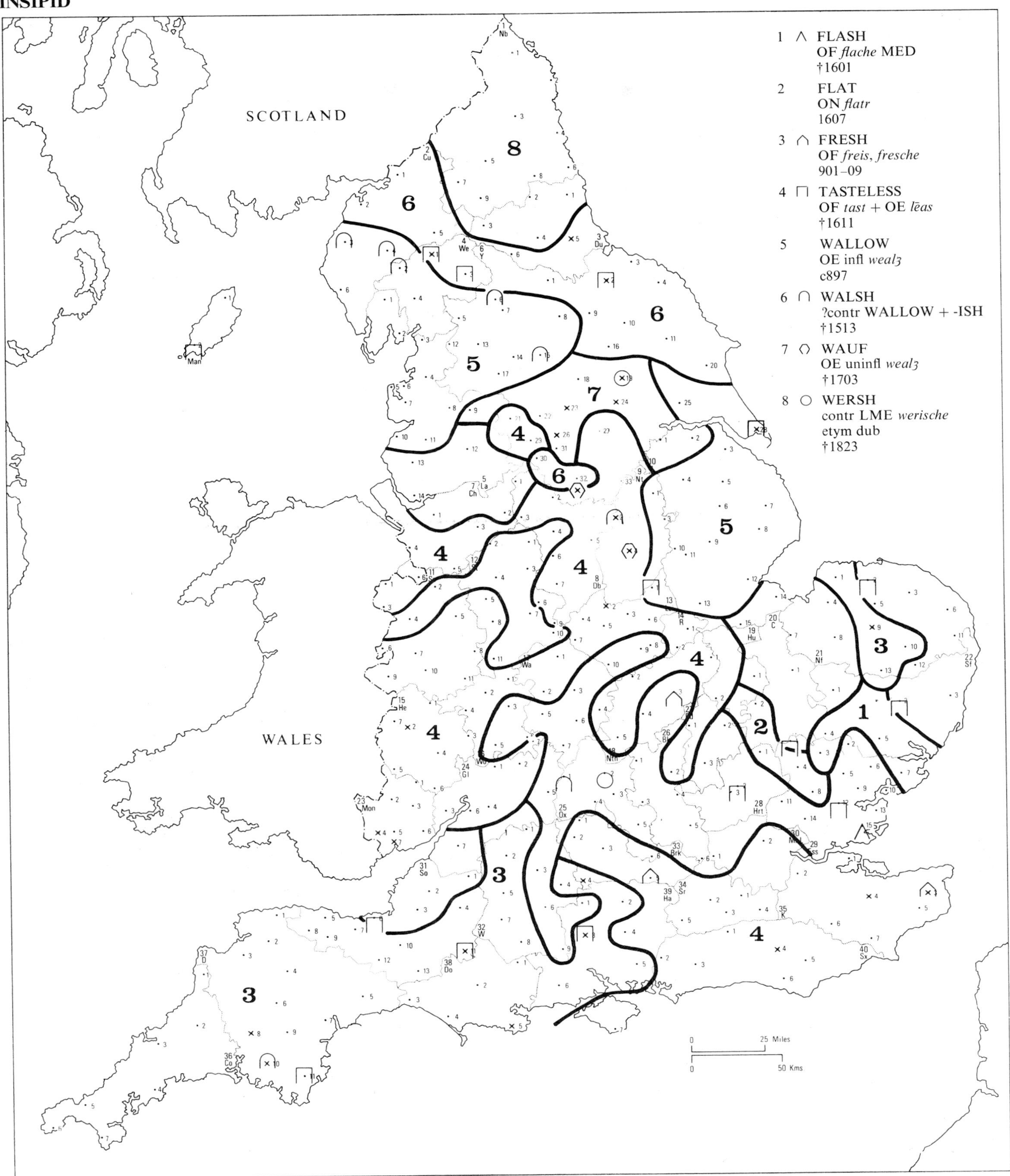

TOO(OE *tō*) FRESH 21Nf 10, 31So 9/10/13, 33Brk $^{+}$5, 35K 3, 37D 5 under FRESH

WALSHY 9Nt 2, WELSH 2Cu 1/2/$^{+}$3/$^{+}$4/5, 4We $^{+}$2/$^{+}$3, 6Y 9, WOLLISH 25Ox 1, WOLSH 6Y $^{+}$1/10/$^{+}$15, 37D 10 under WALSH

WAFFLY 9Nt 4, WAFFY 6Y 18/34, 10L 1/2, WAUGHY 6Y 31 under WAUGH

WAIRISH †1398 25Ox 2, WORRISH 6Y 19 under WERSH

PEA-POD

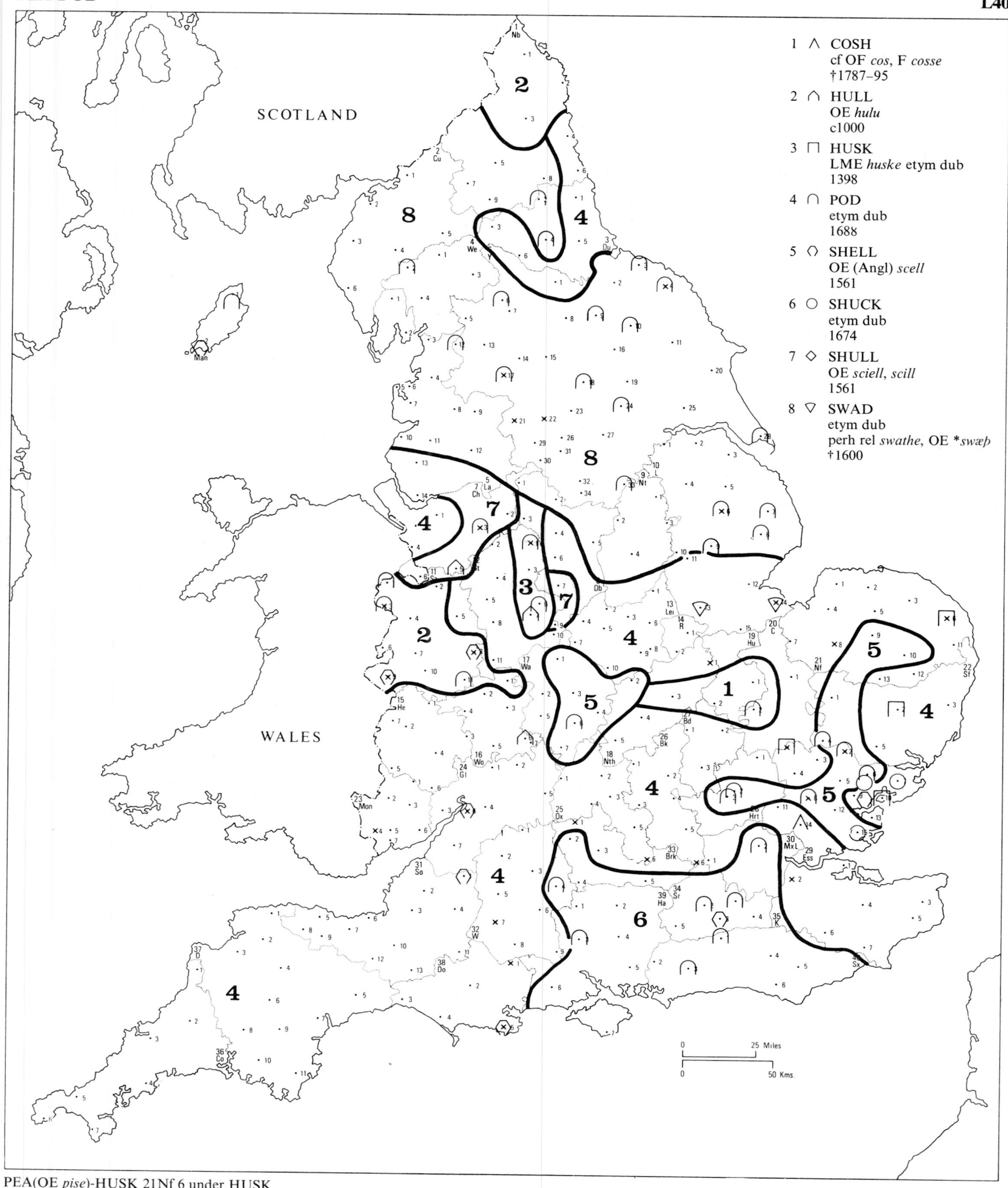

PEA(OE *pise*)-HUSK 21Nf 6 under HUSK
PEA-POD 6Y $^{+}$7/$^{+}$24, 12St 11, 21Nf 1/2/$^{+}$3, 29Ess 3/$^{+}$6/8, 37D 8 under POD
PEA-SHELL †1755 12St $^{+}$2, 24Gl 6, 29Ess $^{+}$6, 31So $^{+}$1, 38Do 5 under SHELL
PEA-SHUCK 30MxL $^{+}$2, 32W $^{+}$4, 33Brk $^{+}$5, 34Sr $^{+}$1, 39Ha $^{+}$1/6 under SHUCK
PEA-SHULL 7Ch $^{+}$2 under SHULL
PEA-SWAD 2Cu $^{+}$6, 5La 6, 6Y $^{+}$3/6/$^{+}$11/$^{+}$18/20/$^{+}$24/26/27/29/30/32/$^{+}$33, SWOD 9Nt 3, 10L 13/14 under SWAD

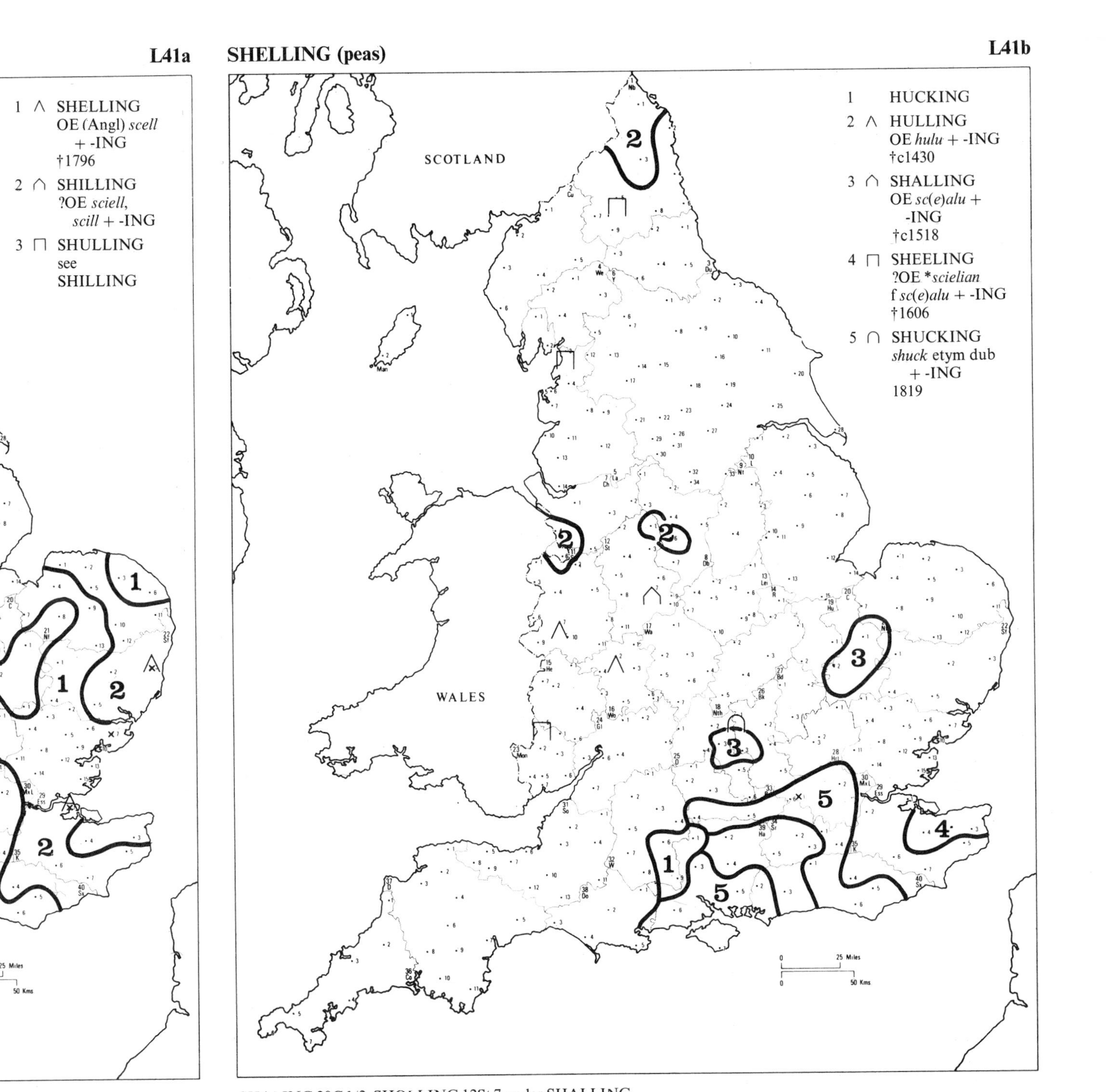

SHELL(ING) OUT 31So 8, 38Do +3 under SHELLING
SHILL OUT 6Y +5 under SHILLING

Forms with ə at 31So 5/9, 37D 2/4 are taken to repr SHELL

SHALING 20C 1/2, SHOLLING 12St 7 under SHALLING

hje·lən 1Nb 3 is taken to repr HULLING

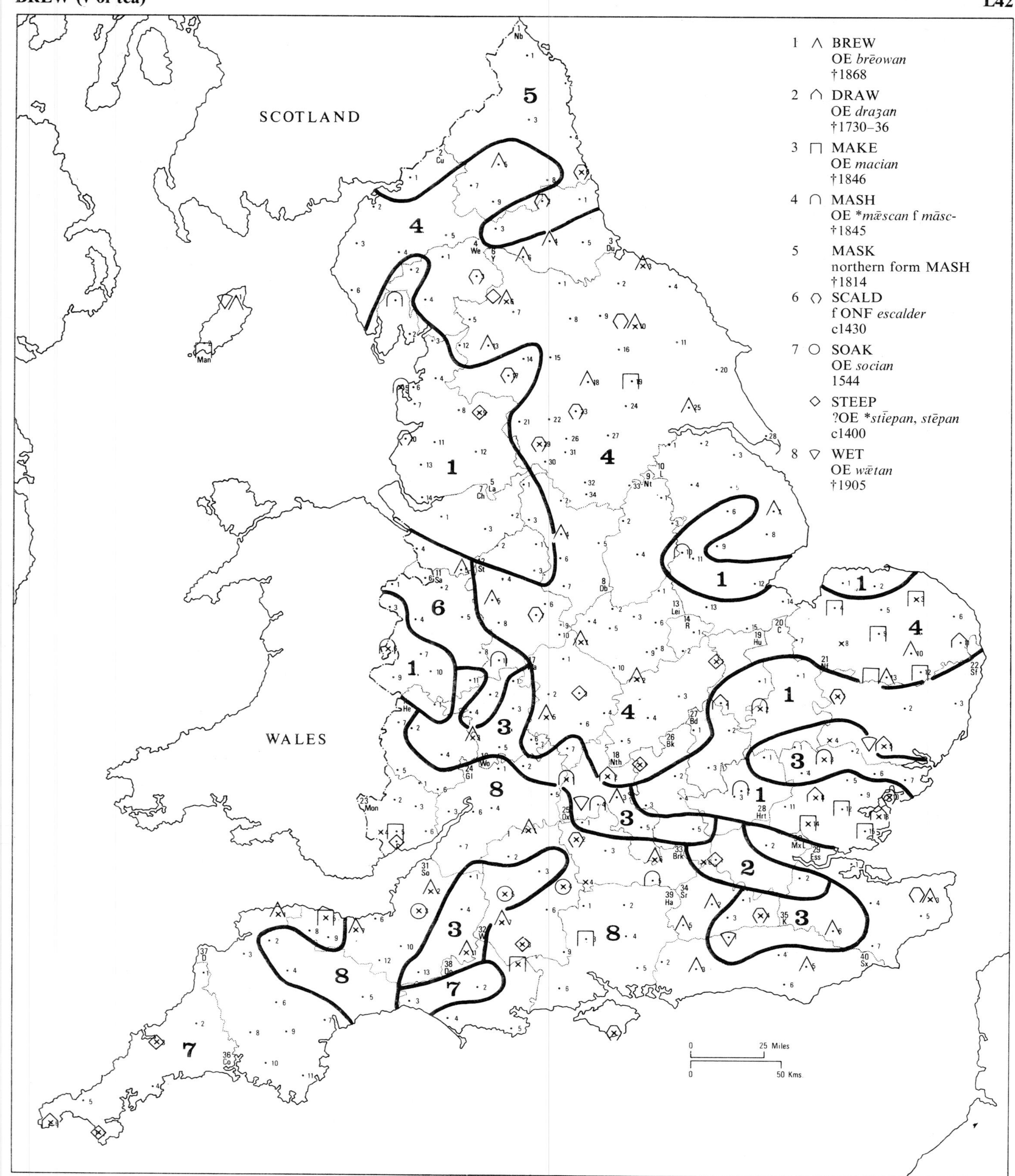

PUT TO DRAW 36Co +6 under DRAW
LEAVE SOAK 36Co 5, LET SOAK 31So 3,
PUT SOAKING 36Co 1,
37D 3/7 under SOAK
MASS 1Nb 8/9, 2Cu 2–6, 4We 1/+3, 5La +1,
MESH 6Y 22 under MASH
MAST 3Du +1/3 under MASK

Although the q specified the pouring of boiling water onto the tea-leaves, the responses included not only words for this, but also for the subsequent process of infusion

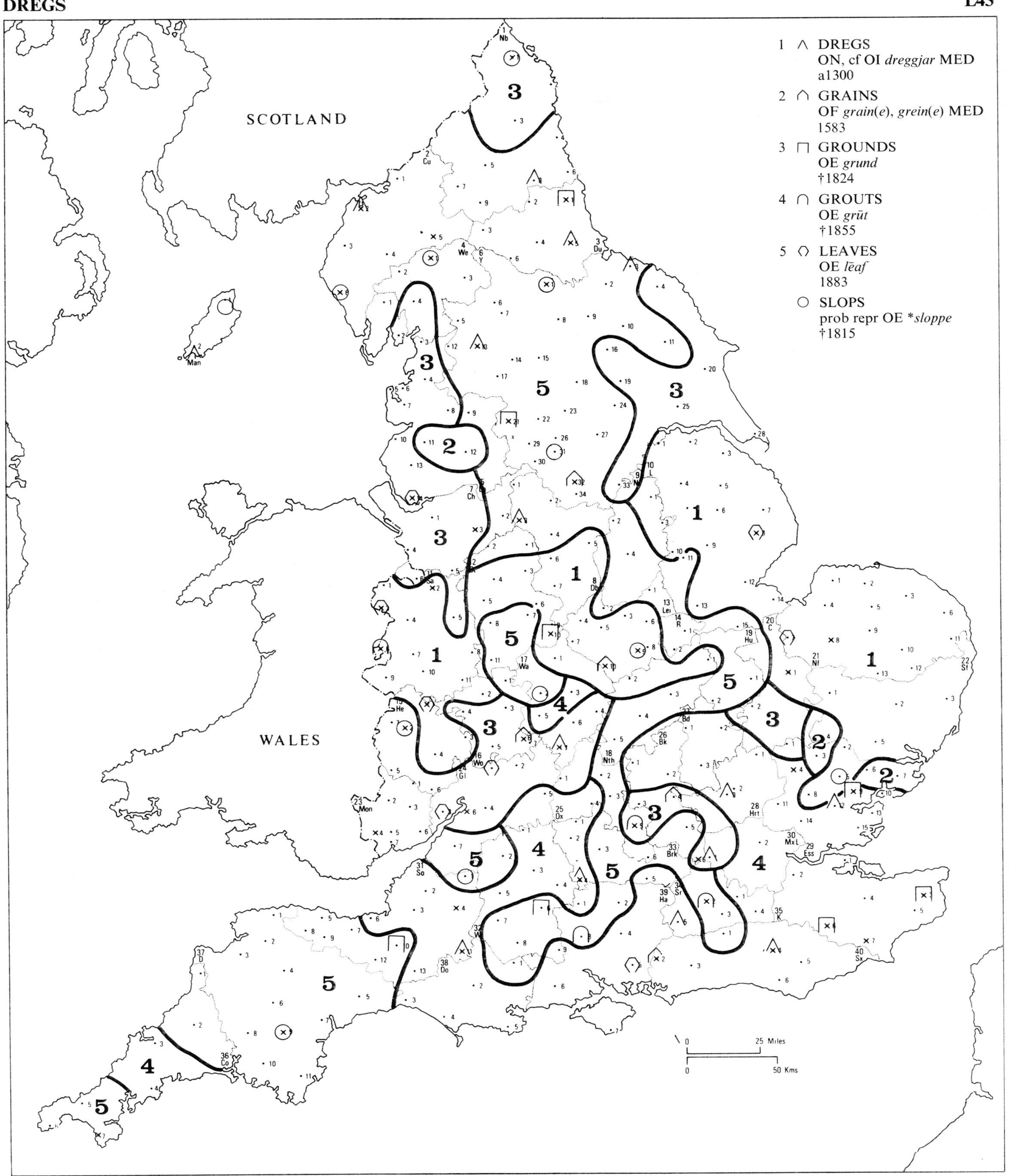

TEA(f Chinese *t'e* 1631)-DREGS 10L 12, 21Nf 4/6 under DREGS
TEA-GRAINS 5La 11/12, 6Y 32, 22Sf 4, 29Ess 6 under GRAINS
TEA-GROUNDS 5La 2–8/10/13, 6Y 4/16/20/21/+25/27/28, 7Ch 4, 11Sa 5, 12St 10, 15He 7, 16Wo +3, 17Wa 4, 23Mon 2/5, 24Gl +1/2/+3/4, 25Ox 1 under GROUNDS
TEA-GROUTS 17Wa 3, 32W +3, 35K 1/4, 36Co 3, 38Do 2, 39Ha 1 under GROUTS

TEA-LEAVES †1756 1Nb 4/5/7/+8/9, 2Cu 1/3/4, 3Du 2–4/6, 4We 2/3, 5La 1/9/14, 6Y 2/5–7/9–12/14/15/17/18/22–24/26/29/30/+31/34, 7Ch 2, 8Db 1/2/4, 9Nt 2/4, 10L 8/11, 11Sa 3, 12St 2/7/11, 13Lei 1/2, 14R 1/2, 15He 1, 17Wa +2, 18Nth 3–5, 19Hu 1/2, 24Gl +1/7, 25Ox 2/3/6, 26Bk 5, 31So 5/7–9/+10/12, 32W 2/+6/7/8, 33Brk 3, 34Sr 3, 36Co 1/2/5/6, 37D 1–8/10/11, 38Do 1, 39Ha 2/+3/+5, 40Sx 1 under LEAVES
SLOP 6Y +31, TEA-SLOPS 4We 1 under SLOPS

gɹɛgz 13Lei 7, gɹɛ̣'gz̥ 29Ess 10 are taken to repr DREGS; gɹɛɪts 26Bk 1 is taken to repr GROUTS

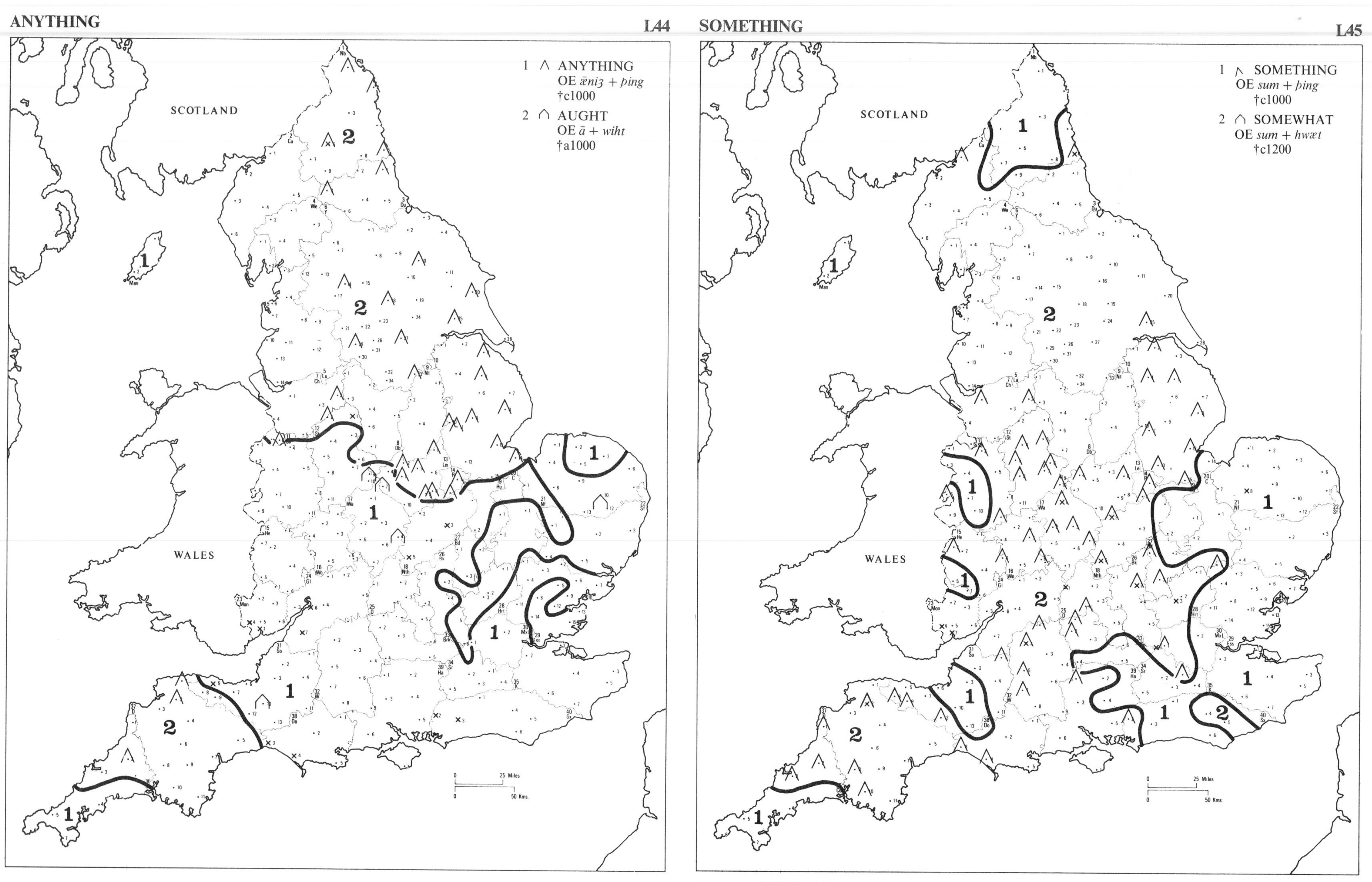

SOMEWHATS 9Nt $^{+}$1,
10L $^{+}$5/$^{+}$10/$^{+}$12 under SOMEWHAT

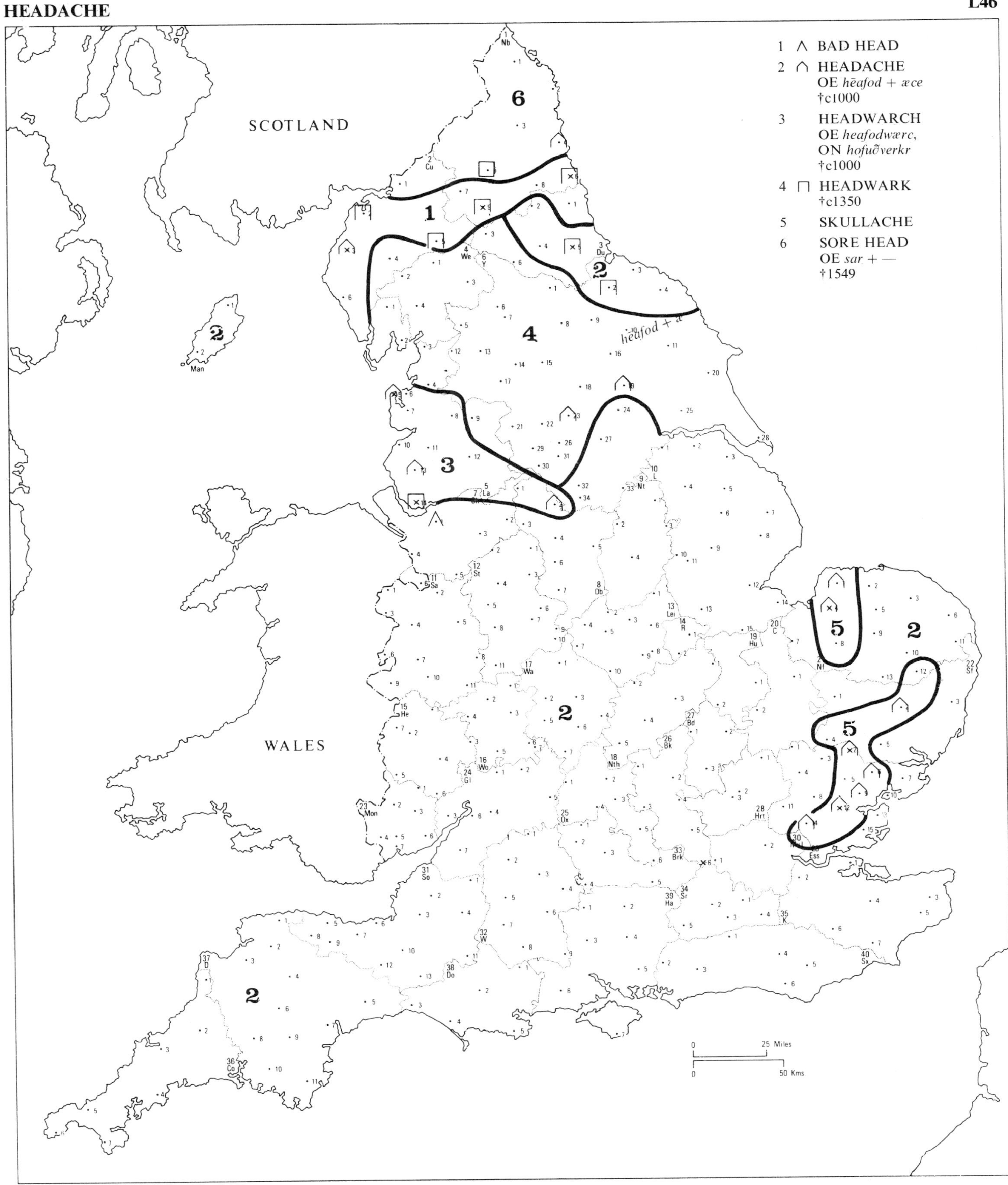

The following pre-modifications were rec:
A (BAD HEAD) 1Nb 7/8, 2Cu $^+$2/$^+$5/6, 7Ch $^+$1
A BIT OF (HEADACHE) 31So 7;
A (HEADACHE) 7Ch 4/6, 9Nt $^+$1/3, 10L 2/10, 11Sa 4, 13Lei 7/9, 17Wa 3/7, 18Nth 2/4/5, 19Hu 1, 20C 2, 21Nf 2/9, 22Sf $^+$2, 23Mon 5, 24Gl 7, 25Ox 3, 26Bk 3–5, 27Bd 1–3, 28Hrt 2, 29Ess 1/$^+$6/8/$^+$10/12/13/$^+$14, 30MxL 2, 31So 3/8, 32W 4, 33Brk 5, 34Sr 2, 37D 9, 38Do $^+$2, 40Sx 1;
A NASTY (HEADACHE) 16Wo 7;
AN (HEADACHE) 9Nt $^+$1, 13Lei 1–6/10, 14R 1/2, 17Wa 7, 23Mon 7;
THE (HEADACHE) 1Nb $^+$4, 3Du 2, 5La 5, 6Y $^+$2/4/$^+$23/24/27/32–34, 7Ch $^+$1/3/5, 8Db 7, 9Nt 4, 10L 8/9/15, 11Sa 1/2/5–11, 12St $^+$9, 15He 1–6, 16Wo 1–6, 17Wa 1/4–6, 18Nth 1/3, 19Hu 2, 20C 1, 21Nf 4/7, 22Sf 1/3/5, 23Mon 1/2/6, 24Gl 1–6, 25Ox 1/2/5/6, 26Bk 2, 28Hrt 1, 29Ess 2/$^+$10/$^+$14, 30MxL 1, 31So 4/6/$^+$9/13, 32W 3/5/6/8, 33Brk 4, 35K 2, 36Co $^+$1/3/5/6, 37D 1/2/5/7/10/11, 38Do $^+$2/3/5, 39Ha 1/3
THE (HEADWARCH) 5La 6/8/10, 8Db 1
A BIT (HEADWARK) 3Du $^+$6;
A (HEADWARK) 2Cu $^+$5, 6Y 1/8/10;
A TERRIBLE (HEADWARK) 6Y 7;
A (SKULLACHE) 29Ess $^+$6/$^+$14;
THE (SKULLACHE) 22Sf 4, 29Ess 5/$^+$14
A (SORE HEAD) 1Nb 1–3/$^+$4, 2Cu 1;

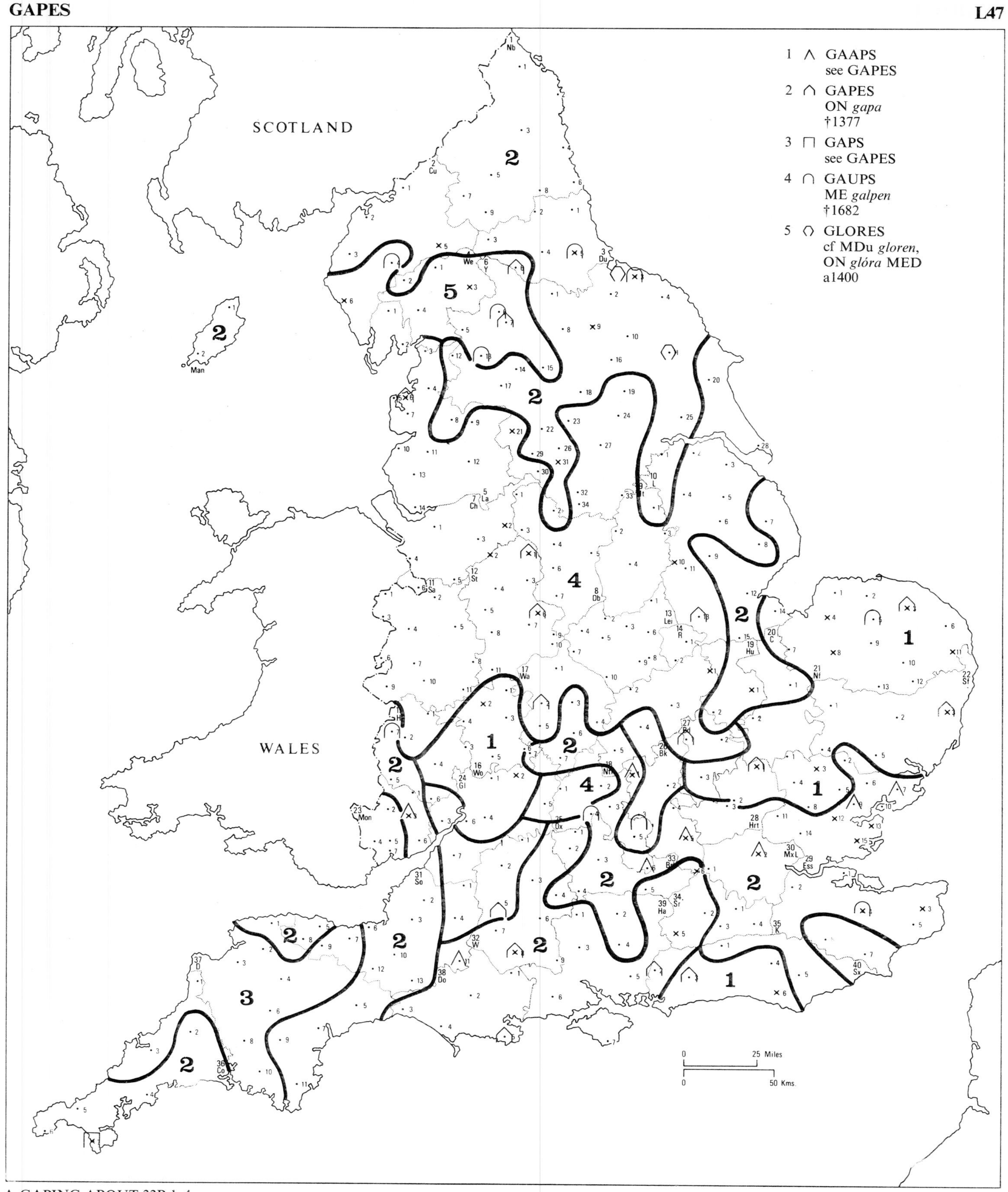

A-GAPING ABOUT 33Brk 4,
GAPING ABOUT 39Ha 2 under GAPES
GAPPING ABOUT 38Do +3 under GAPS

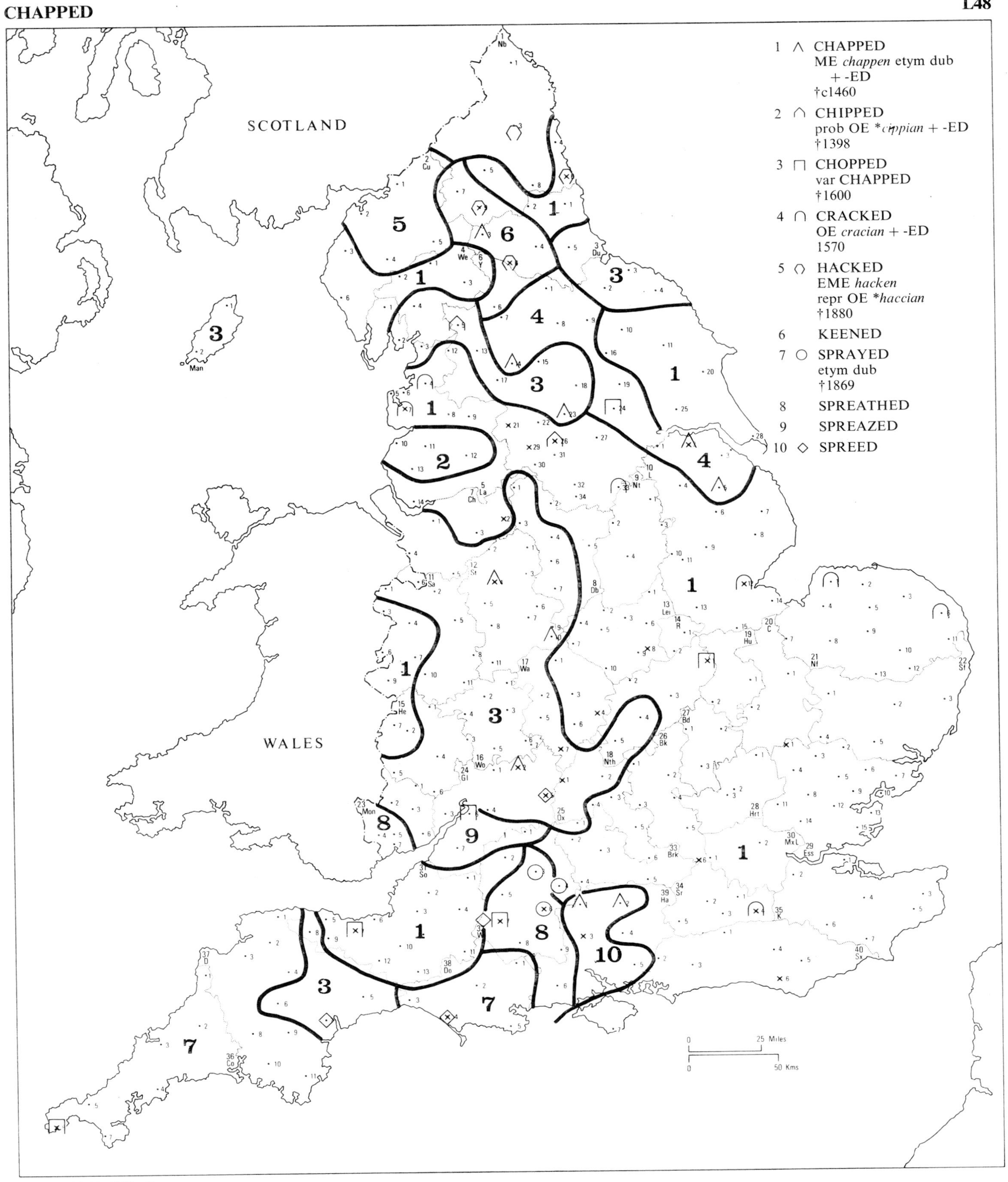

CHAP 6Y 12, 25Ox 3,
CHAPPY 31So $^{+}$1 under CHAPPED
CHIP 5La 11 under CHIPPED
CHOPPY 7Ch 5, 31So 8 under CHOPPED
CRACKED AND SORE(OE *sār*) 6Y $^{+}$14 under CRACKED
HACKY 1Nb 6 under HACKED
SPRAYED UP(OE *up*) 37D $^{+}$11 under SPRAYED
SPREAZE (pres = SPREAZED Edd) 32W 1 under SPREAZED

LOOSE PIECE OF SKIN

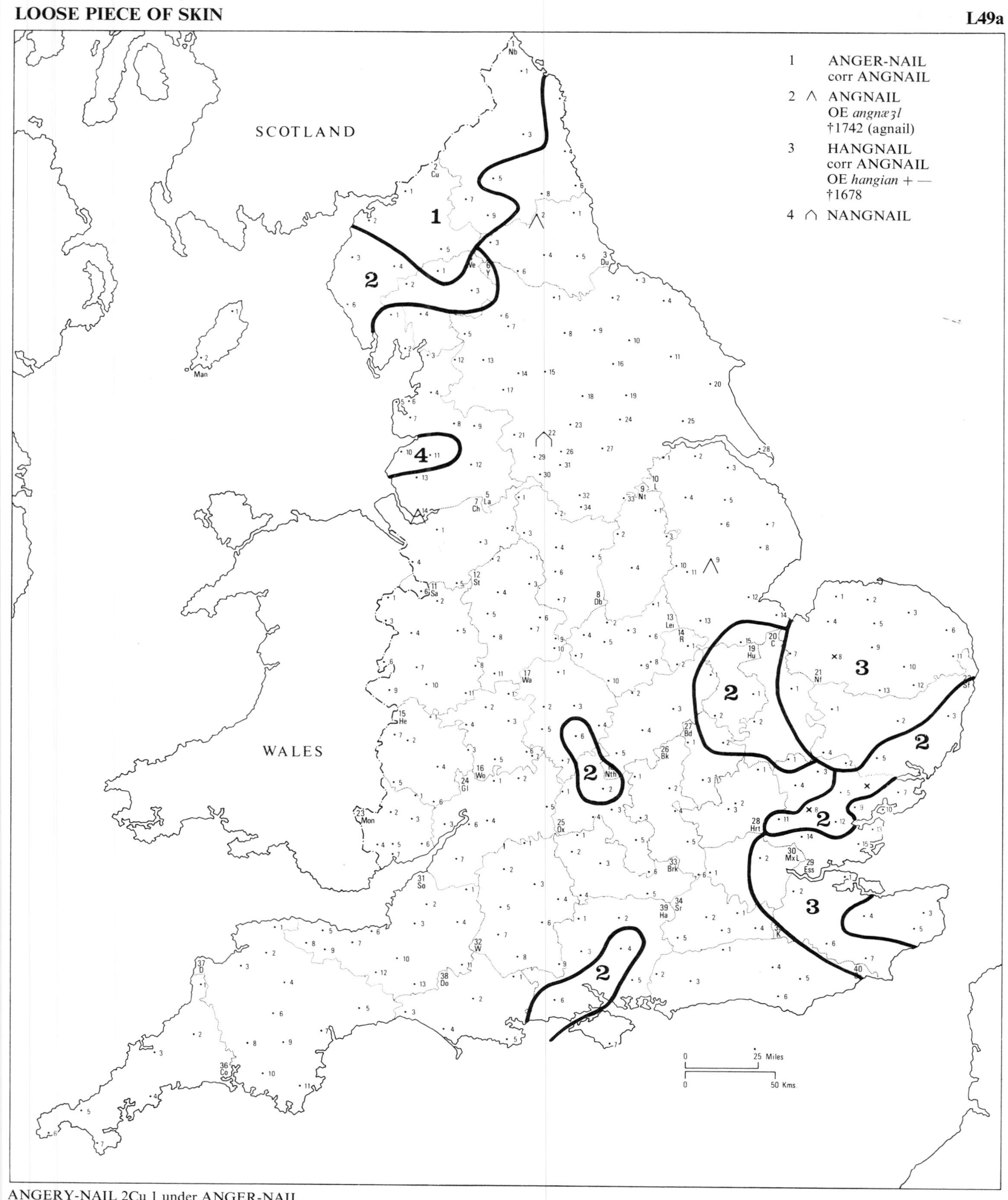

ANGERY-NAIL 2Cu 1 under ANGER-NAIL
ANGERNAIL 22Sf 5,
ANGING-NAIL 18Nth 1 under ANGNAIL

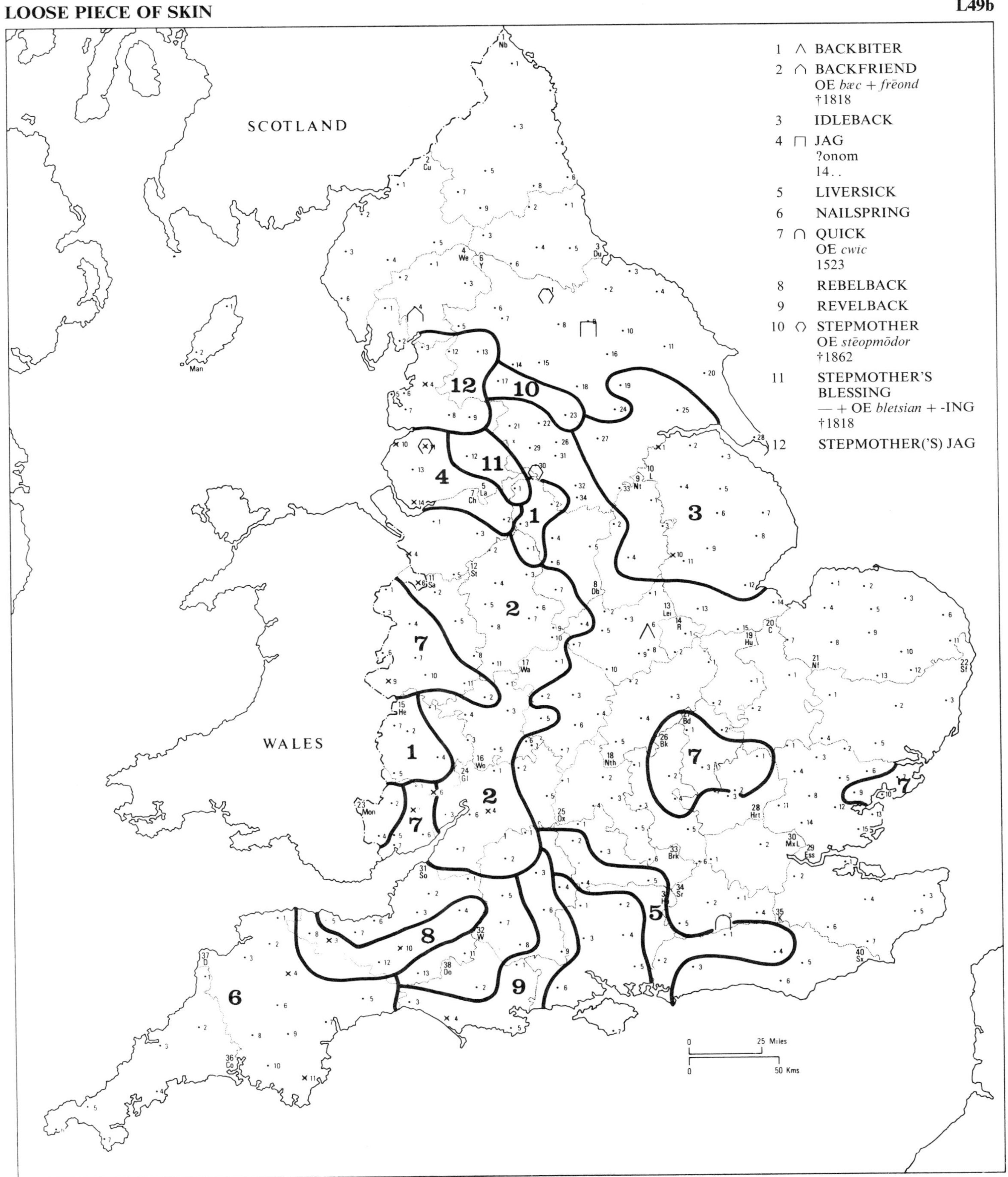

BACKFEEN 17Wa 2, BACKFEN 7Ch 5,
BACKFRAN 11Sa 2 under BACKFRIEND
LIVERKSICK (sic) 40Sx 1,
LIVERSLICK 40Sx 4 under LIVERSICK
RIVELBACK 38Do 5 under REVELBACK
STEPMOTHER JACK 6Y 12,
STEPMOTHER'S JAG 5La 3 under
STEPMOTHER JAG

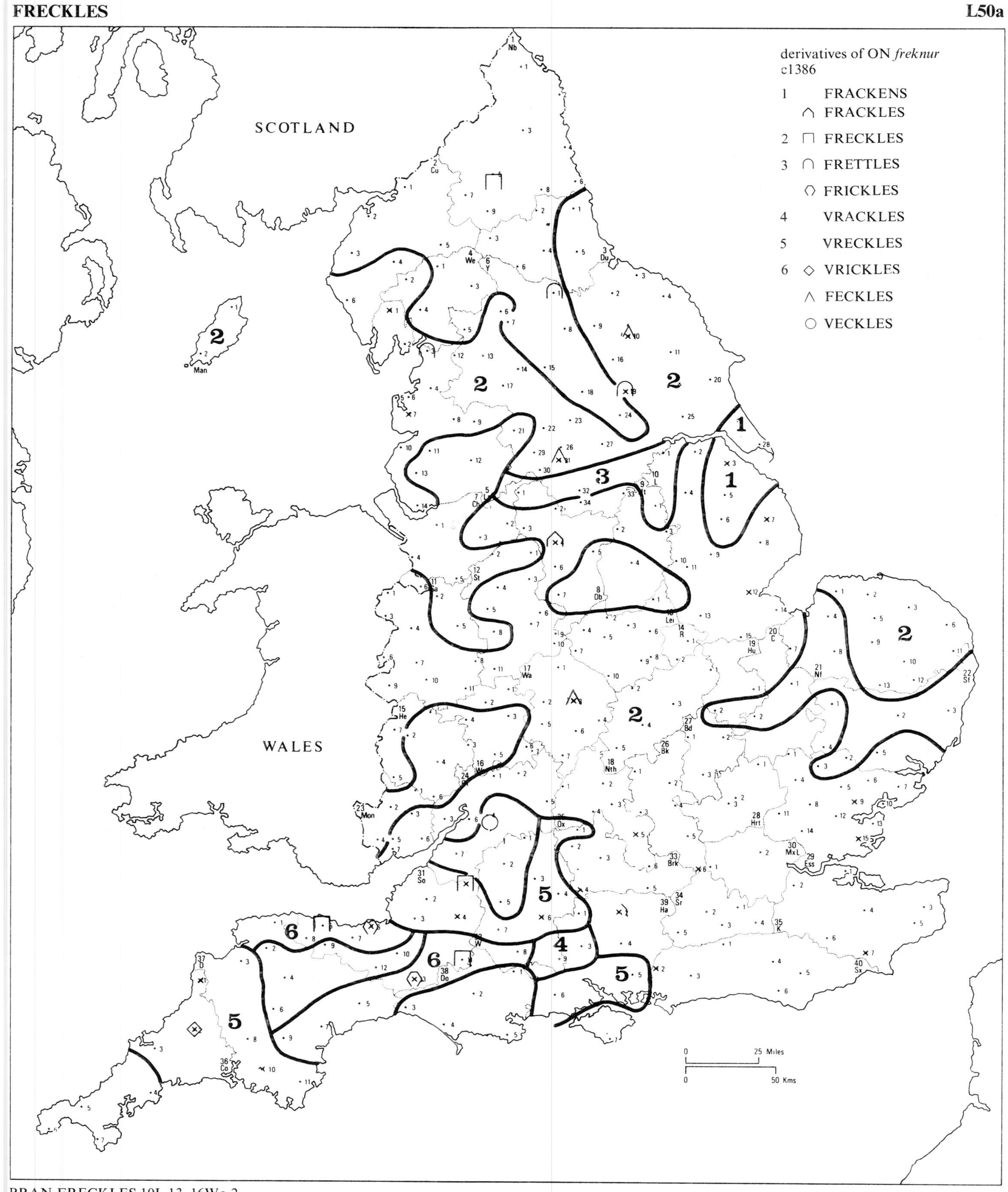

BRAN-FRECKLES 10L 13, 16Wo 2, 19Hu 1, FRAN-FRECKLES 9Nt 3, 10L 10/11, FRON-FRECKLES 6Y 27, SUN(OE *sunne*)-FRECKLES 24Gl ⁺6, 34Sr ⁺1 under FRECKLES
SUMMER(OE *sumor*)-VRACKLES 32W 9 under VRACKLES
SUN-VRECKLES 31So 2 under VRECKLES
FYECKLES 11Sa 5 under FECKLES

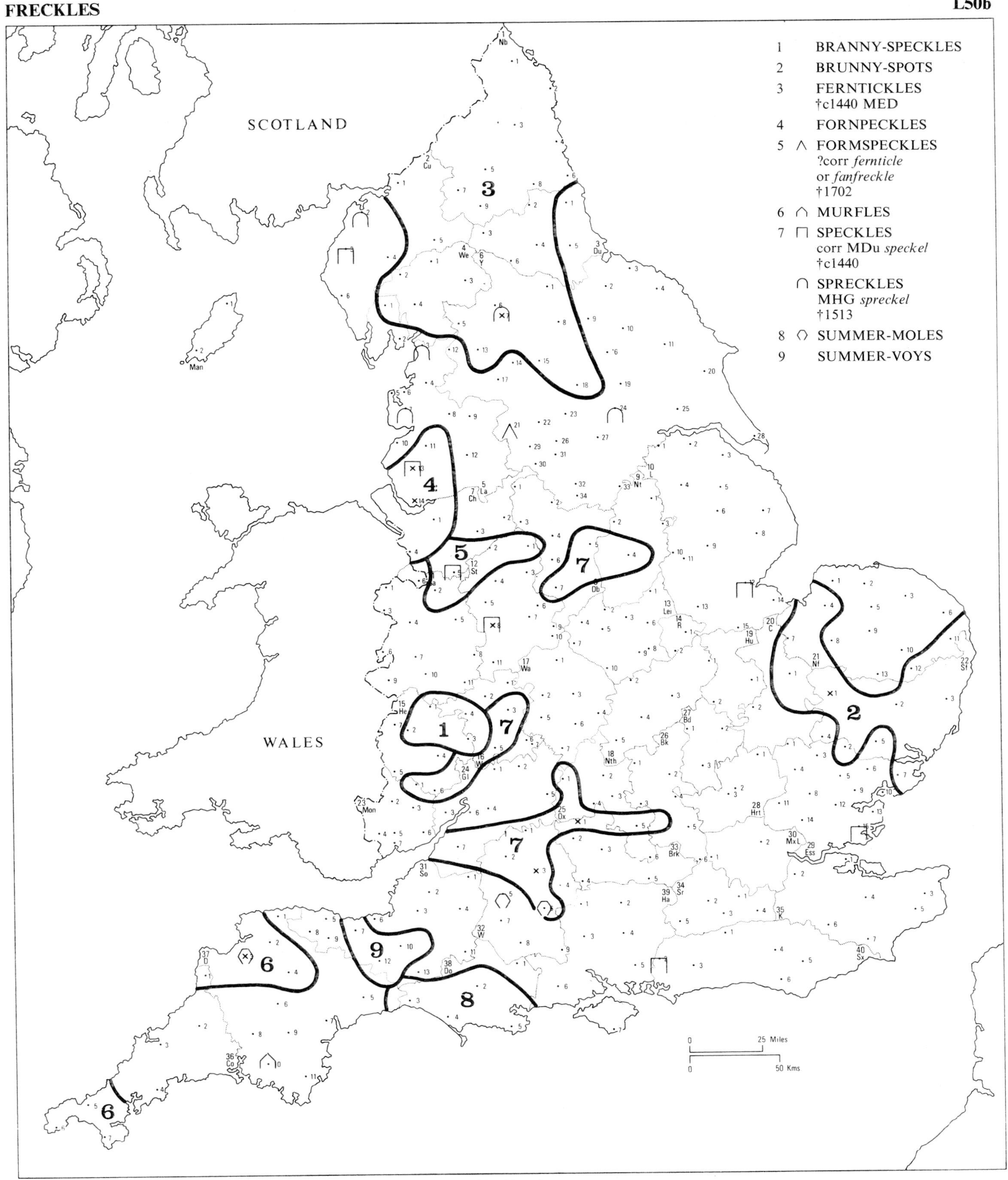

BRANNYSPRECKLES 16Wo 4,
BRANSPECKLES 15He 1 under
BRANNY-SPECKLES
BRUNSPOTS 20C 1, 21Nf 4,
29Ess 2 under BRUNNY-SPOTS
FANTICKLES 1Nb 7/9, 2Cu 5, 3Du 2–4/6,
4We 2–4, 5La 1, 6Y 1/13/15/18,
FARNTICKLES 1Nb 6,
FARNYTICKLES 1Nb 8,
FERNYTICKLES 1Nb 1/3/5,
FRANTICKLES 4We 1,
FRANTITTLES 6Y 8,
FREENYTICKLES 6Y 5,
FRENTICKLES 6Y 6 under FERNTICKLES

FORMPECKLES 5La 11 under
FORNPECKLES
FAAMSPECKLES 6Y 21,
FORMSPECKS 12St 1,
FORNSPECKLES 7Ch $^{+}$5 under
FORMSPECKLES
MUFFLES 36Co 1 under MURFLES
SPETTLES 8Db 7, SUN(OE *sunne*)-SPECKLES
24Gl 7 under SPECKLES
MOLDS 32W $^{+}$5,
SUMMER(OE *sumor*)-MOLDS 32W $^{+}$5/$^{+}$6,
38Do 2/5 under SUMMER-MOLES

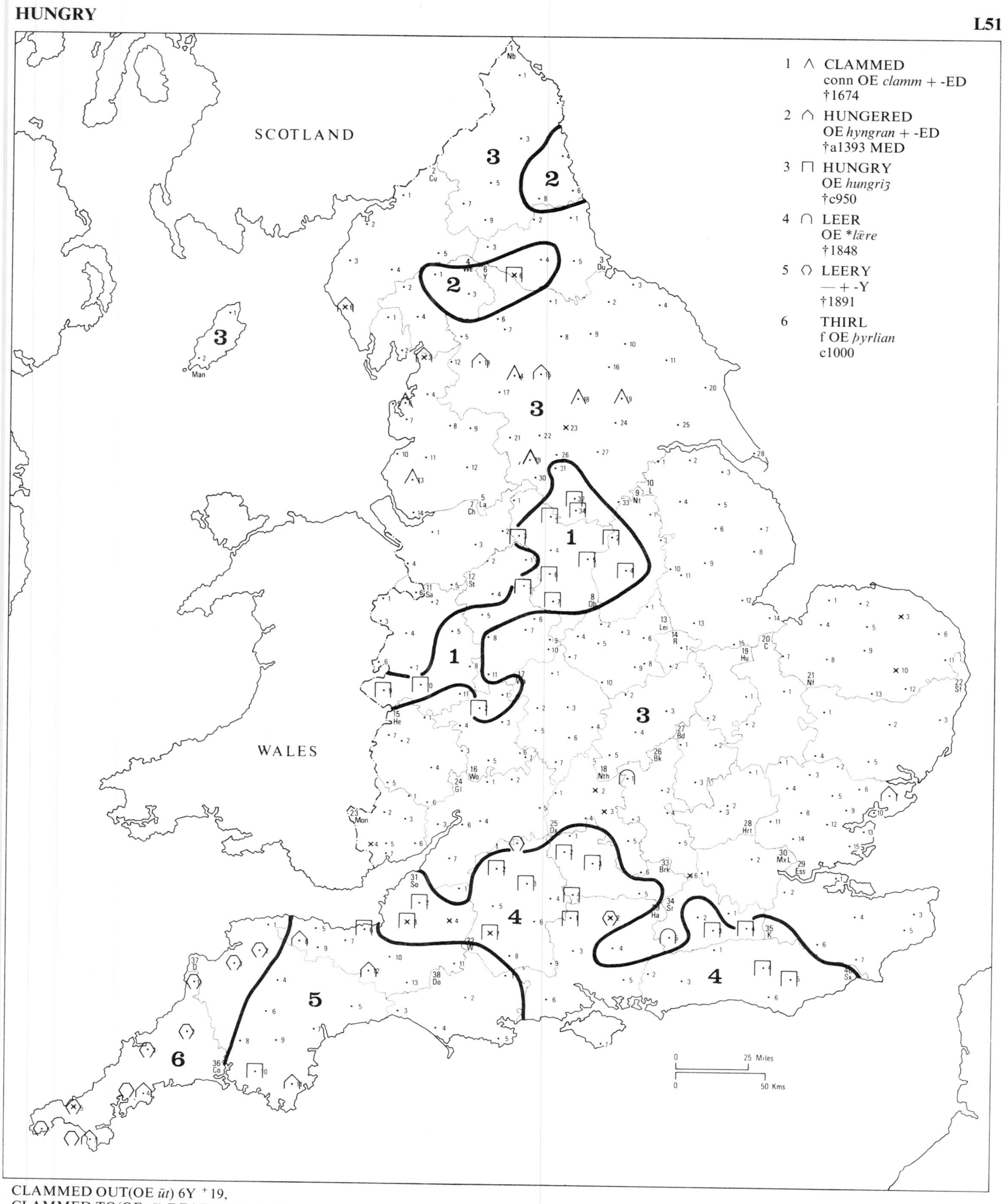

CLAMMED OUT(OE *ūt*) 6Y +19,
CLAMMED TO(OE *tō*) DEATH(OE *dēaþ*)
5La 6im, 6Y 14im/32im, 8Db 4im,
16Wo 1im/+2, CLAMMED TO THE
DEATH 6Y 29im, CLAMMISH 6Y +31,
CLEMMED ?c1540 8Db +6/+7,
11Sa 5/+9, 12St 5,
CLEMMED TO DEATH 8Db +3,
11Sa +10, 12St +3 under CLAMMED
HUNGER (sic) 36Co +7,
HUNGERED TO DEATH 2Cu 6im,
6Y 15im under HUNGERED
THIRDLE 37D 1/+2/+3,
THIRLY 36Co +7 under THIRL

BRIM (of hat)

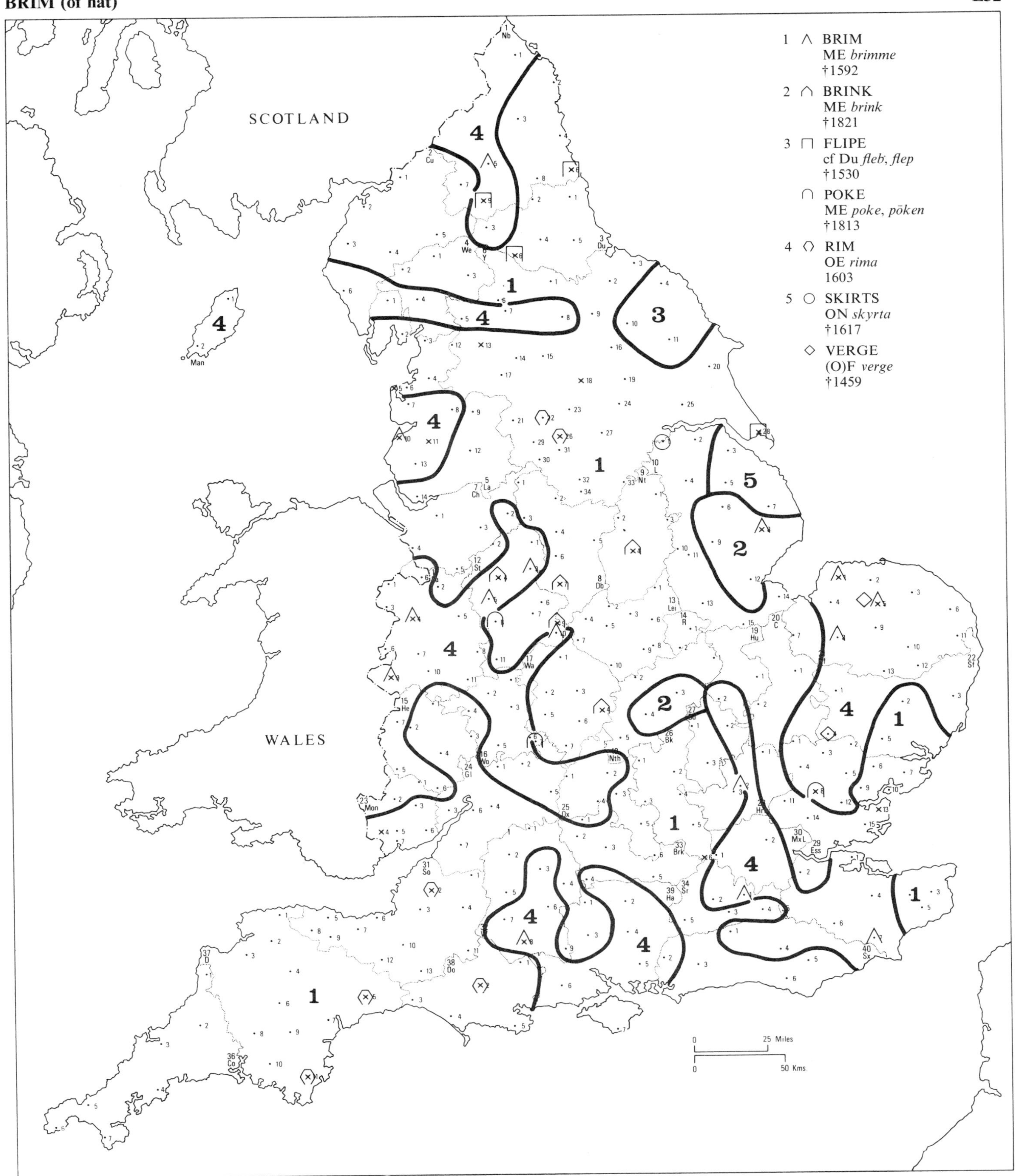

BRINKS 9Nt 4, 10L 9, 18Nth 3/4 under BRINK
HAT(OE *hæt*)-SKIRTS 10L 7,
SKIRT 10L +1 under SKIRTS

JACKET L53 | SHIRT L54

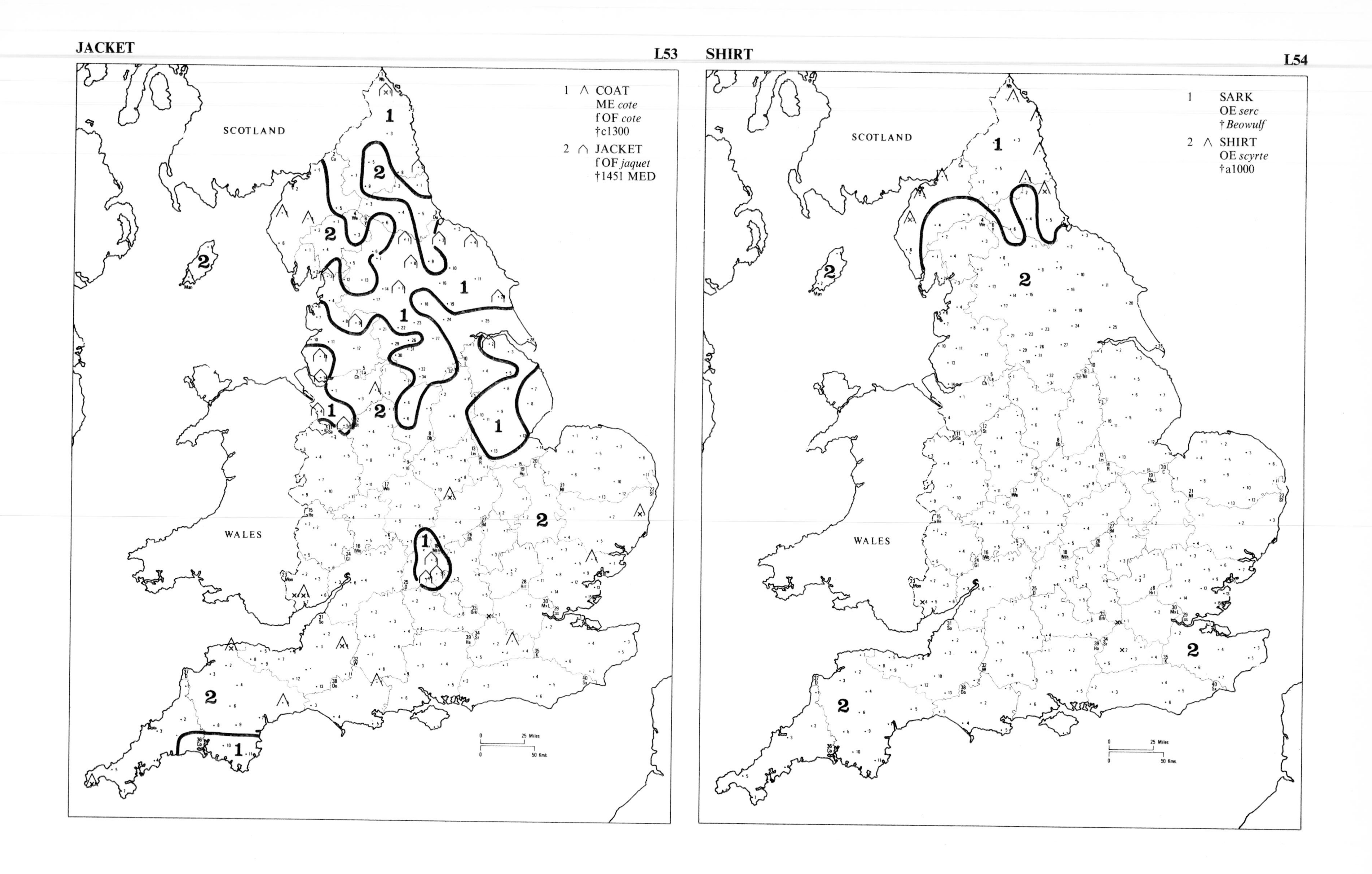

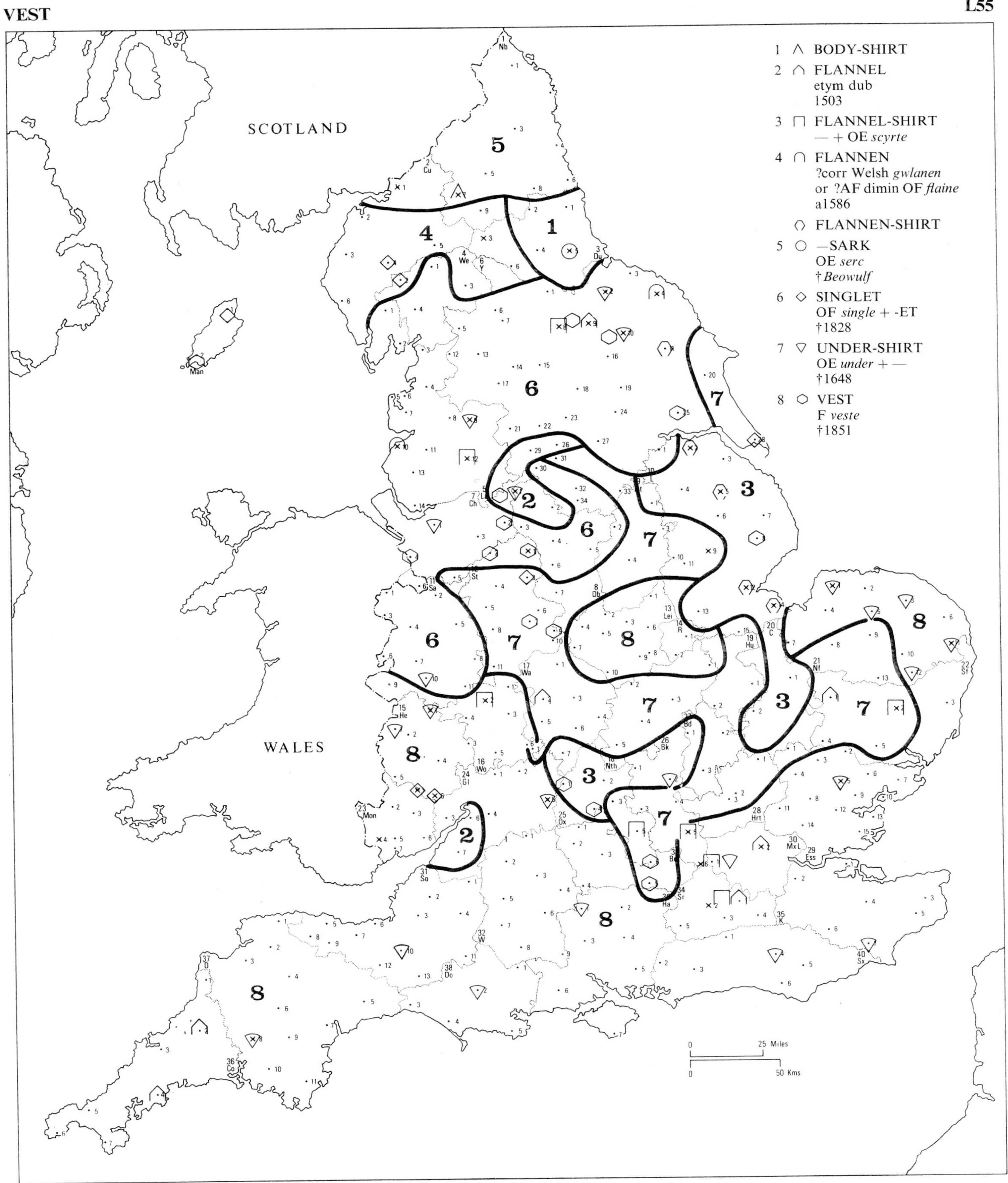

BODY(OE *bodig*)-FLANNEN 1Nb 9, 3Du 6,
4We 3 under FLANNEN
BODY-SARK 1Nb 3/4/6/8, 3Du 5,
FLANNEL-SARK 1Nb 1,
UNDER(OE *under*)-SARK 1Nb 2/5
under -SARK
FLANNEL-SINGLET 5La 8,
SINGLER 11Sa 8 under SINGLET
FLANNEL UNDER-SHIRT 5La 9,
6Y 33, 26Bk 4 under UNDER-SHIRT
UNDER-VEST 7Ch +4, 8Db +1, 12St 1,
18Nth 1, 21Nf 7, 25Ox +4, 29Ess 11, 31So +7,
32W 6, 33Brk 2 under VEST

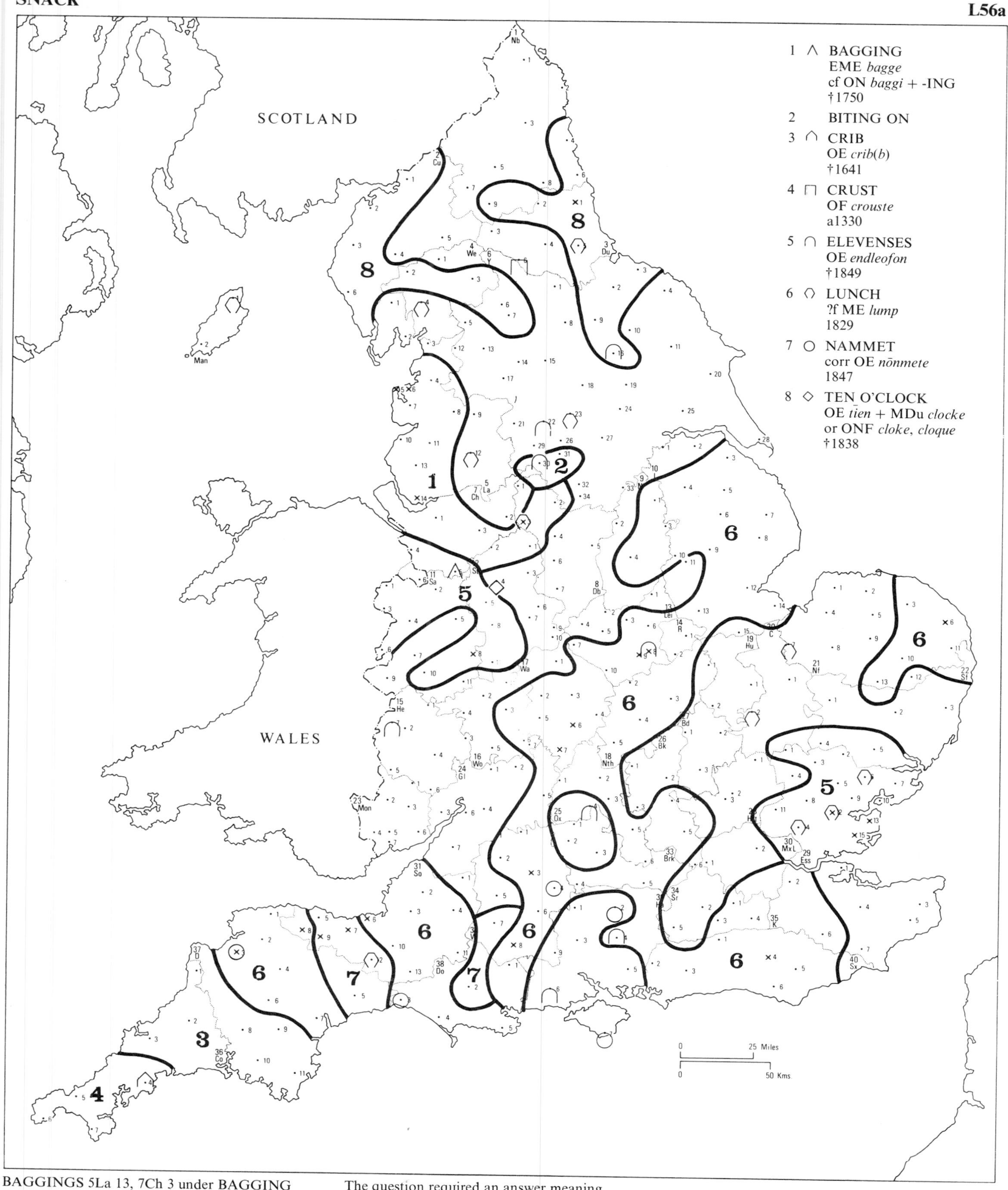

BAGGINGS 5La 13, 7Ch 3 under BAGGING
A BIT(OE *bita*) OF CRIB 37D +9/+11
under CRIB
A LITTLE(OE *lȳtel*) LUNCH 12St +11,
BIT OF LUNCH 38Do 5,
SNACK(etym dub 1757) OF LUNCH
31So +3 under LUNCH
NAMMEK 39Ha 2, NAMMETS 32W +7,
33Brk 2, NOMMET 38Do 2,
NUMMEK 31So 5, NUMMET 31So +12,
37D 5 under NAMMET
BITE OF TEN O'CLOCK 2Cu +3,
TEN O'CLOCKS 2Cu 1/2/6,
6Y 2/3/6/7/9/+16 under TEN O'CLOCK

The question required an answer meaning
"a snack between breakfast and the mid-day meal"

Where the contents of the snack were rec,
bread was always the major constituent

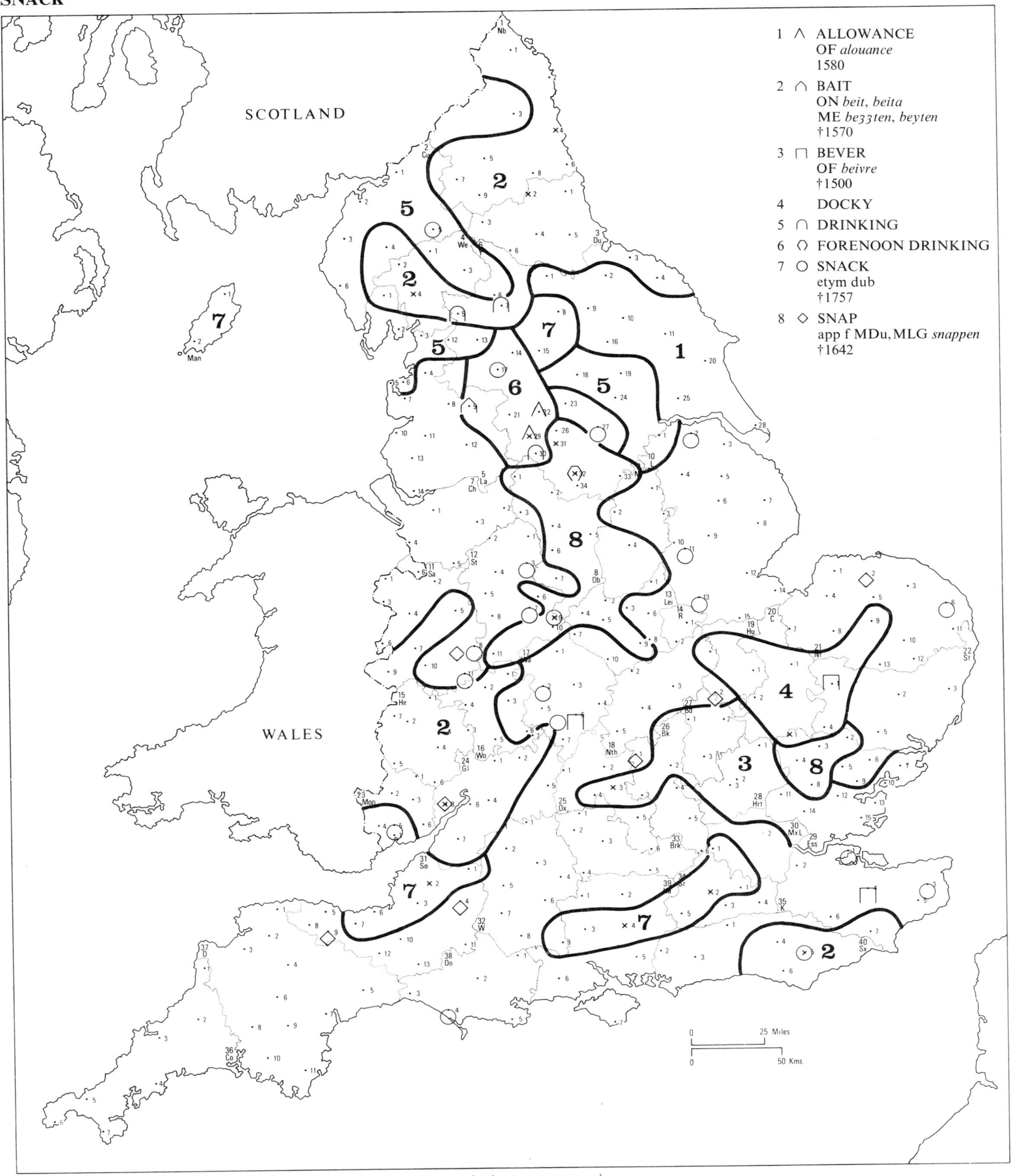

BIT(OE *bita*) BAIT 3Du 1,
BIT OF BAIT 40Sx 4 under BAIT
DRINKINGS 5La 6, 6Y 18/19/24/+30, 10L 1 under DRINKING
FORENOON DRINKINGS 6Y +32 under FORENOON DRINKING
BIT OF A SNACK 6Y 27, SNACK BIT 11Sa +8, SNACK OF LUNCH 31So 3 under SNACK
BIT OF A SNAP 12St 6, SNAPPING 8Db 6, 11Sa +8 under SNAP

The question required an answer meaning "a snack between breakfast and the mid-day meal"

Where the contents of the snack were rec, bread was always the major constituent

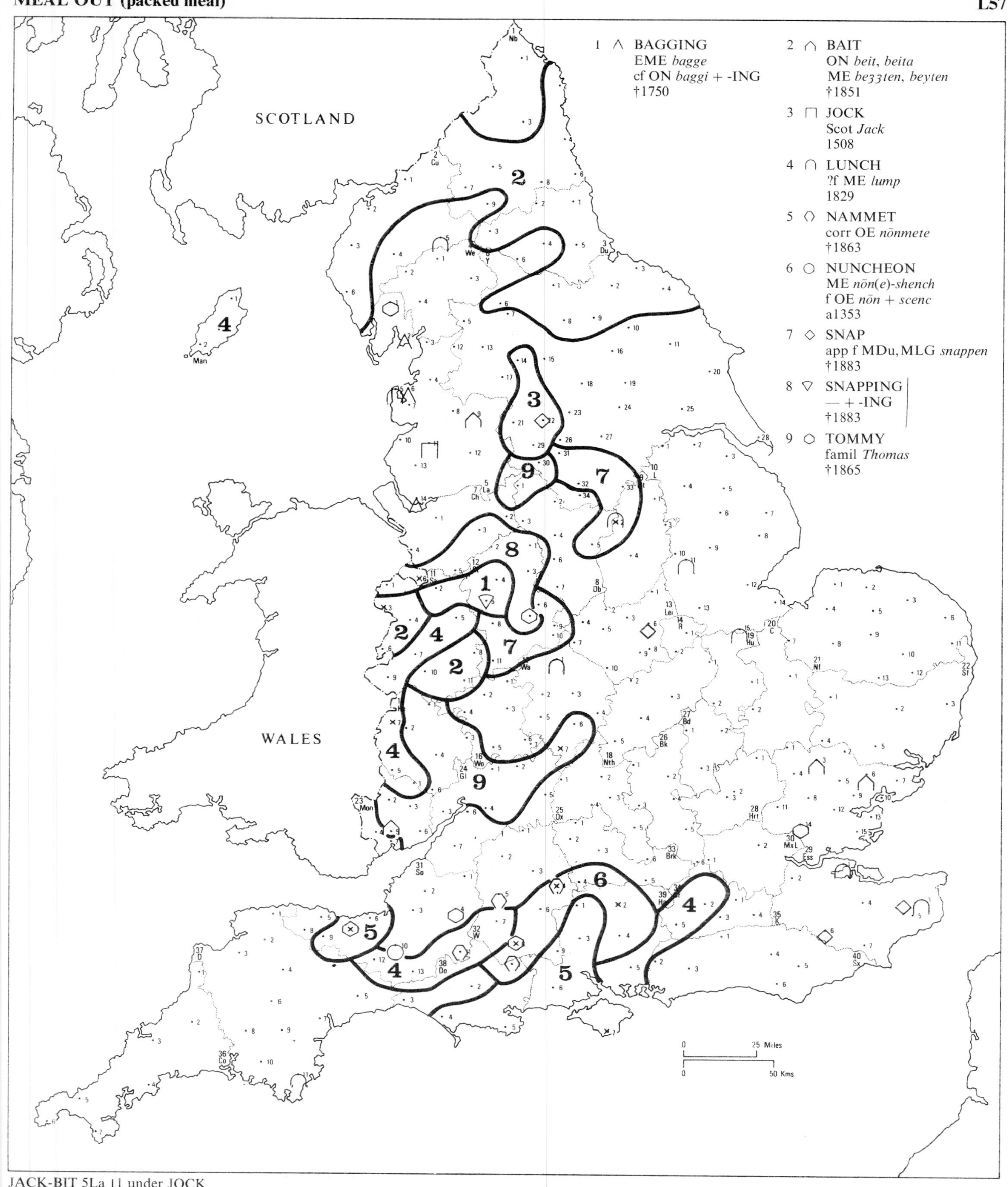

JACK-BIT 5La 11 under JOCK
NAMMEK 39Ha 6, NOMMET 31So 11,
NUMMET †1825 31So 6/9, 38Do $^{+}$1,
under NAMMET
NUNCH 31So 10, 38Do $^{+}$1 under NUNCHEON
FORENOON SNAP 6Y 32 under SNAP

bɪ'gan (sic); ?error for bagɪn, bagging HO 12St 4

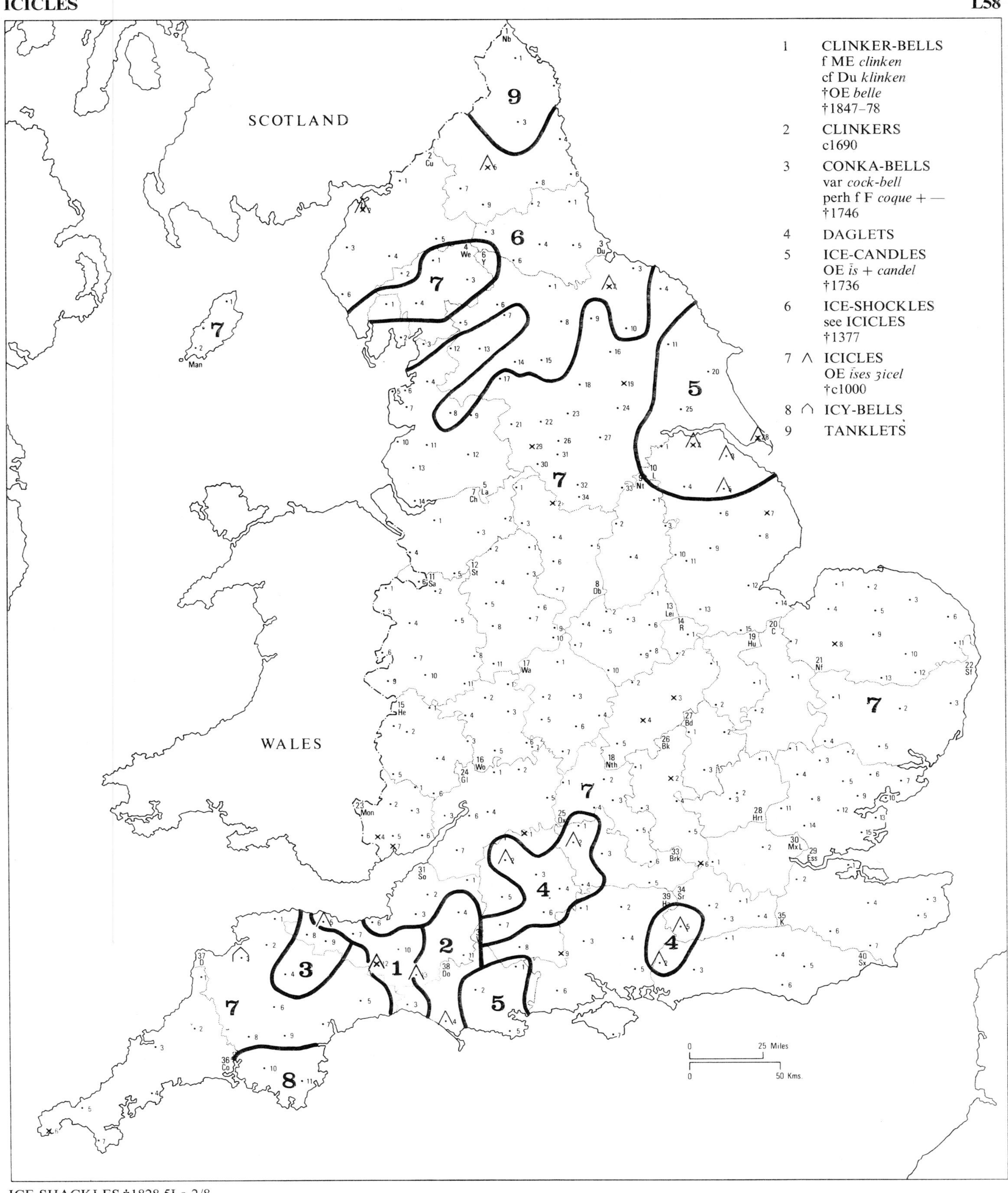

ICE-SHACKLES †1828 5La 2/8,
6Y 14 under ICE-SHOCKLES
SICKLES 29Ess + 10 under ICICLES
TANKLES 1Nb 2 under TANKLETS

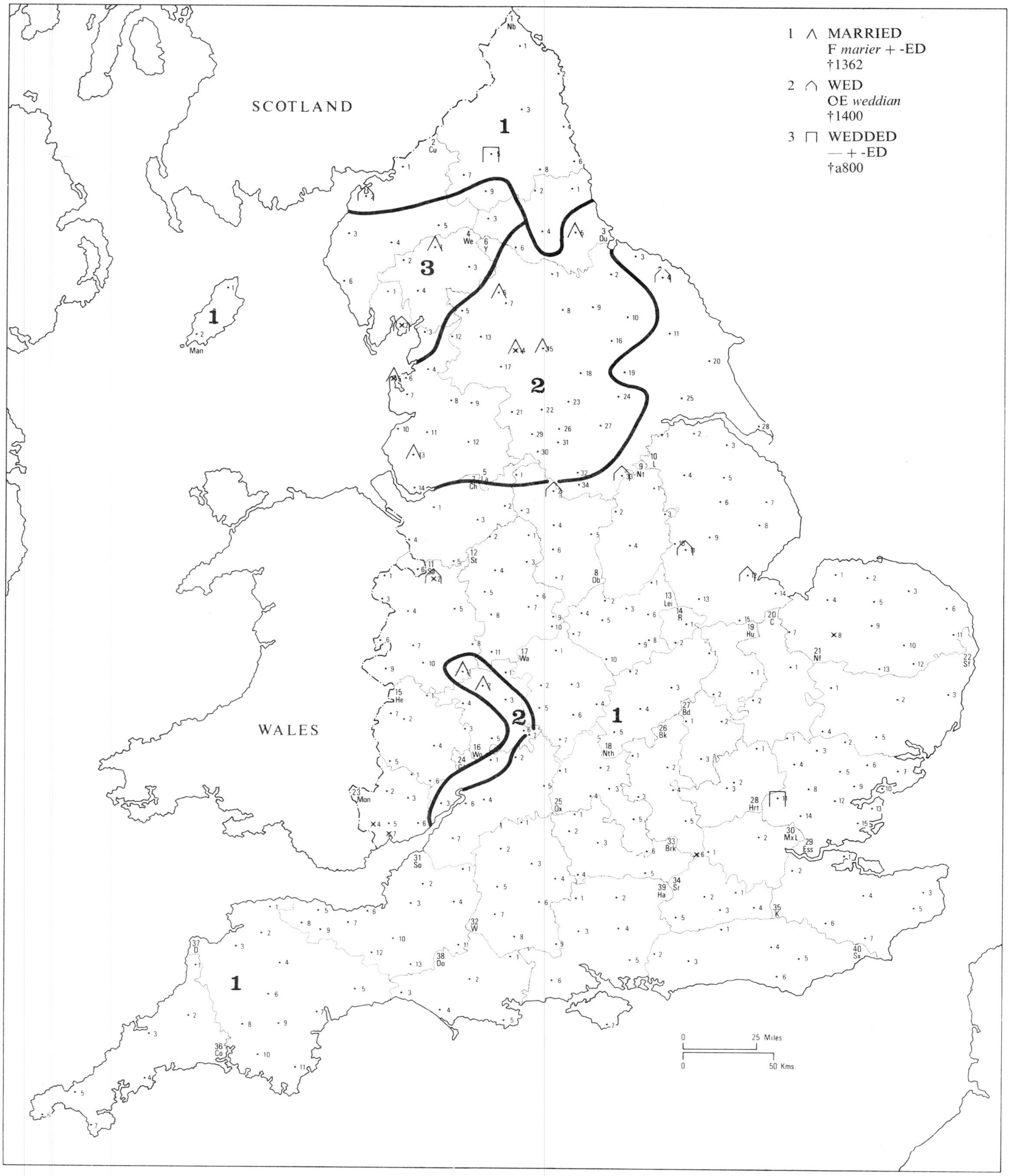

1 ∧ MARRIED
F *marier* + -ED
†1362

2 ∩ WED
OE *weddian*
†1400

3 ⊓ WEDDED
— + -ED
†a800

SCOTLAND

WALES

0 25 Miles

0 50 Kms

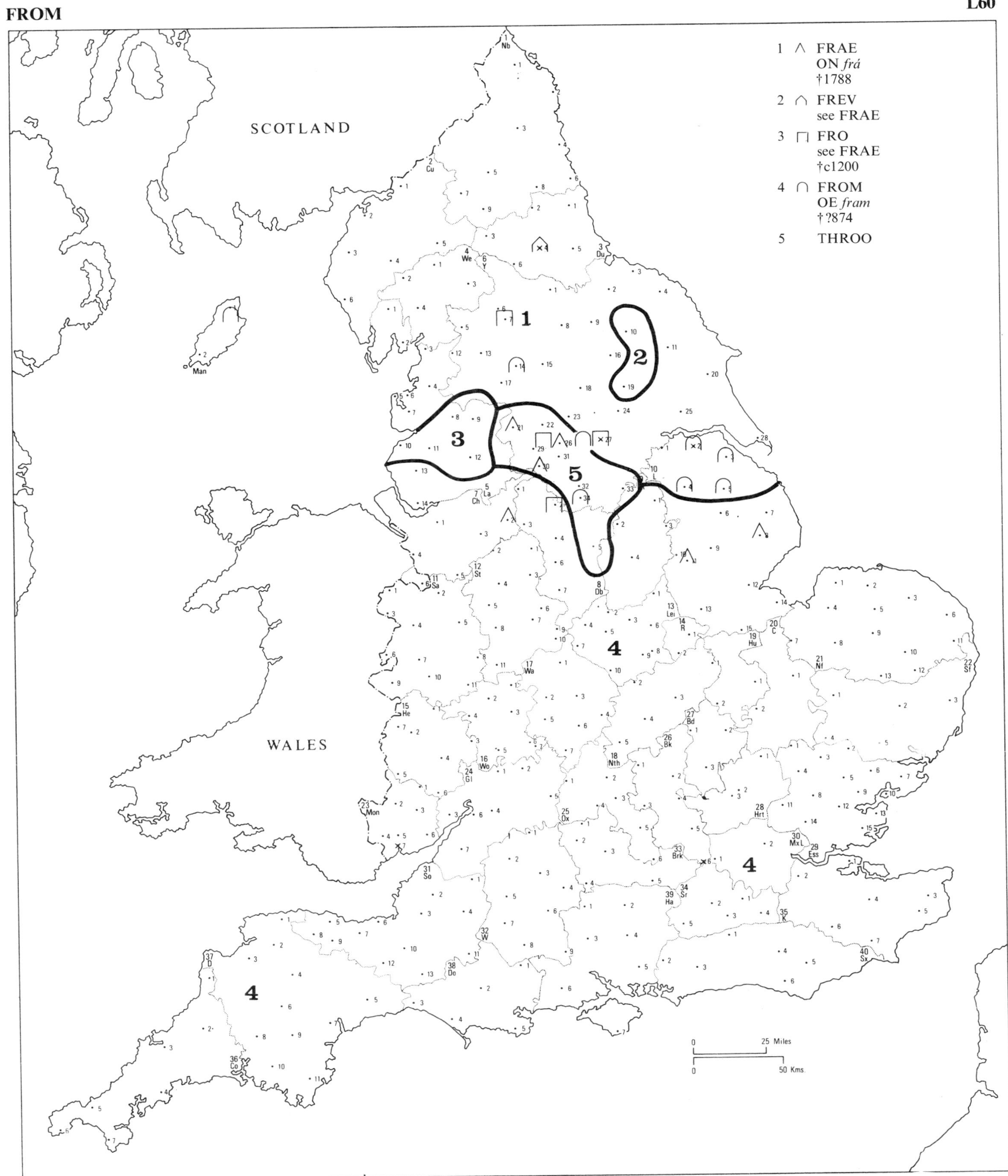

THRAE 5La 2, 6Y $^{+}$30 under FRAE
FROO 5La 10/12, 6Y $^{+}$7/$^{+}$26/$^{+}$27, 8Db $^{+}$2 under FRO

fɹə 6Y $^{+}$6/$^{+}$21/23/$^{+}$24/$^{+}$26, 10L $^{+}$11, θɹə 6Y 30 are taken to repr FRAE

Only forms occurring pre-pausally have been used

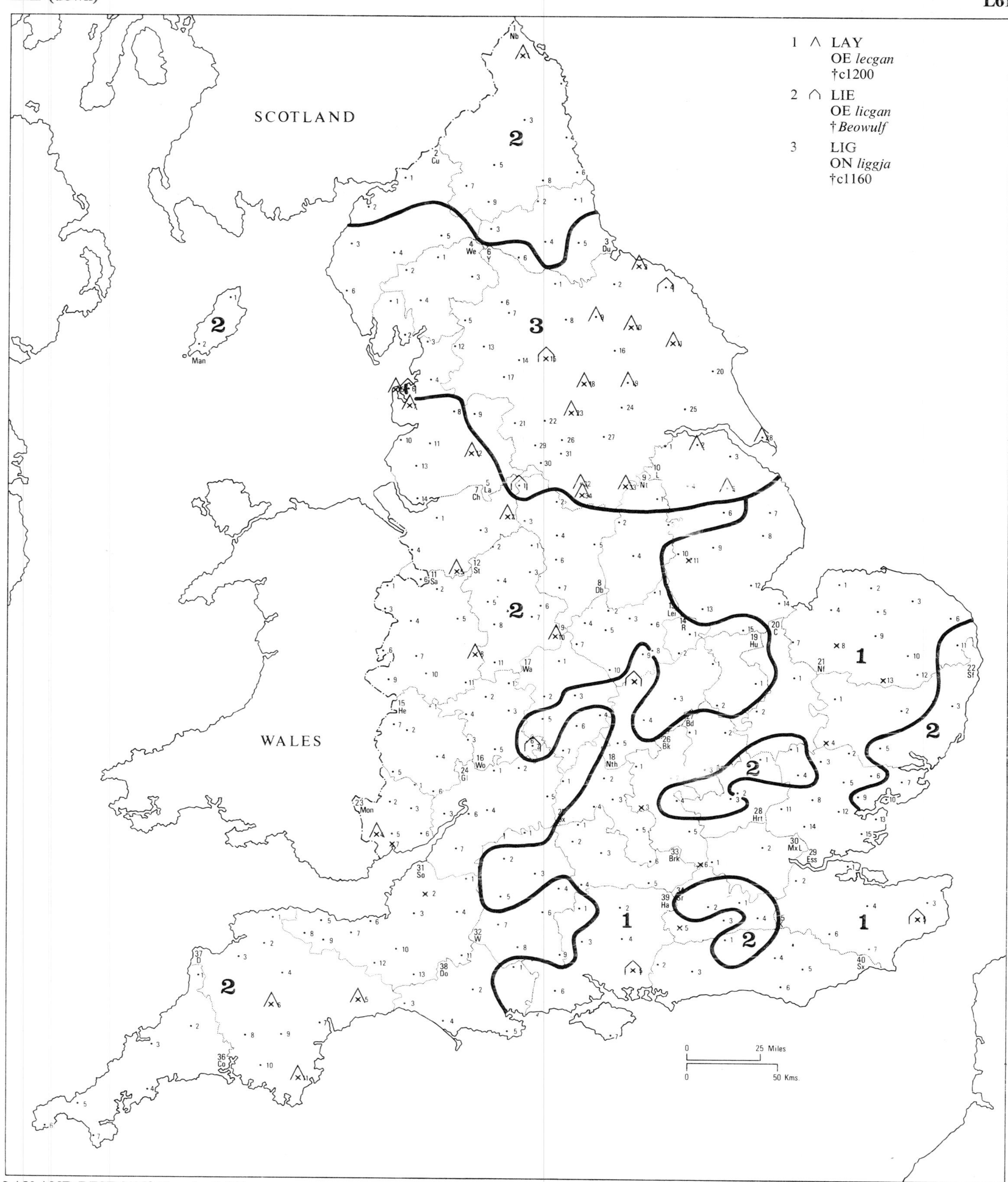

LAY AND REST 21Nf 12 under LAY

Reflexive forms of the verb were rec at:
1Nb 8, 2Cu $^{+}$5, 5La 1/6/7/10–12,
6Y 1/3/6/$^{+}$9/13/14/17/18/21/$^{+}$22/23/24/
26/27/$^{+}$28/29–33, 7Ch $^{+}$2/3, 8Db $^{+}$1/2/3/6/7,
12St 2/3/5

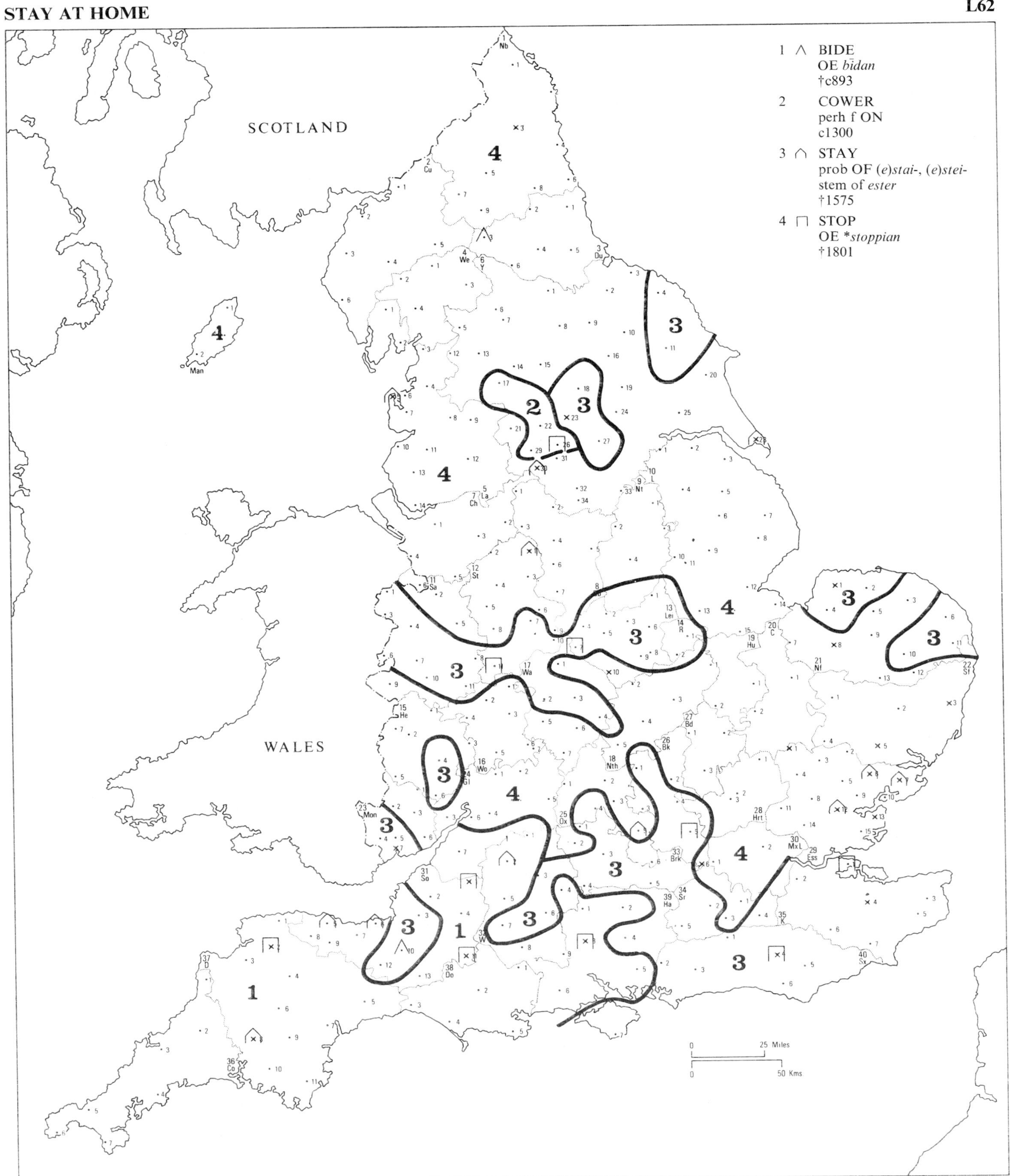

The usual prepositional phrase rec after the verb was AT HOME, but the following were also rec:

(BIDE) HOME 31So +5/+6/7–9/+10/13, 32W 1/+2/4/5/+8/9, 36Co 1–7, 37D 1/3–7/9–11, 38Do 1–5, 39Ha 1/2/5

(STAY) BY HOME 31So 3,
(STAY) HOME Man 2, 23Mon 5, 31So +5/+6/+10, 32W +2/6/7, 33Brk 4, 37D 8, 38Ha 7

(STOP) HOME 31So 1/11, 37D 2,
(STOP) IN 6Y +34

BE STOPPED AT HOME 33Brk 2 under STOP

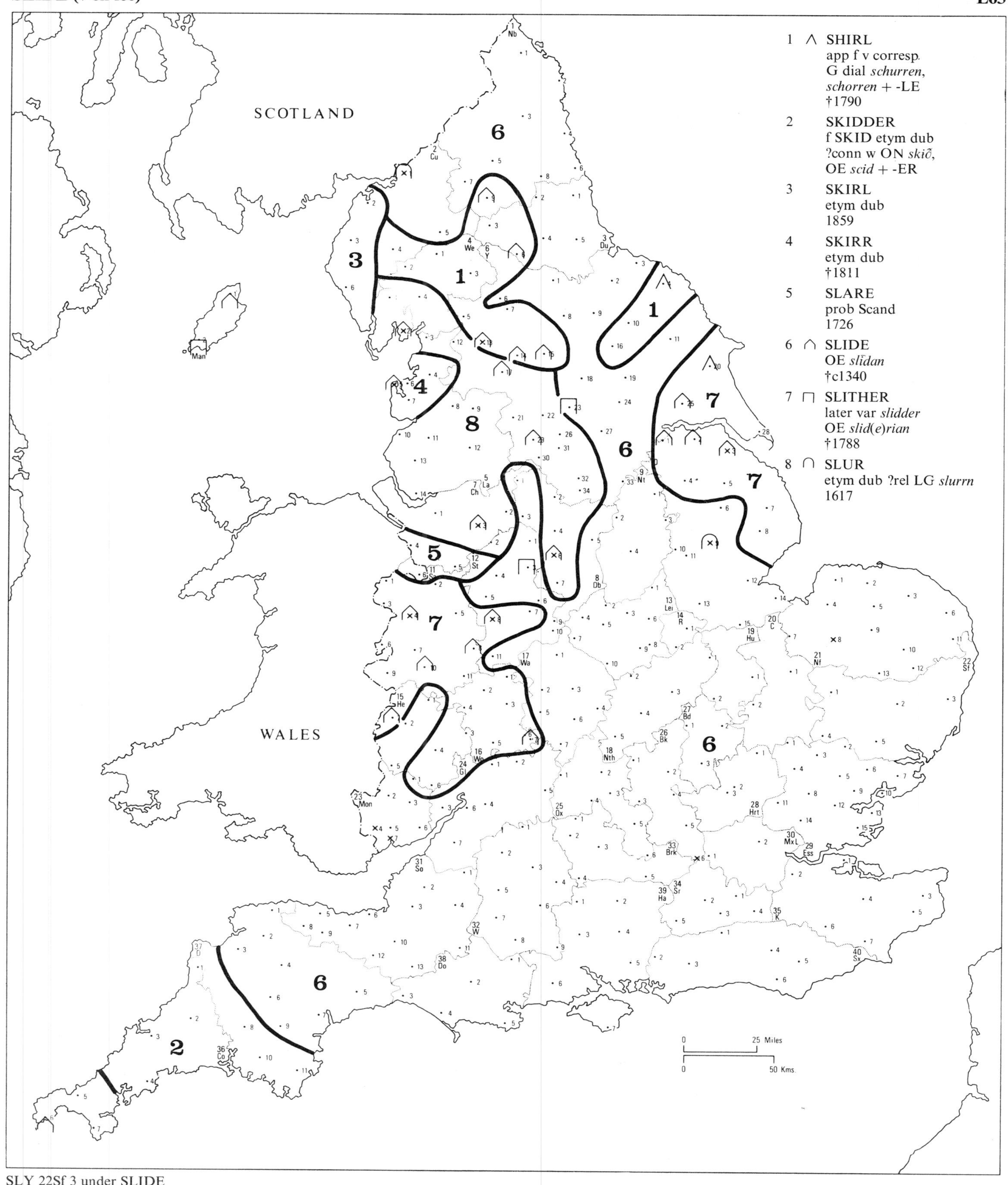

SLY 22Sf 3 under SLIDE
SLIDING AND SLITHERING ABOUT
16Wo 7 under SLIDE and under SLITHER
SLIRE 2Cu 1, SLUR ABOUT 7Ch +2 under
SLUR

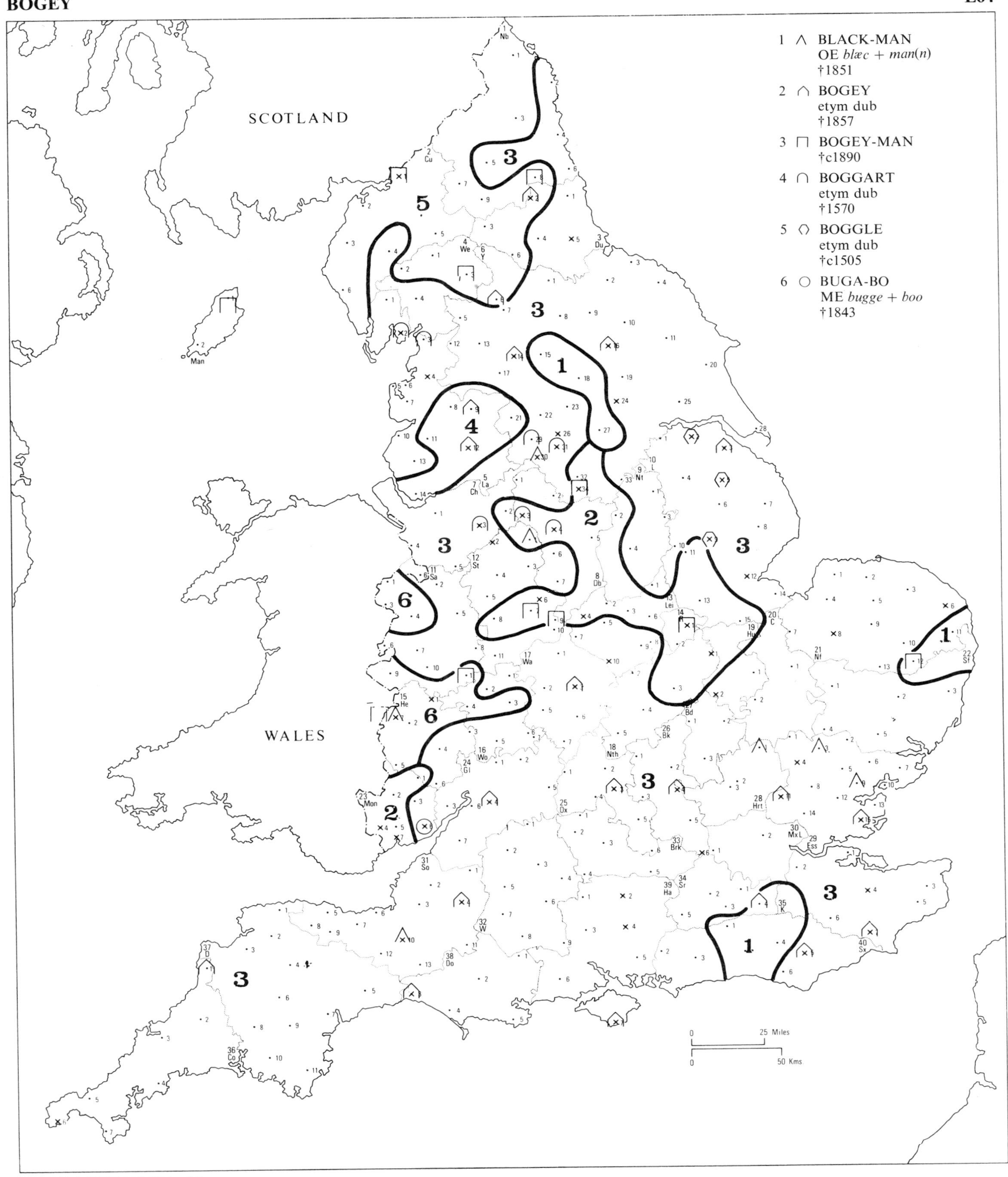

THE BLACKMAN 29Ess $^{+}$9,
40Sx 4 under BLACKMAN
BOOGY 6Y 14, THE BOOGY 36Co $^{+}$1,
THE OLD BOGEY 10L $^{+}$3 under BOGEY
BOGE-MAN 18Nth 2,
BOGGYMAN 37D 7, 39Ha 6,
BOOGYMAN 2Cu 1, 6Y 19, 7Ch 5,
11Sa 6, 12St 3/5, 15He 4, 21Nf 1, 22Sf 2,
24Gl 1, 36Co $^{+}$1/$^{+}$5, 37D 11,
BUGGYMAN 31So 7–9, 32W 4, 36Co $^{+}$2,
37D $^{+}$4/9, THE BOGEYMAN 29Ess $^{+}$9,
32W 6, THE BOOGYMAN 36Co $^{+}$5,
THE BUGGYMAN 36Co $^{+}$2, 37D $^{+}$4,
THE OLD BOGEYMAN 21Nf 10 under
BOGEYMAN
BUGGYBOWL 16Wo $^{+}$3 under BUGA-BO

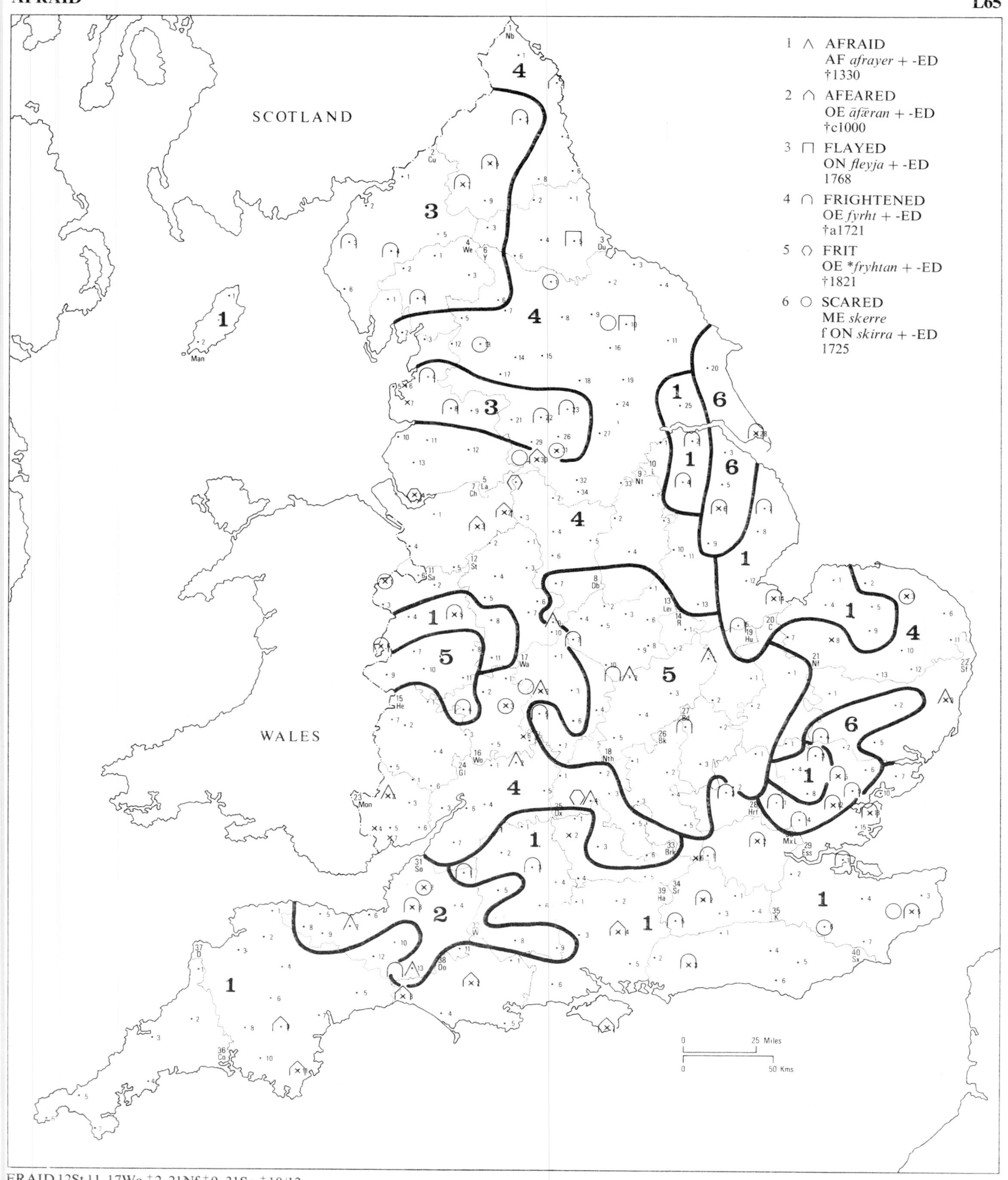

FRAID 12St 11, 17Wa +2, 21Nf +9, 31So +10/12,
34Sr 1/+4/+5, 36Co +1/5–7,
37D +8/10 under AFRAID

FEARED 1Nb 2, 6Y +30, 7Ch 2/3, 31So +13,
37D +11 under AFEARED

FREETENED 2Cu +4, 3Du +4/+5/6,
4We +4, 5La 2/3/+4/+8/10/11/+12,
6Y 2/3/+8/9/12/+13/+14/16–18/+19/+22/
+23/24/28/32–34, 8Db +1/2, 10L 1/+2/+4,
FRITTEN 11Sa 2, FRITTENED 5La +12/13,
7Ch 4–6, 11Sa 5/6,
25Ox +4 under FRIGHTENED

FREET 8Db +1, FRITTED 14R 2 under FRIT

Morphological Maps

(I) AM M1

YOU ARE (2 prsg) M2

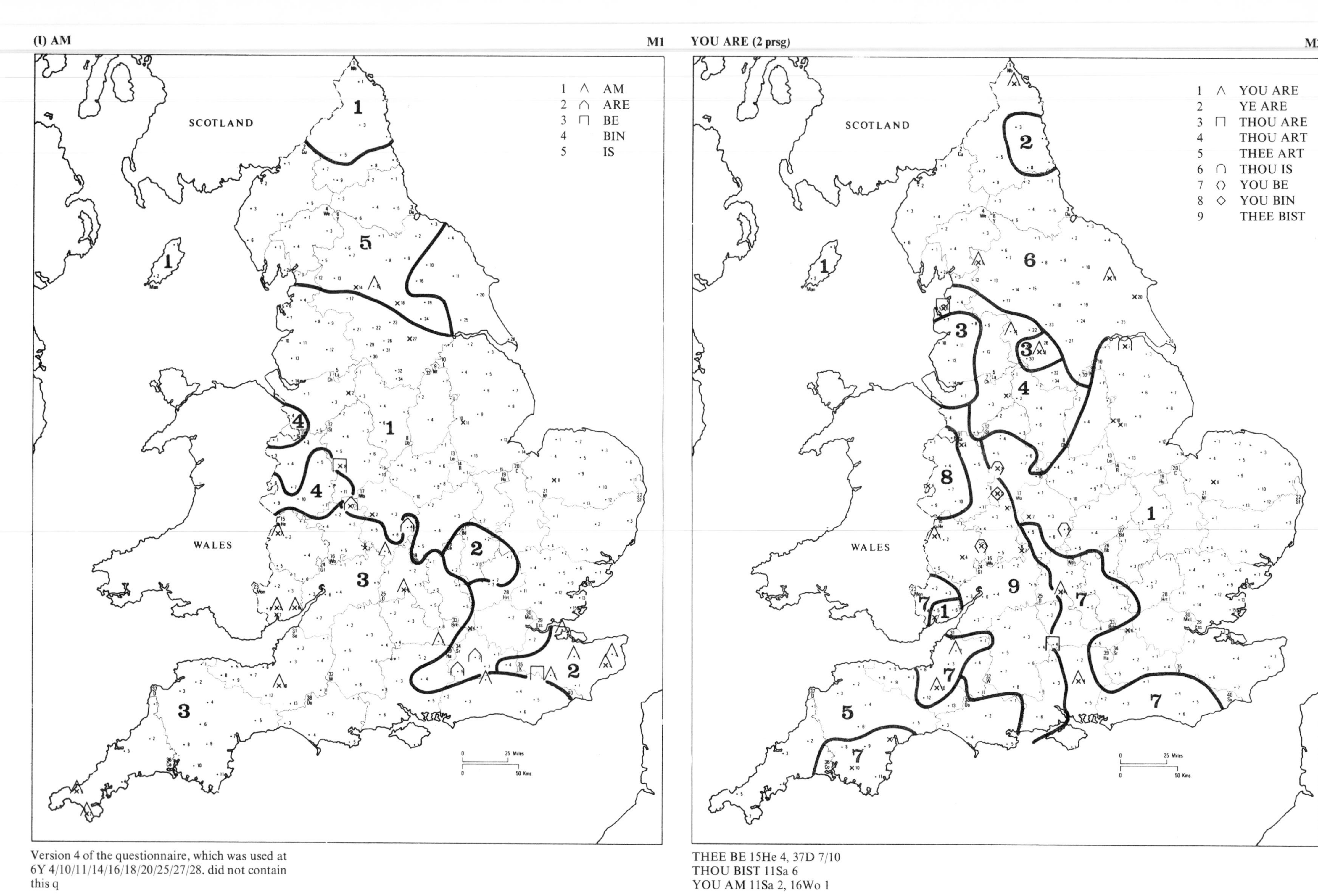

Version 4 of the questionnaire, which was used at 6Y 4/10/11/14/16/18/20/25/27/28, did not contain this q

THEE BE 15He 4, 37D 7/10
THOU BIST 11Sa 6
YOU AM 11Sa 2, 16Wo 1

6Y 21 THOU ART to a friend, YOU ARE to an older person

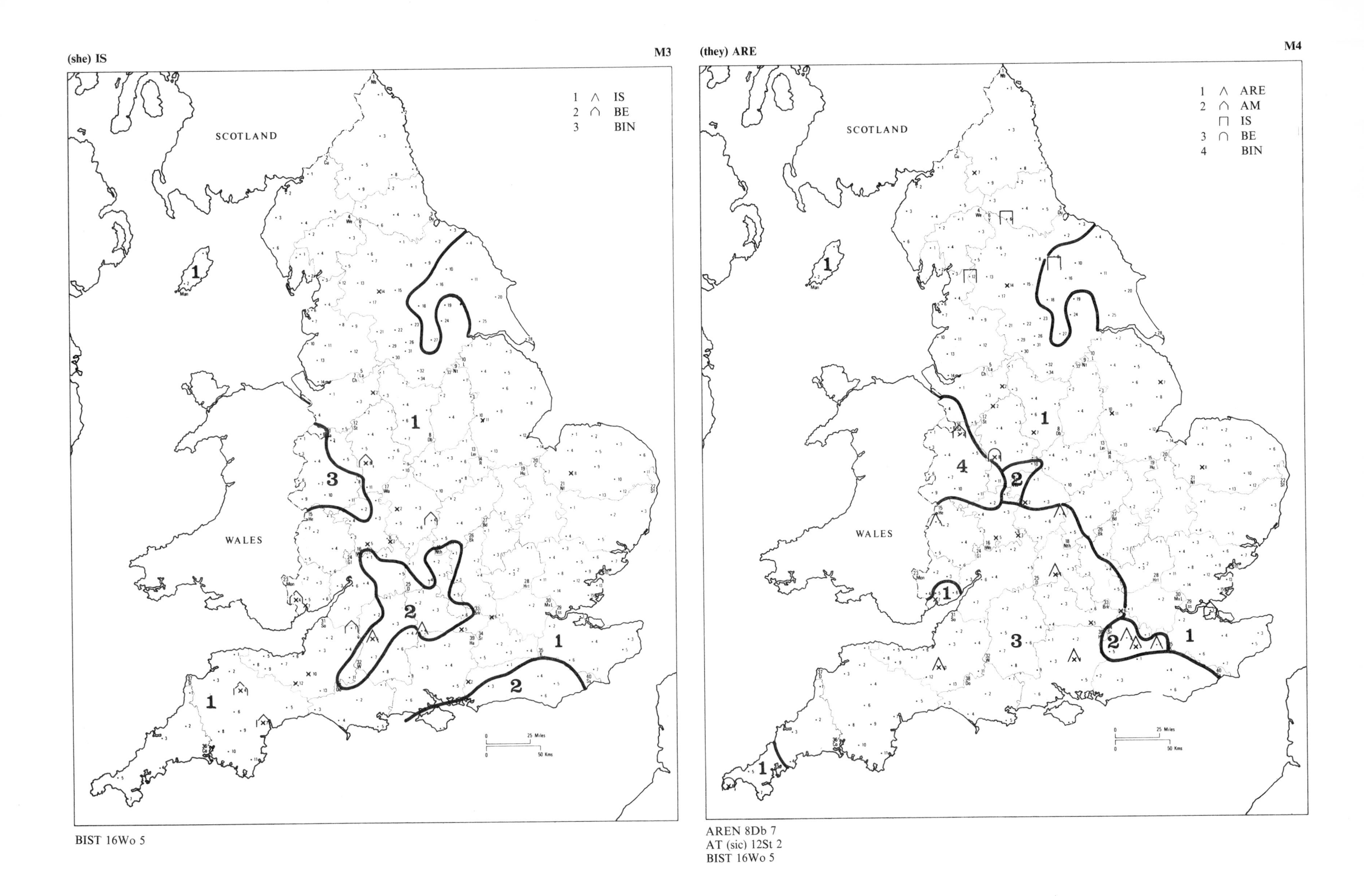

BIST 16Wo 5

AREN 8Db 7
AT (sic) 12St 2
BIST 16Wo 5

(I) AM M5

YOU ARE M6

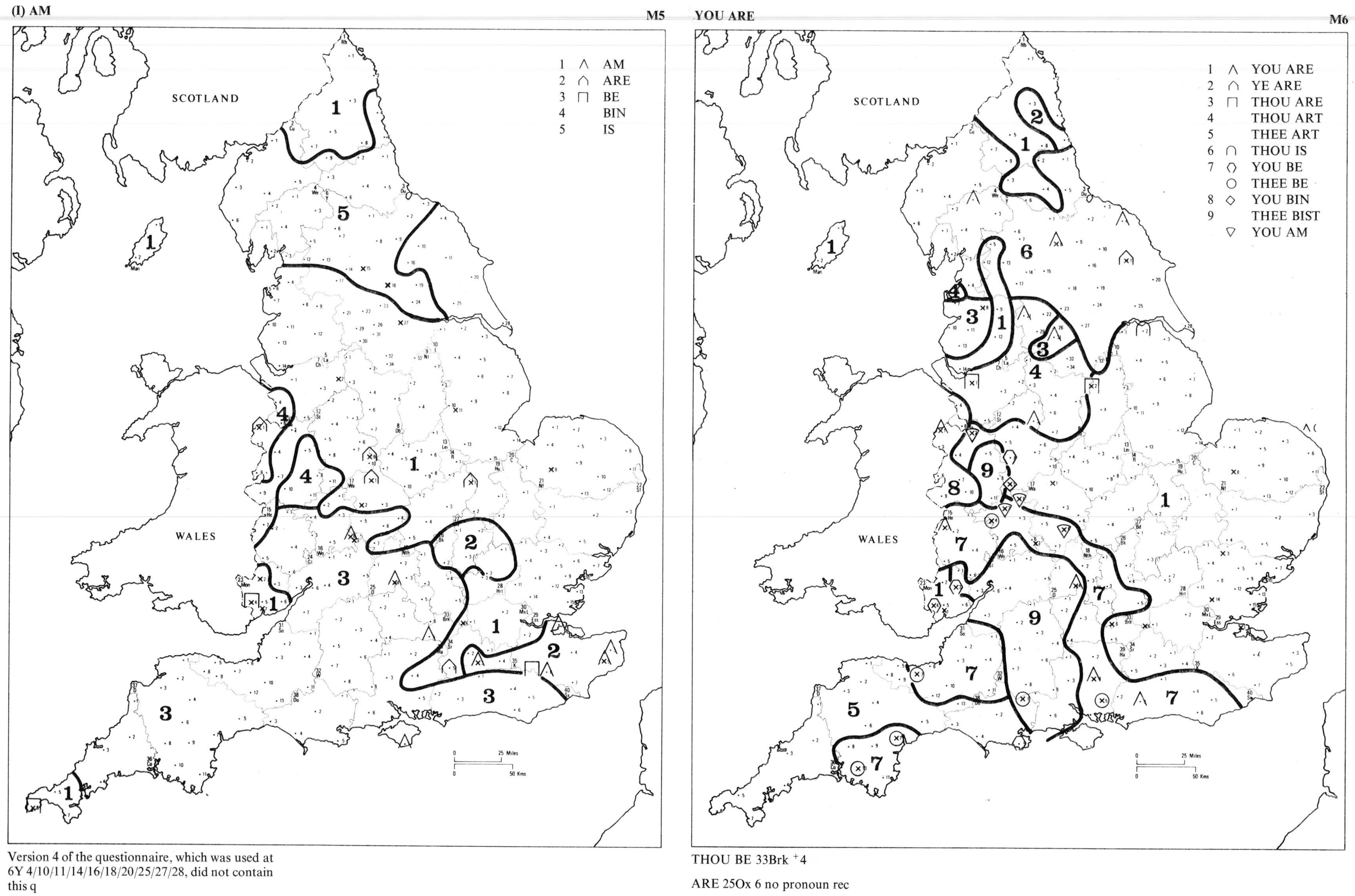

Version 4 of the questionnaire, which was used at 6Y 4/10/11/14/16/18/20/25/27/28, did not contain this q

THOU BE 33Brk $^{+}4$

ARE 25Ox 6 no pronoun rec

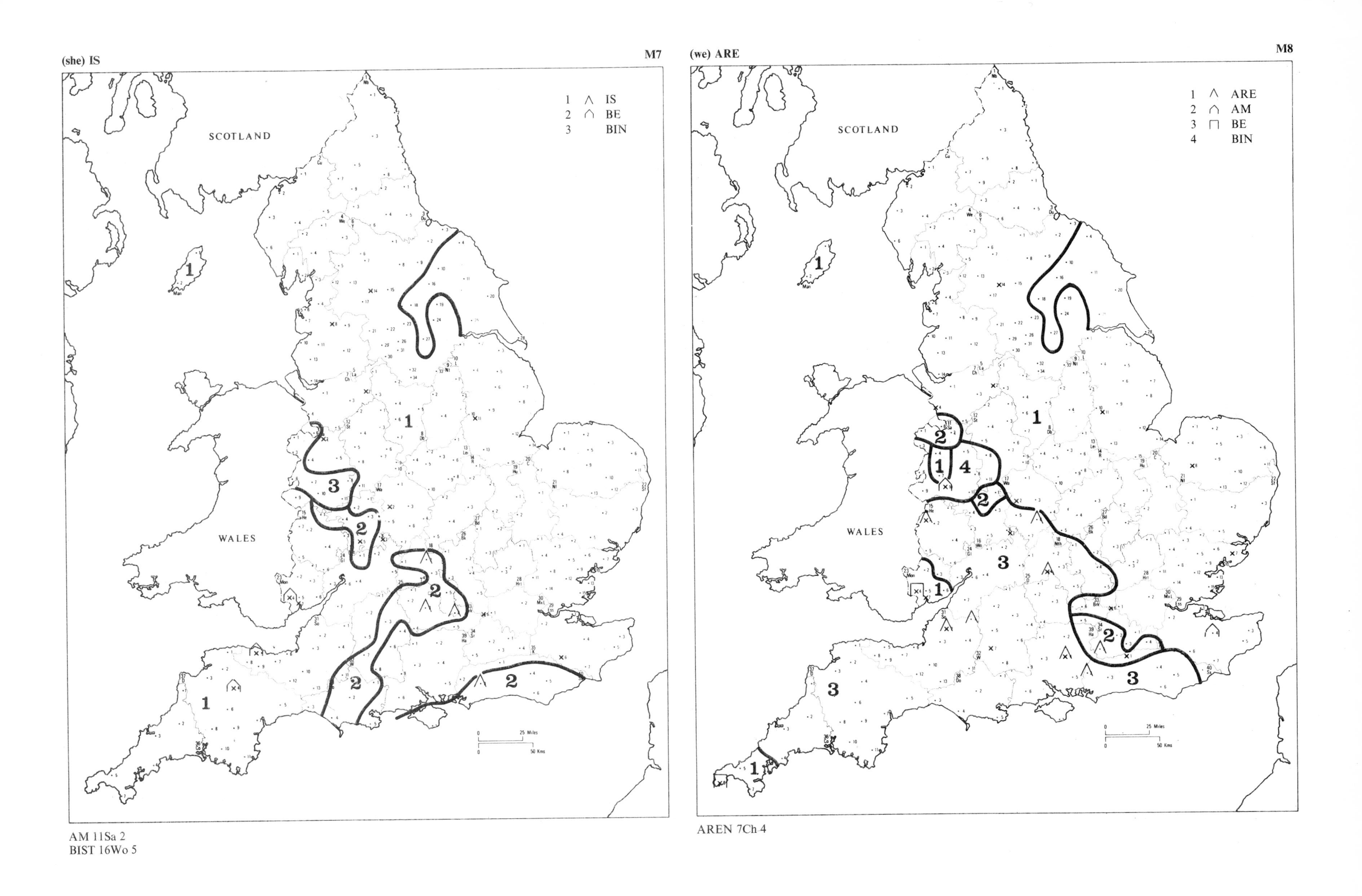

(she) IS
M7
1 ∧ IS
2 ∩ BE
3 BIN
SCOTLAND
WALES
25 Miles
50 Kms
AM 11Sa 2
BIST 16Wo 5
(we) ARE
M8
1 ∧ ARE
2 ∩ AM
3 ⊓ BE
4 BIN
SCOTLAND
WALES
25 Miles
50 Kms
AREN 7Ch 4

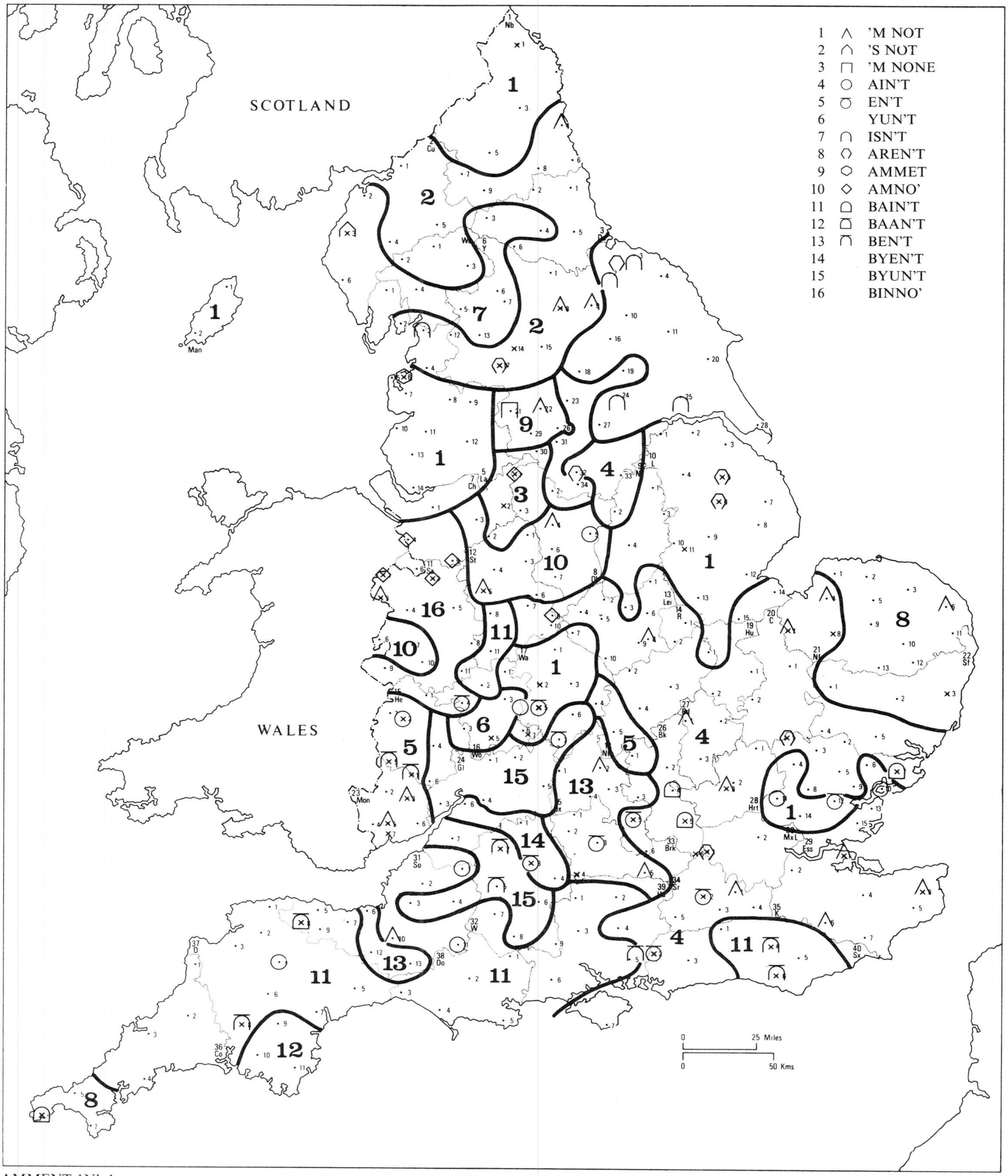

SCOTLAND

WALES

1 ʌ 'M NOT
2 'S NOT
3 'M NONE
4 ○ AIN'T
5 EN'T
6 YUN'T
7 ∩ ISN'T
8 AREN'T
9 AMMET
10 ◇ AMNO'
11 BAIN'T
12 BAAN'T
13 BEN'T
14 BYEN'T
15 BYUN'T
16 BINNO'

0 25 Miles
0 50 Kms

AMMENT 1Nb 1
AM NOT Man +2
AMN' 25Ox +5
BISN'T 16Wo 5
IN'T 22Sf 1/3
'RE NOT 35K +1/+7
'S NOT 6Y +15
YEN'T 33Brk 4

(she) ISN'T

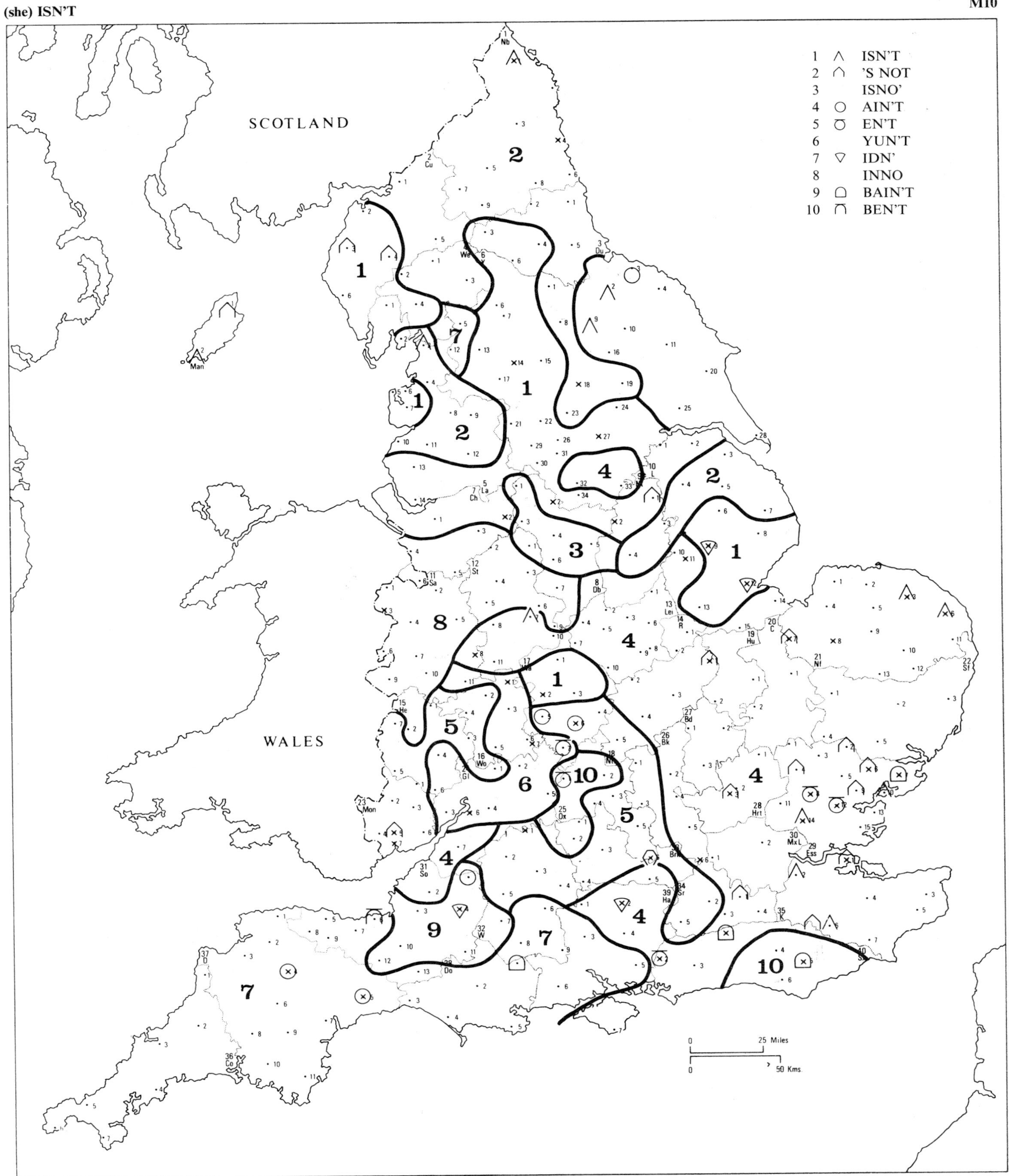

IDN'T 6Y 5/12, 10L 9/12, 39Ha 3/5 under IDN'

BINNO' 11Sa 3/8
BYENT 32W 1
'S NONE 6Y ⁺15
YEN'T 24Gl 6

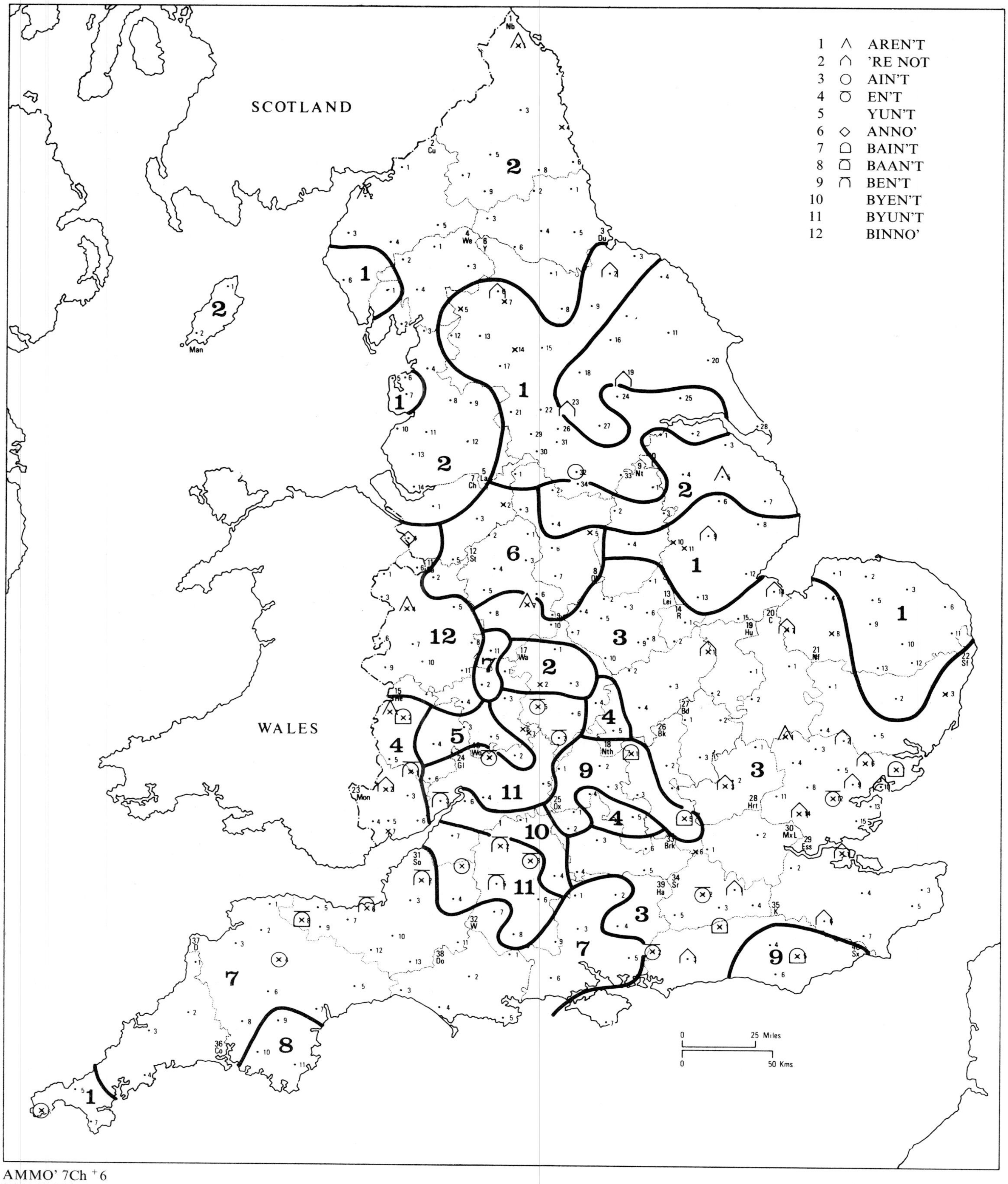

SCOTLAND

WALES

1 AREN'T
2 'RE NOT
3 AIN'T
4 EN'T
5 YUN'T
6 ANNO'
7 BAIN'T
8 BAAN'T
9 BEN'T
10 BYEN'T
11 BYUN'T
12 BINNO'

0 25 Miles
0 50 Kms

AMMO' 7Ch +6
INNO' 8Db 5
IN'T 22Sf 3
ISN'T 6Y 7
'M NOT 16Wo 6
'RE NONE 6Y +15

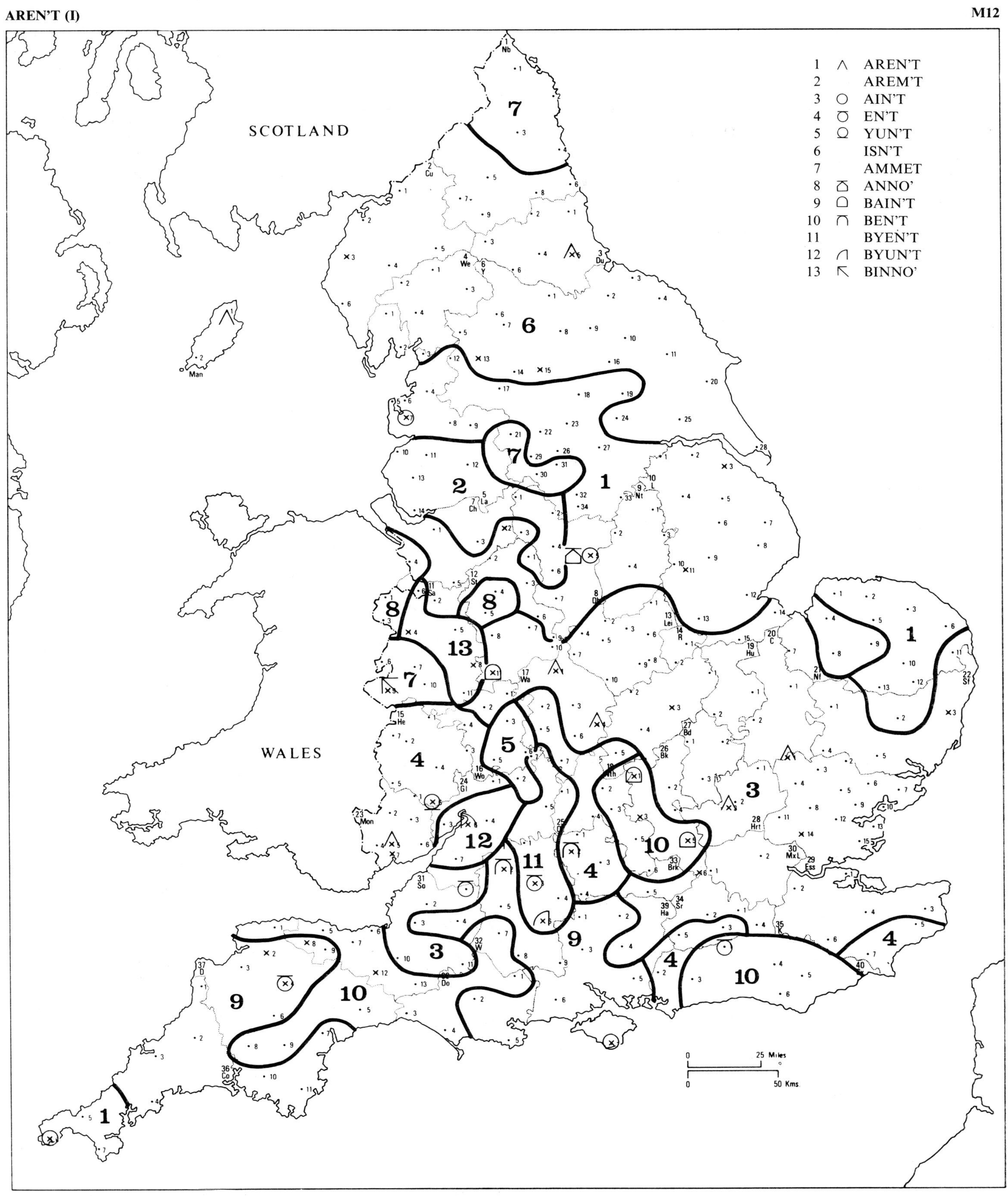

AMMENT 1Nb 1 under AMMET

BAAN' 31So 8
BIN' 26Bk 3
HIN' 22Sf 3
INNO' 11Sa 8
IN'T 6Y 13

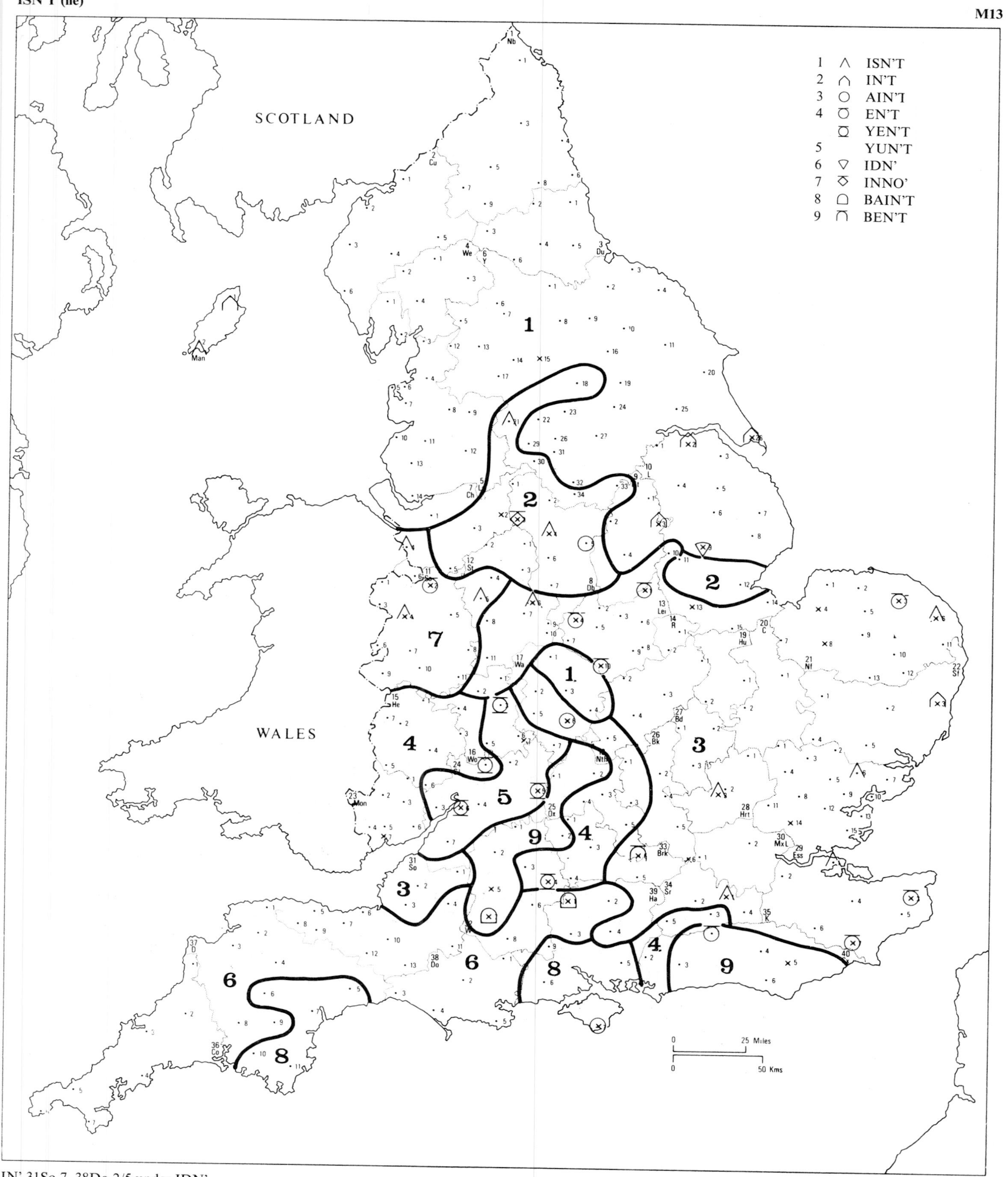

IN' 31So 7, 38Do 2/5 under IDN'
INNOT 11Sa 6/9 under INNO'

BYEN' 32W 1
YAN'T 16Wo 7

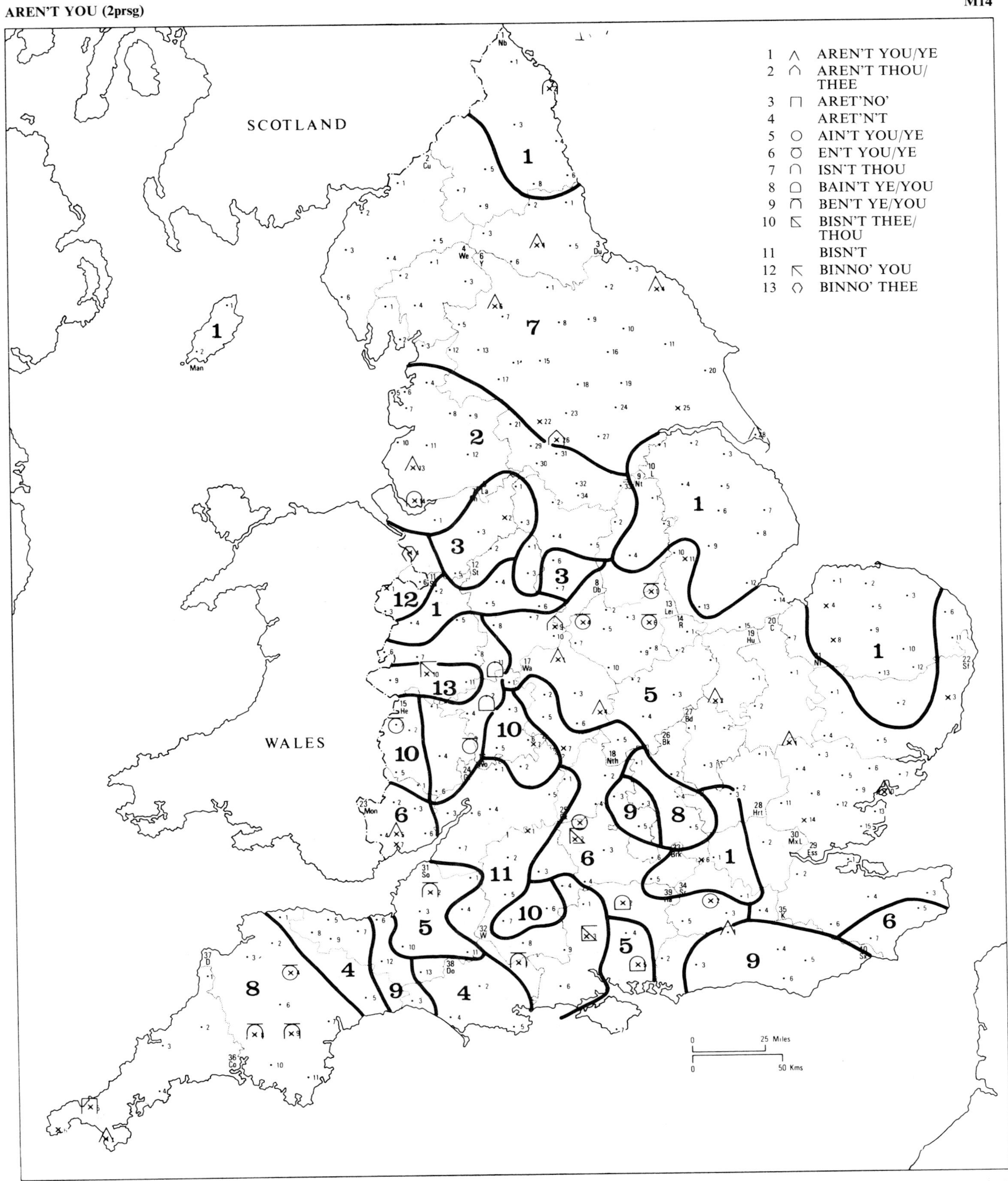

ADN'T THOU 6Y 22
AIN'T THEE 36Co 6
AMMO' YOU 11Sa 6, ANNO' YOU 11Sa 1/7
BIN'T YOU 15He 1
BISNO' 11Sa 5
BYEN'T YE 32W 1, BYEN'T YOU 16Wo 7
BYUN'T YOU 15He 4
EN'T THEE 16Wo 4, EN'T THOU 33Brk +4
HIN'T YOU 22Sf 3
INNO' THEE 11Sa 8
ISN'T YE 35K +6
YEN'T YOU 17Wa 7
YUN'T THOU 15He 6

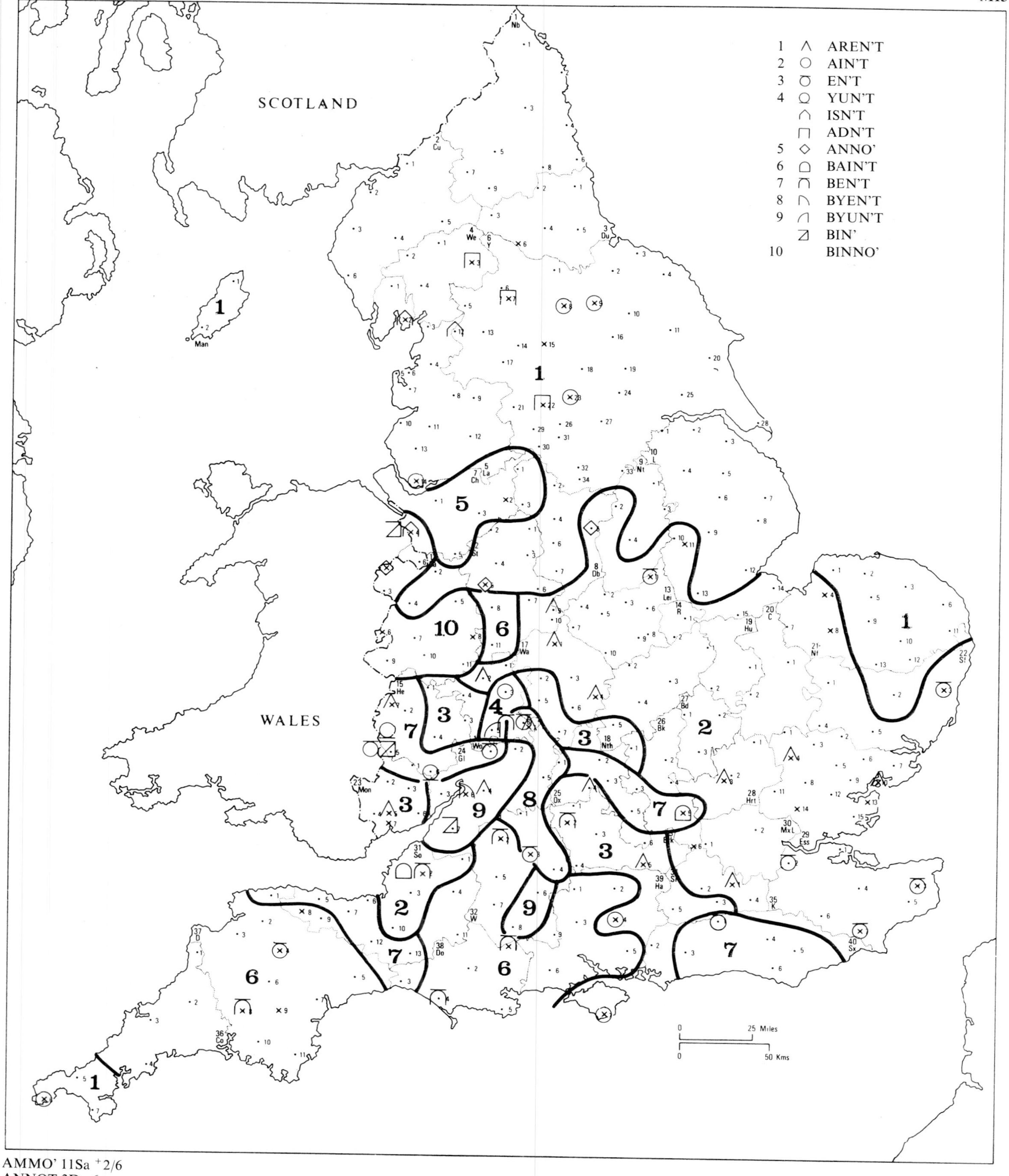

1 ∧ AREN'T
2 ○ AIN'T
3 EN'T
4 YUN'T
ISN'T
ADN'T
5 ◇ ANNO'
6 BAIN'T
7 BEN'T
8 BYEN'T
9 BYUN'T
BIN'
10 BINNO'

SCOTLAND

WALES

0 25 Miles
0 50 Kms

AMMO' 11Sa +2/6
ANNOT 3Du 6
BAAN' 31So 8, 37D 9
INNO' 11Sa 8
YAN'T 16Wo +7
YEN' 24Gl +5

(I) AM — M16

(she) IS — M17

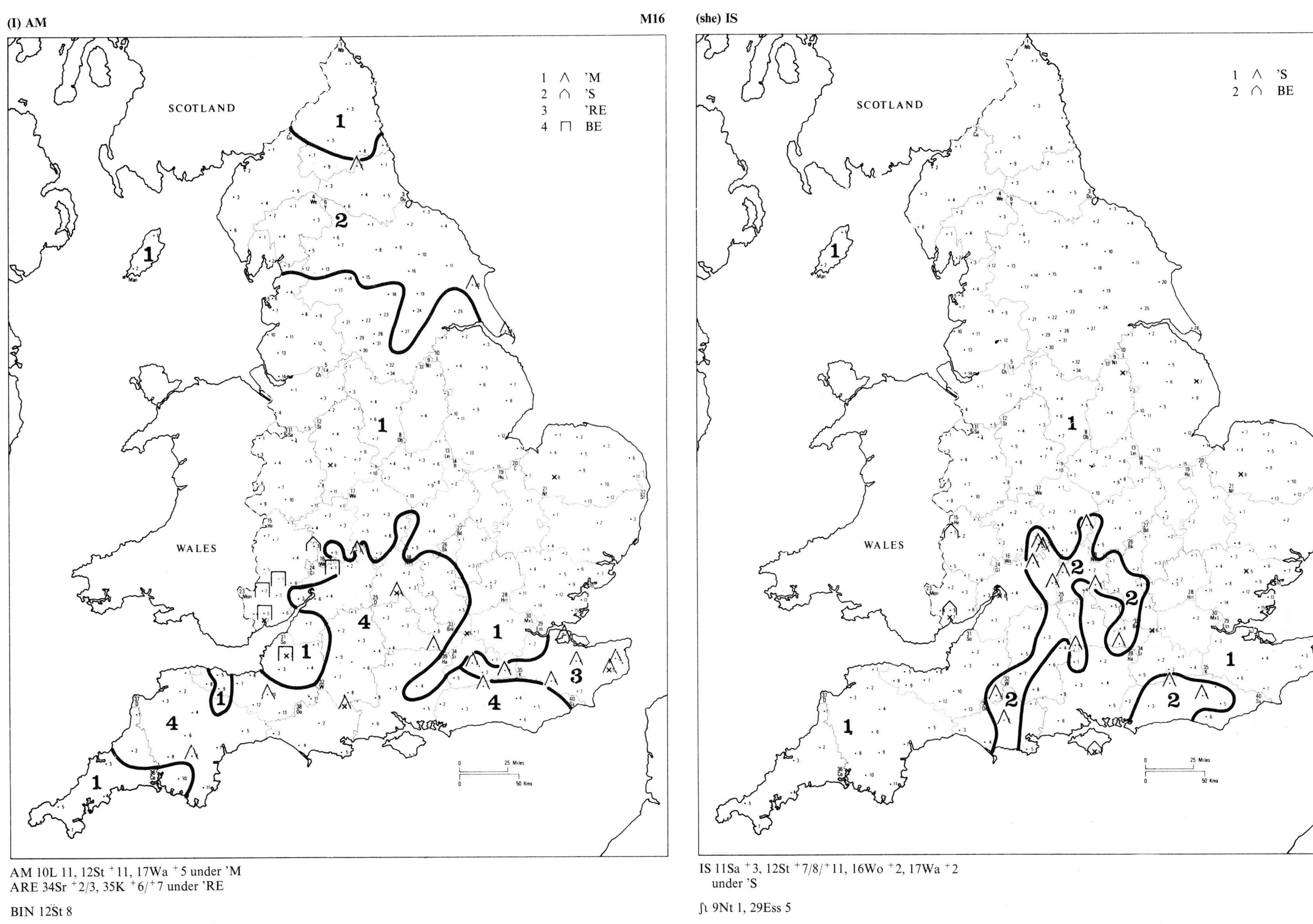

AM 10L 11, 12St ⁺11, 17Wa ⁺5 under 'M
ARE 34Sr ⁺2/3, 35K ⁺6/⁺7 under 'RE

BIN 12St 8

IS 11Sa ⁺3, 12St ⁺7/8/⁺11, 16Wo ⁺2, 17Wa ⁺2
under 'S

ʃt 9Nt 1, 29Ess 5

(we) ARE **M18**

(they) ARE **M19**

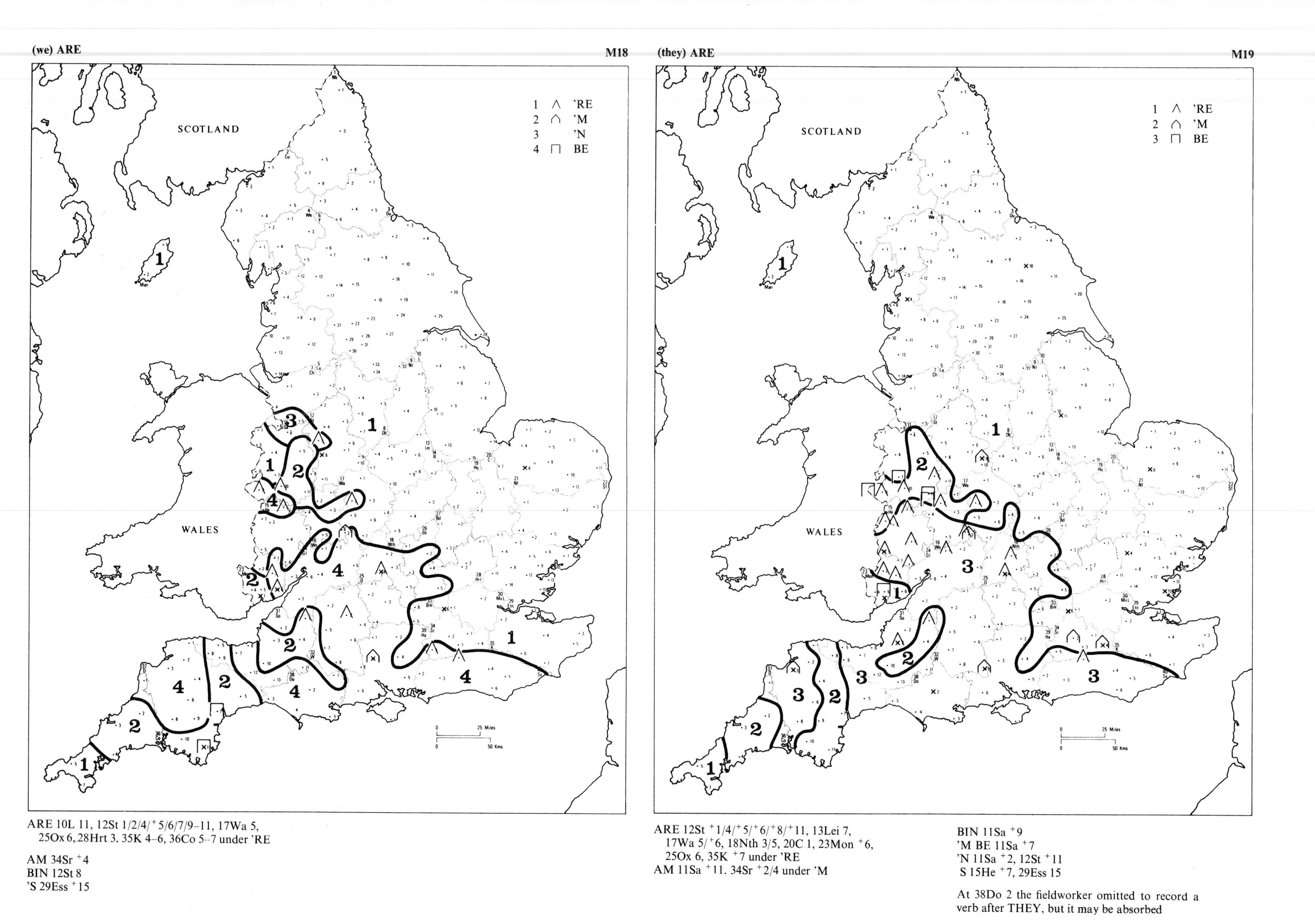

M18:

ARE 10L 11, 12St 1/2/4/$^+$5/6/7/9–11, 17Wa 5, 25Ox 6, 28Hrt 3, 35K 4–6, 36Co 5–7 under 'RE

AM 34Sr $^+$4
BIN 12St 8
'S 29Ess $^+$15

M19:

ARE 12St $^+$1/4/$^+$5/$^+$6/$^+$8/$^+$11, 13Lei 7, 17Wa 5/$^+$6, 18Nth 3/5, 20C 1, 23Mon $^+$6, 25Ox 6, 35K $^+$7 under 'RE
AM 11Sa $^+$11. 34Sr $^+$2/4 under 'M

BIN 11Sa $^+$9
'M BE 11Sa $^+$7
'N 11Sa $^+$2, 12St $^+$11
S 15He $^+$7, 29Ess 15

At 38Do 2 the fieldworker omitted to record a verb after THEY, but it may be absorbed

(I) WAS

M20

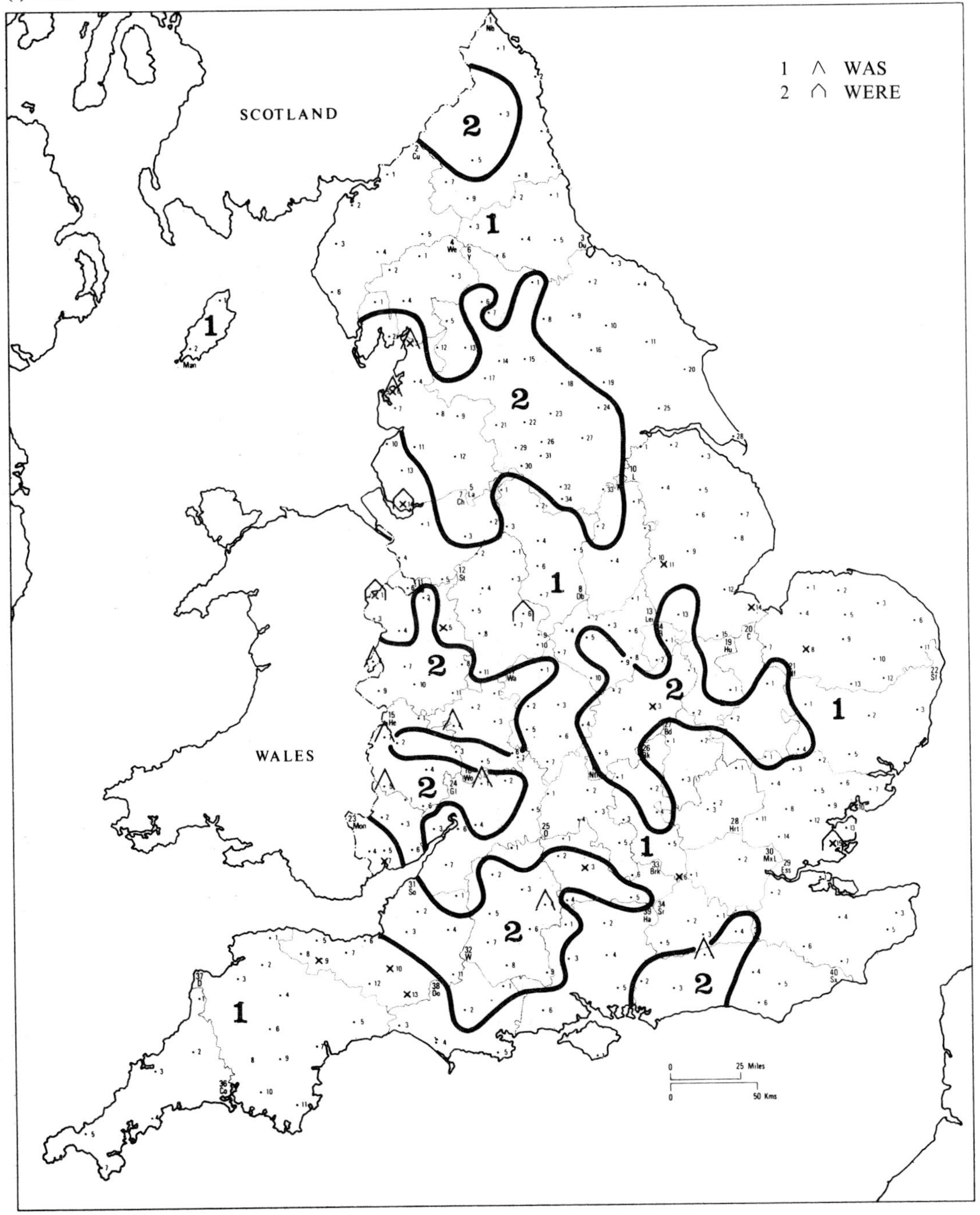

WEREN 11Sa 5

(she) WAS

M21

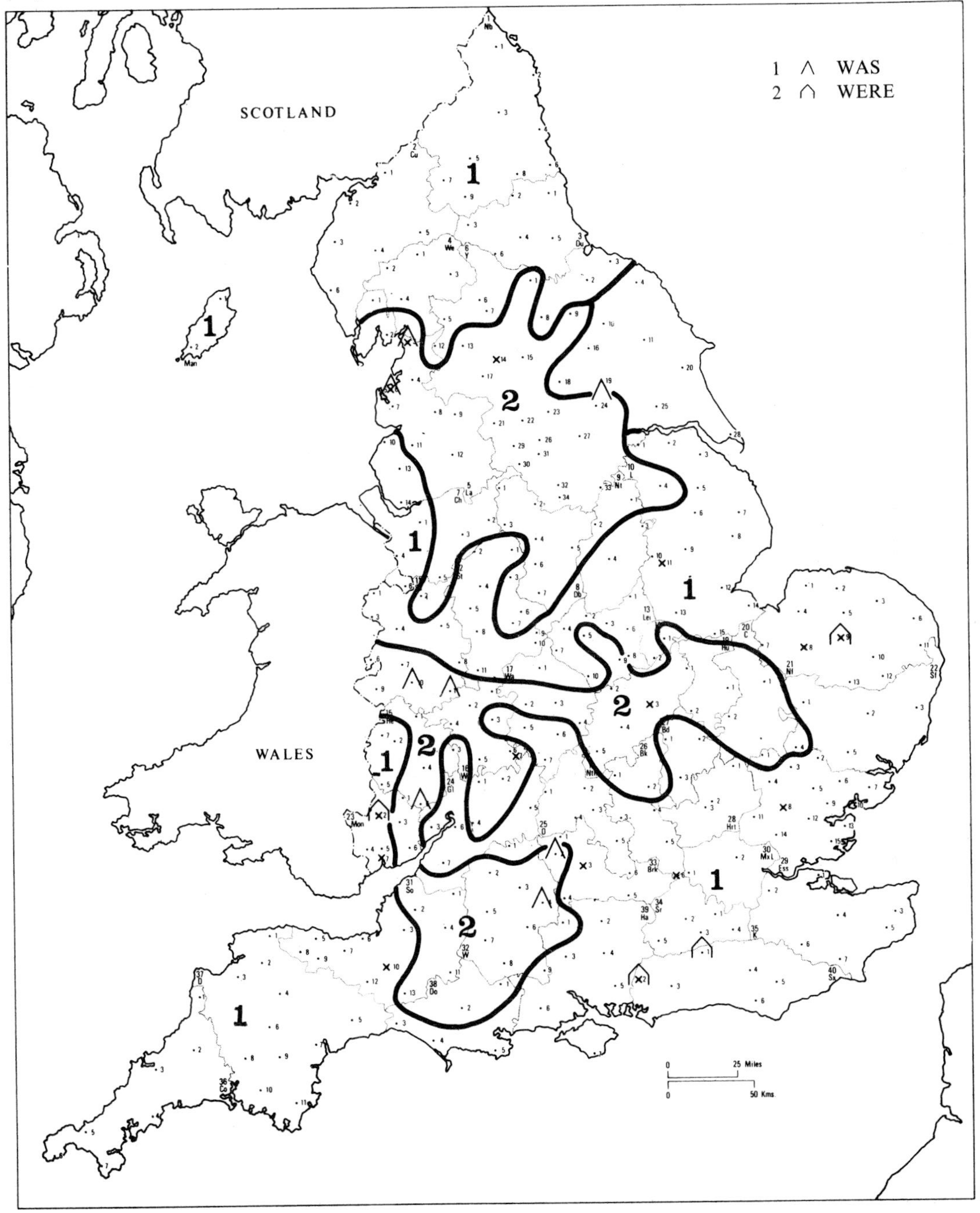

Version 4 of the questionnaire, which was used at 6Y 4/10/11/14/16/18/20/25/27/28, did not contain this q. The 3ptsg fem at 6Y 27 was rec in place of the 3ptsg masc for which the q asked

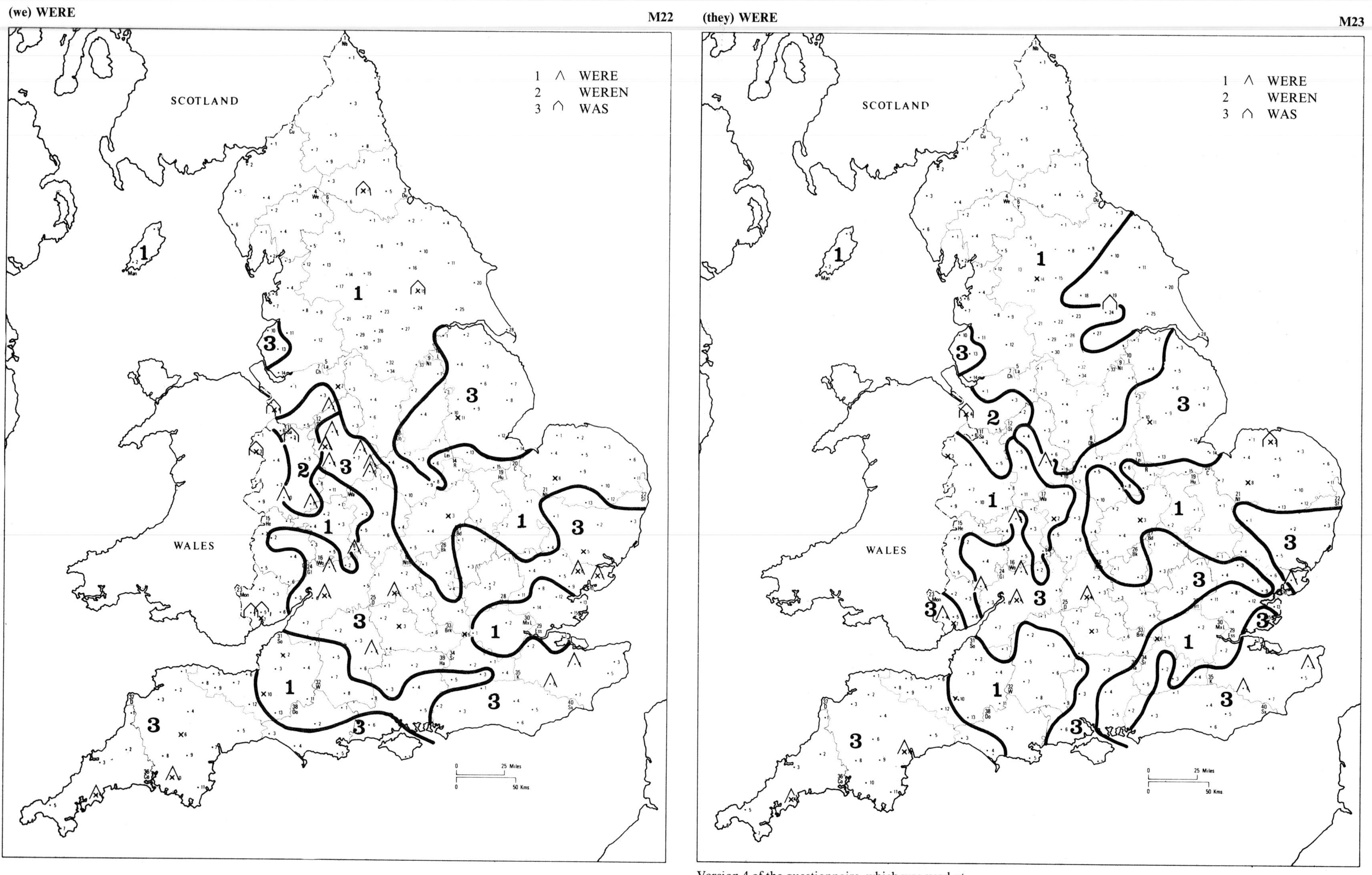

Version 4 of the questionnaire, which was used at 6Y 4/10/11/14/16/18/20/25/27/28, did not contain this q

(if she) WERE

M24

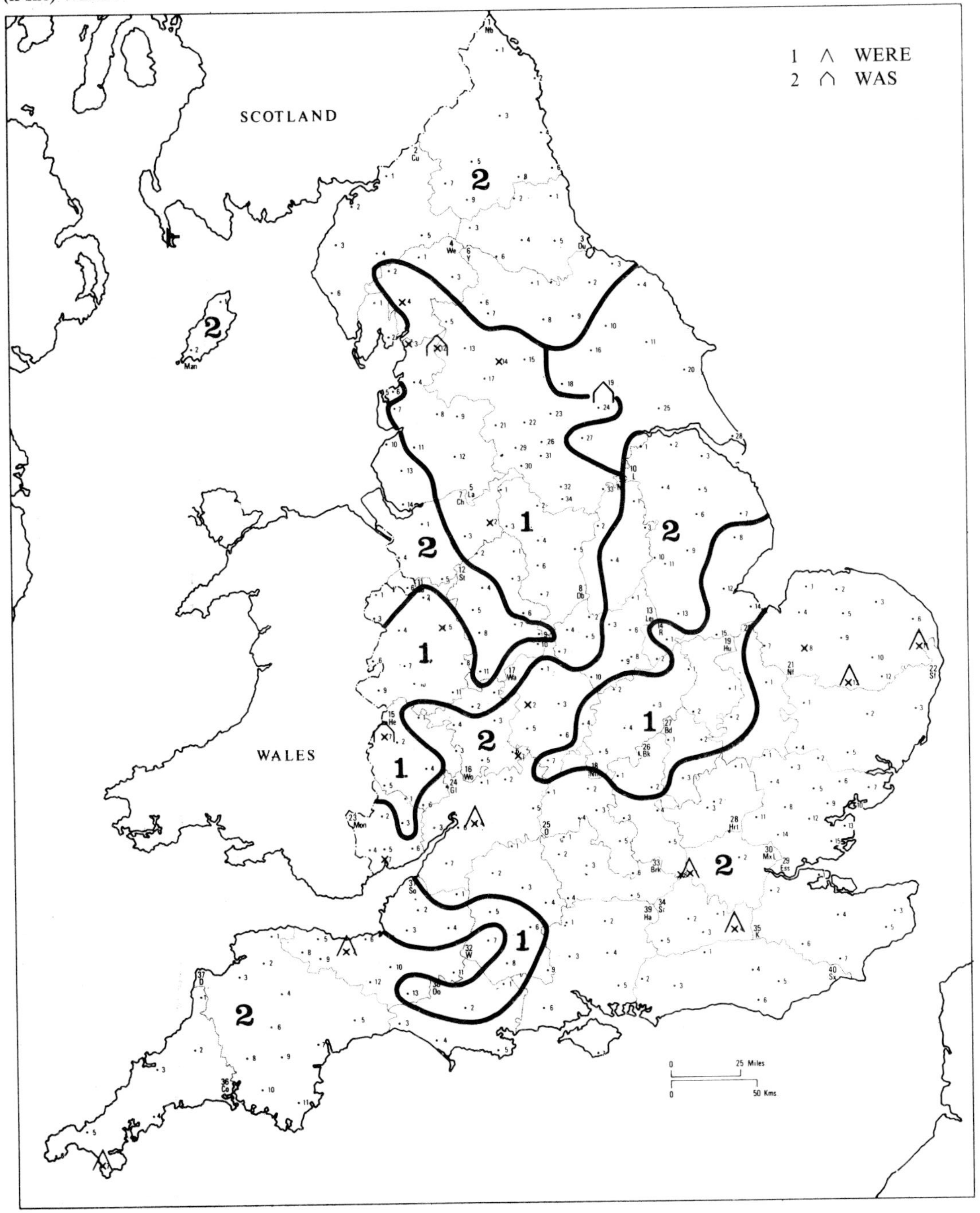

WEREN 11Sa 5

(if we) WERE

M25

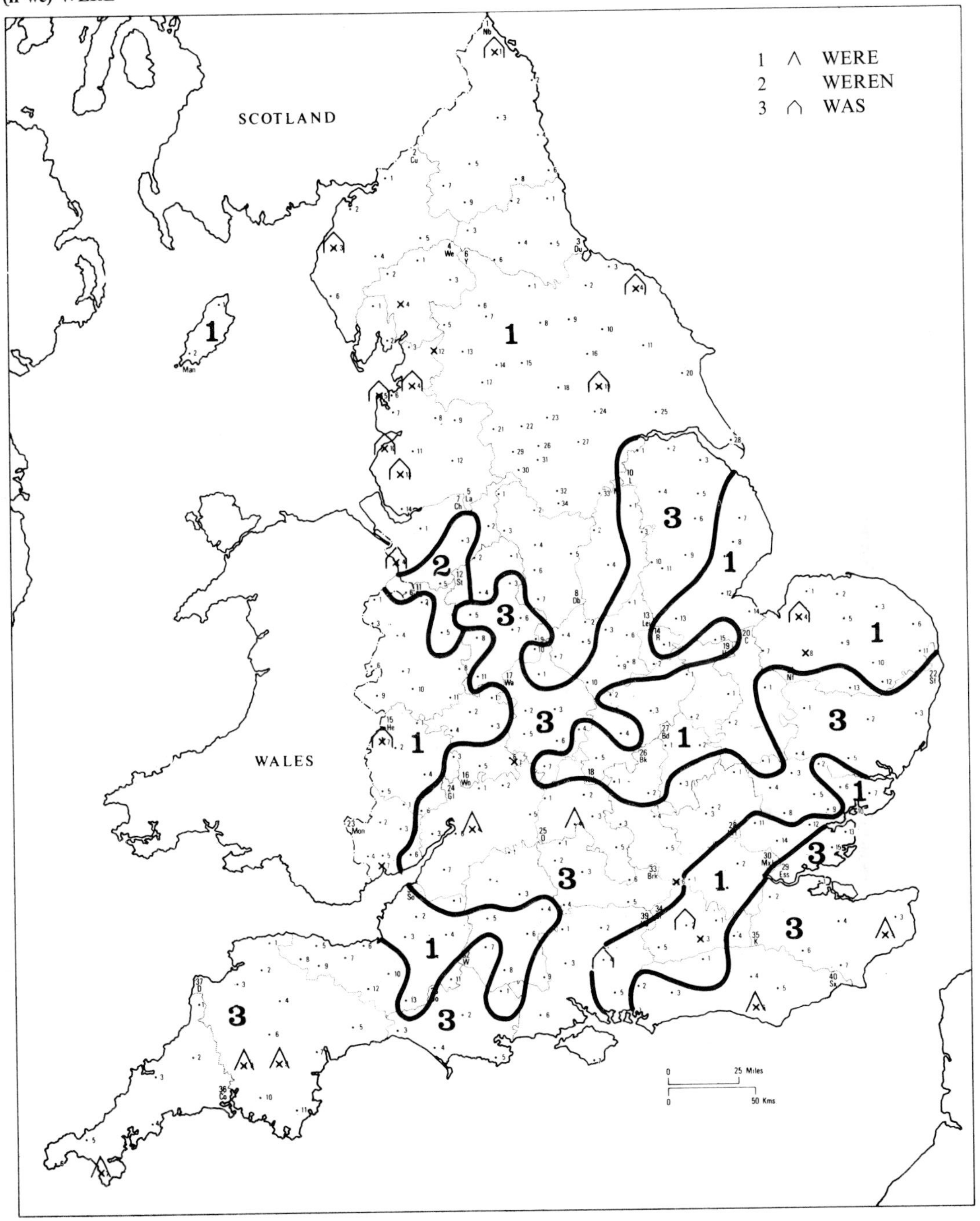

WAR 6Y 12
S 34Sr 3

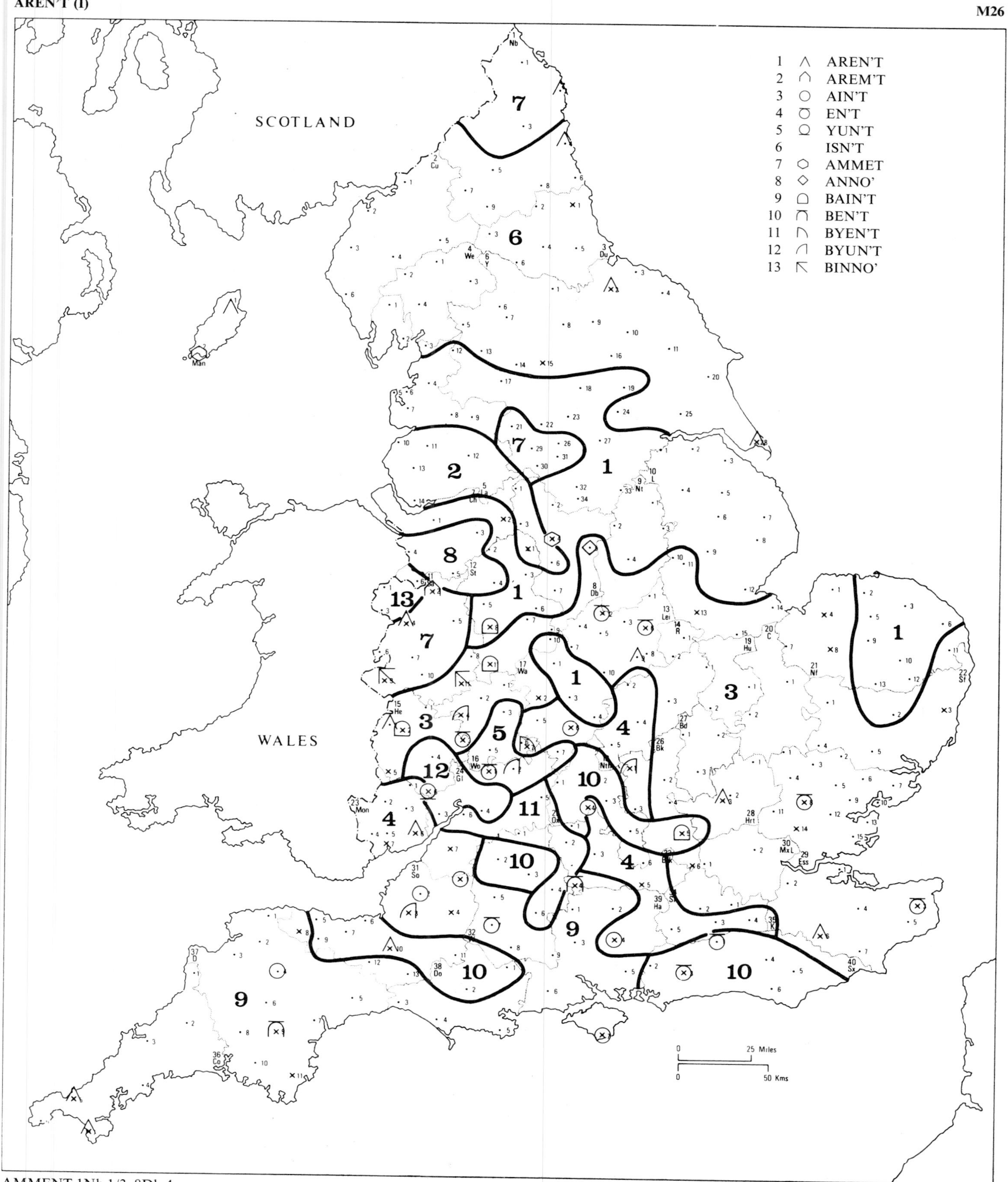

AMMENT 1Nb 1/3, 8Db 4,
AMMEN' Man 2 under AMMET

BAAN'T 31So 8, 37D 11
BIN' 24Gl 7
HIN' 22Sf 3
IN'T 12St 1
IS (I) NOT 3Du 1
YEN'T 15He 5

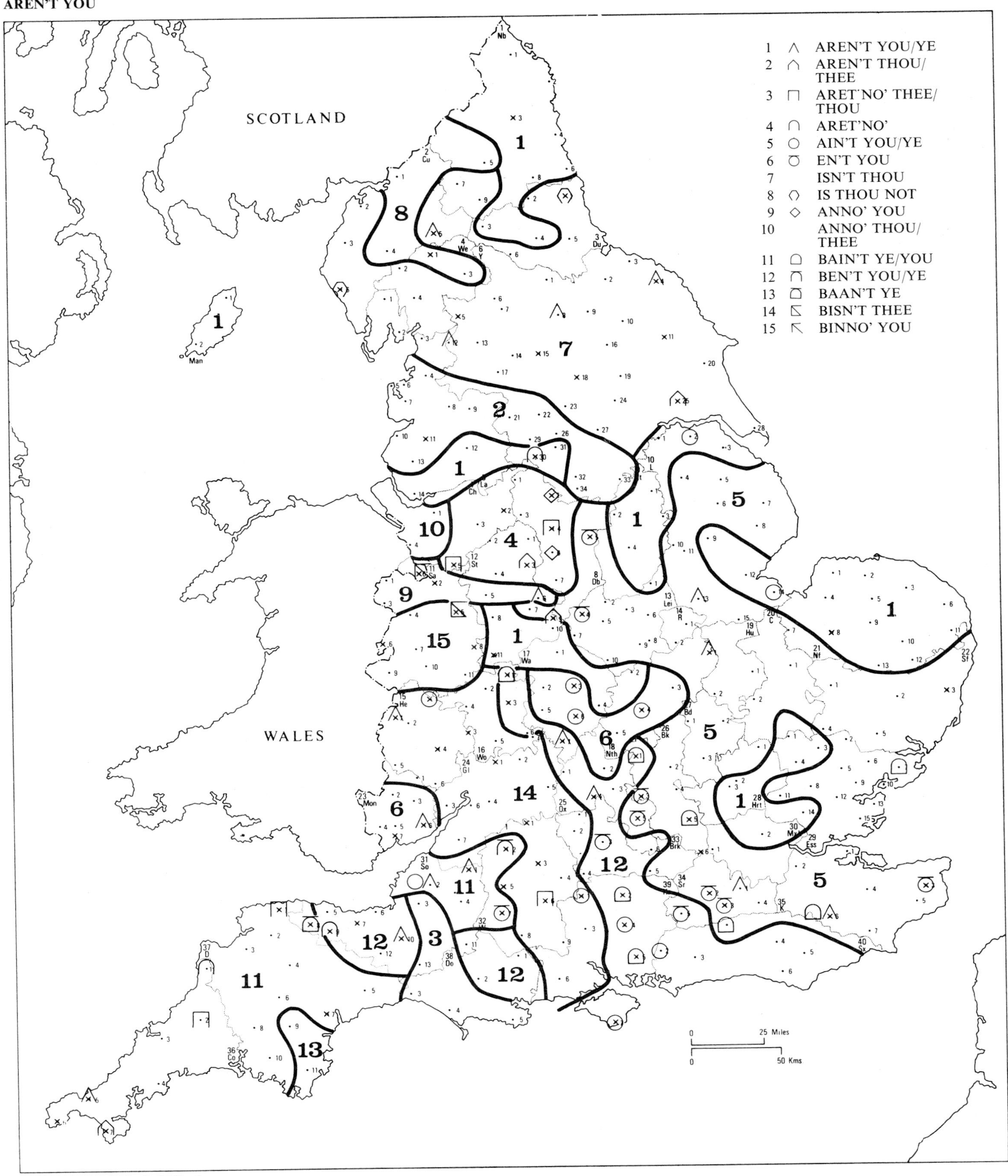

AIN'T THEE 31So 7, 36Co 6
AMMO' YOU 11Sa 2
ARET' NOT 5La 11
ARE YE NOT 1Nb 3, ARE YOU NOT 4We 1
BEN'T THOU 33Brk +4
BINNO' THEE 11Sa 6/8
BISN'T 24Gl +5, 32W 5
BYEN' YE 32W 1
BYUN'T YOU 15He 3, 16Wo 3
BYUN'T THEE 15He 4
BYUSN'T THEE 24Gl 1
EN'T THEE 32W 3/+7
HIN'T YOU 22Sf 3
IN'T THOU 6Y 5/15
ISN'T YOU 8Db +2

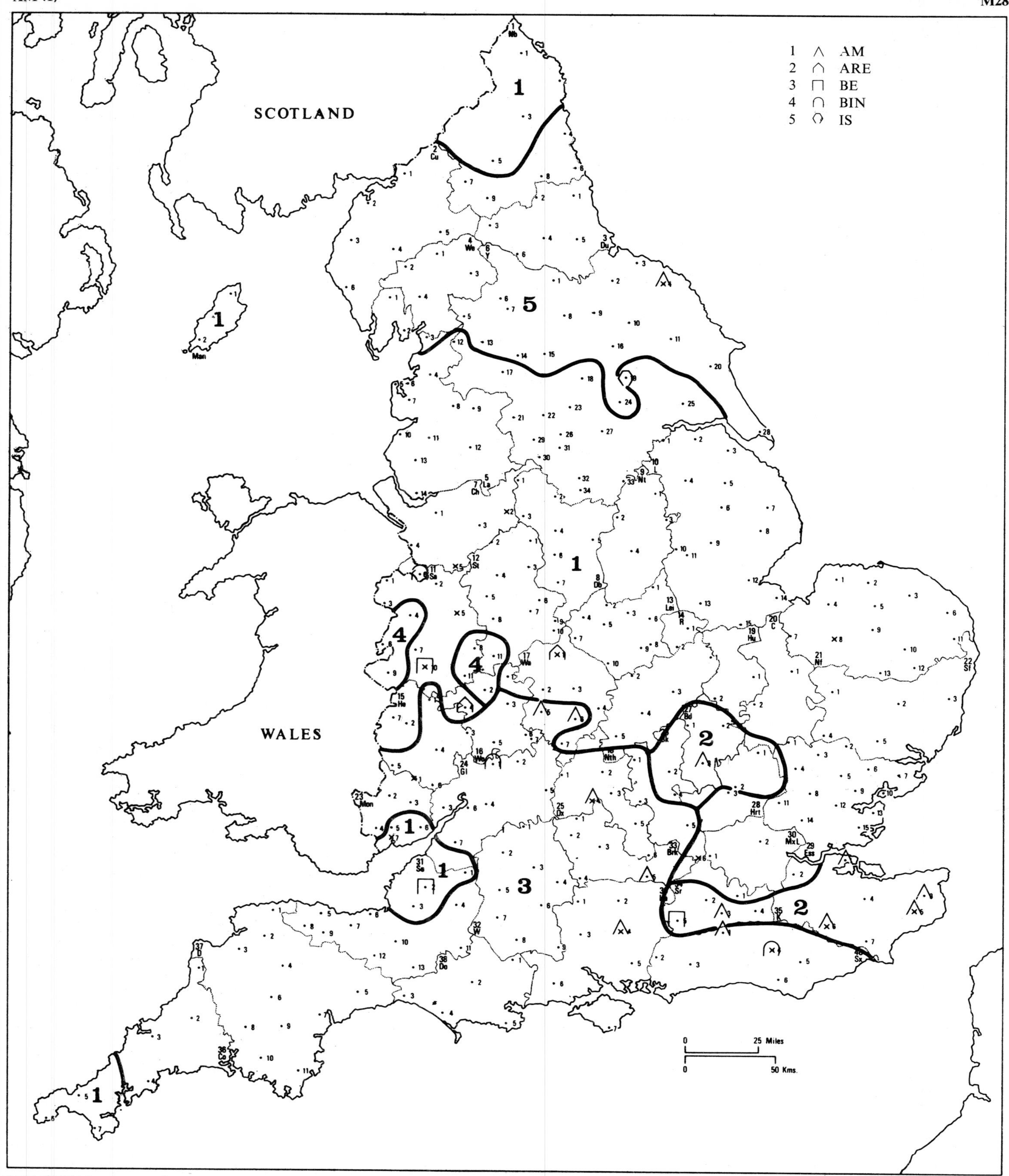

BEN 24Gl ⁺1 under BIN

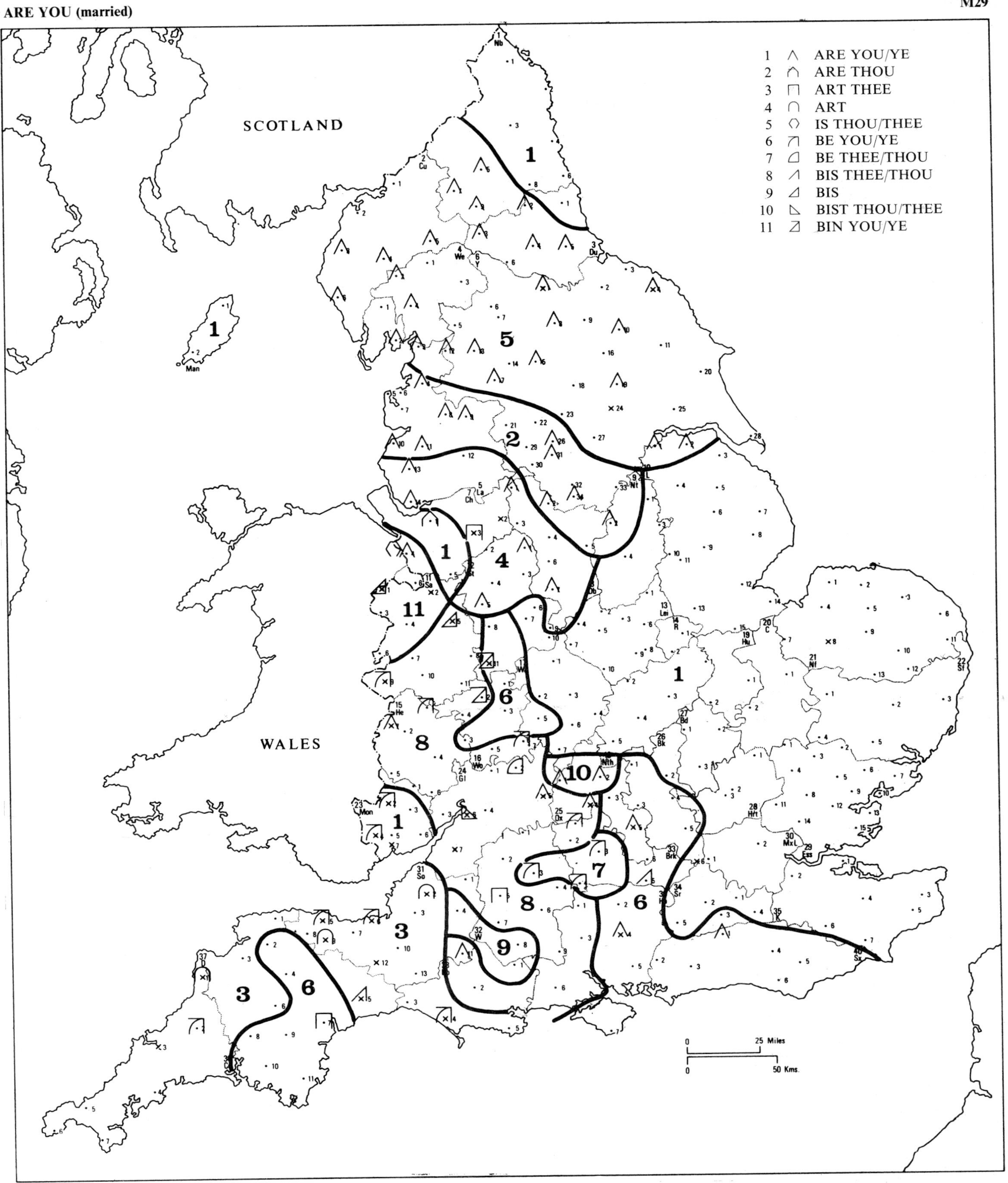

AREN YOU 11Sa 2
BE 31So 12, 36Co 3
BIST 24Gl + 5/7
IST THOU 6Y + 1/24

1	∧	ARE
	∩	ART
	⊓	AM
	∩	IS
2		BE
3		BIN

SCOTLAND

WALES

0 25 Miles

0 50 Kms.

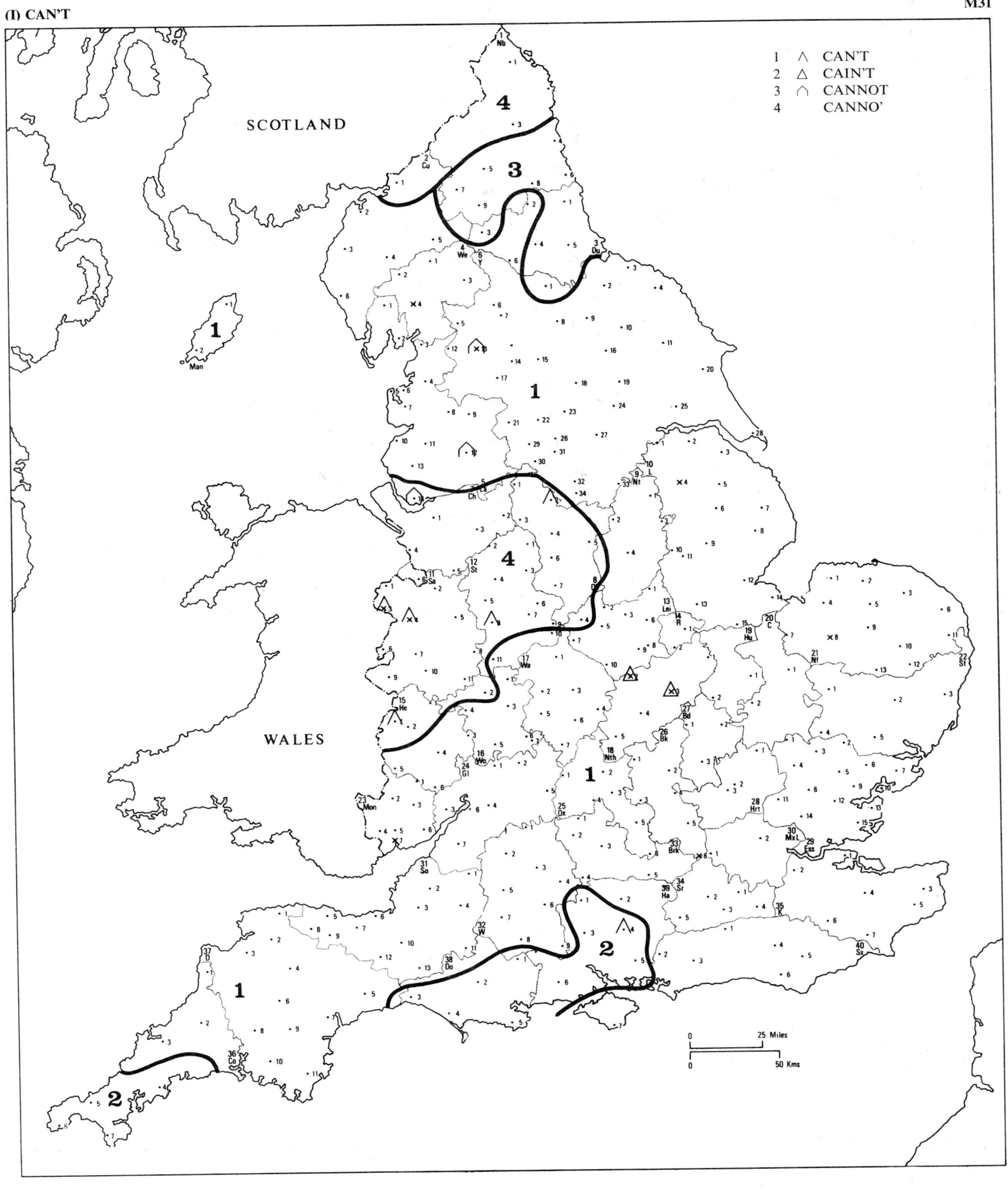
1 ʌ CAN'T
2 △ CAIN'T
3 ∩ CANNOT
4 CANNO'
SCOTLAND
WALES
25 Miles
50 Kms

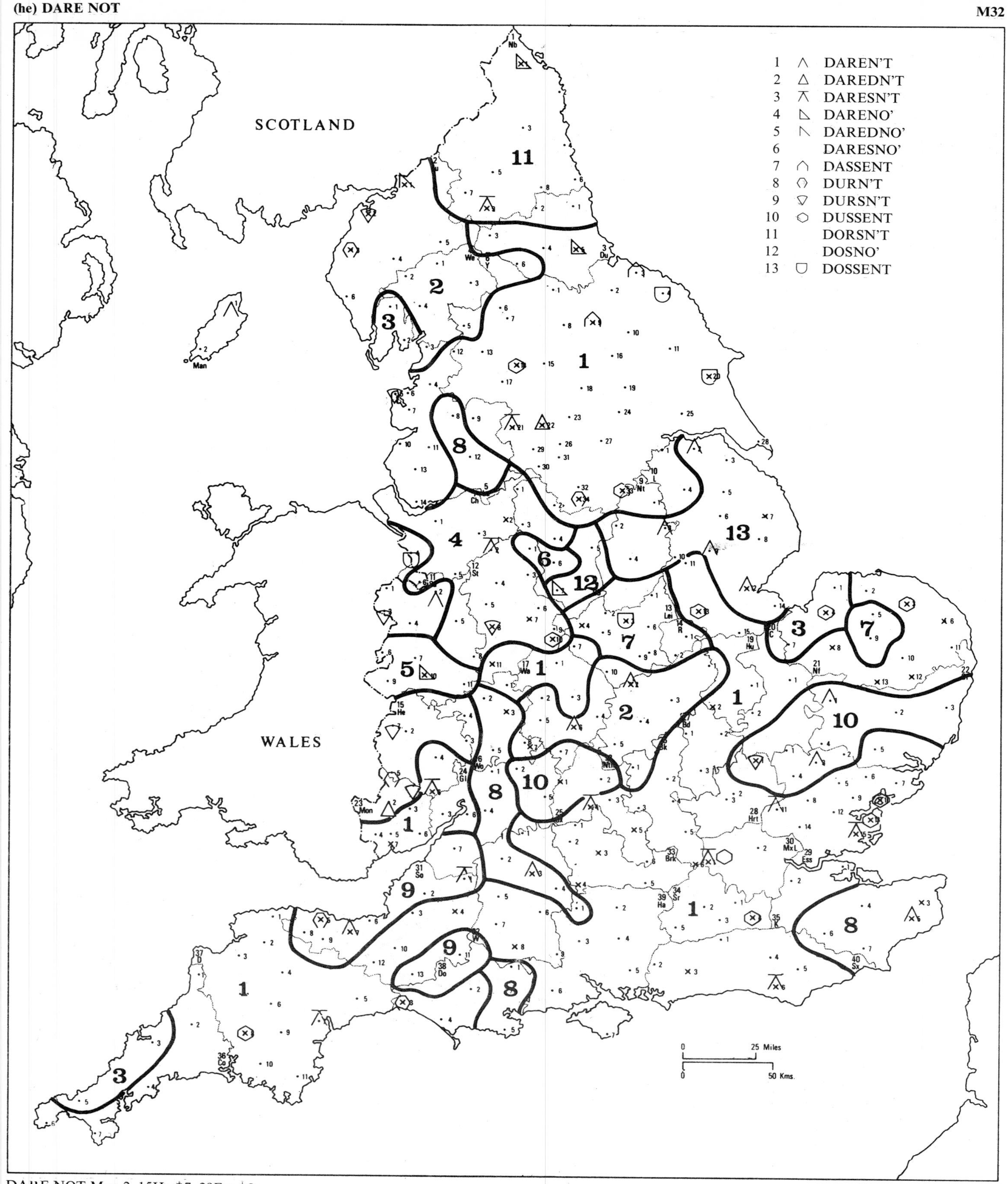

DARE NOT Man 2, 15He +7, 29Ess +8,
DARES NOT 31So 4
DOESN'T DARE 25Ox +4, 32W 8, 33Brk 4
DON'T DARE 33Brk 3, 34Sr +2, 39Ha +3,
40Sx 3, DON'T DARE TO 25Ox 5,
34Sr +3(3prpl)
DURDN'T 12St 11, 25Ox 1
DURDNO' 11Sa 4
DURNO' 11Sa 1
DUSNO' 12St 7, 13Lei 4

(he) DURST NOT M33a

(he) DURST NOT M33b

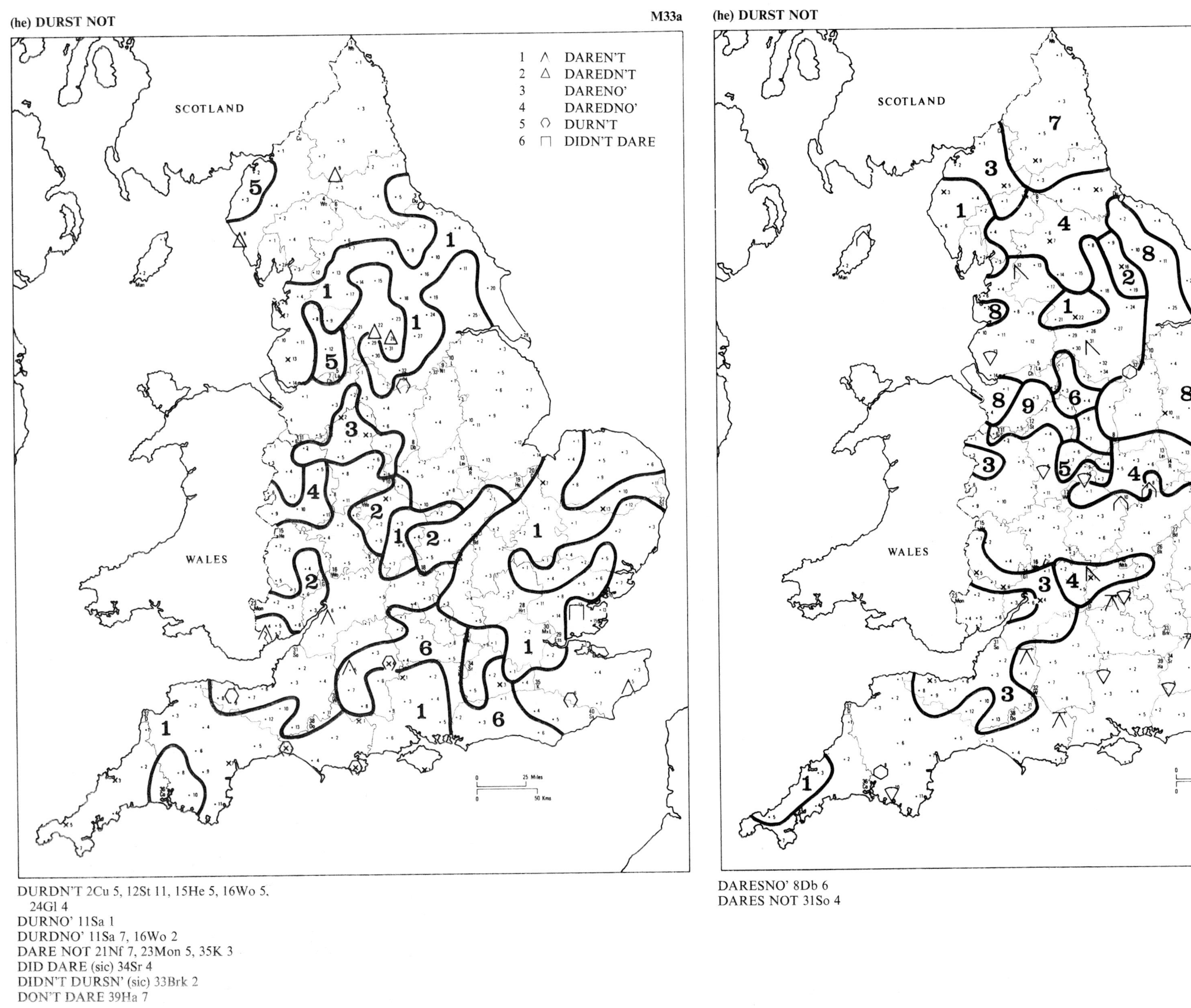

DURDN'T 2Cu 5, 12St 11, 15He 5, 16Wo 5, 24Gl 4
DURNO' 11Sa 1
DURDNO' 11Sa 7, 16Wo 2
DARE NOT 21Nf 7, 23Mon 5, 35K 3
DID DARE (sic) 34Sr 4
DIDN'T DURSN' (sic) 33Brk 2
DON'T DARE 39Ha 7

DARESNO' 8Db 6
DARES NOT 31So 4

(he) DOES M34

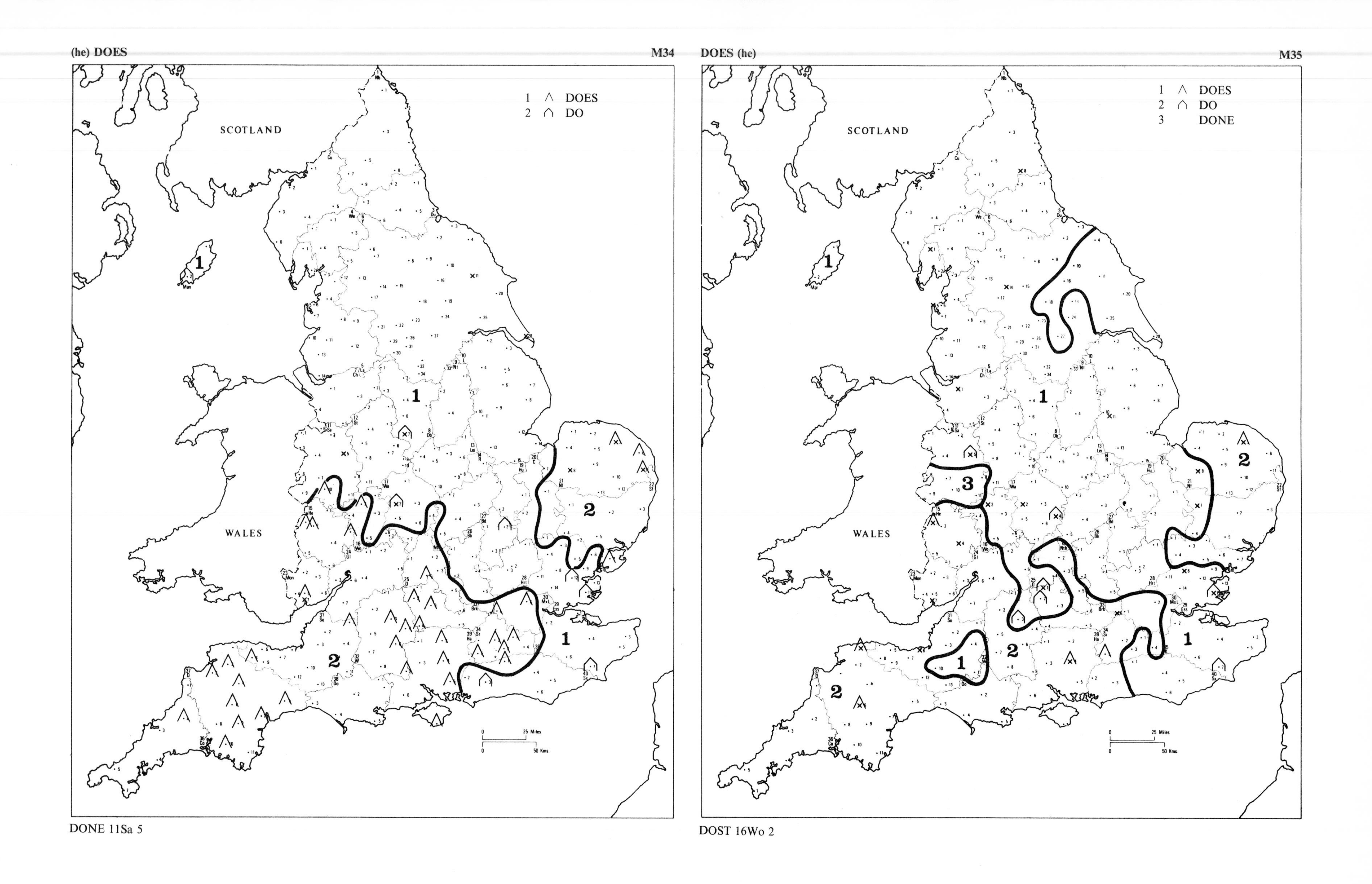

DONE 11Sa 5

DOES (he) M35

DOST 16Wo 2

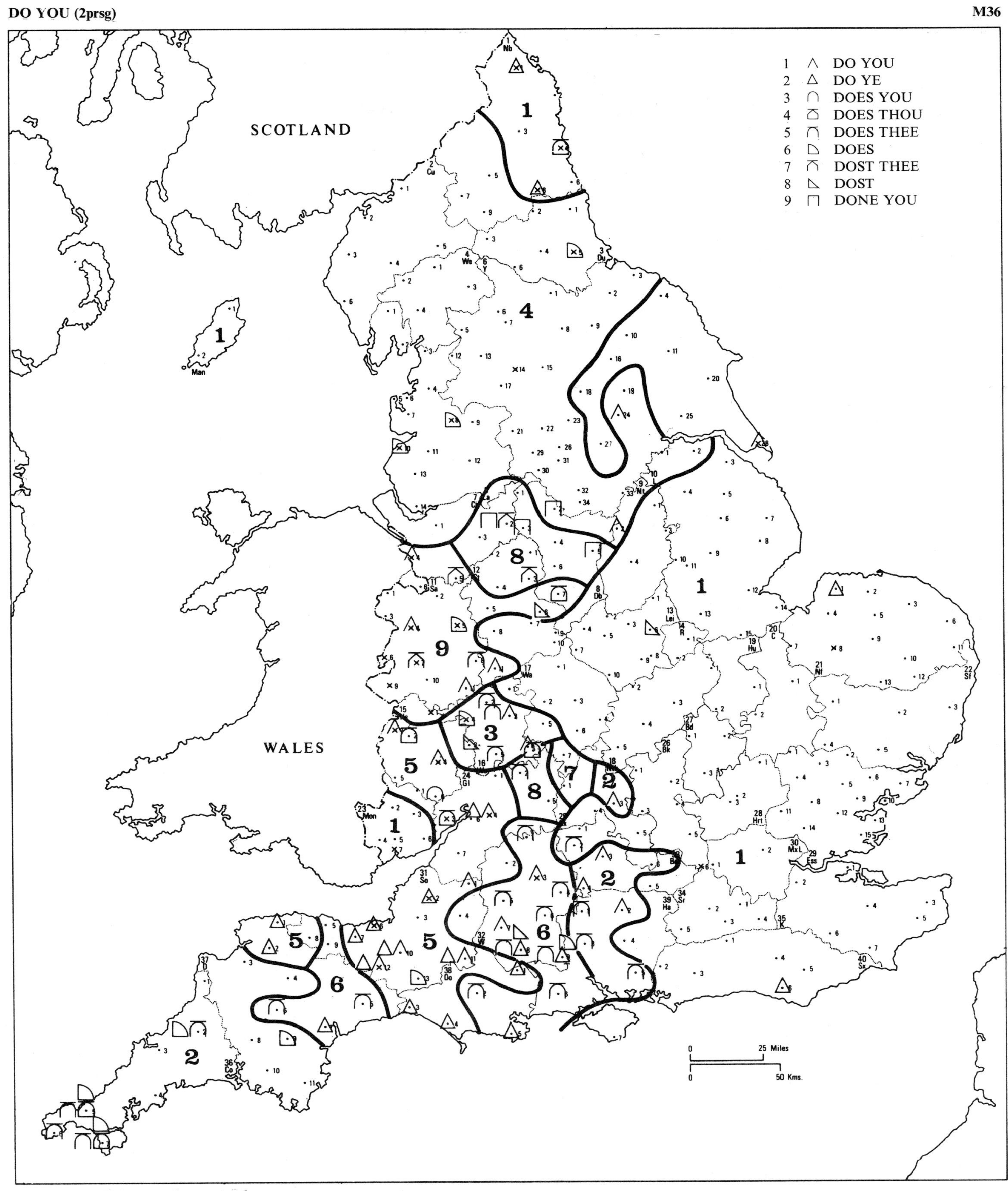

DO THEE 12St +6, 37D +10, 38Do +3
DONE YE 11Sa 6
DONE THEE 7Ch +4, 8Db +3, 12St +3
DOST THOU 11Sa 9, 12St +9
DO YOUM 10L +15
THEE 15He 1

(he) DOESN'T M37

(they) DON'T M38

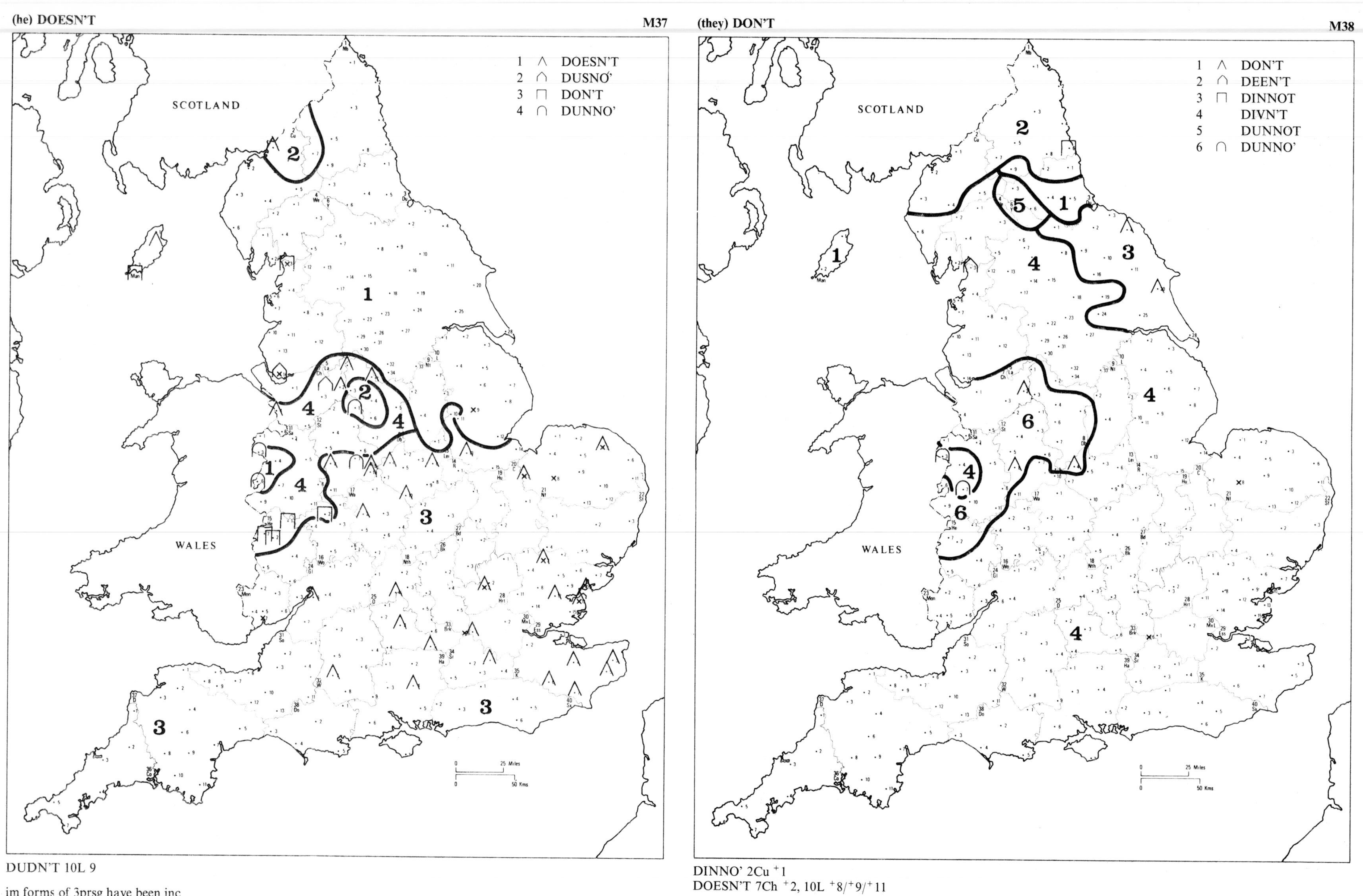

DUDN'T 10L 9

im forms of 3prsg have been inc

DINNO' 2Cu +1

DOESN'T 7Ch +2, 10L +8/+9/+11

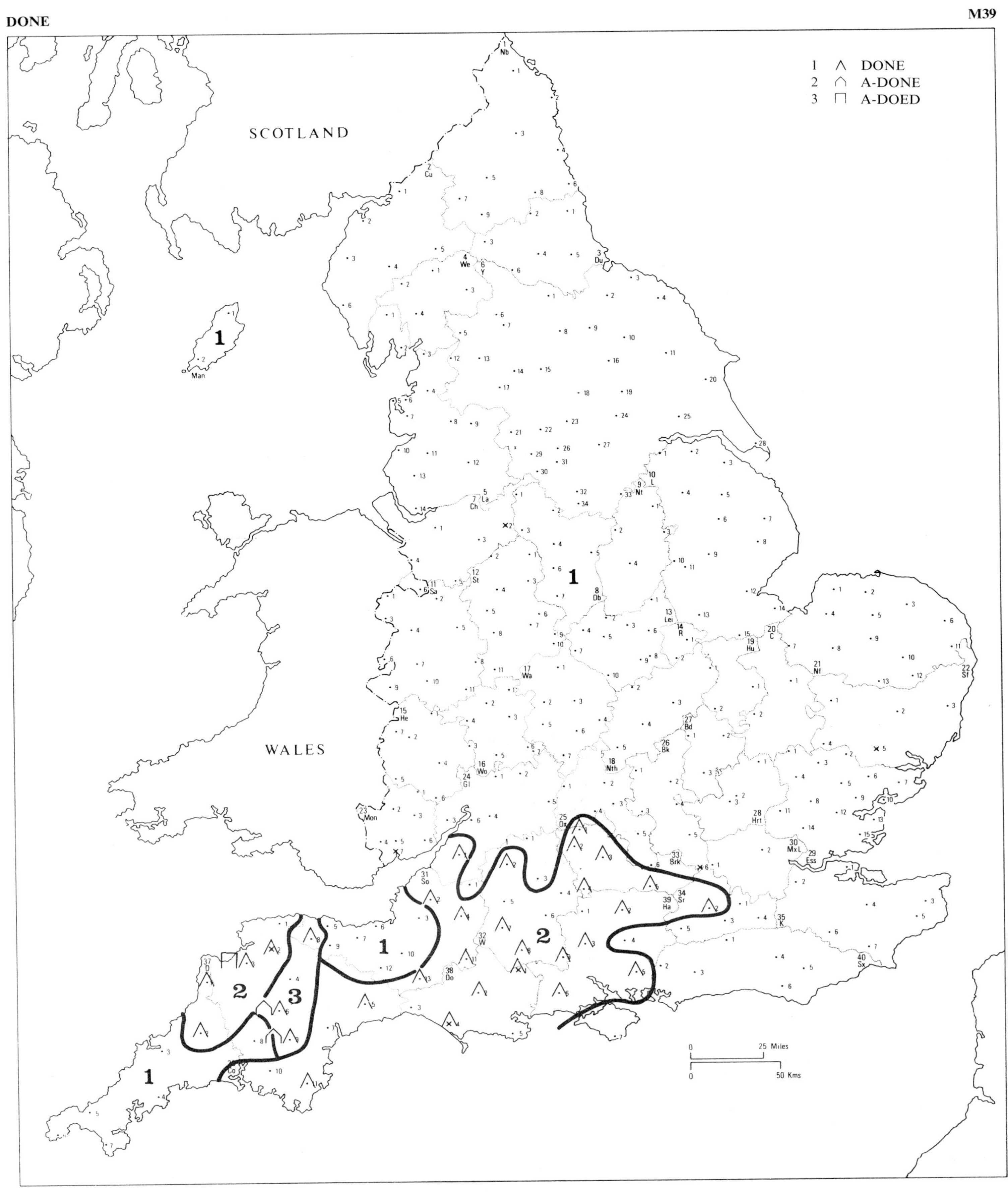

DID Man +1, 33Brk +4
DO 33Brk +3
DOED 31So+8

(I) HAVE — M40

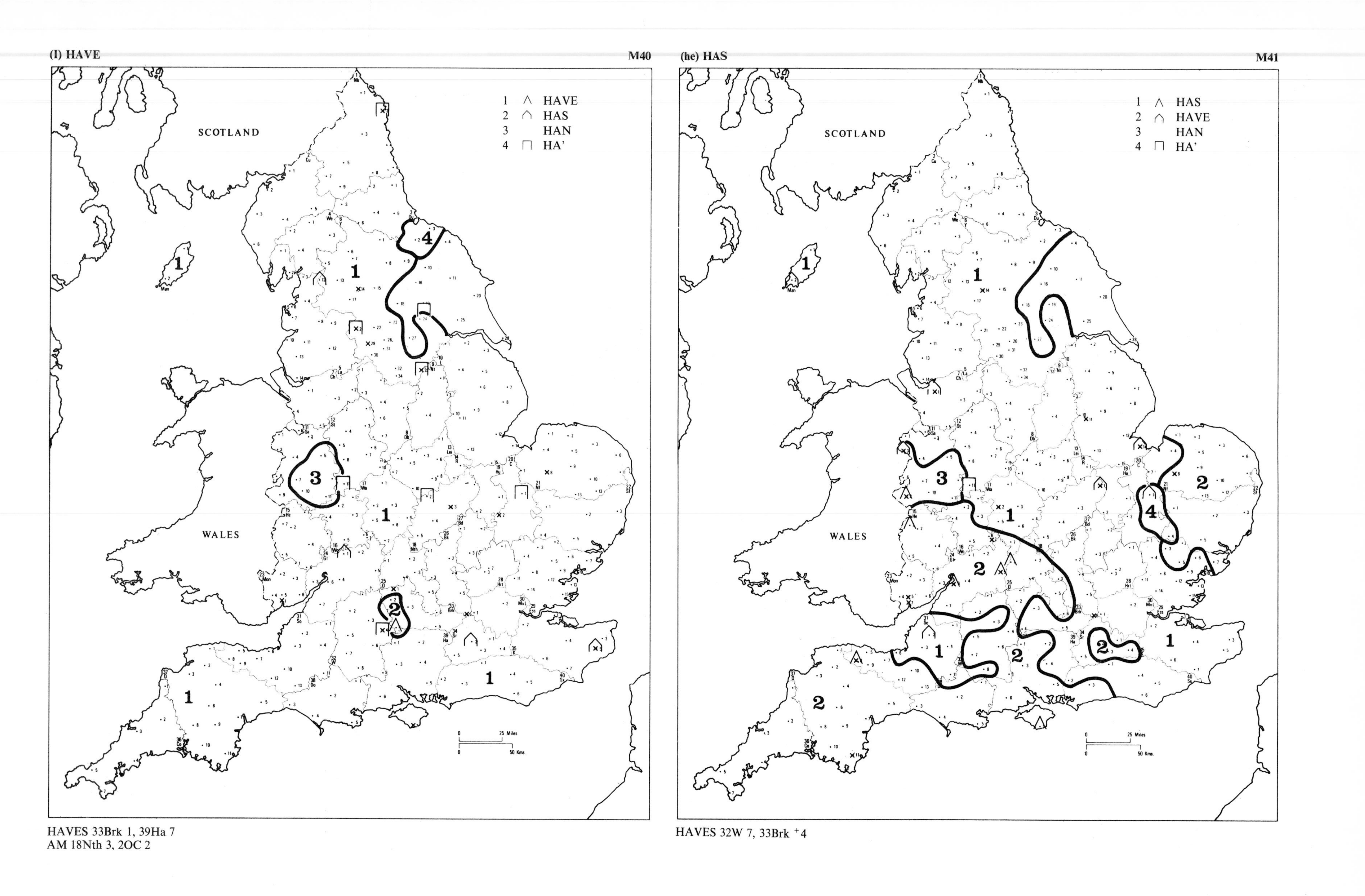

HAVES 33Brk 1, 39Ha 7
AM 18Nth 3, 2OC 2

(he) HAS — M41

HAVES 32W 7, 33Brk +4

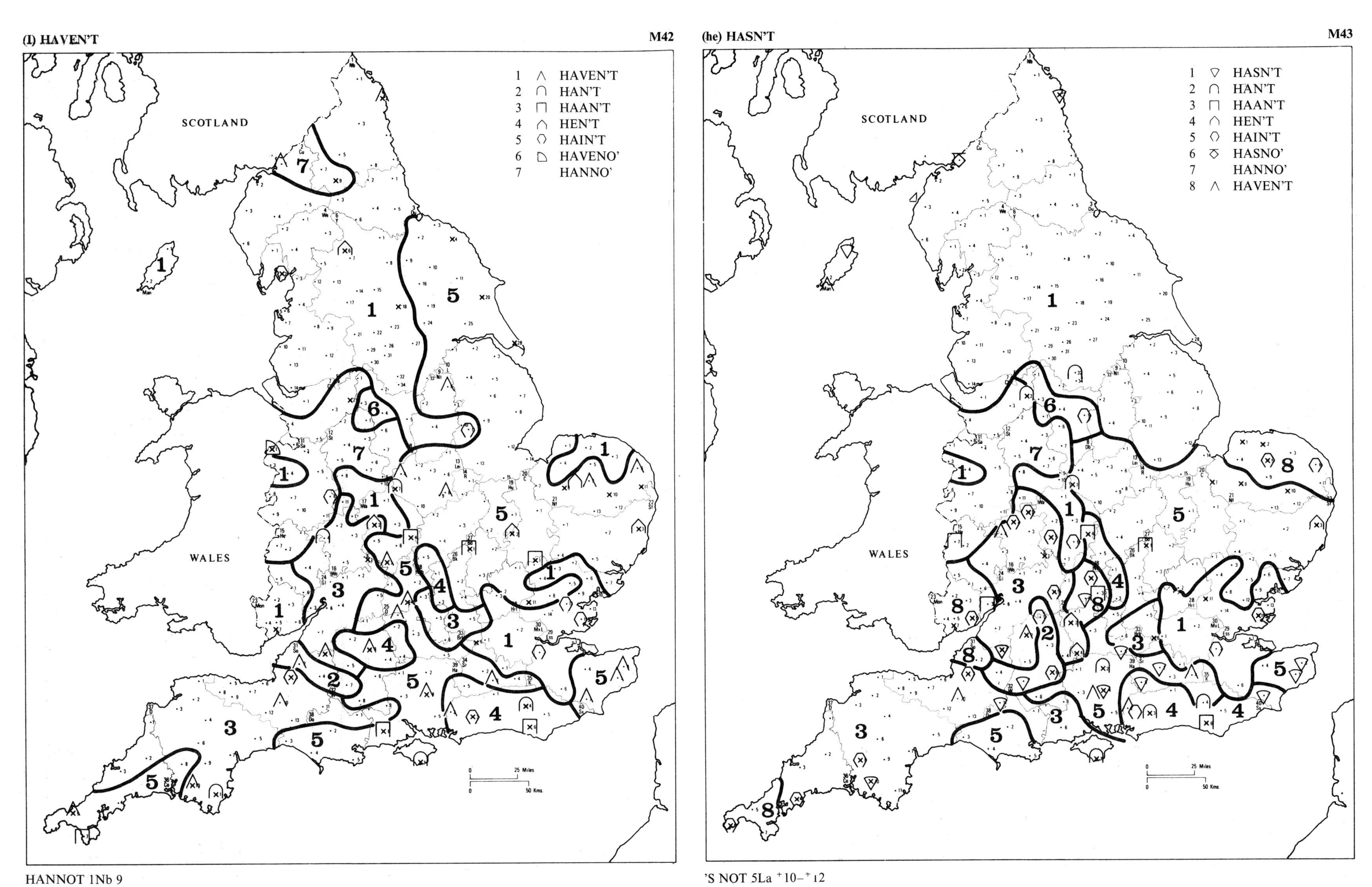

HANNOT 1Nb 9
HASN'T 33Brk $^{+}5$
'VE NOT 5La $^{+}10-^{+}12$

'S NOT 5La $^{+}10-^{+}12$

(we) HAVEN'T — M44

(we) HAVE GOT — M45

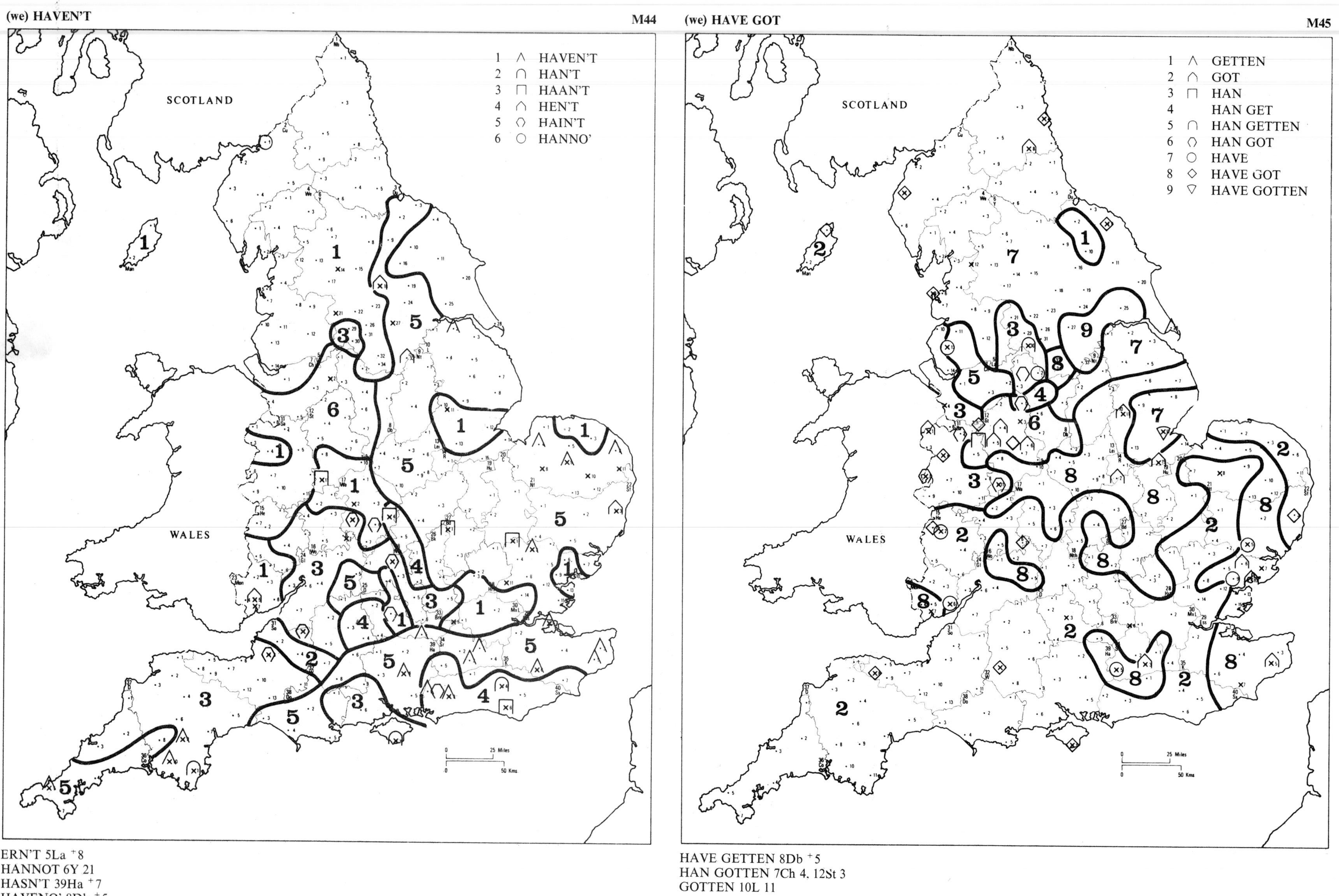

ERN'T 5La $^{+}$8
HANNOT 6Y 21
HASN'T 39Ha $^{+}$7
HAVENO' 8Db $^{+}$5
'N NOT 5La $^{+}$11
'VE NOT 5La $^{+}$10/$^{+}$12

HAVE GETTEN 8Db $^{+}$5
HAN GOTTEN 7Ch 4, 12St 3
GOTTEN 10L 11

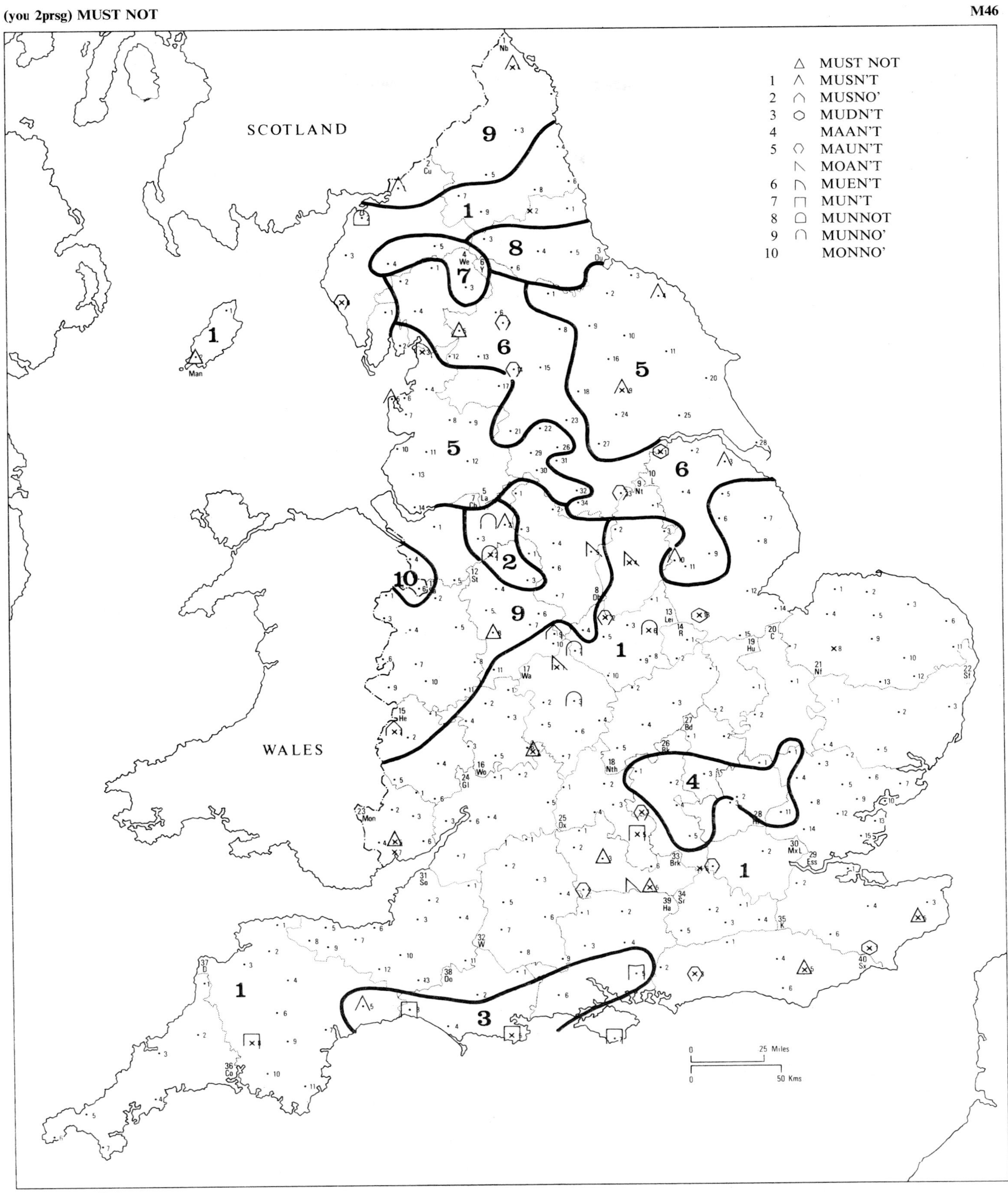

MANNO' 1Nb 2,
MENNO' 2Cu +1 under MUNNO'

MAIN'T 6Y +28, 29Ess +12
MONNOT 5La +7

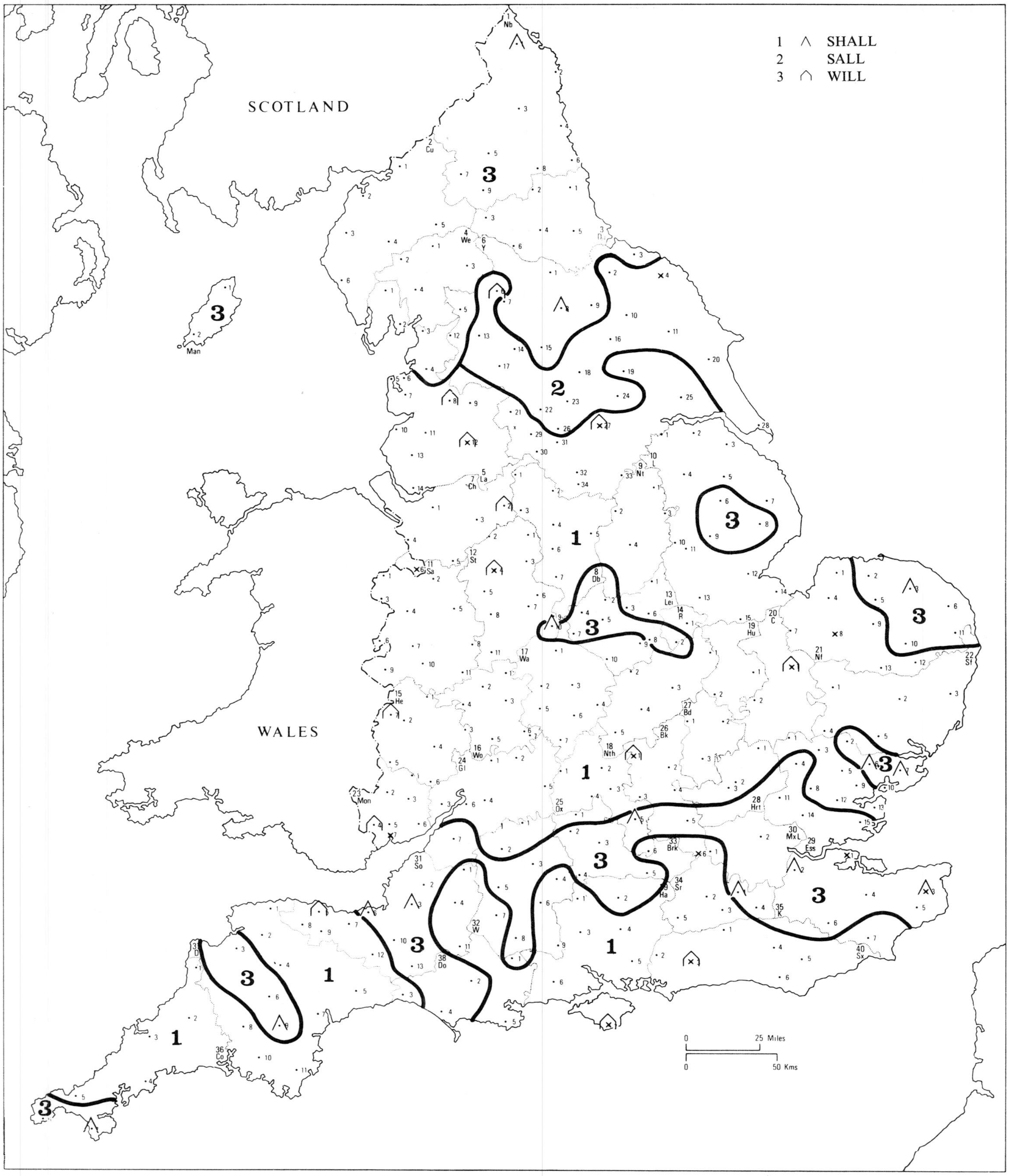

1 ∧ SHALL
2 SALL
3 ∩ WILL
SCOTLAND
WALES
25 Miles
50 Kms

(I) SHALL M48

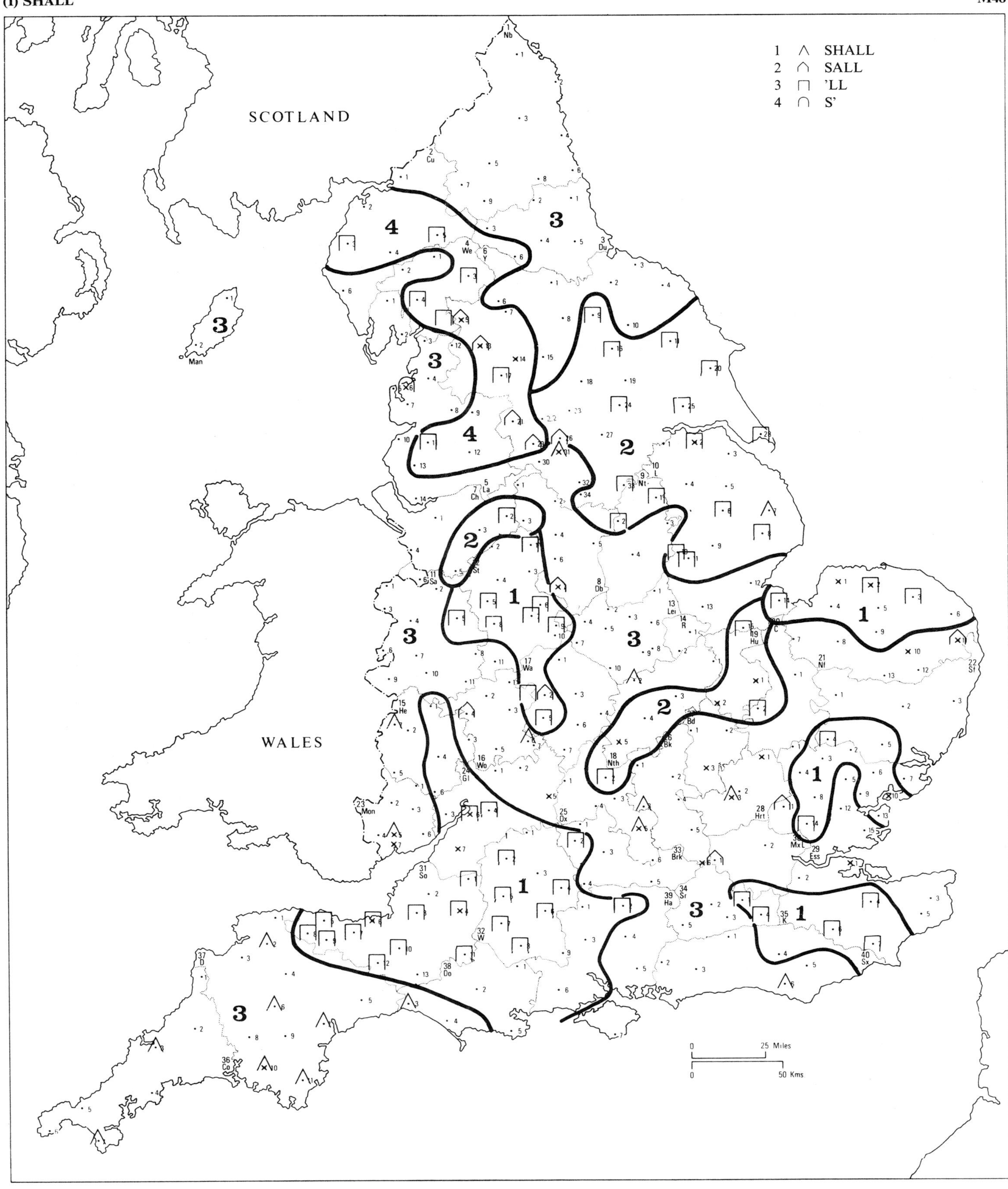

SA' 6Y +6/+17
S'T 5La +10, 6Y +21/+30
WILL Man +2, 12St +11, 29Ess 10
zero 21Nf +7/+9/10/+13, 33Brk +4

S' (+V) 25Ox +4

(I) SHAN'T M49

(I) WON'T M50

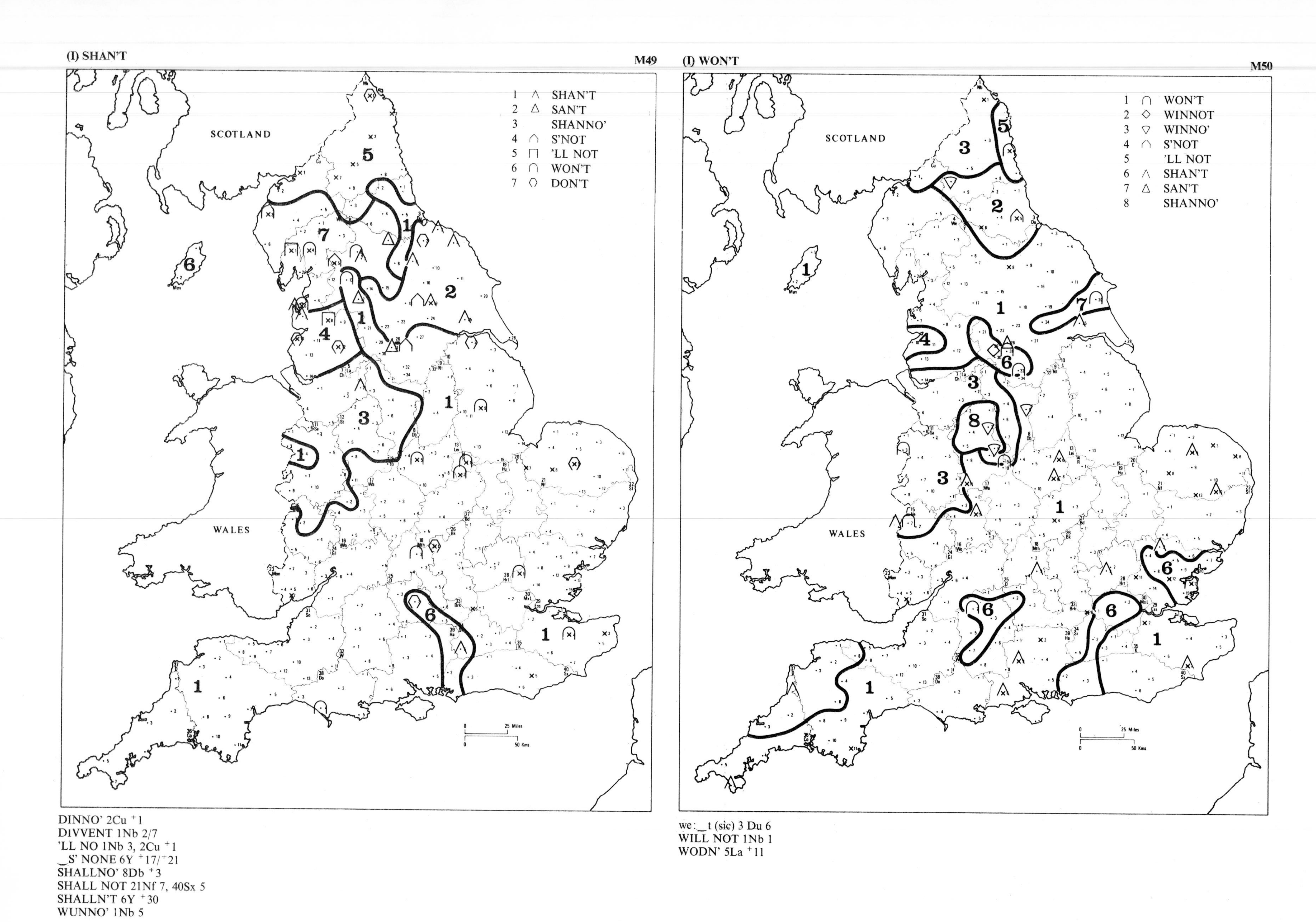

DINNO' 2Cu +1
DIVVENT 1Nb 2/7
'LL NO 1Nb 3, 2Cu +1
_S' NONE 6Y +17/+21
SHALLNO' 8Db +3
SHALL NOT 21Nf 7, 40Sx 5
SHALLN'T 6Y +30
WUNNO' 1Nb 5

ʃɔ:tən app double neg Edd 12St +11

we:_t (sic) 3 Du 6
WILL NOT 1Nb 1
WODN' 5La +11

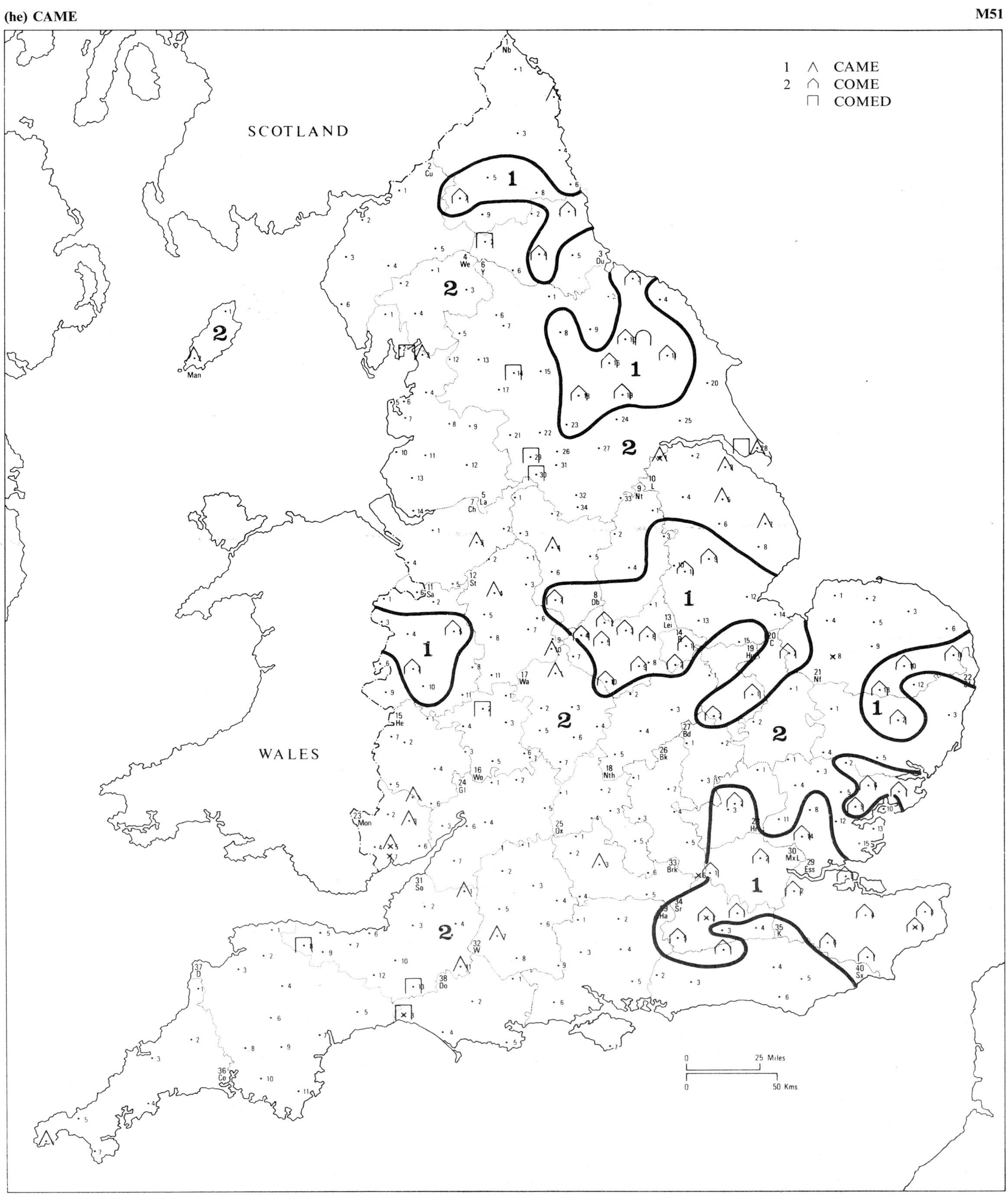

CO' 2Cu +5, 4We +1/+3/+4, 6Y +1/+5/+13
COMEN 7Ch +6

CAUGHT (3ptsg) **M52**

(they) GREW (v intr) **M53**

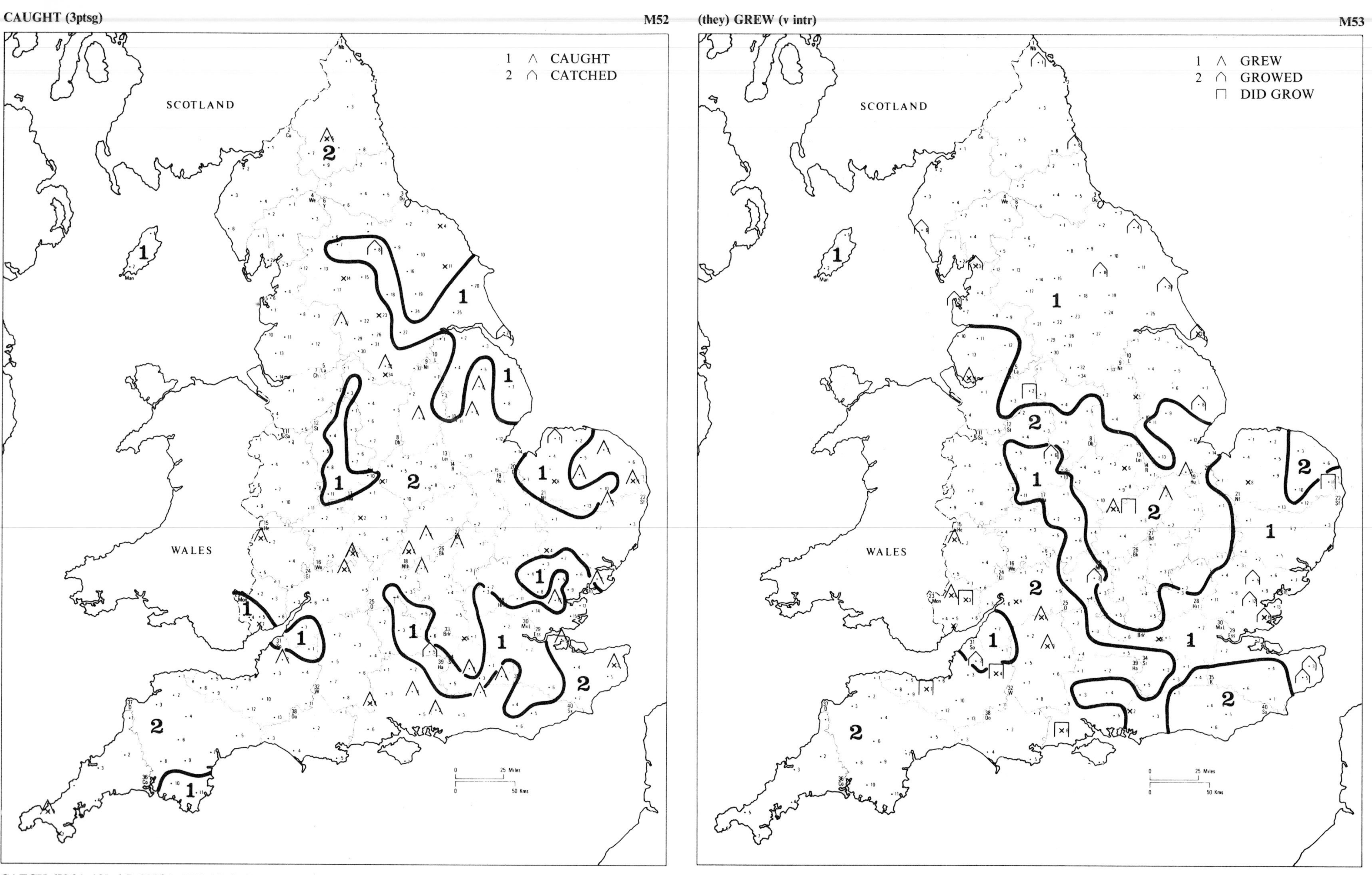

CATCH 6Y 34, 13Lei 7, 22Sf 4, 35K $^{+}$3, 36Co 7

im forms not inc

PUT (pp) M54

TAKEN (pp) M55

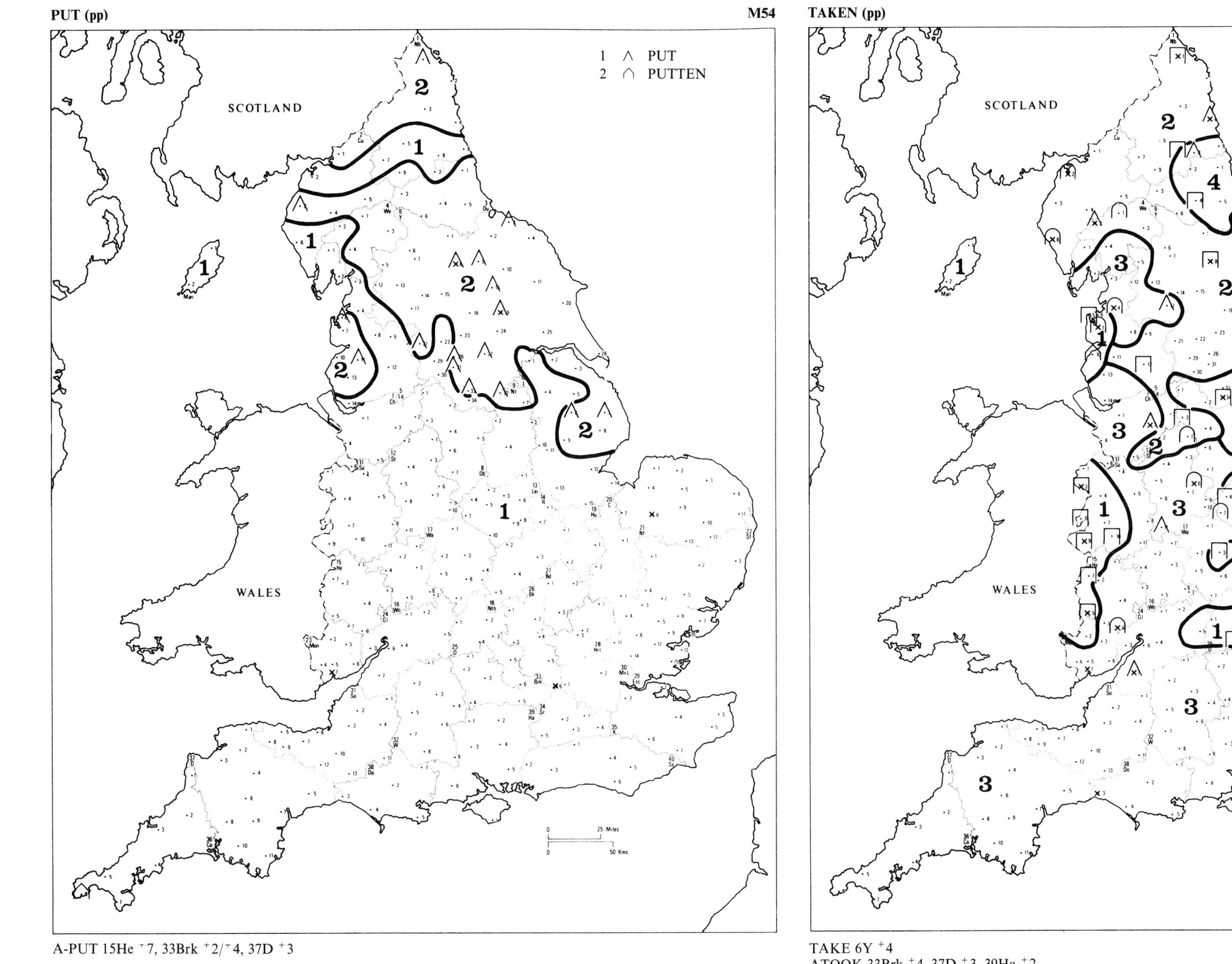

A-PUT 15He $^{+}$7, 33Brk $^{+}$2/$^{+}$4, 37D $^{+}$3

TAKE 6Y $^{+}$4
ATOOK 33Brk $^{+}$4, 37D $^{+}$3, 39Ha $^{+}$2
TOOKED 37D $^{+}$1/$^{+}$4, 38Do 3,
ATOOKED 37D $^{+}$3

CURSING (prp inflection) M56

DOING (prp inflection) M57

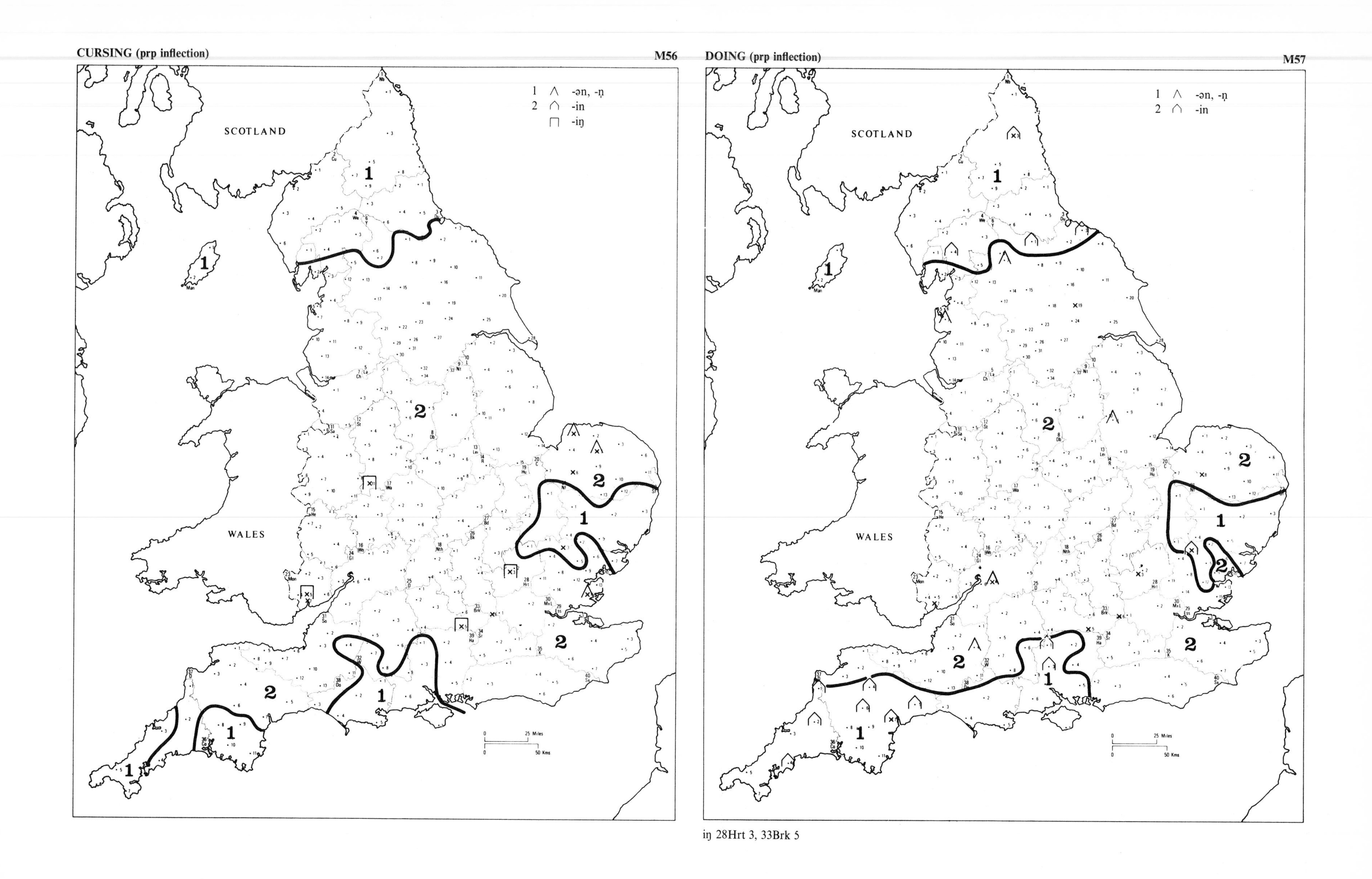

iŋ 28Hrt 3, 33Brk 5

LAUGHING (prp inflection) M58

WRITING (vbl n) M59

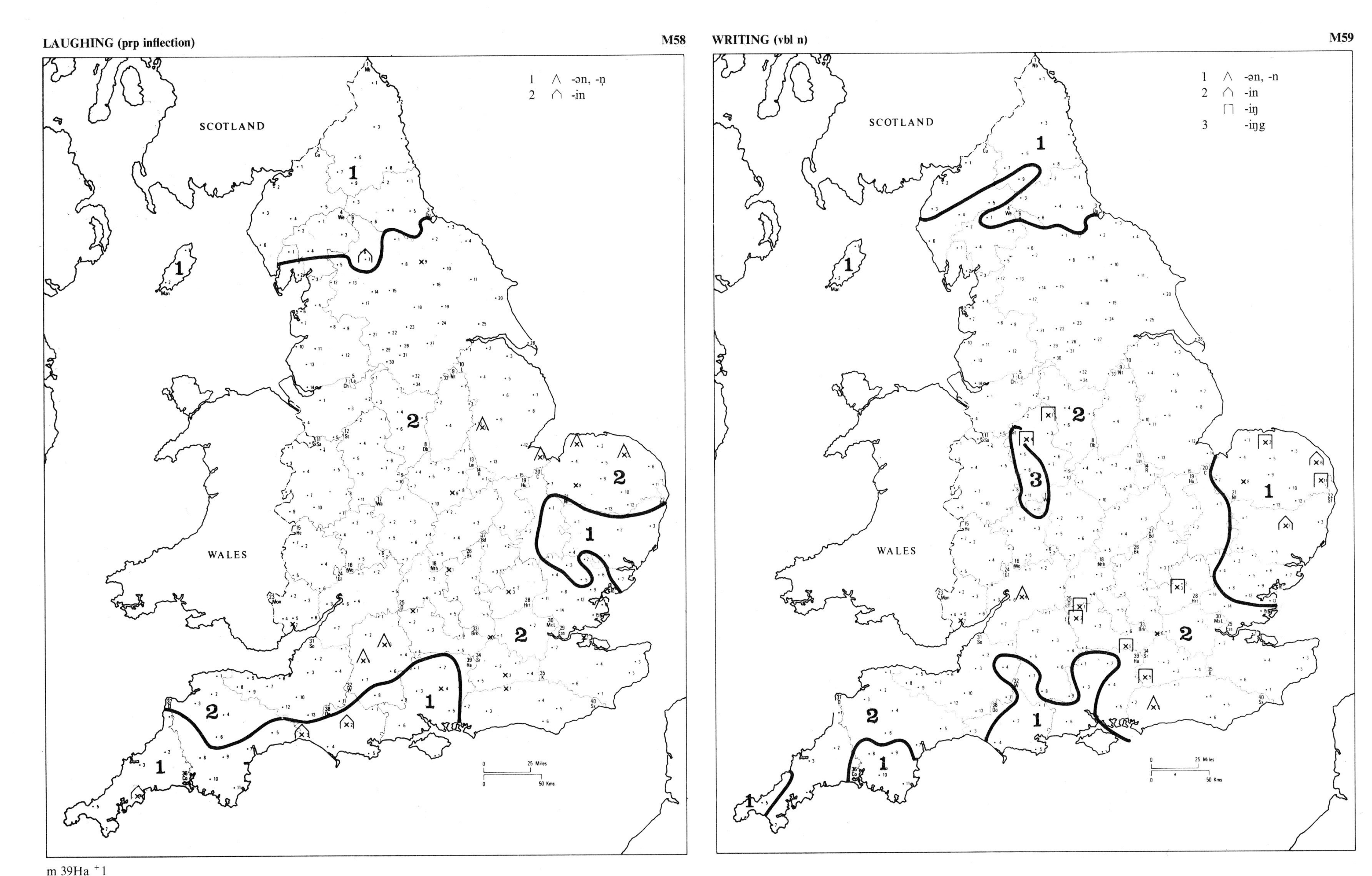

m 39Ha +1
ɩŋ 28Hrt 3, 33Brk 1

lä:ʔṇ (sic) 29Ess +13

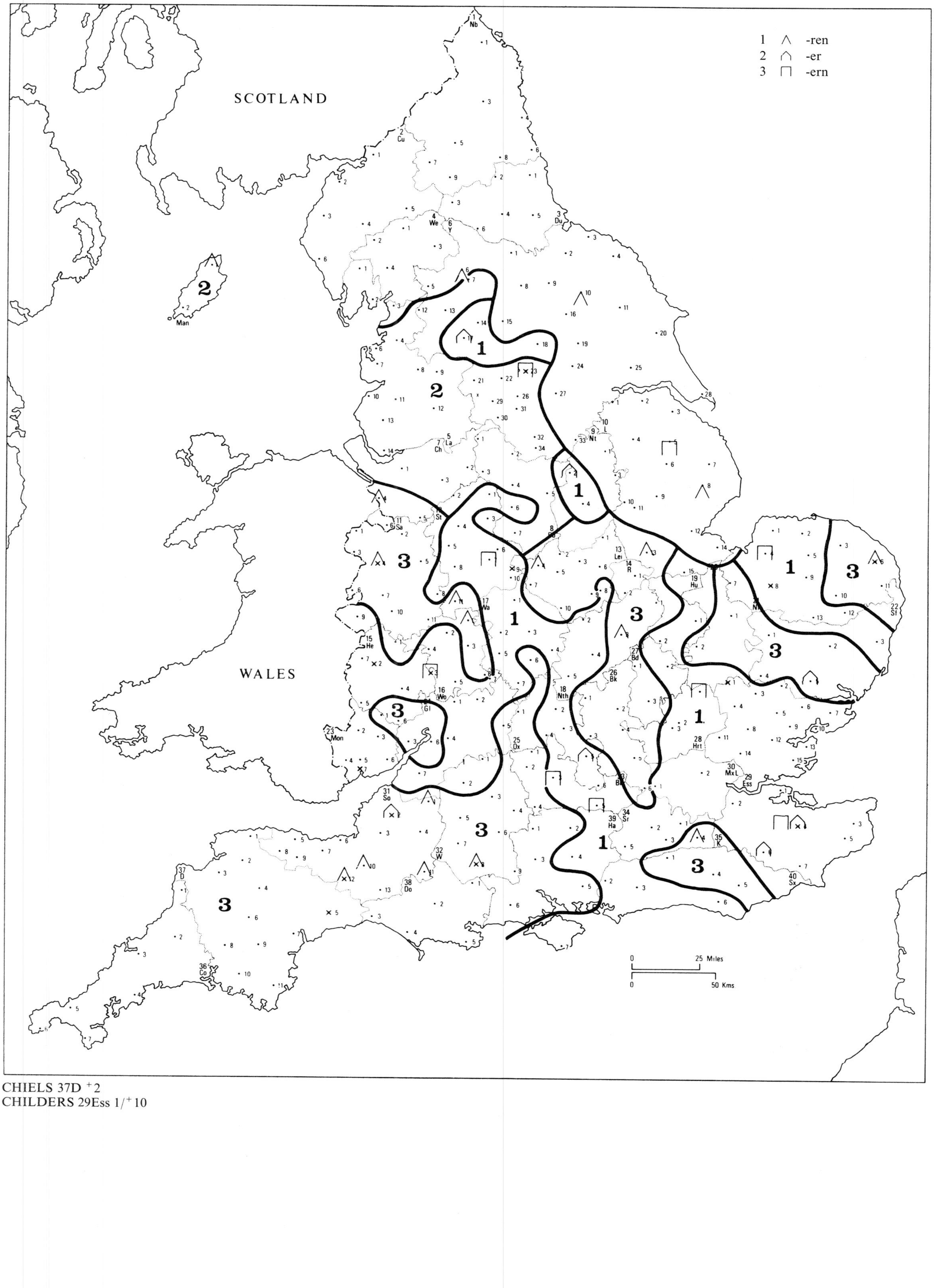

1 /\ -ren
2 ∩ -er
3 ⊓ -ern

SCOTLAND

WALES

0 25 Miles
0 50 Kms

CHIELS 37D +2
CHILDERS 29Ess 1/+10

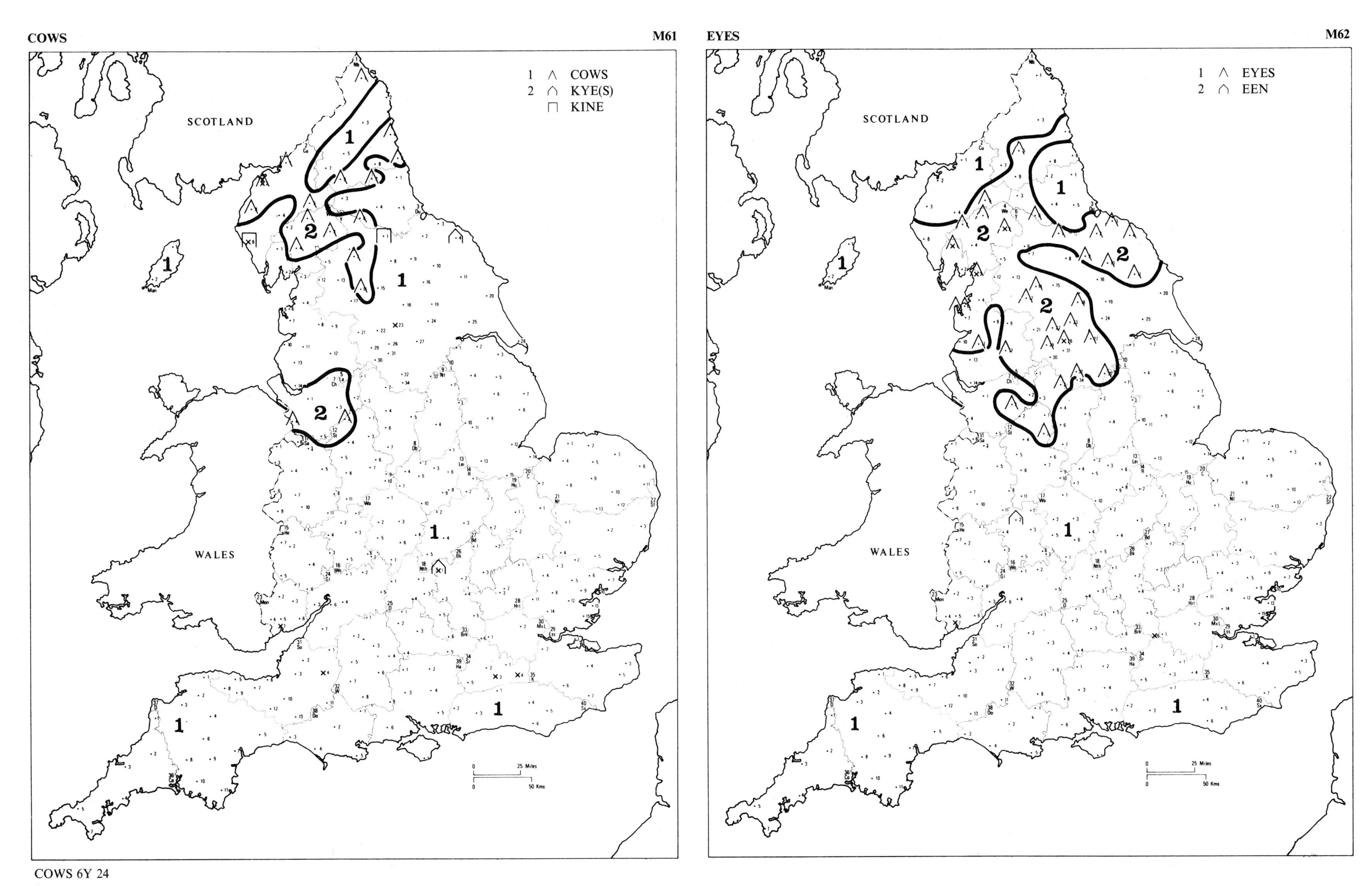

COWS 6Y 24

kɛɪz 7Ch 1/$^{+}$5, kɛ̃ɪz 26Bk 1, k^{ə}i̜:z 7Ch $^{+}$4 pres
repr ME *kies*
"a field of cow" 35K $^{+}$6

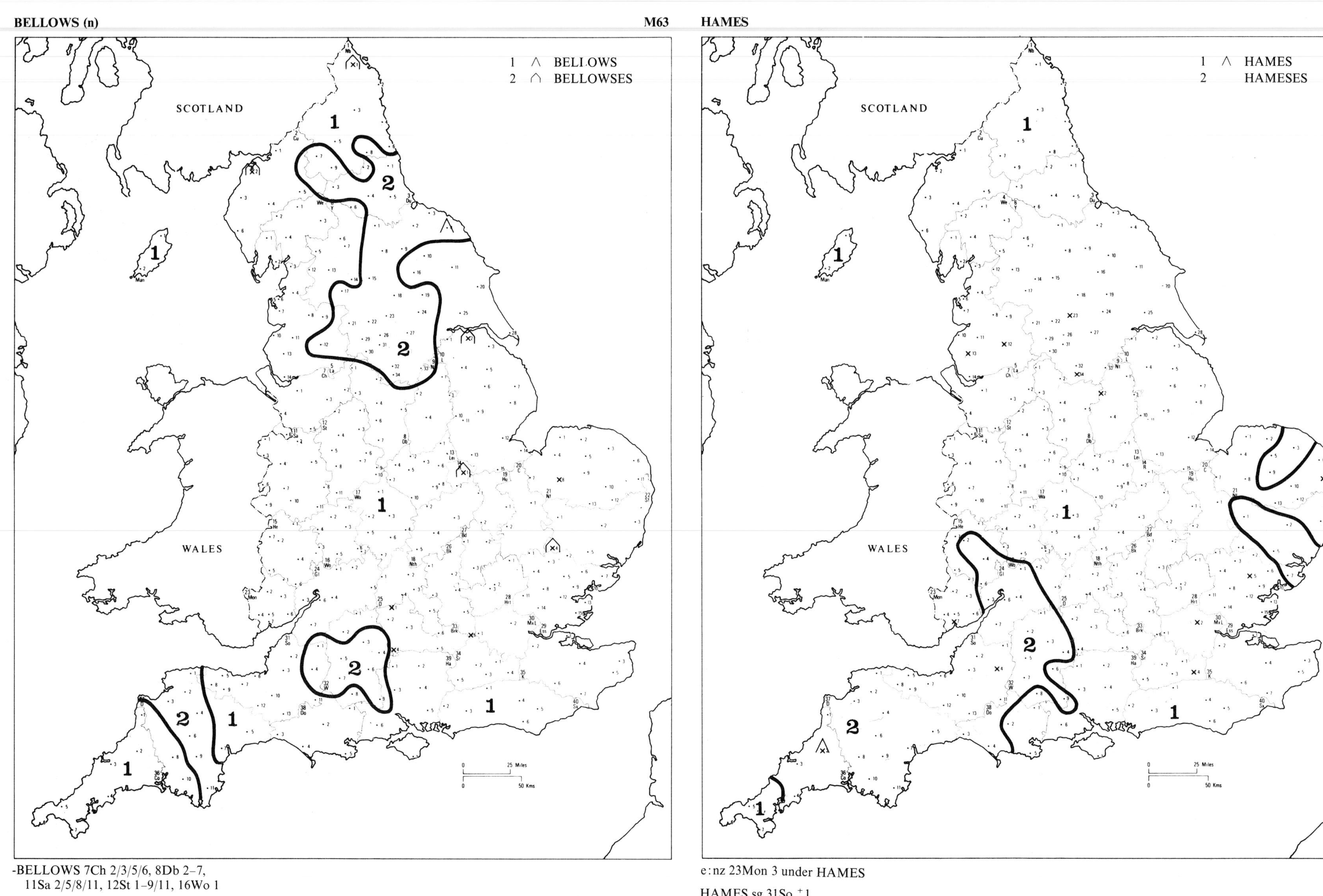

-BELLOWS 7Ch 2/3/5/6, 8Db 2–7, 11Sa 2/5/8/11, 12St 1–9/11, 16Wo 1

BELLOWS = lungs of an animal 6Y +33; BELLOWSES pl 33Brk 4

e: nz 23Mon 3 under HAMES

HAMES sg 31So +1

FATHER'S (boots) M65

COW'S (legs) M66

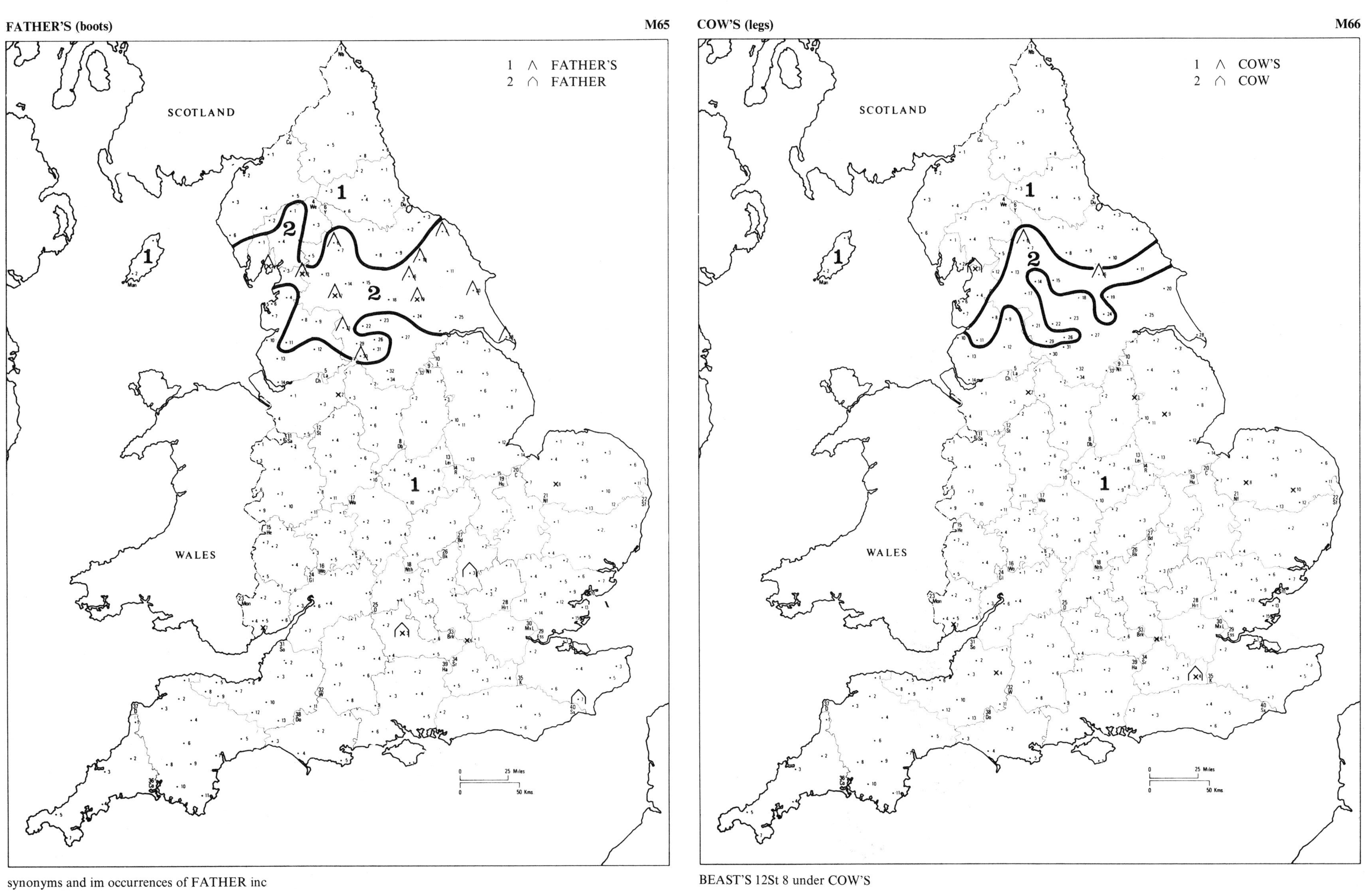

synonyms and im occurrences of FATHER inc

BEAST'S 12St 8 under COW'S

im forms not inc

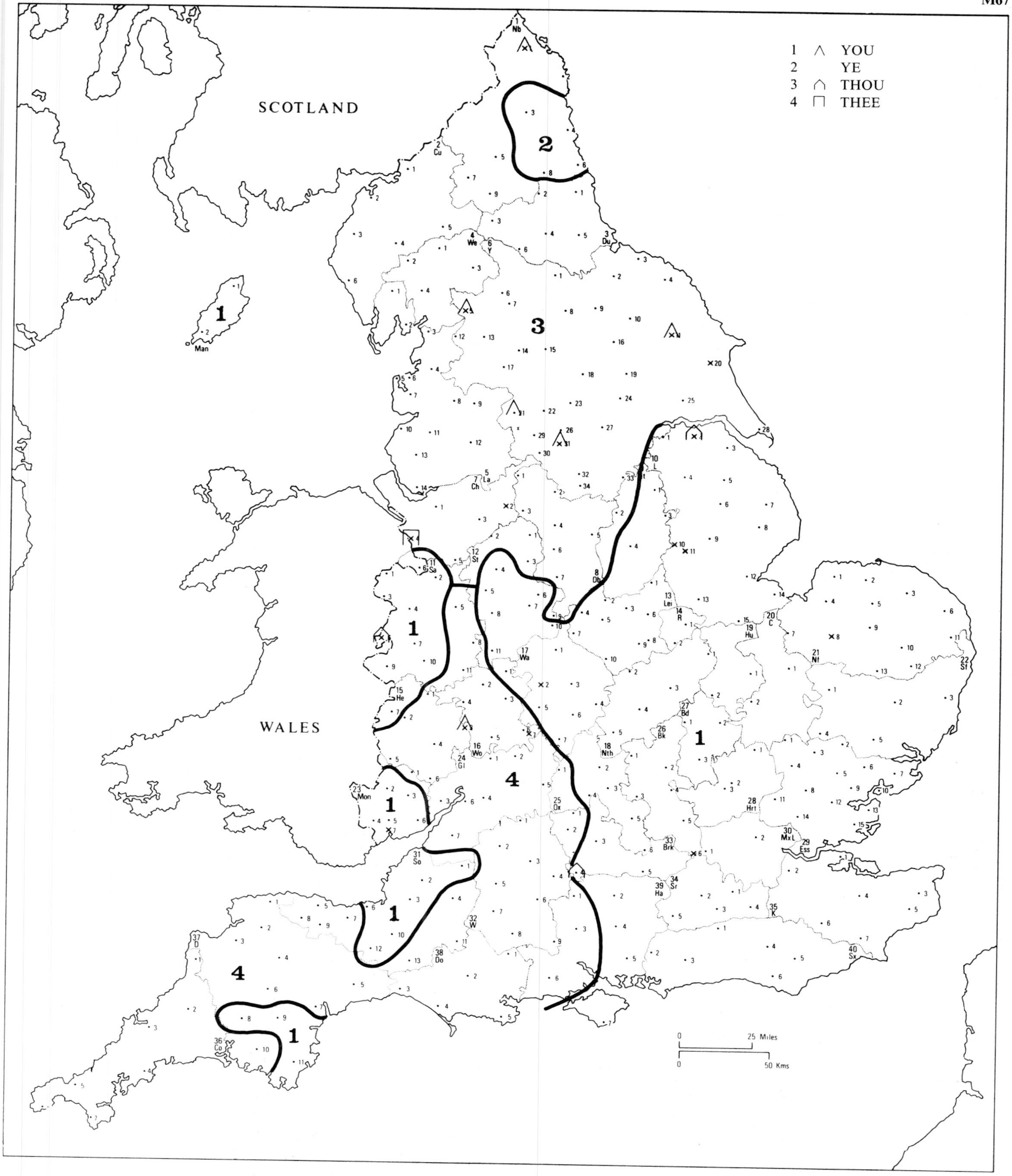

1 ∧ YOU
2 YE
3 ∩ THOU
4 ⊓ THEE

SCOTLAND

WALES

0 25 Miles
0 50 Kms

SHE (is) M68

(is) SHE (married) M69

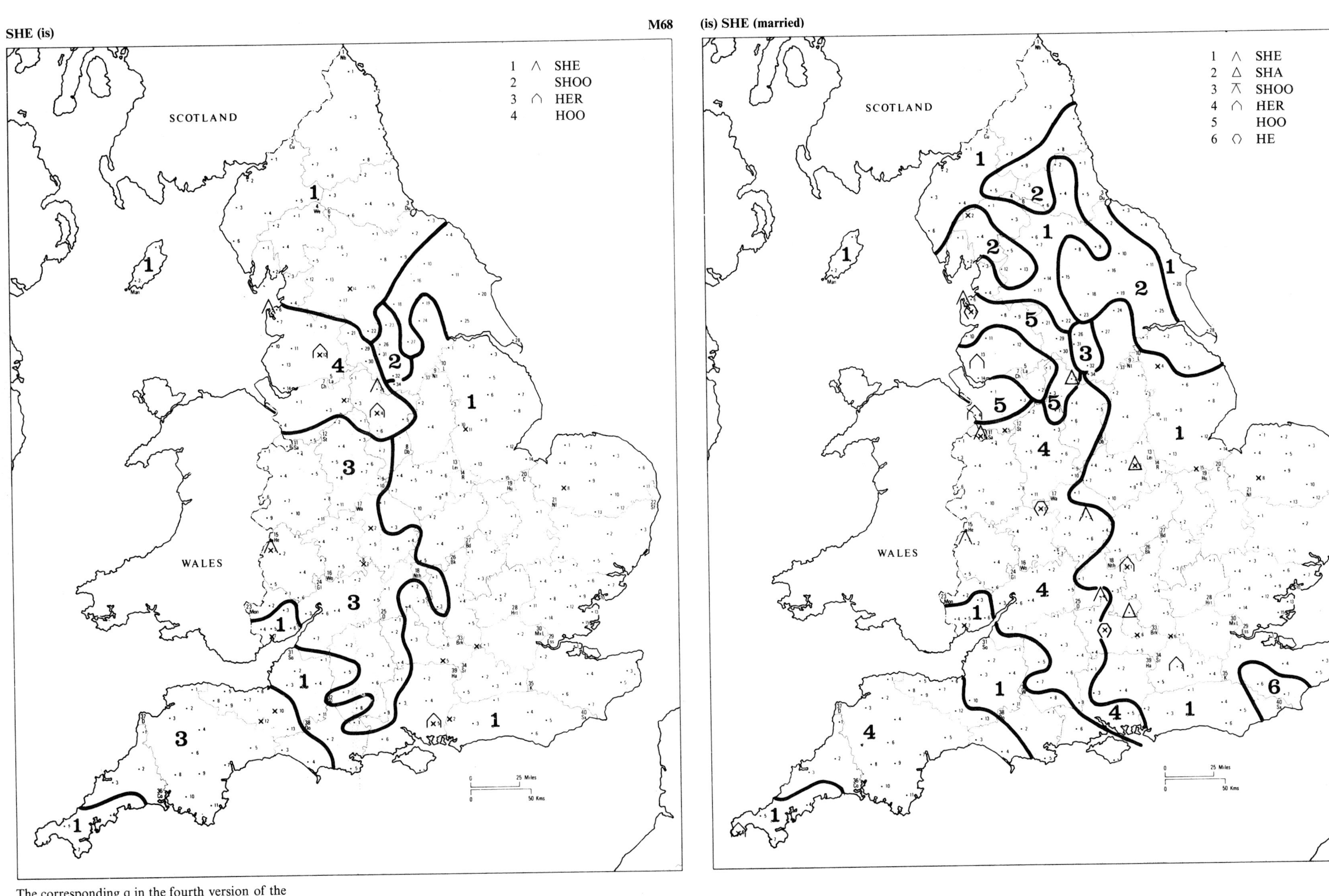

The corresponding q in the fourth version of the questionnaire, which was used at 6Y 4/10/11/14/16/18/20/25/27/28, asked only for the 2prsg YOU ARE. Accordingly, at these localities there is no response to this q

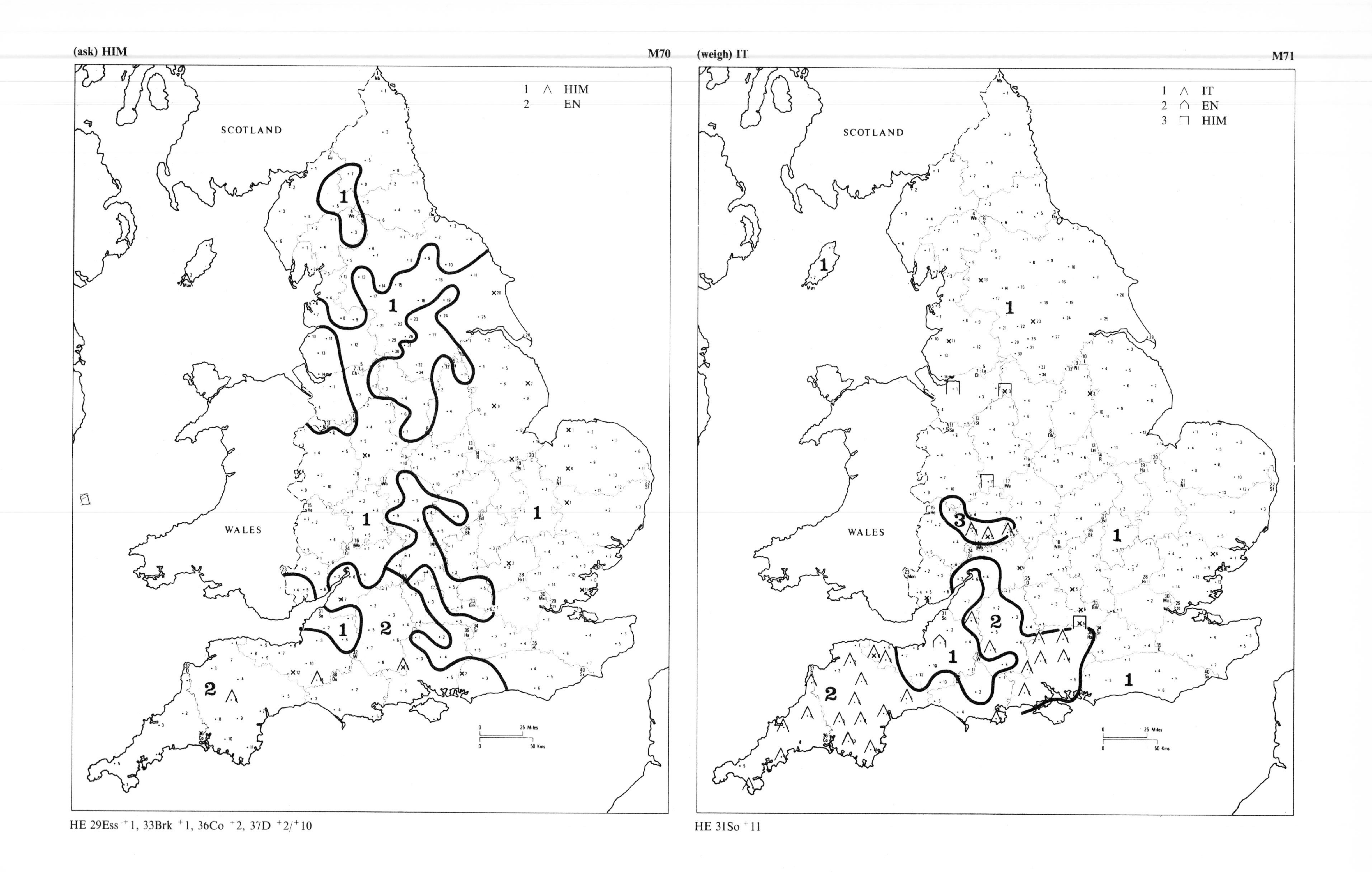

HE 29Ess +1, 33Brk +1, 36Co +2, 37D +2/+10

HE 31So +11

(tasted) IT (of broth) **M72**

IT (is) (of porridge) **M73**

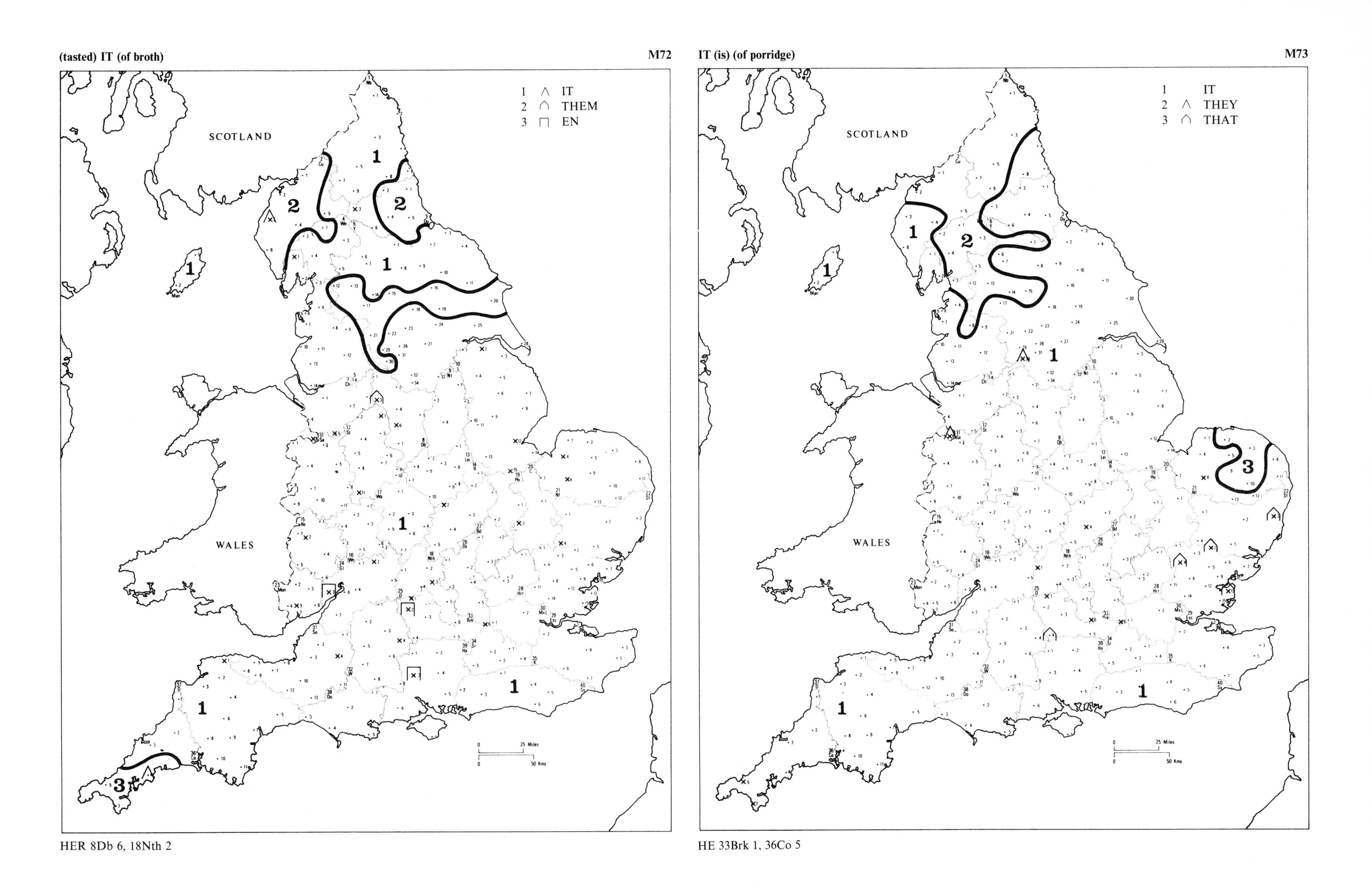

HER 8Db 6, 18Nth 2

HE 33Brk 1, 36Co 5

US M74

(with) OUR (eyes) M75

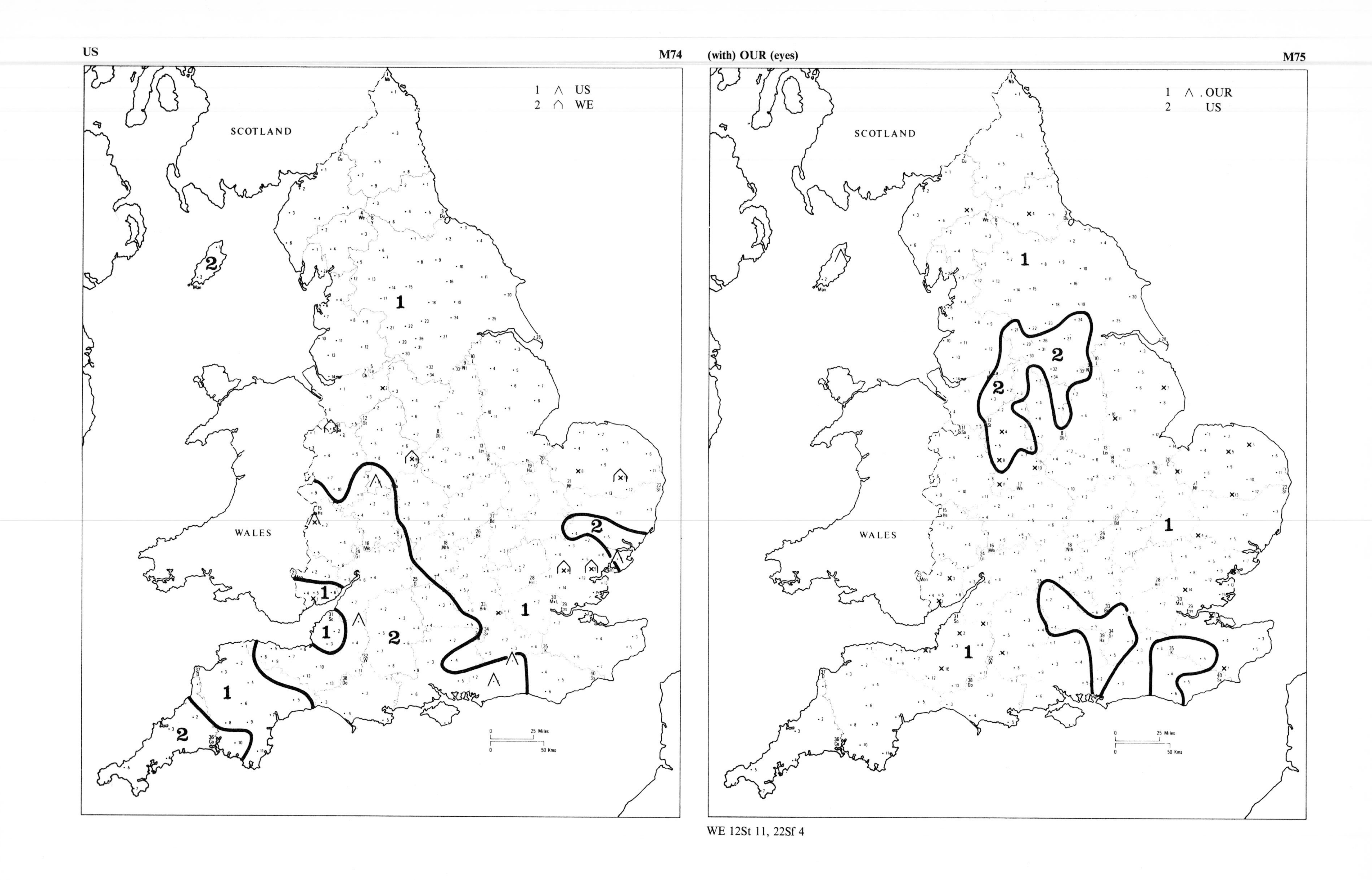

WE 12St 11, 22Sf 4

HIS M76 HERS M77

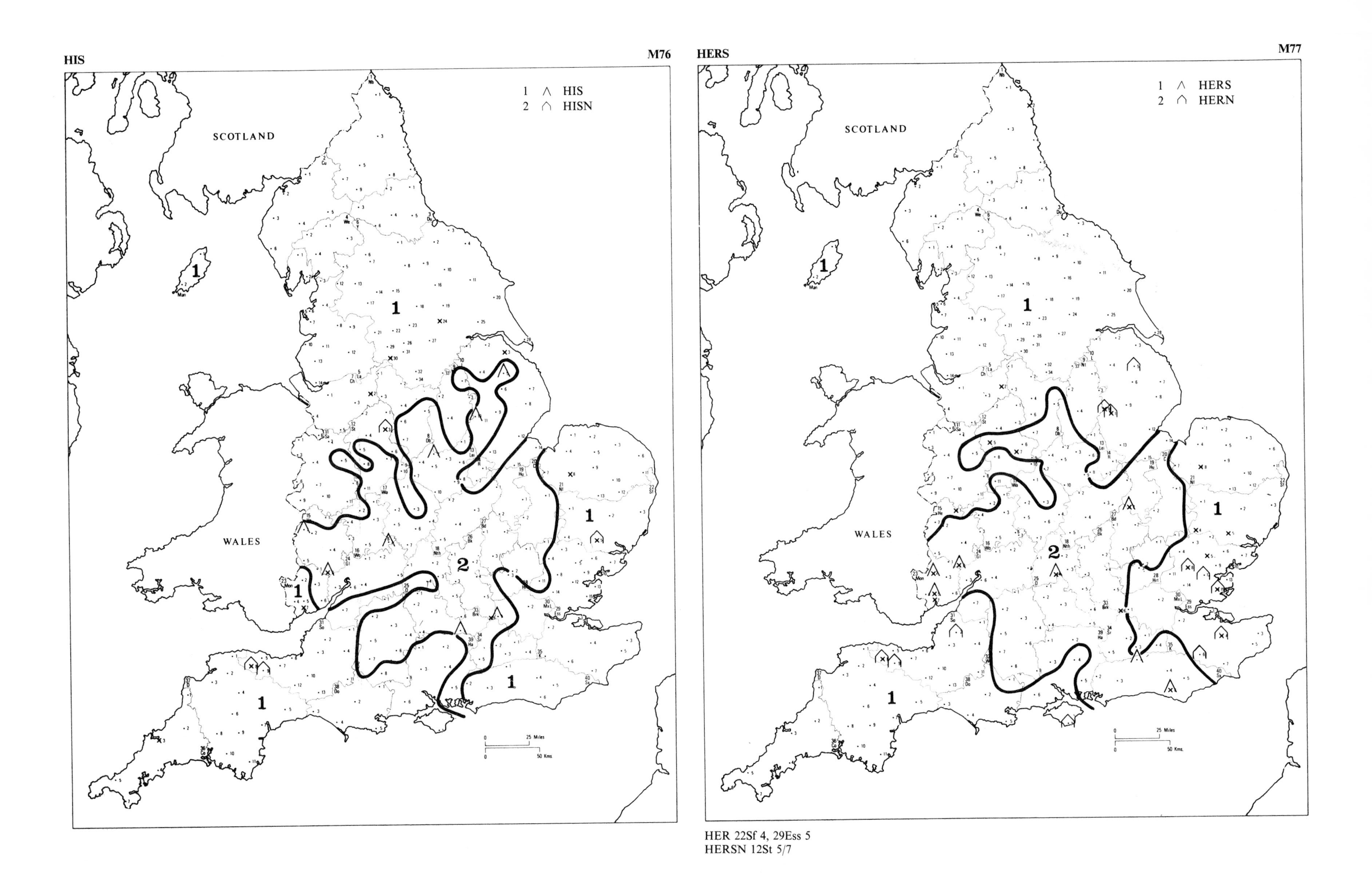

HER 22Sf 4, 29Ess 5
HERSN 12St 5/7

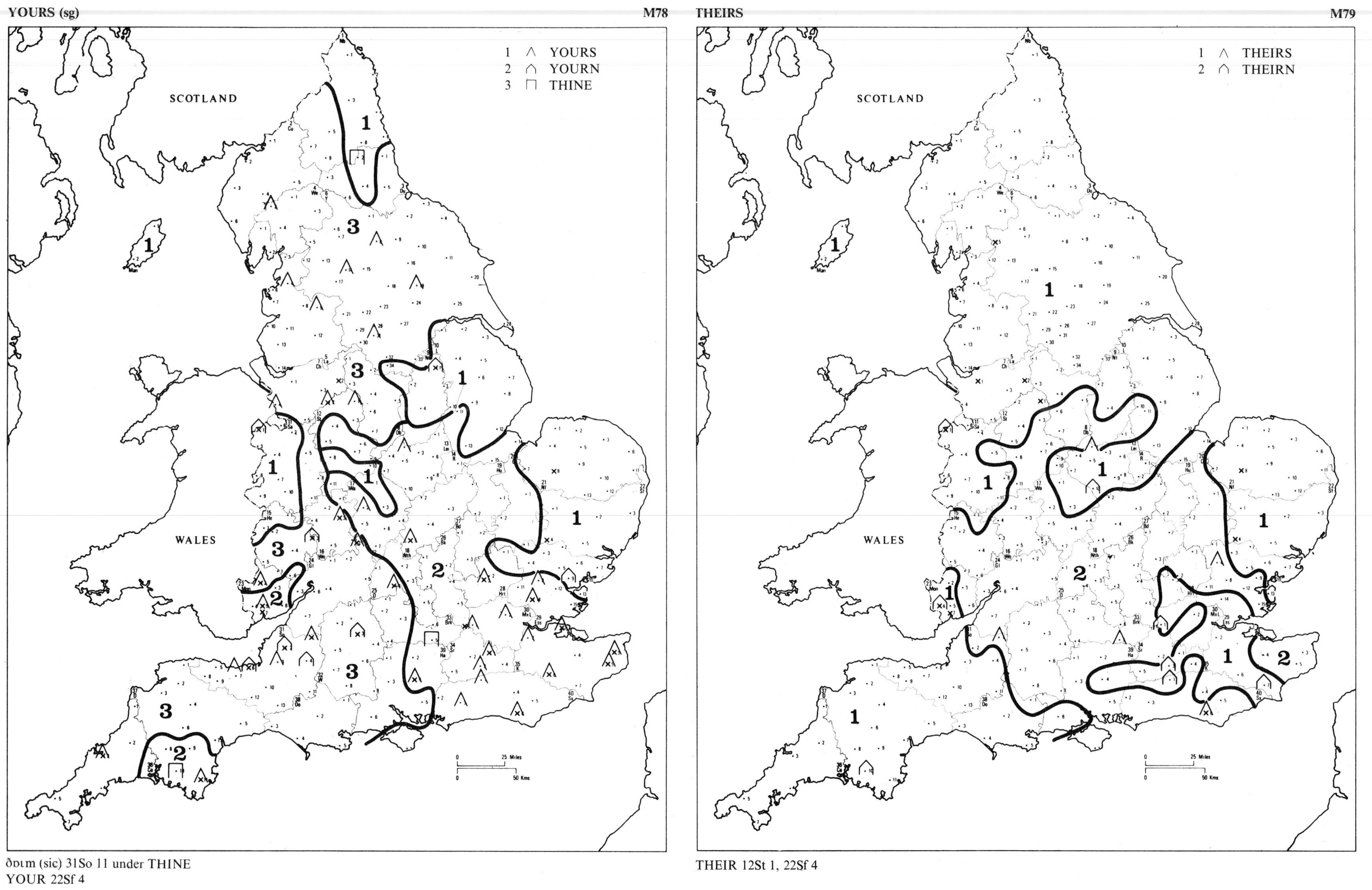

ðɒɪm (sic) 31So 11 under THINE
YOUR 22Sf 4

THEIR 12St 1, 22Sf 4

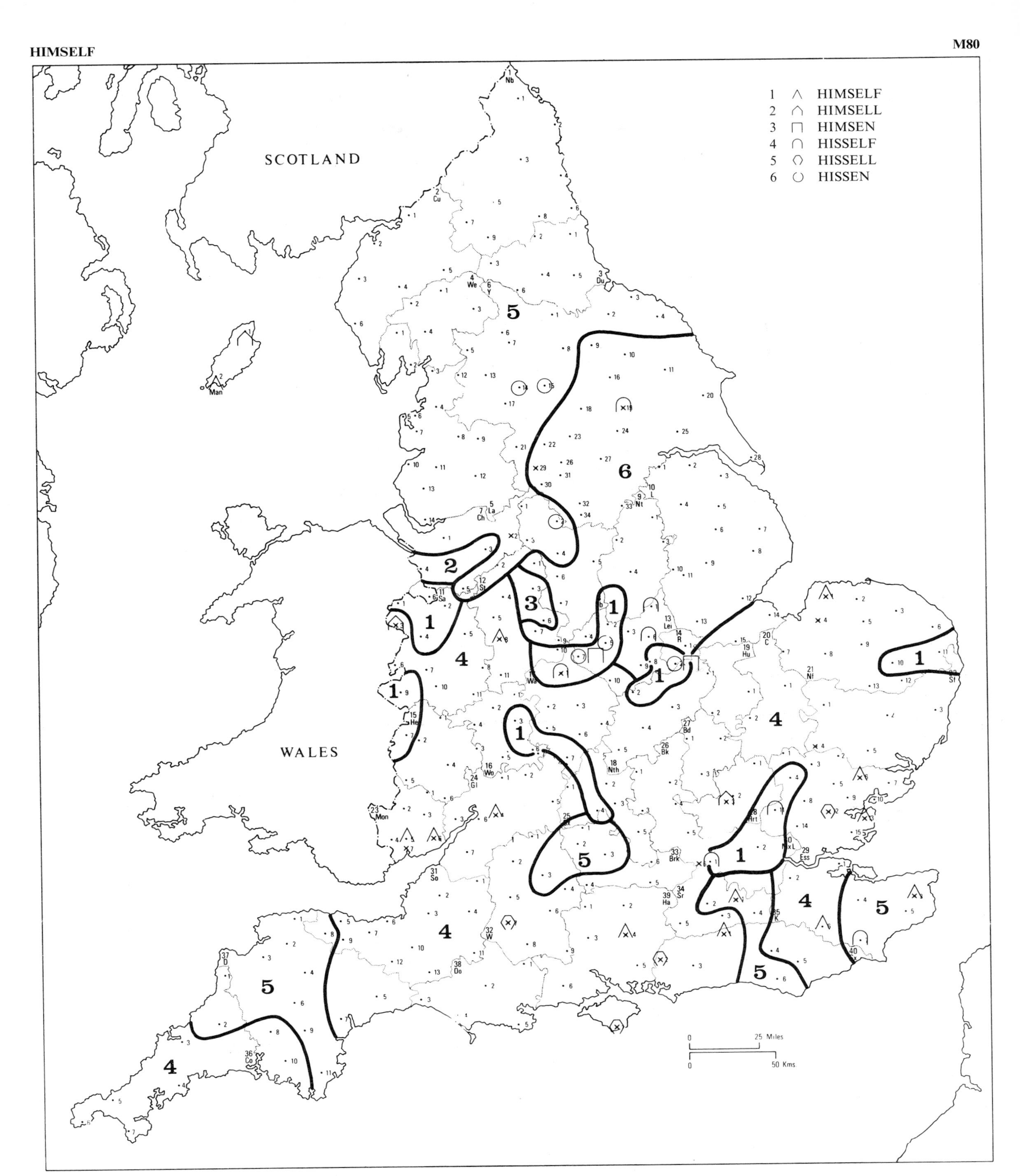

HISSELN 6Y 29
HIS OWN SELF 21Nf [+]4, 22Sf 4

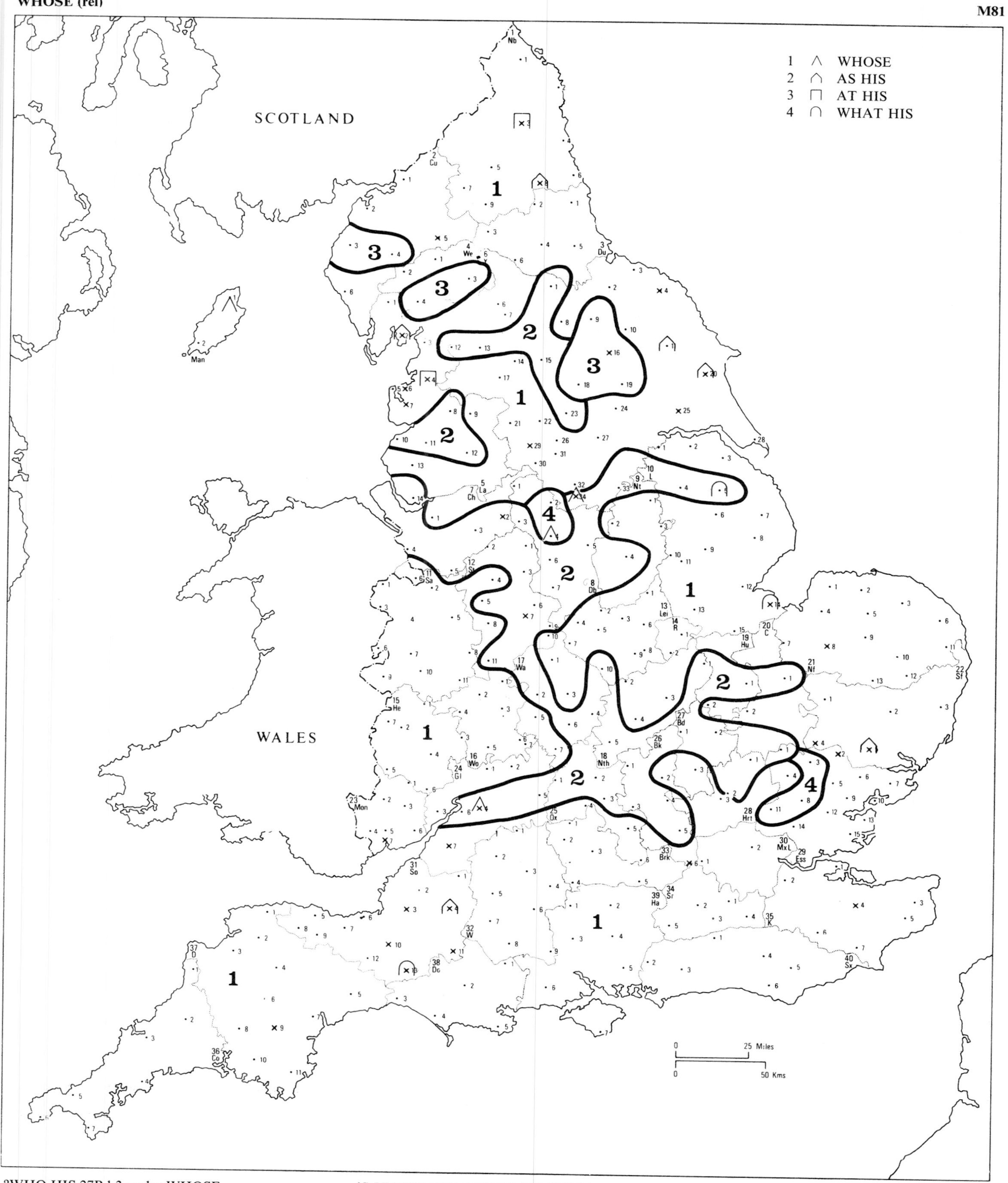

?WHO HIS 27Bd 3 under WHOSE
AT'S 2Cu 3, 5La 4, 6Y 9 under AT HIS
WHAT 29Ess 8, WHAT'S 8Db +4, 28Ess 11, 31So 13 under WHAT HIS

'S UNCLE WHAT WAS DROWNED 31So 10
THAT HIS UNCLE WAS DROWNED Man 2, 37D 9, THAT'S UNCLE WAS DROWNED 29Ess 2, THAT WAS HIS UNCLE DROWNED 35K +7
UNCLE GOT DROWNED 31So 11

əz 13Lei 1–9, 14R 1/2, ɪz 6Y 6/7/22/24/26/27/32, 35K +2 pres repr WHOSE

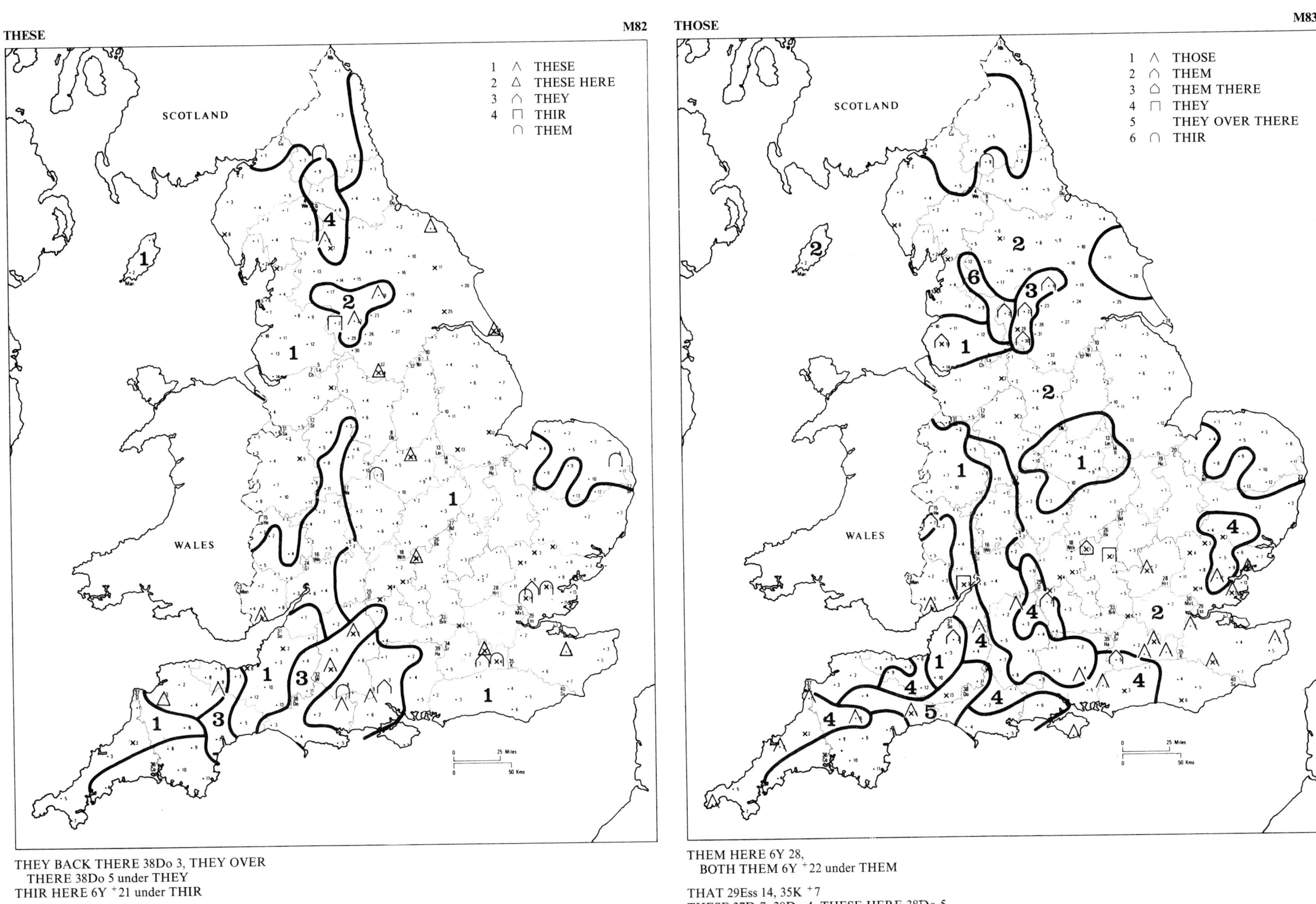

THEY BACK THERE 38Do 3, THEY OVER
THERE 38Do 5 under THEY
THIR HERE 6Y +21 under THIR

THESEUM 32W 4/6, THESEUN 11Sa 5
THIK 24Gl 3
THOSE 10L 13, 28Hrt +3, 31So 6

THEM HERE 6Y 28,
BOTH THEM 6Y +22 under THEM

THAT 29Ess 14, 35K +7
THESE 37D 7, 38Do 4, THESE HERE 38Do 5
THICK OVER THERE 31So 13
THOSEUN 11Sa 5

Syntactical Maps

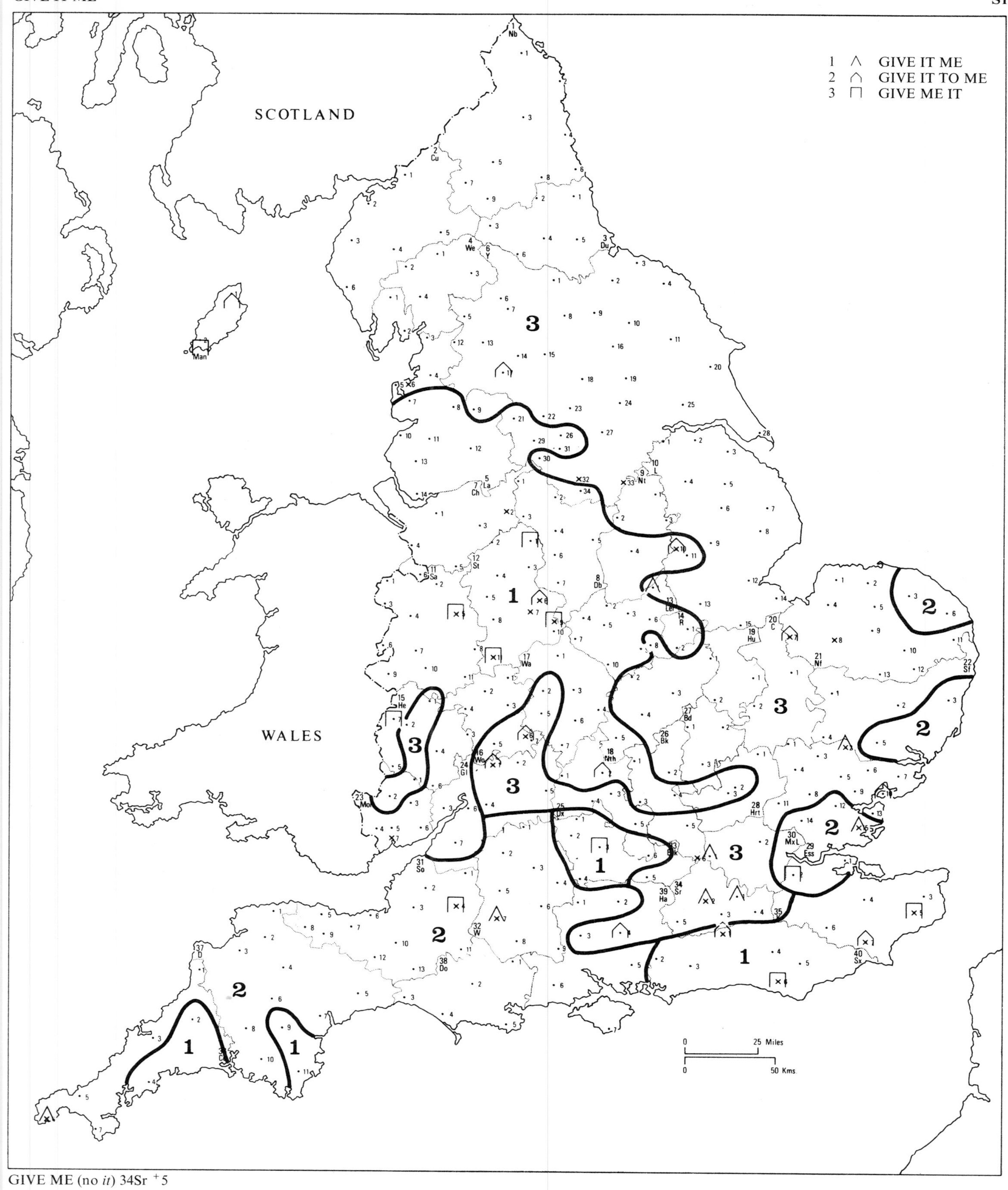

GIVE ME (no *it*) 34Sr +5

The word order alone is taken into account, the direct and indirect object actually used being ignored

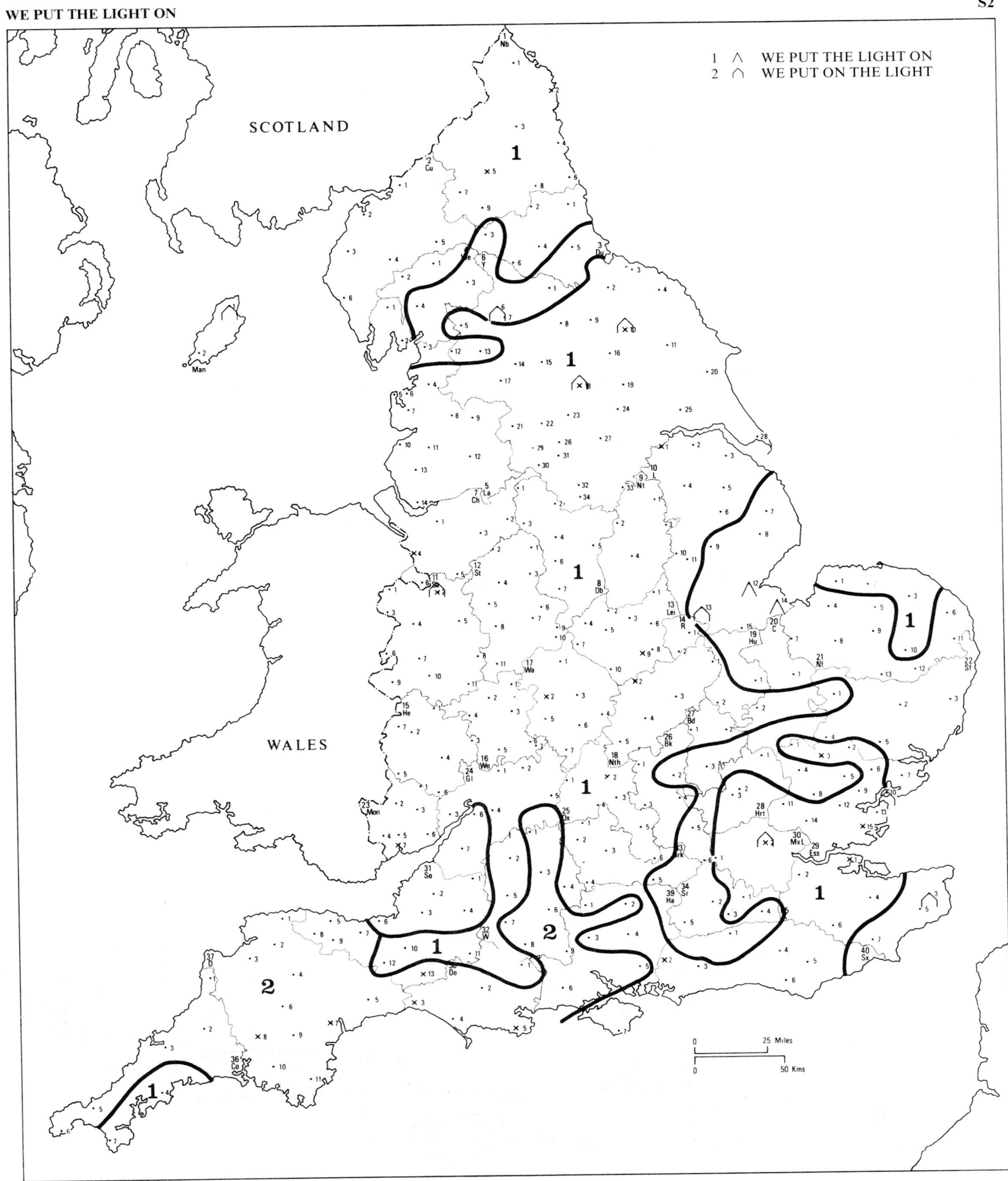

The word order alone is taken into account above, the verb actually used and its form being ignored. Expressions alternative to LIGHT are also disregarded, the position of the object word being the crucial matter

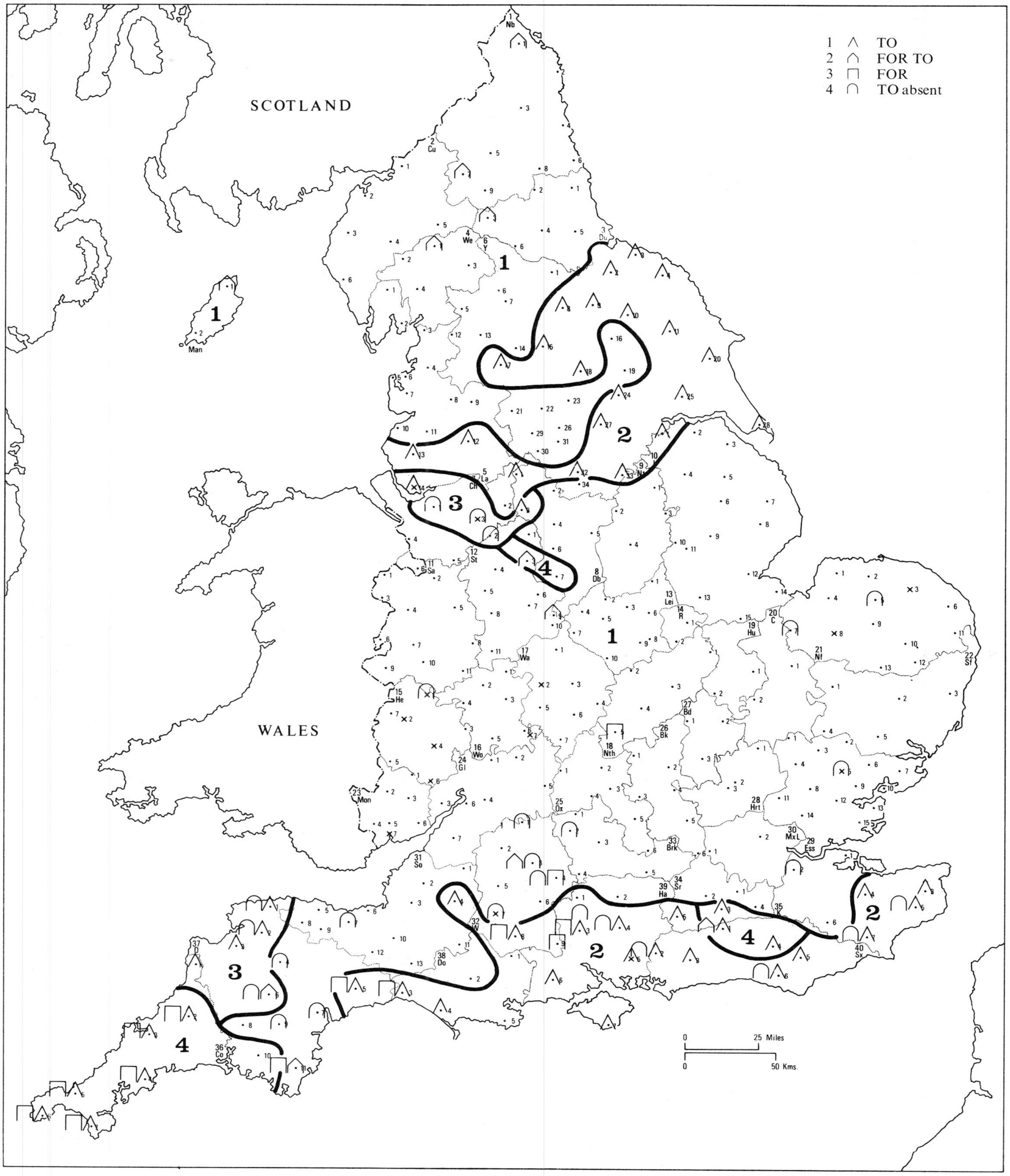

1 ∧ TO
2 ∩ FOR TO
3 ⊓ FOR
4 ∩ TO absent

SCOTLAND

WALES

0 25 Miles
0 50 Kms.

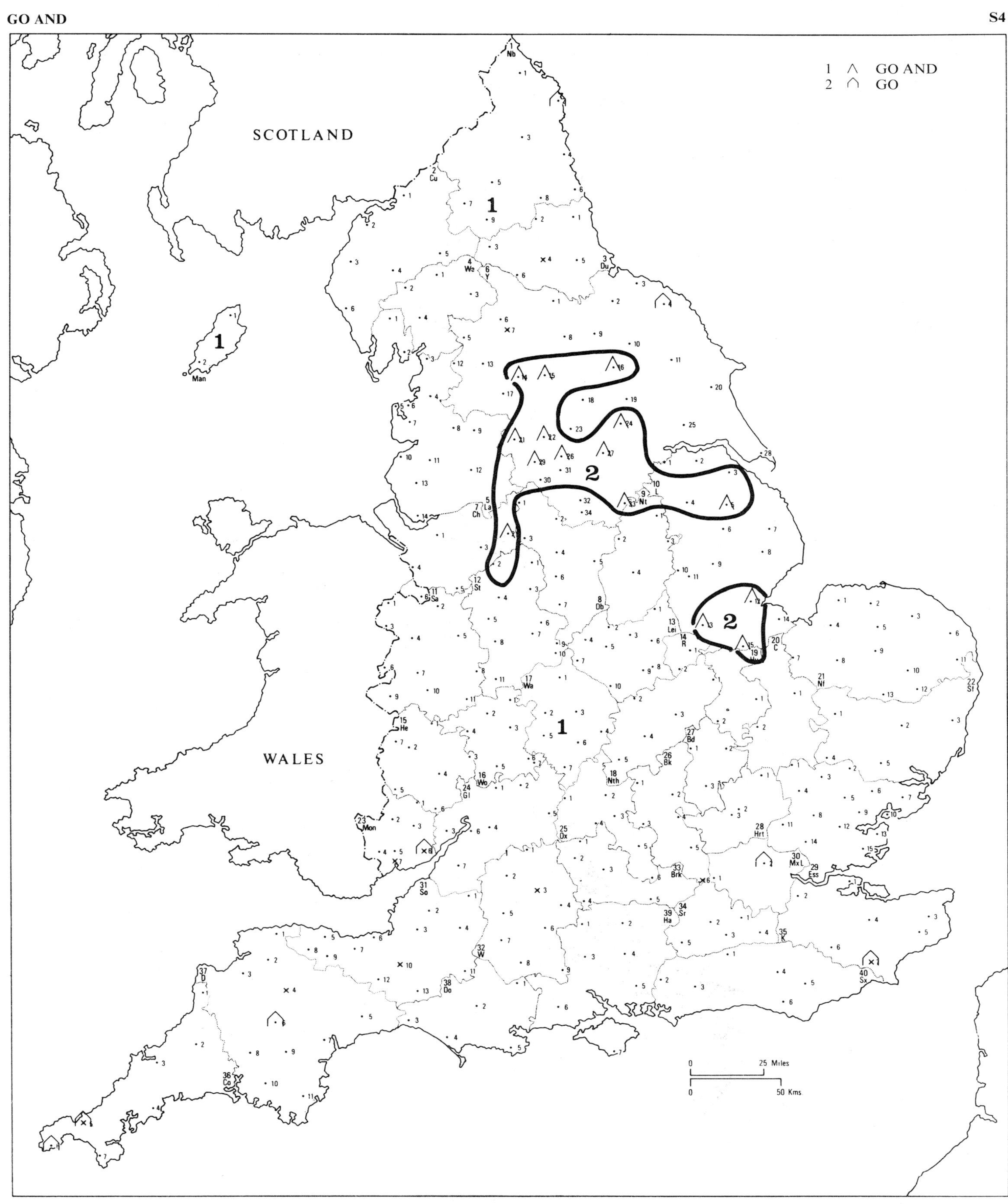
1 ∧ GO AND
2 ∩ GO
SCOTLAND
WALES
0 25 Miles
0 50 Kms

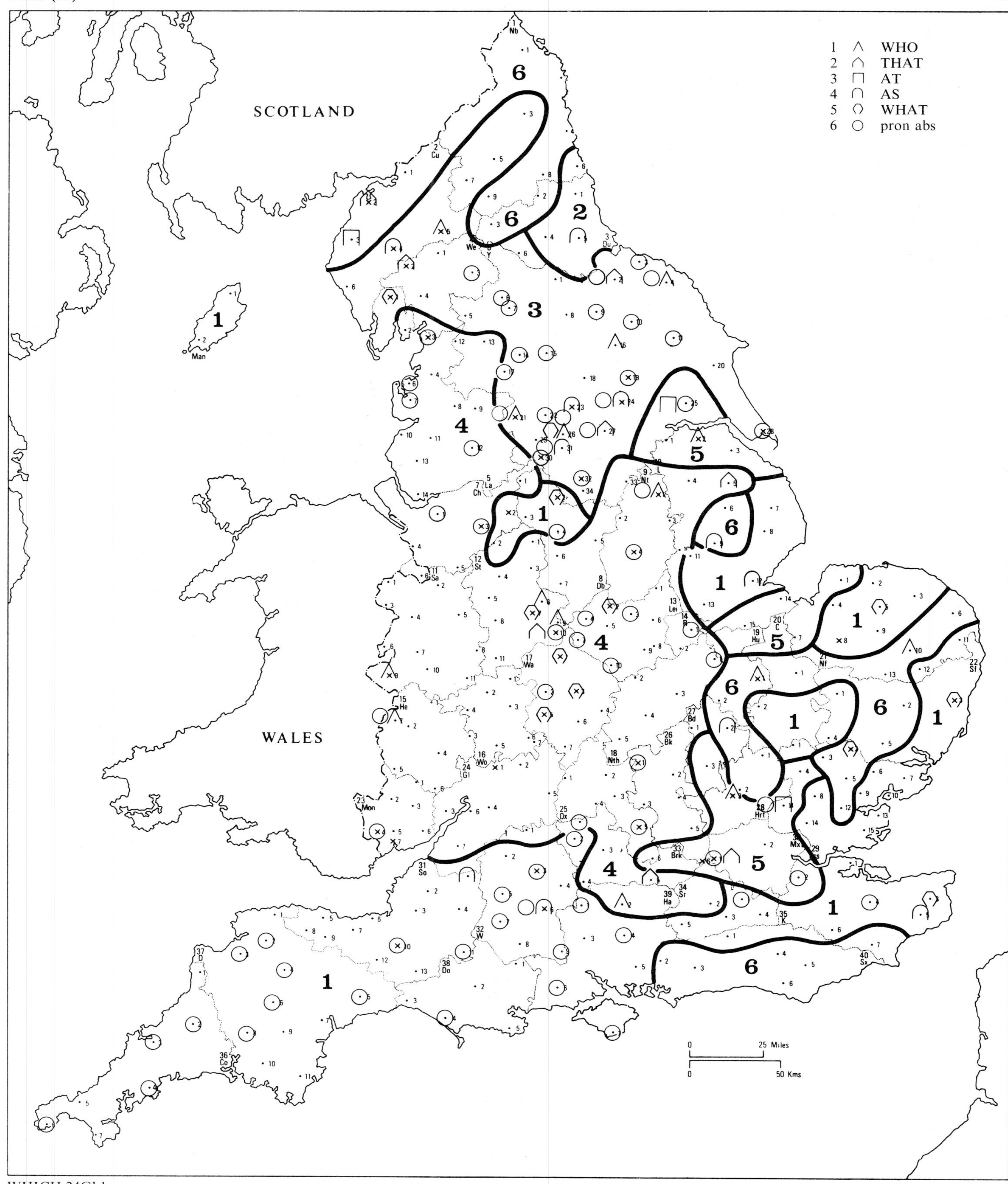

WHICH 24Gl 1

Forms such as əl, əd have been interpr as zero + respectively WILL, WOULD

Only responses where the relative is the subject of the sentence, and where the antecedent is human, have been included

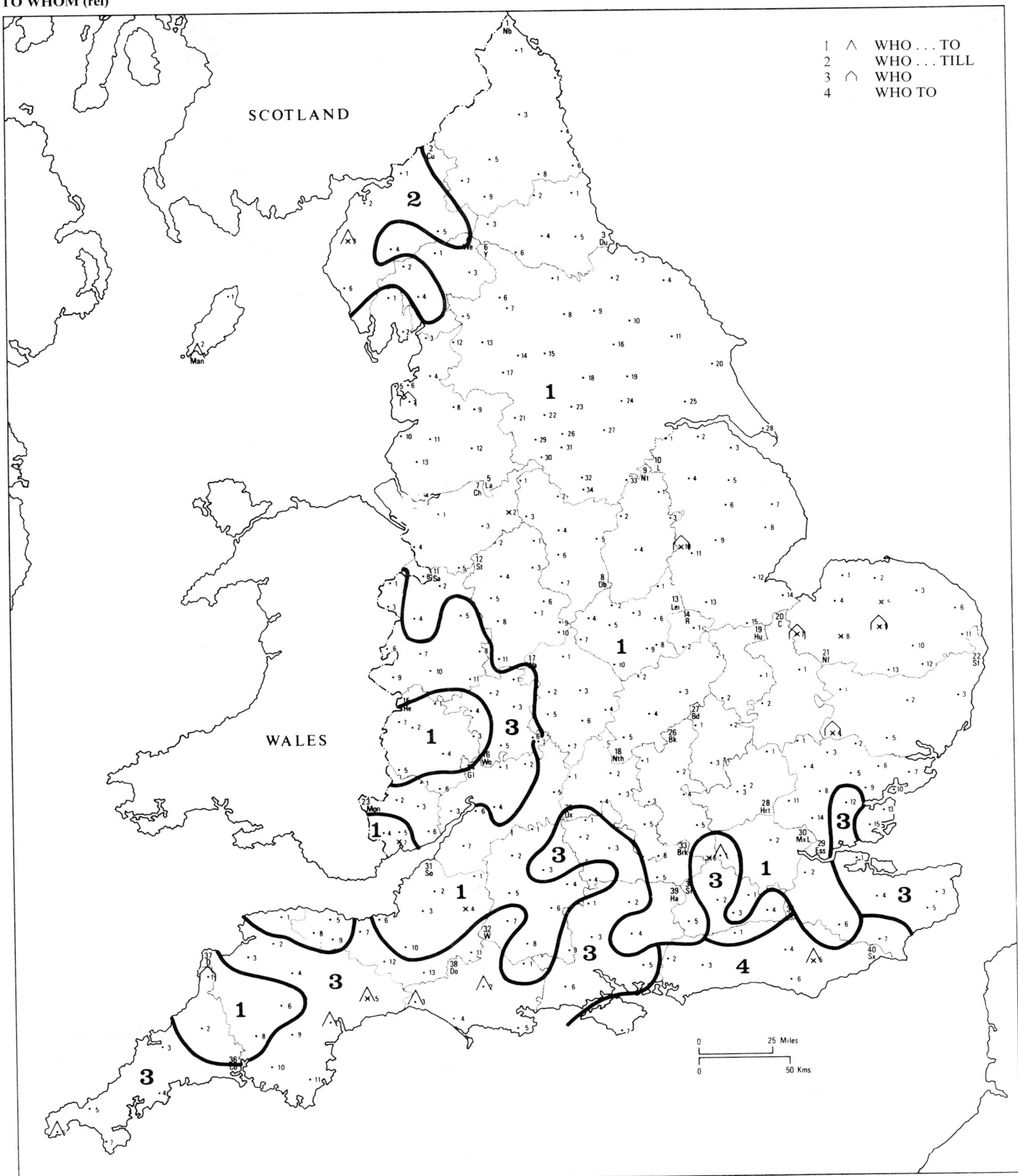

WHICH . . . TO 11Sa 2 under WHO . . . TO

WHO followed by inverted AM I TO 5La 14, CAN I 36CO +6, HAVE I TO 5La 10, 6Y 10, MUN I 5La 13, SHALL I 5La +7, 6Y 27/34, 12St 4, 13Lei 1/3/6/8, 21Nf 11, 22Sf 1/2, 29Ess 8, 31So 6, 33Brk 4, 34Sr +1, 35K 2/6, 36Co +1, 38Do 1, SHOULD I Man 2, 7Ch 1, 21Nf 6, WILL I 6Y 2

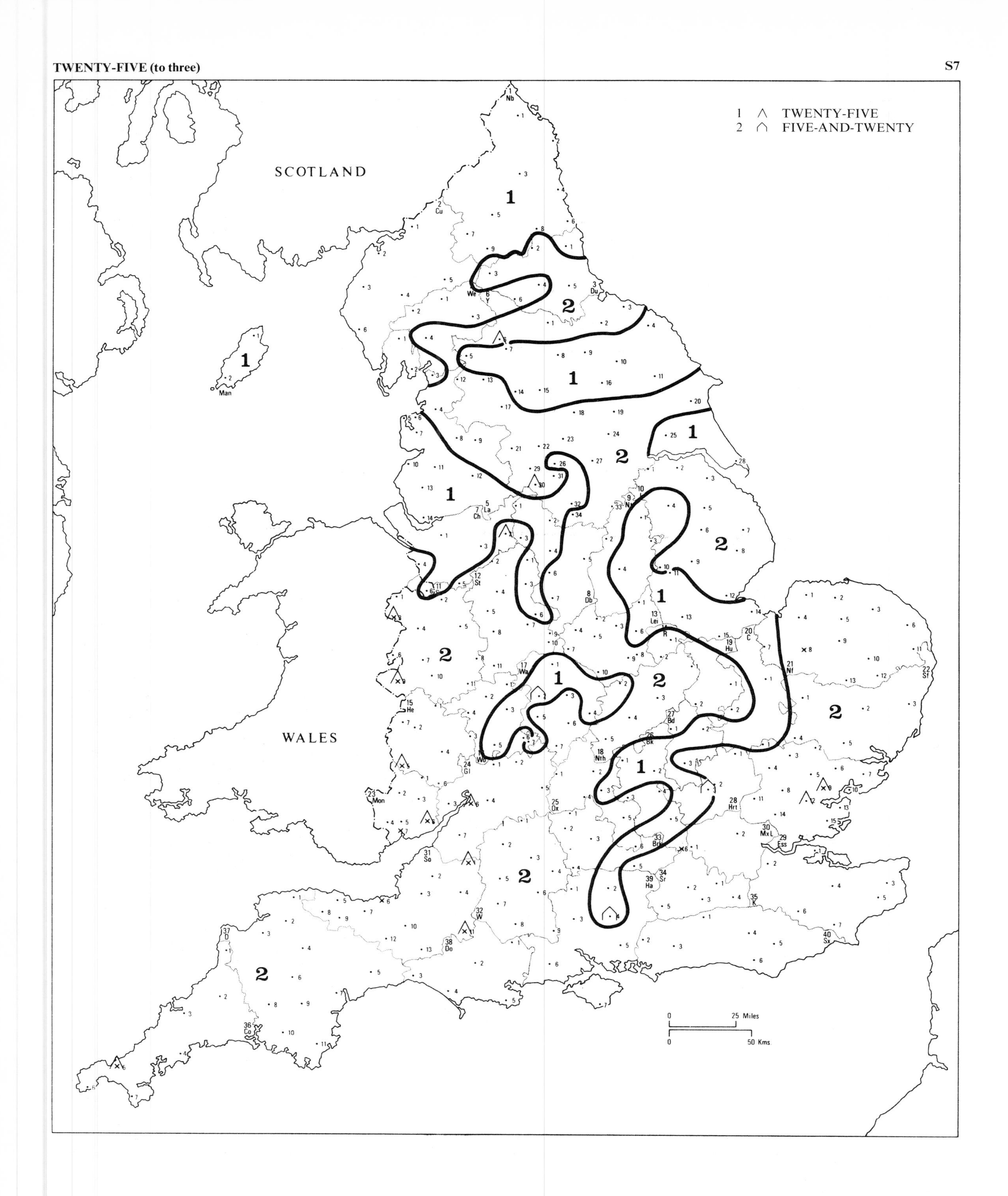
1 ∧ TWENTY-FIVE
2 ∩ FIVE-AND-TWENTY
SCOTLAND
WALES
0 25 Miles
0 50 Kms

ON FRIDAY WEEK

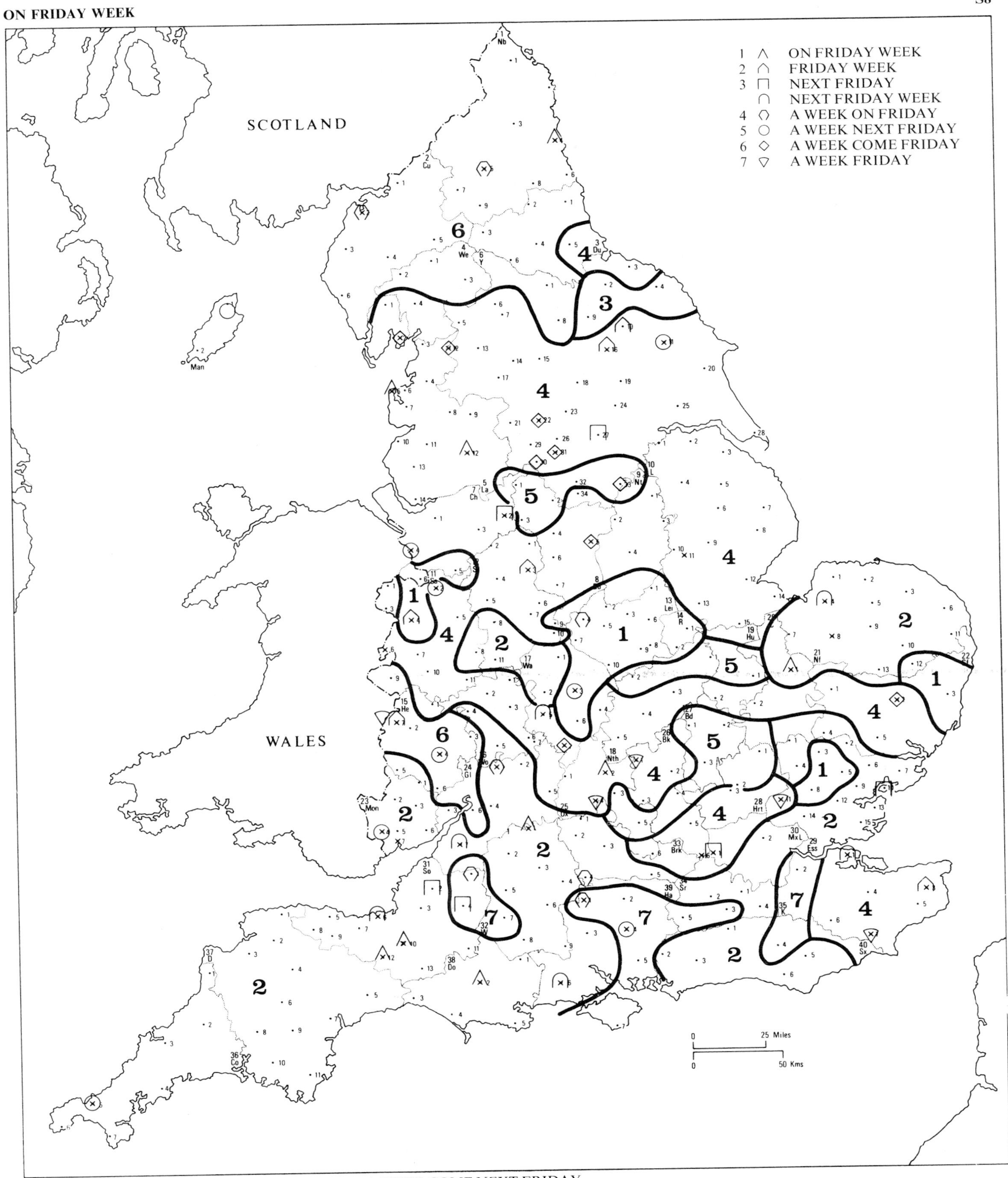

WEEK ON FRIDAY 12St 5, 28Hrt 3, 35 K 6 under A WEEK ON FRIDAY
WEEK NEXT FRIDAY 36Co 5 under A WEEK NEXT FRIDAY
WEEK COME FRIDAY 11Sa 9 under A WEEK COME FRIDAY
WEEK FRIDAY 32W 7, 34Sr 3, 35K 7, 39Ha 2/5/7, 40Sx 4 under A WEEK FRIDAY

A WEEK COME NEXT FRIDAY (/TUESDAY) 6Y $^{+}$3, 30MxL $^{+}$2
A WEEK FOR FRIDAY Man 2
FRIDAY AFTER NEXT 10L 11

Where a fieldworker recorded as a response a day other than Friday, that response has been considered relevant

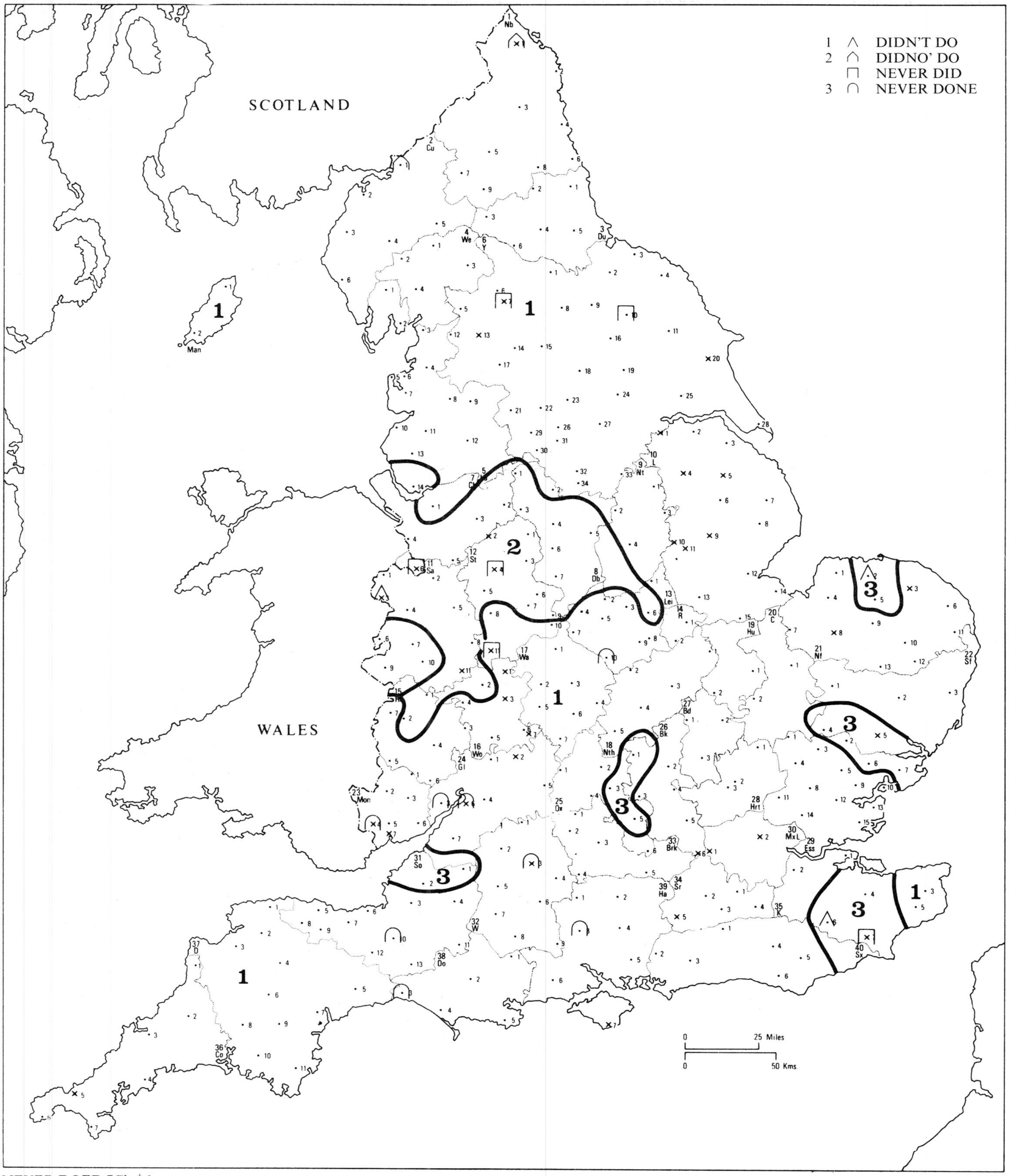

1 ∧ DIDN'T DO
2 ∩ DIDNO' DO
⊓ NEVER DID
3 ∩ NEVER DONE

SCOTLAND

WALES

NEVER DOED 7Ch +6

APPENDIX 1

INDEX TO QUESTIONS

In this Index the map number and atlas keyword are followed by the questionnaire number and the text of the question as presented in the final (1957) version of the Survey's *Questionnaire for a Linguistic Atlas of England*:

Since the import of a specific question sometimes depended on the context of preceding questions within that section of the questionnaire, and sometimes on a general preliminary statement by the fieldworker about the topic to be covered in a particular section, abbreviated contextual information is supplied where necessary in this Index in square brackets directly after the questionnaire number. The symbol □ in the questionnaire instructed the fieldworker to show the informant a photograph or drawing. The symbol ... instructed the fieldworker to ask "What do you call" or "What's your word for" in 'naming' questions, and to pause and allow the informant to complete the sentence in 'completing' questions. The abbreviations g, i, and p were instructions to gesticulate, indicate or imitate, and point, respectively.

The *Questionnaire* included a number of items referred to as 'conversion' type questions. The fieldworkers, having elicited the response for, say, the first person singular of the verb, were instructed to convert the question in order to elicit other numbers and tenses. As the actual conversions used probably varied from one fieldworker to another (though probably without affecting the responses significantly) the editors have printed the questions in the form in which they appear in the *Questionnaire*, together with the instruction to convert for other forms.

Ph1	APPLES	IV.11.8	What common fruits do you grow here?
Ph2	CARROTS	V.7.18	□ ... these garden vegetables?
Ph3	CHAFF	II.8.5	[in threshing corn] ... the light stuff blown away?
Ph4	LAST	VII.2.2	[order of sheep coming through gate (p)] Which is this?
Ph5	MAN	VIII.1.6	A boy grows up into a youth and then into a ....
Ph6	WRONG	IX.7.1a	Am I right or am I ...?
Ph7	AMONG	IX.2.12	Where did you say that rabbit was in the garden? Well, do you see those potatoes? I think it's somewhere ... them.
Ph8	WALK	VIII.7.10	Suppose you missed the last bus or train back to here, then you'd have to set off and ....
Ph9	CALF	III.1.2	[cattle: breeding] ... the young animals just born?
Ph10	HALF	VII.5.4	[□ half past seven] What time is this?
Ph11	ARM	VI.6.8	[p] ... this?
Ph12	ARSE	VI.9.2	[p] ... this, that you sit on?
Ph13	WEDNESDAY	VII.4.2	... the days at the beginning of the week?
Ph14	KETTLE	V.8.7	You boil water for tea in a ....
Ph15	FELLIES	I.9.9	[□ cart] ... these sections of the wooden rim?
Ph16	ELM	IV.10.4	[if informant omits *elm* in listing local trees] ... that other tree with hard wood, which is often used for making coffins and clogs; when old, it's easily blown over?
Ph17	SHELF	V.9.4	[p] ... this, on which you keep your pans?
Ph18	TWELVE	VII.1.10	[show written figure] How many is this?
Ph19	DARNING	V.10.1	... mending socks?

Ph20	FARMER	VIII.4.7	[if informant omits *farmer* in listing trades and occupations] ... the man who works the land?
Ph21	FARTHINGS	VII.7.2	A halfpenny is worth two ....
Ph22	HERRINGS	IV.9.11	... those salt-water fish that kippers are made from?
Ph23	BURIED	VIII.5.11	A grave is a place in which someone has been ....
Ph24	EIGHT	VII.1.7	[ask for the numerals *one* to *nine* by gesture].
Ph25	STRAIGHT	IX.1.2	This line is curved [i], but this one [i] is ....
Ph26	CINDERS	V.4.3	... the red-hot things that fall through the grate when the fire is burning?
Ph27	THIMBLE	V.10.9	[p] ... this?
Ph28	SILVER	VII.7.7	[after eliciting the response *half-a-crown*] What's it made of?
Ph29	BRISTLES	III.9.4	... the short stiff hairs on the back of a pig?
Ph30	THIRD	VII.2.4	[order of sheep coming through gate (p)] And this?
Ph31	BIRDS	IV.6.1	... all those things that fly, with feathers?
Ph32	SQUIRREL	IV.5.8	... that friendly little animal with a bushy tail; it skips about in trees?
Ph33	LIGHT	V.2.12	How do you see in this room when it gets dark? [elicit *we put the light on*]
Ph34	NIGHT	VII.3.11	... the various parts of the day? [elicit *morning, afternoon, evening, night*]
Ph35	RIGHT(-HANDED)	VI.7.13	Of a man who does everything with this [show your left hand], you say he is .... And with the other hand [show your right hand]?
Ph36	SIGHT	VIII.2.9	Some people you know to talk to, but others you just know by ....
Ph37	BONNET	VI.14.1	[to elicit meaning for informant] What do you mean by a bonnet?
Ph38	HOLLY	IV.10.9	At Christmas time we decorate our rooms with branches from what bush?
Ph39	FOX	IV.5.11	... that sly animal that is hunted with hounds?
Ph40	DOG	III.13.1	... that animal that helps you to bring the cattle in?
Ph41	COLT	III.4.3	[horses] And when your male foal is older, you call it a ....
Ph42	GOLD	VII.7.10	[coins] What is a sovereign made of?
Ph43	YOLK	IV.6.5	... the inside of an egg?
Ph44	OFF	IX.2.13	Smith was so bad at riding that he fell ... his horse.
Ph45	CROSS	VIII.5.14	On some graves, there's not a tombstone but a [i] ....
Ph46	BROTH	V.7.20	[to elicit meaning for informant] What do you mean by broth?
Ph47	FORKS	I.7.9	[□ forks of various kinds] What are these?
Ph48	CORN	II.5.1	[to elicit meaning for informant] What do you mean by corn here in these parts?
Ph49	FORD	IV.1.3	[river] Sometimes there is no bridge. What do you call that shallow place where you can walk across?
Ph50	BUTTER	V.5.4	What can you make from milk? [elicit *butter, cheese*]
Ph51	THUNDER	VII.6.21	[weather] ... that loud rumbling noise we often hear on very hot summer days?
Ph52	TONGUE	VI.5.4	[mouth] What am I doing now [i in derision]?
Ph53	BULL	III.1.14	... the male of the cow?
Ph54	WOOL	III.7.5	... the hair of the sheep?

Ph55	SHOULDER	VI.6.6	[p] . . . this?
Ph56	COULTER	I.8.6	[□ plough] . . . this?
Ph57	FURROW	II.3.1	. . . the track made by a plough?
Ph58	WORMS	IV.9.1	[if informant omits *worms* in listing creatures living in and on garden soil] . . . those long red creatures that you turn up with your soil; hens like them?
Ph59	CURSING	VIII.8.9	Of a person who uses a lot of bad language, you'd say: He is always . . . and . . . [elicit *cursing* and *swearing*]
Ph60	SPADE	I.7.6	What do you dig the ground with?
Ph61	NAKED	VI.13.20	By the way, if a person had no clothes on at all, you would say he was . . . .
Ph62	HAMES	I.5.4	[□ harness of cart-horse] . . . this?
Ph63	GRAVE	VIII.5.6	What does the tombstone cover?
Ph64	BACON	III.12.4	[slaughtering pigs] . . . the meat in a flitch?
Ph65	APRIL	VII.3.3	[saying something happened some time back] If in the month before May?
Ph66	APRIL (FOOL)	VII.4.10	On the 1st of April you like to make a person . . . .
Ph67	APRON	V.11.2	. . . the thing that women put on in front to keep their dresses clean?
Ph68	HARE	IV.5.10	. . . that animal like a rabbit, but larger and stronger?
Ph69	MAKE	IX.3.6	You go to a tailor to ask him to . . . a suit.
Ph70	TAKE	IX.3.7	John Smith had the chance to go to college, but didn't . . . it.
Ph71	WAISTCOAT	VI.14.11	[p] . . . this?
Ph72	BEANS	V.7.18	□ . . . these garden vegetables?
Ph73	EAST	VII.6.25	What are the four points of the compass?
Ph74	GREASE	I.11.4	[cart] If you don't want your wheels to squeak, what do you put on?
Ph75	TEAM	I.6.1	[□ two horses in tandem] When you have more than one horse pulling a heavy load, what do you call them?
Ph76	PEAS	V.7.13	[□ peapod with peas] . . . these?
Ph77	PEA	V.7.13	[□ peapod with peas] And one of them?
Ph78	TEA	VII.8.3	[weights and measures; how tea is bought] So, when buying some in a grocer's shop, you might ask for a . . . of . . . . [elicit *pound* of *tea*]
Ph79	SPEAKS	VI.5.5	My brother sometimes behaves as if he were dumb and never . . . .
Ph80	EAT	VI.5.11	When I have an apple, I [i] . . . it.
Ph81	MEAT	V.8.3	Some people eat only vegetables and never touch . . . .
Ph82	MEAL	V.6.1	[what bread is made of] And your brown bread?
Ph83	MARE	III.4.5	[horses] . . . the fully-grown female?
Ph84	PEARS	IV.11.8	What common fruits do you grow round here? [elicit *apples, pears*]
Ph85	BREAK	IX.3.5	Never drop a tumbler on the floor, because it's bound to . . . .
Ph86	DRAIN	IV.1.9	To get water away from land that is wet and boggy, you must . . . it.
Ph87	GREAT	IX.1.6	To marry the wrong woman isn't a little mistake, but a . . . mistake.
Ph88	DEAD	VIII.5.7a	What's inside the coffin? [If he doesn't use *dead*, ask what kind of a body]

Ph89	DEAF	VI.4.5	When a man is hard of hearing, we say he is ....
Ph90	FLEAS	IV.8.4	... those little black insects that jump about and bite you?
Ph91	HEAT	VI.13.6	What makes you sweat? Not the cold, but ....
Ph92	SHEAF	II.6.3	[cutting corn, elicit *to bind*] Into what?
Ph93	GEESE	IV.6.15	... those hissing birds that waddle about in flocks?
Ph94	GREEN	V.10.7	What colour are your reels of thread? [elicit *blue, green, red, white*]
Ph95	CHEESE	V.5.4	What can you make from milk? [elicit *butter, cheese*]
Ph96	WEEDS	II.2.1	... the things that grow in your garden and shouldn't be there?
Ph97	CREEP	IX.1.9	To please the children, I often go down on hands and knees and ....
Ph98	WEEK	VII.3.1	If you wanted to tell me that something happened seven days back from now, you'd say: It happened .... [elicit *a week ago*]
Ph99	SEE	VI.3.2	[eyes] What do we do with them?
Ph100	WHEEL	I.9.5	[□ cart] ... this?
Ph101	HEAR	VI.4.2	[ears] What do we do with them?
Ph102	YEAR	VII.3.18	There's last year, there's next year, and then what do you call the one we're in now?
Ph103	ICE	VII.6.12	When water freezes, it turns into ....
Ph104	KNIFE	I.7.18	[p] ... this?
Ph105	WHITE	V.10.7	What colours are your reels of thread? [elicit *blue, green, red, white*]
Ph106	FIVE	VII.5.6	[□ five to eight] What time is this?
Ph107	FRIDAY	VII.4.4	... the day after Thursday?
Ph108	TIME	VII.5.1	Suppose your watch has stopped and you want to know whether it is 5 or 6, what would you ask someone? [elicit *what time is it?*]
Ph109	BLIND	VI.3.4	A man who cannot see at all is ....
Ph110	FIND	IX.3.2	He was looking for his knife but couldn't ... it.
Ph111	SKY	VII.6.1	What can you see up there?
Ph112	FIRE	V.3.1	What's that burning there?
Ph113	DIED	III.7.2	Sometimes a lamb has to be brought up in the house because its mother has ....
Ph114	EYE	VI.3.1	... these [p]? And one of them?
Ph115	FLIES	IV.8.5	You cover up meat in the pantry, to keep away what?
Ph116	THIGH	VI.9.3	[p] ... this?
Ph117	MICE	IV.5.1	... the small animals that cats are fond of catching?
Ph118	LICE	IV.8.1	When a child scratches its head a lot, what is it likely to have in its hair?
Ph119	BOTH	VII.2.11	What will the very greedy boy have, pudding or pie?
Ph120	COMB	VI.2.4	[p] ... this?
Ph121	LOAF	V.6.9	[to elicit meaning for informant] What do you mean by loaf?
Ph122	SPOKES	I.9.6	[□ cart] ... these?
Ph123	TOAD	IV.9.7	[tadpoles, frogs] ... the other thing like a frog, but ugly?
Ph124	OAK	IV.10.2	[if informant omits *oak* in listing local trees] ... that sturdy tree which gives us our best wood?
Ph125	ONE (pron)	VII.1.1	[Ask for the numerals *one* to *nine* by gesture].

Ph126	ONE (adj)	IX.8.8	You cut an apple in half, and to your little girl you give [g] . . . half.
Ph127	ONCE	VII.2.7	How often a day does the postman come?
Ph128	NONE	VII.1.18	If you had two apples and then ate them both, how many would you have left?
Ph129	HOME	VIII.5.2	[go to church] But some lazy people like to read the Sunday papers, and so they . . . . [elicit *stay at home*]
Ph130	TOES	VI.10.3	. . . these five things?
Ph131	TWO	VII.1.2	[Ask for the numerals *one* to *nine* by gesture].
Ph132	COLD	VI.13.17	What's a room like on a winter's day without a fire?
Ph133	OLD	VIII.1.20	I am a young man, and you are . . . .
Ph134	COAL	IV.4.5	What do miners get out of the ground? [elicit *coal, iron, lead*]
Ph135	FOAL	III.4.1	Now let's talk about horses. What do you call the young animal?
Ph136	COAT	VI.14.6	[jacket] When you go out in very cold weather, what else do you put on?
Ph137	NOSE	VI.4.6	What's your ordinary word for this [p]?
Ph138	BOOTS	VI.14.23	. . . those things that you are wearing?
Ph139	GOOSE	IV.6.15	[geese] . . . one of them?
Ph140	MOON	VII.6.3	What can you see in the sky on a clear night? [elicit *stars, moon*]
Ph141	ROOF	V.1.2	[□ houses] . . . this?
Ph142	HOOF	III.4.10	[□ horse] . . . this?
Ph143	FOOT	VI.10.1	[p] . . . this?
Ph144	SCHOOL	VIII.6.1	Children are not taught to read and write at home, they must . . . . [elicit *go to school*]
Ph145	FLOOR	V.2.7	[interior of house] . . . this?
Ph146	DOOR	V.1.8	[□ houses] . . . this?
Ph147	PLOUGH	I.8.1	□ . . . this?
Ph148	BOUGHS	IV.12.2	[□ tree] . . . these?
Ph149	HOUSE	V.1.1	[houses] . . . one of them?
Ph150	LOUSE	IV.8.1	[lice] . . . one of them?
Ph151	SNOUT	III.9.1	. . . this part of a pig [g]?
Ph152	CLOUDS	VII.6.2	When you can't see the blue sky, then it must be covered with . . . .
Ph153	DROUGHT	VII.6.20	[dry summer] And you say there has been a long and serious . . . .
Ph154	COW	III.1.1	. . . your animals that give milk?
Ph155	FLOUR	V.6.1	What do you make your white bread out of?
Ph156	FLOWERS	VIII.5.13	On graves, people like to put wreaths of . . . .
Ph157	HOUR	VII.5.7	Sixty seconds make a minute, sixty minutes make one . . . .
Ph158	SUCK	III.7.1	How does the newly-born lamb get its milk?
Ph159	DAISY	II.2.10	[□ cowslip, daisy, dandelion] . . . these, they are three common flowers that you find in fields.
Ph160	FAINT	VI.13.7	Sometimes there are so many people in a room and it gets so hot, that you think you are going to . . . .
Ph161	RAIN	VII.6.23	It was quite fine when we left, but then dark clouds gathered and soon it . . . . [elicit *began to rain*]
Ph162	KEY	V.1.10	What do you lock a door with?

Ph163	LAY	IV.6.4	What do you expect hens to do?
Ph164	LIE	VIII.3.6	You might say to your visitor: If you are not feeling well, here's the sofa, why not come and .... [elicit *lie down*]
Ph165	TAIL	III.2.2	[□ cow] ... this?
Ph166	WHEY	V:5.8	[curdled milk] And when the milk does that, what do you call the stuff you get? [elicit *curds, whey*]
Ph167	WEIGH	I.7.1	If you want to know how heavy a thing is, what do you do? [elicit *weigh it*]
Ph168	WEAK	VI.13.2	When you get up after being ill in bed for a long time, you are sure to feel very ....
Ph169	CHAIR	V.2.9	... that you are sitting on?
Ph170	SAWDUST	I.7.17	[sawing wood] What falls to the ground as you saw?
Ph171	SLAUGHTERHOUSE	III.11.4	[butcher killing cattle and sheep] And where does he kill them?
Ph172	STRAW	II.8.2	[threshing] When you've got the grain out, what's left?
Ph173	THAWING	VII.6.15	When it begins to get warm again and the snow begins to melt, what do you say it is doing?
Ph174	AUNT	VIII.1.12	[man's brother is uncle of children] And if he had a sister she'd be their ....
Ph175	BLUE	V.10.7	What colours are your reels of thread? [elicit *blue, green, red, white*]
Ph176	SUET	V.7.6	... that fat that you make a boiled pudding with?
Ph177	EWE	III.6.6	[names of female sheep until first and second shearings] And after that?
Ph178	DEW	VII.6.7	[hoar-frost after cold nights] On other days, especially in late summer, the grass in the early morning is very wet. What has there been during the night?
Ph179	(A) FEW	VII.1.19	You might say to somebody: I'm not going away for long, not even for a week, but just for ... days.
Ph180	(A) FEW	VII.8.21	I might ask you if there are any foxes round here, and you might answer: Yes, but only ....
Ph181	NEW (YEAR'S DAY)	VII.4.8	What specially important days are there during the year? [elicit *Easter, Whitsunday, Christmas, Christmas Eve, New Year's Day*]
Ph182	SUIT	VI.14.21	... jacket and trousers together when they match?
Ph183	TUESDAY	VII.4.2	... the days at the beginning of the week?
Ph184	TUNE	VI.5.19	What am I doing now [i]? Whistling a ....
Ph185	BOILING	V.8.6	When water is heated and is bubbling a lot, you say it is ....
Ph186	OIL	V.2.13	[domestic lighting] Before gas and electricity came in, people had to use what?
Ph187	VOICE	VI.5.17	If you were asked: How did you know it was me talking outside when you couldn't see me? you might reply: .... [elicit *I knew your voice*]
Ph188	ONION	V.7.15	... that vegetable with the thin brown skin that makes your eyes water?
Ph189	MOW	II.9.3	In hay-making, what do you do first?
Ph190	SNOW	VII.6.13	In winter the ground is often all white and covered with ....
Ph191	THROWING	VIII.7.7	What would you say a boy was doing, if you saw him doing this [i]? ... a stone.
Ph192	GROW	IX.3.9	We put potatoes in the ground to make them ....

Ph193	FOUR	VII.1.4	[Ask for the numerals *one* to *nine* by gesture].
Ph194	DAUGHTER	VIII.1.4	[children, parents] He [p] is their ... [elicit *son*], and she is their ....
Ph195	DAUGHTER-IN-LAW	VIII.1.18	If [your son] Jack had married someone called Mary, you'd speak of her as ....
Ph196	BUSHES	IV.10.5	Hawthorns and brambles are not trees, but ....
Ph197	BOOT(-LACES)	VI.14.25	[p] ... these?
Ph198	POCKETS	VI.14.15	[p] ... these?
Ph199	SUET	V.7.6	... that fat that you make a boiled pudding with?
Ph200	TUESDAY	VII.4.2	... the days at the beginning of the week?
Ph201	FRIDAY	VII.4.4	... the day after Thursday?
Ph202	YESTERDAY	VII.3.8	[saying something happened some time back] If not today, but 24 hours ago?
Ph203	EVERY	VII.8.19	You don't milk the cows on Tuesdays and Fridays only, you milk them ... day.
Ph204	READY	VIII.1.16	Jack, waiting to go out with Mary, shouts: Have you got your things on yet? And she answers: Yes, I'm quite ....
Ph205	WINDOWS	V.1.7	[□ houses] ... these?
Ph206	MEADOW	II.9.2	... the field where grass is grown for hay-making?
Ph207	YELLOW	IV.6.6	[yolk of egg] What colour is it?
Ph208	SHILLING	VII.7.5	[show the coins concerned] ... this?
Ph209	MORNING	VII.3.11	... the various parts of the day? [elicit *morning, afternoon, evening, night*]
Ph210	HERRINGS	IV.9.11	... those salt-water fish that kippers are made from?
Ph211	FARTHINGS	VII.7.2	A half-penny is worth two ...?
Ph212	QUICK	VI.7.9	Some boys have a habit of biting their nails down [g] .... [elicit *to the quick*]
Ph213	QUILT	V.2.11	... the top-covering on a bed?
Ph214	FINGER	VI.7.7	[p] ... this?
Ph215	FURROW	II.3.1	... the track made by a plough?
Ph216	FLEAS	IV.8.4	... those little black insects that jump about and bite you?
Ph217	FLOOR	V.2.7	[interior of house] ... this?
Ph218	FROM	VIII.2.11	You might say: Who's that queer-looking stranger over there? I wonder where he comes ....
Ph219	FRIDAY	VII.4.4	... the day after Thursday?
Ph220	HAND	VI.7.1	[p] ... this?
Ph221	HEARSE	VIII.5.9	How is the coffin taken from the house to the churchyard? [elicit *hearse, bier*]
Ph222	WHEEL	I.9.5	[□ cart] ... this?
Ph223	WHITE	V.10.7	What colours are your reels of thread? [elicit *blue, green, red, white*]
Ph224	RAT	IV.5.3	... the animal larger than a mouse, with a long tail; it lives in stacks and sewers?
Ph225	RED	V.10.7	What colours are your reels of thread? [elicit *blue, green, red, white*]
Ph226	SADDLE	I.5.6	[□ harness of cart-horse] ... this?
Ph227	SEVEN	VII.1.6	[Ask for the numerals *one* to *nine* by gesture].

Ph228	SURE	IX.7.12	[after eliciting informant's words for (emphatic) *I am not + adj*] If asked whether the postman had been, and you were somewhat doubtful, you'd say [using his own words]: *I'm not* ....
Ph229	SNOW	VII.6.13	In winter the ground is often all white and covered with ....
Ph230	SWEARING	VIII.8.9	Of a person who uses a lot of bad language, you'd say: He is always ... and .... [elicit *cursing* and *swearing*]
Ph231	SWEAT	VI.13.5	On a very hot day, you [g wiping your forehead] ....
Ph232	THIGH	VI.9.3	[p] ... this?
Ph233	THIMBLE	V.10.9	[p] ... this?
Ph234	THREE	VII.1.3	[Ask for the numerals *one* to *nine* by gesture].
Ph235	THREAD	V.10.2	[p] ... this? [elicit *needle* and *thread*]
Ph236	LADDER	I.7.14	□ ... this?
Ph237	FATHER	VIII.1.1	[□ family group and elicit relationship terms, if necessary using the questions below] Who are the two most important members of a family? [elicit *father, mother*]
Ph238	MOTHER	VIII.1.1	[□ family group and elicit relationship terms, if necessary using the questions below] Who are the two most important members of a family? [elicit *father, mother*]
Ph239	BUTTER	V.5.4	What can you make from milk? [elicit *butter, cheese*]
Ph240	FINGER	VI.7.7	[p] ... this?
Ph241	HUNGRY	VI.13.9	If you haven't eaten any food for a long time, you're bound to be very ....
Ph242	TONGUE	VI.5.4	What am I doing now [i in derision]? [elicit *putting your tongue out*]
Ph243	TONGS	V.3.7	[p] . . this?
Ph244	BUTTER	V.5.4	What can you make from milk? [elicit *butter, cheese*]
Ph245	FARMER	VIII.4.7	[if informant omits *farmer* in listing trades and occupations] ... the man who works the land?
Ph246	UNCLE	VIII.1.12	[of children's father] If this man had a brother, he'd be their ....
Ph247	WEASEL	IV.5.6	... that small animal, reddish brown, white throat, short legs and tail, about half as big as a ferret; it kills rabbits?
Ph248	CABBAGE	V.7.18	□ ... these garden vegetables?
Ph249	DROUGHT	VII.6.20	[of very dry summer] And you say there has been a long and serious ....

L1	FARMSTEAD	I.1.2	[□ farmstead and fields] ... this?
L2	CARTMAN	I.2.2	[of farm-workers] ... the man in charge of the vehicles?
L3	TROUGH	I.3.6	[□ cowhouse interior] ... this?
L4	STRETCHER	I.5.11	[□ cart-horse harness] ... the wooden rod that keeps the traces apart?
L5	TRACEHORSE	I.6.3	[□ two horses in tandem] ... this?
L6	SHAFT	I.9.4	[□ cart] ... these? And one of them?
L7	TIRE	I.9.10	[□ cart, parts of wheel] ... this iron thing round it?
L8	TIP	I.11.6	How do you empty a cart the quickest way?
L9	DUNG	II.1.4	... getting dung from the dung-heap to the field?
L10	COUCH-GRASS	II.2.3	□ ... this?
L11	BINDWEED	II.2.4	□ ... this?

L12	GOOSE-GRASS	II.2.5	□ . . . this?
L13	TOP AND TAIL	II.4.3	In gathering swedes, what do you do to each after you have pulled it out of the ground?
L14	CARTING	II.6.6	. . . taking the corn from the field?
L15	RIDGE	II.7.2	[□ stacks] . . . this?
L16	RIDGE	V.1.2a	[□ houses] . . . this?
L17	PEGS	II.7.7	[thatching stacks] What do you fasten it down with? [elicit *pegs, twine/ropes*]
L18	ROPES	II.7.7	[thatching stacks] What do you fasten it down with? [elicit *pegs, twine/ropes*]
L19	NOT IN CALF	III.1.8	[breeding cattle] And so you can say that the cow at that time is . . . . Does that mean that she can have no more calves?
L20	DONKEY	III.13.16	. . . the animal that makes a noise like *hee-haw*?
L21	TRIM	IV.2.3	When you take the rough growth off your hedges, what do you say you do to them?
L22	PLASH	IV.2.4	But if your hedge is overgrown and there are gaps in the bottom of it, what do you do to it?
L23	SHEEP-HOLE	IV.2.8	. . . the small opening made in the bottom of a wall or fence or hedge to let the sheep through?
L24	HANGING-POST	IV.3.3	[□ gate and posts] . . . this, to which the gate is attached?
L25	PATH	IV.3.11	. . . a track made by cows or sheep or human beings through a field?
L26	MOLE	IV.5.4	. . . the animal that throws up small mounds of earth in the fields?
L27	(KEEP) HENS	IV.6.2	Some people have a shed and a wire-netting run at the bottom of their garden in which they . . . .
L28	CHIP	IV.6.10	When the young birds show signs of hatching out, you say the eggs are beginning to . . . .
L29	GOSLING	IV.6.17	[geese] . . . the young bird?
L30	ANTS	IV.8.12	. . . these fussy little insects that crawl about quickly all over the place and seem to be working hard?
L31	THRESHOLD	V.1.12	[door of house] . . . the slab of stone or piece of wood across the bottom?
L32	EARTH-CLOSET	V.I.13	. . . the old-fashioned W.C.?
L33	KINDLING-WOOD	V.4.2	What do you light your fire with in the morning? [elicit *kindling-wood*, not merely *sticks*]
L34	SLICE	V.6.10	. . . the thin piece you cut off from the loaf with the bread-knife?
L35	SAD	V.6.12	When your bread or pastry has not risen, you say it is . . .
L36	GIRDLE	V.7.4	[as distinct from *gridiron*] And [. . .] that iron plate that cakes were baked on over the fire?
L37	DRIPPING	V.7.5	. . . the fat from roasting meat?
L38	BACON FAT	V.7.5	And [. . . the fat] from bacon?
L39	INSIPID	V.7.8	If you haven't put enough salt into your food, you say it is . . . .
L40	PEAPOD	V.7.12	[□ peapod with peas] . . . this?
L41	SHELLING	V.7.14	. . . taking the peas out of the pod?
L42	BREW	V.8.9	When you pour the boiling water onto the leaves in the tea-pot, what do you say you do?
L43	DREGS	V.8.15	What is left at the bottom of your teacup when you've finished drinking the tea?

L44	ANYTHING	V.8.16	If you come in very late for a meal and are wondering whether the food is all eaten up, you'd ask: Is there ... left?
L45	SOMETHING	VII.8.15	But in this one [show a full pocket] there's not *nothing*, there's ....
L46	HEADACHE	VI.1.6	When you don't feel too well here [p head], what do you say you've got?
L47	GAPES	VI.3.7	If someone looks steadily in astonishment with his mouth open, you say he ....
L48	CHAPPED	VI.7.2	In frosty weather, your hands sometimes get all dry, red and sore, and you say your hands are ....
L49	LOOSE PIECE OF SKIN	VI.7.11	[the hand] ... this, at the bottom of the nail?
L50	FRECKLES	VI.11.1	... the brownish marks or spots that some people have in the skin on their faces, and especially ginger-haired people?
L51	HUNGRY	VI.13.9	If you haven't eaten any food for a long time, you're bound to be very ....
L52	BRIM	VI.14.3	[p] ... this part of a hat?
L53	JACKET	VI.14.5	[p] ... this?
L54	SHIRT	VI.14.8	[p] ... this?
L55	VEST	VI.14.9	[clothing] ... the thing next to the skin?
L56	SNACK	VII.5.11	Tell me, do you have anything to eat between meals? [elicit *snack*; informant to state what and when]
L57	MEAL OUT	VII.5.12	... the food you take to work with you as a meal?
L58	ICICLES	VII.6.11	In winter when water freezes, what can you sometimes see hanging down from the spouts?
L59	MARRIED	VIII.1.17	If your son Jack is not single, he must be ....
L60	FROM	VIII.2.11	You might say: Who's that queer-looking stranger over there? I wonder where he comes ....
L61	LIE DOWN	VIII.3.6	You might say to your visitor: If you are not feeling well, here's the sofa, why not come and ....
L62	STAY AT HOME	VIII.5.2	[good people go to church on Sunday] But some lazy people like to read the Sunday papers, and so they ....
L63	SLIDE	VIII.7.1	When children find the footpaths or the playground covered with ice, they will at once begin to ....
L64	BOGEY	VIII.8.1	Sometimes, when children are behaving very badly, their mother will tell them that someone will come and take them away. What do you call this mysterious person?
L65	AFRAID	VIII.8.2	[frightening children with threat of bogey] Nowadays, of course, that trick doesn't work, for some children are not ....
M1	I AM	IX.7.7	Which of you is English here? For yourself you could answer: .... [elicit *I am*]
M2	YOU ARE	IX.7.7	Which of you is English here? For yourself you could answer: .... [convert for 2prsg *you are*]
M3	SHE IS	IX.7.7	Which of you is English here? For yourself you could answer: .... [convert for *she is*]
M4	THEY ARE	IX.7.7	Which of you is English here? For yourself you could answer: .... [convert for *they are*]
M5	I AM	IX.7.9	If I say: You people aren't English, you can contradict and say: Oh yes, ... [elicit *we are*. Convert for *I am*]
M6	YOU ARE	IX.7.9	If I say: You people aren't English, you can contradict and say: Oh yes, ... [convert for *you are*]

M7	SHE IS	IX.7.9	If I say: You people aren't English, you can contradict and say: Oh yes, ... [convert for *she is*]
M8	WE ARE	IX.7.9	If I say: You people aren't English, you can contradict and say: Oh yes, ... [elicit *we are*]
M9	I'M NOT	IX.7.10	If I said to you: You're drunk, you would answer: Oh no, ... [elicit *I'm not*]
M10	SHE ISN'T	IX.7.10	If I said to you: You're drunk, you would answer: Oh no, ... [convert for *she isn't*]
M11	THEY AREN'T	IX.7.10	If I said to you: You're drunk, you would answer: Oh no, ... [convert for *they aren't*]
M12	AREN'T I	IX.7.5	You can say: We're all right here, aren't we? Now speaking of that man over there, you can say: He's all right there, ...? [elicit *isn't he*? Convert for *aren't I*?]
M13	ISN'T HE	IX.7.5	You can say: We're all right here, aren't we? Now, speaking of that man over there, you can say: He's all right there, ...? [elicit *isn't he*?]
M14	AREN'T YOU	IX.7.5	You can say: We're all right here, aren't we? Now, speaking of that man over there, you can say: He's all right there, ...? [convert for 2prsg *aren't you*?]
M15	AREN'T THEY	IX.7.5	You can say: We're all right here, aren't we? Now, speaking of that man over there, you can say: He's all right there, ...? [convert for *aren't they*?]
M16	I AM	VIII.9.5	We drink water when ... thirsty. [elicit *we are*. Convert for *I am*]
M17	SHE IS	VIII.9.5	We drink water when ... thirsty. [convert for *she is*]
M18	WE ARE	VIII.9.5	We drink water when ... thirsty. [elicit *we are*]
M19	THEY ARE	VIII.9.5	We drink water when ... thirsty. [convert for *they are*]
M20	I WAS	VIII.9.5	We drank water because ... thirsty. [elicit *we were*. Convert for *I was*]
M21	SHE WAS	VIII.9.5	We drank water because ... thirsty. [convert for *she was*]
M22	WE WERE	VIII.9.5	We drank water because ... thirsty. [elicit *we were*]
M23	THEY WERE	VIII.9.5	We drank water because ... thirsty. [convert for *they were*]
M24	(IF SHE) WERE	IX.7.8	Talking about being well-off, we could say: We'd all buy lots of things if we ... rich. [elicit *were*. Convert for *she were*]
M25	(IF WE) WERE	IX.7.8	Talking about being well-off, we could say: We'd all buy lots of things if we ... rich. [elicit *were*]
M26	AREN'T (I)	IX.7.4	Of a man who has just won a thousand pounds, you would say: Isn't he lucky? And if it was you, you'd say of yourself: ... lucky?
M27	AREN'T YOU	IX.7.3	If you saw me wheeling a pram and then gathered from our conversation that I was not married, you might ask me in some surprise: But ... married?
M28	AM (I)	IX.7.1	To find out whether you're right, you ask quite simply: ... right?
M29	ARE YOU	IX.7.2	To find out whether I had a wife, you'd ask me: ...? [elicit *are you married*?]
M30	ARE THEY	IX.7.2	To find out whether I had a wife, you'd ask me: ...? [convert for *are they*?]
M31	CAN'T	IX.4.16	Yes, tomorrow I could, but today ....
M32	DARE NOT	IX.4.17	Your neighbour would like to go and have a drink of beer, but he is so henpecked that he ....
M33	DURST NOT	IX.4.18	He wanted to go for a drink, but was so henpecked that he ....

M34	(HE) DOES	IX.5.1	You don't care for things like that, but I .... [convert for *he does*]
M35	DOES (HE)	IX.5.4	If you want to know how much rent Jack pays for his house, you ask him: Jack, how much rent ... pay? [convert for *does he*?]
M36	DO YOU	IX.5.4	If you want to know how much rent Jack pays for his house, you ask him: Jack, how much rent ... pay?
M37	(HE) DOESN'T	IX.5.2	I do care for it, but he ....
M38	(THEY) DON'T	IX.5.2	I do care for it, but he ... [convert for *they don't*]
M39	DONE	IX.5.6	[of a broken vase] Tell me then, who has ... it?
M40	(I) HAVE	IX.6.1	Have you got a match? Yes, I ....
M41	(HE) HAS	IX.6.1	Have you got a match? Yes, I .... [convert for *he has*]
M42	(I) HAVEN'T	IX.6.2	I have a match but he .... [convert for *I haven't*]
M43	(HE) HASN'T	IX.6.2	I have a match but he ....
M44	(WE) HAVEN'T	IX.6.2	I have a match but he .... [convert for *we haven't*]
M45	(WE) HAVE GOT	IX.6.4	You say to a friend: Shall I give you one of these pups? But he answers: No thanks, we ... one.
M46	MUST NOT	IX.4.12	To tell her child not to play with the fire, a mother might say: You ... play with the fire.
M47	SHALL	IX.4.2	I'm old-fashioned; I've always done it that way and I think I always ....
M48	I SHALL	IX.4.1	I like walking. Yesterday I walked to X, this morning I walked to Y, and tomorrow ... walk to Z.
M49	I SHAN'T	IX.4.4	You can't have my spade today because I want it, but you can have it tomorrow, because then ... want it.
M50	WON'T	IX.4.5	If asked to do something and you don't wish to do it, you say: No, I ... do it.
M51	CAME	IX.3.4	Afterwards Father went out, but then he remembered that he had forgotten something else, so back he ....
M52	CAUGHT	IX.3.8	Our cat saw a mouse and very quickly ... it.
M53	GREW	IX.3.9	[potatoes] Last year it was astonishing how quickly they ....
M54	PUT	IX.3.3	Father says: June, I've lost my collar studs. Where have you ... them?
M55	TAKEN	IX.3.7	[chance to go to college] If their sister had had the same chance, she certainly would have ... it.
M56	CURSING	VIII.8.9	Of a person who uses a lot of bad language, you'd say he is always ... and .... [elicit *cursing* and *swearing*]
M57	DOING	IX.5.3	You see a child very busy with something out there; so you ask: What's that child ... there?
M58	LAUGHING	VIII.8.7	What am I doing now [i]?
M59	WRITING	VIII.6.6	If, as a boy, you wrote badly, you could say: I used to be bad at ....
M60	CHILDREN	VIII.1.2	[members of a family] In the olden days, families often had up to five or six ....
M61	COWS	III.1.1	... your animals that give milk?
M62	EYES	VI.3.1	[p] ... these?
M63	BELLOWS	V.3.10	[p] ... this?
M64	HAMES	I.5.4	[□ harness of cart-horse] ... this?
M65	FATHER'S	IX.8.6	If these boots belong to your father, then you could say: These are my ....
M66	COW'S	IX.8.7	□ These are the legs of this cow. So you can say, in a shorter way: These are this ....

M67	YOU	IX.7.7	Which of you is English here? For yourself you could answer: .... [convert for 2prsg *you are*]
M68	SHE	IX.7.7	Which of you is English here? For yourself you could answer: .... [convert for *she is*]
M69	SHE	IX.7.2	To find out whether I had a wife, you'd ask me: .... [elicit *are you married*? Convert for *is she*?]
M70	HIM	IX.2.4	If you've lost your way and someone comes along, you'd go up to him and .... [elicit *ask him*]
M71	IT	I.7.1	If you want to know how heavy a thing is, what do you do? [elicit *weigh it*]
M72	IT	V.7.20	Before your wife brings you the broth, she is certain to have [g] .... [elicit *tasted it*]
M73	IT	V.7.3	You can burn your mouth in eating porridge, if ... too hot.
M74	US	IX.8.1	You hear voices upstairs and call out: Who's there? Your children up there answer back: It's only ....
M75	OUR	VI.3.3	Again. How do we see? [elicit *with our eyes*]
M76	HIS	IX.8.5	I have my troubles and you have .... [convert for *his*]
M77	HERS	IX.8.5	I have my troubles and you have .... [convert for *hers*]
M78	YOURS	IX.8.5	I have my troubles and you have ....
M79	THEIRS	IX.8.5	I have my troubles and you have ... [convert for *theirs*]
M80	HIMSELF	IX.11.4	I know he wants to sell his house because he told me ....
M81	WHOSE	IX.9.6	That man's uncle was drowned last week. In other words, you might say, that's the chap .... [elicit *whose uncle was drowned*]
M82	THESE	IX.10.5	[stand at informant's side; put two coins close to him, two a little further away, two at some distance from him; p and ask him to choose one pair from the set] Or [p] .... [elicit *these*]
M83	THOSE	IX.10.4	[stand at informant's side; put two coins close to him, two a little further away, two at some distance from him; p and ask him to choose one pair from the set] Now you can choose [p] .... [elicit *those*]
S1	GIVE IT TO ME	IX.8.2	Jack wants to have Tommy's ball and says to him, not: Keep it! but [g] ....
S2	WE PUT THE LIGHT ON	V.2.12	How do you see in this room when it gets dark?
S3	(CAME) TO (SEE)	IX.5.9	If I asked: Why did you come to X last week? And suppose your reason was a visit to the doctor, you'd say: I came ....
S4	GO AND	IX.5.8	You hear a noise in the yard and you want your boy to find out what the trouble is, so you say: Johnny, will you [g] ... see what is the matter?
S5	WHO	IX.9.5	The woman next door says: The work in this garden is getting me down. You say: Well, get some help in. I know a man ... will do it for you.
S6	TO WHOM	IX.9.3	You have something to give away and before deciding on the person to be given it, you might ask yourself: I wonder ... I shall give it?
S7	TWENTY-FIVE TO THREE	VII.5.5	[□ twenty-five to three] What time is this?
S8	ON FRIDAY WEEK	VII.4.7	When you know that a week after this Friday you'll be back here again, you could say: I'll be back again ....
S9	DID NOT DO	IX.5.5	Your wife suddenly says to you: This vase is broken, and you at once say: Well, I can truthfully say I ... it.

APPENDIX 2

NOTES ON THE MAPPED LEXICAL RESPONSES

These notes, which amplify the information printed on the map pages, are based for the most part on the *Basic Material* volumes and therefore on Harold Orton's interpretation of the Survey's incidental material.

Words in capital letters are represented in that form on the maps, while associated but unmapped forms are printed in lower-case italics. The use of quotation marks indicates the informant's own words as noted by the fieldworkers. Phrases not in quotation marks are either the fieldworker's or the *Basic Material* editors' comments. The responses follow the order of the legends for each map, compound forms being listed alphabetically under the appropriate elicited form. The range of variant forms is given in the numerical county order used in the Survey.

L1 FARM farmstead plus land 6Y 5 im/16 im, 20C 1 im, 33Brk 3 im, 40Sx 2 im/4 im; consisting of *homestead* (= farmhouse) and *farmbuildings* 18Nth 4; most common 29Ess $^{+}$10
FARMHOUSE 6Y 26 im
FARMSTEAD not much used 6Y 31 im; not used 9Nt 3, 29Ess $^{+}$8; big 29Ess $^{+}$1; occ 34Sr $^{+}$1
HOMESTEAD small 29Ess $^{+}$1

L2 CARTER does light carting work 3Du 4 im; man who drives a cart 5La 9 im, 6Y 14 im, 17Wa $^{+}$3; in old days 29Ess $^{+}$14
WAGONER driver of horse-drawn wagon 4We 1 im; in charge of two horses 7Ch 5; older word than *horseman* 8Db $^{+}$5; drives wagon 17Wa $^{+}$3; in charge of wagon when in use 22Sf 1; in old days 29Ess $^{+}$14

A big farm had a first, a second, and a third horseman, as well as a wagoner who did wagon work only 6Y 9 im

No-one was specially employed to look after the vehicles 10L 11, 21Nf 3/5/6/9/11

A labourer was used 23Mon 5

L3 BOOSING older than MANGER 17Wa $^{+}$1
COW-CRIB circular feeding-trough divided into sections 28Hrt 3 im. CRIB moveable feeding-trough in the bullock-yard 17Wa 3 im
MANGER not found locally 6Y 6; fieldworker marks "irr r" 39Ha $^{+}$7. SWING (OE *swingan*)-MANGER hung on chains 19Hu 1 im
COW-TROUGH modern 6Y 30. STONE(OE *stān*)-TROUGH for drinking-water in farmyard 6Y 26 im. TROUGH later word than COW-TUB 4We 1; formerly removed after feed 5La 4; (water-) trough outside the cow-house 5La 8 im; now used 5La 11; not used 5La 14 im; a cement utensil in regular use today 6Y $^{+}$3; for pigs and hens 17Wa $^{+}$1; for pigs or sheep 29Ess $^{+}$8; for drinking only 29Ess $^{+}$10; for horses 31So $^{+}$1; elliptical 35K 3; for outside use 35K 4 im; longer and larger than a *pat* 35K 6

The food is placed at the *boose*(= stall)-*head* 6Y 5/6/13 and on the floor of the *boost*(= stall) 1Nb 7

A bucket was used 8Db 3 and used formerly before the "modern" TROUGH 23Mon 5 im

L4b SPREAD-BAT pref to POLE 35K 7

L5a FIRST-HORSE two in a three-horse team 6Y 11
FORE-HORSE the front horse in a team of three 10L 11, 33Brk 3 im

L6 SHARP more common than SHAFT 39Ha 3
STANG old 2Cu $^{+}$3; older than SHAFT 4We 2

L7 BAND two on most cart-wheels 24Gl $^{+}$6; two make one tire 24Gl $^{+}$7
BOND two on most cart-wheels 24Gl $^{+}$6

HOOP older than TIRE 3Du 2; very old 3Du +6; old 6Y +26
RIM pref to TIRE 40Sx 4
STRAKES sections of a tire 11Sa +8/+10, 15He +2, 16Wo +4; on a broad-wheeled cart 11Sa +8/+10; nailed on outside of wheel 24Gl +7; a tire made of four short portions of iron 39Ha +7. STREAKS older than TIRE 22Sf 5, 29Ess 13. STRIGS an older tire made in sections 33Brk +4
TIRE very modern 6Y +26; pref to HOOP 6Y +28; modern 16Wo +7; older than BAND 25Ox 4; older than RIM 26Bk 1

L8a SKELL older than TIP up 6Y 15

L8b GIVE A TIPUP 6Y +6

Verb + BACK(OE *on bæc* 37D 9; + OUT(OE *ūt*) 22Sf +5, 28Hrt +3, 40Sx 6 im; + OVER(OE *ofer*) 31So 6

L10 COUCH older than SQUITCH 25Ox 1; pref to SQUITCH 25Ox 6; pref to COUCH-GRASS 39Ha 5
QUICK not local 21Nf +13. QUICKS pref to TWITCH 21Nf 9
SCUTCH pref to TWITCH-GRASS 7Ch 2; old 12St +11; pref to COUCH 25Ox 5. SCUTCH-GRASS from informant's wife, native 15He +7
SQUITCH older than COUCH 25Ox 2/3; rare 25Ox +6
TWITCH pref to WICKS 6Y 25; pref to WICK-GRASS 6Y 33; not local 21Nf +13; usual 29Ess +9. TWITCH-GRASS modern 7Ch +2
WICKS older than TWITCH 5La 8; pref to TWITCH 6Y 28; couch-grass roots 6Y 32 im

L11a BELL-BIND pref to LILY 40Sx 1
WITHY-WIND older than BIND-WEED 31So 12, 33Brk 4

L11b BIND-WEED pref to BEAR-BIND 34Sr 3

L12a GOOSE-GRASS informant thinks it is different 10L 15 im
HAIRIF does not have burrs 8Db 4; proper name 8Db +5; usual 11Sa 5
ROBIN-RUN-IN-THE-HEDGE from informant's wife, native 5La +7
SWEETHEARTS children's name 6Y 11; "the little old boys that stick to you" 21Nf 1 im

In L11 ROBIN-RUN-IN-THE-HEDGE at 5La +4/6 and ROBIN-RUN-THE-DIKE at 1Nb 1 rec for BINDWEED

L12b CLEAVERS older than *goose-grass* 11Sa 7; "real name" 26Bk 6

L13 FASH ref top of turnip 7Ch +1; pref to TOP AND TAIL 7Ch 3
ROOT AND TOP pref to TOP AND TAIL 34Sr 2
SNAG pref to ROOT AND TOP 1Nb 8
SNOUT trim off root 20C 2; cutting off roots only 28Hrt 2
TOP ref the whole operation 23Mon 2; both ends 23Mon 3

L15 RIDGE very rare 29Ess 7; pref to COMB 29Ess 15; not used 34Sr 4, 40Sx 6

L17 BROACHES made of hazel or elder 21Nf 1; made of hazel 21Nf 2/9–11/13, 22Sf 1–3/+5; made of willow, hazel or elder 21Nf 5; made of willow 21Nf 6; made of elm 21Nf 8; made of hazel or willow 21Nf 12; a rod of bent wood, sharpened at both ends, Edd, "At each end of rick, to tie ropes to" 36Co 5 im; "3ft long, four or five to a rick, driven in each end of rick to moor main ropes. Smaller ropes across roof were secured by stones, and at narrow end by *wind-spur* (a rope tied along *broaches*)" 36Co 6 im; "secured long ropes at each end of rick". Ropes across ridge were weighted with ?*cottar-stones* 36Co 7 im
PEGS made of hazel 6Y 26, 7Ch 4/6, 12St 6, 17Wa 3, 30MxL +1; split-wood 8Db 1; wooden 8Db 2/7, 17Wa 5/7; made of hazel or ash 9Nt +1; of ash or elm 9Nt +4; usually of elder 12St 10; made of willow 17Wa 1, 31So +3. STACK-PEGS wooden, 15ins long 6Y 22; made of willow 21Nf 7. THACK-PEGS made of ash 10L 7; older than STACK-PEGS 10L 15. THATCH-PEGS made of hazel 8Db 6, 9Nt 2. THATCHING-PEGS wooden 6Y 29; split willow 15He 7
PRODS made of hazel 5La 3/6, 6Y 10, 7Ch 6; made of sticks from *withen-*(= willow) *trees* 5La 7. STACK-PRODS wooden sticks, 2ft long, often of willow 6Y 16; hazel sticks 2ft long 6Y +18
SPARS of hazel-wood, nut-wood or willow 31So 5/7/9/+11/12, 32W 7/9, 38Do 2–4; of willow 31So 10, 32W 6; used for building and not ricks 32W 3 im; of hazel-wood or nut-wood 32W 4, 38Do 1/5, 39Ha 4, 40Sx 4; "the spars are laid vertically and horizontally. And binders (5ft long pegs) are also driven in." 34Sr 1 im
SPEARS made of hazel-wood, nut-wood or willow 37D 3; made of hazel-wood or nut-wood 37D 6
SPELKS wooden, about 2ft long 6Y 27. STACK-SPELKS made of hazel 6Y 24
SPICKS withies or hazel 24Gl 7; usually made of nut-wood 32W 2
SPITS made of hazel 18Nth 3, 2OC 2, 27Bd 1; made of willow 27Bd 2

SPRAYS of wood 17Wa 4; pointed sticks 17Wa 6; made of hazel or willow 24Gl 5; i.e. withy sticks 25Ox +4; used in thatching houses 26Bk 2 im/3 im
STACK-STOBS wooden sticks 21ins long 6Y 3; straight branches, 3ft long, cut from hedges, and usually hazel 6Y 9. STOBS pegs made from hazels 6Y 2

not rec—pieces of split hazel-wood were used 34Sr 3

L18 BANDS bought string 8Db 2. BILLY-BANDS usual 6Y +16. BINDER-BANDS usual 6Y +18. HAY-BANDS straw rope 11Sa 11, 16Wo 1; obsolete 23Mon 6. HAZEL-BANDS about 6 ft long, the ends being thrust into the stack to secure the "rope" firmly 5La 8. STACK-BANDS of coconut fibre 6Y 7. STRAW-BANDS of wheat-straw 6Y +10; straw ropes 34Sr 2. TAR-BANDS formerly 6Y +18. THACKING-BANDS matting-type string 8Db 5
BONDS fibre 11Sa 8; spun from wet hay 13Lei 3; of hay 16Wo 4/5, 21Nf 12; of straw or twine 16Wo 6; of straw 21Nf 8/9, 39Ha 2/5, 40Sx 2; hayrope 31So +3, 39Ha 7. STRAW-BONDS of straw 21Nf 3/6/10/11, 26Bk 4, 27Bd 2, 28Hrt 3, 32W 4–8, 35K 1–3/6; older than *tarred line* 21Nf 3; old-fashioned 21Nf 6; older than *binder-twine* 21Nf 10. THUMB-BONDS made of straw, older than *string* or *tarred line* 21Nf 2. REEDEN-ROPES of straw 37D +6. REED-ROPES of straw 37D 2. ROPES of straw 1Nb +9, 31So 8, 36Co 1, 37D 11; of hay 3Du 3. STRAW-ROPES of straw 34Sr 5, 37D 4/7 (but "they have cord now")/11. THATCH-ROPES made of hay 8Db 3

Straw pres ref straw-rope, Edd. 24Gl 7

"Some would thwart-rope them and long-rope them" 36Co 4 im

L19 BARREN can conceive again 5La 14, 6Y 12/21/+24/26/32, Man 1, 7Ch 1/3–6, 8Db 2–7, 9Nt 2, 11Sa 1–3/5/7/9/11, 12St 1/3/5/8, 15He 1/3–5, 16Wo 2/4/5, 17Wa 1/4–7, 18Nth 1/2/4/5, 22Sf 1, 23Mon 1–3/5, 24Gl 1/3/4, 25Ox 3/6, 26Bk 1–3/+6, 27Bd 1/2/+3, 28Hrt 1/2, 29Ess 11, 31So 2/3/10/11, 32W 1/5/8, 34Sr 1, 35K 1, 36Co 1, 38Do 3/5; cannot conceive again 6Y +7/33, 15He 2/6, 16Wo 1, 17Wa +2, 19Hu +1/+2, 20C +2, 23Mon 6, 24Gl 2, 25Ox 1/2, 26Bk 5, 28Hrt 3, 29Ess 7, 33Brk 3/5, 34Sr 2/4, 35K 3/5/6, 38Do 2, 40Sx 3/5/6; infertile, of a cow 6Y 1 im; older than GELD 6Y 12; "when it can't be put in calf" 10L 11; of a sow 13Lei 7 im; *barren mare*, ie "a mare that will not breed" 18Nth 1 im; pref to *out of calf* 22Sf 1; "has neither calf nor milk" 30MxL +1; unlikely to conceive again 34Sr 5, 35K 4/7
BARRENER cannot conceive again 25Ox +4, 29Ess 12, 30MxL +1, 32W 9, 39Ha 1/4/7, 40Sx 2/4; unlikely to conceive again 33Brk 1, 40Sx +1; can conceive again 34Sr 3
EMPTY can conceive again 19Hu +1, 20C 1/+2, 27Bd +3, 32W 2; older than BARREN 26Bk 6, 27Bd 3
GELD can conceive again 1Nb 4/8, 2Cu 1/6, 3Du 3/6, 4We 3, 5La 1/4/7/9, 6Y 2/6/13/15/17/22/29; pref to *not in calf* 2Cu 3; cannot conceive again 3Du 5, 6Y 1/+7/+24

L20a CUDDY older than DONKEY 2Cu 5, 3Du 2, 4We 2, 6Y 6; rare 3Du +1, 6Y +3; "proper name" 3Du 6 im; of a person 6Y +6/+8; pref to DONKEY 6Y 14
DICKY old-fashioned 21Nf +13; older than *ass* 22Sf +5; older than DONKEY 29Ess 6; female 21Nf +7
DONKEY male 21Nf +7; older than *ass* 22Sf +5
NEDDY older than DONKEY 10L 15; pref to DONKEY 39Ha 4

JACK DONKEY male, JENNY DONKEY female 39Ha 6 im. JENNY female 6Y 3 im

L20b ASS half-bred donkey 6Y 5 im; usual 10L +9; older than *donkey* 18Nth 5, 20C 2, 26Bk 1; proper name 21Nf 7
FUSSOCK often 6Y 7; older than *donkey* 6Y 8; pref to *donkey* 6Y 20/28
MOKE pref to *donkey* 6Y 25; children's word 6Y 29; older than *donkey* 8Db 6, 26Bk 4, 27Bd 3, 28Hrt 2; usual 12St 1, old 12St +9; pref to *donkey* or *dicky* 29Ess 10
MOKUS local 38Do +2

L21a BROWSE to trim down to about 18ins or 2ft 31So 1; cutting off overhanging branches 31So 9
BRUSH one year's growth 21Nf 3; topping and siding 21Nf 5; older than TRIM 16Wo 2
CUT of rough work 6Y 28
TOP ref top 7Ch 1; one year's growth 10L 10; older than CUT 35K 6

BROWSING = brushwood 37D 3 im. BROWSE = brushwood 37D 4 im

L21b CLIP pref to CUT 7Ch 2. CLIPPING = pruning 6Y 22 im
SHEAR pref to TRIM 31So 3. SHEARING = pruning, of privet hedges 6Y 22 im
SLASH of beech hedges only, thorn hedges are *faced* 4We 1; of light growth 6Y 28; trimming one or two years' growth 26Bk 1
SPLASH older than *dress* 2Cu 6; along the top 18Nth +4
SWITCH refined 6Y +9
TRIM up sides 18Nth +4

"You go a-hedge-trimming" 32W 6 im; "trim out the ditches" 32W 9 im
"Hedge-paring us used to call it" 36Co 2 im
SWITCHINGS(= trimmings) off the hedge-backs 6Y 2 im

L22 LAY usual 16Wo 4/5; rec but not found—hedges usually cut right down 22Sf 2;
buck older than LAY 29Ess 1; *brail* older than LAY 29Ess 5; *splay* older than LAY 34Sr 2
LIG older than LAY 6Y 12
PLEACH older than LAY 16Wo 2/4, 40Sx 2
PLUSH common 34Sr +5. PLUSH DOWN "very little done locally" 36Co 4

6Y 7 not known—"not done"

"They cut them down low and lay them" 9Nt 2 im; "they have them cut and laid" 32W 2 im;
"just cuts it down and lays it" 39Ha 7 im
"Have them laid" 38Do 1 im; "you do lay some of it" 38Do 3 im
"Build the hedge up first, then pleach the wood or lay it" 37D 8 im; "pleach down that hedge" 37D 10 im
"He've plushed thick there stick", "that's the plusher" (nd) 38Do 2 im; "go out and plush down thick hedge—plush it down or lay it with stakes" 38Do 5 im

LIGGERS = partly severed branches laid horizontally 6Y 25 im, 6Y 28 im
PLEACHERS npl 11Sa 2 im. PLEACHES npl ie hedge branches pulled down and laid horizontally 12St 5 im

L23 CATTLE(ME *catel* f ONF *catel*)-CREEP 21Nf 5 im. CREEP made to allow young sheep through only 31So 9. CREEP-HOLE ref small holes in a pigsty through which only the piglets go to feed 25Ox 4 im
GAP made by sheep 1Nb 2 im, 6Y 32 im; open at top 6Y 16; made by sheep and cattle 6Y 33 im; made by animals 11Sa 2 im/7 im, 15He 7 im, 16Wo 2 im/6 im; rare 11Sa 3; man-made 11Sa 8; old 12St 6; in hedges 32W +7; in a hedge but not found 34Sr 4. GAP-WAY wider than a SHARD-WAY 39Ha +5
GLAT man-made 11Sa 5; made by animals 11Sa 7 im/9 im/11 im, 15He 7 im (a complete break in the hedge), 23Mon 3 im; usual 15He +2; older than GAP 15He 3
SHARD larger than GLAT 23Mon +5; in hedge or wall 24Gl 4; hole made by cattle through hedges 31So 1 im; made by animals 31So 9 im; in hedges 31So +10; place in hedge trodden down by cows 31So 13 im; not defined 32W 5
SMOOT made by hares 2Cu 4 im, 3Du 5 im, 4We 2 im, 6Y 16 im; made by rabbits 5La 1 im (RABBIT-SMOOT)/2 im; for rabbits or for overflow water to run through 6Y 6 im; hole in hedge-bottom 6Y 18 im; made by animals 6Y 25 im, SMOOT-HOLE made by hares and rabbits 6Y 13 im/31 im (*smoose-hole*), 8Db 4 im; made by hares and sheep 6Y 18 im; made by animals 6Y 25 im

7Ch 1 not rec—used *slip-rail* (i.e. low rail placed across a gateway); 12St +8 also used *slip-rails* (pres low bars placed across gateway, Edd)
39Ha 7 not found—"generally a gate"

GLATTING stopping up holes in a hedge 23Mon 3 im

L25 COW-PAD made by cows 11Sa +11, 12St +3. PAD for people 6Y +3; an uncovered passage between two houses 19Hu 2 im; made by any animals 21Nf +7. SHEEP-PAD made by sheep 12St +1
CATTLE-PATH made by cows 30MxL +2. FOOT-PATH for people 39Ha +4; if made by human beings 40Sx +5. PATH = *gangway*, in cow-shed 21Nf 3 im; of human beings 31So +5; made by men 34Sr +2; made by human beings 35K +1
BEAST-TRACK made by cows 10L +10. COW-TRACK for cows 6Y +32; made by cows 7Ch +2, 12St +8, 15He +7, 16Wo +7, 25Ox +4, 27Bd +2, 29Ess +11, 30MxL +1. FOOT-TRACK older than PATH 1Nb +7, 33Brk +1; pref to PATH 35K +7. SHEEP-TRACK made by sheep 7Ch +2, 10L +10, 12St +9, 15He +7, 16Wo +7, 17Wa +5, 25Ox +4, 27Bd +2, 29Ess +11/+12, 30MxL +1. TRACK for cows and humans 6Y +14; for cows and sheep 6Y +16; for cattle 6Y +28, 39Ha +4; for people 6Y +30; more general than FOOT-PATH Man +2; made by any animals 7Ch +3, 10L +8, 18Nth +5, 21Nf +2/+4/+8/+9, 26Bk +1/+3; made by cows 12St +2, 30MxL +1; of sheep or cows 31So +5; made by animals 35K +1; made by cows or sheep 35K +2
FOOT-TROD for people 6Y +28, 21Nf +2. TROD for sheep, cattle, people 6Y 4/6; for people 6Y +7/+11/+25; older word for FOOT-PATH 6Y +20; made by a trespasser 6Y +21

L26 MOUDY rare 5La +9; pref to MOULY 6Y +10

MOULDS = mole-hills 32W 6 im

L27 CHICKEN = hens 35K 7 im, 39Ha 1 im/4 im
CHICKENS pref to HENS 40Sx 3
HENS ref females only 29Ess +2

L28 BILL pref to HATCH OUT and CHIP 35K 3
CHIP from informant's daughter 5La 6 im
PIP pref to HATCH 31So 7
SPRING pref to *chick* 21Nf 13

"That hen, she hatched them all out but one" 6Y 6 im

L29 GIB older than GOSLING 9Nt 2
GULL pref to GOSLING 15He 7

L30 ANTS pref to *pismires* 10L 5; brown and black (*pismires* red) 21Nf 5; rec but not used 38Do +3
EMMETS older than ANTS 34Sr 4/5, 35K 3, 39Ha 4, 40Sx 1

1Nb 9 informant considers *pissymires* and ANTS differ, app in size: *ant-heaps* are much bigger than *pissymire-heaps*

L31 FRESHOL made of cement 29Ess 3. THRASHOL from wife, native of Andover, 16 miles north-west. THRESHOL not used 29Ess 6. THRESHOLD rare 6Y 9; rec but not found 18Nth 4. THRESHOLT but doubtful 2Cu 6
DRAISHOL older than THRAISHOL 31So +11. DRASHOLT older than *step* 31So 8
TRASHOL old-fashioned 21Nf +9. TROSHOL older than THRASHOL 21Nf 6/10; old 21Nf 11
FRESSOL older than THRESSOL 29Ess +1

L32a CLOSET more modern than SHIT-HOLE or NESSY 6Y 26; modern 7Ch +2; polite 8Db +6, 25Ox +4; older than PETTY 16Wo 2; more polite than SHIT-HOUSE 27Bd 2. EARTH-CLOSET pref to PRIVY 35K 4
NECESSARY older than PRIVY 6Y 1. NESSY older word than CLOSET or *shit-hole* 6Y 26
NETTY commoner than PRIVY 3Du 5; polite 6Y +9; older than CLOSET 6Y 34
PETTY more polite than SHIT-HOUSE 6Y 2; older than CLOSET 6Y 19, 9Nt 4, 18Nth 3/5, 19Hu 1; older than PRIVY or CLOSET 7Ch 3; polite 8Db +6; older than PRIVY 10L 6/8; old 12St +4; usual 17Wa +3. PETTY-HOUSE polite 15He 6
PRIVY polite 6Y 3/+9; old 6Y 10; older than CLOSET 6Y 11; more vulgar than PETTY 6Y 28; better than CLOSET or SHIT-HOUSE 26Bk 1; older than CLOSET or PETTY 27Bd 1; more polite than DUNNEKIN 27Bd 3; pref to CLOSET 35K 5

L32b DIKE old 24Gl 7; older than SHIT-HOUSE (both ref pail-closet) 29Ess +5
DUNNEKIN older than CLOSET or PETTY 6Y 34; older than PRIVY or DIKE 26Bk 5; older than PRIVY 29Ess 12; ref the whole building 32W 9
SHIT-HOUSE vulgar 5La 6, 6Y 17; usual 6Y 9, 8Db 7; commoner than NESSY but vulgar 6Y 22; old 8Db 5/6, 24Gl 1; pref to CLOSET and PETTY 19Hu 2; pref to CLOSET 31So 9

21Nf 7 im "double-barrelled shit-house" ie closet with two holes

L33a KINDLING from other informants 6Y 11; not used 18Nth 5, 29Ess 14; rare 25Ox 3, 35K 2; older than *wood* 31So 1
KINDLING-STICKS rare 17Wa 3

"Kindle (= lay) the fire" (for lighting later) 6Y 23 im; "kindling stuff" 36Co 6 im

L33b BAVINS larger wood than FAGGOTS 33Brk 4; bigger than KINDLING-WOOD 34Sr 2; larger than KINDLE-WOOD or *pimps* 40Sx 3
COW-FAGGOTS older than BAVINS 35K 7. FAGGOT larger bundle than *pimp* 28Hrt 2
FAGGOTS older than KINDLING-WOOD 40Sx 4. FAGGOT-WOOD pref to BAVINS, but applies to bigger wood 33Brk 1. SCRAP-FAGGOTS pref to KINDLING or BAVINS 29Ess 7
SPRAY-FAGGOTS older than *spray-wood* 34Sr 3
MORNING-WOOD pref to KINDLING(-WOOD) 35K 5

L34 ROUND older than SLICE 21Nf 5/11
SHIVE rare 3Du +2, 4We +2; old, rare 4We +1; pref to SLICE 7Ch 2

"Cut us a shive of bread off" 6Y 2 im; "jam-shive and treacle-shive" 6Y 30 im; "shive" (to cut bread in slices) 8Db 5 im

L35a FLAT commoner than *hasn't rose* Man 2; pref to SAD 33Brk +4
SAD pref to FLAT 1Nb 8, 4We 4; commoner than FLAT Man 1; pref to FLAT or SODDEN 12St 3; from informant's wife, native 21Nf 13; pref to *sunk* 29Ess 11; rec but not used 33Brk +4
SODDEN pref to SAD 5La 4. SODDENED if cake 33Brk +4

"SAD-cake" = "a pastry, not risen, eaten at allowance-time in harvest", 6Y 11 im
SAD ref boiled potatoes; pres soapy, Edd 13Lei 2 im

L35b DOUGHY pref to *dumpy* 7Ch 2
HEAVY older than SAD 18Nth 5, 24Gl 6; pref to SAD 39Ha 7

L36 BACKSTONE for baking oat-cakes 5La 3/8, 6Y 6/14; for baking both oat-cakes and other cakes 6Y 7; for baking *haver-bread* = oat-cakes 6Y 14 im; older than GIRDLE 6Y 15, 7Ch 3; not made of stone 11Sa 6; older than *gridiron* 12St 7

FRYING-PAN "had short sides, was hung on the reckan (= crane), and used for making pancakes and girdle-cakes" 6Y 24; "an iron plate . . . with no handle and no sides" 17Wa 2
GIRDLE rarely used 5La 6; rec but not found locally 6Y 19/28, 30MxL 2, 34Sr 1; informant uncertain 6Y 25; not used 24Gl 5
GRIDDLE hesitantly 2Cu $^{+}$6; older than GIRDLE 3Du 3; for meat 31So 13 im

9Nt 3 not found, used oven or frying-pan; 16Wo 7 not known, used a frying-pan "with sides"

"BACKSTONE-cake" = "girdle-cake without currants" 6Y 6 im. "BACKSTONE-cakes" 31So 2 im
"GIRDLE-cake" 6Y 2 im/17 im (but not made locally). "GIRDLE-cakes" 2Cu 4 im, 6Y 9 im/10 im/33 im, 25Ox 4 im. "GIRDLE-scones" 6Y 18 im

L37 DRIP pref to DRIPPING 40Sx 5. DRIPPING from beef (*fat* from mutton) 1Nb 5
GRAVY ref meat-juice found at bottom of jar of dripping 11Sa 6 im; oldest 16Wo $^{+}$3; "when warm" 16Wo $^{+}$6

L38 BACON ?error for BACON-FAT, Edd 13Lei $^{+}$7. BACON-FAT if solid 6Y $^{+}$31
DIP older than BACON-FAT 3Du 1; when soaked up in bread 8Db 5 im. DIPPO very old 17Wa $^{+}$4
GREASE very old 17Wa $^{+}$4

"DIPPING-bread" = bread dipped in bacon-fat 6Y 10 im, "drop of DIP" 6Y 24 im

L39 WALLOW also heard by informant 2Cu 4 im
WAFFLY informant hesitant 9Nt 4
WOLSH older than WALSH 6Y 1

" 'Tis main fresh—wants some more salt" 32W 4 im
"Taties is terrible wallow" 6Y 7 im

L40 COSH rare 29Ess $^{+}$14
HULL older than POD 11Sa 1
HUSK when empty 29Ess $^{+}$10
POD when full 6Y $^{+}$18; polite 6Y $^{+}$28; ref beans 29Ess 5 im; when growing 32W 8; pref to SHUCK 34Sr 2
PEA-SHELL when empty 29Ess $^{+}$6
PEA-SHUCK pref to POD 34Sr 1. SHUCK when empty 29Ess $^{+}$10; older than SHELL 29Ess 15, 34Sr 3; pref to POD 40Sx 1; older than POD 40Sx 3
PEA-SWAD when empty 6Y $^{+}$18. SWAD old 3Du $^{+}$2; older than POD 4We 2, 6Y 12, 10L 7/9; pref to POD 6Y 10

L41a SHILL pref to SHELL 6Y 10
SHULLING older than SHELLING 7Ch 1

"Shell those peas" 6Y 10 im; "shell thick peas" 31So 3 im; "shell they peas" 32W 3 im, 39Ha 2 im; "shell them peas" 32W 5 im; "shell they peas out" 37D 5 im
"You shill them" 6Y 19 im; "shill yon peas, will ter" 6Y 22 im; "shill they peas" 37D 9 im

L41b HULLING older than SHELLING 16Wo 2
SHUCKING pref to SHELLING 33Brk 4, 40Sx 1; pref to SHILLING 40Sx 2

"Huck they peas" 32W 9 im, 39Ha 1 im
"Shuck the peas" 39Ha 7 im; "shuck they peas" 40Sx 2 im

L42 BREW ?older than MASH 3Du 4; pres ref beer, Edd 25Ox $^{+}$4
MAKE polite 25Ox $^{+}$4
MASH rarer than BREW 3Du 6; pref to BREW 6Y 25; old 12St $^{+}$11; from informant's wife, born Goodenstone, 12½ miles south-east 21Nf $^{+}$4; not used 21Nf $^{+}$10; older than DRAW 21Nf 11; older than MAKE 25Ox $^{+}$4; older than BREW 28Hrt 2; older than WET 33Brk 5.
MASS old 4We $^{+}$3; older than BREW 5La 1
MASK older than BREW 1Nb 5; old 4We $^{+}$3. MAST older than MASK 3Du 1
SCALD older than MASK 3Du 2; very old 4We $^{+}$3; older than BREW 5La 10, 6Y 10
STEEP modern 17Wa $^{+}$3
WET common Man $^{+}$1; pref to MAKE or MASH 25Ox $^{+}$4; older than BREW 34Sr 5, 40Sx 3/5; older than MAKE 40Sx 1

39Ha 6 im "let it bide and draw"
31So 9 im "is the tea soaked?"; 36Co 4 im "the tea must soak a bit"; 37D 7 im "I've soaked the tea"; 38Do 3 im "you be soaking yer tea"
31So 10 im "have ye wet the tea?"; 37D 2 im "have ye wetted the tea?"; 39Ha 1 im "wet that tea"; 39Ha 5 im "I wetted the tea and let it draw"

L43 DREGS older than TEA-LEAVES 1Nb 8
TEA-GROUNDS older than TEA-LEAVES 24Gl 6
GROUTS older than DREGS 29Ess 12, 34Sr 5
SLOPS usual 29Ess +5

L44 AUGHT older than ANYTHING 7Ch 6

L45 SOMEWHAT uncommon 2Cu +1; pref to SOMETHING 17Wa 2

L46 HEADWARCH older than HEADACHE 5La 13; used at Bradwell, 2½ miles south-east 8Db +2
HEADWARK = mental arithmetic 2Cu 6 im; pref to HEADACHE 6Y 2; sw, reluctantly 6Y +23
SKULLACHE older than HEADACHE 29Ess 6/9
SORE HEAD rarely used 1Nb +5

"I's a bit thick in the head" = I have a headache 6Y 3 im; "you get headache" 29Ess 6 im

L47 GAAP old 25Ox +6. GAAPING older than GAPING 29Ess 7
GAPING = shouting 2Cu 6 im; pref to GAPPING 40Sx 2
GAPPING older than GAPING 38Do 5
GAUPING older than GAPING 15He 7
GLORING older than GAUPING 6Y 13

"Got the gaaps" ie is gawping 21Nf 1 im
"Birds gapes for worms" ie birds crane with open beaks (of young birds) 3Du 6 im;
"got the gapes" 33Brk 3 im
"He's a great gaup" ie stupid fellow 18Nth 2 im; sw "gauping" = shouting 26Bk 2 im
"Catching flies" ie gaping 33Brk 2 im

L48 CHAPPED known but not local 1Nb +5; sore and red 3Du +3; "that's proper" 5La +4;
with deep cuts 6Y +14; older than *chashed* 6Y 31; of faces and backs of hands 6Y +33;
chilblained pref 10L 15; heard, but not used 21Nf +6; *chafed* older 26Bk 3
CHIPPED hesitantly 6Y +5
CRACKED older than CHOPPED 6Y 24; with cuts 6Y +33
KEENED = cracked 3Du +3
SPREAZED older than CHOPPED 24Gl 6
SPREED older than CHOPPED 32W 7

L49a ANGER-NAIL = sore caused by an ingrowing nail 1Nb 5 im
HANGNAIL rec but ref a broken nail 29Ess 7
NANGNAIL pref to STEPMOTHER 5La 11; = corn on the foot 6Y 29 im

L49b BACKBITER from informant's wife, native 8Db 3; a sore chap in corner of nail 15He 7 im

"They revel back" 32W 6 im

L50a FRECKLES hesitantly 7Ch 2; older than SPECKLES 25Ox 1
VRICKLES pref to FRECKLES 31So 5; older than FRECKLES 31So 11

"Frackny-faced" adj 10L 5 im/7 im
"Freckled-face" 6Y 11 im; "freckle-faced" 6Y 34 im, 10L 4 im/15 im; "freckled" adj 17Wa 2 im;
"freckle-face" 25Ox 4 im; "freckle-faces" 10L 14 im; "freckly" adj 35K 7
"Frickly-faced" 36Co 4 im
"Sun-vreckled" 39Ha 5 im
"Vrickle-face" 31So 7 im; "vrickly-faced" 36Co 2 im, 37D 9 im
"They're feckled" 6Y 10 im

L50b BRUNNY-SPOTS older than FRECKLES 21Nf 11
FANTICKLES older than FRECKLES 6Y 13. FERNYTICKLES older than FRECKLES 1Nb 5;
FRENTICKLES from informant's father 6Y 6
FORNSPECKLES older than SPECKLES 7Ch 5
SPRECKLES older than FRECKLES 5La 3

"Bran-faced" adj 10L 2 im; "branny" = freckled, adj 11Sa 8 im/11 im, 19Hu 1 im, 33Brk 4 im;
"old bran-face" (of person with freckles) 10L 13 im; "branny-faced" adj 29Ess 14 im;
"branface", "we used call them old branfaces" 38Do 1 im
"Brunny-faced" adj 20C 1 im/2 im, 21Nf 8 im, 22Sf 5 im, 29Ess 5 im; "he's wholly brunny" ie very
freckled 22Sf 2 im; "brunny" adj 22Sf 4 im, 29Ess 2 im/10 im; "brunny-face" adj 27Bd 2 im
"Farntickled" = freckled 3Du 2 im; "fantickled" = freckled 4We 3 im
"Formpeckled" = freckled 5La 11 im
"Murfly" 36Co 6 im, 37D 10 im; "murfly-faced" 37D 4 im
"Speckledy" 32W 1 im/6 im; "speckly-faced" 32W 2 im

L51 CLAMMED starving 5La 11 im; very hungry 6Y 18 im; old 9Nt +2. CLAMMED OUT older than HUNGRY 6Y 19. CLAMMED TO DEATH very hungry 5La 6 im, 6Y 14 im/32 im. CLEMMED pref to HUNGRY 8Db 7; older than HUNGRY 11Sa 9

HUNGERED TO DEATH very hungry 2Cu 6 im, 6Y 15 im

HUNGRY *famished* older 6Y 5; of animals 37D +9

LEER older than HUNGRY 26Bk 1, 40Sx 4/5; sw = empty 31So 4 im; pref to HUNGRY 33Brk 3; very hungry 34Sr +4; *sinking* pref 40Sx 1; rare 40Sx +5

LEERY nd 31So 1 im; pref to HUNGRY 31So 6

THIRL especially of cattle 36Co +1

"Clamming's (ie starving's) doing without having aught to eat" 6Y 17 im; "it's clamming (ie famished)" †1773 of an animal 6Y 29 im; "if there's aught in the house, I shan't clam (= starve)" 6Y 31 im

L52 BRIM older than RIM 1Nb 5; ref bowler hat 6Y 22 im

FLIPE ref peak of cap 3Du 3 im

POKE old 12St +8

RIM pref to *ridge* 7Ch 2; older than VERGE 22Sf 4; older than BRIM 28Hrt 2; pref to BRIM 35K 7

VERGE older than BRIM 21Nf 5

"Brimmer" ie hat with a brim 17Wa 2 im

"Double-fliped cap" ie having a peak at front and back 6Y 4 im

L53 COAT older than JACKET 5La 9/13/14, 6Y 1/4/8/15, 7Ch 4/5, 29Ess 6

JACKET older than COAT 1Nb 6, 25Ox 4; pref to COAT 7Ch 2, 34Sr 1

"I'll warm thy jacket" ie give you a thrashing 6Y 29 im

"Bairns has jackets, the old men has coats" 6Y 4 im

L54 SARK older than SHIRT 1Nb 2/4; very old 1Nb +8

SHIRT *shift* pref 33Brk 2

L55 FLANNEL older than UNDER-SHIRT 17Wa 2

FLANNEL-SHIRT very old 25Ox +1; formerly worn 25Ox +4; older than UNDER-SHIRT 25Ox 5; worn by men 30MxL +1

FLANNEN-SHIRT older than SINGLET 6Y 11

SINGLET older than FLANNEN 4We 2; older than VEST 6Y 25, 12St 2; older than UNDER-VEST 7Ch 4

UNDER-SHIRT pref to VEST 6Y 10, 35K 7, 40Sx 4; old-fashioned 6Y +28; older than SINGLET 7 Ch 1; older than UNDER-VEST 8Db 1; of flannel 15He +7; rarer than VEST 25Ox 6; older than VEST 30MxL +1, 33Brk 5, 38Do 2; worn by men 30MxL +1

VEST modern 7Ch +2, 34Sr +1; of wool 15He +7; old-fashioned 21Nf 10; worn by woman 30MxL +1

"He had a flannel up" ie he wore a vest 36Co 6 im; "flannels" †1722 ie vest and pants 39Ha 4 im

"Has thou a flannen (= vest) on under thy shirt?" 6Y 4 im

L56a BAGGING includes butter 7Ch +5; includes cheese 8Db 2, 12St 1/2; BAGGINGS includes cheese, also taken at 4pm 7Ch 3; pref to LUNCH 7Ch 5

BITING-ON taken about 6am in fields 6Y +30

A BIT OF CRIB tea and cake 37D +9/+11; CRIB bread and cheese 36Co 2/3; tea and cake 36Co +4, 37D +9/10/+11; sandwiches 37D 8

CRUST oldest 3Du 6; tea and cake 36Co +4/5–7

ELEVENSES modern 6Y +16/+30, 15He 7, 25Ox 4; modern, of factory breaks 6Y 22; bread and cheese 13Lei 8 (plus onion), 29Ess 1/5, 39Ha 6; dry bread 22Sf 5; includes cheese 25Ox 4; builder's labourer's word 29Ess 11; in modern factories, consisting of a sandwich and a cup of tea 39Ha +4

LUNCH unspecified constituents 7Ch 4, 12St 8; includes butter 7Ch +5; includes cheese 7Ch 6, 11Sa 1–4/6/10, 16Wo 3/6, 17Wa 2/3/5; bread and cheese 9Nt 1 (or jam pastry)/3/4, 10L 8/10 (or pasties), 13Lei 3/6 (plus onion)/7/10, 14R 1, 18Nth 2/3 (or bread and bacon)/4 (or bread and meat)/5, 21Nf 7 (plus pork pie)/10, 26Bk 4/5, 32W 1/6 (with bacon and onions), 34Sr 1, 35K 2/6, 37D 1/4/7, 38Do 1; older than SNAP 9Nt 4; bacon and bread 10L 6/8/9 (or bread and beef), 13Lei 7, 14R 1/2 (plus cheese); bacon 10L 7; only bread 17Wa 4; *nunch* older 18Nth 2; cake 21Nf 7/13 (plus bread and butter); biscuits 21Nf 11; *jawer* older and pref 24Gl 5; SNACK OF LUNCH older 31So +3; a pasty 37D 6; in fields 39Ha +4; *nuncheon* older 40Sx 1; pref to SNACK 40Sx 5

NAMMEK bread and cheese 39Ha 2; *nuncheon* pref to NAMMETS 33Brk 2; NAMMET a pasty 37D 3; tea and cake 39Ha 7; NOMMET bread and cheese 38Do 2

TEN O'CLOCK includes cheese 12St 4; TEN O'CLOCKS modern 6Y 9

"Crust-time" 36Co 5 im

"Let's have a bit of lunch" 37D 7 im

"Nammet-time" 37D 3 im

L56b ALLOWANCE oldest 6Y 2; older than TEN O'CLOCKS 6Y 9; consumed in harvest-field or hay-field 6Y 10/25/+28; prob older than FORENOON DRINKING 6Y 22
BAIT older than TEN O'CLOCK 1Nb 9; older than LUNCH 3Du 5; includes cheese 11Sa 5/7/9, 15He 1–7, 16Wo 1/2/4/5, 23Mon 1–3/6; includes bacon 11Sa 7; in afternoon 40Sx 6
BEVER bread and cheese 22Sf +1, 27Bd 3, 28Hrt 1/3, 29Ess 11/13; includes cheese 25Ox 4; bacon and bread 26Bk 2 (plus onion)/3; a dumpling containing bacon and potato 27Bd 1; bread and pork plus onion 27Bd 2; taken only during harvest-time 27Bd 3; bread and meat 28Hrt 2; sandwiches 29Ess 7; taken after mid-day 29Ess 7/10; farm-labourer's word 29Ess 11
DOCKY bread and cheese 18Nth 1 (or bread and onion), 19Hu 1 (plus meat), 20C 1 (or bread and meat)/+2, 21Nf 9, 22Sf +1; older than LUNCH 20C +2
DRINKING more usual than BAIT 6Y 5; consumed in harvest-field or hay-field 6Y +7. DRINKINGS consumed in harvest-field or hay-field 6Y 19
FORENOON DRINKING older than BAIT 5La 9; consumed in harvest-field or hay-field 6Y 21
SNACK commoner than LUNCH Man 1; includes cheese 11Sa 11 (or bacon), 12St 3 (plus cake), 17Wa +6 (plus onion), 23Mon 5 (or biscuits), 24Gl 1 (plus onion)/2/4/6/7; pref to LUNCH 17Wa 2; shortcake 21Nf 6; ref a sandwich 30MxL 1; pork, cheese, cold pudding 34Sr 1; bread and cheese 39Ha 3
BIT OF A SNAP includes cheese 12St 6. SNAP consumed in mine 6Y 26; unspecified constituents 8Db 1; includes cheese 8Db 2/4; includes bacon 8Db 5; usual 12St 11; a pasty 13Lei 1; bread and butter 19Hu 2; ref any snack 29Ess 2; snack taken at any time of day 29Ess 8. SNAPPING unspecified constituents (plus pasty) 8Db 6

"Baiting-time" 15He 17 im
"Bever-time" 17Wa +6, 25Ox 4
"Snap-clout", in which the snap is wrapped 6Y 26 im; "snapping-time" 12St 11 im; "snap-time" 12St 10

BEVER was rec in "bever-time" 17Wa +6, 25Ox 4; SNAP was rec in "snap-time" 12St 10

L57 BAGGING usual 12St +5
BAIT railwaymen's term 2Cu 1; a miner's word 6Y 2
JOCK rare 6Y 14; farmer's word 6Y +22
LUNCH modern 5La 5; *dinner* pref 34Sr 5; rare 35K 1
NAMMET at tea-time 38Do 4/5
SNAP collier's word 6Y +22; coal-miner's term 35K +3

"Bait-time" 6Y 9 im
"Nummet-time" 31So 6 im; the meal was tied up in a "nammet-bag" 32W 8 im
"Snap-bag", which contains the meal 6Y 33 im
"Tommy-bag" 15He 1 im

L58 CLINKERS pref to ICICLES 31So 13
Iceles pref to DAGLETS (sw) 33Brk 2. DAGLETS pref to *ice-daggles* 33Brk 4; older than ICICLES 34Sr 5, 40Sx 2

L59 MARRIED usual 6Y +33
WED older than MARRIED 3Du 5, 8Db 2, 11Sa 11; sw 6Y +33

"If her'd a-married en" 37D 4 im
"A wedded fellow" 4 We 4 im; "what's thou going to get wed to?" 6Y 4 im

L60 FRAE older than FROM 6Y +14
THROO older than FROM 6Y 34

L61 LIG DOWN older than LIE DOWN 6Y 4; older than LAY DOWN 6Y 19/32
LIG DOWN to a dog 6Y 25 im; LIG THISEN DOWN sometimes 6Y +28; LIG THEE DOWN old 8Db +1
LIE DOWN not used 19Hu +2

"Lig thy head down" 6Y 6 im

HAVE A LAY-DOWN 10L 11, 18Nth +3, 19Hu +2, 21Nf +1/+7/+11/13, 22Sf +5, 25Ox +6, 26Bk 3, 27Bd +2, 29Ess +2/+8/+11, 34Sr 5
HAVE A LIE-DOWN 2Cu +5, 6Y 25, 7Ch +2, 22Sf 4, 31So +1/2; HAVE YOU A LIE-DOWN 16Wo +5
HAVE A LIG-DOWN 6Y +22

L62 BIDE HOME older than STAY HOME 31So 5/10
SIT AT HOME more usual than STOP AT HOME 2Cu 2
STOP AT HOME older than STAY AT HOME 26Bk 5; STOP rec second visit, pref to STAY 35K 1

L63 SHIRL older than SLIDE 1Nb 9, 3Du 6, 6Y 15, ie on their buttocks 6Y +4
Glirry older than SLIDE 25Ox 1
SLITHER pref to SLIDE (sw) 6Y 25

"A shirl on the ice" 4We 2 im; "they're shirling in the street" 6Y 16 im
"Skiddering about" 37D 11 im
"They call it skirring" 5La 4 im; "let's go a-skirring on the pit (= pond)" 5La 6 im
"Make a slidie (= slide)" 1Nb 6 im
"They call it slurring" 6Y 12 im; "they start a-slurring" 6Y 26 im; "set a-slurring" ie begin sliding 6Y 3 im; "have you slurred them boots out?" 10L 9 im

L64 BLACKMAN sw 6Y 30, pref to BOGEY 34Sr 4
BOGEY modern 6Y +6, not used 6Y 32
BOGEYMAN sw but not used 3Du 5; sw 6Y +9/16/+29, 18Nth 5 (*Old Harry* pref), 34Sr 3; older than *policeman* 6Y 20; "a spirit of the dark" 19Hu 1; = scarecrow 26Bk 4 im; *Old Nick* older 31So 1
BOGGART pref to BOGEY 5La 9; *scug* pref 7Ch 3
BOGGLE = ghost 3Du +6; rare 10L 9

L65 FEARED older than FRIGHTENED 1Nb 2
FLAYED older than FRIGHTENED 1Nb 3
FREETENED pref to FRIGHTENED 6Y 14; older than FRIGHTENED 8Db +1
FRIT older than AFRAID 12St 9; pref to AFRAID and FRIGHTENED 18Nth 2
SCARED usual 29Ess +9

"It takes summat to flay (= frighten) them" 2Cu 3 im; "flay" = frighten 5La 9 im
"Frighten" v Man 1 im, 29Ess 4 im, 33 Brk 2 im; "fritten" v 7Ch 5 im
"Scaring" prp 31So 2 im

APPENDIX 3

UNMAPPED LEXICAL RESPONSES

The responses mapped in the lexical section were selected from the total range of responses to illustrate, amongst other things, variation in usage, the developments of different historical forms, loan-words, and the distinction between areas which have conserved regional dialect forms and areas more strongly influenced by Standard forms.

In order to provide the reader with the full range of lexical material for each notion, those responses not selected for mapping, and not listed in the map footnotes as subsumed under a mapped form, are listed here under the appropriate map number and headword. Fuller details of the unmapped responses, including their distribution, may be found by reference to the Survey's *Basic Material* volumes. In this Appendix the responses are listed for each map in alphabetical order. The spellings occasionally differ from those in the *Basic Material* headwords. The *LAE* Eds have preferred in doubtful instances to represent the fieldworkers' transcriptions orthographically rather than retain the original *Basic Material* headword spellings, which sometimes suggest etymologies or Standard forms; eg L49 *wick-flo* for wɪkflo: rather than *SED* Edd *quick-flaw*; L64 *jinny-wisp* rather than Edd *jenny-wisp*.

The use of brackets in eg L13 *pull* (*swedes*), indicates that both *pull* and *pull swedes* were elicited. It will be noted that elements of compounds may combine in more than one set of compound variation, eg L17 *mow-pins* and *stack-pins*; *stack-brods*, *stack-pins*, and *stack-pricks*; *stack-pricks* and *thatch-pricks*.

L1 FARMSTEAD

farm-house and buildings
farm-place
farm premises
farm-spot
farm-steading
house and buildings
living-house
place
steading

L2 CARTMAN

bailiff
clodhopper
draughtsman
foreman
head carman
horsechap
ploughman
yardman

L3 TROUGH

bing
bodge
boother
boskin
box
cooler
cow-kit
cow-tub
feeding-pan
?forebay
gangway
gutter
neat-tree
pat
piggin
provin-bucket
provin-tub
stock
tub
tumbler
tumbril
water-stock
water-trough
yusen

L4 STRETCHER

breast-plate
coupling-stick
cratch-stick
cross-pole
cross-stick
drawing-stend
jib
pole
rack-stick
set-staff
sling
spat
stend
stretch-stick
swingle-tree
taw-tree
team-stick
trap-stick
truss-stick
tween-stick
whipper

L5 TRACE-HORSE

body-horse
chain-tit
crippin-horse
harness-horse
pin-horse
sling-tit
string-horse
tandem-horse

L6 SHAFT

blade
draught
pole
sill
till

L7 TIRE

bend
rind
strope
tirl

L8 TIP

cave (up)
chuck up
empt
ent
kelt
let up
skelp
slot up
spring up
throw (up)
trip up
untinge

L9 DUNG

manure
shit

L10 COUCH-GRASS

cockle
crouch-grass
dog's-foot-grass
fowl-grass
kesh
spear-grass
strap-grass
stroil
stroily-grass
twicks
wrack

L11 BIND-WEED

arse-smart
bear-wind
bell-wind
canary creeper
columbine
cornflower
devil's gut
devil's nightcap
devil's twine
ground-lily
lily
morning-glory
?oxberry root
reed-bind
robin-run-in-the-hedge
robin-run-the-dike
sheep-bind
shoelaces
sweethearts
vine
wandering willy
way-bind
wheat-bind
white runners
wild woodbine
willy-wind
woodbine

L12 GOOSEGRASS

beggar-lace
beggar's lice
billy-buttons
bunks
burdock
burr(s)
?carky-mawkins
claggy-buttons
claggy-jack
clives
cly
cockle-buttons
cockles
cogwheels
creeping jinny
crotch-joy
crotch-weed
cuddle-me-close
devil-guts
furbobs
gosling-grass
gully-grass
gum-weed
hair-weed
jack-by-the-hedge
meg-many-feet
nut-grass
policeman's buttons
pricklies
prickly-back
soldier's buttons
sticky-back
sticky bobs
sticky-buttons
sticky-dick
sticky-grass
sticky-jack
sticky-stinking-joe
swine-grass
teasels
tongue-weed

L13 TOP AND TAIL

chop (off)
chop the spurns and tops off
chop the tops and tails off
clean (off)
cut (off)
cut the green off and cut the
root off
cut the swedes off
cut the top and bottom off
cut the top off
cut the tops and roots off
cut the tops and tails off
dress
knock the top off and the tail
loop
lop
pull (swedes)
slash the muck off
slike
sned
snip
snuff
swede-clean
thresh
wrench
wring (the tops off)

L14 CARTING

draw
dray (in)
gather in
get
pull
put in

L15 RIDGE

back
comb
crest
eave-end
heading
head of the rick
rib
roof
top
top-corner
top of the roof

L16 RIDGE

barge
breekin
coping
crease
crest(-tile)
easing
house-crease
pinnacle
roof
top (of the slates)

L17 PEGS

briars
buckles
mow-pins
nibs
prickers
?rawters
scollops
spats
spilks
spindles
splint(er)s
sporrels
sprindles
springers
springles
stack-brods
stack-pins
stack-pricks
stakes
sticks
thatch-pricks

L18 ROPES

bind
binder-string
binder-twine
binding
binding-cord
binding-twine
cocoa-string
coconut-string
coir
cord
corn-yarn
hop-string
manilla
reed-beams
rods
ropekin
scuds
spars
spunyarn
stack-twine
straps
straw
stretchers
string
suggan
tar-cord
tar(red) line
tarmarl (string)
tar(red) twine
tar-string
thack-cord
thacking-string

thatch(ing)-cord
thatch(ing)-line
thatch(ing)-rods
thatching-string
thick rough string
thimes
thumb-beams
thumb-binds
thumble-beams
thumble-binds
towt
twine
walching
wattles

L19 NOT IN CALF

a drape
a segg
broken
drape
eald
gast
gone over
hasn't held
leased
light
not by calf
not fit
not in calf
not proved in calf
not served
not taken
not with calf
out of calf
returned

L20 DONKEY

bronkaw
bunkus
?cornutor
dinky
?hick-horse
jasock
jason
jerusalem
mule
nazareth
nussock
yoke

L21 TRIM

barge (down)
barge out
brow
buck(-head)
bush-hedge
clean
dike
dub
face in
flash
furbish
hedge
hone
lob
lop
nip
rid back
scotch
shave down
shred
side
slansh
snag
snaze
split (up)
stag
swap
trounce
twig

L22 PLASH

block the gaps
braid
brail
buck(-head and braid in)
build up
bung the holes up
cast (the hedge)
cast up
clat up the gaps
crook down
cut and fill the gaps up
cut and make
cut down
cut off and braid down
dike
fell
fill up
gap(-stop)
hedge up
hook
lace
line
make (a hedge)
make up
raze the hedge
reave
set up the gap
slash
slipper
spale gaps up
splash
splawter
splay
splet
splice
splish(er)
split down
split the hedge
steep (down)
steep the hedge (down)
stop
stop the gaps up
stop (the) shards
stop up (gaps)
wreath down

L23 SHEEP-HOLE

bank-hole
bolt-hole
ditch-hole
draw-way
gote
hole
loop-hole
pop-hole
run(-through)
sheep-gate
sheep-hole
sheep-run
sheep-walk
sheep's hole
wash

L24 HANGING-POST

hanger
harr-tree
head of the gate
heel
hurl
slinger
standard

L25 PATH

cattle-walk
cow-run
cow-walk
field-way
foot-gate
foot-road
foot-walk
rack
road-way
sheep-run
sheep-walk
stile-road
towpath
trail
walk

L26 MOLE

?yule

L27 HENS

hen

L28 CHIP

beak
break (shell)
chick
chit
come off
come out
crack
peck
pick
pop
scrat(ch)
spletch
spurt
?stretch
turn

L29 GOSLING

golling
gozzy
gutling
swaddling

L30 ANTS

muryans
pismires
pissy-beds

pissy-mices
pissy-mires
pissy-motes
pissy-mothers

L31 THRESHOLD

board
cross-piece
curb
door-board
door-sill
door-step
draught-board
draught-stopper
flag(-stone)
ground-sill
plat
saddle
sill
slab(-stone)
sole
step(-board)
stone
?stoo
thres(h)-board
thresh-foot
weather-board

L32 EARTH-CLOSET

bumby-hole
bog
crap-house
crapper
earth-lavatory
garden-house
house of commons
houses of parliament
lavatory
lavvy
littlehouse
lobby
middy
mizen
piss-house
out-house
shit-hole
thyeveg
vault

L33 KINDLING-WOOD

a bit of furze
bavin-wood
birns
bit of stick
brash(nachs)
brush-wood
bunts
chats
chips
chop(ped)-sticks
colons
dried wood
elding
faggot(s)
fire-lighting(wood)
fire-sticks
firewood
firing
gorse-birns
hedge-sticks
kids
kinders
kindle(r)
light-fire
lighting-wood
lords
nickies
pimp(s)
puffs
small-wood
some stick
spray(-sticks)
spray-wood
stick(s)
tindlers
top wood off the hedges
twigs
wood

L34 SLICE

bit
butty
hunch
hunk
junk
morsel
piece
slab
slash
slipe
slive(r)
square
slithag
stull

L35 SAD

clabby
clammy
clingy
close
clutchy
dazed
dead
down
dull
dumpy
fallen
gone flop
hasn't rose
isn't rose
kisty
?non-high
not risen
pluffy
pudding-bread
slack-baked
soggy
sour
sunk

L36 GIRDLE

baking-tin
cake-plate
cake-tin
cake-tree
crock(-pot)
flat-jack
grid(iron)
grill
hang-on-oven
hot-plate
oven-shelf
pan
plate
pot
shelf

L37 DRIPPING

beef-fat
dip
fat
lard

L38 BACON FAT

bacon
fat bacon
lard
pork-fat
skimmings

L39 INSIPID

a bit weak
bitter
bout kick
bout salt
dufty
flavourless
got no taste
grummy
insipid
mawkish
mush
nasty
no taste (in it)
no taste to it
not enough salt (in)
not proper taste
not put enough salt in
not salt
not salt(ed) enough
not salty enough
putrid
raw
rotten
saltless
sappy
short of salt
short of seasoning
sipid
swaffy
tame
tastes of nowt
unseasoned
wants salt
watery

L40 PEAPOD

huck
hud
pea-cod
pea-huck
pea-hod
pea-hud
pea-posh

pea-pusket
pease-cod
pea-swath
posh
slough

L41 SHELLING

burst open
cosh
flirt open
hod
hud
husk
peel
pick
pod
posh
swad

L42 BREW

damp
put the tea to stand
stew

L43 DREGS

bottoms
chaff
drains
drugs
grogs
groushans
grummets
monkeys
tea-wiffs

L44 ANYTHING

any (food)
any grub
any layings
any more
any victuals
a thumb bit
nothing

L45 SOMETHING

—

L46 HEADACHE

a big fat head
(a) sick head

L47 GAPES

flabbergasted
gaums
gauves
gawks (about)
gazes
geeks
glapes
glares
glops
gnatcatching
gollied
is glaring
looks agazed
looks aghast
looks amazed
skoons about
stags
stares (with his chops open)
stares with his mouth open
yaaps
yaums
yawns about

L48 CHAPPED

chafed
charked
chashed
chilblain(ed)
chilled
flied (open)
?flue
fly
frayed
frostbitten
frosted
full of keens
hazled
sore
spithey

L49 LOOSE PIECE OF SKIN

angry-wheal
back-feen
back-flee
back-fringe
bit loose skin
bit of loose skin
bit of skin
dry skin
ever-slit
feather
finger-friend
friggan
godmother's wish
grandmother jag
granny
idle-feg
idle-wheal
lazy-back
lazy-flake
loose bit of skin
loose piece of skin
loose skin
nail-hang
peel(er)
piece of loose skin
proud flesh
quick-back
quick-nail
ravel-back
ravelling-back
rebbling
ring-nail
rivel(ling)
rough skin
ruggle-back
scurf
skinning
snag
spring(-wart)
step-father
wart-spring
warty-wheal
wick-flo

L50 FRECKLES

bran
bran-mash
branny
brans
bran-spots
brun
brunnies
brunny
paw(m) pettles
reckles
summer-spots
sun-spots

L51 HUNGRY

empty
famished
famishing
fammelled
gant
hearty
hollow
peckish
pined
sinking
starved
starving
wallow
yap

L52 BRIM

breward(s)
flap
peak
ridge

L53 JACKET

swinger

L54 SHIRT

shift

L55 VEST

body-jacket
gansey
semmit

L56 SNACK

bagging
biting on
break
clocking
clocks
dew-bit
dowan
drum-up
eleveners
forenoons
four o'clock
fourses
jawer
minning-on
morsel
nineses
nunch(eon)
packing
progger
putting-on

sandwich(es)
scran
sup-and-a-bite
tenner
tenses
threeses
tommy

L57 MEAL OUT

bever
bite of eating
boiled beef
bread and cheese
breakfast
chuck
dinner (out)
docky
drinkings
eating
food for the day
grub
hunch of bread and cheese
lunch
meal out
meat
packing(-up grub)
sandwich(es)
snack
victual(s)

L58 ICICLES

cockle-bells
cocky-bells
daggers
dagglers
ice-bugs
ice-daggles
iceles
icelets
ice-lick
ickles
snipes

L59 MARRIED

tied up

L60 FROM

L61 LIE

have a doss
quat down
rest thyself for a bit

L62 STAY AT HOME

keep at home
lop about home
set at home
sit at home

L63 SLIDE

glirry
skid
slider
slip

L64 BOGEY

bobby
bo-boy
boggin
bo-man
boogy-sam
copper
elf
hang-man
high sprite
hooker-man
jinny-wisp
old Harry
old Nick
police(man)
scug
sprite
the constable
the devil
the old lad
the old man
the old Nick
thick (= that) old man
willy-with-the-wisp

L65 AFRAID

afraint
duberous
freckened
frickened
fright
gallied
gliffed

INDEX

The index lists, for each mapped questionnaire notion, the Standard forms used as headwords for the maps and the relevant map numbers preceded by the code Ph for phonological, L lexical, M morphological, S syntactical, to indicate the aspect treated and the section of the atlas in which the map is to be found. The listing is alphabetical with the exception of the parts of the verb *to be* whose complex forms have suggested special treatment. These are all grouped under *be* in the following order: 1st, 2nd and 3rd persons singular and plural, positive present tense forms followed by interrogative forms, followed by negative forms, followed by past tense forms in the same order, followed by conditional forms.